[redacted]

[redacted]

[redacted]

[redacted]

THEOLOGICAL DICTIONARY
OF THE
OLD TESTAMENT

THEOLOGICAL DICTIONARY

OF THE

OLD TESTAMENT

EDITED BY

G. JOHANNES BOTTERWECK

AND

HELMER RINGGREN

Translated by

DAVID E. GREEN

Volume VI

יָתַר ־ יוֹבֵל

yôḇēl – yāṯar I

WILLIAM B. EERDMANS PUBLISHING COMPANY

GRAND RAPIDS, MICHIGAN

Translated from
THEOLOGISCHES WÖRTERBUCH ZUM ALTEN TESTAMENT
Band III, Lieferungen 5-9
Published 1980-1982 by
VERLAG W. KOHLHAMMER GMBH STUTTGART, W. GERMANY

Library of Congress Catologing-in-Publication Data

Botterweck, G. Johannes
Theological dictionary of the Old Testament
Translation of Theologisches Wörterbuch zum Alten Testament.
Includes rev. ed. of v. 1-2.
Includes bibliographical references.
1. Bible. O.T.—Dictionaries—Hebrew. 2. Hebrew language—Dictionaries—English.
I. Ringgren, Helmer, 1917— joint author. II. Title.
BS440.B5713 221.4′4′0321 73-76170

ISBN 0-8028-2338-6 (set)
Volume VI 0-8028-2330-0

Printed in the United States of America

CONSULTING EDITORS

George W. Anderson
Henri Cazelles
David Noel Freedman
Shemaryahu Talmon
Gerhard Wallis

CONTRIBUTORS

L. Alonso-Schökel, Rome
G. André, Uppsala
†C. Barth, Basel
A. Baumann, Wolfsburg
J. Bergman, Linköping
†G. J. Botterweck, Bonn (Editor)
R. D. Branson, Lake Wales
R. E. Clements, Cambridge
W. Dommershausen, Davos
H.-J. Fabry, Bonn
D. N. Freedman, Ann Arbor / San Diego
H. F. Fuhs, Würzburg
M. Görg, Bamberg
G. F. Hasel, Berrien Springs
B. Johnson, Lund
D. Kellermann, Tübingen
T. Kronholm, Madla
N. Lohfink, Frankfurt am Main
J. R. Lundbom, Marburg
G. Mayer, Zornheim
W. Mayer, Rome
R. Mosis, Eichstätt
M. J. Mulder, Badhoevedorp
R. G. North, Rome
M. Ottosson, Uppsala
B. Otzen, Århus
H. D. Preuss, Neuendettelsau
H. Ringgren, Uppsala (Editor)
L. Ruppert, Bochum
M. Sæbø, Sandviken
J. F. Sawyer, Newcastle-upon-Tyne
J. Schreiner, Würzburg
J. Schüpphaus, Königswinter
W. von Soden, Münster
J. A. Soggin, Rome
M. Tsevat, Cincinnati
S. Wagner, Leipzig
G. Wallis, Halle am Saale
H.-J. Zobel, Greifswald

CONTENTS

ABBREVIATIONS

AANLR	*Atti dell' Academia Nazionale dei Lincei, Rendiconti,* Rome
AASOR	*Annual of the American Schools of Oriental Research,* New Haven, Ann Arbor, Philadelphia
AAWLM	*Abhandlungen der Akademie der Wissenschaften und der Literatur in Mainz,* Wiesbaden
AB	*The Anchor Bible,* ed. W. F. Albright and D. N. Freedman, Garden City
AbB	*Altbabylonische Briefe in Umschrift und Übersetzung,* Leiden
ABR	*Australian Biblical Review,* Melbourne
abs.	absolute
acc.	accusative
ACLing-SémCham	*Actes du premier congrès internationale de linguistique sémitique et chamito-sémitique,* Paris, 16-19 July, 1969. *Janua linguarum,* 159 (The Hague, 1974)
act.	active
AcThD	*Acta theologica danica,* Århus, Copenhagen
adj.	adjective
adv.	adverb
AfO	*Archiv für Orientforschung,* Graz
ÄgAbh	*Ägyptologische Abhandlungen,* Wiesbaden
AGWG	*Abhandlungen der Gesellschaft der Wissenschaften zu Göttingen,* Berlin
AHAW	*Abhandlungen der Heidelberger Akademie der Wissenschaften*
AHDO	*Archives d'histoire du droit oriental,* Brussels
AHw	W. von Soden, *Akkadisches Handwörterbuch* (Wiesbaden, 1959—)
AION	*Annali dell'Istituto Universitario Orientali di Napoli*
AIPH	*Annuaire de l'Institut de Philologie et d'Histoire Orientales et Slaves,* Brussels
AJSL	*The American Journal of Semitic Languages and Literatures,* Chicago
AJT	*American Journal of Theology,* Chicago
AKGW	*Abhandlungen der Königlichen Gesellschaft der Wissenschaften zu Göttingen*
Akk.	Akkadian
AKM	*Abhandlungen zur Kunde des Morgenlandes,* Leipzig, Wiesbaden, Hildesheim
ALUOS	*Annual of the Leeds University Oriental Society*
Amhar.	Amharic
AN	J. J. Stamm, *Die akkadische Namengebung. MVÄG,* 44 (1939, ^{2}1968)
AnAcScFen	*Annales Academiae Scientarum Fennicae,* Helsinki
AnBibl	*Analecta biblica,* Rome
AncIsr	R. de Vaux, *Ancient Israel: Its Life and Institutions* (Eng. trans., New York, 1961, ^{2}1965)
ANEP	*The Ancient Near East in Pictures,* ed. J. B. Pritchard (Princeton, ^{2}1955, ^{3}1969)
ANET	*Ancient Near Eastern Texts Relating to the OT,* ed. J. B. Pritchard (Princeton, ^{2}1955, ^{3}1969)
AnOr	*Analecta orientalia,* Rome
ANVAO	*Avhandlinger utgitt av det Norske Videnskaps-Akademi i Oslo*
AOAT	*Alter Orient und AT,* Neukirchen-Vluyn
AOB	*Altorientalische Bilder zum AT,* ed. H. Gressmann (Berlin and Leipzig, ^{2}1927)

AOS	*American Oriental Series,* New Haven
AOT	*Altorientalische Texte zum AT,* ed. H. Gressmann (Berlin and Leipzig, ^{2}1926, repr. 1953)
AP	A. E. Cowley, *Aramaic Papyri of the Fifth Century B.C.* (Oxford, 1923)
APNM	H. B. Huffmon, *Amorite Personal Names in the Mari Texts* (Baltimore, 1965)
Arab.	Arabic
ARAB	D. D. Luckenbill, *Ancient Records of Assyria and Babylonia,* 2 vols. (Chicago, 1926-27)
Aram.	Aramaic
ArbT	*Arbeiten zur Theologie,* Stuttgart
ARM	*Archives royales de Mari,* Paris
ArOr	*Archiv orientâlní,* Prague
ARW	*Archiv für Religionswissenschaft,* Freiburg, Leipzig, Berlin
AS	*Assyriological Studies,* Chicago
ASAW	*Abhandlungen der Sächsischen Akademie der Wissenschaften in Leipzig*
ASTI	*Annual of the Swedish Theological Institute in Jerusalem,* Leiden
AT	Altes Testament, Ancien Testament, etc.
ATD	*Das AT Deutsch,* ed. V. Herntrich and A. Weiser, Göttingen
AThANT	*Abhandlungen zur Theologie des Alten und Neuen Testaments,* Zurich
ATS	*Arbeiten zu Text und Sprache im AT,* Munich
AUM	*Andrews University Monographs,* Berrien Springs
AuS	G. Dalman, *Arbeit und Sitte in Palästina,* 7 vols. (1928-1942, repr. Hildesheim, 1964)
AUSS	*Andrews University Seminary Studies,* Berrien Springs
AWA	*Anzeiger der Wiener Akademie,* Vienna
BA	*The Biblical Archaeologist,* New Haven, Ann Arbor, Philadelphia
Bab.	Babylonian, Babylonian Talmud
BAH	*Bibliothèque archéologique et historique,* Paris
BAR	*Biblical Archaeology Review,* Washington
BASOR	*Bulletin of the American Schools for Oriental Research,* New Haven, Ann Arbor, Philadelphia
BAT	*Die Botschaft des ATs,* Stuttgart
BBB	*Bonner biblische Beiträge*
BDB	F. Brown–S. R. Driver–C. A. Briggs, *A Hebrew and English Lexicon of the OT* (1907; Peabody, Mass., ^{2}1979)
BDBAT	*Beiheft zur Dielheimer Blätter zum AT*
Benz	F. L. Benz, *Personal Names in the Phoenician and Punic Inscriptions. StPohl,* 8 (1972)
BeO	*Bibbia e oriente,* Milan
BET	*Beiträge zur biblischen Exegese und Theologie,* Frankfurt am Main, Las Vegas
BethM	*Beth mikra,* Jerusalem
BETL	*Bibliotheca ephemeridum theologicarum lovaniensium,* Paris, Gembloux
BEvTh	*Beiträge zur evangelische Theologie,* Munich
BHHW	*Biblisch-Historisches Handwörterbuch,* ed. L. Rost and B. Reicke, 3 vols. (Göttingen, 1962-1966)
BHK	*Biblia hebraica,* ed. R. Kittel (Stuttgart, ^{3}1929)
BHS	*Biblia hebraica stuttgartensia,* ed. K. Elliger and W. Rudolph (Stuttgart, 1966-1977)
BHTh	*Beiträge zur historischen Theologie,* Tübingen
Bibl	*Biblica,* Rome
bibliog.	bibliography
BietOr	*Biblica et orientalia,* Rome

BiLe	*Bibel und Leben,* Düsseldorf
BiOr	*Bibliotheca orientalis,* Leiden
BJRL	*Bulletin of the John Rylands Library,* Manchester
BK	*Biblischer Kommentar AT,* ed. M. Noth and H. W. Wolff, Neukirchen-Vluyn
BL	*Bibel-Lexikon,* ed. H. Haag (Einsedeln, 1951, ^{2}1968)
BLe	H. Bauer–P. Leander, *Historische Grammatik der hebräischen Sprache des ATs* (1918-1922, repr. Hildesheim, 1962)
BMAP	E. G. Kraeling, *The Brooklyn Museum Aramaic Papyri* (New Haven, 1953)
BN	*Biblische Notizien,* Bamberg
BRA	*Beiträge zur Religionsgeschichte des Altertums,* Halle
BRL	K. Galling, *Biblisches Reallexikon* (Tübingen, 1937, ^{2}1977)
BS	*Bibliotheca sacra,* Dallas
BSAW	*Berichte über die Verhandlungen der Sächsischen Akademie der Wissenschaften zu Leipzig*
BSt	*Biblische Studien,* Neukirchen-Vluyn
BT	*The Bible Translator,* London
BuA	B. Meissner, *Babylonien und Assyrien,* 2 vols. (Heidelberg, 1920-25)
BWANT, BWAT	*Beiträge zur Wissenschaft vom Alten (und Neuen) Testament,* Leipzig, Stuttgart
BWL	W. G. Lambert, *Babylonian Wisdom Literature* (Oxford, 1960)
BZ	*Biblische Zeitschrift,* Paderborn
BZAW	*Beihefte zur ZAW,* Berlin
ca.	*circa,* about
CAD	*The Assyrian Dictionary of the Oriental Institute of the University of Chicago,* 1956—
CAH^{3}	*Cambridge Ancient History,* ed. I. E. S. Edwards *et al.* (Cambridge, 1970—)
CahRB	*Cahiers de la RB,* Paris
Can.	Canaanite
CB	*Coniectanea biblica, OT Series,* Lund
CBC	*Cambridge Bible Commentary on the New English Bible,* Cambridge
CBQ	*Catholic Biblical Quarterly,* Washington
CBSC	*The Cambridge Bible for Schools and Colleges,* Cambridge
CD A,B	Damascus document, manuscript A, B
cf.	compare, see
ch(s).	chapter(s)
CH	Code of Hammurabi
CIH	*Corpus inscriptionum himyariticarum* (= *CIS,* IV)
CIS	*Corpus inscriptionum semiticarum* (Paris, 1881—)
CJT	*Canadian Journal of Theology,* Toronto
CML	G. R. Driver, *Canaanite Myths and Legends* (Edinburgh, 1956; ^{2}1978, ed. J. C. L. Gibson)
comm(s).	commentary(ies)
ComViat	*Communio viatorum,* Prague
conj.	conjecture
const.	construct
ContiRossini	K. Conti Rossini, *Chrestomathia arabica meridionalis ephigraphica* (Rome, 1931)
Copt.	Coptic
CSD	R. Payne Smith, *A Compendious Syriac Dictionary* (Oxford, 1903, repr. 1957)
CT	*The Egyptian Coffin Texts,* ed. A. de Buck and A. H. Gardiner. *OIP* (1935-1947)
CTA	A. Herdner, *Corpus des tablettes en cunéiformes alphabétiques découvertes à Ras Shamra-Ugarit,* I/II (Paris, 1963)

CThM	*Calwer Theologische Monographien,* Stuttgart
DAWS	*Denkschriften der Österreichischen Akademie der Wissenschaften in Wien, Sonderband,* Vienna
D	Deuteronomistic source
DB	*Dictionnaire de la Bible,* ed. F. Vigouroux (Paris, 1895-1912)
DBS	*Dictionnaire de la Bible, Supplement,* ed. L. Pirot *et al.* (Paris, 1926—)
DISO	C. F. Jean–J. Hoftijzer, *Dictionnaire des inscriptions sémitiques de l'ouest* (Leiden, 1965)
diss.	dissertation
DissAbs	*Dissertation Abstracts* (*International*), Ann Arbor
DJD	*Discoveries in the Judean Desert* (Oxford, 1955—)
DMOA	*Documenta et monumenta orientis antiqui,* Leiden
DN	Deity name
DS	*Dictionnaire de spiritualité, ascétique et mystique,* ed. M. Viller (Paris, 1937—)
E	Elohistic source
EA	Tell el-Amarna tablets
EB	*Die Heilige Schrift in deutscher Übersetzung. Echter-Bibel,* Würzburg
Egyp.	Egyptian
EH	*Europäische Hochschulschriften,* Frankfurt am Main, Bern
Einl.	Einleitung
EMiqr	*Enṣiqlōpedyā miqrāʿit* (Jerusalem, 1950—)
EncJud	*Encyclopedia judaica,* 16 vols. (Jerusalem and New York, 1971-72)
EnEl	Enuma Elish
Eng.	English
ErfThSt	*Erfurter Theologische Studien,* Erfurt, Leipzig
ErJB	*Eranos-Jahrbuch,* Zurich
esp.	especially
EstBíb	*Estudios bíblicos,* Madrid
ÉtB	*Études bibliques,* Paris
Ethiop.	Ethiopic
ETL	*Ephemerides theologicae lovanienses,* Louvain
EvTh	*Evangelische Theologie,* Munich
ExpT	*Expository Times,* Edinburgh
fem.	feminine
fr.	fragment
Fr.	French
FreibThSt	*Freiburger Theologische Studien,* Freiburg im Breisgau
FreibZPhTh	*Freiburger Zeitschrift für Philosophie und Theologie,* Fribourg
FRLANT	*Forschungen zur Religion und Literatur des Alten und Neuen Testaments,* Göttingen
FThS	*Frankfurter Theologische Studien,* Frankfurt am Main
FuF	*Forschungen und Fortschritte,* Berlin
FzB	*Forschung zur Bibel,* Würzburg
GaG	W. von Soden, *Grundriss der akkadischen Grammatik. AnOr,* 33 (1952)
gen.	genitive
Ger.	German
GesB	W. Gesenius–F. Buhl, *Hebräisches und aramäisches Handwörterbuch* (Berlin, ^{17}1921)
Gilg.	Gilgamesh epic
Gk.	Greek
GK	W. Gesenius–E. Kautsch, *Hebräische Grammatik* (Halle, ^{28}1909) (= Kautsch–A. E. Cowley, *Gesenius' Hebrew Grammar* [Oxford, ^{2}1910])

GöttThArb	*Göttinger Theologisch Arbeit*
GSAT	*Gesammelte Studien zum AT,* Munich
GUOST	*Glasgow University Oriental Society Transactions*
H	Holiness Code
HAT	*Handbuch zum AT,* ed. O. Eissfeldt, ser. 1, Tübingen
Heb.	Hebrew
Herm	Hermeneia, Philadelphia
Hitt.	Hittite
HKAT	*Handkommentar zum AT,* ed. W. Nowack, Göttingen
HNT	*Handbuch zum NT,* Tübingen
HSM	*Harvard Semitic Monographs,* Cambridge, Mass.
HThR	*Harvard Theological Review,* Cambridge, Mass.
HThS	*Harvard Theological Studies,* Cambridge, Mass.
HTSt	*Hervormde Teologiese Studies,* Pretoria
HUCA	*Hebrew Union College Annual,* Cincinnati
IB	*The Interpreter's Bible,* ed. G. A. Buttrick, 12 vols. (Nashville, 1952-57)
ICC	*The International Critical Commentary,* Edinburgh
IDB	*The Interpreter's Dictionary of the Bible,* ed. G. A. Buttrick, 4 vols. (Nashville, 1962); *Sup.,* ed. K. Crim (Nashville, 1976)
IEJ	*Israel Exploration Journal,* Jerusalem
IJT	*Indian Journal of Theology,* Serampore
ILC	J. Pedersen, *Israel: Its Life and Culture,* 4 vols. in 2 (Eng. trans., Oxford: 1926-1940, ^{5}1963)
ILR	*Israel Law Review,* Jerusalem
impf.	imperfect
impv.	imperative
inf.	infinitive
in loc.	on this passage
Int	*Interpretation,* Richmond
Intro(s).	Introduction(s) (to the)
IPN	M. Noth, *Die israelitischen Personennamen. BWANT,* 46[3/10] (1928, repr. 1966)
ITC	*International Theological Commentary,* ed. F. C. Holmgren and G. A. F. Knight (Grand Rapids and Edinburgh)
J	Yahwist source
Ja	Enumeration according to A. Jamme (Old South Arabic)
JANES	*Journal of the Ancient Near Eastern Society of Columbia University,* New York
JAOS	*Journal of the American Oriental Society,* Boston, New Haven
Jastrow	M. Jastrow, *A Dictionary of the Targumim, the Talmud Babli and Yerushalmi, and the Midrashic Literature* (1903; repr. 2 vols. in 1, Brooklyn, 1975)
JB	*The Jerusalem Bible* (Garden City and London, 1966)
JBC	*Jerome Biblical Commentary,* ed. R. E. Brown, J. A. Fitzmyer, and R. E. Murphy (Englewood Cliffs, 1968)
JBL	*Journal of Biblical Literature,* New York, New Haven, Philadelphia, Missoula, Chico, Atlanta
JCS	*Journal of Cuneiform Studies,* New Haven, Cambridge, Mass.
JE	*The Jewish Encyclopedia,* ed. I. Singer, 12 vols. (New York and London, 1901-6)
JEA	*Journal of Egyptian Archaeology,* London
Jer.	Jerusalem (Palestinian) Talmud
JESHO	*Journal of Economic and Social History of the Orient,* Leiden
JNES	*Journal of Near Eastern Studies,* Chicago

JNSL	*Journal of Northwest Semitic Languages,* Stellenbosch
Joüon	P. Joüon, *Grammaire de l'hébreu biblique* (^{2}1947, repr. Rome, 1965)
JQR	*Jewish Quarterly Review,* Philadelphia
JSOT	*Journal for the Study of the OT,* Sheffield
JSS	*Journal of Semitic Studies,* Manchester
JTS	*Journal of Theological Studies,* Oxford
Jud	*Judaica,* Zurich
K	*Kethibh*
KAI	H. Donner–W. Röllig, *Kanaanäische und aramäische Inschriften,* 3 vols. (Wiesbaden, ^{2}1966-69, ^{3}1971-76)
KAT	*Kommentar zum AT,* ed. E. Sellin and J. Herrmann, Leipzig, Gütersloh
KB	*Keilschriftliche Bibliothek,* ed. E. Schrader (Berlin, 1889-1900)
KBL	L. Koehler-W. Baumgartner, *Lexicon in Veteris Testamenti Libros* (Leiden, ^{1}1953, ^{2}1958, ^{3}1967—)
KD	C. F. Keil and F. J. Delitzsch, *Comm. on the OT,* 10 vols. (Eng. trans., repr. Grand Rapids, 1954)
KHC	*Kurzer Handcommentar zum AT,* ed. K. Marti, Tübingen, Leipzig
KJV	King James Version
KlSchr	*Kleine Schriften* (A. Alt, Munich, 1953-59, ^{3}1964; O. Eissfeldt, Tübingen, 1962-1979; K. Elliger, *ThB,* 32 [1969])
KTU	*Die keilalphabetischen Texte aus Ugarit,* I, ed. M. Dietrich, O. Loretz, and J. Sanmartín. *AOAT,* 24 (1976)
KUB	Staatliche Museen zu Berlin, Vorderasiatische Abteilung (later Deutsche Orient-Gesellschaft), *Keilschrifturkunden aus Boghazköi* (Berlin, 1921—)
KuD	*Kerygma und Dogma,* Göttingen
Kuhn	K. G. Kuhn, *Konkordanz zu den Qumrantexten* (Göttingen, 1960); Nachträge, *RevQ,* 4 (1963-64), 163-234
l(l).	line(s)
L	Lay source
Lane	E. W. Lane, *An Arabic-English Lexicon,* 8 vols. (London, 1863-1893, repr. 1968)
Lat.	Latin
LD	*Lectio divina,* Paris
Leslau, *Contributions*	W. Leslau, *Ethiopic and South Arabic Contributions to the Hebrew Lexicon* (Los Angeles, 1958)
LexÄg	W. Helck–E. Otto, *Lexikon der Ägyptologie* (Wiesbaden, 1972—)
LexHebAram	F. Zorrell, *Lexicon hebraicum et aramaicum Veteris Testamenti* (Rome, 1958, repr. 1968)
LexLingAeth	A. Dillmann, *Lexicon linguae aethiopicae* (Leipzig, 1865)
LexLingAram	E. Vogt, *Lexicon linguae aramaicae Veteris Testamenti documentis antiquis illustratum* (Rome, 1971)
LexSyr	C. Brockelmann, *Lexicon syriacum* (Halle, 1928, ^{2}1968)
lit.	literally
LThK	*Lexikon für Theologie und Kirche,* ed. M. Buchberger, 10 vols. (Freiburg im Breisgau, 1930-38); ed. J. Höfer and K. Rahner, 10 vols. with index, 3 sups. (^{2}1957-1968)
LXX	Septuagint (LXX^A, Codex Alexandrinus; LXX^B, Codex Vaticanus; $LXX^{S[1,2]}$, Codex Sinaiticus, correctors 1, 2, etc.)
MAB	*Mémoires de l'académie royale de Belge,* Brussels
Mand.	Mandaic
MarThSt	*Marburger Theologische Studien*
masc.	masculine

MdD	E. S. Drower–R. Macuch, *Mandaic Dictionary* (Oxford, 1963)
MGWJ	*Monatsschrift für Geschichte und Wissenschaft des Judentums,* Breslau
MIO	*Mitteilungen des Instituts für Orientforschung,* Berlin
MKAW	*Mededelingen der Koninklijke Nederlandse Akademie van Wetenschapen,* Amsterdam
MPL	J. P. Migne, *Patrologia latina,* 221 vols. (Paris, 1844-1864)
ms(s).	manuscript(s)
MSU	*Mitteilungen des Septuaginta-Unternehmens,* Göttingen
MT	Masoretic Text
MUSJ	*Mélanges de l'Université St. Joseph,* Beirut
MVÄG	*Mitteilungen der Vorderasiatisch-Ägyptischen Gesellschaft* (Berlin), Leipzig
n(n).	note(s)
N	name
NAB	*The New American Bible* (Paterson, N. J., 1970; Collegeville, Minn., and Grand Rapids, ²1988)
NAWG	*Nachrichten der Akademie der Wissenschaften in Göttingen*
NC	*La Nouvelle Clio,* Brussels
NCBC	*The New Century Bible Commentary,* ed. R. E. Clements and M. Black, Grand Rapids and London
NEB	*The New English Bible* (Oxford, 1961-1970, ²1970—)
NedGTT	*Nederduitse Gereformeerde Teologiese Tydskrif,* Kaapstad
NIDNTT	*The New International Dictionary of NT Theology,* ed. C. Brown, 3 vols. (Eng. trans., Grand Rapids, ²1971-75)
no(s).	number(s)
NPN	I. J. Gelb, P. M. Purves, and A. A. McRae, *Nuzi Personal Names. OIP,* 57 (1943)
N.S.	New Series
NT	New Testament, Neues Testament, etc.
NTT	*Norsk teologisk Tidsskrift,* Oslo
obj.	object
OBO	*Orbis biblicus et orientalis,* Fribourg, Göttingen
obv.	obverse of a papyrus or tablet
OIP	*Oriental Institute Publications,* Chicago
OLZ	*Orientalistische Literaturzeitung,* Leipzig, Berlin
Or	*Orientalia,* Rome
OrAnt	*Oriens antiquus,* Rome
OrNeer	*Orientalia neerlandica,* Leiden
OSA	Old South Arabic
OT	Old Testament, Oude Testament, etc.
OTL	*The Old Testament Library,* Philadelphia
OTS	*Oudtestamentische Studiën,* Leiden
p(p).	page(s)
P	Priestly source
PAAJR	*Proceedings of the American Academy for Jewish Research,* Philadelphia
par.	parallel/and parallel passages
pass.	passive
PCIS	*Inscriptiones phoeniciae* (= *CIS,* I/3)
PEQ	*Palestine Exploration Quarterly,* London
perf.	perfect
Phil.-hist. Kl.	Philosophische-historische Klasse
Phoen.	Phoenician
PJ	*Palästinajahrbuch,* Berlin

pl(s).	plate(s)
pl.	plural
PLO	*Porta linguarum orientalium,* Wiesbaden
PN	Personal name
PN	H. Ranke, *Die ägyptischen Personennamen,* 2 vols. (Glückstadt, 1935-1952)
PNPI	J. K. Stark, *Personal Names in Palmyrene Inscriptions* (Oxford, 1971)
PNU	F. Grondähl, *Die Personennamen der Texte aus Ugarit. StPohl,* 1 (1967)
POS	*Pretoria Oriental Series,* Leiden
prep.	preposition
PRU	*Le Palais royal d'Ugarit,* ed. C. F.-A. Schaeffer and J. Nougayrol, Paris
PSBA	*Proceedings of the Society of Biblical Archaeology,* Bloomsbury
ptcp.	participle
PW	A. Pauly-G. Wissowa, *Real-Encyclopädie der classischen Altertumswissenschaft,* 11 vols. (Stuttgart, 1839-1852; sups. 1903-1956); ser. 2, 10 vols. (1914-1948)
Pyr.	K. Sethe, *Die altägyptischen Pyramidentexte,* 4 vols. (Leipzig, 1908-1922)
Q	*Qere*
Q	Qumran scroll (preceded by arabic numeral designating cave)
Qat.	Qatabanian
QuadSem	*Quaderni di semitistica,* Florence
QuaestDisp	*Quaestiones disputatae,* ed. K. Rahner and H. Schlier (New York, 1961—)
RA	*Revue d'assyriologie et d'archéologie orientale,* Paris
RAC	*Reallexikon für Antike und Christentum,* ed. T. Klauser (Stuttgart, 1950—)
RÄR	H. Bonnet, *Reallexikon der ägyptischen Religionsgeschichte* (Berlin, 1952, ²1971)
RB	*Revue biblique,* Paris
RdM	*Die Religionen der Menschheit,* ed. C. M. Schröder, Stuttgart
REJ	*Revue des études juives,* Paris
repr.	reprint, reprinted
RÉS (with number of text)	*Répertoire d'épigraphie sémitique,* Paris
rev.	revised, revision
RevQ	*Revue de Qumrân,* Paris
RGG	*Die Religion in Geschichte und Gegenwart* (Tübingen, ²1927-1931, ed. H. Gunkel–L. Zscharnack, 5 vols.; ³1957-1965, ed. K.Galling, 6 vols.)
RHPR	*Revue d'histoire et de philosophie religieuses,* Strasbourg, Paris
RHR	*Revue de l'histoire des religions,* Paris
RivBibl	*Rivista biblica,* Rome, Brescia
RS	Ras Shamra text
RScR	*Recherches de science religieuse,* Paris
RSF	*Rivista di studi fenici,* Rome
RSO	*Rivista degli studi orientali,* Rome
RSP	*Ras Shamra Parallels: The Texts from Ugarit and the Hebrew Bible,* ed. L. R. Fisher *et al.,* I, *AnOr,* 49 (1972); II, *AnOr,* 50 (1975); III, *AnOr,* 51 (1981)
RSPT	*Revue des sciences philosophiques et théologiques,* Paris
RSV	*Revised Standard Version* (New York, 1946, 1952)
rto.	recto, on the obverse of a papyrus or tablet
RTP	*Revue de théologie et de philosophie,* Lausanne
RyNP	G. Ryckmans, *Les noms propres sud-sémitiques,* 3 vols. *Bibliothèque de muséon,* 2 (Louvain, 1934-35)
SaBi	*La sacra bibbia,* Turin

SAHG	A. Falkenstein and W. von Soden, *Sumerische und akkadische Hymnen und Gebete* (Zurich, 1953)
Sam.	Samaritan
SAW	*Sitzungsberichite der Österreichischen Akademie der Wissenschaften in Wien,* Vienna
SBAW	*Sitzungsberichte der Bayerischen Akademie der Wissenschaften,* Munich
SBFLA	*Studii biblici franciscani liber annuus,* Jerusalem
SBL	Society of Biblical Literature
SBS	*Stuttgarter Bibel-Studien*
SBT	*Studies in Biblical Theology,* London, Naperville
SchThU	*Schweizerische theologische Umschau,* Bern
SchThZ	*Schweizerische theologische Zeitschrift,* Zurich
ScrHier	*Scripta hierosolymitana,* Jerusalem
SDAW	*Sitzungsberichte der Deutschen Akademie der Wissenschaften zu Berlin*
SEÅ	*Svensk exegetisk åarsbok,* Lund
Sem	*Semitica,* Paris
ser.	series
sg.	singular
SHAW	*Sitzungsberichte der Heidelberger Akademie der Wissenschaften*
ShnatMikr	*Shenaton le-mikra ule-ḥeker ha-mizraḥ ha-kadum* (*Shnatioṇian Annual for Biblical and Ancient Near Eastern Studies*), Jerusalem
SJT	*Scottish Journal of Theology,* Edinburgh
SKAW	*Sitzungsberichte der phil.-hist. Kl. der Kaiserlichen Akademie der Wissenschaften,* Vienna
SNVAO	*Skrifter utgitt av det Norske Videnskaps-Akademi i Oslo,* II. Hist.-ph. Kl.
Sond	Sonderband, Sonderheft
Soq.	Soqoṭri
SPAW	*Sitzungsberichte der Preussischen Akademie der Wissenschaften zu Berlin*
SPIB	*Scripta Pontificii Instituti Biblici,* Rome
SSAW	*Sitzungsberichte der Sächsischen Akademie der Wissenschaften zu Leipzig*
SSN	*Studia semitica neerlandica,* Assen
StANT	*Studien zum Alten und Neuen Testament,* Munich
St.-B.	H. L. Strack–P. Billerbeck, *Kommentar zum NT aus Talmud und Midrasch,* 6 vols. (Munich, 1922-1961)
StBTh	*Studia biblica et theologica,* Pasadena, New Haven
StDI	*Studia et documenta ad iura orientis antiqui pertinentia,* Leiden
STDJ	*Studies on the Texts of the Desert of Judah,* Leiden, Grand Rapids
StFS	*Studia Francisci Scholten,* Leiden
StOr	*Studia orientalia,* Helsinki
StPohl	*Studia Pohl,* Rome
StR	*Studies in Religion/Sciences religieuses,* Toronto
StT	*Studi e testi,* Rome
STT	O. R. Gurney and J. J. Finkelstein, *The Sultantepe Tablets,* I (London, 1957); Gurney and P. Hulin, II (London, 1964)
StTh	*Studia theologica,* Lund, Århus
StUNT	*Studien zur Umwelt des NTs,* Göttingen
subj.	subject
subst.	substantive
suf.	suffix
Sum.	Sumerian
Sup	Supplement(s) (to)
s.v.	*sub voce* (*vocibus*), under the word(s)

SVT	*Supplements to VT,* Leiden
Synt	C. Brockelmann, *Hebräische Syntax* (Neukirchen-Vluyn, 1956)
Syr.	Syriac
Syr.	*Syria. Revue d'art oriental et d'archéologie,* Paris
TAik	*Teologinen aikakauskirja,* Helsinki
Targ.	Targum
TCL	*Textes cunéiformes du Musée du Louvre,* 31 vols. (Paris, 1910-1967)
TDNT	*Theological Dictionary of the NT,* ed. G. Kittel–G. Friedrich, 10 vols. plus index (Eng. trans., Grand Rapids, 1964-1976)
TDOT	*Theological Dictionary of the OT,* ed. G. J. Botterweck–H. Ringgren (Eng. trans., Grand Rapids, 1974—)
ThArb	*Theologische Arbeiten,* Berlin
THAT	*Theologisches Handwörterbuch zum AT,* ed. E. Jenni–C. Westermann, 2 vols. (Munich, 1971-79)
ThB	*Theologische Bücherei,* Munich
ThLZ	*Theologische Literaturzeitung,* Leipzig, Berlin
ThPh	*Theologie und Philosophie,* Freiburg im Breisgau
ThR	*Theologische Rundschau,* Tübingen
ThRv	*Theologische Revue,* Münster
ThSt	*Theologische Studien,* Zurich
ThStKr	*Theologische Studien und Kritiken,* Hamburg, Gotha, Leipzig
ThV	*Theologische Versuche,* Berlin
ThViat	*Theologia Viatorum,* Berlin
ThW	*Theologische Wissenschaft,* Stuttgart
ThZ	*Theologische Zeitschrift,* Basel
Tigr.	Tigriña
TigrWb	E. Littmann–M. Höfner, *Wörterbuch der Tigre-Sprache* (Wiesbaden, 1962)
TR	Textus Receptus
trans.	translation, translated by
TrThSt	*Trierer theologische Studien*
TrThZ	*Trierer theologische Zeitschrift*
UF	*Ugarit-Forschungen,* Neukirchen-Vluyn
Ugar.	Ugaritic
UH	C. H. Gordon, *Ugaritic Handbook. AnOr,* 25 (1947)
UNHAI	*Uitgeven van het Nederlands Historisch-Archæologisch Institut in het Nabije Oosten,* Istanbul
Urk.	*Urkunden des ägyptischen Altertums,* ed. G. Steindorff (Leipzig, Berlin, 1903—)
UT	C. H. Gordon, *Ugaritic Textbook. AnOr,* 38 (1965, [2]1967)
UUÅ	*Uppsala universitetsårsskrift*
v(v).	verse(s)
V	vowel
VAB	*Vorderasiatische Bibliothek* (Leipzig, 1907-1916)
VAWA	*Verhandelingen der Koninklijke Akademie van Wetenschappen Amsterdam, Afdeling Letterkunde*
VD	*Verbum domini,* Rome
VG	C. Brockelmann, *Grundriss der vergleichenden Grammatik der semitischen Sprachen,* 2 vols. (1908-1913, repr. Hildesheim, 1961)
VT	*Vetus Testamentum,* Leiden
Vulg.	Vulgate
WbÄS	A. Erman–H. Grapow, *Wörterbuch der ägyptischen Sprache,* 6 vols. (Leipzig, 1926-1931, repr. 1963)

WBTh	*Wiener Beiträge zur Theologie,* Vienna
WdF	*Wege der Forschung,* Darmstadt
Wehr	H. Wehr, *A Dictionary of Modern Written Arabic,* ed. J. M. Cowan (Ithaca, 1961, ^{3}1971)
Whitaker	R. E. Whitaker, *A Concordance of the Ugaritic Language* (Cambridge, Mass., 1972)
WMANT	*Wissenschaftliche Monographien zum Alten und Neuen Testament,* Neukirchen-Vluyn
WO	*Die Welt des Orients,* Göttingen
WTM	J. Levy, *Wörterbuch über die Talmudim und Midraschim,* 4 vols. (Leipzig, ^{2}1924, repr. 1963)
WUS	J. Aistleitner, *Wörterbuch der ugaritischen Sprache. BSAW,* Phil.-hist. Kl., 106/3 (1963, ^{4}1974)
WZ	*Wissenschaftliche Zeitschrift*
WZKM	*Wiener Zeitschrift für die Kunde des Morgenlandes,* Vienna
ZA	*Zeitschrift für Assyriologie,* Leipzig, Berlin
ZÄS	*Zeitschrift für ägyptische Sprache und Altertumskunde,* Leipzig, Berlin
ZAW	*Zeitschrift für die alttestamentliche Wissenschaft,* Giessen, Berlin
ZBK	*Zürcher Bibelkommentare,* Zurich, Stuttgart
ZDMG	*Zeitschrift der Deutschen Morgenländischen Gesellschaft,* Leipzig, Wiesbaden
ZDPV	*Zeitschrift des Deutschen Palästina-Vereins,* Leipzig, Stuttgart, Wiesbaden
ZKTh	*Zeitschrift für katholische Theologie,* Innsbruck
ZNW	*Zeitschrift für die neutestamentliche Wissenschaft,* Giessen, Berlin
ZRFOP	Zion Research Foundation, *Occasional Publications*
ZS	*Zeitschrift für Semitistik und verwandte Gebiete,* Leipzig
ZThK	*Zeitschrift für Theologie und Kirche,* Tübingen
→	cross-reference within this Dictionary
<	derived from
>	whence derived, to
*	theoretical form

TRANSLITERATION

VOWELS

ַ	a
ֲ	^{a}
ָ	ā
ָה	â
ָיו	āw
ַי	ay
ָי	āy
ֶ	e
ֱ	^{e}
ֶי	ey
ֵ	ē
ֵי	ê
ְ	^{e}
ִ	i
ִי	î
ָ	o
ֳ	^{o}
ֹ	ō
וֹ	ô
ֻ	u, ū
וּ	û

CONSONANTS

א	ʾ
בּ	b
ב	ḇ
גּ	g
ג	ḡ
דּ	d
ד	ḏ
ה, הּ	h
ו	w
ז	z
ח	ḥ
ט	ṭ
י	y
כּ, ךּ	k
כ, ך	ḵ
ל	l
מ, ם	m
נ, ן	n
ס	s
ע	ʿ
פּ	p
פ, ף	p̄
צ, ץ	ṣ
ק	q
ר	r
שׂ	ś
שׁ	š
תּ	t
ת	ṯ

יוֹבֵל *yôḇēl*

Contents: I. 1. Occurrences; 2. Egyptian; 3. Akkadian; 4. Arabic/Phoenician; 5. LXX. II. 1. Connection with the Sabbath Year; 2. Forty-ninth or Fiftieth? 3. Particular or Universal? III. Apparent Stages of Jubilee Legislation. IV. Year of Yahweh's Good Pleasure.

I. 1. *Occurrences.* The word *yôḇēl* never appears in the sense of a (ram's) horn unless accompanied by a word unambiguously meaning "horn" or "trumpet (blast)." In no biblical context is there any indication that *yôḇēl* is a material horn or an allusion to the most notable use of such a trumpet, the Jubilee, thus *šôpᵉrôṯ (hay-)yôḇᵉlîm* (Josh. 6:4,6,8,13). In Josh. 6:5 *qeren hayyôḇēl* is introduced by *mᵉšōḵ,* "blast," so that one may well say that even in Ex. 19:13 *mᵉšōḵ* stands for "trumpet blast" and leaves *yōḇēl* undetermined. Apart from these 6 occurrences, *yôḇēl* (also written *yōḇēl*) is found only 21 times, always for the institution of the release year, either with (Lev. 25:13,28a,40,50,52,54; 27:17,18b,23,24) or without (Lev. 25:10,11,12,15,28b,30,31,33; 27:18a,21; Nu. 36:4) *šᵉnaṯ,* "year." Josh. 6 and Ex. 19:13 are E;[1] Lev. 27 is P, as is Lev. 25 (or H).

---

yôḇēl. J. Bottéro, "Désordre économique et annulation des dettes en Mésopotamie à l'époque paléo-babylonienne," *JESHO,* 4 (1961), 113-146; D. Correns, *Die Mischna Schebiit (vom Sabbatjahr)* (diss., Göttingen, 1954); J. D. Eisenstein, "Sabbatical Year and Jubilee," *JE,* X (1905), 605-8; M. Elon, *Freedom of the Debtor's Person in Jewish Law* (Jerusalem, 1964) [Heb.]; F. Horst, *Das Privilegrecht Jahwes. FRLANT,* 28[45] (1930) = *Gottes Recht. GSAT. ThB,* 12 (1961), 79-103: "Brachjahr und Schuldverhältnisse: 15, 1-18"; *idem,* "Das Eigentum nach dem AT," *Kirche im Volk,* 2 (Essen, 1949), 87-102 = *Gottes Recht,* 203-221; *idem,* "Eigentum. Biblisch," *RGG*³, II, 363ff.; E. Kutsch, "Erlassjahr," *RGG,* II, 568-69; *idem,* "Erwägungen zur Geschichte der Passafeier und des Massotfestes," *ZThK,* 55 (1958), 1-35; N. P. Lemche, "The Manumission of Slaves—The Fallow Year—The Sabbatical Year—The Jobel Year," *VT,* 26 (1976), 38-59, esp. 38-41; E. Neufeld, "Socio-economic Background of Yōbēl and šᵉmiṭṭâ," *RSO,* 33 (1958), 53-124; R. G. North, *Sociology of the Biblical Jubilee. AnBibl,* 4 (1954) [with earlier literature]; N. Sarna, "Zedekiah's Emancipation of Slaves and the Sabbatical Year," *Orient and Occident. Festschrift C. Gordon. AOAT,* 22 (1973), 143-49; E. E. Urbach, "The Laws Regarding Slavery: As a Source for Social History in the Period of the Second Temple, the Mishnah, and Talmud," *Papers of the Institute of Jewish Studies,* 1 (1964), 1-94 = *Zion,* 25 (1960) [Heb.]; G. Wallis, "Das Jobeljahr-Gesetz, eine Novelle zum Sabbatjahr-Gesetz," *MIO,* 15 (1969), 337-345; R. Westbrook, "Jubilee Laws," *ILR,* 6 (1971), 209-226; *idem,* "Redemption of Land," *ILR,* 6 (1971), 367-375; W. Zimmerli, "Das 'Gnadenjahr des Herrn,'" *Archäologie und AT. Festschrift K. Galling* (Tübingen, 1970), 321-332 = *Studien zur Alttestamentlichen Theologie und Prophetie. Gesammelte Aufsätze,* 2. *ThB,* 51 (1974), 222-234; → דרור *dᵉrôr*.

1 O. Eissfeldt, *Hexateuch-Synopse* (²1962; repr. Darmstadt, 1973).

2. *Egyptian.* Egyp. *ḥb śd* is often rendered "jubilee (year)," and there are certain similarities: a universal nationwide jubilation over a lengthy period after a solemn proclamation. But the *ḥb śd* could occur only after some thirty regnal years, and then several times after that for the same Pharaoh. It had nothing to do with a seven-year cycle or with liberation from social injustice or grievances. Such a reform is indeed supposed to have taken place under Horemheb *ca.* 1320 B.C., but unrelated to any *ḥb śd* "once for all," as later also under Bocchoris in 720, which was the precedent for Solon's *seisáchtheia* in 594 B.C.[2]

3. *Akkadian.* Akk. *biltu,* "load, tribute, harvest(-gift),"[3] is linked with *wabālu* and is thus admitted as a quasi-infinitive of *ybl.*[4] According to Gordon,[5] *šūdûtu* could have some remote similarity to the Jubilee or (more likely) the *šᵉmiṭṭâ.*[6] A fragment speaking of a *šᵉmiṭṭâ* or *andurāru* type moratorium has even been claimed to fit the lacunas in CH §68.[7] Bottéro[8] sees the edict of Ammi-ṣaduqa[9] as a kind of *seisáchtheia.* The fallow period in Assyria is discussed by Opitz.[10]

4. *Arabic/Phoenician.* South Arabic inscriptions speak of the deity as owner of the land, as in the legitimation of the jubilee release in Lev. 25:23.[11] Akiba (A.D. 130) claims to have heard in Arabia (or "Gaul," perhaps = "Galatia"[12]) the word *yubla* used for a ram.[13] This was considered a "groundless Jewish myth"[14] until the discovery in 1846 of the Marseilles tariff,[15] where a list of the prices of sacrificial animals includes the line: *bybl ʾm bʿz kll ʾm ṣwʿt ʾm šlm kll lkhnm ksp šql,* "in (the case of) a *ybl* or a goat, a whole offering or a sin offering or a substitutionary offering, the priests (receive) one shekel of silver."[16] Here "sheep" or "ram" fits *ybl* far better than "release year."[17] It is now denied

---

[2] Diodorus Siculus *Library of History* i.79.4; not mentioned in M. Floss, "Σεισάχθεια," *PW,* IIA/1 (1921), 1118; J. Pirenne, "La restauration monarchique en Égypte aux VIIIe-VIe s. av. J.C. et les réformes de Bocchoris et d'Amasis," *AHDO,* 4 (1949), 12.

[3] *AHw,* I (1965), 126; *CAD,* II (1966), 228.

[4] N. Nicolskij, "Die Entstehung des Jobeljahres," *ZAW,* 50 (1932), 216 [commonly ignored], with reference to the "votive gifts" of Lev. 27:17.

[5] C. H. Gordon, "Parallèles nouziens aux lois et coutumes de l'AT," *RB,* 44 (1935), 39.

[6] Sumerian antecedent cited by J. A. van Dijk, review of W. Hallo, *Early Mesopotamian Royal Titles* (Chicago, 1955), *ZA,* N.S. 21[55] (1963), 272.

[7] S. H. Langdon, "A Fragment of the Hammurapi Code," *PSBA,* 36 (1914), 100.

[8] P. 145.

[9] *Ein Edikt des Königs Ammi-Ṣaduqa von Babylon,* ed. F. R. Kraus. *StDI,* 5 (1958), 158; new part from J. J. Finkelstein, "The Edict of Ammiṣaduqa: A New Text," *RA,* 63 (1969), 45-64.

[10] D. Opitz, "Eine Form der Ackerbestellung in Assyrien," *ZA,* N.S. 3[37] (1927), 104-6.

[11] N. Rhodokanakis, "Die Bodenwirtschaft im alten Südarabien," *AWA,* 54 (1916), 176, 190.

[12] P. Benoit, "Rabbi Aqiba ben Joseph sage et héros du judaïsme," *RB,* 54 (1947), 85.

[13] *WTM*; *Roš Haš.* 26b; also 8b, 27a; *ʿArak.* 12b; Jer. Ber. 9, 13e.

[14] J. G. K. Kranold, *De anno Hebraeorum jubilaeo* (Göttingen, 1838), 18.

[15] *KAI,* 69.

[16] *KAI,* 69, 7.

[17] → יבל *ybl.*

that the correspondence between *šôpār,* and Akk. *šapparu,* "wild goat," confirms the use of the same term for "ram" and "horn."[18] More rarely an attempt is made to link the ram as "leader" with the Hebrew (Arabic, Ugaritic) verb *wabala/ybl.*[19]

5. *LXX.* It is nevertheless worth noting that the LXX always renders *yôḇēl* as *áphesis,* "sending away" or "sending back";[20] only in Lev. 25:15 do we find *sēmasía,* "proclamation," alone; in 25:10ff. it is used together with *áphesis.* This agrees with the normal meaning of Heb. *yāḇal,* "bring back," "send back solemnly or abundantly," used of returning exiles (Jer. 31:9; Isa. 55:12), victorious armies (Ps. 60:1[Eng. v. 9] par. 108:11[10]), a funeral cortege (Job 10:19; 21:32), or solemn offerings (Zeph. 3:10; Ps. 68:30[29]; 76:12[11]); cf. also the noun forms (*y*ᵉ)*ḇûl,* "produce of the earth" (Lev. 26:4; Isa. 44:19 [Job 40:20; 37:12 and often *tēḇēl,* "earth"[21]), *yāḇāl,* "stream" (Isa. 30:25; 44:4 [Lev. 22:22; Jer. 17:8; Dnl. 8:2]), possibly also meaning "music" as "that which flows" (Gen. 4:21). On *biltu* as "harvest offering" see I.3 above, as "intercalation," see II.2 below. There is no relationship with "jubilation," Lat. *jubilare,* "shout during harvest."[22] Gk. *híēmi* of itself does not imply solemnity or abundance, and *ybl* does not share the nuance of "back" or "away" explicit in *aphíēmi.* Nevertheless, all occurrences of *áphesis* have overtones of solemnity or abundance as the "restoration of former well-being."

II. 1. *Connection with the Sabbath Year.* Ultimately then, the meaning of Heb. *yôḇēl* must be determined solely from Lev. 25:10.[23] There, in the closest possible relationship to the Sabbath Year, it is a kind of solemn homecoming together with liberation from vague or previously mentioned economic disadvantages; it is a → דרור *d*ᵉ*rôr,* "freeing, freedom of movement." This homecoming must be proclaimed by a blast of the ram's horn (*šôp̱ār*; in other verses *qeren* or *t*ᵉ*ruʿâ*; never *yôḇēl*) in the "fiftieth" year.

2. *Forty-ninth or Fiftieth?* "Fifty" is put in explicit relation with the seventh Sabbath Year, the forty-ninth year, whether as a round number standing for forty-nine itself or as an extra year interrupting the sabbatical cycle (a survival of the earlier "pentecontads" or seven fifty-day periods of the agricultural years).[24] Lev. 25:11 speaks explicitly of one

---

18 B. Landsberger, *Die Fauna des alten Mesopotamien. ASAW,* 42/6 (1934), 96; see now "Tin and Lead: the Adventures of Two Vocables," *JNES,* 24 (1965), 296; W. Heimpel, *Tierbilder in der sumerischen Literatur. StPohl,* 2 (1968), 251.

19 D. Baldi, *Giosué. SaBi* (1956), 46, following E. König, *Historisch-kritisches Lehrgebäude der hebräischen Sprache,* II (Leipzig, 1895), 105; E. Power, "Annus jubilaeus," *VD,* 4 (1924), 353-58.

20 Cf. Josephus *Ant.* iii.12.3 (283): "freedom."

21 → תבל *tbl.*

22 *KBL*³, following J. T. Milik, "De vicissitudinibus notionis et vocabuli iubilaei," *VD,* 28 (1950), 167, contra K. Lokotsch, *Etymologisches Wörterbuch der europäischen . . . Wörter orientalischen Ursprungs* (Heidelberg, 1927), 76.

23 Contra J. Morgenstern, "Jubilee, Year of," *IDB,* II, 1001; W. F. Albright, review of North, *Bibl,* 37 (1956), 490.

24 H. Lewy and J. Lewy, "The Origin of the Week and the Oldest West Asiatic Calendar," *HUCA,* 17 (1942/43), 91.

year's harvest that must serve for three years, seeming to imply two successive fallow years; but this very passage perplexingly calls the years the sixth, seventh, and eighth rather than the forty-eighth, forty-ninth, and fiftieth.

Earlier authors inclined to take this apparent equating of the forty-ninth year with the fiftieth year as an intercalation (*ybl,* "*pro-ducere,* lengthen,"[25] or *epakta,* "intercalary year"[26]) either of a whole year or of forty-nine days (Lev. 25:8),[27] or of just the ten days between the actual beginning of the year and the proclamation "on the tenth of the month" (Tishri, Lev. 25:9).[28]

3. *Particular or Universal?* Relatively unimportant in comparison to the social prescriptions of the Jubilee is the question of whether a "release of the land" was to be celebrated in the forty-ninth year, the fiftieth year, or both. More important is the fact that in any case the Jubilee is a special instance of the "seventh" year (Lev. 25:4,8). This poses the inescapable question whether this "seventh" year is to be identified with the release of a "Hebrew" slave in *his* seventh year as a slave, mentioned in Ex. 21:2, or with Dt. 15:12, where the seventh year of the individual slave seems somehow equated with the universal *šᵉmiṭṭâ* (LXX *áphesis*) immediately preceding. There are indeed differences among these three Sabbath Year prescriptions, but these differences are so slight and ambiguous that it is impossible to say when we are dealing with a seventh year of the universal calendar and when we are dealing with a seventh year that varies with the individual. These three laws share the goal of improving the socio-economic status of the individual and thus of the whole community. This goal is so dominant that it justifies seeing a later idealization or adaptation in the universal year presupposed in some of the details. The ideal picture of a general release taking place at regular intervals was developed from the practice of individual release.

III. Apparent Stages of Jubilee Legislation. Despite the many unanswered questions, it seems profitable to attempt a synthesis of the elements of a striving for socio-economic justice that are found in the Jubilee chapter.

1. Above all, the starting point is probably not the purely agricultural fallow year, as Lev. 25:6 might suggest, but the misery, poverty, weakness, and catastrophes that made life unbearable for some Israelites, as they must for people of any time and place.

2. If these sufferers and their families were not simply to die the cruel death of starvation, they had to get a loan and contract a debt.

---

25 A. Klostermann, "Ueber die kalendarische Bedeutung des Jobeljahres," *ThStKr,* 53 (1880), 723.

26 North, 126.

27 S. Zeitlin, "Notes relatives au calendrier juif," *REJ,* 89 (1930), 354.

28 Cf. J. Wellhausen, *Die Composition des Hexateuchs und der historischen Bücher des ATs* (Berlin, ³1899), 165.

3. Hardly any wealthy person would grant such a loan, not merely because remission of the debt in some "seventh" year was already foreseen from the outset, but in general because the risk of loss was out of all proportion to the expected profit.

4. Instead, the debtor or his son would become the "slave" of the creditor, either as a "live gage" instead of a "mort-gage"[29] or more likely in order to work off the debt gradually.[30] Such a person no longer enjoyed freedom of movement or freedom to earn his livelihood so long as the entire wages of his toil had to be applied to the debt.

5. The duration of individual servitude was limited and prescribed. Hammurabi tolerated only three years;[31] the biblical six years may be not less humane but more realistic. In both cases the principal goal was liberation after a specified period.[32] Unquestionably we are dealing here with accidentally preserved examples of widespread usage, not with mutually dependent practice or independent innovation. Whether some historical occasion of implementation of these laws is to be seen in Jer. 34:14 and Neh. 5:5 is disputed.[33]

6. Even if the poor freedman was likely to fall back at once into debt slavery, this was not to be tolerated more than seven times. Since these fifty adult years constitute a normal life span, it seems obvious that this "liberation" or rather the recovery of free title to landed property was more in the economic interest of the community than of the aged debtor. Much as in the case of Naboth (1 K. 21), the inherited field could never pass totally from the small family into the hands of large landowners (Nu. 36:7).

7. The motive clause in Lev. 25:23, "all the land belongs to me [Yahweh]" (which could originally have been Canaanite and referred to Baal[34]), does not mean that private ownership was either excluded or unrestricted, but rather that property relationships among individuals were to be so regulated that all, rather than just a few, could live in true freedom.

IV. Year of Yahweh's Good Pleasure. These true goals of the various pieces of social legislation, long normative, are summarized in the Jubilee chapter. Jubilee is above all a special kind of emancipation of slaves and land in the seventh year (Lev. 25:1-12).

---

29 H.-M. Weil, "Gage et cautionnement dans la Bible," *AHDO,* 2 (1938), 171; A. Abeles, "Der Bürge nach biblischem Recht," *MGWJ,* 66 (1922), 285.

30 P. Koschaker, "Über einige griechische Rechtsurkunden aus den östlichen Randgebieten des Hellenismus," *ASAW,* 42 (1931), 107.

31 CH §117.

32 H. U. Cazelles, *Études sur le code de l'alliance* (Paris, 1946), 150.

33 On Mic. 2:4, see A. Alt, "Micha 2, 1-5: ΓΗΣ ΑΝΑΔΑΣΜΟΣ in Juda," *Interpretationes ad Vetus Testamentum Pertinentes. Festschrift S. Mowinckel. NTT,* 56 (1955), 13-23 = *KlSchr,* II (1953), 373-381.

34 Horst, *GSAT,* 220.

Undoubtedly it is connected more directly with landed property than with slavery (Lev. 25:10,13,23), but both are seen in concrete relation to debt and loan (Lev. 25:25,35,39; Dt. 15:2,7,12; Neh. 5:7f.). Regulation of various sales contracts with respect to the proximity of the Jubilee release (Lev. 25:28-55; 27:17-24; Nu. 36:4; Ezk. 46:17; personal transactions like *gōʾēl* redemption: Lev. 25:25; Jer. 32:8; the levirate: Dt. 25:5; Ruth 3:13) is spelled out far more minutely than is the case with those prescriptions that superficially seem concerned with agricultural fallow but always have more to do with economic benefits to the underprivileged (Lev. 25:8,12,24). These painfully detailed and hardly realistic norms, whether of fallow or of sale, are probably adjustments added by the compiler in an (exilic) period when the primal conditions demanding economic liberation were no longer experienced in daily life.

One must even admit that this P compiler, with his canonical, casuistic, and liturgical orientation, was thinking more of the ideal or even eschatological overtones of the texts he was transmitting. The colorful and solemn "jubilant streaming toward one's (spiritual) homeland" (more or less like the jubilee pilgrimages to Rome), the "year of the Lord's grace" as an anticipation of the heavenly liberation (Isa. 61:2; Lk. 4:19) or the restoration of all things (Acts 3:21),[35] interested him more than the barely perceptible improvement in the economic lot of one individual after another in little villages over the course of years.

This is not to deny that a universal proclamation of release may have been handed down as part of the primitive legislation: the earliest debt slavery would all have taken place more or less in the first years of Israel's occupation of Canaan and would thus have come to a definitive end in roughly the same year. A solemn proclamation could also be considered to have heralded those emancipations that were to take place only some years later. Thus "this H legislation for the Jubilee Year represents an attempt by early postexilic legislators to solve in an altogether unprecedented manner . . . two problems, of distinctly social character, which had found no effective solution throughout the entire pre-exilic period, and which had presumably become acute once again."[36] "But then we are compelled to conclude that the exilic prophets knew the Jubilee Year as a traditional institution, which the predecessor of Isa. 61 had taken over as a vehicle for his astonishing message of salvation."[37]

North

---

35 H. Wildberger, "Israel und sein Land," *EvTh,* 16 (1956), 419.

36 Morgenstern, *IDB,* II, 1002.

37 Zimmerli, 327 = *Studien,* 228f.

יוֹם *yôm*; יוֹמָם *yômām*; יוֹם יהוה *yôm YHWH*

Contents: I. Ancient Near East: 1. Akkadian; 2. Egyptian. II. 1. Etymology and Occurrences; 2. Forms and Distribution; 3. Phrases; 4. Related Words and Expressions. III. General Usage: 1. Literal Usage; 2. Extended Usage. IV. Theological Usage: 1. Creation; 2. Cult; 3. History. V. Qumran. VI. LXX.

I. Ancient Near East.

1. *Akkadian.* a. The common Semitic noun *yaum,* which does not derive from any verbal root, appears in Akkadian as *ūmu(m)*, in Old Akkadian as *yūmum.* The plural is

---

yôm. S. Aalen, "אוֹר *'ôr,*" *TDOT,* I, 147-167; *idem, Die Begriffe 'Licht' und 'Finsternis' im AT, im Spätjudentum und im Rabbinismus. SNVAO,* 1951/1; J. Barr, *Biblical Words for Time. SBT,* 33 (²1969); J. Bergman, H. Ringgren, and C. Barth, "בֹּקֶר *bōqer,*" *TDOT,* II, 217-228; L. Černý, *The Day of Yahweh and Some Relevant Problems. Práce z vědeckých ústavů,* 53/V (Prague, 1948); G. Dalman, *Aus,* I/2 (1928), 594-642; S. J. DeVries, *Yesterday, Today and Tomorrow* (Grand Rapids, 1975); J. Finegan, *Handbook of Biblical Chronology* (Princeton, 1964); E. Jenni, "יוֹם *yōm* Tag," *THAT,* I, 707-726; M. P. Nilsson, *Primitive Time-Reckoning* (Lund, 1920); G. von Rad and G. Delling, "ἡμέρα," *TDNT,* II, 943-53; M. Sæbø, *Sacharja 9–14. WMANT,* 34 (1969); *idem,* "אוֹר *'ōr Licht,*" *THAT,* I, 84-90; R. de Vaux, *AncIsr,* 178-194, esp. 180-83; J. R. Wilch, *Time and Event* (Leiden, 1969).

On II.1: H. Birkeland, *Akzent und Vokalismus im Althebräischen. SNVAO,* 1940/3; T. Nöldeke, *Neue Beiträge zur semitischen Sprachwissenschaft* (Strasbourg, 1910), 133-35; A. F. Rainey, "The Word 'Day' in Ugaritic and Hebrew," *Lešonénû,* 36 (1971/72), 186-89 [Heb.; Eng. summary].

On II.3: G. W. Buchanan, "Eschatology and the 'End of Days,'" *JNES,* 20 (1961), 188-193; B. S. Childs, "A Study of the Formula, 'Until this Day,'" *JBL,* 82 (1963), 279-292; G. Gerleman, "'Heute', 'Gestern' und 'Morgen' im Hebräischen," *TAik,* 72 (1967), 84-89; H. Kosmala, "'At the End of the Days'," *ASTI,* 2 (1963), 27-37 = *Studies, Essays, and Reviews,* I (Leiden, 1978), 73-83; A. Lefèvre, "L'expression 'En ce jour-là' dans le livre d'Isaie," *Melanges bibliques. Travaux de l'institut catholique de Paris, 4. Festschrift A. Robert. Travaux de l'Institut Catholique de Paris,* 4 (1957), 174-79; E. Lipiński, "באחרית הימים dans les textes préexiliques," *VT,* 20 (1970), 445-450; P. A. Munch, *The Expression bayyôm hāhū'. ANVAO,* II, 1936/2; J. Schreiner, "Das Ende der Tage," *BiLe,* 5 (1964), 180-194; H. Seebass, "אַחֲרִית *'aḥ^arîṯ* ['*ach^arîth*]," *TDOT,* I, 207-212; W. Staerk, "Der Gebrauch der Wendung באחרית הימים im at. Kanon," *ZAW,* 11 (1891), 247-253.

On III.1: J. M. Baumgarten, "The Beginning of the Day in the Calendar of Jubilees," *JBL,* 77 (1958), 355-360; P. J. Heawood, "The Beginning of the Jewish Day," *JQR,* N.S. 36 (1945/46), 393-401; E. Kutsch, "Chronologie. III. Israelitisch-jüdische Chronologie," *RGG³*, I, 1812-14; J. Morgenstern, "The Three Calendars of Ancient Israel," *HUCA,* 1 (1924), 13-78; *idem,* "Supplementary Studies in the Calendars of Ancient Israel," *HUCA,* 10 (1935), 1-148; *idem,* "The Calendar of the Book of Jubilees, its Origin and its Character," *VT,* 5 (1955), 34-76; F. S. North, "Four-month Seasons of the Hebrew Bible," *VT,* 11 (1961), 446-48; J. B. Segal, "Intercalation and the Hebrew Calendar," *VT,* 7 (1957), 250-307; H. R. Stroes, "Does the Day Begin in the Evening or Morning? Some Biblical Observations," *VT,* 16 (1966), 460-475; S. Talmon, "The Calendar Reckoning of the Sect from the Judaean Desert," *Aspects of the Dead Sea Scrolls. ScrHier,* 4 (²1965), 162-199; S. Zeitlin, "The Beginning of the Jewish Day During the Second Commonwealth," *JQR,* N.S. 36 (1945/46), 403-414.

usually *ūmū,* rarely the feminine form *ūmātu(m).* Derivatives include *ūmtum/ūndu,* "specific day"; *ūma(m),* "today"; *ūmakkal,* "(for) one day"; *ūmiš,* "like the bright day"; *ūmišam(ma),* and (only Neo-Bab.) *ūmussu,* "daily"; *ūmšu(m),* "to this day."[1] In the sense of "storm," a meaning not deriving from Proto-Semitic and found only in literary texts, *ūmu* is a loan translation from Sumerian, where *u(d)* means both "day" and "storm." As a term for a mythical lion, *ūmu* occurs only in lexical lists. A purely poetical synonym is *immu(m);*[2] *urru(m)* refers primarily to the dawning day (*urra[m],* "in the morning, tomorrow").

b. Not even the lexica can provide a full listing of the tens of thousands of occurrences. A few illustrations must suffice here. As in other Semitic and Indo-European languages, "day" is understood both in contrast to "night" and as a term including both daytime and nighttime, each divided into six double hours (*bīl/ēru,* lit., "interstice"), the length of which depends on the season. As elsewhere, the primary divisions of the day are morning, midday, and evening.[3] "Day" is used in contrast to "night" in the astronomical omen

---

On IV.1: W. H. Schmidt, *Die Schöpfungsgeschichte der Priesterschrift. WMANT,* 17 (^{2}1967), 67-73; O. H. Steck, *Der Schöpfungsbericht der Priesterschrift. FRLANT,* 115 (1975), 158-177.

On IV.3.b-d (selective bibliog., primarily recent, on the theme of the Day of Yahweh): J. Bourke, "Le Jour de Yahvé dans Joël," *RB,* 66 (1959), 5-31, 191-212; C. Carniti, "L'espressione 'il giorno di Jhwh': origine ed evoluzione semantica," *BeO,* 12 (1970), 11-25; F. Couturier, "Le 'Jour de Yahvé' dans l'AT," *Revue de l'Université d'Ottawa,* 24 (1954), 193-217; G. Eggebrecht, *Die früheste Bedeutung und der Ursprung der Konzeption vom "Tage Jahwes"* (diss., Halle/Wittenberg, 1966/67); A. J. Everson, *The Day of Yahweh as Historical Event* (diss., Union Theological Seminary, Richmond, 1969); *idem,* "The Days of Yahweh," *JBL,* 93 (1974), 329-337; F. C. Fensham, "A Possible Origin of the Concept of the Day of the Lord," *Biblical Essays 1966* (Potchefstroom, 1967), 90-97; J. Gray, "The Day of Yahweh in Cultic Experience and Eschatological Prospect," *SEÅ,* 39 (1974), 5-37; H. Gressmann, *Der Ursprung der israelitisch-jüdischen Eschatologie. FRLANT,* 6 (1905); G. N. M. Habets, *Die grosse Jesaja-Apokalypse (Jes 24–27)* (diss., Bonn, 1974), esp. 334-352; J. Héléva, "L'origine du concept prophétique du 'Jour du Yahve'," *Ephemerides Carmeliticae,* 15 (1964), 3-36; J. Jeremias, *Theophanie: Die Geschichte einer alttestamentlichen Gattung. WMANT,* 10 (^{2}1977), 97-100; E. Kutsch, "Heuschreckenplage und Tag Jahwes in Joel 1 und 2," *ThZ,* 18 (1962), 81-94; R. Largement and H. Lemaître, "Le Jour de Yahweh dans le contexte oriental," *Sacra pagina,* I. *BETL,* 12f. (1959), 259-266; C. van Leeuwen, "The Prophecy of the *Yōm YHWH* in Amos v 18-20," *OTS,* 19 (1974), 113-134; H.-M. Lutz, *Jahwe, Jerusalem und die Völker. WMANT,* 27 (1968); E. G. Medd, *A Historical and Exegetical Study of the "Day of the Lord" in the OT, with Special Reference to the Book of Joel* (diss., St. Andrews, 1968/69); S. Mowinckel, " 'Jahves dag'," *NTT,* 59 (1958), 1-56, 209-229; *idem, Psalmenstudien,* II: *Das Thronbesteigungsfest Jahwäs und der Ursprung der Eschatologie* (1922; repr. Amsterdam, 1961); H.-P. Müller, *Ursprünge und Strukturen alttestamentlicher Eschatologie. BZAW,* 109 (1969), 72-85; H. D. Preuss, *Jahweglaube und Zukunftserwartung. BWANT,* 87[5/7] (1968), 170-79; G. von Rad, "The Origin of the Concept of the Day of Yahweh," *JSS,* 4 (1959), 97-108; K.-D. Schunck, "Strukturlinien in der Entwicklung der Vorstellung vom 'Tag Jahwes'," *VT,* 14 (1964), 319-330; *idem,* "Der 'Tag Jahwes' in der Verkündigung der Propheten," *Kairos,* N.S. 11 (1969), 14-21; J. M. P. Smith, "The Day of Yahweh," *AJT,* 5 (1901), 505-533 = *The Day of Yahweh. University of Chicago Divinity School Studies,* 2 (1901); M. Weiss, "The Origin of the 'Day of the Lord'—Reconsidered," *HUCA,* 37 (1966), 29-71.

1 Citations for all these words will be found in *AHw.*

2 *AHw,* I (1965), 378b; *CAD,* VII (1960), 135a.

3 → בקר *bōqer,* צהרים *ṣoh°rayim,* ערב *ʿereḇ.*

texts and in the astronomical texts of the late period generally; elsewhere this usage is primarily found in literary texts, especially poetry. It is noteworthy that the hymns to Šamaš, the sun-god, who gives light to the darkness, speak only rarely of the bright daytime. In one great hymn,[4] for example, Šamaš is called "illuminator of the day" in one passage[5] but "shortener of the (winter) day" in another.[6] As a result of the intense heat of the summer day, the Babylonians preferred nighttime for many activities, especially marches. Sometimes other gods, for instance Nabû, are called "bright day." The darkening of the day by storm and rain is ascribed to the storm-god. The even more intense darkness brought about by eclipses of the sun was thought a serious disaster; such eclipses, along with eclipses of the moon, were among the major themes of astrology. Curses occasionally include the wish that someone's days be darkened.

c. The day in contrast to the night is also involved in the determination of auspicious and inauspicious days, which played a very important role in Babylonia and Assyria. The hemerologies themselves[7] indicate for every day of the month and year what should be undertaken and what should not. Not even cultic acts are recommended for every single day. Generally unfavorable days include the phases of the moon (seventh, fifteenth [*šapattu*], twenty-second, and twenty-ninth), as well as the nineteenth day, which counted as the forty-ninth day of the preceding month. The omen calendars[8] state the good or evil consequences of specific acts on particular days. Constellations and other ominous occurrences are not equally favorable or unfavorable on all days.

d. Much more often the "day" is a unit of time, e.g., in all kinds of documents. In the cult there were sacrifices and ceremonies to be performed every day, as well as those prescribed only for certain days. We often find *ūmu* in the sense of "festival," albeit usually preceding the name of the festival, e.g., *ūm akīti,* "New Year's day"; *ūm eššēši,* "month festival"; *ūm issini,* "feast day"; *ūm kispi,* "day of sacrifice for the dead"; *ūm tēlilti,* "day of purification"; *ūm rimki,* "day of ablutions"; etc. But we also find such expressions as "day of the god," "day of worshipping the god," and "day of serving the goddess,"[9] as well as "day of wrath," "day of fate," etc.

e. Even more frequently than the pl. *šanātu(m)*, "years," the pl. "days" serves as a term for "time,"[10] in the first instance a lifetime, which the gods can lengthen or shorten. A Neo-Assyrian school tablet containing the terms for the fourth through the ninth decades of life (obviously calculating backward from the end) calls the fifth decade *ūmē kurûti,* "short days," and the seventh *ūmē arkūti,* "long days."[11] For those who did not look for life after death, long days were a major hope, even though the subsequent stages

---

4 *BWL,* 126ff.

5 L. 178.

6 L. 180.

7 E.g., P. C. A. Jensen, *Texte zur assyrisch-babylonischen Religion,* I. *KB,* VI/2 (1915; repr. 1970), 8ff.; R. Labat, *Hémérologies et ménologies d'Assur* (Paris, 1939).

8 Cf. R. Labat, *Un calendrier babylonien des travaux des signes et des mois* (Paris, 1965).

9 Cf. *BWL,* 38, 16, 25f.

10 → עת *ʿēṯ*.

11 *STT,* 400, 45f.

of *šībūtu,* "old age," and *littūtu,* "great old age," were unattainable for most. "Distant days" *(ūmū rūqūtu)* or *ūm(ū) ṣiātim/ṣâti,* "days of distant time," may lie in the past or future, *ūmū ullûtu* or later *ūmē pāni* only in the past. The future is denoted, for example, by such expressions as *ūmū dārûtu(m)* and *warkiāt/arkât ūmī* and adverbial expressions like *aḫriātiš, dāriš,* or *labāriš ūmī,* "for later time." Only rarely do we find in references to an evil fate the expression *ina lā ūmī-šu,* "in his 'not' days," "at a bad time."[12]

f. Finally, *ūmu* is used (early in the pl. only, later in the sg.) in the sense of "weather"; cf., e.g., *ūmū dannū,* "the weather is bad";[13] *kī ūmū iṭṭībū,* "as soon as the weather has improved."[14]

Von Soden

2. *Egyptian.* a. Of the Egyptian words for "day,"[15] *hrw*[16] is the most important noun. In dates we find from the Middle Kingdom on the special word *św.*[17] The word *dny.t* (*ḏny.t*[18]) denotes the day of the first and third quarter of the moon, while *ʿrky*[19] means the last day of the month or of the year (in the phrase *ʿrḳy rnp.t*). In the later period, special names developed for most of the days of the month.[20] For "every day" the expression *rʿ nb* (lit., "every sun") is used more often than *hrw nb.* "Day by day" is *hrw ḥr hrw.* "Today" is *hrw pn* or in Late Egyptian *p3 hrw.* For the formula "by day and night," we find *m hrwm grḥ* or *grḥ my hrw.*[21] The dawn is called *ḥḏ-t3,* "the brightening of the land"—cf. the verb *ḥḏ-t3,* "dawn"—and the beginning of the day is *wp-hrw*.

b. The noun *hrw,* which derives etymologically from *hrw,* "be content, calm, happy," has as its determinative sign a sun. It refers to the day as brightness, the period when the sun shines. But *hrw* can also stand for "day and night." The day begins in the morning at or after dawn. Night (*grḥ,* connected with *grh,* "cease," and *gr,* "be silent") stands for the other period, between one sun and the next or between yesterday and the morrow. In the calendar the night goes with the preceding day, but in the cult it introduces the coming festival. The date changes at sunrise, and hours are counted from the beginning of the day. Day and night each have twelve hours, which accordingly vary in length with the seasons. A month comprises thirty days. The year with its twelve months totals 360 days, to which are added five intercalary days, "those (days) outside (time)."

c. The observation of time and the determination of each day's character began early in Egypt. The *horoskopoi* ("time observers") of the temples are famous. Hemerologies became popular. From the Middle Kingdom on, we find entries for each day of the month;

---

12 *BWL,* 132, 114.

13 *AHw,* I, 159a on 4b.

14 J. A. Knudtzon, *Die El-Amarna-Tafeln. VAB,* 2 (1915), 7, 59.

15 *WbÄS,* VI, 153.

16 *WbÄS,* II, 492ff.

17 *WbÄS,* IV, 58.

18 *WbÄS,* V, 465.

19 *WbÄS,* I, 212.

20 *WbÄS,* VI, 153; H. K. Brugsch, *Thesaurus inscriptionum aegyptiacarum,* I (Leipzig, 1883), 46-52.

21 *WbÄS,* II, 499, 1.

from the New Kingdom, for each day of the year. The categories are "good" and "bad," often subdivided more precisely into the three possibilities of "dubious," "bad," and "adverse." Each day usually has three entries, which probably stand for morning, midday, and evening. The nature of the days is often given a mythical explanation, and specific advice (concerning such matters as sacrifice, food, travel, and sexual intercourse) is appended. "On these bad days do not work on grain and clothing; do not begin anything," we read with reference to the intercalary days, which were of special importance as the birthdays of the five deities Osiris, Seth, Horus, Isis, and Nephthys.[22] Special protective books were composed for guidance during them. Besides the simple names reflecting the birth of the deities (e.g., "Birth of Osiris"), strange terms appear in the New Kingdom ("Nile perch in its pond," "Child in its nest," etc.). We are assured: "Whoever knows the names of the intercalary days will neither hunger nor thirst. He will not fall victim to the annual plague. Sachmet has no power over him."[23] The hemerology of the Egyptians exercised great influence in the ancient world, as the mention of the *dies Aegyptica* in the calendars of late antiquity attests.[24]

d. Fundamental for the Egyptians was the rhythm of day and night, called the "two times" *(tr.wy)*. The polar formula "day and night" can express totality by merism. The statement "You have power by day, you cause trembling in the night"[25] attests the total sovereignty of the god. The notion of the sun and moon as the two eyes of the god of heaven (e.g., Khenti-Irti) bears witness to a god who moves into day through night in an eternal cycle. The daily renewal of life, based on a conception repeated every night and a rebirth that takes place each day, is the primary theme of the Egyptian hymns to the sun.[26] "Praise to you, arising day by day, bringing yourself forth every morning"—this is the basic tone of the important Egyptian morning worship in the temple.[27] Therefore the god can be addressed: "O lord of the day, who creates the night,"[28] but also: "O lord of the darkness, who creates the light." More commonly, however, we find a polarity in which light and life appear as positive counterparts to darkness and death. A typical saying of the dead reads: "It is my dread to go forth in the night; I will go forth in the day. I am begotten in the night, but born during the day."[29] The expression *pr.t m hrw,* "going forth by day," is familiar as the title of the Egyptian Book of the Dead; it expresses the highest yearning of the dead. "The day at its coming forth" appears also as a royal title.[30]

e. The phrase *hrw nfr,* "good, perfect day," is very common, and may be translated "festival."[31] From the Old Kingdom on, it even appears as a personal name,[32] possibly

---

22 S. Schott, *Altägyptische Festdaten. AAWLM,* 1950/10, 887ff.
23 Book of Intercalary Days, 2, 6-7; cited by Schott, 889.
24 Cf. T. Hopfner, *Fontes historiae religionis aegypticae* (Bonn, 1922), 521ff., 561ff., 647.
25 *Pyr.,* 2110.
26 Cf. J. Assmann, *Liturgische Lieder an den Sonnengott,* I (Berlin, 1969), 118ff., 180f.
27 → בקר *bōqer* I.1.
28 *Urk.,* VI, 119.
29 *CT,* VI, 86.
30 *Urk.,* III, 60.
31 Cf. H. te Velde, *De goede dag der oude Egyptenaren* (Leiden, 1971).
32 *PN,* I, 231, 4.

because the person in question was born on a festival. The phrase refers to the appropriate time to celebrate festivities and to drink. A hymn to Isis begins thus: "Beautiful day! Heaven and earth rejoice, since Isis gave birth in Chemmis. . . ."[33] A wonderful description of the "beautiful day," i.e., well-ordered time, appears in a hymn recited by Thoth during the battle between Horus and Seth.

O beautiful day, when Horus is lord of this land!
O beautiful day on this day, which is divided into its minutes!
O beautiful day in this night, which is divided into its hours!
O beautiful day in this month, which is divided into its fifteen-day periods!
O beautiful day in this year, which is divided into its months!
O beautiful day in this age, which is divided into its years!
O beautiful day of this eternity. . . .[34]

A love song contains the following variation:

O beautiful day in this night!
Tomorrow we shall say anew, how fresh is the morning!
It is more beautiful than yesterday!
Because it is so beautiful, let us celebrate a very beautiful day![35]

f. The festival calendars of both the various temples and court of the king include a series of festivals.[36] Several of them have names based on *hrw*, e.g., "day of the great going forth of Osiris," "day of the purification of the nonad," "day of setting up the *djed* pillar," "day of the hazard festival." The great celebrations lasted several days. Under Ramses III, the famous festival of Opet ran for twenty-seven days! In addition, there were various commemorative days in the family sphere: "birthday," "this day of landing (= death)," "the day of judgment," etc.[37]

The Egyptians do not speak of a "day of God." Instead they can speak of "the time of the God" (e.g., Seth) as the culmination of his power.[38] Both persons or gods and natural phenomena have their times, but these are expressed by different words (*ꜣ.t* for persons, *tr* for natural phenomena).

Bergman

II. The Hebrew noun *yôm*, "day," which belongs primarily to everyday language, is very common.[39] It has a wide range of usage, which will here attract most of our attention.[40]

1. *Etymology and Occurrences.* The etymology of the word, which is found

---

33 H. Junker and E. Winter, *Das Geburtshaus des Tempels der Isis in Philä. DAWS* (1965), 13f.
34 E. Chassinat, *Le temple d'Edfou,* VI (Paris, 1931), 61.
35 S. Schott, *Altägyptische Liebeslieder* (Zurich, 1950), no. 92, p. 130.
36 *RÄR,* 184-87, *s.v.* "Feste"; Schott, *Altägyptische Festdaten,* 959-993.
37 *WbÄS,* II, 500, 1ff.
38 S. Morenz, *Egyptian Religion* (Eng. trans., Ithaca, N.Y., 1973), 76ff.
39 See II.2 below.
40 Cf. Černý, 5-26.

throughout the Semitic languages,[41] is unexplained. Akk. *ūmu,* "day," also has the meaning "storm"; but the extent to which this may cast light on the etymology[42] remains unclear.[43] Etymological analysis is even more difficult because the root from which the word is derived is obscure.

Some scholars such as Nöldeke have assumed a biliteral root *ym;* the majority, however, favor a triliteral *ywm.*[44] In this case, the pl. *yāmîm (*yam-),* which diverges from the sg. **yaum,* is usually explained as assimilation to the similar word *šānîm,* "years."[45] In the individual Semitic languages, however, we find a complex alternation of *ym* and *ywm* in the singular, as well as an *o* vowel in the plural alongside the basic form **yam-;*[46] this raises the question of whether this complex situation is not better explained by structural and phonological considerations, but the evidence has not been examined from this perspective. (Sperber[47] sees here only a reflection of two different Hebrew dialects.) In this case, however, it would be reasonable to assume that the weak /*w*/ of a basic form **yaum*(*u*) was elided or contracted.[48] This form was then realized differently in the various languages, in both singular and plural.

From this point of view we need not be surprised at the common pl. *yāmîm* or other plural forms (*yāmîn,* Dnl. 12:13; *yᵉmôṯ,* Dt. 32:7; Ps. 90:15, in each case par. the unusual pl. *šᵉnôṯ,* "years"[49]), or treat them as "divergent" in comparison to the singular. Because of the linguistic variety on this point, the forms can be understood as different realizations of the single root **yaum*(*u*), whether the variation is between dialects or individual languages.

2. *Forms and Distribution.* The word group that derives most probably from **yaum*(*u*) does not contain any verbs, but is represented almost exclusively by the subst. *yôm,* "day." With 2,304 Hebrew occurrences and 16 Aramaic, it is the fifth most frequent noun in the OT;[50] *yôm* is thus also by far the most common expression of time (in comparison

---

41 G. Bergsträsser, *Introduction to the Semitic Languages* (Eng. trans., Winona Lake, 1983), 214f.; *BDB; KBL*³.

42 Cf. G. R. Driver, "Isaiah I-XXXIX: Textual and Linguistic Problems," *JSS,* 13 (1968), 46f., on Isa. 21:1.

43 Cf. Černý, 10f.; I.1.a above.

44 Cf. J. Barth, "Formangleichung bei begrifflichen Korrespondenzen," *Orientalische Studien. Festschrift T. Nöldeke* (Giessen, 1906), II, 791f.; *BLe,* §618n; *VG,* I, 74, 430; Joüon, 140; *GesB; KBL*³.

45 Most recently *KBL*³; cf. also D. Michel, *Grundlegung einer hebräischen Syntax* (Neukirchen-Vluyn, 1977), 1, 90.

46 R. Meyer, *Hebräische Grammatik* (Berlin, ³1969), II, §83; also references to the variants in *DISO,* 107f.; F. M. Cross and D. N. Freedman, *Early Hebrew Orthography. AOS,* 36 (1952; repr. 1981), 50, 53; *KAI,* III, 10; *BDB; KBL*³.

47 A. Sperber, *A Historical Grammar of Biblical Hebrew* (Leiden, 1966), 140.

48 Birkeland, 41ff.

49 See M. Dahood and T. Penar, "Ugaritic-Hebrew Parallel Pairs," *RSP,* I, 207; M. Dahood, *Psalms,* II. *AB,* 17 (³1979), 326.

50 Jenni, 707f., 714; *idem,* "עֵת *ʿēṯ* Zeit," *THAT,* II, 371; cf. → עת *ʿēṯ.* A very different count is found in Černý, 5; and *KBL*³.

to *ʿôlām,* "long time," "eternity," with 440 Hebrew and 20 Aramaic occurrences,[51] and *ʿēṯ,* "time," with 296 occurrences[52]). The only other derivative is the adverbial *yômām,* "by day,"[53] with 51 occurrences including Nu. 10:34.[54]

Jenni[55] has included in his statistics the disputed passage Isa. 54:9, but without good reason.[56] It is noteworthy that the singular is always written plene except possibly in Jer. 17:11, where the *qere* form *ymyw* is usually read.[57] There are weighty arguments against the proposed emendation of *ywm* in Job 3:8 to *ym,* "sea,"[58] and the opposite change of *ym,* "sea," to *ywm* in Zec. 10:11.[59] The defectively written plural in Nu. 6:5 is unique.

The singular (1,452 occurrences in Hebrew, 5 in Aramaic) appears in all the books of the OT; it is especially common in the historical books, followed by the prophetic books (above all Isaiah, Jeremiah, and Ezekiel, as well as Zephaniah and Zechariah) and the Psalms. The plural (847 occurrences in Hebrew, 11 in Aramaic) appears in all the books except Obadiah, Haggai, and the Song of Songs. The dual *yômayim/yômāyim* (or *yōmayim/yōmāyim*) appears only 5 times: Ex. 16:29; 21:21; Nu. 9:22; 11:19; Hos. 6:2.[60] There is also a strange plural form with the ending *-â* (*yāmîmâ*) found 5 times: Ex. 13:10; Jgs. 11:40; 21:19; 1 S. 1:3; 2:19.[61] It always follows *miyyāmîm,* with which it constitutes a fixed adverbial formula meaning "year by year."[62]

3. *Phrases.* This formal survey has contributed little to the meaning of *yôm/yāmîm/yômām.* The semantic content of the words can be seen more directly and more clearly in their various combinations with other words and their extended semantic field, since *yôm* and *yāmîm,* and to an extent also *yômām,* are seldom syntactically independent. They are usually associated closely with another word or word element, more frequently than as subject (182 times) or as object (81 times).[63] The compound expressions are multiform and can express various shades of meaning.

a. The repetition of the indefinite sg. *yôm yôm,* "daily," expresses distribution (e.g., Gen. 39:10;[64] possibly also in Ugaritic[65]). The repeated words can also (esp. in later documents) be linked (*yôm wāyôm,* Est. 3:4) or expanded by the addition of a preposition

---

51 E. Jenni, "עוֹלָם *ʿōlām Ewigkeit,*" *THAT,* II, 228-243.

52 *Idem, THAT,* II, 370-385.

53 For the form, see *GK,* §100g; *BLe,* §529y; Meyer, II, §39; *DISO,* 108, 55.

54 S. Mandelkern, *Veteris Testamenti Concordantiae Hebraicae atque Chaldaicae* (New York, ²1955); Jenni, *THAT,* I, 708; *KBL*³ has a different count.

55 *THAT,* I, 708; also G. Lisowsky, *Konkordanz zum hebräischen AT* (Stuttgart, ²1966).

56 Mandelkern; *BHS,* but not *BHK.*

57 Cf. K. Rudolph, *Jeremia. HAT,* 12 (³1968), 114.

58 Cf. G. Fohrer, *Das Buch Hiob. KAT,* XVI (1963), 110; *KBL*³, 396a.

59 Cf. Sæbø, *Sacharja 9–14,* 222.

60 Cf. Meyer, II, §43.

61 Cf. *GK,* §90h.

62 See II.4 below.

63 Lisowsky, 594ff.

64 *Synt,* §129a.

65 Cf. *UT,* 2062:A (= *PRU,* V, 88), 10 (lower edge), and no. 1100; but negatively, *KTU,* 2.47.

(*yôm b^eyôm,* Neh. 8:18; expanded in turn to *l^{eʿ}eṯ-yôm b^eyôm,* 1 Ch. 12:23[22]; cf. *d^eḇar-/biḏbar-/liḏbar-yôm b^eyômô,* "as each day requires," e.g., Ex. 5:13/2 Ch. 8:13/8:14; also *l^eyôm b^eyôm,* 2 Ch. 24:11; cf. *k^eyôm b^eyôm,* "as on every day," 1 S. 18:10).[66] Similar in meaning is *kol-yôm,* "every day" (Ps. 140:3[2]), expanded to *b^eḵol-yôm* (e.g., Ps. 7:12[11]).[67]

b. As the preceding section has already shown, the word is used frequently with prepositions, as is also true of other words connected with time.[68] The prepositional phrases, some of which appear to be formulaic, usually function adverbially to convey temporal meaning; precise differentiation is often difficult.[69] Of 2,304 occurrences of *yôm/yāmîm* in the Hebrew OT, 1057 (45.9%) involve a preposition (esp. with the singular). The most common is *b^e* (as is also true for *ʿēṯ*[70]), which appears 728 times (68.9%), 590 times with the singular and 138 with the plural. We find *ʿaḏ* 121 times (7 times *w^eʿaḏ,* each time following *min* to indicate a period of time), *l^e* 71 times, *k^e* 76 times (in this context not a comparative particle in the strict sense[71]), and *min* 66 times. By contrast, *yômām* is used with a preposition only once: with *b^e* in Neh. 9:19.[72]

c. The meaning "day" is more or less weakened when a prepositional phrase with *yôm* (or occasionally *y^emê*) is itself linked with a verb. The most important usage of this type is *b^eyôm* with an infinitive (almost 70 times) as a general indication of time or a temporal conjunction meaning "when," although the basic meaning "day" need not be totally absent (cf. the important passage Gen. 2:4b following the seven-day schema of creation[73]). Other prepositions than *b^e* are also found (*ʿaḏ, k^e, l^e, min*), as are other forms of the verb (perfect and imperfect).[74] In Lev. 14:57, with the meaning "when" in a noun clause, *yôm* has lost all trace of the meaning "day."

d. In addition, important common formulas expressing time are composed of prepositional phrases with *yôm* (rarely *yāmîm*) and a demonstrative pronoun. These formulas also have a variety of adverbial meanings.

The formula *ʿaḏ-hayyôm hazzeh,* "to this day," "until now," appears 84 times.[75] It also appears in an abbreviated form (*ʿaḏ-hayyôm,* "until now," Gen. 19:38) and an emphatically expanded form (*ʿaḏ-ʿeṣem hayyôm hazzeh,* "until this very day," Lev. 23:14; Josh. 10:27; Ezk. 2:3; cf. the corresponding formula *b^{eʿ}eṣem hayyôm hazzeh,* which appears 13 times and often in a shorter form). In this formula, the definite sg. *hayyôm,* which is very frequent (some 350 occurrences[76]) with a variety of meanings, constitutes the

---

66 See also *BDB,* §7e; Jenni, *THAT,* I, 716, §4; *KBL*³, 382; cf. *DISO,* 108, §9, 11; *KAI,* III, 10.
67 Cf. *GK,* §127b.
68 Cf. Jenni, *THAT,* II, 228-235, 372-77 on *ʿôlām* and *ʿēṯ*.
69 Cf. *BDB,* 399b-401a; Jenni, *THAT,* 711-721; *KBL*³, 383f., §10.
70 See Jenni, *THAT,* II, 372f.
71 *Ibid.,* 373.
72 *BDB,* 401, §1.
73 C. Westermann, *Genesis 1–11* (Eng. trans., Minneapolis, 1984), 198.
74 Jenni, *THAT,* I, 711, with full citations; also *BDB,* 400a, §7d.
75 Childs, 280.
76 Jenni, *THAT,* I, 714.

semantic focus.[77] The formula *ʿaḏ-hayyôm hazzeh* thus emphasizes the present status of the narrator (or redactor) or of what is narrated,[78] but also—through the prep. *ʿaḏ*—the continued existence of a situation into this present. When the prep. *min,* "from," also appears, it increases the sense that an important span of time is involved (e.g., Ex. 10:6; Jgs. 19:30; 1 S. 12:2).[79] This formula serves to express the importance of some historical datum for the present, or else to confirm it with the aid of the present (e.g., Dt. 6:24; 10:15; 29:27[28]; 1 K. 3:6; 8:24; elsewhere primarily in Deuteronomy, Deuteronomistic literature, and the Chronicler's history).

When the formula establishes a connection with an event in the distant past, it sometimes serves to explain a name or a present phenomenon (as in Gen. 26:33; Josh. 7:26; Jgs. 18:12; 2 Ch. 20:26). Under such circumstances, scholars are not agreed as to how to treat the etiological question. Disagreeing with Alt[80] and—with some modification—Noth,[81] Childs[82] concludes that this formula "seldom has an etiological function of justifying an existing phenomenon, but in the great majority of cases is a formula of personal testimony added to, and confirming, a received tradition."[83]

Another formula, even more important theologically, is *bayyôm hahûʾ*, "on that day," which occurs much more frequently than the one just discussed (208 times according to Mandelkern).[84] Of these occurrences, 69 (33%) are in the Deuteronomistic history and 109 (52.4%) in the prophets. Of the latter, 45 are in Isaiah and 17 in Zec. 12–14. The only occurrence in the Psalms is Ps. 146:4.[85] The formula can sometimes be shortened to *bayyôm* (Jgs. 13:10) or expanded by the addition of prepositional and adverbial elements.[86] In the first instance it denotes a specific point in time, a "day" that can be emphasized ("on the same day") or reduced to a mere "then." This affects primarily the use of the formula as an adverb of time in texts referring to the past,[87] in which it can refer to a specific "day" in the past (e.g., Gen. 15:18 [J[88]]; Ex. 14:30; Josh 9:27), the simultaneity of two events (e.g., Gen. 26:32; Dt. 21:23), or even some future "day" (e.g., Dt. 31:17f.). In future-oriented (primarily prophetic) texts,[89] the formula often gives the impression that the "day" can refer not just to some short period but equally well to a

---

77 See above all DeVries, 139-277, with a discussion of all the relevant texts.

78 M. Noth, *Könige 1–16, BK,* IX/1 (1968), 180.

79 Childs, 280.

80 A. Alt, "Josua," *Werden und Wesen des ATs. BZAW,* 66 (1936), 13-29 = *KlSchr,* I (1953), 176-192.

81 M. Noth, "Der Beitrag der Archäologie zur Geschichte Israels," *Congress Volume, Oxford 1959. SVT,* 7 (1960), 262-282 = *Aufsätze zur biblischen Landes- und Altertumskunde* (Neukirchen-Vluyn, 1971), I, 34-51.

82 P. 292.

83 See also B. O. Long, *The Problem of Etiological Narrative in the OT. BZAW,* 108 (1968), 6-8, 90-93.

84 Cf. H. Gressmann, *Der Messias. FRLANT,* 26[43] (1929), 83; Sæbø, *Sacharja 9–14,* 261.

85 Cf. Lefèvre.

86 Jenni, *THAT,* I, 715.

87 DeVries, 57-136.

88 Cf. Munch, 8.

89 DeVries, 281-331.

lengthy period of indefinite duration (e.g., Isa. 2:20; 3:18; 4:2; 7:18; Jer. 4:9; Am. 8:3,9; Zec. 14:6f.), which is otherwise generally expressed by the pl. *yāmîm,* "days."[90] Here the formula approaches such similar formulas as *bayyāmîm hāhēm(mâ),* "in those days" (e.g., Jer. 3:16; 5:18; Zec. 8:6)[91] or *bā'ēṯ hahî',* "in that time" (e.g., Isa. 20:2; Jer. 3:17; 4:11).[92] Here it also comes close to the special prophetic expression *yôm YHWH,* "day of Yahweh."[93] In the prophetic texts, *bayyôm hahû'* appears to be used especially in later strata of tradition and largely for redactional purposes: sometimes to link,[94] sometimes to interpolate passages,[95] sometimes to construct a framework (esp. in Zec. 12f.).[96] Without losing its nature as a temporal adverb, the formula thus takes on functions that lend it the character of an "eschatological term"; in later prophetic traditions it became a characteristic of eschatological style.[97]

Contrary to Gressmann,[98] who attempted to demonstrate that "the expression 'on that day' is presupposed as an [eschatological] *terminus technicus* even before Amos,"[99] Munch seeks to show that the eschatological interpretation is totally unnecessary because the formula can be understood in all contexts as a temporal adverb. Although his view has found general acceptance, a certain one-sidedness in his analysis and his insistence on posing the question as an either/or have been criticized.[100] What had been a sharp controversy over this question seems now to have been replaced by a more judicious and nuanced functional description.

e. Semantically important are the genitive phrases defining *yôm/yāmîm,* which are many and various.[101] In construct phrases the noun appears most frequently as *nomen regens* (*yôm/y^emê*) but also not uncommonly as *nomen rectum* (*yôm, hayyôm/yāmîm, hayyāmîm*) qualified by other nouns or phrases. It can also further define other nouns or circumstances.

As *nomen regens, yôm* usually refers to a specific day, the nature of which is defined by the following *nomen rectum.* Either *yôm* or *y^emê* can be defined more precisely in calendrical terms (e.g., *yôm-haḥōḏeš,* "day of the new moon," "first day of the month" [Ex. 40:2]; *yôm hakkese',* "day of the full moon" [Prov. 7:20]; [*šešeṯ*] *y^emê hamma'^aśeh,* "[six] workdays" [Ezk. 46:1]), a usage especially typical of the cultic sphere (e.g., *yôm haššabbāṯ,* "day of rest," "Sabbath" [Ex. 20:8,11]; *yôm mô'ēḏ,* "festival day," par. *yôm*

90 See below.

91 Cf. Gressmann, *Der Messias,* 83-84; also used of the past; cf. Jenni, *THAT,* I, 720.

92 Cf. Gressmann, *Der Messias,* 83f.; Wilch, 47-104; J. G. Plöger, *Literarkritische, formgeschichtliche und stilkritische Untersuchungen zum Deuteronomium. BBB,* 26 (1967), 218-225.

93 See IV.3.b-e below.

94 Munch, 15-20; DeVries, 310-14.

95 DeVries, 297-310.

96 Sæbø, *Sacharja 9–14,* 264-66.

97 Cf. IV.3.e below.

98 *Der Messias,* 82-87; cf. *idem, Der Ursprung,* 336.

99 *Der Messias,* 86.

100 See the review by W. Rudolph, *OLZ,* 40 (1937), 621ff.; Sæbø, *Sacharja 9–14,* 262-63; De Vries, 57-58, 285f.

101 Full citations in Jenni, *THAT,* I, 711-14, 718-720; cf. *BDB, KBL*³.

ḥag YHWH, "day of the festival of Yahweh" [Hos. 9:5]; also further defined, e.g., *yôm t^{e}rû'â,* "day of blowing the trumpets" [Nu. 29:1]; *yôm ṣôm,* "day of fasting" [Isa. 58:3]).[102]

The *nomen rectum* can also define the nature of the day meteorologically (e.g., *yôm haggešem,* "day of rain" [Ezk. 1:28]; *yôm haššeleg,* "day with snow" [2 S. 23:20]; *yôm qāḏîm,* "day with an east wind" [Isa. 27:8]), with reference to human activities (e.g., *yôm qāṣîr,* "harvest day" [Prov. 25:13]; *yôm milḥāmâ,* "day of battle" [Hos. 10:14]; *y^{e}mê śāḵîr,* "days of a hireling" [Job 7:1], "time of service" [Lev. 25:50]; *y^{e}mê 'ēḇel,* "days/time of mourning" [Gen. 27:41]) or important events of the past (e.g., *yôm ṣē'ṯ^{e}ḵâ,* "the day of your departure [from Egypt]" [Dt. 16:3]; *yôm-hammaggēp̄â,* "day of the plague" [Nu. 25:18]) or the future (e.g., Isa. 22:5; Jer. 46:10; Zeph. 1:15f.; and other passages referring to the day of Yahweh[103]). Historical events are also involved when the *nomen rectum* is a proper name, whether geographical (*yôm miḏyān,* "day of Midian" [Isa. 9:3[4]; cf. Jgs. 7:9ff.]; *yôm y^{e}rûšāla[y]im,* "day of Jerusalem" [Ps. 137:7; cf. Lam. 2:16,21; 4:18,21f.; also *yôm yizr^{e}'e'el,* "day of Jezreel" [Hos. 2:2(1:11)[104]]; *yôm massâ,* "day of Massah" [Ps. 95:8]) or personal (*y^{e}mê dāwiḏ,* "days of David" [2 S. 21:1, with reference to David's reign]), or divine (above all in the prophetical expression *yôm YHWH,* "day of Yahweh," with reference to God's future intervention in history[105]).

In more general terms, the noun can also be connected with something negative (for either the community as a whole or an individual, e.g., *yôm 'êḏ,* "day of calamity" [Dt. 32:35; Prov. 27:10];[106] *yôm ṣārâ,* "day of distress" [Gen. 35:3; Ob. 12]; *yôm rā'â,* "day of trouble" [Ps. 27:5][107]) or something positive (*yôm ṭôḇâ,* "day of prosperity" [Eccl. 7:14, in contrast to "day of adversity"][108]). With respect to a particular individual, it can be used in the sense of "birth" (e.g., *yôm hulleḏeṯ* [Gen. 40:20; cf. also Hos. 2:5(3); Eccl. 7:1] or just *yômô,* "his day," i.e., the day of his birth [Job 3:1]) or "death" (*yôm hammāweṯ* [Eccl. 7:1]; *yôm môṯô,* "day of his death" [Jer. 52:34] or just *yômô,* "his day," i.e., the day of his death [1 S. 26:10]). The plural construct *(y^{e}mê),* usually linked with *ḥayyîm,* "life," can denote the life span of an individual.[109]

As *nomen regens, yôm* (more than 20 times) or *y^{e}mê* (3 times: Lev. 13:46; Nu. 6:5; 9:18; otherwise absolute [12 times]) can also be qualified by a subordinate clause with *'^{a}šer* (3 times with *še-*).[110] The qualification is usually historical, the subordinate clause naming the event that marks the particular day (e.g., the exodus [Dt. 9:7], the occupation [Dt. 27:2], or the laying of the cornerstone of the temple [Hag. 2:18]; with reference to God, the day of creation [Dt. 4:32] or the coming day of intervention [Mal. 3:17,21(4:3)]).

102 Cf. Jenni, *THAT,* I, 712f.; also IV.2 below.
103 Cf. Jenni, *THAT,* I, 724; also IV.3.b-e below.
104 H. W. Wolff, *Hosea. Herm* (Eng. trans. 1974), 28.
105 See IV.3 below.
106 Cf. M. Sæbø, "אֵיד *'ēḏ* Unglück," *THAT,* I, 123f.
107 Additional citations in Jenni, *THAT,* I, 713f.
108 But see IV.3.e below.
109 Cf. Jenni, *THAT,* I, 718f.
110 *Ibid.,* 712, 719.

The reference can also be personal, as when Jeremiah curses the day of his birth (Jer. 20:14; cf. Job 3:3). In some passages, even the sg. *yôm* goes beyond "day" and means something like "time"; this meaning is clear in the passages with the plural. Nevertheless, the phrase *yᵉmê/(hay)yāmîm ʾᵃšer* always represents no more than the conj. "as long as" (cf. Lev. 13:46).

As *nomen rectum, yôm* can be used to qualify other words, e.g., in the phrase *gᵉnuḇtî yôm,* "stolen by day" (Gen. 31:39;[111] cf. also the strange form *bᵉrîṯî hayyôm,* "my covenant with the day" [Jer. 33:20]). It can also qualify other words having to do with time, e.g., *bᵉʿereḇ yôm,* "in the eve of the day" (Prov. 7:9).[112] The temporal qualification can become spatial when travel and distance are involved, as in *dereḵ yôm,* "a day's journey" (Nu. 11:31; 1 K. 19:4).[113] The singular can also sometimes be used in the extended sense of a human lifetime, e.g., Job 30:25, where *qᵉšēh-yôm,* "one whose day is hard," stands in parallel to *ʾeḇyôn,* "poor." But an extended period of time is more usually expressed by the pl. *(hay)yāmîm* (cf. also such idioms as *ʿûl yāmîm,* "an infant a few days old" [Isa. 65:20]; *(lᵉ)ʾōreḵ yāmîm,* "length of days," "as long as I live" [Ps. 21:5(4); 23:6; *mērôḇ yāmîm,* "after many days" [Isa. 24:22]), especially with respect to human life.[114] The formulaic expression *bᵉʾaḥᵃrîṯ hayyāmîm* is generally used in the sense "time to come" (e.g., Gen. 49:1),[115] then the "future" and the "end of time" (e.g., Isa. 2:2/Mic. 4:1; Hos. 3:5; Ezk. 38:16; Dnl. [2:28;] 10:14).[116]

The construct phrase can sometimes be broken down and represented by the prep. *lᵉ*,[117] even when *yôm* is *nomen regens* (*yôm lᵉYHWH* [Ezk. 30:3; cf. Isa. 2:12; 34:8; in Zec. 14:1 in the context of the verb *bôʾ* often used in connection with *yôm* or *yāmîm*).[118]

f. Closer to the genitive qualification is the relatively rare qualification by an attributive adjective, as in such formulas as *(kᵉ)yôm tāmîm,* "(about) a whole day" (Josh. 10:13, as a measure of time, "the bright portion of the day"[119]), or *yôm ṭôḇ,* "a good [happy] day" (1 S. 25:8; also Est. 8:17; 9:19,22), as descriptive of a festival (cf. *mōʿᵃḏîm ṭôḇîm,* "cheerful feasts" [Zec. 8:19]). There are also negative expressions like *yôm ʾānûš,* "day of disaster" (Jer. 17:16; cf. v. 17), *yôm rāʿ,* "evil day" (Am. 6:3), and *yôm mar,* "bitter day" (Am. 8:10), in the sense of a day of disaster for the people. The connection with the *yôm YHWH* is clear; it is also called "bitter" or *gāḏôl,* "great," or described predicatively as being *qārôḇ,* "near" (Zeph. 1:7,14; cf. Ezk. 7:7).[120]

g. As one might expect, a word like *yôm* or *yāmîm* appears relatively often with

---

111 *GK,* §90l; *Synt,* §77c.

112 See also Jenni, *THAT,* I, 709.

113 Cf. *BDB,* 398, §2a.

114 See the detailed citations in Jenni, *THAT,* I, 718f.

115 Seebass, 224-28.

116 Gressmann, *Der Messias,* 84; Staerk; more recently Buchanan, Kosmala, Lipiński, Schreiner; see also IV.3.e below.

117 *Synt,* §74a.

118 E. Jenni, "בוא *bôʾ* kommen," *THAT,* I, 266f.

119 For a different view, see *KBL*³, §2.

120 E.g., H. W. Wolff, *Joel and Amos. Herm* (Eng. trans. 1977), 275; see also IV.3 below.

numbers,[121] especially to indicate a date. Events may be dated (e.g., Ex. 16:1), as may prophetic revelations (e.g., Hag. 1:1). Above all, however, in cultic and legal contexts we find references to the "seventh day" of the week and other times of festival (e.g., Gen. 2:2; Nu. 28f.; Josh. 5:10; 1 K. 12:32f.). In these cases, the word *yôm* can sometimes be omitted (e.g., Hag. 2:1,10 and in the statements in Ezekiel concerning revelations). In 1 S. 27:1, *yôm-ʾeḥāḏ* means simply "one [indefinite] day"; elsewhere (*bᵉ*)*yôm ʾeḥāḏ* is an adverbial phrase indicating a particular day or simultaneity (cf., e.g., Gen. 27:45; Lev. 22:28; 1 K. 20:29; Isa. 9:13[14]; Zec. 14:7 is unique[122]). In 5 passages, *yō/yômayim* is used for "two days."[123]

4. *Related Words and Expressions.* a. Strictly speaking, the opposite of *yôm* is → לילה/ליל *layil/laylâ,* "night" (233 occurrences[124]). The two words, however, often constitute an hendiadys denoting a 24-hour "day" (*yôm wālaylâ,* "day and night," or adverbially "by day and night" [e.g., Gen. 8:22; Isa. 28:19; also with *yômām* instead of *yôm,* e.g., Ex. 13:21[125]] or in the opposite order with the same meaning *laylâ wāyôm* [e.g., 1 K. 8:29]), which can also be expressed by *yôm* alone (e.g., when counting days, as in *šᵉlōšeṯ yāmîm,* "three days" [Est. 4:16], or in the distributive phrase *yôm yôm,* "day by day," "daily"[126]). It is therefore appropriate to call "night" the "correlate of day."[127]

b. In addition, *yôm* also appears with a series of other words relating to time, often to complete the sense. It can be used, for example, with the terms designating the nearest days to the present: *ʾeṯmôl,* "yesterday"[128] (*yôm ʾeṯmôl* [Ps. 90:4]), and *māḥār,* "tomorrow"[129] (*yôm māḥār* [e.g., Prov. 27:1]; cf. *hayyôm ûmāḥār,* "today and tomorrow" [Ex. 19:10]; *bayyôm hāʾaḥēr,* "next day" [2 K. 6:29]), or with words referring to distant times, as in the expressions *yᵉmê qeḏem,* "days of old" (e.g., Isa. 23:7; Mic. 7:20 [cf. *yāmîm miqqeḏem* (Ps. 77:6[5]), and *yāmîm qaḏmônîm,* "former days" (Ezk. 38:17), and *yᵉmê ʿôlām,* "days of the past" (e.g., Am. 9:11; Mic. 5:1(2) [cf. *yᵉmôṯ ʿôlām* (Dt. 32:7)]), which relate to the past (cf. the general expression *yāmîm riʾšōnîm,* "former days" [e.g., Dt. 4:32]). Other expressions refer to the future (e.g., *lᵉʾōreḵ yāmîm* and *bᵉʾaḥᵃrîṯ hayyāmîm*[130]) or its conclusion (e.g., *lᵉqēṣ hayyāmîn,* "at the end of days" [Dnl. 12:13]; cf. *ʿēṯ-qēṣ,* "time of the end" [e.g., Dnl. 8:17]).[131]

c. We also find *yôm* associated (often pleonastically) with terms for divisions of time such as *šāḇûaʿ,* "week" (e.g., *šᵉlōšâ šāḇuʿîm yāmîm,* "for three weeks" [Dnl. 10:2f.]),

---

121 See the exhaustive references in Jenni, *THAT,* I, 710f., 716f.; cf. also *GK,* §129; *Synt,* §§84b, 86.

122 See IV.3.c below.

123 See II.2 above.

124 Jenni, *THAT,* I, 708; for a different count, see *KBL*³, 502.

125 See Mandelkern, 473f.; cf. *BHK/BHS* on Jer. 33:20,25.

126 See II.3.a above.

127 *AuS,* I/2, 630.

128 *KBL*³, 99.

129 *KBL*³, 541.

130 See II.3.e above.

131 See also Jenni, *THAT,* I, 721.

ḥōḏeš, "month" (e.g., *ḥōḏeš yāmîm,* "for a month" [e.g., Gen. 29:14]; cf. *yeraḥ yāmîm* [e.g., Dt. 21:13]), and *šānâ,* "year" (e.g., *y^emê šānâ,* "days of the year" [Job 3:6]; *š^enāṯayim yāmîm,* "two full years" [e.g., Gen. 41:1]).[132]

The parts of the day themselves are expressed by related words like → בקר *bōqer,* "morning" (214 occurrences), *ṣoh^orayim,* "midday" (23 occurrences), and *ʿereḇ,* "evening" (134 occurrences), not sharply differentiated. The phrase *bên hāʿarbayim,* "between the evenings" (Ex. 12:6, plus 10 other occurrences in Exodus and Numbers), probably means "at dusk."[133] Sometimes *yôm* can be replaced by words of this sort (cf. the circumlocution *ʿereḇ bōqer,* "evening morning," for "day" [Dnl. 8:14]) or be linked with one of them (e.g., *b^eʿereḇ yôm,* "in the evening of the day," *b^enešep,* "at dusk" [Prov. 7:9]). More frequently, however, *yôm* is connected with other more descriptive words (e.g., *b^eyôm ʾôr,* "bright day," "broad daylight" [Am. 8:9]; *ḥōm hayyôm,* "the heat of the day" [e.g., Gen. 18:1]; *ʿaḏ-n^eḵôn hayyôm,* "until full day" [Prov. 4:18]; *min-hāʾôr ʿaḏ-maḥ^aṣîṯ hayyôm,* "from light to the half of the day," i.e., "from morning to midday" [Neh. 8:3]; *r^eḇiʿîṯ hayyôm,* "quarter of the day" [Neh. 9:3]).[134]

d. Finally, we must mention certain passages where the pl. *yāmîm* takes the place of *šānâ,* the usual word for "year" (876 occurrences[135]). Thus *t^equpôṯ hayyāmîm* (1 S. 1:20) alternates with *t^eqûpaṯ haššānâ* (Ex. 34:22; 2 Ch. 24:23) to designate the "turning of (the days of) the year" (cf. also *miqqēṣ yāmîm layyāmim,* "at the end of each year" [2 S. 14:26]). Annual repetition is probably also meant by the phrase *zeḇaḥ hayyāmîm,* "yearly sacrifice" (e.g., 1 S. 1:21).[136] More general in sense are the expressions *miyyāmîm yāmîmâ*[137] and *layyāmîm,* "annually" (Jgs. 17:10; cf. also 1 S. 27:7; 29:3).[138]

III. General Usage. This survey of the forms of *yôm/yāmîm* together with its phrases and semantic field has brought to light its wide range of usage. The formal and syntactic manifestations of the singular and plural have been seen to be analogous, so that it is not necessary to treat the singular and plural separately. There is nevertheless a significant difference: *yôm* always designates some fixed point in time, while *yāmîm* often expresses temporal duration by indicating periods of time of various sorts. The plural can also sometimes mean "time" in general, as Kimchi already observed;[139] cf. also *kol-hayyāmîm,* "for all time, forever" (e.g., Dt. 4:40),[140] in 1 S. 2:32 negated with *lōʾ,* to mean "never."[141]

---

132 See also *GK,* §131d.

133 Cf. Jenni, *THAT,* I, 709; for a different view, see *BLe,* §518; *AuS,* I/1 (1928), 619f., 628f.; *AncIsr,* 182.

134 See III.1 below.

135 Jenni, *THAT,* I, 722.

136 See M. Haran, "Zeḇaḥ hayyamîm," *VT,* 19 (1969), 11-22; also P. Joüon, "Locutions hébraïques," *Bibl,* 3 (1922), 71f.; for a different view, North, 446-48.

137 See II.2 above.

138 See *BHK/BHS; KBL*³, 383.

139 C. von Orelli, *Die hebräischen Synonyma der Zeit und Ewigkeit* (Leipzig, 1871), 52f.; Barr, 106, citing Nu. 9:22.

140 Cf. *BDB,* 400, §7f.; Jenni, *THAT,* I, 718.

141 Cf. *BDB,* 399, §6.

The plural can thus move in the direction of a general (and abstract) notion of time, although it is usually held that such a notion does not appear to be present in the OT.[142] However this may be, the word *yôm* is central to the Hebrew understanding of time. Not only is it the fundamental word for division of time according to the fixed natural alternation of day and night, on which are based all other units of time (as well as the calendar),[143] but it also exhibits a wealth of extended and metaphorical meanings, as we have to some extent already seen above. These two usages will provide the general outline for our further semasiological discussion,[144] which will be followed in turn by a discussion of the various theological aspects based on both major divisions.[145] It is important in this regard not to make to sharp a distinction between "secular" and "religious" usage.

The word *yôm* and its narrower semantic field appear (for no great reason) to have taken second place in scholarship to other important words related to times such as → עולם *ʿôlām*, "eternity,"[146] and → עת *ʿēṯ*.[147] A substantial portion of the *yôm* material has been analyzed by DeVries, but there is still no detailed monograph discussing all the material against the background of the other words having to do with time. There are widely divergent opinions about the Hebrew notion of time in general.[148]

1. *Literal Usage.* The fixed natural basis of *yôm* is "light."[149] "Day" in the narrow sense refers to the daylight period[150] in contrast to "night."[151] The relationship of "day" to "night" is essentially that of "light" to "darkness,"[152] although night is not totally without light. The sun,[153] which is superior in strength to the moon and the stars,[154] gives the day not only light but heat; the middle of the day (cf. Neh. 8:3), when the day is "full" (cf. Prov. 4:18), is also the "hot time" (Gen. 18:1; Neh. 7:3).[155] Jgs. 19:4-16,20,25-27 is instructive with respect to the periods making up the day.[156]

The day as "daylight" is the temporal center to which the other major words of time relate in two sequences. The first starts with the beginning of the day in the "morning" (*bōqer*[157]), marked by sunrise and the (morning) light preceding it (cf. Neh. 8:3) and the

---

142 E.g., DeVries, 39; for a different view, see Barr, 100-6.

143 Jenni, *THAT,* I, 722; DeVries, 42; also Aalen, *Begriffe,* 10-20.

144 See IV.1-2 below; DeVries, 343-46, makes a different but similar distinction.

145 See IV below.

146 E. Jenni, "Das Wort *ʿôlām* im AT," *ZAW,* 64 (1952), 197-248; 65 (1953), 1-35.

147 Wilch; see also II.2 above.

148 See the survey by Wilch, 2-19. Cf. now also DeVries, as well as H. H. Schmid, "Das Verständnis der Geschichte im Deuteronomium," *ZThK,* 64 (1967), 1-15.

149 → אור *ʾôr*; Sæbø, *THAT,* I, 84-90.

150 *KBL*³, 382.

151 See II.4.a above.

152 Aalen.

153 → שֶׁמֶשׁ *šæmæš*; cf. T. Hartmann, "שמש *šemeš* Sonne," *THAT,* II, 987-89.

154 See IV.1 below.

155 See also II.4.c above.

156 See Dalman and *AncIsr*.

157 See II.4.c.

"dawn" (*šaḥar*).[158] It moves backward to "last night" or "yesterday evening" (*ʾemeš* [e.g., Gen. 19:34]), then to "yesterday" (*ʾeṯmôl* [e.g., 1 S. 4:7]; *tᵉmôl* [e.g., 2 S. 15:20]) and "day before yesterday" (*šilšôm*, "three days ago" [e.g., Ex. 5:8]), and finally to the far-off past, the days that lie "before" (*qeḏem*).[159] The other starts with the end of the day in the evening (*ʿereḇ*), with "dusk" (*nešep̱* [e.g., 2 K. 7:5]).[160] It moves forward to "tonight" (*hallaylâ* [e.g., Gen. 19:5], as correlate to *hayyôm*, "today") and "night" (*laylâ* [e.g., Ex. 13:21]), then to "tomorrow" (*māḥār* [e.g., Ex. 8:25(29)]) and "day after tomorrow" ([*hayyôm*] *haššᵉlîšîṯ*, "the third day" [e.g., 1 S. 20:12]), and finally to the distant future, the days that lie "after" (*ʾaḥar*; cf. *ʾaḥᵃrîṯ*, "that which comes after," "future").[161] It is noteworthy that only the days immediately before and after the present "day" have special names, while even the next but one are merely enumerated, as is true in general.[162] Neither the days of the month nor the days of the week have special names, but only numbers; the exception is the Sabbath (*šabbāṯ* [e.g., Isa. 1:13] or *yôm haššabbāṯ* [e.g., Ex. 20:8]).[163] This merely underlines the fundamental importance of the "day" even for longer units of time.

When longer units are involved, however, we are not dealing with the day as "daylight" but with the calendar day of twenty-four hours, for which Hebrew (unlike Aramaic and Syriac[164]) does not have a special word. This "full day" includes "night" as a temporal complement; the "night" belongs to the preceding day (cf., e.g., Gen. 19:33f.; 1 S. 19:11, and such phrases as *yôm wālaylâ* and *hallaylâ*, "tonight").[165] From its outset at creation (Gen. 1:3-5),[166] *yôm* as "full day" had the same beginning as *yôm* in the narrower sense, namely morning, and the "minor temporal sequence" remains the same: *ʾeṯmôl, ʾemeš, bōqer-(hay)yôm-ʿereḇ, (hal)laylâ, māḥār.*

The evidence on this point, however, is rendered ambiguous by the cultic regulations governing observance of the Sabbath and other festivals. Lev. 23:32 stipulates that the Day of Atonement shall be a day of absolute rest (*šabbāṯ šabbāṯôn*[167]) on the tenth day of the seventh month (Lev. 23:27); it is noteworthy that v. 32 expressly sets this observance on the "*ninth* day of the month, beginning at evening," that it may last "from evening to evening." Thus we find a kind of competition between a calendrical enumeration of days beginning in the morning and a cultic determination of the festival (Sabbath) that begins on the evening of the preceding day. But the cult also reckoned days as beginning with the morning (cf. the sacrificial regulations in Lev. 7:15; 22:30; the mitigation proposed by

---

158 Hartmann, 990f.

159 E. Jenni, "קֶדֶם *qædem* Vorzeit," *THAT*, II, 587-89.

160 See II.4.c. above.

161 E. Jenni, "אחר *ʾḥr* danach," *THAT*, I, 110-18; also II.3.e above.

162 See II.3.g above.

163 See IV.2 below.

164 See J. Levy, *Chaldäisches Wörterbuch über die Targumim und einen grossen Theil des rabbinischen Schriftthums* (Leipzig, 1867), I, 329f., 336; A. S. van der Woude, "אמץ *ʾmṣ* stark sein," *THAT*, I, 209.

165 *AncIsr*, 181.

166 See IV.1 below.

167 K. Elliger, *Leviticus. HAT*, IV (1966), 303.

Stroes[168] is not valid). In the cultic realm, however, the vespertine beginning of the day gradually increased in importance, although certain irregularities show that a long process was involved: compare Lev. 23:5f. with Ex. 12:8,18; also Nu. 33:3 and Neh. 13:19f. with reference to the Sabbath.[169] Starting from the cultic sphere, this manner of defining days gradually extended throughout Jewish life until it became normative. For a long time, however, there were nonconformists, as Talmon has shown.[170]

There is yet another factor, however, that complicates the evidence respecting the "day" as a "full day" in its temporal calendrical function in the context of larger units of time. The "full day" is determined not only by daylight and the light of the sun,[171] but also by the moon (*yārēaḥ, ḥōḏeš*).[172] This is not especially apparent in the case of the "week" (*šāḇûaʿ*), whose seven-day period is hard to reconcile with the lunar cycle of about 29 1/2 days, or with the 50-day period comprising seven weeks plus a holiday, which has left traces in the calculation of the Feast of Weeks and the Jubilee Year (cf. Lev. 23:15f. [compare with Ex. 23:16; 34:22; Dt. 16:9]; Lev. 25:8-13) and has influenced later apocalyptic writings like Jubilees and 1 (Ethiopic) Enoch as well as the Qumran documents.[173] The moon instead exhibits its calendrical significance primarily in the "month" (*yeraḥ,* → ירח *yārēaḥ,* "moon"; → חדש *ḥōḏeš* [*chōdhesh*], "new moon," "first day of the lunar month," "month"), above all in the cultic sphere (including not only the "new moon" but also the "full moon"[174]). The moon also enters into the computation of the "year" (*šānâ,* also *yāmîm*[175]). This latter is based on much more complex observations than the simple alternation between day and night: there is a conflict between the solar year (of 365 days and some "hours" [Aram. *šāʿâ,* "short interval of time,"[176] e.g., Dnl. 3:6; not in the Hebrew OT]) and the lunar year (of some 354 days [plus additional intervals spread out over an extended period to reconcile the discrepancy with the solar year]). In the OT, these different ways of calculating the year are combined in a "luni-solar" year.[177] One can also observe influences from Israel's neighbors, especially Mesopotamia and Egypt;[178] but this would raise the larger question of the calendar in the ancient Near East.[179]

---

168 P. 470.

169 Morgenstern, *HUCA,* 10 (1935), 15-28; *AncIsr.*

170 Pp. 187-198.

171 See above.

172 See II.4.c above.

173 Morgenstern, *VT,* 5 (1955), 34-76; Segal, Baumgarten, and *AncIsr*; also A. Jaubert, "Le calendrier des Jubilés et de la secte de Qumrân: Ses origines bibliques," *VT,* 3 (1953), 250-264; *idem,* "Le calendrier des Jubilés et les jours liturgiques de la semaine," *VT,* 7 (1957), 35-61; E. Kutsch, "Der Kalender des Jubiläenbuches und das Alte und das Neue Testament," *VT,* 11 (1961), 39-47.

174 See IV.2 below.

175 See II.4.d above.

176 *GesB:* "hour"; *KBL:* "moment."

177 Segal; *AncIsr.*

178 See I above.

179 Nilsson; Kutsch; J. van Goudoever, *Biblical Calendars* (Leiden, ²1961); M. Weippert, "Kalender und Zeitrechnung," *BRL*², 165-68; J. Licht, "Calendar," *EncJud,* 5, 43-53; also S. Mowinckel, *Zum israelitischen Neujahr und zur Deutung der Thronbesteigungspsalmen. ANVAO,* II, 1952/2.

Besides general questions having to do with the calendar, in the modern period the question touched on above of whether the day begins with morning or evening has been the subject of lively discussion. The so-called "morning theory" was revived by Dillmann[180] and has been supported most vigorously by Cassuto.[181] It has been developed, with various modifications and historical nuances, by many scholars.[182] Zeitlin and Stroes, on the other hand, have attempted to defend the traditional "evening theory" to the widest extent possible. The question deserves further traditio-historical analysis.

2. *Extended Usage.* The chronological and calendrical usage of *yôm/yāmîm* is naturally central. But the word has also been used in many extended senses, in which it may take on a special meaning or lend its meaning to characterize other objects.

If we start from the observation that *yôm* refers in the first instance to "daylight,"[183] the meaning "full day" (twenty-four hours) is itself an extended temporal sense. More important, however, are the cases in which the focus of the meaning is not on the "day" as such, but on a "time" or situation characterized in a particular way. This holds true primarily for the pl. *yāmîm,* which not rarely has the meaning "time," often in combination with some additional attribute (e.g., *kîmê ʿôlām,* "as in the days of old" [Am. 9:11]; *yᵉmê ʾēḇel,* "days/time of mourning" [Gen. 27:41]).[184] It is also true, however, for the sg. *yôm* (e.g., *yôm qāṣîr,* "day/time of harvest" [Prov. 25:13]; *yôm ṣārāṯî,* "day/situation of my distress" [Gen. 35:3]).[185] Something similar is probably involved in the more or less stereotyped adverbial use of both *yôm* and *yāmîm/yᵉmê* in the sense of "when."[186] In addition, *(hay)yāmîm/yᵉmê* with reference to an historical period or epoch can be linked with the name of a king (e.g., *bîmê dāwid,* "in the days/reign of David" [2 S. 21:1]; cf. also Jgs. 8:28; 1 K. 16:34); it also appears relatively often in the titles of books (*sēp̱er diḇrê hayyāmîm,* "chronicles"; cf. 1 K. 14:19; Neh. 12:23; 1 Ch. 27:24; Est. 6:1).[187] Similarly, *yôm* can refer to an historic event defined more closely by the context (e.g., *yôm yᵉrûšāla[y]im,* "the day/catastrophe of Jerusalem" [Ps. 137:7]; cf. Ob. 12-14; with reference to Babylon: *kî bāʾ yômᵉḵā ʿēṯ pᵉqaḏtîḵā,* "for your day has come, the time when I will punish you" [Jer. 50:31]).[188]

Especially noteworthy is the use of *hayyôm,* "today,"[189] alone or in compound phrases

---

180 A. Dillmann, *Die Genesis* (Leipzig, ⁶1892), 22.

181 U. Cassuto, *A Commentary on the Book of Genesis* (Jerusalem, ⁴1965), I, 28-30.

182 E. König, "Kalenderfragen im althebräischen Schrifttum," *ZDMG,* 60 (1906), 605-644, esp. 605-612; B. Jacob, *Das erste Buch der Tora, Genesis* (1934; repr. New York, 1974), 35-37; *idem, The First Book of the Bible, Genesis* (abridged Eng. trans., New York, 1974), 4; *AncIsr*; Heawood; most recently DeVries, 42, and Steck, 175.

183 See III.1 above.

184 See also Jenni, *THAT,* I, 719-721.

185 Additional citations in II.3.d-f above; also Jenni, *THAT,* I, 712f.; DeVries, 44f.

186 For details, see II.3.a-d above; Jenni, *THAT,* I, 711f., 718f.

187 Further discussion in *BDB,* 399a.

188 Further discussion in Jenni, *THAT,* I, 713, and IV.3.a below; on the important term *yôm YHWH,* "day of Yahweh," see IV.3.b-e below.

189 See II.3.d above.

to refer not to a single day but to the present time of the speaker in contrast to a past situation or past events (e.g., *lannābî hayyôm yiqqārē' lᵉpānîm hārō'eh,* "he who is now called a prophet was formerly called a seer" [1 S. 9:9]) or, more commonly, to convey actuality. This latter usage is especially common in Deuteronomistic exhortation (e.g., Dt. 11:1-9,13,26,32; 28:1; total renewal is emphasized in 27:9);[190] the crucial importance of "today," the present, for the future is revealed (cf. Josh. 24:15).

In the personal realm, *yôm* can also be a time of special importance for an individual. The single word *yômô,* "his day," can refer not only to the day of someone's birth or death,[191] but also to the day/time that marks the end and judgment of the wicked (Ps. 37:13; Job 18:20; cf. also *bᵉlō'-yômô,* "prematurely" [Job 15:32]). The pl. *yāmîm* frequently refers to the days of someone's life[192] and can thus be a term meaning "lifetime" or occasionally "advanced age" (Job 32:7).

Furthest removed from the temporal sense is the use of *yôm/yāmîm* in a spatial sense, to indicate distance in the form of a journey.[193]

As a general rule, it is often difficult to make precise distinctions among the extended uses of the word.

IV. Theological Usage. We have seen that the word *yôm/yāmîm* is the fundamental term for time, with a wide and varied range of uses.[194] The transition from what might be called "secular" usage (in temporal and extended senses) to explicitly religious or theological usage is also fluid and therefore difficult to define precisely. The information cited in the preceding discussion has often contained a "theological" element. It is theologically significant, for instance, that the days do not have names but are simply counted,[195] for this deprives them of any independent significance. In the OT, "days"—or the opposites "day" and "night"—are not expressions of divine powers; instead of being deified, they are made entirely subject to Yahweh, the God of Israel.[196] "Days"—and "time," to the extent that "time" can be spoken of in the OT—belong to God; this finds various forms of theological expression.

1. *Creation.* God is lord of days and time because he is the creator of light and darkness, day and night and seasons (cf. Ps. 74:16f.; Isa. 45:7; also Ps. 139:11f.; Jer. 33:20). We have here a universal creative causality on the part of God comprehending both day and night that does not find corresponding expression in Gen. 1, a passage of central importance for the theology of creation. In the latter, there seems instead to be a certain polarity of light and darkness, in which light is the first thing created by God. Like the rest of his creation, it is viewed with approval and called "good" (*ṭôḇ* [Gen.

---

190 See also DeVries, 139-277, esp. 252-277, 337.
191 See II.3.e above.
192 For citations see Jenni, *THAT,* I, 718f., also II.3.e above.
193 See II.3.e above; *BDB,* 398, §2b.
194 See also Jenni, *THAT,* I, 722 [4.a]; DeVries, 337.
195 See III.1 above.
196 Cf. Aalen, *Begriffe,* 16; Schmidt, 100; Jenni, *THAT,* I, 723; I. Ta-Shma, "Day and Night," *EncJud,* V, 1374-76.

1:3-4a]),[197] while the same is not said of darkness.[198] There is then a "separation" *(hiḇdîl)* between light and darkness (v. 4b), and above all a "calling" of the light "day" and the darkness "night," which can be seen as further acts in the process of creation.[199] This incorporates darkness/night at least functionally into God's creation, but the "day" as "daylight" when the sun gives its light maintains its precedence.

The other important theological point of Gen. 1:3-5 is the constant alternation of day and night as a fundamental element of creation.[200] It is confirmed after the Deluge (Gen. 8:22; cf. Jer. 33:20), and will not come to an end until the eschaton, in the glorious final revelation of Yahweh (Zec. 14:7).[201] Thus "time takes precedence over space in P's presentation of creation; creation does not begin with the division of space, but with the division of night and day as the basis of time."[202] This also makes it possible to present the seven-day schema of the first account of creation and to link it with history.[203]

The division between day and night is also the subject of important statements in Gen. 1:14-18 (see also Ps. 136:7-9), this time in connection with *meʾōrōṯ,* "lights" (Gen. 1:14-16), or "light" and "darkness" (v. 18). The tension between this section and vv. 3-5 has been variously judged.[204] It is noteworthy in any case that there is no longer any trace of the light/day versus darkness/night polarity; there also seems to be a neutral balance between sun and moon. Their temporal functionality is emphasized, not just with respect to "days and years" but also with respect to "seasons/festivals" (*môʿaḏîm*), so that we find here an element of cultic theology. The same is true at the end of the account (2:2f.), which deals with the seventh day, on which God "rested" (*šāḇaṯ*).[205]

Ultimately the "lights" and stars in Gen. 1:14-18 are presented only as instruments for measuring time; they are robbed of their traditional power to affect human destiny. As parts of God's creation, they are servants rather than masters of time.[206]

God's sovereignty over time as Creator extends from the cosmic level to the "days" of each individual, as we see above all in texts that have been influenced by Wisdom Literature (e.g., Ps. 39:5-7[4-6]; 90:9f.,12,14; 102:4,12,24f.[3,11,23f.]; Job 7:6; 8:9; 10:20; 17:1,11; also Ps. 31:16[15]: *beyāḏeḵā ʿittōṯāy,* "My times [future] are in thy hand."

2. *Cult.* God's sovereignty over the time of each individual finds expression in the theology of the cult, an important element of which is the division and arrangement of days and seasons.[207]

---

197 N. J. Stoebe, "טוֹב *ṭôḇ* gut," *THAT,* I, 659f.

198 See, e.g., von Rad, *TDNT,* II, 943; Westermann, *Genesis 1–11,* 124; *idem, Isaiah 40–66. OTL* (Eng. trans. 1966), 161f.; Sæbø, *THAT,* I, 88.

199 Steck, 158, 163, 165, contra Schmidt, 95-100.

200 See esp. Steck, 166-177.

201 Sæbø, *THAT,* I, 89.

202 Westermann, *Genesis 1–11,* 114.

203 *Ibid.,* 112f.; Steck, 173-75.

204 Cf. Schmidt, 109-120; Westermann, *Genesis 1–11,* 126-134; for a different view see Steck, 95-118.

205 See IV.2 below.

206 See I above.

207 On the effects of the cult on the calendar, see III.1 and IV.1 above.

Special days belong to God and are therefore "holy" (*qāḏôš*; cf. Neh. 8:9; also *yᵉmê habbᵉʿālîm,* "(feast) days of the Baals" [Hos. 2:15(13)]); they are therefore governed by certain regulations or rituals. In addition to days set apart by special circumstances (e.g., *yᵉmê niddâ,* "days of [menstrual] uncleanness" [Lev. 12:2]) or events in the life of the family (e.g., Gen. 21:8) or the community (e.g., Isa. 58:3; Zec. 7:1ff.),[208] there were regularly recurring festivals throughout the year with various cultic observances.[209]

First there is the most frequent festival, the Sabbath; as the day of rest concluding a seven-day week, it defines the smallest cultic temporal unit. This festival is merely described in Ex. 23:12; 34:21; in the Decalog (Ex. 20:8-11 and Dt. 5:12-15) and elsewhere it is mentioned by name (*yôm haššabbāṯ*).[210] It became much more important with the passage of time.[211]

Alongside the Sabbath, Am. 8:5; Hos. 2:13(11); Isa. 1:13 speak of the "(day of the) new moon" (*ḥōḏeš*; see also Nu. 10:10; 1 S. 20:5,18f.,26f.).[212] This bespeaks a cultic rhythm regulated by the moon,[213] which was considered "lord of the calendar"[214] in Mespotamia and is mentioned before the sun in Ps. 104:19 in its function "for the festivals" (*lᵉmôʿᵃḏîm*). The moon had a cultic significance that cannot be overlooked, as is attested by the ritual in the latest cultic calendar (Nu. 28f.) for the "day of the new moon" (Nu. 28:11-15) (cf. Lev. 23:24; Nu. 29:1; and such late texts as Neh. 10:34[33] and 2 Ch. 2:3[4]).

The cultic calendars (Ex. 23:14-17; 34:18-23; Lev. 23; Nu. 28f.; Dt. 16:1-17; cf. Ezk. 45:18-25[215]) regulate primarily the three great pilgrimage festivals. It is noteworthy that the earlier calendars (Ex. 23, 34) are entirely agrarian, while the later (that of H in Lev. 23 and that of P in Nu. 28f., as well as Ezk. 45) reveal a calendrical interest in certain fixed days. The day of the new moon on the first day of the first month and half a year later on the first day of the seventh month was especially important, but so was the fifteenth day of the same months. This may indicate that the "day of the full moon" (*yôm hakkēseʾ*, e.g., Ps. 81:4[3]; Prov. 7:20) was also of great cultic importance.

Thus in the calculation of "days" (and more generally of time) we find not only an observable tension between the sun (or daylight) and the moon (or evening/night), but also a certain element of competition between them in the theologies of creation and the cult.

3. *History.* God is lord of time, not only because he created the constant alternation between day and night, thus laying the foundation for the course of history, but because he

---

208 Cf. *AncIsr,* 468; DeVries, 46f.; see also II.3.e above.

209 See G. B. Gray, *Sacrifice in the OT* (²1971), 271-284; H.-J. Kraus, *Worship in Israel* (Eng. trans., Richmond, 1966), 26-92; *AncIsr,* 468-517; J. B. Segal, "The Hebrew Festivals and the Calendar," *JSS,* 6 (1961), 74-94.

210 → שבת *šabbāṯ*.

211 Kraus, *Worship in Israel,* 78-88; *AncIsr,* 475-483; F. Stolz, "שבת *šbt* aufhören, ruhen," *THAT,* II, 863-69, with bibliog.

212 Kraus, *Worship in Israel,* 76-78; *AncIsr,* 469f.

213 See III.1 above.

214 Kraus, *Worship in Israel,* 43.

215 *AncIsr,* 468-474; presented somewhat differently by Kraus, *Worship in Israel,* 26-36.

also intervenes mightily in the course of history. In the context of the theology of history, the most important expression of his activity is the genitive phrase *yôm YHWH,* "day of Yahweh." It occurs 16 times, all in the prophets (from the southern kingdom): Isa. 13:6,9; Ezk. 13:5; Joel 1:15; 2:1,11; 3:4(2:31); 4:14(3:14); Am. 5:18(twice),20; Ob. 15; Zeph. 1:7,14(twice); Mal. 3:23(4:5). In 3 passages the genitive is replaced by *l*ᵉ: Isa. 2:12; Ezk. 30:3; and (expanded by the addition of *bāʾ*, "comes") Zec. 14:1. In 8 passages there is an additional qualification: *yôm ʿeḇraṯ YHWH* (Ezk. 7:19; Zeph. 1:18) and *yôm-ʾaḇ YHWH* (Zeph. 2:2,3; Lam. 2:22), "the day of the wrath of Yahweh"; *yôm nāqām lᵉYHWH* (Isa. 34:8), "the day of vengeance of Yahweh" (cf. Jer. 46:10); *yôm zeḇaḥ YHWH* (Zeph. 1:8), "the day of sacrifice of Yahweh"; also *yôm mᵉhûmâ . . . laʾdōnāy* (Isa. 22:5), "a day of confusion . . . for the Lord Yahweh." Apart from Lam. 2:22, which is retrospective, these citations also are all from the prophets. Oddly enough, the expression does not occur in Daniel.

Modern scholars have interpreted these observations very differently. Early on, the primary question concerned the (pre-prophetic) origin of the "notion" or "idea" of a special "day of Yahweh." Gressmann hypothesized a very ancient complex of eschatological ideas involving salvation and deliverance, rooted in nature mythology, which underwent further development in the OT. In opposition to this theory, Mowinckel explained the eschatology of the prophets and their talk of the "day of Yahweh" on the basis of the Israelite cult, especially the enthronement festival of Yahweh; many have followed his lead.[216] More critically, Černý and Herrmann[217] have suggested Israel's traditions of (theological) history as a better interpretative background, as have Couturier and most recently Preuss and van Leeuwen. Von Rad, on the other hand, has proposed interpreting the particular phraseology of the "day of Yahweh" primarily on the basis of traditions associated with the ancient holy war. He has been followed more or less by Müller and Schunck, while Lutz has modified von Rad's theory substantially.[218] Jeremias has studied the relationship of the day of Yahweh to ideas associated with theophany.[219] In contrast to the earlier approach,[220] scholars today generally attempt to understand the "day of Yahweh" within the terms of the OT itself. Scholars (still) often inquire into the origin of the expression; but, despite many theories, they know almost nothing about what (if anything) it was before Amos, but only what it developed into among the prophets. And the picture is puzzlingly varied.

a. As we saw above, *yôm* as *nomen regens* can take on an historical aspect in the context of an attributive *nomen rectum*:[221] one might speak, for example, of "the day that the LORD spoke to you at Horeb out of the midst of the fire" (Dt. 4:15) or "the day when

216 See, e.g., C. J. Lindblom, *Prophecy in Ancient Israel* (Philadelphia, 1962), 316-322; A. S. Kapelrud, *Joel Studies. UUÅ,* 1948/4; Gray, *Sacrifice in the OT*.

217 S. Herrmann, *Die prophetischen Heilserwartungen im AT. BWANT,* 85[5/5] (1965), 120-24.

218 See also Héléwa, who also cites the notion of the covenant; also Fensham, who speaks also of ancient Near Eastern "treaty-curses"; the most negative is Weiss, who prefers to see the concept as Amos' invention (cf. also Carniti).

219 Cf. also Bourke, as well as Wolff, *Joel and Amos,* 33f.

220 But cf. Largement and Lemaître.

221 See II.3.e above.

you came out of the land of Egypt" (Dt. 16:3; to be "remembered" [*zāḵar*[222]] cultically; cf. the frequent use of actualizing *hayyôm* in Deuteronomy[223]). In this way special times were indicated that had important (transforming) significance for the life of the people; what was important, however, was not the actual point in time, but the event recorded. "The concept 'day' describes the eventful historical character of a mighty happening and its effects.[224] This is also true when the *nomen rectum* is a toponym ("day of Midian" [Isa. 9:3(4)]; "day of Jezreel" [Hos. 2:2(1:11)]; "days of Gibeah" [Hos. 9:9; 10:9]).[225]

When *YHWH* is the *nomen rectum* associated with *yôm* he has a time to act, a time to intervene in "history"; what will take place then, he alone determines. The relative chronology is necessarily not uniquely defined (e.g., future), being defined in each instance by usage and context; but the future is most common. The most important element, however, is God's act.

b. The earliest passage is Am. 5:18-20, which states metaphorically that Yahweh has appointed a "day" when he will intervene, from which no one can escape. This "day" will bring the opposite of what the people hope for from Yahweh, namely disaster ("darkness") rather than deliverance ("light").[226] Amos' speech is a judgment discourse linked with history (v. 27); it constitutes an integral part of his general message of judgment, in which he proved in many ways to be breaking new ground (cf., e.g., what he says about the *qēṣ,* "end," of Israel in 8:2).

In like fashion, the form and phraseology of Isaiah's discourse concerning the "day of Yahweh" in Isa. 2:(6-11), 12-17(18-22) is part of his proclamation of judgment for the people in the present day. The same is true in 22:5, where the mention of the "day" is followed at once by "a concrete description with reference to his historical moment."[227]

The "day of Yahweh" of which Amos and Isaiah speak, each in his own historical setting, thus refers to the immediate future of the people, which will be radically altered.

c. In the prophets that follow Amos and Isaiah, mention of the "day of Yahweh" appears to have become a prophetic theologoumenon of a very different kind. Highly informative in this regard are both Zeph. 1:7–2:3[228] and Ezk. 7:2-4,5-27,[229] the latter being a literary composite. In Zeph. 1:7f.,14-16; 2:2f., a series of attributes (some synonymous) describing the "day," referring in part to changes in the natural realm, in part to God's wrath and human fear, and in part to the "nearness" (*qārôḇ*) of the "day," gives the impression of more or less stereotyped phraseology. In Ezk. 7:2-4,5ff., similarly, terms like *haqqēṣ,* "the end," *rāʿâ,* "disaster," and *hayyôm,* "the day," which appear elsewhere in various contexts, are juxtaposed in baroque abundance. The "day of

---

222 H. Eising, "זכר *zāḵar* [*zākhar*]," *TDOT,* IV, 64-82; W. Schottroff, "זכר *zkr* gedenken," *THAT,* I, 507-518.

223 Mandelkern, 466.

224 Herrmann, 121.

225 See II.3.e above; also Jenni, *THAT,* I, 720; Preuss, 173.

226 Sæbø, *THAT,* I, 89.

227 H. Wildberger, *Jesaja. BK,* X/1 (1972), 106.

228 A. S. Kapelrud, *The Message of the Prophet Zephaniah* (Oslo, 1975), 27-33; cf. 80-87.

229 W. Zimmerli, *Ezekiel 1. Herm* (Eng. trans. 1979), 193-214.

Yahweh" is still a coming day of God's judgment upon Israel, albeit upon other nations as well; but it is no longer just an "application" of the prophets' message: it has in large measure become an independent didactic theme.[230]

In a sense the exile marked a turning point. Now—in Lam. 1:12; 2:1,21f., for example—people look back upon the "day of the wrath of Yahweh." With the fall of Jerusalem and the temple, the "day" has already come and the prediction has been fulfilled (cf. also Ob. 15; Ps. 137:7). But the "history" of the "day of Yahweh" has not thereby come to an end.

In postexilic prophecy, the formation of the didactic tradition continues. The "day of Yahweh" gradually becomes the nucleus around which crystallizes a complex eschatological drama, as we see above all in Joel 1–4(1–3) and Zec. 12–14. The "day of Yahweh" can bring both disaster and deliverance; it can come to both Israel and the "nations."[231] The final stage is the apocalypticism of Daniel, where *yôm YHWH* is replaced by *qēṣ*, "end," and other fixed terminology.[232]

d. Although with the passage of time the eventful nature of the "day of Yahweh" came increasingly to be emphasized, along with other attributes, its temporal nature still was preserved. This is shown by the various words for time that cluster about the "day of Yahweh": *bayyôm hahû'*, "on that day"; *bayyāmîm hahēm,* "in those days"; *bā'ēṯ hahî'*, "in that time"; *hinnēh yāmîm bā'îm,* "behold, days are coming"; *b^{e}'aḥ^{a}rîṯ hayyāmîm,* "at the end of the days."[233] Most of these formulas, which have undergone some development and take on eschatological character only in the later texts, not only define an eventful point in time, but refer to actual "days" or "time," the "time of the end."

e. Within the context of prophetic eschatology, which is largely a question of definition among the preexilic prophets, too much importance should not be attached to the *yôm YHWH*;[234] nevertheless, the expression makes an essential contribution to the theocentric emphasis of the prophetic (eschatological) message: it is God who holds the initiative in doing mighty acts, it is God who holds dominion over time, over the "history" of the people of Israel and of the nations.

V. Qumran. Usage in the Qumran documents, including eschatological usage, agrees essentially with that of the OT.[235] We can observe, however, a greater interest in calendrical questions.[236]

---

230 See, e.g., Müller, 74-76.

231 See Lutz; Sæbø, *Sacharja 9–14,* 252-317; also Preuss, 178f.

232 For citations see von Rad, *TDNT,* II, 946.

233 See II.3.d above; also Gressmann, *Der Messias,* 83f.; Preuss, 174-76, with citations and bibliog.

234 Von Rad, *TDNT,* II, 944.

235 For citations see Kuhn, 86f.; also P. Benoit, J. T. Milik, and R. de Vaux, *Les grottes de Murabb'ât, DJD,* II (1961), 292; M. Baillet, Milik, and de Vaux, *Les 'petites grottes' de Qumrân. DJD,* III (1962), 306 (315); J. A. Sanders, *The Psalms Scroll of Qumrân Cave 11 (11QPs^{a}). DJD,* IV, 96; J. Allegro, *Qumrân Cave 4. DJD,* V (1968), 99; and J. Maier, *Die Texte vom Toten Meer* (Munich, 1960), II, 216.

236 Talmon.

VI. LXX. In the LXX, *yôm* is almost always rendered by *hēméra,* which emphasizes the chronological character of the word.[237] Most of the other words used to translate *yôm* appear only once; exceptions include *bíos* (12 times) and *kairós* (3 times).[238]

Sæbø

---

[237] See Delling, *TDNT,* II, 947; Jenni, *THAT,* I, 726; and esp. DeVries, *passim* (cf. 367c).
[238] See G. Delling, "καιρός," *TDNT,* III, 458f.

יוֹנָה *yônâ*; תּוֹר *tôr* II; גּוֹזָל *gôzāl*; יְמִימָה *yᵉmîmâ*

Contents: I. Terminology and Etymology: 1. *yônâ*; 2. *tôr* II; 3. *gôzāl*; 4. *yᵉmîmâ*; 5. LXX. II. Ancient Near East: 1. Natural History; 2. Representations on Cultic Objects; Goddess and Dove; 3. Akkadian Literature; 4. Egyptian Literature. III. OT: 1. Symbolic Usage; 2. Gen. 8; 3. Gen. 15; 4. Sacrifice; 5. Ps. 56:1; 6. Ps. 68:14.

I. Terminology and Etymology. Hebrew has several terms for "dove"; their distribution varies in the OT and the Semitic dialects.

1. *yônâ.* The noun *yônâ* is usually associated[1] with the root *ynh* > *ʾnh* (EA *a-un-nu,*[2] Ugar. *tant* < **ʾny* "the [rain?] [of the heavens],"[3] OSA *ʾny*[4]). This root refers to a soft

---

yônâ. F. S. Bodenheimer, *Animal and Man in Bible Lands* (Eng. trans., Leiden, 1960); *idem, Animal Life in Palestine* (Jerusalem, 1935); B. Brentjes, "Nutz- und Hausvögel im Alten Orient," *WZ Halle-Wittenberg,* 11 (1962), 635-702; E. D. van Buren, *The Fauna of Ancient Mesopotamia as Represented in Art. AnOr,* 18 (1939), 88-89; *idem, Symbols of the Gods in Mesopotamian Art. AnOr,* 23 (1945); G. S. Cansdale, *Animals of Bible Lands* (Exeter, 1970); M. E. Cohen, "The Identification of the *kušû,*" *JCS,* 25 (1973), 203-210; G. Dalman, *AuS,* VII (1942), 256-290; G. R. Driver, "Birds in the OT, II. Birds in Life," *PEQ,* 87 (1955), 129-140; J. Feliks, *The Animal World of the Bible* (Eng. trans., Tel Aviv, 1962); H. Greeven, "περιστερά," *TDNT,* VI, 63-72; O. Keel-Leu and U. Winter, *Vögel als Boten. OBO,* 14 (1977), esp. 11-91; S. Krauss, *Talmudische Archäologie,* II (1911; repr. Hildesheim, 1966), 138-140; W. S. McCullough, "Dove," *IDB,* I, 866f.; *idem,* "Pigeon," *IDB,* III, 810; *idem,* "Turtledove," *IDB,* IV, 718f.; S. Mowinckel, "Den kurrende due," *NTT,* 65 (1965), 187-194; A. Parmelee, *All the Birds of the Bible* (New York, 1959), 53-58, 236ff.; W. Pinney, *The Animals in the Bible* (Philadelphia, 1964); G. M. Rinaldi, "Nota [*jwnh* (*jônâ*)]," *BeO,* 8 (1966), 10; A. Salonen, *Vögel und Vogelfang im Alten Mesopotamien. AnAcScFen,* ser. B, 180 (1973); A. Steier, "Taube," *PW,* IV A/2 (1932), 2479-2500; W. Wessely, *Die symbolische, mythische und allegorische Bedeutung der Taube bei den alten Hebräern. Wiener israelitisches Jahrbuch,* 1846.

[1] *GesB,* 295; *KBL*³, 384; Driver, 129.
[2] EA 116, 11.
[3] *WUS,* no. 304; *UT,* no. 2507.
[4] W. W. Müller, *Die Wurzeln mediae und tertiae Y/W im Altsüdarabischen* (diss., Tübingen, 1962), 26.

murmuring sound like that of falling rain.[5] In the OT, the root *ynh* (par. *'āḇal,* Isa. 3:26; 19:8) appears as a verb of lamentation and mourning for the dead; here, too, the murmuring sound of the mourners probably preceded the formation of the descriptive verb. The onomatopoetic background can still be seen when the cooing of doves is used as an image for mourning (cf. Isa. 38:14; 59:11). In Nah. 2:8(Eng. v. 7) "moaning like doves" appears in parallel with "beating their breasts."[6] The name of the prophet Jonah is also associated with the dove and interpreted metaphorically as referring to his personal nature or message.

There are few occurrences of *yônâ* outside the OT. The word does not appear at all in East or South Semitic, being found only in Northwest Semitic. The earliest usage is in Ugaritic. Whitaker[7] lists 7 passages,[8] the meaning of which is disputed. In *KTU,* 1.39, we have a list of sacrifices[9] that includes sheep, doves, cattle, lambs, and heifers. Line 1 (*dqṭ š' ynt š'm dqṭ š'm*), however, which contains our term *ynt,* has been interpreted by Dussaud[10] as a rubrical superscription, "Ritual of rejoicing, lament of rejoicings, ritual of rejoicings." This would make *ynt* a term for a mourning rite. In *KTU,* 1.41, too, we are dealing with a list of sacrifices, but the text can hardly be made coherent; cattle and sheep, among other animals, are mentioned as being the usual creatures taken from flocks and herds for sacrifice. The role played by *ynt.qrt* (ll. 10, 16) in this context cannot be defined more precisely.[11] The same context appears in *KTU,* 1.87; Herdner[12] adopts Gordon's earlier suggestion that *ynt* be taken as a by-form of *yn,* "wine." The text of *KTU,* 1.109 is identical with *KTU,* 1.46 in ll. 1-23. In short, Aistleitner's statement[13] that *ynt* means "dove" needs further clarification. All that can be said with confidence is that all the occurrences are in sacrificial formularies listing the sacrifices specific to the individual gods of the Ugaritic pantheon.

In Jewish Aramaic we find *yônā'* and *yōnā'*; in the Galilean dialect we also find *yawnā'* (cf. Syr. *yauna,* "dove"[14] and Mand. *yaunā*).[15] Here it is a preferred sacrifice and is therefore blessed. In Targum and Midrash, the spirit of God at creation is likened to a dove;[16] the Targum contains polemic against a divine image like a dove on Mt. Gerizim.[17] In Midrash *Qinnim,* the dove serves as a purification sacrifice for a woman after childbirth. The term has not yet appeared in the Qumran documents.

---

5 Cf. *KTU,* 1.3 III, 24; also *KTU,* 1.1 III, 14.

6 See also P. Seethaler, "Die Taube des Heiligen Geistes," *BiLe,* 4 (1963), 115-130, esp. 120.

7 Pp. 313f.

8 *KTU,* 1.39, 1; 1.41, 10, 21; 1.46 I, 12; 1.87, 11, 23; 1.109, 6.

9 E. P. Dhorme, *CTA;* cf. M. Dijkstra and J. C. de Moor, "Problematical Passages in the Legend of Aqhâtu," *UF,* 7 (1975), 171-215.

10 R. Dussaud, "Brèves remarques sur les tablettes de Ras Shamra," *Syr,* 12 (1931), 70.

11 Also *KTU,* 1.46 I, 12; cf. J. C. de Moor, "Studies in the New Alphabetic Texts from Ras Shamra II," *UF,* 2 (1970), 317.

12 A. Herdner, "Un nouvel exemplaire du rituel RS 1929, No. 3," *Syr,* 33 (1956), 110f.

13 *WUS,* no. 1185.

14 *LexSyr*², 300.

15 *MdD,* 185b.

16 *Ḥag.* 15a.

17 See the citations in *WTM,* II, 229.

The word *yônâ* occurs 33 times in the OT: 5 times in Genesis (J's account of the Deluge), 9 in Leviticus, and once in Numbers (sacrificial regulations), 6 times in the Song of Songs, 3 in Psalms, twice each in Hosea and Trito-Isaiah, and once each in 2 Kings, Isaiah, Jeremiah, Ezekiel, and Nahum.

2. *tôr II.* The word *tôr* II is likewise an onomatopoetic term for the "turtle"-dove.[18] This word has found its way into all the languages of the Mediterranean world; cf. Akk. *turtu,* Gk. *trygṓn* or *trygṓs,* Lat. *turtur.* Egyptian, however, in *gry* has developed a different onomatopoetic term for the dove.[19] The word *tôr* also does not appear at Qumran. It occurs 14 times in the OT, primarily in connection with sacrificial regulations and in parallel with *yônâ*: 9 times in Leviticus and once in Numbers. It also appears once each in Gen. 15:9 (J), Psalms, the Song of Songs, and Jeremiah.

3. *gôzāl.* The word *gôzāl* means "young bird" and hence "young dove" (Gen. 15:9); cf. Arab. *ǧauzal* and Syr. *zūgallā,* "young dove." In Dt. 32:11, *gôzāl* also means "young eagle." The word appears in the OT only in these 2 passages.

4. *y^emîmâ.* Job's daughter is named *y^emîmâ* (Job 42:14). This word is analogous to Arab. *yamāmatun,* "dove." According to Driver,[20] *y^emîmâ* (like Akk. *summatu,* "dove," and Arab. *ḥamamātun,* "dove") is based on the voiced *m* that is characteristic of roots that refer to soft sounds; he claims it is a dialect word from Arabic.

Often *y^emîmâ* is explained on the basis of Ugar. *ymmt. lỉmm* as an epithet of the goddess ʿAnat,[21] a variant of the more common *ybmt. lỉmm.* But the meaning of the latter phrase is itself obscure. It is interpreted as "mother of nations" by Albright,[22] Cassuto,[23] Dahood,[24] and others; "lover" by van Selms;[25] "beautiful sister of princes" by Driver (similarly Gray); "relative [sister] of Baal" by Ginsberg[26] and de Moor;[27] and "progenitress of heroes" (cf. Heb. *y^eḇāmâ*) by Kaiser;[28] cf. → יבם *ybm.*

5. *LXX.* The LXX uses *peristerá* 32 times to render *yônâ.*[29] Ps. 56:1 (superscription) (*ʿal-yônaṯ ʾēlem r^eḥōqîm*), which is probably corrupt (read *ʾēlîm* instead of *ʾēlem*), was not understood by the LXX: *hypér toú laoú toú apó tṓn hagíōn memakrymménou* (LXX 55:1). In Zeph. 3:1, the LXX renders the proper name with *peristerá.* In Jer. 46:16(26:16);

---

18 *GesB,* 874; *KBL*², 1023; Driver, 130.
19 *WbÄS,* V, 181.
20 Pp. 129ff.
21 *KTU,* 1.3 II, 33.
22 W. F. Albright, "Recent Progress in North-Canaanite Research," *BASOR,* 70 (1938), 19n.6.
23 U. Cassuto, *The Goddess Anath* (Eng. trans., Jerusalem, 1971), 64f.
24 M. Dahood, *Ugaritic-Hebrew Philology. BietOr,* 17 (1965), 60.
25 A. van Selms, *Marriage and Family Life in Ugaritic Literature* (London, 1954), 70.
26 H. L. Ginsberg, "The North-Canaanite Myth of Anath and Aqhat," *BASOR,* 97 (1945), 9ff.
27 J. C. de Moor, "Studies in the New Alphabetic Texts from Ras Shamra I," *UF,* 1 (1969), 183.
28 W. C. Kaiser, Jr., *The Ugaritic Pantheon* (diss., Brandeis, 1973), 154f.
29 Only 29 are counted by E. C. dos Santos, *An Expanded Hebrew Index for the Hatch-Redpath Concordance to the Septuagint* (Jerusalem, 1973), 79.

50:16(27:16), the LXX renders *hayyônâ* as *Hellēnikós,* while Aquila and Symmachus presume *yônâ.*

All 14 occurrences of *tôr* II are rendered by *trygṓn.* The common Greek terms *phássa, pérdix* (= *qōrēʾ*), etc., are not used by the LXX.

In Gen. 15:9, the LXX uses *peristerá* for *gôzāl.* The name *yᵉmîmâ* is a hapax legomenon in Hebrew; the LXX calls Job's daughter *Hēméra.*

II. Ancient Near East.

1. *Natural History.* As early as the fourth millennium B.C., numerous species of dove or pigeon are found throughout the ancient Near East.[30] Paleological evidence going back to the Pleistocene has even been found in the prehistoric caves of Zuttiyeh.[31] The most common species are the slate-blue rock pigeon (*Columba livia*), the domesticated white pigeon (*C. livia domestica*), the ringdove (*C. palumbes*) with its white neck ring, the red stock dove (*C. oenas*), and the ash-gray turtledove (*C. turtur*).[32] Many columbaries (dovecotes) have been found, primarily from the Greco-Roman period.[33] As a rule, these contained a series of niches for nests, but Galling doubts that they were used for raising doves. Such structures have repeatedly been interpreted as housing burial urns, even in regions where cremation was demonstrably not customary.[34] In any case, the frequent identification of dovecotes with funerary columbaria is not sufficient basis for concluding that doves served as vehicles for the soul.[35]

2. *Representation on Cultic Objects; Goddess and Dove.* The dove is often taken as an attribute of Ishtar (cf. the Greek etymology *peristerá perah-Ištar,* "birds of Ishtar." Scholars cite a terra-cotta dove found in the Asherah temple at Nahariyah (17th century B.C.) and the lead doves from the Ishtar temple of Ashur (13th century);[36] cf. also the dove figurines from the vicinity of the Ninmaḫ temple of Babylon and the dove-shaped attachments of gold and lapis lazuli from the royal cemetery at Ur. The earliest representation of a dove dates from the Ubaid period (4th millennium) at Tell Arpachiyah.[37]

The dove motif appears frequently on cultic objects as early as the beginning of the third millennium (miniature terra-cotta house from the Ishtar temple at Ashur, stratum IX[38]), on cultic vessels from the shrine of Astarte (?) at Beth-shan, at Nuzi, and in Phoenician temple replicas.[39] There is an important connection between the dove and the rosette of Ishtar.[40]

---

30 Salonen, 85.
31 Bodenheimer, *Animal and Man,* 2, 3.
32 *Idem, Animal Life in Palestine,* 171.
33 *AuS,* VII, 256-290.
34 Cf. Y. Yadin, *Masada* (Eng. trans., New York, 1966), 134-39.
35 Greeven, 65.
36 Keel-Winter, 41-47.
37 Van Buren, *Fauna,* 88.
38 *Ibid.,* 89.
39 See W. Fauth, *Aphrodite Parakyptusa. AAWLM,* 1967/6, 356.
40 E. D. van Buren, "The Rosette in Mesopotamian Art," *ZA,* N.S. 11[45] (1939), 99-107.

When a goddess is depicted with birds, the identification of the birds with doves is usually disputed. There is little doubt, however, about the dove on the shoulder of a (war-)goddess wearing a cloak and carrying a seven-headed club depicted on a cylinder seal from Alalakh VII (1800-1650).[41] This goddess with a dove, attested iconographically from the beginning of the second millennium, might be identified with the *bʿlt šmm rmm,* "lady of the high heavens," of Ugaritic literature.

At a very early date the "Syrian" form of the goddess with a dove spread west through Asia Minor to Greece, where the dove became an attribute of Aphrodite and Eros/Adonis, and then of Atargatis/Derketo. Doves were worshipped as sacred to Atargatis at Ashkelon, Paphos (Cyprus), and Dodona.

Botterweck

3. *Akkadian Literature.* Salonen[42] lists (with citations) several possible Akkadian words for doves or pigeons of various kinds. Of these, the only certain ones are *summatu/summu* (the masculine is much rarer), *sukannīnu/šukannunnu,* and *amursānu/uršānu* II/*araššannu*(?), "wild dove" or "ring dove." The latter, found primarily in lexical lists and omen texts, is called a forest bird and is associated with the god Dumuzi, since its call was interpreted as *rēʾû,* "shepherd." According to one text,[43] someone sighs like an *uršānu.* The terms *summatu* and *summu*[44] appear primarily in literary texts of all kinds, especially in similes (someone weeps or mourns like a dove).[45] In the account of the deluge in the Gilgamesh Epic, a dove is the first animal sent forth from the ark, as in Gen. 8:8f.[46] Dove droppings are used medicinally as a drug. The most common word for "dove" in letters, documents, and sacrificial rituals is *sukannīnu.*[47] Pigeons were popular as food—according to an Old Babylonian letter,[48] three hundred cost two shekels of silver—and were often used for sacrifice during the first millennium, especially in the period of the Chaldean kings. In early Babylonian documents, a few women are named *summatum,* "Dove." A special association with the goddess Ishtar has been suggested on the basis of certain monuments, but to the best of my knowledge there is no evidence for it in the texts.

Von Soden

4. *Egyptian Literature.* The dove (Egyp. *wš3t, pẖt mnwt*) does not play an important role in Egypt. As a domestic fowl it is almost unknown. Together with geese and ducks, however, doves are common in the ceiling decoration of palaces and burial chambers. Doves also appear in sacrificial lists, and their eggs were part of the food provided for

---

41 D. Collon, *The Seal Impressions from Tell Atchana/Alalakh. AOAT,* 27 (1975), no. 12, 180.
42 Pp. 114ff., 250ff.
43 *STT,* 52, 52.
44 Cf. also *AHw,* II (1972), 1058a.
45 For examples, see Salonen, 255ff.
47 Gilg. XI, 146-47; read *summatu.*
47 *AHw,* II, 1055a.
48 F. R. Kraus, *Briefe aus dem British Museum (CT 52). AbB,* 7 (1977), 159.

the dead, so that they were popular as funerary offerings.[49] Like anything that flies, the dove could be looked on as a soul-bird, the form taken by the ba of the departed as it rises to the heavens.[50] The fact that the dark ringdove was considered an attribute of Persephone, the goddess of the dead, may provide a religio-historical parallel. The dove had special significance in connection with the enthronement of Osiris and Horus. When the ceremony was completed, doves (identified in part with the sons of Horus) were released in all directions to proclaim this enthronement "to the whole world."[51]

III. OT.

1. *Symbolic Usage.* In the language of the OT, the dove appears as a symbol of love. Their attractive billing and cooing, as well as their supposed fidelity, probably helped shape the image of the dove. In Cant. 2:14, for instance, the bridegroom addresses his beloved: "O my dove, in the clefts of the rock, in the covert of the cliff, let me see your face, let me hear your voice." In Cant. 5:2; 6:9, the bridegroom extols his bride as a perfect dove. She uses the same figure in describing the beauty of his eyes: they are "like doves beside springs of water, bathed in milk" (5:12). The turtledove appears in 2:12 as a harbinger of spring; its voice is heard when the flowers appear on the earth.

In the Song of Hezekiah (Isa. 38:14), the sick king likens his moaning to that of a dove; a similar statement is made concerning the people who moan looking for justice (Isa. 59:11). The queen and her entourage who have gone into captivity are described as lamenting and moaning like doves (Nah. 2:8[7]). Ezk. 7:16 compares the fearful survivors to doves moaning on the mountains.

Those who are called back from exile hasten home eagerly like doves (Hos. 11:11). In Isa. 60:8, too, the speed with which doves fly to their cotes provides an image for the westerners hastening home. In Ps. 55:7(6), the psalmist wishes for the wings of a dove in order to escape the enemy and find rest. In Hos. 7:11, the vacillation of Ephraim is likened to "a dove, silly and without sense"; Israel has been running to and fro between Egypt and Assyria, to its own destruction (cf. also Hos. 8:1; 9:15).

Since doves are birds of passage, their instinct and sense of order surpasses that of human beings, who do not know what they owe Yahweh (Jer. 8:7).

According to Jer. 48:28, Moab is to leave the city and dwell like doves that nest in the clefts of the rock or in the desert, rather than being captured in the cities by the enemy.

2. *Gen. 8.* In the story of the Deluge (Gen. 8:6-12,13a), a raven (*ʿōrēḇ*) and dove (*yônâ*) help Noah pilot the ark on the high seas. Noah first sends forth a raven and then a dove to find out whether the water has receded from the earth so that he and his passengers can leave the ark. The second time the dove returns with a freshly plucked olive twig (*zayiṯ ṭārāp̱*) in its mouth. The sending forth of birds is a widespread motif in stories of

49 R. A. Caminos, "Ei," *LexÄg*, I, 1186.

50 Cf. H. Kees, *Der Götterglaube im alten Ägypten. MVÄG,* 45 (³1977), 46f., 407.

51 *Ibid.,* 128ff.

shipwreck or flood.[52] In contrast to Gen. 8, in the Gilgamesh Epic[53] first a dove (Akk. *summatu*) was sent forth and then a swallow (*sinūntu*), both of which returned. The raven (*āribu*) saw the water was ebbing; he "ate, fluttered, croaked . . . and did not return."[54]

The different sequences of birds and several other features have led to the conclusion that there were two versions. According to Westermann,[55] an earlier form of the bird episode included three sendings of a dove; the single sending of a raven (v. 7) represents only the remnant of a variant of 8:6-12. According to this theory, the Yahwist merely gave narrative form to an already extant tradition. On the other hand, Keel[56] and others maintain that the threefold sending of the dove has replaced an earlier variant with the raven. Keel raises the question whether the dove's displacement of the raven could have resulted from the popularity of the dove as the bird of ʿAnat/Astarte; the stronger raven would have served primarily as an aid to navigation. Cassuto emphasizes the cultic contrast between raven and dove: the raven is unclean, the dove clean. The dove's return with the olive twig announces deliverance.

3. *Gen. 15.* In Gen. 15:7-12,17-21, a turtledove (*tôr*) and young pigeon (*gôzāl*) play a sacrificial role within a rite of self-obligation and solemn covenantal promise of the land: Abraham is to take a heifer, a goat, and a ram, each three years old, cut them in two, and lay the halves out to form a passage. He is also to take a turtledove and a young pigeon, but he is not to cut them in two. In a deep sleep, Abraham sees a smoking firepot and a flaming torch passing between the pieces. Much evidence (e.g., Jer. 34:18 and the treaty between Bargaʾyah of Ktk and Matiʿ-ʾel) suggests that the undivided *tôr* and *gôzāl* and the provision of three sacrificial animals were not part of the original rite of dividing animals and walking between the halves but were intended to reshape the rite as a sacrificial ritual without eliminating the self-deprecation. The date of the passage is hotly debated. Westermann thinks in terms of a "late stage in the history of the patriarchal promises . . . a period when the possession of the land (vv. 7-21) and the survival of the people (vv. 1-6) was [sic] in danger, and the old patriarchal promises were newly revived so as to give surety to God's promise in a time of national danger."[57] According to Zimmerli, however, "there is much to suggest . . . that the narrator is here reproducing an ancient tradition long antedating the Deuteronomic period, with its distanced talk of Yahweh's presence in the holy place."[58]

4. *Sacrifice.* Among all the birds, only the pigeon was used for sacrificial purposes: Lev. 1:14; 5:7,11; 12:6,8; 14:22,30; 15:14,29; Nu. 6:10. This may be connected with the

---

52 Cf. A. Heidel, *The Gilgamesh Epic and OT Parallels* (Chicago, ^{2}1963); C. Westermann, *Genesis 1–11* (Eng. trans., Minneapolis, 1984), 399ff., 444ff.; Keel, 79ff.

53 XI, 145-154.

54 Line 154.

55 *Genesis 1–11,* 445.

56 Pp. 90-91.

57 *Genesis 12–36* (Eng. trans., Minneapolis, 1985), 217.

58 W. Zimmerli, *1. Mose 12-25: Abraham. ZBK,* I/2 (1976), 56.

fact that pigeons were the first birds to be domesticated. There is no way to determine precisely when sacrifice of pigeons became an element of Israel's cult.

According to Elliger,[59] in the case of the burnt offering of birds in Lev. 1:14ff.—obviously added by a later hand—we cannot even say whether such a sacrifice was actually practiced. Possibly it was not considered a fully sufficient burnt offering, and was not accepted until much later under the pressure of social conditions. The question is whether we are dealing with an ancient sacrificial practice "that was not accepted until relatively late . . . in the priestly circles of the exilic period"[60] or with a postexilic attempt to regulate the sacrifice of pigeons "occasioned by the altered economic situation" of the postexilic community. The other legislation dealing with indigence (Lev. 5:7ff.,11ff.; 12:8; 14:21ff.) suggests postexilic origin or acceptance. Originally a substitute for costly sacrifices, intended to help the needy of the postexilic period, pigeon sacrifice finally became a full-fledged burnt offering with a ritual analogous to that of the great burnt offerings.

The indigence clause in Lev. 5:7-10 allows turtledoves (*tōrîm*) or young pigeons (*b^e^nê-yônâ*) to serve for a sin offering: "If he cannot afford a lamb, then he shall bring, as his guilt offering . . . , two turtledoves or two young pigeons for Yahweh, one for a sin offering and the other for a burnt offering" (v. 7). If even the two pigeons are more than he can afford (v. 11), he can offer—according to a further clause in vv. 11-13—a tenth of an ephah of fine flour as a sin offering.[61] In any case, however, the bloody sacrifice of a pigeon is superior to the cereal offering. That the sacrificial animal may be offered as an intact surrogate, the head of the pigeon is not to be severed when it is used for a sin offering (v. 8). In the sacrifice offered for the purification of a woman who has given birth, a year-old lamb is brought to the priest at the entrance to the tent of meeting as a burnt offering and a young pigeon or turtledove as a sin offering (Lev. 12:6). Here, too, an indigence clause (v. 8; cf. Luke 2:24) commutes the year-old lamb to the burnt offering of two turtledoves or young pigeons (cf. Lev. 1:14; 5:7; 14:22; [15:30]).

When someone who is poor (*dal*) offers a purification offering, in cases of indigence (Lev. 14:21-32) the two lambs are commuted to two turtledoves or young pigeons (v. 22) and the amount of flour from three tenths to one tenth (v. 21b); one pigeon serves as a sin offering, the other as a burnt offering. The regulations governing purification sacrifice for a man (Lev. 15:13-15) or a woman (vv. 28-30) on the eighth day after the cessation of his discharge or of her flow of blood provide for a sin offering and burnt offering of two pigeons (*tôr* or *yônâ*) each (vv. 14,29). In like manner, a Nazirite who has accidentally come in contact with or close to a dead body (Nu. 6:6-12) offers a purification sacrifice of two turtledoves or young pigeons as a combined sin offering and burnt offering at the entrance to the tent of meeting, after a seven-day waiting period (Nu. 19:11,14,16) following the shaving of his head (Nu. 6:9). This determined the conditions for the reinstitution of his dedication as a Nazirite. Since purification sacrifice became increasingly common, pigeons (*peristerá*) were later offered for sale in the courtyard of the temple (Mt. 21:12 par.).

---

59 K. Elliger, *Leviticus. HAT,* IV (1966), 32.

60 *Ibid.,* 33.

61 Cf. *ibid.,* 74f.

5. *Ps. 56:1.* A minor textual change (*ʿal-yônaṯ ʾēlîm* instead of *ʾēlem*) connects the "dove" of the superscription in Ps. 56 as "dove of the far-off gods" with the Syro-Canaanite deity ʿAnat/Astarte/Atargatis.[62] Winter[63] discusses the statuettes of doves, their representations on miniature terra-cotta houses and pots, and the association between dove and goddess.

6. *Ps. 68:14.* The interpretation of *kanpê yônâ neḥpâ bakkesep* in Ps. 68:14bc(13bc) is obscure. Since Gunkel, many have interpreted the dove with wings covered with silver and gold as a valuable item of booty; others[64] interpret the dove as an image of Israel or as a symbolic name for the the paredra of Yahweh (ʿAnat/Astarte). Keel[65] has argued convincingly that the dove is a messenger of victory: "Even if Israel—like Reuben in the past (cf. Ps. 68:14a[13a] with Jgs. 5:16)—refrains from battle [to wit, stays among the saddlebags], the wings of the dove are covered with silver and gold to proclaim the victory of Yahweh . . . to all the world."[66] The parallelism between *meḇaśśerôṯ* (Ps. 68:12b[11b]) and *yônâ* (v. 14[13]) is enlightening.[67]

On the NT use of the dove as a symbol of the Holy Spirit, see Greeven[68] and the comms.

Botterweck

---

62 Greeven, Caquot, Lipiński, Winter, etc.
63 Pp. 37-80.
64 Delitzsch, Mowinckel, Caquot, etc.
65 Pp. 34ff.
66 *Ibid.*, 34.
67 Already pointed out by B. D. Eerdmans, *The Hebrew Book of Psalms. OTS*, 4 (1947), 328.
68 Pp. 67ff.

יָחַד *yāḥaḏ*; יַחַד *yaḥaḏ*; יָחִיד *yāḥîḏ*; יַחְדָו *yaḥdāw*

Contents: I. 1. Etymology and Extrabiblical Occurrences; 2. Semantic Development. II. 1. OT; 2. LXX; 3. Qumran. III. The Term and Its Meanings: 1. Noun and Verb; 2. Adjective and Adverb. IV. Ecclesiological Usage at Qumran.

---

yāḥaḏ. H. Bardtke, "Der gegenwärtige Stand der in Palästina neu gefundenen hebräischen Handschriften: 44. Die Rechtsstellung der Qumrān Gemeinde," *ThLZ*, 86 (1961), 93-104; A. M. Denis, "Die Entwicklung von Strukturen in der Sekte von Qumran," in J. Giblet, *Vom Christus zur Kirche* (Ger. trans., Vienna, 1966), 21-60; B. W. Dombrowski, "היחד in 1QS and τὸ κοινόν: An Instance of Early Greek and Jewish Synthesis," *HThR*, 59 (1966), 293-307 (cf. *idem*, diss., Basel, 1962/63); Y. M. Grintz, "Die Männer des Yaḥad–Essener," *Sinai*, 32 (1953), 11ff., repr. in A. Schalit, ed., *Zur*

I. 1. *Etymology and Extrabiblical Occurrences.* Although the root *y/wḥd* is found in almost all the Semitic languages, its etymology has always been disputed. On the basis of a relationship with → אחד *'eḥāḏ* [*'echādh*], the meaning "one," "single," "unique" has been suggested.[1] This traditional theory postulates a triliteral root, such as appears in the majority of instances. But the biliteral form *ḥad,* fem. *ḥ^e^ḏā',* "one," found primarily in Aramaic, must then be explained as a consequence of the loss of a compound *shewa* before *ḥ,*[2] or, less probably, on the basis of a biliteral root, as suggested by Christian: "Etymologically, the word belongs to the root *ḥd,* 'separate' (cf. Arab. *ḥadda,* '(de)limit,' 'distinguish,' *ḥā(i)da,* 'diverge,' 'move away')."[3]

The earliest occurrences of the root *yḥd* are found in Ugaritic texts. Here *yḥd* means "alone," "sole,"[4] or (as in later usage at Qumran) "community"[5] in the religious sense. Also ancient is the Canaanite gloss *yaḫudunni* in the El Amarna tablets, which undoubtedly means "together with (me)."[6] The root is attested in such Amorite personal names as *yaḫadu,* in which it functions as an appellative or even as a theophorous element.[7] This usage does not appear in the OT, even as a monotheistic term. The root appears as a verb in the Old Aramaic Zakir inscription[8] in the haphel form *hwḥd;* here it means the

---

Josephus-Forschung. WdF, 84 (1973), 294-336; M. D. Goldman, "Lexical Notes on Exegesis," *ABR,* 1 (1951), 57-67, esp. 61ff.; E. Koffmahn, "Rechtsstellung und hierarchische Struktur des יחד von Qumran," *Bibl,* 42 (1961), 433-442; "Die staatsrechtliche Stellung der essenischen Vereinigungen in der griechisch-römischen Periode," *Bibl,* 44 (1963), 46-61; J. Maier, "Zum Begriff יחד in den Texten von Qumran," *ZAW,* 72 (1960), 148-166 (cf. *idem, Erscheinung, Wesen und Ideologie der Assoziation von Hirbet Qumran nach dem "Manual of Discipline" (1QS)* [diss., Vienna, 1958]); R. Marcus, "Philo, Josephus and the Dead Sea *Yaḥad,*" *JBL,* 71 (1952), 207-9; J. Mauchline, "The Uses of *YAḤAD* and *YAḤDĀW* in the OT," *GUOST,* 13 (1947-49 [1951]), 51-53 (cf. P. Nober, "Nota brevis a J. MAUCHLINE [pp. 51-53] edito de *yaḥad* et *yaḥdaw* cum concordantia Mandelkern contra dictionaria moderna consentit," *VD,* 30 [1952], 371); J. C. de Moor, "Lexical Remarks Concerning *Yaḥad* and *Yaḥdaw,*" *VT,* 7 (1957), 350-55; L. Rost, *Die Vorstufen von Kirche und Synagoge im AT. BWANT,* 78[4/24] (1938, ²1967); *idem,* "Zur Struktur der Gemeinde des Neuen Bundes im Lande Damaskus," *VT,* 9 (1959), 393-98; P. Seidensticker, "Die Gemeinschaftsform der religiösen Gruppen des Spätjudentums und der Urkirche," *SBFLA,* 9 (1958/59), 94-198; S. H. Siedel, *Qumran. Bibliotheca Carmelitica,* II/2 (1963); W. R. Stegner, *The Self-Understanding of the Qumran Community Compared with the Self-Understanding of the Early Church* (diss., Drew, 1960); E. F. Sutcliffe, "The General Council of the Qumran Community," *Bibl,* 40 (1959), 971-983; S. Talmon, "The Sectarian יחד—a Biblical Noun," *VT,* 3 (1953), 133-140; P. Wernberg-Møller, "The Nature of the *Yaḥad* According to the *Manual of Discipline* and Related Documents," *Dead Sea Scroll Studies 1969. ALUOS,* 6 (1966-68), 65-81; D. Yellin, "Forgotten Meanings of Hebrew Roots in the Bible, 9: יחד," *Jewish Studies,* 1 (1927), 449.

1 Goldman; de Moor; G. Sauer, "אחד *æḥād* einer," *THAT,* I, 104.

2 *VG,* I, 257.

3 V. Christian, *Untersuchungen zur Laut- und Formenlehre des Hebräischen. SAW,* 228/2 (1953), 173.

4 *WUS*⁴, no. 1153.

5 *UT,* no. 1087; cf. M. Dahood, "Hebrew-Ugaritic Lexicography III," *Bibl,* 46 (1965), 318: *pqr yḥd,* "overseer of the (religious) community."

6 *CAD,* VII (1960), 321; *RA,* 19 (1922), 108; rendered by *DISO,* 106, as "moi seul," "me alone."

7 *APNM,* 210.

8 *KAI,* 202 A, 4.

"assembly" or muster of military forces. Jewish Aramaic uses the pael in the sense "leave alone," "define," and the hithpael in the sense "be alone together," with reference to a husband and wife.[9] In South Semitic the root is very common. In Arabic alone it has given rise to more than ten different formations, all of which center on the meaning "one," "unique," "together"; cf. the verb *waḥada,* "be unique," "be incomparable," II "unite," V "be alone," "constitute a unit," VIII "be one."[10] These meanings are already attested in Old South Arabic, e.g., Qat. *wḥd,* "together,"[11] and Thamudic. Ethiopic has *wēḥada,* "be little," declaratively "belittle," and Tigr. *waḥada,* "be united,"[12] found later in Geʿez and Amhar. *and* and the other dialects of the northern coast of Africa[13] and in Meḥri *ṭād.*[14] In Syriac, overtones of "separated," "eremitical," "monastic" are clearly present in the meaning.[15] Finally, several derivatives appear in Middle Hebrew and Christian Palestinian: *yāḥad,* "be joined," piel "join"; *yiḥûd,* "uniqueness," "aloneness" (= *yiḥûdā*ʾ etc.).[16]

Akk. *(w)ēdu(m),* "unique," "alone," "sole,"[17] is undoubtedly connected etymologically with our root, as the Phoenician and Punic form *yad*[18] and Amharic[19] may suggest. Semantically, Akk. *ištēn,* "one," rarely "unique," and its numerous derivatives is similar to our root,[20] but is closer to *ʾeḥāḏ.*

2. *Semantic Development.* Of the proposed attempts to trace the semantic development of the root, that of de Moor is most convincing. According to this theory, the basic meaning is not "together," nor does it develop via "all"—"all one" to "alone," as suggested by Goldman; it is in fact "one": as a verb, "be one," as a noun, "unity," "entirety." The semantic development then moves from corporative "be together" through "together (apart from others)"[21] to "alone."

To this form can be appended the old Semitic locative *-aw* (originally *-u*[22]), giving *yaḥdāw* (variant *yaḥdāyw* [Jer. 46:12,21; 49:3]).[23] Most recently, Aartun[24] has interpreted

---

[9] *KBL*³, 387.

[10] Wehr, 1054.

[11] *RÉS* 3566, 7; cf. ContiRossini, 136, "one," "single," "unique"; *RyNP,* I (1934), 7.

[12] *TigrWb,* 433; W. Leslau, *North Ethiopic and Amharic Cognates in Tigre. AION,* 42/2, Sup. 31 (1982), 82.

[13] Leslau, *Etymological Dictionary of Harari* (Berkeley, 1963), 22.

[14] *VG,* I, 484.

[15] *LexSyr,* 300; cf. also Mand. *iahid*; *MdD,* 185.

[16] *WTM,* II, 232-35.

[17] *CAD,* IV (1958), 36ff.; cf. *GaG,* § 71c.

[18] Cf. Plautus *Poenulus* 932.

[19] See above.

[20] Cf. *CAD,* VII, 275-78.

[21] Cf. Christian.

[22] *VG,* I, 465; Mauchline.

[23] For a different view, see Joüon; cf. *BLe,* §65ᵉ, where the ending is interpreted as a pronominal suffix: "together with him."

[24] K. Aartun, "Die hervorhebende Endung -*w*(V) an nordwestsemitischen Adverbien und Negationen," *UF,* 5 (1973), 1-5.

the form as a compound of *waḥda (originally a noun in the accusative) + *-w(V) (emphatic particle), synonymous with the simple form *yaḥaḏ*. Finally, after the OT period the *waw* was lost once more; now the adverb is simply *yḥd* or (par. *lpnyw*) *yḥyd*. We must remember in this discussion that the semantic development exhibits bipolarity: the elements "alone"[25] and "together" run in parallel.[26] Subsequent development within the context of the OT and at Qumran is discussed below.

II. 1. *OT.* In the OT, *yḥd* occurs 154 times (plus 4 conjectural emendations and 7 occurrences in Sirach). The verb occurs 3 times (qal: Gen. 49:6 [J]; Isa. 14:20; Job 3:6 [conj.]; piel: Ps. 86:11; Sir. 34:24 [conj.]), the noun only twice (Dt. 33:5; 1 Ch. 12:18[Eng. v. 17]).[27] As an adverb, *yaḥaḏ* occurs 43 times (plus 1 conjecture and 1 occurrence in Sirach), *yaḥdāw* 96 times (plus 4 occurrences in Sirach), and *yāḥîḏ* 12 times.

The Dead Sea scrolls exhibit quite the opposite distribution: among 133 occurrences (115 according to Kuhn), we find the verb 6 (7) times, the adverb 22 (25) times, but the noun *yaḥaḏ* 101 (87) times and *yāḥîḏ* 4 times. The form *yaḥdāw* has totally vanished from use and may therefore be considered a purely OT form, preserved at Qumran only in 1QIs^a.[28]

The distribution of the root in the OT does not exhibit any peculiarities. It is found from J (for E, cf. Gen. 22 [6 times]) to Chronicles, and is especially frequent in Isaiah (34 times), Jeremiah (19 times), the Psalms (32 times), and Job (16 times). It appears only 24 times in Deuteronomy and the Deuteronomistic history.

2. *LXX.* The LXX is unable to provide a uniform rendering for the verb and the noun; it also misreads *yāḥîḏ* 7 times as *yāḏîḏ,* translating it *agapētós*; elsewhere it uses (correctly) *monogenḗs* (4 times) and *monótropos.* Aquila prefers *monachós.*[29] The most common rendering of *yaḥaḏ* is *epí tó autó* (13 times) in the sense "as a whole, in all"[30] or "together, at the same place."[31] For this usage cf. also the parallelism with *en ekklēsía* in 1 Cor. 11:18,20.[32] Also common—especially in Job—are *homothymadón,* "of one mind," "together," and *háma,* which is etymologically related to *homós, homoú,*[33] but is more spatial in meaning. The adv. *yaḥdāw* is translated *háma* (39 times), *epí tó autó* (29

---

25 Mauchline, Goldman.

26 A different view is taken by Sauer, *THAT,* I, 105; the ambivalence is also discussed by Koffmahn, 434f.

27 Cf. Talmon, 134ff., who finds the noun also in Ps. 2:2 and Ezr. 4:3.

28 The problem is discussed by de Moor, 352f.

29 The history of the two Greek terms is discussed by F.-E. Morard, "Monachos, Moine: Histoire du terme grec jusqu'au 4e siècle," *FreibZPhTh,* 20 (1973), 332-411, esp. 347-357; cf. also *idem,* "Histoire du terme grec jusqu'au 4e siècle," *Archiv für Begriffsgeschichte,* 18 (1974), 167ff.

30 De Moor, 335.

31 Bauer.

32 See also E. Ferguson, "'When You Come Together': *Epi To Auto* in Early Christian Literature," *Restoration Quarterly,* 16 (1973), 202-8.

33 → אחד *'eḥāḏ* (*'echādh*).

times), and *homothymadón* (7 times). Only once do we find *mónos* (Isa. 10:8), probably a misreading; we may therefore assume that the numerical element of the basic meaning was hardly felt in actual usage (cf. *katá mónas* in Ps. 141:10[LXX 140:10] and the translation of *yāḥîḏ*).

3. *Qumran.* The occurrences cited by Kuhn[34] are clearly concentrated in the Manual of Discipline: the verb occurs 5 times in 1QS; the noun *yḥd* occurs 62 times in 1QS, 8 times in 1QSa, 3 times in 1QSb; *yḥyd* occurs only in CD; the adverb occurs 9 times in 1QS and once in 1QSa (additional occurrences in 1QH and 1QM). In the OT the derivatives of *yḥd* are used absolutely for the most part; in the Dead Sea scrolls, however, the noun enters into a wide variety of constructions. We find *yḥd* as *nomen rectum* in the phrases *sereḵ hayaḥaḏ,* "rule of the community"; *ʿēṣeṯ hayyaḥaḏ,* "council of the community" (1QS 3:2);[35] *ʾanšê hayyaḥaḏ,* "men of the community" (5:1,3); *sôḏ hayyaḥaḏ,* "council of the community" (6:19); *mišᵉṭê hayyaḥaḏ,* "laws of the community" (6:15); *bᵉrîṯ hayyaḥaḏ,* "covenant of the community" (8:16f.); *bêṯ hayyaḥaḏ,* "house of the community" (9:7); *šulḥān hayyaḥaḏ,* "table of the community" (1QSa 2:18); *ʿēḏaṯ hayyaḥaḏ,* "congregation of the community" (1QSa 2:21), and finally *môreh hayyaḥaḏ,* "teacher of the community" (CD 20:1). Of particular importance for the understanding of *yaḥaḏ* are the phrases in which it functions as *nomen regens*: *yaḥaḏ ʾemeṯ,* "community of faithfulness" (1QS 2:24); *yaḥaḏ ʿēṣâ,* "community of the council (of God)" (3:6); *yaḥaḏ ʿôlāmîm,* "community of the eternal ones" (3:12); *yaḥaḏ qôḏeš,* "community of holiness" (9:2), and especially *yaḥaḏ ʾēl,* "community of God" (1:12; 2:22).

III. The Term and Its Meanings.

1. *Noun and Verb.* Dt. 33:5 and 1 Ch. 12:18(17) are generally considered the only OT occurrences of the noun,[36] with the meaning "community," "agreement." In the difficult verses of the Blessing of Moses, *yaḥaḏ šiḇṭê yiśrāʾēl* probably means something like an "ancient Hebrew Parliament,"[37] which meets when the leaders (*rāʾšîm*) of the tribes are gathered (Dt. 33:4f.). According to 1 Ch. 12:18(17), David proposes to form a *yaḥaḏ* at Ziklag with thirty followers, assuming that they have come in friendship. In both cases, *yaḥaḏ* denotes a political entity, a preinstitutional confederation.

The verb does not appear in political contexts. In the Blessing of Jacob (Gen. 49), the patriarch renounces fellowship with the *qāhāl* of Simeon and Levi; his *kāḇôḏ* will not be joined with them because of their cruelty (v. 6).[38] This "joining" (par. *bōʾ bᵉ*; cf. Job 3:6) obviously brings blessing, whereas its refusal entails curses and scattering (Gen. 49:7). Because of his wicked deeds, the king and ruler of Babylon will not be "joined" with the

---

34 Kuhn, 87ff.; *Nachträge,* 198.

35 See G. Vermès, " 'Car le Liban, c'est le conseil de communauté': Note sur le pésher d'Hab 12,3-4," *Festschrift A. Robert. Travaux de l'Institut Catholique de Paris,* 4 (1957), 316-325.

36 But cf. *LexHebAram; GesB;* Talmon, 134ff.

37 M. Sulzberger, *The Am ha-aretz, the Ancient Hebrew Parliament* (Philadelphia, 1910).

38 M. Dahood, "A New Translation of Gen. 49,6a," *Bibl,* 36 (1955), 229, takes *tēḥaḏ* even here from *ḥdy,* "fix (one's gaze)," and translates: "let not my liver be seen in their assembly."

dead in the grave but will remain unburied and alone (Isa. 14:20;[39] the usual term for "being gathered to one's fathers" is the niphal of *'āsap* [cf. Gen. 25:8]).

The piel of *yḥd* in Ps. 86:11 is especially difficult because it is unique. Only from the use of the hiphil of *yārâ,* "instruct," "teach," in syntactic parallelism in v. 11a can one arrive at the meaning "direct toward a single goal" (contra the LXX and Syr.).[40] The oppressed psalmist prays for renewed concentration: *yaḥēḏ leḇāḇî leyir'â šemeḵā,* "Make my heart solely fear thy name!"

The emendations are not universally accepted. Vogt[41] reads *dāḥâ* in Sir. 31:14. In Ps. 122:3, contra Gunkel, the adverb should probably be read. Job 3:6 (reading *yēḥaḏ* with the LXX[42]) uses the verb metaphorically: cursing himself, Job wishes no longer to "share" in the days of the year, i.e., he does not want to live any longer.

2. *Adjective and Adverb.* The adverb and adjective qualify an activity by lending it the connotation "together," "simultaneously," "in all."

a. When applied to impersonal objects, *yaḥaḏ* and *yaḥdāw* are often synonymous with *kol,* "all" (esp. Isa. 10:8; cf. 40:5). Vegetation may lie together on the ground or be burned up together (Isa. 18:6; 27:4; 60:13); a variety of trees may be planted together (Isa. 41:19). Mixed fabric of linen and wool may not be worn (Dt. 22:11). It is forbidden to plow with an ass and an ox together (Dt. 22:10), but the peaceful coexistence of otherwise hostile animals is a favorite image to represent cosmic peace (Isa. 11:6f.). The OT speaks of various objects as going together: fields and furrows (Job 31:38), ramparts and walls (Lam. 2:8), houses, fields, and wives as the spoil of war (Jer. 6:12). The simultaneous appearance of chariots and horses characterizes the judgment of God (Isa. 43:17). All flesh perishes together (Job 34:15) or finds salvation together (Isa. 40:5). In the technical description of how the *miškān* is built, *yaḥdāw* has a technical architectural sense that is hard to define precisely; it probably refers to the solid mortising of boards (Ex. 26:24; 36:29). Metaphorical usage is found in Dt. 33:17; Job 6:2; 17:16; Prov. 22:18; Isa. 45:8.

b. In the interpersonal realm, the adjective and adverb have a wide range of usage. A military context is especially common: "to be together against someone" (Isa. 9:20[21]), conspire (Neh. 4:2[8]), encamp together (Josh. 9:2; 11:5; Jgs. 6:33; 2 S. 10:15), plunder (Isa. 11:14) and kill (2 S. 14:16), take flight together (Isa. 22:3; Jer. 46:21; cf. Ps. 48:5f.[4f.]; 141:10 conj.), be captured together (Isa. 22:3; Jer. 48:7; 49:3; Am. 1:15), or perish together (1 S. 31:6; 2 S. 2:16; 21:9; 1 Ch. 10:6; Jer. 46:12). We often find *yaḥaḏ* in descriptions of hostile conspiracy (Job 16:10; Ps. 2:2; 31:14[13]; 41:8[7]; 71:10; 74:6 conj.,8; 83:6[5]). When God intervenes they will be put to shame together (Ps. 35:26; 40:15[14]; 70:3[2] conj.) and be destroyed together (Ps. 37:38). In all these cases, *yaḥaḏ* has the meaning "together against others"; only rarely does it clearly mean "against one another" (Dt. 25:11; 1 S. 17:10; 2 S. 2:13).

---

39 Cf. Talmon, 138.

40 Cf. H.-J. Kraus, *Psalmen. BK,* XV (⁵1978), *in loc.*; E. Jenni, *Das hebräische Pi'el* (Zurich, 1968); *KBL*³, 387; etc.

41 E. Vogt, "Einige hebräische Wortbedeutungen," *Bibl,* 48 (1967), 72-74.

42 Cf. F. Horst, *Hiob. BK,* XVI/1 (1968), 37.

In the forensic realm, *yaḥad* refers to the joint status of the parties, equality before the law and identity of punishment (cf. Isa. 43:9; 50:8; Jer. 6:11,21; 13:14; 51:38). In everyday life people live together, go together, meet together, build a house together, and eat together (Gen. 13:6 [twice]; 22:6,8,19; 36:7; Dt. 25:5; Jgs. 19:6; Ezr. 4:3; Job 2:11; Jer. 41:1; Am. 3:3).[43] Common action is also important in the liturgical and cultic sphere: it is possible for people to transgress the law together (Jer. 5:5; cf. Isa. 66:17), but it is also possible to respond together to God's word (Ex. 19:8; cf. 24:3) and praise his name (Ps. 34:4[3]). Frequently *yaḥad* expresses common human fate (Job 3:18; 21:26; 40:13; Ps. 49:11[10]; 62:10[9]; Isa. 1:31; 42:14). In the prophetic notion of the reunited kingdom, *yaḥad* describes the new community of the people of God (Ps. 102:23[22]; 122:3; Jer. 3:18; 50:4; Hos. 2:2[1:11]).

A few passages, especially where the adj. *yāḥîḏ* occurs, bring out the numerical aspect of the basic meaning. In the context of the sacrifice of Isaac (Gen. 22), it is repeatedly emphasized that he is Abraham's *ben-hayyāḥîḏ,* "only son" (Gen. 22:2,12,16), especially beloved by his father (cf. Prov. 4:3). The specifically sacrificial context of the expression *ben-hayyāḥîḏ* and its development in the NT are discussed by Cocchini.[44] In Jgs. 11:34, the reference to Jephthah's "only" daughter, reinforced by the statement "beside her he had neither (*'ên*) son nor daughter" (v. 34bβ), emphasizes the dramatic weight of Jephthah's oath.

"Mourning for an only son" (*'ēḇel yāḥîḏ*) is almost proverbial as a metaphor for the situation at the eschatological judgment (Jer. 6:26; Am. 8:10; Zec. 12:10).[45] In Akkadian, the loss of an only son could be mourned through the use of the personal name *ḫabilwedum,* "the only son is dead," which indicates clearly that the later son who bears it is a substitute for the departed.[46]

In prayer, being "alone,"[47] like being "small"[48] or "poor,"[49] is reason to expect one's prayer to be heard (Ps. 25:16), because God cares especially for the desolate (Ps. 68:7[6]). Metaphorically, *yāḥîḏ* can also stand for the sole human good, one's life (par. *nep̱eš*: Ps. 22:21[20]; 35:17), and thus by synecdoche for a human person under the aspect of helplessness. It has been suggested that *hayyāḥîḏ* was later used as a messianic title for Bar Kochba.[50]

c. The transition to the use of the the adjective and adverb in religious and theological

---

43 On Neh. 6:2, see also R. Schiemann, "Covenanting with the Princes: Neh VI 2," *VT,* 17 (1967), 367ff., who suggests the meaning "let us covenant together" on the basis of the par. *y'ṣ yḥdw* in Neh. 6:7. On Ps. 133:1, see A. Y. Brawer, *BethM,* 18/1 (1972/73), 62ff., 134.

44 F. Cocchini, "Il figlio unigenito sacrificato e amato," *Studi sotrica-religiosi,* 1 (1977), 301-323.

45 According to W. W. Graf von Baudissin, *Adonis und Esmun* (Leipzig, 1911), 89ff., the *yāḥîḏ* lament preserves a remnant of the cult of Adonis.

46 *AN,* 296f.

47 → בדד *bāḏāḏ* [*bādhādh*]; also H. Seidel, *Das Erlebnis der Einsamkeit im AT. ThArb,* 29 (1969), esp. 29f.

48 → קטן *qāṭān.*

49 → דל *dal.*

50 M. Philonenko, "Un titre messianique de Bar Kokheba," *ThZ,* 17 (1961), 434f.

contexts is not sharp. People are called on both individually and together to know God, to recognize and understand his works (Job 34:29; Isa. 41:20; 45:20f.). At the same time, it is a source of dismay and terror to see the works of idols (Isa. 41:23), for they are powerless. Therefore the idols shall be put to shame together (Isa. 44:11; 45:16), and the whole Babylonian pantheon will bow down together (Isa. 46:2). Their worshippers call on them in vain (*qāra' yaḥaḏ,* "call on together" [Hos. 11:7], probably denotes a cultic act; cf. the similar expression in Ps. 55:15[14]), and their priests and princes will go into captivity together (Jer. 48:7). The God of Israel, on the other hand, is powerful. He calls all things and they stand forth together (Isa. 48:13); he fashions the hearts of all and observes all their deeds (Ps. 33:15). God forgives (Isa. 65:7) and shows mercy (Hos. 11:8) in the immediacy of his decrees. God and human beings can draw near for judgment together (*špt,* Job 9:32; Isa. 41:1; 43:26). Since God's judgment is universal, both the helper and the one who is helped will perish together (Isa. 31:3; cf. Jer. 50:33); but he delivers his own and gathers the remnant together (*yaḥaḏ śîm,* Mic. 2:12; *qāḇaṣ,* Jer. 31:8). When he delivers, all are joyful together (Jer. 31:13), and the praise of God unites the human and material world in a cosmic community of praise (*rnn,* Job 38:7; Isa. 52:8). When fortunes are reversed, according to Deutero-Isaiah, the *k^eḇôḏ YHWH* will be revealed (Isa. 40:5), and all flesh (*kol . . . yaḥdāw*) will see it.[51] The ordinances of the Lord are both true and righteous (Ps. 19:10[9]), thus fulfilling a norm that cannot be met by human works.

IV. Ecclesiological Usage at Qumran. In the postexilic period, there formed within the Jewish religious community a variety of groups[52] espousing the fulfillment of the Torah of Moses as completely as possible. Many *ḥaḇûrôṯ,* "associations,"[53] are known to us, preeminently that of the Pharisees. Following traditional ecclesiological terminology, such groups called themselves *b^erîṯ, qāhāl, ʿēḏâ, ʿam, sôḏ,* and *ʿēṣâ;*[54] there was a group of Pharisees, for example, who called themselves the "holy congregation (*qahalā'*) of Jerusalem."[55] The Essene groups also had a variety of names for themselves. The Damascus group, for example, called themselves the "new covenant" (*b^erîṯ haḥ^aḏāšâ* [CD 8:21]), while the group with the rule 1QSa preferred the term "community of Israel (*ʿēṣaṯ yiśrā'ēl*) at the end of days" (1QSa 1:1); the Qumran group merely called themselves *yaḥaḏ* (always in the sg.), a term the Damascus group borrowed for themselves after recension B (CD 20:1,14,32).

---

51 It is inappropriate to treat *yaḥdāw* here as a noun deriving from *ḥy,* meaning "face," as suggested by M. Dahood, "Some Ambiguous Texts in Isaias," *CBQ,* 20 (1958), 46ff., or to render it by an irrelevant "above all," as suggested by K. Elliger, *Deuterojesaja. BK,* XI/1 (1978), 1, 21; it stands in emphatic synthetic parallelism with *kol.*

52 Cf. Seidensticker.

53 → בחר *bāḥar* [*bāchar*]; J. Neusner, "ḤBR and N'MN," *RevQ,* 5 (1964/-66), 119-122 [reply to G. W. Buchanan]; J. A. Fitzmyer, "The Aramaic Inscriptions of Sefire I and II," *JAOS,* 81 (1961), 188f.

54 Cf. Rost, *passim;* G. W. Anderson, "Israel: Amphictyony: ʿAM; ḲAHAL; ʿEḎÂH," *Translating and Understanding the OT. Festschrift H. G. May* (Nashville, 1970), 135-151.

55 Bab. *Yoma* 69a.

Various explanations have been put forward to account for the choice of this particular term, which became absolutized as the central ecclesiological concept at Qumran. Dombrowski attepted to demonstrate that *yaḥaḏ* translated Hellenistic Gk. *tó koinón,* a term of religious and cultic provenience (but cf. Phoen. *gaw,* → גויה *g^ewiyyâ* [*g^eviyyāh*]). Since, however, the essential core of what is referred to is borrowed with the term, the process of hellenization would have had to have been much further advanced than was actually the case. Furthermore, the equivalence between *yaḥaḏ* and *tó koinón* could not have escaped the ancient historiographers Philo and Josephus, who obviously had difficulty finding a Greek equivalent for the term the Essenes of Qumran used to describe themselves (*thíasos, hómilos*).[56] As a corporate body recognized by civil law, the *yaḥaḏ* may have been comparable to a Hellenistic association.[57]

The element of "being one," "being a community" inherent in the root may have given the Essenes of Qumran occasion to breathe new life into the word by turning it into a noun, since it embodied programmatically the essence of their new community of faith. The noun *yaḥaḏ* was able to express not only the "communal solidarity" of the group but also the "unity" of its members and the "uniqueness" of the community as the "only source of blessing."[58] This *yaḥaḏ* presents itself as an organized body, clearly esoteric and cut off from the outer world, distinguished internally by its well-defined hierarchy and cenobitic way of life, realized in daily life through the purity of the *sacra communio.* But *yaḥaḏ* can refer not only to the monastic group of insiders but also to nonmonastic groups affiliated with the Qumran community.[59] It is their stated purpose to return (→ שׁוב *šûḇ*) to God (1QS 3:1) "in gracious humility, in merciful love and concern for righteousness, each toward his neighbor" (1QS 2:24), in strict obedience to the Torah of Moses (CD 15:7ff.). In the hostile environment of the desert by the Dead Sea (cf. Isa. 40:3), this *yaḥaḏ* shaped an internal structure that was able to take ancient prophetic traditions (Jer. 31:31ff.) and fill them with new spirit, in clear contrast to the hellenizing tendency of orthodox Judaism.[60]

Fabry

---

56 Cf. Marcus.
57 Bardtke, Hengel.
58 Koffmahn.
59 Wernberg-Møller, Sutcliffe, et al.
60 Cf. also Maier, Koffmahn, Siedl, and J. Murphy-O'Connor, "The Essenes and Their History," *RB,* 81 (1974), 215-244.

יָחַל *yāḥal*; תּוֹחֶלֶת *tôḥelet̠*

Contents: I. 1. Root; 2. Derivatives; 3. Etymology; 4. Versions. II. 1. Occurrences; 2. Object; 3. Stems; 4. Semantic Field. III. 1. "Wait for God"; 2. "Endure"; 3. Forms.

I. 1. *Root.* The root *yḥl* is not definitely attested outside of Hebrew. The proper name *yḥlbʿl*[1] may indicate its occurrence in Phoenician, but more likely this name is only a by-form of *yḥnbʿl*[2] occasioned by a phonetic shift. In Arabic, *wḥl* would be the best equivalent phonetically, but the meanings attested so far suggest that this is a different root.[3] The meaning of Syr. *ʾauḥēl*[4] also points elsewhere. On the other hand, *yḥl*, "wait," is found in the Dead Sea scrolls[5] and in later Middle Heb. *yiḥûl*, "expectation."[6] The supposed by-form *ḥyl* is discussed below.[7]

2. *Derivatives.* From the hiphil we have the derived noun *tôḥelet̠*, "expectation," "hope"; cf. the form *tôḥelâ* in the Dead Sea scrolls (1QH 9:14) and Middle Heb. *yiḥûl*. An adj. *yāḥîl*, "expectant," "patient" has been proposed[8] on the basis of a single occurrence in Lam. 3:26, but it is better to read this word as a verbal form.[9] Whether the name *yaḥleʾēl* derives from *yḥl*[10] is dubious.[11]

3. *Etymology.* Various hypotheses have been proposed with respect to the fundamental meaning of the root. In *KBL*[2,3], the meanings of *wḥl* in Arabic ("be stuck in the mud," "be in a bind") and Old South Arabic ("be undecided," "grant a respite") are cited, together with Syr. *ʾauḥēl*, ("despair"), so that the basic meaning is sought primarily in objective and subjective affliction, from which arises an attitude of waiting (for help, deliverance, etc.). Kopf, however, seeks to explain the root on the basis of the Arabic

---

yāḥal. R. Bultmann, "ἐλπίς," *TDNT,* II, 517-521; E. Jenni, *Das hebräische Piʿel* (Zurich, 1968), 249f., 256ff.; L. Kopf, "Arabische Etymologien und Parallelen zum Bibelwörterbuch," *VT,* 8 (1958), 176f. = *Studies in Arabic and Hebrew Lexicography* (Jerusalem, 1976), 133ff.; A. Weiser, "πιστεύω," *TDNT,* VI, 182-196; C. Westermann, "Das Hoffen im AT," *ThViat,* 4 (1952/53), 19-70 = *Forschung am AT, I. ThB,* 24 (1964), 219-265; *idem,* "יחל *yḥl* pi./hi. warten," *THAT,* I, 727-730; H. W. Wolff, *Anthropology of the OT* (Eng. trans., Philadelphia, 1974), 149f.; W. Zimmerli, *Man and His Hope in the OT. SBT,* N.S. 20 (Eng. trans. 1971), 5-10.

1 *KAI,* 49, 15.
2 *KAI,* 80, 2.
3 Cf. *KBL*³, 389.
4 *LexSyr,* 301a.
5 See II.1. below.
6 *WTM,* II, 235.
7 See I.3.
8 *GesB, KBL*².
9 See II.1. below; *KBL*³.
10 *KBL*².
11 *KBL*³; *IPN,* 204.

noun *ḥawl*, "power," claiming that other verbs of waiting have etymologies connected with being strong, firm, and powerful.[12] Similarly, he connects → קוה *qāwâ*, "hope," "await," with Arab. *quwwa*, "strength," and postbiblical *hmtn*, "wait," with Arab. *matīn*, "firm," "strong." The root *ḥyl*,[13] formerly considered a by-form of *yḥl*, he identifies with Heb. *ḥayil*, "strength," "might," and Arab. *ḥawl*, "power." In other words, Kopf considers *ḥyl* the true root and *yḥl* the by-form. Weiser takes still another approach, deriving *yḥl* from *ḥyl*, "be in labor," "give birth";[14] the basic meaning of *yḥl* would thus be "a state of painful expectation." So far none of these etymologies has been able to carry the day.

4. *Versions.* The Greek Bible usually translates *yḥl* with *hypoménein* (7 times), *elpízein* (13 times), *epelpízein* (6 times, limited to Ps. 119), or *dialeípein* (twice). The noun *tôḥeleṯ*, "expectation," is rended by such words as *elpís* (twice), *hypóstasis*, or *kaúchēma* (once each). It seems that the LXX interpreted the root primarily in the sense of future hope, but we must remember that in the LXX *elpízein* emphasizes the element of personal devotion and confidence.[15] For the Vulg., the element of future hope is primary:[16] it usually translates *expectare* (13 times, plus 19 times in the Psalms *iuxta Hebraeos*) or (*super*)*sperare* (19 times in the Psalms *iuxta LXX* and Lam. 3:21), only rarely *praestolari*, "wait," *sustinere*, or *perseverare*. The Latin rendering of *tôḥeleṯ* agrees with these observations.

II. 1. *Occurrences.* The root occurs 48 times in the MT: there are 41 occurrences of the verb (24 in the piel, 15 in the hiphil, and 2 in the niphal), 6 occurrences of the noun, and 1 of the "adjective." A more detailed picture of its frequency and distribution depends on examination of the numerous forms assigned by emendation to another root (e.g., *ḥîl*, "be in labor," "tremble," or *ḥll* I hiphil, "begin") or added to the statistics.

a. Jer. 4:19 must certainly be excluded: the *kethibh* *'āḥûlâ*, "I must writhe,"[17] is supported by many manuscripts and the ancient versions; it is clearly preferable in the context to the *qere* *'ôḥîlâ*.

In 2 S. 18:14, Joab's statement *lō'-ḵēn 'ōḥîlâ lᵉpāneyḵā* yields no understandable sense as recorded in the text;[18] it should probably be read *lāḵēn 'āḥellâ*, "thus I will make a beginning" (from *ḥll*).[19]

In Ezk. 19:5, the *nôḥᵃlâ* (usually understood as a niphal of *yḥl*) of the text contradicts the immediately following statement *'āḇᵉḏâ tiqwāṯāh;* it is therefore best to follow Zimmerli[20] in emending it to *nô'ᵃlâ*, "was destroyed" (niphal of *y'l* I).

---

12 Cf. → בטח *bāṭaḥ* [*bāṭach*] I; → חכה *ḥāḵâ* [*chākhāh*] I.2.a.
13 *GesB*: חיל III.
14 *GesB*: חיל I.
15 Zimmerli, 9f.
16 → חכה *ḥāḵâ* [*chākhāh*] I.3.
17 Rudolph.
18 Cf. H. W. Hertzberg, *I & II Samuel. OTL* (Eng. trans. 1964), 354.
19 See *KBL*³.
20 W. Zimmerli, *Ezekiel 1. Herm* (Eng. trans. 1979), 389, following Cornill.

b. In 5 passages (Gen. 8:10; Jgs. 3:25; Job 35:14; Ps. 37:7; Mic. 1:12), we find verbal forms from an otherwise unattested root *ḥyl*[21] identical in meaning with *yḥl*. These forms are probably distorted forms of the latter root (to be read as *wayᵉyaḥēl* [Gen. 8:10], *yiḥᵃlâ* [Mic. 1:12], *wayyôḥîlû* [Jgs. 3:25], and *wᵉhôḥēl lô* [Job 35:14 and Ps. 37:7; hiphil]). Another piel results if the unexpected niphal *wayyiyyāḥel* in Gen. 8:12 is taken like the piel *wayᵉyaḥēl* in v. 10. There are 2 additional hiphil forms if the *qere wayyôḥel* is read in 1 S. 13:8 and *wᵉyōḥîl* in Lam. 3:26[22] instead of the difficult "adj." *wᵉyāḥîl*.

When these emendations are included, the data concerning *yḥl* change accordingly: the verb appears 44 times (27 times in the piel and 17 times in the hiphil), the noun 6 times, for a total of 50 occurrences of the root. The root appears in such early texts as J's narrative of the Deluge (Gen. 8:10,12), the story of Ehud (Jgs. 3:25 conj.), the tradition of Saul's rise and fall (1 S. 10:8; 13:8), and the cycle of Elisha legends (2 K. 6:33). The noun *tôḥeleṯ* appears frequently in the first collection of the Proverbs of Solomon (Prov. 10:28; 11:7; 13:12). Ezk. 13:6 appears to date from around 587 B.C.,[23] but there is no certain occurrence of the root in the prophetic traditions of the monarchy (possibly Mic. 1:12). The occurrences in Deutero-Isaiah (Isa. 42:4; 51:5) and Lamentations (Lam. 3:21,24,26; noun in 3:18) are exilic, and the occurrences in the secondary Micah passages (Mic. 5:6[Eng. v. 7]; 7:7) are postexilic. Also probably postexilic are most of the 20 occurrences (21 including an emendation) in the Psalter (Ps. 31:25[24]; 33:18,22; 37:7 conj.; 38:16[15]; 42:6,12[5,11]; 43:5; 69:4[3]; 71:14; 119:43,49,74,81,114,147; 130:5,7; 131:3; 147:11; noun in 39:8[7]), as well as the 9 (10 including an emendation) in Job (Job 6:11; 13:15; 14:14; 29:21,23; 30:26; 32:11,16; 35:14 conj.; noun in 41:1[9]). There are at least 6 occurrences in the Dead Sea scrolls (1QH 7:18; 9:10; 11:31; fr. 4:17; CD 8:4; for the noun, cf. 1QH 9:14).

2. *Object.* As in the case of other verbs of waiting and hoping,[24] *yḥl* frequently has an object or goal in view.

a. In the majority of cases, the object waited or hoped for is mentioned explicitly (30 times with *lᵉ*, 3 times with *'el*). One may wait or hope for Yahweh or God (2 K. 6:33; Ps. 31:25[24]; 33:22; 37:7 conj.; 38:16[15]; 42:6,12[5,11]; 43:5; 69:4[3]; 130:7; 131:3; Lam. 3:24; Mic. 7:7; also Job 13:15 conj.; 35:14 conj.), God's word (Ps. 130:5; 119:74,81,114,147), ordinances (Ps. 119:43), law (Isa. 42:4), steadfast love (Ps. 33:18; 147:11; cf. 1QH 9:10; 11:31), arm (Isa. 51:5), help (Lam. 3:26), or fulfillment of the prophetic word (Ezk. 13:6). With *tôḥeleṯ,* too, Yahweh can be named as the object of expectation (Ps. 39:8[7]; negatively in Lam. 3:18). Elsewhere expectation can have as its object other human beings (Job 29:21,23; Mic. 5:6[7]), human speech (Job 32:11), or a change of fortune that will bring light (Job 30:26) or good (Mic. 1:12 conj.).

b. In a smaller group of texts there is no reference to an object. What matters is not

---

21 See I.3 above.

22 Following *BHS* and Rudolph.

23 Zimmerli, *Ezekiel 1,* 298.

24 → חכה *ḥāḵâ* [*chākhāh*], קוה *qāwâ,* שׂבר *śbr,* צפה *ṣāp̱â.*

who or what is awaited but how long someone must wait. Noah twice (thrice?) waits "seven days" (Gen. 8:10,12); the receding of the waters (8:11) is the end and goal of his waiting, but the passage is clearly stressing Noah's inactivity during each seven-day period. Saul, too, waits "seven days" and is forced to watch the people begin to scatter (1 S. 10:8; 13:8); his waiting for Samuel (*ʿaḏ-bôʾî* [10:8]; *lammôʿēḏ* [13:8]) is clearly in the background, but the main point is equally clear, namely that Saul must wait seven days with the burnt offering, doing nothing. Similarly, the servants of Eglon have to wait for him "until they are utterly at a loss" (Jgs. 3:25 conj.).[25] Job 14:14 probably is an example of waiting for a certain period: a word from God (v. 13) would enable Job to wait out all the days of his service, "till my release should come" (*ʿaḏ-bô ḥªlîp̄āṯî*).[26]

c. Even smaller is the group of passages in which neither the object waited for nor the duration of the waiting is mentioned. In this "absolute" usage even more than in the second group the attitude of "waiting" itself becomes the focus of attention. According to Ps. 71:14, the psalmist will "hope continually" in the midst of "scorn and disgrace" (v. 13). The same patient endurance and waiting is expressed in both Lam. 3:21 ("therefore I have hope"; cf. 3:24: "therefore I will hope in him") and Job 6:11 ("What is my strength, that I should wait?"). Ps. 119:49 is probably also an instance of absolute usage: "while I have hope" (*yiḥāltî* should probably be read instead of the MT *yiḥaltānî,* usually taken as a causative). In Job 32:16, the context suggests silent, submissive "waiting" on the part of Elihu. Job 13:15 is not included here, since *lô ʾªyaḥēl* should be read and there is an object waited for.

3. *Stems.* As our initial survey has shown, the verb *yḥl* actually appears only in the piel and hiphil. The distinction between the piel meaning "wait" and the hiphil meaning "adopt a waiting attitude"[27] has been supported and elaborated by Jenni.[28] His thesis is based on observation that the usage focuses sometimes on the object waited for, sometimes on the subject doing the waiting.[29] On this criterion the distinction must stand or fall.

The piel of *yāḥal* regularly names a specific object or at least implies such an object;[30] it "always involves a specific expectation."[31] This is true to the extent that 19 of the 24 instances of the piel in the MT mention an object waited for. It appears to be true therefore that emphasis on the object is characteristic of the piel. But it is also true that the piel can be used without an object, and there are occasions when the hiphil is used with stress on the object. The piel appears without an object in Job 6:11; 14:14; Ps. 71:14; 119:49; and probably[32] in Gen. 8:10,12. The context does not support the claim that an object of expectation is "implied."[33]

---

25 See II.1 above.
26 Cf. F. Horst, *Hiob. BK,* XVI/1 (1968), 179, 210.
27 *KBL*², 377f.; *KBL*³, 389.
28 Pp. 249f., 256ff.
29 See II.2 above.
30 Jenni, 257.
31 *Ibid.,* 249.
32 See II.2 above.
33 Jenni, 257.

The hiphil of *yāḥal*—like the hiphil of all transitive verbs—designates an "internal causative action";[34] this would imply as a rule that it should mean "cause oneself to adopt an expectant attitude." When the hiphil forms are interpreted in this way, the subject should be the focus of interest and the object should stand in the background. The first point is well illustrated by passages like 1 S. 10:8; 13:8 conj.; Job 32:16, which speak of a "temporary waiting with no specified object."[35] The only problem is that the piel can also be used to express this very type of waiting. Further doubts are raised by 3 passages of theological importance (2 K. 6:33; Lam. 3:24; Mic. 7:7) in which, despite the clear focus of expectation on Yahweh, the "modal nature" (1st person sg. impf.) of the hiphil forms is used as evidence that a determination on the part of the subject is emphasized. At least Ps. 71:14 (piel) exhibits the same "modal nature," and hiphil passages emphasizing the object that do not exhibit the same modality include Ps. 38:16(15); 42:6,12(5,11); 43:5; 130:5, as well as the conjectural forms in Job 35:14; Ps. 37:7; and Lam. 3:26.

We may conclude that it is no longer possible to demonstrate a clear semasiological or syntactic distinction in usage between the piel and the hiphil of *yāḥal*. If the proposed differentiation ever did exist, the "interpenetration of the two meanings"[36] must have begun long before theological usage appeared. Whether the accent is on the waiting subject or the object awaited must now be determined in each case from the context.

4. *Semantic Field*. The semantic field of *yḥl* includes above all the synonymous verbs that appear in parallelism, in the larger context, or in semantically related contexts. The root is especially common in conjunction with → קוה *qāwâ*, "wait, hope" (Job 30:26; Ps. 130:5; Isa. 51:5; Mic. 5:6[7]; Lam. 3:26 [cf. v. 25]; 1QS 11:31). For the use of *tôḥelet* in parallelism with *tiqwâ*/*miqweh*, "hope," see Ps. 39:8(7); Prov. 10:28; 11:7; 1QH 9:14. Ps. 33 ends with a confession expressing confident hope in Yahweh; here *yḥl* appears (vv. 18 and 22) in conjunction with *ḥākâ* (v. 20) and *bāṭaḥ* (v. 21). In 1QH 7:18, too, *yḥl* is used in parallel with a verb expressing confidence: → שׁען *šāʿan*, "rely on." In more detail:

a. In several passages, the context exhibits a semantic relationship between *yḥl* and → דמה *dāmâ* [*dāmāh*] II/*dmm*/*dwm*, "be silent."[37] This is clearest in Job 29:21 (cf. v. 23), where *šmʿ*, "hear," *yḥl*, "wait," and *dmm*, "be still," stand in series; the same is true in Ps. 37:7 ("be still before Yahweh and wait for him" [reading *hôḥēl*]). This usage suggests reading *ṭôḇ yôḥîl dûmām*, "it is good to wait in silence," in Lam. 3:26 (cf. v. 28) and *dîm lᵉpānāyw wᵉhôḥēl lô*, "be still before him and wait for him," in Job 35:14. The same cluster of ideas appears in Ps. 39:3(2); 62:2,6(1,5) and possibly also in Ps. 65:2(1).

b. The usage of *yḥl* often involves the notion of expectant "looking." In Mic. 7:7, for example, *yḥl* stands in parallel with *ṣāp̄â*, "look," a verb that by itself can have the connotation of "waiting" (cf. Ps. 5:4[3]). The same cluster of ideas appears in a lament in Ps. 69:4(3): "My eyes grow dim with waiting (reading *miyyaḥēl*) for my God." In other passages, too, "my eyes grow dim" expresses expectant waiting (Ps. 119:82,123; Jer. 14:6).

---

34 *Ibid.*, 256.
35 *Ibid.*, 257.
36 *Ibid.*, 258.
37 IV.1, 3.

c. All waiting expects as its object something good; the corresponding concepts therefore also belong in the semantic field of *yḥl*. But not all waiting is fulfilled. That someone awaits good only to receive evil is a frequent complaint: "When I waited for light, darkness came" (Job 30:26) (*yḥl*; similarly Mic. 1:12 conj.); cf. Job 3:9; 30:26; Ps. 69:21(20); Isa. 5:7; 59:9,11; Jer. 8:15; 13:16; 14:19 (*qwh*); Job 3:21 (*ḥkh*). In the light of such disappointment one can speak of "lost" expectation (Lam. 3:18 [*tôḥeleṯ*]) or hope (Job 8:13; Ps. 9:19[18]; Prov. 10:28; 11:7; Ezk. 19:5; 37:11 [*tiqwâ*]).[38] Lost hope turns to humiliation (Isa. 30:3); cf. the contrary in Ps. 22:6(5) (*bṭh*); 25:3; Isa. 49:23 (*qwh*).

III. 1. *"Wait for God."* We find theologically relevant usage in the first instance when waiting has God as its object.[39] The formulaic expression "wait for Yahweh" refers to God as the source of all good for which one can hope: God alone is the source and reality of what is awaited; cf. the motivations in Ps. 130:4,7: "For with you/Yahweh is. . . ." Because Israel knows Yahweh to be such a God on the basis of the past, it waits "for Yahweh"; because it can never possess him as such a God, it "waits" for Yahweh.

It is surprising how infrequently in this context we find any statement of what is expected from Yahweh. Lam. 3:26 speaks of waiting for his saving intervention (*litᵉšûʿaṯ YHWH*; cf. Isa. 51:5 [*ʾel-zᵉrōʿî*]); Ps. 33:18; 147:11 speak of waiting for his *ḥeseḏ* (translated by Kraus as "gracious favor and saving faithfulness"). According to Ps. 119:74,81,114,147; 130:5, what is awaited is God's "word" (*dāḇār*); according to Ps. 119:43, it is God's "ordinance" (*mišpāṭ*); according to Isa. 42:4, it is his "law" (*tôrâ*). In all three cases, an actual utterance (oracle of salvation?) is probably intended. But if expectation focuses on an event, specifically the "saving intervention" of Yahweh,[40] in the majority of passages this "intervention" seems to consist in a favorable reply. The formula seems to have this same meaning in 2 K. 6:33. After all the disasters that have befallen him (2 K. 6:24-30), the king of Israel considers it pointless to "inquire" (2 K. 3:11)[41] again of Yahweh through Elisha: "This trouble is from Yahweh! Why should I wait for Yahweh any longer?" Elisha's immediately following oracle of salvation (2 K. 7:1) shows that the expression of despair is unjustified.

As a participle, the formula appears in the phrase *mᵉyaḥᵃlîm lᵉYHWH/lᵉḥasdô* (Ps. 31:25[24]; 33:18; 147:11 (frequently par. *yirʾê YHWH*[42]). Ps. 31:25(24) makes it clear that "waiting for Yahweh" does not refer to an inherent characteristic of the devout: truly to wait for Yahweh requires special strength and courage.

2. *"Endure."* The use of *yḥl* without an object, often too quickly termed "secular," also has theological relevance.[43] In several instances the "waiting" is motivated by a specific relationship between the one who waits and God. It is at least open to debate

38 → אבד *ʾāḇaḏ* [*ʾābhadh*], IV.2.
39 See II.2.a. above.
40 Westermann, *THAT,* I, 728.
41 → דרשׁ *dāraš* [*dārash*], III.1.
42 → ירא *yārēʾ*.
43 See II.2.b, c above.

whether the seven-day wait of Gen. 8:10,12; 1 S. 10:8; 13:8 is purely a narrative motif or represents a traditional display of patient expectation (cf. Vulg. *expectare*). Clearly theological usage is found in Ps. 71:14 and Lam. 3:21 (cf. also Ps. 119:49 conj.): the "endurance" of the devout in the face of alienation, persecution, and suffering is grounded in an ongoing relationship with God. This meaning is also present in Job 6:11 and 14:14.

3. *Forms.* The question of the formal setting of *yḥl* in its theological usage has been answered by Westermann through his reference to the "confession of trust" in individual laments.[44] In fact, confessions of the type "I hope/wait for Yahweh" are common in individual laments (Ps. 119:43,49,74,114,147; 38:16[15]; 39:8[7]; 130:5; with *qwh*: Ps. 39:8[7]; 40:2[1]; 71:5; 130:5; with *bṭḥ*: Ps. 13:6[5]; 25:2; 26:1; 31:7,15[6,14]; 52:10[8]; 56:5,12[4,11]; 119:42; 143:8; with *ḥsh*: Ps. 7:2[1]; 11:1; 16:1; 31:2[1]; 71:1; etc.).

It must not be overlooked, however, that *yḥl* is used in other sections of the lament. The "confession of trust" is often preceded by a passage lamenting disappointed hope or expectation (cf. Job 6:11; 30:26; Ps. 69:4[3]; Lam. 3:18 [also Ps. 69:21(20)]). The question *mah-qqiwwîṯî YHWH* (Ps. 39:8[7]) should possibly be understood as a lament, like *māh-ʾôḥîl lᵉYHWH ʿôḏ* in 2 K. 6:33 and *mah-kkōḥî kî-ʾᵃyaḥēl* in Job 6:11. One may exhort oneself to wait; cf. Ps. 42:6,12(5,11); 43:5; Lam. 3:21,24; Mic. 7:7; and the Qumran fragment 1QH fr 4:14. Waiting appears as a vow (with *qwh*) in Ps. 52:11(9); cf. Job 14:14. One may also exhort others to wait (Ps. 130:7; 131:3; Lam. 3:26). The whole congregation is called to follow the example of the individual. The "confession of trust" thus reflects a trajectory of experience moving from lament through reflexive exhortation to a confession that is joyous albeit still in need of ratification.

Barth

---

44 Cf. H. Gunkel and J. Begrich, *Einl. in die Psalmen. HKAT,* sup. (1933; ⁹1975), with respect to "statements of confidence."

יָחַשׂ *yāḥaś*; יַחַשׂ *yaḥaś*

Contents: 1. Occurrences; 2. Meaning; 3. Theological Implications.

1. *Occurrences.* Biblical Heb. *yḥś,* like the common corresponding Jewish Aram. *yḥs,*[1] is traditionally rendered "enter one's name in the family register, be enrolled," or, as a

---

yāḥaś. F. Schulthess, "Zwei etymologische Versuche," *ZAW,* 30 (1910), 61f.

1 *WTM, s.v.*

noun, "registration, genealogy."[2] Schulthess is probably right in connecting it with Arab. *wḥš*, "wild beast, being solitary in contrast to domestic animals," as a verb "grow savage, alienated," assuming an original meaning "isolated."[3] But his identification of those who are "isolated" with the Jewish "diaspora" is highly improbable. The actual usage of *yḥś* certainly admits some connection with Arab. *wḥš* but does not involve any element of "foreignness" in the sense of "diaspora."[4] The root is unattested in other Semitic languages.

The root *yḥś* appears 21 times in the OT, only once as a noun (*sēp̱er hayyaḥaś,* Neh. 7:5b, if this form is not in fact to be read as a hithpael inf.[5]). Elsewhere it is a verb, always in the hithpael; finite forms appear only in 1 Ch. 5:17; 9:1 and possibly 2 Ch. 31:19; Ezr. 8:3 (if the form in these 2 passages is not in fact also the hithpael inf.[6]). The plural participle with the definite article occurs twice (Ezr. 2:62 par. Neh. 7:64). But even here 1 Esd.(LXX Esd. A) 5:39 *en tṓ katalochismṓ* appears to read the Hebrew hithpael infinitive (the noun *katalochismós* also represents the hithpael inf. of *yḥś* in LXX 1 Ch. 4:33; 5:17; 9:22; 2 Ch. 31:17).[7] Here, too, therefore, the plural participle could be a corruption of an original hithpael infinitive. In the other 14 passages (19 if we include Ezr. 2:62 par. Neh. 7:64; Ezr. 8:3; Neh. 7:5b; 2 Ch. 31:19)—in other words, the vast majority—we find the hithpael infinitive of *yḥś*.

The word occurs only in the Chronicler's history, and always in the context of a list of names; the only exception is the uncertain 2 Ch. 12:15. With good reason, therefore, many scholars deny or doubt that the word or the entire unit in which it appears belonged to the original form of Chronicles–Ezra–Nehemiah.[8] The occurrences are not distributed evenly through the (secondary) units of the Chronicler's history, appearing in only a small fraction of them, sometimes in high concentration (e.g., 1 Ch. 7:5-9; 2 Ch. 31:16-19). Often within these (secondary) texts *yḥś* itself appears to be a secondary addition, primarily to introduce or conclude an existing list (1 Ch. 4:33; 5:17; 7:5,40; Ezr. 8:1; also 1 Ch. 5:7[?]; 9:1[?]). If the list in Nehemiah 7 is in fact borrowed from Ezra 2,[9] the occurrences in Neh. 7:5a,b are also secondary, added to introduce the list. The Vulg. has no equivalent for the 4 occurrences in 2 Ch. 31:16,17,18,19, probably bearing witness to an earlier Hebrew text in which *yḥś* did not appear, so that here too *yḥś* is

---

2 Cf. *KBL*³, *s.v.*

3 Cf. also *KBL*³, *s.v.*

4 See 3 below.

5 A. Kropat, *Die Syntax des Autors der Chronik. BZAW,* 16 (1909), 57; A. B. Ehrlich, *Randglossen zur hebräischen Bibel* (1908-1914; repr. Hildesheim, 1968), *in loc.*; W. Rudolph, *Esra und Nehemia. HAT,* XX (1949), 11, n. 2; and others.

6 See, e.g., *KD* on Ezr. 8:3.

7 On Esdras A as a direct translation of a Hebrew prototype see Rudolph, *HAT,* XX, xv-xvi; R. Hanhart, "Text und Textgeschichte des 1. Esrabuches," *MSU,* 12 (1974), 11; and others.

8 See, e.g., M. Noth, *Überlieferungsgeschichtliche Studien* (1943) (first part translated as *The Deuteronomistic History. JSOTSup,* 15 [Eng. trans. 1981]); Rudolph, *HAT,* XX; *idem, Chronikbücher. HAT,* XXI (1955; ³1968), *in loc.*

9 Cf. U. Kellermann, *Nehemia: Quellen Überlieferung und Geschichte. BZAW,* 102 (1967), 24-26, with bibliog.

probably a secondary addition. In 1 Ch. 5:1, *yḥś* is probably part of a secondary gloss. In 2 Ch. 12:15 and possibly also in 1 Ch. 7:5,[10] *yḥś* is a gloss, as it probably is in Ezr. 8:3, since it does not appear in the sentences of 8:4-14 that have a structure parallel to that of 8:3. The syntactically awkward introduction of *yḥś* in several passages also suggests its secondary nature.

The late and abrupt appearance of *yḥś,* the fact that most of its occurrences are literarily or textually secondary, its highly uneven distribution in the Chronicler's history, and finally its pregnant, almost technical meaning[11] are most readily explained by the hypothesis that *yḥś* belonged initially to the language of a separate self-contained group responsible for (some of) the passages where the word has been interpolated secondarily. The language and ideology of this group were incorporated into postbiblical rabbinic Judaism.

The LXX renders the noun *yaḥaś* in Neh. 7:5(LXX 17:5) as *synodía.* For the hithpael of *yḥś* we find *katalochismós* (5 times), *arithmós* (4 times), *synodía* (twice), *katalochía, enkatalogízein, syllochismós,* and *katarithmeín* (once each). The ptcp. *mityaḥśîm* in Ezr. 2:62 was not understood and was transcribed as *methōesím* (Lucian: *genealogoúntes*). It is noteworthy that only once (1 Ch. 5:1) do we find the translation *genealogeísthai.*

2. *Meaning.* The genealogy of the sons of Simeon (1 Ch. 4:24-27) and the list of their settlements (vv. 28-32) are summarized by 1 Ch. 4:33; *môšᵉḇōṯām* in v. 33bα clearly refers to vv. 28-32, and *hiṯyaḥśām* in v. 33bβ to vv. 24-27. Although the genealogy in vv. 24-27 lists successive generations, *hiṯyaḥśām* alongside *môšᵉḇōṯām* can no longer express the genealogical relationship of the individual members in a temporal sequence of generations; it expresses a relationship that is present and timeless. Our word interprets the true genealogy of successive generations as a list of those who are counted among the sons of Simeon without regard for their temporal sequence. Elsewhere, too, the relationship ascribed by *yḥś* involves membership in a family or group of families (cf. *lᵉmišpᵉḥōṯāyw . . . lᵉṯōlᵉḏôṯām* [1 Ch. 5:7]; *wa'ᵃḥêhem . . . mišpᵉḥôṯ* [1 Ch. 7:5]; *ûḇᵉnê N* [1 Ch. 7:7]; *lᵉṯōlᵉḏôṯām . . . bêṯ 'ᵃḇôṯām* [1 Ch. 7:9]; etc.). But nowhere does *yḥś* document the temporal succession of generations in a genealogy; it assigns someone to a specific circle with reference to the present and therefore timelessly. Thus although *yḥś* almost always involves the notion of genealogical membership, the "enrollment" referred to is not meant diachronically but synchronically.

The nominalized hithpael inf. *yiṯyaḥēṣ* usually refers no longer to the process of registration but by metonymy to its result: not the list, genealogy, or the like that is produced,[12] but concretely "that which is written down in the genealogical registers,"[13] "those who are inscribed genealogically,"[14] i.e., the individuals or clans recorded. This

---

10 Cf. *BHK.*

11 See 2 below.

12 Cf. *KBL*³; E. König, *Hebräisches und aramäisches Wörterbuch zum AT* (Leipzig, 1910; ⁶,⁷1937), *s.v.*

13 *GesB, s.v.*

14 *LexHebAram, s.v.*

is easy to see in all the noun clauses where the infinitive as subject or predicate noun corresponds to another noun that is logically or grammatically plural. It is "their enrolled"—not "their enrollment" or "their genealogical register"—that number so and so many (1 Ch. 7:5,7,9,40).

In 1 Ch. 4:33, *hiṯyaḥśām* occurs in parallel with the concrete pl. *môšeḇōṯām*. Just as *môšeḇōṯām* refers to the settlements listed in vv. 28-32, so *hiṯyaḥśām* refers to the sons of Simeon named in vv. 24-27. It does not mean "their genealogical register"[15] but concretely those who are reckoned among the sons of Simeon.[16] The same is true in Ezr. 8:1 (*hiṯyaḥśām* in conjunction with the concrete *rā'šê 'aḇōṯêhem*). In Ezr. 8:3, also, the hithpael infinitive probably has the concrete metonymic meaning (cf. the parallel statements in Ezr. 8:4ff.). In 2 Ch. 31:16-19, the concrete translation "those recorded" is probably preferable to the traditional rendering, as also in 1 Ch. 5:1 ("but not for those recorded as having the right of primogeniture") and 1 Ch. 5:7 ("among those recorded in the genealogical register"). The concrete metonymic meaning of the infinitive in most passages also explains why the conjectured original infinitive was replaced by the participle in Ezr. 2:62 par. Neh. 7:64 and by the noun *hayyaḥaś* in Neh. 7:5b. Only rarely, then, does the hithpael infinitive mean the process of registration or enrollment (possibly in Neh. 7:5a); it usually conveys the result, the fact that specific individuals or groups are among those enrolled.

Nevertheless, the finite verb always looks back to the completed process of enrollment; with the possible exception of 1 Ch. 5:17, it is resultative or factitive in character (1 Ch. 9:1 and, if the finite verb is actually used, 2 Ch. 31:19; Ezr. 8:3).

We sometimes find → כתב *kāṯaḇ* or → ספר *sēper* in conjunction with *yḥś* (1 Ch. 9:1; 2 Ch. 12:15; Ezr. 2:61 par. Neh. 7:64; 7:5b), so that *yḥś* probably always evokes the idea of a written document. Therefore the notion associated with *yḥś* probably had its setting in some institution, although we cannot give any details of its form.

3. *Theological Implications.* The enrollment in Israel or one of its subdivisions referred to by *yḥś* is not intended as a registration of all those actually present, as is clear above all from Ezr. 2:62 par. Neh. 7:64. This enrollment has both a positive element of inclusion and a negative element of separation. When a person is enrolled in Israel or a group within Israel, that person is also differentiated and separated from others. This establishes an unforced association with Arab. *wḥš,* "be alienated," etc.

It is also clear that the enrollment referred to by *yḥś* does not serve to impose obligations on those who are enrolled, but to recognize their rank and privilege and to give them certain rights. For example, those who cannot demonstrate that they are enrolled among the priests lose their priestly rights (Ezr. 2:62 par. Neh. 7:64), while enrollment results in the recogntion of priestly rights (2 Ch. 31:16-19). Similarly, enrollment among the warriors no longer has the demands of a real battle in view, in which those enrolled would have to perform certain duties; it is a distinction of honor

---

15 *LexHebAram*; *KBL*³, *s.v.*

16 *GesB, s.v.*

(1 Ch. 7:5,7,9,40). Those who are enrolled in Israel (1 Ch. 9:1) or the returned exile community (Ezr. 8:1; Neh. 7:5b) are singled out thereby as full members of the people of God.

The enrollment referred to by *yḥś* therefore has little to do with a numbering of the people like that related in 2 S. 24 or with a registration like that involved in the Roman tax census. It is connected instead with the OT notion of an enrollment in a list entailing and guaranteeing certain rights and privileges for those so enrolled and setting them apart from others (cf., e.g., Ex. 32:32f.; Ps. 87:6; Isa. 4:3; Ezk. 13:9.).[17]

In *yḥś,* therefore, we catch sight of an understanding according to which if one is fully to belong to "Israel" a personal enrollment in Israel or one of its subdivisions is required over and above one's membership by birthright. In this view, membership in Israel by birth is no longer automatically identical with "Israel" as a theological entity.

Mosis

---

17 See L. Koep, "Buch, IV," *RAC,* II (1954), 725-731, with bibliog.; E. Zenger, "Ps 87,6 und die Tafeln vom Sinai," in *Wort, Lied und Gottesspruch. Festschrift J. Ziegler. FzB,* 1f. (1972), II, 97-102.

יַיִן *yayin*

Contents: I. 1. Root; 2. LXX. II. Cultural History of Wine: 1. Manufacture; 2. Storage; Varieties. III. Appreciation: 1. Nourishment; 2. Pleasure; 3. Comfort. IV. Drunkenness and Abstinence. V. Cult. VI. Metaphorical Usage.

---

yayin. N. Avigad, "Two Hebrew Inscriptions on Wine-Jars," *IEJ,* 22 (1972), 1-9; L. Bauer, *Volksleben im Lande der Bibel* (Leipzig, 1903); G. I. Beridzé, *Les vins et les cognacs de la Géorgie* (Fr. transl., Tbilisi, 1964); J. P. Brown, "The Mediterranean Vocabulary of the Vine," *VT,* 19 (1969), 146-170; E. Busse, *Der Wein im Kult des AT. FreibThSt,* 29 (1922); G. Dalman, *AuS,* IV (1935), 291-413; M. Delcor, "De l'origine de quelques termes relatifs au vin en hébreu biblique et dans les langues voisines," *ACLingSémCham,* 223-233 = *Études bibliques et orientales de religions comparées* (Leiden, 1979), 346-356; A. Demsky, " 'Dark Wine' from Judah," *IEJ,* 22 (1972), 233f.; J. Döller, "Der Wein in Bibel und Talmud," *Bibl,* 4 (1923), 143-167, 267-299; W. Dommershausen, "Der Wein im Urteil und Bild des ATs," *TrThZ,* 84 (1975), 253-260; A. Drubbel, "Der Wein in der Heiligen Schrift," *Heilige Land,* 9 (1956), 74-76, 82-84; E. Ferguson, "Wine as a Table-Drink in the Ancient World," *Restoration Quarterly,* 13 (1970), 141-153; K. Galling, "Wein und Weinbereitung," *BRL*^{2}, 362f.; V. Hehn, *et al., Kulturpflanzen und Haustiere in ihrem Übergang aus Asien nach Griechenland und Italien sowie in das übrige Europa* (^{8}1911; repr. Hildesheim, 1963); M. E. Jastrow, "Wine in the Pentateuchal Codes," *JAOS,* 33 (1913), 180-192; K. Kircher, *Die sakrale Bedeutung des Weines im Altertum* (Giessen, 1910); J. Limbacher, *Weinbau in der Bibel* (Bratislava, 1931); H. F. Lutz, *Viticulture and Brewing in the Ancient Orient* (Leipzig, 1922); J. Megrelidzé, "Sur l'origine du culte de Dionysos Vaky-Bacchus-Aguna et du mot du vin," *Bedi*

I. 1. *Root.* The original meaning of *yayin* cannot be determined. Derivation from a root *vei* (Lat. *vieo*), "wind,"[1] is totally hypothetical. Also uncertain is the derivation from *yānâ*, "oppress," with a basic meaning "press."[2] The word obviously came into common usage with the cultivation of wine grapes.[3] Since the Akkadian word for wine is *karānu*, the Hebrew word can hardly have a Semitic origin. Rabin[4] suggests Hittite or Anatolian origin, probably correctly. Cf. Heb. *yayin, yên*, Ugar. *yn*, Arab. and Ethiop. *wain* (also meaning "grape"), OSA *wyn, yyn* ("vineyard"), Akk. *īnu* (a loanword), Hitt. *wiyāna* ("grape"), Gk. *oínos*, Lat. *vinum*, and the analogous Indo-European terms. As synonyms we find *sōḇe'*, "fine wine"[5] (Isa. 1:22) and Aram. *ḥamar* (Ezr. 6:9; 7:22; Dnl. 5:1,2,4,23).

2. *LXX.* The LXX almost always translates *yayin* as *oínos* (144 times), thus interpreting it as synonymous with *tîrôš*. Three other words are each used once: *gleúkos* (Job 32:19, more specific than the MT), *oinopótēs* (Prov. 23:20, for *sōḇē' yayin*), and *sympósion* (Est. 7:7, for *mištēh hayyayin*).

II. Cultural History of Wine.

1. *Manufacture.* The pre-Israelite inhabitants of Canaan undoubtedly knew how to make wine. In a document written *ca.* 1780 B.C., an Egyptian named Sinuhe, a friend of King Sesostris I (*ca.* 1980-1935), relates his adventures in Palestine. In his description, he writes: "There were figs there and wine grapes and more wine than water. . . . I had bread to eat every day and wine as an everyday drink."[6] The patriarchal narrative of the Bible also presupposes the presence of wine in Canaan (Gen. 14:18; 27:25,28,37); from the time of the monarchy on, the use of wine was common.

The actual process of winemaking began with the grape harvest in August and September. The clusters were cut off with special knives and collected in baskets. Sometimes they were then spread out in the sun (usually in the vineyard itself) for up to fourteen days in order to increase the sugar content of the fruit. Usually, however, the grapes were dumped at once into the winepress. This consisted of two round or rectangular basins, the press itself and a catch basin, both hewn out of rock or dug in the ground, covered with stones, and coated with pitch. The pressing basin (*gaṯ*) covered an

---

Karthlisa, 19f. (1965), 109-111; S. M. Paul, "Classifications of Wine in Mesopotamian and Rabbinic Sources," *IEJ*, 25 (1975), 42-44; C. Rabin, "Hittite Words in Hebrew," *Or*, 32 (1963), 113-139; E. Schürer, *A History of the Jewish People in the Age of Jesus Christ*, II (Eng. trans., Edinburgh, ²1979); A. van Selms, "The Etymology of *yayin*, 'Wine'," *JNSL*, 3 (1974), 76-84; C. Seltman, *Wine in the Ancient World* (London, 1957); N. Shapira, "The Wine Industry as to the Ancient Hebrew Sources," *Koroth*, 3 (1962), 40-75; A. A. Wieder, "Ben Sira and the Praises of Wine," *JQR*, N.S. 61 (1970), 155-166; V. Zapletal, *Der Wein in der Bibel. BSt*, 20/1 (1920).

1 Hehn, 93.

2 Van Selms, 82.

3 → גפן *gepen* (*gephen*).

4 Pp. 138f.

5 *KBL*²: "beer of wheat."

6 *AOT*, 57.

area of about 16 square meters (172 sq. ft.); it was 20 to 30 centimeters (8 to 12 in.) deep, and tilted toward one side or corner. The catch basin[7] was lower and smaller, about 1 meter (40 in.) deep; it was connected to the press by a channel. The grapes were trodden by barefoot men or boys (*dāraḵ yayin bayᵉqāḇîm* [Isa. 16:10; cf. Jer. 48:33]) or weighted down with large stones. There were also pressing beams with one end inserted into the rim of the basin, so that large round stones lashed to them could be pressed down on the grapes by lever action. The resulting grape juice was poured into earthenware pots (*nēḇel* [Jer. 13:12]) or wineskins made from skins of goats or lambs (*nō'ḏ* [Josh. 9:4,13]); within six to twelve hours it would begin to ferment.

This must is referred to in the OT as → תירוש (*tîrôš*), from the Semitic root *wrṯ*, "press out." Cf. Mic. 6:15: "You shall tread must, but not drink wine." This term includes both unfermented must and the alcoholic must that has begun to ferment, which, like wine, can "take away the understanding" (Hos. 4:11).[8] It is often associated with grain (*dāgān*) and oil (*yiṣhār*), especially in the context of firstfruits and tithes (Dt. 14:23; 18:4; Neh. 10:40[Eng. v. 39]; 13:12; etc.). A poetic synonym is *ʿāsîs*, "sweet must." At Qumran, *tîrôš* was drunk with the community meals, probably mixed with water (1QS 6:4ff.; 1QSa 2:17f.,20; 1QH 10:24); possibly *yayin* has here been replaced by *tîrôš*.

After fermentation, the wine must not be left on its lees (cf. *šᵉmārîm* in Ps. 75:9[8]); it should be drawn off into other containers. Often a kind of siphon was used, and the wine was filtered through a sieve or a piece of cloth. Sometimes the jugs were labeled with the kind of wine or place of origin. Special wine regions included Lebanon (Hos. 14:8[7]), Helbon near Damascus (Ezk. 27:18), Samaria (1 K. 21:1; Jer. 31:5), Heshbon, Sibmah, and Jazer in Transjordan (Isa. 16:8f.; Jer. 48:32), En-gedi (Cant. 1:14), and Eshcol near Hebron (Nu. 13:23).

2. *Storage; Varieties.* Wine was stored in a cellar near the house. The abundance of limestone made the region well adapted for such cellars. There were also special storage chambers for wine in the wine cellars of the kings, in fortresses, and in the temple (1 Ch. 27:27; 2 Ch. 11:11). Wines that had been aged were preferred to younger wines. In ancient Palestine, it was probably a dark blue variety of grape that was cultivated, from which was made the common red wine (Prov. 23:31; cf. Isa. 63:2 or "blood of the grape" in Dt. 32:14; Sir. 50:15; 1 Mc. 6:34).

To fortify wine or give it a more pleasing taste it was mixed with pepper, wormwood, or incense; it was then called mixed or spiced wine (*māsaḵ/meseḵ* [Ps. 75:9(8); Prov. 9:2,5; 23:30; Isa. 5:22; 65:11] or *reqaḥ* [Cant. 8:2]). Wine mixed with myrrh was used as a narcotic (cf. Ps. 60:5[3]). The wine recovered from the skins was made into vinegar (*ḥōmeṣ*), considered a good thirst quencher when diluted with water (Ruth 2:14). The custom of drinking wine mixed with water—probably in the ratio of two or three to one—seems to have made its first appearance in the Hellenistic era (cf. 2 Mc. 15:39). In Isa. 1:22, at least, the watering of wine is looked on as something bad. "Strong drink"

---

7 → יקב *yeqeḇ*.

8 Cf. W. Rudolph, *Hosea. KAT,* XIII/1 (1966), 110.

(*šēḵār*), probably a kind of beer, was distinguished from wine (Lev. 10:9; Nu. 6:3; Dt. 29:5; Jgs. 13:4; 1 S. 1:15).

III. Appreciation.

1. *Nourishment.* Water was drunk with food, but at a full meal wine was normally passed (Gen. 27:25; 1 Ch. 12:40f.[39f.]; Isa. 22:13). Wine is therefore often mentioned in conjunction with bread (Gen. 14:18; 1 S. 16:20; 25:18). It formed part of the diet of both governor (Neh. 5:15,18) and laborer (2 Ch. 2:9,14[10,15]). Wine was taken among the provisions for a journey (Jgs. 19:19), and it was stored in the garrison cities (2 Ch. 11:11; 32:28). Jesus Sirach includes "the blood of the grape" with grain, milk, honey, and oil as the most important foodstuffs (Sir. 39:26).

2. *Pleasure.* Wine cheers "gods and men" (Jgs. 9:13; Ps. 104:15; Eccl. 10:19; Sir. 31:27); it was considered a source of pleasure that was a necessary part of any feast (Isa. 5:12). In a luxurious house, the room in which banquets were held was called the "wine-drinking room" (*bêṯ mištēh hayyayin* [Est. 7:8]). There were plenty of occasions for festive celebration: the weaning of a son (Gen. 21:8), a wedding (Jgs. 14:10), the vintage (Jgs. 9:27), sheep shearing (1 S. 25:2,36f.), the building of a house (Prov. 9:1-6), the enthronement of a king (1 Ch. 12:40[39]), the making of a covenant (2 S. 3:20f.), a visit from friends or others one desires to honor (2 K. 6:23; 1 Mc. 16:15). The Temple scroll even mentions a special festival devoted to wine. Wine was drunk after the meal, and the atmosphere of celebration was heightened by singing, music, and the garlanding of guests with flowers (Isa. 5:12; 28:1; Wis. 2:7f.). Exchange of toasts was not unknown.[9] Women usually did not take part in these festivities (2 S. 13:23-32), although they were allowed to drink wine. Wine was drunk from earthenware cups or bowls; only the wealthy could afford drinking vessels or precious metal. Glass goblets came into extensive use in the Hellenistic period.

3. *Comfort.* Because wine cheers people up, it is especially recommended for those who are sad (Eccl. 2:3,10,24; Zec. 10:7; cf. the "cup of consolation" for those who mourn [Jer. 16:7]). It was also thought that wine was helpful to those in despair or distress, helping them forget their sorrows (Prov. 31:6f.). "The wine is for those who faint in the wilderness to drink," was Ziba's response to King David when the latter was seeking refuge (2 S. 16:2).

IV. Drunkenness and Abstinence. In the earliest period of Israel, the effects of overindulgence in wine were considered offensive at worst; the prophets and wisdom teachers, however, warned vigorously against heavy drinking and pointed out its terrible consequences. Isaiah hurled his invective against those who are heroes at drinking wine and strong drink (Isa. 5:11,22), and Tobit counseled his son not to let drunkenness accompany him on his way (Tob. 4:15). Various harmful effects are listed: drunkenness

[9] Döller, 272.

causes people to reel and stagger (Ps. 107:27; Prov. 23:34), it causes them to be ill and vomit (Isa. 28:8; Jer. 25:27), it reddens the eyes (Prov. 23:29), brings unconsciousness (Jer. 51:39,57), encourages mockery (Hos. 7:5) and wrath (Sir. 31:30), lessens modesty (Lam. 4:21), takes away understanding (Hos. 4:11), impoverishes the drinker (Prov. 23:21; cf. 21:17), and makes leaders incapable of executing their office (Prov. 31:4f.). Horrible examples are recounted involving the drunkenness of Noah (Gen. 9:21), Lot (Gen. 19:31-38), Nabal (1 S. 25:36-39), David (2 S. 11:13), Absalom (2 S. 13:28), Elah (1 K. 16:9f.), Belshazzar (Dnl. 5:2), Holofernes (Jth. 12:20; 13:4-10), and Simon (1 Mc. 16:15f.).

Abstention from wine was unusual. It involved in the first instance wine with any relationship to pagan religion (Dnl. 1:8; cf. Dt. 32:38). We are also told that Daniel drank no wine for three weeks because he was mourning (Dnl. 10:2f.). The cultic functions of the priests must not be endangered by intoxication; officiating priests were therefore forbidden to drink wine under penalty of death (Lev. 10:8-11; Ezk. 44:21). Nazirites, too, had to renounce any beverage made from grapes for the duration of their oath (Nu. 6:3; cf. Jgs. 13 and Am. 2:12). Finally, the Rechabites drank no wine because they sought to preserve their nomadic way of life without fixed dwellings, agriculture, or viticulture (Jer. 35).

V. Cult. Wine was not incorporated into the cult until it had become a daily beverage. In the nomadic and desert period, water was probably used as a drink offering. The Rechabites' avoidance of wine probably points in this direction. All the passages in the law pertaining to the use of wine in the cult belong to P (Ex. 12:1-20; 29:38ff.; Nu. 15:5; also Dt. 26:1-8). The first evidence for the use of wine during the celebration of Passover dates from the Hellenistic period (Jub. 49:6). The Samaritan Passover, in which wine is not used, is also an argument that the association of wine with Passover is late.

The phrase *nāsak yayin* denoted both the offering of drink offerings to foreign gods (Dt. 32:38) and the offering of wine as part of the cult of Yahweh (Ex. 29:40; Lev. 23:13; Nu. 15:5,10; 28:7,14; Hos. 9:4). With the exception of Gen. 35:14, however, the offering of wine alone or the use of an altar intended solely for this purpose was not a customary cultic act, either public or private. Wine was instead a complement to the sacrifice. A precisely prescribed amount accompanied all burnt offerings: with the sacrifice of a lamb, 1/4 hin; of a ram, 1/3 hin; of a bull, 1/2 hin (Nu. 15:5-10; 28:14; Lev. 23:13). The daily morning and evening sacrifice also ended with a libation of wine, as did the concluding sacrifice for Nazirites. The table for the bread of the Presence also held flagons of wine (Nu. 4:7), and wine was a necessary part of sacrificial meals. The sacrificial wine kept by the Levites was poured out of bowls at the foot of the altar of burnt offering (Sir. 50:15) or sprinkled over the sacrifice with which it was burned ("a pleasing odor" [Nu. 15:7; Jub. 7:5]). Wine is mentioned as a beverage of the gods in Dt. 32:37f. and Jgs. 9:13. In the ancient Near East, sacrifice represented actual food and drink for the deity.[10] This notion may lie behind Ezk. 44:7, where Yahweh speaks of *laḥmî,* "my food" (cf. Nu. 25:2).

---

10 Cf. *KTU,* 1.14 II, 66-79, etc.

VI. Metaphorical Usage. The importance of wine in the life of Israel is clear also from its metaphorical language, in which "wine" can symbolize both joyous and disastrous circumstances. The abundance of God's blessing is seen when those who are delivered from Babylon can buy wine and milk without money (Isa. 55:1). The wisdom teacher equates wine with life (Sir. 31:27), and the consumption of wine with the inward strength given by wisdom instruction (Prov. 9:2,5; Sir. 40:20). The thoughts that arise in the breast are like new wine, still fermenting, which looks for an exit and bursts even new wineskins (Job 32:19), whereas wine on its lees symbolizes the quiet life of Moab, far from the bustle of the world (Jer. 48:11). In Zec. 9:15, "drinking blood like wine" means victory over Israel's enemies; in Ps. 78:65f., God is compared to a warrior rising from wine. In the Song of Songs, the caresses of the bridegroom and the love of the bride are sweeter than wine (Cant. 1:2,4; 4:10; 5:1; 7:10[9]). In Dt. 32:32, wine stands for the salvation or peace of the gentile world. Finally, the paradisal age to come will be so abundant that people can wash their clothes in wine (Gen. 49:11), the mountains and winepresses will overflow with must (Joel 2:24), and Yahweh will provide for all nations a banquet with the best wines (Isa. 25:6).

The cup of wine in the hand of Yahweh signifies God's judgment of wrath upon Israel and other nations. Sinners must drink this cup to the dregs (Ps. 75:9[8]). In Jeremiah's vision of the cup (Jer. 25:15ff.,27), he is to address all the nations, that they may drink and stagger and fall before the sword that Yahweh is sending. At Yahweh's instigation, disaster comes upon the nations because they have drunk the wine from the golden cup of Babylon, i.e., the cup of luxurious Babylon (Jer. 51:7; cf. Zec. 12:2, where a similar image is applied to Jerusalem). To drink of God's cup means to bring misfortune upon oneself (Jer. 49:12; Lam. 4:21; Ezk. 23:31ff.; Hab. 2:16). When God gives his people wine to drink, he is treating them harshly (Ps. 60:5[3]) or destroying them totally (Jer. 13:12ff.).

In the Dead Sea scrolls, *yayin* appears only 4 times, always metaphorically. In a quotation from Dt. 32:33, the wine of the wicked is the poison of serpents (CD 8:9; 19:22), interpreted allegorically as the the sinful path of all who are far from God (CD 8:10; 19:23).

Dommershausen

יכח *yk̲ḥ*; תּוֹכַחַת *tôk̲aḥaṯ*; תּוֹכֵחָה *tôk̲ēḥâ*

Contents: I. Verb: 1. Etymology and Basic Meaning; 2. LXX; 3. Forensic Usage; 4. Pedagogical Usage; 5. Derived Usage. II. Noun: 1. Forensic Usage; 2. Pedagogical Usage. III. Qumran.

---

ykḥ. H. J. Boecker, *Redeformen des Rechtsleben im AT. WMANT,* 14 (²1970), esp. 45-47, 177; F. Büchsel, "ἐλέγχω," *TDNT,* II, 473-76; L. Dürr, *Das Erziehungswesen im AT und im antiken*

I. Verb.

1. *Etymology and Basic Meaning.* The root *ykḥ* occurs in Hebrew and in Jewish Aramaic. It is related to Ethiop. *wakaḥa* and Arab. *wakaʿa* as well as the root *nkḥ.*[1] The basic meaning is "set right,"[2] "show what is right."[3] The verb is found in the niphal (3 times), hiphil (54 times), hophal (once), and hithpael (once). Most of the occurrences are in the prophets (13), Psalms (7), Job (17), and Proverbs (10). There are two derived nouns: *tôḵēḥâ* (4 occurrences) and *tôḵaḥaṯ* (24 occurrences).

2. *LXX.* The LXX translates the 3 occurrences of the niphal by *alētheúein, dielénchein,* and *élenchos.* The hiphil is usually translated by *elénchein* (41 times). The double translation with *elénchein* and *paideúein* reflects the variety of meanings conveyed by the hiphil of *ykḥ.*[4] Other translations include *exelénchein* (3 times), *élenchos* (twice), and *hetoimázein* (twice). Once each we find *dielénchein, blasphēmeín,* and *oneidízein.* The hophal is translated by *elénchein* and the hithpael by *dielénchein.*

3. *Forensic Usage.* A. Forensic usage has its setting in judgment in the gate (Isa. 29:21; Am. 5:10) and its preparatory stages. This "normal procedure" provides the basis for other forms of legal dispute. We find *ykḥ,* for example, in the context of the king's judicial function (Isa. 11:3f.; Hab. 1:12)[5] and the seeking of a legal decision from the deity in the temple (Isa. 2:4; Mic. 4:3).[6] In particular, E pictures a resolution of conflicts in the patriarchal period, where one of the parties has the status of a *gēr,* leading up to a *bᵉrîṯ* after the analogy of judgment in the gate (Gen. 21:25ff.; 31; cf. also Gen. 20:1-17, but

---

Orient. MVÄG, 36/2 (1932); K. Elliger, *Studien zum Habakuk-Kommentar vom Toten Meer. BHTh,* 15 (1953), 50; A. Gamper, *Gott als Richter in Mesopotamien und im AT* (Innsbruck, 1966); B. Gemser, "The *Rîb-* or Controversy-Pattern in Hebrew Mentality," *Wisdom in Israel and in the Ancient Near East. Festschrift H. H. Rowley. SVT,* 3 (1955), 120-137 = *Adhuc Loquitur. POS,* 7 (1968), 116-137; A. Guillaume, *Hebrew and Arabic Lexicography* (repr. Leiden, 1965), 9; F. Horst, "Recht und Religion im Bereich des AT," *EvTh,* 16 (1956), 49-75 = *Gottes Recht. GSAT. ThB,* 12 (1961), 260-291, esp. 289; *idem, Hiob. BK,* XVI/1 (1968), 85f.; G. Liedke, "יכח *jkḥ* hi. feststellen, was recht ist," *THAT,* I, 730-32; V. Maag, *Text, Wortschatz und Begriffswelt des Buches Amos* (Leiden, 1951), 152-54; G. Many, *Der Rechtsstreit mit Gott (RIB) im Hiobbuch* (diss., Munich, 1971), 91-100; W. Richter, *Recht und Ethos. StANT,* 15 (1967), 166-186; I. L. Seeligmann, "Zur Terminologie für das Gerichtsverfahren im Wortschatz des biblischen Hebräisch," *Hebräische Wortforschung. Festschrift W. Baumgartner. SVT,* 16 (1967), 251-278; R. de Vaux, *AncIsr*; R. R. Wilson, "An Interpretation of Ezekiel's Dumbness," *VT,* 22 (1972), 91-104, esp. 98-102; H. W. Wolff, *Hosea. Herm* (Eng. trans. 1974), 76, 113; E. Würthwein, "Der Ursprung der prophetischen Gerichtsrede," *ZThK,* 49 (1952), 1-16 = *Wort und Existenz* (Göttingen, 1970), 111-126.

1 *KBL*³, 391f.

2 Horst.

3 Liedke.

4 Cf. G. Bertram, "παιδεύω," *TDNT,* V, 621.

5 Cf. J. Jeremias, *Kultprophetie und Gerichtsverkündigung in der späten Königszeit Israels. WMANT,* 35 (1970), 101f.

6 Cf. H. Wildberger, *Jesaja. BK,* X/1 (1972), 84.

without explicit mention of a *b^erîṯ*). There is good reason to include in our study the passages mentioned in these texts.

B. The ptcp. *môḵîaḥ* obviously refers to the one who oversees the procedure. In Job 9:33 (cf. Prov. 24:24f.), the *môḵîaḥ* delivers the judgment that is binding upon both parties, functioning as an umpire. This is brought out very clearly by the LXX, which uses *elénchōn* in parallel with *mesítēs.* In Am. 5:10, the *môḵîaḥ* must have a different function. If we follow Wolff[7] and Rudolph[8] in reading the passage in the light of Am. 5:7 and 12, the reference cannot be to a judge, since it is the judges who are accused of perverting justice. In Isa. 29:21, for the same reason, the *môḵîaḥ* can only be someone who demands justice, whether by making an accusation (cf. Job 40:2; Ezk. 3:26) or by defending his own cause. The term *môḵîaḥ,* therefore, can denote both judge or mediator and the parties involved. The use of the same term for a variety of functions is not accidental, but is rooted in the nature of the proceedings. This peculiarity also explains why modern translations must often be remarkably vague.

C. a. The finite forms of the verb can describe the function of the *môḵîaḥ* in the 3rd person. When the party doing the judging is the subject, we often find *ykḥ* following → שׁפט *špṭ* in synonymous parallelism (Isa. 2:4; 11:3f.; Mic. 4:3; Hab. 1:12). Gen. 21:25 uses *ykḥ* for the action of the plaintiff. The nature of the Israelite lawsuit as an interaction between parties is reflected in the use of the hithpael (Mic. 6:2) or niphal (Job 23:7, where a nominal clause using the ptcp. takes the place of the 3rd person impf.).

b. In addition to this general narrative usage, the finite forms appear in the rhetorical forms associated with the preparatory and official stages of a lawsuit, as detailed most recently by Boecker.

(1) In the appeal of the defendant, the accused uses the 3rd person jussive to appeal to the court for justice[9] after denying the charge (Gen. 31:36f.) or declaring his innocence with the formulaic cry *lō' ḥāmās b^ekappay* (1 Ch. 12:18[Eng. v. 17]; Job 16:17,21).

(2) A witness who wishes to bring a charge before the court (Ps. 50:7) announces his intention in the 1st person (*ʿal . . . 'ôḵîḥeḵā,* Ps. 50:8). Such a witness also uses the 1st person within the indictment to conclude the list of circumstances justifying the accusation (Ps. 50:21). Hos. 4:4, an obscure passage, also involves the introduction to an indictment, in which the proposed punishment follows the charge (cf. the emendations proposed in the comms.). The present text at least shows that the negative jussives *'al-yārēḇ w^e'al-yôḵaḥ,* by expressly rejecting charges against other parties, bring their entire force to bear on the one attacked.

Regardless of whether it is possible to recover complete forensic discourses in Job 13, the chapter is full of juristic terminology.[10] Job is accused unjustly; he seeks to demonstrate his innocence in a formal proceeding, two phases of which are recorded: vv. 3-12 and 13-27. In the first section, he seeks to defend himself against the charges of

---

7 H. W. Wolff, *Joel and Amos. Herm* (Eng. trans. 1977), 246.

8 W. Rudolph, *Amos. KAT,* XIII/2 (1971), 194.

9 Boecker, 44.

10 Horst, *BK,* XVI/1, 186.

his friends, who presume to speak for God. In the second, God himself is the plaintiff; Job, sensible of his innocence, demands to know the meaning of the accusations. The court to which he appeals—God in both cases—appears in the 3rd person, introduced by the prep. *'el* (vv. 3 and 15). A comparison with Ps. 50 is illuminating. As in Ps. 50:8,21, the adversary is addressed in the 2nd person. It is therefore reasonable to assume that in Job 13:3, as in Ps. 50:8, the plaintiff voices his accusation in the 1st person, albeit in the periphrastic form *hôḵēaḥ 'eḥpāṣ.*[11] Job 13:15 corresponds to Ps. 50:21. In Ps. 50:16b-20, the plaintiff lists the charges in detail and summarizes the accusation in v. 21, whereas in Job the plaintiff simply summarizes the charges as *darkî.* The list of charges in the indictment has been replaced by the counterstatement of the defense. It will be seen from this discussion that we have in Job 13:3 and 15 elements of an indictment: the exordium in v. 3 and the summary of the charges in v. 15.

(3) Distinct from the indictment is the stipulative complaint,[12] which has as its purpose the demonstration that one of two sides is correct. It, too, can be preceded by an appeal. An exhortative niphal plural is used to address the opponent, urging that both parties present their dispute together to a court for decision (Isa. 1:18).

(4) In the defendant's response, the accused dismisses the plaintiffs with a question that expects a negative answer, in order to go on to present his own side of the case. When referring to the action of the plaintiff, the question uses *ykḥ* in the 2nd person; apart from this, the formulation exhibits considerable variation (Job 6:25f.; 19:5).

(5) Abimelech's inclusion of Sarah in his harem (Gen. 20) is objectively a *ḥᵃṭa'â gᵉḏōlâ* (v. 9), although he considers himself innocent (cf. v. 5) and considers Abraham the true offender. Through God's special providence he has avoided sleeping with a married woman, a crime punishable by death according to Dt. 22:22 (cf. Gen. 20:3), but there remains an act of defamation impugning Sarah's honor. According to Gen. 20:16, this is righted by payment of a sum referred to as a "covering of the eyes" and a declaration of Sarah's innocence on the part of Abimelech. The 1,000 shekels are for reparation to her; but they are given to Abraham as her *ba'al,* just as in Dt. 22:19,29 the fine imposed on the offender is given to the father as the head of the family. The payment of this fine and the further declaration *wᵉlô-ṯihyeh lᵉ'iššâ* (v. 19) are easy to visualize in a procedure that restores honor, as in Gen. 20:16. In Gen. 20, the clause introduced by *hinnēh* and its continuation, a noun clause incorporating a niphal participle (the pronoun is not needed in this case[13]), represents the decision resolving the conflict. It constitutes a formal judgment of innocence, pronounced by the opponent.[14]

c. The action denoted by *ykḥ* is verbal (Job 13:3,13; Ps. 50:7), taking the form of argument and counterargument (Job 13:22). The plaintiff charges the defendant with offenses against the law and morality: he has forgotten the torah of God (Hos. 4:6), which

11 On the use of the infinitive, see *BLe,* §§332t, 382.

12 Boecker, 68f.

13 Cf. *GK,* §116s; the emendation proposed there, reading the 2nd person perfect, is unnecessary.

14 Boecker, 124.

has a special interest in protecting the interests of one's neighbor (compare Ps. 50:18-20 with Ex. 20:14-16; Gen. 21:25 with Lev. 5:23[6:4] and 19:13; Job 22:6-9 with Ex. 22:25[26]; Dt. 24:6; Ex. 22:1f.[2f.]; Dt. 24:17ff.). The defendant seeks to be declared innocent; his complaint is characterized by the question of the nature and extent of the offense (Job 13:23; cf. Gen. 20:9; 31:36; 1 K. 18:9; Jer. 37:18). The plaintiff, having described his own ways (Job 13:15), must respond. The concluding verdict of the judge restores the broken relationship of the two parties (Job 16:21; cf. Isa. 2:4 par. Mic. 4:3). It helps establish justice (Isa. 11:4). Therefore a verdict of innocence can be brief (Gen. 20:16), whereas a different verdict stated with equal brevity would be vacuous. It must be pronounced as a directive that reshapes the world (Isa. 2:3f.). Anyone refusing to submit to this authoritative word must bear the consequences, since it ultimately means death (Isa. 11:4).

D. Yahweh (El, Eloah, Elohim) is the source of justice; he is supreme plaintiff and judge, not only on behalf of his people Israel (Ps. 50:8,21; Isa. 1:18; Mic. 6:2) and individuals (Gen. 31:42; 1 Ch. 12:18[17]; Job 13:10; 16:21; 22:4) but also on behalf of the nations of the world. Therefore God appears repeatedly as subject of *ykḥ* or with the verb in his mouth (cf. the passages listed above). As source of justice he is the final court of appeal, to which one turns in utmost need (1 Ch. 12:18[17]; Job 16:21). Since God does not hold court when the outcome is unknown, the meaning of *ykḥ* often moves in the direction of "punish." But it is not just isolated rhetorical forms that are assigned to God. These forms can also be integrated into other forms having a different setting. In the prophetic judgment discourse, which can be spoken by a prophet as mediator (2 K. 19:4),[15] Yahweh calls on his people to show wisdom. Ps. 50 exhibits a further development of the prophetic judgment discourse; it is a festival psalm in which Israel is charged with its sins, probably by a Levite.[16]

4. *Pedagogical Usage.* a. To the extent that the hiphil of *ykḥ* has pedagogical import, it usually appears in conjunction with *ysr/mûsār*[17] (Job 5:17; Ps. 6:2[1]; 38:2[1]; 94:10; Prov. 9:7; Jer. 2:19). The object is introduced directly as a noun or suffix (2 S. 7:14; Job 5:17; Ps. 6:2[1]; 38:2[1]; 141:5; Jer. 2:19) or by the prep. *bᵉ* (Prov. 30:6) or *lᵉ* (Prov. 9:7f.; 15:12; 19:25). As can be seen from Prov. 9:8, the variation in construction is semantically irrelevant. It is nevertheless striking that the prepositional construction appears only in Proverbs, where there are just 2 occurrences of a direct object; the relative clause introduced by *ʾēṯ* should probably be included with the prepositional constructions. This cannot be more than a stylistic peculiarity, especially since there is no discernible correlation between the form of the verb and the syntax of the object. The hophal provides the passive. In this usage, *ykḥ* belongs to the vocabulary of wisdom. Its locus is primarily the aphorism stating a lesson from experience. Very rarely it is recorded as professional instruction in the form of advice (compare Prov. 9:8 with 9:7) or as a liturgical petition

---

15 Cf. Jeremias, 141.

16 *Ibid.*, 127.

17 → יסר *yāsar*.

in sickness and distress (Ps. 6:2[1]; 38:2[1]). In 2 S. 7:14; Jer. 2:19, also, where the word appears in the mouth of a prophet in a promise or threat, we note a sense of the connection between guilt and punishment.

b. The activity denoted by *ykḥ* is a function of a father, the natural disciplinarian of his sons (2 S. 7:14; Prov. 3:12), or a teacher (Ps. 94:10)—in general, of a sage whose company is sought (Prov. 15:12; 25:12; cf. 13:20; 15:31). Although it is a mark of love and affection (Job 5:17; Prov. 3:12), it is devoid of pity. Its words are harsh (Prov. 28:23)—no less so than the beatings designed to reinforce them. The rod is the instrument of discipline (2 S. 7:14; Ps. 141:5); even when it does not achieve its intended purpose it is worthwhile, since it cannot fail to have a beneficial effect in the eyes of an unsophisticated third party (Prov. 19:25).[18] What provokes *ykḥ* is a mistake on the part of the learner, transgression of a commandment (hiphil of *ʿwh,* 2 S. 7:14). The nature of the response is revealed by Prov. 30:6, an admonition that in its original form (as preserved, e.g., by the Egyptian Instruction of Ptah-hotep [from the time of the Middle Kingdom, 2150-1750 B.C.])[19] demanded that the learner perform every task exactly as stated.[20] The biblical version may be aimed at someone copying sacred texts, inculcating absolute accuracy (cf. Dt. 4:2; 13:1[12:32]). Although the mistake is specific, it is also typical, so that it must be prevented from becoming habitual. This is true even when the situation changes from a specific sociological context to something broader. In Jer. 2:18, the error consists in relying on treacherous political coalitions instead of Yahweh. The act of *ykḥ* itself reveals and specifies the mistake. The intensity of the attack on the self-esteem of the person involved is shown by the conclusion of Prov. 30:6: ". . . and you be found a liar." The disciplinary rigor that unmasks the transgressor is inescapable. But this is just one side of the situation. The other side is the resulting increase of *daʿaṯ,*[21] knowledge and insight (Ps. 94:10; Prov. 19:25; Jer. 2:19) into the order that determines the course of the world and the connection between an act and its consequences. What Israel suffered in 721 and Judah in 701 was the consequence of apostasy from Yahweh (Jer. 2:19).

c. There are two typical responses to the act of *ykḥ* (Prov. 9:8): one may accept it with love (*ʾāhaḇ*) or reject it with hate (*śānēʾ*). These attitudes are fundamentally unalterable. As experience shows, they are inherent in the person of the "scoffer" (*lēṣ,*[22] Prov. 9:7; 15:12; 19:25) or the "wicked" (*rāšāʿ,*[23] Prov. 9:7) and the "wise" person (Prov. 9:8), who has "understanding" (*nāḇôn,*[24] Prov. 19:25). The nature of the *lēṣ* is revealed in his stubbornness (Prov. 13:1; cf. 23:9; 27:22), whereas a joyful willingness to learn characterizes the *ḥāḵām* or *nāḇôn* (Prov. 1:5; 14:6; 19:25; 21:11). Therefore the teacher is

---

18 W. McKane, *Proverbs. OTL* (1970), 525f.

19 *ANET*^{3}, 414.

20 For a different interpretation, see S. Morenz, *Egyptian Religion* (Eng. trans., Ithaca, N.Y., 1973), 223f.

21 → ידע *yāḏaʿ*.

22 → ליץ *lîṣ*.

23 → רשע *rāšāʿ*.

24 → בין *bîn*.

counseled to act according to this observation and not even bother to reprove a scoffer, but to devote his attention to the *ḥāḵām* (Prov. 9:8). In the ideal relationship between student and teacher, the latter finds a receptive ear for his reproofs: "A golden ring, a costly jewel—a wise reprover to a listening ear" (Prov. 25:12).

d. Yahweh as the subject of *ykḥ* is a special case of a more general process, the "theologizing" of wisdom; Prov. 30:6 has already provided an eloquent example. Yahweh acts as a father acts toward his son (Prov. 3:12); he is the sage who teaches knowledge (Ps. 94:10). The reproof that issues from love may take the form of sickness or some other disaster, which can take on the role of subject (Jer. 2:19). As a result, sickness and distress can be interpreted as the consequence of error, as an act of reproof on the part of Yahweh (Job 5:17f.; 33:19; and esp. Ps. 38). In this case they do not represent a final punishment, but convey the possibility of a new beginning (Job 5:18) realized through joyous public confession of sin (Job 33:27-29; cf. Ps. 38:19[18]). This "theologized" wisdom entered into the second stratum of Nathan's prophecy,[25] providing the interpretive schema that makes history bearable (2 S. 7:14).

5. *Derived Usage.* a. In wisdom disputations *ykḥ* designates the argumentative refutation of the position taken by the other party. There are certain formal requirements for such a discourse if the opponent is to accept it (Job 15:3; 32:12).

b. In one instance *ykḥ* designates the revelation of the divine will in an oracle, which is recognized when a previously announced sign comes to pass.[26] The person in question appears as the immediate object of the verb, so that the translation "appoint" is appropriate (Gen. 24:14,44).

II. Noun.

1. *Forensic Usage.* All the discussion concerning the meaning and usage of the verb applies also to the nouns *tôḵaḥaṯ* and *tôḵēḥâ,* which are derived from the hiphil.[27] In forensic usage, *tôḵaḥaṯ* refers to a formal statement of one's position (Job 13:6; 23:4; Ps. 38:15[14]; Hab. 2:1). From God's mouth it is the verdict that effects punishment, through which justice is accomplished (Ezk. 5:15; 25:17). The form *tôḵēḥâ,* found only 4 times, is restricted to the latter meaning (2 K. 19:3 par. Isa. 37:3; Ps. 149:7; Hos. 5:9).

2. *Pedagogical Usage.* In pedagogical usage, the noun *tôḵaḥaṯ,* often used with *mûsār* (Prov. 3:11; 5:12; 6:23; 10:17; 12:1; 13:18; 15:5,10,32), means "reproof, rebuke, censure"; it belongs to the genre of threat and invective (1:23,25,30; 5:12),[28] addressed to the learner by the teacher (5:13). The rod reinforces the words (29:15). If the reproof is not heeded—cf. such expressions as "ignore" (*lō' 'āḇâ*; 1:25), "despise" (*nā'aṣ*; 1:30;

---

[25] L. Rost, *The Succession to the Throne of David. Historic Texts and Interpreters,* 1 (Eng. trans., Sheffield, 1982), 50f.

[26] Cf. P. van Imschoot, *BL*², *s.v.* "*Orakel.*"

[27] *GK,* §85p; *BLe,* §61n.

[28] Cf. C. Kayatz, *Studien zu Proverbien 1–9. WMANT,* 22 (1966), 119ff., 61f.

5:12), "be weary of" (*qûṣ*; 3:11), "reject" (*ʿāzaḇ*; 10:17), "hate" (*śānēʾ*; 12:1; 15:10), "stiffen the neck" (*hiqšâ ʿōrep̱*; 29:1)—the consequences are stupidity (12:1), error (10:17), misfortune (5:9-12), and death (15:10). Obedience, however—described by such terms as "return" (*šûḇ*; 1:23), "heed" (*šāmar*; 13:18; 15:5), and "hear" (*šāmaʿ*; 15:31)—brings wisdom (29:15), the spirit of wisdom (1:23), prudence (15:5,32), honor (13:18), and life (6:23; 15:31). Moreover, *tôḵaḥaṯ* is true love (27:5). God's *tôḵaḥaṯ* is heard by the psalmist in his sickness (Ps. 39:12[11]; 73:14).

G. Mayer

III. Qumran. The verb *ykḥ* appears at least 18 times in the Dead Sea scrolls, almost exclusively in the hiphil, with the meaning "reprimand." The noun *tôḵaḥaṯ* appears 9 times. Its meaning ranges from a "reprimand" in the presence of witnesses in the sense of *correctio fraterna* (1QS 6:1) through "corrective punishment" as an act of God's judgment (1QH 7:29; 9:24,33; 12:31) to the torturing, "chastisement" (and execution?) of the Teacher of Righteousness by the "man of lies" (1QpHab 5:10).

The situation is reversed at the eschaton, when the Essene of Qumran becomes the instrument of God's vengeance, undertaking the "chastisement" (= punitive extermination) of the wicked (1QpHab 5:4).[29]

Fabry

---

[29] Cf. H. Fabry, *Die Wurzel ŠÛB in der Qumran-Literatur. BBB*, 46 (1975), 166.

יָכֹל yāḵōl

Contents: I. 1. Etymology, Occurrences, LXX; 2. Meaning. II. Phoenician and Aramaic. III. OT Usage: 1. Human Beings; 2. God; 3. Without Infinitive; 4. Jacob; 5. Qumran.

---

yāḵōl. W. Grundmann, "δύναμαι," *TDNT,* II, 284-317.

On Gen. 32: R. B. Coote, "The Meaning of the Name Israel," *HThR,* 65 (1972), 137-142; O. Eissfeldt, "Non dimittam te, nisi benedixeris mihi," *Mélanges bibliques. Festschrift A. Robert. Travaux de l'Institut catholique de Paris,* 4 (1957), 77-81 (= *KlSchr,* III, 412-16); K. Elliger, "Der Jakobskampf am Jabbok," *ZThK,* 48 (1951), 1-31 = *KlSchr. ThB,* 32 (1966), 141-173; G. Gevirtz, "Jacob at the Ford (Gen. 32,23-33)," *HUCA,* 46 (1975), 50-53; H.-J. Hermisson, "Jakobs Kampf am Jabbok (Gen. 32,23-33)," *ZThK,* 71 (1974), 239-261; J. L. McKenzie, "Jacob at Peniel: Gn 32,24-32," *CBQ,* 25 (1963), 71-76; F. van Trigt, "La signification de la lutte de Jacob près du Yabboq," *OTS,* 12 (1958), 280-309.

On Hos. 12: P. R. Ackroyd, "Hosea and Jacob," *VT,* 13 (1963), 245-259; F. Diedrich, *Die Anspielungen auf die Jakob-Tradition in Hosea 12,1–13,3. FzB,* 27 (1977); M. Gertner, "An

I. 1. *Etymology, Occurrences, LXX.* The verb appears in Northwest Semitic, probably (according to the most commonly accepted interpretation) as early as the Phoenician Karatepe inscription (*ca.* 720 B.C.).[1] It also appears in Egyptian, Biblical, and Nabatean Aramaic, as well as in the Aramaic of Qumran, the Targum, and the Talmud. The root is probably based on the biliteral *kl,* expanded by the prefix *y* or the interpolation of *h* (Aram. *khl*). The verb appears 193 times in the Hebrew OT, 4 times in Sirach, 8 times in the Dead Sea scrolls, and 12 times in Biblical Aramaic, always in the qal. The LXX usually translates it with *dýnamai* and its derivatives, but sometimes with *ischýō* or *poiéō* and their derivatives.

2. *Meaning.* The most frequent meaning is "be able" or "succeed";[2] other meanings include "be allowed," "be superior," "be victorious over," "grasp," "bear," and "endure." According to Köhler and Elliger, the latter three constitute the primary meaning; but their rarity makes this highly unlikely.

II. Phoenician and Aramaic. In Phoenician we find the sentence *wbymty ʾnk ʾšt tkl hdy dl . . . ,*[3] "In my [the king's] days a woman was able. . . ." The rest is left untranslated by *KAI,* but is rendered most recently:[4] "In my days a woman was able to rejoice in spinning the spindle"—i.e., the image of a land at peace. A different division of the consonants in which *ykl* does not occur, and therefore a different translation, has been proposed by van den Branden.[5]

The verb appears frequently in the Aramaic of the OT, Hermopolis, Qumran, the Talmud, and the Targum; it is often identical with the semantically related verb *khl.* Here, too, its meaning is usually "be able." Once, in Dnl. 7:21, it means "prevail."

The verb has a specialized juristic sense in the Aramaic of Elephantine: when negated it means "waive the right to go to court" (Vogt: *non habere jus . . .*).[6]

Soggin

III. OT Usage.

1. *Human Beings.* In OT Hebrew, *yāḵōl* is usually used with the infinitive construct (usually with *lᵉ,* sometimes without). It is noteworthy that in most instances the verb is negated or otherwise represented as being uncertain (conditional clause: Gen. 15:5; 1 S.

Attempt at an Interpretation of Hosea XII," *VT,* 10 (1960), 272-284; E. M. Good, "Hosea and the Jacob Tradition," *VT,* 16 (1966), 137-151; W. L. Holladay, "Chiasmus, the Key to Hosea XII 3-6," *VT,* 16 (1966), 53-64; J. Vollmer, *Geschichtliche Rückblicke und Motive in der Prophetie des Amos, Hosea und Jesaja. BZAW,* 119 (1971), 105-115.

1 *KAI,* 26.

2 *GesB*[17], *BDB, LexHebAram,* contra *KBL*[2.3].

3 *KAI,* 26 II.5.

4 E. Lipiński, "From Karatepe to Pyrgi," *RSF,* 2 (1974), 48.

5 A. van den Branden, "Inscriptions phéniciennes de Karatepe," *Melto,* 1 (1965), 44f.

6 Cf. the waiving of this right in *BMAP,* 3, 12; and in *BMAP,* 10, 15; a contract for the transfer of a house; and *AP,* 15, 31, a marriage contract.

17:9; Isa. 47:12; question: Ps. 78:19f.; 2 Ch. 32:13f.; with *'ûlay*, "perhaps": Nu. 22:11; unreal condition: Jer. 13:23; but positive in Ex. 18:23; 1 K. 3:9). In 2 K. 16:5, for example, we read: "they were not able to do battle with [the enemy]." We also find: "they could not conquer it" (Isa. 7:1; cf. 1 S. 17:9 [*'im*]; Nu. 22:11 [*'ûlay*]); Jgs. 2:14 [*'āmaḏ*]; Josh. 7:12f. [*qûm*; cf. Ps. 18:39(Eng. v. 38); 36:13(12), where *qûm* more likely means "rise up"]); "they could not drive them out" (Dt. 7:17; Josh. 15:63); "he could not see" (etc.) (because he was blind: Gen. 48:10; 1 S. 4:15; 1 K. 14:4; because it was dark: 1 S. 3:2; cf. also Ps. 40:13[12], describing suffering as a consequence of sin). Moses cannot "carry the people" alone (Nu. 11:14; Dt. 1:9); because of his age he could not longer "go out and come in" (Dt. 31:2). The descendants of Abraham cannot be counted (Gen. 13:16; cf. 15:5; both passages use conditional clauses). Jephthah cannot take back his vow (Jgs. 11:35). The king of Assyria boasts that no one can be saved from his hand (2 K. 18:29 par. Isa. 36:14; the parallel in 2 Ch. 32:13-15 is more expansive: even the gods canot save). The wicked are like a sea that cannot rest (Isa. 57:20; Jer. 49:23). Often human impotence before God is stressed: when God has acted, Laban and Bethuel can do nothing (Gen. 24:50). David cannot bring back his dead child (2 S. 12:23). Job cannot (stand) before God's majesty (Job 31:23, without inf.). Balaam cannot say anything except what is put in his mouth by God (Nu. 22:18,37,38). Cf. also 1 S. 6:20: "Who is able to stand before Yahweh?" (the answer is "no one"). Ecclesiastes in particular emphasizes human impotence: no one can make straight what God has made crooked (Eccl. 7:13; cf. 1:15). "All things are full of weariness; no one can utter it" (1:8). No one can find out the work of God (8:17), and therefore no one can dispute with God (6:10). Isa. 47:11 states that Babylon cannot avert (*kpr* piel, par. *lō' ṯēḏeʿî šaḥᵉrāh*) the threatened disaster. The idols of Babylon "cannot save the burden" (Isa. 46:2). Gold cannot deliver on the day of Yahweh's wrath (Ezk. 7:19; Zeph. 1:18).

We see another aspect of impotence when custom or tradition forbids something. Jacob's sons cannot give their sister Dinah to be the wife of someone uncircumcised (Gen. 34:14). The Egyptians cannot or may not eat with Hebrews (Gen. 43:32). Because of a vow, the other Israelites cannot give their daughters to a Benjaminite (Jgs. 21:18). Ruth's *gō'ēl*[7] cannot redeem the field from Naomi because to do so would impair his own inheritance (Ruth 4:6).

In a further specialization, *yāḵōl* becomes a legal term meaning "be permitted by law": "you may not put a foreigner over you" as king (Dt. 17:15); a man who has two wives "may not treat the son of the loved as first-born in preference to the son of the disliked" (21:16); "you may not evade" the duty of restoring something lost by your neighbor (22:3); "she shall be his wife and he may not put her away all his days" (22:19,29). Cf. the cultic law in Dt. 12:17: one may not eat within the towns the tithe of grain or wine or oil, but only before Yahweh in the sanctuary.

Cultic prohibitions use negated *yāḵōl*. The Israelites must not come up to Mt. Sinai (Ex. 19:23); the Passover must not be sacrificed within any of the towns of the land (Dt. 16:5); someone who is unclean must not keep the Passover (Nu. 9:6); Joshua states that

---

7 → גאל *gā'al*.

the people cannot serve Yahweh, for he is a holy and jealous God, who will not forgive their transgressions (Josh. 24:19); Moses cannot or must not see the face of God (Ex. 33:20); Moses could not enter the *ʾōhel môʿēḏ* "because the cloud abode upon it, and the *kāḇôḏ* of Yahweh filled the tabernacle" (Ex. 40:35); cf. 1 K. 8:11: the priests could not enter to minister because of the cloud, because the *kāḇôḏ* of Yahweh filled the temple (par. 2 Ch. 5:14; cf. 7:2).

Ringgren

2. *God.* Theologically, the verb should be especially appropriate to the omnipotent God of Israel; it is rarely so used, however, and then often in negative expressions: Nu. 14:16; Dt. 9:28; 2 Ch. 32:14; Job 42:2; Ps. 78:19f.; Jer. 18:6; 20:7; 44:22; Hab. 1:13. In the 2 passages from the Pentateuch, Moses in his prayer supports the theory that the nations might doubt God's omnipotence if Israel perished in the desert instead of entering the promised land. In Jer. 44:22, God cannot bear the evil doings of his people; Habakkuk states that his eyes are so pure that he cannot look on wrong. In the 2 Psalms passages and in 2 Chronicles, God is the subject of a blasphemous statement casting doubt on his omnipotence. Only in 3 passages does *yāḵōl* appear in a positive context with God as its subject: Jer. 18:6 underlines his omnipotence with the image of the potter, who can do whatever he wants with his clay; in Jer. 20:7, he deceives and prevails over the prophet; and according to Job 42:2, God can do all things and no purpose of his can be thwarted.

In the Aramaic portion of Daniel, God appears 4 times as the subject of *ykl:* 3:17,29; 4:34(37); 6:21(20). The 6 passages where angels or human beings are the subject stress that they can do nothing without God, not to speak of acting against him (2:10,27,47; 4:15[18]; 6:5[4]; 7:21). Even Daniel can interpret dreams only with God's help (5:16 *Q*). The frequent use of *ykl* with God as subject, rare elsewhere, is characteristic of Daniel.

Soggin

3. *Without Infinitive.* Without an infinitive, *yāḵōl* sometimes means "bear" or "endure," sometimes "be superior," "prevail over." The former meaning is found in several passages. God cannot endure "iniquity and solemn assembly" (Isa. 1:13). Neither can he endure (par. *ṣmt* hiphil) the haughty and arrogant (Ps. 101:5). According to Hos. 8:5, the Israelites cannot be pure by their own efforts (*niqqāyôn* as obj.). Jer. 38:5 says, "The king can do nothing against you." Cf. also Job 42:2, mentioned above (*kōl*).

The meaning "prevail" appears in the following passages: Gen. 30:8 (Rachel at the naming of Naphtali: "I have wrestled with my sister, and have prevailed"); Gen. 32:26[25] and Hos. 12:5(4) (Jacob at the Jabbok, discussed below); Jer. 20:7 (discussed above); Isa. 16:12 ("when Moab comes to his sanctuary to pray, he will not prevail"); Ps. 21:12(11) ("if they devise mischief, they will not prevail"); Ps. 13:5(4) (the enemy says, "I have prevailed over him"); Nu. 13:30 (Caleb encourages the people, saying, "We are well able to overcome it"); Jgs. 16:5 ("that we may bind him [Samson] to subdue him"); Jer. 1:19 ("they shall not prevail against you"); Jer. 20:10 ("perhaps he will be deceived, then we can overcome him"; cf. v. 11: "my persecutors will not succeed"); Jer. 38:22 (the women deported to Babylon lament: "Your trusted friends have deceived [*hissîṯû*] you [the king of Judah] and prevailed against you"); Ob. 7 ("all your allies have deceived [*nš'* hiphil] you [Edom] and prevailed against you"); Ps. 129:2 (enemies have afflicted me, but "have not prevailed against me"); Est. 6:13 (Haman cannot prevail against Mordecai).

Ringgren

4. *Jacob.* In Gen. 32:23-33(22-32), a narrative ascribed to J, the subject of *ykl* in v. 26(25) is not God but a mysterious "man," who did not prevail against Jacob. This is confirmed in v. 29(28) by the popular etymology of Jacob's new name "Israel."[8] Hos. 12:4b-5(3b-4) refers to the "man" first as *'ᵉlōhîm,* "God," then as → מלאך *mal'āḵ* a "messenger" or "angel," probably the earliest identification of the "man." Note, however, the different prepositions (*'eṯ* and *'el*) and the different verbs (*śārâ* and *śārar* [or *swr,* in which case *wayyāśar* should be read]); cf. the discussions cited in the bibliography. We need not devote space to the problems posed by the second verb.[9] While the text in Gen. 32:26(25) is quite clear ("When the man saw that he did not prevail against Jacob, he touched the hollow of his thigh . . ."), v. 29(28) is replete with problems. The usual translation is: ". . . for you have striven with God [or "gods"] and with men, and have prevailed." A different translation is possible, however: ". . . for you have striven with God [or "gods"]—indeed, you have prevailed over men." This rendering, reading the *waw* in *wᵉ'im* as asseverative, is supported by Coote, although the verb at the end of the clause with *waw*-consecutive is peculiar. Another possibility would be to delete "with men," but this would yield a *lectio facilior.*

In any case, the meaning of our verb in this context is clear: on one occasion a human being strove with a divine being and prevailed. It need not concern us whether the divine being was a form of → אל *'ēl*[10] or some other divine being, as suggested already by Hosea. What is important is that, although Jacob did not finally emerge victorious, he nevertheless was able in some measure to impose his will on his opponent. Of course this bald statement could not be allowed to stand: the divine being becomes a human "man" in J; and in Hosea, who was probably closest to the original tradition, the entire episode is a further sign of the sin of Jacob, which lives on in the sin of Israel.

Soggin

5. *Qumran.* In the Dead Sea scrolls, *ykl* occurs some 10 times (to the extent that the texts are intact), only negated. It appears in statements representing the anthropology of the Essenes at Qumran. By themselves, human beings are not able (*ykl*) to perform any actions: to understand God's glory (1QS 11:20), to tell of his wonders (1QH 11:24), to stand before him (1QH 7:29), to guide their own steps (1QH 15:13,14,21). The expression *lw' ykl* becomes the term for human impotence as God's creatures.

Fabry

---

8 → ישראל *yiśrā'ēl.*

9 *Ibid.*

10 Eissfeldt.

יָלַד yālaḏ; יֶלֶד yeleḏ; יַלְדָּה yaldâ; יַלְדוּת yalᵉḏût; יָלִיד yālîḏ; תּוֹלְדוֹת tôlᵉḏôt

---

Contents: 1. Etymology, Occurrences, Meaning; 2. Birth and Descendants in OT Theology; 3. Genealogies; 4. Verb with God as Subject; 5. yeleḏ and yālîḏ; 6. Figurative Usage; 7. Qumran.

1. *Etymology, Occurrences, Meaning.* The root *wld (Akk. walāḏu alongside later alāḏu, Arab. and Ethiop. walada) is copiously attested in the Semitic languages,[1] mostly as yld (Syr. īleḏ). The basic meaning, "bring forth (children)," is universal; its variants in the corresponding verbal stems are roughly the same.

The verb (including the piel ptcp.) occurs 492 times in the OT, most often in the qal and hiphil. It is relatively most frequent in Genesis and Chronicles, where it is found primarily in genealogies and in the patriarchal narratives of Genesis. The detailed distribution is as follows:[2] Genesis, 170; 1 Chronicles, 117; Isaiah, 23; Jeremiah, 22; Exodus and Job, 15; Ruth, 14. Of the occurrences, 237 are in qal (90 in Genesis, 26 in 1 Chronicles, 17 in Jeremiah, 15 in Isaiah), 38 in the niphal (10 in 1 Chronicles, 7 in Genesis), 10 in the piel (8 in Exodus, 2 in Genesis), 27 in the pual (11 in Genesis), 176 in the hiphil (80 in 1 Chronicles, 59 in Genesis, 9 in Ruth, 6 in Isaiah), 3 in the hophal (Gen. 40:20; Ezk. 16:4f.), and 1 in hithpael (Nu. 1:18).

Nouns derived from yld include wālāḏ, "child" (Gen. 11:30); yeleḏ, "child, boy" (89 times); yaldâ, "girl" (3 times); yalᵉḏût, "youth" (3 times); yillôḏ, "born" (5 times); yālîḏ,

---

yālaḏ. F. Büchsel, "γεννάω," *TDNT,* I, 670-75; M. David, *Die Adoption im altbabylonischen Recht. Leipziger rechtswissenschaftliche Studien,* 23 (1927); H. Donner, "Adoption oder Legitimation?" *OrAnt,* 8 (1969), 87-119; G. R. Driver and J. C. Miles, *The Babylonian Laws,* I (Oxford, ²1956); K. Galling, "Goliath und seine Rüstung," *Volume de Congrès, Genève 1965. SVT,* 15 (1966), 150-169; P. Humbert, "Yahvé dieu géniteur?" *Asiatische Studien,* 18/19 (1965), 247-251; B. Jacob, *Der Pentateuch* (Leipzig, 1905); E. Jenni, *Das hebräische Piʿel* (Zurich, 1968); J. Kühlewein, "ילד jld gebären," *THAT,* I, 732-36; T. Lescow, "Das Geburtsmotiv in den messianischen Weissagungen bei Jesaja und Micha," *ZAW,* 79 (1967), 172-207; E. Lipiński, "Le récit de 1 Rois XII 1-19 à la lumière de l'ancien usage de l'hébreu et de nouveaux textes de Mari," *VT,* 24 (1974), 430-37; E. C. B. Maclaurin, "ANAK/᾽ ANAΞ," *VT,* 15 (1965), 468-474; A. Malamat, "Organs of Statecraft in the Israelite Monarchy," *BA,* 28 (1965), 34-65 (repr. in E. F. Campbell and D. N. Freedman, ed., *BA Reader,* III [Garden City, 1970], 163-198); idem, "Kingship and Council in Israel and Sumer: A Parallel," *JNES,* 22 (1963), 247-253; P. D. Miller, Jr., "Yeled in the Song of Lamech," *JBL,* 85 (1966), 477f.; G. Sauer, "Bemerkungen zu 1965 edierten ugaritischen Texten," *ZDMG,* 116 (1966), 235-241; J. Scharbert, "Der Sinn der Toledot-Formel in der Priesterschrift," *Wort–Gebot–Glaube.* Festschrift W. Eichrodt. *AThANT,* 59 (1970), 45-56; R. de Vaux, *AncIsr;* P. Wernberg-Møller, "The Contribution of the *Hodayot* to Biblical Textual Criticism," *Textus,* 4 (1964), 133-175; P. Weimar, "Die Toledot-Formel in der priesterschriftlichen Geschichtsdarstellung," *BZ,* N.S. 18 (1974), 65-93; F. Willesen, "The Yālīḏ in Hebrew Society," *StTh,* 12 (1958), 192-210.

[1] KBL³.
[2] Kühlewein, 732f.

"son" (13 times); *lēḏâ,* "birth" (4 times); *môleḏeṯ,* "descendants" (22 times); *tôl^eḏôṯ,* "offspring, generation" (39 times); the personal names *'^aḥîlûḏ* (father of Jehoshaphat; 2 S. 8:16, etc.) and *môlîḏ* (1 Ch. 2:29); and the toponyms *môlāḏâ* (Josh. 15:26, etc.) and *tôlāḏ* (1 Ch. 4:29) or *'eltôlāḏ* (Josh. 15:30; 19:4), which means "place of prayer for a child."[3] The following forms are found in the Dead Sea scrolls: *yālaḏ* (6 times); *yālûḏ* (5 times); *lēḏâ* (1QH 3:7; cf. Jer. 13:21); *môlāḏîm* (4 times); *tôl^eḏôṯ* (8 times).

The LXX translates as follows (in order of frequency): qal: *tíktein, gennán, gí(g)nesthai, gennētós (gynaikós), tékna poieín, teknopoieín, paidíon, toketós mḗtēr*; niphal: *tíktein, gennán* passive, *gí(g)nesthai, apógonos eínai, génnēsis, gennētós;* pual: *apógonos gennán, tíktein* passive, *gí(g)nesthai*; hiphil: *gennán, gí(g)nesthai, (ek)tíktein, teknopoieín*; hophal: *tíktein* passive, *génesos*; hithpael: *epaxoneín (episképtein) katà génesin*; *yeleḏ*: *país, huiós, paidíon, paidárion, téknon, neanías, neanískos, árs(r)ēn, neṓteros, n(e)ossós*; *yaldâ*: *país, paidískē, korásion*; *yillôḏ*: *gennán, tíktein; yālîḏ*: *huiós, ék(g)gonos, geneá*; + *bêt*: *oikogenḗs*; *lēḏâ*: *tókos, tíktein*; *yal^eḏûṯ*: *(ek)-gennán, neótēs*; *môleḏeṯ*: *gí(g)nesthai*; + *'ereṣ*: *patrís, génesis, geneá, syngéneia*; + *bêṯ*: *endogenḗs*; + *'āḇîḵā*: *homopátrios, phylḗ*; *tôl^eḏôṯ*: *génesis, syngéneia, geneá*.

In line with the basic meaning "bring forth," the qal is used with a male subject in genealogies (Genesis, 1 Chronicles), but also in Prov. 17:21; 23:22,24; in these instances it means "beget." Since, however, the causative hiphil was available for the meaning "beget," the qal with the meaning "bear" is reserved for women, as Jer. 30:6 suggests. Animals can also be the subject of *yld* (Gen. 30:39; 31:8; Job 39:1f.; Jer. 14:5; Ezk. 31:6; also Jer. 17:11 [the partridge, which lays eggs]); this usage expresses an element that human beings and beasts have in common. The qal and hiphil are also used figuratively. The niphal and pual function as passives to the qal, meaning "be born." In the construction "N was born to (*l^e*) A.," the niphal appears in Gen. 4:18; 21:5; Nu. 26:60 with *'eṯ* before the name of the son; this probably signifies an impersonal construction,[4] emphasizing the relationship between father and son. The piel means "assist at birth" (Ex. 1:16);[5] its participle came to mean "midwife" (Ex. 1:15). The hophal is represented only by the infinitive in the expression "day of birth." The hithpael means "gain recognition by having onself entered in the genealogical registers."[6]

2. *Birth and Descendants in OT Theology.* For Israel, the patriarchal period is dominated by the motifs of land and offspring, which are accented variously by the different strata of the Pentateuch. While J stresses the theme of the land, E emphasizes the people. The Yahwist, to whom recent scholarship ascribes a substantial portion of the pre-P texts of Genesis, reshapes the traditions concerning the patriarchs into a family history, in which procreation and birth play an essential role. In these processes J already

---

3 G. R. Driver, "Problems of the Hebrew Text and Language," *Alttestamentliche Studien. Festschrift F. Nötscher. BBB,* 1 (1950), 58f.

4 *KBL*³, 97b.

5 Jenni, 210f.

6 *KBL*³.

sees Abraham, Isaac, and Jacob/Israel, the representatives of related tribes looking for a place to settle, as constituting a sacral lineage that merges into the people of Israel through the twelve sons of Jacob. In them is fulfilled the divine promise of descendants, a promise developed also by P and other late strata along with the promise of the land. God's promise of (many) descendants, fulfilled in their birth, is probably a heritage from the earliest nomadic history of Israel as attested in the patriarchal narratives. It is not limited to regions settled by seminomads. In the Ugaritic legend of Keret, King Keret, having lost wives and children and then taken a mate according to El's counsel, receives El's promise: "She will bear you seven sons,"[7] and "she will bear you a daughter."[8] The promise is fulfilled.

Schreiner

Also, *yld* appears some 40 times in Ugaritic with the meaning "bear," in the causative "beget."[9] It refers both to the realm of the gods (ʿAnat bears Baʿal an ox;[10] the wives of El bear attractive deities[11]) and to the human world (a son is born to Keret[12] and to Danel[13]).

Botterweck

In addition to the birth of the patriarchs (Isaac: Gen. 21; Ishmael: Gen. 16; Jacob and Esau: Gen. 25:19-26; the sons of Jacob: Gen. 29f.), the birth of deliverers (Moses: Ex. 2:1-10; Samson: Jgs. 13; Samuel: 1 S. 1) can be variously emphasized and traced to Yahweh's will. The savior belonging to the Davidic dynastic (Isa. 9:5f.[Eng. vv. 6f.]) and the son of the *ʿalmâ* (Isa. 7:14) are also born in response to God's word and act. Thus God guides the history of the nation as it continues and develops. At the same time, the fate of the individual shows that it is ultimately God who bestows life. It is true that the OT depicts procreation and birth quite straightforwardly as purely human activities, in contrast, for example, to the divine origin of the king described by the royal ideology of the ancient Near East.[14] But it is well known that human birth is also God's gift and a demonstration of his favor. P describes it as the result of divine blessing (Gen. 1:28; 5:1-3).

In the pre-P strata this conception finds two forms of expression: in the interpretation of names and in the motif of the patriarch's barren wife. Eve says, "I have gotten a man with the help of Yahweh" (Gen. 4:1) and "God has appointed for me another child instead of Abel" (4:25). In the names they give their children, Jacob's wives proclaim that Yahweh has seen their misery and heard their prayer, that God has brought justice,

---

7 *KTU,* 1.15 II, 13.
8 *Ibid.,* III, 7ff.
9 *WUS,* no. 1166; *UT,* no. 1097.
10 *KTU,* 1.10 III, 21.
11 *KTU,* 1.23, 58ff.
12 *KTU,* 1.14 III, 43.
13 *KTU,* 1.17 II, 14.
14 Cf. 4 below.

bestowed riches and reward, and taken away their shame (Gen. 29:31–30:24). Sarah (Gen. 16:1) and Rachel (30:1-7,22-24), both barren—a reproach (30:23) or even a divine punishment (20:17f.)—give birth only when Yahweh speaks his effective word or God remembers them. In the case of such a birth, God's intervention is plain to see: it is a sacral event of history. The Deuteronomistic history interprets the birth of Samson (Jgs. 13:2f.) and Samuel (1 S. 1:5,17) similarly (cf. Lk. 1:7,13). In this context, the formula "she conceived and bore N" (Gen. 4:1, etc.) takes on special significance (Jgs. 13:3-7; 1 S. 2:21); it occupies a central place in the fulfillment of God's promise (Gen. 21:2; 2 K. 4:17) and, in a different form, in the promise itself (Gen. 16:11; Isa. 7:14; cf. also Lk. 1:31).

Schreiner

In Hos. 1:2, the prophet is to take a prostitute as his wife and with her beget *yalᵉḏê zᵉnûnîm,* because Israel has committed harlotry, forsaking Yahweh and following Baʿal. The names of the children—Jezreel, Not pitied, and Not my people (vv. 4,6,9)—symbolize concretely Israel's sin and Yahweh's judgment. At the nadir of his prophetic ministry Jeremiah curses the day of his birth (Jer. 15:10; 20:14; cf. Job 3:3).

Botterweck

3. *Genealogies.* Various stems (qal, hiphil, niphal, pual) of *yld* occur most often in genealogies, especially in Genesis and 1 Chronicles. P uses the hiphil for "beget"; the pre-P material, introduced at the earliest by the Yahwist, also uses the qal in this sense. The variation does not support the conclusion that the hiphil "designates the true physical father and progenitor," whereas the qal "evades or avoids any guarantee of actual fatherhood and legitimacy."[15] The hiphil seems to be preferred in vertical genealogies traced from father through son, grandson, etc. (Gen. 5; Ruth 4:18-22); the qal, in horizontal genealogies that attempt to list all the offspring of a patriarch (cf. Gen. 10; 22:20-24). In the present form of the text, the latter are structurally hybrid. They may be introduced by a passive ("A was born to B": Gen. 4:18; 10:1; etc.), list offspring ("the sons of C are": Gen. 10:22f.; etc.), and include matriarchs ("D bore E": Gen. 22:20ff.; etc.); they are intended to express relationships between tribes and clans. Vertical genealogies trace the line of descent from the patriarch to an important descendant (Gen. 5; 6:10; 11:10-27). Both may be used for historical purposes, especially when expanded by the interpolation of narrative elements. It is an open question whether they were "circles of narratives"[16] that developed out of them or ancient materials linked by means of genealogical traditions.

P uses the term *tôlᵉḏôṯ,* "generations," "begettings," in combination with the genealogies in the sense of "tribal history," as a structural signal that the sacral history leading up to the people of Israel is being dealt with. Especially frequent in the Creation Narrative and the story of Jacob, the formula *ʾēlleh tôlᵉḏôṯ* expresses the fact that both

---

15 Jacob.

16 C. Westermann, *Genesis 1–11* (Eng. trans., Minneapolis, 1984), 12.

stand within God's blessing, which finds expression in fertility and increase.[17] The import of Gen. 2:4a is: "This sums up the 'genealogy' . . . of heaven and earth, after they were created"; "heaven and earth" are, as it were, the patriarchal ancestor, and the *tôl^e^d̠ôṯ* are the creatures formed during the seven days of creation. Thus any theogony or divine cosmogony that views creation as an act of begetting and birth is rejected, and the relationship existing among all creatures is emphasized.[18]

4. *Verb with God as Subject.* Begettings and births of deities like those recorded (sometimes in coarse detail) in Ugaritic mythology[19] are foreign to Yahwism; according to the OT, Yahweh has neither mate nor children. The few passages (Dt. 32:[15],18; Ps. 2:7; LXX 110:3[LXX 109:3]) in which God appears as subject of *yld* must be interpreted figuratively against a mythological background.[20] This is shown by the fact that Dt. 32:18 takes *ṣûr,* "rock," as its subject (cf. also Jer. 2:27), and in Ps. 2:7 Yahweh says during the enthronement of the king: "*Today* I have begotten you." The MT of Ps. 110:3 is pointed as *yal^e^d̠uṯeyk̠ā,* "your youth," blurring the mythological image. The king is not a son of Yahweh physically, nor even formally adopted by him.[21] His special relationship to and legitimation by God[22] are declared by allusion to the formulary of adoption, of which the OT says nothing in narrative, law, or treaty: "You are my son" (Ps. 2:7; cf. 2 S. 7:14; Ps. 89:27[26]); "I will make the nations your heritage, and the ends of the earth your possession" (Ps. 2:8).[23]

Schreiner

Boecker, however,[24] maintains that Ps. 2:7 and 2 S. 7:14 do refer to the institution of adoption. Precisely because there is no other evidence for this institution in the OT, the statement in Ps. 2:7 in which God installs the Davidic king in office by declaring him to be his son attracts special attention for ears attuned to the language of the OT through its use of this unusual legal form.

Botterweck

The OT has even less to say about the human race in general being the physical offspring of God. Isa. 66:9 (*yld* hiphil) says only that Yahweh "causes to bring forth," opening the womb. The same is probably true of 1QSa 2:11.[25] And Gen. 5:3 together

---

17 Weimar, 92f.

18 Scharbert, 53-56.

19 Esp. in *KTU,* 1.28, but also in the Baʿal texts: *KTU,* 1.5 V, 22; 1.15 III, 5; and the hymn to Nikkal: *KTU,* 1.24, 5.

20 Humbert, 250.

21 → בן *bēn.*

22 Donner, 113f.

23 Cf. CH §§ 4f. and the treaties cited by David.

24 H. J. Boecker, "Anmerkungen zur Adoption im AT," *ZAW,* 86 (1974), 86-89, esp. 89.

25 See, however, D. Barthélemy and J. T. Milik, *Qumran Cave I. DJD,* I (1955), 117; J. Maier, *Die Texte vom Toten Meer* (Munich, 1960), II, 158.

with 1:26 makes it clear that the human "likeness to God" is transmitted through ordinary procreation.[26]

5. *yeled and yālîd.* The *ye lādîm* whose counsel Rehoboam follows (1 K. 12:1-19) are not children but—as the LXX (*sýntrophoi*) shows—friends who have grown up with him or possibly an institution contrasting with the "elders (of Israel)," comprising the royal princes.[27] The reference in Gen. 4:23 may also be to young men or warriors. It is theologically significant that Jer. 31:20 refers to Ephraim as Yahweh's favorite child, and that Ezr. 10:1; Neh. 12:43 include women and children in the congregation of Yahweh.

Like Bab. [*w*]*ilid bîtim,*[28] the *ye lîd bayit* is a "homeborn" slave, required by Gen. 17 to be circumcised. This group of dependents ("retainers") could have special duties, e.g., military service (Gen. 14:14). The "children of Anak" (Nu. 13:22,28; Josh. 15:14; cf. Dt. 9:2) and the "children of Raphah" (2 S. 21:16,18) are probably such a "troop." Jer. 2:14 denies that Israel is a slave or a homeborn servant of Yahweh, and is therefore not totally within his care and protection.

6. *Figurative Usage.* Sometimes the basic meaning "bring forth" appears in figurative usage: the wicked bring forth lies (Ps. 7:15[14]), mischief and evil (Job 15:35), and that which does not endure ("straw," Isa. 33:11). The proverbial pain of those "giving birth" is cited in similes (Isa. 13:8; Jer. 22:23; Mic. 4:9f.; etc.; 1QH 3:7,11; 5:31). Finally, when the city of Jerusalem (Zion) gives birth (Isa. 51:18; 66:7), the people's increase through God's grace is both image and reality.

Schreiner

7. *Qumran.* In the Dead Sea scrolls, *yld* appears some 16 times, *ylwd* 5 times (4 in 1QH), and *twldwt* 8 times (4 in 1QS). The verb *yld* appears in various contexts (bearing children: CD 7:7; 19:3; cattle giving birth on the Sabbath: CD 11:13; God's bringing forth the Messiah: 1QSa 2:11; birth pangs as a sign of the end: 1QH 5:31), but *ylwd* is limited to the phrase *ylwd 'šh,* "born of woman," referring to the creaturely vulnerability of human beings (cf. Sir. 10:18: *gennḗmasin gynaikṓn*; Matt. 11:11: *gennētoí gynaikṓn*). The noun *twldwt* usually refers to human generations (1QS 3:13; 4:15), the generations of Israel (CD 4:5), or the generations of the Qumran community (1QM 3:14; 5:1; 10:14). In a more general sense, however, it can also mean "origin" (of truth or wickedness, 1QS 3:19).

Botterweck

---

26 Cf. EnEl I, 15f.; *AOT*², 109.

27 Malamat.

28 Driver-Miles, 222.

ילל yll; יְלֵל yᵉlēl; יְלָלָה yᵉlālâ

Contents: I. 1. Etymology; 2. Meaning, Occurrences. II. Original Usage: 1. Death and Catastrophe; 2. Communal Day of Prayer. III. Prophetic Usage: 1. Judgment against Foreign Nations; 2. Judgment against Israel.

I. 1. *Etymology.* The root *yll,* both verb and noun, occurs in various Semitic languages (Aramaic, Syriac, Mandaic). It is also closely related to Arab. *walwala* and Amhar. *wailawa,* "wail" (cf. *waile,* "alas!"; *walale,* "cry of pain"). There is a possible occurrence in Neo-Punic,[1] but no immediate analog in Akkadian[2] or Ugaritic. The phonetic similarity to Gk. *ololýzō* or *alalázō* (cf. Lat. *ululo*) need not indicate etymological relationship: it is probably due primarily to the often-suggested onomatopoetic nature of the root. This probably accounts also for the similarity to → הלל *hll* II: if the latter originally designated peals of joy, *yll* denotes exactly the opposite, a shrill scream of agony.

The verb appears 30 times (always in the hiphil); *yᵉlēl* occurs once, *yᵉlālâ* 5 times.

2. *Meaning, Occurrences.* The verb *yll* is usually translated "wail, lament." This rendering seems appropriate for the polished language of the postbiblical period—Middle Hebrew, together with contemporary Syriac and Aramaic documents. For the biblical period, however, it must be clear that we are dealing with an extraordinary phenomenon: an inarticulate, shattering scream such as is found in primitive funerary laments[3] and in the face of sudden catastrophe.

The related root *'ll* II,[4] its derived interjection *'alᵉlay,* "woe is me!" (similar to Amhar. *'allē,* Akk. *allū,* and Egyp. Aram. *alla/ī*), and the associated root *'ll* II (if the single occurrence in Joel 1:8 is not to be emended to a form of *yll*[5]) all belong to the same semantic field.

Semantically related words include above all → זעק *zʿq* (e.g., Isa. 14:31; 15:4f.; Jer. 25:34; 47:2; 48:20,31; Ezk. 21:17[Eng. v. 12]; Hos. 7:14; cf. *zᵉʿāqâ* [Isa. 15:8]) and its

---

yll. A. Baumann, "Urrolle und Fasttag," *ZAW,* 80 (1968), 350-373; H. W. Heidland, "ὀλολύζω," *TDNT,* V, 173f.; H. Jahnow, *Das hebräische Leichenlied im Rahmen der Volksdichtung. BZAW,* 36 (1923), 2-57; W. Janzen, *Mourning Cry and Woe Oracle. BZAW,* 125 (1972), 89f.; E. Peterson, "ἀλαλάζω," *TDNT,* I, 227f.; M. Saebø, *Sacharja 9–14. WMANT,* 34 (1969), 229-233; H. Wildberger, *Jesaja. BK,* X/2 (1978), 514; H. W. Wolff, "Der Aufruf zur Volksklage," *ZAW,* 76 (1964), 48-56 = *GSAT. ThB,* 22 (²1973), 392-401.

1 *KAI,* 161, 2.

2 The *alālu,* "work cry," "work song," cited by *KBL*³ and its derivatives belong with → הלל *hll* II.

3 Jahnow, 40.

4 Cf. *KBL*³.

5 Cf. H. W. Wolff, *Joel and Amos. Herm.* (Eng. trans. 1977), *in loc.*

variant *ṣʿq* (e.g., Isa. 65:14; cf. *ṣᵉʿāqâ* [Jer. 25:36; 48:3; Zeph. 1:10]), → ספד *spd* (e.g., Jer. 4:8; 49:3; Joel 1:13; Mic. 1:8; cf. *mispēḏ* [Mic. 1:8]); → אבל *ʾāḇal* [*ʾābhal*] (e.g., Joel 1:10; Mic. 1:8), and other terms denoting mourning customs such as putting on *śaq,* shaving the head, and covering oneself with ashes. The occasion evoking lamentation is described by means of → שדד *šdd* (e.g., Isa. 23:1,14; Jer. 25:36; 48:20; 49:3; Joel 1:10; Zec. 11:2f.) and similar words denoting destruction and devastation. This observation confirms the usage described above. In Isa. 65:14, *rnn* is used as an antonym of *yll.*

The only occurrence of *yᵉlēl,* Dt. 32:10, is unrelated to the other occurrences of the root in both form and content and poses substantial problems of interpretation. What is clear is that the word describes the horror of the desert. The various translations proposed ("auditory hallucinations," "howling of wild beasts") are not really convincing; the text is very possibly corrupt.

The occurrences of *yᵉlālâ,* by contrast, are all in the same semantic realm as the verb; this is underlined by the observation that *yᵉlālâ* always appears in immediate conjunction with verbal forms of *yll* (compare Isa. 15:8 with 15:2f.; Jer. 25:36 with 25:34; Zeph. 1:10 with 1:11; Zec. 11:3 with 11:2).

Isa. 52:5 should be dropped from the list of occurrences of the verb *yll;* the verb here is a form of *hll* III.[6] Joel 1:8 should probably be added; the original text likely read *hêlîlû,* as in Joel 1:5,11,13.[7] The proposed inclusion of *wᵉṯôlālênû* in Ps. 137:3 as an additional occurrence is to be rejected.

The LXX translates *yll* and its derivatives primarily by means of *ololýzō* (18 times) or *ololygmós* (twice) (throughout Isaiah; Jer. 48:20,31[LXX 31:20,31]; Ezk. 21:17[Eng. v. 12], Hos. 7:14; Am. 8:3; Zec. 11:2), 5 times by means of *alalázō* (Jer. 4:8; 25:34[LXX 32:34]; 47:2[29:2]; 49:3[30:19]) or *alalagmós* (Jer. 25:36[32:36]), and 7 times by means of *thrēnṓ* (Jer. 51:8[28:8]; Joel 1:5,[8],11,13; Mic. 1:8; Zeph. 1:11; Zec. 11:3). The meaning described above is confirmed above by Ezk. 30:2, where *yll* is translated by the lament *ṓ, ṓ.* The verb *ololýzō* is used almost exclusively to translate *yll,* whereas *alalázō* (representing the hiphil of *rwʿ*) and even more *thrēnṓ* (above all for the pilpel of *qyn*) are more widely used for other purposes.

II. Original Usage.

1. *Death and Catastrophe.* From the preceding discussion, one would expect to find *yll* and *yᵉlālâ* primarily in the context of lament for the dead. Strangely enough, however, the root appears only in prophetic texts (with the exception of the single occurrence of *yᵉlēl* in Dt. 32:10, which probably involves another root[8]). In the few accounts of mourning for departed individuals there is no occurrence of *yll.* Neither does it occur in similar contexts in the prophetic books. This observation demands explanation, although the lack of direct evidence makes any theory hypothetical. In fact, *yll* appears not to have been a term commonly used for lamenting the dead; it must have had a specialized usage.

---

6 *KBL*³.
7 See above.
8 See I.2 above.

It has often been noted that the OT is much more reticent about mourning rites than the rest of the ancient Near East. This is due to theological reservations about many manifestations of the cult of the dead. Now in Hos. 7:14, *yll* occurs in a context where it denotes a form of idolatry that Israel should avoid. This might explain why *yll* does not appear in OT accounts describing mourning for individuals.

There is more involved, however. Later Judaism, though having fewer reservations about the funerary customs of its neighbors, made hardly any use of the root *yll* in this context. In the prophetic books the root always appears in contexts involving major catastrophes affecting a whole land or people, whether Israel or some other nation. Is this perhaps what distinguishes *yll*—its use only when the entire community is affected, not just an individual? If so, it would never have been part of normal lamentation for the dead, because it expresses affliction in the face of unimaginable catastrophe, moving everyone to pity. The very use of *yll* would then suggest the ultimate degree of lamentation, an extraordinary wail of agony.

2. *Communal Day of Prayer.* The extraordinary nature of this lamentation would allow *yll* to signalize total catastrophe. In such situations it was important to assemble all the people, the entire community affected, as quickly as possible in order that they might jointly make a final effort to obtain the aid of the deity and thus avert disaster. The term "communal lament" has come to designate such assemblies in Judah. Since, however, their purpose was not merely to lament the disaster at hand but above all to avert catastrophe through prayer, the term "communal day of prayer" would be more accurate and will be used in the following discussion.

Wolff was the first to point out that there were fixed rhetorical forms for the opening phase of such a day of prayer; they have been preserved in the prophetic books, but must have been usable originally without the participation of prophets. In the context of this "summons to lament" the root *yll* plays a crucial role: it appears in 8 of the 11 texts Wolff assembles to define this genre (Isa. 14:31; 23:1-14; Jer. 25:34; 49:3; Ezk. 21:17[12]; Joel 1:5-14; Zeph. 1:11; Zec. 11:2; absent only in Isa. 32:11-14; Jer. 6:26; and—significantly—in 2 S. 1:24, a lament for a departed individual). It appears also in 4 of the 8 texts Wolff cites as partial example (Isa. 13:6; Jer. 4:8; 51:8; Ezk. 30:2f.; absent in Jer. 7:29; 22:10,20; and—again a lament for an individual—2 S. 3:31). The root *yll* is thus one of the most regular elements of the "summons to communal lament."

Taking the term "communal lament" as his point of departure, Wolff examined the genre to determine whether it involved elements of lamentation for the dead. This is indeed the case, as he showed convincingly. But more is involved than an expression of grief or pain over the disaster. The "summons to communal lament" serves primarily to introduce the "communal lamentation" that follows.

This signalizing purpose appears, for instance, in the motivation (introduced by *kî*) for lamentation, which almost always follows the "summons to lament." Visual signals were also addressed to those who were not yet informed: torn clothing, *śaq,* ashes sprinkled on the head, etc. Above all, however, there were auditory signals that could not be missed: weeping, wailing, the sounding of the lament (*spd*). But shrill, earthshaking keening, *y*[e]*lālâ,* was probably the first thing to catch attention, followed perhaps by the sound of the *šôpār,* which appears in conjunction with *yll* in Jer. 4:5; Joel 2:1; Zeph. 1:16.

The course of events may be pictured somewhat as follows. First the catastrophic occasion was recognized through some circumstance as being imminent or already at hand. Then individuals would begin to lament and observe the customs of mourning, attracting the attention of others. Their questions would evoke the motivation just mentioned, conveyed in short, abrupt sentences, describing the disaster that had come to pass (often expressed by means of *šdd*; cf. Isa. 23:1,14; Jer. 25:36; 48:20; 49:3; Zec. 11:3) or was coming (often expressed by means of forms of *bw'*; cf. Isa. 13:6; 14:31; 23:1). As a result, the populace would assemble at their sanctuary or some other appropriate spot. In this context, Wolff makes the interesting observation that the impv. *hêlîlû,* "wail," is usually addressed to specific groups. This chimes completely with the situation during the opening phase of a communal day of prayer: as a rule, it was impossible to address the entire populace immediately but only a portion, whose first task was to spread the news of the catastrophe by summoning the rest to a day of communal prayer. This is clearly the situation behind Joel 1, where first the sleeping drunkards are awakened (v. 5), then another group (v. 8; probably not specified because of textual corruption, as discussed in the comms.), and finally the vinedressers (v. 11) and priests (v. 13). In Zeph. 1:10f., the same situation is reflected in the naming of places in Jerusalem.

This discussion should make it clear that *yll* has a substantial range of usage in the "summons to communal lament." It is also reasonable to assume that most of the instances not included by Wolff have their original *Sitz im Leben* here. This holds above all for the occurrences of *y^elālâ* in Isa. 15:8; Jer. 25:36; Zeph. 1:10; Zec. 11:3; but also the occurrences of the verb in Isa. 15:2f.; 16:7; Jer. 47:2; 48:20,31,39; Am. 8:3; Mic. 1:8 seem to fit in this context. Thus *yll* appears to be a characteristic word for the initial phase of a communal day of prayer. This may also explain the relative rarity of the root: it denotes something truly extraordinary.

III. Prophetic Usage.

1. *Judgment against Foreign Nations.* The original usage, still discernible in prophetic texts, must be distinguished from the special usage of the prophets. Their purpose is to proclaim judgment. This purpose can be well served by using *yll* to describe a catastrophe or even by employing the forms associated with a "summons to communal lament" in direct address, thus involving the listeners immediately in a catastrophic situation.

The root appears primarily in proclamations of judgment against foreign nations, above all in the so-called "oracles against the nations." Is it that *yll* was more to be expected in the case of foreign nations, familiar with the cult of the dead, than in the case of Israel? Or do we find an echo of treaty language like that of an eighth-century Aramaic treaty,[9] which threatens *y^elālâ* instead of the music of the harp if the treaty is broken? In any case, there are 19 occurrences of the verb or *y^elālâ* in the context of judgment against foreign nations.

---

9 *KAI,* 222A, 30.

Several entities are threatened with "wailing": all the nations (Jer. 25:34,36), Babylon (Isa. 13:6; Jer. 51:8), Egypt (Ezk. 30:2), the Philistines (Isa. 14:31; Jer. 47:2), Moab (Isa. 15:2f.,8; 16:7; Jer. 48:20,31,39), Ammon (Jer. 49:3), Tyre (Isa. 23:1,6,14). Sometimes particular representatives of the people in question are addressed, e.g., the "shepherds" (i.e., leaders: Jer. 25:34), or particular cities (Jer. 49:3); a foe may be introduced in symbolic terms (Isa. 23:1,6,14).

The threats of judgment are pronounced by the prophets in the name of Yahweh, even though not usually in the immediate context of the threat of wailing. In Isa. 13:6; Ezk. 30:2, the judgment is referred to explicitly as the "day of Yahweh."[10] It is always assumed, however, that those addressed are to seek refuge not in Yahweh but with their own gods (cf., e.g., Isa. 15:2). This means that from the standpoint of the prophet these nations have no chance, even if in face of imminent catastrophe they assemble for a kind of day of prayer and call upon their gods. Fundamentally, then, there is a note of irony in the summons to foreign nations to "wail": all their crying will be to no avail.

2. *Judgment against Israel.* There are 15 passages where Israel is threatened with "wailing" (9 if we do not count repetitions in the same section). But the motivation is sometimes entirely different than in the case of foreign nations. In Isa. 65:14; Hos. 7:14, for example, it is the idolatry of the people that will lead to catastrophe. Hos. 7:13-15 contrasts right with wrong conduct toward Yahweh: here *yll* appears primarily as a sign of idolatry.[11] In Isa. 65:13-15, the fate of those who have remained faithful is contrasted with the fate of those who have fallen away. Such a charge of idolatry obviously makes sense only in the case of the people of Yahweh.

In the case of Israel, too, particular representatives may be addressed,[12] e.g., the "shepherds" (Zec. 11:3) or princes (Ezk. 21:17[12]), as may symbolic figures (Zec. 11:2). As we have already seen,[13] the call to "wail" can be addressed sequentially to various groups among the people (Joel 1:5,[8],11,13) or various areas of the city (Zeph. 1:10f.). Am. 8:3 probably refers to female singers (*šārôṯ*) who are to break forth in lamentation instead of their usual songs.[14]

It is obvious that the threats of judgment spoken by the prophets against their own nation should be uttered in the name of Yahweh, in Jer. 4:8 with explicit reference to Yahweh's wrath. Unlike the oracles against the foreign nations, however, these threats express a conscious solidarity of the prophet with those addressed. This finds explicit expression in Ezk. 21:17(12); Mic. 1:8, where the prophet calls upon himself to begin the lament, thus involving himself in the imminent catastrophe. Here we see that threats of judgment against Israel have a function fundamentally different from that of oracles against the nations. In the latter, the coming catastrophe is irreversible; in the former, there is always the chance for repentance. By identifying himself with those who lead

---

10 → יום *yôm*.

11 Cf. II.1 above.

12 See III.1 above.

13 See II.2 above.

14 Cf. the comms.

the lamentation, the prophet calls his people to communal lament. If they then assemble for a communal day of prayer, there is still hope for change.

Baumann

יָם *yām*

Contents: I. Etymology. II. Ancient Near East: 1. Egypt; 2. Mesopotamia; 3. Ugarit. III. OT: 1 Geographical Names; 2. Neutral Usage; 3. Mythology; 4. The Exodus; 5. Jonah; 6. Tyre; 7. Idioms; 8. Summary. IV. 1. LXX; 2. Qumran. V. The Bronze Sea.

I. Etymology. Heb. *yām* (< *yamm*) corresponds etymologically to Ugar. *ym,* Phoen. *ym,* and Aram. *yam(māʾ)*. Akk. *yāmi*[1] is a West Semitic loanwoard. The normal word for "sea" in Akkadian is *tâmtu* (earlier *tiāmtu*), corresponding to Heb. → תהום *tᵉhôm.* Arabic uses *baḥr*; cf. Ethiop. *bāḥr.* Arab. *yamm* appears already in the Koran (for the Red Sea and the Nile), but is nevertheless to be considered an Aramaic loanword.[2] Egyp. *ỉm* and Copt. *eiom* are likewise Semitic loanwords.[3]

II. Ancient Near East. 1. *Egypt.* The native Egyptian term for "sea" is *w3d wr,* "the great green";[4] from the New Kingdom on, the Semitic loanword *ỉm* is also found. Egyptian religion also speaks of the primal ocean, *nnw,* Nun, the cosmic sea from which the creator-god came forth at the beginning, which still surrounds the world, and from which the sun emerges every morning;[5] it is embodied by the Nile.[6] There is no clear distinction between the sea and the primal ocean. As early as the Pyramid texts, *w3ḏ wr*

---

yām. A. H. W. Curtis, "The 'Subjugation of the Waters' Motif in the Psalms; Imagery or Polemic?" *JSS,* 23 (1978), 245-256; E. P. Dhorme, "Le désert de la mer (Isaïe, XXI)," *RB,* 31 (1922), 403-6 = *Recueil Édouard Dhorme* (Paris, 1951), 301-4; G. R. Driver, "Mythical Monsters in the OT," *Studi orientalistici in onore di Giorgio Levi Della Vida,* I (Rome, 1956), 234-249; O. Eissfeldt, "Gott und das Meer in der Bibel," *Studia orientalia Ioanni Pedersen septuagenario* (Copenhagen, 1953), 76-84 (= *KlSchr,* III [1966], 256-264); H. Gunkel, *Schöpfung und Chaos in Urzeit und Endzeit* (Göttingen, ²1921); A. Heidel, *The Babylonian Genesis* (Chicago, ²1963); O. Kaiser, *Die mythische Bedeutung des Meeres in Ägypten, Ugarit und Israel. BZAW,* 78 (²1962); H. G. May, "Some Cosmic Connotations of *MAYIM RABBÎM,* 'Many Waters'," *JBL,* 74 (1955), 9-21; S. I. L. Norin, *Er Spaltete das Meer. CB,* 9 (Ger. trans. 1977); P. Reymond, *L'eau, sa vie, et sa signification dans l'AT. SVT,* 6 (1958); A. J. Wensinck, *The Ocean in the Literature of the Western Semites. VAWA,* N.S. 19/2 (1918; repr. 1968).

1 *AHw,* I (1965), 514.

2 S. I. Fraenkel, *Die aramäischen Fremdwörter im Arabischen* (Leiden, 1886), 231.

3 See II.1 below.

4 *WbÄS,* I, 269; also *km wr,* "the great black," *ibid.,* V, 126.

5 → תהום *tᵉhôm.*

6 Kaiser, 10-32.

refers to the cosmic sea.[7] Usually, however, *w3ḏ wr* refers concretely to the open sea, as in the Story of the Shipwrecked Sailor,[8] where we read, for example: "We were at sea when the storm broke loose," and: "I was cast up on an island by a wave of the sea."[9] When the sailor wakes up the next morning, he sees a gigantic serpent coming out of the sea—an echo of mythological notions associated with the primal ocean.[10] In ch. 175 of the Book of the Dead, we find the notion that the world will some day return to its initial state, so that only the primal ocean (Nun) will be left.[11]

There are also scattered suggestions that the sea is a power hostile to life.[12] The Instructions for Merikare do not mention the sea explicitly, but include among the good deeds done by the creator-god the destruction of the "greedy creature of the water" (*snk n mw*). And in proverb 11.13 of Papyrus Hearst,[13] we read: "As Seth charmed the sea (*w3ḏ wr*) so Seth will charm you, disease of the Asiatics." This passage probably refers to Seth as the helper of the sun-god, in which role he every evening slays the serpent that bars the path of the sun-bark.[14] The same idea is found also in incantation 189 of the great Berlin Medical Papyrus: "They [the incantations] are beneficial to him [the sick person] . . . as when the sea (*ỉm*) hears the voice of Seth."[15] This last example uses the Semitic loanword *ỉm* as does the Astarte papyrus,[16] which is unfortunately poorly preserved. In it we read how the sea demands tribute from the gods, whereupon the goddess Astarte comes against him naked and probably overcomes him.[17] Obviously the influence of West Semitic (Ugaritic?) mythology is at work here.[18]

2. *Mesopotamia.* Akk. *tâmtu,* "sea,"[19] is used as a general geographical term: *tâmtu elītu,* "the upper sea," refers to the Mediterranean; *tâmtu šaplītu,* "the lower sea," is the Persian Gulf. The phrase "from the upper sea to the lower sea" denotes the entire known world. A memorial preserved in a Neo-Assyrian copy lists the lands that King Sargon "conquered three times by his own hand"; these include lands "beyond the upper sea" and "beyond the lower sea."[20]

---

7 *Pyr.* 902, 1505a; cf. Kaiser, 33.

8 A. Erman, *The Ancient Egyptians: A Sourcebook of Their Writings* (Eng. trans., New York, ²1966), 29ff.

9 Kaiser, 34.

10 G. Lanczkowski, "Die Geschichte des Schiffbrüchigen," *ZDMG,* 103 (1953), 363, 368.

11 Following H. Kees' translation; see S. Morenz, *Egyptian Religion* (Eng. trans., Ithaca, N.Y., 1973), 169.

12 Kaiser, 31ff.

13 A. Gardiner, "Notes and News," *JEA,* 19 (1933), 98; see G. Posener, "La légende égyptienne de la mer insatiable," *AIPH,* 13 (1953/55), 469ff.

14 Book of the Dead, 108; Kaiser, 87f.

15 W. Wreszinski, *Der grosse medizinische Papyrus des Berliner Museums* (Leipzig, 1909), 44, 102.

16 *ANET,* 17f.

17 Kaiser, 81ff.

18 See II.3 below.

19 *AHw,* II (1972), 1353f.

20 *BuA,* II, 377f.

Historical inscriptions often mention kings who reach the Mediterranean ("the great sea": Ashurbanipal[21]) and there wash or purify their weapons (Sargon;[22] Ashurnasirpal[23]). Tiglath-pileser kills a *naḫiru* in the midst of the sea;[24] Shalmaneser boards a ship and sails to the midst of the sea.[25] The sea in its concrete sense is mentioned, for example, in a hymn to the sun: "You pass over the sea, broad and wide, whose inmost interior is unknown even to the Igigi-gods. Your rays descend into the ocean; even those . . . of the sea behold your light."[26] This passage emphasizes both the breadth of the sea (cf. the hymn to the moon:[27] "Your divinity is like the distant heavens, awesome as the broad sea") and its depth: the rays of the sun reach even into the depths of the sea.

The sea is mentioned together with other parts of the cosmos to express the totality of the world: Šamaš is said to pass every day over sea, ocean, mountains, earth, and sky;[28] the Erra epic lists land, cities, mountains, seas, days, life, and animals to express universal judgment.[29] Expressions like "birds of the sky" and "fish of the sea" are common.

In Sumerian cosmogony, heaven and earth emerge from the primal sea, Nammu, also called *abzu.* A Babylonian didactic poem describing creation[30] says that when "Apsû had not yet been created," "all the lands were sea." According to EnEl, however, the freshwater ocean Apsû and the saltwater sea Tiamat were separate from the beginning, although they both "mingled their waters." Ea puts Apsû to sleep through a spell and establishes his dwelling place upon it: Apsû is the fresh water that is under the earth. Tiamat, however, creates discord and is finally beaten and slain by Marduk. He divides Tiamat's body into two parts, making the firmament of the heavens out of the upper part; then he places guards to see that the heavenly waters are not let out. Over Apsû he sets the earth like a heavenly throne. Nothing more is said of the lower half of Tiamat; Heidel[31] thinks that it provided the material for the creation of the earth.

The earth thus rests upon Apsû and is surrounded by water. A Neo-Babylonian world map,[32] which claims to be a copy of an earlier original, shows a circular continent surrounded by a "river," the so-called *nâru marratu,* "bitter river" or "circular river."[33] There is also a text extolling a river (*nâru*) as creator of all;[34] this river appears to be the Euphrates, and the text served as an incantation.

---

21 *AOT,* 340.
22 *BuA,* II, 368.
23 *AOT,* 340.
24 *Ibid.,* 339.
25 *Ibid.,* 342.
26 *BuA,* II, 167; *BWL,* 128, 35f.
27 *BuA,* II, 165 = Å. Sjöberg, *Der Mondgott Nanna-Suen in der sumerischen Überlieferung* (Uppsala, 1960), 167, 14.
28 *AOT,* 245, ll. 27ff.
29 *Ibid.,* 222, ll. 37ff.
30 *Ibid.,* 130f.
31 P. 116.
32 *BuA,* II, 378f.
33 *Ibid.,* 111.
34 *AOT,* 130.

The largest reservoir in the temple, which served various cultic purposes, is called *apsû,* but not *tâmtu*; it is often likened to the Euphrates or Tigris.[35] There is obviously a mental association connecting water, *apsû,* river, incantation, and life.

3. *Ugarit.* The Ugaritic texts speak occasionally of the sea in the literal sense. One text[36] speaks of El's going along the shore of the sea (par. "the shore of the ocean [*thm*]"); the same text[37] speaks of the fish from the sea (par. "the birds of the heavens"); finally, the length of El's phallus is compared to the sea.[38] In one passage we find the pair *qdm*/*ym* in the sense "east"/"west."[39] The other occurrences either refer to the goddess called "Athirat of the sea" (*ʾṯrt ym*)[40] or use *ym* as the name of a god who contends with Baʿal.[41]

The narrative goes roughly as follows: "Lord Sea" (*zbl ym*) reigns as king, with the approval of El; he is also called *tpṭ nhr,* "Judge River,"[42] an epithet recalling the Babylonian practice of ordeal by water[43] and the notion that the river of creation has healing powers.[44] Yam sends messengers to the assembly of the gods, demanding that Baʿal be handed over to him. El agrees and declares Yam to be lord (*bʿl*) and master (*ʾdn*).[45] But Baʿal refuses and attacks Yam. Kothar-wa-Ḫasis promises him victory and makes weapons for him with which to conquer Yam.[46] Yam finally collapses and falls to the earth. Astarte rejoices at the victory: "Yam indeed is dead! Baʿal will be king!"[47] This victory is alluded to in another text.[48]

What enemy arose against Baʿal,
what foe against the rider of the clouds?
Have I not conquered Sea, El's favorite?
Have I not destroyed River, the great god?
Have I not curbed the dragon (*tnn*), curbed him indeed?
I have conquered the sinuous serpent,
šlyṭ with seven heads.
I struck El's favorite, the earth,
I destroyed the young bull of El, Atak. . . .

The question is whether sea/river is identical with the "dragon," "serpent," and *šlyṭ* that

---

35 *BuA,* II, 77.
36 *KTU,* 1.23, 30.
37 L. 63.
38 Ll. 33f.
39 *KTU,* 1.4 VII, 34.
40 *Ibid.,* 1.4 I, 14, 21; III, 25, 27, 29; 1.6 I, 44, 45, 47, 53.
41 Kaiser, 44ff.
42 *KTU,* 1.2, *passim.*
43 E.g., CH, § 2.
44 See II.2 above; Heidel, 75; Kaiser, 57f.
45 *KTU,* 1.2 I, 36f., 45.
46 *Ibid.,* IV, 1-5.
47 L. 32.
48 *Ibid.,* 1.3 III, 37-44.

follow (one text[49] identifies the serpent with *šlyṭ* and both with Lotan/Leviathan). The text is not clear. A plurality of sea monsters is suggested by the fact that the whole passage is a list of vanquished enemies; it goes on to list several others that cannot possibly be identical with Yam. It is also worth noting that the battle between Baʿal and Yam does not issue in the creation of the world, which instead appears to lie already in the past. What is at stake in the contest is sovereignty.

III. OT.

1. *Geographical Names.* As a purely geographical term *yām* occurs alone and in various phrases.

a. Simple *yām* or *hayyām* refers to the Mediterranean Sea (Jgs. 5:17 even uses the pl. *yammîm*), which can be further described as *hayyām haggāḏôl* (Josh. 1:4), *yām pᵉlištîm* (Ex. 23:31), *hayyām hā'aḥᵃrôn* (Dt. 11:24), or *yām yāp̄ô'* (Ezr. 3:7). Since this sea constitutes the entire western boundary of the land, *yām* became the term for the direction "west": *miyyām* means "from the west," *yāmmâ* means "westward."

b. The phrase *yām hammelaḥ* refers to the Dead Sea (Gen. 14:3); it is also called *yām hāʿᵃrāḇâ,* "sea of the steppe" (Dt. 3:17; cf. simple *hayyām* in Ezk. 47:8, a context that also speaks of *hāʿᵃrāḇâ*) or *hayyām haqqaḏmônî,* "the eastern sea" (Ezk. 47:18).

c. The phrase *yām-sûp̄,* "sea of reeds," sometimes denotes the body of water where the Israelites were delivered from the Egyptians (Ex. 13:18), sometimes the Elamite seacoast (Gulf of Aqaba: Ex. 23:31; Nu. 14:25; 1 K. 9:26).

d. The sea of Chinnereth is called *yām kinnereṯ/kinnᵉrôṯ* (Nu. 34:11; Josh. 12:3; 13:27).

e. Isa. 21:1 speaks of a *miḏbar-yām,* "wilderness of the sea"; since Babylon is the subject of the oracle, the reference may be to the Persian Gulf or the "river" (*nāhār*) Euphrates.[50]

2. *Neutral Usage.* The only completely neutral usage of *yām* is in the expressions *miyyām,* "from the west," and *yammâ,* "westward," as well as a few strictly geographical passages, e.g., *lip̄'aṯ-yām,* "on the west side," "toward the west" (Ex. 27:12; 38:12), rafts on the sea (1 K. 5:23[Eng. v. 9]; 9:27; 10:22), the islands of the sea (Est. 10:1; Isa. 11:11; cf. Jer. 25:22: "beyond the sea"), Carmel by the sea (Jer. 46:18), *ḥôp̄ yammîm/hayyām,* "the shore of the sea" (Gen. 49:13; Jgs. 5:17; Jer. 47:7; Ezk. 25:16), sending messengers across the sea (Isa. 18:2), or the phrase *dᵉgaṯ/dᵉgê hayyām,* "fish of the sea" (Gen. 1:26,28; 9:2; Nu. 11:22; Job 12:8; Ps. 8:9[8] [par. *ʿōḇēr 'orḥôṯ yammîm*]; Ezk. 38:20; Hos. 4:3; Hab. 1:14; Zeph. 1:13; cf. also Lev. 11:9f.: "creatures in the sea").

The sea is spoken of quite naturally as part of the world created by God, but it does not enter into fixed phrases like "heaven and earth." The Creation account of P speaks of the heavens, earth, and the sea (Gen. 1); Ex. 20:11 refers to this account in its motivation for the Sabbath commandment (cf. Ex. 20:4: heaven, earth, water). The psalm in 1 Ch. 16:31f. calls on heaven, earth, sea, and fields to rejoice; Ps. 98:7f. speaks of sea,

---

49 *Ibid.,* 1.5 I, 103.

50 See Dhorme and the comms.

floods, and hills; Hos. 4:3 says that the beasts of the field, the birds of the air, and the fish of the sea mourn and languish. Other combinations also occur: Eccl. 1:3-7 speaks of earth, heaven, wind, and sea (Reymond[51] finds here echoes of Egyptian and Sumerian cosmology); Ps. 135:6 speaks of heaven, earth, sea, and deeps (*t^e^hômôṯ*); and Job 11:8f. lists heaven, Sheol, earth, and sea. These are clearly instances of random combinations of elements vividly representing the whole.

3. *Mythology.* According to the Creation account in P, the earth was originally covered by the primal sea (*t^e^hôm*), called "waters" in Gen. 1:2. On the second day, God created the firmament to divide the waters into an upper and a lower portion; on the third day, he distinguished the earth ("the dry land," *hayyabbāšâ*) from "the seas" (*yammîm*; Gen. 1:10).

Ever since, the earth has rested in the cosmic sea upon its foundations, the mountains. God founded (*yāsaḏ*)[52] the earth upon "the seas" and established (*hēḵîn*)[53] it upon the rivers (Ps. 24:2). Even here we find a certain confusion with respect to the terms "primal sea," "physical sea," and "cosmic ocean," a confusion that recurs in various contexts. The words *t^e^hôm, yām,* and *nāhār*[54] are used interchangeably for the cosmic ocean that surrounds the earth. For example, we read in Ps. 72:8; Zec. 9:10 that the king will have dominion "from sea to sea" (*miyyām ʿaḏ-yām*) and "from the River to the ends of the earth" (*ʿaḏ-ʾap̱sê-ʾāreṣ*). The parallelism suggests that *yām* and *nāhār* refer to the cosmic ocean and the worldwide rule of the king, but as they stand *yām* could refer to the Mediterranean or the Persian Gulf[55] and *nāhār* to the Euphrates. Joel 2:20 speaks of the eastern (*qaḏmōnî*) and western (*ʾaḥ^a^rôn*) seas as the extreme limits to which the "northerner" will be driven. The same meaning may be found in Zec. 14:8 (water flowing to the eastern and western seas), but there the reference could also be to the Mediterranean Sea and the Dead Sea.

This "sea" appears as a power hostile to God and to the world, confronting God at the beginning of the world. At Yahweh's rebuke,[56] the deep (*t^e^hôm*) or the waters (*mayim*) covering the earth fled (Ps. 104:6f.). Thus he set a bound (*g^e^ḇûl*) for the sea, which it can no longer pass; cf. Jer. 5:22, where a bound or *ḥōq* is set for the sea (*yām*), and Job 38:8-10, where Yahweh sets the sea doors and *ḥōq*.

The Psalms and other poetic texts contain references to this primal event that sound more or less mythological. "By his power he stilled the sea; by his understanding he smote Rahab. By his wind the heavens were made fair; his hand pierced the fleeing serpent" (Job 26:12f.). "Thou dost rule the raging of the sea; when its waves rise, thou stillest them. Thou didst crush Rahab like a carcass" (Ps. 89:10f.[9f.]). "Thou didst divide

51 P. 167, n. 1.
52 → יסד *yāsaḏ*.
53 → כון *kûn*.
54 → נהר *nāhār*.
55 See II.2 above.
56 → גער *gāʿar*.

the sea by thy might; thou didst break the heads of the dragons (*tannînîm*) on the waters. Thou didst crush the heads of Leviathan" (Ps. 74:13f.). With the exception of Rahab, the same figures are involved as in the Ugaritic texts:[57] dragon, Leviathan (Lotan), the fleeing serpent. Again, the question is whether these are identical with Yam (the sea) or are Yam's helpers. In Job 26:12f., the serpent even seems to be associated with the clouds that darken the heavens (cf. the Egyptian serpent Apophis[58]).

Allusions to this myth appear in various contexts. Hab. 3:8 asks: "Was thy anger against the rivers, or thy indignation against the sea?" Nah. 1:4 speaks of Yahweh's rebuking the sea and drying up all the rivers. Isa. 50:2, "By my rebuke I dry up the sea, I make the rivers a desert," may refer to the exodus, as may Ps. 77:17(16), "When the waters saw thee, O God, . . . the deep (*t^ehōmôṯ*) trembled," since v. 20(19) goes on: "Thy way was through the sea, thy path through the great waters (*mayim rabbîm*)." This last verse recalls Isa. 43:16: "Yahweh makes a way in the sea, a path in the mighty waters (*mayim ʿazzîm*)," but this passage has no explicit connection with the exodus.

Although the primal sea has been vanquished, it is a real and ever-present threat. Ps. 46:3f.(2f.) considers what would happen were the mountains to fall into the midst of the sea (*b^elēḇ yammîm*): the psalmist would have no fear, because Yahweh is his refuge. According to Ps. 68:23(22), Yahweh's enemies may be in the depths of the sea (*m^eṣulôṯ yām*), but he will draw them out and shatter (*māḥaṣ*, v. 22[21], as in the mythological texts) their heads.

Job 38:16 speaks of the the springs of the sea (*niḇ^ekê yām*) and the recesses of the deep (*t^ehôm*) as distant places that no human being can ever reach. In Job 28:14, *yām* and *t^ehôm* stand in parallel, expressing the idea that wisdom is not found anywhere in the world, but is found only with God.

The sea also plays a role in apocalyptic literature: the four beasts of Daniel 7 come up out of the sea (v. 3; possibly an allusion to passages like Isa. 17:12f.; Jer. 6:23, where the raging of the nations is compared to the roaring of the sea, but more likely a reference to the primal sea[59]). An eagle emerges similarly from the sea in 2 Esd. 11:1, and a human being (the Messiah) in 2 Esd. 13:2f. (cf. 13:25,51,52f.: the depths of the sea are unsearchable).

Ever since Gunkel's *Schöpfung und Chaos in Urzeit und Endzeit* (1895), scholars have generally assumed that there was an Israelite creation myth describing Yahweh's battle with a sea monster, an account that came into being through the influence of the Babylonian creation myth. Against this theory, Heidel has pointed out that Tiamat is never explicitly called a dragon,[60] that the word *t^ehôm* cannot be derived directly from "Tiamat," although the two words may share a common origin,[61] and that the passages cited by Gunkel do not refer specifically to creation and therefore cannot be derived

---

57 See II.3 above.
58 Kaiser, 144.
59 O. Plöger, *Das Buch Daniel. KAT,* XVIII (1965), 108.
60 Pp. 83ff.
61 *Ibid.*, 98f.

directly from the myth of Marduk and Tiamat.[62] Kaiser[63] cites the Ugaritic parallels and points out that several passages are connected unambiguously with the motif of creation, while others clearly locate the battle with the sea monster in the period after creation (cf. Ugarit). Norin theorizes that the battle myth is West Semitic in origin, was known in Egypt (Astarte papyrus), and thence found its way into the exodus theme of the Israelites.

Since the battle motif does not appear in the Sumerian account of creation, it is even conceivable that the battle with the "dragon" derives from West Semitic mythology, whence it was borrowed by the Babylonian creation epic, which is relatively late. In any case, the greatest similarity is between the Israelite and Ugaritic ideas.

4. *The Exodus.* The sea plays a crucial role in the narratives describing the deliverance of Israel from Egypt. The Israelites arrive at the shore of the *yam-sûp̱* (Ex. 13:18 [E]); they encamp by the sea opposite Baal-zephon (14:2 [P]), where the pursuing Egyptians find them (v. 9). At the command of Yahweh, Moses stretches out his hand over the sea and divides it (*bāqaʿ*; v. 16 [P]). According to E, the division of the sea is brought about by a strong wind (v. 21a; cf. v. 21b: the sea becomes dry land and the waters are divided). Thus the Israelites pass through the sea (v. 22) and the Egyptians pursue them into the midst of the sea (*beṯôḵ hayyām*). Again Moses stretches out his hand over the sea, and the sea returns (v. 27), killing the Egyptians (cf. 15:19).

This narrative is interpreted in the Song of the Sea (Ex. 15:1-18), where the sea appears as an instrument in the hand of Yahweh: he throws horse and rider into the sea (v. 1 par. v. 21); he casts the army of Pharaoh into the sea (v. 4); the blast of his rage makes the waters of the sea congeal (*qp*ʾ; v. 8); he blows on the enemy and the sea covers them (v. 10). Then v. 12 strangely says that the *earth* swallowed them up (v. 12), but *ʾereṣ* here probably refers to the underworld.

The Psalms often refer to these fundamental salvific events. The division of the sea is often depicted in terms of the battle myth described above. Ps. 74:13a, for example, says: "Thou didst divide the sea by thy might"; v. 13b speaks of the "dragons on the waters," and v. 14 of Leviathan. Verse 12, however, speaks of salvation "in the midst of the earth." It is therefore not clear whether the passage is referring to creation or the exodus; v. 15 speaks of drying up the streams, which could allude to the exodus, but vv. 16f. speak quite clearly of the order imposed on the world by creation. Ps. 78:13, however, is clear: "He divided the sea and let them pass through it, and made the waters stand like a heap (*nēḏ*)." Verse 53 of the same psalm states that the sea overwhelmed their enemies. Ps. 33:7, however, is ambiguous: "He gathered the waters of the sea like a *nēḏ* (wineskin?)"; since Ps. 78:13 uses the same word in referring to the exodus miracle, the present verse may also allude to this deliverance as evidence of Yahweh's power. The preceding verse in Ps. 33, however, clearly speaks of the creation of the world. Ps. 77:20(19) is ambiguous on its face: "Thy way was through the sea. . . , yet thy footprints

62 *Ibid.,* 104ff.
63 Pp. 140ff.

were unseen." The next verse, however, shows that the reference is to the deliverance of the people through Moses and Aaron.

Ps. 66 speaks of the wonderful deeds of Yahweh (v. 5); more specifically: "He turned the sea into dry land; men passed through the river (*nāhār*) on foot" (v. 6). Here, then, the miracle of the exodus parallels the crossing of the Jordan. The same is true in Ps. 114:3,5, where the sea is personified: it sees God and flees. The context exhibits theophanic features. Ps. 106:7 states straightforwardly that the Israelites rebelled (*wayyamrû*) against God at the *yam-sûp*.[64] Verse 9, however, uses the verb *gāʿar*[65] for Yahweh's intervention against the Sea of Reeds. The same juxtaposition of *gāʿar* and "drying up" appears also in Nah. 1:4.[66] Despite the rebellion of the Israelites' fathers, Yahweh came to their aid "for his name's sake" (Ps. 106:8).

Deutero-Isaiah occasionally uses similar expressions to allude to these same events. He looks for the imminent deliverance of Israel as a new exodus, and cites the deliverance from Egypt as an proof of Yahweh's power: "Thus says Yahweh, who makes a way in the sea, a path in the mighty waters, who brings forth chariot and horse . . ." (Isa. 43:16f.). Now he will do something new, something even more wonderful (v. 19). In Isa. 50:2, the words "by my rebuke I dry up the sea" do not refer unambiguously to the exodus event; in 51:10, however, the same expression is clearly associated with the exodus, for the verse goes on to speak of a redeemed people passing through the sea. The preceding verse clearly alludes to the battle myth, mentioning the slaying of Rahab and the dragon in the *yᵉmê qeḏem* and *dōrôṯ ʿôlāmîm*.[67]

Trito-Isaiah also refers to the exodus miracle: Yahweh brought Moses, the shepherd of his flock, out of the "sea" (Nile?); he divided the waters and led his people through the depths (*tᵉhōmôṯ*) "to make for himself an everlasting name" (Isa. 63:12).[68]

5. *Jonah.* The sea also plays an important role in the story of Jonah, who, we are told, wanted to flee from Joppa to Tarshish in order to evade the command of Yahweh. Yahweh, however, causes a great storm upon the sea (Jon. 1:4), so that the mariners throw the cargo into the sea to lighten the ship (v. 5). When the crew makes inquiry, Jonah responds that the storm was sent by Yahweh, the God of heaven, who made the sea and the dry land (v. 9). They then ask what they should do to still the sea (v. 11), and Jonah replies that they should throw him into the sea (v. 12). The storm continues (v. 13), but subsides when the mariners throw Jonah into the sea (v. 15). The sea is thus not simply a geographical entity; it obeys Yahweh and serves his purposes. In ch. 2, an interpretive psalm, Jonah says that Yahweh cast him into the sea (v. 4[3]). The choice of the words *mᵉṣûlâ, yām,* and *nāhār* points up the cosmic signficance of the sea; v. 6(5) also uses *tᵉhôm,* and v. 7(6) speaks of the underworld.

---

64 For discussion of the text, see *BHS*.
65 → גער *gāʿar*.
66 See above.
67 For a discussion of the time referred to, see Kaiser, 141f.
68 On the text, see *BHS*.

6. *Tyre.* A third concentration of passages involving *yām* appears in Ezekiel's oracles concerning Tyre, the great Phoenician seaport. It is mighty on the sea (Ezk. 26:17), dwells at the entrance to the sea and trades with the peoples on the coastlands (27:3), is built in the heart of the seas (27:4), and is the place to which all the ships of the sea resort to trade (27:9). Ezekiel likens Tyre to a ship heavily laden in the heart of the seas (27:25); now, however, the east wind comes and wrecks it *b^e lēḇ yammîm* (v. 26), so that it sinks (v. 27). Now it lies silent (*k^e ḏumâ*; or should we read *niḏmâ*, "destroyed"?) in the heart of the sea (v. 32). "Once your wares came from the seas. . . , now you are wrecked by the seas, in the depths of the waters" (*b^e ma^{ca}maqqê-māyim*; vv. 33f.). In ch. 28, the prince of Tyre says that he is enthroned "in the seat of the gods, in the heart of the seas" (v. 2); but in his arrogance he will be thrust down by his enemies into the Pit, and will "die the death of the slain in the heart of the seas" (v. 8). Thus the sea, formerly the source of Tyre's wealth, will also be its destruction. Here we also note the motifs of the netherworld and the realm of the dead. Similar notions appear in Isaiah's oracle concerning Tyre (Isa. 23:2,4,11); cf. also Zec. 9:4.

7. *Idioms.* The notion of the sea in general is illuminated by various idioms making use of the word *yām*.

The wideness of the sea is proverbial. Ps. 104:25 speaks of the "great and wide sea" (*hayyām gāḏôl ûr^e ḥaḇ yāḏāyim*). Job 11:9 states that the nature of God is "longer than the earth, and broader than the sea." Isa. 11:9 also probably alludes to the compass of the sea: just as the waters fill the sea in enormous volume, so the knowledge of God will fill the land or the earth.

"Beyond the sea" (*mē^cēḇer layyām*) is the greatest possible distance, comparable to "high in the heavens" (Dt. 30:13). When the psalmist says that he cannot flee from God in the "uttermost parts of the sea" (*'aḥ^a rîṯ yām*; Ps. 139:9), he is speaking of the most remote place he can imagine. Both passages contain overtones of the sea as a cosmic entity, since the heavens and the dawn appear as parallels.

The depths of the sea challenged the imagination even more. The word *yām* alternates with synonyms like *t^e hôm* and *m^e ṣûlâ*, "depth"; we even find the phrase *m^e ṣûlôṯ yām* (Mic. 7:19: God will cast sins into the depths of the sea, i.e., he will forgive them totally; Ps. 68:23[22]: God will bring his enemies back from the depths of the sea). The bottom (*qarqa^c*) of the sea is for Amos the most distant hiding place he can seek (Am. 9:3, par. heaven, Sheol, and the top of Mt. Carmel); as in Ps. 139,[69] he cannot escape God even there. The roots of the sea (*šoršê hayyām*) and the clouds (Job 36:29f.) represent the extent of God's dominion. The phrase "the springs of the sea" (Job 38:16) also refers to the depths of the sea, for it stands in parallel with "the recesses (*ḥēqer*) of the deep (*t^e hôm*)." "The heart of the sea(s)" (*lēḇ yam*[*îm*]; Ps. 46:3[2]; Prov. 23:34; Ezk. 28:2,8) also refers to its depths; cf. Jon. 2:4(3), "Thou didst cast me into the *m^e ṣûlâ*, into the heart of the sea."

The motion of the sea naturally attracted attention. Its waves[70] and breakers[71] are often

69 See above.
70 → גלל *gll.*
71 → משברים *mišbārîm.*

mentioned; the two words sometimes appear together (Ps. 42:8[7]; Jon. 2:4[3]). Figuratively they refer to death and suffering. In Job 9:8, the "heights of the sea" (*bomºṯê-yām* may refer to its waves—or is the reference to the heavenly ocean?

The thunderous roar of the sea is sometimes mentioned. Ps. 65:8(7) speaks of the *šā'ôn* of the sea and its waves, parallel to the *hāmôn* of the peoples: both will be silenced by Yahweh (cf. Ps. 46:4[3]; 89:10[9]). In Isa. 17:12f., the two roots *šā'â* and *hāmâ* refer again to the roaring of the sea, this time as an image for the tumult of the attacking nations. Isa. 5:30 uses *nahᵃmaṯ-yām,* "the roaring of the sea," as an image of impending doom.

The sea can "thunder" (*rā'am*; Ps. 96:11 = 1 Ch. 16:32; Ps. 98:7), "be tempestuous" (*sā'ar,* Jon. 1:11), "boil" (*rāṯaḥ,* Job 41:23[31]), "be stirred up" (*rāḡa'*; Isa. 51:15, with God as agent; the result is the roaring [*hāmâ*] of the waves), and "storm" (*hitgā'aš,* Jer. 5:22). Jon. 1:15 speaks of the sea's "rage" (*za'ap*). The wicked are like the tossing (*nigrāš*) sea, which cannot rest (*hašqēṭ lō' yûḵal*) and whose waters toss up mire and dirt (Isa. 57:20).

But the sea can also quiet down (*šāṯaq,* Jon. 1:11), "stand up" (*'āmaḏ*) and "be congealed" (*qp',* Ex. 15:8), or "stand up in a heap" (*nṣb*; Ex. 15:8; Ps. 78:13).

Other verbs used with *yām* include *rā'aš,* "shake" (Hag. 2:6), *rāḡaz,* "be afraid," *ḥyl,* "tremble" (Ps. 77:17[16]), *nûs,* "flee" (Ps. 104:7; 114:3,5), and *ḥpz* niphal, "take flight" (Ps. 104:7). The sea can rise (*'ālâ,* Ezk. 26:3; *ṣûp,* Dt. 11:4), return to its normal level (*šûḇ,* Ex. 14:27), or sink ("depart": *hālaḵ,* Ex. 14:21; *'āzal,* Job 14:11).

8. *Summary.* It is impossible to summarize the theological significance of the sea in a simple formula, for OT usage is not uniform and consistent. In many cases, *yām* simply refers to the sea as a geographical entity; in other cases, however, it is associated by both language and context with the primal sea *tᵉhôm,* which clearly continues to exist in the sea of the present, or with the cosmic sea surrounding the circle of the earth, which is occasionally also called a "river" (*nāhār*). It follows that the context in which the sea occurs is rarely neutral theologically. On the one hand, the sea is a negative entity, a hostile element tamed by God, a chaotic world in opposition to the civilized world. Remarkably, it shares this feature with the dry and barren desert. We can even be told that the sea comes upon Babylon and covers it with its tumultuous waves, but with the result that the cities become a desert and the land a land of drought (Jer. 51:42f.). Desert and sea are the two elements of the world that are hostile to life.[72]

On the other hand, the sea is subordinate to God and must obey him. He has "made" it (Ps. 95:5; Jon. 1:9), and set it a bound that it cannot pass.[73] He calls for the waters of the sea and pours them out upon the surface of the earth (Am. 9:6). Not only attacking enemies[74] but also the majesty of Yahweh can be compared to the waves of the sea (Ps.

---

72 Cf. *ILC,* I–II, 471-74.

73 See above.

74 See above.

93:4). Not only destruction and death but also the unfathomable nature of Yahweh can be symbolized by the depths of the sea (Job 11:9).[75]

IV. 1. *LXX.* In the LXX, *yām* is almost always translated by *thálassa*; only rarely do we find such circumlocutions as *parálios* (Gen. 49:13; Dt. 1:7; Josh. 11:3; Job 6:3) or *parathalássios* (2 Ch. 8:17). Josh. 15:46 reads a proper name *Iemnai* or *Gemai*; Ex. 36:27,32 are based on a different text.

2. *Qumran.* The Dead Sea scrolls use *yām* several times in a purely geographical sense, especially in the Habakkuk commentary (1QpHab 5:12; 6:1; 11:14f. [all quotations]; 3:10f., in the commentary, referring to the Kittim; also 1QM 11:10 [*yām sûp*]). Elsewhere it usually appears in metaphors and similes, together with *tᵉhôm* and/or *mᵉṣûlôṯ*, often with verbs referring to the raging or roaring of the sea. Examples include: "They made my soul like a ship on the high sea (*bimᵉṣûlôṯ yām*)" (1QH 3:6f.); "Their sages are like sailors on the deep sea (*mᵉṣûlôṯ*), for their wisdom is swallowed up by the raging of the seas (*bahᵃmôṯ yammîm*) when the depths (*tᵉhômôṯ*) foam up" (1QH 3:14f.); "I was like a sailor on a ship in the raging of the seas (*zaʿap yammîm*)" (1QH 6:22f., followed by an allusion to Ps. 42:18[17]). Another passage (1QH 2:12) states that the wicked rage like tempests (*naḥšôlê*, a word found in the Mishnah) of the seas, and then quotes Isa. 57:20. God is also called the creator of the sea and the primal deep (1QH 1:14; 13:9; cf. 1QM 10:13). We are told in 1QS 3:4 that the wicked cannot even be purified or "sanctified" by the water of the sea and rivers.

V. The Bronze Sea. The bronze sea (*yam hannᵉḥōšeṯ*: 2 K. 25:13; 1 Ch. 18:8; Jer. 52:17), sometimes called *hayyām mûṣāq*, "the molten sea" (1 K. 7:23; 2 Ch. 4:2), or simply *yām* (1 K. 7:24; 2 K. 16:17), was a container for water in the temple of Solomon, used by the priests for their ablutions (2 Ch. 4:6). It had a diameter of ten cubits and was five cubits high. Originally it rested on twelve bronze bulls, but Ahaz removed them and set it upon a stone pediment (2 K. 16:17). It was destroyed by the Babylonians when they took Jerusalem (2 K. 25:13). If the vessel is comparable to the bronze laver of the tabernacle (Ex. 30:18), it probably stood at the entrance to the temple, in front of the altar.

Although it is never expressly so stated, the bronze sea probably corresponded to the "sea" in the Babylonian temple,[76] which represented the *apsû.*[77]

Ringgren

---

[75] See above.

[76] See II.2 above.

[77] Cf. W. F. Albright, *Archaeology and the Religion of Israel* (Garden City, ⁵1968), 144f.

יָמִין yāmîn; ימן ymn hiphil; יְמָנִי y^e^mānî; יְמִינִי y^e^mînî; יָמִינִי yāmînî; יִמְנָה yimnâ; תֵּימָן têmān

Contents: I. 1. Etymology; 2. Occurrences; 3. Meaning. II. Usage: 1. Right Hand; 2. South; 3. Joy. III. Theological Usage. IV. Qumran.

I. 1. *Etymology.* The noun *yāmîn,* from which the verb appears to be a denominative, is attested in Akkadian (*imnu, imittu*),[1] Ugaritic,[2] the Siloam inscription,[3] and Aramaic (Imperial Aramaic, Nabatean, Palmyrene,[4] Syriac), as well as Arabic, Old South Arabic (both verb and noun),[5] and Ethiopic (*yamān*). It does not appear in Biblical Aramaic and has not yet been found in Phoenician or Punic. It thus belongs to the stock of common Semitic words.[6] In Egyptian, we find *ỉmn,* "right," and the synonymous *wnmy,* as well as *ỉmnt(y),* "west(ward)"; in Egypt the direction of orientation is toward the south, where the sources of the Nile are found.

2. *Occurrences.* The noun *yāmîn* appears 139 times in the Hebrew OT; it occurs once in the Siloam inscription, 3 times in the Hebrew text of Sirach, and 10 times (Kuhn) in the Dead Sea scrolls. From the noun comes the denominative verb, found only in the hiphil (5 occurrences). Other derivatives include the adj. *y^e^mānî,* "right," "south," found 33 times in the OT and once in the Dead Sea scrolls, and the gentilics *y^e^mînî* (13 times), *yāmînî* (once), and *yamnâ* (4 times). The word *têmān* appears 24 times as noun or adjective and 10 times as a toponym, from which derives the gentilic *têmānî* (8 occurrences). The LXX usually translates the word with *dexiós* and its derivatives.

In antithetic parallelism *yāmîn* appears primarily with *ś^e^mō'l,* "left";[7] in synonymous parallelism it appears with → יד *yād,* "hand," or → זרוע *z^e^rōaʿ,* "arm," twice in Ps. 144:8,11 with *peh,* "mouth" (word and action).

Similar parallelisms are found at Ugarit, e.g., *ymn* par. *šm'l,*[8] *yd* par. *ymn,*[9] and *ymn* par. *p.*[10]

---

yāmîn. H. Cohen and L. I. Rabinowitz, "Right and Left," *EncJud,* XIV, 177-180; M. Dahood, "Congruity of Metaphors," *Hebräische Wortforschung. Festschrift W. Baumgartner. SVT,* 16 (1967), 40-49; W. Grundmann, "δεξιός," *TDNT,* II, 37-40; G. M. Rinaldi, "Nota [*jmjn* (*jāmîn*) 'la destra']," *BeO,* 10 (1968), 162.

1 *AHw,* I (1965), 377-79.

2 *WUS,* no. 1179.

3 *KAI,* 189, 3.

4 *DISO,* 109.

5 ContiRossini.

6 Cf. P. Fronzaroli, "Studi sul lessico comune semitico," *AANLR,* N.S. 20 (1965), 258, 265, 268.

7 See below.

8 *KTU,* 1.2 I, 40; 1.23, 63f.

9 *KTU,* 1.2 I, 39; 1.4 VII, 40f.; 1.10 II, 6f.; 1.14 II, 14f.; 1.15 II, 17f.; 1.16 I, 41f., 47f.; 1.19 IV, 56-58.

10 *KTU,* 1.23, 63f.; cf. M. Dahood and T. Penar, "Hebrew-Ugaritic Parallel Pairs," *RSP,* I

3. *Meaning.* Three meanings may be observed in the use of *yāmîn.* (1) The first and most common is "right" (side, hand, etc.) or "to the right." When associated with "hand," it frequently takes on the figurative meaning of "might" or "power." (2) Frequently the word and its derivatives mean "south." (3) Less common (but implicit in personal names) is the meaning "favorable side" (*latus faustum*). The connection between the first two meanings is obvious: the south is to the right when one looks in the direction of sunrise ("orienting oneself"). The relationship, if any, between the first two meanings and the third can no longer be determined; it may suffice to point out that in many ancient and modern cultures the right-hand side is also the "good" or "favorable" side, so that the right hand is extended in greeting and things are passed from right to left. The fact that most people are right-handed may have played a part. There is no good reason to postulate two homophonous roots.

II. Usage.

1. *Right Hand.* In both biblical and extrabiblical usage, the most frequent meaning of *yāmîn* and *y^{e}mānî* is the "right" hand or side. In this sense *yāmîn* often appears with *ś^{e}mō'l,* either literally, to indicate that something is located to the right or left of a person or object (Ex. 14:22,29; 2 S. 16:6; 1 K. 22:19; Neh. 8:4; Zec. 4:3,11), or in the extended sense of "in all directions," negatively "in no direction," "not at all" (Isa. 9:19[Eng. v. 20]; 54:3; Ezk. 21:21[16];[11] Zec. 12:6). Especially noteworthy is the phrase "turn to the right or to the left" (*pānâ*: Gen. 24:49; *nāṭâ*: 2 S. 2:21) and the negated expression "turn aside to the right or to the left," i.e., "not turn aside at all" (*nāṭâ:* Nu. 20:17; 22:26; 2 S. 2:19; *sûr:* Dt. 2:27; 1 S. 6:12; metaphorically of a judge's verdict: Dt. 17:11; of careful observance of the law: Dt. 5:32; 17:20; Josh. 1:7; 2 K. 22:2 = 2 Ch. 34:2; Isa. 30:21; cf. 1 Mc. 2:22; with reference to idolatry, Dt. 28:14; Josh. 23:6). The verb conveys the same meaning in 2 S. 14:19. A choice is presupposed in Gen. 13:9 (verbal in part). The inability of the Ninevites to tell left from right indicates their lack of judgment (Jon. 4:11).

Sometimes we are told quite neutrally that someone uses the right or the left hand for a particular purpose. The men of Gideon hold torches in their left hands and trumpets in their right (Jgs. 7:20). The Song of Deborah states that Jael held the tent peg with her (left?) hand and the mallet with her right hand (Jgs. 5:26). The left hand holds the bow; the right hand holds the arrows and draws the bow (Ezk. 39:3). When lepers are cleansed, the priest holds oil in his left hand and with his right hand sprinkles it before Yahweh. Then he touches the leper on the tip of the right ear, on the thumb of the right hand, and on the great toe of the right foot (Lev. 14:15f.,26f.). The blood of the guilt offering is applied similarly (Lev. 14:14,25). In the Song of Solomon, the bridegroom supports the head of his beloved with his left hand and embraces her with his right (Cant. 2:6; 8:3).

(1972), Intro. 7d, nos. 218a,d, 239a, 240a,d, 461a; M. Dahood, "Hebrew-Ugaritic Pairs," *RSP,* II (1975), no. 54a.

[11] The text is discussed by W. Zimmerli, *Ezekiel I. Herm* (Eng. trans. 1979), 430.

With like neutrality we are sometimes told that the right hand is used for some action: to give bribes (Ps. 26:10), to hold an idol (Isa. 44:20), to restrain a contentious woman (Prov. 27:16), to give victory (Job 40:14), or to cast lots (Ezk. 21:27[22]). A signet ring is worn on the right hand (Jer. 22:24; Sir. 49:11). God's right hand bestows blessing (Ps. 16:11) and bears the cup of his wrath (Hab. 2:16). In some cases there is no special emphasis on the right hand, in others there are overtones of the preeminence associated with it.

When both "left" and "right" are mentioned, "right" almost always comes first (22 times). The exceptions are Gen. 13:9; Ezk. 4:4; 16:46. In some sense the right hand is privileged. Jacob blesses Ephraim with hs right hand and Manasseh with his left, implying that the younger son receives the greater blessing (Gen. 48:14,19). The right hand is thus the place of honor: the queen mother sits at the king's right hand (1 K. 2:19), as does the king's bride (Ps. 45:10[9]). The king is to sit at Yahweh's right hand (Ps. 110:1), and is the "the man of Yahweh's right hand" (Ps. 80:18[17]), with the possible suggestion that the king is the channel for Yahweh's power. The text of Dt. 33:2 is corrupt: *'ēš dāṯ* is at Yahweh's right hand. The proposed emendations are not convincing.[12]

Since the right hand is used to carry out actions, raising someone's right hand means increasing his power (Ps. 89:43[42]). When Yahweh grasps someone by the right hand, the person whose hand is grasped is strengthened (Israel: Isa. 41:13; Cyrus: Isa. 45:1; cf. Ps. 63:9[8]; 73:23, and Akk. *qāta ṣabātu/aḫāzu* for leadership and guidance[13]). Yahweh causes his glorious arm to go at the right hand of Moses, thus giving him powerful aid (Isa. 63:12). In Eccl. 10:2, the right-hand side is the side of good fortune and success.

Since time immemorial, the "right hand" has been used figuratively in the sense of "power" or "might."

In this sense *yāmîn* may appear (in parallelism or otherwise) with → יד *yāḏ* (Ps. 74:11; 89:14[13]; 138:7; 139:10; Isa. 48:13) or → זרוע *zᵉrôaʿ* (Ps. 44:4[3]; 98:1), or by itself (Ex. 15:6,12; Ps. 18:36[35] [not in the par. 2 S. 22]; 48:11[10]; 63:9[8]; 78:54; 80:16[15]; 118:15f.; Lam. 2:3f.). These passages refer to the right hand (i.e., the might) of Yahweh. But it is also possible to speak of the "right hand" of the king (Ps. 21:9[8], with *yāḏ*) or other human beings (Ps. 144:8, with *yāḏ*; Job 40:14, by itself).

Here, too, the fact that most people are right-handed plays a role. Jgs. 3:15 emphasizes left-handedness as being unusual, although the meaning of the word used (*'iṭṭēr*) is uncertain (cf. the LXX's translation *amphoterodéxios,* which is hardly likely); cf. also Jgs. 20:16. Once (1 Ch. 12:2) the verb has the sense "use one's right hand" (and thus shoot with both hands); elsewhere it always means "go to the right." The right hand, then, is the active or powerful hand.

Soggin

---

12 See the comms.
13 *AHw,* II (1972), 909.

The right hand plays an especially important role in gestures. The raising of the right hand was considered a gesture of affirmation, especially in the context of a treaty (e.g., Ezk. 17:18) or oath (Gen. 14:22).[14] Kopf[15] identifies the right hand used to swear an oath with the oath itself on the basis of terminology, because *yāmîn,* like Arab. *ymn,* can itself also mean "oath."

Fabry

Dahood[16] has asked why the Psalms never mention the left hand, and looks for the explanation in the fact that *yāḏ* and *yāmîn* often appear in parallel. In these cases he takes *yāḏ* to denote the left hand, e.g., Ps. 89:14(13): "Strong is thy (left) hand, high thy right hand" (cf. Isa. 48:12f.: with his [left] hand God formed the earth and with his right hand he stretched out the heavens). This explanation is possible, but more likely is the suggestion[17] that the parallelism is meant to be incremental: might par. great might. But it is also possible to interpret the parallelism as identical, both terms referring to God's might in general. Cf. the similar parallelism between *ṣaḏ,* "side," and *yāmîn* in Ps. 91:7: "A thousand may fall at your side, ten thousand at your right hand." The only passage where the proposed interpretation is likely is Jgs. 5:26.[18]

2. *South.* We find *yāmîn* for "south" in such passages as Josh. 17:7; 1 S. 23:19,24; 2 S. 24:5; 2 K. 12:10(9); Ps. 89:13[12] (opposite *ṣāp̄ôn*); Ezk. 10:3. We find *yᵉmānî* in the same sense in 1 K. 6:8; 7:39; 2 K. 11:11; 2 Ch. 4:10; 23:10; Ezk. 47:1f. (all with *kāṯēp̄* or *keṯep*). Ps. 48:11(10) has also been cited here,[19] but that is unlikely. In many of these passages the translation "right" is also possible, but then the meaning of the expression would be totally uncertain, since the location of the speaker is unknown.

The word *têmān,* on the other hand, found 20 times (plus Sir. 43:16), clearly means "south." In 4 passages it is a technical term for the south wind (Job 39:26; Ps. 78:26; Cant. 4:16; Zec. 9:14). It appears also as a toponym for a region in the northern Hejaz, a usage distinct from that of Modern Hebrew (= Yemen). Aharoni[20] suggests that the region is identical with *ṭāwīlân.*

3. *Joy.* The naming of Benjamin (Gen. 35:18) may be cited to illustrate the meaning "favorable side" (*latus faustum*) and hence "joy." The child, named by his mother (as was customary) *ben-'ônî,* "son of my sorrow," is renamed at once by his father "son of the right hand," i.e., "child of happiness."[21] This double meaning is also found in Arabic,

---

[14] See esp. Z. W. Falk, "Gestures Expressing Affirmation," *JSS,* 4 (1959), 268f.

[15] L. Kopf, "Arabische Etymologien und Parallelen zum Bibelwörterbuch," *VT,* 9 (1959), 257 = *Studies in Arabic and Hebrew Lexicography* (Jerusalem, 1976), 198f.

[16] Pp. 40ff.

[17] M. Dietrich and O. Loretz, "Zur ugaritischen Lexikographie (I)," *BiOr,* 23 (1966), 130.

[18] See above.

[19] M. Palmer, "The Cardinal Points in Psalm 48," *Bibl,* 46 (1965), 357f.

[20] Y. Aharoni, *The Land of the Bible* (Eng. trans., ^{2}1979), 442; cf. F. M. Abel, *Géographie de la Palestine,* I (Paris, 1933), 284.

[21] Noth.

where *yamana* means both "go to the right" and "be happy": cf. the name of the region *al-yaman,* Yemen, *Arabia meridionalis* or *Arabia felix.* Although in Israel the name "Benjamin" also suggests the location of the tribe on the southern edge of an Israel that at the time had nothing to do with Judah, the account of the naming shows that the element of happiness also played a role. Cf. the words *yāmîn, yāmînî,* and *y^e^mînî* used as names for persons and places.

The name "Benjamin" appears some 170 times as *binyāmîn,* 7 times as the variant *ben-yāmîn* (or *ben 'îš y^e^mînî* or *ben hay^e^mînî*). These compounds are ancient, and probably lie behind the name of a seminomadic tribe in the vicinity of Mari (18th–17th centuries): *DUMU^MEŠ^-yamīna,* often read as West Semitic *binū-yamīna.* But it is also possible to read the logogram as Akk. *marū-yamīna,* in which case it would simply mean "southern lands," without any echo of the OT name.[22]

III. Theological Usage. The right hand of Yahweh is "terrible in power" (Ex. 15:6; possibly read *ne'dôrî,* inf. abs.[23]); it "laid the foundation of the earth and . . . spread out the heavens" (Isa. 48:13); it "strengthens" or "supports" the worshipper (Ps. 18:36[35]; the expression does not appear in the parallel text 2 S. 22:36, and is therefore deleted by several comms.[24]). In Ps. 63:9(8), an expression of trust, the worshipper finds himself upheld by the right hand of Yahweh; even in the uttermost parts of the sea, the right hand of Yahweh would hold the psalmist (Ps. 139:10). Yahweh's right hand—together with other parts of his body—rather than the courage or might of God's people effected the occupation of Canaan (Ps. 44:4[3]; 48:11[10]; cf. 78:54; 80:16[15]). Yahweh's "right hand is full of righteousness (or 'renown'?[25])" (Ps. 48:11[10]); when he "holds back" or "withdraws" his right hand, God's people suffer (Ps. 74:11; Lam. 2:3f.). His right hand is "high" (Ps. 89:14[13]); "his right hand and his holy arm have gotten him victory" (Ps. 98:1; cf. 118:15f.; Ex. 15:12).

But the "right hand" of the king can also do wonders (Ps. 21:9[8]; 45:5[4]). The terminology recalls that used for the God of Israel: "Your [the king's] (left) hand will find out all your enemies; your right hand will find out those who hate you" (Ps. 21:9[8]). The verb used in each instance is *timṣā',* which must probably be translated "overtake," "grasp."[26] The second *timṣā'* is often emended to *timḥāṣ,* following Symmachus and the Targum, but without real reason. In Ps. 45:5(4), the king appears as a victorious ruler: "Let your right hand teach you dread deeds (*nôrā'ôt*)!" or[27] "Your right hand takes

---

22 Cf. K.-D. Schunck, *Benjamin. BZAW,* 86 (1963), 3-8.

23 W. L. Moran, "The Hebrew Language in its Northwest Semitic Background," in *The Bible and the Ancient Near East. Festschrift W. F. Albright* (1961; repr. Garden City, 1965), 54-72, esp. 60 and n. 48, with bibliog.

24 For a discussion of the problem see also G. Schmuttermayr, *Psalm 18 und 2 Samuel 22. StANT,* 25 (1971), 147f. Schmuttermayr favors deleting the word, although he cannot provide convincing reasons; see the criticism of E. Zenger's review, *BZ,* N.S. 20 (1976), 265f.

25 → צדק *ṣdq.*

26 M. Dahood, *Psalms I. AB,* XVI (1965), 133, a suggestion already made by G. R. Castellino (*Libro del Salmi* [Turin, 1955]) on the basis of 1 S. 23:17.

27 Castellino.

dreadful aim!" (the text is corrupt). The same image appears where the "right hand" of ordinary mortals is mentioned. Noteworthy is Ps. 144:7f., where deliverance "from the many waters" stands in parallel with deliverance "from the hand of aliens, whose mouths speak lies, and whose right hand is a right hand of falsehood." Also noteworthy are the ironic words of Yahweh in Job 40:14: Job is challenged to equal God in competition; only "then will I [Yahweh] also acknowledge to you, that your own right hand can give you victory." The implicit assumption, as elsewhere in the OT, is that this is beyond the ability of the human right hand.

Soggin

IV. Qumran. The word *ymyn* appears some 13 times in the Dead Sea scrolls; its usage remains by and large identical with that of the OT, referring to the mighty "right hand" of God, which creates (1QH 17:18) and vouchsafes the worshipper protection (1QH 18:7). Thus it is also the first inscription on the standards in the decisive eschatological battle (1QM 4:7). The Essene worshipper at Qumran seems himself protected by God at his right hand (1QS 11:4f.). The negated merismus *lw' ymyn wśm'wl,* "(turning aside) neither to the right nor to the left" (1QS 1:15; 3:10), denotes straightforward obedience to the Torah.

Fabry

יָנָה *yānâ*

Contents: 1. Etymology, Occurrences; 2. Qal; 3. Hiphil.

1. *Etymology, Occurrences.* The root *yānâ* occurs in Middle Hebrew (hiphil, with the sense "take advantage of," "annoy [verbally])," Jewish Aramaic (*aphel,* "oppress," "take advantage of," "annoy"), Old Aramaic[1] ("oppress," "afflict"), Old Assyrian (*wanā'um,* "put pressure on," "afflict"), and possibly also Arabic (*wanā,* "be weak"). In OT Hebrew we find 4 occurrences of the qal participle (in addition to Ps. 123:4, where *ga'ᵃyônîm* should be read for *gᵉ'ê yônîm*) and 14 occurrences of various hiphil forms, limited almost exclusively to laws (Covenant Code and Holiness Code) and prophetic oracles that refer to laws (6 in Ezekiel). The LXX translates the qal participle with (*máchaira*) *Hellēnikḗ* (twice), *megálē* (Jer. 25:38[LXX 32:38]), and *peristerá* (Zeph. 3:1). The hiphil is translated *kakoún,* 4 times *thlíbein.*

2. *Qal.* The qal participle appears primarily in the phrase *ḥereḇ hayyônâ,* "sword of violence." This phrase occurs in 3 passages in Jeremiah, the first being 25:38, which concludes the commentary on the vision of the cup of wrath (25:15ff.) and may not derive

1 Sefire inscription, *KAI,* 223 B, 16.

from Jeremiah. The land (Judah? the land of the enemy?) has become a waste because of the (his?) violent sword (read *haḥereḇ* or *ḥarbô hayyônâ*; *ḥ^a^rôn* has intruded from the following clause) and because of his (Yahweh's? Nebuchadnezzar's?) fierce anger.[2] In Jer. 46:16, an oracle concerning Egypt, the mercenaries say to each other, "Arise, and let us go back to our own people and to the land of our birth, from the violent sword." A similar statement appears in Jer. 50:16, in an oracle concerning Babylon: "From the violent sword every one shall turn to his own people, and every one shall flee to his own land." This verse alludes to Isa. 13:14, and is undoubtedly secondary. Finally, Zeph. 3:1 refers to Jerusalem as a rebellious (*mōr^e^'â*), defiled (*nig'ālâ*), and violent (*yônâ*) city. It is clear from the following verses that the prophet is castigating violent officials, unjust judges, and deceitful prophets.

3. *Hiphil.* The hiphil means "oppress," "do violence to." It appears first in Ex. 22:20(Eng. v. 21), in the Covenant Code, which prohibits "oppressing" or wronging[3] a resident alien (*gēr*). The prohibition is based on the fact that the Israelites themselves were resident aliens in Egypt. This prohibition is repeated in the plural in the Holiness Code (Lev. 19:33) on the same grounds (v. 34b), but with the additional requirement that such a resident alien be treated like a native (*'ezrāḥ*) and loved as oneself. The regulations governing the purchase of property during the Jubilee Year (Lev. 25:14,17) forbid oppressing a neighbor (*'āḥ, 'āmîṯ*), probably on the grounds that an emergency sale is usually involved: it is wrong to take advantage of another's distress.[4]

Dt. 23:17(16) prohibits "oppressing" an escaped slave: he must not be returned to his master but allowed to dwell where he pleases. In the Covenant Code, the law against oppressing a *gēr* is followed by a law against "afflicting" (*'nh* piel) widows or orphans (Ex. 22:21[22]). This combination reappears in Jer. 22:3, where the following admonition in Deuteronomistic prose is addressed to the king and his people: "Do justice and righteousness. . . , and do no wrong (*yānâ* hiphil) or violence (*ḥms*) to the alien (*gēr*), the fatherless, and the widow."

Ezekiel uses a somewhat different vocabulary. In Ezk. 22:7 (and 22:29) we find the charge that "the fatherless and the widow are wronged in you"; but in the discussion of individual responsibility in ch. 18 we are told that the wicked oppresses the poor and needy (*'ānî w^e^'eḇyôn*: v. 12; the language is that of the Psalms) and the righteous does not oppress anyone (vv. 7, 16). In the program at the end of the book, finally, the prince is forbidden to oppress the people (45:8) or to take any of the inheritance of the people, "thrusting them out of their property" (46:18): all are to enjoy their inheritance unmolested.

Outside this tradition stands a passage in Deutero-Isaiah, where God promises to make the people's oppressors (*mônayiḵ*) eat their own flesh, "that all the world may know that

---

2 Against the the reading that finds here the "dove" of Ishtar (proposed by L. Saint-Paul Girard, "La colère de la colombe," *RB*, 40 [1931], 92f.), see A. Condamin in *Bibl,* 12 (1931), 242f.

3 → לחץ *lāḥaṣ*.

4 K. Elliger, *Leviticus. HAT,* IV (1966), 353.

I am Yahweh, your savior and redeemer" (Isa. 49:26). This category also includes Ps. 74:8 if *nînām* is to be emended to either *nînēm* (qal) or *nônēm* (hiphil), so that the enemies are saying, "Let us oppress them."

In the Dead Sea scrolls, *ynh* appears only in 4QpPs37 3:7, in the pesher on Ps. 37:20. Here it is the leaders of wickedness who have "oppressed" the people of God, a clear allusion to the persecuted status of Qumran.

Ringgren

יָנַק yānaq; יוֹנֵק yônēq; יוֹנֶקֶת yôneqeṯ

Contents: I. 1. Etymology; 2. Ugaritic; 3. OT Occurrences. II. OT Usage: 1. Qal; 2. Hiphil; 3. *yônēq*; 4. *yôneqeṯ*.

I. 1. *Etymology.* The verbal root *ynq*, "suck," is attested in various Aramaic dialects,[1] Ugaritic,[2] and Akkadian (*enēqu*);[3] Egyp. *śnk*, "suck(le),"[4] originally a causative, probably belongs here also.

2. *Ugaritic.* The occurrences of this root in Ugaritic are especially interesting. One passage states that the son of King Keret "will suck the milk of Aṯirat and drink (*mss*) from the breasts of virgin ʿAnat."[5] The "merciful" gods Šahar and Šalim are repeatedly said to suck the breasts of Aṯirat and Raḥmai.[6] In the last passage, the text continues: "One lip to the earth and one lip towards heaven, and the birds of the heavens and the fish in the sea go into her mouth, and they hasten from piece to piece as they are ready and from right and left (they are placed) in her mouth, and are not satisfied."

3. *OT Occurrences.* The OT contains 8 occurrences of the qal and 10 of the hiphil; there are also 11 occurrences of the qal ptcp. *yônēq*, "suckling," and 5 occurrences of the hiphil ptcp. *mêneqeṯ*, "wet-nurse." The qal ptcp. *yôneqeṯ*, which means "sucker," "shoot," occurs 6 times. There is also 1 occurrence of *yᵉnîqâ*, "shoot" (Ezk. 17:4).

The LXX usually translates *thēlázein* (Isa. 60:16: with *esthíein*) and often uses *tropheúein* for the hiphil; *yônēq* is rendered *nḗpios*.[7] For *mêneqeṯ* the LXX uses *tróphos*.

---

1 *DISO*, 109; also Syriac and Mandaic.
2 *WUS*, no. 1188.
3 *AHw*, I (1965), 217.
4 *WbÄS*, IV, 174.
5 *KTU*, 1.15 II, 26.
6 *KTU*, 1.23, 24, 59, 61.
7 Cf. G. Bertram, "νήπιος," *TDNT*, IV, 912-14.

II. OT Usage.

1. *Qal.* The qal forms have the primary literal meaning "suck" (Job 3:12: "Why [were there] breasts for me to suck?"; Cant. 8:1: "Oh that you were my brother, who sucked my mother's breasts"). The other occurrences illustrate metaphorical usage. Dt. 33:19, for example, says of Zebulun: "They suck the affluence of the seas," i.e., they enjoy the bounty of the sea; and Isa. 60:16 says of restored Zion: "You shall suck the milk of nations, you shall suck the breast of kings," i.e., draw in the wealth of the gentile world. In Isa. 66:10f., the inhabitants of Jerusalem are summoned to rejoice "that you may suck (*ynq*) and be satisfied with her consoling breasts, that you may drink deeply (*mṣṣ*) and be refreshed (*ʿng* hithpael) at her abundant mother's breast" (in v. 12, *wînaqtem* should be emended to *weyōnaqtām*). Jerusalem is thus depicted as a mother and her inhabitants as suckling children, nourished abundantly by her.

Job 20:16 presents a different image: "He (the wicked) will suck the poison of asps; the tongue of a viper will kill him."

2. *Hiphil.* The hiphil is usually used in the literal sense of "suckle, nurse": Gen. 21:7 ("Who would have said to Abraham that Sarah would suckle children?"); 32:16(15) ("thirty milch camels"); Ex. 2:7,9 (nursing the infant Moses); 1 S. 1:23 (Hannah nurses Samuel); 1 K. 3:21 ("I rose in the morning to nurse my child"); Lam. 4:3 ("even jackals suckle their young"). Only in Dt. 32:13 do we find figurative usage: God "made [Israel] suck honey out of the rock, and oil out of the flinty rock."

The ptcp. *mêneqeṯ* means "wet-nurse" (Gen. 24:59; 35:8; 2 K. 11:2 par. 2 Ch. 22:11), figuratively in Isa. 49:23: "Kings shall be your foster fathers and their queens your nursing mothers."

3. *yônēq.* The word *yônēq* means "suckling," "infant"; it appears frequently with its near synonym *ʿôlēl.*[8] Samuel tells Saul to slay "man and woman, infant and suckling" (*mēʿōlēl weʿaḏ-yônēq*) among the Amalekites (1 S. 15:3). He slays the inhabitants of Nob: "men and women, children and sucklings" (1 S. 22:19). Jeremiah asks whether the Israelites mean through their sins to cut off "man and woman, infant and child" (*ʿôlēl weyônēq*; Jer. 44:7). Lam. 2:11 laments that infants and sucklings faint in the streets of the city, and in Lam. 4:4 *yôneqîm and ʿôlālîm* appear again as victims of hunger and thirst. The combination obviously means that even the littlest are wiped out or fall victim to disaster. Dt. 32:25 uses "the sucking child" and "the man of gray hairs" (*yônēq ʿim-ʾîš śêḇâ*) to stand for the entire population as victims of war. In Joel 2:12-17 (a call to lament), the prophet says: "Gather (*ʾsp*) the people . . . assemble (*qbṣ*) the elders; gather (*ʾsp*) the children, even nursing infants" (v. 16). In other words, the entire populace is to be summoned.

Elsewhere the reference is to little, helpless infants. Moses, for example, asks whether he is expected to care for the people as a nurse carries the sucking child (Nu. 11:12). Isa. 11:8 paints a picture of nature at peace by saying that the sucking child shall play over the hole of the asp. Ps. 8:3(2) is usually interpreted similarly: *mippî ʿôlelîm weyôneqîm yissaḏtā*

---

8 → עול *ʿwl.*

ʿōz, "By the mouth of babes and infants thou hast founded a bulwark," i.e., even the littlest and weakest can protect against the hostile powers of chaos because Yahweh supports them. The LXX and Syriac interpret *ʿōz* as "praise," with the meaning that even the babbled praise of small children is pleasing to God. Both interpretations are problematic, as is the attempt to connect the passage with the preceding verse: "Thou, whose glory above the heavens is chanted (*tᵉnâ* from *tānâ*; Jgs. 5:11) from the mouth of babes. . . ." But the prep. *min* does not normally express agency, although it does appear frequently in the expression "take refuge from (*min*) something." Then *ʿōz* could be taken as *māʿōz,* and the translation would run: "From the mouth of the *yônᵉqîm* thou hast founded a bulwark." In this case, *yônᵉqîm* can only be a reference to the mythological *ynqm* of the Ugaritic text about the "merciful gods."[9] Since Ps. 73:9f. sounds like an echo of the same text,[10] and the verb *mṣh* recalls the *mss* of the Keret text, it is not unlikely that Israel was familiar with the myth. Early Jewish exegesis reinterpreted Ps. 8:3(2): *ʿôlᵉlîm wᵉyônᵉqîm* was understood to refer to Israel as a weak and helpless nation. Rashi even finds a reference to the priests and Levites.[11] The use of *yônēq* in Isa. 53:2 is discussed below.

4. *yôneqeṯ*. Like *yônēq* in Isa. 53:2, *yôneqeṯ* means "sucker," "shoot," "sprout." It is found only in figurative usage.

Ps. 80:9ff.(8ff.) describes Israel as a vine that Yahweh has transplanted from Egypt; v. 12(11) says that it sent out its shoots to the river. Hos. 14 describes the restoration of Israel in terms of fertility, and says in v. 7(6): "His shoots shall spread out." The double allegory of Ezk. 17 speaks twice of an eagle that breaks off the topmost twig of a cedar (v. 4: *yᵉnîqâ*; v. 22: *yôneqeṯ*). The first time he plants it in a "land of trade," the second time on a high mountain. The first image represents the deportation of the king to Babylon as a prisoner, the second represents the restoration of Israel.

The other occurrences are in Job, where images taken from the plant world depict the fate of the wicked: he thrives in the sun and "his shoots spread over his garden" (Job 8:16), but soon he is destroyed (v. 18); he cannot escape his fate: "the flame will dry up his shoots" (15:30). By way of contrast, see 14:7: "There is hope for a tree, if it be cut down, that it will sprout again, and that its shoots will not cease"—but human beings die and are laid low (v. 10).

Finally, *yônēq* appears with this meaning in Isa. 53:2: the servant grew up "before him" (Yahweh?; "before himself," i.e., "privately"?;[12] or emend to *lᵉp̄ānênû,* "before us"?) "like a shoot and like a root out of dry ground"—an image of insignificance and weakness.

Ringgren

---

9 H. Ringgren, "Psalm 8 och Kristologin," *SEÅ,* 37f. (1972-73), 17f.; similarly C. Schedl, "Psalm 8 in ugaritischer Sicht," *FuF,* 38 (1964), 183-85; cf. also W. Rudolph, "'Aus dem Munde der jungen Kinder und Säuglinge. . .' (Psalm 8,3)," *Beiträge zur Alttestamentlichen Theologie. Festschrift W. Zimmerli* (Göttingen, 1977), 388-396.

10 H. Ringgren, "Einige Bemerkungen zum LXXIII. Psalm," *VT,* 3 (1953), 265ff.

11 Cf. Bertram, 921.

12 S. Nyberg, "Smärtornas man," *SEÅ,* 7 (1942), 49.

יָסַד yāsaḏ; יְסוֹד yᵉsôḏ; יְסוּדָה yᵉsûḏâ; יֶסֶד yᵉsuḏ; מוּסָד / מוּסָדָה mûsāḏ(â);
מוֹסָד / מוֹסָדָה môsāḏ(â); מַסָּד massāḏ

Contents: I. General: 1. Root; 2. Cognates; 3. Statistics; 4. Basic Meaning. II. Bible: 1. Nouns; 2. Verb. III. Theological Usage: 1. Yahweh, Layer of the Earth's Foundations; 2. Inaccessibility to Human Knowledge; 3. Foundations Laid by Yahweh; 4. Foundation of the Second Temple; 5. Base of the Altar.

I. General.

1. *Root.* Besides the root *ysd* I, "found," "foundation," the lexica are probably correct in seeing a root *ysd* II, "close together," in Ps. 2:2; 31:14(Eng. v. 13); this root is a secondary formation from → סוד *sôḏ.*[1] It is possible that *ysd* I and *swd/ysd* II go back to a common Semitic ancestor with a basic meaning something like "bind together, join."[2] The actual usage of Heb. *ysd* I and its cognates in other Semitic languages exhibits no traces of this hypothetical basic meaning, however, so that the postulated common ancestor of *ysd* I and *swd/ysd* II is irrelevant to the meaning of *ysd* I.[3]

In the Dead Sea scrolls, the roots *ysd* and *swd* are so confused that it is often impossible to identify distinct meanings.[4] But here we are obviously dealing with a semantic development that is characteristic of Qumran. In any case, "biblical usage exhibits a firmly established semantic distinction between the two words,"[5] so that we cannot draw any conclusions about *ysd* I in the OT from the language of Qumran.

2. *Cognates.* Heb. *ysd* I is the same root as OSA *mwśd,* "base,"[6] and Arab. *wisād* (= Jewish Aram. *ʾissāḏā*), "cushion," "support." It is also connected with Syr. *satta,* "grapevine slip." In Ugaritic, *ysd* I appears as both noun and verb.[7] Whether *ysd* in Ugar.

---

yāsaḏ. B. Couroyer, "Un égyptianisme biblique: 'Depuis la fondation de l'Égypte' (*Exode,* IX, 18)," *RB,* 67 (1960), 42-48; W. Foerster, "κτίζω," *TDNT,* III, 1000-1035; A. Gelston, "The Foundations of the Second Temple," *VT,* 16 (1966), 232-35; P. Humbert, "Note sur *yāsad* et ses dérivés," *Hebräische Wortforschung. Festschrift W. Baumgartner. SVT,* 16 (1967), 135-142; E. Jenni, *Das hebräische Piʿel* (Zurich, 1968), 211f.; H. Muszyński, *Fundament. AnBibl,* 61 (1975), esp. 46-65; W. H. Schmidt, "יסד *jsd* gründen," *THAT,* I, 736-38; K. L. Schmidt, "θεμέλιος," *TDNT,* III, 63f.

[1] Cf. *GesB, KBL³,* etc., *s.v.*

[2] Cf. F. H. W. Gesenius, *Thesaurus philologicus criticus linguae hebraeae et chaldaeae Veteris Testamenti,* II (Leipzig, ²1835), 601-3.

[3] Cf. also H.-J. Fabry, "סוד: Der himmlische Thronrat als ekklesiologisches Modell," *Bausteine biblischer Theologie. Festschrift G. J. Botterweck. BBB,* 50 (1977), 102; a different position is represented by Muszyński, 46f.

[4] Cf. Muszyński, 46, n. 109, with bibliog.

[5] *Ibid.,* 47; cf. 52.

[6] Cf. W. W. Müller, "Altsüdarabische Beiträge zum hebräischen Lexikon," *ZAW,* 75 (1963), 304-316.

[7] *WUS,* no. 1189; *UT,* no. 1117; see II.1.c below.

bn ysd[8] and the Phoenician name *bn ysd*[9] is to be identified with *ysd* I is disputed.[10] Also uncertain is the reading *ysdh* (= Heb. *y^e sôḏâ*) on the stela of Yeḥimilk of Byblos.[11]

Akk. *išdu,* the same root as Heb. *ysd* I,[12] exhibits a range of meanings corresponding quite closely to that of Heb. *ysd* I. It refers first to the foundation of a building, which guarantees its solidity and permanence; it then comes to mean the unshakable foundation of an entire city, land, or kingdom, as well as the firm foundation of human existence and the reliability of some particular human conduct. Finally, it can refer to the lower portion or base of an object such as a jar, or the lower portion of a plant or part of the body.[13] The verb *šuršudu*[14] may be a denominative from *išdu.*

For "foundation," Biblical Aramaic uses *'uššîn,* borrowed from Akkadian. Like Sumero-Akk. *uššū,*[15] it is found almost exclusively in the plural (Ezr. 4:12; 5:16; 6:3).[16] In Jewish Aramaic, however, the root *ysd* I occurs frequently alongside the root *'šš.*[17]

3. *Statistics.* In the OT, *ysd* I appears in a variety of substantives and as a verb. Since Akkadian and Arabic have substantives derived from *ysd* but no verbs, the use of the root as a noun is probably primary. No adjective forms are found. In addition to the 80 occurrences of the root in the MT listed by Lisowsky, *ysd* is found in Sir. 16:19 (*ye sôḏê tēḇēl*) and can be postulated confidently in Sir. 1:15 (*themélion aiṓnos*; cf. *ye sôḏ ʿôlām* [Prov. 10:25]); Sir. 10:16 ("destroy *héōs themelíōn gḗs*"; cf. *ʿaḏ hay^e sôḏ bāh* [Ps. 137:7]); Sir. 50:15 ("pour out *eis themélia thysiastēríou*"; cf. *'el-ye sôḏ mizbaḥ* [Lev. 4:7; etc.]); and probably also Sir. 3:9 (*ekrizoún themélia,* in antithetical parallelism with *stērízein oíkous*). In Jth. 16:15, however, the leaping of the mountains *ek themelíōn* is more likely to reflect Heb. *māqôm* (cf. Job 9:6; 18:4; Isa. 13:13).

Of the 80 occurrences in the MT, roughly half (41) involve the verb. Half of these (20) represent the qal and a quarter (10) the piel; there are 2 occurrences of the niphal, 6 of the pual, and 3 of the hophal. The hiphil and hithpael are not found. Of the 39 occurrences as a noun, about half (19) involve *ye sôḏ* and a third (13) *môsāḏ.*

4. *Basic Meaning.* All occurrences of the Hebrew root *ysd* I and of its Semitic cognates exhibit the same basic meaning: *ysd* reflects the way of life of a settled population accustomed to erecting permanent buildings made of durable materials. It refers in the first instance to the foundation of a permanent building or the laying of such a foundation.

---

8 *WUS,* no. 1190; *UT,* no. 1118.

9 *KAI,* 29, 2.

10 Cf. *PNU,* 102, 146.

11 Cf. *KAI,* 10, 14.

12 *AHw,* I (1965), 393f.; uncertain: *GesB, KBL,* etc.

13 Cf. *AHw.*

14 *Ibid.,* II (1972), 960.

15 Cf. *GaG,* § 61h.

16 Cf. *LexLingAram* and *KBL, s.v.*

17 Cf. *WTM, s.v.*

The primary emphasis is on the element of stability and permanence provided by the foundation or its laying.

This basic meaning can be extended so that *ysd* refers to the "founded" building as a whole or to the construction and "founding" of the whole; it is no longer limited to the foundation or its laying. But the basic meaning can also be restricted so that the element of permanence implicit in the notion of a foundation recedes or vanishes entirely, and what is "below" in contrast to "above" is emphasized, or what is "first" in contrast to what is "last." Occasionally the notion of "beneathness" is augmented by the element of hiddenness, so that it is unexpected and astonishing for this "foundation" to come to light.

In the OT, these various elements appear first of all in the "secular" area of ordinary buildings. Then *ysd* appears in the context of building the sanctuary or Zion, either initially or (in predictions for the glorious future) finally. Like the notion of a structure as a whole, *ysd* can also be transferred to other spheres. It is used metaphorically in hymnic praise of God as the creator and foundation-layer of the earth or in statements about the foundation and creation of the earth. In addition, *ysd* can refer to laws and commandments that are fixed and unalterable.

II. Bible.

1. *Nouns.* a. The sg. *y^esôḏ* appears 9 times in the context of propitiatory consecration of an altar (Ex. 29:12; Lev. 8:15; 9:9; cf. the passages that speak of [re]consecrating an altar without mentioning its *y^esôḏ* [Ex. 30:10; Lev. 16:18f.; Ezk. 43:20; cf. also Ex. 29:36f.]) or in connection with the sin offering (Lev. 4:7,18,25,30,34; 5:9).[18] The priest, in order to (re)consecrate an altar or to offer sacrifice on behalf of himself, the ruler, or the people, is to take the blood of the sacrificial animal and "give" it on the horns of the altar or "sprinkle" (*nzh* hiphil, Lev. 5:9) it on the "side" (*qîr*) of the altar. He is to "pour out"[19] the rest of the blood on the *y^esôḏ*, the base of the altar. In contrast to the "horns" of the altar, which are atop it, and also in contrast to its "side," *y^esôḏ* designates the lower part of the altar, the base or foot that rests upon or is embedded in the earth. The *y^esôḏ* postulated in Sir. 50:15 has the same meaning.[20]

In Ezk. 13:14, the *y^esôḏ* (sg.) is the foundation on which a wall is built; in Hab. 3:13, it is the foundation of a house resting directly on bare rock; in Ps. 137:7, it is the foundation of a city, probably more particularly of the city wall. In Mic. 1:6, the pl. *y^esôḏîm* has the same meaning. Destruction "lays bare" (→ גלה *gālâ* [*gālāh*]) ([Ezk. 13:14; Mic. 1:6]; → ערה *ʿrh* [Hab. 3:13; Ps. 137:7]) the foundation. In these 4 passages, then, the *y^esôḏ* and its plural in *-îm* refer to a deeply buried foundation, which is therefore secure as well as being covered by the structure erected upon it. The "laying bare" of a hidden foundation depicts radical destruction. Sir. 10:16 speaks in similar hyperbole of destruction *héōs themelíōn gḗs* (probably = *ʿaḏ y^esôḏê ṯēḇēl*; cf. Sir. 16:19).

---

18 → חטא *ḥāṭā'* (*chāṭā'*).

19 → שׁפך *šāpak̠*.

20 See III.5 below.

Job 4:19 describes human frailty in terms of a *y^e^sôḏ*, itself the element lending permanence and stability, that rests not upon rock but upon "dust."[21] Job 22:16 depicts the insecurity of the wicked by saying that their *y^e^sôḏ* flows away beneath them like a river. According to Prov. 10:25, on the other hand, the righteous has a *y^e^sôḏ ʿôlām*, a foundation that endures forever and bestows permanence. Sir. 1:15 expresses the enduring presence of wisdom among humankind by stating that she has laid for her dwelling place among them an enduring foundation (*themélios aiṓnos*, probably = *y^e^sôḏ ʿôlām*). These 4 passages use *y^e^sôḏ* as a wisdom metaphor expressing permanence and enduring presence. In Sir. 16:19, the pl. *y^e^sôḏîm*, alongside the "roots of the mountains" (*qiṣḇê hārîm*; cf. Jon. 2:7[6]), refers to the foundation of the earth, on which it rests secure and unshakable. Both the singular and the plural in *-îm* thus always refer, literally or metaphorically, to a concrete structural element: the lowest portion of a building, its foundation.

Twice we find a plural of *y^e^sôḏ* in *-ôṯ*. Lam. 4:11 says that the fire Yahweh has kindled in Zion has destroyed "its foundations" (*y^e^sôḏōṯeyhā*). In contrast to Ezk. 13:14; Hab. 3:13; Mic. 1:6; Ps. 137:7 (and Sir. 10:16), which speak of destruction that "lays bare" or reaches the foundation (sg. or pl. in *-îm*), here the pl. *y^e^sôḏôṯ* itself designates the object of destruction. The word refers therefore not just to the foundation but by metonymy to all the buildings of Zion. The translation "to the ground"[22] is not precise. The plural in *-ôṯ* exhibits the same metonymous extension in Ezk. 30:4, which declares that the *y^e^sôḏôṯ* of Egypt—undoubtedly meaning all its buildings—will be destroyed. Isa. 54:11 is discussed in II.2.a below.

The sg. *y^e^sûḏâ* (Ps. 87:1), like the par. "gates of Zion," is also an example of metonymy; it refers not to the foundation but to the structure as a whole, which belongs to Yahweh (note the masc. suf.).[23] The metonymy of *y^e^sûḏâ* in Ps. 87:1 also supports a common emendation in Isa. 23:13, which replaces *y^e^sāḏāh*, "he founded it," with *y^e^sûḏâ*, "a foundation (laid by seafarers)."[24]

The metonymous meaning "(entire) structure" thus distinguishes the pl. *y^e^sôḏôṯ* from the singular and the plural in *-îm* and associates it with *y^e^sûḏâ*.[25] It also argues against the common emendation in Isa. 40:21 of *môs^e^ḏôṯ* (*haʾāreṣ*) to *miyy^e^sûḏaṯ* or *mîsuḏaṯ* (*haʾāreṣ*).[26] Two other occurrences of *y^e^sôḏ* are textually problematic: 2 Ch. 23:5 (*šaʿar hay^e^sôḏ*; cf. 2 K. 11:6: *šaʿar ṣûr*) and Ezr. 3:12 (*b^e^yosḏô*; qal inf. of *ysd* or scribal error for *bîsōḏô*?). Also textually problematic is *y^e^suḏ* in Ezr. 7:9 (no equivalent in 3 Esd. 8:6, a direct translation, prior to the LXX, of a Hebrew original[27]).

---

21 → עפר *ʿāpār*.

22 Cf., e.g., H.-J. Kraus, *Klagelieder (Threni)*. *BK*, XX (1956), 71; W. Rudolph, *Die Klagelieder, KAT*, XVII/3 (1962), 246; A. Weiser, *Klagelieder. ATD*, XVI/2 (1958), 98.

23 For a different view, see Humbert, 139, and Muszyński, 50.

24 Cf. B. Duhm, *Jesaja. HKAT*, III/1 (1902) and others *in loc.*; for a different interpretation, see *KBL*³, etc., *s.v. ysd* I.

25 Contra Muszyński, 48.

26 See II.1.c below.

27 Cf. W. Rudolph, *Esra und Nehemia. HAT*, XX (1949), xv-xvi; D. Hanhart, *Text und Textgeschichte des 1. Esrabuches. MSU*, 12. *AKGW*, 3/92 (1974), 11; etc.

b. In 2 Ch. 8:16, the "day of the foundation (*mûsāḏ* sg.) of the house of Yahweh" is contrasted with the time of its completion. Here *mûsāḏ* undoubtedly refers not to part of the structure but to an action: the laying of the cornerstone and the start of construction. It is likely that the sg. *mûsāḏ* has the same meaning in the difficult passage Isa. 28:16: not the foundation as a structural entity but the act of laying the cornerstone.[28] Yahweh will lay a "cornerstone of value, of a sure foundation," i.e., a precious cornerstone set after the fashion of a deep foundation. The phrase *mûsāḏ mûssāḏ*, "deep cornerstone-laying," is thus syntactically an adnominal phrase describing the precious cornerstone; but it incorporates the verb *ysd* twice to describe—adverbially—the act of laying the cornerstone, in which the precious cornerstone is set deep so as to be especially secure and unshakable.[29] Isa. 40:21 is discussed in II.1.c below.

The emendation of *mûsāḵ* to *mûsāḏ* in 2 K. 16:18 is arbitrary and unnecessary. In Isa. 30:32, *mûsāḏâ* is undoubtedly a scribal error for *mûsārâ*, "punishment." In Ezk. 41:8, the *qere mwsdwt* is preferable to the *kethibh mysdwt*; but *mwsdwt* is the plural of *môsāḏ*, not of *mûsāḏ*/*mûsāḏâ*.[30] The noun *mûsāḏâ* cited in the lexica[31] is therefore unattested, even through textual emendation.

Our conclusion is that *mûsāḏ* occurs only in the singular and refers to the laying of a cornerstone for a building.

c. The noun *môsāḏ* forms a plural in both *-ôṯ* and *-îm*, without any detectable semantic difference. The singular is not found. According to Jer. 51:26, no stone shall be taken from the ruins of Babylon for use as a cornerstone (*'eḇen l^epinnâ*), no stone *l^emôs^eḏôṯ*. In parallel with *pinnâ*, *môs^eḏôṯ* cannot denote the act of laying a foundation; it must refer to the actual foundations. Similarly *môs^eḏê ḏôr-wāḏôr* in Isa. 58:12, in parallel with *ḥorḇôṯ ʿôlām*, refers to the foundations left standing after buildings are destroyed. According to Ezk. 41:8 (*Q*), the *môs^eḏôṯ* (not *mûs^eḏôṯ*[32]) of the side chambers of the temple are 6 cubits high. In these 3 passages, *môs^eḏîm*/*-ôṯ* refers to the foundations of a structure, raised to a certain height so that the building proper can be erected upon them. The same meaning attaches to the *hapax legomenon massāḏ* in 1 K. 7:9 (in contrast to *haṭṭ^epāḥôṯ*, "corbel"?).

The notion of "foundations on which the structure as a whole is built" is then extended to the structure of the cosmos. One may speak of the "foundations of the mountains" (*môs^eḏê hārîm*: Dt. 32:22; Ps. 18:8[7]) and the "foundations of (the vault of) heaven" (*môs^eḏôṯ haššāmayim*: 2 S. 22:8 if the text is correct; cf. Ps. 18:8[7]). Most commonly, however, we hear of the "foundations of the earth" (*môs^eḏê 'āreṣ*: Ps. 82:5; Prov. 8:29; Isa. 24:18; Jer. 31:37; Mic. 6:2; *môs^eḏôṯ tēḇēl*: 2 S. 22:16 par. Ps. 18:16[15]). It is noteworthy that in these phrases not only *tēḇēl* but also *'ereṣ* and *hārîm* always appear without the article.

---

28 Contra Humbert, 140; Muszyński, 50.
29 See III.3 below.
30 See II.1.c below.
31 Cf. also Humbert, 140f.
32 See II.1.b above.

There is a precise parallel in Ugaritic. The costly materials of which certain objects are made for a goddess are called *dbbm d msdt ʾrṣ.*[33] The *msdt ʾrṣ* are thus the rocky foundations of the earth from which valuable materials are recovered and on which the earth or land rests.

The text of Isa. 40:21 (*môsᵉd̲ôt̲ hāʾāreṣ*) is undoubtedly corrupt (*mērōʾš* as a parallel term; *ʾereṣ* with an article; *môsᵉd̲ôt̲* used in a concrete sense). The emendation *miyyᵉsud̲at̲* or *mîsud̲at̲ hāʾāreṣ* is often proposed, but runs against the familiar metonymous usage of *yᵉsûd̲â/yᵉsôd̲ôt̲.*[34] A possible reading is (*hᵃlōʾ hᵃb̲înōt̲em*) *mimmûsad̲ hāʾāreṣ,* "from the foundation of the earth," assuming haplography of one of the three adjacent *mems* and assimilation of *mûsād̲,* read as *môsād̲,* to the otherwise common plural.[35]

When "foundations" are mentioned in a cosmic context, there are often overtones of permanence and solidity lent by such "foundations" to the mountains, the vault of heaven, or the earth. Just as Yahweh assigns a limit to the sea, which its waters cannot pass, so he establishes "the foundations of the earth" (Prov. 8:29). Therefore the cosmic order is disturbed when the foundations of the earth (Ps. 82:5; Isa. 24:18), the heavens (2 S. 22:8), or the mountains (Ps. 18:8[7]) tremble. Usually, however, the emphasis is on the inaccessibility of the cosmic "foundations."[36]

Finally, the cosmic "foundations" can be used in merismus. Such double expressions as "foundations of the mountains/earth" (Dt. 32:22; Ps. 18:8[7]), "foundations of the heavens/earth" (2 S. 22:8), "foundations of the earth/mountains" (Mic. 6:2), "foundations of the earth below/heavens above" (Jer. 31:37), and "foundations of the earth/bottom of the sea" (2 S. 22:16 par. Ps. 18:16[15]) include the extreme poles of the cosmos or the inhabited world, in order to express the totality of the world or its "bases" (cf. also 1 K. 7:9: the temple of Solomon is built entirely of hewn stones *mibbayit̲ ûmiḥûṣ,* "inside and outside," and *ûmimmassād̲ ʿad̲-haṭṭᵉpāḥôt̲,* "from the foundation to the top layer under the roofbeams"). In these expressions the idea of permanence originally associated with "foundations" vanishes totally. They resemble similar meristic expressions without *môsᵉd̲ôt̲/-îm* that speak simply of heaven and earth or earth and sea.

2. *Verb.* a. Ps. 102:26(25) states that Yahweh founded (*ysd* qal) the earth and that the heavens are the work of his hands (*maʿᵃśēh yād̲eyk̲ā*). The qal of *yāsad̲* stands in chiastic parallelism with *maʿᵃśeh* and therefore cannot refer to the laying of the foundations of the earth, but must designate the completed work of its creation as a whole. The same is true in all passages where *yāsad̲* with the "earth" as object stands in parallel with the "spreading out" (*ṭpḥ, nṭh*) or "establishing" (*kwn*) of the heavens (Ps. 104:5 ["heavens" in v. 2]; Prov. 3:19; Isa. 48:13; 51:13,16; Zec. 12:1; cf. Ps. 78:69). The meristic double construction comprehends the creation of the entire cosmos, and *yāsad̲* comprehends the whole creation of the earth.

---

33 *WUS,* no. 1189; *UT,* no. 1117.

34 See II.1.a above.

35 On *mûsād̲,* see II.1.b above.

36 See III.2 below.

When the heavens are not mentioned, *yāsaḏ* refers to the entire process of creation. In Ps. 24:2, it alternates with *kônēn*. In Ps. 89:12(11), it refers not only to the circle of the earth (*tēḇēl*) but also to all that is in it (*mᵉlō'āh*); it stands in parallel with *bārā'* in v. 13(12). In Job 38:4, it introduces the entire process of creation, the individual aspects of which are detailed in the following verses. According to Am. 9:6, Yahweh has built (*bānâ*) his upper chambers in the heavens and founded (*yāsaḏ*) his vault upon the earth—i.e., he has built it as a whole upon the earth as its foundation.

Even in the few passages where *yāsaḏ* refers not to the creation of the earth by Yahweh but to some other activity, it denotes the activity as a whole. According to 2 Ch. 31:7, they began in the third month to lay up (*yāsaḏ*)[37] many heaps of provisions (*ᶜᵃrēmôṯ*: 6b) and finished the work in the seventh month. The number of heaps precludes taking *yāsaḏ* as being limited to "setting out the bottom layer" (of a heap).[38] Furthermore, *killû*, "they finished," does not contrast with *yāsaḏ* but with *hēḥēllû*, "they began." Here, therefore, *yāsaḏ* refers to the entire act of piling up the heaps, from the first to the last. In 2 Ch. 24:27, *yāsaḏ* refers to construction work on the existing temple, and therefore cannot be limited to the laying of foundations.

This evidence must be taken into account when we determine the precise sense of *ysd* qal in figurative usage. Ps. 104:8 means not just that Yahweh "appointed" (as most translations say) the mountains and valleys a place, but rather that he prepared (*yāsaḏ*) this place. According to Ps. 119:152, Yahweh not only gave the law (*ᶜēḏûṯ*) permanence, but created and established it (*yāsaḏ*). According to Hab. 1:12, he did not merely "assign" an existing enemy for punishment but created (*yāsaḏ*) it for this very purpose. Isa. 23:13 is discussed elsewhere.[39]

In Isa. 54:11, *wîsôḏōṯayik*, "and your foundations," "and your newly built buildings," should probably be read (with 1QIs*ᵃ* and the LXX and in chiastic parallelism with *'ᵃḇānayik*, "your stones") for *wîsaḏtîk*, "and I will found you." Yahweh is promising to encrust the buildings of rebuilt Zion with sapphires (cf. Tob. 13:16; Rev. 21:18-20). The noun *yᵉsôḏôṯ* has already been discussed.[40]

The niphal of *ysd*, which appears twice, has the same comprehensive meaning. The "founding of Egypt" (Ex. 9:18) refers to the entire process of establishing the Egyptian kingdom. In Isa. 44:28, the niphal of *ysd* stands in parallel with *bānâ* and means the entire rebuilding of the temple.

Although *ysd* qal and niphal—unlike the piel, pual, and hophal—refers to the entire process of construction, it differs clearly from general, unspecific verbs of "making" such as *ᶜāśâ*. Two semantic elements present in the basic meaning of the root *ysd*, "foundation (laying)," modify and characterize the construction referred to by *ysd* qal and niphal. The first is that of building "from the ground up," which implies something new, even something unique and primordial. This element is obviously determinative

---

37 *GK*, §§ 69n, 71.
38 W. Rudolph, *Chronikbücher. HAT*, XXI (1955), 304.
39 See II.1.a above.
40 See II.1.a above.

when the qal of *ysd* is used to describe creation.[41] But it cannot be overlooked in the other passages as well (with the possible exception of 2 Ch. 24:27).

Second, there are overtones of solidity and permanence in many passages where the qal or niphal of *ysd* appears; this is almost always true in connection with the creation of the earth (cf. Ps. 24:2 and [figuratively] 119:152). Often, however, this element is not dominant. In parallel with the "creation" (→ ברא *bārā'*), "spreading" (*nāṭâ*), or "making" (*'āśâ*) of the heavens, the OT can speak of the "founding" (*ysd* qal) of the earth, as well as its being "spread out" (→ רקע *rq'*: Ps. 136:6; Isa. 42:5; 44:24), "made" (*'āśâ*), "established" (→ כון *kwn*), or "formed" (→ יצר *yṣr*: Isa. 45:18). Other verbs are substituted for the qal of *ysd* without changing the meaning or function of the expression as a whole.

b. Josh. 6:26 pronounces a curse upon anyone who rebuilds the destroyed city of Jericho: he will lay its foundation (*ysd* piel) at the cost of his first-born and set up its gates at the cost of his youngest son (cf. 1 K. 16:34, quoting Josh. 6:26). According to 1 K. 5:31(17), great and costly stones are quarried so that the foundations of the First Temple can be laid (*ysd* piel) with dressed stones. Here the laying of a foundation is distinguished from the subsequent construction (*bānâ*: 1 K. 5:32[18]). In 1 K. 6:37, the pual of *ysd* refers to the laying of the foundation for the temple, in contrast to its completion (→ כלה *kālâ*) in v. 38; a similar usage appears in 1 K. 7:10. According to Zec. 4:9, the hands of Zerubbabel have laid the foundations (*ysd* piel) of the Second Temple and will also complete (*bṣ'*) it.

The laying of the foundation for the Second Temple to mark the beginning of construction is described in Ezr. 3:10 with the piel of *ysd*, in Ezr. 3:6; Hag. 2:18; Zec. 8:9 with the pual. In Ezr. 3:11, the hophal has the same meaning, and possibly also in 2 Ch. 3:3 (text?).

In all these passages, then, the piel, pual, and hophal of *ysd* have the precise technical meaning of "laying the foundations" on which the building can then be built and completed.[42] This usage is clearly distinct from that of the qal and niphal, which refer to the construction of the entire building.[43] In these passages, the element of permanence also retreats into the background. The laying of the foundation is mentioned solely to mark the beginning of construction, in contrast to the completion of the building.

The situation is different in Isa. 14:32; 28:16; and probably also Ps. 8:3(2), where Yahweh is the subject of the piel or hophal of *ysd*. Here the emphasis is primarily on the trustworthiness and permanence of the building, because Yahweh has laid its foundation.[44]

The precise meaning of *ysd* piel, "lay foundations," argues against the common conjectural emendation of *yissaḏ* in Isa. 28:16 to *yōsēḏ* (qal ptcp.). The participle expected after *hinn*[e]*nî*[45] has to be the piel ptcp. *m*[e]*yassēḏ* (as in 1QIs[a], but not 1QIs[b]).

---

41 Cf. also CD 2:7.
42 Cf. Jenni, 212.
43 Contra Schmidt, 736.
44 See III.3 below.
45 Cf. *GK*, §§ 116p,q, 155-56.

After *ny,* which can easily be confused in Phoenician script with *m,*[46] the *m* of the piel participle was omitted by haplography.

The notion of "making secure" also explains the metaphorical usage of the piel to mean "command" in Est. 1:8: by his orders, the king has laid an unshakable foundation, which must govern the actions of his officials. Also similar is 1 Ch. 9:22: the appointment of the gatekeepers of the temple by David and Solomon is such that this institution will last like an unshakable foundation through ages to come. Ezr. 7:9 is discussed in II.1.a above.

The metaphor in Cant. 5:15—legs "founded" (pual ptcp. of *ysd*) upon "bases of fine gold" (*ʾaḏnê-pāz*)—probably serves simply to express the distinction below/above, together with the notion of security (cf. Sir. 26:18).

III. Theological Usage.

1. *Yahweh, Layer of the Earth's Foundations.* Ps. 24:2 states that it is Yahweh who "founded" (*ysd* qal) the earth upon the seas. The compound noun clause, as is generally true of this type of construction,[47] does not describe the (past) act of creation, but depicts Yahweh as founder of the earth, who as such possesses fundamentally and for all time proprietary rights over the earth and its inhabitants (Ps. 24:1). The mention of Yahweh's "foundation" (*ysd* qal) of the earth in Ps. 89:12(11) has the same import. Isa. 48:13 also uses a compound noun clause to speak of Yahweh's "founding" (*ysd* qal) the earth. Here, too, then, the reference is not to creation as an event of the past; v. 13, continuing v. 12b, declares what Yahweh (or his hand) is: the one who founds the earth and spreads out the heavens.

Ps. 102:26(25) likewise does not use the qal of *ysd* to describe a former act in which Yahweh laid the foundations of the earth; rather, it describes the earth as having been "previously" (*lᵉp̄ānîm*) "founded" by him and the heavens as the work of his hands in order to make it clear that Yahweh—unlike what he has made—remains forever himself. The qal of *ysd* speaks here directly about the earth, but indirectly about Yahweh himself. In Ps. 78:69, the permanence of the sanctuary Yahweh has built upon Zion is illustrated by the heights of the heavens and by the earth, "which he has founded for ever" (*ysd* qal). Here, too, *yāsaḏ* does not describe the act through which the earth was founded, but as in Ps. 102:26(25) characterizes the earth as something founded by Yahweh and therefore permanent.

The doxology in Am. 9:6 confesses Yahweh as "building his upper chambers in the heavens and founding (*ysd* qal) his vault upon the earth." The "founding" ascribed here to Yahweh refers directly to his heavenly sanctuary, but this is understood primarily as a part of the cosmos (cf. the similar statements about creation in the doxologies of Am. 4:13; 5:8), so that Am. 9:6 also speaks of Yahweh as "founder" of (part of) creation. Ps. 8:3(2) is discussed in III.3 below.

---

46 Cf. *ANEP,* no. 286, esp. ll. 7, 13, 17.

47 See, e.g., B. D. Michel, *Tempora und Satzstellung in den Psalmen. Abhandlungen zur evangelischen Theologie,* 1 (Bonn, 1960), 177-182; also *GK,* §§ 142a-e, etc.

The ptcp. *yōsēḏ* appears in Isa. 51:13; Zec. 12:1; Ps. 104:5. Isa. 51:16 uses the gerundive infinitive with *l*ᵉ- in apposition with Yahweh. Here *ysd* does not denote the act of creation but describes Yahweh in his nature as founder of the earth and creator of the cosmos.

Thus none of the creation passages involving *ysd* speaks of a prior act of creation; all describe Yahweh, present either speaking or addressed, as the one who founded the earth and stretched out the heavens, i.e., created the cosmos and its order.

In all these passages it is clear that Yahweh's "attribute" of being founder of the earth and creator of the universe explains why he acts in the history of Israel, why he acts on behalf of Zion, the house of David, the psalmist—choosing, building, delivering, saving. This association with acting in history does not detract in the least from the description of Yahweh expressed by *yāsaḏ* and other creation terminology. The earth and heavens as the product of divine "foundation" and creation are not replaced by Israel as the beneficiary of Yahweh's saving acts in history; neither does Yahweh the creator of the world vanish into the God who deals with Israel in history. Quite the contrary: the nature of God as creator of the universe manifests itself anew in his historical treatment of Israel. When Yahweh acts in the history of Israel, he does so fundamentally in his nature as creator of the universe.

Furthermore, in these passages (with the possible exception of Ps. 104:5) Yahweh is not described as the "founder" of the earth and creator of the universe with the naive simplicity of spontaneous praise, but in the sense of a confession demanded (when Yahweh presents himself as Creator) or offered (when one speaks of Yahweh as Creator), to which the person addressed by Yahweh must assent or to which the worshipper feels called upon to assent. In this assent one decides to acknowledge Yahweh as "founder" of the earth and creator of the universe, while acknowledging also that, as Creator, he is also the God who deals with people in history.

2. *Inaccessibility to Human Knowledge.* Like the "planting" (*ṭbʿ*) of the mountains and the "establishing" (*kwn*) of the heavens, according to Prov. 8:29 the "marking out" (*ḥwq*; text?) of the "foundations of the earth" (*môsᵉḏê ʾāreṣ*) is among the works of God done "from the beginning" (*mēʾāz*; *mēʿôlām*; *mērōʾš*; *bᵉṭerem*). Although the earth's foundations support the human world, the laying of these foundations is set in that primordial "age" accessible only to Yahweh and his wisdom, but beyond the ken of human beings.

In Prov. 3:19, the discourse praising wisdom and calling on those listening to seek it out is interrupted by the emphatic statement that it is Yahweh who is primarily concerned with wisdom: it is by wisdom that he "founded" (*ysd* qal) the earth and established the heavens. In this context, emphasis on the association of wisdom with Yahweh and on its fundamental role in the creation of the universe (compound nominal clause!) can only serve to restrict the accessibility of wisdom to human beings. Only in part and only indirectly can one gain the wisdom that belongs completely and directly to Yahweh alone, which is found in his work of creation.

According to Job 38:4, the laying of the earth's foundations (*ysd* qal) together with the sinking of its bases (*ṭbʿ*), etc., took place in a primordial age inaccessible to human thought. Jer. 31:37 says it is simply impossible for mortals to measure the heavens and explore the "foundations of the earth" (*môsᵉḏê-'ereṣ*). On the other hand, Yahweh's theophany lays bare (→ גלה *gālâ* [*gālāh*]) these foundations and lets the channels of the sea be seen (→ ראה *r'h*: 2 S. 22:16 par. Ps. 18:16[15]). When the fire of God's wrath burns "to the depths of Sheol" (*ʿaḏ-šᵉ'ōl taḥtîṯ*) and sets on fire the "foundations of the mountains" (*môsᵉḏê hārîm*), it reaches to the farthest and deepest limit of the cosmos, inaccessible to mortals, so that there can be no refuge (Dt. 32:22).

In these passages the founding of the earth or the laying of its foundations denotes a "time" and "place" reserved to Yahweh alone as the "beginning" and "base" of the human world. It is simply inaccessible to mortals and thus illustrates the limits imposed upon them.

3. *Foundations Laid by Yahweh.* According to Isa. 14:32b, it is Yahweh who laid the foundations of Zion. This fundamental act on Yahweh's part makes it possible for the "afflicted of his people," i.e., the afflicted who are his people, not only to have a sense of security but also to find in Zion a secure and indestructible refuge (→ חסה *ḥāsâ*: v. 32bβ).

The precise meaning of Isa. 28:16 has been extensively debated.[48] The concluding clause, which probably states both the result and the purpose of what precedes, speaks of "one who makes himself secure," "one who believes" (*hamma'ᵃmîn*). The key word of the first clause is *ysd,* which appears in 3 variants. Yahweh presents himself as laying a foundation stone in Zion (*mᵉyassēḏ* [emended][49]). It is a precious stone—probably not a gemstone, but rather a stone exceptionally well suited for the foundation of a building, i.e., one especially solid and well shaped (cf. "precious stone" in this sense also in 1 K. 5:31[17]; 7:9-11). Yahweh will lay this foundation stone, which is of particular excellence, as a "sure foundation."[50] Besides the special quality of the stone, there is thus also the extraordinary care with which Yahweh himself will lay the foundation. The whole statement built around the root *ysd* thus emphasizes not the hiddenness and invisibility of the foundation stone[51] but the solidity and security given Zion by Yahweh's work.

Thus the element of security expressed in the second clause of Isa. 28:16 by the root *'mn* parallels the same element expressed in the first clause by the root *ysd.* The security of faith is a response to the security of Yahweh's saving work, visible and concentrated in Zion, which precedes faith and makes it objectively possible.

Ps. 8:3(2) is also debated. If the first three words are appended to the preceding verse and *ʿōz* can be taken like *māʿôz* to mean "fortress,"[52] the passage states that Yahweh has

---

48 → בחן *bḥn,* III; → אבן *'eḇen* (*'ebhen*); → אמן *'āman,* V.5.

49 See II.2.b above.

50 See II.1.b above.

51 Cf. e.g., Duhm, 175.

52 A. Deissler, "Zur Datierung und Situierung der 'kosmischen Hymnen' Pss 8; 19; 29," *Lux Tua Veritas. Festschrift H. Junker* (Trier, 1961), 47-58; J. A. Soggin, "Textkritische Untersuchung von Ps. VIII vv.2-3 und 6," *VT,* 21 (1971), 568-570; etc.

laid the foundations (*ysd* piel) of the heavens, providing for his worldwide dominion a security against which enemies cannot prevail.[53]

4. *Foundation of the Second Temple.* According to Haggai, hardship and want will be replaced by the blessing of Yahweh if Israel sets about building the house of Yahweh (Hag. 1:8; 2:15-19). Hag. 2:18 dates the change of fortune from the day the foundation was laid (*ysd* pual) for the Second Temple. This dating, however, is most likely a later gloss, added after the laying of the foundation and probably also after the completion of the temple. Therefore the salvation proclaimed by Haggai cannot be considered final and complete. The gloss relativizes the salvation announced while lending precision to its time.

In Zec. 8:9, the prophet proclaims a new age of salvation on the day the foundation of the Second Temple is laid (*ysd* pual). According to vv. 9-13, the promised salvation means that the land will yield a rich harvest and Israel, now despised by the nations, will be honored once more. According to Zec. 4:6b-10a, the day of foundation-laying (*ysd* piel, v. 9) for the Second Temple appears insignificant, but the completion of the temple will assuredly come to pass and be a day of rejoicing (v. 10a).

According to Ezr. 3:8-13, there was great rejoicing (v. 10) when the foundation for the Second Temple was laid (*ysd* piel, v. 10; hophal, v. 11). But this rejoicing and the change for the better it signals are reduced by the fact that sacrifice is offered even before the foundation is laid (*ysd* pual) (v. 6) and above all by the continued weeping of the previous lamentation even during the rejoicing (vv. 12f.).

In all these passages, then, the beginning of work on the Second Temple marked by the piel, pual, and hophal of *ysd* inaugurates a new age of salvation and prosperity, but it is clearly represented as provisional and imperfect.

5. *Base of the Altar.* The blood placed on the horns of the altar when it is consecrated and in the course of a sin offering represents an essential element of the propitiatory rite, but the pouring out (→ שׁפך *šāpak̲*, not *zāraq* or the like!) of the remaining blood at the base (*y*ᵉ*sôd̲*) of the altar probably serves primarily to dispose of the additional blood properly[54] and return it to God, its proper owner (cf. Dt. 12:16,23-27; 15:23; Lev. 17:10-14).

Unlike the horns[55] of the altar, therefore, the *y*ᵉ*sôd̲* is (at least originally) not a ritually significant part of the altar. In Sir. 50:15, however, "blood of the grape" is poured out at the base of the altar "for a sweet-smelling savor"; this is therefore a sacrificial ritual and the *y*ᵉ*sôd̲* of the altar is here ritually significant.

The same may be true in Lev. 5:9, where the remainder of the blood is not poured out at the *y*ᵉ*sôd̲* but "drained out" upon it (*mṣh* niphal; cf. Lev. 1:15, where the blood is drained on the "side" of the altar).

---

53 Cf. → ינק *yāanaq.*

54 R. Rendtorff, *Studien zur Geschichte des Opfers im alten Israel. WMANT,* 24 (1967), 145-47, 218-220.

55 → קרן *qeren.*

Rev. 6:9f. (cf. 16:6f.) says that the souls of those slain "for the word of God and for the witness they have borne" are "under the altar" (*hypokátō toú thysiastēríou*) and cry out to God. This notion appears to assume that the base of the altar was included in the sacrificial ritual as suggested by Sir. 50:15 (and Lev. 5:9?) and to be connected with the idea that blood unjustly shed "cries out"[56] to God (cf. Gen. 4:10, etc.).

Mosis

56 → זעק *zāʿaq*.

יָסַף *yāsap̱*

Contents: I. Etymology, Occurrences. II. Independent Verb: 1. "Add"; 2. Canon Formula; 3. "Increase"; 4. Oaths; 5. Used Absolutely. III. Auxiliary Verb: 1. With Infinitive Construct; 2. Parataxis. IV. *ysp/ʾsp/sph/swp.* V. Qumran. VI. LXX.

I. Etymology, Occurrences. The verbal root *ysp* is found in Phoenician ("add"),[1] Moabite ("add"),[2] and various Aramaic dialects.[3] It also appears in Old South Arabic as *wśf,* ("add," "increase")[4] and in Soqotri as *scf,* "augment."[5] Akk. *(w)aṣābu,* "add," "increase,"[6] and *ṣibtu,* "interest," are semantically comparable, although the sibilant raises problems.

There are 214 occurrences of the root in the OT: 33 in the qal, 6 in the niphal, and 176 in the hiphil.

II. Independent Verb.

1. *"Add."* The independent verb (qal and hiphil) is usually found with an object plus *ʿal,* with the meaning "add something to something."

When restitution is made for holding back property, a fifth of its value is to be "added" (*wᵉḥᵃmîšiṯô yôsēp̱ ʿal*: Lev. 5:16,24[Eng. 6:5]; Nu. 5:7). Likewise when something sacred to Yahweh is redeemed, e.g., tithes, a fifth of the value is "added" (qal: Lev. 22:14; 27:13,15,19,27; hiphil: Lev. 27:31). To the three cities of refuge three others (*ʿôḏ*) are to be "added" (Dt. 19:9; cf. Nu. 36:3f. [niphal]). Yahweh "adds" years to a human life (2 K.

1 *KAI,* 10, 11; 14, 19.

2 *KAI,* 181, 21, 29.

3 Dnl. 4:33(Eng. v. 36); *DISO,* 109, always in the haphel or aphel, "add."

4 ContiRossini, 141; E. Ullendorff, "The Contribution of South Semitics to Hebrew Lexicography," *VT,* 6 (1956), 196 = *Is Biblical Hebrew a Language?* (Wiesbaden, 1977), 195.

5 Leslau, *Contributions,* 24.

6 *CAD,* I/2 (1968), 352f.

20:6; Ps. 61:7[6]; Isa. 38:5 [hiphil]), but it is also possible to say that someone "adds year to year" in the sense of letting the years run their course (Isa. 29:1 [qal]). Yahweh says through Jeremiah that it does not matter how many sacrifices are offered ("add your burnt offerings to your sacrifices": Jer. 7:21 [qal]) because he requires obedience (vv. 22-28; cf. 6:20).

The expression *ysp ʿal* sometimes means "do something even worse." Samuel is to pray for the people because they have added to all their sins the evil of asking for a king (1 S. 12:19 [qal]). Elihu accuses Job of having added rebellion (*pešaʿ*) to his sins (*ḥaṭṭāʾṯ*) (Job 34:37 [hiphil]). Baruch says that Jeremiah has added sorrow to his pain (Jer. 45:3 [qal]). In the concluding section of the Holiness Code, Lev. 26, vv. 14-17 state the punishment for transgressing the law; whoever refuses to obey despite the punishment will be punished an additional sevenfold (*weyāsaptî ʿalêḵem makkâ šeḇaʿ*: v. 21; cf. v. 18: *ysp* + inf.; vv. 24 and 28: *šeḇaʿ* without *ysp*). The same construction is used in the positive sense of "surpass" in Eccl. 1:16: *higdaltî wehôsaptî ḥoḵmâ ʿal kol-ʾašer-hāhâ lepānay,* "I have acquired great wisdom, surpassing all who were before me." Compare Eccl. 2:9: *wegāḏaltî wehôsaptî mikkōl . . . ,* i.e., "(although) I became greater and surpassed (in riches) all who were before me, I retained my wisdom" (summarizing 2:4-8[7]). Solomon's wisdom and wealth surpassed the rumors that the queen of Sheba had heard (*hôsaptā ḥoḵmâ wāṭôḇ ʾel haššemûʿâ* [1 K. 10:7]; the construction with *ʾel* is rare; the par. 2 Ch. 9:6 has *yāsaptā ʿal*).

The hiphil of *ysp* with *ʿal* can be expanded with *ke,* "add just as much again." In Dt. 1:11, for example, Moses wishes that Yahweh will make the Israelites a thousand times as many as they are (*yōsēp ʿalêḵem kāḵem ʾelep peʿāmîm*). In 2 S. 24:3, Joab wishes similarly for a hundredfold increase of the people in the light of the census (with *ʾel*; cf. 1 Ch. 21:3 with *ʿal*).

2. *Canon Formula.* The hiphil of *ysp* with *ʿal* is used as the opposite of *gāraʿ min* (→ גרע *gāraʿ*) in Dt. 4:2; 13:1(12:32): *lōʾ ṯōsipû ʿal-haddāḇār . . . welōʾ ṯigreʿû mimmennû,* "You shall not add to the word which I command you, nor take from it" (the so-called canon formula). The formula has an Egyptian parallel: the conclusion of the Instruction of Ptahhotep reads: "Take away (*ỉty*) no word (*md.t*), add (*ỉny*) no word, replace none (*k.t*) with another (*k.t*)." It is dubious, however, whether the formula refers to the actual number of words. It can also be translated: "Do not say one time this and one time that, and do not confuse one matter with another." In this case the formula guards against a change in wording.[8] The 2 passages in Deuteronomy refer to the commandments given by God. The prohibitions are actualized with a warning against idolatry. Obedience to the commandments given by Yahweh—and only to them—is required of those who would live in and possess the promised land. The warning against apostasy indicates that in its present literary context the formula defends the substance of Yahwism and is not intended to define a canon.

Prov. 30:6 says that it would be deceitful to add anything to the words of God, using

---

7 W. Zimmerli, *Prediger. ATD,* XVI/1 (1962), 154.

8 S. Morenz, *Egyptian Religion* (Eng. trans., Ithaca, N.Y., 1973), 224.

only the first part of the formula. The prohibition against taking anything away appears by itself in Jer. 26:2, where Yahweh enjoins Jeremiah to speak *kol-hadd^e^ḇārîm.* From the reaction of those listening, we may conclude that this refers to the content of the words, not their extent. On the other hand, Jer. 36:32 (niphal) says that the scroll written by Baruch to replace the one burned by Jehoiakim received additions. We are not told whether these were made by Jeremiah himself, were written at his dictation, or represented later expansion.

In Eccl. 3:14, a similar formula appears in a totally different context. The work of God cannot be affected by anyone. Everything goes its familiar course, and no one can either add to it or take away from it.[9] Referring to the Decalog, Moses says in Dt. 5:22: "These are the words that Yahweh spoke, *w^e^lōʾ yāsāp̱ wayyiḵt^e^ḇēm*" ("he added no more, and he wrote them . . ."), i.e., he wrote them after he stopped speaking. The idiom is probably short for *ysp* + *ʿal haddāḇār* or *ysp l^e^ḏabbēr.*[10]

3. *"Increase."* Addition that results in an increase in size or number can be expressed by means of the hiphil of *ysp* + object or with *ʿal* and no object. Ezra, for example, says that the men who married foreign women have "increased the guilt of Israel" (*l^e^hôsîp̱ ʿal-ʾašmaṯ yiśrāʾēl*: Ezr. 10:10; cf. Prov. 23:28). When the northern Israelites took prisoners from Judah during the Syro-Ephraimite war, certain Ephraimite chiefs said it would be bad enough to attack Judah and Jerusalem (*rabbâ ʾašmâ lānû*), but to take kinsfolk as prisoners of war would add to the guilt (*l^e^hōsîp ʿal-ḥaṭṭōʾṯênû weʿal-ʾašmāṯênû*: 2 Ch. 28:13). Isaiah says that the people have forsaken (*ʿāzaḇ*) their God and increased their rebellion (*tôsîpû sārâ*: Isa. 1:5). According to Ezk. 23:14, the harlotry of Oholibah (i.e., Jerusalem) exceeded that of her sister (Samaria) (*wattôsep̱ ʾel-taznûṯêhā*). Rehoboam threatens to lay upon the people an even heavier yoke than that laid by Solomon (*ʾôsîp̱ ʿal-ʿull^e^ḵem*: 1 K. 12:11,14 par. 2 Ch. 10:11,14). Nehemiah laments that by breaking the Sabbath the people have increased the wrath of Yahweh against Israel (hiphil ptcp.: Neh. 13:18; cf. Nu. 32:14: *lāsep̱eṯ* [conj.]).

In Wisdom Literature, the hiphil of *ysp* often appears in connection with "wisdom," "knowledge," or the like. The person who is already wise may increase in wisdom by listening to the proverbs (*leqaḥ*: Prov. 1:5). "Give instruction to a wise man, and he will be still wiser (*w^e^yeḥkam-ʿôḏ*); teach a righteous man and he will increase in learning (*w^e^yôsep leqaḥ*)" (Prov. 9:9). In the group of 4 sayings that discuss the speech of the wise (Prov. 16:21-24), *yōsîp̱ leqaḥ* (vv. 21, 23; cf. Sir. 6:5) appears instead to mean "increase persuasiveness."[11] One who is wise increases the persuasiveness of his speech by speaking pleasantly. The emendation of *weʿal* to *ûḇaʿal,* "an expert speaker promotes learning," in Prov. 16:23[12] is unnecessary.

---

9 For a discussion of this passage and the canon formula, see W. Herrmann, "Zu Kohelet 3,14," *Festschrift A. Alt. WZLeipzig,* 3 (1953/54), 23-95.

10 G. Vermès, "The Decalogue and the Minim," *In Memoriam Paul Kahle. BZAW,* 103 (1968), 236.

11 B. Gemser, *Sprüche Salomos. HAT,* XVI (^{2}1963), 70f.; Ringgren, *Sprüch. ATD,* XVI/1, 67, 70.

12 R. B. Y. Scott, *Proverbs-Ecclesiastes. AB,* XVIII (1965), 105; W. McKane, *Proverbs. OTL* (1970), 490.

The commandments of wisdom lengthen life and give increase of *šālôm* to those who do not forget them (Prov. 3:2; cf. 9:11 [hiphil, conj. niphal][13]). But increased knowledge brings increased sorrow (Eccl. 1:18; Dahood[14] takes *yôsîp̱* as the hiphil inf. const. and suggests a Phoenician background for the proverb "to increase knowledge is to increase sorrow"). The fear of God prolongs life (*tôsîp̱ yāmîm),* while wickedness shortens it (Prov. 10:27). The upright are appalled at a fate like that of Job, but the righteous holds to his way and "increases in strength" (Job 17:9).

Sometimes *ysp* is linked with *b^erāḵâ* and great success. We see this most clearly in Ps. 115:14, where *yôsēp̱ YHWH ʿal* is interpolated between the *brk*-clauses (vv. 12f., 15). Unlike idols (vv. 4-8), the God of Israel, the Creator (vv. 15f.), can increase the family. In Gen. 30, the name "Joseph" is given two explanations. According to E (v. 23), the name derives from *ʾsp*: God has taken away the reproach of Rachel, since she has finally borne a son. According to J (v. 24), the name is connected with the hiphil of *ysp* and looks forward to the birth of another son, Benjamin.

Trees will increase their yield (Lev. 19:25) if certain rules are observed when they are planted and when the harvest is gathered. No one can increase his own wealth; it depends completely on the blessing of Yahweh (Prov. 10:22). When Job humbled himself before Yahweh and was blessed by him, among the results was a doubling of his possessions (Job 42:10). In his castigation of David, Nathan says that Yahweh, who has given David so much, could have added "this or that" (*kāhēnnāh w^eḵāhēnnāh*: 2 S. 12:8). In the first of 3 sayings concerning generosity (Prov. 11:24-26), we are told that the spendthrift grows all the richer (*ysp* niphal + *ʿôḏ*), but one who withholds only becomes the poorer; it is clear from vv. 25f. that the spendthift is one who gives freely and is blessed in return (cf. Prov. 19:4). An oracle of favor addressed to Hezekiah (Isa. 37:31 par. 2 K. 19:30 [qal]) states that the surviving remnant of Judah will "add roots" below and bear fruit above, i.e., will flourish once more. The lament in Isa. 26 contrasts Yahweh's ability to increase the land and the nation with the inability of the people themselves to do so (vv. 16-18). Isa. 29:17-24, an oracle of salvation, says that after the destruction of the enemy the meek will increase their joy in Yahweh (v. 19). Pharaoh was afraid that if the Israelites multiplied (*rbh*: Ex. 1:10,12,20) they could "join" (*ysp* niphal: v. 10) the enemies of Egypt in case of war. The psalmist in his lament says confidently that, just as he has always praised God (Ps. 71:5f.), he will have further occasion to do so (v. 14). Ezk. 5:16 states that Yahweh for punishment will bring more and more famine upon the people (absent from the LXX). According to the version of the Chronicler, David provided a great portion of the material for building the temple, and he exhorts his son to add to it (1 Ch. 22:14). Isa. 15:9a,b is a crux. Kaiser[15] is certainly right in saying "even more" is a highly abstract way of referring to additional disasters. There is the further problem that the form *nôsāp̱ôṯ* (niphal ptcp., fem. pl.) stands unique; substantive forms of *ysp* are not found elsewhere.

---

13 Ringgren, 41; Scott, 74; McKane, 224.

14 M. Dahood, "Qoheleth and Northwest Semitic Philology," *Bibl,* 43 (1962), 349-365, esp. 350f.

15 O. Kaiser, *Isaiah 13–39. OTL* (Eng. trans. 1974), 69f.

4. *Oaths.* The oath formula *kōh ya'aśeh 'elōhîm/YHWH le . . . wekōh yôsîp̄,* "may God do thus and so to," "may God punish,"[16] is most often spoken of oneself: *lî* or *le* + a personal name: Saul (1 S. 14:44), Jonathan (1 S. 20:13), Abner (2 S. 3:9), David (2 S. 3:35; 19:14[13]), Solomon (1 K. 2:23), Jezebel (1 K. 19:2), Ben-hadad (1 K. 20:10), the king of Israel (2 K. 6:31), Ruth (Ruth 1:17). It may be noted that in 1 K. 19:2; 20:10 the verbs are in the plural because *'elōhîm* refers to foreign gods, not Yahweh. In 2 instances (1 S. 3:17; 25:22), the oath refers to someone other than the speaker. In 3:17, Eli adjures Samuel not to conceal a word of what Yahweh has said to him during the night. In 25:22, David pronounces the oath against his enemies, promising to slay every male member of the house of Nabal (*'ōyeḇê,* "enemies of," does not appear in the LXX[17]).

Perhaps this formula lies behind the questions in Ps. 120:3: "What will he do to you and what more, you deceitful tongue?"

5. *Used Absolutely.* The hiphil of *ysp* is occasionally used absolutely with a negative, sometimes to emphasize the niphal of *hāyâ* (*kāmōhû lō' nihyāṯâ wekāmōhû lō' ṯôsîp̄,* "such as there has never been, nor ever shall be again": Ex. 11:6; cf. Joel 2:2), sometimes to indicate that the action of the immediately preceding verb has ceased (*'ayin šezāp̄attû welō' ṯôsîp̄,* "the eye which saw him will see him no more": Job 20:9). We find this most clearly in Dt. 25:3: "forty stripes may be given him, but not more (*lō' yôsîp̄*); lest, if one should go on to beat him with more stripes, your brother be degraded in your sight." Cf. also Job 34:32: "If I have done iniquity, I will do it no more" (cf. Nu. 11:25). The hiphil of *ysp* also appears in the context "thus far and no farther": *'aḏ-pōh ṯāḇô' welō' ṯôsîp̄,* "thus far the sea shall come, but no farther" (Job 38:11). At the end of the book of Job, Job humbles himself and says that he has answered God twice, but will not do so a third time (Job 40:5). Prov. 19:19 may contain an instance of the absolute hiphil used positively, but the text is difficult and certainty is impossible.

III. Auxiliary Verb.

1. *With Infinitive Construct.* The verb *ysp* is often used as an auxiliary with the infinitive construct in the sense "continue to do something," "do something again" (once in the qal, 21 times in the hiphil; with *le* + the qal inf. 12 times, with the hiphil 64 times). The idiom is often underlined by the addition of *'ôḏ.* Of the 98 occurrences, 53 are negated and come at the end of a passage. The main verb in these cases rarely appears earlier in the passage. For example, Gen. 38:26 reads *welō'-yāsap̄ 'ôḏ leḏa'tâ,* but v. 18 reads *wayyāḇô' 'ēleyhā.* The exceptions are: Gen. 8:12; Jgs. 13:21; 1 S. 27:4 (qal); Dt. 19:20; Josh. 23:13; Jgs. 10:13; Isa. 51:22; Am. 7:13 (hiphil). The situation is generally reversed in the case of positive *ysp* with the infinitive: in 25 cases the main verb appears earlier, as in Nu. 22:23, which reads *wayyak bil'ām eṯ-hā'āṯôn,* and v. 25, which reads *wayyôsep̄ lehakkōṯah.* In 20 cases the verb is different.

---

16 Cf. J. Pedersen, *Der Eid ben den Semiten* (Strasbourg, 1914), 117f.; South Arabic parallels are cited by Ullendorff, *VT,* 6 (1956), 196.

17 H. J. Stoebe, *Das erste Buch Samuelis. KAT,* VIII/1 (1973), 448.

2. *Parataxis.* The hiphil sometimes appears in parataxis with the main verb, e.g., Gen. 25:1: *wayyōsep̱ ʾaḇrāhām wayyiqqaḥ ʾiššâ,* "Abraham took another wife"; cf. also Gen. 38:5; 1 S. 19:21; 2 S. 18:22; 1 Ch. 14:13; Est. 8:3; Job 36:1; Dnl. 10:18. The two verbs can also be juxtaposed asyndetically, as in Hos. 1:6: *lōʾ ʾôsîp̱ ʿôḏ ʾaraḥēm,* "I will no more have pity." Cf. also Jgs. 11:14; Prov. 23:35; Isa. 52:1. The main verb and the auxiliary can have different subjects: *lōʾ ṯôsîpî yiqreʾû-lāḵ,* "you shall not continue that they call you," i.e., "you shall not continue to be called" (Isa. 47:1,5).

IV. ysp/ʾsp/sph/swp. The infinitive construct of *ysp* should be *sepeṯ.*[18] In some cases the Masoretes have apparently vocalized *spt* as *sepôṯ,* from *sāp̄â,* "throw away" (Nu. 32:14; Isa. 30:1), which would give a very strange meaning. In Isa. 30:1, the context demands something like "add sin to sin." In Nu. 32:14, "increase anger" is a natural expression after the mention of anger in vv. 10,13.

The weak impf. *yōʾsēp̱,* from *ʾāsap̱,* "collect," can be written without the *aleph,* in which case it can be confused with the hiphil imperfect of *ysp.* In Nu. 11:25, *welōʾ yāsāp̄û* has been read as both *ʾsp* and *swp* (cf. vv. 16,24,30, and BHS), but the Masoretic pointing is quite possible, i.e., *ysp* qal used absolutely, "they did not continue," namely to prophesy.[19] The episode of Eldad and Medad in Nu. 11:26-29 is an independent passage interrupting the continuity between vv. 25 and 30, which say that Moses and the seventy elders returned to the camp when the period of ecstasy was over.[20] The text of 2 S. 6:1 begins with *wayyōsep̱ ʿôḏ* + *ʾeṯ* + object + *be,* a construction not found elsewhere. The LXX reads *ʾsp,* which fits the context better.[21] On the other hand, we also find the hiphil imperfect of *ysp* written with an *aleph* (Ex. 5:7; 1 S. 18:29).

Some passages are very obscure. In 1 S. 15:6, *ʾōsip̱ḵā* was read by the LXX as the qal imperfect of *ʾsp* (*prosthṓ met' autoú*), while many modern commentators prefer to read *ʾespeḵā,* from *sph.* Lisowsky lists the same form *ʾōsip̱ḵā* (*ʾel-ʾaḇōṯeyḵā*) in 2 Ch. 34:28 under *ysp* (= LXX *prostíthēmi*) although it is followed by *ʾsp* (*weneʾesaptā ʾel-qiḇrōṯeyḵā* [= LXX *prostethḗsē*]) and the construction does not favor *ysp.*

V. Qumran. The Dead Sea scrolls exhibit certain peculiarities. The object is introduced by *ʾeṯ* (1QpHab 6:1: *hôn*; 11:15: *qālôn*?). The hiphil infinitive construct is contracted to *lôsîp̱* (1QpHab 8:12; 11:15). In the 3 occurrences of the niphal (1QS 6:14; 8:19; CD 13:11), *ysp* refers to one who joins the community. The only instance of *ysp* as an auxiliary (1QS 2:11) uses an asyndetic construction. In 1QH 1:35, *hôsîpû* appears as an antonym of *šbt* hiphil. The semantic distinction between *ysp* and *ʾsp* is obscured: *weyôsîpû* (1QpHab 6:1) is the pesher of *weyaspēhû* (5:14); cf. *weyaʾasp̄ēhû* (Hab. 1:15); compare also *qbṣ hôn* (1QpHab 8:11) with *ysp ʿawôn ʾašmâ* (8:12).

---

18 Cf. *BLe,* § 379q, and the Mesha inscription, *KAI,* 181, 21.
19 Cf. II.5.
20 In part contra M. Noth, *Numbers. OTL* (Eng. trans. 1968), 86-91.
21 Cf. *ysp* in 1 S. 5:22 and J. Blenkinsopp, "Kiriath-Jearim and the Ark," *JBL,* 88 (1969), 151.

VI. LXX. The LXX usually uses *prostithénai* to translate *ysp,* which it also uses to translate *'sp* (17 times) and *sph* (6 times). In Prov. 11:24, the niphal is rendered by *pleíona poieín* (active). The second hemistich uses *synágein (ḥśk?),* which represents *ysp* in 2 S. 3:34 and *'sp* in 2 S. 6:1,[22] while *s^e pû* in Isa. 29:1 and Jer. 7:21 was read as *sph.* Other translations of *ysp* include *prósthema* (Lev. 19:25), *dýnasthai* (Isa. 24:20), *analambánein* (Job 17:9), *hyperbaínein* (Job 38:11), *analískein* (Prov. 23:28), and *érchesthai* (Prov. 23:35). In Job 40:32(41:8), *mēkéti ginésthō* shows that the LXX took *'al-tôsap̱* (in pause) in an absolute sense: "it will not happen again"; the Vulg.'s translation *nec ultra addas loqui* assumes the addition of *l^e ḏabbēr.* Free translation or hebraizing paraphrase are found in Gen. 8:10 (*pálin exapostéllein*), Ex. 10:29 (*opthḗsomai*; cf. v. 28: *prostheínai ideín*), Prov. 1:5 (*sophṓteros ésthai*), Prov. 16:21 (*hoi dé glykeís en lógō pleíona akoúsontai*) and 16:23 (*phorései epignōmosýnēn* [hapax legomenon]), Isa. 29:19 (*agalliásthai*[?]), and Jer. 38(31):12 (*peinán éti*). The LXX leaves *ysp* untranslated in Gen. 37:5; Isa. 15:9; 37:31; Ezk. 5:16 (cf. 2 S. 19:14[13]: *prostithénai*).

André

22 Cf. IV above.

יָסַר *yāsar;* מוּסָר *mûsār*

Contents: I. 1. Etymology; 2. Occurrences; 3. LXX. II. *yāsar*: 1. Semantic Field; 2. Instruction; 3. Correction; 4. Punishment. IV. *mûsār*: 1. Semantic Field; 2. Body of Knowledge; 3. Content; 4. Discipline, Punishment. IV. Theological Usage.

I. 1. *Etymology.* Cognate forms of the root *wsr* are found in Akkadian, Ugaritic, and Arabic. Akk. *eseru* in 4 places has the meaning "to instruct."[1] Two Ugaritic occurrences

yāsar. G. Bertram, "παιδεύω," *TDNT,* V, 596-625; R. D. Branson, *A Study of the Hebrew Term* שנא (diss., Boston, 1976); G. R. Driver, "Studies in the Vocabulary of the OT. VIII," *JTS,* 36 (1935), 293-301; L. Dürr, *Das Erziehungswesen im AT und im antiken orient. MVÄG, 36/2* (1932); G. Gerleman, "Bemerkungen zum alttestamentlichen Sprachstil," *Studia Biblica et Semitica. Festschrift T. C. Vriezen* (Wageningen, 1966), 108-114, esp. 112; H.-J. Kraus, "Geschichte als Erziehung: Biblisch-theologische Perspektiven," *Probleme biblischer Theologie. Festschrift G. von Rad* (Munich, 1971), 258-274, esp. 267-272 = *Biblisch-theologische Aufsätze* (Neukirchen-Vluyn, 1972), 66-83; *idem,* "Paedagogia Dei als theologischer Geschichtsbegriff," *EvTh,* 8 (1948/49), 515-527; M. Sæbø, "יסר *jsr* züchtigen," *THAT,* I, 738-742; J. A. Sanders, *Suffering as Divine Discipline in the OT and Post-Biblical Judaism* (Rochester, 1955); D. Yellin, "חזק, אמץ, יסר," *Sinai,* 65 (1969), 139f.; R. B. Zuck, "Hebrew Words for 'Teach,'" *BS,* 121 (1964), 228-235.

1 *AHw,* I (1965), 249; Sæbø (728) associates *ysr* with *ašāru, AHw,* I, 79.

in ritual texts[2] have the meaning "instruct"; a third forms part of a personal name.[3] The association of *wsr* with the Arabic root *šwr*[4] is supported by the existence of OSA *yšrn,* "explain," which also derives from the root *šwr*.[5] The root appears 6 times in the Dead Sea scrolls, with the meaning "instruct."[6] This meaning is retained in later Hebrew.[7] The basic meaning of the root, "instruct," is therefore attested in all the comparative material.

2. *Occurrences.* The verb appears 43 times in the MT, and the noun 51 times. The hapax legomenon *yissôr* (Job 40:2), despite its formal parallelism with *gibbôr*,[8] most likely derives from *swr*.[9] The nouns in Job 12:18; Prov. 7:22 should be read as forms of *'sr*.[10] Thus we arrive at a total of 92 occurrences. The verb appears most often in the piel (32 times), 5 times in the niphal, 4 times in the qal, and once each in the hiphil and in a late form (Ezk. 23:48) that combines the niphal and hithpael.[11]

More than a third of the occurrences are found in Proverbs (39 nouns, 5 verbs). There are 15 (8,7) in Jeremiah, 10 (1,9) in Psalms, 6 (1,5) in Deuteronomy, 5 (4,1) in Job, 4 (4,0) in 1 Kings (2 of which are repeated in 2 Chronicles), 1 (1,0) in 1 Chronicles, 4 (2,2) in Isaiah, 3 (3,0) in Leviticus, 2 (1,1) in Ezekiel, 4 (1,3) in Hosea, and 2 (0,2) in Zephaniah.

Neither noun nor verb is found in the earliest literature of the OT, and both are rare in postexilic texts.[12] The root is found primarily in texts from the period of the monarchy, but is also common in exilic texts. The dating of the earliest passages of Hebrew literature is connected with the problem of dating the earliest strata of Proverbs and Deuteronomy and the question of whether 1 K. 12:11,14 are the *ipsissima verba* of Rehoboam. When *yāsar* and *mûsār* first appear, the word has already developed a range of meanings somewhat removed from the basic meaning "instruct."

It is most common in Wisdom Literature, which appears to be its natural *Sitz im Leben*; but its use in cultic texts from Ugarit cautions against supposing that the word had a single point of reference in Hebrew society from which it penetrated into others. Its late appearance could in fact suggest that it already covered a wide semantic range when it was borrowed from Canaanite.

Branson

---

2 *KTU,* 1, 5 V, 4; 1, 16 VI, 16.

3 *KTU,* 4, 281, 29.

4 J. Barth, *Etymologische Studien zum semitischen insbesondere zum hebräischen Lexicon* (Leipzig, 1893), 55.

5 W. W. Müller, "Altsüdarabische Beiträge zum hebräischen Lexikon," *ZAW,* 75 (1963), 304-316, esp. 310.

6 Cf. J. Murphy-O'Connor, "A Literary Analysis of Damascus Document VI,2–VIII,3," *RB,* 78 (1971), 210-232, esp. 221.

7 Jastrow, 583.

8 S. R. Driver and G. B. Gray, *Job. ICC* (1921, repr. 1977), 325.

9 M. H. Pope, *Job. AB,* XV (^{3}1979), 318.

10 *Ibid.,* 89; W. McKane, *Proverbs. OTL* (1970), 340.

11 *GK,* § 55k.

12 On the dating of Prov. 1–9, see R. J. Clifford, "Proverbs IX: A Suggested Ugaritic Parallel," *VT,* 25 (1975), 298-306.

3. *LXX.* Except in 1 Ch. 15:22 (*árchōn*), the LXX always uses *paideúein* to translate *yāsar.* The noun *mûsār* is usually rendered by *paid(e)ía*; from the same root we find *apaídeutos* for *ʾên mûsār* in Prov. 5:23, *paideúein* in Prov. 13:24; 23:13, and *paideutḗs* in Hos. 5:2. In Prov. 8:33, *mûsār* is translated *sophía* and identified with *ḥoḵmâ.*

Botterweck

II. yāsar.

1. *Semantic Field.* The semantic field of *yāsar* is relatively restricted, since it is associated with only a few words in any significant number of occurrences. It appears 5 times with → יכח *ykḥ,* "rebuke." Except in Ps. 94:10(Eng. v. 9), the words are used in synthetic parallelism (Ps. 6:2[1]; 38:2[1]; Prov. 9:7; Jer. 2:19). Ps. 6:2(1); 38:2(1) are identical: each psalm is an individual lament, and the verse is part of the introductory cry for help.[13] The psalmist prays that Yahweh will not "rebuke" (*ykḥ*) him in his anger (*ʾap*) nor "chasten" (*yrs*) him in his wrath (*ḥēmâ*). Jer. 10:24 prays similarly that Yahweh will not "correct" (*ysr*) the prophet in his anger (*ʾap*). The association of Yahweh's anger with *ysr* is feared by the one to be corrected, for the result is destructive. On the other hand, *yāsar* can be limited by *mišpāṭ,* in which case it refers to controlled punishment "in just measure," which is not destructive but constructive and helpful (Isa. 28:26; Jer. 10:24; 30:11; 46:28).

2. *Instruction.* The primary purpose of instruction (*yāsar*) is to communicate knowledge in order to shape specific conduct. It is usually addressed to a child. Proverbial wisdom requires parents to fulfill this duty zealously to assure that the child will develop properly as a productive member of society (Prov. 19:18; 29:17). A slave (Prov. 29:19) or a fool (Prov. 9:7) can be instructed, but with them mere words are ineffectual. It is nevertheless appropriate to strengthen the weak through instruction (Job 4:3).[14] Yahweh instructs in many ways and on various topics. He instructs the farmer in his work (Isa. 28:26) and the prophet in the perspective of God rather than the human (Isa. 8:11). Yahweh instructs both nations and individuals (Ps. 94:10,12); "his heart"[15] can instruct his people even in the middle of the night (Ps. 16:7). Dt. 4:36 states that Yahweh instructed Israel directly from heaven when he made known his commandments at Sinai. Instruction can come through observation; the rulers of the earth are admonished to be instructed by Yahweh's support of the Israelite king and not to be rebellious (Ps. 2:10). The nations are also to understand that the destruction of Judah the harlot is Yahweh's punishment for her idolatry (Ezk. 23:48).

3. *Correction.* The verb *yāsar* often appears with the meaning "correct," i.e., instruct someone by using punishment to "correct" what has been done. The responsibility of parents to employ this kind of instruction was considered obvious (Dt. 21:18).

---

13 Cf. C. Westermann, *Praise and Lament in the Psalms* (Eng. trans., Atlanta, 1981), 68ff.
14 Pope, 35, contra the root *ysr* II proposed by *KBL*^{3}, 400.
15 M. Dahood, *Psalms I. AB,* XVI (1966), 87.

There is a series of passages in which Yahweh "corrects" or punishes those who have sinned against him. According to Hosea, Israel is "chastised" for wicked deeds (Hos. 7:12; 10:10); there is no suggestion that this chastisement is intended to instruct and restore the nation.[16] In the Psalms, sickness is often looked upon as a punishment from God, intended to bring the psalmist to repentance (Ps. 6:2[1]; 38:2[1]; 39:12[11]). Jeremiah (Jer. 10:24) prays that God's punishment will come upon the people for the purpose of restoration, but he knows that God's intervention is destructive when not modified by *mišpāṭ*.

God's chastising influence is revealed in historical events; they can also point to even worse actions should the people reject instruction and chastisement. Chastisement (*yāsar*) can come through the tribulations of the wilderness (Dt. 8:5), siege (Jer. 6:8), or the dispersal of Ephraim (Jer. 31:18).

The consequences of God's rigorous discipline can include preservation of life (Ps. 118:18) and the strengthening of the people (Hos. 7:15; here the more common verb *ḥāzaq* in parallel with *yāsar* explicates the unusual meaning of the latter rather than suggesting an unusual root[17]).

4. *Punishment.* The verb appears 3 times in the last chapter of the Holiness Code (Lev. 17–26). Twice God seeks through harsh treatment to correct the people's error (Lev. 26:18,23). The third passage (v. 28) speaks of punishment for lack of repentance in the face of earlier chastisement. An exilic interpolation in Jer. 30:10f.[18] similar to one found also in Jer. 46:27f.[19] speaks likewise of punishment. "Instruction" in these verses comes through punishment, which is intended to be remedial.

Evil itself (*raʿ*) can be the driving force of punishment. In Jer. 2:19, Judah is condemned for making alliances with foreign nations, thereby breaking their covenant with Yahweh. These new alliances will rebound upon Judah; instead of the security they are intended to bring, they will be the instrument of Judah's destruction. Their act of infidelity toward their God initiates a disastrous chain of events that leads eventually to the punishment of Judah.

The use of *yāsar* in the sense of "punish," with no suggestion of remediation, could derive from the concept of corporal punishment of students (cf. *mûsār* below). In this case it refers more to the act of discipline than to its result, namely instruction. The next step was the loss of any pedagogical connotations. Dt. 22:18 says that corporal punishment shall be inflicted on a man who falsely charges his wife with not having been a virgin. Here there can be no pedagogical overtones, since the man obviously cannot bring the charge a second time. The elders of the city are to whip the offender.

Rehoboam's response to the Israelites' request to have their obligations toward the royal court lessened is contained in 1 K. 12:11,14 (par. 2 Ch. 10:11,14). Although this

---

16 H. W. Wolff, *Hosea. Herm* (Eng. trans. 1974), 99, 127, 184f.

17 Contra Driver, *JTS,* 36 (1935), 295.

18 J. P. Hyatt, "The Book of Jeremiah: Introduction and Exegesis," *IB,* V, 1024f.

19 J. G. Janzen, *Studies in the Text of Jeremiah. HSM,* 6 (1973), 94.

speech is recorded in an exilic work, it may record the authentic words of Rehoboam. It uses *yāsar* in the sense of "oppress," speaking figuratively of "chastising" with whips and scorpions to describe oppression of the people. There are no pedagogical overtones in this speech.[20]

III. mûsār.

1. *Semantic Field.* In Proverbs, *mûsār* is associated directly with *tôḵaḥaṯ*,[21] "reproof," in 9 passages (Prov. 3:11; 5:12; 6:23; 10:17; 12:1; 13:18; 15:5,10,32). In 3:11; 5:12, the reproof is a source of affliction for its recipient; in all the other passages, *tôḵaḥaṯ* represents verbal censure or oral reproof.[22] The connection between affliction and *mûsār* is obvious when blows are involved (*nkh*: Prov. 3:11; Jer. 2:30; 5:3). The verb *lāqaḥ*, "receive," is used with *mûsār* 6 times in Jeremiah (Jer. 2:30; 5:3; 7:28; 17:23; 32:33; 35:13), as well as in Prov. 1:3; Zeph. 3:2,7. Those who receive *mûsār* learn from experience and conform their conduct to acceptable standards. Not to receive *mûsār* means to reject the proffered instruction. In addition, *mûsār* is associated with *ḥoḵmâ* (Prov. 8:10f.; 23:23), *bînâ* (4:1; 23:23), *ṣeḏeq ûmišpāṭ* (1:3), *daʿaṯ* (19:27; 23:12), and *tôrâ* (1:8; 4:1f.; 6:23). It can be identified with *yirʾaṯ YHWH* (15:33) and derived from Yahweh (3:11).

2. *Body of Knowledge.* The noun *mûsār* can be used for a body of knowledge to be assimilated. In 4 passages it refers to the totality of a father's instruction (Prov. 1:8; 4:1; 13:1; 15:5). The "father" can be a parent (1:8) or a professional teacher whose authority derives from a store of practical wisdom gained through experience (4:1; 13:1).[23] The son (or pupil) must learn (*šāmaʿ*) the instruction of his father so as to profit from it.

As the body of knowledge to be learned, *mûsār* can take on the meaning of a necessary quality that is needed to master the problems of life. One is urged to acquire *mûsār* at any price (Prov. 8:10; 23:23), since it provides the basis for wise conduct in the future (Prov. 19:20). It is therefore closely associated with "knowledge" (*daʿaṯ*: Prov. 8:10; 12:1; 19:27; 23:12) and "wisdom" (*ḥoḵmâ*: Prov. 1:2; 19:20; 23:23): all are necessary if one is to achieve proper standards of behavior. Whoever neglects *mûsār* will have no success in life but will suffer poverty and disgrace (Prov. 5:12; 13:18) and even loss of life (Prov. 15:23). On the other hand, to learn (*šāmaʿ*) *mûsār* is wisdom (Prov. 8:33) and thus the correct way of life (Prov. 6:23; 10:17). It is necessary not only for survival but also for attainment of happiness and prosperity.[24]

In 2 of the latest passages in Proverbs, *mûsār* is associated theologically with *yirʾaṯ YHWH* (Prov. 1:7; 15:33):[25] the fear of God is the source of learning and wisdom. The

---

20 E. L. Curtis and A. A. Madsen, *Chronicles. ICC* (1910, repr. 1952), 362f.

21 → יכח *ykḥ*.

22 Sanders, 38.

23 McKane, 303; R. N. Whybray, *The Book of Proverbs. CBC* (1972), 77.

24 McKane, 307.

25 *Ibid.*, 487.

incorporation of Wisdom Literature into the religion of Yahweh gave rise to an awareness that the knowledge needed to deal successfully with life must ultimately be religious knowledge. Thus *mûsār* represents the content of religion which is necessary to lead a life that is pleasing to Yahweh.

3. *Content.* In one series of passages, *mûsār* refers to a specific point to be learned rather than the entire body of knowledge. One who is wise gains insight into the results of idleness while observing the poor condition of a vineyard belonging to a sluggard (Prov. 24:32). The same notion is used by the prophets Ezekiel (Ezek. 5:15) and Zephaniah (Zeph. 3:7) to describe the desired effect of God's punishment on sinners.

In Ps. 50:17, the wicked are punished for refusing to learn, a notion that agrees with the Deuteronomistic interpolation in Jer. 17:23.[26] In both instances the commandments of the Decalog are not observed and thus the covenant is broken.[27] Refusal to accept instruction includes failure to observe the requirements of the covenant.

In 3 passages, prophets accuse the people of not hearkening to Yahweh's voice or word (Jer. 7:28; 35:13; Zeph. 3:2). The same notion appears in Jer. 32:33, where it is the message of the prophet that is involved. In all 4 passages, Yahweh or the prophet is rejected. The prophet's message is identified with the voice of Yahweh, so that rejection of the former means rejection of the latter also. The teaching of their message (*mûsār*) is rejected, i.e., there is no alteration in the conduct of the people based on the prophet's appeal.

In the difficult passages Job 20:3; Jer. 10:8, *mûsār* appears also to mean verbal instruction. In Job 20:3, Zophar states that Job's words represent an "insulting censure," which he cannot accept. In Jer. 10:8, which is obscure, Jeremiah seems to be saying that the sages of other nations either instruct others on the basis of what their wooden idols have said to them or that they teach others to worship idols. In either case, what they teach is worthless.

4. *Discipline, Punishment.* The noun *mûsār* is associated not only with the content but also with the method of instruction. According to the wise, education of the young requires strict discipline. Deliverance from folly comes through the rod (Prov. 22:15). Life itself is assured by discipline reinforced by corporal punishment (Prov. 23:13).[28] In fact, a father who dotes on his son by not disciplining him neglects his covenant obligations to him (Prov. 13:24).[29]

Lack of *mûsār* brings death, the worst punishment (Prov. 5:23). Those who busy themselves with wickedness (15:10) and folly (16:22) find chastisement in their self-chosen way of life, for the harsh discipline they sought to evade is replaced by destruction and death.

---

26 W. W. Nicholson, *The Book of the Prophet Jeremiah, Chapters 1–25. CBC* (1973), 154.
27 Branson, 109f.
28 C. H. Toy, *Proverbs. ICC* (1904, repr. 1977), 433.
29 Branson, 80f.

Only twice is *mûsār* in the sense of "punishment" associated with Yahweh without any overtones of correction or redemption. In Hos. 5:2, Yahweh announces that he is about to chastise the house of Israel, and to become himself their complete punishment. Jer. 30:12-17 speaks of healing the incurable wounds of Judah, but in the meantime the people must for their sins accept a terrible punishment at the hands of their enemies (v. 14).

In most cases *mûsār* is redemptive when it comes as Yahweh's punishment. It is intended to restore the one on whom it is inflicted to proper conduct. Yahweh expects that Israel will learn from everything experienced and suffered at the time of the exodus and wilderness wanderings, and that they will be true to the covenant (Dt. 11:2). Nevertheless, Jer. 2:30; 5:3 show that the people remained disobedient even when Yahweh multiplied their anguish with repeated discipline.

The sage likens the *mûsār* of Yahweh to the way a father disciplines his beloved son: it is an expression of love, seeking to make the believer even better (Prov. 3:11f.).[30] A similar usage is found in Job 5:17.[31] The punishment inflicted by Shaddai is pedagogical (Job 33:16; 36:10). The latest passage in which this notion is found is Isa. 26:16,[32] where Yahweh's chastening of his people awakens repentance.

Isa. 53:5 contains an unusual use of *mûsār,* combining two different meanings. First, the kings or nations (52:15b) learn through observation and experience. In addition, they receive this instruction through the suffering of the one who suffers their punishment. This act works redemptively in that the punishment occasioned by sin is borne (vicariously) by a third party, for the sake of those who are instructed by the suffering.[33]

IV. Theological Usage. For the sage, discipline was an essential element in the process of educating a pupil. Folly and wickedness pave the way for destruction (Prov. 5:23). The only way for the pupil to save his life consisted in willingness to bear the rigorous discipline of instruction (Prov. 6:23). The pragmatic approach of the sage is based on the doctrine of the double way: the way of life is secured by wisdom, insight, and prudence; but the path of disgrace and death lies before the undisciplined fool who follows his own inclinations (Prov. 4:13; 10:17; 15:10). When the wisdom school came increasingly under the influence of Yahwistic theology,[34] wisdom was looked upon as Yahweh's gift, which could be acquired through study of the law. The way to succeed was associated with the proper understanding of the One who ordains creation. Therefore *mûsār* was associated with the fear of Yahweh, i.e., an understanding of the rules for a successful life depends on learning the principles of true religion (Prov. 1:7; 15:33).

Yahweh instructs people—a common function of the deity in the religions of the ancient Near East. He teaches things that bear on everyday life (Isa. 28:26), but his

30 McKane, 294; Whybray, 25.

31 Toy, 65.

32 Cf. B. Otzen, "Traditions and Structures of Isaiah XXIV–XXVII," *VT,* 24 (1974), 196-206, esp. 204.

33 Sanders, 15f.

34 Cf. M. V. Fox, "Aspects of the Religion of the Book of Proverbs," *HUCA,* 39 (1968), 55-69.

greatest revelation is contained in his covenant. The covenant goes beyond the limits of a written law code; it includes all the liberating acts before and after the Sinai event. The history of Yahweh's redemption is both instructive for his people and binding upon them (Dt. 4:36; Ps. 50:17; 94:12; Jer. 17:23). Yahweh can teach through a variety of means: the law (Dt. 4:36), direct communication (Isa. 8:11), dreams (Ps. 16:11), prophets (Jer. 7:28; 32:33; 35:13; Zeph. 3:2), suffering (Prov. 3:11), observation of the suffering of others (Zeph. 3:7). Recipients of his instruction may be individuals, the people of Israel and Judah, or even the larger collective of the nations (Ps. 2:10; 94:10; Ezk. 5:15). On the international plane, Yahweh uses historical events to teach not only Israel but also the other nations to fear him (Ezk. 5:15; 23:48).

One series of passages presents Yahweh as using corrective discipline to convey or repeat a specific teaching. He confronts the people in order to engender repentance, i.e., ready obedience to his commandments. This confrontation can take place through the preaching of a prophet (Jer. 7:28; Zeph. 3:2), but usually comes through a form of suffering imposed on the sinner (Lev. 26:18,23; Job 5:17; 36:10; Ps. 6:2[1]; 38:2[1]; 39:12[11]; Isa. 26:16; Jer. 2:30; 5:3; 6:8; 10:24; 31:18). Suffering itself does not necessarily effect forgiveness; it works as a spur to repentance. This educational and beneficial punishment is part of God's righteousness; as long as it leads to correction, it is part of the operation of the covenant (Ps. 6:2[1]; Jer. 10:24).[35] In 3 passages, something is learned through observation of the suffering of others (Ezk. 5:15; 23:48; Zeph. 3:7). Only in 1 passage does the suffering of an individual appear to be redemptive: it works vicariously on behalf of those who observe the suffering (Isa. 53:5).[36]

Those who reject correction experience Yahweh's actions as punishment rather than restoration. Acceptance of correction is not a matter of insight but an act of will: refusal to obey provokes Yahweh's anger (Jer. 10:24). Only in a few passages does *yāsar* or *mûsār* involve the notion of punishment without pedagogical overtones (Lev. 26:28; Jer. 30:11,14; 46:28; Hos. 5:2; 10:10). Yahweh can even use the destruction of one nation to instruct another; the sentence of condemnation can touch one nation and be instructive, i.e., redemptive, for another (Ezk. 5:15; Zeph. 3:7).

The use of *yāsar/mûsār* tells us something not only about Yahweh, but also about human beings. It is a fundamental notion that people need instruction not only to deal with the complexities of life but also to serve Yahweh. This instruction can come through observation (Zeph. 3:7), revelation (Dt. 4:3), or suffering (Prov. 3:11). In response, one can choose between learning obedience to Yahweh on the one hand and refusal to be instructed on the other. The concept denoted by *yāsar/mûsār* thus becomes a matter of the will and of the intellect, since people have the ability to resist Yahweh. Yahweh can employ corrective discipline, but human beings can resist it (Lev. 26). As a final possibility, when someone rejects Yahweh's plans for salvation and is therefore punished, that punishment can become an object lesson to warn others (Ezk. 5:15).

Branson

---

35 A. A. Anderson, *The Book of Psalms,* I. *NCBC* (1972, repr. 1981), 88.
36 Sanders, 15f.

יָעַד yā'aḏ

→ מוֹעֵד *mô'ēḏ;* → עֵדָה *'ēḏâ*

Contents: I. Distribution: 1. Semantic Description; 2. West Semitic Derivatives; 3. OT. II. With Human Subject: 1. Appointment of Others; 2. Collective Self-Appointment; 3. Self-Appointment in P. III. Relationship Between God and Human Beings: 1. God as Object; 2. God as Subject; 3. "Meeting."

I. Distribution.

1. *Semantic Description.* The root *w'd,* apparently part of the common Semitic stock, consists morphologically of a biliteral root *'d* together with the augment *w,* a combination that Akkadian suggests has fientic significance in its semantic structure.[1] It sets off an independent section of the complex system of the preformative and afformative compounds based on the root element *'d,* whose "original semantic connotation"[2] has to do with "recurrence." Whether this meaning is really inherent in the hypothetical basic word is dubious, especially since the Akkadian lexemes based on *'d,* like the prep. *adi,* "up to," or the noun *adānum,* (*'ad-ān*),[3] "term," have more to do with the semantic element of "termination" than "iteration." While *adānum* (= Ugar. *'dn*) cannot be taken as an Aramaic loanword,[4] since it is found in Old Babylonian, an Aramaic origin for Akk. *adû* (pl. *adê*), "oath,"[5] "*adû*-agreement,"[6] suggested by several,[7] is definitely possible although not certain, especially because a terminative sememe can be discerned in the semantic modification found here. This certainly does not contradict the hypothesis of a primary expansion of the element *'d,* or, more likely, a secondary derivation from the root *w'd.*[8] There would be further evidence for the notion of spatial and temporal limitation as the semantic content of primary compounds of *'d* if there

---

yā'aḏ. B. W. Dombrowksi, "The Meaning of the Qumran Terms 'T'WDH' and 'MDH,' " *RevQ,* 7 (1969-71), 567-574; M. Görg, *Das Zelt der Begegnung. BBB,* 27 (1967); J. Hoftijzer, "Ex. xxi 8," *VT,* 7 (1957), 388-391; L. Rost, *Die Vorstufen von Kirche und Synagoge im AT. BWANT,* 78[4/24] (1938; ²1967); G. Sauer, "יעד *j'd* bestimmen," *THAT,* I, 742-46; R. Schmitt, *Zelt und Lade als Thema alttestamentlicher Wissenschaft* (Gütersloh, 1972); J. A. Thompson, "Expansions of the עד Root," *JSS,* 10 (1965), 222-240; W. P. Wood, *The Congregation of Yahweh* (diss., Union Theological Seminary, Richmond, 1974).

1 Cf. *GaG,* § 103b.

2 Thompson, 223.

3 *AHw,* I (1965), 10b; cf. *GaG,* § 26r.

4 Contra G. R. Driver, "Hebrew Roots and Words," *WO,* 1/5 (1950), 412.

5 *AHw,* I, 14a.

6 *CAD,* I/1 (1964), 131-34.

7 J. A. Fitzmyer, "The Aramaic Inscriptions of Sefire I and II," *JAOS,* 81 (1961), 187; *idem, The Aramaic Inscriptions of Sefire. BietOr,* 19 (1967), 23f.; Thompson, 236f.; T. Veijola, "Zu Ableitung und Bedeutung von *hē'īd* I im Hebräischen," *UF,* 8 (1976), 347f.

8 Cf. Thompson, 236.

were contamination with the Sumerian loanword *á-dú/adû,* Akk. *adû,* "(daily) job,"[9] but this is uncertain.

2. *West Semitic Derivatives.* Derivatives of *wʿd* are found above all in West Semitic. Ugaritic texts contain the synonymous nouns *ʿdt*[10] and *mʿd,*[11] "assembly." Another possible derivative is *tʿdt,* meaning "plenipotentiary."[12] There is a Canaanite word *mwʿd(t),* "council," found in the Egyptian story of Wen-amon,[13] but neither it nor the Ugaritic evidence permits us to draw any direct conclusions about the distribution and semantics of the root in the Canaanite area. It is clear, though, that here also the semantic contribution involves termination. In spite of all contextual variation, purposive determination is the characteristic semantic element even in the later dialects, including Syr. *waʿdā,* "appointed time, signal or place," with denominative forms in the pael and ethpael meaning "meet";[14] Middle Heb. and Aram. *w/yʿd,* "appoint,"[15] and related nouns.[16] Whether *ʿiddān,* "time," belongs here is a matter of debate.[17] Analogous usage appears in Old South Arabic, Amharic, and Arabic.[18] This root is also an element in the Phoenician personal name *šmnyʿd.*[19]

3. *OT.* The OT exhibits extensive use of the nominal derivatives → עדה *ʿēḏâ*[20] and → מועד *môʿēḏ,* to which → עדות *ʿēḏûṯ* should possibly be added,[21] and, with certain reservations, → עת *ʿēṯ* (<* *ʿidt*),[22] but almost certainly not *ʿēḏ.*[23] There are also 2 hapax legomena: *môʿaḏ,* "place of assembly(?)" (Isa. 14:31),[24] and *mûʿāḏâ,* "agreement" (Josh. 20:9).[25] In contrast to the early dialects, the various verbal stems occur with remarkable frequency: *yʿd* qal 5 times, niphal 19 times, hiphil 3 times, and hophal twice.

Proposed emendations find *yʿd* in 1 S. 21:3(Eng. v. 2); 22:6; Ps. 132:6. In 1 S. 21:3(2), MT *ywdʿty* is usually emended on the basis of LXX *diamemartýrēmai* to *hwʿdty,*[26] but

---

9 *AHw,* I, 14a.
10 → עדה *ʿēḏâ.*
11 → מועד *môʿēḏ.*
12 *WUS,* no. 1195; interpreted differently by *UT,* no. 1832. See Veijola, 346.
13 ii.71.
14 *CSD,* 108b; cf. Thompson, 230.
15 Jastrow, 583f.
16 Cf. Thompson, 230; *KBL*³, 400b.
17 *GesB,* 918b (negative); *KBL*³, 400b (positive); but cf. I.1 above for a discussion of the earlier equivalents, and Thompson, 232, for a different view.
18 Cf. Thompson, 230ff.; *KBL*³, 400; Sauer, 742.
19 *BDB,* 416; cf. Benz, 178f., 324.
20 But see Thompson, 230.
21 See III.3 below.
22 Cf. *BLe,* § 61j; also E. Jenni, "עֵת *ʿēt Zeit,*" *THAT,* II, 371.
23 → עוד *ʿwd*; cf. Driver, 412.
24 *KBL*³, 529; cf. Rost, 7, and esp. the discussion by Wildberger, *Jesaja. BK,* X/2 (1978), 574.
25 *KBL*³, 529b; cf. M. Noth, *Das Buch Josua. HAT,* VII (³1971), 122f.; Rost, 7.
26 S. R. Driver, Budde, *et al.*

nwʿdty[27] and *yʿdty*[28] have also been proposed.[29] Certainty is impossible, especially in the light of still other conjectures.[30]

The proposed reading *nwʿd* for *nwdʿ* in 1 S. 22:6 is unnecessary.[31] Instead of MT *yʿr* (usually taken as a poetic form of the toponym *qryt yʿrm*[32]), the qal form *yāʿaḏ,* appended asyndetically to *bśdh,* has been suggested recently ("In the field he appointed").[33] There is no real need for emendation, however.[34]

Attention should also be called to the personal name *nwʿdyh* (Ezr. 8:33; Neh. 6:14), which represents an additional occurrence of the niphal.[35] Whether the personal names *mʿdyh* (Neh. 12:5) and *mwʿdyh* (Neh. 12:17) also belong here is uncertain.[36]

The Greek renderings of the LXX exhibit such a variety[37] that it is impossible to speak of a specific sememe. Only the translation *gnōsthēsomai* (Ex. 25:22; 29:42; 30:6,36; Nu. 17:19[4]) requires special notice: it is clearly based on confusion with *ydʿ*. In the Dead Sea scrolls, only *ywm yʿwd* in 1QM 1:10 adds to the forms found in the OT; it refers to the predetermined day for the destruction of the sons of darkness (cf. also 1QM 13:14,18).

II. With Human Subject.

1. *Appointment of Others.* In the casuistic law of female slaves (Ex. 21:7-11), the qal of *yʿd* plays a double role as a verb. The interpolated relative clause *ʾašer-lōʾ yᵉʿāḏāh* (v. 8) in the first subcase defines a circumstance that is legally significant but is not the immediate object of the protasis. It is not necessarily legitimate formally to equate the procedure referred to here by *yʿd* with that which follows in v. 9.[38] The construction with *lᵉ* supports the semantic orientation: purposive appointment.

The word *lōʾ* should not be deleted; it is an orthographic variant of *lô*.[39] In order to retain the negative particle, an emendation to *ydʿh* has been proposed.[40]

No less problematic are semantic interpretations like those proposed by Cazelles and de Boer,[41] but without sufficient supporting evidence.[42] Hoftijzer himself would extend

---

27 Klostermann, Dhorme.

28 Boström.

29 See the discussion by H. J. Stoebe, *Das erste Buch Samuelis. KAT,* VIII/1 (1973), 392f.

30 See, e.g., D. W. Thomas, "The Root ידע in Hebrew," *JTS,* 35 (1934), 299f.

31 Stoebe, 409, contra *KBL*³, 400b.

32 Cf. H.-J. Kraus, *Psalms* 60–150 (Eng. trans., Minneapolis, 1989), 480, *et al.*

33 A. Robinson, "Do Ephrathah and Jaar Really Appear in Psalm 132 6?," *ZAW,* 86 (1974), 221.

34 The passage is also discussed by E. Vogt, "Benjamin geboren 'eine Meile' von Ephrata," *Bibl,* 56 (1975), 35.

35 Cf. III.3 below.

36 M. Noth (*IPN,* 250) knows "no convincing etymology" for either form, but cf. *KBL*³, 529, 576.

37 Cf. Rost, 107ff.

38 Contra M. Noth, *Exodus. OTL* (Eng. trans. 1962), 169.

39 Contra *GesB,* 306a; cf. similar examples in *KBL*³, 487a.

40 K. Budde, "Bemerkungen zum Bundesbuch," *ZAW,* 11 (1891), 99-114.

41 H. S. Cazelles, *Études sur le code de l'alliance* (Paris, 1946), 48 ("épouser"); P. A. H. de Boer, "Some Remarks on Exodus xxi 7-11: The Hebrew Female Slave," *OrNeer,* 1948, 165 ("keep").

42 Cf. Hoftijzer, 389.

the relative clause in Ex. 21:8 to include the following *wehep̄dāh* with an implied logical subordination: "who is not taking the decision about her to let her be redeemed." This interpretation does not take sufficient account of either the function or the construction (cf. v. 9!) of the verb; it is therefore best to retain the translation "who has appointed her for himself,"[43] in the sense of "appoint for sexual intercourse."[44]

The second subcase, which follows, uses the prefix conjugation of *yʿd* (long form) in the protasis to indicate a circumstance that is now immediately relevant legally, reflecting the change of the person who is the indirect object (with *le*) of *yʿd* (Ex. 21:9). Here the verb functions extratemporally.[45] In contrast to v. 8, where it is the owner who is displeased with his slave, this verse deals with appointment of the woman for the purchaser's son. In this case she is have the same legal rights as her owner's daughters, whereas v. 8 enjoins her sale to another party (redemption), albeit not a foreigner. Emancipation is out of the question (v. 7), regardless of whether the "rights of a daughter" (*mišpaṭ habbānôṯ*) are "to some extent identical to the rights of a wife."[46]

The expression *yʿd* (qal) *le* is thus used for a formal appointment or assignment to a particular person. More specifically, its semantic force in a legal context involves authority over a woman for the purpose of incorporating her into a marriagelike relationship. This shows that from a very early date *yʿd* was used in legal terminology.[47]

The juridical significance of *yʿd* qal also finds expression in the position of the paronomastic relative clause *ʾšer yeʿāḏô* appended to the noun *môʿēḏ* in 2 S. 20:5. The reference is to a period of three days within which Amasa must call the men of Judah together (v. 4). The requirement laid down by David is apparently aimed at defining a kind of martial law during mobilization. Amasa's delay beyond the appointed time gives rise to the official assumption that he is siding with the rebellious Benjaminite Sheba, which settles his fate. To go beyond the time limit set by the king is in itself an offense of lese majesty, which does not require independent conviction. Note the skillful way in which vv. 6-10 present the consequences of disregarding *yʿd*.[48]

2. *Collective Self-Appointment.* The earliest occurrence of the niphal of *yʿd* is in the proverbial question recorded in Am. 3:3: *hayēleḵû šenayim yaḥdāw biltî ʾim-nôʿāḏû.* The emendation of *nôʿāḏû* to *nôḏāʿû* (following the LXX) is problematic not only formally (being based on the analogy of *yāḏaʿtî* in v. 2) but also semantically.[49] The position of the verbal phrase indicates its extratemporal and substantiating function: going together

---

43 Cf., e.g., Noth, *Exodus,* 169; B. S. Childs, *The Book of Exodus. OTL* (1974), 448; and also *BHS, in loc.*

44 Noth, *Exodus,* 179.

45 Cf. G. Liedke, *Gestalt und Bezeichnung alttestamentlicher Rechtsätze. WMANT,* 39 (1971), 38.

46 Noth, *Exodus,* 179.

47 Cf. Görg, 168.

48 Cf. also Rost, 6.

49 Cf. H. W. Wolff, *Joel and Amos. Herm* (Eng. trans. 1977), 179-188; W. Rudolph, *Amos. KAT,* XIII/2 (1971), 151; *et al.,* contra D. W. Thomas, "Note on נוֹעָדוּ in Amos III,3," *JTS,* N.S. 7 (1956), 69f.

is inconceivable without prior meeting. The semantic connotations are limited to the realm of everyday life;[50] despite the climax of the series of questions in v. 8, there are no compelling grounds for broader interpretations such as would see here an allusion to the relationship between Yahweh and the prophet.[51] Amos' initial purpose is clearly just to seek acceptance of an obvious truth;[52] there is no need to suggest a formal appointment.[53] In spite of Rudolph's argument,[54] however, we should not think in terms of a chance meeting, precisely because it is not chance that leads people to go together, but rather their having "appointed" themselves to do so: the niphal of *yʿd* suggests a "constructive" meeting. The characterization of the saying in v. 3 as part of a "didactic disputation"[55] is supported by the evidential argumentation, which reflects the language of legal discourse.[56]

In Job 2:11, the construction of the narrative tense *wayyiwwāʿᵃḏû* with *yaḥdāw* followed by *lᵉ* + infinitive indicates a collective purpose that Job's friends, who have arrived from various places, intend to carry out. Horst's statement[57] that it is "of little consequence" whether the niphal of *yʿd* is meant to emphasize the element of "common agreement" or of "(agreed-upon) meeting" is somewhat off the mark. The meeting of the friends is not an end in itself. It is not based on a formal agreement to meet, but is oriented toward the purpose of the visit. The emphasis of the niphal of *yʿd* is therefore in this case also on the final purpose, which is also a manifestation of the terminative semic nucleus.

Collective self-appointment can also be directed against others. The aggressive concentration of Canaan's forces to do battle with Israel finds literary expression in a cumulative series of narrative verbs (Josh. 11:4f.), in which *wayyiwwāʿᵃḏû* with its summary mention of the kings paves the way for the confrontation (v. 5). Here, too, the niphal of *yʿd* implies less a meeting by appointment than agreement for the purpose of making an active threat; in other words, it points forward. The more this menacing opposition dominates the narrative, the more impressively can the scenario of the Yahweh war unfold (vv. 6ff.). In Ps. 48:5(4)ff., poetic transformation places the niphal of *yʿd* in the stative (*nôʿᵃḏû*) in order to document the enormous threat. It is true that early traditions are here elevated "to the level of a visionary demonstration"; but the passage represents not so much a "historicizing variant to the primordial battle of chaos in creation myths"[58] as a threat on the part of those who agree to "appoint" themselves Israel's enemies, a threat based on historical experience but raised to a higher plane as the enemy in the wars of Yahweh and finally given cosmic overtones.

In Neh. 6:2, the aspect of collective conspiracy can still be heard in the apparently

---

50 Rudolph, 154.
51 Wolff, 184.
52 *Ibid.*
53 Cf. also Rudolph, 155.
54 P. 151.
55 Wolff, 183.
56 Görg, 168.
57 F. Horst, *Hiob. BK,* XVI/1 (³1974), 33.
58 H.-J. Kraus, *Psalms 1-59* (Eng. trans., Minneapolis, 1988), 475.

neutral voluntative message *lᵉḵâ wᵉniwwāʿᵃḏâ yaḥdāw,* with its designation of a specific rendezvous, concealing the true purpose of Nehemiah's opponents. What seems to be an offer to talk matters over is in fact a malicious ultimatum. The intended meeting is even glossed as a calculated ambush (v. 2b). In any case, a purposive meeting is intended, as Schiemann's rendering ("let us covenant together," citing the parallel phrase *yʿṣ yaḥdāw* in Neh. 6:7)[59] brings out.

Shemaiah's suggested meeting in the *bêṯ-hāʾᵉlōhîm* in order to capitalize on the right of asylum (Neh. 6:10) also makes use of the formula *niwwāʿēḏ ʾēl* (future punctiliar); in this case, too, the element of purpose is semantically significant. At the same time, of course, the words of this counselor are no less deceitful: Nehemiah considers Shemaiah an ally of his opponents, who seek to embarrass him (vv. 11ff.). For all that, the niphal of *yʿd* appears even in this passage in the context of legal usage expressive of purpose.

3. *Self-Appointment in P.* The occurrences of the niphal of *yʿd* in contexts dealing specifically with cultic law constitute a distinct group. The alternatives of "designating" oneself (i.e., deciding) for or against the cultic community are brought out especially in those passages that have been influenced by the terminology of P.

In Nu. 14:35, in a "general oath"[60] placed in the mouth of Yahweh, P states that rebellion against the leaders of the people (cf. 14:2f.) is also rebellion against Yahweh. Judgment will overtake the entire congregation (*ʿēḏâ*), characterized as *rāʿâ* and paronomastically with the appositional phrase *hannôʿāḏîm ʿālāy*; their reprobation follows from their collective opposition to Yahweh. This self-appointment, too, has a purpose: a total reversal of course; it therefore meets with radical judgment. In Nu. 16:11, a secondary text of P, the rebellion is again formally against the leadership (Aaron), "but indirectly against Yahweh."[61] Above all, the group around Korah is represented here as a revolutionary cell, which—undoubtedly with "opposition to the Jerusalem priesthood" in the background[62]—is described in the words of Moses (vv. 8-11) as an "anti-congregation," an *ʿēḏâ* within the *ʿēḏâ,* with the judgmental phrase *hannôʿāḏîm ʿal-YHWH* in apposition, again by way of paronomastic explanation. The same holds true for what is probably an even later interpolation in Nu. 27:3,[63] where the noun *ʿēḏâ* is also accompanied by the explanatory phrase *hannôʿāḏîm ʿal-YHWH.* Here Baentsch interprets the act of rebellion "not as a revolt of the Levites (as in P^s), but (as in P) as a movement within the community, involving members of all the tribes";[64] but the text does not provide any compelling grounds for such a distinction.

Although in P^g and P^s the niphal of *yʿd* with *ʿal* appears to indicate hostile self-appointment, 1 K. 8:5 (par. 2 Ch. 5:6) represents a special case. The text is part of the exposition of Solomon's so-called dedication prayer; among other things, its language

59 R. Schiemann, "Covenanting with the Princes: Neh VI 2," *VT,* 17 (1967), 368f.
60 S. E. McEvenue, *The Narrative Style of the Priestly Writer. AnBibl,* 50 (1971), 113.
61 B. Baentsch, *HAT,* I/2 (1903), 546.
62 M. Noth, *Numbers. OTL* (Eng. trans. 1968), 125.
63 Cf. *ibid.,* 211.
64 Baentsch, 636.

has many elements typical of P. The congregation accompanying Solomon, called *kol-ʿaḏaṯ yiśrāʾēl,* is described as *hannôʿaḏîm ʿālāyw.* Here *ʿal* does not indicate opposition. Nevertheless—as in the constructions just discussed—the priestly language is unmistakable;[65] there is no reason to break up v. 5 and assign *hannôʿaḏîm ʿālāyw* to an earlier stratum.[66] Nu. 10:3f., which contains instructions relating to the function of the trumpet signal, also betrays a late phase of priestly redaction,[67] involving an association of the "petitive"[68] *nôʿāḏû* with the terms *ʿēḏâ* and *ʾōhel môʿēḏ* (v. 3), further evidence of the semantic interdependence typical of the P tradition.

III. Relationship Between God and Human Beings.

1. *God as Object.* The semantic affinity with legal language is both clear and distorted in those passages where the hiphil of *yʿd* touches the relationship between God and human beings. In the parallel threats of Jer. 49:12-21 (against Edom) and 50:44-46 (against Babylon), we find the rhetorical question *mî yôʿîḏennî* as a "formulaic phrase"[69] in the mouth of Yahweh. Using words that in each case follow a variant of the incomparability formula (*mî kāmônî*), likewise in the form of a question, Yahweh refuses "all responsibility for his violent acts"[70] and at the same time discredits all alien ambition for power of whatever provenience. Here it is the foreign nations of Edom and Babylon (the oracle against Edom probably having been composed later after the model of the oracle against Babylon[71]) whose aggressive self-importance leads to their own destruction. The causative interpretation of the hiphil of *yʿd* eliminates all possibility of human influence on God's authority to decide.

This incompetence in the face of God's omnipotence is especially clear in Job 9:19, where the formula in question reappears in the context of Job's lament. Horst finds here a function different from that in the Jeremiah passages: it "does not mean that God cannot be summoned because he refuses to be summoned, but that Job himself, who wishes to be summoned, will not be."[72] It is unnecessary, however, to distinguish two different functions for the formula, since the entire context of v. 19 addresses the question of divine autonomy. It is this unfathomable autonomy with its absolute omnipotence to which Job objects in his despair. God is not a legal authority open to human claims. Instead he stands above any rebuke and determines his own justice (*mišpāṭ*).

2. *God as Subject.* Yahweh's legal function finds its most graphic expression in the judgment signalized by the traditional image of his "sword." Against Ashkelon and the

---

[65] E. Würthwein, *Das erste Buch der Könige. ATD,* XI/1 (1976), 86.

[66] M. Noth, *Könige 1–16. BK,* IX/1 (1968), 178.

[67] The literary question is discussed by D. Kellermann, *Die Priesterschrift von Numeri 1* 1 bis 10 10. *BZAW,* 120 (1970), 146f.

[68] Cf. M. Görg, review of W. Gross, *Bileam. StANT,* 38 (1974), *ThRv,* 73 (1977), 19.

[69] Horst, 149.

[70] *Ibid.*

[71] W. Rudolph, *Jeremia. HAT,* XII (³1968), 269.

[72] Horst, 149.

seashore, there (*šām*) Yahweh has appointed (*yʿd* qal) his sword (Jer. 47:7); the instrument of death has become, as it were, "a living entity, an organ of the deity," and Nebuchadnezzar is the "agent" of Yahweh's will, "like his sword."[73] The second part of the "Song of the Sword" in Ezk. 21:13-22(8-17)[74] apostrophizes the sword's function, addressing it directly as an "instrument of judgment."[75] The hophal of *yʿd* in v. 21(16)[76] describes the "mysterious" directing of the sword, more specifically the turning of its "face," in a kind of personification.[77]

Mic. 6:9 also involves the threat of punishment; here it is a "rod" (*maṭṭeh*) that Yahweh has appointed (*yʿd* qal). There is no need to emend the text.[78] Neither is it necessary to interpret the feminine suffix of the form *yʿdh* as a "neuter."[79] The much-debated occurrence in Jer. 24:1 (MT) can also be interpreted against the background of fixed legal idiom. The hophal *mûʿāḏîm* serves not only to describe the position of the two symbolic baskets of figs before the *hêḵal YHWH* but also to indicate their mysterious provenience. Yahweh appoints this sign for salvation and for disaster. According to Driver,[80] derivation from the root *yʿd* causes it "to bear a sense alien to its whole usage." Like the interpretations of Driver ("ripe" or "test figs") and Thomas[81] (derivation from a hypothetical root *yʿd,* "place"), the alternatives suggested by Rudolph[82] (based on the root *ʿmd*) are not convincing. But the forensic context allows for a corresponding dimension in *yʿd.* The fate of the deportees and that of those remaining in Jerusalem is symbolically appointed or determined: according to Jer. 24:10, the sword is among the disasters that will come upon the Jerusalemites.

3. *"Meeting."* The relationship to Yahweh takes on specific nuances when the niphal of *yʿd,* otherwise used collectively, is used at the very heart of P's theology for a mode of revelation of the deity.

The passages can be categorized on the basis of the conjugation used and the nature of the clause. The main clauses in Ex. 25:22; 29:43 use the suffix conjugation; the subordinate relative clauses in Ex. 29:42; 30:6,36; Nu. 17:19(4) use the prefix conjugation. In both cases the verbs clearly refer to future time. The main clauses are also short and imitate the formulaic style of the pre-P rituals so as to gain a share in their authority.

---

73 Rudolph, 237.

74 For a discussion of the structure of this passage, see W. Zimmerli, *Ezekiel 1. Herm* (Eng. trans. 1979), 431.

75 *Ibid.,* 432.

76 There is no compelling reason to emend *muʿāḏôṯ* to *mûʿeḏeṯ* (fem. sg.), as proposed by G. R. Driver, "Ezekiel: Linguistic and Textual Problems," *Bibl,* 35 (1954), 154f.

77 Zimmerli, 434.

78 For the various suggestions, all of which are rightly rejected, see W. Rudolph, *Micha. KAT,* XIII/3 (1975), 115.

79 *Ibid.*

80 G. R. Driver, "Hebrew Notes on the 'Wisdom of Jesus ben Sirach'," *JBL,* 53 (1934), 288.

81 D. W. Thomas, "A Note on מוּעָדִים in Jeremiah 24,1," *JTS,* N.S. 3 (1952), 55.

82 *HAT,* XII, 134.

According to Koch,[83] one of the two short clauses in Ex. 25:22 (with *wᵉ* + suf. conjugation) belongs to the prototype used by P; but a group of five units can be reconstructed even without including v. 22,[84] so that v. 22 may be thought of as originating with P. The local reference of the niphal of *yʿd* is indicated by *šām* in the first short clause, but is detailed only in the following clause, where the locative phrases *mēʿal hakkappōreṯ* and *mibbên šᵉnê hakkᵉruḇîm* are added. These undoubtedly reflect the layout of the Jerusalem temple with its cherubim throne.

Despite P's interest in defining the locus of the niphal of *yʿd* in the words of Yahweh, the semantic weight must not be shifted to a one-sided "emphasis on place."[85] As elsewhere in P, there is equal emphasis on those addressed and above all on the element of purpose: the event of "meeting" takes place in order that the parties to the "meeting" may speak together. This relationship is documented in Ex. 25:22 on the one hand by the association of the niphal of *yʿd* with *lᵉḵā* and on the other by the verbal phrase with the piel of *dbr* and *ʾittᵉḵā* following after *šām.* Last but not least, the locative orientation is influenced by P's readily observable love of paronomasia, reflected here at least from the perspective of P—probably not without reason[86]—in the relationship between *yʿd* and *ʿēḏûṯ* (v. 21b).

Furthermore, P obviously does not insist that the meeting takes place exclusively above the ark, since the second occurrence of the niphal of *yʿd* in an independent clause (Ex. 29:43) uses *šāmmâ* to refer back to the entrance to the *ʾōhel-môʿēḏ,* a locality that already plays a role in the tabernacle tradition outside of P.[87] The use of short clauses here, which is also undoubtedly imitative, includes a collective group addressed by Yahweh *nôʿaḏ,* as one would expect from the public position of the entrance to the tent of meeting. Similarly, the relative clause in v. 42, which links the niphal of *yʿd* with a term of address (*lāḵem*), the locative *šāmmâ,* and an expression of purpose (*lᵉḏabbēr ʾēleyḵā šām*), probably involves an effort to bring the "collective" and "individual" uses of *yʿd* niphal under a single roof. With the statement of purpose, P once again does justice to the basic terminative aspect of the root. The interest in a paronomastic correspondence (*yʿd—môʿēḏ*) is again obvious.

Despite the impression the passage gives of combining heterogenous elements, the context of the *yʿd* niphal occurrences in Ex. 29:43-46 "in its present form represents a pointed summary of P's ideas about the significance of the sanctuary as a whole together with its priesthood."[88] The thematic line is formally discernible in the series of 1st person singulars of the suffix conjugation. It leads from *nôʿaḏtî* (v. 43) through *qiddaštî* (v. 44) to *šāḵantî* (v. 45), demonstrating simultaneously the need to understand the dynamism

---

83 K. Koch, *Die Priesterschrift von Exodus 25 bis Leviticus 16. FRLANT,* N.S. 53[71] (1959), 12f.

84 M. Görg, "Eine neue Deutung für *kăpporet,*" *ZAW,* 89 (1977), 115; *idem,* "Kerubin in Jerusalem," *BN,* 4 (1977), 17f.

85 Schmitt, 227.

86 Cf. M. Görg, "Zur 'Lade des Zeugnisses'," *BN,* 2 (1977), 14.

87 Cf. Görg, *Das Zelt der Begegnung,* 60, etc.

88 Koch, 31.

of both *qdš* piel and *škn* from the perspective of *y'd* niphal, i.e., from the programmatic self-appointment Yahweh undertakes for the sake of the meeting. To interpret *y'd* niphal from the perspective of *škn,* as Schmitt proposes,[89] seems inappropriate to the internal logic of vv. 43-45. The niphal of *y'd* signalizes the fixed point of contact, the necessary precondition for Yahweh's "sanctifying" and "dwelling," acts that are certainly not to be understood as being restricted to the temporal plane, but advise against the assumption of permanent static presence.

The other occurrences of *y'd* niphal with the deity as subject do not diverge fundamentally from the aspectual correlation observed here, although formal variations appear: the change of addressee from *lᵉḵā* (Ex. 30:6,36) to *lāḵem* (Nu. 17:19[4]) at the same place within the sanctuary; paronomastic reference to *'ēḏûṯ* alone (Ex. 30:6) or in conjunction with *'ōhel mô'ēḏ* (30:36; Nu. 17:19[4]). Even in the fixed idioms of P, then, the terminative semic nucleus can still be seen.

Görg

89 P. 227.

יעל *y'l*

Contents: I. Occurrences, Etymology, Semantic Field, LXX. II. 1. Prophetic Polemic; 2. Wisdom Texts.

I. Occurrences, Etymology, Semantic Field, LXX. The verb *y'l* appears grammatically only in the hiphil, semantically only in theological usage, never in secular usage. It occurs 23 times within the OT, as well as twice in Sirach (Sir. 5:8; 38:21) and once in the Dead Sea scrolls (1QH 6:20). The OT occurrences divide neatly into two groups:[1] a prophetic group, which includes the single Deuteronomistic text (1 S. 12:21; Isa. 30:5 [twice],6; 44:9f. [twice]; 47:12; 48:17; 57:12; Jer. 2:8,11; 7:8; 12:13; 16:19; 23:32 [twice]; Hab. 2:18); and a Wisdom group (Job 15:3; 21:15; 30:13; 35:3; Prov. 10:2; 11:4). The proposed emendation in Ps. 16:2f.[2] has found few supporters and is therefore disregarded. The verb usually means "profit" or "benefit" someone; it is used intransitively in the sense "profit from something" only in Job 21:15; 35:3; Jer. 12:13.

y'l. H. D. Preuss, *Verspottung fremder Religionen im AT. BWANT,* 92 [5/12] (1971), 161, 170, 208f., 224, 239; M. Sæbø, "יעל *j'l* hi. nützen," *THAT,* I, 746-48.

1 Cf. Sæbø.

2 *KBL*³, 401.

The word's etymology is disputed.[3] Guillaume[4] proposes a metathetic form of Arab. *ʿalā,* "prosper." Possible derivatives include only *tʿlh* and *twlʿt* in Sir. 30:23; 41:14, and probably also the form → בליעל *bᵉliyyaʿal;*[5] it was formerly common to suggest a connection with *yāʿēl,* "mountain goat,"[6] but most scholars today rightly reject this etymology.

The verb usually appears in the imperfect, negated by *lōʾ,* being used primarily[7] to say that something does *not* profit. Besides *lōʾ,* the negatives *bal, biltî,* and *ʾayin* also appear. The verb is used affirmatively only in Isa. 48:17 (with the explanatory term → דרך *drk* in the niphal) and Jer. 2:11 (with a positive reference to → כבוד *kāḇôḏ*); in these cases, as might be expected, it is associated with Yahweh.

Among other words that refer to the futility of idols or one's own human efforts, *yʿl* is associated especially with the hiphil of → נצל *nṣl,* the nouns → עזר *ʿzr* (cf. Isa. 30:5), and → תהו *tōhû* (1 S. 12:21; Isa. 44:9), as well as *bōšeṯ* and *ḥerpâ* (Isa. 30:5). Other verbs used like *yʿl* include *ytb, yšʿ,* and *skn;* they appear commonly in conjunction with *yʿl.*[8] In Wisdom passages, the semantic field includes both → בצע *bṣʿ*[9] and *yiṯrôn,* used affirmatively and in implicitly negative questions.

The LXX usually uses *ōpheleín* for the hiphil of *yʿl,* as well as *ōphéleia;* rarely we find *ōphélēma* (Jer. 16:19), *óphelos* (Job 15:3), or *anōphelḗs* (Isa. 44:10; Jer. 2:8). Occasionally *symphérein* is used.[10] The only noteworthy exceptions are 1 S. 12:21 with *peraínein* and Job 35:3 with *poieín.*

II. 1. *Prophetic Polemic.* The primary use of *yʿl* hiphil is prophetic criticism and polemic. Isa. 30:5, a woe oracle with motivation,[11] calls Egypt a people that cannot profit. Verse 6, which begins a new section, picks up the theme of v. 5.[12] According to Jer. 12:13, Israel will not profit from what it has sown.[13]

Starting with Jeremiah (although the idea appears earlier; cf. Hos. 8:6; 10:5-7; 13:2), the futility of idols becomes a common theme, often expressed by means of *yʿl.* Deutero-Isaiah, the Deuteronomistic history, and the isolated late text Hab. 2:18 stand in the line of tradition that begins here.

---

3 Cf. Sæbø, 746.

4 A. Guillaume, "Hebrew and Aramaic Lexicography," *Abr-Nahrain,* 1 (1959/1960 [1961]; repr. Leiden, 1965), 26.

5 B. Otzen, *TDOT,* II, 131-36.

6 Cf. still E. König, *Hebräisches und aramäisches Wörterbuch zum AT* (Leipzig, 1910; 6,7 1937), 154.

7 See II below.

8 For a discussion of the semantic field with references see Preuss, 239 and 161.

9 D. Kellermann, *TDOT,* II, 205-8.

10 Cf. K. Weiss, "φέρω," *TDNT,* IX, 69-78.

11 O. Kaiser, *Isaiah 13–39. OTL* (Eng. trans. 1974), *in loc.*

12 For analysis of the argument, see F. Huber, *Jahwe, Juda und die anderen Völker beim Propheten Jesaja. BZAW,* 137 (1976), 116f., 120f., 139; W. Dietrich, *Jesaja und die Politik. BEvTh,* 74 (1976), 139ff.

13 → זרע *zrʿ.*

Jer. 7:8 states that deceptive words[14] will be of no avail (cf. Job 15:3). According to Jer. 23:32, these are the words of the false prophets; according to 2:8, they are spoken by prophets who prophesy in the name of Ba'al[15] and go after[16] idols that do not profit. One must not trust[17] in these words. Israel has even managed to exchange its mighty Yahweh for an idol (Jer. 2:11: sg.!) that does not profit—possibly a reference to the calf at Samaria. According to Jer. 16:19b, the nations will recognize that their fathers have inherited lies, worthless gods[18] in which there is no profit. This statement takes on special importance for being placed in the mouth of the nations themselves.

False gods cannot profit and therefore neither can their images, since the mocking and polemic texts of the OT explicitly identify the false gods with their lifeless and powerless images. This is the argument of Isa. 44:9f.,[19] which states that the idol in which the heart of its maker delights and its products are profitless. So are Babylon's enchantments (Isa. 47:12), to which people have looked for help. In Isa. 57:12, too, the "works" (*ma'^aśeh*[20]) that will not help are probably idols, as the continuation in v. 13 shows, which uses affirmation (elsewhere only in Isa. 48:17) alongside the negative. Isa. 57:3-13 resembles the judgment scenes in Deutero-Isaiah. The only true refuge is in Yahweh, who bestows his promise.

It is wrong to turn aside after[21] idols of vanity (*tōhû*: 1 S. 12:21; Isa. 44:9), since they cannot profit or save, warns the Deuteronomist, echoing the words of the prophets (cf. also Deut. 13:14).

The vigorous polemic of Hab. 2:18, a late exilic interpolation comparable in content to Isa. 2:18; 19:3; Mic. 5:12f.(Eng. vv. 13f.), cannot avoid emphasizing the helplessness of idols, asking what profit there is in a deceitful idol, the work of human hands. Such rhetorical questions (cf. Job 21:15; 35:3, where the questions are not rhetorical!), where the answer is already known, are common in texts that make fun of idols: questions of this type are typical of hymns, and mockery of idols is equivalent to hymning Yahweh.

Isa. 48:17 is the only prophetic text (not without reason put in the mouth of Yahweh) to say that it is Yahweh alone who teaches Israel what profits, by being a God who leads the people.[22]

As a consequence, the verb *y'l* is used from the time of Jeremiah on to state the futility of idols. Deutero-Isaiah and the Deuteronomistic history extend the theme. But this development merely conceptualizes what is already implicit in narrative form in the earlier OT texts discussed above, which recount the futility of foreign idols without using

---

14 → שקר *šqr*.

15 → בעל *ba'al*.

16 → אחרי *'aḥ^arê* (*'ach^arê*), → הלך *hālak* (*hālakh*).

17 → בטח *bāṭaḥ* (*bāṭach*). The hiphil of → אמן *'āman* is never used of idols, but only of Yahweh.

18 → הבל *hebel* (*hebhel*).

19 → פסל *psl*; for a discussion of Isa. 44:9-20 and its literary analysis, see Preuss, 208ff.

20 → עשׂה *'śh*.

21 → אחרי *'aḥ^arê* (*'ach^arê*); → סור *sûr*.

22 → דרך *drk* hiphil; cf. K. Koch, "דֶּרֶךְ *derek* (*derekh*)," *TDOT*, III, 290.

yʿl.[23] The word itself appears at the moment when the Babylonian threat and subsequent exile raise the question whether other gods can "help" when Yahweh seemed defeated. In this time of distress and temptation, when people need "help," Jeremiah explicitly rules out one such source of help. Other exilic texts and authors follow his lead. This prophetic criticism and polemic is thus linked with the prophets' view of history and their message of judgment; it is quite distinct from the other realm in which *yʿl* is used,[24] namely Wisdom Literature, where the argument and train of thought involving *yʿl* are far different. But it is clear likewise that the prophetic polemic texts mocking false gods and idols are not to be derived from Wisdom tradition,[25] which indeed makes use of *yʿl* but never in the context of polemic against idolatry (Wis. 13–15 is late both historically and traditio-historically, and exhibits a mixture of forms).

2. *Wisdom Texts.* Alongside the texts illustrating prophetic polemic, whose purpose is a call to repentance, there is a group of Wisdom texts using *yʿl* that includes 2 passages from Proverbs and 4 from Job. They all speak likewise of what does *not* profit, using *yʿl* only in grammatical negations or with negatively critical meaning. A favorite theme of Wisdom is to ask what brings profit.

Prov. 10:2; 11:4 are wisdom aphorisms enshrining the knowledge that treasures gained by wickedness (10:2) and riches (11:4; cf. Eccl. 11:4) do not profit on the day of wrath; only *ṣᵉḏāqâ*[26] can do so. "Day of wrath" refers here not to some last judgment but to an earthly crisis, in which—because of the world order established and maintained by Yahweh—injustice cannot bring forth good.

In the book of Job, where Satan himself indirectly asks what "profit" there is in Job's piety (Job 1:9), Eliphaz charges that Job's words, which are in fact the words of a sage, cannot bring any profit, any good (15:3; cf. Sir. 5:8). Job raises the meaning and usage to a new level by insisting that even praying to → שׁדי *šadday* is profitless (Job 21:15, with the pl. "we"; cf. 22:2f. with *skn*; Mal. 3:14) and that his opponents are aiding (*yʿl* without negation but in a negative sense) his fall (Job 30:13). Job 34:9, in the second speech of Elihu, uses *skn* in critical—albeit distorted—reference to Job's words in 21:15; and 35:3 also criticizes Job's position that there is nothing left to help or profit him. In both passages, Job's statements appear in the form of a quotation, intended to remind him once more of his words, which Elihu considers culpable and erroneous. In addition, the discussion on the theme of "profit" underlines the Wisdom roots of the book of Job.

The infinitive of *yʿl* with *lᵉ* is used in 1QH 6:20 in a sense somewhat different from OT usage: God has ordained what "profits" or "promotes" the way of his holiness (cf. Isa. 48:17 with reference to the corrupt text).

Preuss

---

23 See Preuss, 161.

24 See II.2 below.

25 G. Fohrer, *Intro. OT* (Eng. trans., Nashville, 1968), 382, and esp. G. von Rad, *Wisdom in Israel* (Eng. trans., Nashville, 1972), 177-185.

26 → צדק *ṣdq*.

יעף *yʿp* I; יָעֵף *yāʿēp̱*; עיף *ʿyp* II; עָיֵף *ʿāyēp̱*

Contents: I. 1. Etymology, Basic Meaning; 2. Statistics and Distribution; 3. Synonyms; 4. Dead Sea Scrolls; 5. LXX. II. Semantic Domain: 1. Physical Usage; 2. Figurative Usage; 3. Religious Usage.

I. 1. *Etymology, Basic Meaning.* Etymological studies of the verbal and adjectival derivatives of the roots *yʿp* I and *ʿyp* II in Biblical Hebrew yield the following picture:

a. The root *yʿp* I is among the triliteral roots with an original *yodh* as the first radical;[1] it should be considered in parallel with → יגע *yāgaʿ*, "be (become) tired." It therefore has nothing to do with the root *yʿp* II, a variant of the root *ʿwp* I[2] with an original *waw* as the middle radical. Unlike *ygʿ*, *yʿp* I is not part of the common Semitic root stock. Apart from Biblical Hebrew and its Middle Hebrew piel form meaning "tire,"[3] it is found also in the Arabic forms *waġaga* and *waʿafa*, "run, hurry." It is still unclear whether it really occurs in Christian Palestinian Aramaic.[4]

On the basis of Akkadian, Arabic, and Old South Arabic parallels, Zolli has proposed distinguishing *yʿp* I from a hypothetical *yʿp* II,[5] which arose by metathesis from *ypʿ* and means "rise up," "shine." The uncertainty in assigning the Semitic cognates to the different roots makes this theory less than convincing. The Arabic forms *yafaʿa*, "grow up," "rise up," and *wafʿu(n)*, "height (of land)," "tall building,"[6] as well as OSA *yfʿ*, "get up,"[7] to which may be added Ugar. *ypʿ*, "arise (?),"[8] "be exalted,"[9] seem to be connected with the hypothetical Hebrew root *ypʿ* II, which must be distinguished from the Hebrew root *ypʿ* I,[10] "cause to shine," "shine forth," "reveal oneself,"[11] with its Akkadian cognates *(w)apû*, "be visible,"[12] and *šûpû*, "make visible." It is therefore improbable to

---

yʿp I. M. Z. Kaddari, "The Double Meaning of '*ʿAyef*' (עיף) in the Bible," *Tarbiz,* 34 (1965), 351-55 [Heb.], VI [Eng. summary]; S. Segert, "Zur Habakkuk-Rolle aus dem Funde vom Toten Meer, III," *ArOr,* 22 (1954), 444-459, esp. 452f.; E. Zolli, "Note di lessicografia biblica: II יעף," *Bibl,* 27 (1946), 127f.

1 Cf. R. Meyer, *Hebräische Grammatik,* II (Berlin, ³1969), 138; W. Gesenius–G. Bergsträsser, *Hebräische Grammatik,* II (²⁹1926; repr. Hildesheim, 1962), 126.

2 Cf. *KBL*³, 402.

3 G. Dalman, *Aramäisch-neuhebräisches Handwörterbuch zu Targum, Talmud und Midrasch* (³1938; repr. Hildesheim, 1967), 185; Jastrow, 585.

4 Cf. F. Schulthess, *Lexicon Syropalaestinum* (Berlin, 1903), 85a.

5 Not identical with *yʿp* II in *KBL*³, 403.

6 Cf. G. R. Driver, "Ezekiel: Linguistic and Textual Problems," *Bibl,* 35 (1954), 158.

7 ContiRossini, 164.

8 *UT,* no. 1133.

9 *WUS,* no. 1215; cf. F. L. Moriarty, "A Note on the Root YPʿ," *CBQ,* 14 (1952), 62; *PNU,* 144f.; J. Maier, *Die Texte vom Toten Meer* (Munich, 1960), II, 149f.

10 → יפע *ypʿ*.

11 *KBL*³, 405; cf. E. Jenni, "יפע *jpʿ* hi. aufstrahlen," *THAT,* I, 753-55.

12 *CAD,* I/2 (1968), 201-4; cf. *GaG,* §§ 103b, 106o. See also *APNM,* 212f.

think in terms of a single root *ypʿ* in the Semitic languages from which *yʿp* can be derived by metathesis.

Isa. 8:23(Eng. 9:1) contains the hophal ptcp. *mûʿāp̱*, which can hardly come from *yʿp* I.[13] It is derived traditionally from *ʿwp* II, "be dark,"[14] but has recently been associated with **ʿyp*, "gleam."[15] Others derive it from → עוף *ʿwp* I, "fly," and associate it with Syrian Arab. *ʿawwafa*, "release, let go," so that it has the meaning "escape" (Vulg. reads: *et non poterit avolare de angustia sua*).[16]

In Dnl. 9:21, we find the difficult phrase *muʿap̱ bîʿāp̱*, traditionally rendered "totally exhausted" (lit., "exhausted in exhaustion") and associated etymologically with *yʿp* I. It is reasonably certain, however, that the hophal ptcp. *muʿāp̱* (written *mûʿāp̱* in many Hebrew manuscripts) should be considered an instance of the root *yʿp* II,[17] which probably represents a by-form of *ʿwp*, I, "fly," and is connected with Arab. *wġf*, "run, hasten." Zolli[18] has proposed treating this hophal as a metathesis of *ypʿ*, "rise up," "shine," but this is problematic. The noun *y^eʿāp̱* has been considered an aramaism,[19] but it is preferable to consider it as a type of a native Hebrew noun form.[20] It appears to derive from *yʿp* II and mean "flight," so that the phrase *muʿāp̱ bîʿāp̱* should be translated "in swift flight" (lit., "in flying flight"; cf. LXX, Theodotion, Vulg., and Syr.).[21]

b. The adj. *yāʿēp̱* is certainly a *qaṭil* form.[22] Apart from emendations (Jgs. 4:21; 1 S. 18:28; 2 S. 21:15) it is relatively rare (Jgs. 8:15; 2 S. 16:2; Isa. 40:29; 50:4) and undoubtedly derives from *yʿp* I.

c. The Hebrew root *ʿyp* II appears to have developed by metathesis from *yʿp* I.[23] It may have a cognate in the Syriac verb *ʿāp̱*, "be tired."[24] Kaddari's attempt on the basis of Ps. 63:2(1) to associate *ʿyp* II with *ʿyp* I, "be dark,"[25] which appears to be a by-form

---

13 S. Mandelkern, *Veteris Testamenti Concordantiae Hebraicae atque Chaldaicae* (²1955; repr. 1971), 491.

14 Cf. *BLe*, § 490d.

15 H. L. Ginsberg, "An Unrecognized Allusion to Kings Pekah and Hoshea of Israel (Isa 8:23)," *Festschrift B. Mazar. Eretz-Israel*, 5 (1958), 62*, 64*; *KBL*³, 529.

16 Cf. A. Guillaume, "Paronomasia in the OT," *JSS*, 9 (1964), 290; G. R. Driver, "Isaianic Problems," *Festschrift W. Eilers* (Wiesbaden, 1967), 46, 49; H. Wildberger, *Jesaja. BK*, X/1 (1972), 356.

17 *KBL*³, 402.

18 P. 128.

19 E. Kautzsch, *Die Aramäismen im AT* (Halle, 1902), 37; M. Wagner, *Die lexikalischen und grammatikalischen Aramäismen im alttestamentlichen Hebräisch. BZAW*, 96 (1966), 122; *KBL*³, 402.

20 Cf. Meyer, II, 24, § 34.6.

21 Cf. J. A. Montgomery, *Daniel. ICC* (1927), 372; O. Plöger, *Das Buch Daniel. KAT*, XVIII (1965), 133f. Keil and Meinhold take a different approach, retaining "totally exhausted" and letting the phrase refer to Daniel.

22 Meyer, II, 25.

23 Cf. J. Barth, *Die Nominalbildung in den semitischen Sprachen* (²1894; repr. Hildesheim, 1967), 19, § 106; *GesB*, 583.

24 *LexSyr*, 516.

25 Cf. *KBL*², 700.

of ʿwp II (cf. Akk. *upû,* "clouds")[26] and had an original *waw* as its middle radical,[27] is not convincing, because all the evidence suggests that ʿyp II developed by metathesis from *y*ʿ*p* I, preserving an original etymological *yodh.* The same problem affects Kopf's proposal[28] to derive → **תועבה** *tôʿēḇâ* from the double root ʿyp II and *y*ʿ*p* I.

All 5 occurrences of the verbal derivatives of the qal form of the root ʿyp II (Jgs. 4:21; 1 S. 14:28,31; 2 S. 21:15; Jer. 4:31) are disputed. In each instance with the exception of Jer. 4:31, the MT reads *wayyāʿap̱,* which is usually emended to *wayyiʿap̱* (defective writing of *wayyîʿap̱*[29]) and treated as a verbal form of *y*ʿ*p.* Proposed emendations in Jgs. 4:21 include *wᵉʿāyēp̱,* "tired, exhausted,"[30] and *wayyāʿep̱,* "and he fainted."[31] More substantial emendations are *wayyiḡwaʿ,* "and he died,"[32] and *wayyāʿap̱* (from ʿwp), "he twitched convulsively."[33] Others find these conjectures contrived[34] and suggest (more appropriately to the text) *wᵉyāʿēp̱,* "he went to sleep exhausted," i.e., "he went to sleep from exhaustion."[35]

The context makes the MT of 1 S. 14:28 difficult: *wayyāʿap̱,* from ʿyp II, "and the people were faint." Some scholars[36] eliminate the statement as a gloss, others propose substantial emendation: *wᵉyaʿᵃṭōp,* "languish," as part of a curse formula;[37] *wayyāʿaḏ,* "take as witnesses";[38] *wayyôḏaʿ,* "cause to know";[39] *wayyereḇ,* "agree."[40] Since the major versions support the MT, these proposals appear arbitrary. The MT *wayyāʿap̱* can easily be derived from ʿyp II (not with Ehrlich from ʿ*ûp̱,* "fly"), so that the vocalization *wayyîʿap* (from *y*ʿ*p* I) is unnecessary. The words do not appear to belong to the curse formula;[41] they can also be retained as the MT in v. 31 with the meaning "but the people were utterly exhausted" (*wayyāʿap̱*),[42] because the context states that Saul made the people swear not to eat any food (v. 24).

---

26 Cf. *KBL*², 689.

27 Cf. J. Barth, *Etymologische Studien zum Semitischen insbesondere zum hebräischen Lexicon* (Leipzig, 1893), 33.

28 L. Kopf, "Arabische Etymologien und Parallelen zum Bibelwörterbuch," *VT,* 8 (1958), 188f. (= *Studies in Arabic and Hebrew Lexicography* [Jerusalem, 1976], 160f.).

29 Cf. *GK,* § 72t.

30 *BDB,* Moore.

31 Bertheau.

32 Ehrlich.

33 G. R. Driver, "Problems of Interpretation in the Heptateuch," *Mélanges bibliques. Festschrift A. Robert. Travaux de l'Institut Catholique de Paris,* 4 (1957), 74; cf. R. G. Boling, *Judges. AB,* VI A (1975), 98.

34 W. Richter, *Traditionsgeschichtliche Untersuchungen zum Richterbuch. BBB,* 18 (²1966), 48.

35 Keil, Budde, Gray, *BHS.*

36 Wellhausen, Ehrlich.

37 Caspari and others.

38 H. P. Smith, S. R. Driver, Budde.

39 Dhorme.

40 Klostermann.

41 Keil, van den Born, Hertzberg, Stoebe.

42 Cf. H. J. Stoebe, *Das erste Buch Samuelis. KAT,* VIII/1 (1973), 265, 268.

The emendations in 2 S. 21:15 proposed by Wellhausen[43] eliminate the *lectio difficilior* of the MT (*wayyāʿap̱ dāwiḏ,* "and David grew weary") in part on the basis of the LXX, with the suggestion that the name of the Philistine should stand here. His conjecture *wayyāqom dôḏ,* "and Dod rose up," accepted by many[44] but rightly rejected by Ehrlich,[45] is as arbitrary as the proposed *wayyîʿap̱.*[46] On the other hand, Joüon takes *ʿāyēp̱* in 2 S. 17:29 as a perfect.[47]

In Jer. 4:31, the qal perf. *ʿāyᵉp̱â,* which appears without particular difficulty in the statement "my soul is faint before the murderers," has been emended conjecturally to *ʿᵃyēp̱â,*[48] i.e., changed into a feminine adjective. The versions, however, support the MT, and the conjecture is unnecessary.[49]

In short, there seem to be no compelling reasons to eliminate the readings of the MT in these passages and treat the forms otherwise than as derivatives of *ʿyp* II.

d. Like its synonym *yāʿēp̱,* the adj. *ʿāyēp̱,* "tired," is a *qaṭil* form. Whether it is a primary adjective[50] or a derivative of the verb depends on whether one recognizes the existence of a verb *ʿyp* II. Since there are no compelling reasons to reject this root, it seems reasonable to assume that the adjective derives from the verb. This appears to agree with Syriac, in which the adj. *ʿayîfāʾ,* "weary," appears alongside the verb from which it derives.[51]

e. A survey of the semantic relationships between the roots *yʿp* I and *ʿyp* II in Biblical Hebrew and their mutual relationships as well as their meanings in their contexts makes it difficult to come up with a clear definition of their basic meaning. The sense "(be or become) weary" appears to stand in the foreground, giving rise to such meanings as "(be or become) faint," "(be or become) powerless," "(be or become) exhausted."

2. *Statistics and Distribution.* The root *yʿp* I appears in its verbal and adjectival forms in only five of the books of the OT. The verb appears in the qal in three of the literary prophets (4 times in Isa. 40–66, 3 times in Jeremiah, once in Habakkuk); the adjective appears in two historical books (once each in Judges and 2 Samuel) and in Isaiah (twice). The derivatives of *ʿyp* II are distributed among ten of the OT books. The verb appears in the MT of the historical books (4 times) and in one of the literary prophets (Jeremiah); the adjective appears in the Pentateuch (twice in Genesis, once in Deuteronomy), in historical books (twice each in Judges and 2 Samuel), in hymnic poetry (twice in the Psalms), in Wisdom Literature (once each in Job and Proverbs), and in the literary prophets (4 times in Isa. 1–39, once each in Isa. 40–55 and Jeremiah).

---

43 J. Wellhausen, *Der Text der Bücher Samuelis untersucht* (Göttingen, 1871), 210.
44 H. P. Smith, Dhorme, Englert, *et al.*
45 A. B. Ehrlich, *Randglossen zur hebräischen Bibel,* III (repr. Hildesheim, 1968), 331.
46 Cf. W. Caspari, *Die Samuelbücher. KAT,* VII (1926), 649.
47 P. Joüon, "Notes philologiques sur le texte hébreu de 2 Samuel," *Bibl,* 9 (1928), 312.
48 *GesB, KBL*².
49 E. König, *Hebräisches und aramäisches Wörterbuch zum AT* (Leipzig, 1910; ⁶˒⁷1931), 326.
50 Meyer, II, 25.
51 *LexSyr,* 516.

3. *Synonyms.* As a synonym of *'āyēp* in the sense of "tired" we find the adj. *yāgēa'*;[52] in the sense of "exhausted," the semantic nuance conveyed by the verb → תמם *tmm,* "exhausted, be wasted," or the like, is comparable. In one instance (Job 22:7), *'āyēp* seems to have been used instead of → צמא *ṣāmē',* "thirsty" (cf. Job 5:5),[53] although here, too, a nuance of physical fatigue seems to be included.

4. *Dead Sea Scrolls.* The literature from Qumran uses *'yp* in the form of its orthographic variant *''p* (cf. Isa. 50:4)[54] in the context of words that refresh someone who is "tired" (1QH 8:36).[55] If the difficult reading *l'pym* in 1QH 7:10 stands for either *l'ypym*[56] or *ly'pym* and is neither a qal participle of *'wp,* "those who fly,"[57] nor the plural of an Aramaic loanword *'opî,* "branches,"[58] which simply does not yield an intelligible sense, it is a further instance of the word group *y'p* I and *'yp* II. In this case, it would be a statement depicting God as the one who uses the Teacher of Righteousness to lead the "tired" on the right path (cf. Isa. 50:4).[59]

5. *LXX.* The LXX uses a surprising variety of Greek terms to translate the Hebrew roots. The verbal forms of *y'p* I are rendered 4 times (Isa. 40:28,30f.; 44:12) by means of the common term for being hungry, *peinán.*[60] The terms *oligopsycheín,* "be exhausted" (Hab. 2:13),[61] *kopián,* "become tired" (Jer. 2:24),[62] and *ekleípein* (Jer. 51:58[LXX 28:58])[63] are used once each. For the adjective derivative *yā'ēp,* the translators twice chose *eklýein,* a term for being powerless (Jgs. 8:15; 2 S. 16:2), and once *peinán* (Isa. 40:29). The translation *en kairṓ hēníka deí* in Isa. 50:4 does not correspond to the Hebrew text.

The five MT verbal forms of *'yp* II are translated 3 times by *eklýein* (1 S. 14:28; 2 S. 21:15; Jer. 4:31) and once each by *ekpsycheín* (Jgs. 4:21 [LXX^{A}]) and *kopián* (1 S. 14:31). The adjective is rendered once each by *kopián* (Isa. 46:1), *oligopsycheín* (Jgs. 8:4 [LXX^{A}]), *ánydros,* "waterless" (Ps. 143:6[LXX 142:6]), and *ábatos,* "inaccessible" (Ps. 63:2[1][LXX 62:2]), twice by *eklýein* (2 S. 16:14; 17:29), 3 times by *ekleípein* (Gen. 25:29f.; Jgs. 8:5 [LXX^{B}]), and 5 times each by *peinán* (Dt. 25:18; Jgs. 8:4

---

52 → יגע *yāga'.*

53 É. P. Dhorme, *A Comm. on the Book of Job* (Eng. trans. 1967; repr. Nashville, 1984), 328.

54 M. Wallenstein, *The NEẒER and the Submission in Suffering Hymn from the Dead Sea Scrolls. UNHAI,* 2 (1957), *in loc.*

55 Cf. M. Mansoor, *The Thanksgiving Hymns. STDJ,* 3 (1961), 158.

56 G. Jeremias, *Der Lehrer der Gerechtigkeit. StUNT,* 2 (1963), 181, n. 10; S. Holm-Nielsen, *Hodayot: Psalms from Qumran. AcThD,* 2 (1960), 131f., n. 10, etc.

57 T. H. Gaster, *The Dead Sea Scriptures* (Garden City, ^{3}1976), 246.

58 Cf. the translations of Bardtke, Dupont-Sommer, Maier, Lohse, and Ps. 104:12; Wagner, 92f.

59 J. S. Licht, ed., *Megilat ha-hodayot (The Thanksgiving Scroll)* (Jerusalem, 1957) [Heb.], *in loc.*

60 Cf. L. Goppelt, "πεινάω," *TDNT,* VI, 12-22.

61 Cf. D. Lys, "The Israelite Soul according to the LXX," *VT,* 16 (1966), 225.

62 Cf. F. Hauck, "κόπος," *TDNT,* III, 827f.

63 Cf. *BHS,* Segert.

[LXX^B], 5 [LXX^A]; Isa. 5:27; 28:12) and *dipsḗn,* "thirsty" (Job 22:7; Prov. 25:25; Isa. 29:8; 32:2; Jer. 31:25[24][LXX 38:25]).[64] The appearance of these nine Greek terms does not reveal any particular system of translation, but suggests conceptual points of contact and overlap within the group of Hebrew roots. Each occurrence must be examined individually.

II. Semantic Domain.

1. *Physical Usage.* In the early part of the Jacob-Esau cycle in Genesis (Gen. 25:27-34), there appears in the context of of the rivalry between the two brothers a statement about Esau's fatigue brought about by physical exertion while hunting (vv. 29f.), which led him to sell his birthright. In addition to the objective physical tiredness or exhaustion of the individual, there is the physical exhaustion of large groups. The strenuous journey through the desert left all Israel "tired (*'āyēp̱*) and weary" (Dt. 25:18), and those who lagged behind out of weakness fell victim to a vicious attack by the Amalekites (cf. Ex. 17:8-16). Military operations cause real physical weariness and exhaustion to those who engage in them (Jgs. 4:21;[65] 8:4 with *'āyēp̱* and v. 15 with *yā'ēp̱*; 1 S. 14:28,31; 2 S. 16:2 with *yā'ēp̱* and v. 14 with *'āyēp̱*; 17:29 with *'āyēp̱* and v. 2 with *yāḡēa'*; 21:15[66]). By contrast, Isaiah describes the outstanding physical condition of a rapidly advancing army and its constant readiness for battle as follows: "None is weary [for MT *'yp,* 1QIs^a reads the synonymous *y'p,* further evidence for the synonymy of the two adjs.[67]], none stumbles" (Isa. 5:27). Eichrodt comments: "Even if we grant extensive poetic license, such language does not apply to any earthly people, but suggests a superhuman foe that will put an end to Israel."[68]

In a number of passages, it is clear that physical fatigue is occasioned by actual bodily weakness caused by lack of food (Gen. 25:29f.; Jgs. 8:4f.; 1 S. 14:28,31; 2 S. 16:2,14) and/or drink (2 S. 16:2; Job 22:7; Prov. 25:25; Isa. 29:8; 44:12). Here the sequence in 2 S. 17:29—"hungry, weary, thirsty" (*rā'ēḇ*[69] *w^e'āyēp̱ w^eṣāmē'*[70])—is informative, showing that in some contexts "tired" is similar to the other two terms (cf. Job 5:5[71]). The phrase *nep̱eš '^ayēp̱â* in Prov. 25:25 (cf. Jer. 31:25) is more appropriately translated "tired throat"[72] than the traditional "thirsty throat,"[73] because both dust and thirst tire the throat, which is rejuvenated totally by cold water (cf. Isa. 29:8). Isa. 44:12 demonstrates that *y'p* can also refer to someone wearied by thirst; the text, formerly often emended to *'yp,* is now supported by 1QIs^a also.

---

64 Cf. G. Bertram, "διψάω," *TDNT,* II, 227-29.
65 See I.1.c above.
66 See I.1.c above.
67 Contra Ehrlich, IV (repr. 1968), 23.
68 W. Eichrodt, *Der Heilige in Israel, Jesaja 1–12. BAT,* 17/1 (1960), 117.
69 → רעב *r'b.*
70 → צמא *ṣāmē'.*
71 G. Fohrer, *Das Buch Hiob. KAT,* XVI (1963), 357.
72 Cf. W. McKane, *Proverbs. OTL* (1970), 590.
73 B. Gemser, *Sprüche Salomos. HAT,* XVI (²1963), 113.

2. *Figurative Usage.* Ps. 63:2(1) uses the phrase "dry and thirsty [lit., weary] land"; on the masculine form *ʿāyēp̱* following the fem. *ṣiyyâ,* cf. 1 S. 15:9; 1 K. 19:11; Jer. 20:9.[74] The expression is a simile describing the yearning of the praying one, who seeks longingly God's help. Ps. 143:6 states similarly that the worshipper praying for Yahweh's help (cf. Ps. 42:3[2]) yearns for God like a parched land thirsting for water (11QPs[a] reads *bʾrṣ ʿyph*).

Prophetic texts employ the image of a weary, exhausted land.[75] The image of the shadow of a massive rock in a "weary land" (Isa. 32:2) symbolizes the protection and help that, in the coming age of salvation, each will give those in national or social need. Quite different are the images of the hopeful who run or walk toward the future with and through Yahweh, never growing weary (Isa. 40:31).[76] But Jeremiah can represent the daughter of Zion (Jerusalem) symbolically as a woman attacked by murderers, painfully crying out in fear, "Woe is me! My soul is exhausted before murderers" (Jer. 4:31).[77]

3. *Religious Usage.* The exclamation "Give rest to the weary" (Isa. 28:12) provides a summary insight into the Yahweh message found in the prophet Isaiah. The "weary" one (*ʿāyēp̱*) refers not just to "city dweller and peasant"[78] but collectively to every Israelite of Isaiah's time, exhausted by all the chaos of war and exploitation. The motif of giving rest[79] calls on natural and supernatural forces to give the weary rest by bringing about a state of peaceful and wholesome well-being (Isa. 30:15; cf. Ex. 33:14; Dt. 3:20; 12:10; 25:19). In the final analysis, the change in the condition of the weary is a divine act of salvation.

The prophesied deliverance upon Zion (Isa. 29:1-8)[80] is a divine eschatological event, illustrated by the image of a dreamer who "awakes faint, with his thirst not quenched; so shall the multitude of all the nations be that fight against Mount Zion" (v. 8). The futility of the politics of power practiced by the nations, which amass wealth, honor, and security through exploitation and forced labor, is sharply attacked by Yahweh's judgment saying: "Nations weary themselves only for fire" (Hab. 2:13 par. Jer. 51:58; cf. 1QpHab[81]; in Jer. 51:58, most scholars follow M[K455], LXX, Theodotion, and Syr., reading *yîʿāp̱û* instead of MT *wᵉyāʿēp̱û,* which is repeated unnecessarily in v. 64).

Some of the most profound theological statements using our catchwords are found in

---

[74] Cf. also *GK,* § 132d; E. König, *Historisch-comparative Syntax der hebräischen Sprache* (Leipzig, 1897; repr. 1981), §§ 334f.; Kaddari, 354f. Arbitrary emendation like that of M. Dahood, *Psalms II. AB,* XVII ([3]1979), 97, is therefore unnecessary.

[75] Cf. *AuS,* VI (1939), 122f.

[76] See II.3 below.

[77] See I.1.c above.

[78] B. Duhm, *Jesaja. HKAT,* III/1 ([4]1922, [5]1968), 198.

[79] Cf. G. von Rad, "There Remains Still a Rest for the People of God," *The Problem of the Hexateuch and Other Essays* (Eng. trans. 1966; repr. London, 1984), 94-102.

[80] Cf. H.-P. Müller, *Ursprünge und Strukturen alttestamentlicher Eschatologie. BZAW,* 109 (1969), 86-101.

[81] Discussed by K. Elliger, *Studien zum Habakuk-Kommentar vom Toten Meer. BHTh,* 15 (1953), 56; Segert, 452.

Isa. 40–55. Yahweh is the Creator and the Lord of history; he shows himself as one who "does not faint (*yʿp*) or grow weary (*ygʿ*)" (Isa. 40:28). He is therefore an inexhaustible source of strength for the faint (*yāʿēp̄* v. 29), whom he constantly succors. Even youths and young men, the very symbols of robust physical strength, become "faint and weary" (v. 30). Unlike them, those who hope in Yahweh will constantly renew their strength through their God (cf. Ps. 84:8[7]; 103:5): "they shall run and not be weary (*ygʿ*), they shall walk and not faint (*yʿp*)" (Isa. 40:31). The images of running and walking without fatigue show that those who hope are traveling the way with Yahweh (cf. v. 27); their fundamental stance of faith rests on the promise that their strength will constantly be renewed, so that they can always go forward toward the future with confidence. This promise shows that the Lord of history is also Lord of the future of each one who hopes in faith. This notion is very close to the promise in Jer. 31:25 that the "weary soul" will be refreshed and replenished.

The taunt song mocking idols in Isa. 44:9-20[82] presents an enormously stark contrast to the description of the untiring God of Israel in Isa. 40:28-31. Just as the craftsman who makes idols himself grows weak and weary in the process (44:12), so the god he makes can have no attributes superior to those of its maker.[83] Furthermore, the god of the idolator becomes itself a burden in the hour of need (Isa. 46:1).[84] The contrast could not be more pointed: the images of the great gods of Babylon must be carted off in disaster[85] and are only burdens, unable to save; Yahweh, the unimaged God of Israel, has borne his people in the past[86] and will continue to carry, bear, and save them (vv. 3f.). These contrasts furnish their distinctive component of the biblical image of Yahweh's incomparability[87] and represent an essential element of the polemic against idols in the message of Isa. 40–55.

The third Servant Song (Isa. 50:4ff.) states that the servant of God knows he is sent to the weary (*yāʿēp* in v. 4 is to be taken collectively)[88] to sustain them with a word (1QIs[a] and 1QIs[b] support the MT with *lʿwt*).[89] As in Isa. 40:28-31, the weary here appear to include those who hope,[90] i.e., those who do not give up waiting and hoping, those whose

---

82 Cf. J. C. Kim, *Verhältnis Jahwes zu den anderen Göttern in Deuterojesaja* (diss., Heidelberg, 1963), 53-61; H. D. Preuss, *Verspottung fremder Religionen im AT. BWANT,* 92[5/12] (1971), 208-215.

83 Cf. G. A. F. Knight, *Servant Theology. ITC* (1984), 79.

84 C. F. Whitley, "Textual Notes on Deutero-Isaiah," *VT,* 11 (1961), 459, deletes *maśśāʾ laʿᵃyēpâ* as a gloss; but see C. Westermann, *Isaiah 40–66. OTL* (Eng. trans. 1969), 177.

85 Cf. Preuss, 217ff.

86 Cf. J. J. Rabinowitz, "A Note on Isa 46 4," *JBL,* 73 (1954), 237.

87 Cf. C. J. Labuschagne, *The Incomparability of Yahweh in the OT. POS,* 5 (1966).

88 The LXX is discussed in I.5 above. The proposed emendations are arbitary: *ḥānēp,* "the doubting" (Duhm, 379); *ḥōrᵉpay,* "those who despise me" (J. Morgenstern, "The Suffering Servant—a New Solution," *VT,* 11 [1961], 294, 311); cf. H. S. Cazelles, "Les poémes du Serviteur," *RScR,* 43 (1955), 53f.

89 Cf. C. R. North, *The Second Isaiah* (London, 1964), 201; P. E. Bonnard, *Le Second Isaïe. ÉtB* (1972), *in loc.;* contra the many proposed emendations.

90 Contra F. W. Praetorius, "Bemerkungen zu den Gedichten vom Knechte Jahwes," *ZAW,* 36 (1916), 12f.; Cazelles, 54.

relationship to God is exposed to seemingly perpetual danger. With the word that he himself receives from his God, the servant gives to the weary sustaining and life-giving strength.

Hasel

יָעַץ *yāʿaṣ*; עֵצָה *ʿēṣâ*; מוֹעֵצָה *môʿēṣâ*

Contents: I. 1. Etymology; 2. Occurrences. II. General Usage: 1. Qal; 2. *ʿwṣ;* 3. Niphal; 4. Hithpael; 5. *yôʿēṣ*; 6. *ʿēṣâ*; 7. Distribution of *ʿēṣâ* in the OT; 8. *ʿēṣâ*: The Function of Sages? 9. Verbs with *ʿēṣâ*; 10. Phases and Results of *ʿēṣâ*; 11. The Counsel of Ahithophel and the Counsel of the "Old" vs. "Young" Men; 12. Semantic Nuances of *ʿēṣâ*; 13. *môʿēṣâ*; III. Theological Usage: 1. Isaiah and Prov. 19:21; 2. "Counsel"; 3. "Plan"; 4. Isaiah; 5. Deutero-Isaiah; 6. Isaiah Apocalypse; 7. Jeremiah; 8. Ezekiel; 9. Book of the Twelve; 10. Psalms; 11. Job; 12. Chronicler's History. IV. 1. Sirach; 2. Dead Sea Scrolls.

---

yāʿaṣ. P. A. H. de Boer, "The Counsellor," *Wisdom in Israel and in the Ancient Near East. Festschrift H. H. Rowley. SVT,* 3 (1955), 42-71; G. R. Driver, "Mistranslations," *ExpT,* 57 (1945/46), 192f.; J. Fichtner, *Gottes Weisheit. Gesammelte Studien zum AT. ArbT,* 2/3 (1965); *idem,* "Jahwehs Plan in der Botschaft des Jesaja," *ZAW* 63 (1951), 16-33 (= *Gottes Weisheit,* 27-43); J. R. Irwin, *The Revelation of* עצה *in the OT* (diss., Drew, 1965; cf. *DissAbs,* 26f. [1965/66], 7470 A); S. Mowinckel, "Zwei Qumran-Miszellen," *ZAW,* 73 (1961), 297-99; H.-P. Müller and M. Krause, "חָכָם *ḥāḵam* (*chākham*)," *TDOT,* IV, 364-385; G. Schrenk, "βούλομαι," *TDNT*, I, 633-37; H. P. Stähli, "יעץ *jʿṣ* raten," *THAT,* I, 748-753.

I: W. F. Albright, *The Proto-Sinaitic Inscriptions and their Decipherment. HThS,* 22 (1969); W. W. Müller, "Altsüdarabische Beiträge zum hebräischen Lexikon," *ZAW,* 75 (1963), 304-316; M. Wagner, *Die lexikalischen und grammatikalischen Aramaismen im alttestamentlichen Hebräisch. BZAW,* 96 (1966).

II and III: J. Begrich, *Studien zu Deuterojesaja. BWANT,* 77[4/25] (1938) (repr. *ThB,* 20 [1963]); R. Bergmeier, "Zum Ausdruck עצת רשעים in Ps 1 1; Hi 10 3; 21 16 und 22 18," *ZAW,* 79 (1967), 229-232; M. Dahood, "Accusative *ʿēṣāh,* 'Wood', in Isaiah 30,1b," *Bibl,* 50 (1969), 57f.; W. Dietrich, *Jesaja und die Politik. BEvTh,* 74 (1976); G. R. Driver, "Problems of the Hebrew Text and Language," *Alttestamentliche Studien. Festschrift F. Nötscher. BBB,* 1 (1950), 46-61; W. Eichrodt, *Der Herr der Geschichte: Jesaja 13–23 und 28–39. BAT,* 17/2 (1967); J. Fichtner, "Jesaja unter den Weisen," *ThLZ,* 74 (1949), 75-80 (= *Gottes Weisheit,* 18-26); F. Huber, *Jahwe, Juda und die anderen Völker beim Propheten Jesaja. BZAW,* 137 (1976); O. Mury and S. Amsler, "Yahweh et la sagesse du paysan: Quelques remarques sur Esaïe 28,23-29," *RHPR,* 53 (1973), 1-5; J. Pedersen, *ILC,* I–II, 128-133; L. Rost, *The Succession to the Throne of David. Historic Texts and Interpreters,* 1 (Eng. trans., Sheffield, 1982); W. Rudolph, "Jesaja 23,1-14," *Festschrift F. Baumgärtel. Erlanger Forschungen,* ser. A, 10 (1959), 166-174; H. Wildberger, "Die Thronnamen des Messias, Jes. 9,5b," *ThZ,* 16 (1960), 314-332 (= *Jahwe und Sein Volk. ThB,* 66 [1979], 56-74); *idem,* "Jesajas Verständnis der Geschichte," *Congress Volume, Bonn 1962. SVT,* 9 (1963), 83-117 (= *ThB,* 66, 75-109).

IV. D. Barthélemy and O. Rickenbacher, *Konkordanz zum hebräischen Sirach* (Göttingen, 1973); J. Carmignac and P. Guilbert, *Les textes de Qumran,* I (Paris, 1961); J. Carmignac,

I. 1. *Etymology.* The root on which *yʿṣ* is based appears in West Semitic but not in East Semitic. It is found already in Proto-Sinaitic (*yʿẓ*, "advise, give counsel/oracle"),[1] in Arabic (*waʿaẓa,* "admonish, advise, warn"; *wāʿiẓ,* "preacher"; *ʿiẓa,* "sermon, instruction, admonition"; *waʿẓ* and *waʿẓa,* "admonition, sermon, exhortation"),[2] in Old South Arabic (*ʿẓt,* "admonition"),[3] in Punic (*yʿṣ,* "counselor"),[4] in Imperial Aramaic (peal ptcp. *yʿṭ,* "counselor": Ahikar 12; *ʿṭh,* "counsel": Ahikar 28; etc.), in Biblical Aramaic (peal ptcp. *yʿṭ,* "counselor": Ezr. 7:14f.; ithpeal, "take counsel": Dnl. 6:8[Eng. v. 7]; *ʿēṭāʾ*, "counsel": Dnl. 2:14), and in Jewish Aramaic.[5] The cognate Ethiop. *maʿada*[6] is similar. In East Semitic (Akkadian) the verb for "counsel" is *malāku,*[7] which appears as *mlk* II niphal in Neh. 5:7 ("take counsel with oneself"), as well as in Biblical Aramaic in Dnl. 4:24(27) (**mᵉlēḵ,* "counsel").[8]

In Biblical Hebrew, the verb appears in the qal, niphal, and hithpael. The by-form *ʿwṣ* also occurs. Since this latter appears only twice in the imperfect plural (*ʿuṣû*),[9] it might represent instead an erroneous pointing (instead of *ʿᵃṣû*) on the part of the Masoretes, influenced by the Jewish Aramaic by-form *ʿwṣ,*[10] especially since no imperative forms of *yāʿaṣ* occur in the OT.[11] There are 2 nominal derivatives: *ʿēṣâ* and *môʿēṣâ.*

The basic meaning is usually taken to be "advise," but this does not account for the observation that in nearly half (!) of its occurrences the noun *ʿēṣâ* can mean "plan." Apart from the qal participle, which means "counselor," the same is true for the verb: in the qal, there is a rough balance between the meaning "advise" on the one hand and "determine, plan" on the other. The common translation "counsel" (rather than "plan") merely glosses over the difficulty. It would be legitimate only if there were both an objective connection between the two meanings[12] and this connection proved to be etymologically and linguistically probable for *yʿṣ* and *ʿēṣâ.* There is etymological evidence, however, only for the meaning "advise, admonish"/"advice, admonition," not

É. Cothenet, and H. Lignée, *Les textes de Qumran,* II (Paris, 1963); G. Jeremias, *Der Lehrer der Gerechtigkeit. StUNT,* 2 (1963); K. G. Kuhn, Nachträge; E. Lohse, *Die Texte aus Qumran* (Munich, ²1971); J. Maier, *Die Texte vom Toten Meer* (Munich, 1960); M. H. Segal, *Sefer Ben Sira* (Jerusalem, ³1972) [Heb.]; J. Worrell, "עצה: 'Counsel' or 'Council' at Qumran?" *VT,* 20 (1970), 65-74.

1 Albright, 43.

2 Wehr, 1082a.

3 Müller, 310, citing *CIH,* 541, 56, 64, 94, "*admonitio*"; erroneously cited in *KBL*³, 403a, with the meaning "order."

4 *DISO,* 110; but *RÉS,* 906, l. 1, has *yʾṣ*!

5 *KBL*², 1082b; Jastrow, 585a, 1101b; *WTM,* II, 252a: "advise"; pael: "take counsel."

6 *LexLingAeth,* 210: "counsel, exhort, esp. with reference to what the future may bring."

7 *AHw,* II (1972), 593f.

8 See Wagner, no. 170.

9 See below.

10 Cf. Jastrow, 1056a; *WTM,* III, 628b.

11 Cf. *BLe,* § 383: "after the analogy of the ע״ין verbs"; similarly W. Gesenius–G. Bergsträsser, *Hebräische Grammatik,* I (²⁹1918; repr. Hildesheim, 1962), § 26d, n.d.

12 Fichtner, *Gottes Weisheit,* 29: "insofar as a counselor initiates a 'plan' through his 'counsel,' thus prompting a specific 'decision.'"

"intend, determine, plan"/"purpose, plan." Did the root in Biblical Hebrew undergo a unique semantic development?

Although it is correct to say that Isaiah was the first to use *ʿēṣâ* for Yahweh's "(historical) plan,"[13] it is unlikely that the usage that speaks of Yahweh's plan in general derives from this prophet, not to mention the use of *ʿēṣâ* with the meaning "plan." Both meanings of *ʿēṣâ* are found in early proverbial literature; in Prov. 19:20f., they even occur in two adjacent proverbs (v. 20: "advice"; v. 21: Yahweh's "plan"). In Jgs. 20:7, which is traditio-historically early,[14] the context shows clearly that *ʿēṣâ* (par. *dāḇār*) does not mean "counsel" but denotes the "plan" that, in the words of the Levites, the Israelites assembled at Mizpah are to "come up with" (*hāḇû lāḵem dāḇār weʿēṣâ halōm*). Even 2 S. 16:20, where the same formula or idiom occurs, *can* at least be taken in this sense.[15]

Even more noteworthy is the fact that in the literarily early framework of the Balaam narrative (Nu. 24:14 [J]) the qal of *yāʿaṣ* can have the meaning "utter an oracle," which Albright[16] furthermore notes as a meaning of the root in the Proto-Sinaitic inscriptions.[17] It is therefore quite possible that the original meaning of *yāʿaṣ* was "utter an oracle." Since people seeking advice would make use of the oracle, the root could take on the meaning "advise" and the person uttering the oracle could become an "adviser"; the substance of the oracle, the revealed *plan* of the deity for the future, could become "advice," in that it would show the correct course of action in accord with the plan of the deity. This hypothesis at least does justice to the importance evidence of Nu. 24:14.

In this case Isaiah, by using *ʿēṣâ* regularly in the sense of "purpose, plan," would be hearkening back to the original meaning of the noun, in the sense that a divine "plan" was revealed in the oracle. Since there is no clear evidence for use of the verb to mean "determine, plan" before Isaiah (!), this meaning would accordingly not be original, but would derive from the noun ("plan"). Thus the semantic development would be: "utter an oracle" > "give/receive advice" > "plan." The meaning "advise" would then (contra Irwin) not be secondary to that of "conceive a plan." We must probably follow Irwin, however, in taking the primary meaning of *ʿēṣâ* to be "plan" rather than "advice."

2. *Occurrences.* The verb *yʿṣ* occurs 57 times in the OT in the qal (22 of which are the act. ptcp. as a technical term for "adviser" or "counselor"), 22 times in the niphal, and once in the hithpael. The by-form *ʿwṣ* occurs twice (Jgs. 19:30; Isa. 8:10). Of the nominal derivatives, *ʿēṣâ* occurs 86 times and *môʿēṣâ* 7 times. Not counting the 4 occurrences in Aramaic passages, the root occurs a total of 175 times in the OT. This

---

13 See III below.
14 Irwin, 57-61.
15 Cf. *ibid.*, 63f.
16 See above.
17 Cf. already F. H. W. Gesenius, *Lexicon manuale hebraicum et chaldaicum in Veteris Testamenti Libros* (Leipzig, 1833) [Lat.], 432: "predict, announce what is to come; Num. 24, 14. Jes 41,28"; also *LexHebAram,* 319, citing Arab. *waʿaẓa,* "in the broader sense, announce something to someone with authority in order to give counsel, with the accusative of the person and thing: Nu 24,14."

does not include the occurrences of ʿēṣâ II, "disobedience, rebellion" (Ps. 13:3[2]; 106:43),[18] or ʿēṣâ III, "wood" (Jer. 6:6).

The occurrences are distributed very unevenly, being concentrated primarily in Isaiah (36, of which 27 are in Isa. 1–35), 2 Chronicles (19), 2 Samuel, Psalms, and Proverbs (17 each), Jeremiah (13), and 1 Kings and Job (12 each), so that eight OT books account for 80 percent of the occurrences. In view of the root's meaning, it is remarkable that only 29 occurrences (scarcely 17%) are in Wisdom Literature (Job, Proverbs).

II. General Usage.

1. *Qal.* When the 22 occurrences of *yôʿēṣ* as a technical term are omitted, we are left with 35 occurrences of the qal. Of these, only 5 appear in narrative (2 S. 16:23; 17:7; 1 K. 12:8 [par. 2 Ch. 10:8], 13); the other 30 appear in direct discourse or (like Prov. 12:20) wisdom aphorisms. The occurrences in direct discourse include words of Jethro (Ex. 18:19), Balaam (Nu. 24:14), Hushai (2 S. 17:11,15), Ahimaaz and Jonathan (2 S. 17:21), Nathan (1 K. 1:12), Jeremiah (Jer. 38:15), the psalmist (Ps. 16:7; 62:5[4]), and Job (Job 26:3), as well as 18 instances of Yahweh's words, all (except for Ps. 32:8) in prophetic discourse (10 in Isaiah, 3 in Jeremiah, plus 2 Ch. 25:16; Ezk. 11:2; Mic. 6:5; Hab. 2:10). This surprising observation is explained in part by the fact that in the 17 prophetic passages (beginning with Isaiah) *yāʿaṣ* does not mean "advise" but "plan," whereas in 16 of the other passages (excluding Nu. 24:14: "proclaim [the future]"; Ps. 62:5[4]: "plan") it means "advise."

The following constructions deserve notice: *yāʿaṣ* introducing direct discourse (2 S. 17:11); with *lᵉ*, "advise someone" (Job 26:3); with the accusative of the person, "advise or counsel someone" (Ex. 18:19; 2 S. 17:15; Jer. 38:15). There is frequent use (11 times) of the *figura etymologica*[19] *yāʿaṣ ʿēṣâ*, 5 times meaning "give advice" (4 with double acc.: "give advice to someone" [1 K. 1:12; 12:8 (par. 2 Ch. 10:8), 13]) and 5 times meaning "plan" (4 having Yahweh at least as the logical subj. [Isa. 14:26 (pass.); 19:17; Jer. 49:20; 50:45]). With only a single exception (Isa. 32:8), *yāʿaṣ* in the sense of "plan" has negative connotations, which are underlined by the use of the conjunctions *ʾel* and *ʿal*, "against" (*ʾel*: Jer. 49:20; 50:45; *ʿal*: Isa. 7:5; 14:26; 19:12,17; 23:8; Jer. 49:30). As the object planned we find *rāʿâ*, "evil" (Isa. 7:5); *ʿᵃṣaṯ-rāʿ*, "evil plan" (Ezk. 11:2); *zimmâ*, "wicked devices" (Isa. 32:7); *bōšeṯ*, "shame" (Hab. 2:10); and the infinitive constructions *lᵉhaddîaḥ*, "to thrust down" (Ps. 62:5[4]) and *lᵉhašḥîṯeḵā*, "to destroy you" (2 Ch. 25:16).

The distribution of the Hebrew "tenses" of *yʿṣ* is also interesting. The vast majority of occurrences of the finite verb involve the x-*qāṭal* tense, used for making direct statements. Only 4 times (each 1st person sg.) do we find the x-*yiqṭōl* form, which indicates a certain future: once in the introduction to an oracle (Nu. 24:14), twice in the introduction to advice (Ex. 18:19; 1 K. 1:12), and once in a temporal subordinate clause with conditional overtones (Jer. 38:15). Only once each do we find the forms *qāṭal*-x (Hab. 2:10) and *yiqṭōl*-x (Ps. 32:8; 1st person sg.). There are also 3 instances of qal

---

18 *KBL*², 726f.; cf. Driver, *ExpT*, 57 (1945/46), 192f.

19 Cf. *GK*, § 117p.

participial forms, 3 active (2 verbal [Isa. 19:17; Ezk. 11:2] and 1 substantival [Prov. 12:20: *yōʿaṣê šālôm*]) and 1 passive (Isa. 14:26: *hāʿēṣâ hayyeʿûṣâ*). Remarkably, the narrative tense is not found.

2. *ʿwṣ*. The by-form *ʿwṣ* qal appears in only 2 passages (Jgs. 19:30; Isa. 8:10), with the meaning "conceive a plan," each time in the imperfect plural (*ʿuṣû*). Like *yʿṣ*,[20] *ʿwṣ* can appear in *figura etymologica* with the cognate object *ʿēṣâ* (Isa. 8:10); the same situation may have obtained originally in Jgs. 19:30.[21] In Jgs. 19:30, there are positive connotations to "framing a plan" (cf. also Jgs. 20:7), whereas the connotations in Isa. 8:10 are negative. Mere advice is not the point of either passage: the Levite to whom the original text of Jgs. 19:30 probably assigned the words[22] is not looking for mere advice but for a concrete plan to avenge the crime of the people of Gibeah.

3. *Niphal*. The niphal relates to the meaning "advise" of the qal. The reflexive sense "seek advice for onself" appears only once (Prov. 13:10); the reciprocal sense "take counsel together" predominates. Only in 1 passage (1 K. 12:28) do we find the meaning "take counsel with oneself." In 4 passages (1 K. 12:6,9 [par. 2 Ch. 10:6,9]) the meaning is "recommend after consultation,"[23] with emphasis on the result of the consultation; in this specific instance, the presence of a superior authority (King Rehoboam) allows only advice, not a decision. Only in 1 passage (2 Ch. 30:23) is the meaning clearly "decide"; this meaning is no more appropriate to 1 K. 12:28 than to 2 Ch. 25:17; 30:2; 32:3.[24]

The niphal of *yʿṣ* is used with a great variety of prepositions: *yaḥdāw*, "together with" (Isa. 45:21; Ps. 71:10; 83:6[5] [+ *lēḇ*]; Neh. 6:7); *ʾēṯ* (1 K. 12:6,8 [par. 2 Ch. 10:6,8]; Isa. 40:14); *ʿim* (1 Ch. 13:1; 2 Ch. 32:3); *ʾel* (2 K. 6:8; 2 Ch. 20:21). It can also be followed by a finite verb (1 K. 12:28; 2 Ch. 25:17) or by an infinitive, whether it means "decide" (2 Ch. 30:23) or "take counsel" (2 Ch. 30:2; 32:3). The latter usage suggests that the consultation has as its subject matter a plan that can become a firm decision with the agreement of all concerned, especially the authorities (cf. 2 Ch. 30:4; 32:3). A following finite verb (1 K. 12:28; 2 Ch. 25:17) indicates that the consultation has resulted in a decision.

The niphal of *yʿṣ* can be used in both positive and negative senses. Positive usage appears in 1 K. 12:6 (par. 2 Ch. 10:6); 1 Ch. 13:1; 2 Ch. 20:21; 30:2,23; 32:3; negative usage in 1 K. 12:8,9 (par. 2 Ch. 10:8,9), 28; 2 K. 6:8; 2 Ch. 25:17; Neh. 6:7; Ps. 71:10; 83:6(5); Isa. 45:21.

Syntactically, the narrative tense predominates (13 occurrences). The asseverative past (x-*qāṭal*) appears twice (Ps. 71:10; 83:6[5]), the optative future (x-*yiqṭōl*) once (Isa. 45:21). There are also 6 verbal constructions with the participle indicating simultaneity (sg.: Isa. 40:14; pl.: 1 K. 12:6,9 [par. 2 Ch. 10:6,9]; Prov. 13:10).

---

20 See above.
21 Cf. *BHK*^{3}, *BHS, in loc.*
22 Cf. *BHK*^{3}, *BHS, in loc.*
23 *KBL*^{3}, 403a.
24 Contra *KBL*^{3}, 403a.

4. *Hithpael.* The reciprocal sense "take counsel together" can also be expressed by the hithpael (Ps. 83:4[3]). In this single passage and interestingly also in the single occurrence of *yʿṭ* ithpael (Dnl. 6:8[7])—a negative accent is heard: in each case, the subject is enemies who "take counsel together" against the devout or the worshippers of Yahweh (like Daniel). In Dnl. 6:8(7), the result is a request to the king. In both passages the reflexive stem of *yʿṣ/yʿṭ* suggests conspiracy.

5. *yôʿēṣ.* The qal ptcp. *yôʿēṣ* occurs 23 times, including the conjectured *yôʿᵃṣāyiḵ* in Isa. 47:13.[25] It always involves the meaning "advise, counsel." Like Aram. *yāʿēṭ* in Ezr. 7:14f., it has acquired more or less the nature of a technical term for "counselor" or "adviser." A semantic development is clearly observable. The wise are convinced that "in an abundance of counselors" (*bᵉrōḇ yôʿēṣ*) there is safety (Prov. 11:14; 24:6). The first passage clearly refers to political advisers (e.g., of a king). The originally political meaning of Prov. 11:14 is shifted to the private sphere by the identical words in 24:6: "war" (v. 6a) is now a metaphor for "the battle of life."[26] Yet another passage in the book of Proverbs (Prov. 15:22) speaks of a multitude of counselors: "Without counsel (*sôḏ*) plans (*maḥᵃšāḇôṯ*) go wrong, but with many advisers (*bᵉrōḇ yôʿᵃṣîm*) they succeed." Since Proverbs never speaks elsewhere of a single counselor, the preference of the sages for "an abundance of counselors" is all the more significant, especially since the masterdisciple relationship would naturally make us think of the sages as individualists. But instead of finding success in the advice of a single sage, they recommend consulting "an abundance of counselors," who obviously (as in Prov. 15:22) assemble for "counsel" or to form a "council" (*sôḏ*).

Of course, as the advice of Ahithophel (2 S. 16:20-23; 17:1-3) shows, an individual can also give advice, i.e., propose a plan. Such advice, however, at least according to the passages from Proverbs, does not absolutely guarantee success (cf. the advice of Hushai in 2 S. 17:5-14, which is, to be sure, deliberately misleading). The plan advised by a single individual will not miscarry, however, if it is approved in a "consultation" involving "an abundance of counselors" (Prov. 15:22). It is therefore not absolutely necessary that the "counselors" who gather in "council" themselves have a plan to propose as their counsel. Their primary function is to arrive at a positive or negative decision about a plan. When a plan is under discussion, it is clearly important that as many "counselors" or "advisers" as possible be involved (Prov. 15:22; cf. 11:14; 24:6), else the plan can miscarry. The account in 2 S. 17, where contradictory advisers give contradictory advice, could almost be read as a cautionary tale illustrating Prov. 15:22.

The 3 passages from Proverbs reveal two further points about the nature of a *yôʿēṣ*. The term *yôʿēṣ* ("adviser") does not in the first instance designate an official function; any competent and experienced male could act as *yôʿēṣ* in a specific case. He need not necessarily belong to the class of "sages"; it is hard to imagine that in a specific case a private individual (cf. Prov. 24:6!) could have had recourse to "an abundance" of sages as counselors.

---

25 *KBL*[2], 390a; *KBL*[3], 385b.

26 Cf. Gemser, *in loc.*

The first official "counselor" mentioned is Ahithophel, David's adviser, who went over to David's rebellious son Absalom (2 S. 15:22) and became the latter's personal adviser (cf. 2 S. 15:34; 16:20-23; 17:1-23). According to the Chronicler, David had his own uncle Jonathan as "counselor" (1 Ch. 27:32) in addition to Ahithophel, whose place was taken by Jehoiada, the son of Benaiah (1 Ch. 27:34). Hushai appears instead as the king's "friend" (2 S. 16:16; 1 Ch. 27:33), probably a position of trust. The Chronicler likewise states that the queen mother Athaliah served as "counselor" (*yô'eṣeṯ*) to her son Ahaziah (2 Ch. 22:3). She and other members of his house became for the young king "counselors to his undoing" (2 Ch. 22:4; cf. v. 3). These latter (except for the queen mother) do not appear, however, to have functioned as official royal counselors. The existence of such an office is also assumed by 2 Ch. 25:16, where King Amaziah says to a prophet of Yahweh who appears uninvited: "Have we made you a royal counselor?" Perhaps this passage reveals one of the Chronicler's biases: prophets of Yahweh are spurned, and as a result poor advisers are allowed to function within the Davidic court, to its downfall. The Chronicler does not reject the office of royal counselor in itself, as the example of David's uncle Jonathan shows (1 Ch. 27:32). In addition, Zechariah, a gatekeeper toward the end of David's reign, is rather surprisingly called a "shrewd counselor" (1 Ch. 26:14), an expression that can hardly refer to official office. The Chronicler also emphasizes that the Davidic kings, when faced with important decisions, took counsel (for good or ill) with the men surrounding them and even with the people as a whole (*y'ṣ* niphal: 2 Ch. 10:8f.; 25:17 [for ill]; 1 Ch. 13:1; 2 Ch. 10:6; 20:21; 30:2; 32:3 [for good]).

Isaiah implies that the office of counselor in Jerusalem and Judah antedates his own period (Isa. 3:3). The counselor is named with other officials (such as judges, prophets, elders, and men of rank) and representatives of a variety of seemingly indispensable or influential professions, whether serious or trivial (such as mighty men, soldiers, diviners, magicians, and experts in charms); they are referred to collectively as "stay and staff," i.e., the guarantors of social and political order in the human world—wrongly, as the oracle in Isa. 3:1-7 reveals. Yahweh, whose support people have forgotten, will remove these false props (v. 1). Similar statements appear in Isa. 19:11 with reference to the "wise counselors of Pharaoh," in Deutero-Isaiah (Isa. 47:13) with reference to the counselors of Babylon, and in Mic. 4:9 with reference to the counselors of Zion.

The mention of counselors in immediate conjunction with the (somewhat dubious) magicians in Isa. 3:3 might suggest that Isaiah was rejecting the office of counselor. This is by no means the case. According to Isaiah's oracle in Isa. 1:24-26, after the judgment upon Jerusalem Yahweh will restore the judges of that city as at the first and its counselors (councils) as at the beginning (v. 26). By "beginning" Isaiah clearly means the period of David, when the office of royal counselor (Ahithophel!) was of the utmost importance to the monarchy and the state. Something similar is expected for the counselor of the eschaton. Thus in Isaiah the office of counselor takes on eschatological overtones.

Like Isaiah and the later prophets already mentioned, Job also bears witness to God's power over the (mighty) counselors (Job 12:17). The fascination in which they were held by ordinary citizens can also been seen in the words of the very same Job (3:14), who would like to exchange his wretched life for the rest they enjoy in Sheol.

The word *yô'ēṣ/yā'ēṭ* appears for the first time as a clear term for a formal office in Ezra (Ezr. 4:5; 7:28; 8:25; cf. 7:14f.). Ezr. 4:5 speaks of the venality of the Persian king's counselors, who used the enemies of the Jews to frustrate the rebuilding of the temple. The few passages of clearly theological significance (Isa. 9:5[6]; 41:28) will be discussed in greater detail below.

6. *'ēṣâ*. Two of the 86 occurrences of *'ēṣâ* I are to be rejected: in Isa. 47:13, *yô'aṣāyiḵ* (*yô'ēṣ*) should be read,[27] and in Prov. 27:9 probably *'aṣṣeḇeṯ*.[28] The conjectural emendation *'aṣbô* in Hos. 10:6,[29] however, is not convincing, since the MT yields good sense.[30]

Semantic ambiguity is characteristic of *'ēṣâ* ("advice" or "plan"); the two meanings appear with roughly equal frequency in the total number of passages (84). The picture changes at once, however, when we consider the narrative and poetic passages in isolation. In the poetic and prophetic passages, "plan" dominates "advice" by roughly two to one. Only Proverbs is exceptional, where 7 passages have the meaning "advice" (Prov. 1:25,30; 8:14; 12:15; 19:20; 20:18; 21:30) and only 2 the meaning "plan" (19:21; 20:5). In narrative (nonprophetic) texts, the meaning "advice" occurs 22 times; the meaning "decision, purpose, plan" is found only 5 times with some assurance (Jgs. 20:7; Ezr. 4:5; 10:8; Neh. 4:9[15]; 1 Ch. 12:20[19]). Here the ratio is roughly four to one.

7. *Distribution of 'ēṣâ in the OT.* The distribution of *'ēṣâ* between the poetic/prophetic portions of the OT on the one hand and the narrative portions on the other is itself interesting. Of the total of 84 occurrences, only 27, roughly one third, appear in narrative texts outside the prophetic books. The noun *'ēṣâ* is thus a term associated with poetic literature. Of these latter 57 occurrences, 9 each appear in Proverbs and Job, again roughly one third; there are 11 occurrences in the nonapocalyptic sections of Isa. 1–35 and 4 additional occurrences in Isa. 40–66, for a total of 15. The noun *'ēṣâ* also appears frequently (8 times) in Jeremiah, but much less often in the other prophetic books (twice in Ezekiel, once each in Hosea, Micah, and Zechariah). With 28 occurrences, therefore, *'ēṣâ* appears much more frequently in the prophets than in Wisdom Literature (18 occurrences). The ratio shifts somewhat in favor of Wisdom when one realizes that of the 9 occurrences in Psalms, 5 are in psalms that are influenced by Wisdom (Ps. 1:1; 33:10f.; 73:24; 119:24). Even so, however, prophetic texts predominate over Wisdom Literature (28 occurrences to 23). In a certain sense, the evidence specific to *'ēṣâ* confirms our general observations about the occurrences of *y'ṣ* and its derivatives.[31] Even though there is a certain association of *'ēṣâ* with Wisdom Literature, our findings are surprising.

8. *'ēṣâ: The Function of Sages?* If, as is usually assumed, *'ēṣâ* and *y'ṣ* were typical

---

27 See above.

28 B. Gemser, *Sprüche Salomos. HAT,* XVI (²1963), *in loc.*; *KBL*², 726b.

29 Cf. *KBL*², 726b.

30 Cf. de Boer, 49f.; H. W. Wolff, *Hosea. Herm* (Eng. trans. 1974), *in loc.*

31 See I.2 above.

examples of Wisdom terminology, it would be hard to account for the statistical evidence. This relationship is all the more surprising, since the often-cited passage Jer. 18:18 seems to prove the opposite: "For the law shall not perish from the priest, nor counsel from the wise, nor the word [of revelation] from the prophet." Do these words not establish the prerogatives of counsel for "the wise," the sages who, as a class, were established relatively late in comparison with the priests and the prophets? Can this really apply to those who composed Wisdom proverbs (cf. Prov. 22:17; 24:23) or those who collected such proverbs, the "men of Hezekiah" (Prov. 25:1)? If so, it would be very strange that the authors of Prov. 10–29 came to speak only 3 times of the source, function, and meaning of "counsel" (*ʿēṣâ*: Prov. 12:15; 19:20; 21:30; cf. also 22:22 [*môʿēṣâ*]) and in 3 other passages of a human or divine "plan" (*ʿēṣâ*: 20:5,18; 19:21). Prov. 21:30 even denigrates the importance of human counsel: "No wisdom, no understanding, no counsel can avail against Yahweh." Strange "sages" indeed who so downplay the significance of their most important task, the giving of counsel and advice! Their emphasis on the need to have an abundance of advisers if successful decisions are to be made (Prov. 11:14; 15:22; 24:6: all the instances of *yôʿēṣ* as a technical term in the book of Proverbs) points in the same direction, as does the total absence of *yʿṣ* as a finite verb in Proverbs (in Prov. 12:20 we find only the ptcp. in the construct phrase *yôʿᵃṣê šālôm*).

This also puts Ezk. 7:26b in a new light: "They seek a vision from the prophet, but the law perishes from the priest, and counsel from the elders." At first glance, the "sage" in this triplet of offices appears to have been replaced by the "elders" (*zᵉqēnîm*),[32] especially since the Ezekiel passage draws on the beginning of Jer. 18:18. Fichtner has suggested[33] that "the 'sages,' influential and diplomatically important in the preexilic period, had exhausted their energies and left the field to the elders," assuming of course that the elders had previously played a less significant role.

The reality of the situation is probably rather different. It is true that the "elders" (*zᵉqēnîm*) to whom Rehoboam turns for advice in 1 K. 12:6-8 should not be taken as official representatives of the tribes of Israel; but they could very well—in the service of the king—have taken the place of the tribal elders, who ceased to be consulted during the absolute monarchy of Solomon (cf. v. 6: "who had stood before Solomon his father"). In the narrative of the Davidic succession, we are told that the "elders of Israel" passed favorable judgment on the counsel of Ahithophel (2 S. 17:4; cf. v. 15). Already in the time of David, therefore, it was their duty to judge the quality of advice given by a royal counselor! Both cases involve *political* advice, for which one would better turn to people who, like the "elders" in the time of David or the elders at the court of Rehoboam—or even the elders in the days of Ezekiel—were more familiar before the destruction of Jerusalem with affairs of state than to the "wise," whose primary duty was training future officials.

Even Jer. 18:18 fits in this context. The three groups mentioned are to be understood as enemies "united in their common hatred of Jeremiah."[34] Unlike the officials beholden

32 → זָקֵן *zāqēn*.

33 P. 77 = *Gottes Weisheit*, 21; cf. also Stähli, 751f.

34 W. Rudolph, *Jeremia. HAT*, XII (³1968), 125.

to King Jehoiakim, the temple priesthood, and the cult prophets, the nonpolitical sages had no vital interest in eliminating Jeremiah. Jer. 18:18 probably refers to them hyperbolically as "the wise" because they had been through the school of their Wisdom teachers and could draw on the experience of these sages in reaching their decisions.

We may conclude, therefore, that in the OT period "giving counsel" was the task of political officials who had been trained in Wisdom, not of the "sages" as such, who were not directly concerned with concrete political decisions. There is no evidence that they were consulted like oracles in specific cases. Their relationship to the real political world, where good advice and good advisers were important, was only indirect, since they had charge of training future officials. Only for this reason, then, did they occasionally find it necessary to speak of (political) "counsel" in their proverbs. This understanding of the *zᵉqēnîm* as those responsible for giving *ʿēṣâ,* developed above all by Irwin, makes it necessary to revise at least in large part the standard theory "that the root *yʿṣ* belongs in the realm of Wisdom."[35] The role played by "advice" and "advisers" in the Proverbs of Ahikar[36] cannot be cited as evidence to the contrary, for Ahikar, "the wise and skillful scribe . . . , the counselor of all Assyria,"[37] is not represented as an ordinary sage but as a high state official. In this role he functions as "counselor." Ahikar's "wisdom," which in that relatively early work of Wisdom Literature is understood to be a prerequisite for such office, obviously is intended to serve as an example for the sages' disciples, who were themselves seeking political office. Only in this sense is there an affinity between the root *yʿṣ* and wisdom or Wisdom Literature, an affinity already suggested by the appearance in the semantic field of *yʿṣ* of the roots *byn, ḥkm, śkl,* and their derivatives. It was the task of "the wise" (as a professional class) to theorize about "advice" and "advisers," but not to be available as advisers in specific cases. The latter function was most likely performed by a different professional class, the "elders," whose education probably qualified them to be called "wise" in the *broader* sense of the word (cf. Jer. 18:18).

Unlike the revelation of the divine plan through seers like Balaam (cf. Nu. 24:14!), the advising done by the elders is to be understood as a secular function. To interpret *ʿēṣâ* as a term for revelation after the analogy of the prophetic *dāḇār*[38] is to overinterpret Jer. 18:18; Ezk. 7:26. Furthermore, Irwin overlooks the fact that, in contrast to the prophetic *dāḇār, tôrâ* as specific "instruction" on the part of the priests (Jer. 18:18; Ezk. 7:26) could hardly have been a term for revelation. In later times, it is true, the entire *tôrâ* was considered to have been revealed to Moses; but concrete priestly *tôrâ* is to be understood as the application of priestly sacral traditions to specific cases. The two passages under discussion mention the three groups together not because they were thought to be (in varying degree) bearers of revelation, but because they were most influential in the political arena. If the giving of *ʿēṣâ* originally had anything to do with revelation of a

35 Stähli, 751.
36 See I.1 above.
37 Ahikar 1f.; *AOT,* 454.
38 Irwin, 199, etc.

divine *plan,* the reference here is not to the institution of the "elders" but to the ancient system of seers and oracles (cf. Balaam!). At best, one may think of the "elders" charged with giving advice as secular "successors," trained in the school of the wise, to seers like Balaam. The revelation of a divine plan would then have been replaced by communication of appropriate human advice, arrived at with the help of wisdom, not divine revelation. Ahithophel, the official counselor of David and later of Absalom, was a kind of secular seer, for his contemporaries ascribed to his counsel the significance of a (prophetic) oracle (2 S. 16:23).

9. *Verbs with ʿēṣâ.* In discussing the usage and meaning of *ʿēṣâ,* it is instructive to examine the verbs with which it appears as object. There are no fewer than 21 of them. Of these, 4 can be used with both meanings ("advice" and "plan") of *ʿēṣâ: yāʿaṣ,* "advise," "decide" (11 times in *figura etymologica,* as discussed above); *yhb,* "give, present" (only pl. impv. *hāḇû*: Jgs. 20:7 [a plan]; 2 S. 16:20 [advice]); *šāmaʿ,* "hear" (Prov. 19:20 [advice]; Jer. 49:20; 50:45 [Yahweh's plan]); *prr* hiphil, "frustrate" (2 S. 15:34; 17:14 [Ahithophel's advice]; Ps. 33:10; Ezr. 4:5; Neh. 4:9[15] [a plan or plans]).

Three verbs take *ʿēṣâ* as an object only with the meaning "advice": *ʿāzaḇ,* "forsake," i.e., "not follow" (1 K. 12:8,13 [par. 2 Ch. 10:8,13] [the advice of the elders: subj. Rehoboam]); *pāraʿ,* "ignore" (Prov. 1:25 [the advice of Wisdom]); *skl* piel, "make foolish" (2 S. 15:31 [Ahithophel's advice: subj. Yahweh]).

There are 14 verbs that take *ʿēṣâ* as object only with the meaning "plan." Of these, 7 have human beings as the subject; in the case of the other 7, God or Yahweh is the subject. The first group comprises: *ʿûṣ,* "decide" (Isa. 8:10); *bôʾ* hiphil, "get" (Isa. 16:3 [*Q*]); *str* hiphil, "hide" (Isa. 29:15); *bôš* hiphil, "confound" (Ps. 14:6 [the plans of the poor]); *bîn,* "understand" (Mic. 4:12 [Yahweh's plan]); *ḥšk* hiphil, "darken" (Job 38:2 [= 42:3] [God's plan: subj. Job]); *nʾṣ,* "spurn" (Ps. 107:11 [the plan of the Most High]).

The second group, with Yahweh as subject, comprises: *blʿ* piel, "confound" (Isa. 19:3 [Egypt's plan]); *bqq,* "make void" (Jer. 19:7 [the plan of Judah and Jerusalem]); *yāḏaʿ,* "know" (Jer. 18:23 [the murderous plans of Jeremiah's enemies]); *mlʾ* piel, "fulfill" (Ps. 20:5[4] [the plans of the Davidic king]); *šlm* hiphil, "accomplish" (Isa. 44:26 [the plan announced by Yahweh's messenger]); *ʿāśâ,* "bring about" (Isa. 25:1 [a wonder of planning:[39] subj. Yahweh]; Isa. 30:1 [a plan that does not come from Yahweh:[40] subj. the people of Judah]); *plʾ* hiphil, "have wondrous plans," "prove oneself wondrous in plans" (Isa. 28:29).[41]

10. *Phases and Results of ʿēṣâ.* The passages cited illustrate the following phases and results of advice: it is "advised" (*yāʿaṣ*) or given (*yhb*); it may be "heard" (*šāmaʿ*), "ignored" (*pāraʿ*), or "forsaken" (*ʿāzaḇ*). A third party, human or divine, may also "frustrate" someone's advice (*prr* hiphil).

---

39 Cf. *BHK*³, *BHS;* in the MT, *ʿēṣôṯ* is the direct object.

40 Needlessly read by Dahood, 57f., as an archaic accusative of *ʿēṣ,* "wooden idol."

41 Cf. *KBL*², 726b, contra *KBL*², 760a; for additional discussion, see Mury-Amsler.

The range of possibilities is even richer with respect to the phases and results of a plan. It may be "determined" or "decided" (*yāʿaṣ, ʿwṣ*); it may also be "presented" (*yhb*), "gotten" (*bôʾ* hiphil), "understood" (*bîn*), or "known" (*yādaʿ*). It may be "hidden" from a third party (*str* hiphil), "carried out" (*ʿāśâ*), or "accomplished" (*šlm* hiphil), for example when God "fulfills" it (*mlʾ* piel). But a plan can also be "spurned" (*nʾṣ*) or "confounded" (*bôš* hiphil), not to speak of being "confounded" (*blʿ hiphil*), "laid waste" (*bqq*), or "frustrated" (*prr* hiphil) by Yahweh.

11. *The Counsel of Ahithophel and the Counsel of the "Old" vs. "Young" Men.* Like a plan, advice can either succeed or fail—the latter often not for internal reasons but because a third party, human or divine, intervenes.

How this can happen when advice is given is illustrated by the two narratives that focus on the different outcomes of two such incidents: 2 S. 16:15–17:23 and 1 K. 12:1-19 (par. 2 Ch. 10:1-19).

The similarity of the two stories is immediately apparent: in both cases poor advice supplants good advice, although only in the case of Hushai's advice to Absalom (2 S. 17:5-14) is there malicious intent. The story of the Davidic succession (2 S. 9–20; 1 K. 1f.), in which Ahithophel's double advice (2 S. 16:20-22; 17:1-4) and Hushai's counterproposal constitute the focus of a crucial episode (2 S. 16:15–17:23), was probably known to the author of 1 K. 12:1-19 within the framework of the Deuteronomistic history;[42] but the literary dependency is probably not so great that this author could have used "the actual events of this still familiar but nevertheless 'private' and possibly even 'naive' narrative"[43] to invent the contradictory advice of the "old men" and the "young men." The differences between the two stories are too great. In each case Absalom requests advice from a single individual: Ahithophel the Gilonite (2 S. 15:12), David's former official adviser, who had gone over to Absalom's side, and Hushai the Archite (2 S. 15:32-37; 16:15-19), David's "friend," who was only feigning his shift of allegiance. The contradictory advice of each in turn is accepted by the king's son and the "elders of Israel" (2 S. 17:4; cf. vv. 1-3) or Absalom and "all the men of Israel" (2 S. 17:14; cf. vv. 5-13). Rehoboam, on the other hand, asks the advice of the "old men" and the "young men" (1 K. 12:6-11), i.e., two groups of advisers. On the surface, it seems that in each case the king accepts the advice that flatters him the most. Hushai flatters Absalom the military leader, who can already see himself at the head of a victorious army of all Israel (cf. 2 S. 17:11-13). The "young men" similarly flatter the boastful and ambitious Rehoboam (cf. 1 K. 12:11 [par. 2 Ch. 10:11]). The narrators, however, see Yahweh's governance of history at work here: it is Yahweh who saw to it that Ahithophel's wise advice was not followed, because he had already determined Absalom's downfall (2 S. 17:14). David's prayer that Yahweh would turn the advice of Ahithophel into foolishness (2 S. 15:31; cf. 1 K. 22:20-23) was answered; and Hushai, whom David had sent to Absalom for this purpose, thus served as the instrument of both

---

42 Cf. Rost, 136-38 (= *Das kleine Credo,* 242ff.).

43 M. Noth, *Könige 1–16. BK,* IX/1 (1968), 270.

David and Yahweh. The foolish advice of the "young men" served likewise in Rehoboam's case to realize a prophetic oracle of judgment against the house of David (1 K. 12:15 [par. 2 Ch. 10:15]). Human advice is subordinate to the divine plan of history. To overstate the case: in the last analysis, Hushai's advice was accepted and acted upon not because it was appealing but because it was in conformity with Yahweh's plan; the same is true of the advice given by the "young men" to Rehoboam. Whether or not a plan is successful depends on whether or not it agrees with Yahweh's plan. Thus both narratives, which seem to speak in quite secular terms of contradictory advice, carry overtones of theological notions articulated explicitly above all in Isaiah but also in Prov. 19:21.[44]

12. *Semantic Nuances of ʿēṣâ.* There are several points to be made with regard to the semantic nuances of *ʿēṣâ*. In the realm of "advice," when used in parallel with *ʾimrê-ʾēl* (Ps. 107:11), *tôkaḥaṯ* (Prov. 1:25,30), or *mûsār* (Prov. 19:20), it can take on the sense of "admonition." In some passages, where it occurs in parallel with *ḥokmâ* or *tᵉḇûnâ,* what is involved is not so much advice as the ability to discover the proper ways and means (Prov. 21:30; Jer. 49:7; less certainly Dt. 32:28; Job 12:13).[45]

Isa. 19:11 calls "the wise counselors of Pharaoh" *ʿēṣâ niḇʿārâ,* "stupid counsel," using abstract for concrete ("counsel" for "counselors").[46] The emendation *ḥakmê parʿōh yāʿᵃṣû ʿēṣâ niḇʿārâ*[47] has little support, not least because the qal and niphal of *bāʿar* are used exclusively of persons.[48] Bergmeier proposes similarly to take the abstract expression *ʿᵃṣaṯ rᵉšāʿîm* (Job 10:3; 21:16; 22:18; Ps. 1:1), usually translated "counsel of the wicked" (Ps. 1:1) or "plan of the wicked" (Job), concretely in the sense "company of the the wicked." It is questionable, however, to base a translation on the relatively late and restricted usage of the Qumran community (discussed in IV below) and simply disregard the 4 other OT passages with *hālaḵ bᵉʿēṣâ* (2 Ch. 22:5) or *bᵉmôʿēṣâ* (Ps. 81:13[12]; Jer. 7:24; Mic. 6:16). These very passages show that *hālaḵ bᵉʿēṣâ* means "follow some specific counsel or decision." Neither can we ignore the climactic progress in Ps. 1:1 noted by Kraus[49] (→ *hālaḵ* → *ʿāmaḏ* → *yāšaḇ*): the "company," one might say, is not reached until the third stage, the *môšaḇ lēṣîm.* Furthermore, "follow the company of the wicked" would not really fit the imagery of Ps. 1:1. The 3 passages from Job are textually and literarily too problematic (glosses?) to cast further light on Ps. 1:1. Bergmeier[50] translates Job 21:16: "Do they not have their prosperity in their own hand, is the company of the wicked not far from him?" The argument presented elsewhere by Job or the author of the book would lead us rather to expect: "Is (the avenging) God not far from the wicked?" It is therefore correct to retain the traditional rendering of *ʿēṣâ* as "advice,

---

44 See III below.
45 *GesB,* § 610b.
46 Cf. B. Duhm, *Jesaja. HKAT,* III/1 (⁴1922, ⁵1968), 143.
47 Noted in *BHS* and accepted by O. Kaiser, *Isaiah 13–39. OTL* (Eng. trans. 1974), *in loc.*
48 Cf. Duhm.
49 H.-J. Kraus, *Psalms 1–59* (Eng. trans., Minneapolis, 1987), 115.
50 P. 231.

counsel" or (in the Job passages) "plan." In Ps. 1:1, however, it is reasonable to understand *ʿaṣaṯ rᵉšāʿîm* more precisely as "the maxims or ethical principles of the wicked."[51]

In the sense of "plan," *ʿēṣâ* can take on the specific meaning "decision." This is true, for instance, when *ʿēṣâ* is the result of deliberation (cf. Ezr. 10:8). In 1 Ch. 12:20(19), *bᵉʿēṣâ* is used almost adverbially in the sense of "purposely";[52] there is no reason to find a reference to asking a sage for advice.[53] The phrase *ʾîš ʿēṣâ* can mean not only "adviser, counselor" (Isa. 40:13; Ps. 119:24) but also—when "plan" is the underlying meaning—"man of the plan," i.e., the one who carries out or performs a function in a plan (Isa. 46:11). Another construct phrase with specialized meaning is *ʿaṣaṯ šālôm* (Zec. 6:13), which can be interpreted as either "agreement in plans"[54] or (in a weakened sense) "peaceful understanding."[55]

Like the verb *yāʿaṣ,* the noun *ʿēṣâ,* whether it means "decision, plan" or "advice," does not belong to the purely intellectual sphere. This is suggested by the phrase *ʿēṣâ ûgᵉḇûrâ,* "counsel and strength," which occurs 3 times (2 K. 18:20 [par. Isa. 36:5]; Isa. 11:2; cf. Job 12:13). In the first passage it is the opposite of *dᵉḇar śᵉp̄āṯayim,* "mere words." In Isa. 29:15, similarly, *ʿēṣâ* stands in parallelism with *maʿaśeh,* "work," and in Prov. 8:14 with *tûšiyyâ,* "success." Pedersen rightly says with respect to this specific element of *ʿēṣâ*: "It means that the carrying into effect is the normal expansion of the counsel. Therefore counsel and action are identical."[56] De Boer, Kaiser, and Irwin have accepted Pedersen's view.[57]

13. *môʿēṣâ.* The noun *môʿēṣâ* appears 7 times in the MT, always in the plural. Only once (Prov. 22:20) does it mean "advice"; elsewhere it always means "plan, decision," with universally negative overtones. With only 2 exceptions (Jer. 7:24; Prov. 22:20), it appears with 3rd person plural suffixes. There are 3 occurrences of the formulaic expression *hālaḵ bᵉmôʿaṣôṯ,* "follow (evil) decisions" (Ps. 81:13[12]; Jer. 7:24; Mic. 6:16). Prov. 22:20 also uses the prep. *bᵉ* with *môʿēṣâ*; 3 other passages (Ps. 5:11[10]; Prov. 1:31; Hos. 11:6) use *min.* Oddly, *môʿēṣâ* never appears as subject or as accusative object.

Even more than *ʿēṣâ, môʿēṣâ* is a favorite term of poetic and prophetic literature; it is not found in narrative. Only in Prov. 22:20 does it appear in a nontheological context. Once it occurs in an individual lament, in a petition against the enemies of the psalmist (Ps. 5:11[10]). It occurs 4 times in oracles (Ps. 81:13[12]; Jer. 7:24; Hos. 11:6; Mic. 6:16) and once in the words of divine Wisdom (Prov. 1:31)—a total of 5 times in the mouth of a nonhuman speaker. Hos. 11:6 and Mic. 6:16 are prophetic judgment discourse; the

---

51 *GesB,* § 610b; cf. Kraus, 116.
52 *KBL*², 726b.
53 De Boer, 54.
54 *GesB,* § 610b.
55 *KBL*², 726b.
56 P. 129.
57 De Boer, 56; O. Kaiser, *Isaiah 1–12. OTL* (Eng. trans. ²1983), 255f.; Irwin, 192f.

closely related passages Jer. 7:24 and Ps. 81:13(12) are prophetic invective based on a theological interpretation of history. All the passages except Prov. 22:20 associate *môʿēṣâ* directly or indirectly with God's judgment—even Prov. 1:31, which threatens punishment for rejecting the counsel of Wisdom. The wicked are punished not only for their (evil) "plans" (Hos. 11:6) but also in such a way (Ps. 5:11[10]) that they fall "through" their own evil plans; their punishment can even consist in having to be sated with their "plans" (Prov. 1:31, par. "the fruit of their way"). In Ps. 5:11(10), *môʿēṣâ* has overtones of malice. In Mic. 6:16, the personal suffix refers to the house of Omri and Ahab, whose (evil) decisions have been followed by the inhabitants of Zion. An element of stubbornness can be noted in Jer. 7:24; Ps. 81:13(12), where *šᵉrîrûṯ libbām* appears as a parallel term.

The MT of Hos. 11:6 (*mimmōʿᵃṣôṯêhem,* "on account of their plans") is disputed, since the motivation of the judgment oracle seems to be an afterthought, in conflict with v. 5 and not really appropriate to the context, where one would expect a further punishment (like that stated in v. 6a). But the various emendations proposed in the comms. (most recently Rudolph: a garbling of *maʿᵃśōṯêhem* from *maʿᵃśâ,* "preparation") are even less satisfactory, since they involve major alterations in the text. It is more attractive to follow Driver[58] in his conjecture of a previously unattested noun *maʿᵃṣâ,* "disobedience,"[59] so that the text would mean "for their disobedience." Driver[60] finds this noun also in Ps. 81:13(12). Since, however, "on account of their plans" fits the context of Hos. 11:6,[61] the MT should probably be retained (cf. also Hos. 10:6).

On the other hand, *lᵉmô ʿᵃṣāṯî* in Job 29:21 is often emended to *lᵉmôʿᵃṣāṯî,*[62] a reading found in many manuscripts. There is no compelling reason, however, to accept the conjectural emendation, although many support it.[63] Furthermore, the prep. *lᵉmô* as a longer poetic form of *lᵉ* appears in 3 other passages in Job (and only there): Job 27:14; 38:40; 40:4; it has cognates in other West Semitic languages (Ugaritic and Amorite).[64] If we disregard the special case of Prov. 22:20, *môʿēṣâ* in Job 29:21 would have a positive sense that it does not have in its other 6 occurrences. Finally, the fact that *môʿēṣâ* appears elsewhere only in the plural (even in Prov. 22:20, where it means "advice") argues against the emendation. The variant reading of the manuscripts is probably best explained as an inadvertent combination of two words either orally or in writing, which led in turn to a pointing based on *môʿēṣâ.*

In Isa. 41:21, Begrich[65] has proposed emending *ʿᵃṣumôṯêḵem* to *môʿᵃṣôṯêḵem,* postulating on the basis of the context an additional meaning of *môʿēṣâ* ("proof"). This emendation has little to recommend it: it is unclear how the meaning "proof" could develop out of "advice" or "plan." Furthermore, *ʿᵃṣumôṯêḵem* is appropriate, with the

---

58 *Festschrift F. Nötscher,* 54.
59 Cf. *ʿēṣâ* II, discussed in I.2 above.
60 *Festschrift F. Nötscher,* 54.
61 Wolff, 200.
62 E.g., G. Hölscher, *Das Buch Hiob. HAT,* XVII (^{2}1952), *in loc.*
63 *KBL*^{2}, 504b; *KBL*^{3}, 529b; Stähli, 751.
64 *KBL*^{3}, 505b, with bibliog.
65 P. 44; cf. now also *KBL*^{3}, 529b.

meaning "your strong ones" in the sense of "your arguments,"[66] so that no emendation is needed. *BHS* therefore omits the conjectural reading still found in *BHK*[3] on the basis of the Peshitta, whose rendering is best explained as deliberate alteration of a Hebrew word no longer understood by the translators of the Syriac version.

On the other hand, an emendation of *ba'ᵃṣûmāyw* in Ps. 10:10 to *bᵉmô'ᵃṣōṯāyw* deserves serious consideration,[67] since "through his plans" is much more appropriate to the context, dominated by verbs referring to malicious conduct, than is the reading of the MT ("through his [use of] violence"?). The emendation also fits the negative connotations of *mô'ēṣâ,* "plan," and the standard usage of prepositions with this noun. Finally, the entire MT of Ps. 10:10 is corrupt.

III. Theological Usage.

1. *Isaiah and Prov. 19:21.* Fichtner's study of Yahweh's plan in the message of Isaiah shows that Isaiah, as the first of the writing prophets, came to speak of Yahweh's plan and developed a corresponding theology. This insight on Fichtner's part must not be generalized to mean that *y'ṣ* "was first used theologically by Isaiah."[68] The theologically significant statement about Yahweh's "plan" (*'ēṣâ*) in Prov. 19:21 must not be overlooked or treated as having been influenced by Isaiah: "Many are the plans (*maḥᵃšāḇôṯ*) in the mind of a man, but it is the plan of Yahweh (*'ᵃṣaṯ YHWH*) that will be established." Of course this proverb does not provide grounds for thinking of an historical plan on the part of Yahweh like that in Isaiah's message, but it can be understood to mean a divine providence that can interact with human plans. The sages were well aware of Yahweh's plan and the discrepancy between human plans and the plan (or decision) of Yahweh. A similar idea appears in Prov. 21:30f., as well as in Gen. 50:20 (the Joseph story). If Isaiah was trained among the sages, as Fichtner has suggested convincingly in his essay, it is even easier to understand his repeated prophetic references to Yahweh's (historical) plan, which is clearly universal. As we have seen,[69] the sages themselves had precursors who spoke implicitly of a divine plan: seers like Balaam, who revealed to Balak, the Moabite king, the future of his people in an oracle from Yahweh (Nu. 24:14: *yā'aṣ!*).

2. *"Counsel."* The noun *'ēṣâ* appears in theological contexts with both meanings: "counsel, advice" and "plan, decision." The same is true of the verb *yā'aṣ* (*yô'ēṣ*). It is noteworthy, however, that the meaning "counsel" for both verb and noun is relatively rare in theological contexts. The earliest text is undoubtedly 2 S. 17:14. Here the author of the history of the Davidic succession (2 S. 9–20; 1 K. 1f.) gives the theological reason why Ahithophel's undoubtedly superior advice did not prevail over the advice of Hushai, which was to be fateful for Absalom (and Ahithophel!): "Yahweh had ordained to defeat (*prr* hiphil) the good counsel of Ahithophel, so that Yahweh might bring evil upon

66 Cf. *KBL*², 728b; also C. Westermann, *Isaiah 40–66. OTL* (Eng. trans. 1969), 81, as well as *GesB,* § 611b.

67 Gunkel, Kraus, *in loc.*; *KBL*², 504b; *BHK*³; cf. *BHS*.

68 Stähli, 752.

69 See II.8 above.

Absalom." What appears superficially to be a clever intrigue on the part of Hushai, indirectly occasioned by David himself—war carried on by other, underground means—is understood theologically to be the earthly manifestation of a mysterious divine providence, a concrete act of historical intervention on the part of Yahweh. As most commentators emphasize, the defeated Ahithophel may well have committed suicide because he saw clearly that Absalom's cause (and his) was lost after Hushai's advice was accepted (2 S. 17:23); from the historico-theological perspective of the narrator, however, this was merely the final result of the fact that Ahithophel's plan was brought to nought by Yahweh himself, who thus demonstrated his superiority to the cunning adviser of kings and princes. Both the wise counsel of Ahithophel and the counselor himself were defeated by Yahweh, who governed the fate of David, his chosen king.

The tragic fate of Ahithophel and his famous counsel, later realized to be correct (cf. 2 S. 17:14), were long remembered in Israel. Perhaps it lies behind Prov. 21:30, which is probably the next earliest text and may or may not antedate Isaiah: "No wisdom, no understanding, no 'counsel' can avail against Yahweh." The best and wisest counsel, the counsel of Ahithophel, was doomed to failure in the face of Hushai's appealing but basically foolish counsel, because Yahweh willed it so.

It is therefore easy to understand why Isaiah expects that in the age of salvation Yahweh will give the king *rûaḥ ʿēṣâ ûgᵉḇûrâ* (Isa. 11:2; cf. Prov. 8:14). The parallel noun *gᵉḇûrâ* makes it clear that Isaiah is not thinking of *ʿēṣâ* that remains in the realm of theory but of *ʿēṣâ* that leads to acts of power (cf. 2 K. 18:20 [par. Isa. 36:5]). He means the God-given ability that enables the king to find ways and means to carry out his purposes,[70] not the ability to advise others. The throne name *peleʾ yôʿēṣ* of the expected king (Isa. 9:5[6]) could be understood as "who (himself) knows wonderful counsel" (cf. Mowinckel:[71] "the wonderfully endowed ruler, who always 'knows counsel'") rather than "who counsels wonders."[72] Probably, however, Isaiah's preference for *ʿēṣâ* in the sense of "plan" means that we should follow Wildberger[73] in accepting the translation "who plans wonders." In practice there is little difference. And since this king will enjoy the charisma of this mighty "counsel" (or better: "plan"), which is in conformity with the will of Yahweh, he will not fail like an Ahithophel (or an Absalom). Of course the prophet was probably thinking primarily of the title *yôʿēṣ* borne by the kings of Judah (cf. Mic. 4:9)—often, as he was to discover, with no basis in fact. In a similar vein, he promises in an oracle that, after a purifying judgment (Isa. 1:25), Yahweh will once against restore to Jerusalem "counselors" as at the beginning (v. 26: *yōʿᵃṣayiḵ*).

Isa. 19:11, possibly not from Isaiah but quite in agreement with his thought, calls "the wise counselors of Pharaoh" a "stupid counsel" (*ʿēṣâ niḇʿārâ*; cf. also vv. 3,12). According to Isa. 3:3, a threat that is authentically Isaianic, Yahweh will remove from Jerusalem and Judah the "counselors" (*yôʿēṣ*) along with other officials and dignitaries (cf. also Job 12:17).

---

70 See the discussion of Jer. 49:7; Prov. 21:30 in II.12 above.

71 Mowinckel, 298.

72 *KBL*³, 386a.

73 P. 316.

In Jeremiah, too, in an oracle against Edom (Jer. 49:7-22), Yahweh asks ironically (v. 7; cf. v. 8) whether the prudent there have lost the gift of "counsel," i.e., the ability to recognize that Edom is ripe for judgment and to draw the appropriate conclusions (such as the need to take flight). An oracle of Ezekiel (Ezk. 7:26) states that in the last phase of Jerusalem's downfall counsel (*'ēṣâ*) perishes from the "elders" (*z^eqēnîm*) of Judah—those who by virtue of their office, so to speak, are responsible for giving counsel in political questions (cf. also Jer. 18:18).[74]

Deutero-Isaiah speaks no more of Yahweh's counsel than does his great prototype Isaiah, although he speaks all the more of Yahweh's plan.[75] He makes it clear nevertheless that there is no one Yahweh need "consult" (Isa. 40:14: *yā'aṣ* niphal). Furthermore, among the (so-called) gods there is none able to "counsel" him (41:28: *w^e'ên yô'ēṣ*), i.e., address and answer him.[76] The "survivors of the nations," however, must take counsel together (*yā'aṣ* niphal), i.e., those who have escaped from a Babylon already seen as fallen, in order to understand their desperate situation, brought about by Yahweh (45:21). Babylon cannot be helped by many "counselors" (47:13: conj. *yô'^aṣayik*[77]).

When human counsel fails, who can give counsel? In Jer. 32:19, a later writer reinterpreting Jeremiah's prayer (32:17-25)[78] gives a clear answer: Yahweh alone is great in counsel (*'ēṣâ*) and mighty in deed (*'^alîliyyâ*). A similar statement appears in Job 12:13 (*'ēṣâ* par. *t^eḇûnâ*), after Job has just questioned the wisdom of the aged (v. 12). In general, later Wisdom passages speak with some frequency of God's counsel, or more precisely the counsel of (divine) Wisdom. Personified Wisdom says of herself in Prov. 8:14: "I have 'counsel' (*'ēṣâ*) and 'help' (*tušiyyâ*), I have 'insight' (*bînâ*) and I have 'strength' (*g^eḇûrâ*)." According to Prov. 1:25,30, on the other hand, people have ignored or refused the "counsel" of Wisdom. In contrast to them stands the wise and devout poet of Ps. 119, who states in v. 24 that Yahweh's testimonies are his delight and his "counselors" (*'anšê '^aṣāṯî*). Two passages in the Psalter speak of counsel given directly to the petitioner. In Ps. 32:8, the psalmist cites a divine promise that he obviously has received in the form of a priestly oracle of salvation:[79] "I will 'instruct' (*śkl* hiphil) you and 'teach' (*yārâ* hiphil) you the way you should go; 'I will counsel [you]' (*'î'^aṣâ*), my eye is upon you." Ps. 16:7a appears also to allude to such an oracle: "I bless Yahweh 'who gives me counsel' (*y^e'āṣānî*)." According to Kraus,[80] this counsel consists in Yahweh's showing the psalmist the path of life (v. 11).

In Ps. 83, a communal lament, the verb *y'ṣ* (hithpael and niphal) appears twice with clearly negative meaning. "Against thy people they lay a 'crafty plan' (*sôḏ*), 'they consult together' (*y'ṣ* hithpael) against thy protected ones" (v. 4[3]). As v. 6(5) shows, this conspiracy is directed against God (or Yahweh) himself: "For they [the gentile nations]

74 See II.8 above.
75 See below.
76 Westermann, *in loc.*
77 Cf. *KBL*³, 385b.
78 Rudolph, *HAT,* XII, 211.
79 Cf. Kraus, 371.
80 *Ibid.,* 241.

'conspire with one accord' (*yʿṣ* niphal, *lēḇ yaḥaḏ*); against thee 'they make a covenant' (*kāraṯ bᵉrîṯ*)." A specific historical reference is most unlikely. What is recorded here is rather the article of faith, well supported by the evidence of Israel's history, that the very existence of God's people is constantly threatened by other nations. Israel's understanding of itself as God's people leads it to interpret this threat also as a threat against Yahweh.

3. *"Plan."* The focus of theological usage of *yāʿaṣ* and its derivatives rests indisputably in the meaning "determine, plan." Of the 27 passages that speak of the plan of Yahweh or God, more than half (15) are in the book of Isaiah (verb: Isa. 14:24,26,27; 19:12,17; 23:8,9; noun: 5:19; 14:26; 19:17; 25:1; 28:29; 44:26; 46:10,11). These passages are concentrated in Isa. 1–39. In 11 additional passages, 3 of which are in Isaiah, human "plans" (verb or noun) are associated directly with Yahweh (Neh. 4:9[15]; Job 5:13; 10:3; 22:18 conj.; Ps. 33:10; Isa. 19:3; 29:15; 30:1; Jer. 18:23; 19:7; Nah. 1:11 [*yôʿēṣ*]). Finally, 8 additional occurrences of *yʿṣ, ʿwṣ,* and *ʿēṣâ* in the writing prophets speak of human plans in the context of a divine oracle (*yʿṣ*: Isa. 9:5[6]; Jer. 49:30; Ezk. 11:2; Hab. 2:10; *ʿwṣ*: Isa. 8:10; *ʿēṣâ*: Isa. 8:10; Jer. 49:30; Ezk. 11:2; outside of oracles, cf. also Isa. 16:3; Hos. 10:6).

Outside the writing prophets, the *yʿṣ* and *ʿēṣâ* of human beings associate with God or Yahweh in only 8 passages (2 Ch. 25:16; Neh. 4:9[15]; Job 5:13; 10:3; 22:18 conj.; 38:2 [par. 42:3]; Prov. 19:21). Since we may assume that these passages with only one exception (Prov. 19:21) were influenced by the writing prophets, it is appropriate to speak in the case of *yāʿaṣ* and *ʿēṣâ* of typically prophetic semantic variations, but not—at least in the case of *ʿēṣâ* (cf. Prov. 19:21!)—of language created by Isaiah. It is quite conceivable that Isaiah was the first to take the step from *ʿēṣâ* ("plan") to *yāʿaṣ* in the sense of "determine, plan," doing so in the service of his special kerygma concerning the plan(ning) of Yahweh. His point of departure, both linguistically and theologically, could well have been the experience of the sages articulated in the the dictum of Prov. 19:21.[81] Of course he could also have arrived at the new usage of *yāʿaṣ* via the royal title *yôʿēṣ* ("the one who gives counsel"; cf. Mic. 4:9), thanks especially to his experience in the temple, where he had a vision of Yahweh as king (Isa. 6:3). But it is dubious to conclude on the basis of Jer. 49:20; 50:45 (*yāʿaṣ ʿēṣâ*) not only that it was a traditional royal prerogative and duty to frame a plan,[82] but that this planning was already expressed by *yāʿaṣ* even before Isaiah, since the 2 Jeremiah passages could have been influenced by Isaianic usage and the royal title in Mic. 4:9 does not yet have such a specialized meaning.

4. *Isaiah.* Even in the early phase of Isaiah's ministry the notion of Yahweh's plan played an important role in his preaching. We may come to this conclusion on the basis of an invective against Isaiah's detractors among his own people (Isa. 5:18f.), to which the commentators assign an early date.[83] It contains an apposite quotation from the words

---

81 See III.1 above.

82 H. Wildberger, *Jesaja. BK,* X/1 (1972), 189.

83 Cf. Kaiser, Wildberger.

of the scoffers: "Let him make haste, let him speed 'his work' (*maʿaśēhû*) that we may see it; let the 'plan' (*ʿēṣâ*) of the Holy One of Israel draw near" (v. 19). According to Wildberger, the "plan" that is mocked refers to Yahweh's governance of history, "to the extent that it involves Yahweh's judgment against his people."

When Isaiah speaks of human plans in connection with Yahweh (Isa. 7:5; 8:10; 29:15; 30:1), he always has in mind intentions and actions that oppose Yahweh's plan or at least are not shared by Yahweh. Therefore these human plans are bound to fail when they encounter Yahweh. The evil plan (*yāʿaṣ . . . rāʿâ*) of Aram (and Ephraim) against King Ahaz and Judah (Isa. 7:5) is doomed to failure: "It shall not stand, and it shall not come to pass" (v. 7b). Isaiah says something similar in the oracle against the nations (8:9f.; genuineness disputed), which may be dated in the early period of the Syro-Ephraimite war:[84] "'Frame a plan' (*ʿuṣû ʿēṣâ*), but it will come to nought; 'make an agreement' (*dabbᵉrû dāḇār*), but it will not stand, for God is with us" (v. 10). The plan devised by the nations against Jerusalem and Judah is bound to fail, because Yahweh is in league with Jerusalem and Judah.

But even the plans of the authorities in Jerusalem and Judah must fail if they are contrary to Yahweh's historical plan. Isa. 29:15; 30:1 bring us to the period of the anti-Assyrian revolt against Sennacherib led by Hezekiah (703-702 B.C.). The woe oracle 29:15f. is directed at those "who hide deep from Yahweh their 'plan' (*ʿēṣâ*), whose 'deeds' (*maʿaśeh*) are in the dark" (v. 15). This secret plan that is contrary to God's will is also the theme of the woe oracle in 30:1-5: "Woe to the rebellious children—an oracle of Yahweh—who carry out a 'plan' (*ʿēṣâ*), but not mine, who pour out a libation, but without my spirit, that they may add sin to sin" (v. 1).[85] Verse 2 defines this plan more precisely as the policy, doomed to failure, of making alliance with Egypt.

In the context of Isaiah's message, these passages present a problem: it would seem that only Yahweh's plans for judgment and disaster upon his people and the nations are inevitable and bound to defeat human plans, whereas Yahweh's plans for salvation for Jerusalem and Judah can be "crossed" by human actions. What is left of the conclusion to the prophet's parable of the peasant (Isa. 28:23-29; authenticity disputed): "He [i.e., Yahweh] is wonderful in his plan, excellent in his success" (v. 29b[86])? What are we to think of the effectiveness of Yahweh's wisdom as depicted by this parable, wisdom which Mury and Amsler describe by saying that Yahweh "is no less wise, no less inventive, no less skillful than a peasant. His action in history is no less confusing in its diversity than the various operations demanded by agriculture. But it is no less effective precisely because, like these operations, it varies according to the particular times and circumstances in order to achieve its purpose"?[87]

The solution probably lies along the lines suggested by Dietrich:[88] "When Yahweh has said 'No,' there are no longer any 'ifs' or 'buts.' The situation is quite different when

---

84 Cf. Wildberger, *BK*, X, *in loc.*, with bibliog.
85 Following Kaiser's translation.
86 Cf. Mury-Amsler, 2.
87 *Ibid.*, 5.
88 P. 242.

Yahweh's 'No' to one nation means 'Yes' to another. Such promises remain irrevocably in force only when those concerned act according to the promise." This does not indicate vacillation on the part of Yahweh, as Dietrich emphasizes in the same passage: "To think so would indicate a failure to see that, according to Isaiah, Yahweh never plans disaster against anyone without cause; there is always antecedent human sin, i.e., abuse of the freedom to choose between right and wrong." Although "Yahweh always plans disaster in response to previous human misconduct, he never plans salvation as a response to antecedent right conduct."[89] Assyria's conquest of Israel is due to Israel's sin, not Assyria's merit; similarly, the promise of salvation to Judah (Isa. 7:4-9; cf. v. 7b) is rooted in the evil plans of Aram and Ephraim (cf. v. 5), not in the virtuous conduct of Judah and Ahaz.[90]

The degree to which Isaiah's theologoumenon of "Yahweh's plan" influenced the prophet's "school" can be seen in the frequency with which other parts of the book of Isaiah use *yāʿaṣ* and *ʿēṣâ* theologically in the sense of "plan." Before turning our attention to Deutero-Isaiah, we shall examine the other occurrences in Isa. 13–23. The chapters in question (Isa. 14, 19, 23) are today held by some (e.g., Kaiser) to be totally inauthentic, by others (e.g., Wildberger) to derive only in part from Isaiah.

The first and third sections (vv. 1b-4, 11-15) of the prophecy against Egypt (Isa. 19:1-15) are relevant here; according to Wildberger,[91] both may be Isaianic. Intervening in history, Yahweh empties out the spirit (*rûaḥ*) of the Egyptians and confounds their plans (*ʿēṣâ*) (v. 3). The confusion of Egypt's "plans" (or better: "planning") results in a general sense of helplessness, articulated in the need to consult idols and the spirits of the dead. Pharaoh's wisest counselors are at a loss (cf. v. 11). Thus the prophet can ask ironically (v. 12): "Where then are your wise men? Let them tell you and make known what Yahweh of hosts 'has determined' (*yāʿaṣ*[92]) against Egypt." What is new is that Yahweh's "plan" no longer affects either directly or indirectly segments or political divisions of the people of God. It has become a pure historical plan directed against a foreign nation; the text at least makes no mention of Judah or Jerusalem. In addition, Yahweh's plan serves to put the foreign sages to shame (v. 12). In a first supplement to this oracle against Egypt (vv. 16f.), a later hand has constructed a remarkable association between Yahweh's "plan" against Egypt and the land of Judah (v. 17): "The mere mention of this land will provoke terror, because it will recall immediately the irrevocable decision of Yahweh of hosts."[93] If this interpretation is correct, v. 17 must be considered in part a correction of v. 12, where the wise (i.e., the political advisers of the country) are incapable of understanding the substance of Yahweh's plan against Egypt (i.e., the course of history). In v. 17, however, mention of the land of Judah makes the Egyptians tremble in fear at Yahweh's plan. They know that irrevocable disaster with Yahweh as its source threatens them or has already overtaken them.

---

89 *Ibid.,* 243.
90 Cf. *ibid.*
91 *BK,* X, 704-8.
92 Following Kaiser's translation.
93 Wildberger, *BK,* X, 732.

The prophecy of disaster against Assyria on the basis of Yahweh's irrevocable decision (Isa. 14:24-27) bears clearer marks of Isaianic authorship than Isa. 19, although Kaiser[94] disputes its authenticity also. Duhm[95] and Wildberger[96] date the passage in the time of Sennacherib's invasion of Judah (701). We are told 3 times (Isa. 14:24,26f.) that Yahweh has "determined" (*yā'aṣ*) his "plan" (*'ēṣâ*). Yahweh's historical plan for Assyria is irrevocable. Significantly, it will be realized "in my land" (v. 25), i.e., in Judah. This plan extends to more than Assyria: it is "purposed concerning the whole earth" (v. 26). This probably means that the plans for world dominion of Assyria, which was once Yahweh's instrument (cf. Isa. 10:7-11) but has grown arrogant through misunderstanding its function, will be shattered in Judah, Yahweh's land. It is an overreading to find in Isa. 14:26 a universal plan of world history or "the establishment of a new order over the nations";[97] Yahweh's planning is "guided by each particular hour of history."[98]

Despite the opinion of Rudolph[99] and Eichrodt[100] to the contrary, it is unlikely that Isaiah was the author of the oracle over desolate Phoenicia (Isa. 23:1-14), which speaks of Yahweh's plan against Tyre (vv. 8f.). The entire section gives the impression of being a retrospective lament rather than a prophecy. In addition, the alternation of question and answer in vv. 8f. has cultic overtones (cf. Ps. 24:3f.,8,10). The author interprets the catastrophe that has befallen Tyre (Isa. 23:5-11) as the realization of what Yahweh "planned" (*yā'aṣ*) against that city. The passage distantly recalls Isa. 19:11-15, except that in ch. 19, as is typical of Isaiah, Yahweh's plan destroys the (political) wisdom of Egypt (cf. vv. 11f.), whereas in ch. 23 it destroys the glory and renown of the Phoenician trade center (vv. 8f.).

5. *Deutero-Isaiah.* In the context of the Cyrus oracle in Isa. 44:24–45:7, Deutero-Isaiah says in 44:26 that Yahweh "confirms" (*qwm* hiphil) the "word" (*dāḇār*) of his servants (conj.) and "performs" (*šlm* hiphil) the "plan" (*'ēṣâ*; not "counsel") of his messengers. This refers to Yahweh's concrete historical plan for his people, which he has proclaimed through "his messengers" (*mal'āḵāyw*), i.e., his prophets. It is easy to see how Isaiah's great "disciple" borrowed and developed his predecessor's approach: Isaiah spoke repeatedly of Yahweh's historical plan;[101] Deutero-Isaiah thinks of all the prophets as "messengers" of Yahweh's plan. It is their function to disclose Yahweh's plan for history—now no longer a plan for judgment, but a plan for salvation (cf. 44:26-28). Cyrus himself appears as the fulfiller of Yahweh's purpose (v. 28); he is the human instrument who carries out the divine plan proclaimed by the prophets.

Deutero-Isaiah speaks a second time of Yahweh's *'ēṣâ* in connection with Cyrus (Isa.

---

94 *Isaiah 13–39,* 46f.
95 P. 123.
96 *BK,* X, 568.
97 Eichrodt, 31.
98 Wildberger, *BK,* X, 569.
99 *Festschrift F. Baumgärtel,* 173f.
100 Pp. 111f.
101 See above.

46:9-11, esp. 10f.). Yahweh declares that his "plan" will stand (*qwm*) and that he will accomplish all his purpose (*kol-ḥepṣî,* v. 10; cf. 44:28). He will do this by bringing from a far country "the man of his plan" (*ʾîš ʿaṣāṯî* [*Q*]), i.e., Cyrus (46:11). As *ʾîš ʿēṣâ,* as Yahweh's chosen instrument, Cyrus will accomplish the divine plan proclaimed by Yahweh's messengers (prophets; cf. 44:26). For Deutero-Isaiah, then, Yahweh's historical plan takes the concrete form of a plan of salvation for the people of God; a foreign ruler—and here is a change from Isaiah—is charged with bringing to the people of God not judgment but salvation.

6. *Isaiah Apocalypse.* In the context of a proleptic hymn of thanksgiving (Isa. 25:1-5) within the great Isaiah Apocalypse (Isa. 24–27), the author gives thanks to Yahweh for having destroyed "the city" (25:2), "a symbol of the whole concentration of power hostile to God."[102] He sees in this event the fulfillment of "wonderful plans (*peleʾ ʿēṣôṯ*[103]) formed of old, faithful and sure" (v. 1). Probably the author sees in the expected fall of the city that is hostile to God the fulfillment of such oracles against foreign nations as Isa. 13, 14, and 21.[104] Probably he also thinks of Yahweh's *peleʾ ʿēṣôṯ* in terms of the *peleʾ yôʿēṣ* of 9:5(6); this would be tantamount to an apocalyptic reinterpretation of the Davidic expectations enshrined in 9:1-5(2-6). Here for the first time one might speak of God's "universal plan," described as "wonderful plans" (25:1).

7. *Jeremiah.* There are no clear allusions to Yahweh's "plan" or "planning" in Jeremiah. The references to his historical plan (*ʿaṣaṯ-YHWH ʾašer yāʿaṣ*) against Edom (Jer. 49:20) and Babylon (50:45) occur in the context of inauthentic oracles against foreign nations. Jer. 49:20f. is identical in part with 50:45f. and is literarily dependent on the latter.[105] In the oracle against Edom in 49:30-32, however, which Rudolph considers authentic, the prophet says that Nebuchadnezzar has "made a plan" (*yāʿaṣ ʿēṣâ*; v. 30) against the inhabitants of Hazor, a plan of conquest, behind which Yahweh himself ultimately stands (cf. v. 32). Yahweh's situation is quite different in Jer. 18:13-17, an individual lament of the prophet; here there is a "plan" to murder Jeremiah, a plan "known" (*yāḏaʿ*; v. 23) to Yahweh. It is therefore appropriate for Jeremiah to pray for vengeance against his enemies. Jer. 19:7 (in the context of the Deuteronomistic supplement 19:2b-9) distantly recalls Isa. 19:3; Yahweh will make void (lit., "devastate," *bqq*) the "plan" of Judah and Jerusalem on account of the sin committed in Topheth. Since no concrete plan on the part of Judah and Jerusalem is mentioned, this probably means that Yahweh will reduce them to a state in which it is impossible to frame a reasonable plan, a state of total bewilderment.

8. *Ezekiel.* In a judgment oracle addressed to the leading men of Jerusalem (Ezk. 11:1-13), Ezekiel calls twenty-five men assembled at the east gate of the temple, "men

---

102 Kaiser, *Isaiah 13–39,* 197.
103 Cf. *BHS.*
104 Kaiser, *Isaiah 13–39,* 198.
105 Cf. Rudolph, *HAT,* XII, 291ff.

who devise iniquity" (*haḥōšeḇîm ʾāwen*) and "give counsel of iniquity" (*hayyōʿaṣîm ʿaṣaṯ-rāʿ*) (v. 2). This refers to unpatriotic inhabitants of Jerusalem (cf. v. 3), not the elders from whom "counsel" (*ʿēṣâ*) perishes (7:26).

9. *Book of the Twelve.* In the Book of the Twelve there is only 1 reference to Yahweh's "plan" (*ʿēṣâ*), and that in a passage whose authenticity is disputed. Mic. 4:12 states that the nations assembled against Jerusalem do not "know" (*yāḏaʿ*) "the thoughts of Yahweh" (*maḥšeḇôṯ YHWH*) and do not "understand" (*bîn* hiphil) "his plan" (*ʿaṣāṯô*), which consists in having gathered them like sheaves to the threshing floor, i.e., to their own judgment. Unsuspecting, therefore, they do their part before Jerusalem to accomplish Yahweh's historical plan against them. In Hos. 10:6, it is the (political) "plan" of Israel (i.e., the northern kingdom) that brings about its shame. The prophet Nahum (Nah. 1:11) encourages his fellow citizens with a reference to Sennacherib, who had to retreat from Jerusalem: "who plotted evil against Yahweh (*ḥōšeḇ ʿal-YHWH rāʿâ*), and counseled villainy (*yōʿēṣ beliyyāʿal*)." For Nahum, the prophet of salvation, the plan of conquest directed against Jerusalem was ultimately directed against Yahweh himself.

Habakkuk stands in the wisdom tradition when he speaks of the anonymous world power (probably Babylon) in his second woe oracle (Hab. 2:9-11): "You have 'devised' (*yāʿaṣtā*) shame to your house" (v. 10a). The imperialistic plans of the foreign ruler bring his dynasty to shame because he fails in his intended purpose, namely "to be safe from the reach of harm" (v. 9).[106] Indeed, he "forfeits" his own life (v. 10).[107]

We can summarize what the writing prophets (outside the book of Isaiah) say concerning human plans or planning by stating that human planning, above all political planning, must generally fail and indeed turn to shame when (as in Jer. 49:30-32) it does not agree with Yahweh's historical plan. Thus the usage of *yāʿaṣ* and *ʿēṣâ* in the non-Isaianic writing prophets keeps fundamentally within the theological region already defined by Proto-Isaiah. In later prophecy of course, in contrast to Isaiah, the plans of the foreign nations against Judah and Jerusalem no longer fall in any sense within the framework of Yahweh's historical plan. It is astonishing that, except for Mic. 4:12 and the 2 secondary passages Jer. 49:20; 50:45, Isaiah's theologoumenon of "Yahweh's plan" did not have any influence outside the book of Isaiah.

10. *Psalms.* Only 4 Psalms (Pss. 14, 33, 73, 106), 3 of them exilic or postexilic, speak of Yahweh's "plan" or of a human "plan" associated with Yahweh.

Ps. 14 is a relatively early lament with a hopeful conclusion; it has been influenced by prophecy and wisdom.[108] It states that evildoers (cf. v. 4) will be put to shame (*bôš* hiphil) "through the plan of the poor one" (*ʿaṣaṯ-ʿānî*; probably in the sense of "their plan against the poor one"), "for Yahweh is his refuge" (v. 6). If the hiphil of *bôš* is understood

106 Translation following W. Rudolph, *Habakuk. KAT,* XIII/3 (1975), *in loc.*

107 Cf. *ibid.*

108 Cf. H.-J. Kraus, *Psalmen. BK,* XV (^{4}1972), 105; cf., however, *Psalms 1–59,* 220: "The lament, which certainly is comparable to prophetic indictment, reaches its climax in the question of despair in v. 4."

transitively, it would refer to a (vain) attempt to bring "the plan of the poor one" to shame; another possible meaning is "act shamefully on account of the plan against the poor one."[109] Perhaps the most likely interpretation of *ʿaṣaṯ-ʿānî* is that supported, for example, by Kraus: "breviloquence." However one translates, we are dealing with another passage where a plan with which Yahweh is not in agreement fails. The special element here is that this plan is directed against the poor, i.e., those who are especially dependent on Yahweh for protection.

Ps. 33, a hymn, contrasts "the plan of the nations (*ʿaṣaṯ-gôyîm* par. *maḥšeḇôṯ ʿammîm*)" and "the plan of Yahweh (*ʿaṣaṯ YHWH*)" (vv. 10f.). Yahweh "frustrates (*prr* hiphil)" the plan (or better, collectively: "plans") of the nations (v. 10), but his plan "stands (*ʿāmaḏ*) for ever," and "the thoughts of his heart (*maḥšeḇôṯ libbô*) to all generations (*leḏōr wāḏōr*)" (v. 11). The context (v. 12) suggests that the reference is to plans of the nations that affect the people of God. They are therefore bound to be defeated by Yahweh's universal historical plan, in which the people of God play a central role. There is a similarity to Proto-Isaiah (the subordination of the plans of the nations to the sovereign historical plan of Yahweh), but there is an even greater difference: Yahweh's historical plan has become eternal, independent of concrete historical situations; there is no longer any possibility that even a limited attack of a foreign nation upon the people of God could be in harmony with Yahweh's historical plan as a plan of judgment against Israel (cf. Isa. 10:5f.).

Ps. 106 is an historical psalm exhibiting the influence of Deuteronomy. Verse 13 states that the fathers in the desert, greedy to satisfy the desires of the flesh, quickly "forgot" (*šāḵaḥ*) Yahweh's "(saving) works" (*maʿaśāyw*) and did not "wait for" (*ḥkh* piel) his "plan" or "counsel" (*ʿēṣâ*), i.e., its fulfillment. Yahweh's *ʿēṣâ* here takes on the contours of a plan of salvation for God's people. The disaster springs from the inability to wait patiently for the salvation determined in Yahweh's plan.

Ps. 73:24 is exceptional in that it speaks of Yahweh's "plan" (not "counsel"!) for the individual believer: "According to thy plan (*baʿaṣāṯeḵā*) thou dost guide me, and afterward thou wilt receive me in glory." Here *ʿēṣâ* does not mean "counsel," despite the arguments of Irwin, who, taking the interpretation of *ʿēṣâ* in v. 24 as "advice" (which he rightly sees to be highly problematical), concludes that the basic meaning of *ʿēṣâ* is "purpose,"[110] revealed as God's purpose in the political arena by the "elders" (Ezk. 7:26) in concrete cases in the form of advice.[111] In fact, the petitioner has been influenced by wisdom ideology: he is convinced that, in accordance with the divine plan (*ʿēṣâ*) of salvation, Yahweh will guide him through life to his final destiny (being received in glory). The psalmist may possibly have in mind a particular plan of salvation for each individual believer.

Prov. 19:21, which contrasts Yahweh's abiding *ʿēṣâ* to the many "plans" (*maḥašāḇôṯ*) in the mind of a man, has already been discussed.[112]

---

109 *KBL*^{3}, 112b.
110 Irwin, 56.
111 Cf. *ibid.*, 112-132.
112 See III.1 above.

11. *Job.* On the basis of Prov. 19:21, it is easy to see why the book of Job speaks twice of God's "plan" and 5 times of mortal "plans" (God: Job 38:2 [par. 42:3]; mortals: 5:13; 10:3; 18:7; 21:16b [par. 22:18b]).

Following the lead of traditional wisdom, Eliphaz states (Job 5:13) that God "takes the wise in their own craftiness, so that 'the plan of the wily' (*ʿaṣaṯ nipṯālîm*) is brought to a quick end (*mhr* niphal)." Likewise drawing on the notion of actions that lead to their own consequences, Bildad states (18:7) that the wicked is brought low (*šlk* hiphil) by "his own plan" (*ʿaṣāṯô*). But this is just what Job contests (10:3) when Yahweh—in contrast to his conduct toward Job—causes his light to shine on (*ypʿ* hiphil) the "plan of the wicked" (*ʿaṣaṯ rešāʿîm*), probably a reference to the salvific appearance of Yahweh in glory, his epiphany."[113] This passage is not a gloss!

Job 21:16; 22:18, however, are secondary glosses. The statement that "the plan of the wicked is far from him,"[114] i.e., God (21:16b [par. 22:18b]), is only a slight variation of Job 10:3: God does not look with favor on the plan of the wicked but rather ignores it, refuses to countenance it. In a rhetorical question (Job 38:2 [par. 42:3]), God makes it clear that it is Job who "darkens" (*ḥšk* hiphil, 38:2) or "hides" (*ʿlm* hiphil, 42:3) the "plan" (*ʿēṣâ*) by words without knowledge. The "plan" that Job darkens, "turning the clear course of will and action into trackless darkness,"[115] is "God's will and action in creation and governance of the world."[116] This "plan," Fohrer goes on to say, "is on the one hand the order of the universe, which Job calls into question and finds arbitrary, and on the other God's unfathomable will and action, impenetrable to the human eye." What is new is the extension of *ʿēṣâ* from the realm of history to the order of the universe, realized primarily in the natural realm.

12. *Chronicler's History.* Apart from the isolated passage Jgs. 20:7 discussed in I.1 above, it is surprising that in OT narrative it is only in the relatively late Chronicler's history that we find *ʿēṣâ* with the meaning "decision" (1 Ch. 12:20[19]; Ezr. 4:5; 10:8; Neh. 4:9[15]) and *yāʿaṣ* with the meaning "decide" (2 Ch. 25:16). The only passages that are important theologically are Neh. 4:9(15) (*ʿēṣâ*); 2 Ch. 25:16 (*yāʿaṣ*). The earlier passage (Neh. 4:9[15]) occurs in the memoirs of Nehemiah. In it, he glorifies God because the enemies have refrained from their planned attack on the unfinished walls of Jerusalem; he ascribes this respite to God's having "broken," i.e., "frustrated" (*prr* hiphil) "their plan" (*ʿaṣāṯām*) by giving Nehemiah knowledge of it so that he could take preventive measures (cf. Neh. 4:1-8[7-14]). The terminology (*hēp̄er ʿēṣâ*) is conventional (cf. Ezr. 4:5; Ps. 33:10; also Isa. 8:10; 14:27; and 2 S. 15:34; 17:14, where *ʿēṣâ* has the meaning "advice"); what is new is Nehemiah's understanding that the enemies themselves understand their failure as being due to the frustration of their plan through (the) God (of the Jews).

The verse 2 Ch. 25:16 is interesting in that the root *yʿṣ* appears no less than 3 times

113 F. Horst, *Hiob. BK,* XVI/1 (1968), 154f.
114 Conj.; cf. *BHK.*
115 G. Fohrer, *Das Buch Hiob. KAT,* XVI (1963), 499.
116 *Ibid.,* 500.

in it: *yô'ēṣ,* "counselor"; *'ēṣâ,* "counsel"; and *yā'aṣ,* "determine." When King Amaziah haughtily rejects the intervention of the anonymous prophet (cf. 2 Ch. 25:15), the latter recognizes that God has "determined" (*yā'aṣ*) to destroy Amaziah.

IV. 1. *Sirach.* In the extant Hebrew sections of Sirach, the concordance[117] reveals the following occurrences of *yā'aṣ* and its derivatives: The qal appears only 4 times in the form of the ptcp. *yô'ēṣ,* "counselor" (Sir. 37:7[twice],8; 44:3). The niphal ("take counsel") appears once (37:10), since the form *hy'ṣh* in 4:28 derives from another root (LXX *agṓnisai*; cf. *'āṣâ* II).[118] The hithpael likewise occurs once (39:32: *hiṯyā'aṣtî*; LXX *estērı́chthēn*). The noun *'ēṣâ* appears 6 times (30:21 [marginal gloss in manuscript B]; 35:19; 37:13; 41:23 [= 42:1]; 42:8; 47:23). In 11:9, the reading of manuscript A (*'ṣbt*) should be followed rather than that of B (*'ṣh*).

In the "praise of the fathers," Sirach begins (44:3-6) with twelve categories to be included among the famous men of the past. In third place (v. 3), following "rulers of the earth in their royalty" and "famous men in their power," and preceding "seers of all things in their prophetic office," we find "counselors in their understanding" (*hayyô'ᵃṣîm biṯᵉḇûnām*). The mention of "counselors" in third position is significant; it is probably connected with Sirach's admiration of the wise, which is evident in the following six categories (vv. 4f.). He also devotes an entire section to counselors and the advice they give (37:7-18). All the more surprising, therefore, is the skepticism revealed by the introductory statements concerning contemporary "counselors" (vv. 7f.): "Every counselor 'points with the hand (*yānîp yāḏ*),' " i.e., points the way to the one seeking advice; "but there is *yô'ēṣ dereḵ 'ālāyw.*" Hamp,[119] whose translation is generally followed here, emends *'ālāyw* to *'awlâ* (v. 7): "counselors who point the wrong way." The ambivalent nature of the "counselors" is underscored by a reference to their price: "Be careful before the 'counselor' and find out in advance what he requires" (v. 8a-b). The counselor's egoism can also influence the substance of his counsel (vv. 8c-9). Verses 10f. are summarized in v. 10 with a double warning: "Do not take counsel" (*'al tiwwā'ēṣ,* niphal) and "Keep your plans secret." Several categories of those who are inappropriate counselors are named: (v. 10) someone who is envious (*ḥmyk,* with the 2nd person sg. suf.; the parallelism with *mqn'* makes Segal's translation[120] "father-in-law" unlikely); (v. 11) a woman (concerning her rival); a merchant (concerning business); a man of ill will (*'îš ra'*) (concerning generosity); a lazy man (about his work); a lazy slave (about his hard service). Instead, Sirach recommends (v. 12, still echoing the niphal of *yā'aṣ* in v. 10) seeking a counselor who is extremely conscientious and devout, who is devoted to the interests of the inquirer and will stand helpfully by his side. The "counselor's" ethical and religious qualities are therefore crucial.

The most important source of counsel, however—and this is new vis-à-vis the OT

117 Barthélemy-Rickenbacher, 159f., 309.

118 Cf. also Driver, *ExpT,* 57 (1945/46), 193: "made himself stubborn, resisted."

119 V. Hamp, "Das Buch der Sprüch," *EB,* IV (1959), *in loc.*

120 *In loc.*

tradition—is one's own conscience: "But heed the 'counsel of conscience' (*'ᵃṣaṯ lēḇāḇ*), for there is nothing more faithful to you than this" (Sir. 37:13). As a sage, Sirach warns vigorously (41:12 [= 42:1]) against the indiscretion of "revealing any secret counsel (*kol sôḏ 'ēṣâ*)." The noun *'ēṣâ* can also refer to something disreputable; 42:8, for example, speaks in passing of the lustful old man who "takes counsel with himself" (*nwṭl 'ṣh*) concerning unchastity, i.e., is looking for sex.

The other 3 occurrences of *'ēṣâ* fall within the spectrum of "consideration—decision." The sage cautions against doing anything "without consideration" (*bᵉlō' 'ēṣâ*), if only for selfish reasons (35:19). But consideration must not degenerate into "scrupulosity": *wᵉ'al taḵšîlᵉḵā ba'ᵃṣāṯᵉḵā* (30:21, manuscript B, first marginal reading). As a fateful "decision" (*'ēṣâ*) of the past 47:23 speaks of the decision of Rehoboam (cf. 1 K. 12), through which (*ba'ᵃṣā[ṯô]*) he "plunged the people into depravity [disunion?]" (*hiprîa'*). The only occurrence of the hithpael is in Sir. 39:32, in a hymn of praise (vv. 16-35): *'al kēn mērō'š hiṯyā'aṣtî wᵉhiṯbônantî ûḇiḵtāḇ hinnaḥtî.* Here the meaning is somewhat different. The statement could be translated literally: "Therefore from the beginning 'I came to a decision' and turned my attention [to what I had decided] and set [it] down in writing [as a hymn of praise]." In other words, God's wonders in creation and history (39:16-30) evoked from the sage the decision to celebrate them in a hymn.

There is no trace of *'ēṣâ* used in the sense of "plan," above all in the theological sense of "God's historical plan" after the manner of Isaiah. Despite the "praise of the fathers," therefore, Sirach does not appear to have developed a more profound view of history.

2. *Dead Sea Scrolls.* The Dead Sea scrolls use *'ēṣâ* with impressive frequency. Kuhn's concordance and its supplement[121] list no fewer than 83 occurrences. The verb, however, is suprisingly rare, with only 4 occurrences: 2 of the qal active participle (1QH 3:10; 6:21) and 2 of the niphal (1QS 6:3; CD 3:5).

It is uncertain whom *pele' yô'ēṣ* in 1QH 3:10 refers to: the male child born of the pregnant woman[122] or God, who is to be understood as the implicit subject of *ygyḥ* (read as a hiphil: "causes to break forth").[123] Maier[124] also connects *pele'* with God, but does not do justice to the echo of the title in Isa. 9:5(6), separating *yô'ēṣ* from *pele'* and interpreting the former as a predicate: "The wonderful one takes counsel with his power." Furthermore, the niphal would seem to be impossible. The most likely interpretation appears to be that of Mowinckel; as he points out,[125] *gbwr* in 1QH 6:29ff. is a second divine title that recalls Isa. 9:5(6). The painful birth does not look forward to the Messiah but rather symbolizes "the coming deliverance of the Qumran community."[126] According to Jeremias,[127] it is the "Teacher of Righteousness" who is speaking here, saying that

---

121 Nachträge, 216.
122 Ll. 9f.; cf. Carmignac-Guilbert, 194f.; Lohse, 121.
123 Mowinckel, 297f.
124 *In loc.*
125 Mowinckel, 298.
126 *Ibid.*
127 P. 17.

God himself, as *peleʾ yôʿēṣ* (1QH 3:10), "one who plans wonders,"[128] will bring this (eschatological) deliverance of the community to pass "with his mighty power" (*ʿim geḇûrāṯô,* likewise an allusion to Isa. 9:5[6]). In other words, the imminently expected deliverance of the community appears to be the realization of a wonderful plan on the part of God. But Belial, too, is at work. He is present to "counsel" (*yôʿēṣ*) or "plan(?)" "with their hearts" (*ʿim leḇāḇām*), i.e., with the apostate (1QH 6:21f.). The outcome of this counsel or plan is *maḥšeḇeṯ rišʿâ,* "a wicked plan" (1QH 6:22).

Like the qal, the niphal is used ambivalently (1QS 6:3; CD 3:5). In the Community Rule, 1QS 6:2f. requires that members of the community share common meals, common prayer, and common "advising" (*yḥd ywʿṣw*), which will be discussed below. According to CD 3:5f., the Israelites in Egypt demonstrated their hardness of heart by "taking counsel together" (*lhyʿṣ*) against the commandments of God.

Because of the wealth of occurrences, we can discuss *ʿēṣâ* only cursorily. Remarkably, it has the meaning "advice" or "admonition" in only 8 passages: 1QS 9:9,17 ("the admonition of the law"); 1QS 6:4 (the "counsel" of members of the community); 1QS 6:22; 9:2 (the "counsel" of an individual member); 1QS 8:23,25 (in case of his temporary exclusion); 4QpNah 2:9 (of those who "lead Ephraim astray"). In CD 5:17, citing Dt. 32:28, *ʿēṣôṯ* in effect means "insight." In 4 passages we find the adverbial phrase *beʿēṣâ,* "upon consideration" (1QpHab 3:6[twice]; 4:11; 1QS 7:11; CD 12:8). Some 16 times we find the meaning "decision" or "plan": 13 times as God's decision (1QS 1:13; 2:23 [*ʿôlāmîm*]; 3:6; 6:9; 11:18,22; 1QH 1:5; 4:13; 6:10; 16:8; 1QH fr. 13:7; 1QSb 5:25), 3 times as a plan contrary to God (1QM 13:11; 4QpNah 1:2; 2:6).

In the rest of the passages (more than 50), the meaning of *ʿēṣâ* ranges from "consultation" through "council" to "assembly" as a term for a specific form of community. We find the sense of "community" with negative overtones in 4QpNah 3:7f. Unique to 1QSb 3:28 is the phrase "assembly of all flesh" (*ʿaṣaṯ kôl bāśār*) as a term for the human race. Several constructions with *ʿēṣâ* refer to the Qumran community and its organs or at least to functions of the community and its organs; the precise meaning cannot always be determined in each instance. In 1QS 6:16, *ʿaṣaṯ hārabbîm* probably denotes an actual assembly of the total community. Aspects of the community are mentioned in 1QS 1:8,10, "the assembly of God" (*ʿaṣaṯ ʾēl*); 1QS 10:24, "the assembly of understanding" (*ʿaṣaṯ tûšiyyâ*); and 1Q38 8:1, "the (inner) circle of thy assembly" (*sôḏ ʿaṣāṯeḵâ* [with reference to God]). The community is frequently called the "holy assembly" (*ʿaṣaṯ [haq]qōḏeš*: 1QS 2:25; 8:21; 1QM 3:4; 1QH 6:5[?]; 7:10; 1QSa 2:9; CD 20:24). Above all, however, no fewer than 23 passages call it *ʿaṣaṯ [hay]yaḥad,* "assembly of the community" (1QpHab 12:4; 1QS 3:2; 5:7; 6:3,10,12,14,16; 7:2,22,24; 8:1,5,22; 11:8; 1Q14 10:6; 1QSa 1:26f.; 2:2,11; 1QSb 4:26; 4QpIs^d 1:2; 4QFlor 1:17). One passage (1QS 8:11) speaks of the "assembly of the men of the community" (*ʿaṣaṯ ʾanšê hayyaḥaḏ*), another (1QS 3:6) of the "community of his counsel" (*yaḥaḏ ʿaṣāṯô*), i.e., the community that realizes God's plan.[129]

---

128 See III.2 above.

129 See above.

This last passage casts some light on the community's understanding of itself as *ʿēṣâ.* It considered itself to be a *yaḥaḏ,* "community," i.e., an intimate society, based on an *ʿēṣâ,* a "decision" or "plan" of God. Since the community was reminded repeatedly of the plan when it met in council (*ʿēṣâ* in the sense discussed above), it could think of itself as the "community council/counsel." Thus *ʿēṣâ* does not mean simply "community" but rather a concrete *act* of community associated with the councils of the group. In this respect, Worrell's description of the Qumran *ʿēṣâ* as a "reciprocal consultation in a prescribed setting"[130] is accurate.

Finally, we must discuss briefly the meaning and usage of another phrase that is characteristic of Qumran: *ʾanšê ʿēṣâ* (+ suf. or gen.). The expression does not refer (as in Isa. 40:13) to "advisers," but to persons who are "advised" or (better) "determined" by the one whose *ʿēṣâ* they belong to, so that they constitute his followers or together with him form an active community. On the one hand, we hear of *ʾanšê ʿēṣâ* who are associated with God (1QpHab 6:11,13; 1QSb 4:24; also *ʾnwšy ʿṣhtw,* 1QSa 1:3) or with the "Teacher of Righteousness" (1QpHab 9:10; 4QpPs 37:2,18[19])—ultimately the Qumran community. On the other hand, *ʾanšê ʿēṣâ* are mentioned who belong to the "house of Absalom," the apostates (1QpHab 5:10) or (4QpNah 1:5) the "lion of wrath" (possibly Alexander Jannaeus). It is typical of the dualistic thought of the Qumran community that *ʾanšê ʿēṣâ* in conjunction with differentiating terms should be used as the community's self-designation and also as its designation of its apostates and opponents.

Thus the noun *ʿēṣâ*—obviously on account of its inherent double meaning (both theological and anthropological), found already in the OT—was especially appropriate for the Qumran community to use as a linguistic expression of their unusual self-understanding.

Ruppert

130 P. 74.

יַעֲקֹב / יַעֲקוֹב *yaʿaqōḇ/yaʿaqôḇ*

Contents: I. 1. Occurrences and Meaning; 2. Etymology. II. Jacob in the Pentateuch: 1. The Jacob Tradition in J, E, and P; 2. Interpretation of the Figure of Jacob; 3. Jacob and Israel. III. The God of the Fathers: 1. El; 2. "The Mighty One of Jacob"; 3. "The God of Jacob." IV. Historical Considerations. V. Jacob in the Prophetic Canon: 1. Jacob the Individual; 2. Jacob as a Designation of the People. VI. Jacob in the Psalms: 1. Jacob the Individual; 2. Jacob as a Designation of the People. VII. Jacob in Deuteronomy. VIII. Summary.

yaʿaqōḇ/yaʿaqôḇ. P. R. Ackroyd, "Hosea and Jacob," *VT,* 13 (1963), 245-259; W. F. Albright, "Northwest-Semitic Names in a List of Egyptian Slaves from the Eighteenth Century B.C.," *JAOS,*

I. 1. *Occurrences and Meaning.* According to Lisowsky-Rost, the name "Jacob" occurs 349 times in the OT, according to Mandelkern 345 times. Kuhn cites 9 occurrences

---

74 (1954), 222-233; *idem, Yahweh and the Gods of Canaan* (1968; repr. Winona Lake, 1978); A. Alt, "The God of the Fathers," in *Essays on OT History and Religion* (Eng. trans. Garden City, 1966), 1-100 = *KlSchr,* I (1953), 1-78 [German]; *idem,* "Erwägungen über die Landnahme der Israeliten in Palästina," *PJ*, 35 (1939), 8-63 = *KlSchr,* I, 126-175; J. Bright, *A History of Israel,* (Philadelphia, 1959; [3]1981); W. Caspari, "Der Name Jaqob in israelitischer Zeit." *Festschrift G. Jacob* (Leipzig, 1932), 24-36; P. Diepold, *Israels Land.* BWANT, 95[5/15] (1972); M. Dietrich and O. Loretz, "Zur ugaritischen Lexikographie (I)," *BiOr,* 23 (1966), 127-133; H. Eising, *Formgeschichtliche Untersuchung zur Jakobserzählung der Genesis* (diss., Münster, 1940); O. Eissfeldt, "Religionshistorie und Religionspolemik im AT," *Wisdom in Israel and in the Ancient Near East. Festschrift H. H. Rowley. SVT*, 3 (1955), 94-102 = *KlSchr,* III (1966), 359-366; *idem, Die Genesis der Genesis* (Tübingen, 1958, [2]1961); *idem,* "Jahwe, der Gott der Väter," *ThLZ,* 88 (1963), 481-490 = *KlSchr*, IV (1968), 79-91; *idem,* "Jakobs Begegnung mit El und Moses Begegnung mit Jahwe," *OLZ,* 58 (1963), 325-331 = *KlSchr,* IV (1968), 92-98; *idem,* "Palestine in the Time of the Nineteenth Dynasty. (a) The Exodus and Wanderings," *CAH*[3], II/2. XXVI(a), 307-330; *idem,* "Jakob-Lea und Jakob-Rahel," *Gottes Wort und Gottes Land. Festschrift H. W. Hertzberg* (Göttingen, 1965), 50-55 = *KlSchr,* IV, 170-75; *idem,* "Der kanaanäische El als Geber der den israelitischen Erzvätern geltenden Nachkommenschaft- und Landbesitzverheissungen," *Festschrift C. Brockelmann. WZ Halle-Wittenberg,* 17 (1968), 45-53 = *KlSchr,* V (1973), 50-62; *idem,* "Renaming in the OT," *Words and Meanings. Festschrift D. W. Thomas* (Cambridge, 1968), 69-79 = *KlSchr,* V, 68-76 [Ger.]; D. N. Freedman, "The Original Name of Jacob," *IEJ,* 13 (1963), 125f.; T. E. Fretheim, "The Jacob Traditions," *Int,* 26 (1972), 419-436; J. C. L. Gibson, "Light from Mari on the Patriarchs," *JSS,* 7 (1962), 44-62; A. Goetze, "Diverse Names in an Old-Babylonian Pay-List," *BASOR,* 95 (1944), 18-24 (cf. W. F. Albright in 19, n. 6a); E. M. Good, "Hosea and the Jacob Tradition," *VT,* 16 (1966), 137-151; C. H. Gordon, "The Story of Jacob and Laban in the Light of the Nuzi Tablets," *BASOR,* 66 (1937), 25-27; *idem,* "The Patriarchal Narratives," *JNES,* 13 (1954), 56-59; H. Gressmann, "Sage und Geschichte in den Patriarchenerzählungen," *ZAW,* 30 (1910), 1-34; W. Gross, "Jakob, der Mann des Segens," *Bibl,* 49 (1968), 321-344; H. Gunkel, "Jacob," *What Remains of the OT and Other Essays* (Eng. trans., New York, 1928), 151-186; A. H. J. Gunneweg, *Geschichte Israels bis Bar Kochba, ThW,* 2 ([3]1979); M. Haran, "The Religion of the Patriarchs: An Attempt at a Synthesis," *ASTI*, 4 (1965), 30-55; S. Herrmann, *A History of Israel in OT Times* (Eng. trans., Philadelphia, [2]1981); J. M. Heuschen, "Jacob of de genadevolle uitverkiezing," *ETL,* 45 (1969), 335-358; G. Hölscher, "Zur jüdischen Namenskunde," *Vom AT. Festschrift K. Marti. BZAW,* 41 (1925), 148-157; J. Hoftijzer, *Die Verheissungen an die drei Erzväter* (Leiden, 1956); W. L. Holladay, "Chiasmus, the Key to Hosea XII 3-6," *VT,* 16 (1966), 53-64; H. B. Huffmon, *APNM*; G. Jacob, "Der Name Jacob," *Litterae orientales,* 54 (1933), 16-19; A. Jepsen, "Zur Überlieferung der Vätergestalten," *Festschrift A. Alt. WZ Leipzig,* 3 (1953/54), 265-281 = *Der Herr ist Gott* (Berlin, 1978), 46-75; J. O. Lewis, *An Analysis of Literary Forms in the Jacob Narratives* (diss., Southern Baptist Theological Seminary, Louisville, 1964); V. Maag, "Jakob—Esau—Edom," *ThZ,* 13 (1957), 418-429 = *Kultur, Kulturkontakt und Religion* (Göttingen, 1980), 99-110; *idem,* "Der Hirte Israels: Eine Skizze von Wesen und Bedeutung der Väterreligion," *SchThU,* 28 (1958), 2-28 = *Kultur, Kulturkontakt und Religion,* 111-144; E. Meyer, *Die Israeliten und ihre Nachbarstämme* (1906; repr. Darmstadt, 1967), 271-287; J. G. Mitchell, *A Study of the Jacob Tradition in the OT* (diss., Southern Baptist Theological Seminary, Louisville, 1970); S. Mowinckel, " 'Rahelstämme' und 'Leastämme'," *Von Ugarit nach Qumran. Festschrift O. Eissfeldt. BZAW,* 77 ([2]1961), 129-150; M. Naor, "יַעֲקֹב und יִשְׂרָאֵל," *ZAW,* 49 (1931), 317-321; E. Nielsen, *Shechem: A Traditio-Historical Investigation* (Copenhagen, [2]1959), 222-240; M. Noth, *IPN*; *idem, A History of Pentateuchal Traditions* (Eng. trans. 1972; repr. Chico, Calif., 1981), 54-58, 79-101, 198-201; *idem,* "Mari und

in the Dead Sea scrolls, and Stark[1] lists 3 additional occurrences of *yʿqwb* in Palmyrene texts, where it is interpreted as a Jewish masculine name.[2] The form *yaʿᵃqōḇâ* in 1 Ch. 4:36 is also the name of a Simeonite with the suffix *-â*.[3] In the Jewish diaspora and "from the final period of the temple, the name 'Jacob' was quite common among scholars . . . , and in the first century A.D. it was not uncommon among others."[4] In the NT, the personal name is used in the form *Iakṓb* for the son of Isaac (Mt. 1:2; Lk. 3:34; Jn. 4:5f.; etc.) and the father of Joseph (Mt. 1:15f.; cf. Lk. 3:23) and in the hellenized form *Iákōbos* for the son of Zebedee (Mt. 4:21; etc.), the son of Alphaeus (Mt. 10:3; etc.), the son of Mary

---

Israel: Eine Personennamenstudie," *Geschichte und AT. Festschrift A. Alt. BHTh,* 16 (1953), 127-152 = *Aufsätze zur biblischen Landes- und Altertumskunde* (Neukirchen-Vluyn, 1971), II, 213-233; *idem, The History of Israel* (Eng. trans., New York, ²1960); M. Oliva, *Jacob en Betel. Institución San Jerónimo,* 3 (1975); E. Otto, "Jakob in Bethel," *ZAW,* 88 (1976), 165-190; A. de Pury, *Promesse divine et légende cultuelle dans le cycle de Jacob,* I-II. *ÉtB* (1975); W. Richter, "Das Gelübde als theologische Rahmung der Jakobsüberlieferungen," *BZ,* N.S. 11 (1967), 21-52; L. Rost, "Die Gottesverehrung der Patriarchen im Lichte der Pentateuchquellen," *Congress Volume, Oxford 1959. SVT,* 7 (1960), 346-359; H. H. Rowley, "Recent Discovery and the Patriarchal Age," *BJRL,* 32 (1949/50), 44-79 = *The Servant of the Lord and Other Essays on the OT* (²1965), 283-318; L. Ruppert, "Herkunft und Bedeutung der Jakob-Tradition bei Hosea," *Bibl,* 52 (1971), 488-504; L. Sabourin, "La lutte de Jacob avec Elohim," *Sciences ecclésiastiques,* 10 (1958), 77-89, 256f.; J. Scharbert, "Patriarchentradition und Patriarchenreligion," *Verkündigung und Forschung. BEvTh,* 19 (1974), 2-22; J. B. Schildenberger, "Jakobs nächtlicher Kampf mit dem Elohim am Jabbok (Gn 32, 23-33)," *Miscellanea Biblica. Festschrift B. Ubach. Scripta et documenta,* 1 (Montserrat, 1953), 69-96; L. Schmidt, "Überlegungen zum Jahwisten," *EvTh,* 37 (1977), 230-247; W. H. Schmidt, *The Faith of the OT: A History* (Eng. trans., Philadelphia, 1983), 5-27; H. Seebass, *Der Erzvater Israel und die Einführung der Jahweverehrung in Kanaan. BZAW,* 98 (1966); *idem,* "Die Stämmeliste von Dtn. XXXIII," *VT,* 27 (1977), 158-169; *idem,* "Landverheissungen an die Väter," *EvTh,* 37 (1977), 210-229; W. Staerk, *Studien zur Religions- und Sprachgeschichte des ATs* (Berlin, 1899), I, 21-53, 77-83; II, 1-13; J. K. Stark, *PNPI*; C. Steuernagel, *Die Einwanderung der israelitischen Stämme in Kanaan* (Berlin, 1901); W. H. Stiebing, Jr., "When Was the Age of the Patriarchs?" *BAR,* 1/2 (1975), 17-21; T. L. Thompson, *The Historicity of the Patriarchal Narratives. BZAW,* 133 (1974); R. de Vaux, "Les patriarches hébreux et les découvertes modernes," *RB,* 53 (1946), 321-347; 55 (1948), 321-347; 56 (1949), 5-36; *idem,* "The Hebrew Patriarchs and History," *The Bible and the Ancient Near East* (Eng. trans., London, 1971), 111-121; *idem, The Early History of Israel* (Eng. trans. Philadelphia, 1978); T. C. Vriezen, "La tradition de Jacob dans Osée XII," *OTS,* 1 (1942), 64-78; L. Wächter, "Israel und Jeschurun," *Schalom: Studien zu Glaube und Geschichte Israels. Festschrift A. Jepsen. ArbT,* 1/46 (1971), 58-64; G. Wallis, "Die Geschichte der Jakobtradition," *WZ Halle-Wittenberg,* 13 (1964), 427-440 = "Die Jakobtradition und Geschichte," *Geschichte und Überlieferung. ArbT,* 2/13 (1968), 13-44; *idem,* "Die Tradition von den drei Ahnvätern," *ZAW,* 81 (1969), 18-40; H. Weidmann, *Die Patriarchen und ihre Religion im Lichte der Forschung seit Julius Wellhausen. FRLANT,* N.S.[94] (1968); P. Weimar, "Aufbau und Struktur der priesterschriftlichen Jakobsgeschichte," *ZAW,* 86 (1974), 174-203; H. Wuthnow, *Die semitischen Menschennamen in griechischen Inschriften und Papyri des vorderen Orients. Studien zur Epigraphik und Papyruskunde,* 1/4 (Leipzig, 1930); S. Yeivin, "Yaʿqobʾel," *JEA,* 45 (1959), 16-18.

For additional bibliog., see → אַבְרָהָם *ʾaḇrāhām* (*ʾabhrāhām*) and → יִשְׂרָאֵל *yiśrāʾēl.*

[1] *PNPI,* 26.

[2] *Ibid.,* 91.

[3] *IPN,* 38.

[4] Hölscher, 152f.

(Mt. 27:56; etc.), and for others.[5] The name also occurs in a variety of forms in Greek inscriptions and papyri.[6]

The other OT passages refer either to the patriarch Jacob or to all or part of the people of Israel who claim him as their genealogical ancestor. Even though it is sometimes difficult or impossible to determine which meaning is intended, the majority of the occurrences refer to the patriarch: the individual Jacob is clearly meant in 208 OT passages and 5 passages in the Dead Sea scrolls. Most occurrences are concentrated in Genesis (180 total, 178 individual), Deuteronomy (11/7), Psalms (34/1), Proto-Isaiah (15/0), Deutero-Isaiah (23/0), Trito-Isaiah (4/1), Jeremiah (16/0), Lamentations (3/0), Hosea (3/2), Amos (6/0), Obadiah (3/0), Micah (11/0), and Malachi (4/0); the name does not appear at all in Judges, Ruth, Ezra, Nehemiah, Job, Proverbs, Ecclesiastes, Song of Songs, Joel, Habakkuk, Zephaniah, Haggai, or Zechariah.

2. *Etymology.* The name "Jacob" is always derived by popular etymology in the OT. Gen. 25:26a, assigned by Eissfeldt[7] to the source stratum L but by Noth[8] and others to J, associates the name "Jacob" with *'eqeḇ,* "heel," because Jacob took hold of Esau's heel when he was born. The story that recounts the blessing of Esau and Jacob by their almost blind father Isaac tells how Esau was cheated of the blessing due him as first-born and has him say: "He is indeed rightly named Jacob, for he has defrauded (*'āqaḇ*) me two times: he took away my birthright, and behold, now he has taken away my blessing" (Gen. 27:36 [J]). Here Jacob's action is to be taken positively, as a reason for Israel to rejoice over its superiority to Edom. The popular etymology reappears in Hos. 12:4(Eng. v. 3), which incorporates both Genesis traditions but with a clearly negative perspective: the fact that Jacob (among other things) "defrauded (*'āqaḇ*) his brother in the womb" is used by the prophet as grounds for threatening judgment. In Jer. 9:3(4), finally, "Every brother is a defrauder" (*kol-'āḥ 'āqôḇ ya'qōḇ*) can be seen as an allusion to the name "Jacob" and its interpretation as "defrauder." Rudolph, following Erbt, actually translates: "Every brother defrauds like Jacob."[9]

Thus the OT associates the name "Jacob" exclusively with the root *'qb,* meaning "heel" as a noun and "defraud" as a verb.[10] This leads Ackroyd to say that *'qb* literally means "overtake, supplant," figuratively, "deceive."[11] It is noteworthy, as Ackroyd points out, that neither Hosea nor the Pentateuch tradition was aware of what is generally accepted today as the true etymology of the name "Jacob."

According to this theory, the name is a hypocoristic form of what was originally a theophorous name belonging to the class of statement-names made up of a divine name

---

5 W. Bauer, *A Greek-English Lexicon of the NT and Other Early Christian Literature* (Chicago, ²1979), 367f.

6 Wuthnow, 55f., 159.

7 O. Eissfeldt, *Hexateuch-Synopse* (²1962; repr. Darmstadt, 1973), 44*.

8 Noth, *A History of Pentateuchal Traditions,* 29.

9 W. Rudolph, *Jeremia. HAT,* XII (³1968), 64, citing W. Erbt, *Jeremia und seine Zeit* (Göttingen, 1902), *in loc.*

10 Cf. also Ugar. *'qb*: *UT,* no. 1907; *WUS,* no. 2086.

11 P. 249.

and the imperfect of a verb. Its full form, not found in the OT, was "Jacob-El." By means of textual emendation, Freedman finds this full form in Dt. 33:28:

Israel dwells in safety,
By himself Jacob-"El" [reading *ʾēl* for *ʾel* and shifting the word to this stich] "settles" [reading *ʿān* for *ʿên*]:
(His is) a land of grain and must,
[yea,] His skies also drip with dew.

Outside the OT, however, occurrences of this name are plentiful.[12] At Ašnakkum (Chagar Bazar) in Upper Mesopotamia, the name *ia-aḫ-qú-ub-el* is found in texts of the eighteenth century B.C. In texts from Kish, the name appears in the forms *ia-aḫ-qú-ub-el* and *ia-qú-ub-el.* In the form *ia-qú-ub-el* it appears among the texts found at Tell Ḥarmal. Texts from the first dynasty of Babylon contain the name *ia-qu-úb-el* and even the hypocoristicon *ia-qú-bi.* On Egyptian scarabs of the Hyksos period we find *iaʿqob-ʾr* and *iaʿqob-hr,* probably to be read "Jacob-El."[13] Lists of Thutmose III, Rameses II, and Rameses III include a Palestinian toponym *iaʿqob-el.*

This survey shows that "Jacob" was from the outset a masculine personal name, a hypocoristic form of "Jacob-El," and that this name was familiar among the Arameans but uncommon among the Canaanites and Phoenicians.[14] Etymologically, it is of a type that is especially common in Mesopotamian West Semitic onomastics;[15] it is in fact "a simple personal name like German 'Hinz' or 'Kunz'."[16] Since the root *ʿqb* appears in a whole series of such names (cf. *Aqbi-il, [Ḫ]aqba-aḫum, [Ḫ]aqba-ḫammu]*), but also in the Egyptian slave names *ʿqbʾ* and *ʿqbtw,*[17] the Aramaic name *ʿaqûbaʾ,*[18] and in several cuneiform names from Ugarit (*abdi-ia-qub-bu, ia-qub-buʿal, ia-qub-bi-nu, ia-qub-ia-nu*),[19] we may second Noth's statement that "the name 'Jacob' . . . is a typically Mesopotamian West Semitic name."[20]

As to the interpretation of the name, the attempt to understand it as a divine name[21] may be judged a failure, especially since the Ugaritic name *Abdi-iaqubbu* cited above must be considered "pseudo-theophorous."[22] Jacob (who cites the earlier literature) proposes to interpret the name on the basis of *yaʿqûb,* "heath cock," with the meaning "he follows after (the heath cock)"; this suggestion has rightly found no support. Today Noth's interpretation[23] is generally accepted. Citing the root *ʿqb,* "guard, protect," found

12 Cf. already Gressmann, 6-9; now Rowley, *The Servant of the Lord,* 290f.; Gibson, 51; de Vaux, *The Early History of Israel*; *APNM,* 203f. (with citations).

13 For a different interpretation, see Albright, *Yahweh,* 50, n. 10; 133, n. 1.

14 R. de Vaux, *Die Patriarchenerzählungen und die Geschichte. SBS,* 3 (^{2}1968),4.

15 Noth, *Aufsätze,* II, 225.

16 Gressmann, 9.

17 Albright, *JAOS,* 74 (1954), 231.

18 *KAI,* 241, 1.

19 Cf. *PRU,* III, 241, 261; also *PNU,* 111f., 317, 337.

20 *Aufsätze,* II, 225.

21 Meyer, 282, 286f.

22 *PRU,* III, 261.

23 *IPN,* 177f., 197.

in Old South Arabic and also in Ethiopic, he translates the name "Jacob" as "the deity has protected"[24] or "may (the deity) protect."[25] Similar translations are proposed by other scholars.[26] This interpretation has recently been questioned by Dietrich and Loretz[27] on the basis of a Ugaritic text containing the root *ʿqb* with the meaning "follow closely, be near."[28] This root is also found in Amorite and Phoenician; it confirms the proposed translation of *ʿqb* in a Phoenician inscription as "continuation."[29] In this case, our name would mean "He (El) is near," which is very attractive.

At this point a further observation is necessary. The OT tradition makes a distinction between the names "Jacob" and "Israel," in that the former, "neutral"[30] name is solemnly changed to the theophorous name "Israel," which contains the element "El." This is hard to reconcile with the form "Jacob-El," however, whether "El" is taken as an appellative or as a proper name, because this theory presents us with a name that is formally and semantically indistinguishable from "Israel." Furthermore, if (as is universally assumed) the "El" in "Israel" is the name of the well-known Canaanite deity, there are additional difficulties with the traditional understanding of the pre-Palestinian patriarchal religion. There are two possibilities: either (1) the seminomads did not come to know El only when they settled in Palestine, but already called their patriarchal God by this name;[31] or (2) the name "Jacob," although theophorous in origin, in its hypocoristic form had long lost its religious associations and was nothing more than a neutral personal name in the OT period. The latter possibility is the easiest to reconcile with the OT tradition.

II. Jacob in the Pentateuch. The interpretation of the name "Jacob" as a common masculine personal name has not been without influence on the interpretation of the OT Jacob traditions.

1. *The Jacob Tradition in J, E, and P.* As even our cursory survey shows, the focus of these traditions is in Genesis. In it, or in part of it, the figure of Jacob is in fact thematic: Gen. 27–36 or 25:19–35:22. The assignment of these chapters by literary criticism to J, E, and P—in other words, the documentary hypothesis—is generally accepted by OT scholarship, although this does not mean that the observations of what is called the new documentary hypothesis are rejected. But this means that we must deal with Jacob figures characteristic of J, E, and P, not to mention the possibility of an equivalent Deuteronomistic figure. The Yahwist has special importance in the context of these considerations

---

24 *Ibid.,* 178.

25 *Ibid.,* 197.

26 Gibson, 51; J. J. Stamm, "Ein ugaritisch-hebräisches Verbum und seine Ableitungen," *ThZ,* 35 (1979), 9; de Vaux, *Die Patriarchenerzählungen,* 4; *idem, The Early History of Israel,* 199; Herrmann, 54, n. 36; Freedman, 125; Bright, 78.

27 P. 131.

28 *KTU,* 4.645, 1: "the field of the *snr* people, which adjoins [the territory of] *ayly.*"

29 *KAI,* 37B, 1; II, 55.

30 So described repeatedly by Eissfeldt, most recently in *KlSchr,* V, 74.

31 Cf. most recently W. H. Schmidt, 25ff.

because, as far as we know, he was the first in history to write a connected account of the patriarchal tradition.[32] In the Joseph narrative, J may call the father of the brothers "Israel" rather than "Jacob" (Gen. 37:3,13; 43:6,8,11; etc.) because in the course of J's narrative the people of Israel already begins to emerge distinct from the patriarch.[33]

The question of J's own achievement—its extent and nature—can be answered only tentatively because the texts often do not admit clear answers. It is highly probable that the association of the patriarchal deities with Yahweh goes back to J precisely because E and P do not follow his lead, and it is likewise reasonable to ascribe the association of the traditions with Israel to him, because it coincides in the realm of political history with the union for the first time of all the "Israelite" tribes in the empire of David.[34] We may therefore also possibly ascribe to J the genealogical association of the patriarchs as grandfather, father, and son. But it remains an open question whether J linked the tradition of the patriarchs with that of the exodus and occupation or found them already so linked. Last but not least, the question of J's "intention," of his overall theme or kerygma, is variously answered.

As to the linking of the patriarchal tradition with that of the exodus and entry into Canaan, von Rad in particular has looked on J as the author of this connection,[35] while Wolff[36] and probably also Smend,[37] following Noth,[38] ascribe this linkage to the pre-J tradition. We must probably accept the latter view that the motif of the entry into Canaan belonged historically to the bedrock of the patriarchal tradition;[39] as Alt has shown,[40] the promise of the land and the fulfillment of this promise were a central element of the patriarchal religion. But at this early stage in the history of traditions, the two themes were very closely associated: they referred to the individual patriarch. In its present form, however—and here we may follow von Rad—J not only presents the patriarchs as genealogically related (a notion that may be ascribed to J because it is easiest to understand against the background of the Davidic period, i.e., the period of J) but also describes the fulfillment of the promises to the patriarchs, which did not come about until the early days of David, when the process of occupation was complete. J is therefore more likely to have forged this connection than to have incorporated it as it stood,[41] although this does not mean that J also linked the exodus tradition with the tradition of the entry into Canaan.

---

32 Cf. most recently L. Schmidt.

33 Cf. H. Donner, *Die literarische Gestalt der alttestamentlichen Josephsgeschichte. SHAW,* 1976/2, 39; also Jepsen, *Festschrift A. Alt,* 277.

34 See esp. Wallis, *Geschichte und Überlieferung,* 20ff., who identifies characteristic features of the early J, J, and E in the Jacob-Esau tradition.

35 G. von Rad, *OT Theology,* I (Eng. trans., New York, 1962), 168ff.; *idem, Das formgeschichtliche Problem des Hexateuch. BWANT,* 78[4/26] (1938), 54f. = *Gesammelte Studien,* I. *ThB,* 8 (1958), 67f. Cf. Weidmann, 148.

36 H. W. Wolff, "Das Kerygma des Jahwisten," *EvTh,* 24 (1964), 73-98 = *GSAT. ThB,* 22 (^{2}1973), 345-373, esp. 347.

37 R. Smend, *Yahweh War and Tribal Confederation* (Eng. trans., Nashville, 1970), 114f.

38 *A History of Pentateuchal Traditions,* 40ff.

39 *Ibid.,* 54ff.; most recently, de Pury.

40 Alt, *KlSchr,* I, 64.

41 Cf. Mitchell.

It is not so easy to answer the question of J's purpose, at least with respect to the Jacob tradition. According to von Rad,[42] J's message may be found in his addition of the birth oracle (Gen. 25:23) at the beginning of the Jacob narrative, in his inclusion of the powerful Bethel and Penuel narrative (Gen. 28, 32), and finally in his placing the prayer of Gen. 32:9-12 in the mouth of Jacob himself. The meaning of J's Jacob narrative is therefore that "God is concerned with Jacob; he is to be the ancestor of the people of God, and therefore God desires to lead him wherever he goes." Jepsen also suggests that "belief in the divine guidance of Jacob" is the work of J.[43] But it remains an open question whether this really describes the unique contribution of J, because both the birth oracle (Gen. 25:23) and the blessing of Isaac (27:27ff.) do not derive from J and may even antedate J's work, although both presuppose the identification of Jacob with the people of Israel and Esau with the Edomites.[44] No one doubts that by including these passages J incorporates their message and makes it his own; the only question is whether J does not have something of his own to add.

On the basis of Gen. 12:1-4, Wolff has identified the catchword "blessing" as J's characteristic term for "interpreting the overall history of Israel from Abraham's departure down to the empire of David."[45] This word, of course, is also found in the tradition, associated both with Jacob (Gen. 27:29) and with Israel (Nu. 24:9); and, if Jepsen is right, the central theme of the pre-J Jacob tradition was "the struggle to be blessed by the deity."[46] But the deliberate transformation of the word in Gen. 12 and its climactic position in the final clause, "In you all the families of the earth will bless themselves," are the work of J. For the Jacob tradition this means[47] that J can trace the blessing to a second generation through the genealogical linkage of Jacob (and Esau) with Isaac (Gen. 27). There is also an element of tension: the blessing can be lost (Gen. 25, 27). Furthermore, because Gen. 28:14 clearly alludes to Gen. 12:3 and therefore must derive from J, the expansion of Jacob in all directions means for J the realization of the blessing. Finally, Wolff points to Gen. 30:27,31, which speaks of Jacob's blessing in the form of large flocks and of the blessing that extends to Laban indirectly through these flocks. The covenant between Jacob and Laban at the conclusion of these narratives is also ascribed to J, who, Wolff maintains, is concerned to establish friendly relations between Israel and its neighbors, even "economic aid based on the model of Jacob."[48] Even if these expressions sound all too modern, in the catchword "blessing" Wolff has indeed put his finger on an important—possibly the most important—theme of J.[49] For J, Jacob epitomizes Israel standing unique in the world, happy because richly blessed.[50]

---

42 I, 171f.

43 *Festschrift A. Alt,* 279-281.

44 For a different view, see Wolff, *GSAT,* 349, n. 20; cf. also Maag.

45 P. 356.

46 *Festschrift A. Alt,* 274.

47 Wolff, 364f.

48 P. 365.

49 On the sources of the Pentateuch, see also Rost, 347-350.

50 See also J. Coppens, "La bénédiction de Jacob," in *Volume du Congrès, Strasbourg 1956. SVT,* 4 (1957), 97-115.

In addition, Fohrer points out[51] that in the patriarchal narratives J seeks to represent the relationship between God and humankind, both saying that God does not desert the sinner but stays with him, speaking to him and guiding him with his grace, and also seeking to describe the attitude such a person should have toward God: he should be faithful like Abraham, patiently accepting like Isaac, hopefully expectant like Jacob, and humble like Joseph.[52] Whether these deep theological statements really belong to J remains an open question, even if it is correct to say that all the features typical of the entire Jacob complex or even the whole complex of the patriarchal narratives are most likely J's interpretative contribution. J linked the patriarchs genealogically, subsuming them all under the theme of "blessing promised and bestowed" (and possibly also "blessing mediated"). He also gave thematic shape to each individual patriarchal figure, emphasizing in Jacob the resoluteness and obstinacy that leads to outstanding success, as well as Jacob's trust in God's help that prevents him from forfeiting the blessing. The figure of Jacob as depicted by J glows with joy and satisfaction, and even with a kind of pride.

In E, as the thematic unity of the total work would lead us us to expect, the Jacob tradition is shaped stylistically by the notion of an oath[53] and the figure of Jacob is refined ethically and morally. Unlike J, E does not ascribe Jacob's wealth to a shepherd's trick (Gen. 30:25-43) but to divine intervention (Gen. 31:2-12), and indicates similarly that the blessing of children (Gen. 33:5) and great riches (v. 11) come from God. We may note in general that E repeatedly theologizes secular material (cf. Gen. 31:50 with v. 48; also 30:6,8,18,20,23).[54]

A final step in the interpretation of the Jacob figure is taken by P, who substantially abbreviates the tradition he incorporates. For the most part, P's patriarchal narrative comprises nothing more than lists and summary statements. It is impossible to construct from these a Jacob figure typical of P. Furthermore, Gross has pointed out that for P Jacob represents merely a passing phase between the covenant with Abraham and the people of Israel. Only in Gen. 27:46–28:9 does P become more expansive.[55] Here he recounts Isaac's solemn sending of Jacob to Aram in order to find a legitimate wife, turning J's account of Jacob's flight into a formal mission. P also continues the process of purifying the ancient tradition of all its objectionable elements[56] and makes the relationship between Esau and Jacob more harmonious. Finally, the patriarch is significant for P as a witness in the disputes of his own period concerning mixed marriages. Outside of Genesis, P cites the covenant with Abraham, Isaac, and Jacob (Ex. 2:24) and the oath sworn to the three patriarchs to give them the land (Ex. 6:8). It must remain an open question, however, whether we can follow Weimar[57] in saying that for P Jacob is the man of the blessing as Abraham is the man of the covenant.

---

51 *Intro. OT* (Eng. trans., Nashville, 1968), 150.
52 See also O. Kaiser, *Intro. OT* (Eng. trans., Minneapolis, 1975), 85-91.
53 Richter.
54 See also G. von Rad, *Genesis. OTL* (Eng. trans. 1961), 25f.
55 Cf. C. Houtman, "What Did Jacob See in His Dream at Bethel?" *VT,* 27 (1977), 337-351.
56 Von Rad, *Genesis,* 282.
57 P. 202.

2. *Interpretation of the Figure of Jacob.* When we address the problem of how the figure of Jacob was interpreted in the oral tradition, we must face two questions: (1) Is the figure of Jacob an individual, or does it represent a tribe or some similar group? (2) What is the meaning of the change of Jacob's name to "Israel"?

Today it is generally recognized that the figure of Jacob is human, not divine, a conclusion supported by the etymology of the name. This means that we should be able to equate Jacob with others who bear the same name and treat him as an individual.[58] Alt's examination of the form and substance of the patriarchal religion led to the same conclusion. If each patriarch received a revelation and founded a cult, then he must have been a human individual.[59] And it would even be legitimate to follow Gunkel[60] in exploring the oral tradition. Gen. 25:27, which describes Jacob as a quiet man, dwelling in tents, suggests that he was a herdsman, Esau a hunter.[61] We might therefore interpret the Jacob-Esau narratives as a legend of class conflict and even question its historical value.[62] Those who interpret the figure of Jacob along these or similar lines are therefore forced to deal with the question of how the legendary figure of Jacob could become the ancestor of the historical people of Israel. Gunkel[63] thinks this happened in the latest stage of the tradition, on the grounds that the element of tribal history is secondary with respect to the element of legend.[64] Albright[65] even thinks that very ancient ethnic traditions have been incorporated into the patriarchal narratives.

Even today, however, there are still those who support the tribal interpretation of the patriarchs, first proposed by Steuernagel but later greatly modified in detail. We shall not go into the problems this theory presents with respect to Abraham and Isaac. It claims that behind the figure of Jacob—at least in the Genesis narratives—there stands a group, so that we should in fact speak of the "Jacob tribe,"[66] the "Jacob people,"[67] the "proto-Israelite Jacob group,"[68] or the like.[69] This interpretation is supported by the observation that at least in the extant sources Jacob represents less a nomadic individual than a seminomadic group trying to achieve permanent settlement. Furthermore, unlike the name "Abraham," which is never used for the people, and the name "Isaac," which appears in parallel with "Israel" only in Am. 7:9,16, the name "Jacob" (as seen above) is used constantly as a parallel term for Israel. Elsewhere in the OT, too, we note that

---

58 De Vaux, *Die Patriarchenerzählungen,* 5f.; Albright, *Yahweh,* 56; etc.

59 Alt, *KlSchr,* I, 47f.

60 Pp. 169-181.

61 Most recently Noth, *A History of Pentateuchal Traditions,* 95-99; Maag, *ThZ,* 13 (1957), 423ff.

62 Already Gressmann, now Thompson.

63 P. 181.

64 P. 154.

65 *Yahweh,* 56.

66 Eissfeldt, *Die Genesis der Genesis,* 61; *KlSchr,* V, 74.

67 Mowinckel, 132; Gunneweg, 18f.

68 Wallis, *Geschichte und Überlieferung,* 17.

69 Similar conclusions are reached by de Vaux, *The Early History of Israel,* 266; Seebass, *EvTh,* 37 (1977), 212.

groups are personified; the sons of Jacob, for example, stand for the Israelite tribes bearing their names. It is therefore probably also legitimate to look on Jacob as representing a group. This is not to deny that this group preserved a memory that their ancestor had functioned as recipient of a revelation, even though it is scarcely possible to say more on this point, since it lies beyond the horizon of the present narratives in Genesis, which now deal with the residence of the patriarchs in Canaan.

3. *Jacob and Israel.* We must accordingly interpret "Jacob" as the "Jacob group," distinct from the later twelve sons of Jacob. Similarly, in order to deal with the relationship between "Jacob" and "Israel" within the tradition of the Pentateuch, we might interpret "Israel" as an originally independent group that later merged with "Jacob." That Jacob and Israel were originally "two legendary figures" was already suggested by Georg Jacob.[70] Mowinckel[71] also saw in them two originally independent entities of the tradition, reflecting the history of two different groups. Seebass, finally, attempted to demonstrate the independence of the patriarch Israel, who was especially associated with Shechem.[72] Without going into the problems connected with the name Israel, we note only that according to Gen. 32:23-33(22-32) the change of Jacob's name to Israel[73] takes place at the threshold of the settled territory of Canaan and in the context of what is therefore Jacob's first encounter with the god El. According to Gen. 33:18-20, it leads to the formal introduction of El-worship among this group, now called Israel; the altar set up at Shechem to commemorate the event bears the confessional name "El is the Elohim of Israel."[74] This means that we may see in "Israel" a new name for the Jacob group, with religious associations connected with the worship of El, but not a tribal group originally independent of the Jacob people and later merging with them.

The next question is whether we can determine more precisely who belonged to the entity called "Jacob." The tradition that Jacob was the father of twelve sons who embody Israel as a whole means that as an entity Israel includes Jacob, but that Jacob and his twelve sons—i.e., Israel—are not identical. They are identified, it is true, in Gen. 25:23; 27:29,40, where "Jacob" means the people of Israel and "Esau" means the Edomites; but

70 P. 18.

71 P. 132.

72 *Der Erzvater Israel*; *EvTh*, 37 (1977), 212f.

73 Cf. O. Eissfeldt, "Non dimittam te, nisi benedixeris mihi," *Mélanges bibliques. Festschrift A. Robert. Travaux de l'Institut Catholique de Paris,* 4 (1957), 77-81 = *KlSchr,* III (1966), 412-16; F. van Trigt, "La signification de la lutte de Jacob près du Yabboq: Gen xxxii.23-33," *OTS,* 12 (1958), 280-309; J. L. McKenzie, "Jacob at Peniel: Gn 32,24-32," *CBQ,* 25 (1963), 71-76; R. Barthes, "The Struggle with the Angel: Traditional Analysis of Genesis 32:23-33," in *Structural Analysis and Biblical Exegesis,* ed. Barthes, *et al.* (Eng. trans., Pittsburgh, 1974), 21-33; K. Elliger, "Der Jakobskampf am Jabbok," *ZThK,* 48 (1951), 1-31 = *KlSchr. ThB,* 32 (1966), 141-173; H.-J. Hermisson, "Jakobs Kampf am Jabbok (Gen 32, 23-33)," *ZThK,* 71 (1974), 239-261; G. Hentschel, "Jakobs Kampf am Jabbok (Gen 32, 23-33)—eine geunin israelitische Tradition?" *ErfThSt,* 37 (1977), 13-37; A. de Pury, "Jakob am Jabbok, Gen. 32, 23-33," *ThZ,* 35 (1979), 18-34.

74 Eissfeldt, *KlSchr,* III, 412-16; IV, 96-98; *Festschrift D. W. Thomas,* 75f.; on Gen. 33:20, cf. also M. H. Pope, *El in the Ugaritic Texts. SVT,* 2 (1955), 15; I. Mihalik, "Some Thoughts on the Name of Israel," *Theological Soundings,* 1973, 11-19, esp. 15.

these national aphorisms belong to a later stage of the tradition.[75] That both sayings, or at least the verses mentioned, are anachronistic in the context of the Jacob-Esau narratives is shown by the clear distinction made elsewhere between Jacob and his sons, who represent this very Israel (cf. also the awkward formulations in 1 K. 18:31; 2 K. 17:34), both with respect to living conditions and political circumstances and also with respect to religion.

In terms of living conditions, Jacob is described as a tent dweller (Gen. 25:27; 32:22[21]; 33:18; etc.) and a prosperous shepherd (Gen. 29:1ff.; 30:25ff.; etc.); this is also the way he lives in Canaan. Jacob's sons, however, take up agriculture during the course of the occupation, just as the "Jacob" who represents the people in Gen. 27:27-29 is described as a farmer. It is true that transhumance can account not only for the entry of the patriarchs into Canaan but also for its occupation by the Israelite tribes and even the migration of Israelite groups to Egypt, suggesting that these three complexes of events, although historically distinct in the OT tradition, all belong to the extended phenomenon of "Israel's" occupation of the land.

There is nevertheless an important distinction to be preserved. The patriarchs, including Jacob, are concerned to establish peaceful coexistence with the Canaanites, whom they recognize as rulers of the land and from whom Jacob purchases a piece of land near Shechem (Gen. 33:19). The OT tradition, however, despicts the later occupation proper as a military operation, expressing the claim of the Israelites to rule the land of Canaan, which actually belongs to them. There is also a religious difference. The patriarchs, again including Jacob, worship El as their God. Gen. 31:53 also mentions the *paḥaḏ* of Isaac, by whom Jacob swears, and Gen. 49:24 speaks of an *ʾāḇîr* of Jacob. For the later Israelites, however, Yahweh alone is God. We must necessarily conclude that Jacob is not identical with Israel, and the Jacob people are not the sons of Israel. To this point the argument is relatively clear.

If we go on to ask who these Jacob people were or into what familiar groups they were absorbed, any answer must be hypothetical. We observe that the Abraham tradition centers on Hebron, the Isaac tradition on Beer-sheba, and the Jacob tradition on central Palestine and Transjordan; the traditions do not overlap but generally cover the later territory of Israel. This observation suggests associating Jacob with the Israelite groups dwelling in the vicinity of Shechem and Bethel as well as Mahanaim and Penuel. For the historical period, this means the tribes of Ephraim and Manasseh and possibly Benjamin, as well as the tribe of Gad in Gilead. Following Alt, Noth[76] therefore designates the "house of Joseph" as the locus of the Jacob traditions. Since Abraham and Isaac are associated with southern Judah and the Negeb, this would mean that there is no patriarch associated with Judah itself.[77] In addition, the "house of Joseph" was quite probably the locus of the exodus and occupation traditions, which makes its identification with Jacob unlikely. According to Gen. 34, finally, Simeon and Levi formerly (i.e., before

---

[75] Cf. H.-J. Zobel, *Israel und die Völker* (inaugural diss., Halle, 1967).
[76] *A History of Pentateuchal Traditions,* 107-9.
[77] So W. H. Schmidt, 23.

the entry of the "house of Joseph") dwelt at Shechem; this almost rules out the "house of Joseph" as the original locus of the Jacob tradition.

The tribes just mentioned are in fact possible candidates. Since the birth narrative assigns both sons to Leah, distinguishing them from the Rachel sons Joseph and Benjamin, one might also consider the other children of Leah: Reuben, Judah, Issachar, and Zebulun.[78] This hypothesis is supported by the observation that, besides the special tradition associated with Simeon and Levi in Gen. 34, tribal traditions connected with Reuben (Gen. 35:21f.) and Judah (Gen. 38) have been interwoven with the Jacob narrative; this might indicate that these traditions, which go back to the patriarchal period, deal with earlier events than the traditions associated with the other Israelite tribes. As concerns Issachar, Alt[79] has shown on the basis of several Amarna letters that this tribe could have settled in the plain of Jezreel much earlier, possibly as early as the fourteenth millennium B.C. This conclusion is probably also applicable to the other Leah tribes. As concerns the tribe of Reuben, Reuben's genealogical status as the first-born and his association with the Transjordan indicates that this tribe dwelt originally in the territory of Gilead and may even have been the locus of the Jacob tradition, as Jepsen[80] assumes; indeed, Jacob's tomb was at one time located in the Transjordan.[81]

Last but not least, it may be pointed out that these archaic traditions still reflect the seminomadic life of these tribes, as seems appropriate for the Jacob people. Gen. 35:21f. speaks of pitching tents and locates Reuben's transgression at Migdal-eder, "Flock Tower," probably in the Transjordan. Gen. 34 assumes that Simeon and Levi are not yet permanently settled (vv. 10, 17), possess herds of cattle (vv. 5, 23), and take flocks and herds and asses when they plunder Shechem (v. 28). Gen. 49:6 says that they both hamstring oxen, suggesting a way of life that has no use for oxen. Finally, Gen. 38 also depicts Judah as a herdsman.

III. The God of the Fathers.

1. *El.* The Genesis narratives associate Jacob with Shechem and Bethel[82] west of the Jordan and with Mahanaim and Penuel or Peniel east of the Jordan. In our tradition, this association is established in each instance by a revelation of the local deity. At Bethel it is El-bethel who appears to Jacob, promising him descendants and possession of the land, whereupon the patriarch sets up a massebah, which he calls Bethel (Gen. 28:10-22); another version has him build an altar and call the place El-bethel (Gen. 35:1-7). At Shechem Jacob sets up an altar or, more likely, a massebah, which he names *'ēl 'elōhê yiśrā'ēl* (Gen. 33:20). After Jacob had been blessed by Elohim (or better: El) and renamed Israel, he called the place Penuel or Peniel, "Face of El" (Gen. 32:31[30]). We may confidently assume that here, too, Jacob worshipped El. With regard to Mahanaim, E

---

78 Eissfeldt, *CAH,* II/2. XXVI(a) (³1975), 316f.; *idem, KlSchr,* IV, 170-75; Jepsen, *Festschrift A. Alt,* 274, 276; for a different conclusion, see Mowinckel, 129ff.

79 *KlSchr,* I, 165-68.

80 *Festschrift A. Alt,* 270-73.

81 Noth, *A History of Pentateuchal Traditions,* 88, n. 260.

82 On the transfer of the tradition from Shechem to Bethel, see Otto, 165ff.

speaks of the "angels of Elohim," and the toponym is interpreted as meaning "Camp of Elohim" (Gen. 32:2f.[1f.]), so that one might ask whether these hints suggest a tradition that Jacob worshipped El at Mahanaim.[83] As Eissfeldt has repeatedly pointed out,[84] all this evidence suggests that Jacob or the Jacob group in Palestine worshipped the Canaanite god El; the local El deities there are hypostases of the one El. Furthermore, it was this El who promised Jacob descendants and possession of the land. Up to this point the situation is relatively clear.

2. *"The Mighty One of Jacob."* Problems arise when one attempts to define the relationship between El and the god(s) of the fathers in our tradition. We owe to Alt the observation, still generally accepted, that each of the patriarchs was associated with a particular patriarchal god, the "god of the father."[85] Over the objections of Hoftijzer, Rost[86] finds a reference to this type of religion in Gen. 31:53 (E): two seminomadic groups, represented by Jacob and Laban, agree to delimit their grazing area and reinforce this agreement through an oath. Jacob calls on the Elohim of Abraham and Laban on the Elohim of Nahor as witnesses to the treaty. In the same context we are told that Jacob swore "by the *paḥaḏ* of his father Isaac." Verse 42 makes it clear that the word *'āḇîw,* "of his father," is secondary: the original name of this god is *paḥaḏ yiṣḥāq.*[87] The same verse also indicates that this deity seems to have been an independent entity alongside the God of Abraham.

The situation is made even more complex by the mention of the *'āḇîr* of Jacob in Gen. 49:24.[88] We thus have two divine appellatives associated with Jacob, each made up of a noun followed by the name of the patriarch, since we are certainly justified in assuming that the "Mighty One of Jacob" was worshipped by the Jacob people just as the *paḥaḏ* of Isaac was worshipped by the Isaac people. To the extent that the figure of Jacob was individualized and appended to the (Abraham-)Isaac narratives, the divine appellatives had to be included in the process. Thus the *paḥaḏ* of Isaac became the God of Jacob's father Isaac, worshipped by Jacob. In the same way, Abraham, the father associated with Isaac, became the ancestor of Jacob, and the God of Abraham became a "god of the father" worshipped by Jacob. This shows that the Mighty One of Jacob was the patriarchal deity of the Jacob people, and at an early stage may have been called only "the god of my/our father."[89]

On the basis of this terminology, Alt demonstrated convincingly that this religion is

---

[83] Cf. C. Houtman, "Jacob at Mahanaim: Some remarks on Genesis xxxii 2-3," *VT,* 28 (1978), 37-44.

[84] Most recently in *Die Genesis der Genesis,* 63-64; *KlSchr,* V, 50-62.

[85] *Essays,* 17ff.

[86] P. 353.

[87] On *paḥaḏ yiṣḥāq,* see J. Becker, *Gottesfurcht im AT. AnBibl,* 25 (1965), 177ff.; N. Krieger, "Der Schrecken Isaaks," *Jud,* 17 (1961), 193ff.; D. R. Hillers, "*paḥad yiṣḥāq,*" *JBL,* 91 (1972), 90-92; → פחד *pḥd.*

[88] → אביר *'āḇîr* (*'ābhîr*).

[89] Cf. W. H. Schmidt, 19f.

associated with a nomadic society; the deity is linked not to a place but to a person. The deity goes with the group. Gen. 31 agrees with this observation in that it deals with "delimitation of the grazing areas of two nomadic tribes" on the fringe of the settled territory.[90] But if this type of religion is associated with seminomadic groups, then the promises of descendants and territorial possession are substantially earlier; they were made to the fathers not at the sanctuaries of the settled territory but in the open countryside.[91] This is only natural: on the one hand, the substance of what is promised corresponds to the needs of nomadic shepherds in search of land; on the other, the acceptance of these promises and their realization by the El deity at the sanctuaries of the settled territory is quite comprehensible after the fathers settled there and ceased their nomadic existence.

Now Rost points out[92] furthermore that Gen. 46:1 also speaks of "the God of his father Isaac," who thereupon introduces himself: "I am El, the God of your father" (v. 3). Whatever questions the text may raise, it is important that it sees worship of the fathers' God and worship of El as identical. The sanctuaries of the deity El in Canaan antedate the arrival of the patriarchal groups, and the patriarchs did not come to know El in the desert but in Canaan. Rost therefore concludes[93] that for at least a period the fathers' God and El must have been worshipped side by side. A part of the people that had already settled worshipped El with the Canaanites, while another part, still nomadic, held fast "to the God of the fathers, whom they brought with them from their desert wanderings."[94] Attractive as this theory is, it founders on the identification of the God of the fathers with El in Gen. 49:25, as well as Gen. 48:3; Ex. 15:2.[95] This is also the primary objection to Eissfeldt's view that the renunciation of foreign gods alluded to in Gen. 35:4; Josh 24:2,14f. refers to the pre-Canaanite patriarchal deities.[96] He is correct in recognizing that the deities and symbols involved are not merely pre-Mosaic but pre-Canaanite. It is most unlikely, however, that the term "foreign gods" (Gen. 35:4) or "the gods which your fathers served" (Josh. 24:14f.; cf. 24:2) refers to the "God of the fathers" identified by Alt, since Gen. 35:4 speaks of earrings in the same breath as foreign gods, which are much more apt to have been something like the teraphim of Rachel (Gen. 31:30ff.).[97] It is true that Gen. 49:24 speaks of the *ʾāḇîr* of Jacob in parallel with the Shepherd of the Rock of Israel, who, as the locative particle *šām* shows, is associated with a particular site and that in v. 25 the parallelism between "El Shaddai"[98] and "the God of your father" identifies the God of the fathers with El. This does not prove, however, that El and the

---

90 Rost, 354.

91 Noth, *A History of Pentateuchal Traditions,* 54-56; *idem, The History of Israel,* 133-35; cf. Jepsen, 270; W. H. Schmidt, 20-22; Gunneweg, 18.

92 Pp. 354f.

93 *Ibid.,* 355.

94 *Ibid.,* 355.

95 Cf. Haran, 35-37.

96 *KlSchr,* III, 363; IV, 97; *CAH,* II/2. XXVI(a) (^{3}1975), 311.

97 Cf. also Weidmann, 159, 172f.

98 Following *BHS.*

God of the fathers were originally the same deity.[99] Instead, the pre-Canaanite cult of the "Mighty One of Jacob" coalesced with the worship of El at various local sanctuaries during the occupation of the land by the Jacob people; more precisely, the "Mighty One of Jacob" absorbed El and as a result of this process acquired local ties. The fact that the patriarchs occupied the ancient sanctuaries and finally came to be looked on as founders of the local cults demonstrates their inner vitality and explains how El could be absorbed by the God of the fathers.[100]

3. *"The God of Jacob."* The same process is suggested by the phrase "the God of Jacob,"[101] which appears 16 times (17 counting the LXX of Ps. 24:6[LXX 23:6], or even 18 if we read "the God of 'Jacob' " in 2 S. 23:3[102]). It is also possible that a *y* has dropped out by haplography in Ps. 114:7 and that we should read *'ᵉlōhê ya'ᵃqōḇ*.[103] The phrase "El of Jacob" appears uniquely in Ps. 146:5; it is an open question whether "El" is a proper name or an appellative. If the latter, the meaning would be the same as that of the common expression "the God of Jacob."

It is noteworthy that this phrase appears only 4 times in narrative passages (Ex. 3:6,15f.; 4:5), and then always in association with "the God of Abraham" and "the God of Isaac" (3:6,15; 4:5) or in the expression "the God of Abraham, Isaac, and Jacob" (3:16). The other occurrences are all in poetic texts. The Psalms have the most, with 10 occurrences (Ps. 20:2[1]; 24:6; 46:8,12[7,11]; 75:10[9]; 76:7[6]; 81:2,5[1,4]; 84:9[8]; 94:7). Two more are found in the last words of David (2 S. 23:1,3) and 1 each in Isaiah (Isa. 2:3) and Micah (Mic. 4:2), identical late postexilic passages. This survey is not very encouraging as to the independence and antiquity of the phrase. The earliest occurrence that can be dated with some confidence is 2 S. 23:1,3, where David calls himself "the anointed of the God of Jacob" and "the favorite of the songs of Israel" and affirms that "the God of 'Jacob' " and "Rock of Israel" has spoken to him and promised him an eternal dynasty. The language points clearly to Jerusalem and perhaps to the time of David. One gains the impression that this terminology for Yahweh is a Jerusalemite theologoumenon, an impression confirmed by the Psalms passages, the majority of which appear to be preexilic and—like Isa. 2:3 par. Mic. 4:2—to be associated with Jerusalem. Protection is ascribed to the "God of Jacob" in Ps. 20:2(1), help in 75:10(9), strength in 81:2(1), and military might in 76:7(6); in Ps. 46:(4),8,12([3],7,11), we are told that "Yahweh Sabaoth is with us, the God of Jacob is our fortress," and in Ps. 84:9(8) "Yahweh Sabaoth" appears in parallel with "the God of Jacob," probably expressing the element of power associated with this term for God. We should give serious consideration, therefore, to Kraus's theory[104] that "the Mighty

---

99 Contra Eissfeldt.

100 Cf. Herrmann, 48, 50; also W. H. Schmidt, 22-25.

101 Cf. also G. Wanke, *Die Zionstheologie der Korachiten in ihrem traditionsgeschichtlichen Zusammenhang. BZAW,* 97 (1966), 54-58.

102 With *BHS.*

103 See the comms.

104 H.-J. Kraus, *Psalms 1–59* (Eng. trans., Minneapolis, 1988), 280.

One of Jacob," the ancient name for the God of the patriarchs, established the tradition of mighty protection provided by "the God of Jacob."[105] More particularly, it is possible that the term "God of Jacob" is an extension of the archaic phrase "Mighty One of Jacob," which also appears in the Psalms (Ps. 132:2,5; cf. 24:6); their similarity in usage and meaning make this a reasonable assumption. The parallelism "Yahweh" par. "Mighty One of Jacob" (Ps. 132) is equivalent to the parallelism "Yahweh" par. "God of Jacob" (Pss. 20, 24, 46, 84, 94; cf. 114, 146), and both express strength and help, protection and assistance, reinforced by the use of "Sabaoth" with "Yahweh" (Pss. 46, 84). But the term "Sabaoth" itself points to Jerusalem. All this evidence makes it likely that the title "God of Jacob" represents a Jerusalemite equivalent to "Yahweh," first used in the time of David. J adopted the expression in Ex. 3:16; 4:5 to summarize the pre-Yahwistic worship of the God of the fathers and El, and this usage was followed by E in Ex. 3:6,15.

Finally, Wildberger[106] suggests that both the earlier term "Mighty One of Jacob" and the later term "God of Jacob" were associated with the ark (cf. Pss. 24, 132) and were brought to Jerusalem with it.

IV. Historical Considerations. A nomadic group of herdsmen from the region around Safa[107] tracing its origins back to Jacob and worshipping the "Mighty One of Jacob" as its god settles on both sides of the central Jordan, obviously during transhumance. This process is entirely peaceful and encompasses the region surrounding the cities of Mahanaim and Penuel, Shechem and Bethel. Its date is entirely a matter of guesswork. Since the events of Gen. 34 take place before the arrival of the Moses group and since Gen. 49:14f. can be dated around the period of Labaiah, we can assume that the Jacob people came into Canaan a century or two before the entrance of the Moses group, although several features appear to go back to an earlier date.[108] The period around 1800-1500 B.C. is supported by many.[109] Because the archaeological evidence is ambiguous, it will not be discussed here. For the OT tradition, the most important element of this process is the adoption of the indigenous worship of El. This deity incorporates and lends appropriate support to the immigrants' desire for land and offspring already aroused by the Mighty One of Jacob. Thus the pre-Canaanite worship of the Mighty One of Jacob coalesces with the Canaanite cult of El. Henceforth El is solemnly proclaimed to be the God of Jacob or (because the change of Jacob's name to "Israel" is also involved) the God of Israel. The patriarchs attract to themselves the local traditions of Canaan, reshaped so that they themselves appear as the heroes.

---

105 Also H. Wildberger, *Jesaja. BK,* X/1 (1972), 63.

106 *Ibid.*

107 Wallis, *ZAW,* 81 (1969), 35f.

108 See above the histories of Israel: Noth, *The History of Israel,* 135f.; Bright, 67-72; Eissfeldt, *Die Genesis der Genesis,* 6-10; de Vaux, *The Early History of Israel,* 265f.; Herrmann, 45, 49-51; Gunneweg, 17-20; also Gordon, *JNES,* 13 (1954), 56-59, changing his position presented in *BASOR,* 66 (1937), 25-27.

109 Albright; Rowley, 305.

V. Jacob in the Prophetic Canon. When we examine the appearances of the name "Jacob" in the prophetic literature, we note that it is used for both the patriarch and the people (or part of the people) of Israel.

1. *Jacob the Individual.* "Jacob" as the name of the patriarch appears very rarely in the prophets. Isa. 58:14 speaks of him as the father of God's people; Ezk. 28:25; 37:25 state that Yahweh gave the land to his servant Jacob; Ob. 10 speaks of Jacob as the brother of Esau/Edom; and Mal. 1:2 states that Yahweh loved Jacob but not Esau. All of these passages allude to the familiar tradition. It is also possible that the phrase "the pride of Jacob" in Am. 8:7 ("Yahweh has sworn by the pride of Jacob"); Ps. 47:5(4) ("He chose our heritage for us, the pride of Jacob whom he loves") alludes to the Jacob tradition reduced to proverbial dimensions.[110]

The Jacob tradition is clearly drawn upon by Hosea.[111] Hos. 12:4a(3a) ("In the womb he outwitted his brother") alludes to Gen. 25:26 in conjunction with v. 23 and also Gen. 25:28-34 in conjunction with 27:36. Hos. 12:4b(3b) ("In his manhood he strove with Elohim") recalls Gen. 32:23-33(22-32); both use the verb *śārâ.* Hos. 12:5a(4a) ("He strove with an angel and prevailed") might also suggest the event at the Jabbok,[112] but Gen. 32 speaks of a "man" (Gen. 32:25, 29[24,28]) or "Elohim" (vv. 29,31[28,30]), not an "angel." Gen. 32:2(1), however, does speak of angels. It is hard to decide whether Hosea was familiar with still other Jacob traditions, these narratives had not yet taken on fixed form, or Hosea was simply alluding to them freely.[113] The next clause of Hos. 12:5(4) ("He wept and sought his favor") is likewise hard to interpret, even if Jacob rather than the angel is the subject. Good[114] thinks the reference is to Gen. 35:8; Holladay[115] suggests Gen. 33:4 (weeping) and Gen. 32:6(5); 33:8,10,15 (seeking favor). Others, like Wolff,[116] find a free reference to Gen. 32 or "a special element of the Penuel tradition."[117] The continuation (Hos. 12:5b[4b]) goes on to say that God "met him at Bethel and there spoke with 'him'," once again making quite free use of Gen. 28:10-22; 35:1-7.[118] Finally, Hos. 12:13(12) speaks of Jacob's fleeing to Laban (Gen. 27:41-45; 29:1-14), as well as his doing service for Leah and Rachel (Gen. 29:15-28). For the sake of topicality, in this last passage Hosea calls Jacob "Israel." All in all, the prophet exhibits extensive familiarity with major portions of the Jacob tradition, which he draws on freely to

---

110 H. W. Wolff, *Joel and Amos. Herm* (Eng. trans. 1977), 328.

111 See also I. H. Eybers, "The Use of Proper Names as a Stylistic Device," *Semitics,* 2 (1971/72), 84; F. Diedrich, *Die Anspielungen auf die Jakob-Tradition in Hosea 12,1–13,3. FzB,* 27 (1977).

112 W. H. Schmidt, 33.

113 See esp. Good, 140-151; Rudolph (*Hosea. KAT,* XIII/1 [1966], 222) deletes the statement on unconvincing grounds.

114 Pp. 147ff.

115 Pp. 56f.

116 H. W. Wolff, *Hosea. Herm* (Eng. trans. 1974), 212.

117 Otto, 176, n. 60.

118 Good, 146, 149.

emphasize his message of judgment. Like E,[119] he interprets these negatively,[120] as does the allusion in Jer. 9:3(4).[121]

2. *Jacob as a Designation of the People.* Hosea and Jeremiah both draw on the Jacob tradition for the purpose of identifying the nation with its ancestor, so that the sin of the people is prefigured in the misconduct of the patriarch. Now we come to the numerous passages in which "Jacob" is used to refer to the people. This occurs most frequently where "Israel" and "Jacob" are used in parallelism, usually with Jacob mentioned first (Isa. 9:7[8]; 10:20; 14:1; 27:6; 40:27; 41:8,14; 42:24; 43:1,22,28; 44:1,5,21,23; 45:4; 46:3; 48:1,12; 49:5f.; Jer. 2:4; 30:10 par. 46:27; 31:7; Ezk. 20:5; 39:25; Mic. 1:5; 2:12; 3:8f.; Nah. 2:3[2]; exception: Isa. 41:8). Other names appearing in parallelism with "Jacob" include Jeshurun (Isa. 44:2), Judah (Isa. 65:9; Jer. 5:20; Hos. 12:3[2]), Ephraim and Judah (Hos. 10:11), Samaria (Mic. 1:5), Zion (Isa. 59:20), Abraham (Mic. 7:20), and Joseph (Ob. 18).

Each instance must be examined to determine to which portion of the nation the name "Jacob" refers. When only Judah or Joseph is mentioned, it is clear that the name refers to the southern or the northern kingdom. It is not clear what is meant by "Jeshurun."[122] The name can also be used for the people of the Exile (Deutero-Isaiah) or the postexilic community (Trito-Isaiah), but the real problem is that "Jacob" can refer to both the entire nation and to individual parts of it.

This observation is confirmed by the passages in the prophetic canon where "Jacob" appears independently without a parallel expression. For example, "house of Jacob" (Isa. 2:5f.; 8:17; 14:1; 29:22; 58:1; Ezk. 20:5; Am. 3:13; 9:8; Ob. 17; Mic. 2:7) can refer to the northern kingdom, the southern kingdom, and both components of Israel together. The "pride of Jacob" obviously refers to the arrogant claims of Samaria (Am. 6:8), just as the simple word "Jacob" in Am. 7:2,5 refers to the northern kingdom. In Mic. 5:6f.(7f.), the "remnant of Jacob" refers to the Jewish *gôlâ*; unqualified "Jacob" in Jeremiah (Jer. 10:25; 30:7,10; 31:11; 46:27f.) refers to the people of Judah; the phrase "servant Jacob" without any parallel expression in Isa. 48:20 refers to the exile community (cf. also the "tents of Jacob" in Jer. 30:18; Mal. 2:12); unqualified "Jacob" in Isa. 29:22, "glory of Jacob" in Isa. 17:4 (cf. v. 3: "glory of the sons of Israel"), and "guilt" of Jacob (Isa. 27:9) all probably refer to the entire nation; and the phrase "sons of Jacob" (Mal. 3:6) or "seed of Jacob" (Isa. 45:19,25; Jer. 33:26) has the same meaning as just "Jacob."

Finally, there are various divine appellatives employing "Jacob" and understood as titles of Yahweh: "King of Jacob" (Isa. 41:21), "Holy One of Jacob" (Isa. 29:23, par. "God of Israel"), "Portion of Jacob" (Jer. 10:16; 51:19), and of course once again "God of Jacob" (Isa. 2:3 par. Mic. 4:2) or "'God' of the house of Jacob" (Isa. 29:22) and "Mighty One of Jacob" (Isa. 49:26; 60:16, par. "Yahweh"; cf. Isa. 1:24: the "Mighty One

---

119 Cf. Ruppert.

120 Wolff, *Hosea,* 208; Rudolph, *KAT,* XIII/1, 224, contra Ackroyd, 245-259.

121 Rudolph, *HAT,* XII, 64.

122 Cf. Wächter; Seebass, *VT,* 27 (1977), 160f., 166, 169: Judah's associated non-Israelite neighbors Caleb, Cain, Othniel, and Jerahmeel, which is unlikely.

of Israel"). These expressions illuminate the real meaning of the name "Jacob." Just as "Jacob" and "Israel" can stand in parallelism, so the corresponding divine appellatives can be used in parallel construction. This shows that between Yahweh and Jacob there is a correlation like that between Yahweh and Israel. In the visions of Amos, for example, we are told that Jacob cannot stand because he is so small (Am. 7:2,5); Yahweh can be moved to repentance, but finally brings judgment upon Israel (7:8f.; 8:2).

This connection finds even clearer expression in prophetic idioms associated with the semantic field of "Jacob." Isa. 2:6 refers to the "house of Jacob" also as "thy [Yahweh's] people"; Mic. 2:7 addresses the people's rejection of the prophet's message by asking, "Is the house of Jacob 'cursed'?" This question can be understood fully only against the background of the rich blessings associated with the house of Jacob. According to van der Woude,[123] this phrase also reflects the covenant at Sinai, so that "Jacob" is the name of the covenant people. Isa. 14:1 says that Yahweh will again have compassion on and choose Jacob-Israel, so that even aliens will "cleave to the house of Jacob." Like Jeremiah (Jer. 30:10; 46:28), Deutero-Isaiah (Isa. 41:8; 44:1f., 21; 45:4; 48:20) addresses Jacob as the servant of Yahweh. In this context Jeremiah uses the terminology of ransom (Jer. 31:11) and deliverance (30:7,10; 46:27); Deutero-Isaiah speaks of the election (Isa. 41:8; 44:1f.; 45:4), redemption (41:14; 44:23; 49:26 par. 60:16), calling (48:12), creation (43:1), and again the ransom of Jacob (48:20). Trito-Isaiah (Isa. 58:1) refers to Jacob as "my people," and finally Ezekiel (Ezk. 20:5) speaks of the choosing of Jacob in Egypt, reinforced by God's oath.

In the OT prophets, then, the name "Jacob" clearly means Israel as the people of God, the community of Yahweh. This lends support to Wolff's theory[124] that in Hos. 10:11 "Jacob" refers to the old tribal league and in Hos. 12:3(2) to Israel's sacral past.[125] On the one hand, Jacob is held up to the people as a negative example, reflecting their own sinful failure; on the other hand, the patriarch, chosen by God and endowed with the promises of great blessings, is for the prophet the prototype of the blessed people of God. In him the election of Israel is already prefigured, its liberation and redemption, its deliverance and call. Jacob typifies God's faithfulness toward his people, a source of comfort in deepest depression. When the nation as a whole is addressed as a spiritual entity it can be called "Jacob." This name is obviously chosen because there is no danger of its being misunderstood in a political sense; none of the political manifestations of Israel throughout the course of history (with the exception of the original Jacob group) was ever called "Jacob." This is probably also the reason for the usual sequence Jacob/Israel in parallel construction. Finally, when Deutero-Isaiah can say (Isa. 43:1) that Yahweh created Jacob, and when Ezekiel speaks of God's choosing Jacob in Egypt, there is logic in their words: they are speaking of the birth of the people of God in its historical beginnings.

---

123 A. S. van der Woude, "Micah in Dispute with the Pseudo-Prophets," *VT,* 19 (1969), 244-260, esp. 247f.

124 *Hosea,* 185.

125 *Ibid.,* 211.

VI. Jacob in the Psalms.

1. *Jacob the Individual.* The picture of Jacob in the Psalms differs little if at all from that drawn by the prophets.[126] Ps. 105:9f. speaks of Abraham, Isaac, and Jacob/Israel as three individuals with whom Yahweh made a covenant. The Israelites now assembled for worship, called "all the seed of Jacob/Israel" in Ps. 22:24(23), are to remember this covenant and give thanks to Yahweh for it. This worshipping community is addressed in Ps. 105:6 as the "offspring of Abraham, his servant, sons of Jacob, 'his chosen one' " (cf. 1 Ch. 16:13). This form of address expresses Yahweh's fidelity to the covenant and his oath to Israel; Ps. 105:23 goes on to speak of the coming of Israel/Jacob to Egypt, and v. 24 speaks of "his [Yahweh's] people." The same notion appears in Ps. 77:16(15), which calls God's redeemed people "sons of Jacob and Joseph," and in Dt. 33:28, where the "assembly of Jacob" (Dt. 33:4) is called the "fountain of Jacob." Negative features of the Jacob tradition do not appear in Israel's poetry.

2. *Jacob as a Designation of the People.* We have already alluded in passing to the fact that the people of Israel understands itself to be sons of Jacob; this idea will now be examined in detail. In addition to this expression, we also find once again the phrase "house of Jacob," used in Ps. 114:1 for Israel on its departure from Egypt. The notion that we might have here a secular usage of "Jacob" is ruled out by the mention of the "God of Jacob" in v. 7; here, too, "Jacob" is understood in relationship to Yahweh, the God of Jacob.

In the poetry of Israel, too, "Jacob" and "Israel" appear frequently in parallel. In the tribal sayings, the relevant passages are Gen. 49:7; Dt. 33:10. The passage in the Blessing of Jacob that speaks of the scattering of Simeon and Levi in Jacob/Israel originates as a prophetic curse and really belongs under V.2 above. According to the Blessing of Moses, the Levites are to instruct Jacob/Israel in the law; here the reference is roughly equivalent to the congregation of Yahweh. Whether this comprised all Israel is dubious, because the sayings preserved in the Blessing of Moses suggest a North Israelite group of tribes, centering on Tabor.[127] There are also several occurrences in the Balaam oracles of J (Nu. 24:5,7), which have overtones of secular nationalism, and E (Nu. 23:7,10,21,23[twice!]), which bear a much more marked religious stamp, clearly using "Jacob/Israel" to refer to the people of God, blessed, chosen, and protected by Yahweh.

Thus in the early period the name "Jacob" is more nationalistic than religious; in the later period the religious meaning comes to dominate and finally completely displaces the nationalistic meaning.[128] We observe the same phenomenon in the Psalms. Ps. 14:7 par. 53:7(6); 135:4; 147:19, which are probably postexilic, think of Jacob(/Israel) as the congregation of Yahweh, to whom he has given his words and ordinances (147:19), whom he has chosen to be his own possession (135:4). Also in the late Psalms are

---

126 Cf. W. E. Barnes, "A Note on the Meaning of יעקב (אלהי יעקב) in the Psalter," *JTS,* 38 (1937), 405-410.

127 Cf. H.-J. Zobel, "Die Stammessprüche des Mose-Segens (Dtn 33,6-25): Ihr 'Sitz im Leben,' " *Klio,* 46 (1965), 83-92.

128 See also *idem,* "Das Selbstverständnis Israels nach dem AT," *ZAW,* 85 (1973), 281-294.

passages that speak of Jacob alone. Ps. 47:5(4) calls the land given to the people by God "the pride of Jacob whom he loves"; Ps. 79:7 (par. Jer. 10:25) describes the fall of the nation in 586 B.C. by saying that the heathen "have devoured Jacob" (cf. also Lam. 1:17; 2:2f.); Ps. 85:2(1) (*Q*) bears witness to the "restoration of the fortunes of Jacob" in the exilic period, ascribing the reversal to God's forgiveness of his people's iniquity (v. 3[2]); Ps. 87:2 states that God "loves the gates of Zion more than all the dwelling places of Jacob"; Ps. 99:4 affirms that God has "executed justice and righteousness in Jacob," and therefore calls on the congregation to extol him.

In preexilic texts, however, it is often not so easy to determine whether "Jacob" refers to a religious or a national entity. Nu. 24:19, a difficult text, says that "one out of Jacob" will exercise dominion over Edom, probably an allusion to David's victory over Edom. This would mean that "Jacob" refers to Davidic Israel, as is the case in the Balaam oracles of J discussed above. The Song of Moses, which is probably also a very early example of Israelite poetry,[129] assigns "Jacob" to be Yahweh's people (Dt. 32:9) when El Elyon apportions the nations to their national deities. In fact, the term "Israel" does not appear in Dt. 32.[130] And if we read vv. 14f. as " 'Jacob ate and was satisfied,' Jeshurun waxed fat, and kicked,"[131] we have a reference to the apostasy of the people once they settled in Canaan. Here the national and religious elements are so interwoven that neither can be said to dominate; both are present in the name "Jacob." Ps. 78, also probably preexilic,[132] uses the doublet Jacob/Israel in vv. 5,21,71. Verse 5 speaks of the "testimony in Jacob" and the "law in Israel" established by Yahweh that the works of God and his commandments might not be forgotten (v. 7); v. 21 speaks of Yahweh's anger at Jacob's lack of faith in the desert, and v. 71 mentions David's reign over "Jacob his [Yahweh's] people and Israel his inheritance." Here, too, the element of nationalism—the importance of the people constituting the Davidic state—is intimately associated with the religious element implicit in the concept "people of Yahweh." This is also true in Ps. 44:5(4), where God's favor finds expression in ordaining "victories for Jacob,"[133] and in Ps. 59:14(13), which speaks of God's ruling "in Jacob."

We come finally to the divine appellatives compounded with "Jacob" in the poetry of Israel; the most important is the expression "God of Jacob." It has been shown above[134] that this is clearly a Jerusalemite theologoumenon appearing around the time of David. It must be recalled here that in 2 S. 23:1,3 our name refers to the people of the Davidic state, who worship Yahweh as the God of this state (cf. v. 2), thereby giving it a religious cast. This is quite consonant with the references to the "God of Jacob" in the preexilic psalms Ps. 20:2(1); 46:8,12(7,11), 76:7(6); 81:2,5(1,4); 84:9(8), and (with textual emendation) Ps. 24:6; 114:7. To these should be added the postexilic passages Ps. 75:10(9);

---

129 O. Eissfeldt, *Das Lied Moses Deuteronomium 32,1-43 und das Lehrgedicht Asaphs, Psalm 78. BSAW,* 104/5 (1958), 41-43.

130 On v. 8, cf. *BHS*.

131 Cf. *BHS*.

132 Eissfeldt, *Das Lied Moses,* 31-37.

133 On the text, cf. *BHS*.

134 III.3.

94:7, as well as Ps. 146:5, which speaks of the "El of Jacob." We have already discussed the theory that this phrase is a further development of the divine appellative "Mighty One of Jacob," which is also found in the Psalter (Ps. 132:2,5; cf. 24:6 LXX [LXX 23:6]) and conveys the same meaning.

VII. Jacob in Deuteronomy. The name "Jacob" does not occur in the legal corpus of Deuteronomy; it appears, however, in the introduction and conclusion, always in combination with the two other names "Abraham" and "Isaac." It clearly refers to the patriarch. In Dt. 9:27, the patriarchs are called "thy [Yahweh's] servants," a phrase used also in Jeremiah and Deutero-Isaiah. They are depicted in a positive light, in contrast to the rebellious people. This suggests two characteristics of Deuteronomy: it has only good to say of the patriarchs, and it distinguishes them from Israel, because they belong to the pre-Egyptian era of Israel's history. Dt. 29:12(13) goes on speak of a covenant between Yahweh and Israel in the land of Moab, which he promised to the people and swore to the patriarchs, a concept found nowhere else in the OT.

In Deuteronomy we frequently find (with minor grammatical variations dependent on the context) the expression "the land that Yahweh swore to your fathers, Abraham, Isaac, and Jacob, to give them" (Dt. 6:10; 34:4; similarly 9:5; without naming the patriarchs individually: 6:18,23; 7:13; 8:1; 10:11; 11:9,21; 26:3,15; 28:11; similarly 19:8; 31:7,20ff.). In 1:8; 30:20, the fathers are also described as recipients of the land, which probably reflects the ancient tradition. The description of the land "which Yahweh swore to Abraham, Isaac, and Jacob, to give to their seed" also appears in the Pentateuch (Ex. 33:1 [J?]; similarly Gen. 50:24 [J?]); the land promised to the patriarchs is also mentioned in Nu. 32:11 as well as in P (Ex. 6:8; cf. 2:24) and Lev. 26:42. Whether there was any mutual influence and how it might have operated will not be discussed here. For our purposes it is more important to note that Deuteronomy pictures the patriarchs as recipients of Yahweh's solemn promise of the land, formulated as an oath; the fulfillment of this promise is the gift of the land to the people of Israel.[135] We also find in passages that do not mention the patriarchs by name but speak of them summarily the further statement that Yahweh swore a covenant oath with them, which he will now keep with Israel (Dt. 7:8,12; 8:18; etc.). Such a covenant is also presupposed in 2 K. 13:23; Ps. 105:9f. Its substance, according to Deuteronomy, is the election of Israel and the enduring nature of Yahweh's mercy expressed in this election. This affirmation of Yahweh's faithfulness clearly represents the core of what Deuteronomy considers the theme of the "patriarchs." They are powerful witnesses to God's faithfulness to his word, to God's love toward his people, and to their unmerited election.

VIII. Summary. In conclusion, we may say that the significance of Jacob in the poetry of Israel is substantially the same as in the prophetic literature and that Deuteronomy differs only in reserving the name exclusively for the patriarch. The earliest evidence for the use of "Jacob" to designate the people goes back to the early Davidic

---

135 Cf. Diepold, 77-81, 86f.

period, or—if Eissfeldt is correct in dating the Song of Moses around the middle of the eleventh century B.C.—even to the pre-Davidic period, a dating that would also be supported by the tribal sayings. This evidence suggests that both national and religious notions were associated with the name "Jacob" and that the national element even predominated on occasion. With the passage of time, however, the religious meaning came increasingly to the fore. "Jacob" became a term incorporating something like the historical idea of Israel. And if it is correct to say that in parallel constructions the second element defines the first more precisely, since "Jacob" usually comes first and "Israel" appears to be a term with much stronger religious overtones, the name "Jacob" probably came once more to express the element of national unity and solidarity.

Zobel

יַעַר *yaʿar*

Contents: I. Forests in the Syro-Palestinian Region. II. Etymology and Meaning: 1. "Forest" or "Thicket"; 2. "Honey"? III. OT Usage: 1. Proper Names and Geographical Terminology; 2. General Usage. IV. Theological Usage.

I. Forests in the Syro-Palestinian Region. In the prehistoric era, extensive forests covered large portions of the Mediterranean region.[1] It is possible to reconstruct the former presence and nature of these forests in Syria and Palestine, in part on the basis of scattered studies in paleobotany and paleogeography,[2] in part on the basis of some

yaʿar. D. Baly, *Geographical Companion to the Bible* (New York, 1963); H. Bardtke, "Die Waldgebiete des jordanischen Staates," *ZDPV,* 72 (1956), 109-122; G. Dalman, *AuS,* I (1928), 73-89, 254-261; A. Eig, *On the Vegetation of Palestine* (Tel Aviv, 1927); H. Gilead, "היער המקראי," *BethM,* [61] (1974/75), 276-282 [Heb.]; G. Giordano, "The Mediterranean Region," in S. Haden-Guest, J. K. Wright, and E. M. Teclaff, eds., *A World Geography of Forest Resources* (New York, 1956), 317-352; R. Gradmann, *Die Steppen des Morgenlandes in ihrer Bedeutung für die Geschichte der menschlichen Gesittung* (Stuttgart, 1934); *idem,* "Palästinas Urlandschaft," *ZDPV,* 57 (1934), 161-185; C. Houtman, "De jubelzang van de struiken der wildernis in Psalm 96:12b," *Loven en geloven. Festschrift N. H. Ridderbos* (Amsterdam, 1975), 151-174; B. S. J. Isserlin, "Ancient Forests in Palestine: Some Archæological Indications," *PEQ,* 86 (1955), 87f.; H. F. Mooney, "Southwestern Asia," in Haden–Guest–Wright–Teclaff, 421-440; M. Nadel, "שמות הררים התלויים בשערה," *Lešonénû* Sond, 5714 (1954), 51-60 [Heb.]; E. Orni and E. Efrat, *Geography of Israel* (Jerusalem, [3]1971); L. Rost, "Jüdische Wälder," *PJ,* 27 (1931), 111-122; M. B. Rowton, "The Topological Factor in the *Ḫapiru* Problem," *Festschrift B. Landsberger. AS,* 16 (1965), 375-387; *idem,* "The Woodlands of Ancient Western Asia," *JNES,* 26 (1967), 261-277; W. van Zeist and J. A. H. Heeres, "Paleobotanical Studies of Deir ʿAlla, Jordan," *Paléorient,* 1 (1973), 21-37; M. Zohary, *Plant Life of Palestine: Israel and Jordan. Chronica Botanica,* 33 (1962); *idem,* "שרידי יערות קדומים שנמציאו בארץ ישראל," *EMiqr,* III (1958), 726-735 [Heb.].

1 Rowton, *JNES,* 26 (1967), 263ff.

2 Gradmann, *ZDPV,* 57 (1934), 174; van Zeist-Heeres, 35ff.

evidence found in ancient literature and documents[3] as well as graphic evidence,[4] and in part on the basis of very meager remains of earlier vegetation.[5] A brief outline of botanical geography will help define the meaning of the term "forest" in the OT.

The flora of Palestine comprise no less than 718 genera and 2,250 species of plants (cf. Germany with 2,680, Great Britain with 1,750),[6] which vary depending on the climate and type of soil from forests with dense stands of trees to clumps of desert grass.[7] The botanist A. Eig has attempted to define three phytogeographic regions in Palestine:[8] (1) the Mediterranean region, comprising the greater part of Cisjordan and a broad area in Transjordan from Yarmuk to Petra, with an annual precipitation in excess of 350 millimeters (14 inches); (2) the Irano-turanic region, comprising a narrow strip of Cisjordan to the southeast of the Mediterranean region, delimited by the Hebron-Jerusalem-Nablus-Tiberias watershed, and the part of Transjordan described above with extensions to the northeast into the Syrian desert; it receives 150 to 350 millimeters (6 to 14 inches) of precipitation annually, has a continental climate, and loessial soil; (3) the Saharo-sindic region, the largest of the three, comprising about half of Palestine together with Edom and large portions of the Negeb, with an annual precipitation of only 25 to 150 millimeters (1 to 6 inches). Apart from a few smaller regions (e.g., the Sudanic penetration zone in the vicinity of the Dead Sea) and transition zones, and areas edaphically unsuited to forest growth, the first of these three regions is characterized by forest and maquis (e.g., Carmel and Galilee[9]). The remains of prehistoric vegetation indicate that the mountains and valleys of Palestine were formerly covered with a variety of growth, including forests of pine and oak and savanna woodland, as well as evergreen maquis.[10] The human (cf. Isa. 14:8; 37:24; 60:13) and animal (Isa. 7:25; 27:10) populations were important ecological factors, clearing and killing forests at an early date; the regenerative strength of vegetation later replaced these forests in part by a cover of maquis and garigue.[11] In part, however, the human population put the soil to other use, adding the destructive effects of erosion to the mix.[12]

If one takes "forest" to mean a dense growth of trees, one must picture the forests of the Mediterranean region, and especially Syria and Palestine, differently than those of Europe or America. They include maquis, Mediterranean woodland or scrub, made up of hardwood, low evergreens, and bushes 4 meters (12 to 15 feet) tall. Without human

---

3 *ANET*³, 227, 240, 268f., 307, 477; cf. 25f. (the story of Wen-amon); M. Broshi, "יַעַר," *EMiqr,* III, 724f.; Rowton, *JNES,* 26 (1967), 261-277.

4 *ANEP,* nos. 350, 374, etc.

5 *AuS,* I, 76; Gradmann, *ZDPV,* 57 (1934), 171; Zohary, *Plant Life,* 71ff.

6 Cf. Zohary, *ibid.,* 39.

7 For maps, see Baly; Zohary, *Plant Life*; Survey of Israel, *Atlas of Israel* (Jerusalem, 1970), ch. VI.

8 Zohary, *Plant Life,* 50ff., 232f. (studies of Eig); Orni-Efrat, 164-174; M. du Buit, "Palestine: Écologie végétale," *DBS,* VI, 1044-1050; *Atlas of Israel* (Jerusalem, ²1970), ch. VI.

9 *AuS,* I, 75.

10 Zohary, *Plant Life,* 67ff.

11 Gradmann, *Die Steppen des Morgenlandes,* 44; *idem, ZDPV,* 57 (1934), 171.

12 Rowton, *Festschrift B. Landsberger,* 378.

interference, under suitable ecological conditions maquis can revert to forest; the trees may belong to a single species or to several (cf., e.g., the pine forests of Aleppo with their maquis and garigue shrubbery[13]). It is therefore impossible to make a clear distinction between evergreen forests and maquis.[14] A forest with tall trees often may have a dense understory of bushes and shrubs.[15] "Garigue" is scrubland with a rich groundcover of plants reaching a height of 1 meter (3 feet). Finally, besides these "forests" there is *batha* (*bāṯâ* [Isa. 5:6]), a word coined by Eig in 1927 for low Mediterranean shrubbery no taller than 50 centimeters (20 inches);[16] such terrain is also called moorland. Today, apart from the remnants of ancient forests on Mt. Carmel, in the Lebanon, in Transjordan, etc., and the extensive reforestation projects in Israel,[17] garigue and *batha* predominate in large areas of Palestine; for the OT period, however, one should think in terms of substantially more dense and tall forest. In contrast to the situation in Syria and Palestine, nothing like the forests of the Syrian and Canaanite mountains was known in Mesopotamia,[18] Egypt,[19] or Arabia.[20]

II. Etymology and Meaning.

1. *"Forest" or "Thicket."* The word *ya῾ar* occurs in only a few Ugaritic texts[21] and some toponyms and personal names.[22] The translation varies between "forest," "scrub," etc., on the one hand[23] and "razor" on the other.[24] In *KTU,* 1.5 VI, 17-19,[25] many scholars rightly translate *y῾r* in *ġr. bʾbn ydy. psltm. by῾r yhdy. lḥm. wdqn* as "razor."[26] In *KTU,* 1.4 VII, 36, however, *y῾r* clearly involves the notion of a forest: *b. b῾l. t3ẖd y῾rm šn3. hd. gpt ġr,* "the enemies of Ba῾al attacked the forests, those who hated Hadad the cliffs of the rocks." Here, as occasionally in the OT, there is a close relationship between "forest" and "mountain." Synonymy, however, is not implied;[27] there is no

---

13 Zohary, *Plant Life,* 111; *idem, EMiqr,* 726ff.; Rowton, *Festschrift B. Landsberger,* 380f.

14 Zohary, *Plant Life,* 83.

15 Rowton, *Festschrift B. Landsberger,* 376.

16 Eig, 37-49, esp. 37ff.

17 J. Weitz, "State of Israel: Afforestation," *EncJud,* IX, 787-790.

18 Mooney, 428.

19 Giordano, 341.

20 Mooney, 433ff.

21 *KTU,* 1.4 VII, 36; 1.5 VI, 18; 1.6 I, 2; 4.609, 18.

22 *PNU,* 30, 142.

23 E.g., *UT,* no. 1126; WUS, no. 1200.

24 *WUS,* no. 2097; cf. Heb. *ta῾ar* and *môrâ* I.

25 Cf. *KTU,* 1.6 I, 2.

26 J. Aistleitner, *Die mythologischen und kultischen Texte aus Ras Schamra* (Budapest, ²1964), 17; J. C. de Moor, review of A. S. Kapelrud, *The Violent Goddess* (Oslo, 1969), *UF,* 1 (1969), 227; *idem, The Seasonal Pattern in the Ugaritic Myth of Ba῾lu. AOAT,* 16 (1971), 190, 193; M. Dahood and T. Penar, "Ugaritic-Hebrew Parallel Pairs," *RSP,* I, 135; for other approaches, see, e.g., A. Jirku, *Kanaanäische Mythen und Epen aus Ras Schamra-Ugarit* (Gütersloh, 1962), 63 ("forest"); T. L. Fenton, "Ugaritica-Biblica," *UF,* 1 (1969), 70 (reading *bydm* instead of *by῾r*).

27 Cf. M. Dahood, *Proverbs and Northwest Semitic Philology. SPIB,* 113 (1963), 18, n. 2; Nadel, 57; also E. Lipiński, *La royauté de Yahwé dans la poesie et le culte de l'ancien Israël* (Brussels, 1965), 105, n. 2; P. J. van Zijl, *Baal. AOAT,* 10 (1972), 148.

reason to translate *y'r* as "hill." Neither is it certain that *ġr* should be translated "forest" or "woods."[28]

The common Akkadian word for "forest" is *qištu(m)*;[29] we also find the loanword *a-ar*,[30] which is probably not related to West Semitic *y'r*.[31] In other Northwest Semitic languages, there are only scattered occurrences of *y'r* in the earlier periods. Punic is said to have used *iar* for "wood" (*lignum*),[32] and a Numidian-Punic bilingual[33] has *hḥršm šyr*, "carpenters." The element *y'r* also occurs in personal names.[34] In the Moabite Mesha inscription,[35] we find *ḥmt hy'rn*, "wall of the 'forests'," along with *ḥmt h'pl*, "wall of the acropolis." In this case we are probably dealing with one of the walls of a Moabite city, which was so named either because it surrounded a park (cf. Eccl. 2:5f.) or because it was made of (cedar) wood.[36] In Syriac, *ya'rā*, "thicket," often translates *šāmîr* in the alliterative pair *šāmîr* and *šayiṯ* (Isa. 5:6; 7:23ff.; 9:17[Eng. v. 18]; 10:17; 27:4; 32:13 [without *šayiṯ*]; also Job 38:27; Prov. 24:31; Hos. 10:4). In the Aramaic Targ. Onqelos, *ya'rā'* translates Heb. *sûp̱*, "reed" (Ex. 2:3,5, etc.); this language uses other words to translate Heb. *ya'ar*.[37] Scholars generally suggest that Heb. *ya'ar* is related to Arab. *wa'r*, "impassable (way)," "undulating (terrain)";[38] (in Ethiopic, this word means "rocky and forested terrain"). There may be an etymological relationship, but depending on whether such a *ya'ar* is located in the dry Syro-Arabian desert or the moist Syro-Palestinian mountains the meaning of the word can change: in the first case it refers to rocky ground, in the second to a forest made impassable by dense scrub.

2. *"Honey"?* In some OT passages, *ya'ar* is translated "honeycomb" (1 S. 14:26 [conj. v. 25: *wayᵉhî ya'ar dᵉḇaš*, following LXX]; Cant. 5:1; cf. 1 S. 14:27: *ya'ᵃrâ*). Caquot has rightly pointed out[39] that *ya'ᵃrâ* "is an obscure hapax legomenon whose established translation by 'honeycomb' is by no means certain." The same is true of *ya'ar* = "honeycomb." The only passage where the word comes close to this meaning is Cant. 5:1, where the LXX translates *ya'ar* as Gk. *ártos*, "bread" (cf. Vetus Latina *panis*; Syr. translates "sweetness," Symmachus Gk. *drymós*). On the basis of Ex. 2:3,5 (Targ. Onqelos), Rashi suggests that the word means something like "sugar cane."[40] In 1 S. 14:25f. there is even less reason to assume that *ya'ar* means "honeycomb"; the translation

---

28 J. C. de Moor, "Frustual Ugaritica," *JNES*, 24 (1965), 362f.; van Zijl, 149f.; also *WUS*, no. 2166; *UT*, no. 1953; J. M. Sasson, "Flora, Fauna and Minerals," *RSP*, I, 435.

29 *AHw*, II (1972), 923b.

30 *CAD*, I/2 (1968), 209a; cf. *ayaru*, *CAD*, I/1 (1964), 230, and **yaru*, *CAD*, VII (1960), 326.

31 *GesB*, *s.v.* *y'r*.

32 Augustine *Enarratio in Ps. 123*. *MPL*, 37, 1644.

33 *KAI*, 100, 6.

34 Benz, 324.

35 *KAI*, 181, 21f.

36 See III.1 below on 1 K. 7:2, etc.

37 See III.2.b below.

38 Lane, *s.v.*

39 A. Caquot, "דְּבַשׁ *dᵉḇaš* (*dᵉbhash*)," *TDOT*, III, 129.

40 Cf. E. Nestle in P. Joüon, *Le Cantique des Cantiques* (Paris, ²1909), 226: "bee bread."

"forest" is quite appropriate. The meaning of *ya'ar* in Cant. 5:1 is therefore uncertain, and so is its etymology. Some scholars consider it a homonym of *ya'ar* = "forest," implying a different origin.[41] Others think that the words derive from the same root.[42] However the case may be, it is possible that *ya'ar* in Cant. 5:1 (like Ugar. *'r*) refers to a sweet plant; in the Palestinian environment, this suggests a connection with *ya'ar* = "forest."

III. OT Usage.

1. *Proper Names and Geographical Terminology.* As an element of a name, *ya'ar* occurs most frequently in Kiriath-jearim, "Forest City"[43] (Josh. 9:17; 15:9f. [= Baalah],60 [= Kiriath-baal]; 18:14 [*idem*],15; Jgs. 18:12 [twice]; 1 S. 6:21; 7:1f.; 1 Ch. 2:50,52f.; 13:5f.; 2 Ch. 1:4; Neh. 7:29; Jer. 26:20 [Kiriath-hajjearim!]; also in the form Kiriath-arim in Ezr. 2:25 and Kiriath in Josh. 18:28 [haplography?[44]]). This is a Benjaminite city (modern Deir el-Azhar[45]) some 14 kilometers (9 miles) west-northwest of Jerusalem on the border of Judah. There are also other passages in which *ya'ar* is to be taken as part of a toponym: Josh. 15:10, describing the boundaries of Judah, calls the northern shoulder of *har-y^e'ārîm* ("Forest Mountain"[46]) *k^esālôn* (also interpreted as a toponym by LXX, Vulg., Syr., and Targ.); 1 S. 22:5 states that David is to go to *ya'ar ḥereṯ* (=Kharās, some 4 kilometers [2.5 miles] east of Keilah [cf. 1 S. 23:1-13]);[47] 2 S. 18:6 (cf. vv. 8,17) speaks of a battle with Absalom in *ya'ar 'eprayim.* Here we are probably dealing with a forest in Transjordan.[48]

There are also passages in which the forest is located with some precision. Josh. 17:15,18 speaks of Joseph's descendants clearing a forest in the land of the Perizzites and the Rephaim. The location of of this forest is disputed, however, primarily because scholars[49] see in Josh. 17:14f.,16ff. two different but parallel narratives; the first is only a later variant of the second, which is not associated with Transjordan. Along with those who think the reference is to Transjordan[50] are others who prefer the territory west of

---

41 Cf. *KBL*³, *s.v.*, 404; A. Guillaume, *Hebrew and Arabic Lexicography* (repr. Leiden, 1965), 7: Arab. *'ary*, Ethiop. *ma'ar*; J. C. de Moor, "*'ar* 'Honey-Dew'," *UF*, 7 (1975), 591, n. 1, comments on the uncertainty of this etymology.

42 W. Gesenius, *Thesaurus philologicus criticus linguae hebraeae et chaldaeae Veteris Testamenti* (Leipzig, 1858), *s.v.*, 611; for another view, see F. Delitzsch, "Philologische Forderungen an die Hebräische Lexikographie," *MVÄG*, 20/5 (1917), 26ff.

43 *AuS*, I, 76.

44 J. J. Simons, *The Geographical and Topographical Texts of the OT. StFS*, 2 (1959), §327 (II/14).

45 *Ibid.*, §§ 314, 319 (F/1), 326, 1016, etc.

46 Cf. A. Alt, "Das Taltor in Jerusalem," *PJ*, 24 (1928), 28ff.

47 Simons, §700; Rowton, *Festschrift B. Landsberger*, 380, n. 32.

48 Simons, §785; M. Noth, *The History of Israel* (Eng. trans., New York, ²1960), 60, 201; but cf. D. Leibel, "Mt. Rephaim—The Wood of Ephraim?" *Yediot*, 31 (1966/67), 136-39 [Heb.]: "forest of the Rephaim."

49 Cf. O. Eissfeldt, *Hexateuch-Synopse* (1922; repr. Darmstadt, 1973), 77; M. Noth, "Das Land Gilead als Siedlungsgebiet israelitischer Sippen," *PJ*, 37 (1941), 75 = *Aufsätze zur biblischen Landes- und Altertumskunde* (Neukirchen-Vluyn, 1971), IV, 368.

50 Noth, *ibid.*; J. Mauchline, "Gilead and Gilgal: Some Reflections on the Israelite Occupation

the Jordan.[51] A forest in the vicinity of Bethel is mentioned in 2 K. 2:24, and we are told of forests on Mt. Carmel,[52] in Lebanon,[53] and once (Zec. 11:2) in Bashan. Ezk. 21:2f.(20:46f.) states that there was a forest in the Negeb, but it is possible (aside from textual emendation[54]) that the word merely means "the south."[55] It would be risky to look for a forest in Assyria on the basis of Isa. 10:17ff. or in Egypt on the basis of Jer. 46:23, because both passages are speaking figuratively. In Ps. 132:6, *śᵉḏê-ya'ar,* in parallel with Ephrathah, should be taken as a toponym referring to Kiriath-jearim, although the ancient versions do not support this interpretation.[56] In 1 K. 7:2; 10:17 (par. 2 Ch. 9:16), 21 (par. 2 Ch. 9:20), one of the buildings built by Solomon is called *bêṯ ya'ar hallᵉḇānôn*; in Isa. 22:8 it is called *bêṯ hayya'ar* (cf. also Jer. 21:14; 22:7[57]). The reference here is to a building made of cedar, whose original purpose is not revealed by the sources. It has been suggested that the building was an armory (cf. the texts cited, plus Neh. 3:19 and Vulg. 2 Ch. 9:16; Isa. 22:8 [Lat. *armamentarium*]); it is more likely, however, that the "House of the Forest of Lebanon" was originally a royal reception hall.[58]

There is no clear evidence that *ya'ar* was used as an element in personal names (cf. *ya'râ* in 1 Ch. 9:42 [*ya'dâ* according to some LXX manuscripts]).

2. *General Usage.* a. Apart from the toponym Kiriath-jearim[59] and Cant. 5:1,[60] *ya'ar* occurs 59 times in the OT (with the meaning "forest" or the like). The following passages are involved: Dt. 19:5; Josh. 15:10; 17:15,18; 1 S. 14:25f.; 22:5; 2 S. 18:6,8,17; 1 K. 7:2; 10:17,21; 2 K. 2:24; 19:23; 1 Ch. 16:33; 2 Ch. 9:16,20; Ps. 29:9; 50:10; 80:14(13); 83:15(14); 96:12; 104:20; 132:6; Eccl. 2:6; Cant. 2:3; Isa. 7:2; 9:17(18); 10:18f.,34; 21:13; 22:8; 29:17; 32:15,19; 37:24; 44:14,23; 56:9; Jer. 5:6; 10:3; 12:8; 21:14; 26:18; 46:23; Ezk. 15:2,6; 21:2f.(20:46f.); 34:25; 39:10; Hos. 2:14(12); Am. 3:4; Mic. 3:12; 5:7(8); 7:14; Zec. 11:2. The syntactic position of the word is in a sense characteristic of its role in the books of the OT: in about half of its occurrences it is in the construct (usually as *nomen rectum*); only rarely is it subject (2 S. 18:8; Isa. 32:19; Zec. 11:2) or object (Ps. 29:9; 83:15[14]; Eccl. 2:6; Jer. 10:3; 46:23); it is often the object of a preposition. Twice

---

of Palestine," *VT,* 6 (1956), 31; J. R. Bartlett, "Sihon and Og, Kings of the Amorites," *VT,* 20 (1970), 269, n. 3.

51 H. W. Hertzberg, "Wald," *BHHW,* III (1966), 2134; J. Gray, *Joshua, Judges, Ruth. NCBC* (^{2}1986), 151.

52 → כרמל *karmel.*

53 → לבנון *lᵉḇānôn.*

54 J. Reider, "Etymological Studies in Biblical Hebrew," *VT,* 2 (1952), 119f.

55 W. Zimmerli, *Ezekiel 1. Herm* (Eng. trans. 1979), 420, 422-24.

56 Cf. also A. Robinson, "Do Ephrathah and Jaar Really Appear in Psalm 132 6?" *ZAW,* 86 (1974), 220ff.

57 A. Weiser, *Das Buch Jeremia 1–25,14. ATD,* XX (^{8}1981), 189; W. Rudolph, *Jeremia. HAT,* XII (^{3}1968), 139.

58 M. J. Mulder, "Einige Bemerkungen zur Beschreibung des Libanonwaldhauses in I Reg 7 2f.," *ZAW,* 88 (1976), 99ff.

59 See III.1 above.

60 See II.2 above.

(apart from Josh. 15:10) it appears as a plural in *-îm* (Ezk. 34:25 [in some manuscripts as the *kethibh*: *y'wrim*[61]]; 39:10), once in *-ôṯ* (Ps. 29:9[62]). The word is found once with *he*-locale (Josh. 17:15) and 4 times with a suffix (Isa. 10:18f.; Jer. 21:14; 46:23). A vocative appears in Isa. 44:23.

Apart from these grammatical observations, there is considerable contextual information that helps clarify the meaning of *ya'ar*.

The word often occurs in immediate association with *'ēṣ(îm)* (Dt. 19:5; Isa. 7:2; 10:19; 44:14; etc.). Trees may be cleared (*br'* piel: Josh. 17:15,18), felled (*ḥṭb*: Dt. 19:5; Jer. 46:22f.; Ezk. 39:10), or cut down (*krt*: Isa. 44:14; Jer. 10:3; 46:23); they may also be planted (*nt'*: Isa. 44:14). In Isa. 10:34, *nqp,* "cut down," can be taken as either a piel or a niphal.[63] Forests can be destroyed by fire (Ps. 83:15[14]; Isa. 9:17[18]; 10:17; Jer. 21:14; Ezk. 39:10 [cf. 15:6]), storm (Ps. 29:9, although the translation "forest" is dubious here), or hail (Isa. 32:19[?]); the wind causes trees to "shake" (Isa. 7:2). The end of a forest's "glory" (Isa. 10:18) can also be signified by the verbs *kālâ* and *yāraḏ* (Isa. 10:18; 32:19; Zec. 11:2). Besides the dense and wild forests (2 S. 18:8,17; Jer. 26:18; Mic. 3:12; etc.; cf. 1 Mc. 9:45), there were apparently also cultivated forests, parks, and gardens (Isa. 44:14; Eccl. 2:6 [cf. v. 5]; Cant. 2:3).[64] Orchards, however, can be laid waste and revert to forest (Hos. 2:14[12]), and forest can appear in the midst of garden land (or: "on Carmel") (Mic. 7:14). Besides "all the trees of the forest" (Ps. 96:12; etc.), the following trees are mentioned by name: *'ēlâ* (2 S. 18:9) and *'allôn* (Isa. 44:14; Zec. 11:2), "oak" or "terebinth"; *'ōren* (Isa. 44:14), "laurel"; *'erez,* "cedar" or "tall conifer," and *b^erôš,* "juniper" (2 K. 19:23; Isa. 37:24; Zec. 11:2); and *tirzâ* (Isa. 44:14), an unidentified species. Forests provide firewood (Isa. 44:15; etc.), but also *d^eḇaš* (1 S. 14:25ff.) and fruit trees (Eccl. 2:6 mentions a kind of orchard), of which *tappûaḥ* (Cant. 2:3), "apple tree," and *gep̄en* (cf. *z^emôrâ,* "branch": Ezk. 15:2,6; Hos. 2:14[12] [here along with *t^e'ēnâ,* "fig tree"]), "(grape) vine," are singled out, possibly just because they are not trees usually found in a forest.

Because "forest" includes maquis, thorns and thistles (Isa. 9:17[18]; 10:17) are found there, as well as underbrush or thickets (*śôḇeḵ*: 2 S. 18:9; *s^eḇaḵ*: Isa. 9:17[18]; 10:34), which provide easy concealment for fugitives (1 S. 22:5)[65] but can also prove fatal (2 S. 18:8f.). Forests are in fact not places where people normally dwell, although one can spend the night there if necessary (Isa. 21:13; cf. *mālôn* in 2 K. 19:23 [par. *mārôm* in Isa. 37:24]; Ezk. 34:25; Mic. 7:14). The inhospitable terrain of many forests is attested by such words as *'^aḇānîm* and *paḥaṯ* (2 S. 18:17); some passages speak of *ya'ar* in the desert (Isa. 21:13; Ezk. 21:2f.[20:46f.]).

Now and then the semantic field of *ya'ar* includes such words as *har* (Josh. 15:10 [in

---

61 Cf. Gesenius, 612; P. Wernberg-Møller, "The Noun of the *qṭl* Class in the Massoretic Text," *RevQ,* 2 (1959-60), 448; not noted in *BHS* (possibly an oversight).

62 G. R. Driver, "Studies in the Vocabulary of the OT. II," *JTS,* 32 (1931), 255, suggests a plural of **ya'^arā,* "kid"; but double forms of plural endings are not uncommon (cf. *GK,* §87m).

63 E. Jenni, *Das hebräische Pi'el* (Zurich, 1968), 237.

64 → גן *gan.*

65 Cf. P. Hoftijzer, "Two Notes in the Ba'al Cyclus," *UF,* 4 (1972), 156, n. 13.

a name]; 17:15,18; Ps. 50:10; 83:15[14]; Isa. 44:23; Mic. 3:12 [par. Jer. 26:18; with *bāmôṯ*]; cf. 2 K. 19:23 [par. Isa. 37:24]); *miḏbār,* "steppe" (Ezk. 34:25; cf. Isa. 32:15); *ᶜᵃrāḇ,* "desert" (Isa. 21:13; cf. *zᵉ'ēḇ ᶜᵃrāḇôṯ* in Jer. 5:6); and *śāḏeh* (1 S. 14:25; 2 S. 18:6; Ps. 50:10; 96:12 [par. 1 Ch. 16:33]; Isa. 56:9; Ezk. 21:2[20:46]; 39:10; Hos. 2:14[12]; etc.). But one should not conclude, for example, that *har* and *ya'ar* are identical.[66] In mountainous regions, forests are naturally found on the mountains (e.g., in Lebanon: 2 K. 19:23; Isa. 10:34; etc.).

The wild and sinister character of forests is often intensified by the presence of beasts of prey and other wild animals (Ps. 50:10; 104:20; Isa. 56:9; cf. Ezk. 34:25; Hos. 2:14[12]; 1QH 8:8), among which lions (Jer. 5:6 [par. "wolf from the steppe"]; 12:8; Am. 3:4; Mic. 5:7[8]), bears (2 K. 2:24), and wild boars (Ps. 80:14[13])[67] are mentioned by name. In addition to *ḥayyâ,* the word *bᵉhēmâ* is used for forest animals (Mic. 5:7[8]; cf. Ps. 50:10).[68]

This discussion shows that in the OT the word *ya'ar* is not a sharply limited technical term for a well-defined type of "forest." Its meaning, however, does approximate the Mediterranean forest described by Eig, Zohary, and other botanists.[69] In exceptional cases the forest may be composed entirely of tall trees, but it usually includes the maquis found under and among these trees, with grass (cf. 1 Mc. 4:38) and other plants, which is a home for both wild and domesticated animals and often renders the forest impenetrable. To this context belong such words as *ḥōreš* (2 Ch. 27:4; Ezk. 31:3; cf. 1 S. 23:15-19; Isa. 17:9); *ḥᵃrōšeṯ* (cf. Jgs. 4:2,13,16); *sᵉḇaḵ* (Gen. 22:13; Isa. 9:17[18]; 10:34); *sᵉḇoḵ* (Ps. 74:5; Jer. 4:7); *śôḇeḵ* (2 S. 18:9); and *ᶜāḇ* (Jer. 4:29).

b. The LXX uses Gk. *drymós* some 50 times to translate *ya'ar*; in the books that do no have a Hebrew original, this word appears in Bar. 5:8; Ep.Jer. 6:63[LXX 61]; 1 Mc. 4:38; 9:45; Ps.Sol. 11:5; T.Sol. 11:7 (cf. 14:6); T.Abr. A 10 (2); B 6 (2). The same word is sometimes used to translate such Hebrew words as *ḥōreš* (2 Ch. 27:4), *ḥᵃrōšeṯ* (Jgs. 4:16 [A]), and *sᵉḇōḵ* (Ps. 74:5[LXX 73:6]), while in other passages different manuscripts have different translations. Sometimes it is not clear what Hebrew word is being translated by the LXX. In the Vulg., we find Lat. *saltus* 36 times and *silva* 19 times (and *saltus* in *Psalmos ad. Heb.* in Ps. 29:9[Vulg. 28:9]; 96:12[95:12]; 132:6[131:6]). Only in 2 Ch. 9:16 is *nemus* used (found in Gen. 21:33; 1 S. 22:6; 31:13 translating Heb. *'ešel,* in Jgs. 6:25f.,30 translating *'ᵃšērâ*). In the Vulg., the usual translation of *'ᵃšērâ* is *lucus* (in the LXX, Gk. *álsos*). This term refers to the sites of pagan cults, a "sacral grove" as the KJV and other early modern translations, influenced by the LXX and Vulg., erroneously render the text.

Of the two translations in the Aramaic tradition, the Syr. almost always uses *ᶜabā* for *ya'ar* (50 times; cf. for *ya'rā,* etc., Job 38:27; Prov. 24:31[70]), and the Targ. commonly

66 See II.1 above.

67 Cf. O. Keel, *The Symbolism of the Biblical World* (Eng. trans., New York, 1978), 108f.

68 J. Botterweck, "בְּהֵמָה *bᵉhēmâ* (*bᵉhēmāh*)," *TDOT,* II, 6-20; the passage may not refer to wild animals.

69 See I above.

70 See II.1 above.

uses *ḥuršā'* (39 times). In the context of the midrashic nature of the latter translation, other renderings often appear (*mšyryyt'*, "army," in Isa. 9:17[18]; 10:18f.; etc.; *byt mqryt mlk'*, "cool house of the king," in 1 K. 7:2; etc.).

In the ancient versions, as in the Hebrew original, the boundary between *ya'ar* on the one hand and *har* or *śāḏeh* on the other is sometimes vague: Gk. *drymós* for *har* (Josh. 17:18) and *śāḏeh* (2 S. 18:6); Lat. *saltus* for *śāḏeh* (2 S. 17:8; 2 K. 14:9; Ezk. 31:6); Lat. *silva* for *śāḏeh* (2 S. 2:18; 2 Ch. 25:18) and *s^eḇoḵ-'ēṣ* (Ps. 74:5). This confirms the theory that in the OT, although *ya'ar* means "forest" in the secular sense, it is not a technical term for a particular kind of forest.

IV. Theological Usage. The word *ya'ar* may play a lesser role in the theological language of the OT than do → גן *gan*, → עץ *'ēṣ*, and similar words.[71] No sacral meaning can be associated with the word. Nevertheless, *ya'ar* does occur in theological discourse, especially in the prophetic books. Sometimes it is only a secondary element in a simile, as in Isa. 7:2 (the heart of the king and his people shook as trees in the forest shake before the wind); 9:17(18) (wickedness burns like fire that kindles the forest); Ezk. 15:6 (like the wood of the vine among the trees of the forest, which God gives to the fire as fuel, so . . . etc.). It is dubious whether a grapevine can even grow in the forest (cf. Hos. 2:14[12][72]). The noun *gep̱en* (in the general sense of "vine" or "shrub"[73]) and especially *z^emôrâ* may mean "young green twigs." Ezk. 15:2 might be translated as follows: "Son of man, how does the wood of the grapevine surpass any wood, (and) the branch which is among the trees of the forest?" (reading the *h* before *z^emôrâ* as an interrogative particle).

Besides these similes, there are passages that speak of the beasts of the forest (Ps. 50:10; 80:14[13]; 104:20 [nocturnal]; Isa. 56:9; Jer. 5:6; 12:8; Am. 3:4; Mic. 5:7[8]; 1QH 8:8; cf. Hos. 2:14[12]), which either appear to execute judgment or symbolize isolation and judgment (cf. also 2 K. 2:24). Although robbers and impenetrable thickets can make the forest an inhospitable region, it has a kind of "glory" (*kāḇôḏ*: Isa. 10:18). This "glory" (cf. *g^e'ôn hayyardēn*: Jer. 12:5; 49:19; Zec. 11:3[74]) is not primarily aesthetic; it derives from the sovereign power of God, because the forest is part of God's creation (Ps. 50:10: every beast in the forest is God's; Ps. 29:9: God's "voice" strips the forests bare [unless a different interpretation is preferred[75]]; cf. Ep.Jer. 6:63: God's fire consumes the forests).

The notion of the "garden of God"[76] may appear in Isa. 37:24 (par. 2 K. 19:23), where Sennacherib is said to have gone up to the heights of Lebanon, "into the forest of its garden (*karmillô*)." This is the only passage in which the close connection between *ya'ar* and *karmel* does not signify a clear antithesis. Isa. 29:17; 32:15, however, clearly

---

71 See III.2.b above on the translation of *'ašērâ*.

72 See III.2.a above.

73 See R. Hentschke, "גֶּפֶן *gep̱en* (*gephen*)," *TDOT,* III, 57; cf. Zimmerli, *Ezekiel 1,* 319.

74 D. Kellermann, "גָּאָה *gā'â* (*gā'āh*)," *TDOT,* II, 347.

75 See III.2.a above.

76 H. Gressmann, *Der Messias. FRLANT,* 26[43] (1929), 179ff.; B. Jacobs-Hornig, "גַּן *gān*," *TDOT,* III, 37f.; O. Kaiser, *Der Prophet Jesaja: Kapitel 13–39. ATD,* XVIII (²1976), 314.

illustrate this contrast: Lebanon will be turned into a garden and the garden (*karmel*) will be regarded (*ḥāšaḇ*; cf. also 1 K. 10:21 for this meaning) as a forest. God's sovereignty over the forests is denied by the conduct of idolators, who search out the forests for their idols (Isa. 44:14; Jer. 10:3),[77] letting a tree grow strong among the trees of the forest and finally carving it into a god, the work of human hands.

The perils of a forest were often more important to the Israelites than its advantages; a few prophecies of disaster therefore use the forest to symbolize an inhospitable place. Mic. 3:12 (cited in Jer. 26:18) predicts that Jerusalem will become a heap of ruins and that the temple mountain will become wooded heights (LXX: *álsos drymoú*; sg. in Syr. and Targ.; cf. 2 K. 23:8 and → במה *bāmâ* [*bāmāh*]). Hos. 2:14(12) declares that the God of Israel will lay waste her vines and her fig trees and make them a forest (cf. Cant. 2:3: the friend of the bride is like an apple tree among the trees of the forest). But a forest is more than a symbol of devastation: it is itself devastation. This is depicted graphically in 2 S. 18:8: Absalom met his death in a forest that devoured more people than the sword (cf. also 2 K. 2:24). But in their prophecies of disaster the prophets also proclaim the destruction of the forests themselves: Isa. 10:18f.,34; Jer. 21:14 (possibly with a reference to the "house of the forest of Lebanon"[78]); 46:23 (the forest should probably not be localized in Egypt[79]); Ezk. 21:2f.(20:46f.; "toward the south"[80]). In Zec. 11:2, agony over the destruction of the forests culminates in a summons to lament: "Wail, O cypress, for the cedar has fallen . . . , wail, oaks of Bashan, for the thick forest has been felled."

On the other hand, optimistic prophecies also speak of forests. This is not so clear in Isa. 29:17; 32:15;[81] it is clearer, however, in Ezk. 34:25: the good shepherd will enable his flock to sleep even in the woods. Ezk. 39:10 declares that the inhabitants of the cities of Israel will be able to build their fires for seven years from the weapons of the king of Magog, so that it will not be necessary to cut down any wood from the forest. And joy at God's deliverance culminates in a summons calling on the forests to rejoice and give thanks (Ps. 96:12 [par. 1 Ch. 16:33];[82] Isa. 44:23; Bar. 5:8). At the eschaton, the forest, often so sinister, will become a place of peace and security as it was at creation (Gen. 2).

Mulder

---

77 On the polemic against idols, see H. D. Preuss, *Verspottung fremder Religionen im AT. BWANT,* 92[5/12] (1971), 211ff.

78 See III.1 above and Jer. 22:6f.

79 See III.1 above.

80 See III.1 above.

81 See above.

82 Cf. Houtmann.

יָפָה yāp̱â; יָפֶה yāp̱eh; יְפִי yᵉp̱î; יְפֵיפֶה yᵉp̱êp̱eh

Contents: I. Ancient Near East: Egyp. *nfr.* II. 1. Etymology and Occurrences; 2. Semantic Field, Meaning, Human Beauty; 3. Zion, the King, Trees; 4. Song of Songs; 5. Other.

I. Ancient Near East: Egyp. nfr. The Egyptian word *nfr,* usually translated "beautiful" or "good," has a wide range of special meanings.[1] The phrase *ỉnr nfr* means a "beautiful" stone, but also a stone "suitable" for building; a *ṯ3w nfr* is a "favoring" wind; a *pẖr.t nfr* is an "effective" remedy.[2] In many cases, *nfr* means "young": young people, young soldiers, young recruits. Osiris' name *wnn-nfrw* (Onnophris) probably means that he is a god who is perpetually renewed or rejuvenated.[3] Similarly, the phrase *nṯr nfr* as an epithet of the king may refer to him as the perpetually renewed incarnation of the god Horus. The "beautiful paths" are the paths to the great god taken by the departed; the "beautiful west" is the place where life is renewed. Attempts to use these special meanings to discover an original meaning of *nfr* ("something that leads to the goal or end";[4] "undergoing renewal";[5] "passage" or "transition" [to life][6]) are of solely theoretical interest in this context.

II. 1. *Etymology and Occurrences.* Cognate with *yāp̱â/yāp̱eh* are Syr. *p'y,* "be beautiful" (and possibly also *ip̄āʾ,* "be able," "be sufficient"[7]); Arab. *wafā,* "be whole," "be complete";[8] OSA *wpy,* "be whole"; and possibly Ethiop. *wafaya,* "be complete." In the Amarna letters, we find Can. *yapu* glossed by *ḫamudu* (cf. Heb. → חמד *ḥāmaḏ chāmadh*); Akk. *wapû,* "become visible," may also belong here.

In the case of the verb, the qal occurs 5 times, the piel once, and the hithpael once; there is also a reduplicating form *yop̱yāp̱îṯā* (Ps. 45:3[Eng v. 2]). The adj. *yāp̱eh* occurs 42 times, together with the reduplicating form *yᵉp̱êp̱eh* (Jer. 46:20 and possibly Jer. 11:16, reading *yᵉp̱êp̱eh* instead of *yᵉp̱ēh-pᵉrî*). The subst. *yᵉp̱î/yōp̱î* occurs 19 times.

2. *Semantic Field, Meaning, Human Beauty.* The frequent association of our word with *toʾar,* "form" (Gen. 41:18; Dt. 21:11; 1 S. 25:3; Est. 2:7), or *marʾeh,* "appearance" (Gen. 12:11; 41:2,4; 1 S. 17:42; 2 S. 14:27), or both (Gen. 29:17; 39:6; cf. Est. 2:7: *tôḇaṯ*

---

yāp̱â. M. Mannati, "Ṭûb-Y. en Ps XXVII 13: *Le bonté de Y.,* ou *Les biens de Y.?*" *VT,* 19 (1969), 488-493; H. W. Wolff, *Anthropology of the OT* (Eng. trans., Philadelphia, 1974), 69-73.

1 *WbÄS,* II, 253ff.

2 Cf. H. Stock, *Nṯr nfr—der gute Gott?* (Hildesheim, 1951), 4ff., with additional examples.

3 See G. Jéquier, *Considérations sur les religions égyptiennes* (Neuchâtel, 1946), 51-54.

4 Stock, 8.

5 Jéquier.

6 J. Bergman, "Quelques reflexions sur *nfr-nfr.t-nfrw,*" *Actes du XXIXᵉ Congrès international des Orientalistes, Section Égyptologie* (Paris, 1975), 8-14.

7 See below.

8 Leslau, *Contributions,* 24.

mar'eh) shows that beauty refers to outward appearance. In parallel we find *nā'wâ* (Cant. 6:4, describing a city), *nā'am* (Cant. 7:7[6], describing the beloved), *bar*[9] (Cant. 6:10, describing the sun and moon), and *ḥēn*[10] (Prov. 31:30).

Both men and women are called beautiful: Joseph (Gen. 39:6), the youthful David (1 S. 16:12: *yᵉpēh 'ênayim,* also *ṭôḇ rō'î*; 17:42: *yᵉpēh mar'eh*), Absalom (2 S. 14:25), the king (Ps. 45:3[2]; the king of Tyre: Ezk. 28:12,17; the messianic king: Isa. 33:17), Sarah (Gen. 12:11); Rachel (Gen. 29:17), Abigail (1 S. 25:3), Tamar, Absalom's sister (2 S. 13:1), Tamar, Absalom's daughter (2 S. 14:27), Abishag the Shunammite (1 K. 1:3f.), Vashti (Est. 1:11), Job's daughters (Job 42:15), the royal bride (Ps. 45:12[11]), women in general (Prov. 11:22; Am. 8:13). The term is applied metaphorically to Israel as a woman (Ezk. 16:13-15,25) and to the "strange woman" (Prov. 6:25). There are numerous additional examples in the Song of Songs.[11] A woman's beauty is emphasized by her clothing (Jer. 4:30).

Other beautiful things include cows (Gen. 41:2,4,18), a heifer symbolizing Egypt (Jer. 46:20), trees (Jer. 11:16; Ezk. 31:3,7-9), the human voice (Ezk. 33:32), Zion (Ps. 48:3[2]; 50:2; Lam. 2:15), and Tyre (Ezk. 27:3f.,11). We are told with surprising frequency how beauty awakens love in the opposite sex. This is sometimes stated explicitly by the use of *'āhaḇ* (Gen. 29:18; 2 S. 13:1) or *ḥāšaq* (Dt. 21:11) immediately afterwards (cf. also *ḥāmaḏ* in Prov. 6:25, *hiṯ'awwâ* in Ps. 45:12[11]), but is elsewhere implied by the context (Gen. 12:10ff.; 39:6ff.; 1 K. 1:1ff.; also in the allegory of Ezk. 16). Twice the verb *hll* is used to represent beauty as being laudable (Gen. 12:15; 2 S. 14:25).

Physical beauty is usually taken as positive, but it can also lead to arrogant disregard of God (Tyre: Ezk. 27:3ff.; the king of Tyre: Ezk. 28, esp. v. 17; the women of Jerusalem: Isa. 3:16-24, with *yōp̄î* in v. 24). With respect to women, it is sometimes pointed out that beauty alone is insufficient; only when accompanied by prudence or the fear of God does it represent the feminine ideal. Abigail is *ṭôḇaṯ-śeḵel* and physically beautiful (1 S. 25:3); a beautiful woman without discretion (*sāraṯ ṭā'am*) is an absurdity (Prov. 11:22). "Charm (*ḥēn*) is deceitful (*šeqer*), and beauty is vain (*heḇel*), but a woman who fears Yahweh is to be praised" (Prov. 31:30).

3. *Zion, the King, Trees.* Unlike Egyp. *nfr,* "beautiful," "good," *yph* is never used of God. But Zion, God's dwelling place, is occasionally called beautiful: "beautiful in elevation, the joy of all the earth" (Ps. 48:3[2]); "out of Zion, the perfection of beauty, God shines forth" (Ps. 50:2). Lam. 2:15 alludes to these two passages: "the perfection of beauty" and "the joy of all the earth" are now laid low.

The beauty of Tyre, depicted in the form of a ship, is condemned, however, because it is the occasion of arrogance toward God (Ezk. 27:3f.,11).

In 1 isolated passage (Ps. 45:3[2], an epithalamion), the king of Israel is praised for his beauty. Isa. 33:17 refers to the beauty of the messianic king. The king of Tyre, however, boasts of his beauty (Ezk. 28:12,17) and is therefore punished.

Jer. 11:16 speaks of a beautiful tree as a symbol of Israel: "a green olive tree and fair

---

9 → ברר *bārar.*
10 → חנן *ḥānan.*
11 See below.

[conj. yᵉp̱êp̱eh] Yahweh has called you." Now, however, the tree will be consumed. The same theme is used by Ezekiel in an allegorical discourse with Egypt as its subject: the land is represented as a beautiful cedar (Ezk. 31:3,7-9) brought down by its pride.

4. *Song of Songs.* The love poetry of the Song of Songs naturally refers often to the beauty of the lovers (masc. in 1:16, otherwise fem.). Such expressions as "you are beautiful" (1:15f.; 4:1), "fairest among women" (1:8; 5:9; 6:1), "my fair one" (2:10,13) are formulaic. Noteworthy are the comparison to Tirzah and Jerusalem (6:4) and to the moon and sun (6:10: "fair as the moon, bright as the sun"). Other passages include 4:10 (*dôḏayiḵ,* "your love"), 7:2(1) ("your feet"), 7(6) ("how fair you are" [verb par. *nāʿam,* reading *ʾahuḇâ*]).

In ch. 16, Ezekiel applies the bride motif to Israel in an allegorical discourse. He tells how the foundling Israel grows up to be a beautiful woman, magnificently clothed by Yahweh and "exceedingly beautiful" (Ezk. 16:13); she is renowned for her beauty (v. 14). But she trusts in her beauty and commits harlotry (i.e., idolatry; v. 15), and will therefore be punished. A similar motif also appears in isolation in Jer. 4:30: in vain she beautifies herself (hithpael); her lovers despise her.

5. *Other.* Jer. 10:4 speaks of using gold and silver to "beautify" (piel) idols, which nevertheless have no power. Zec. 9:17 describes the excellence (*ṭûḇ*) and beauty of restored Israel (the suffixes refer to *ʿam* [v. 16], not Yahweh).

The adj. *yāp̱eh* is obviously used figuratively in 2 passages in Ecclesiastes. According to Eccl. 3:11, God "has made everything beautiful in its time." The translation "good" might be possible here;[12] in any case, there is probably an allusion to Gen. 1:31 and similar passages. In Eccl. 5:17(18), *ṭôḇ* and *yāp̱eh* appear to be almost synonymous; eating and drinking and enjoyment of life are called "good" and "beautiful."

Ringgren

---

12 W. Zimmerli, *Prediger. ATD,* XVI/1 (³1980), 168, 171.

יָפַע *yāp̱aʿ*; יִפְעָה *yip̱ʿâ*

Contents: I. Root. II. 1. Statistics; 2. "Shine Forth"; 3. "Appear"; 4. Ancient Versions. III. 1. Literary Forms; 2. Ancient Near East; 3. Sinai; 4. Ambivalence; 5. Theophany and Epiphany.

---

yāp̱aʿ. E. Jenni, "יפע *jpʿ* hi. aufstrahlen," *THAT,* I, 753-55; J. Jeremias, *Theophanie. WMANT,* 10 (²1977), 8-10, 62-64, 77f.; F. Schnutenhaus, "Das Kommen und Erscheinen Gottes im AT," *ZAW,* 76 (1964), 1-22, esp. 8f.

I. Root. The Hebrew root *yp'*, "shine forth," has only one likely cognate: Akk. *(w)apû,* "become visible," usually found in the causative stems *šūpu* and *šutāpû/šutēpû,* "show forth," "cause to appear," or "become visible," "appear" (of planets), "become famous."[1] Arab. **yf'* "rise up," "grow up" (with its derived noun *yafa'*, "building"), OSA **yf'*, "arise," and Ugar. *yp'* ("be exalted" or "rise up"?[2]) appear to involve a different root.[3] Albright[4] has suggested a semantic relationship between *yp'* I and → יפה *yāpâ,* "be beautiful." The root *yp'* I is found in Jewish Aramaic,[5] as well as in Middle Hebrew and the Targums,[6] with the meaning "appear."

II. 1. *Statistics.* The verb *yp'* appears 8 times in the OT (Dt. 33:2; Job 3:4; 10:3,22; 37:15; Ps. 50:2; 80:2[Eng. v. 1]; 94:1). There is a ninth occurrence if we follow the versions in Ps. 12:6(5), reading *yôpîa'* or *'ôpîa'* instead of the difficult *yāpîaḥ.*[7] The noun **yip'â,* "brilliance,"[8] appears only twice (Ezk. 28:7,17). It is uncertain whether or not the personal name *yāpîa'* derives from this root.[9] The hiphil *hôpîa'* (as in the MT, the only stem found) is very popular in the Dead Sea scrolls, with 18 occurrences, of which 9 are in 1QH and 3 each in 1QM and CD.[10]

2. *"Shine Forth."* When *hôpîa'* is used, some phenomenon involving light is usually prominent. This is clear on the one hand from the use in synonymy or parallelism of the verbs → אור *'ôr* (hiphil), "make bright" (Ps. 80:2[1]; cf. vv. 4,8,20[3,7,19]; 1QH 9:26; cf. v. 27), and → זרח *zāraḥ,* "light up" (Dt. 33:2; cf. also → נגה *nāgâ*), and on the other from the frequent appearance in the same context of words for "light" (Job 3:4f.; 37:15; 1QS 10:2; 1QH 7:24; 9:26; "dawn" in 1QH 4:6) and "darkness" (Job 3:4f.; 10:21f.; 1QS 10:2; 1QH 9:26; Job 37:15[?]). Only in a few cases, however, does the "shining forth" refer to a physical source of light (1QS 10:2: the stars in the sky at night). Job 3:4; 10:22; 37:15 are discussed immediately below.

Of the three verses in Job, only 3:4 is clear: Job curses the day of his birth, wishing that it may be darkness and that no light may shine upon it. Job 10:22, which refers to the cheerless darkness of the realm of the dead, is almost certainly corrupt; despite many suggestions,[11] it is not clear who or what is the subject of *wattōpa'*, "and she/it shone

---

1 *CAD,* I/2 (1968), 201-4; for passages using the derived adj. *šûpû,* "brilliant, glorious," see K. L. Tallqvist, *Akkadische Götterepitheta. StOr,* 7 (1938 [repr. 1974]), 89; C. Mullo Weir, *A Lexicon of Accadian Prayers in the Rituals of Expiation* (Oxford, 1934), 29, 253; *AHw,* III (1981), 1281.

2 Cf. *UT,* no. 1133; *WUS,* no. 1215.

3 Jenni, 753.

4 W. F. Albright, "Notes on Assyrian Lexicography and Etymology," *RA,* 16 (1919), 177, n. 1.

5 T. Nöldeke, *Neue Beiträge zur semitischen Sprachwissenschaft* (Strasbourg, 1910), 198f., 203f.

6 *WTM,* II, 254.

7 See 4 below.

8 *KBL*³.

9 See *KBL*³.

10 Kuhn.

11 See the comms.

forth." Job 37:15 is equally problematical. Whether the causative *wᵉhôpîa'* is taken normally ("and he causes to shine forth") or internally ("and it shines forth"), it is unclear what is referred to in the shining forth of the "light of his cloud" (lightning?).

The meaning is figurative when the subject that "shines forth" cannot be a physical source of light. This is the case in all the passages in which Yahweh or God "shines forth" (Dt. 33:2; Ps. 50:2; 80:2[1]; 94:1).[12] The Dead Sea scrolls in particular illustrate how a "spiritual" rather than physical source of light can "shine forth" or cause human subjects to "shine." In 1QM 18:10; 1QH 18:6, the damaged text does not reveal who or what made the beleaguered worshipper "shine." In 1QM 9:26f. ("in thy glory my light shone forth, for thou hast caused a lamp to shine forth from the darkness for me"); 1QH 11:26f. ("thy truth shone forth for eternal glory"), however, it is clearly God's salvation and truth that constitute the "light."[13] Thus enlightened, the worshipper can say that he himself "shines forth": 1QH 7:23-25, "My [G]od, thou hast helped me. . . , I have shone forth with sevenfold li[ght]. . . . For thou didst become an [et]ernal light to me." We may note also the hymnic summons to Jerusalem in 1QM 12:13: "Shine forth in joy!"

3. *"Appear."* There is another usage of *hôpîa'* not characterized by either a physical or a spiritual "shining," but by the "appearance" of something previously hidden or invisible. The notion of light is still more or less consciously present, but the central element is not this "shining" but rather a visible "appearance" or "coming."

The use of words meaning "come" in the immediate context is characteristic of this usage of the verb. In Dt. 33:2, *hôpîa'* is synonymous not only with *zāraḥ*[14] but also with → *bô'* and *'āṯâ,* "come." In Ps. 50:2, *hôpîa'* corresponds to *bô'* in v. 3; in Ps. 80:2(1), to *hālaḵ* in v. 3(2); and in Ps. 94:1, to *nāśā'*, "rise up," in v. 2. In Job 10:3, also, *hôpîa'* comes close to meaning "appear" or "come."[15]

In the Dead Sea scrolls, too, *hôpîa'* often has the meaning "come," "appear visibly." This is certainly the case in 1QpHab 11:7, which speaks of the appearance of the Wicked Priest: "On the Day of Atonement he appeared to them in order to destroy them." Since the verb here has no positive connotations, the translation "shine forth" is out of the question. The translation "come," "appear," or "be present" is also appropriate in 1QH 4:6 ("Like the dawn . . . thou didst appear to me"), 23 ("Thou didst appear to me in thy might for perfect illumination"); 9:31 ("From my youth thou didst appear to me in insight into thy judgment"). Although the notion of a "spiritual" illumination and enlightenment is certainly not far distant here (especially in 4:6,23), the central point is the "coming" of God to the devout or their experience of God's presence.

We see yet another semantic nuance of *hôpîa'* when its subject is an invisible (or even concealed) reality; the Dead Sea scrolls furnish many examples. The destructive "designs" of the wicked "appear" to the devout "as bitterness" (1QH 5:32; cf. 7:3), and when the community is purified (CD 20:27) the deeds of the wicked will "appear" (CD

12 See 3 below.
13 S. Aalen, "אוֹר *'ôr,*" I, 166f.
14 See 2 above.
15 See III.1 below.

20:3,6). In the same "apocalyptic" sense, "the glory of God for Israel" appears (CD 20:25f.). Neither "shine forth" or "come" would translate *hôpîa'* correctly here; the best translation is "be seen/revealed."

4. *Ancient Versions.* The ancient versions exhibit a striking uncertainty in translating *hôpîa'*. Only in 2 passages does the LXX use Gk. *emphaínomai,* "appear" (Ps. 80:2[1][LXX 79:2]; 50:2[LXX 49:2]); in the latter passage *emphanṓs hḗxei* is a conflation of Heb. *hôpîa'* (v. 2) and *yāḇō'* (v. 3) in the MT. The Vulg. follows the LXX in 80:2(1)(Vulg. 79:2) with Lat. *manifestare* and 50:2(Vulg. 49:3) with *manifeste veniet*; in the former, Jerome translates *ostendere,* and in the latter correctly gives *apparuit* in v. 2 and *veniet* in v. 3. The LXX takes a different tack in Ps. 94:1(LXX 93:1) with *parrēsiázomai,* "speak or appear freely" (the same verb in Ps. 12:6[5][Vulg. 11:6]); the Vulg. adopts this translation with *libere egit,* which Jerome corrects to *ostendere.* In Job 3:4, the LXX prefers the meaning "come" with *élthoi,* whereas the Vulg. emphasizes "shining" with *inlustret.*

In some cases the meaning of *hôpîa'* seems to have been guessed at, with varying success. In Dt. 33:2, for example, the LXX reads *katéspeusen,* "hurried down" (from Mt. Paran); the Vulg. correctly translates *apparuit.* The difficult passage Job 10:3 is translated by the LXX as *prosésches,* "thou dost approach" or "thou art troubled by" (the counsel of the wicked); the *adiuves* of the Vulg. is also a free rendering. No equivalent to *hôpîa'* can be found in the LXX versions of Job 10:22; 37:15; the Vulg. has *ostenderunt* in 37:15, but reads totally differently in 10:22. In Ezk. 28:7,17, the noun *yip'â* is translated *kállos,* "beauty," by the LXX and *decus,* "ornament," by the Vulg., clearly on the basis of an erroneous etymology (from *yāpâ*).[16]

In summary, we may say that the LXX and Vulg.—to the extent the root was known to them—almost always took it in the sense of "come" or "appear," never (with the single exception of the Vulg. in Job 3:4) in the sense of "shine forth."

III. 1. *Literary Forms.* The verb *hôpîa'* takes on theological significance primarily when it is used to describe the appearance of the deity. This is clearly the case in 4 passages belonging to cultic poetry: Dt. 33:2; Ps. 50:2 occur at the beginning of hymnic sections, and Ps. 80:2(1); 94:1 occur at the beginning of communal laments. Job 10:3 (Job's response to Bildad's first speech) probably speaks ironically of God's appearance. But it would be unwise to conclude that the natural setting of *hôpîa'* was sacral language, where it was used as a technical term for "appearance" in a theophany; such a conclusion is contradicted by the "secular" usage in Job 3:4; 10:22; 37:15, which continues in the Dead Sea scrolls (cf. esp. 1QpHab 11:7; 1QH 5:32; CD 20:3,6). Furthermore, a specifically theological usage of *hôpîa'* did in fact develop at Qumran, by no means restricted to the appearance of God.[17]

2. *Ancient Near East.* To the extent that Yahweh or God is the subject who "appears,"

16 See I above.
17 See II.2, 3 above.

hôpîa' belongs to the realm of theophany. Like *zāraḥ* and *nāgâ,* it depicts theophany as a blinding light. In order to understand this "visual" element, we must first recall the religio-historical background of theophany in the ancient Near East.[18] The Egyptians, too, thought that consuming fire—or at least blinding light—was associated with the coming of the gods in their "true" (i.e, incapable of graphic representation) form.[19] It would be erroneous to derive this type of theophany description from the cult of solar deities.[20] We agree with Stein[21] that "primitive" religion should be considered the common root: here fire and light are inseparable components of the notion of the divine.[22]

3. *Sinai.* Of the OT texts that speak of God's "radiant" appearance, Dt. 33:2 is by general consensus the earliest; the analogous use of *hôpîa'* (Ps. 50:2; 80:2[1]; 94:1) and *zāraḥ* is probably traditio-historically dependent on this passage. The statement in Dt. 33:2 that Yahweh appeared "from Sinai" suggests a connection with the Sinai tradition, but it must be noted that the descriptions of the Sinai theophany before P know nothing of the "radiant" appearance of Yahweh/Elohim.[23] It is therefore wrong to suggest any literary influence of these accounts on Dt. 33:2. The passage emphasizes the extraordinary importance of the Sinai tradition, but it depicts the theophany in its own unique way.

4. *Ambivalence.* As in the case of other verbs used to describe a theophany, when *hôpîa'* is used the purpose and effect of God's coming or appearance must be determined from the context. God's timely intervention in human affairs is always involved, but the purpose ranges from punishment and death for God's enemies to deliverance and life for God's people. The focus is on judgment (*n^eqāmôṯ*) in Ps. 94:1f., on salvation (*y^ešû'â*; cf. *'ēzer* in 1QM 1:16) in Ps. 80:2f.(1f.). In the hymnic framework surrounding the Blessing of Moses (Dt. 33:2-5,26-29), the emphasis is also on the help (*'ēzer,* v. 26) provided by God's coming. The solemn description of a theophany in Ps. 50:1-6 is followed by a divine address in two parts, "in which Yahweh enters into judgment with his people."[24] This "prophetic" usage of *hôpîa'* is all the more noteworthy because the word never came to be used in the prophets' message of judgment and salvation. The double symbolism (consuming fire and radiant light) of *hôpîa'* vividly expresses the ambivalence of God's appearance.

5. *Theophany and Epiphany.* The appearance of Yahweh must be thought of in both

---

18 On Sum. *me-lám,* Akk. *melammu* and *šalummatu,* "terrifying brilliance," see Jeremias, 77f.; on the use of Akk. (*w*)*apû,* "shine forth," and *šûpû,* "brilliant," see I above.

19 E. Hornung, *Der Eine und die Vielen: Ägyptische Gottesvorstellungen* (Darmstadt, 1971), 117-124.

20 Cf. Schnutenhaus, 9, who thinks that the appearance of the sun-god may also have been transferred to Yahweh.

21 B. Stein, *Der Begriff K^ebod Jahweh und seine Bedeutung für die alttestamentliche Gotteserkenntnis* (Emsdetten, 1939), 75-79.

22 W. Schmidt, *Der Ursprung der Gottesidee,* VI (Münster, 1935), 299f., 419.

23 Jeremias, 100-111, 154f.

24 H. Gunkel, *in loc.*

historical and cultic terms, as suggested by Westermann's distinction between "epiphany" and "theophany."[25] In Ps. 80:2(1); 94:1, intervention is primarily historical; in Ps. 50:2, it is cultic. Only in cultic rite and ceremony, however, is the historical event recognized as Yahweh's appearance; conversely, cultic appearance takes on substance only as it makes the past or future acts of Yahweh in history present reality. The two "loci" of Yahweh's appearance are inseparable. Both focus on the experience of Yahweh's mighty presence, which can be described only in symbolic words. The verb *hôpîaʿ* characterizes this experience as an event beyond the control of God's people, explicable only on the basis of Yahweh's sovereign faithfulness, in each instance immediately terrifying and only thus seen also as an act of deliverance and a fulfillment of hope.

Barth

---

25 C. Westermann, *Praise and Lament in the Psalms* (Eng. trans., Atlanta, 1981), 99f.

יָצָא *yāṣā'*; מוֹצָא *môṣā'*; תּוֹצָאוֹת *tôṣā'ôṯ*

Contents: I. General. II. Qal in General Usage. III. Theological Usage. IV. The Exodus (Qal). V. Hiphil in General Usage. VI. The Exodus (Hiphil). VII. Dead Sea Scrolls.

---

yāṣā'. P. P. Boccaccio, "I termini contrari come espressioni della totalità in ebraico (I)," *Bibl,* 33 (1952), 173-190, esp. 178ff. on *bô'* and *yṣ'*; H. J. Boecker, *Die Beurteilung der Anfänge des Königtums in den deuteronomistischen Abschnitten des 1. Samuelbuches. WMANT,* 31 (1969), 39-42; L. Boisvert, "Le passage de la Mer des Roseaux et la foi d'Israel," *Science et Esprit,* 27 (1975), 147-159; H. Cazelles, "Rédactions et Traditions dans l'Exode," *Studien zum Pentateuch. Festschrift W. Kornfeld* (Vienna, 1977), 37-58; B. S. Childs, "Deuteronomic Formulae of the Exodus Traditions," *Hebräische Wortforschung. Festschrift W. Baumgartner. SVT,* 16 (1967), 30-39; D. Daube, *The Exodus Pattern in the Bible* (London, 1963), esp. 31-35 on the exodus formula and 39ff. on the release of slaves; A. Eitz, *Studien zum Verhältnis von Priesterschrift und Deuterojesaja* (diss., Heidelberg, 1969/70), 62-71; S. Esh, "Note on יצא," *VT,* 4 (1954), 305-7; J. P. Floss, *Jahwe dienen, Göttern dienen. BBB,* 45 (1975); G. Fohrer, *Überlieferung und Geschichte des Exodus. BZAW,* 91 (1964); M. Görg, "Ausweisung oder Befreiung," *Kairos,* N.S. 20 (1978), 272-280; W. Gross, *Bileam. StANT,* 38 (1974), 257-58; *idem,* "Die Herausführungsformel—Zum Verhältnis von Formel und Syntax," *ZAW,* 86 (1974), 425-453; P. Humbert, "Dieu fait sortir," *ThZ,* 18 (1962), 357-361, 433-36; E. Jenni, "יצא *jṣ'* hinausgehen," *THAT,* I, 755-761; J. Jeremias, *Theophanie. WMANT,* 10 (^{2}1977), 7f.,9,24,52ff.,61,148; K. Kiesow, *Exodustexte im Jesajabuch. OBO,* 24 (1979); L. Köhler, "Hebräisches *jāṣā'* und Markus 8,11," *ThZ,* 3 (1947), 471; J. Kühlewein, *Geschichte in den Psalmen. CThM,* 2 (1973), N. Lohfink, *Das Hauptgebot. AnBibl,* 20 (1963), 161f.; *idem,* "Zum 'kleinen geschichtlichen Credo,' Dtn 26, 5-9," *ThPh,* 46 (1971), 19-39; H. Lubsczyk, *Der Auszug Israels aus Ägypten. ErfThSt,* 11 (1963); R. Meyer, *Gegensinn und Mehrdeutigkeit in der althebräischen Wort- und Begriffsbildung. SSAW,* Phil.-hist. Kl., 120/5

I. General. The Semitic root *yṣ'*[1] is used primarily to refer to various forms of going out or in (qal) or leading out or in (hiphil). The root appears also in Akkadian as *(w)aṣû*[2] (cf. Ezr. 6:15), in Ugaritic,[3] in Phoenician and Punic,[4] and in Aramaic (although the more common Aramaic word for "go out" is *npq,* with 11 occurrences in Biblical Aramaic).[5] In Arabic, *ḫrǵ* is more common.[6] The name 'I-ṣa-Yà has been found at Ebla.[7]

The semantic field of *yṣ'* includes: → בוא *bô'* (like *yṣ'*, found only in qal, hiphil, and hophal), → שלח *šālaḥ* piel, → שוב *šûḇ*, → נסע *nāsaʿ*, and → זרע *zāraʿ*. In descriptions of theophanies we also find *ṣāʿaḏ* (Jgs. 5:4f.) and → ירד *yāraḏ*. For *bô'* as the antonym of *yṣ'*, see *TDOT,* II, 21, 24, 30, 46, 49.

The verb *yāṣā'* occurs 781 times in the qal (counting multiple occurrences within a single

---

(1979), 9f.; E. W. Nicholson, *Exodus and Sinai in History and Tradition* (Richmond, 1973); S. I. L. Norin, *Er Spaltete das Meer. CB,* 9 (Ger. trans. 1977); M. Noth, *A History of Pentateuchal Traditions* (Eng. trans. 1972; repr. Chico, Calif., 1981), 47-51; J. G. Plöger, *Literarkritische, formgeschichtliche und stilkritische Untersuchungen zum Deuteronomium. BBB,* 26 (1967), 100-115, 174-184; H.-D. Preuss, *Deuterojesaja* (Neukirchen-Vluyn, 1976); W. Richter, "Beobachtungen zur theologischen Systembildung in der alttestamentlichen Literatur anhand des 'kleinen geschichtlichen Credo'," *Wahrheit und Verkündigung. Festschrift M. Schmaus,* I (1967), 175-212; *idem,* Die sogenannten vorprophetischen Berufungsberichte. *FRLANT,* N.S. 83[101] (1970), 112; H. Rücker, *Die Begründungen der Weisungen Jahwes im Pentateuch. ErfThSt,* 30 (1973), 40ff., 52ff.; L. Ruppert, "Gottes befreiendes Handeln in der Geschichtstheologie des ATs," in L. Hödl, *et al., Das Heil und die Utopien* (Paderborn, 1977), 67-81; W. H. Schmidt, "Jahwe in Ägypten," *Sefer Rendtorff. Festschrift R. Rendtorff. BDBAT,* 1 (1975), 94-112 = *Kairos,* N.S. 18 (1976), 43-54; R. Schmitt, *Exodus und Passah: Ihr Zusammenhang im AT. OBO,* 7 (1975); F. Schnutenhaus, "Das Kommen und Erscheinen Gottes im AT," *ZAW,* 76 (1964), 1-22, esp. 2-5; J.-L. Ska, "La sortie d'Égypte (Ex 7-14) dans le récit sacerdotale (P^g) et la tradition prophétique," *Bibl,* 60 (1979), 191-215; D. E. Skweres, *Die Rückverweise im Buch Deuteronomium. AnBibl,* 79 (1979), 110ff., 213ff.; H. Vorländer, *Die Entstehungszeit des jehowistischen Geschichtswerkes. EH,* ser. 23, 109 (1978), 82ff.; H.-E. von Waldow, *Die Bedeutung der Erwählungstraditionen Israels für die Eschatologie der alttestamentlichen Propheten* (diss., Heidelberg, 1956), 24ff.; P. Weimar, *Untersuchungen zur priesterschriftlichen Exodusgeschichte. FzB,* 9 (1973); *idem* and E. Zenger, *Exodus. SBS,* 75 (1975) (esp. with regard to historical questions); J. Weingreen, "הוצאתיך in Genesis 15:7," *Words and Meanings. Festschrift D. W. Thomas* (Cambridge, 1968), 209-215; J. N. M. Wijngaards, *The Formulas of the Deuteronomic Creed* (Tilburg, 1963), 22-27; *idem,* "הוציא and העלה, a Twofold Approach to the Exodus," *VT,* 15 (1965), 91-102; E. Zenger, "Funktion und Sinn der ältesten Herausführungsformel," *ZDMGSup,* 1 (1969), 334-342.

See also the bibliog. on the theme of "theophany" in H. D. Preuss, "בּוֹא *bô'*," *TDOT,* II, 20.

1 Cf. Jenni, 755; G. Bergsträsser, *Introduction to the Semitic Languages* (Eng. trans, Winona Lake, 1983), 218f.

2 *CAD,* I/2 (1968), 356-385.

3 *UT,* no. 1138; *WUS,* no. 1222; Whitaker, 317; D. G. Pardee, "Attestations of Ugaritic Verb/Preposition Combinations in Later Dialects," *UF,* 9 (1977), 214; here also in the shafel with the meaning "cause to come forth, escape," as well as a verbalized substantive and a military term for "move out"; see also M. Dijkstra and J. C. de Moor, "Problematical Passages in the Legend of Aqhâtu," *UF,* 7 (1975), 206.

4 *DISO,* 110, 164 (noun); cf. KBL^3, 406a.

5 KBL^2, 1082b; *LexSyr,* 304f.; also the citations in *KAI,* III, 38.

6 Cf. Jenni, 755.

7 G. Pettinato, "The Royal Archives of Tell Mardikh-Ebla," *BA,* 39 (1976), 50.

verse, including use in *figura etymologica*) and 278 times in the hiphil. There are only 4 clear occurrences of the hophal: Gen. 38:25; Jer. 38:22; Ezk. 38:8; 47:8. Both occurrence of a hophal and overall meaning are disputed in 2 S. 18:22 (reading *muṣē'ṯ* [cf. Gen. 38:25; Dt. 14:28] with Wellhausen and Caspari as "paid out"; cf. "distribute" in 1QS 6:20); Cant. 8:10; Ezk. 14:22; 44:5. The prepositions used with *yṣ'* are discussed by *GesB,* §310b.

Ginsberg and above all Dahood[8] have proposed for Job 23:10b; 28:11 (cf. v. 1); Prov. 25:4 a meaning "shine" similar to that of Arab. *waḍu'a* or *waḍa'a* (cf. also Ugaritic[9]).

Nominal derivatives of the verb include: *yôṣē'ṯ,* "miscarriage" (?) in cattle (Ps. 144:14; cf. Ex. 21:22); *yāṣî',* "descendant" (only 2 Ch. 32:21 [*Q*][10]); and *ṣe'ᵉṣā'îm,* "growth," "offspring" (11 occurrences, plus 2 in Sirach[11]).

The noun *môṣā'* (an abstract formation[12]) has a range of meanings similar to that of the verb: "exit," "going out," "intention," "point of departure," "rising" (of the sun), "utterance" (what "goes out" of someone's lips [Yahweh's: Dt. 8:3; Sir. 39:17]), and even "spring" (2 K. 2:21; etc.); special note should be taken of Ps. 19:7(Eng. v. 6) (cf. Ps. 75:7[6] and the proper name in 1 Ch. 2:46); Hos. 6:3. Note also *môṣā'â* in the sense of "origin" (exit = beginning) in Mic. 5:1(2), but "latrine" in 2 K. 10:27 (*Q*) (the place to which one goes out?).

Like *môṣā',* *tôṣā'ôṯ* (23 occurrences) has a wide range of meanings: "exits," "sources," "terminus"; also "way out," "escape" (Ps. 68:21[20]). Whether *ṣō'n* derives from the root *yṣ'* is disputed.[13]

The most important equivalents in the LXX are Gk. *exérchomai,*[14] *ekporeúomai,*[15] *éxodos,*[16] and *exágō* (for the hiphil). Altogether, however, the LXX uses more than 100 equivalents for the root.[17]

In addition to the disputed hophal passages, the reading of Prov. 25:4; Hos. 6:5 is uncertain.

II. Qal in General Usage. a. Of the 781 occurrences of the verb in the qal, the majority (almost 400) involve the meaning of someone's going or coming forth (or not

---

8 M. Dahood, *Proverbs and Northwest Semitic Philology. SPIB,* 113 (1963), 52; *idem,* "Hebrew-Ugaritic Lexicography III," *Bibl,* 46 (1965), 321; *idem,* "Hebrew-Ugaritic Lexicography IV," *Bibl,* 47 (1966), 416, on *môṣā'* = "star"; cf. also Neh. 4:15; Job 38:7; Ps. 65:9; Cant. 8:10; *idem, Psalms I. AB,* XVI (1965), 93f., 267; on Job 28:11, cf. also A. C. M. Blommerde, *Northwest Semitic Grammar and Job. BietOr,* 22 (1969), 106f.; also J. Barr, *Comparative Philology and the Text of the OT* (Oxford, 1968), 328.

9 *KTU,* 1.16 I, 53.

10 Cf. *KBL*³, 408f.

11 Cf. D. Barthélemy and O. Rickenbacher, *Konkordanz zum hebräischen Sirach* (Göttingen, 1973), 161f.

12 Cf. R. Meyer, *Hebräische Grammatik* (Berlin, ³1966-1972).

13 Cf. *KBL*², 790a.

14 J. Schneider, "ἐξέρχομαι," *TDNT,* II, 678-680.

15 F. Hauck and S. Schulz, "ἐκπορεύομαι," *TDNT,* VI, 578f.

16 W. Michaelis, "εἴσοδος," *TDNT,* V, 103-9.

17 See E. C. dos Santos, *An Expanded Hebrew Index for the Hatch-Redpath Concordance to the Septuagint* (Jerusalem, 1973), 83f.

doing so) to or from a place, departing, setting forth, or escaping, and sometimes even returning; cf. → שׁוּב *šûḇ* but above all → נסע *nāsaʿ* and → הלך *hālaḵ* (*hālakh*). The meaning is thus "dislocative, separative, ingressive,"[18] and the verb is therefore used most often with *min.* Not uncommonly the point of departure is implied (cf. 2 S. 16:7: "Begone!"), while the antonym → בוא *bôʾ* focuses more on the goal (also true of the hiphil). Most often, the qal of *yāṣāʾ* appears in the perfect or as a participle. Like *bôʾ*,[19] it can be used as an auxiliary verb, e.g. 2 S. 24:20; 1 K. 2:46; 19:11 ("step outside"); 2 K. 8:3; 10:9; Isa. 30:22; Mal. 3:20(4:2). Some texts clearly use *yāṣāʾ* as a catchword: Ex. 8f.; 11:8; 16:4ff.; Jgs. 11:31ff.; 1 S. 11:1-11; 1 K. 20:13ff.

One important aspect of this range of meanings is the release of slaves (→ חפשי *ḥopšî*) or property (*šᵉmiṭṭâ*): Ex. 21:2,5; cf. especially 21:7; this represents a fixed idiom, which serves as a catchword in Ex. 21:2-11. The verb can also be used without the addition of *ḥopšî,* since the meaning is clear even without this qualification (Lev. 25:28,30f.; cf. also Lev. 25:33; 27:27; Dt. 15:16; 2 K. 13:5 [or is this a hiphil?]). This usage will be discussed again under V.c and VI.

b. Another large group of occurrences (over 50) involves things or objects (e.g., rivers, years, boundaries[20]) that go forth from some beginning, or go to (*ʾel*) or end at some destination.[21] This meaning also appears in negative constructions. The word can also refer to "necessities" (2 K. 12:13[12]), and can mean "undertake" or "succeed" (2 K. 18:7; Prov. 25:4). A sword is "drawn" (Ezk. 21:9[4]), a river "flows" (Gen. 2:10; Ezk. 47:8), something "comes" to light (Job 28:11; cf. Ps. 17:2; Hab. 1:4) or "sprouts" (1 K. 5:13[4:33]; Isa. 11:1; 14:29; etc.). A person "comes forth" from the womb (Jer. 1:5; 20:18; Sir. 40:1; cf. the derivatives discussed under I above).

This "birth" or "descent" is of special importance[22] in the context of the promise to David and P's version of the promise of descendants to Abraham (probably modeled on the promise to David) in Gen. 17:6 (cf. v. 16; 35:11), which speaks of "kings."[23] In a contrasting sense we find the verb used for a miscarriage (Ex. 21:22; Nu. 12:12; cf. Dt. 28:57) or an emission of semen (Lev. 15:16,32; 22:4).[24] In Mic. 5:1(2), the absence of a subject and the unclear reference of *lî* make it difficult to translate both *yāṣāʾ* and *môṣāʾ*,[25] but the problems hardly justify translating *yṣʾ* here as "subject, (go out in order to) surrender" (as in 1 S. 11:3,10; 2 K. 18:31 par. Isa. 36:16; Jer. 38:2,17,18,21), in the sense

18 H. Schweizer, *Elischa in den Kriegen. StANT,* 37 (1974), 151.

19 → בוא *bôʾ*, II, 21.

20 On the latter, see M. Ottosson, "גבול *gᵉḇûl (gᵉbhûl),*" *TDOT,* II, 364.

21 See also E. Kutsch, "'. . . am Ende des Jahres': Zur Datierung des israelitischen Herbstfestes in Ex 23 16," *ZAW,* 83 (1971), 15-21.

22 → זרע *zāraʿ*, IV, 157; also the combination with *yāṣāʾ* in 2 S. 7:12; 16:11 and the contrast with 1 K. 8:19 par. 2 Ch. 6:9, as well as the negative statement in 2 K. 20:18 par. Isa. 39:7. See also E. von Nordheim, "König und Tempel: Der Hintergrund des Tempelbauverbotes in 2 Samuel vii," *VT,* 27 (1977), 450f.

23 See M. Weinfeld, "ברית *bᵉrîṯ (bᵉrîth),*" *TDOT,* II, 270-72; also R. Clements, *Abraham and David. SBL,* N.S. 5 (1967), 72.

24 See also M. Tsevat, "חקר *ḥāqar,*" *TDOT,* IV, 148.

25 See W. Rudolph, *Micha. KAT,* XIII/3 (1975), 90; also *UF,* 9 (1977), 358ff.

that the future ruler subjects himself totally to Yahweh (= *lî*) (cf. Mic. 5:3[4]).[26] Above all, Mic. 5:1c(2c) contradicts this interpretation.

c. In a third group of occurrences (more than 120), *yāṣāʾ* is used as a technical military term (often with → צבא *ṣāḇāʾ*)[27] meaning "go forth to battle," "move out" (e.g., Gen. 14:8, with v. 17 possibly meant as a deliberate contrast; Ex. 17:9; Nu. 1:3,22ff.; Jgs. 21:21 in contrast to peaceful "coming forth"; Nu. 26:2 with reference to everyone qualified for military service; and so on through 1–2 Chronicles). It is noteworthy that both Yahweh and the militia of Israel "go out" to battle (Jgs. 4:14; cf. 5:4), although the use of the same verb is (deliberately?) avoided (→ ירד *yāraḏ*; but cf. 1 Ch. 14:15!). Usage in the Chronicler's history has been discussed by Welten.[28]

d. This usage in military terminology leads to a first, relatively frequent, combination of the opposites *bôʾ* and *yāṣāʾ* to mean "go out and come (back) in" (a usage found also at Ugarit and in the Dead Sea scrolls):[29] Nu. 21:23; 27:17,21 (reinterpreted in a cultic sense; cf. e below); Dt. 20:1; 21:10; 23:10f.(9f.) (close to being cultic); 24:5; 31:2(?); Josh. 11:4; 14:11; 1 S. 8:20; 18:13,16; 29:6; 2 S. 5:2; 1 K. 3:7 (but cf. 2 Ch. 1:10!); also 2 K. 11:7;[30] 1 Ch. 5:18; 20:1; 2 Ch. 1:10; Job 39:21; Isa. 42:13; cf. Prov. 30:27 (locusts).

e. "Come in and go out"[31] is also used (mostly with priests as the subj.) in the sense "perform cultic acts": Ex. 28:35; 33:7-11; 34:34; Lev. 9:23; 16:17f.,23f.; Nu. 27:17,21 (here clearly on the borderline between military and cultic terminology); 1 K. 8:10 (*yāṣāʾ* alone; cf. 2 Ch. 5:11); 2 K. 11:9; Ezk. 42:13f.; 44:3 (cf. v. 19); 46:2,8-10; with → נשׂיא *nāśîʾ* as subject: Ezk. 44:3; 46:2,8,10,12; with → עם *ʿam* as the subject: Ezk. 46:9f. Only in 2 Ch. 23:7 is the king the subject; contrast 2 Ch. 26:18,20. See also 1QSa 1:17 (hiphil in 1:23).

f. In addition to the general meaning of "go out and come in," it is not uncommon for *bôʾ* and *yāṣāʾ* to be used together (with some 15 occurrences) as an inclusive pair of antonyms to indicate totality:[32] "be able to do something/everything," or simply "do something," as in Nu. 27:17(?); Dt. 28:6,19; 31:2; 2 K. 11:8 par.; 19:27; Ps. 121:8; Isa. 37:28; Jer. 37:4; cf. the deliberate contrast and the word order in Gen. 42:15. When negated, this combination means "not know what to do," "be incapable of doing anything" (Dt. 31:2; 1 K. 3:7;[33] cf. 2 S. 3:25 with *môṣāʾ*).

g. As in Akkadian (*ṣit šamši*), Ugaritic,[34] and Egyptian,[35] *yāṣāʾ* not uncommonly means

---

26 This interpretation is also supported by J. T. Willis, "ממך לי יצא in Micah 5.1," *JQR*, N.S. 58 (1967/68), 317-322.

27 See A. S. van der Woude, "צָבָא *ṣābāʾ Heer,*" *THAT*, II, 500ff.

28 P. Welten, *Geschichte und Geschichtsdarstellung in den Chronikbüchern. WMANT*, 42 (1973), 92, 97, 130, 154f.

29 On the antonyms discussed here in sections d-f, see Plöger, 174ff.; also → בוא, II, 21, 44-49.

30 See J. Wellhausen, *Die Composition des Hexateuchs und der historischen Bücher des ATs* (Berlin, ⁴1963), 292f.; also G. Robinson, "Is 2 Kings XI 6 a Gloss?" *VT*, 27 (1977), 56-58.

31 → בוא *bôʾ*, II, 23.

32 Cf. Boccaccio.

33 Contra Plöger, 180.

34 Cf. T. Hartmann, "שֶׁמֶשׁ *Šæmæš* Sonne," *THAT*, II, 993.

35 See, e.g., J. Assmann, *Liturgische Lieder an den Sonnengott*, I (Berlin, 1969), index; *idem, Zeit und Ewigkeit im alten Ägypten. AHAW*, 1975/1, 49ff.

the "going forth" = "rising" of the sun (or other heavenly bodies): Gen. 19:23; Jgs. 5:31; Ps. 19:6f.(5f.); Isa. 13:10;[36] cf. Ps. 65:9(8); 75:7(6).[37] In combination with → בוא *bô'*[38] it refers to the rising and setting of the sun or stars in Neh. 4:15(21); cf. Ezk. 7:10, where the text is obscure. The similarity to military usage is noteworthy. When the sun rises, it enters into sovereignty (Ps. 19); cf. the coming forth of → צדק(ה) *ṣeḏeq/ṣᵉḏāqâ* in Ps. 37:6; Isa. 45:23; 62:1, where noun and verb together describe the "shining forth of salvation" (cf. also "shine").[39] According to Ahlström,[40] *yṣ'* in the Psalms is always associated with the notion of light, although this holds true only in Ps. 19.[41]

h. "Go forth from the mouth" (→ פה *peh*; cf. Akk. *ṣit pī*) can mean "utter" in general (Josh. 6:10; Jgs. 11:36; etc.), but usually more specifically "command" (Nu. 30:3[2]; 32:24; Jer. 44:17; etc.; cf. Lk. 2:1!; also Prov. 2:6 without the verb[42]). From the mouth of Yahweh or God go forth commands and words that can be trusted (esp. Deutero-Isaiah: Isa. 45:23; 48:3; 55:11; also Job 37:2 [thunder]; Ps. 89:35[34]; Dnl. 9:23).

i. Just as water goes forth (Ex. 17:6; Nu. 20:11; Jgs. 15:19; cf. *môṣā'* in the sense of "spring"; also Ezk. 47:1,8,12; Joel 4:18[3:18]; Zec. 14:8, where the notion is developed on the basis of Yahweh's new dwelling in his temple among his people) and light (Hos. 6:5) or fire[43] breaks out (Ex. 22:5[6]; Lev. 9:24; etc.), not uncommonly with Yahweh as the cause, so anger (Nu. 17:11[16:46]) or a curse throughout the whole earth (Zec. 5:3; cf. vv. 5b-6; note here, too, the close association with the antonym *bô'*[44]) may go forth from Yahweh.

j. In combination with → גורל *gôrāl*, *yāṣā'* refers to instruction received by casting lots, especially in questions having to do with assignment of territory: Nu. 33:54; Josh. 16:1 (cf. 18:11); then 19:1,17,24,32,40; 21:4 (possibly P); 1 Ch. 24:7; 25:9; 26:14; also Job 23:10 (all exilic or postexilic passages). In 1 S. 14:4, on the other hand, the verb designates "free passage" that is not determined by lot. Usage in the Dead Sea scrolls is discussed in VII below.

k. Finally, with → נפש *nepeš* or → רוח *rûaḥ* as object, *yāṣā'* means "breathe one's last" (as it does in Ugaritic[45]): Gen. 35:29; Ps. 146:4; cf. Gen. 44:28; Job 14:2; Ezk. 26:18; Sir. 38:23. Use with *lēḇ* also belongs here ("their hearts failed them": Gen. 42:28), as does "be beside oneself" in Cant. 5:6.

III. Theological Usage. The texts already discussed have often had theological overtones, so that here, too, as so often in the OT, the boundary between "secular" and

---

36 → זרח *zāraḥ* (*zārach*).
37 See G. W. Ahlström, *Psalm 89* (Lund, 1959), 127f.
38 → בוא *bô'*, II, 21.
39 Esh, 306f.; Ahlström, 79.
40 *Ibid.*, 127, n. 5.
41 Cf. the criticism by H. Ringgren in "זרח *zāraḥ* (*zārach*)," *TDOT*, IV, 142.
42 But cf. RS 22.439, I, 4f. = *Ugaritica*, V, 277.
43 → אש *'ēš*, I, 418-428; Esh.
44 Cf. → בוא *bô'*, II, 26f.; also → אלה *'ālâ* (*'ālâ*).
45 *KTU*, 1.18 IV, 24f., 36 = *KTU*, 1.16 I, 35.

"theological" is not absolutely clear. The texts to be discussed in this section are those in which the qal of *yṣ*ʾ appears in contexts that are of special theological significance, e.g., those that refer to Yahweh.

a. In the visions of Zechariah (Zec. 2–6), the 14 occurrences of *yāṣāʾ* make it a catchword. Often it is the → מלאך *malʾāḵ* who goes forth (Zec. 2:7[3]; 5:5; similarly in 2 K. 19:35 par. and the restatement in 2 Ch. 32:21!; also Nu. 22:32; Dnl. 9:22). A great narrative arch holds these visions together, defined in part by the frequent repetition of *yāṣāʾ* (cf. also Zec. 5:6,9; 6:1,7), which on the one hand conveys (as it is meant to) an "impression of centrifugal movement"[46] and on the other emphasizes the spatial orientation of the entire section.[47]

In the heavenly court, when Yahweh asks who will entice Ahab, a → רוח *rûaḥ* comes forward (1 K. 22:21f.) declaring its readiness to be → שקר *šeqer* and to work in the mouth of all his prophets. Micaiah states that Yahweh has asked the spirit to do so (cf. 2 Ch. 18:20f.).

From the false prophets of Jerusalem, too, disaster or ungodliness and wickedness go forth into all the land (Jer. 23:15, a verdict spoken by Yahweh). But it is also promised that songs of thanksgiving will once more go forth from this city (Jer. 30:19) and that its ruler[48] will come forth from its midst (v. 21).

From Zion instruction[49] will go forth (Isa. 2:3; Mic. 4:2; cf. Dt. 17:11[?]), defined more closely by the parallel → דבר *dāḇār* (*dābhār*)[50] (cf. Isa. 45:23; 51:4f.; 55:11; Ezk. 33:30) and therefore clearly meaning more than help in resolving specific conflicts. A "remnant"[51] will also go forth from Jerusalem (Isa. 37:32 par.).[52]

Deutero-Isaiah has Yahweh state repeatedly that salvation, help, deliverance, and a trustworthy word go forth from his mouth promising salvation (Isa. 45:23; 51:4f.; 55:11; cf. the restatement in Isa. 62:11, which nevertheless seeks to hold fast to the essential message). There is a certain similarity to Ps. 17:2, which looks for priestly assurance.

The catchword → משפט *mišpāṭ* in Ps. 17:2 recalls Hos. 6:5, a verse that is textually and literarily difficult; some light may be cast on the passage by Hab. 1:4, 7, where the same idea is expressed negatively. The imperfect tense describes the expected outcome.

The people in exile wish indeed to hear from the prophet the word that goes forth from Yahweh, but they do not act according to it (Ezk. 33:30). Therefore in a symbolic action the prophet proclaims proleptically the removal into exile of the remaining population of Jerusalem and their king (Ezk. 12:4; cf. v. 12; also with the hiphil in v. 14; on the pl. *môṣāʾê,*

---

46 K. Seybold, *Bilder zum Tempelbau. SBS,* 70 (1974), 34.

47 *Ibid.,* 36, 41; cf. W. A. M. Beuken, *Haggai—Sacharja 1–8. SSN,* 10 (1967), 248; G. Wallis, "Die Nachtgesichte des Propheten Sacharja," in *Congress Volume, Göttingen 1977. SVT,* 29 (1978), 379f.

48 → משל *mšl.*

49 → טורה *tôrâ.*

50 *TDOT,* III, 109.

51 → שארית *šᵉʾēriṯ.*

52 Cf. W. E. Müller–H.-D. Preuss, *Die Vorstellung vom Rest im AT* (Neukirchen-Vluyn, ²1973), 126 and *passim.*

cf. Ps. 65:9[8]). Those who are left will "come forth" to the exiles as witnesses to the judgment that has befallen Jerusalem (Ezk. 14:22; cf. Jer. 15:1; also Ezk. 36:20; Am. 4:3; Mic. 4:10; Zec. 9:14; 14:2, where "going forth" appears in oracles of judgment).

b. The antonym of *yāṣā'*, → בוא *bô'*,[53] is often used in Wisdom Literature to indicate the connection between conduct and reward. Although an analogous statement of this notion with *yāṣā'* is not found in Proverbs or Ecclesiastes, it does occur in Sir. 16:14 (cf. 42:13). And 1 S. 24:14(13) cites a proverb to the effect that wickedness "comes forth" from the wicked. The deliberate repetition of *yāṣā'* in 2 K. 2:23f. also shows that this usage, although rare, did occur.

c. A small group of texts uses *yāṣā'* to express Yahweh's governance of history. This recalls the similar use of → בוא *bô'*[54] in a larger group of texts. When something "comes from Yahweh," its course and above all its end are determined (Gen. 24:50; Ruth 1:13[?]; Isa. 28:29; Lam. 3:38 [with v. 37]; also 2 K. 18:7; Ps. 109:7, where "from Yahweh" is implicit).

d. There are 18 occurrences of the qal of *yāṣā'* with Yahweh as subject. Here it is Yahweh who comes forth in a theophanic or epiphanic event, which usually leads up to an action (cf. also the use of → בוא *bô'*,[55] → ירד *yāraḏ*, and → צעד *ṣ'd*.[56] The focus is not so much on Yahweh's starting point in these cases as on his goal and purpose in coming forth.[57] As a subset of the many passages that speak of God's coming,[58] the texts using *yāṣā'* do not focus on heaven or the earthly temple or some other place, which might be seen as correlates,[59] but rather define his coming forth as being warlike.[60] Yahweh comes forth to battle, usually on behalf of his people but in prophetic oracles of judgment also against them (cf. Jgs. 5:4f.; 2 S. 5:24!; Isa. 42:13a; also Hos. 6:3 [*môṣā'*]). Yahweh probably starts from Sinai, as Dt. 33:2; Hab. 3:3 show. Mic. 1:3 (cf. literally Isa. 26:21, but for judgment against the nations) describes Yahweh's coming forth without indicating his starting point precisely (*māqôm*: his heavenly palace?), merely stating that he comes for judgment (Mic. 1:5; also Jer. 4:7; 15:1; 21:12; 23:19; 25:32). The natural phenomena consequent on Yahweh's coming are often mentioned. Hab. 3:13[61] also speaks of Yahweh's warlike coming to aid his people. Drawing on motifs of the Yahweh war (cf. Jgs. 5:4f.), Zec. 14:3 promises that Yahweh will go forth to fight against the nations. But Yahweh's → כבוד *kāḇôḏ* also went forth from the Jerusalem temple as a sign of judgment (Ezk. 10:18f.). The verb *yāṣā*, as a technical term associated with theophany, appears also, for example, in 1 (Eth.) En. 1:3; As.Mos. 10:3.[62] Yahweh also

---

53 II, 25ff.
54 *Ibid.*, III, VII on the hiphil; also → דבר *dāḇar* (*dābhar*), III, 109.
55 II, 46f.; also the bibliog., 20.
56 The subject is discussed by Schnutenhaus, 2-5.
57 Jenni, 759.
58 → בוא *bô'*, II, 49.
59 M. Metzger, "Himmlische und irdische Wohnstatt Jahwes," *UF*, 2 (1970), 139-158.
60 See II.c above.
61 Omitted by G. Lisowsky.
62 See Jeremias, 52f.

goes forth as a warrior in Ex. 11:4 (J) (cf. 2 S. 5:24 par.; Ps. 81:6[5]; Mic. 7:15). These passages are already somewhat close to the texts that use the qal of *yāṣā'* for the exodus from Egypt.[63]

Several Psalms lament that Yahweh has not gone out with Israel's armies[64] (Ps. 44:10[9]; 60:12[10] par. 108:12[11]; cf. Mic. 7:15; Ps. 68:8[7] in its context), illustrating once more that Yahweh's going forth as a warrior to help his people was an integral part of Israel's faith and hope.

IV. The Exodus (Qal). In comparison to the hiphil of *yṣ'* ("cause to go out," "bring out," with Yahweh as subj.),[65] the qal ("go out," with Israel as subj.) is used much less frequently with reference to the exodus. It appears some 40 times, and not at all in Leviticus, Hosea, Amos, Joel, Jonah, Nahum, Zephaniah, Obadiah, or Sirach.[66] This usage must be treated separately, because it exhibits certain peculiarities. In addition, the use of the hiphil in this context can then be defined more precisely.

a. The only occurrence in Genesis is 15:14, in the historical summary of vv. 13-16. Verses 13f.,16 are often assigned to E; this cannot be correct, however, since P is already familiar with the summary. These words spoken by God are a masterpiece of OT historical theology,[67] but presuppose by their very nature a developed historical perspective. The ease with which v. 12 leads into vv. 17f. likewise reveals vv. 13-16 to be an interpolation. History is interpreted here as being shaped by Yahweh's promise and its fulfillment, guided by his purpose and plan. The exodus of Israel from Egypt is "foreseen." It is possible that *yṣ'* in 15:14 (cf. vv. 4f.,7) echoes 14:17f.;[68] this would also imply a late date for Gen. 14 in its final form.

The clear relationship of *yṣ'* to the description of Yahweh's liberating act begins with the book of Exodus. Yahweh sets his oppressed people free from their slavery in Egypt. Here, too, there is a striking similarity to military usage of *yāṣā'*.[69] Yahweh acts as a warrior in order to liberate. Against the background of Ex. 11:4, v. 8, with three repetitions of *yṣ'*, marks a first focal point. According to Ex. 12:31, Moses and Aaron are to give the command to depart, so that the people may serve Yahweh.[70] Verse 37 uses *ns'* instead of *yṣ'*, thus illustrating the relatively undeveloped terminology of this chapter: the hiphil of *yṣ'* does not appear at all in Ex. 13:17–14:31. Ex. 12:41 describes in this context the carrying out of the command: "all the hosts" (military terminology!) of Israel went out from the land of Egypt.[71]

Ex. 13:3 (with its doublet in v. 14), 8 are among the first texts to associate a specific

---

63 Cf. IV below.
64 → צבא *ṣāḇā'*.
65 See VI below.
66 On the passages using the qal, see Humbert, 433-36; his list, however, is incomplete.
67 See G. von Rad, *Genesis. OTL* (Eng. trans.[2]1972), *in loc.*
68 Cf. N. Lohfink, *Die Landverheissung als Eid. SBS,* 28 (1967), 85ff.
69 Cf. II.c, III.d above.
70 → עבד *'bd.*
71 → ארץ *'eres* (*'erets*); → מצרים *miṣrayim.*

date with the exodus ("coming out" [qal]) from Egypt; cf. Ex. 19:1; Nu. 1:1; 9:1; 33:38; 1 K. 6:1 (usually with the inf.); also 26:4; Nu. 33:1 (before the list of stages). Ex. 23:15; 34:18 also connect the appointed time for the Feast of Unleavened Bread with the exodus from Egypt (cf. Dt. 16:3,6).[72] The texts that use the qal of *yṣ'* for the exodus from Egypt are thus in fact[73] more interested in the event than in its chronology;[74] this means that their *Sitz im Leben* is literary. Israel is to "remember"[75] (Ex. 13:3, with Moses speaking; cf. the catechetical element in v. 8) the day of the exodus, on which they came "out of the house of bondage."[76]

b. The phrase *mibbêṯ ʿᵃḇāḏîm*[77] describes Egypt negatively and Israel positively, as having been delivered by its God from this form of existence (esp. with the hiphil of *yṣ'*).[78] This phrase, which occurs 13 times, is used 3 times with → פדה *pāḏâ* (Dt. 7:8; 13:6[5]; Mic. 6:4), once with the hiphil of → עלה *ʿālâ* alone (Josh. 24:17), and once in combination with the hiphil of *yṣ'* (Jgs. 6:8). If Mic. 6:4 is authentic, one can argue[79] that the verb *pāḏâ* was associated originally with the "house of bondage," although the evidence is scanty. Only here in Ex. 13:3 is the qal of *yṣ'* used with "out of the house of bondage," but the hiphil appears 10 times (Ex. 13:14; 20:2; Dt. 5:6; 6:12; 7:8; 8:14; 13:6,11[5,10]; Jgs. 6:8; Jer. 34:13). Plöger[80] points out also that the hiphil is used in combination with both "out of the land of Egypt" and "Yahweh your God," while another stratum uses the hiphil with "Egypt" and "Yahweh" alone. This latter stratrum, furthermore, never uses the otherwise common phrase "with a strong hand" in combination with "out of the house of bondage." He concludes[81] that the usage of the exodus formula reveals different strata. It is dubious, however, whether it is correct to speak of a clear "formula,"[82] and it not clear how the content of such a formula should be explained and what its historical roots might be. The hiphil passages should be examined once more from this perspective. In any case, the use of *yṣ'* with "out of the house of bondage" reveals a degree of theological reflection and penetration that is further underlined by the command to "remember that you were a slave in the land of Egypt" (Dt. 5:15; 15:15; 16:12; 24:18,22). This point, too, will be taken up again later.[83]

c. Ex. 14:8 (and Nu. 33:3 [secondary; the common stratum of P]) states that the

---

72 For a discussion of the association and the style of argumentation, see J. Halbe, "Erwägungen zu Ursprung und Wesen des Massotfestes," *ZAW,* 87 (1975), 324-346; and (with different conclusions) E. Otto, *Das Mazzotfest in Gilgal. BWANT,* 107[6/7] (1975).

73 Jenni, 761.

74 Cf. Görg, 272.

75 → זכר *zāḵar* (*zākhar*).

76 See d below.

77 See Floss, 56ff., 526ff.; Plöger, 113, n. 204.

78 See VI below.

79 Cf. Floss.

80 Pp. 108f.

81 Cf. Lubsczyk, 83ff.; Gross, *ZAW,* 86 (1974), 425-452, with more precision.

82 Cf. Gross.

83 See VI below.

Israelites went out of Egypt "with a high/mighty hand"; Nu. 11:20 says that Yahweh will continue to give them meat in spite of their rebellious question ("Why did we come forth out of Egypt?").

In the Balaam story, Nu. 23:22; 24:8 will play a role later in our discussion of the hiphil passages. Nu. 22:5 (cf. the hiphil in v. 11), must be mentioned here. It describes Israel as a people that has come out of Egypt. By alluding to this act of deliverance, the verse "introduces Yahweh into the reckoning from the very outset; the tension can only increase."[84] There is no trace of a developed formula, but there are echoes of similar statements and obvious points of contact.

d. In Deuteronomy, the passages referring to the exodus are 4:45f.; 9:7; 11:10; 23:5(4) (cf. 24:9; 25:17); at least half of these are Deuteronomistic. Most of these texts enshrine the commandments imposed upon Israel by the exodus and the God who delivered his people in that event, which therefore demand (newly) heightened obedience (4:45f.: v. 46 refers to the victory over Sihon, whom Moses and the Israelites defeated as they were brought up from Egypt, thus involving chronology in the broader sense;[85] other broadly chronological Deuteronomic or Deuteronomistic texts include Dt. 9:7; 23:7[6]; Josh. 2:10; 1 K. 8:9; 2 K. 21:15; Ps. 114:1; Jer. 7:25; Mic. 7:15).

Also Deuteronomistic is the reference to Israel's faithlessness "from the day you came out of the land of Egypt" (Dt. 9:7; cf. 2 K. 21:15; Jer. 7:25 [Deuteronomistic, with the additional element of a prophetic call; cf. also the context of 2 K. 21:15]). Here the solidarity of Israel in sin and apostasy is emphasized in order (e.g., Jer. 31:29; Ezk. 18:2) to justify solidarity in guilt and punishment.[86] In 1 K. 8:9 (cf. Ex. 20:2 par.), the association of the ark and the law tablets of the → ברית b^e^rîṯ (b^e^rîth) with the exodus is Deuteronomistic.[87]

The people of the exodus had been circumcised (Josh. 5:5: a restrospective reference like that in v. 4 [Deuteronomistic], albeit establishing a connection between the occupation of Canaan and the exodus[88]; v. 6 is a doublet with a Deuteronomistic reference to the forty years in the wilderness). According to Josh. 2:10, Rahab tells the spies that the inhabitants of Jericho had heard what Yahweh did "when you came out of Egypt," attesting to the fundamental significance of this event for Israel. Even Egypt rejoiced when Israel departed (Ps. 105:38). Mic. 7:15, in the liturgy of vv. 8-20, prays that Yahweh will do wonders "as in the days when you [!] came out of Egypt," underlining the importance of this event by referring to it in a different context. And Hag. 2:5 states that Yahweh's promise of salvation pronounced when Israel came out of Egypt, which is not only primary chronologically but also fundamentally constitutive, is still in force. Yahweh's going forth is also that of his people, just as the deliverance of Israel is Yahweh's epiphany (cf. Ps. 114:1 and Josh. 2:10; the connection between the exodus and

84 Gross, *Bileam*, 258.
85 See IV.a above.
86 → אב *'āḇ* (*'ābh*), I, 13-16.
87 On the Deuteronom(ist)ic evaluation of the exodus, see Skweres.
88 For a discussion of the subject, see Otto.

the "miracle at the sea" is rarely explicit but is more common than is sometimes assumed[89]). This is probably also the background of Ps. 81:6(5), where the use of *ʿal* is unique and the context requires "out of Egypt."

In the Deuteronom(ist)ic descriptions of the promised land in Deuteronomy, which deliberately describe it in exaggerated terms as a paradise (probably to present it to the eyes of the exile community as the substance of a new promise), the land "which you are entering"[90] is placed in exaggerated contrast to the land of Egypt "from which you have come": in the promised land irrigation will be unnecessary (Dt. 11:10).[91]

When the motivation clauses of the Deuteronomic laws use the qal of *yṣʾ*, they are more concerned with the chronology of the exodus, echoing the chronological interest of the expansive Deuteronomic and Deuteronomistic style mentioned above[92] (Dt. 16:3,6; cf. the hiphil in v. 1; also 23:5[4]; 24:9 expanding on v. 8; 25:17[93]).

e. Deutero-Isaiah frequently uses the qal of *yāṣāʾ* in promises and descriptions of the new exodus (Isa. 48:20; 52:11f.; 55:12);[94] it appears in 52:11 as a double imperative, which is typical of Deutero-Isaiah.

V. Hiphil in General Usage. "In the hiphil of the verb, most of the usages of the qal reappear with a corresponding causative meaning."[95] The 278 occurrences of the hiphil therefore can be categorized analogously to section II. In this case, too, the so-called "exodus formula" will be treated separately.[96]

a. The primary meaning of the hiphil, with one person or a group as object, is "cause to go out, lead out, bring out, send out, drive out," then also "deliver." Here, too,[97] the verb can function as a kind of auxiliary with the sense "go on to do (something)" (some 40 occurrences, including Gen. 19 where it appears as a catchword suggesting deliberate contrasts). People are brought out, for example, to be killed (Gen. 38:24; cf. v. 25 [hophal]; also Lev. 24:14,23; Nu. 15:36; etc.), and a corpse is brought out (Am. 6:10).

Troops are led out to battle[98] (2 S. 5:2; 10:16; Isa. 43:17; etc.). Use in conjunction with the hiphil of *bôʾ* in Nu. 27:17 also has military overtones (cf. 2 S. 5:2; 1 Ch. 11:2; more general usage is found in Ex. 4:6).

Just as the qal of *yāṣāʾ* (often in conjunction with *bôʾ*;[99] cf. 1 Ch. 9:28) can mean

---

89 See G. W. Coats, "The Traditio-historical Character of the Reed Sea Motif," *VT*, 17 (1967), 258-260; also VI below.

90 → בוא *bôʾ*, IV.

91 → זרע *zāraʿ*, IV, 149.

92 See IV.b and d.

93 See Rücker, 40ff., and Skweres.

94 See D. Baltzer, *Ezechiel und Deuterojesaja. BZAW*, 121 (1971), 12-26; Preuss, *Deuterojesaja*, 42-45; Kiesow.

95 Jenni, 758.

96 See VI.

97 → בוא *bôʾ*, II, 21.

98 Cf. II.c above.

99 Cf. II.e above.

"perform a cultic act," so too can the hiphil (Gen. 14:18; Dt. 14:28; Jgs. 6:18; probably also Ex. 19:17).[100]

b. The hiphil can also have things rather than persons as its object, with the meaning "carry out, bring out, take out, lift out, take away, release, produce, get rid of." Jenni[101] rightly emphasizes that when Yahweh is the subject[102] the verb refers to a specific act rather than a general way of acting.

Yahweh brings forth water, fire, and wind (Nu. 20:8,10; Dt. 8:15; Ps. 78:16; etc.), gnats (Ex. 8:14[18]), and stars (Job 38:32; Isa. 40:26).

The tithe is to be brought forth (Dt. 14:28), as are various implements, foodstuffs, cultic objects, and idols. The red heifer is taken outside the camp (Nu. 19:3); the remains of a sacrificial animal are taken away (Lev. 4:12,21; etc.), as are the ashes of a burnt offering (Lev. 6:4[11]; cf. Ezk. 46:20; Lev. 14:45). Something is brought to light (Jer. 51:10), a work is completed (Isa. 54:16), a pledge is brought out (Dt. 24:11; cf. Jgs. 16:18f., etc.; cf. what 2 Ch. 34:14 adds to 2 K. 22:8). Evidence is brought forth in the course of judicial proceedings (Dt. 21:19; 22:15; cf. Isa. 43:8). Articles can be given out or used (2 K. 12:12[11]; cf. 15:20 and the conjectured hophal in 2 S. 18:22).

Slander and anger can also be brought forth (Prov. 10:18; 29:11; Proverbs uses the hiphil of *yṣ'* only with fools as the subj.; cf. the admonition in Eccl. 5:1[2]). In the conduct-reward nexus that is fundamental to Wisdom Literature,[103] the hiphil of *yṣ'* appears in Prov. 30:33.

For the "uttering" of words—usually negative—see Nu. 13:32; 14:36f.; Dt. 22:14,19; Neh. 6:19; Job 8:10; 15:13; Prov. 10:18; Eccl. 5:1(2); Jer. 15:19.

Several texts, mostly late, use the hiphil of *yṣ'* to mean "bring forth," "yield" (Gen. 1:12,24;[104] Nu. 17:23[8]; Dt. 28:38; Isa. 61:11; 65:9; cf. Job 10:18; Ps. 104:14; Sir. 38:4).

Finally, some texts in Ezekiel speak of the judgment or curse that Yahweh causes to go forth (cf. Jer. 38:23 and the opposite statement in 51:10 regarding salvation); Ezekiel also represents the deportation of Jerusalem as a symbolic action (Ezk. 11:7,9; 12:4-7;[105] cf. Zec. 5:3f.).

c. A small but significant group comprises texts that use the hiphil of *yṣ'* for the "deliverance" of prisoners (Gen. 40:14; 43:23; Isa. 42:7; Jer. 20:3; 51:44; 52:31 [deliverance from Babylon; cf. Deutero-Isaiah]; in Jer. 52:31 there is important material not found in 2 K. 25:27;[106] see also Ps. 142:8[7]; cf. 68:7[6]; 107:14). Because, as we shall see in VI below, the so-called "deliverance formula" with the hiphil of *yṣ'* makes its appearance as a special aspect of "deliverance" or "liberation," the passages cited here are of some importance.

---

100 For a list of the occurrences of *yṣ'* hiphil in P, see K. Elliger, *Leviticus. HAT,* IV (1966), 301, n. 22.

101 Pp. 759f.

102 For additional details, see VI.k, n below.

103 See again → בוא *bô'*, III.

104 The notion of "Mother Earth" is discussed by C. Westermann, *Genesis 1–11* (Eng. trans., Minneapolis, 1984), 125f.

105 Not to be emended to the qal; cf. W. Zimmerli, *Ezekiel 1. Herm* (Eng. trans. 1979), 268f.

106 But cf. *BHK, in loc.*

VI. The Exodus (Hiphil). a. There are 91[107] occurrences of the hiphil of *yṣ'* associated with the exodus from Egypt.[108] We shall first state several common and generally accepted observations.

The language used for the "bringing out" does not constitute a clear and fixed "formula." The subject is usually Yahweh,[109] sometimes Moses and/or Aaron. The object is usually the Israelites, sometimes the fathers or the people (with appropriate suffixes). The place from which they are brought out is Egypt or the land of Egypt. The verb appears in the perfect (1st, 2nd, and 3rd person), as a participle, and as an infinitive, in main and subordinate clauses, with and without other words in apposition, and with a variety of functions. The imperfect is not found.[110]

The use of the hiphil of *'ālâ* for the "bringing up" out of Egypt[111] is earlier, as Ex. 3:8,17 (J); Am. 9:7 show.[112] The hiphil of *yṣ'* in this sense is not found in Isaiah 1–39, Hosea, Joel, Amos, Obadiah, Micah, Nahum, Habakkuk, Zephaniah, Haggai, Zechariah.[113] For the use of the two verbs together, see also Jer. 10:13.

It is usually also stated that the prophetic use of the hiphil of *yṣ'* for the exodus begins with Jeremiah[114] or that it first appears in Dt. 1:27[115] and finds heavy use in Deuteronomy and in other legal texts,[116] where it is common in the motivations of laws.[117] It is said to have taken on increasing importance in the postexilic period. Furthermore—Gross notwithstanding, on the basis of insufficient evidence[118]—we also find in the use of *yṣ'* an implication that the exodus is an act of deliverance on the part of Yahweh, especially since the hiphil (which appears frequently, e.g., in divine discourse) more than the qal emphasizes Yahweh's initiative. It will be our task to verify these observations, elaborate them, and above all set them in a chronological framework. We must therefore begin with texts that can be dated with certainty.

b. It is true that references to the exodus play an important role in the motivation clauses of laws. But the Covenant Code still uses the qal of *yāṣā'*, and with the people as subject (Ex. 23:15; cf. 34:18). The Holiness Code, however, when referring to the exodus characteristically uses only the hiphil with Yahweh as subject (Lev. 19:36; 22:33; 23:43; 25:38,55; 26:45). Of these passages, Lev. 25:38; 26:45 are statements of fundamental purpose: the goal of the exodus is the gift of the land, where Yahweh will be "your God" (cf. the end of 22:33; Ex. 29:46 [P], with a more developed statement of purpose; also Nu. 15:41 [P]). Deliverance from bondage in Egypt enables Israel to live

---

107 Humbert: 76; Wijngaards: 83/84.
108 For a literature survey, see Gross, *ZAW,* 86 (1974), 425-27.
109 See k and n below.
110 For further details, see Gross, *ZAW,* 86 (1974), 425-453.
111 See G. Wehmeier, "עלה *'lh* hinaufgehen," *THAT,* II, 272-290, with bibliog.
112 These texts are discussed by Schmidt, *Festschrift R. Rendtorff,* 96.
113 On the various verbs used for the "exodus," see Fohrer, 1, n. 1.
114 Jenni, 760.
115 *KBL*³, 407b.
116 Wijngaards, *VT,* 15 (1965), 92.
117 See now Rücker, 40ff. (on Deuteronomy), 52ff. (on the Holiness Code).
118 See below.

under the sovereignty of Yahweh. Those whom Yahweh has delivered have not merely been set free (cf. Deuteronomy) but are now his servants (Lev. 25:42,55; 26:13;[119] cf. 20:26; cf. "serve Yahweh" in Dt. 6:12f.; 13:6,11[5,10]). Particular laws also lead up to this fundamental statement of purpose; they are connected by deliberate use of the catchword → עבד *'āḇaḏ,* and Yahweh describes himself ("I am Yahweh, who . . .") as the God who brought the Israelites out and set them free (Lev. 19:36; 22:33; cf. the shorter equivalent in Deuteronomy). The motivations are both theohistorical and theocentric. Yahweh acts for his own sake (cf. Ezekiel).

This emphasis on the end of bondage, on the gift of the land, and on "serving" under the sovereignty of Yahweh as the purpose of deliverance must be seen against the background of the exile, from which the final recension of the Holiness Code dates (cf. only Lev. 26:45; Ex. 20:2). The "bringing out" from Egypt as an act of deliverance on the part of Yahweh, with the gift of the land as its goal, is a theohistorical and theocentric message to the exilic community, living in hope that it, too, will be similarly "brought out," so that Yahweh may once again be the God of his people in the land (cf. P). The participles and perfects describing what Yahweh does emphasize his ability to "bring out." Whereas the nucleus of the Holiness Code uses brief clauses to motivate the individual laws (Lev. 19:36; 23:43), later strata present more developed theological statements to those addressed by the Holiness Code in its exilic form. A survey of other groups of texts will confirm these observations.

c. A second major focus for the "bringing out of Egypt" is the Deuteronomistic corpus. This includes in the first instance all the occurrences in Jeremiah (Jer. 7:22; 11:4; 31:32; 32:21; 34:13).[120] Here, too (cf. Lev. 26:45), covenant, exodus, and deliverance from bondage go together (Jer. 34:8ff.; cf. v. 13; Dt. 15:1,12). The chronology of sacred history is introduced (Jer. 7:22; 11:4; 31:32; 34:13; cf. also 11:7; "the day that I brought out" appears only in Deuteronomistic texts in Jeremiah[121]). Jer. 32:21 is also clearly Deuteronomistic. Jer. 10:13, like vv. 12-16,[122] is not authentic. Yahweh is described as a deliverer (Jer. 32:21), and the new exodus from Babylon will make possible the new obedience that the exodus from Egypt and its associated *b^e^rîṯ* could only demand (31:32).

This same train of thought is followed by the other Deuteronomistic texts: Josh. 24:5f.; Jgs. 2:12; 1 K. 9:9 (cf. 2 Ch. 7:22); Jgs. 6:8 (clearly secondary in conjunction with the hiphil of *'ālâ*);[123] also 1 K. 8:16 (cf. 2 Ch. 6:5). The Deuteronomistic theme is especially clear in 1 K. 8:21,51 (cf. Dt. 29:24[25] [Deuteronomistic]; Jer. 11:3f.; 31:32 [Deuteronomistic]). Yahweh's deliverance was a military act (Josh. 2:10). Apostasy from

---

119 See M. A. Anat, "Determinism and Redemption," *BethM,* 23[75] (1978), 425-29 [Heb.], *525 [Eng. summary].

120 See M. Weinfeld, "Jeremiah and the Spiritual Metamorphosis of Israel," *ZAW,* 88 (1976), 39-52.

121 W. Thiel, *Die deuteronomistische Redaktion von Jeremia 1–25. WMANT,* 41 (1973), 122; for a somewhat different approach, see P. K. D. Neumann, *Hört das Wort Jahwäs* (diss., Hamburg, 1975), 296ff., 308, 312f.

122 Cf. H.-D. Preuss, *Verspottung fremder Religionen im AT. BWANT,* 92[5/2] (1971), 166-170.

123 For the addition of "out of the house of bondage," see IV.b above and VI.e below.

this God has brought judgment (Jgs. 2:12; cf. Dt. 13:6,11[5,10]). The verb *yṣ'* occurs 6 times in 1 K. 8:1–9:9, usually (esp. in 8:46-53; cf. 2 K. 21:1-15) interwoven with other motifs traceable to the exile.[124]

d. The texts in Deuteronomy, which is now extant in a markedly Deuteronomistic recension, also agree with these observations.[125] For the exodus from Egypt or the land of Egypt,[126] Deuteronomy uses only *yṣ'*.[127] Most of the occurrences are in the Deuteronomistic framework of the book; *'ālâ* hiphil appears only in Dt. 20:1, apparently a quotation from an ancient military regulation.[128] The subject of the verb "bring out" is always Yahweh, with the single deliberate exception of Dt. 9:12, a Deuteronomistic retrospect in which Yahweh consciously distances himself from the people.[129]

Dt. 4:20,37 are among the latest (late exilic) Deuteronomistic texts of the book. The former looks back to the time when Yahweh brought forth his people from the "iron furnace" of Egypt (elsewhere only Jer. 11:4 [Deuteronomistic]; cf. 1 K. 8:51 [Deuteronomistic]), that they might serve him and be his people (as in the Holiness Code and P; "take" appears elsewhere only in Dt. 4:20,34; 30:4 [Deuteronomistic]). The addition in 4:20 is intended to emphasize the uniqueness of Yahweh and strengthen confidence in his power. Here, then, we find the later Deuteronomistic stratum, which uses the hiphil of *yṣ'* without "your God," speaks only of "Egypt," and uses the phrase "with a mighty hand" to emphasize Yahweh's power (Dt. 4:20,37; 6:21,23; 9:26,28f.; 26:8). A different stratum adds the qualifier "your God" to "Yahweh," speaks of the "land of Egypt," and adds the interpretive phrase "out of the house of bondage." In this earlier (albeit still exilic) stratum, the exilic situation, its theological interpretation, and the attempt to come to terms with it are somewhat clearer.[130] Yahweh's bringing out of Israel (cf. P in Gen. 17 and → זרע *zāra'*) is interpreted in Dt. 4:37 as a demonstration of Yahweh's love (v. 34; 7:8) toward the fathers and their descendants(!). It was done with great might through Yahweh's → פנים *pānîm*. The element of mercy in this divine act is essential (cf. Dt. 5:15; 11:1-9; also 6:20-25), so that new hope for an analogous act can consciously be awakened. Herein Dt. 1–4 resembles P^g; like P, it deliberately depicts the exodus from Egypt in transparent terms reflecting the hope that Yahweh with mercy and might will bring his people out of Babylon. Therefore Dt. 1:27 can only suggest in a confession of doubt[131] that this act did not reflect Yahweh's love but rather his hate (cf. 9:28): within Dt. 1–3, the exodus is mentioned only here and only in these terms (cf., however, the references elsewhere in the Deuteronomistic history and their relationship to prophecies of judgment: Jgs. 2:12; 1 K. 8:51,53; 9:9; 2 K. 21:15).

---

124 See also Lubsczyk, 115.

125 See Skweres.

126 On the distinction, see Plöger, 110-15.

127 On the qal, see IV.c above.

128 On the situation in Deuteronomy, cf. Childs; also Lubsczyk, 79ff., who claims to distinguish two strata: one "priestly," the other "prophetic."

129 On the special nature of this passage, see also Lohfink, *Das Hauptgebot,* 207ff.

130 On the strata, see Lubsczyk; also Plöger, 111f.; but cf. the combination in Ex. 13:14 (Deuteronomistic).

131 N. Lohfink, "Darstellungskunst und Theologie in Dtn 1,6–3,29," *Bibl,* 41 (1960), 105-134.

Dt. 5:6 (cf. Ex. 20:2)[132] presents Yahweh's law as the reflex and consequence of his gift; Yahweh, the giver, defines himself theologically as deliverer. In a kind of general clause, Yahweh declares himself to be the God who acts in history to deliver and thus imposes an obligation on those who are delivered. The first and second commandments are the immediate focus, but the theological argument applies to the entire Decalogue. In Dt. 5:6, as in Ex. 20:2, the language is clearly Deuteronomistic.[133] The lawgiver is first the liberator, and Israel's primary experience with this God determines the present and future of the people, since it is always possible and necessary to hope that Yahweh will once again set his people free. The God who imposes demands is first characterized and legitimized as the God who sets free; it is typical of the OT to interpret "your God" in historical terms. "Other gods" cannot claim this historical demonstration. During the exile this line of argument was important as a source of hope (cf. Deutero-Isaiah).[134]

In the actual legal corpus of Deuteronomy, only 13:6,11(5,10) (Deuteronomistic); 16:1 use the hiphil of *yṣ'* (Dt. 26:8, a unique text, is discussed below); here (in contrast to the usage of the qal[135]) the fact of deliverance is more important than its chronology.[136] For the emphasis on Yahweh as agent, compare the hiphil in Dt. 16:1 with the qal in Ex. 23:15; 34:18. From this God the Israelites must not turn away (again), as the Deuteronomistic additions in 13:6b,11a(5b,10a) state, taking their material from Dt. 5:6; 6:12; 7:8; 8:14.

The people brought forth by Yahweh from the "iron furnace" of the exile (Dt. 4:20; 1 K. 8:51; Jer. 11:4 [all Deuteronomistic]) are once again to be Yahweh's own people and heritage (1 K. 8:51,53 [Deuteronomistic]). The exilic situation of the Deuteronomistic texts and certain others explains why the return, pictured in terms of a hopeful exodus from Egypt, is described as leading up to the (renewed) gift of the land, and as such is promised once more (Lev. 25:38; Dt. 6:23; 26:8; 1 S. 12:8 [Deuteronomistic]; Ezk. 20:34f.,41; 34:13 [all probably exilic]; also Ps. 105:37ff.; 114:1f. [postexilic]).

The additional material in Dt. 5:15 (not found in Ex. 20) motivating the extremely detailed and central Sabbath commandment also goes on to qualify Yahweh's act as having been done "with a mighty hand[137] and an outstretched arm"[138] (on the so-called priestly stratum, cf. here Dt. 4:34; 5:15; 6:21; 7:8,19; 9:26,29; 11:2; 26:8; cf. 1 K.

---

132 On the terminology, see Lohfink, *Das Hauptgebot,* 98ff.; *idem,* "Die These vom 'deuteronomischen' Dekaloganfang—ein fragwürdiges Ergebnis atomischer Sprachstatistik," in *Festschrift W. Kornfeld,* 99-109.

133 G. Fohrer, "Die sogenannte apodiktisch formulierte Recht und der Dekalogue," *Studien zur alttestamentlichen Theologie und Geschichte (1949-1969). BZAW,* 115 (1969), 130, n. 28 (contra Lohfink). Cf. in the Holiness Code Lev. 19:36; 25:38; 26:13; also Nu. 15:41.

134 On the theological argument presented in Dt. 5:6, see esp. H. Schüngel-Straumann, *Der Dekalog, Gottes Gebote? SBS,* 67 (1973), 99-101, with bibliog.; W. Keszler, "Die literarische, historische und theologische Problematik des Dekalogs," *VT,* 7 (1957), 15f.; J. J. Stamm, "Dreissig Jahre Dekalogforschung," *ThR,* N.S. 27 (1961), 234-37.

135 See IV.a above.

136 Cf. Rücker, 41, and Skweres.

137 → יד *yāḏ;* cf. Childs, 31.

138 → זרוע *zᵉrôaʿ;* on the phrase "with signs and wonders," see Childs, 31.

8:9,16,21; 9:9; 2 K. 21:15; also Josh. 5:4-6—again with motifs that reflect the exile). Experienced in this way, Yahweh is unique; he desires obedience and can grant fertility. Accordingly, Israel should not (again) forget this God (Dt. 6:12; cf. 8:14; on the prophetic "stratum": Dt. 5:6f.; 6:12; 7:8; 8:14; 13:6,11[5,10]: the clear distinction between "strata" is problematic; previously distinct emphases are recognizable). Yahweh now expects much more grateful obedience, and the Sabbath commandment in its full foundation and elaboration leads us to suppose an exilic setting also for Dt. 5:15.

Dt. 6:21 (based on an earlier text?) also is a paradigmatic parenetic historical retrospect emphasizing the act through which Yahweh set his people free; the "us" expresses the solidarity of the generations. The recounting of God's mighty acts is here the beginning of theology. Bondage under Pharaoh and liberation through Yahweh stand in sharp contrast. The relationship between liberation and law is treated above in the discussion of Dt. 5:6. The catechetical text Dt. 6:21 is then also related to Ex. 13:3,9,14,16 (surely not pre-Deuteronomic). The Deuteronomistic addition in Dt. 7:7-8b also indicates that Yahweh's act of deliverance has meaning for the future history of Israel (on → פדה *pāḏâ* in v. 8c, cf. 9:26; 2 S. 7:23 [both Deuteronomistic]). This mighty act is also military in nature and makes it possible for Israel to confront the nations without fear (Dt. 7:19). In the Deuteronomistic prayer of Moses, Dt. 9:28f. (cf. Israel's own words in 1:27!; cf. Ex. 32:11f. [Deuteronomistic]) likewise reflects the exilic situation: Yahweh will not stand historically impotent before the nations (cf. Deutero-Isaiah). But the proof of his power is the exodus (Dt. 9:29): he will not let his people perish "in the wilderness." Only for a short while will the nations be able to say that Yahweh's anger was upon his people because they had forsaken his *bᵉrîṯ*, which he established when he brought them out (Deuteronomistic understanding of *bᵉrîṯ* and argument from history). Here, too, the exilic community is attempting a theological explanation of its fate (cf. 1 K. 8:21; Jer. 11:4; 31:32; 34:13 [Deuteronomistic]; in 2 Ch. 7:22 only with reference to the exodus, without *bᵉrîṯ*).

Finally, Dt. 26:8, which unlike Nu. 20:15f. is Deuteronomistic and not early, once more uses Deuteronomistic language and the exilic categories of distress, lament, and intervention to develop the theme of Yahweh's bringing Israel out as an act of deliverance and of guidance into the land. It summarizes the deuteronomistic texts Dt. 1:27; 4:34,37; 5:6; 6:22; etc. in a statement (cf. 6:21) confessing that Yahweh is known in his acts and is recognized as a God who acts historically to deliver, who shapes history purposefully and therefore here looks toward the (new) occupation of the land.[139]

e. Dt. 5:6 includes the (Deuteronomistic) addition "out of the house of bondage,"[140] not found in J or E. This addition is fully understood only when seen as a transparent description of the exilic situation addressed by the Deuteronomistic history. Its purpose is to strengthen hope for liberation and return through Yahweh's promises and Israel's new obedience in the land. (Note this difference: Deuteronomy speaks more of obedience

---

139 On the Deuteronomistic character of Dt. 26:8, see Lohfink, *ThPh*, 46 (1971), 19-39; Richter, *Festschrift M. Schmaus*, I, 175-212.

140 See IV.b above, with bibliog.

that the people may continue to dwell in the land; the Deuteronomistic texts in Deuteronomy speak of obedience that the people may come [back] into the land!) The phrase "out of the house of bondage" appears in Dt. 5:6; 6:12; 7:8; 8:14; 13:6,11(5,10)—in other words, only in passages that have been Deuteronomistically shaped or edited (not Deuteronomically, and hence dating from the book of Deuteronomy[141]) and are therefore exilic. Another 6 of the 13 occurrences are in Ex. 13:3 (qal),14; 20:2; Jer. 34:13 (all the product of Deuteronomistic editing); cf. also Josh. 24:17; Jgs. 6:8; Mic. 6:4 with *pāḏâ*. The function of this qualifying phrase is to describe the land pejoratively,[142] but also to define the situation of Israel in this "Egypt." (In Dt. 14, too, "Egypt" is a transparent term for Babylon; cf. also P and the Holiness Code.) In Ex. 13:3, *yṣ'* appears in the qal; elsewhere it is always in the hiphil: the point is that Yahweh will bring his people out of (always *min*) this house of bondage, that Yahweh's act of deliverance will put an end to this way of life.

f. It has been suggested[143] that the *hôṣî'* formula referred originally not to the exodus but to the miracle at the Sea of Reeds and was only later extended to the former. This theory cannot be maintained.[144] The formula speaks rather of Yahweh's total act of deliverance described in Ex. 1–15, expressing an analogous theology of deliverance and hope of liberation. Daube[145] has proposed that the verb *yṣ'* belongs to the realm of social law and is associated with the redemption of slaves; there is much to say for this theory in the context of the "deliverance from Egypt" and later references to this event, but the historical setting is more conditioned by the exilic situation and its hopeful interpretation than Daube realizes. Extension of his theory to other textual complexes such as the Jacob-Laban stories is unconvincing.

According to Otto,[146] the themes of exodus and occupation had a (single!) locus in the Feast of Unleavened Bread at the sanctuary of Gilgal (citing Josh. 4:21-23; 5:9; Ps. 114; Mic. 6:4f.). He does not, however, claim that the exodus theme was linked exclusively with this sanctuary.

Norin, on the contrary, distinguishes (unjustifiably) the prose tradition of the exodus from the poetic tradition found in the Psalms and Ex. 15, which he considers earlier. He connects the latter with a cult that was not linked with Passover and the Feast of Unleavened Bread until the Deuteronomistic period. It is significant, however, that even Norin[147] speaks of an exilic focus for the theme, even though he does not make a more nuanced analysis of its conceptuality.

g. Besides the exilic texts of the Holiness Code and those deriving from the Deuteronomistic school, there is a further exilic focus for the deliverance theme: the

---

141 Humbert, 360.

142 Floss, 56.

143 Wijngaards, *VT*, 15 (1965), 91ff.

144 See the criticisms by Childs, 30ff.; Nicholson, 53ff.; D. Patrick, "Traditio-History of the Reed Sea Account," *VT*, 26 (1976), 248f.; Weimar-Zenger, 36, 44f., 130.

145 Pp. 33-38.

146 Otto, 186-191 (actually pp. 295ff. of the original typescript of the diss.).

147 Pp. 199ff.

basic stratum of P, which likewise uses only the hiphil of *yṣʾ* for the "deliverance from Egypt" (exceptions: Lev. 11:45; Nu. 14:13 [both P^s]). Only here do we find the participial self-predication "who brought you out of the land of Egypt," uttered by Yahweh in conjunction with several variants of the self-introduction formula (Ex. 6:7; Lev. 11:45; cf. 22:33 [Holiness Code];[148] different construction: Dt. 8:14; 13:6,11[5,10]; Jgs. 2:12 [all Deuteronomistic]). Again the relative form appears (besides the Deuteronomistic Ex. 20:2; Dt. 5:6) only in P texts (in conjunction with the grace formula "I am Yahweh your God"): Ex. 6:6f.,13,26; 7:4f.; 12:17,39,42,51; 16:6,32; 29:46. Here the exodus is defined theologically as a judgment upon Egypt,[149] an act of redemption (*gāʾal*), an act of deliverance (*nṣl*; Ex. 6:6). The important statement in Ex. 29:46 likewise describes the theological goal of the exodus as renewed community with God in the land. Ex. 6:6 further interprets the exodus as a deliverance "from under the burdens" (*siḇlâ*; elsewhere J in Ex. 1:11; 2:11; 5:4f.; cf. the Deuteronomistic "house of bondage" and Lev. 26:13) imposed by the Egyptians.[150] The purpose of the whole event is knowledge of the nature, greatness, and power of Yahweh (Ex. 6:6f.), who shows his power to intervene in history by bringing his people out (cf. the Holiness Code, the Deuteronomistic history, Ezekiel, and Deutero-Isaiah!). He will bring them out from the midst of the "Egyptians," who shall thereby know him (Ex. 7:5; cf. Deutero-Isaiah). Of course all these statements are deliberately framed as divine discourse (Ex. 6:2-8; 7:1-5). The fact that Moses and Aaron are then set apart by Yahweh to lead Israel out merely comports with equivalent status of these two persons in P and their position as mediators between Yahweh and the people (on 6:13, cf. vv. 26f.). By the exodus Yahweh will once again make Israel his people, whereas according to J and E Israel is already the people of Yahweh. P's shift of emphasis, occasioned by the exile (Ex. 6:7; again in 29:46, an important statement of purpose), is noteworthy (cf. Dt. 4:20; 1 K. 8:53; also 2 S. 7:23).[151] Yahweh will once again be Israel's God. He can and will deliver Israel in battle (Ex. 7:4; cf. also 6:26)—that is the assurance of P^g.

The association of exodus, Passover, and the Feast of Unleavened Bread in Ex. 12:17,42a,51 exhibits the priestly interest in chronology of a later period (additions to P^g, i.e., P^s or R^p; cf. also P's use of the qal in Ex. 12:41; 14:8; 16:1; 19:1; Nu. 1:1; 9:1; 33:1,38).[152] For P, see finally also Ex. 16:3,6,32, where the deliberate contrast between vv. 3 and 6 is noteworthy.

h. Ezekiel—likewise exilic—speaks of the exodus in ch. 20, a focal passage (elsewhere only Ezk. 11:7,9 [oracles of judgment]; 34:13 [promise of salvation]). This discourse, spoken by Yahweh, is a comprehensive summary of Israel's history from

---

148 See Elliger, *HAT,* IV, 301, n. 22.

149 Cf. Ska.

150 On the syntax, see Weimar, 94, 113-131; elsewhere P says "out of the land of Egypt": *ibid.*, 121, n. 109.

151 See R. Smend, *Die Bundesformel. ThSt,* 68 (1963), 21; N. Lohfink, "Beobachtungen zur Geschichte des Ausdrucks עם יהוה," *Probleme biblischer Theologie. Festschrift G. von Rad* (Munich, 1971), 304.

152 See Schmitt; on the chronology, see Gross, *ZAW,* 86 (1974), 437-442.

retrospect to promise; it shows that this history is a history of sin (cf. the Deuteronomistic history). The exodus is grounded on Yahweh's oath (cf. the Deuteronomistic texts in Deuteronomy with reference to the oath to the fathers and the gift of the land); its purpose was (and is!) the gift of the land and the worship of Yahweh alone in this land (Ezk. 20:6,34,38,41; cf. Ex. 29:46 [P]). It is not without reason that the formula of majesty expressing divine self-demonstration should appear in this context (Ezk. 20:5; cf. P). Everything leads to knowledge of Yahweh in the presence of the nations (vv. 9f.,14,22) for the sake of Yahweh's name (v. 9). Again exodus and law are associated (vv. 9f.,11f.; cf. the Deuteronomistic history), and vv. 23f. reflect the exilic situation. Verses 34,38,41 (cf. 34:13) promise that Yahweh will once again bring his people out, assemble them from among the nations (never using *he'ᵉlâ*!) and bring them into the land. Yahweh the king will show himself once more to be the Holy One before the eyes of the nations. It is likely that these texts derive from the school of Ezekiel (20:33 betrays a Deuteronomistic hand). The similarity to Deutero-Isaiah is clear and the exilic situation obvious.[153]

i. Deutero-Isaiah, also exilic, uses → נחם *nḥm,* "comfort," and → רחם *rḥm,* "have mercy," to interpret *yṣ'* more specifically. The qal is used 14 times, 5 of which refer to the "going out" of Yahweh or the people (Isa. 42:13; 48:20; 49:9; 52:11; 55:12). There are 8 occurrences of the hiphil (40:26; 42:1,3,7; 43:8,17; 48:20; 54:16). The use in parallel with → גאל *gā'al* and → פדה *pāḏâ* is theologically significant. "Salvation" goes forth from Yahweh and from his word (45:23; 48:3; 51:4f.; 55:11; cf. 42:1,3; Jer. 51:10!). The prisoners (!) are to go out (Isa. 49:9). As Yahweh brings out the stars (40:26) and his servant brings forth *mišpāṭ* (42:1,3), so will Cyrus (who is probably alluded to in 42:7[154]) bring forth the prisoners (!) (cf. 45:13). This is interpreted and promised as a mighty military victory on the part of Yahweh (43:17), with conscious allusion to the "first" exodus from Egypt. The second exodus from Babylon is seen as being analogous but superior to the first. Yahweh himself will lead the people out and bring them back to Zion (52:11f.).[155]

j. It is thus indisputable that the usage that speaks of "bringing Israel out of Egypt" has its focal point in the situation and literature of the exile.[156] Before we develop this conclusion in greater detail, we must ask whether there are any clearly preexilic occurrences of the hiphil in the context of "bringing out of Egypt." It is immediately noteworthy that the earlier sources in Ex. 13:17–14:31 do not use the term; the central word in Ex. 1–15 is rather → שלח *šlḥ.* Here, too, descriptive narrative came before defining formulas, and the origin and development of the more formulaic language can be traced.

---

153 Cf. Gross, *ibid.,* 439; W. Zimmerli, "Der 'neue Exodus' in der Verkündigung der beiden grossen Exilspropheten," in *Gottes Offenbarung. Gesammelte Aufsätze,* 1. *ThB,* 19 (^{2}1969), 192-204; Baltzer, 1-26 on Ezekiel and Deutero-Isaiah (also with reference to the next section); also F. L. Hossfeld, *Untersuchungen zu Komposition und Theologie des Ezechielbuches. FzB,* 20 (1977), 309-314.

154 Cf. K. Elliger, *Deuterojesaja. BK,* XI/1 (1978), 228.

155 Cf. Preuss, 42-46; Kiesow.

156 Now cf. also S. Hidal, "Some Reflections on Deuteronomy 32," *ASTI,* 11 (1977/78), 18.

J uses *yṣ'* only in the qal (Ex. 12:31).[157] No text that clearly comes from the Yahwist uses the "bringing out" formula (cf. instead Ex. 3:8,17 [J]), which makes the recently proposed exilic dating of J unlikely. Ex. 20:2 cannot be assigned to E. Nu. 20:15f. (E?), possibly an ancient credal text, speaks of an angel as the subject. Both 2 S. 7:6; 1 K. 12:28 have been subject to Deuteronomistic revision and therefore cannot be considered clearly early texts.[158] In Josh. 24:5f., v. 5 at most may represent an early text, but there are good reasons to doubt that the formula itself is original there. Ex. 13:3,9,14,16 have also been subject to Deuteronomistic revision. Gen. 15:7 (cf. 11:31 [P])[159] is also not an early text, as its similarity to Ex. 6:6 (P); Lev. 25:38 shows. It has been framed deliberately after the analogy of the "bringing out of Egypt," reveals the problems posed by the exile (cf. also Ezk. 33:24), and reflects P's estimation of Abraham (Gen. 17, 23), including the promise to him and his occupation of the land (Gen. 11:31!).

This leaves only Nu. 23:22 (E?); 24:8 (J?), which Zenger considers very early.[160] Here the subject is not Yahweh and the object is not Israel (but cf. 23:20; 24:5): the subject is El, and in each case the verb is a hymnic participle with a suffix in a descriptive clause ("this is what God is like"). Furthermore, 23:22 probably echoes 24:8.[161] The God who blesses is also the God who saves, and this God is probably called El because a non-Israelite is speaking. Loretz[162] claims that the verse is a secondary interpolation; so, too, and with better reason does Müller,[163] arguing that the connection between El and Balaam holds also for Israel. It is possible, however, that 24:8 has preserved an ancient formula, describing an act of God with which Yahweh was not associated until later. It is even more likely that within the nation of Israel several "exodus traditions" coalesced, among which the one with Yahweh as subject proved to be the most important (for whatever reasons and in whatever contexts). In any case, the new material assembled by Strobel[164] must be mentioned here; it could be both helpful and suggestive. The two texts from Nu. 23f. therefore cannot be cited in support of Richter's theory[165] that the *ḥôṣî'* formula and the *heʿelâ* formula are equally early, especially since the language here is not yet formulaic. The passages using *heʿelâ* are earlier; those with *ḥôṣî'* do not take

---

157 For an explanation of why *ʿālâ* is not used here, see Gross, *ZAW,* 86 (1974), 447. See also Nu. 22:5,11 (JE?); Nu. 11:20 qal (secondary); the hiphil in Ex. 18:1b is also secondary (see Noth's *OTL* comm. on each passage).

158 Contra Richter, *Festschrift M. Schmaus,* I, 180.

159 On these texts, see the important discussion by J. Van Seters, *Abraham in History and Tradition* (New Haven, 1975), 263-65; on the Deuteronomistic language, see also O. Kaiser, "Traditionsgeschichtliche Untersuchung von Genesis 15," *ZAW,* 70 (1958), 119; M. Köckert, "Die Väterverheissungen," *ThV,* 10 (1979), 16; Westermann, *Genesis 1–11, in loc.*; *idem, Genesis 12–36* (Eng. trans., Minneapolis, 1985), *in loc.*

160 D. Vetter, *Seherspruch und Segensschilderung. CThM,* A/4 (1974), 24f.; also Gross, *Bileam,* 258; *idem, ZAW,* 86 (1974), 427, n. 14, rightly critical of Zenger's syntactical analysis.

161 Cf. M. Noth, *Numbers. OTL* (Eng. trans. 1968), *in loc.*

162 O. Loretz, "Die Herausführungsformel in Num 23,22 und 24,8," *UF,* 7 (1975), 571f.

163 H.-P. Müller, "Einige alttestamentliche Probleme zur aramäischen Inschrift von *Dēr ʿAllā,*" *ZDPV,* 94 (1978), 63f.

164 A. Strobel, *Der spätbronzezeitliche Seevölkersturm. BZAW,* 145 (1976).

165 *Festschrift M. Schmaus,* I (1967), 175-212.

shape until the exile and do not become formulaic until after the exilic period. Neither can it be demonstrated, as suggested by Zenger,[166] that the theme of "bringing out of Egypt" has its original *Sitz im Leben* (what would this expression mean here in any case?) in the acclamation of Yahweh as king, found from the time of the occupation onward, or that there was a connection between "bringing out," "covenant formulary," and "Jerusalem ritual."[167]

The few texts that are probably preexilic thus show that a "bringing out" formula comprising the elements listed above had not developed before the exile. The relevant statements remained very rare until the exile, and only then—albeit for very good reasons—took on importance and received their full development. None of the possibly preexilic texts uses the full formula. Furthermore, they prefer the qal to the hiphil, which means that they have not completed the theological shift of emphasis signalled by the hiphil.

k. A brief survey of the grammatical subjects can underline these observations. When the statement has developed into a formula, Yahweh is always the subject (125 times according to *KBL*[3], although this count includes general usage). The earlier texts still have the *mal'aḵ* as subject (Nu. 20:15f.; cf. Ex. 14:19; cf. the use of "El" discussed above with reference to Nu. 23f.). When Moses is the subject, we are dealing with a later theological intention. His mention in the mouth of the people deliberately articulates a charge against him in the murmuring narratives (Ex. 17:3; Nu. 16:13; 20:5; 21:5 [J]; cf. Ex. 14:11 [E?]). E uses Moses positively as subject in Ex. 3:10-12, as P later uses Moses in conjunction with Aaron (Ex. 6:13,26f.; 16:3).[168] Among the Deuteronomistic texts, Dt. 9:12 is likewise a deliberate exception;[169] cf. also Josh. 24:5f.; 1 S. 12:8 (both Deuteronomistic); also Ex. 33:1-3; Nu. 21:5; and the juxtaposition in Ex. 32:1,23 alongside vv. 4,8; then 32:11f. with Moses as subject, although deliverance is not mentioned explicitly; 32:1,23 as the voice of the people; finally 33:12; and then Dt. 4:37 (Deuteronomistic) with the subject *pānîm*. The choice of subjects developed toward a preference for Yahweh, and this with the purpose of making a clear theological distinction. That Yahweh is clearly the subject who does the "bringing out"—an idea expressed in a fixed formula and based on clear theological reflection—was not brought to full consciousness until after the exile. It is therefore not by chance that Yahweh is much more often the subject of *hôṣî'* than of *he'ᵉlâ* (42 times).

l. The use of *yṣ'* hiphil with Yahweh as subject accordingly says more about this God as liberator and redeemer than is the case with *he'ᵉlâ*. It is he above all who who liberates Israel from the house of bondage of the exile.[170] It is not only the legislative texts that focus on this statement,[171] but the exilic textual complexes of Ezekiel, the

166 *ZDMGSup*, 1 (1969), 340.

167 As proposed by N. Lohfink, "Dt 26,17-19 und die 'Bundesformel'," *ZKTh*, 91 (1969), 517f., 542, 549f.

168 This stage of reflection is discussed in VI.g above.

169 Cf. VI.d above.

170 Cf. H. A. Brongers, "Das Zeitwort '*'ālā*' und seine Derivate," in *Travels in the World of the OT. Festschrift M. A. Beek. SSN*, 16 (1974), 35.

171 Wijngaards.

Deuteronomistic history, P, Deutero-Isaiah, and the Holiness Code (cf. also the contrast in Ezr. 1:7). Deliverance from Egypt stands transparently for deliverance from the house of bondage of the exile in Babylon. There the new deliverance, the new exodus, is hoped for and promised through reference to the former act of liberation and its emphatic interpretation as such. The postexilic texts exhibit the effective history of this primarily exilic idea; the few preexilic texts lead up to it. Liberating "bringing out" from exile was the newly established accent demanded by the ancient faith in Yahweh, who had been Israel's God since Egypt (Hos. 12:10[9]; 13:4); therefore when we survey the semantic field, this "bringing out" is defined in more details by *pdh, gʾl, qbṣ, yšʿ*, and *nṣl.*

Some 75 of the 91 occurrences involving "bringing out" are therefore exilic, and 10 belong to postexilic texts. Since they also speak of this "bringing out" in very different ways, it is best to follow Gross[172] in speaking of a developed idea rather than a "formula." It is no accident that the hiphil participle is found as Yahweh's self-predication only in the exilic texts of the Holiness Code, P, and the Deuteronomic/Deuteronomistic history. The *Sitz im Leben* was where such theological argumentation was needed: oral and written "preaching" to the exilic community. The hiphil of *yṣʾ* as a statement about a God whose act of deliverance one recounts and hopes for is amply attested in this more soteriological aspect,[173] but it can be examined properly only in the context of the further usage of "out of Egypt," and also against the background of the wider semantic field, above all the other uses of *yṣʾ* hiphil with Yahweh as subject.[174] The verb *heʿᵉlâ* spoke more explicitly in geographical and topographical terms from the perspective of the land; its antonym is *yrd.* The most important antonym of *yṣʾ*, however, both in the qal and in the hiphil, is *bôʾ*, which establishes the connection with Yahweh's gift of the land and his leading of the people into the land.[175] Thus the perspective that looks to a future determined by Yahweh's deliverance appears not only in passages where it is explicit (e.g., Isa. 52:12; 55:12; Jer. 51:10,45; Ezk. 14:22; 20:34; 34:13; 38:8; Mic. 7:15; Hag. 2:5), but also implicitly in many other texts, especially those that are exilic.

m. There are several postexilic texts. Ps. 105:37,43 (cf. the qal in v. 38[176]) are narrative verse extolling the great deeds done by Yahweh, leading up to the gift of the land. The same is true of Ps. 136:11 (with a Deuteronomistic variant in v. 12). The exodus is cited as justifying a plea for help or a prayer for forgiveness in Ps. 107:14,28; Dnl. 9:15 (Deuteronomistic language). It is unclear whether Ps. 66:12 refers to the exodus.[177] For comparison, we may cite passages in the Psalms that use the qal: Ps. 68:8(7); 105:38; 114:1; also 81:6(5), where *ʿal* must be emended. In the Psalter, which is predominantly exilic or postexilic in origin and final form, it is characteristic that *heʿᵉlâ* should appear

172 *ZAW,* 86 (1974), 451.
173 Contra Gross, *ibid.,* 427.
174 Cf. n below.
175 Cf. Wijngaards, *Formulas,* 35-43.
176 See S. Holm-Nielsen, "The Exodus Traditions in Psalm 105," *ASTI,* 11 (1977/78), 22-30.
177 Cf. Kühlwein, 108; also (differently) 137.

only in Ps. 81:11(10), since this verb was little used in this context after the exile.[178] The situation in Chronicles has already been discussed.[179]

n. The exile with its theological and historical situation and the need to come to terms with it led to the dominant use of *yṣʾ* hiphil to mean deliverance, liberation from Babylon, the exilic house of bondage. This usage is further underlined by a survey of the passages in which Yahweh appears as subject of a hiphil form where nothing is said about "bringing out of Egypt."[180]

It has often been pointed out that the hiphil of *yṣʾ* is not used for the initial work of creation, although Gen. 1:12,24 make this statement not quite true. Besides a few minor passages (Gen. 15:5; Ps. 135:7; Jer. 10:13; 50:25; 51:16; Ezk. 37:1), there are several of more significance: on the journey through the desert on the way to the promised land (!) Yahweh brought forth water out of the rock (Dt. 8:15; Neh. 9:15; Ps. 78:16; cf. Ex. 17:6 [qal]; note the variety of ways in which Moses appears as agent). Gen. 15:7 is patterned deliberately on the exodus from Egypt (cf. Neh. 9:7 and the discussion at VI.j above). Yahweh also brings forth descendants (Isa. 65:9) and brings out stars (Isa. 40:26; cf. Neh. 4:15[21]; Job 38:32[181]), which supports Israel's faith in its own liberation (cf. Isa. 43:17). He also brings forth human "creators" (Isa. 54:16; cf. 10:13). Yahweh brings forth to judgment (Ezk. 11:7,9; 21:8,10[3,5]; 28:18; cf. 38:4 [military usage]; also Jer. 10:13; 50:25; 51:16) and lets a curse take its course (Zec. 5:4). Almost all the important passages stress Yahweh's sovereignty over history.

Especially important are the texts that use a hiphil form of *yṣʾ* to describe Yahweh as liberating prisoners, as delivering those who are oppressed. These passages are closely related to those that speak of "deliverance from Egypt" or support the notion that the exodus was a liberation from slavery.[182] Yahweh delivers from enemies (2 S. 22:49), sets free from Babylon (Jer. 51:44), brings forth from among the nations (Ezk. 20:34; cf. vv. 38,41; 34:13). Many Psalm texts illustrate this assurance (Ps. 25:15; 37:6) on the part of the Israelites that Yahweh will bring them to the light so that they may see salvation (Ps. 37:6; Mic. 7:9; cf. Job 12:22). They give thanks to Yahweh as the deliverer who "brought" them out of distress (Ps. 18:20[19] par. 2 S. 22:20; Ps. 66:12; 68:7[6]) or pray that he will so act (Ps. 25:17; 31:5[4]; 142:8[7]; 143:11). The frequently mentioned deliverance of prisoners fits well with the exilic focus of the hiphil (Ps. 68:7[6]; 107:14,28: 142:8[7]; cf. 18:20[19] par.; 66:12). And the attributes ascribed to God show that Yahweh was known as a God who "brings forth" (Ps. 68:7[6]; 135:7; cf. 104:14).

VII. Dead Sea Scrolls. Among the more than 60 occurrences of the root in the Dead Sea scrolls, there are several semantic foci. The only apparent reference to the exodus from Egypt is in 4QDibHam 5:10 (also 1Q14 12:3; 1Q22 1:1; 2:6 [?]). Military "going

---

178 Cf. Gross, *ZAW,* 86 (1974), 439, 450.

179 See VI.c above.

180 See Humbert, 358f.; according to Jenni, 759f., this usage denotes a specific act done by Yahweh, not a constant activity.

181 On the text, see G. Fohrer, *Das Buch Hiob. KAT,* XVI (1963), 492.

182 See V.c above.

forth" to the (eschatological) battle appears in 1QM 1:4,13; 2:8; 3:1,7; 4:9; 6:1,4,9,11; 7;3,9,13f.,16f.; 8:3; 9:3,11,13; 16:4,12; cf. 1QH 6:31. Yahweh can bring forth (1QH 1:29; 4:25); instruction (or the lot) goes forth (1QS 5:3; 6:16,18,21; 9:7; 1QSa 1:16; CD 13:4). There are cultic regulations prescribing what one may (not) bring forth (e.g., CD 11:8). "Go out and in" can be used generally to mean "do something," "conduct oneself" (CD 11:10f.; 20:27; with cultic overtones in CD 13:4). All these meanings are suggested or attested in OT usage.

In the Dead Sea scrolls, there is also a group of texts in which the Qumran community refers to itself as "those who have gone out of the land of Judah" (CD 4:3; 6:5; also 20:22 ["from the holy city"]). But one can also depart from this community (1QS 7:23f.).

Preuss

יצב *yṣb* → **נצב** *nṣb*

יצג *yṣg*

Contents: I. Occurrences, Meaning, LXX. II. Literal Usage: 1. With Inanimate Objects; 2. With Persons; 3. With Cult Objects. III. Figurative Usage.

I. Occurrences, Meaning, LXX. The root *yṣg* appears 16 times as a verb in the OT; it occurs also in Sir. 30:18. The verb is found primarily in the hiphil (hophal in Ex. 10:24; Sir. 30:18). The hiphil follows the paradigm of verbs *primae nun,* and several earlier lexicographic works list it as *nāṣag.*[1]

The verb is found only in Hebrew; it has the general meaning "set, place." Both its relative rarity and above all the contexts in which it occurs often lend it an emphasis not found in other verbs for "set, place."

The root obviously is related to → **יצק** *yṣq,* "pour out," which also has the meaning "place" or "lay down" in the hiphil. Therefore most modern scholars emend *wayyaṣṣiqû*

---

yṣg. W. R. Arnold, *Ephod and Ark. HThS,* 3 (1917); K. Budde, "Ephod und Lade," *ZAW,* 39 (1921), 1-42; J. J. Rabinowitz, "Neo-Babylonian Legal Documents and Jewish Law," *Journal of Juristic Papyrology,* 13 (1961), 131-175; S. Rin, "Ugaritic–OT Affinities," *BZ,* N.S. 7 (1963), 22-33; E. Sellin, "Das israelitische Ephod," *Orientalische Studien. Festschrift T. Nöldeke* (Giessen, 1906), II, 699-717.

1 Cf. J. Cocceius, *Lexicon et commentarius sermonis hebraici et chaldaici Veteris Testamenti* (Leipzig, ^{5}1793); and F. H. W. Gesenius, *Thesaurus philologicus criticus linguae hebraeae et chaldaeae Veteris Testamenti* (Leipzig, ^{2}1839).

in 2 S. 15:24 to *wayyaṣṣiḡû,* and in Josh. 7:23 the meaning of *wayyaṣṣiqum* is close to *yṣg,* "lay down," "spread out" (cf. Jgs. 6:37). The close relationship between *g* and *q,* found also in Ugaritic, is stressed by Rin[2] in this context.

The LXX renders the verb in a variety of ways; the individual passages were understood and translated according to their context.

II. Literal Usage.

1. *With Inanimate Objects.* Literally, the hiphil *hiṣṣîḡ* means to set something in place. The object may be set up or laid down: both are possible in Gen. 30:38 with reference to the peeled rods Jacob lays or places in the runnels. The spoiled woman in Dt. 28:56 does not set her foot upon the earth, and in Jgs. 6:37 Gideon lays the fleece upon the threshing floor.

2. *With Persons.* With a personal object, *hiṣṣîḡ lip̄nê* means "present" or "bring forward": in Gen. 43:9, Judah wishes to bring his brother Benjamin back and set him before his father; in Gen. 47:2, Joseph presents five of his brothers to Pharaoh. On the basis of 43:9, Rabinowitz[3] even proposes to interpret the formula *hiṣṣîḡ lip̄nê* as a technical term for "set before" or "produce" in the juristic sense. The argument, however, is not compelling—if this were the case, one would expect to find the formula in legal contexts elsewhere in the OT.

Another meaning of *hiṣṣîḡ* is "leave behind." Esau wishes to leave some of his men with Jacob (Gen. 33:15), and Gideon is to set apart everyone who laps the water with his tongue (Jgs. 7:5). This is also the sense in Ex. 10:24: the flocks and herds are to be left behind.

3. *With Cult Objects.* When *hiṣṣîḡ* is used in cultic contexts, the question arises whether the cult object is merely being set out on a particular occasion or whether the sense of "establishing a cult" is also involved. Sir. 30:18 speaks of a food offering placed before an idol (*mṣgt lpny glwl*; the LXX took the last word as *gwll,* the stone closing a tomb, and translated: "precious foods placed upon a tomb"). Here we are dealing with the solemn presentation of an offering. In Jgs. 8:27 it is the ephod and in 1 S. 5:2; 2 S. 6:17 (cf. 1 Ch. 16:1) the ark of the covenant that is put in a special place. Discussing Jgs. 8:27, Sellin[4] vigorously defends the translation "he deposited" and rejects any notion that has to do with setting up an idol. Cf. Keil[5] and Friedrich:[6] "The basic meaning of *hiṣṣîḡ* is 'place' or 'set' something so that it has a fixed location."[7]

---

2 P. 26.

3 Pp. 144ff.

4 Pp. 707f.

5 *Judges. KD,* II, *in loc.*

6 I. Friedrich, *Ephod und Choschen im Lichte des Alten Orients. WBTh,* 20 (1968), 17.

7 Cf. also K. Elliger, "Ephod und Choschen: Ein Beitrag zur Entwicklungsgeschichte des hohepriesterlichen Ornats," *VT,* 8 (1958), 19-35 = *Festschrift F. Baumgärtel. Erlanger Forschungen,* ser. A, 10 (1959), 9-23; → גורל *gôrāl.*

Burney,[8] however, takes a different position: "What the writer wishes to express is that it was there that the Ephod-cult was 'established'; and any alternative expression, such as 'he placed' or 'kept it at Ophrah,' would scarcely have been possible." Still others prefer to understand the ephod as a later substitute for an earlier word. Arnold thinks of → ארון *'arôn*; Budde proposes → אביר *'āḇîr* (*'ābhîr*), emphasizing[9] that *hiṣṣîg* can mean not only "set down on the ground" but also "set up."

The beginning of a cult is certainly referred to in 2 S. 6:17, which tells how the ark was set in its place inside the tent. In this passage only, the LXX uses the verb *anatithénai* to translate *hiṣṣîg*. This verb is used in Greek for the placing of votive offerings in a temple. In 1 S. 5:2, however, we are told how the ark is set up in the temple of Dagon. The common element in these narratives is the ceremonious placing of the ark, not the cultic arrangements that follow. Schreiner, emphasizing the difference between 1 S. 5:2 and 2 S. 6:17 in this respect, rightly notes:[10] "In most cases, the hiphil of *yṣg* has the force of a deliberate or purposeful placement." Of course the purpose can be to establish a cult, but this is not stated explicitly. The choice of *hiṣṣîg* in a particular context means only that the speaker sees a special importance in the act of placing.

III. Figurative Usage. In figurative usage, *hiṣṣîg* has the same emphatic overtones: "He (truly) made me a byword of the peoples" (Job 17:6). In Jer. 51:34, the speaker is "placed" as an empty vessel—here the meaning "leave behind" may also be involved. Where the emphasis lies in Hos. 2:5(Eng. v. 3) is open to question. The threat "I will strip her naked and set her as on the day of her birth" can mean refusal to support an unfaithful wife and readiness to leave her. But there is also a suggestion of exposing her to public disgrace (cf. v. 12[10]).

In Am. 5:15, the prophet demands that justice (*mišpāṭ*) be "set up" in the gate. This is in contrast to the work of those who "cast down (*hinnîḥû*) righteousness to the earth" (v. 7), as Hammershaimb[11] notes. Here, too, the prophet's words take on a special emphasis: in vv. 14f. he summarizes what God requires of his people.

B. Johnson

---

8 C. F. Burney, *The Book of Judges* (1918; repr. New York, 1970), 241.
9 Pp. 30f.
10 J. Schreiner, *Sion-Jerusalem Jahwehs Königssitz. StANT,* 7 (1963), 43, n. 118.
11 *Amos* (Copenhagen, 1946), *in loc.*

יִצְהָר yiṣhār

Contents: 1. Etymology, Meaning, Occurrences; 2. "Grain, Wine, and Oil"; 3. Used Alone.

1. *Etymology, Meaning, Occurrences.* The noun *yiṣhār* is usually derived from the root *ṣhr,* "shine"; it is said to describe olive oil as "shining." But this etymology contributes little to an understanding of the term, which seems to be synonymous with *šemen,* "oil." In Dt. 8:8, *zêṯ šemen* means "olive tree," as does *zêṯ yiṣhār* in 2 K. 18:32.

With only one exception, *yiṣhār* always appears in the fixed sequence *dāḡān, tîrôš,* and *yiṣhār* (18 times; the same words appears in a different order in Nu. 18:12).

2. *"Grain, Wine, and Oil."* This sequence appears in several contexts. It is not peculiar to any particular literary genre, but is rooted in the ecology of Palestine. It serves to summarize the produce of the land, which is a result of God's blessing. Dt. 11:14, for example, promises increase of grain and wine and oil. In Dt. 7:13, Yahweh promises to bless the fruit of the land if the people keep his commandments; in addition to grain and wine and oil, the verse speaks of the young of sheep and cattle. On the other hand, Dt. 28:51 threatens that if the commandments are not kept these same resources will be destroyed by enemy invasion. Jer. 31:12 (Deuteronomistic) similarly looks forward to a rich harvest of grain, wine, and oil, as well as sheep and cattle, when Israel is restored.

The propagandistic speech of the Rabshakeh is formulated in somewhat different terms: if the Israelites will reach a peaceful accommodation with the king of Assyria, he will give them a land that, like the land of Canaan, provides grain and wine, bread and vineyards, olive trees and honey (2 K. 18:32). In the same context, 2 Ch. 32:28 speaks of storehouses for grain, wine, and oil, as well as stalls for cattle. Haggai speaks of a drought that will come upon the grain, wine, oil, and other produce because the people have procrastinated in rebuilding the temple (Hag. 1:11).

The list takes on special importance in Hosea and Joel. Hosea emphasizes that it is Yahweh, not Baʿal, who gives corn and wine and oil, as well as silver and gold (Hos. 2:10[Eng. v. 8]); he looks forward to a time of restoration when the heavens will "hear" the earth and the earth will "hear" the grain, wine, and oil (2:24[22]), i.e., the heavens will send rain and the earth will bring forth its increase. The formula is further developed in Joel, where it appears 3 times. First, the prophet laments that the fields and ground mourn[1] "because the grain is destroyed, the wine fails, the oil languishes" (Joel 1:10). After the lament, Yahweh responds with a promise: "I am sending to you grain, wine, and oil, and you will be satisfied" (2:19). And at the end of the oracle of salvation, Yahweh

---

yiṣhār. L. Köhler, "Archäologisches. Nr. 23: Eine archaistische Wortgruppe," *ZAW,* 46 (1928), 218-220; V. Maag, *Text, Wortschatz und Begriffswelt des Buches Amos* (Leiden, 1951), 192f.

1 → אבל *'āḇal* (*'ābhal*).

says: "The threshing floors shall be full of grain, the vats shall overflow with wine and oil" (2:24). Thus the formula in its various manifestations serves almost as a leitmotif in Joel.

The formula appears several times in cultic legislation, sometimes expanded to include sheep and cattle. Some of these laws deal with the firstfruits to be given to the priests (Nu. 18:12 [with *ḥēleḇ,* "the best of . . ."]; Dt. 18:4; cf. also 2 Ch. 31:5; Neh. 10:38,40[37,39]), others with tithes (Dt. 12:17; 14:23; cf. Neh. 13:5,12).

3. *Used Alone.* The only passage in which *yiṣhār* appears without *dāg̱ān* and *tîrôš* is Zec. 4:14, which speaks of two "sons of oil" (*b*ᵉ*nê-hayyiṣhār*), i.e., "anointed ones," obviously a reference to a king and a high priest anointed to lead the people.[2]

Ringgren

---

[2] See A. S. van der Woude, "Die beiden Söhne des Öls (Sach. 4:14): Messianische Gestalten?" in *Travels in the World of the OT. Festschrift M. A. Beek. SSN,* 16 (1974), 262-68; W. Rudolph, *Sacharja 1–8. KAT,* XIII/4 (1976), 108f.

יָצַק *yāṣaq;* צוּק *ṣûq* II; יְצֻקָה *y*ᵉ*ṣuqâ;* מָצוּק *māṣûq*

Contents: I. Occurrences and Meaning. II. Literal Usage: 1. Secular; 2. Cultic or Sacral; 3. Casting Metal. III. Figurative Usage.

I. Occurrences and Meaning. The root *yṣq,* with its by-form *ṣûq,* is one of the Semitic words for "pour (out)." Besides Biblical and Postbiblical Hebrew, it appears in Ugaritic[1] and Phoenician.[2] When it is compared with other roots of similar meaning (such as *nsk, ntk,* and *špk*), the semantic fields are often found to overlap. What primarily distinguishes *yṣq* is its reference to pouring upon or into something. While *nsk* is especially common with a drink offering as its object, *špk* refers to pouring in general; what is poured out is not collected in some kind of vessel, but falls upon the ground and drains away. The root *yṣq,* on the other hand, is used primarily in cases where the liquid being poured has a particular destination such as a container or a part of the body to be anointed. Other terms, however, are used for the act of anointing itself: primarily *mšḥ* and also *ntn.*

The verb appears 41 times in the qal, 3 times in the hiphil, and 9 times in the hophal. The hiphil ptcp. *môṣāqeṯ (qere)* in 2 K. 4:5 appears in the *kethibh* as *myṣqt,* which can be interpreted as a by-form of the hiphil or as a unique instance of the piel. The meaning

---

[1] *WUS,* no. 1228.
[2] *DISO,* 110.

in either case is "pour (into)." The 2 other instances of the hiphil have the meaning "lay or set down": the messengers laid the objects down before Yahweh (Josh. 7:23), and the Levites set down the ark of God (2 S. 15:24).[3] There may well be confusion here with → יצג *yṣg,* especially in 2 S. 15:24. Hertzberg's proposed interpretation[4] of *wayyaṣṣiqû* here as referring to a drink offering is not convincing.[5] On the other hand, it can be argued that Josh. 7:23 illustrates the conceptual similarity between the pouring of liquids and the laying down of solid objects. We are dealing here with a collection of larger or smaller objects that are "poured out" before Yahweh.

The by-form *ṣûq* appears twice in the qal (Job 28:2; 29:6), in addition to the questionable passage Isa. 26:16.[6]

The verb *yṣq* is used intransitively in 2 passages: the king's blood "flowed" into the bottom of the chariot (1 K. 22:35); the dust "runs" into a mass (Job 38:38). Elsewhere the verb generally appears with an object (oil, water, blood, metal) and a preposition indicating the direction or goal of the pouring. In most passages the preposition is *ʿal,* but in the case of blood it is *ʾel* (perhaps through the influence of the construction used with *špk*). When metal is cast, *lᵉ-* or *bᵉ-* indicates the purpose of the resulting implement.

The LXX uses a variety of translations, often drawing on compounds of the verb *cheín.*

II. Literal Usage.

1. *Secular.* "Pouring" occurs in everyday contexts: oil is poured into vessels (2 K. 4:4); soup and other foods are poured (2 K. 4:40; 2 S. 13:9). Water is to be poured into the pot (Ezk. 24:3). Elisha was the one who poured water over the hands of Elijah (2 K. 3:11). A rock can be said to pour out (*ṣûq*) streams of oil (Job 29:6), either because oil vats have been hewn out of the rock or as a symbol of abundance.[7]

2. *Cultic or Sacral.* Most of the passages, however, are found in cultic or sacral contexts. Jacob poured oil on top of the stone (Gen. 28:18; 35:14). Oil is poured on the cereal offering (Lev. 2:1,6), although not on the "cereal offering of jealousy (*minḥaṯ qᵉnāʾōṯ*)" (Nu. 5:15). When a priest or king is anointed, *mšḥ* refers to the anointing itself and *yṣq* to the associated act of pouring out oil: Moses is to pour (*yṣq*) the anointing oil on Aaron's head and anoint (*mšḥ*) him (Ex. 29:7; Lev. 8:12). In 1 S. 10:1, when Saul is anointed, the concrete act is underlined by mention of the vial of oil. Here, too, as when the disciples of the prophets anoint Jehu in 2 K. 9:3, *yṣq* refers to the act of pouring, which is then interpreted by the *mšḥ* that follows. According to Lev. 14:15ff., when a priest cleanses a leper he is to pour (*yṣq*) some of the offered oil into his left hand and sprinkle (*nzh* hiphil) it with his finger before Yahweh. He then puts oil on various parts

---

3 Cf. J. Hoftijzer, "Een opmerking bij II Sam. 15:24 (*wayyaṣṣīqū*)," in *Travels in the World of the OT. Festschrift M. A. Beek. SSN,* 16 (1974), 91-93.

4 H. W. Hertzberg, *I & II Samuel. OTL* (Eng. trans. 1964), *in loc.*

5 Cf. R. A. Carlson, *David the Chosen King* (Eng. trans., Stockholm, 1964), 172f.

6 See below.

7 Cf. G. Fohrer, *Das Buch Hiob. KAT,* XVI (1963), *in loc.*

of the leper's body as well as pouring it on his head; for these actions the passage uses not *mšḥ* but *ntn.*

Blood is also poured out in the cult. In this case the most common verb is *špk.* Only in Lev. 8:15; 9:9, in the narrative of Aaron's consecration and first sacrifice, is *yṣq* used in the same construction as the usual *špk.* Perhaps this is meant to emphasize that the blood is poured out on (rather than beside) the foot of the altar, as an act by which the altar is sanctified (cf. Lev. 8:15).

The verb is used with water as its object in 1 K. 18:34a(33b), in the story of the judgment on Mt. Carmel.

3. *Casting Metal.* Metal can also be "poured" or "cast." In the account of how the sacred paraphernalia of the sanctuary were made, we are told that Moses and Bezalel cast gold rings and silver or bronze bases for various cultic objects (Ex. 25:12; 26:37; 36:36; 37:3,13; 38:5,27). In like manner the temple of King Solomon was furnished with cast metal objects (1 K. 7:16,23f.,30,33,46; 2 Ch. 4:2f.,17). The by-form *ṣûq* also appears in this sense in Job 28:2.

III. Figurative Usage. When metal is poured, the result is a permanent casting. Therefore *yṣq* can be used metaphorically not only of liquids but also in connection with solid objects. In Job 38:38, the poet describes how the clods cleave fast together in the time of rain, when the dust "pours" into a mass (*b*ᵉ*ṣeqeṯ ʿāp̄ār lammûṣāq*). As modern commentaries point out, this undoubtedly refers to the state of the ground before a rain. It is hard as stone, solid "as though cast." The firmament of heaven is solid as a cast mirror (Job 37:18). Leviathan is described as having the folds of his flesh cleave together as though cast upon him; his heart is hard as though cast of stone, fixed as a cast nether millstone (Job 41:15f.[Eng. vv. 23f.]).

A human being, too, if righteous, can be "cast solid" and need not fear (Job 11:15). This image of firmness and solidity is often used of God's persecuted messengers: in the face of all attacks, God makes them hard as stone or a wall of bronze (Isa. 50:7; Jer. 1:18; 15:20; Ezk. 3:9).

In contrast to solidity and permanence, Job 22:16 uses *yṣq* to describe the destruction of the wicked. The words *nāhār yûṣaq y*ᵉ*sôḏām* can be interpreted variously, e.g., "a river poured over their foundation" or "their foundation washed away as a river," but the image of something permanent that washes away remains the same. The context suggests the story of the Deluge, but this may not be intentional. It is more likely that the same image is being drawn upon as in Mt. 7:24ff.

In figurative usage, *yṣq* with an object appears in both positive and negative contexts. Isa. 44:3 uses water and spirit in parallelism: "I will pour water on the thirsty land, and streams on the dry ground; I will pour out my Spirit upon your descendants, and my blessing on your offspring." By inserting *kên,* 1QIsᵃ already takes the pouring of water as a symbol representing the outpouring of the Spirit: ". . . so I will pour out my Spirit. . . ."

The meaning of *ṣāqûn* (*lāḥaš*) in Isa. 26:16 is obscure. The form could derive from *ṣûq* II, and figurative usage is quite possible after the analogy of *yṣq.* But the root *ṣûq* I, "oppress," also fits the context. Others propose the emendation *ṣāʿaqnû,* "we cried out."

In Ps. 41:9(8), the psalmist's enemies say: *d^e^ḇar-b^e^lîya'al yāṣûq bô,* "A deadly thing has been poured in him." The use of the prep. *b^e^-* (rather than *'al,* for example), suggests interpreting the image to mean that the disaster is already present within him rather than being poured upon him. Delitzsch[8] takes the expression to mean "poured like cast metal," but this is less likely. The same preposition (*b^e^-*) appears also in Ps. 45:3(2): "Grace (*ḥēn*) is poured upon your lips." On the basis of Ugaritic, Dahood suggests[9] interpreting *b^e^-* here as meaning "from, out of": "Charm flows from your lips." This argument remains dubious, but there is still the question what *b^e^-* (instead of *'al,* for example) means in this passage. Both prepositions appear several times in conjunction with *ś^e^pat*: *'al* always has the locative meaning "upon, over"; *b^e^-* has either the locative meaning "upon, within" or the agential meaning "through, by means of." In Ps. 45, therefore, the prep. *b^e^-* could suggest the translation "grace flows through your lips" (cf. Eccl. 10:12) as well as "grace is (already present) poured within your lips."[10]

B. Johnson

---

8 *The Psalms. KD,* V, *in loc.*
9 M. Dahood, *Psalms I. AB,* XVI (1965), *in loc.*
10 For further discussion, see → חנן *ḥānan.*

יָצַר *yāṣar*; יֵצֶר *yēṣer*; צוּר *ṣûr*; צִיר *ṣîr*; צוּרָה *ṣûrâ*

Contents: I. Etymology, Related Terms, Distribution. II. Craftsmanship; Pottery. III. The Potter. IV. God's Creative Handiwork: 1. Creation of the Human Race; 2. Creation of the World. V. Deutero-Isaiah: 1. Creation and Election of Israel; 2. Creation of the World; 3. Creation and Election of the Servant. VI. God's "Shaping" of History. VII. *yṣr,* "Purpose." VIII. *yṣr* in Later Judaism.

---

yāṣar. R. Albertz, *Weltschöpfung und Menschenschöpfung. CThM,* A/3 (1974); H. A. Brongers, "Schöpfer und Schöpfen im alttestamentlichen Sprachgebrauch," *Persica,* 7 (1975-78), 84-131 (§ IV of F. M. T. de Liagre Böhl and Brongers, "Weltschöpfungsgedanken in Alt-Israel," *ibid.,* 69-136); W. Foerster, "κτίζω," *TDNT,* III, 1005-15; P. Humbert, "Emploi et portée bibliques du verbe yāṣar et de ses dérivés substantifs," *Von Ugarit nach Qumran. Festschrift O. Eissfeldt. BZAW,* 77 (1958), 82-88; R. E. Murphy, "*Yēṣer* in the Qumran Literature," *Bibl,* 39 (1958), 334-344; G. von Rad, "The Theological Problem of the OT Doctrine of Creation," *The Problem of the Hexateuch* (Eng. trans. 1966; repr. London, 1984), 131-143 (= *Werden und Wesen des ATs. BZAW,* 66 [1936], 138-147; repr. *GSAT,* I. *ThB,* 8 [^4^1971], 136-147); R. Rendtorff, "Die theologische Stellung des Schöpfungsglaubens bei Deuterojesaja," *ZThK,* 51 (1954), 3-13 = *GSAT. ThB,* 57 (1975), 209-219; W. H. Schmidt, *Die Schöpfungsgeschichte der Priesterschrift. WMANT,* 17 (^3^1973); *idem,* "יצר *jṣr* formen," *THAT,* I, 761-65; C. Westermann, *Genesis 1–11* (Eng. trans., Minneapolis, 1984).

I. Etymology, Related Terms, Distribution. The basic meaning of the Semitic root *yṣr* is "shape, form." In West Semitic (Ugaritic, Phoenician), we find nouns with the meaning "potter."[1] Driver finds some Ugaritic verbal forms from the same root, but this is not certain.[2] In Akkadian we find the analogous root *eṣēru,* meaning "form, sketch," or the like, but also with the secondary meaning "plan, determine."[3] In the many Akkadian creation texts, this word is not used for the divine work of creation; other verbs, especially *banû,* are used instead. Ringgren[4] lists the various Akkadian verbs for "create," with special emphasis on those used in Enuma Elish. We may note furthermore that the verb *eṣēru* also appears in this context, but with the meaning "mark out" ("he also marked out the paths of the earth"[5]). From the same root we find the Akkadian noun *ēṣiru,* "potter."[6] Another word for "potter," *paḫāru* I, is used to describe the gods Marduk and Ea in their function as creator-gods.[7]

Forms derived from the root *yṣr* occur some 70 times in the OT. The verbal forms are almost entirely in the qal; the niphal, pual, and hophal are found once each.[8] There are also a few niphal forms in Sirach, of which the occurrence in Sir. 37:3 is not listed in *KBL*[3]. Lexica vary widely in distinguishing between noun and adjective forms of the participle. There are clearly some 20 occurrences of the qal participle that must be translated "potter." Besides verbal forms, there are also about 10 occurrences of the noun *yēṣer* meaning "form" or "purpose." Unique to Job 17:7 is the noun *y*^{e}*ṣûrîm,* "members." There are also a few personal names based on this root (see the lexica). The root *yṣr* is probably related to the root *ṣwr* III, "form," and its derivatives.

The root and its derivatives appear for the most part in preexilic prophetic texts (about 20 times), in postexilic prophetic texts (about 30, of which more than 20 are in Deutero-Isaiah), and in the Psalms (about 10). There are 5 occurrences in the Yahwistic portions of the primeval history. Elsewhere it is very rare.[9] The most important parallel terms—especially in creation texts—are *ʿāśâ* and *bārāʾ*.[10]

In the LXX, most of the verbal forms of *yṣr* are rendered by forms of *plássō.*[11] The nominalized participle is usually represented by *kerameús* and Heb. *yēṣer,* "thought, intent" (6 occurrences), by various Greek words.

II. Craftsmanship; Pottery. The basic meaning of *yṣr* allows it to designate various

---

1 See *WUS,* no. 1229; *DISO,* 110; cf. Humbert, 83; Brongers, 92.

2 See *CML,* 148.

3 *AHw,* I (1965), 252.

4 H. Ringgren, "ברא *bārāʾ*," *TDOT,* II, 244.

5 EnEl VI, 43; see G. Pettinato, *Das altorientalische Menschenbild und die sumerischen und akkadischen Schöpfungsmythen. AHAW,* Phil.-hist. Kl., 1971/1, 106f.; cf. 57-61, 147.

6 *AHw,* I, 253.

7 H. Wildberger, *Jesaja. BK,* X/3 (1982), 1130.

8 See the analysis by Humbert, 83; *KBL*[3], 409f.

9 See Humbert, 82, 87.

10 See *ibid.,* 85-87; Brongers, 92f.; K.-H. Bernhardt, *TDOT,* II, 246-48.

11 See H. Braun, "πλάσσω," *TDNT,* VI, 256f.; Foerster, 1007f., esp. n. 57, which suggests different translations.

forms of craftsmanship. The satire against idols in Isa. 44:9-20 (possibly very late[12]) provides a good sense of the range of meanings inherent in the root. In v. 9, the craftsmen are called "idol makers"; the ptcp. *yōṣēr* is linked with *pesel,* an image that may be carved, cast, or chiseled. The next verse then asks who can fashion (*yāṣar*) a god or cast (*nāsaḵ*) an image (*pesel*). Finally, v. 12 describes the fabrication of idols by a smith: the craftsman shapes (*yāṣar*) his material with hammers. Among the parallel synonyms are *ʿāśâ* and *pāʿal.* (Note also Ex. 32:4, where *ṣûr* is used in connection with fashioning the golden calf, and 1 K. 7:15, where it is used for the casting of the two bronze pillars at the entrance to the temple). In a similar context, Hab. 2:18 describes a *yōṣēr* making a *pesel*; the result of his labor is called *yēṣer* (the text does not require emendation[13]). The cognate root *ṣûr* has a derived noun *ṣîr,* which clearly means "idol" in Isa. 45:16. The noun *ṣûrâ* from the same root appears only in Ezk. 43:11 (but 4 times in that single verse!); it probably is an abstract noun meaning "form" (of a structure). Finally, Isa. 54:16f. speaks of the weapons produced (*yûṣar*) by a smith (*ḥārāš*). These passages make it clear that *yṣr* and *ṣûr* refer to all kinds of shaping and forming: metalworking, casting, carving, chiseling.

This insight has recently illuminated some obscure passages. On the basis of Zec. 11:13 together with 2 K. 12:11(Eng. v. 10); 22:9, it has been shown that the Jerusalem temple probably housed the shop of a metalworker (*yōṣēr*) whose official job it was to melt down (*ṣûr* and *nāṯaḵ*) the silver that was offered and pay the craftsmen employed by the temple; there is no need to emend these passages, as often suggested by earlier scholars.[14]

The craft most often referred to by words based on the root *yṣr* is pottery. A common household vessel can be called *kᵉlî (hay)yôṣēr,* "potter's vessel" (2 S. 17:28; Ps. 2:9, Jer. 19:11) or more specifically *baqbuq yôṣēr ḥāreś,* "jar of a clay-former" (Jer. 19:1) or *nēḇel yôṣᵉrîm,* "potter's jar" (Isa. 30:14; cf. Lam. 4:2)—ceramic jars. In these passages, *yôṣēr* clearly means "potter," as it does also in Isa. 29:16; 41:25; 45:9; Jer. 18:2,3,4,6 (twice in each of the last 2). This may also be the case in 1 Ch. 4:23, where certain clans of Judah are called "potters."

III. The Potter. It is striking that the passages listed rarely mention the potter in an everyday context; almost all employ the term in a theological context. The potter may symbolize the divine Creator and the forming of clay may symbolize creation; or the smashing of pottery may symbolize the execution of divine judgment through the destruction of Israel, the enemy, or the like. Such symbolic language is very common in the OT; it is rooted in the notion, found in both Israelite and non-Israelite religion, that the Creator formed the human race from clay like a potter.[15] Thus the Hebrew verb *yṣr* by itself can refer to the creation of the human race.[16]

---

12 See K. Elliger, *Deuterojesaja. BK,* XI/1 (1970), 421f.

13 See K. Rudolph, *Habakuk. KAT,* XIII/3 (1975), 219-222.

14 See C. C. Torrey, "The Foundry of the Second Temple at Jerusalem," *JBL,* 55 (1936), 247-260; O. Eissfeldt, "Eine Einschmelzstelle am Tempel zu Jerusalem," *FuF,* 13 (1937), 163f. = *KlSchr* (1963), II, 107-9.

15 For parallels, see Westermann, 203-6; Wildberger, 1127-1131; etc.

16 See IV.1 below.

Citing Job 10:9; 33:6 (cf. 4:19), Wildberger suggests that the image of the potter was borrowed from wisdom instruction.[17] But the image is even more frequent and more highly developed in the prophets. Isa. 29:15f. probably deals with political decisions in Jerusalem, which are contrary to Yahweh's will. Isaiah uses the image of the potter to say that human beings as God's creatures are and must be totally subject to God's will. Just as the work (*yēṣer*) of the potter cannot turn against its maker (*yôṣēr*), so human beings cannot turn against the will of the divine Creator. In Jer. 18:1-12, we have the classic picture of the potter in the OT. At first glance, it seems identical to the image in Isaiah: on the basis of what he sees in the potter's house, Jeremiah speaks of Yahweh as a potter, who exercises sovereign authority over what he makes; he can destroy it if he does not like it. The interpretation of the image, however, shows that Jeremiah uses it somewhat differently than does Isaiah. In Isaiah, the image is meant to symbolize the relationship of created human beings to God their Creator. In Jeremiah, however, the emphasis is on the relationship between Yahweh the creator-God and his chosen people Israel as well as between the universal God Yahweh and the other nations, as we see from the extended interpretation in Jer. 18:7-10. Punning on *yôṣēr* and *yāṣar* (ptcp.!), Jeremiah says in vv. 11f. that Yahweh is shaping evil against Judah and Jerusalem and has conceived a plan against them.

The image of the potter reappears in Deutero-Isaiah and Trito-Isaiah. Isa. 45:9-13 is obscure. So much is clear: the image in v. 9 is fairly closely related to Isa. 29:16 (God the Creator of the human race), while 45:11 is more like Jer. 18 (God the Creator of Israel).[18] Isa. 64:7(8) is simpler. In a great communal lament, the petitions are separated from the confession of sin by this single verse, an expression of confidence: Yahweh is the potter (*yôṣēr*), Israel the clay, the work of his hands. A late form of this image is found in the somewhat corrupt Hebrew text of Sir. 33:10,13 (cf. Wis. 15:7; Rom. 9:19-21).

Finally, the image of the potter can be used in a different way, with the emphasis no longer on the relationship between creator and creature but on the fragility of earthenware. Israel is destroyed like a "potter's vessel" (Isa. 30:14); Judah and Jerusalem are shattered like "a potter's earthen flask" (Jer. 19:1-13). Israel's enemies are dashed in pieces "like a potter's vessel" (Ps. 2:9). After the fall of Jerusalem, the sons of Zion are worthless as broken "earthen pots" (Lam. 4:2). And in yet another image, Cyrus tramples rulers as the potter treads the wet clay with his feet (Isa. 41:25).

IV. God's Creative Handiwork. It is not by chance that the work of the potter appears so frequently in religious imagery. We have already alluded to the religio-historical background; and if we note the semantic development of the root *yāṣar,* we see that the image of the potter forms a bridge between the two semantic spheres of the verb, human craftsmanship and divine creation. The OT uses the verb primarily in the latter sense; it refers to the divine activity of creating and shaping, as we have already noted behind the metaphorical language.

---

17 Pp. 1127, 1129.

18 See the discussion in C. Westermann, *Isaiah 40–66. OTL* (Eng. trans. 1969), 164-68.

1. *Creation of the Human Race.* The Yahwistic account of creation is relatively restrictive in its use of *yāṣar,* employing it primarily for the creation of the human race (Gen. 2:7f.). In contrast to the Priestly account, which uses the verbs *ʿāśâ* and *bārāʾ* for the creation of humanity (Gen. 1:26f.), the Yahwistic account explicitly mentions the material used in creation: human beings are made of dust (cf. Ps. 103:14; Sir. 33:10 [Heb.], probably alluding to Gen. 3:19[19]); the work of creation is not complete until the breath of life has been infused.[20] In the Yahwistic account, not only human beings but animals are formed (*yāṣar*) "out of the ground" (Gen. 2:19); the Priestly account uses the verb *ʿāśâ* for the creation of the animals (Gen. 1:25). Even more striking is the use of the verb *bānâ,* "build," instead of this verb for the creation of woman (Gen. 2:22). The verb *bānâ* is cognate with *banû,* the usual Akkadian "creation verb";[21] in addition, the stress on the man's rib as the material used by God in creating woman is intended to express the intimate relationship between male and female.[22]

This idea of how God formed the human race, which dominates the Yahwistic account of creation, undoubtedly had a long history in Israel, although it probably reflects foreign influence. It gave rise to the notion, found in texts of various periods, that Yahweh is the Creator of specific parts of the human body, such as the heart (Ps. 33:15), the eye (Ps. 94:9), or the spirit (Zec. 12:1).[23] In Ps. 103:14, the noun *yēṣer* designates the human body as a whole, and the hapax legomenon **yāṣûr* in Job 17:7 probably refers to members of the body.

2. *Creation of the World.* Secondary to the idea that God formed the human race is the notion that he shaped the whole world.[24] For theological reasons, the Priestly account of creation (Gen. 1:1–2:4), which focuses on the creation of the world, uses the verb *bārāʾ* exclusively.[25] This verb in fact replaced the other "creation verbs" in creation texts that were edited theologically.[26] Along with *bārāʾ* the "totally neutral verb" *ʿāśâ* found increasing use in creation texts, so as to avoid the anthropomorphic *yāṣar.*[27] In certain contexts, however, the notion of "forming" the universe survived: the hymnic introductory formula in Jer. 33:2, which has probably been separated from its original context,[28] refers to Yahweh as "shaper" (*yôṣēr*) of the world (ambiguously in the MT, explicitly in

---

19 Schmidt, *THAT,* I, 764; cf. Humbert, 83f.

20 See Schmidt, *Die Schöpfungsgeschichte der Priesterschrift,* 197-99, citing Egyptian and Mesopotamian notions of how the human race was formed out of clay. Similar material is presented by Wildberger, 1127-1131; see also Westermann, *Genesis 1–11,* 205-7. Westermann cites further parallels, but maintains that the element of craftsmanship retreats into the background in the OT.

21 See I.1 above.

22 Schmidt, *Die Schöpfungsgeschichte der Priesterschrift,* 199-201.

23 See Albertz, 121 and 120, citing Ps. 139:13-15, which mentions the creation of other parts of the body, albeit using different verbs.

24 Westermann, *Genesis 1–11,* 22-25; cf. Albertz, 54f.

25 See Bernhardt, 246-48.

26 See Humbert, 85-87.

27 Brongers, 93.

28 *Ibid.,* 95.

the LXX[29]). Jer. 10:16 (par. 51:19; probably not authentic[30]) sums up an account of creation by saying that Yahweh "formed all things." More frequently we find a synecdoche: one of the doxologies of Amos (Am. 4:13) states that Yahweh formed the mountains; according to Ps. 95:5, his hands formed the dry land; according to Ps. 74:17, he formed summer and winter—probably meaning "everything"[31] or, more narrowly, the seasons, the order of the universe (cf. Jer. 31:35; 33:25). In hymns that emphasize the motif of creation, however, such as Ps. 104; 136; 148; 24:1; etc., the verb *yāṣar* is very uncommon; it is found only in Ps. 104:26, which describes the creation of Leviathan in language that is clearly polemic, with antimythological overtones.[32]

V. Deutero-Isaiah. We have seen that the notion of creation—expressed by *yāṣar* as well as other verbs—is relatively diffused in early OT texts. Only in two groups of texts does the idea of creation actually play a major role: the hymns found in Psalms (together with hymnic fragments in other texts) and Deutero-Isaiah. Recent study has demonstrated the close relationship between these two groups of texts.[33]

1. *Creation and Election of Israel.* It is striking that Deutero-Isaiah uses the verb *yāṣar* almost exclusively in contexts that speak of the creation (and election) of Israel. The many passages that speak of the creation of the world in general make use of other verbs.[34] The restricted use of *yāṣar* is connected with the complex development of the creation texts in Deutero-Isaiah: the passages that speak of Yahweh as Creator of the world find their function in disputations, where they establish Yahweh's power in contrast to the impotence of idols; the passages that speak of Yahweh as Creator of Israel, however, find their function in oracles of salvation, where they establish Yahweh's salvific will.[35] In addition, the former originated in OT hymns and the latter in the salvation oracles or laments of the individual.[36] We see, therefore, that the verb *yāṣar* in Deutero-Isaiah appears almost exclusively in passages that speak of the creation of Israel and therefore originate in the individual salvation oracle or lament.

Isa. 43:1-7; 43:16-21; 44:1-5 are typical salvation oracles; 44:21f. is at least closely related to a salvation oracle,[37] and 44:24a must probably be considered the fragmentary introduction of a salvation oracle.[38] These passages do not mention the creation of the world, but they do refer to Yahweh as the *yōṣēr,* "former," of Israel (Isa. 43:1; 44:22,24;

---

29 See B. Duhm, *Das Buch Jeremia. KHC,* XI (1901), 271; Albertz, 103.

30 Brongers, 95; see also W. Thiel, *Die deuteronomistische Redaktion von Jeremia 1–25. WMANT,* 41 (1973), 81.

31 Schmidt, *THAT,* I, 763.

32 Brongers, 96f.; Albertz, 92-98.

33 See Rendtorff, 4-6, on the relationship between hymns and creation language in Deutero-Isaiah.

34 See IV.2 above; also Bernhardt, 247.

35 Rendtorff, 8; Albertz, 1-21.

36 Albertz, 50f.

37 Elliger, 443.

38 Albertz, 27, 32f.; for a general discussion of the passages examined here, see 26-33.

perfective form of the verb in 43:21; 44:21). Parallel synonyms are derived from the roots *bārā'* and *'āśâ*; cf. Isa. 43:7, where all three verbs occur together. Here we find features characteristic of the salvation oracles in Deutero-Isaiah: "the doctrine of creation has been fully incorporated into the dynamic of the prophet's doctrine of redemption."[39] In other words, the primordial creation of Israel is seen in the same perspective as its present deliverance; both concepts coalesce in the notion of election.[40] These motifs are expressed by the verbs → **גאל** *gā'al,* "redeem" (Isa. 43:1; 44:22,24), → **עזר** *'āzar,* "help" (44:2), → **בחר** *bāḥar* (*bāchar*), "choose" (43:20; 44:1f.), and → **אהב** *'āhab* (*'āhabh*), "love" (43:4). In addition, Isa. 43:7 states that the chosen nation—"every one who is called by my name"—was created for God's glory. Familiar motifs associated with the idea of salvation and election are joined here with the idea of creation.

2. *Creation of the World.* In addition to passages that speak of the creation of Israel, which characteristically use words derived from the root *yṣr,* there is also a passage in Deutero-Isaiah that uses forms of *yṣr* in connection with the creation of the world. Isa. 45:18f. is a fragment that is hard to categorize as to form, but it is probably to be considered the introduction to vv. 20-25.[41] Verse 18 brings together a remarkable number of verbs for creation, and it is no surprise to find *yāṣar* among them.

3. *Creation and Election of the Servant.* The connection just noted between the idea of creation and notion of election also appears in a totally different form in Deutero-Isaiah. The Servant Songs often make pregnant reference to the relationship between the Servant and Yahweh. Yahweh is the "former" (*yōṣēr*) of the Servant (Isa. 49:5). Similar statements are made by Isa. 49:8 and 42:6.[42] The appearance of words like *qārā',* "call" (Isa. 49:1; 42:6), and *bāḥar,* "choose" (49:7; 42:1), in this context shows that the passages deal with the call and election of the Servant. Inclusion of the idea of creation in this context reflects precisely the correspondence between the creation and election of Israel in Deutero-Isaiah that we have just discussed.[43] If we then compare the passages from the Servant Songs with Jer. 1:5 and Ps. 139:16 (both of which use *yāṣar*), we gain the impression that the notion of creation has yet another function in these texts: election actually precedes creation, so that Yahweh's sovereign elective authority is emphasized. We may also interpret the Servant passages in this sense: just as Jeremiah was "known" and "consecrated" even before being created by Yahweh, so too was the Servant.[44] And just as the petitioner in Ps. 139 knows that he stands under the protection of the omniscient creator-God throughout his entire life, so too does the Servant.[45]

---

39 Von Rad, 136.

40 Rendtorff, 9-12.

41 Westermann, *Isaiah 40–66,* 172f.; Albertz, 9f.

42 The text-critical problems of these passages are discussed by Elliger, 223.

43 See Rendtorff, 12; Albertz, 48-50.

44 See P. Volz, *Der Prophet Jeremia. KAT,* X (^{2}1928), 3f., where the text-critical problem of Jer. 1–5 is also discussed; cf. the Hebrew text of Sir. 49:7, which alludes to Jer. 1:5 and contains a niphal form of *yāṣar.*

45 See H.-J. Kraus, *Psalms 60–150* (Eng. trans., Minneapolis, 1989), 518f.

VI. God's "Shaping" of History. The passages just discussed reflect a kind of predestination. This notion is actually latent in the passages in Deutero-Isaiah that speak of the creation of Israel; elsewhere it appears even more clearly. It is quite explicit in the addendum to the account of Jeremiah's visit to the potter in Jer. 18: Yahweh shapes the destiny of the people of Judah—but not arbitrarily, for if they repent and return to him, he will not send disaster upon them. But if they do not repent, Yahweh will shape (*yāṣar*) evil against them and devise (*ḥāšaḇ*) a plan against them (Jer. 18:11). A similar notion is expressed more radically and independently by the Cyrus oracle in Isa. 45:1-7: following the assertion that there is no God but Yahweh (vv. 5f.), Yahweh describes himself in v. 7 as the one who forms (*yāṣar*) light and creates (*bārā'*) darkness, who makes (*'āśâ*) weal and creates (*bārā'*) woe. One must understand this passage either as an attempt to comprehend the totality of creation, in which case the pairs of opposites are merely merisms meaning "everything" (as in the summary at the end of the verse),[46] or as deliberate polemic against Persian dualism.[47] Whether or not polemic is present, clearly Deutero-Isaiah here pushes his creation theology to its utmost limit.[48] The extended Hebrew text of Sir. 11:4 contains a similar list of opposites, all of which derive from God or were created (*yāṣar* niphal) by God.

Other passages, many using the verb *yāṣar,* state more concretely how Yahweh as Creator "shapes" certain historical situations or events. Isa. 22 probably reflects the political crisis in Jerusalem during Sennacherib's attack in 701 B.C. Isaiah accuses the inhabitants of Jerusalem of worrying about their fortifications instead of looking to him who did (*'āśâ*) it, who planned (*yāṣar*) it long ago (Isa. 22:11); the vague "it" refers to the whole historical situation. In 2 K. 19 (par. Isa. 37), Sennacherib's advance is described in the same terms: Yahweh says that he did (*'āśâ*) it long ago, he planned (*yāṣar*) it from days of old (2 K. 19:25 par. Isa. 37:26). The relationship of these expressions in the Isaiah tradition to Deutero-Isaiah is clear from Isa. 46:11, where Yahweh says of Cyrus' coming: "I have spoken, and I will bring it to pass; I have purposed (*yāṣar*), and I will do (*'āśâ*) it." It is noteworthy that such statements generally do not appear in eschatological contexts and that they are not found in the Deuteronomistic corpus with its highly developed notion of history.[49]

VII. yṣr, **"Purpose."** We have already discussed some occurrences of the noun *yēṣer*: in Isa. 29:16; Hab. 2:18, it designates a product of craftsmanship; in Ps. 103:14, it refers to the human frame. There are 6 passages, however, in which the noun clearly has a meaning closely related to the usage of the verb just discussed. The various statements to the effect that Yahweh has "created" the historical situation of Israel could be rephrased by saying that Yahweh has framed a plan concerning Israel. Jer. 18:11 actually says that Yahweh is shaping evil against Israel and devising (*ḥāšaḇ*) a plan against them. The noun *yēṣer* in conjunction with → לב *lēḇ,* "heart," takes on the meaning

---

46 Elliger, 499-502.

47 Bernhardt, 247f.

48 See Westermann, *Isaiah 40–66,* 161f.

49 Humbert, 85.

"imagination of the heart," the heart's thoughts and purpose (Gen. 8:21); with the addition of *maḥᵃšeḇeṯ* it means "imagination of the thoughts of the heart" (Gen. 6:5; 1 Ch. 29:18; cf. 28:9). When *yēṣer* stands alone, it must be translated as something like "purpose." Its overtones can be negative (Yahweh knows "Israel's nature" [Dt. 31:21][50]) or positive (the righteous nation enters Jerusalem with its "mind stayed" [*yēṣer sāmûḵ*] on Yahweh [Isa. 26:3]).[51]

VIII. yṣr in Later Judaism. In the late Jewish texts from Qumran, the verb *yāṣar* appears 8 times, the noun *yēṣer* some 40 times.[52] In 1 passage (1QpHab 12:13, discussing Hab. 2:18), the verb refers to the manufacture of idols; elsewhere it refers to the creation of the human race (1QH 1:15; 3:21) or the human spirit (1QH 1:8; 4:31; 15:22). The occurrences of the noun can be categorized in three groups:

a. The noun *yēṣer* can mean "created human being," often in conjunction with *ʿāpār*, "dust," *ḥōmer*, "clay," or *bāśār*, "flesh" (1QH 1:21; 3:23; 4:29; 9:16; 10:23; 11:3; 12:26,32; 18:11,13,25,31; 1QH fr. 1:8; 3:5; etc.). Such expressions are connected with the characteristic creation theology of the Qumran hymns.

b. The phrase *yēṣer sāmûḵ* is borrowed from Isa. 26:3 in 1QS 4:5; 8:3; 1QH 1:35; 2:9,36.

c. Reflecting such passages as Gen. 6:5 or 8:21, the noun can have the meaning "purpose" or the like, almost always in the context of human sinfulness (1QS 5:5; 1QH 5:6,31; 6:32; 7:3,13,16; 11:20). These passages are discussed by Murphy.[53]

The most interesting passage is actually a hymn fragment (1QH fr. 3:9f.) that Murphy does not mention. Here, although the context is obscure, *yēṣer* appears in construct with two other nouns: *ʿawlâ*, "wickedness," and *rᵉmiyyâ*, "deception." These 2 formulas are not far removed from the phrase *yēṣer raʿ*, "evil impulse," which to date has been found only in a single passage in the Dead Sea scrolls (the hymnic text "Plea for Deliverance" [11QPsᵃ 19:15f.][54]). The poet prays that Satan and an unclean spirit may not rule over him and that "the evil impulse" may not take possession of his limbs. It is true that Sir. 15:14; 27:6 speak of *yēṣer* and the Greek version of Sir. 37:3 shows that the original may have read *yēṣer raʿ*, although the extant Hebrew text reads simply *yēṣer*.[55] But the Qumran passage (datable by paleography in the first half of the 1st century A.D.) is probably the earliest clear use of the phrase "evil impulse." This concept plays an important role in later rabbinic literature, often in contrast to *yēṣer ṭôḇ*, "good impulse."[56]

Otzen

---

50 G. von Rad, *Deuteronomy. OTL* (Eng. trans. 1966), 190.

51 For a discussion of these passages, see Humbert, 87f.; Westermann, *Genesis 1–11*, 410; Murphy, 334f.

52 Kuhn, 92f.

53 Pp. 339-343.

54 J. A. Sanders, *The Psalms Scroll of Qumrân Cave 11 (11QPsᵃ). DJD*, IV (1965), 40, 77.

55 Murphy, 335-38.

56 Cf. W. Bousset–H. Gressmann, *Die Religion des Judentums im späthellenistischen Zeitalter. HNT*, 21 (³1926; repr. 1966), 402-5; St.-B., IV (1928), 466-483; G. F. Moore, *Judaism in the First Centuries of the Christian Era*, I (1927; repr. Cambridge, Mass., 1958), 479-496.

יצת *yṣt*

Contents: I. Meaning, Occurrences. II. Concrete Meanings in the OT. III. Usage in Theological Contexts.

I. Meaning, Occurrences. Hebrew *yṣt* is another, less common, root used in the OT to mean "kindle" or "burn" (cf. *dlq, ḥrh, ḥrr, yqd, lhṭ, qdh*). The more common roots are → בער *bʿr* and → שרף *śrp*.

The root has no cognates in the other Semitic languages, including Aramaic. In the OT, it appears primarily in Deuteronomic material and in prophetic writings (including Lamentations) from the 8th to the 6th centuries B.C. About half of its 30 occurrences are in Jeremiah, both in the poetry and in the prose. The verb appears later in Neh. 1:3; 2:17, and continues in use into the postbiblical period.[1] In the OT, *yṣt* is used with reference to the burning of land and property, and by metaphorical extension to include the populace (Jer. 11:16), who, especially during war, are tied closely to property and land (Jgs. 9:49). Moreover, when Yahweh pours out his wrath, he does not discriminate between people and land (2 K. 22:13,17). The common word in P for the burning of sacrifices is *śārap̱* (Leviticus). Our root is nevertheless interchangeable with *bʿr* and *śrp*, both of which are used for burning of all kinds.

There are 4 occurrences of the qal. With *bᵉ*, it means "kindle" (Isa. 9:17[Eng. v. 18]); with *bāʾēš*, it means "be kindled with fire" (Isa. 33:12; Jer. 49:2; 51:58). The niphal means "be kindled, burned"; it is found only in the 3rd person. The common form *niṣṣᵉṯâ* (3rd person sg. fem.) appears in 2 K. 22:13,17; Jer. 9:11(12); 46:19, although the 2 occurrences in Jeremiah may be derived from the root *nṣh*, "be ruined, laid waste" (cf. Jer. 4:7). The kethibh of Jer. 2:15, *nṣth*, is an old 3rd person plural feminine, as in Aramaic,[2] although it could also come from *nṣh*.[3] The 3rd person pl. *nṣtw* appears in Jer. 2:15 (*Q*); 9:9(10); Neh. 1:3; 2:17. In the hiphil with *bāʾēš* the meaning is "set on fire" (Josh. 8:8,19); with *ʾēš* alone, it is "set fire to" (Am. 1:14; Jer. 17:27). In Jer. 51:30, *hiṣṣîṯû miškᵉnōṯeyhā* means "they set her houses on fire."

II. Concrete Meanings in the OT. Land and property—fields of grain, pastures, uncultivated groves of trees, and especially cities—are burned by enemies as an act of war. To finish the destruction of the city of Shechem, Abimelech sets fire to the fortified tower with bundles of brushwood he and his people have gathered (Jgs. 9:49). Absalom, too, as an act of war has his servants set fire to the barley fields of Joab (2 S. 14:30f.).

III. Usage in Theological Contexts. In a holy war, Yahweh expressly commands

---

1 Jastrow, 590f.
2 *BLe*, § 55c´; cf. § 42o´.
3 Graf, Duhm, Driver, Peake, and Rudolph.

the burning of cities. Ai (or Bethel?) was thus set on fire after it had been taken by Joshua (Josh. 8:8,19). By the time of Amos, however, Yahweh's judgment is conceived in more universal terms. In his great sermon in Am. 1:2–3:8, Amos prophesies destruction by fire against seven nations, including Judah. Against six of them—Damascus, Gaza, Tyre, Edom, Moab, and Judah—Yahweh says *wᵉšillaḥtî ʾēš,* "and I will send fire" (Am. 1:4,7,10,12; 2:2,5), whereas against the Ammonites he says *wᵉhiṣṣattî ʾēš bᵉḥômaṯ rabbâ,* "and I will kindle a fire in the wall of Rabbah" (Am. 1:14).

Isaiah speaks of thorns and briars (*šāmîr wāšayiṯ*) as symbolizing wicked people who are set afire. One hears echoes of Jotham's parable and the subsequent debacle suggested by Abimelech in his discourse (Jgs. 9). In Isa. 9:17(18), Isaiah speaks of the civil wars that characterized the closing years of the northern kingdom: each is like a fire that consumes briars and thorns and devours the thickets of the forest (*wattiṣṣaṯ bᵉsiḇᵉḵê hayyaʿar*) (Hos. 7:7; 2 K. 15:8-30; cf. Jgs. 9:15-20). Yet through it all, the wrath of Yahweh is manifested (Isa. 9:18[19]; cf. Jgs. 9:56f.). In Isa. 33:10-12 we find the same idea: when Yahweh exalts himself on the day of judgment, the chaff that the nation has conceived and borne will be consumed; people will treat one another "like thorns cut down, that are burned in the fire" (*qôṣîm kᵉsûḥîm bāʾēš yiṣṣattû*) (v. 12). Later, however, when Yahweh sings his new Song of the Vineyard (Isa. 27:2-6; cf. 5:1-7), wrath is gone because the wicked are no more. To emphasize the point, Yahweh says that if only he had some thorns and briars he would trample them and burn them up (Isa. 27:4), but none are left.

Before this can take place, however, judgment must come upon Jerusalem. In 622 B.C., a lawbook was found in the temple and subsequently read to King Josiah. After hearing its contents, he rent his clothes, saying: *kî-gᵉḏôlâ ḥᵃmaṯ YHWH ʾᵃšer-hîʾ niṣṣᵉtâ bānû,* "for great is the wrath of Yahweh that is kindled against us" (2 K. 22:13). A divine oracle confirmed his assessment of the situation. The scroll may have included the Song of Moses found in Dt. 32, vv. 15-22 of which are echoed in the oracle uttered against Judah by the prophetess Huldah.[4] In Dt. 32:22a, Yahweh says: *kî-ʾēš qāḏᵉḥâ bᵉʿappî wattîqaḏ ʿaḏ-šᵉʾôl taḥtîṯ,* "for a fire is kindled by my anger, and it burns to the depths of Sheol"; in Huldah's oracle, he says: *wᵉniṣṣᵉṯâ ḥᵃmāṯî bammaqôm hazzeh wᵉlōʾ tiḵbeh,* "therefore my wrath will be kindled against this place, and it will not be quenched" (2 K. 22:17b).

Jeremiah was chosen to bring this message to both king and people after the time of Josiah. He grieves over the damage already inflicted, while predicting worse in the days ahead. The enemies arising against Judah did not come from within, as in the case of the northern kingdom, but from without. They came and burned the countryside, the cities, and the inhabitants of the land. They came in a steady stream: first the Assyrians, then the Egyptians, followed by various mixed hordes (Jer. 18:22; 2 K. 24:2) possibly including Scythian tribes,[5] and finally the mighty Babylonian army. The lions who burn up the cities of Judah are not named (Jer. 2:15), but are probably the Babylonian kings,

---

4 J. R. Lundbom, "The Lawbook of the Josianic Reform," *CBQ,* 38 (1976), 293-302.

5 Herodotus *Hist.* i.105.

who oppressed Judah for many years. The enemy that burns the pastures (Jer. 9:9[10]) is also unnamed, but he, too, leaves the land without inhabitant. Even the animals and birds are gone. Jeremiah weeps over this destruction (following MT *'eśśā'* in 9:9[10]), but in the following verse Yahweh answers that Jerusalem and what remains of Judah's cities will suffer a similar fate. In Jer. 32:29, Yahweh says explicitly that he is sending Babylonians to set fire to Jerusalem. Behind every particular enemy stands the ominous figure of Yahweh, who has declared holy war on his people. But after the burning of Jerusalem, fires will be set in other nations: Yahweh says he will kindle a fire in the temples of the gods of Egypt (Jer. 43:12); Memphis will be burned and left without inhabitants (46:19). The villages of the Ammonites will be burned with fire (Jer. 49:2). Yahweh will again kindle fire in the wall of Damascus (v. 27; cf. Am. 1:4). When Babylon's time comes, her cities and the surrounding area will be consumed by Yahweh's fire (Jer. 50:32; 51:30,58). Ezekiel speaks on one occasion of Yahweh's kindling a fire among the trees of the Negeb (Ezk. 21:3[20:47]). Whenever Yahweh kindles fire in a foreign land, no reason is given. This stands in stark contrast to the judgment oracles against Israel, in which Yahweh states reasons in almost every case. The message proclaimed by Jeremiah is essentially the same as that of Dt. 32:15-22 and Huldah's oracle: the people have forsaken Yahweh and his law and have provoked his anger by worshipping other gods; therefore Yahweh's wrath will burn against them and their land like an unquenchable fire. The burned cities in Jer. 2:15 are the consequence of forsaking Yahweh (v. 17). In the sapiential comment in Jer. 9:11-13(12-14), the reason given for the burning of the land is that the people have forsaken Yahweh's law and gone after the baʿals. In the sermonic prose of Jer. 11:16f., the prophet says that Israel was once a green olive tree that bore much fruit, but now Yahweh will set fire to her because she has burned incense to Baʿal. In Jer. 17:19-27, he declares that if the people do not keep the Sabbath and desist from bringing burdens through the gates of Jerusalem on the Sabbath, Yahweh will burn those gates along with the palaces of the city (v. 27). The destruction of Jerusalem announced in Jer. 32:29 results from the worship of baʿals and other gods—a clear echo of Huldah's oracle in 2 K. 22:17. When Zedekiah of Judah sins by not practicing justice and by not turning from self-righteous arrogance about Jerusalem's security, Yahweh declares that Israel's forest will be burned (Jer. 21:14). Here, as in Jer. 22, the reference is to the cedar-lined buildings of Jerusalem's royal complex.[6] What finally took place in Jerusalem is summed up in Lam. 4:11: "Yahweh gave full vent to his wrath, he poured out his hot anger; and he kindled a fire in Zion, which consumed its foundations" (*wayyaṣṣeṯ-'ēš beṣiyyôn wattō'ḵal yesôḏōṯeyhā*).

The city was still in the same condition many years later, when Nehemiah inquired about Jerusalem from the visitors who had come to Babylon (Neh. 1:3). The news he received made him weep, but he responded by confessing Israel's sin to Yahweh. Shortly

---

6 J. R. Lundbom, *Jeremiah: A Study in Ancient Hebrew Rhetoric. SBL Diss.,* 18 (1975), 48; cf. G. Vermès, "The Symbolic Interpretation of *Lebanon* in the Targums: The Origin and Development of an Exegetical Tradition," *JTS,* N.S. 9 (1958), 1-12.

afterwards he went to Jerusalem himself to initiate and supervise the great task of rebuilding the city wall upon the burned ruins (Neh. 2:17).

Freedman, Lundbom

יֶקֶב yeqeḇ

Contents: 1. Etymology, Occurrences; 2. Proper Names; 3. General; 4. Figurative Usage.

1. *Etymology, Occurrences.* The noun *yeqeḇ* is connected etymologically with Arab. *waqb,* "depression, hole"; in Hebrew, it refers to a winery.

The word appears 15 times in the OT; it means primarily a receptacle carved in the rock where wine is collected as it is pressed (Isa. 5:2; Jer. 48:33). This meaning appears also to be present in conjunction with → גרן *gōren* (Nu. 18:27,30; Dt. 15:14; 16:13; 2 K. 6:27; Hos. 9:2; Joel 2:24), *gaṯ* (Joel 4:13[Eng. 3:13]), *ʿărēmâ* (Hag. 2:16), and *ʾāsām* (Prov. 3:10). But it also appears as the direct object of *dāraḵ,* where it presumably has the extended sense of "wine press" (Job 24:11; Isa. 16:10; cf. Zec. 14:10).

The word *gaṯ* appears 5 times in the OT, 3 times as the object of *dāraḵ* (Neh. 13:15; Isa. 63:2; Lam. 1:15) and once as the object of *rāḏâ* (Joel 4:13[3:13]). It refers to the actual press where the grapes are trodden. According to Jgs. 6:11, in case of necessity it could also be used for threshing grain.

The word *pûrâ* appears only twice. In Hag. 2:16 it appears to be some kind of measure (if *yeqeḇ* is interpreted as the trough of the winepress), but in Isa. 63:3 it is the object of *dāraḵ* and refers to the press itself.

2. *Proper Names.* Both *yeqeḇ* and *gaṯ* appear in toponyms. Jgs. 7:25 mentions a place called *yeqeḇ-zeʾēḇ.* The name in Neh. 11:25, read by the Masoretes as *yiqaḇṣeʾēl,* might also contain the element *yeqeḇ*.

In the OT, *gaṯ* appears primarily as the name of one of the five Philistine cities (33 times); it also occurs in several compounds. The home of the prophet Micah is identified as *môrešeṯ gaṯ* (Mic. 1:14). It appears in the construct in the toponyms *gaṯ haḥēper* (Josh. 19:13; 2 K. 14:25) and *gaṯ-rimmôn* (Josh. 19:45; 21:24; 1 Ch. 6:54[69]). Similar compounds are found in the Amarna letters (e.g., Ginti-ašna, Ginti-rumna, Ginti-kirmil, Giti-rimunima, Giti-padalla) and in Ugaritic (*gt glʿd, gt ngr, gt ʿṯtrt*).[1] The dual form *gittāyim* appears in 2 S. 4:3; Neh. 11:33 as the name of a city in Benjamin.

---

yeqeḇ. G. W. Ahlström, "Wine Presses and Cup-Marks of the Jenin-Megiddo Survey," *BASOR,* 231 (1978), 19-49; G. Dalman, *AuS,* IV (1935), 354ff.; J. B. Pritchard, *Winery, Defenses, and Soundings at Gibeon* (Philadelphia, 1964).

[1] *WUS,* no. 705; M. Dahood, "Ugaritic Lexicography," in *Mélanges Eugène Tisserant,* I. *StT,* 231 (1964), 86f.; M. Ottosson, *Gilead. CB,* 3 (1969), 17f.

3. *General.* In Palestine, the vintage (*bāṣîr*) occurs in the months of Tammuz, Ab, and Elul (roughly July–September); in good years, however, it might last from the time of harvest to the time of sowing (Lev. 26:5; Am. 9:13). The grapes were picked by hand and placed in baskets (*kᵉlûb̲ qāyiṣ* [Am. 8:1f.]), then brought to the press (*gat̲*) (Neh. 13:15: upon asses). A vineyard (→ כרם *kerem*) would have a wall (*gāḏēr* [Isa. 5:5; Ps. 80:13(12)]) and watchtower (*migdāl* [Isa. 5:2]) as well as a winepress and vat (*yeqeb̲* [Isa. 5:2]).[2]

Archaeological evidence shows that a winery consisted of a press (*gat̲*) hollowed in the rock, connected by ditches with one or more vats (*yeqeb̲*). The vats were often quite deep.[3] They collected the new wine (*ʿāsîs* [Cant. 8:2; Isa. 49:26; Joel 1:5; 4:18(3:18); Am. 9:13] or *tîrôš* [Prov. 3:10; Joel 2:24; Mic. 6:15]), which was drawn (*ḥāsap̱* [Hag. 2:16]) into earthenware jars (*nēb̲el* [1 S. 1:24; 10:3; 25:18; 2 S. 16:1; Jer. 13:12]). Wineskins (*nōʾḏôt̲* [Josh. 9:4,13]) were used to transport wine. At the vintage, the grapes were trodden (*dārak̲* [Jgs. 9:27]). The treading press was large enough for several persons to work at the same time; cf. the picture in the tomb of Nakht at Thebes.[4] At Gibeon, where great quantities of wine were produced, storerooms some 2 meters (6 ft.) deep were hewn in the rock, in which jars of finished wine were stored.[5]

Shouts of joy (*hêḏāḏ* [Jer. 25:30; 48:33]) and singing (*hillûlîm* [Jgs. 9:27]) accompanied the vintage; cf. the superscription *ʿal-haggittît̲* to Pss. 8, 81, 84, which may refer to the vintage, as well as a relief in the tomb of Mereruka at Sakkarah.[6]

4. *Figurative Usage.* The work of the vintage could easily find application in religious imagery. Yahweh himself was represented as treading out the harvest at the great judgment of the nations (Isa. 63:2ff.; Lam. 1:15). The juice of the grapes, which colored the garments of the workers, thus came to symbolize human blood (Isa. 63:3). The overflowing wine vat of Joel 4:13(3:13) symbolizes the wickedness of the nations and indicates the coming judgment (cf. also Am. 8:2; Mic. 4:12).

Ottosson

---

[2] On viticulture in general, see → גפן *gep̱en* (*gephen*), → יין *yayin*; see also *AuS* and Ahlström.

[3] Ahlström.

[4] N. de G. Davies, *The Tomb of Nakht at Thebes* (New York, 1917), pls. 23b, 26, 69f.

[5] Pritchard, 1-27.

[6] Sakkarah Expedition, *The Mastaba of Mereruka*, 2. *OIP*, 39 (1938), pl. 114.

יָקַד yāqaḏ; יְקֹד yᵉqōḏ; מוֹקֵד môqēḏ

Contents: I. 1. Etymology, Meaning; 2. Occurrences. II. Theological Usage: 1. The Perpetual Altar Fire; 2. Yahweh's Burning Wrath.

I. 1. *Etymology, Meaning.* Heb. *yqd* is a less common root used in the OT to mean "be kindled" or "burn" (cf. *bāʿar, ḥārâ, ḥārar, yāṣaṯ, śārap̱*). Akk. *qādu* is attested in Middle and Late Babylonian; while it normally means "light, kindle," it can also mean "burn."[1] Besides *qādu,* Akkadian also has *qalû* and *qamû* (both transitive), which mean "burn," in addition to the more common *šarāpu* (cf. Heb. *śārap̱*). We know that *qādu* and *šarāpu* are synonyms.[2] The former appears frequently in cultic texts, where it denotes the lighting of a torch, lamp, or cultic fire.[3] In "A Nightly Ceremony in the Temple of Anu,"[4] *qādu* alternates with *napāḫ,* which also means "kindle," but more in the sense of "blow into a flame." During this ritual, the high priest "lights" a great torch (*gizillû rabû*) from a fire containing aromatic spices, makes a recitation to Anu, and then carries the torch out into the street; there the other priests "light" their lamps and bring the fire to the outlying temples.[5] In an incantation text from *ca.* 1000 B.C.,[6] the ritual calls for "lighting" a torch in spices and then using it to ignite a brazier where clay images are to be baked. Torches are also kindled for lighting funeral pyres.[7] Assyrian kings burn cities, temples,[8] and cedars.[9] Tukulti-Ninurta I (1243-1197 B.C.) possesses might and energy that "burns the unsubmissive left and right."[10]

In Ugaritic, the root *srp* is attested but not *yqd,* although Dahood reads *mqdm* as "braziers."[11] Arab. *wqd* means "burn," and OSA *mqdn* means "altar hearth." In Aramaic, *yqd* is attested in all periods, which could mean that it comes into Hebrew as a loanword.[12]

---

1 *AHw,* II (1972), 892.

2 B. Meissner, *Beiträge zum Assyrischen Wörterbuch,* I. *AS,* 1 (1931), 71, 14.

3 E. Ebeling, *Tod und Leben nach den Vorstellungen der Babylonier* (Berlin, 1931), 17, 23: *išāta aqâd,* "I kindle the fire"; 93, 16: *gizillâ iqâda,* "[the priest] lights a cultic torch."

4 F. Thureau-Dangin, *Rituels Accadiens* (Paris, 1921), 118ff.; *ANET,* 338f.

5 Thureau-Dangin, *Rituels Accadiens,* 119, 30; 120, 15; cf. *CAD,* V (1956), 114.

6 *AfO,* 18 (1957-58), 297, 8f.

7 M. Streck. *Assurbanipal und die letzten assyrischen Könige bis zum Untergange Ninevehs. VAB,* 7 (1916), 266, 10; E. Ebeling, "Beschwörungen gegen den Fiend und den Bösen Blick aus dem Zweistromlande," *ArOr,* 17 (1949), 187, 17.

8 Sargon II; F. Thureau-Dangin, *Une relation de la huitième campagne de Sargon* (Paris, 1912) = *TCL,* 3; *Zusätze ZA,* 34, 113-122; E. F. Weidner, "Neue Bruchstücke des Berichtes über Sargons achten Feldzug," *AfO,* 12 (1937-39), 144-48; cf. *AHw,* II, 892.

9 Ebeling, *Tod und Leben,* 36, 24.

10 W. G. "Three Unpublished Fragments of the Tukulti-Ninurta Epic," *AfO,* 18 (1957-58), 48A, 11.

11 *KTU,* 4.158, 19; cf. M. Dahood, *Psalms III. AB,* 17A (1970), 11.

12 *KBL*³, 410.

In the Sefire inscriptions,[13] Barga'yā pronounces a curse on Matî'el should he break their treaty: *'yk zy tqd š'wt' z' b'š kn tqd 'rpd w[bnth r]bt,* "just as this wax is burned by fire, so may Arpad be burned and [her gr]eat [daughter-cities]." Again in ll. 37f. we find: *'ykh zy tqd š'wt' z' b'š kn yqd m[t''l],* "just as this wax is burned by fire, so may Matî['el be burned by fi]re."[14] In the Bible, Shadrach, Meshach, and Abednego survive the furnace of *nûrā' yāqiḏtā',* "burning fire," which Nebuchadnezzar has prepared for anyone who refuses to bow down to his image (Dnl. 3:6,11,15,17,20f.,23,26). In Dnl. 7:11, the beast is destroyed and consigned to *lîqēḏaṯ 'eššā',* "the burning fire," which is undoubtedly an unceremonious funeral pyre.

2. *Occurrences.* There are at least 3 occurrences of *yqd* in the qal (Dt. 32:22; Isa. 10:16; 65:5) and 5 in the hophal (Jeremiah and Leviticus). *BDB* takes *yāqûḏ* in Isa. 30:14 to be the qal passive participle ("that which is kindled"; NEB: "glowing embers"), but *KBL*[3] considers it a noun meaning "hearth."[15] Sherds, as we know, were used to take fire from the hearth. In Isa. 10:16, the prophet plays on *y^eqōḏ* and *y^eqôḏ,* which may derive ultimately from the infinitive absolute but are used here as nouns: *w^eṯaḥaṯ k^eḇōḏô yēqaḏ y^eqōḏ kîqôḏ 'ēš,* "and under his glory a burning [fever?] will be kindled, like the burning of fire." The noun *môqēḏ* may mean "burning embers" (Ps. 102:4[Eng. v. 3]; Isa. 33:14), or, as in Rabbinic and Modern Hebrew, simply "hearth" or "fireplace." The *môq^eḏâ* is a "hearth" (Lev. 6:2[9]).

II. Theological Usage. Theological usage of *yqd* in the OT is quite similar to usage in extrabiblical sources. Fires lit by priests in the temple are part of divine worship. Fires also burn when Yahweh the king comes in judgment.

1. *The Perpetual Altar Fire.* The law (Ex. 29:38-42; Lev. 6:2-6[9-13]; Nu. 28:2-8) prescribes both a morning and evening whole burnt offering (*'ōlâ*); the fire from the evening offering is to be kept burning (*tûqaḏ*) on the hearth (*môq^eḏâ*) all night. This allows for a perpetual altar fire. It has been argued, however, that having an *'ōlâ* both morning and evening is a postexilic ritual and that during the monarchy only a morning *'ōlâ* was prescribed.[16] Ahaz, for example, directs his priest to perform a morning *'ōlâ* and an evening *minḥâ* (cereal offering), but no evening *'ōlâ* (2 K. 16:15). Ezekiel, too, mentions only a morning *'ōlâ* (Ezk. 46:13-15). On the other hand, Elijah offers an *'ōlâ* on Mt. Carmel late in the day (1 K. 18:38; cf. v. 29). A schematic view seems to be precluded since different traditions no doubt existed in preexilic times. The 3 passages formally prescribing both a morning and an evening *'ōlâ* are legislative and seek standardization. Furthermore, Ahaz is hardly a model for the preexilic period, since he modified worship in other respects to conform to Assyrian practice.

---

13 *KAI,* 222A, 35f.

14 J. A. Fitzmyer, *The Aramaic Inscriptions of Sefire. BietOr,* 19 (1967), 14f.

15 Also RSV, JB, NAB.

16 W. O. E. Oesterley, *Sacrifices in Ancient Israel* (London, 1937), 221; R. de Vaux, *Studies in OT Sacrifice* (Eng. trans., Cardiff, 1964), 36; R. J. Faley, "Leviticus," *JBC,* 71.

2. *Yahweh's Burning Wrath.* Yahweh's anger burns when his people go after other gods (cf. *ᵉʼlōhîm ʼaḥērîm*). The classic expression of this is found in the Song of Moses, where in response to Israel's apostasy Yahweh declares: *kî-ʼēš qāḏᵉḥâ bᵉʻappî wattîqaḏ ʻaḏ-šᵉʼôl taḥtîṯ,* "For a fire is kindled in my anger, and it burns to the depths of Sheol" (Dt. 32:22). Isaiah and Jeremiah both show familiarity with this song, which goes on to say that after judgment Yahweh will turn to punish the enemy—which has served as his agent of destruction—lest the enemy's own arrogance become too great (Dt. 32:26ff.). This latter part of the song is appropriated in Isa. 10:16 and its context: Assyria, Yahweh's agent of destruction, will now be punished. Assyrian warriors will be smitten with disease, while under the king's glory (splendid attire?) "a burning will be kindled, like the burning of fire" (Isa. 10:16; cf. 37:36-38). Isaiah has in mind the boastfulness of the Assyrian kings, who, as we have seen, were wont to speak of their own glory as "burning the unsubmissive left and right."[17] Isaiah also anticipates later apocalyptic thought in his idea that Yahweh's punishment serves to separate the righteous among his people from the wicked. In Isa. 33:14, the sinners in Zion say: "Who among us can dwell with the devouring fire? Who among us can dwell with everlasting burnings (*môqᵉḏê ʻôlām*)?" The answer is immediate: Those who walk righteously and speak uprightly . . . (Isa. 33:15ff.). They will survive and will see the good times that lie ahead. Their eyes will see Judah's kings arrayed in splendor (v. 17) and Jerusalem a quiet habitation (v. 20).

The influence of Dt. 32 on Jeremiah appears not only in Jeremiah's poetic diction[18] but also in phrases occurring in the sermonic prose. In Jer. 15:14; 17:4, the prophet quotes Dt. 32:22 more closely even than Huldah, who draws upon this verse (and those immediately preceding) for her oracle against Judah (2 K. 22:17).[19] The first colon, *kî-ʼēš qāḏᵉḥâ bᵉʻappî,* is quoted verbatim in Jer. 15:14 and almost verbatim in 17:4 (with *qᵉḏaḥtem* instead of *qāḏᵉḥâ*). The second colon is abbreviated to *ʻaḏ-ʻôlām tûqāḏ* in 17:4, and also in some manuscripts of 15:14 where the MT has *ʻᵃlêḵem tûqāḏ.* For Jeremiah, Yahweh's wrath comes as a perpetual fire causing exile in a foreign land. It looks as though Jeremiah is using *tûqāḏ* to play deliberately on the usage found in Lev. 6, especially since there are no other occurrences of the hophal. In Jer. 17:1-4, too, the sin is clearly illicit worship, engraved "on the horns of their altars" and on "their altars . . . in the open country."

Deutero-Isaiah likewise associates Israel's sin with the cult. Isa. 65:5 quotes the Zadokite priests as saying that they alone may approach Yahweh's altar. As Hanson has shown,[20] these words echo almost precisely those found in the pro-Zadokite statements of Ezk. 44:13,15,19. But Yahweh is not pleased, at least so far as this prophet is concerned. The smoke they send up, which he might normally enjoy (Gen. 8:21; etc.), is now converted by his anger into *ʼēš yōqeḏeṯ kol-hayyôm,* "a fire that burns all the day" (Isa. 65:5). Therefore, the perpetual altar fire evokes a perpetual fire of Yahweh's anger.

---

17 Cf. Lambert, 48A, 11.

18 W. L. Holladay, "Jeremiah and Moses: Further Observations," *JBL,* 85 (1966), 18-21.

19 J. R. Lundbom, "The Lawbook of the Josianic Reform," *CBQ,* 38 (1976), 293-302.

20 P. D. Hanson, *The Dawn of Apocalyptic* (Philadelphia, ²1979), 147-49.

Finally, in Ps. 102:4(3) the psalmist speaks of his bones' burning "like a furnace" (*k^e^môqēḏ*). His sickness and the transitory quality of his life he takes as a divine judgment, showing that Yahweh is angry with him (v. 11[10]). He nevertheless finds enough strength to praise Yahweh, who is enthroned forever (v. 13[12]).

Freedman, Lundbom

יקץ *yqṣ*; קיץ *qyṣ*

Contents: I. 1. Etymology; 2. Semantic Field. II. Human Subjects (General): 1. Awakening from Sleep; 2. Awakening from Intoxication. III. Human Subjects in Theological Contexts: 1. Awakening from Dreaming to Consciousness; 2. God's Intervention to Prevent Awakening; 3. Awakening from Death. IV. Divine Subjects: 1. Gods or Idols; 2. Yahweh.

I. 1. *Etymology.* Koehler and Baumgartner[1] call *yqṣ* a by-form of *qyṣ*, which suggests that the two words came into being through differentiation of an original biliteral root *qṣ*. The homophonous geminate root *qṣ*(*ṣ*), "cut off,"[2] has no connection with *yqṣ* or *qyṣ* hiphil, even though Ezk. 7:6[3] in the LXX^Q^ and Vulg. as well as Ps. 139:18[4] in the LXX and Vulg. appear to contain forms of *qṣṣ* hiphil derived by analogy from the hiphil of *qyṣ*. Koehler and Baumgartner,[5] citing von Soden,[6] also suggest a relationship with Akk. *akāṣu*, "be obdurate, desire violently"; this connection is likewise uncertain, since there is no persuasive semantic relationship. Instead, Heb. *yqṣ* corresponds to Ugar. *yqǵ*.[7] The root *yqṣ* also appears in Arabic as *yqẓ*, "awaken." The equivalence of Arab. *ẓ* to Heb.

---

yqṣ. H. Balz, "ὕπνος," *TDNT,* VIII, 545-556; J. Bergman, M. Ottosson, G. J. Botterweck, "חָלַם *ḥālam* (*chālam*)," *TDOT,* IV, 421-432, with bibliog. on dreams and their interpretation; M. Bittner, "Einige Besonderheiten aus der Sprache der Insel Soqoṭra," *WZKM,* 30 (1917/18), 347-358; *idem,* "Studien zur Laut- und Formenlehre der Mehri-Sprache in Südarabien," *SKAW,* 162/5 (1909), 26; 168/2 (1912), 85; 178/3 (1915), 32; E. L. Ehrlich, *Der Traum im AT. BZAW,* 73 (1953); *idem,* "Traum," *RGG*³, VI (1959), 1001-5; W. Leslau, *Lexique soqoṭri* (Paris, 1938); R. Meyer, *Hebräische Grammatik,* I (Berlin, ³1966); A. Oepke, "ἐγείρω," *TDNT,* II, 333-39; *idem,* "καθεύδω," *TDNT,* III, 431-37; *idem,* "ὄναρ," *TDNT,* V, 220-238; M. Wagner, *Die lexikalischen und grammatikalischen Aramaismen im alttestamentlichen Hebräisch. BZAW,* 96 (1966).

1 *KBL*³, 412a.

2 *KBL*², 848b.

3 Cf. W. Zimmerli, *Ezekiel 1. Herm* (Eng. trans. 1979), 195, with bibliog. on 7:6a.

4 Cf. H.-J. Kraus, *Psalms 60–150* (Eng. trans., Minneapolis, 1989), *in loc.*

5 *KBL*³, 412a.

6 *AHw,* I (1965), 28a.

7 *UT,* no. 1144; contra O. Rössler, "Ghain im Ugaritischen," *ZA,* N.S. 20[54] (1961), 161, according to whom *wtqǵ* must be considered a scribal error for *wtqẓ,* "watch out."

ṣ probably points to a common Semitic root (*y*)*qṯ* also attested by the aramaizing name *yoqṭān.*[8] Also deserving of mention is *yqṭ.*[9]

For our understanding of the root in question, the relationship between Heb. *yqṣ/qyṣ,* Aram. *qyṭ* (?), Soq. *ʾqṭ,* "awaken," on the one hand and Heb. *qyṣ* aramaizing *qyṭ* (Job 8:14),[10] Biblical Aram. *qyṭ* (Dnl. 2:35), Jewish Aram. *qyṭ,* Arab. *qaiẓ,* OSA *qyṭ,* "summer," as well as Heb. *qyṣ* qal, "spend the summer,"[11] may be noted. The Hebrew root *qyṣ,* "be warm, summer," appears to be related to the meaning "awaken, grow conscious." This is easier to account for when we note that Aram. *qyṭ* and Heb. *qyṣ* do not refer to summer itself, but basically mean "(summer-)ripe fruit" and hence the time of ripe harvest. This suggests the semantic shift "(be) ripe" > "be awake, be conscious." Awakening is accordingly the result of a ripening process, gaining consciousness.

2. *Semantic Field.* The root *yqṣ/qyṣ* hiphil appears 11/21 times in the OT. Of these occurrences, *yqṣ* appears 9 times in narrative passages, once in prophetic texts, and once in the Psalms; *qyṣ* appears 10 times in the prophets, 9 in poetic texts, and only twice in narrative passages. Thus *yqṣ/qyṣ* hiphil is found in all genres but with varying distribution. Originally, *yqṣ* appears to have been used primarily for the purely human phenomenon of waking up, while the hiphil of *qyṣ* seems to have been reserved more for "awakening" with theological overtones. Both roots differ distinctly from the synonymous root → עור *ʿwr* III,[12] "be(come) aroused," which is more expressive of emotional excitement (although Akk. *êru* means "awaken"). There is a purely formal difference in that *yqṣ/qyṣ* hiphil is always used intransitively in the sense of "awaken," whereas *ʿwr* III is used transitively at least in the pilel, hiphil, and pilpel, and elsewhere usually reflexively. Semantically, *yqṣ/qyṣ* hiphil has less to do with "be(com)ing aroused" than with the transition from unconsciousness or dreaming to full consciousness and rationality. For this reason, *yqṣ/qyṣ* hiphil is often used with the prep. *min*: "wake up, waken from sleep, from intoxication." This awakening is totally punctiliar, which probably explains the absence of any noun derived from the root. Because of their semantic nuances, *yqṣ/qyṣ* and *ʿwr* III are sometimes used in parallelism.

In rendering *yqṣ/qyṣ* hiphil, the LXX uses *egeírō* or *egeíromai* 3 times,[13] a translation it also uses for *ʿwr* III (once); it uses *exegeírō* or *exegeíromai* 14 times, as well as 19 times for *ʿwr* III, for which it is actually a better translation in its original sense of "rouse, stir up." Other verbs are used in specific contexts: *exanístēmi* (twice), plus once for *ʿwr* III; *exypnízō* (once), plus once for *ʿwr* III. We see that the LXX has no idiomatic root to

---

8 *KBL*³, 413a.

9 Benz, 129; *PCIS,* 3414, 2; on Protosemitic *ṯ* = Aram. *ṭ* = Heb. *ṣ* = Arab. *ẓ,* see S. Moscati, *An Introduction to the Comparative Grammar of the Semitic Languages. PLO,* N.S. 6 (²1969), 8, 14.

10 J. Reider, "Etymological Studies in Biblical Hebrew," *VT,* 4 (1954), 288f.; G. Fohrer, *Das Buch Hiob. KAT,* XVI (1963), *in loc.*; Wagner, 101, no. 165.

11 *KBL*², 837b.

12 *Ibid.,* 690b.

13 See Oepke, *TDNT,* II, 334.

represent *yqṣ/qyṣ* hiphil, using instead a word that better translates *ʿwr* III to render *yqṣ/qyṣ* hiphil as well as → קום *qûm* and → עמד *ʿāmaḏ*.

II. Human Subjects (General).

1. *Awakening from Sleep.* Reflecting general human experience, the word *yqṣ/qyṣ* hiphil has the meaning "awaken from sleep, from unconsciousness or semiconsciousness to full consciousness." Samson, for example, awakens (*yqṣ*) from sleep to free himself (Jgs. 16:14), but also to the clear awareness that the loss of his hair means also the loss of his strength (v. 20). Talk of "awakening" can also be used proverbially in a poetic sense: "Therefore it is said, 'I awoke (*qyṣ*) [and was overjoyed], my sleep was pleasant to me'" (Jer. 31:26). To awaken refreshed from a sound sleep after labor is the order willed by God (Eccl. 5:11[Eng. v. 12]);[14] to awaken is to feel one's life renewed. The "awakening" (*qyṣ*) in Prov. 6:22 is undoubtedly meant in the same sense: one must be fully awake to receive divine instruction. The point is readiness to receive God's commandment. In Ps. 17:15, awakening (*qyṣ*) is associated with the hope of experiencing the presence of Yahweh. Encounter with God is not an unconscious or mystical experience, but an event that can be comprehended clearly and deliberately by the human senses (cf. 1 Th. 5:6).

2. *Awakening from Intoxication.* The sleep from which one awakens can also be the negative consequence of overindulgence in wine, which so disables the sleeper that he is totally unaware of the world around him or even what is happening to him. When drunk with wine, Noah, for example, does not wake up even when his son Ham/Canaan plays a trick on him; he remains oblivious until he finally awakens to consciousness (*wayyîqeṣ miyyênô* [Gen. 9:24 (J)]). Abuse of alcohol has the same disastrous effect in Joel 1:5: the drunkards do not awaken (*qyṣ*) from their stupor until the plague of locusts is past; disaster has befallen them while they were unconscious and unable to save anything. The drunkard is doomed to awaken too late from his sleep. Abuse of wine can have even more terrible consequences if it leads to dependency and the self-destructive state in which even after awakening (*qyṣ*) the drinker is driven by the agony of intoxication to an even stronger need for drink (Prov. 23:29ff.,35). In this case, ultimately, sobriety is never attained again. But woe to those who fall into the clutches of a creditor waking (*qyṣ*) from a drunken sleep, who will be totally merciless in this condition (Hab. 2:7)!

III. Human Subjects in Theological Contexts.

1. *Awakening from Dreaming to Consciousness.* Special importance is attached to the dream state, which is distinct from being either awake or sound asleep. Dreaming provides its own unique experience of reality,[15] which is nonetheless open to criticism. The two states of consciousness—being awake and dreaming—are polar opposites. If a

---

14 See Balz, 545f.

15 → חלם *ḥālam* (*chālam*) II.2; Oepke, *TDNT,* V, 230f.

hungry man dreams that he is eating and awakes (*qyṣ*), he is aware that his hunger is unabated; if a thirsty man dreams that he is drinking and awakes (*qyṣ*), he is faint from thirst (Isa. 29:8).[16] Indeed, "dreams are like bubbles"; the images in dreams are shadowy experiences that melt away upon awakening (Ps. 73:20), since they are not real. Thus "dream" comes to symbolize impermanence and insubstantiality. God lets the wicked in their illusory glory perish like a dream. Such statements presuppose a critical attitude toward dreaming;[17] dreams cannot stand the test of reality.

A dream, nevertheless, can also have positive value. Jacob awakes (*yqṣ*) from a dream knowing that the place where he has spent the night is a *bêṯ ᵓᵉlōhîm* (Gen. 28:16 [J], 17f. [E]). The next morning he sets up the stone on which his head had rested, an act that makes it possible to understand the interpretation of the dream. The dream experience must invade the waking realm, over which it takes precedence, for it is the domain, shrouded in mystery, in which God has free rein.

Dreams can reveal what remains hidden to the corporeal eye. When Pharaoh awakes (*yqṣ* [Gen. 41:4,7,21 (E)]), he is so disquieted by the repeated symbolic dream that he assembles all the oneiromancers and refuses to rest until the meaning of the dream has been interpreted to him (Gen. 41:8ff. [E]; cf. Dnl. 2:2,12; 4:2f.[5f.]). A dream taken by itself without any evaluation when the dreamer is awake must remain meaningless and unsatisfying. Awakening to full rational consciousness and the resulting action in the conscious realm are essential parts of the dream experience.

This observation helps explain the practice of oracular incubation.[18] Preceded by ritual preparation, it is intended to induce such experiences. Solomon awakes (*yqṣ*) from his dream in the temple at Gibeon (1 K. 3:15) and notes that he has had a dream. He thereupon returns to Jerusalem, stands before the ark, and offers a *šᵉlāmîm* sacrifice. The dream experience has made him certain of his divine commission.

2. *God's Intervention to Prevent Awakening.* Instead of revealing himself in a dream, God can make use of sleep in other ways by deliberately delaying awakening, imitating the effect of intoxication.[19] David, for example, is able to sneak unrecognized into Saul's camp at night: no one "saw it, or knew it, nor did any awake (*qyṣ*)" (1 S. 26:12). Yahweh can also punish people—Babylon in Jer. 51:39,57—by forcing them behind this pale of consciousness, exiling them to the dark domain from which they shall never wake (*qyṣ*). "Falling asleep" encompasses the whole realm of unreal existence, from which no one can rise[20] or awaken (*qyṣ* par. *ʿwr* III [Job 14:12]).

3. *Awakening from Death.* Only Yahweh, who guards the pale of death, can break through it and open it to human passage. His omnipotence alone can reopen the gates from death to life. After praying, Elisha is able to restore the son of the Shunammite to

16 Cf. Ehrlich, *Der Traum im AT,* 151f.
17 → חלם *ḥālam* (*chālam*) I.1; III.2.
18 Ehrlich, *Der Traum im AT,* 13ff.
19 See II.2 above.
20 → קום *qûm.*

life, awakening him after he had been unable to awaken (*qyṣ* [2 K. 4:31]) and had to be considered dead (cf. also 1 K. 17:22; 2 K. 13:21; Mk. 5:21-43; Lk. 7:11-17; Jn. 11:1-44).

The later OT period saw the birth of the hope that Yahweh would vouchsafe his elect a reawakening to full consciousness from the night of death, allowing them to arise again from the dust, the element of nonexistence (Gen. 3:19; Isa. 14:9-19), that they might rise (→ קום *qûm*) and sing for joy, that the dwellers in the dust might awake (*qyṣ*) with rejoicing to new life (Isa. 26:19). The dead will not merely return to life; they will attain the highest goal that the concept of awakening could ever provide in the human context, the eschatological dimension of a life in which those delivered from the night of death awaken (*qyṣ*) to a higher form of everlasting life (Dnl. 12:2).[21]

IV. Divine Subjects.

1. *Gods or Idols.* The concept of awakening can extend beyond the human and earthly realm to the supernatural realm. Even though speaking ironically, in the contest on Mt. Carmel Elijah challenges the prophets of Baʿal to awaken Baʿal from his sleep (*qyṣ* [1 K. 18:27]). The notion that a deity must awaken (cf. 1 S. 5:3 [?])[22] may originate in a ritual intended to waken such a god every morning, if we are not in fact dealing with the resurrection of a dead god. The root *qyṣ* is used similarly of an idol in Hab. 2:19 (par. *ʿwr* III), which speaks of an idol made by human hands that is not alive and therefore cannot awaken. It is simply nonexistent.

2. *Yahweh.* On the basis of these observations, it is surprising that the prayers in the Psalter extend the notion of awakening to Yahweh. The petitioner appeals to Yahweh to awaken (*qyṣ*) and no longer cast off (→ זנח *zānaḥ*) his faithful (Ps. 44:24[23]), not to hide his face but to awaken (*qyṣ*) to defend the cause of the faithful (Ps. 35:23), to awaken (*qyṣ*) to help the petitioner and to punish the wicked (Ps. 59:6[5]). Joyfully the psalmist recounts how Yahweh "awakes (*yqṣ*) as from sleep, as a strong man rises from wine" (Ps. 78:65). It is noteworthy that the first 3 passages use *qyṣ* in parallel with *ʿwr* III, and in the latter it even appears in parallel with the hithpolel of *rnn,* "grow sober."[23] The point is not that Yahweh has been asleep or in a drunken stupor; the image is entirely figurative. The awakening of Yahweh at the behest of his worshippers may be associated with the naive imagery of the language used by the Psalms, which insists that Yahweh awakes to help the faithful while false gods sleep and cannot awake. This appears all the more likely when we note that the author of Ps. 121 (v. 3) rejects the very suggestion that Yahweh might be asleep. At worst, Yahweh may withdraw for a time in silence or even in anger (Ps. 30:6a[5a]; Isa. 54:7f.). The notion of Yahweh's awakening thus expresses the joy

---

21 On the problem of the resurrection of the dead, see F. Nötscher, *Altorientalischer und alttestamentlicher Auferstehungsglaube* (1926; repr. with sup. Darmstadt, 1970); A. T. Nikolainen, *Der Auferstehungsglauben in der Bibel und ihrer Umwelt. AnAcScFen,* B 49/3 (1944); R. Martin-Achard, *From Death to Life* (Eng. trans., Edinburgh, 1960); G. W. E. Nickelsburg, *Resurrection, Immortality, and Eternal Life in Intertestamental Judaism. HThS,* 26 (1972).

22 Oepke, *TDNT,* II, 333; *idem, TDNT,* III, 433, 435.

23 KBL^2, 881b.

occasioned by his help after the oppressive sense of having been forsaken by God. The psalmist can comprehend this situation only in terms of Yahweh's awakening and coming deliberately to his aid. Yahweh is by nature unchanging; only in his relationship to human beings is he capable of change. His refusal to show favor, perceived as rejection, is intended to draw the faithful all the closer to him.

Wallis

יָקַר *yāqar*; יָקָר *yāqār*; יַקִּיר *yaqqîr*; יְקָר *y^e^qār*

Contents: I. Root: 1. Etymology; 2. Occurrences; 3. Meaning. II. General Usage: 1. Material Sense; 2. Abstract Sense. III. Theological Usage.

I. Root.

1. *Etymology.* Although the number of occurrences in the OT is relatively small, *wqr* (*yqr*) represents a common Semitic root. It appears in Ugaritic, Akkadian ("be valuable"), East Canaanite, Arabic ("be dignified" > "honor"), Hebrew, and Middle Hebrew ("be heavy, valuable, honored"). It is found also in later Semitic dialects such as Samaritan, Syriac, Modern Syriac, Aramaic, Palmyrene, Jewish Aramaic ("be heavy, precious" > "honor"), Egyptian Aramaic, Biblical Aramaic, Christian Palestinian Aramaic, Mandaean, and Pahlavi.

2. *Occurrences.* The root appears 73 times in the OT, including 10 passages in the Aramaic sections. The forms in the latter appear also in Hebrew texts. There is reason to accept the frequently proposed theory that the forms in Hebrew contexts are Aramaic loanwords.[1]

The root *yqr* appears as verb (qal and hiphil), adjective, and noun. It is noteworthy that the root does not appear in the entire Pentateuch, Joshua, or Judges, or in the Minor Prophets except for 3 late passages in Zechariah. Neither is it found in the Song of Songs, Ruth, or Nehemiah. Although caution is necessary in interpreting the statistics, it is clear that *yqr* appears more frequently in the later literary strata of the OT, e.g., Wisdom Literature (8 occurrences in Proverbs, 3 in Job, 1 in Ecclesiastes), including some of the 9 occurrences in the Psalms. There are 10 occurrences in Esther and 9 in Daniel. The use of *yqr* can also be found in the Chronicler's history (1 occurrence in Ezra, 2 in 1 Chronicles, 5 in 2 Chronicles). If we add in the occurrence in Lamentations, the majority of occurrences appear in OT documents of the postexilic period. We must also ask whether the passages in which *yqr* appears in the Deuteronomistic history (3 in

---

yāqar. G. Fohrer, "Schmuck," *BHHW,* III (1966), 1706-8; W. Frerichs, "Edelsteine," *BHHW,* I (1962), 362-65; H. Weippert, "Edelstein," *BRL*², 64-66.

1 *KBL*³, 412.

1 Samuel, 1 in 2 Samuel, 7 in 1 Kings, 2 in 2 Kings) are late. The same is true of the occurrences in Isaiah (1), Deutero-Isaiah (1), Jeremiah, and Ezekiel (3 each).

3. *Meaning.* The forms of *yqr* express meanings having to do with value, best rendered by such adjectives as "valuable" or "precious" or the intransitive verbal phrases "be valuable, precious." This notion of value easily leads to nuances reflecting quantity rather than quality, always in the sense of a smaller quantity: "(be) rare, scarce." Quality and limited quantity lead to a further semantic development of the root; when used to describe the value or rareness of a person or object, it can indicate importance, fame, or honor. Hebrew also has an impressive ability to use the root in expressing abstractions: forms of *yqr* may denote "dignity," "honor," "glory," "splendor," and such collective notions as "riches," "wealth," and "value." The verb is used intransitively in the qal to make statements about quality; the causative hiphil provides transitive forms of the verb. Finally, *yqr* can express a subjective personal meaning ("precious" in the sense of "beloved" or "esteemed"), as we might expect from the basic meaning associated with value. This value can describe not only material objects but also abstractions such as wisdom, knowledge, speech, a name, and life.

II. General Usage.

1. *Material Sense.* To define what *yqr* means, we may take its usage in material contexts as our point of departure. After David captures Rabbah of the Ammonites, we are told that he put the heavy golden crown of Milcom on his head (2 S. 12:30); the verse states that its weight was due not only to the quantity of gold it contained but also to an *'eḇen yᵉqārâ,* a precious stone or (interpreting the phrase collectively) precious stones. The Targ., Syr., and Vulg. read here the variant found also in 1 Ch. 20:2, which associates the weight solely with the gold and then adds a phrase about the precious stone(s): *ûḇāh 'eḇen yᵉqārâ,* "and in it was a precious stone." The pre-Deuteronomistic narrative of the Queen of Sheba's visit also speaks of precious stones not further defined (1 K. 10:2,10; 2 Ch. 9:1,9).[2] The gifts given to the host include gold, spices, and *'eḇen yᵉqārâ,* "precious stone(s)," probably to be understood collectively (Lagarde's edition of the LXX adds "much" in 1 K. 10:10). There has been interpolated into this story a comment that Solomon imported gold from Ophir and "almug wood" by sea, trading with King Hiram of Tyre (1 K. 10:11; 2 Ch. 9:10). (The differences in language between 1 Kings and 2 Chronicles together with the discrepancy between these passages and 1 K. 9:26-28 need not be discussed here.) The phrase *'eḇen yᵉqārâ* is clearly attested in both passages.

Precious stones turn up in other contexts also. They appear in Ezekiel's lament over the destruction of Tyre, which includes a passage describing the commercial empire of the island state, listing the trading partners and the goods involved. Ezk. 27:22 states that Tyre imported spices and gold and "all kinds (*kol-*[3]) of precious stones." Ezk. 28:11ff. is

2 See M. Noth, *Könige. BK,* IX/1 (1968), 208.
3 See W. Zimmerli, *Ezekiel 2. Herm* (Eng. trans. 1983), 50.

a complex text based on a lament for the fall of the King of Tyre.[4] In v. 13, the description of his former splendor and majesty mentions the precious stones (*kol-ʾeḇen yᵉqārâ*) set in (or constituting?) his royal robes.[5] Nine gems (carnelian, topaz, jasper, etc.; twelve in the LXX) are named epexegetically (probably secondary).[6] In any case, *ʾeḇen yᵉqārâ* is clearly understood as a collective phrase. The same is true in the Chronicler's list of the treasures and wealth of Hezekiah (2 Ch. 32:27) and Daniel's discourse on the unsuccessful and abominable religious policies of Antiochus IV, who refused to honor a God known even to his fathers by means of (*bᵉ*) gold and silver, precious stones and costly gifts (Dnl. 11:38). The only passage in which *yqr* as an adjective is associated with a single kind of gem is Job 28:16, the poem in praise of wisdom, which describes how inaccessible wisdom is to human efforts. It cannot be gotten through payment of gold of Ophir, *bᵉšōham yāqār,* or sapphire (rare, precious carnelian).[7]

In several other Wisdom texts, *yqr* has become an abstract term for wealth in general, without further specification. In Prov. 1:13, *kol-hôn yāqār* stands in parallel with *šālāl.* The proverb cautions against falling in with the *ḥaṭṭāʾîm,* who by doing evil collect as spoil "all kinds of valuable goods." Ps. 49 is a Wisdom psalm on the transitoriness of life. Verse 21(Eng. v. 20) (cf. v. 13[12]) states: *ʾāḏām bîqār wᵉlōʾ yāḇîn nimšal kabbᵉhēmôṯ niḏmû,* "A mortal in his wealth does not realize that he is like the beasts that perish." Here *yᵉqār* alone means "wealth" or "possessions." The notion can also have overtones of "splendor" or "glory."[8] Job 28:10, finally, uses *kol-yᵉqār,* "all kinds of precious things," in the sense of valuable minerals:[9] the miner sees them as he tunnels, but he cannot find wisdom. The same usage of *yᵉqār* appears in 2 judgment oracles, Jer. 20:5; Ezk. 22:25. According to Jeremiah, Yahweh will surrender to the Babylonians as spoil *kol-yᵉqārâ* (the suf. refers to Jerusalem), the treasures (*ʾôṣᵉrôṯ*) of the kings of Judah, the city's gains (*yᵉgîʿāh*) and wealth (*ḥōsen*). Here the parallel terms qualified by *yᵉqār* may refer to art objects or luxury items. Ezekiel names *yᵉqār* in a list of indictments in which he castigates the greed of the Jerusalem upper class (the MT reads "prophets," but exegetes usually prefer the LXX reading "princes"), who like roaring and rending lions devour *nepeš, ḥōsen,* and *yᵉqār.* The phrase *ḥōsen wîqār* has the ring of an idiom meaning "property and possessions."[10]

In conjunction with Solomon's building program (temple and palace), *ʾᵃḇānîm yᵉqārôṯ* are mentioned along with other *ʾᵃḇānîm.* In 1 K. 5:31(17), the account of preparations for building the temple, including quarrying and dressing building stones, *ʾᵃḇānîm gᵉḏōlôṯ ʾᵃḇānîm yᵉqārôṯ* ("great stones, costly stones") are to be quarried, that the

---

4 For a detailed discussion of the traditio-historical problems posed by this passage, see *ibid.,* 87ff.

5 On the interpretation of the obscure *mᵉsuḵāṯeḵā,* see *ibid.,* 82, 92.

6 For a discussion of this passage and its possible association with the breastplate of the high priest, see *ibid.,* 82-85.

7 See *KBL*³; cf. G. Fohrer, *Das Buch Hiob. KAT,* XVI (1963), 389ff.

8 See H.-J. Kraus, *Psalms 1–59* (Eng. trans., Minneapolis, 1988), 479.

9 Cf. Fohrer, 393f., 397.

10 For a different interpretation, see W. Zimmerli, *Ezekiel 1. Herm* (Eng. trans. 1979), *in loc.*: "possessions and treasures."

foundations of the house may be laid with dressed stones (*ʾaḇnê gāzîṯ*). Since rock in Palestine varies in quality, the statement is meant to indicate that the stones to be dressed for the foundation had to be solid and unusually large.[11] Here *yqr* takes on the meaning "suitable." Various sorts of building stone are also mentioned in the description of how specific portions of the palace complex were built. According to 1 K. 7:9-11, it appears that the *ʾᵃḇānîm yᵉqārôṯ* were dressed stones, sawed (*mᵉḡōrārôṯ bammᵉḡērâ*) on at least two faces (*mibbayiṯ ûmiḥûṣ*) (v. 9), that were laid from the foundation.[12] Unfortunately the text is not clear as to how far they were laid. Verse 10 goes on to speak of *ʾᵃḇānîm yᵉqārôṯ* in apposition with *ʾᵃḇānîm gᵉḏōlôṯ* and gives some dimensions: stones of ten and eight cubits (*ʾaḇnê ʿeśer ʾammôṯ wᵉʾaḇnê šᵉmōneh ʾammôṯ*). The verse adds that these were laid as a foundation. Finally, v. 11 gives more detail about the *ʾᵃḇānîm yᵉqārôṯ* by describing them as "hewn according to measurement" (*kᵉmiddôṯ gāzîṯ*). Verse 12, however, like v. 9, states that they were laid in the courses of the wall above the foundation. The phrase *ʾᵃḇānîm yᵉqārôṯ* must therefore refer to large, solid stones suitable for dressing, which could be used either as foundation stones or in other exposed portions of a temple or palace.

The later parallel account in 2 Ch. 3:6 adds yet another variant: the floor, of which 1 Kings gives no details, becomes an ornament (*lᵉṯip̄ʾereṯ*) overlaid (*wayᵉṣap̄*) with *ʾeḇen yᵉqārâ*. Some scholars have identified this as a mosaic,[13] but this theory is not totally convincing. Carefully dressed flagstones are also a possibility.

Also obscure is the statement in 1 Ch. 29:2, in the description of David's preparation for Solomon's building of the temple. These included David's personal contribution of "precious" materials, the description of which is meant to appeal to the generosity of the people. The list includes gold for the things of gold, silver for the things of silver, bronze, iron, wood, and a series of individually named stones, including *kol ʾeḇen yᵉqārâ*. Since carnelian, malachite, marble, and colored stones are mentioned, *ʾeḇen yᵉqārâ* might likewise mean "precious stone." On the other hand, the list also includes expressions that have been interpreted (e.g., by Rudolph[14]) as meaning "filling stones" (*millûʾîm*) and "hard mortar" (*ʾaḇnê-pûḵ wᵉriqmâ*).[15] Whatever its specific meaning may be, the term appears once more to be a collective, this time referring to "precious building materials." There is little to recommend the theory that this statement refers to a plan to finance the building of the temple through contributions of precious metals and stones.

2. *Abstract Sense.* The occurrences in wisdom aphorisms are instructive for our understanding of *yqr* in an abstract sense. Prov. 3:15 praises wisdom (*ḥoḵmâ,* par. *tᵉḇûnâ*) as more precious than jewels (*yᵉqārâ hîʾ mippᵉnînîm* [*Q*]) and incomparably superior to

---

11 See Noth, 93f.

12 On the whole question, see *ibid.,* 130ff.; A. Kuschke, "Tempel," *BRL*², 338-340; C. Watzinger, *Denkmäler Palästinas,* I (Leipzig, 1933), ch. IV.

13 K. Galling, *Die Bücher der Chronik. ATD,* XII (1959), 84; W. Rudolph, *Chronikbücher. HAT,* XXI (1955), 202f.

14 *Ibid.,* 190.

15 Galling, *ATD,* XII, 69: "enclosure stone, malachite stones, and colored stones."

any treasure (see above on Job 28:16). Its value is defined by the context: wisdom brings riches, honor, long life—in short, *šālôm* (Prov. 3:17). The same point is made with somewhat different words in Prov. 20:15, which may possibly be preexilic: "lips of knowledge" (*śipṯê-ḏāʿaṯ*, i.e., intelligent discourse) are here called "a valuable tool" (*keli yeqār*, usually meaning "a precious ornament"), preferable to gold or an abundance of costly stones. The material profit of wisdom (*daʿaṯ*, par. *ḥoḵmâ* and *teḇûnâ*) is extolled in Prov. 24:4; through (*be*) it, treasuries are filled with precious and pleasant riches (*kol-hôn yāqār wenāʿîm*; cf. also v. 3). Probably Eccl. 10:1 (together with its context) means much the same thing, while developing further the idea of wisdom's value by reflecting on how quickly it can be brought to nought. In this aphorism, *yqr* must be translated "outweigh": "a little folly outweighs wisdom and honor" (*yāqār mēḥoḵmâ mikkāḇôḏ siḵlûṯ meʿaṭ*).[16] The reading of the LXX, which says the exact opposite, can hardly be original.

The aphorisms dealing with practical wisdom contain other examples in which types of conduct and situations are weighed against each other, followed by appropriate warnings or advice. Prov. 12:27 states that human diligence is more profitable than sloth, which does not pay off (*wehôn-ʾāḏām yāqār ḥārûṣ*, which should probably be transposed on the basis of the LXX and Syr.: *wehôn yāqār* [*le*]*ʾāḏām ḥārûṣ*, "and diligence is a precious possession for a person"). A reticent person who curbs his speech, referred to as *yeqar-rûaḥ*, is extolled as a man of understanding (*ʾîš teḇûnâ* [Prov. 17:27; *weqar* (*K*), *yeqar* (*Q*)]) by the previous clause: "a cool spirit." In these instructions we find the hiphil of *yaqar* used in the sense "cause to be rare": "Let your foot be seldom in your neighbor's house, lest he become weary of you and hate you" (Prov. 25:17). It is prudent not to risk friendship through importunity.

Forms of *yqr* can also be used in isolation to convey abstract concepts. This is frequently the case in such late books as Esther and Daniel. The concept of "honor" or "recognition" plays an important role in Est. 6:1-13, the account of how Haman, Mordecai's enemy, is forced by the Persian king to reward Mordecai (vv. 3,6 [twice],7,9 [twice],11). The technical term is *ʿaśôṯ yeqār le*. The expression "be pleased to honor someone" is *ḥāpēṣ bîqārô*, with the suffix representing an objective genitive. The context (vv. 7-9, 11) makes it clear how the narrator envisions this recognition: public recognition of the person honored arrayed in royal robes, mounted on a royal horse, crowned with a diadem and made the subject of a formal proclamation, waited on personally by the nobility—in effect, made second only to the king. The parallel term in v. 3 is *geḏûlâ*.[17] The restoration of the Jews to social respectability in the Persian Empire, accomplished by Mordecai and Esther, is interpreted as "honor" (*yeqār*, listed with light, gladness, and joy [Est. 8:16]).[18] The reason given for the rejection of Vashti for her disobedience is not far different in substance. Her punishment is to be exemplary, warning against dis-

---

16 See W. Zimmerli, *Prediger. ATD*, XVI/1 (²1962), 229f.; H. W. Hertzberg, *Der Prediger. KAT*, XVII/4 (1963), 187f.

17 See H. Ringgren, *Das Buch Esther. ATD*, XVI/2 (²1962), 392ff.; H. Bardtke, *Esther. KAT*, XVII/5 (1963), 342ff.

18 Bardtke, 372f.

obedience and inculcating the honor all the women in the empire should show their spouses (*wekol-hannāšîm yittenû yeqār lebaʿalêhen* [Est. 1:20]). Here *yeqār* has the meaning "honor, obedience." In Est. 1:4 *yeqār* is ambiguous. In order to paint a vivid picture of the wealth, glory, and splendor displayed at Ahasuerus' banquet, the narrator uses terminology that is both concrete and abstract: *behar'ōṯô 'eṯ-ʿōšer kebôḏ malkûṯô we'eṯ-yeqār tip'ereṯ geḏûllāṯô.* The construct phrases have both concrete and abstract sense: "the riches of the glory of his kingship and the splendor of the pomp of his majesty." Ideal values are based on material values (cf. Est. 1:6ff.).[19]

Aram. *yeqār* in Daniel has the same meaning as in Est. 6. In addition to material reward, success in interpreting the king's dream brings the interpreter "great honor" (*yeqār śaggî'* [Dnl. 2:6]). In Daniel's interpretation we find a ceremonious official form of address to Nebuchadnezzar, framed in general terms, calling him the king of kings, to whom the God of heaven has given the kingdom, the power, the might, and the "glory" (Dnl. 2:37, repeated almost verbatim in 5:18). In Dnl. 4:27(30), Nebuchadnezzar praises his own deeds, saying that he has done everything for the glory of his majesty (*lîqār haḏrî*). In the same context, the reader learns of Nebuchadnezzar's temporary loss of his kingship and his restoration (Dnl. 3:31–4:34[4:1-37]); in addition to his health, his majesty and splendor for the glory or honor of his kingdom (*lîqār malkûṯî haḏrî weziwî*) are returned to him (4:33[36]). Chapter 5 refers to this story. Verse 20 tells how, as punishment for his pride, Nebuchadnezzar was deprived of the "throne of his kingship *wîqārâ*" (probably also with a suf.; cf. the LXX and the apparatus of *BHK*[3]: *wîqārēh*), i.e., "and his honor (or 'dignity')." Finally, *yeqār* plays the same role in the vision of the son of man (Dnl. 7:14), to whom are given dominion and glory and kingdom. In all the passages in Daniel, *yqr* serves to predicate majesty and exalted status of a person.[20]

Ezr. 4:10 (likewise Aramaic) can be ranked alongside these Daniel passages. According to Galling,[21] the phrase about the "great and noble" (*rabbā' weyaqqîrā'*) Ashurbanipal comes from the Aramaic chronicle of Jerusalem (Ezr. 4:8–6:18).

Of course there are earlier examples illustrating the abstract meaning of *yqr* itself or of terms modified by a form of this root. In Jer. 15:19, a renewal of Jeremiah's call within one of his confessions, he is told that he is to utter only what is "good" or "precious" (in contrast to what is "worthless" [*mizzôlēl*]). Exegetes commonly interpret this passage as a rebuke to Jeremiah on the part of Yahweh. The root *yqr* must then be taken as the opposite of *zôlēl.* In the final analysis, to reproach God and accuse him of injustice is sinful; the appropriate response is to repent, to confess and praise God.[22]

In this context we may cite the "preciousness" of God's word, which has become "rare" (1 S. 3:1), or, in the account of Saul's failures and David's successes, the value of the name of David (1 S. 18:30), which is highly esteemed (*wayyîqar šemô me'ōḏ*). Life

19 Ringgren, 377ff.; Bardtke, 275ff.

20 O. Plöger, *Das Buch Daniel. KAT,* XVIII (1965), 112; A. Bentzen, *Daniel. HAT,* XIX ([2]1952), 62f.

21 *ATD,* XII, 199f.

22 See A. Weiser, *Das Buch Jeremia 1–25,14. ATD,* XX ([6]1969), 134f.; K. Rudolph, *Jeremia. HAT,* XII ([3]1968), 109.

can also be described as precious (*nep̱eš* + adj. or verb from *yqr*), for example in Prov. 6:26, a warning against the adulteress who stalks a man's "precious life" (*nep̱eš y^eqārâ tāṣûḏ*). But the same usage appears already in the traditions of Saul and David just mentioned: after David spares Saul, Saul says to him, "My life has become precious in your eyes this day" (*yāq^erâ nap̱šî b^eʿêneyḵā hayyôm hazzeh*), i.e., "You have spared me this day" (1 S. 26:21). Sparing life is also involved in the plea of Ahaziah's third emissary to Elijah that he not lose his life through Yahweh's punishment like the two before him (2 K. 1:13f.). In v. 13, the captain pleads: *tîqar-nāʾ nap̱šî w^enep̱eš ʿ^aḇāḏeyḵā ʾēlleh ḥ^amiššîm b^eʿêneyḵā.* A similar but shorter variant appears in v. 14. The phrase "let life be precious in the eyes of someone" appears to be a technical term meaning "spare." A parallel expression is found in Ps. 72:14, a preexilic royal psalm: *w^eyêqar dāmām b^eʿênāyw,* "and precious is their blood [i.e., that of the poor and needy] in his sight." The social obligations of the king include providing help and justice for the forsaken and powerless. If Ps. 45:10(9) is not corrupt, *yqr* here even has the meaning "beloved," and has to be interpreted as referring to persons: "daughters of kings are among your beloved (*b^eyiqq^erôṯeyḵā*)." The verse, however, is usually emended.[23] Finally, steadfast love (*ḥeseḏ* [Ps. 36:8(7)]) and thoughts (*rēʿîm* [Ps. 139:17]) can be precious, although this usage, like the "rare" word in 1 S. 3:1, refers to the words, thoughts, and steadfast love of God. It is easy to see that the abstract usage of the root is especially appropriate for expressing theological ideas.

We shall mention in passing Job 31:26; Dnl. 2:11, where the adj. *yāqār,* used abstractly, functions as an adverb (Job) or predicate noun (Daniel). Job extols the shining course of the sun and the splendid path of the moon (*w^eyārēaḥ yāqār hōlēḵ,* "the moon moving in splendor"). The Daniel passage uses *yaqqîr* (Aramaic) in the sense of "weighty," hence "difficult." The interpretation of the dream demanded by the Babylonian king is a difficult matter (cf. 1 S. 3:1, where *yāqār* is also used as a predicate noun for the word of God that has become rare [*hāyâ yāqār*]). It is possible that *yqr* (used as a verb) may also mean "be difficult" in Ps. 139:17 (see III below).

III. Theological Usage. The theological usage of *yqr* is incomparably less frequent than its general usage. Obviously the judgment oracles in Jeremiah and Ezekiel are theologically relevant, in that they bear witness to Yahweh as having the ultimate disposition over wealth and possessions. In order to punish his people, he can give it to Israel's enemies, the Babylonians (Jer. 20:5). But it is also Yahweh who watches over the honest or dishonest acquisition of riches, avenging the violation of the traditional rule of social justice brought about by privilege, oppression, and exploitation (Ezk. 22:25). The Israelites certainly thought that ultimate wisdom and knowledge—for which nothing can substitute, no matter what its value—are ultimately a gift of God, who alone can show the way to them (Job 28:16,23). And Dnl. 2:27; 5:18; 7:14 state explicitly that dignity and honor are bestowed by God. In this broader sense, many of the passages already discussed have direct or indirect theological implications. But there are also a

23 See Kraus, 451f.

few noteworthy passages in which a form of *yqr* refers directly to God. The most significant examples of this usage occur in (relatively late) oracles of salvation, for example the rhetorical question in Jer. 31:20: *h^abēn yaqqîr lî ʾeprayim,* "Is Ephraim (not) my dear son?"[24] Here *yaqqîr* serves to express Israel's faith in divine election, reconfirmed through the declaration of salvation. The verse proclaims Yahweh's love and favor toward his people despite all the catastrophes of historical judgment. The same note is struck, perhaps even a bit more strongly, by Deutero-Isaiah in Isa. 43:4 (cf. vv. 1-7). In the context of a 1st person divine oracle, we find in parallel to *yāqartā b^eʿênay* the clause *nikbadtā waʾ^anî ʾ^ahabtîkā,* "You are precious in my eyes, and honored, and I love you." Here the predication of value in the figurative sense is strongly underlined by the statement that Yahweh will give peoples as ransom (*kōper*) for his people, nations in return for (*taḥat*) Israel and kingdoms for the life (*nepeš*) of God's people. What is possible for Yahweh on behalf of the people as well as on behalf of an individual is not possible for mortals, no matter how rich they may be: *w^eyēqar pidyôn napšô* [following the apparatus] *w^eḥādal l^eʿôlām,* "For the ransom of his life is costly [const. phrase used as an objective gen.], and can never suffice" (Ps. 49:9[8]). Lam. 4:2 bewails the reversal of Israel's election: *b^enê ṣiyyôn hay^eqārîm ham^esullāʾîm bappāz,* "the sons [inhabitants] of Zion, the precious ones worth their weight in fine gold, must now be reckoned as earthen pots." Even in this lament, the idea of election lives on in the image of the precious personal relationship between God and God's people.

The idea is somewhat obscure in a postexilic individual thanksgiving (Ps. 116:15; v. 10 probably begins a new psalm; cf. LXX), which states that the death of those who are devoted to Yahweh is precious in his eyes. The basic meaning is clear from the context: Yahweh loves and protects the *ḥāsîd*. The specific point, however, must be revealed by a kind of "detour." The loss occasioned by death is "costly" to Yahweh, so that he does everything he can to avert it. Indeed, death is *too* costly in Yahweh's eyes,[25] and that is what gives the devout a chance to live. On the other hand, the "wicked" (*r^ešāʿîm*) and the "enemies of Yahweh" (*ʾôy^ebê YHWH*) perish *kîqar kārîm,* "like the glory [or: 'wealth'] of the pastures" that wither (Ps. 37:20; cf. 49:13,21[12,20]). According to this late Wisdom psalm, human beings are a capital resource, like a fertile pasture. But wickedness and hostility to God are like the blazing heat that scorches what is green, until finally everything goes up in smoke (see the apparatus of *BHS* for the variant reading of the LXX). A similar idea appears in a proclamation of judgment in the oracles against Babylon of Isa. 13f. Speaking in the 1st person, Yahweh declares in Isa. 13:12 that he "will make men more rare than fine gold, and mankind than the gold of Ophir" (*ʾôqîr ʾ^enôš mippāz w^eʾādām mikketem ʾôpîr*). The context shows that the judgment consists in an historical catastrophe that will decimate the population (most scholars assign the oracle to the middle of the 6th century B.C.). The hiphil of *yāqar* is used to express judgment, in the sense that when judgment comes anyone who survives will be a precious rarity.

---

24 K. Rudolph, *HAT,* XII, 196f.; A. Weiser, *Das Buch Jeremia 25,15–52,34. ATD,* XXI ([6]1969), 281; S. Herrmann, *Die prophetischen Heilserwartungen im AT. BWANT,* 85[5/5] (1965), *passim.*

25 R. Kittel, *Die Psalmen. KAT,* XIII ([3-4]1922; ed. E. Sellin).

In discussing the theological use of *yqr,* we must also mention the forms of expression or conduct associated with God that are termed "precious" or "rare."[26] An example is 1 S. 3, the account of Samuel's experience of nocturnal revelation in the temple at Shiloh, which is introduced (v. 1) by the statement that in those days the *d^e^bar-YHWH* was precious or rare (*yāqār*) and there was no frequent "vision." Here *yāqār* already has the specific meaning "rare" in a quantitative sense. A different meaning is conveyed by the motif of confidence in Ps. 36:8(7), a psalm of mixed genre,[27] which speaks of the preciousness of God's steadfast love, in the sense that men and women enjoy the blessing of God's favor. We must also cite Ps. 139, an impressive postexilic individual Wisdom psalm. The psalmist, meditating on God's omnipotence and omnipresence, speaks of God's thoughts in a tone of resignation or admiration: *mah-yāq^e^rû rēʿeyḵā ʾēl,* "How precious ['valuable,' or possibly 'weighty, difficult'] are your thoughts, O God!" (Ps. 139:17). Since the parallel stich makes a quantitative statement (*meh ʿāṣ^e^mû rāʾšêhem,* "How vast they are in number!"), the first stich could easily be making a qualitative statement (cf. Ps. 92:6[5]). In any case, the root *yqr* suggests that the subject of discussion is great, profound, and unfathomable.[28]

Finally, we must discuss 2 difficult passages in Zechariah (Zec. 11:13[twice]; 14:6). The text of the latter is uncertain, and is usually emended on the basis of the versions,[29] since the MT does not yield an intelligible sense. The former occurs in the context of an allegory[30] or a symbolic narrative that remains a mere literary form and shades off into allegory.[31] Yahweh is made to state ironically how worthless his people and their leaders esteem him: "Cast it [the 30 shekels of silver in wages mentioned in Zec. 11:12] before the craftsman, the precious price[32] at which I was valued by them" (*ʾeder hayy^e^qār ʾ^a^šer yāqartî mēʿ^a^lêhem*). This passage can be interpreted as the motivation for a declaration of disaster. The passage is interesting because it applies the human concept of value directly to Yahweh, expressing *e contrario* the theological point that Yahweh expects that his people will value him highly. It is possible, as Elliger suggests,[33] that the whole of Zec. 11:4-16(17) (linked by many with 13:7-9) deals intellectually with the Samaritan schism from the theological perspective of the worshippers of Yahweh in Jerusalem. In any case, the text is traditio-historically quite complex.[34]

Wagner

---

26 See II.2 above.

27 G. Fohrer, *Intro. OT* (Eng. trans., Nashville, 1968); cf. Kraus, 397, 399.

28 See S. Wagner, "Zur Theologie des Psalms CXXXIX," *Congress Volume, Göttingen 1977. SVT,* 29 (1978), 357ff.

29 Cf. *BHS.*

30 F. Horst, *Die zwölf kleinen Propheten: Nahum bis Maleachi. HAT,* XIV (^{3}1964), 251ff.

31 K. Elliger, *Das Buch der zwölf kleinen Propheten,* II. *ATD,* XXV (^{7}1975), 160ff.

32 *KBL*^{3}.

33 P. 163.

34 See Horst, 253f.

יָקַשׁ yāqaš; יָקוֹשׁ yāqôš; מוֹקֵשׁ môqēš

Contents: I. 1. Etymology; 2. Occurrences; 3. Semantic Field and Meaning; 4. LXX. II. Usage.

I. 1. *Etymology.* The etymology of *yqš* is disputed. Kopf[1] connects it with Arab. *wṯq* (noun: *wiṯāq,* "fetter"; verb (IV): "enfetter"), but this is unlikely in view of Ugar. *yqšm* found 3 times in lists, which probably means "fowler."[2] *KBL*[3] cites Arab. *waqaš,* which would require *ś* in Hebrew.

2. *Occurrences.* The verb appears 3 times in the qal, 4 times in the niphal, and once in the pual (*yûqāšîm* [Eccl. 9:12], possibly a ptcp. without *m*ᵉ-). The agent noun *yāqôš* or *yāqûš* occurs 4 times; the noun *môqēš,* usually translated "snare," occurs 27 times (and once in Sirach).

3. *Semantic Field and Meaning.* The verb often appears together with *nilkād* (→ לכד *lkd*) (Prov. 6:2; Isa. 8:15; 28:13 [both verbs in the niphal]; Jer. 50:24 [qal of *yqš,* niphal of *lkd*]; Am. 3:5). Eccl. 9:12 conjoins *yûqāšîm, ʾāḥûz,* and *neʾeḥāz.* Semantically related verbs found in the context of *yqš* include *māṣāʾ* and *tāpaś* (Jer. 50:24), *kšl, npl,* and the niphal of *šbr* (Isa. 8:15; 28:13).

There is no consensus as to the precise meaning of *môqēš.* It often appears in conjunction with *paḥ,* "trap" (Josh. 23:13; Ps. 69:23[Eng. v. 22]; 140:6[5]; 141:9; Isa. 8:14; Am. 3:5), without any clear semantic distinction. The noun *paḥ* is also used frequently with the verb *yqš*: *paḥ yāqᵉšû lî* (Ps. 141:9); *paḥ yōqᵉšîm* (Ps. 124:7); cf. also *paḥ yāqôš* (Hos. 9:8; Ps. 91:3). Eccl. 9:12 is also related, but more distantly. It is clear from Ps. 124:7; Prov. 6:5; Am. 3:5 that the context involves fowling. Marti[3] and Driver[4] suggest the meaning "boomerang"; Vogt prefers "bait." According to Gerleman, *paḥ* is a snare that is tripped automatically, whereas *môqēš* is a larger net that is closed by cords (cf. the possible allusion in Jer. 5:26). A different meaning is found in Job 40:24, where *môqēš* refers to a hook through the nose of Behemoth (or Leviathan?[5]). Possibly Ehrlich's reading *qimmōšîm,* "thorns,"[6] is correct here.

---

yāqaš. G. Dalman, *AuS,* VI (1939), 336f.; G. R. Driver, "Reflections on Recent Articles," *JBL,* 73 (1954), 125-136, esp. 131-36: "Heb. MÔQĒŠ, 'Striker' "; H. S. Gehman, "Notes on מוקש," *JBL,* 58 (1939), 277-281; G. Gerleman, "Contributions to the OT Terminology of the Chase," *Bulletin de la Société Royale des Lettres de Lund,* 1945-46, 79-90; E. Vogt, " 'Ihr Tisch werde zur Falle' (Ps 69,23)," *Bibl,* 43 (1962), 79-82.

1 L. Kopf, "Arabische Etymologien und Parallelen zum Bibelwörterbuch," *VT,* 8 (1958), 178 (= *Studies in Arabic and Hebrew Lexicography* [Jerusalem, 1976]).

2 M. Dahood, *Psalms III. AB,* XVII A (1970), 213, discussing Ps. 124.

3 K. Marti, *Das Dodekapropheton erklärt. KHC,* XIII (1904), 174.

4 G. R. Driver, "Linguistic and Textual Problems: Minor Prophets. II," *JTS,* 39 (1938), 262.

5 M. H. Pope, *Job. AB,* XV (^{3}1979), 328.

6 A. Ehrlich, *Randglossen zur hebräischen Bibel* (repr. Hildesheim, 1968), *in loc.*

4. *LXX.* The LXX uses a variety of translations: *thēreúō* (Ps. 124:7[LXX 123:7]), *pagideúō* (Eccl. 9:12; cf. *pagís* in Prov. 6:2); *epitíthēmi* (Jer. 50:24[LXX 27:24]); *synístēmi* (Ps. 141:9[LXX 140:9]); *ptaíō* (Dt. 7:25); *engízō* (Isa. 8:15); untranslated in Isa. 28:13. The commonest translations of *môqēš* are *skándalon* and *pagís;* other renderings include *skṓlon* (Ex. 10:7; Dt. 7:16), *próskomma* (Ex. 23:33; 34:12), *ixeutós* (Am. 3:5), *sklērótēs* (2 S. 22:6; cf. *pagís* in Ps. 18:6[5][LXX 17:6]), etc.

II. Usage. Both the verb and the noun are almost always used figuratively. Jer. 50:24 describes a sudden and unexpected enemy attack: "I [Yahweh] set a snare (*yāqaštî*) for you, O Babylon, and you were taken (*nilkaḏt*) although you did not know it; you were found (*mṣ'* niphal) and caught (*tpś* niphal)." According to Isa. 8:14, Yahweh will become to the inhabitants of Jerusalem "a trap (*paḥ*) and a snare (*môqēš*)"; they shall "stumble (*kšl*) and fall (*npl*) and be broken (*šbr* niphal); they shall be snared (*yqš* niphal) and taken (*lkd* niphal)" (v. 15). Isa. 28:13 warns that those who despise the prophets will be struck by Yahweh's word, so that they will "fall backward, and be broken, and snared, and taken."

Hos. 9:8 uses the phrase *paḥ yāqôš,* "fowler's snare," for Ephraim's attacks on the prophets. Jer. 5:26 speaks of the wicked (*rᵉšāʿîm*) among the people, who "set snares to destroy (*šḥt* hiphil) and to catch (*lkd*) people." In Ps. 141, a lament, the psalmist prays for Yahweh's protection from the traps (*paḥ*) that have been laid (*yqš*) and from the snares (*mōqᵉšîm*) of evildoers (*pōʿᵃlê ʾāwen*) (v. 9). In Ps. 124, a thanksgiving psalm, the psalmist thanks Yahweh for delivering him and his companions from the snare (*paḥ*) of the fowler: "the snare is broken (*šbr* niphal), and we have escaped (*mlṭ*)!" (v. 7). Ps. 64:6(5) speaks in general terms of enemies who lay snares; they are not further characterized, but the context speaks of their cunning and secrecy. In Ps. 140:6(5), the enemies are arrogant men (*gēʾîm*) who set *paḥ, rešet* ("net"), and *môqᵉšîm.* Ps. 91:3 includes *paḥ yāqûš* among the perils from which God delivers the faithful.

Dt. 7:25 contains a warning against the gods of the heathen, on the grounds that the Israelites might covet the silver and gold of the idols and be ensnared (*yqš* niphal) by them. In a similar vein, several passages state that idols can become a *môqēš* (Ex. 23:33; 34:12; Dt. 7:16; Josh. 23:13 [*paḥ* and *môqēš*]; Jgs. 2:3; 8:27; also Ps. 106:36, in the historical retrospect). This usage expresses the perilous temptation of idolatry. In Job 34:30, Elihu states that God will prevent a godless (*ḥānēp*) man from reigning as king and becoming *môqᵉšîm* to the people. According to Prov. 22:25, the company of an angry man can become a snare to others; his ways should therefore be shunned.

One can also speak of the *môqᵉšîm* of death. Ps. 18:6(5) (par. 2 S. 22:6) uses "the cords (*ḥbl*) of Sheol" as a parallel expression for the disaster from which the psalmist has been saved. One can avoid the *môqᵉšîm* of death through wisdom (Prov. 13:14) or the fear of God (14:27) and thus live a happy life.

Foolish speech can also be called a snare (Prov. 12:13 [possibly reading *nôqaš*]; 18:7 [par. *mᵉḥittâ,* "ruin"; cf. also 6:2: "you are snared in the utterance of your lips"), as can the transgression of an evil man (29:6), the fear of man (29:25, in contrast to the safety that comes through trust in Yahweh), and a rash oath (20:25).

In Ex. 10:7, the servants of Pharaoh ask, "How long shall this man [Moses; or: 'this thing,' the problem of the Israelites] be a *môqēš* to us?" The translation "snare" is not quite right; possibly one should use some general term like "ruin" or "danger." When Saul suggests that Michal will be a *môqēš* to David (1 S. 18:21), the proposed translation "bait" deserves serious consideration; but here, too, the meaning is probably "snare."

The text of Ps. 69:23(22) may be corrupt. The psalmist prays that the table of his enemies may be a *paḥ* to them; in the parallel stich we find *wᵉlišlômîm lᵉmôqēš,* which does not make sense. Most scholars follow the Targ., reading *wᵉšalmêhem,* "their sacrificial feasts." This would mean that Yahweh is to judge the psalmist's enemies at their sacrifices, so that what gives them security may be transformed into ruin.

In Am. 3:3ff., the prophet's discourse employs a series of images, all of which express the idea that nothing happens without a cause. Among them is the double question: "Does a bird fall to earth when there is no trap (*môqēš*) for it? Does a snare spring up from the ground when it has taken (*lkd*) nothing?" (v. 5).

Eccl. 9:12 describes humans thus: "like fish which are taken (*'ḥz* hiphil) in an evil net (*mᵉṣôḏâ*), and like birds which are caught (*'ḥz* qal pass. ptcp.) in a snare (*paḥ*), so are human beings snared (*yûqāšîm*) at an evil time, when it suddenly falls upon them."

Finally, Sir. 32/35:20 describes transgression of the law as a snare: "Do not go by a way with snares; avoid the danger and remain faithful to the law."

Ringgren

יָרֵא *yārē'*; יָרֵא *yārē'*; יִרְאָה *yir'â*; מוֹרָא *môrā'*

Contents: I. 1. Etymology; 2. Occurrences; 3. Semantic Field; 4. Contexts and Idioms; 5. LXX. II. Fear in Everyday Life. III. Fear of God: 1. General; 2. Egypt; 3. Mesopotamia; 4. Ugarit. IV. Fear of God as Fear of the Numinous: 1. Holy and Terrible; 2. Yahweh's Presence; 3. Yahweh's Intervention in History and the Natural Realm; 4. Divine Panic; 5. Fear and Joy. V. "Fear Not": 1. Everyday Life; 2. Holy War; 3. Oracles of Salvation; 4. Theophanies. VI. Loyalty to the God of the Covenant: 1. Deuteronom(ist)ic Literature; 2. Psalms; 3. Other Texts. VII. Fear of God as Moral Response: 1. Northern Prophecy; 2. Elohist; 3. Wisdom; 4. Fear of God as Obedience. VIII. Fear of God as Devotion to Torah. IX. Qumran.

---

yārē'. K. Arayaprateep, "A Note on *YR'* in Jos. IV 24," *VT,* 22 (1972), 240-42; K. Baltzer, *The Covenant Formulary in OT, Jewish, and Early Christian Writings* (Eng. trans., Philadelphia, 1971); B. J. Bamberger, "Fear and Love of God in the OT," *HUCA,* 6 (1929), 39-53; E. G. Bauckmann, "Die Proverbien und die Sprüche Jesus Sirach: Eine Untersuchung zum Strukturwandel der israelitischen Weisheitslehre," *ZAW,* 72 (1960), 33-63; J. Becker, *Gottesfurcht im AT. AnBibl,* 25 (1965); *idem,* review of L. Derousseaux, *La crainte de Dieu dans l'AT, Bibl,* 53 (1972), 280-87; P. Biard, *La puissance de Dieu. Travaux de l'Institut catholique de Paris,* 7 (1960); E. Boularand, "Crainte," *DS,* II (1949), 2463-2511; H. A. Brongers, "La crainte du Seigneur (*Jir'at Jhwh, Jir'at 'Elohim*)," *OTS,* 5 (1948), 151-173; C. J. de Catanzaro, "Fear, Knowledge, and Love: A Study in OT Piety," *CJT,* 9 (1963), 166-173; H. Cazelles, "A propos

I. 1. *Etymology.* The etymology of *yrʾ* is still unclear. Růžička[1] derives it from a root *rʿ* with the fundamental meaning "tremble." Oosterhoff[2] agrees, citing Arab. *wariha,* "be short of breath," Aram. *rêʾâ,* "lung," and Heb. *rāʾâ,* "see." Becker[3] sees a connection with *yāraʿ,* "tremble" (Isa. 15:4), and suggests that the verb has this original meaning in Ps. 76:9(Eng. v. 8). Finally, Joüon[4] cites Arab. *waʾara,* "terrify." The use of Arabic parallels, however, is highly suspect. The verb *waʾara* is probably a variant of *waraʾa,* meaning "push (back), strike";[5] cf. Ethiop. *warawa,*[6] as well as Amhar. *wäräwwärä,* Tigr. *wärwära,* and *wärā,* "strike, threaten, proclaim,"[7] and Amhar.

---

d'une phrase de H. H. Rowley," *Wisdom in Israel and in the Ancient Near East. Festschrift H. H. Rowley. SVT,* 3 (1955), 26-32; D. J. A. Clines, "The Tree of Knowledge and the Law of Yahweh (Psalm XIX)," *VT,* 24 (1974), 8-14; L. Derousseaux, *La crainte de Dieu dans l'AT. LD,* 63 (1970); S. J. De Vries, "Note Concerning the Fear of God in the Qumran Scrolls," *RevQ,* 5 (1964-66), 233-37; P.-E. [H. M.] Dion, "The 'Fear Not' Formula and Holy War," *CBQ,* 32 (1970), 565-570; F. Dreyfus, review of L. Derousseaux, *La crainte de Dieu dans l'AT, RB,* 80 (1973), 449-452; J. H. Eaton, "Some Misunderstood Hebrew Words for God's Self-Revelation," *BT,* 25 (1974), 331-38; W. Eichrodt, *Theology of the OT,* I. *OTL* (Eng. trans. 1961); B. J. Engelbrecht, "Die betekenis van die begrip 'Vrees van die Here' in Spreuke, Job en Prediker," *HTSt,* 7 (1951), 191-223; W. Foerster, "σέβομαι," *TDNT,* VII, 168-196; J. Haspecker, *Gottesfurcht bei Jesus Sirach. AnBibl,* 30 (1967); I. Heinemann, "יִרְאַת ה׳ ,יִרְאָה ,יָרֵא," *EMiqr,* III (1958), 768-770; P. van Imschoot, *Théologie de l'AT,* II (Paris, 1958), 98ff.; P. Joüon, "Études de sémantique hébraïque. 1. L'idée de *danger* en hébreu; 4. Locutions pour *craindre de (que)* en hébreu: Étude de lexicographie et de stylistique," *Bibl,* 2 (1921), 336-38, 340-42; *idem,* "*Crainte* et *peur* en hébreu biblique," *Bibl,* 6 (1925), 174-79; N. Kirst, *Formkritische Untersuchung zum Zuspruch 'Fürchte dich nicht!' im AT* (Hamburg, 1968); L. Köhler, "Die Offenbarungsformel 'Fürchte dich nicht!' im AT," *SchThZ,* 36 (1919), 33-39; *idem, Hebrew Man* (Eng. trans., Nashville, 1956); *idem, OT Theology* (Eng. trans., Philadelphia, ²1957), 36ff.; G. van der Leeuw, *Religion in Essence and Manifestation* (Eng. trans., Princeton, ²1986); F. Michaeli, "La sagesse et la crainte de Dieu," *Hokhma,* 2 (1976), 35-44; W. L. Moran, "The Ancient Near Eastern Background of the Love of God in Deuteronomy," *CBQ,* 25 (1963), 77-87; G. Nagel, "Crainte et amour de Dieu dans l'AT," *RTP,* 33 (1945), 175-186; B. Olivier, *La crainte de Dieu, comme valeur religieuse dans l'AT. Études religieuses,* 75 (1960); B. J. Oosterhoff, *De vreze des Heren in het OT* (Utrecht, 1949); R. Otto, *The Idea of the Holy* (Eng. trans., Oxford, ²1950); E. Pfeiffer, "Die Gottesfurcht im Buche Kohelet," *Gottes Wort und Gottes Land. Festschrift H. W. Hertzberg* (Göttingen, 1965), 133-158; R. H. Pfeiffer, "The Fear of God," *IEJ,* 5 (1955), 41-48; S. Plath, *Furcht Gottes. ArbT,* 2/2 (1963); T. Polk, "The Wisdom of Irony," *StBTh,* 6/1 (1976), 3-17; O. Procksch, *Theologie des ATs* (Gütersloh, 1950), 610ff.; G. M. Rinaldi, "Nota [*jāḵeh*]," *BeO,* 10 (1968), 23; K. Romaniuk, "La crainte de Dieu à Qumrân et dans le NT," *RevQ,* 4 (1963/64), 29-38; R. Sander, *Furcht und Liebe im Palästinischen Judentum. BWANT,* 68[4/16] (1935); H.-P. Stähli, "ירא *jrʾ* fürchten," *THAT,* I, 765-778; J. A. Thompson, "Israel's 'Lovers'," *VT,* 27 (1977), 475-481; F. Vigouroux, "Crainte de Dieu," *DB,* II (1899), 1099f.; C. Wiéner, *Recherches sur l'amour pour Dieu dans l'AT* (Paris, 1957); H. W. Wolff, "Zur Thematik der elohistischen Fragmente im Pentateuch," *EvTh,* 29 (1969), 59-72 = *GSAT. ThB,* 22 (²1973), 402-417.

1 R. Růžička, "Die Wurzel *rʿ* in den semitischen Sprachen," *ZA,* 25 (1911), 114-138.

2 P. 8.

3 *Gottesfurcht im AT,* 1.

4 *Bibl,* 6 (1925), 174; also *Mélanges Beyrouth,* 10 (1925), 15.

5 Lane, 2933.

6 *LexLingAeth,* 899; Leslau, *Contributions,* 25.

7 *TigrWb,* 435b.

a-wärra, "proclaim," *wäre,* "news."[8] These all derive from a root *wry,* which is associated with Heb. *yrh* I. In any case, Arab. *wariʿa,* "be pious, God-fearing,"[9] must be considered, although it may well reflect Hebrew influence, especially since it is not attested in Old South Arabic and the otherwise rare Ethiop. *waraʿa*[10] appears to be a loanword from Arabic.

Few traces of *yr'* appear in the other Semitic languages. The association with Akk. *îrû* suggested by *BDB* has been dropped by *AHw* and *CAD.* It may appear as a Canaanite gloss in EA 155, 33 (*ir . . .*, restored by Knudtzon as *irta*). An important instance of *yr'* in the Amarna letters has been pointed out recently by Wilhelm,[11] who claims that the damaged l. 24 of KL 72:600 contains a personal name of the type X-Addu, which is attested elsewhere. The remaining legible signs can be read syllabically as *iri,* corresponding to Heb. *yᵉrē'*. If so, the name would be Iri-Addu, "In Fear of Addu." This name is unrelated to names consisting of "Iri-" followed by a divine name, such as Iri-Teššub, which are Hurrian forms.[12] We may therefore agree that "*yr'* is attested only in Hebrew and Ugaritic."[13] Even the Ugaritic occurrences are rare; the only certain ones are *KTU,* 1.6 VI, 30f., and *KTU,* 1.5 II, 6f.

The Akkadian semantic equivalent is *palāḫu* with its derivatives; *adāru* is used somewhat differently.

2. *Occurrences.* The scanty attestation in other Semitic languages stands in marked contrast to the situation in Hebrew, where *yr'* and its derivatives have an impressive total of 435 occurrences.[14] The verb appears 333 times:[15] in the qal (20 times in Genesis; 11 times in Exodus; 8 times in Leviticus; 4 times in Numbers; 32 times in Deuteronomy; 11 times in Joshua; 6 times in Judges; Ruth 3:11; 21 times in 1 Samuel; 6 times in 2 Samuel; 8 times in 1 Kings; 19 times in 2 Kings; 3 times in 1 Chronicles; 6 times in 2 Chronicles; 6 times in Nehemiah; 8 times in Job; 30 times in Psalms; 5 times in Proverbs; 7 times in Ecclesiastes; 22 times in Isaiah; 21 times in Jeremiah; Lam. 3:57; 5 times in Ezekiel; 3 times in Daniel; Hos. 10:3; Joel 2:21,22; Am. 3:8; 4 times in Jonah; Mic. 7:17; Hab. 3:2; 3 times in Zephaniah; Hag. 1:12; 2:5; 3 times in Zechariah; Mal. 2:5; 3:5); in the piel (2 S. 14:15; 2 Chr. 32:18; 3 times in Nehemiah); and in the niphal (as a verb only in Ps. 130:4; 44 times as a ptcp. [semasiologically an adj.]:[16] Gen. 28:17; Ex. 15:11; 34:10; 6 times in Deuteronomy; Jgs. 13:6; 2 S. 7:23; 1 Ch. 16:25; 17:21; 3

---

8 W. Leslau, *Contributions*; also *idem, Hebrew Cognates in Amharic* (Wiesbaden, 1969), 83.

9 Wehr, 1062.

10 *LexLingAeth,* 899.

11 G. Wilhelm, "Ein Brief der Amarna-Zeit aus Kāmid el-Lōz (KL 72:600)," *ZA,* N.S. 29[63] (1973), 69-75.

12 *Ibid.,* 75, n. 8; cf. *NPN,* 220; *PNU,* 327.

13 Derousseaux, 69; cf. 61. There are no grounds for Becker's demur in his review, 281.

14 Lisowsky; Stähli, 766; *KBL*² and *KBL*³: 429; Plath, 8: 420; Derousseaux, 68: 426; Derousseaux (68, n. 6) explains the differences as representing variant texts and considers them unimportant; for details, see Becker, *Gottesfurcht im AT,* 5f.

15 Stähli; Lisowsky: 332; *KBL*²: 323; *KBL*³: approximately 320.

16 Becker, *Gottesfurcht im AT,* 46; Stähli, 765; Derousseaux, 71.

times in Nehemiah; Job 37:22; 15 times in Psalms; 4 times in Isaiah; Ezek. 1:22; Dnl. 9:4; Joel 2:11; 3:4[2:31]; Hab. 1:7; Zeph. 2:11; Mal. 1:14; 3:23[4:5]).

The verbal adj. *yārē'* appears 45 times:[17] Gen. 22:12; Ex. 18:21; Dt. 20:8; Jgs. 7:3; 1 S. 23:3; 1 Ch. 10:4; 3 times in Job; 27 times in Psalms; Prov. 14:2; 31:30; Eccl. 8:12; Isa. 50:10; 3 times in Malachi.

The nominalized inf. *yir'â* appears 45 times[18]: Gen. 20:11; Ex. 20:20; Dt. 2:25; 2 S. 3:11; 23:3; 2 Ch. 19:9; Neh. 5:9,15; 5 times in Job; 8 times in Psalms; 14 times in Proverbs; 5 times in Isaiah; Jer. 32:40; Ezk. 1:18; 30:13; Jon. 1:10,16. The normal form of the infinitive, *y^erō'* appears only in Josh. 22:15; 1 S. 18:29.[19]

The *maqṭal* noun *môrā'* appears 12 times: Gen. 9:2; 4 times in Deuteronomy; Ps. 9:21(20); 76:12(11); Isa. 8:12,13; Jer. 32:21; Mal. 1:6; 2:5.

The statistics show a clear preponderance of occurrences in Psalms (83), Deuteronomy (44), and Wisdom Literature (48). Also noteworthy are the numerous occurrences in Isaiah (34, of which 22 are in Deutero-Isaiah or Trito-Isaiah) and Jeremiah (23).

3. *Semantic Field.* Besides *yr'* and its derivatives, which cover almost the entire semantic range of "fear," Hebrew has a wealth of terminology to designate specific aspects and situations involving fear, alarm, or terror. These often appear in combination, as in Ex. 15:15f.; Job 4:14f.; Ps. 48:6f.(5f.); 55:5f.(4f.); Isa. 7:2; 13:7f.; Jer. 6:24 (par. 50:43); 49:24; Ezk. 7:17; 21:12(7); Nah. 2:11(10); Hab. 3:16.[20]

The fundamental meaning of *paḥaḏ* is probably "tremble";[21] Oosterhoff[22] suggests "jump up," citing *pḥḥ(?)*, "blow," *paḥ*, "snare," and *paḥaḏ*, "thigh." The root *pḥd* "seems to be quite close to *yr'* because it is used in expressions similar in form and meaning":[23] *paḥaḏ-YHWH* (2 Ch. 19:7) and *paḥaḏ 'elōhîm* (Ps. 36:2[1]) correspond to *yir'aṯ YHWH* and *yir'aṯ 'elohîm.* See below for a discussion of *paḥaḏ yiṣḥāq.*

We find *gwr* used for fear of God in Ps. 22:24(23); 33:8. Becker,[24] following Oosterhoff,[25] proposes the fundamental meaning "bend," citing *gāhar* and *gûr,* "young lion." More likely, however, we should follow the LXX and assume the basic meaning "keep at a distance," "retreat" > "retreat out of fear" > "fear."[26] In Ps. 22:24(23); 33:8, *gwr* stands in parallel with *yr'*. The nouns *māḡôr* and *m^eḡôrâ* refer to fear of divine punishment; cf. *māḡôr* in Jer. 6:25 (= Ps. 31:14[13]); 20:3,4,10; 46:5; 49:29. A cognate noun *yāḡōr* is found in Dt. 9:19.

---

17 Lisowsky, Stähli; Derousseaux, 70: 43.

18 Stähli; Lisowsky and Derousseaux, 69: 46.

19 *GK,* §45d; P. Joüon, *Grammaire de l'Hébreu biblique,* §49d; Becker, *Gottesfurcht im AT,* 3; Derousseaux, 69.

20 Joüon, *Bibl,* 6 (1925), 174; Köhler, *Hebrew Man,* 116ff., 146; Becker, *Gottesfurcht im AT,* 6f.

21 L. Kopf, "Arabische Etymologien und Parallelen zum Bibelwörterbuch," *VT,* 9 (1959), 257; Becker, *Gottesfurcht im AT,* 7; Derousseaux, 74.

22 P. 15.

23 Derousseaux, 74; cf. Becker, *Gottesfurcht im AT,* 8.

24 *Gottesfurcht im AT,* 8.

25 P. 11.

26 Joüon, *Bibl,* 6 (1925), 176; Derousseaux, 74.

The root *ḥwl* or *ḥyl* means primarily "turn in a circle, dance a round dance" (Jgs. 21:21; Ps. 87:7) or "whirl" (Jer. 23:19), hence "writhe in birth-pangs" > "give birth" > "tremble, fear." Following Nöldeke,[27] *KBL* and *GesB* distinguish *ḥwl,* "turn, dance," from *ḥyl,* "tremble, fear." Other etymologies have also been proposed.[28] The root *ḥwl/ḥyl* belongs to the language of theophany and "signifies terror of the holy, the human emotion that serves to mark cosmic phenomena"[29] (cf. Ex. 15:14; Dt. 2:25; Ps. 29:8; 77:17[16]; 96:9 [par. 1 Ch. 16:30]; 97:4; 114:7; Isa. 13:8; Jer. 5:22; 51:29; Ezk. 30:16; Hab. 3:10; Zec. 9:5). For a discussion of the entire topic, see → חול *ḥûl* (*chûl*).

The root *ḥrd* refers to panic terror, especially in the presence of the numinous (Ex. 19:16, 18 [conj.]; Job 37:1; Isa. 19:16; 32:11; 41:5); cf. *ḥerdaṯ ʾelōhîm* (1 S. 14:15; RSV: "great panic"). For further discussion, see → חרד *ḥāraḏ*.

The root *ʿrṣ* in the qal and hiphil means "be terrified, terrify."[30] It appears primarily in Isaiah as a term for fear of Yahweh's omnipotence (Isa. 2:19,21; 8:12f.; 29:23; cf. *maʿarāṣâ* in 10:33). Elsewhere the verb appears only in Job 13:25; Ps. 89:8(7).

The root → חתת *ḥtt* appears in the context of the formula "Fear not" (Dt. 1:21; 31:8; Josh. 8:1; 10:25; Jer. 30:10 [par. 46:27]; Ezk. 2:6; 3:9). It is also found in Isa. 8:9; 30:31; Mal. 2:5. In Gen. 35:5, *ḥittaṯ ʾelōhîm* is used for "terror from God." In Job 7:14; 33:16 the piel of the verb and in Prov. 10:29; Jer. 17:17 the noun *meḥittâ* describe the terrifying effect of God on the individual.

Used as both verb and noun, the root *śʿr* "always refers to the terrible judgment of Yahweh, which appalls everyone"[31] (Job 18:20; Jer. 2:12; Ezk. 27:35; 32:10; cf. Ps. 58:10[9]; Isa. 28:2).[32]

The etymology of *štʿ* is disputed; some authorities[33] derive it from *šʿh,* "look around"; König derives it from *šʿʿ*; Zorell treats *štʿ* as a separate root, citing Arabic and Ugaritic parallels. It is found in Isa. 41:10,14(?),23 in parallel with *yrʾ,* with the meaning "be dismayed."

The root *bʿt* describes the terrifying effect of God on the individual; it is characteristic of the language of Job (Job 6:4; 7:14; 9:34; 13:11,21). Elsewhere it appears only in 1 S. 16:14f.; Ps. 88:17(16). The noun *beʿāṯâ,* "sudden disaster," occurs only in Jer. 8:15; 14:19.

The noun *ṣirʿâ* is a "typical term for terror evoked by God"[34] (cf. Ex. 23:28; Dt. 7:20; Josh. 24:12). The meaning "horror" is proposed by *KBL*²,[35] contra *GesB, BDB,* and Zorell, who prefer "hornets."

The noun *ʾêmâ* likewise refers to the divine terror that befalls the foe (Ex. 15:16;

---

27 T. Nöldeke, "Untersuchungen zur semitischen Grammatik," *ZDMG,* 37 (1883), 536.

28 J. Scharbert, *Der Schmerz im AT. BBB,* 8 (1955), 21-26; Joüon, *Bibl,* 6 (1925), 178.

29 Derousseaux, 75.

30 For proposed etymologies, see G. Hoffmann, "Bibliographische Anzeigen," *ZDMG,* 32 (1878), 762; *GesB*; Becker, *Gottesfurcht im AT,* 12.

31 Derousseaux, 76.

32 On Dt. 32:17, see Becker, *Gottesfurcht im AT,* 13; Derousseaux, 76, n. 24.

33 *GesB*; *BDB*; *KBL*², 999f.; cf. M. Dahood, "Some Ambiguous Texts in Isaias," *CBQ,* 20 (1958), 48f.

34 Becker, *Gottesfurcht im AT,* 16.

35 P. 817.

23:27; Josh. 2:9) but can also strike individuals (Gen. 15:12; Job 9:34; 13:21; 20:25; Ps. 88:16[15]). Jer. 50:38 calls idols *'êmîm.*

A wealth of additional terms appear in the more or less extended context of *yr'*, each of which reflects a different aspect of fear. We can only cite them summarily here: *plṣ,* "reel" (Job 21:6; Ps. 55:6[5]; Isa. 21:4; Ezk. 7:18); *tmh,* "be astounded" (Ps. 48:6[5]), with the derived noun *timmāhôn,* "panic" (Dt. 28:28; Zec. 12:4); → חפז *ḥāpaz,* "hurry away" (Dt. 20:3; Ps. 31:23[22]; 48:6[5]; 116:11); *d'g,* "fear" (Isa. 57:11; Jer. 38:19); *rkk,* "be soft," in combination with *lēḇ*; *r'd,* "tremble"; *mwg,* "lose courage";[36] *rgz,* "tremble in panic" in the presence of the divine (Ex. 15:14; Dt. 2:25), also used of cosmic trembling in the context of theophany (2 S. 22:8 [par. Ps. 18:8(7)]; Ps. 77:17,19[16,18]; 99:1; Hab. 3:7); *nw',* "tremble" (Ex. 20:18); *mwṭ* and *nwṭ,* "quake" (Ps. 99:1); *g'š,* "quake" (2 S. 22:8 par. Ps. 18:8[7]); *r'š,* "be shaken" (of the natural world; cf. Jgs. 5:4; 2 S. 22:8 [par. Ps. 18:8(7)]; Ps. 46:4[3]; 68:9[8]; 77:19[18]; Isa. 24:18; Jer. 4:24; 10:10; 51:29; Ezk. 38:30; Joel 2:10; 4:16(3:16); Am. 9:1; Nah. 1:5); *qwṣ,* "dread" (Ex. 1:12); *zw'* and its derivatives, "tremble";[37] *smr,* "tremble" (Job 4:15 [piel]; Ps. 119:120); *šmm* and its derivatives;[38] *mss* niphal, with *lēḇ,* "dissolve"; *reṭeṭ,* "anguish" (Jer. 49:24); *rᵉṯēṯ,* "trembling" (Hos. 13:1); *ḥāggā',* "terror" (Isa. 19:17); *ša'ᵃrûrâ* (Jer. 5:30; 23:14) and *ša'ᵃrûriyyâ* (Jer. 18:13; Hos. 6:10 [*Q*]);[39] *rhb* and *r''* with the meaning "fear."[40] See also → בהל *bhl,* → המם *hmm.*

4. *Contexts and Idioms.* If we examine the syntax of *yr'* in the qal, we may be content with the regular translation "fear (someone or something)," less often "be afraid (to do something)." But the content of the verb is varied by context-sensitive classificators[41] in such a way as to cover the entire semantic range in all its variety, from alarm in the face of everyday threats through fear of numinous powers to fear of God.

The subject of *yr'* may be an individual such as Isaac (Gen. 26:7), Jacob (Gen. 31:31; 32:8,12[7,11]), Moses (Ex. 2:14), Gideon (Jgs. 6:27); Saul (1 S. 15:24), David (1 S. 21:13[12]), Ishbaal (2 S. 3:11), or Nehemiah (Neh. 6:13). The subject may also be a group, such as David's court (2 S. 12:18); Joseph's brothers (Gen. 43:18), or Israel as a whole (Ex. 14:10; 1 S. 7:7; 17:11; 2 K. 25:26; 2 Ch. 32:18; Jer. 41:18; and esp. Dt. 13:12[11]; 17:13; 19:20; Isa. 57:11; cf. Lev. 19:3). Three passages speak of Israel's enemies as fearing Israel: Dt. 2:4; Josh. 10:2; 2 S. 10:19. The "fear of God" or "fear of Israel" that panics the enemy is discussed below.

Only in comparatively few passages is the object of fear a threatening situation in everyday life: other people or animals, enemies, sickness, or death. The object is usually

---

36 P. Joüon, "Notes de lexicographie hebraïque," *Bibl,* 7 (1926), 165-68.

37 See M. Dahood, "Hebrew-Ugaritic Lexicography, II," *Bibl,* 45 (1964), 405.

38 See N. Lohfink, "Enthielten die im AT bezeugten Klageriten eine Phase des Schweigens?" *VT,* 12 (1962), 267ff.

39 See *KBL*², 1002.

40 See Kopf, 273-76.

41 Cf. G. Wahrig, *Anleitung zur grammatisch-semantischen Beschreibung lexikalischer Einheiten. Linguistische Arbeiten,* 8 (Tübingen, 1973), 146f.; H. F. Fuhs, *Sehen und Schauen. FzB,* 32 (1978), 91ff.

introduced by the prep. *min* (Dt. 1:29; 2:4; 7:18; 20:1; Josh. 10:8) or *mippᵉnê* (Dt. 5:5; 7:19; Josh. 9:24; 11:6; 1 S. 7:7; 21:13[12]; 1 K. 1:50; 2 K. 25:26; Jer. 41:18; 42:11), rarely directly (Gen. 32:12[11]; Lev. 19:3; Nu. 14:9; 21:34; Dt. 3:2,22; Jgs. 6:27; 1 S. 14:26; 15:24; 1 K. 1:51; Ezk. 3:9; 11:8; Dnl. 1:10). Often *yrʾ* is used absolutely, so the the object of fear must be deduced from the context (Gen. 31:31; 32:8[7]; 43:18; Ex. 2:14; 14:10; Dt. 13:12[11]; 17:13; 19:20; 20:3; Josh. 10:2; 1 S. 17:11,24; 28:5; 2 K. 10:4; 2 Ch. 20:3; Neh. 2:2; 6:13; Jer. 26:21; Am. 3:8). In almost 80 percent of the passages, however, the object of fear is God. The nature of this "fear of God" is modified substantially by the particular contextual classificators. A highly differentiated development may be observed, both synchronically and diachronically.

The verb *yrʾ* appears in parallel not only with other verbs meaning "fear,"[42] but also with such expressions as *ʾhb,* "love" (Dt. 10:12); *dbq,* "cleave to" (Dt. 10:20; 13:5[4]); *ʿbd,* "serve" (Dt. 6:13; 10:12,20; 13:5[4]; Josh. 24:14; 1 S. 12:14); *šmr,* "keep (commandments)" (Dt. 5:29; 6:2; 8:6; 13:5[4]; 17:19; 31:12); *hlk bidrākāyw,* "walk in his ways" (Dt. 8:6; 10:12); *hlk ʾaḥᵃrê,* "follow" (Dt. 13:5[4]); *šmʿ bᵉqōlô,* "hearken to his voice" (Dt. 13:5[4]; 1 S. 12:14); *ʿśh haḥuqqîm,* "do the commandments" (Dt. 6:24).

Typical phrases include the formula *ʾal-tîrāʾ* (some 75 occurrences; pl. only in Gen. 43:23; 50:19,21; Ex. 14:13; 20:20; Nu. 14:9; Dt. 20:3; 31:6; Josh. 10:25; 2 S. 13:28; 2 K. 25:24 [par. Jer. 40:9]; Isa. 51:7; Jer. 10:5; 42:11; Joel 2:22; Hag. 2:5; Zec. 8:13,15; Neh. 4:8[14]; 2 Ch. 20:15,17; 32:7; cf. *lōʾ tîrāʾ*: Jgs. 6:10; Isa. 8:12); *yirʾat ʾᵉlōhîm* (Gen. 20:11; 2 S. 23:3; Neh. 5:9,15); *yirʾat YHWH* (Isa. 11:2,3; 33:6; Prov. 1:7, 29; 2:5; 8:13; 9:10; 10:27; 14:26,27; 15:16,33; 16:6; 19:23; 22:4; 23:17; Ps. 34:12[11]; 111:10; cf. Jon. 1:16), often in parallel with *daʿat* (Prov. 1:7,29; 2:5; 9:10; Isa. 11:2; 33:6), *ḥokmâ* (Job 28:28; Prov. 15:33), *tām,* "right," *yāšār,* "upright," *ṣaddîq,* "righteous"; *sûr mēraʿ,* "turn aside from evil," *śnʾ raʿ,* "hate what is evil" (cf. 2 S. 23:3; Job 1:1,8; 4:6; Ps. 34:12,15[11,14]; Prov. 3:7; 8:13; 10:27); *yirʾat šadday* (Job 6:14); *yirʾat ʾᵃdōnāy* (Job 28:28); *yirʾat ʿelyôn* (Sir. 6:37) or *yirʾat ʾēl* (Sir. 32:12); also: *yirʾê YHWH* (Ps. 15:4; 22:24[23]; 115:11,13; 118:4; 135:20; cf. Mal. 3:16) or forms with pronominal suffixes, "those who fear thee/him" (Ps. 22:26[25]; 25:14; 31:20[19]; 33:18; 34:8,10[7,9]; 60:6[4]; 85:10[9]; 103:11,13,17; 111:5; 119:74,79; 147:11).

5. *LXX.* The LXX usually renders *yrʾ* by means of *phobeín* and its derivatives, but attempts to express semantic nuances by using appropriate terminology, e.g., *tromeísthai, sébesthai, trómos, krataiós, thaumastós* for *nôrāʾ* (Ex. 15:11; 34:10; Ps. 45:5[4][LXX 44:5]; 65:6[5][LXX 64:5]; 68:36[35][LXX 67:36]; Dnl. 9:4; Sir. 43:2,8; 48:4; elsewhere rendered *epiphanḗs,* which may represent occasional confusion with *nirʾeh*), *theosébeia, eusébeia.*

II. Fear in Everyday Life. The root *yrʾ* refers to human fear for physical safety in threatening situations and the perils of everyday life. Shepherds are afraid when lions roar in the meadows of the Jordan (Am. 3:8), and farmers fear the destruction of their

42 See above.

seed by wild beasts (Job 5:22). Jacob, fleeing from Laban, has good reason to be afraid when the latter catches up to him (Gen. 31:31); before his encounter with Esau, he takes various precautions because he fears Esau's vengeance (Gen. 32:8,12[7,11]). On their second journey to Egypt, Joseph's brothers are afraid that he will "fall upon us, to make slaves of us" (Gen. 43:18). Gideon tears down the altar of Ba'al at night because he is afraid of his family and the townspeople (Jgs. 6:27). Fear of the king plays an important role: David's courtiers are afraid to report the death of his child to him (2 S. 12:18); Adonijah is afraid of Solomon (1 K. 1:50f.); the prophet Uriah flees out of fear of Jehoiakim (Jer. 26:21); the princes of Ahab are in terror of Jehu (2 K. 10:4). On the other hand, Saul's fear of his people leads him to offer sacrifice himself in a forbidden manner (1 S. 15:24).

In battle it is the enemy that spreads fear and terror. Israel takes fright at the approach of Pharaoh's army (Ex. 14:10) and is afraid of the Philistines (1 S. 7:7), especially Goliath (1 S. 17:11,24). Gideon is afraid of the Midianites (Jgs. 7:10), Saul is afraid of the Philistines (1 S. 28:5), and David is afraid of Achish of Gath (1 S. 21:13[12]). On the other hand, the Gibeonites are afraid of Israel (Josh. 9:24), Adoni-zedek is afraid of Joshua (Josh. 10:2), and fear of Israel makes the Syrians discontinue aiding the Ammonites (2 S. 10:19). This context includes the passages using the formula of reassurance "Do not fear . . . [him/them/the people of the land, etc.]" (Nu. 14:9; 21:34; Dt. 1:29; 3:2,22; 7:18; 20:1,3; Josh. 10:8; 11:6), discussed below under *'al-tîrā'*. Fear of the → חרב *hereḇ,* "sword" (Jer. 42:16; Ezk. 11:8), a metaphor hypostatizing God's judgment against Israel, falls under the heading of numinous fear.

Finally we come to fear of punishment. Because he has killed an Egyptian, Moses is afraid that Pharaoh will kill him (Ex. 2:14). The death penalty for incitement to idolatry (Dt. 13:12[11]), refusal to obey the ruling of a priest or judge (Dt. 17:13), or bearing false witness (Dt. 19:20) is explicitly motivated by its deterrent effect: ". . . that all Israel [or: 'all the people'] shall hear and fear."[43]

III. Fear of God.

1. *General.* "Fear of God" is without question a central concept of OT religion, as of other religions in the ancient Near East; it may be "the earliest term for religion in biblical Hebrew, and indeed in Semitic languages in general."[44] The notion that fear of God is the ultimate source of religion was expressed by Democritus, followed by Epicurus; a fully developed exposition of this theory is found in Lucretius,[45] and it was given pregnant expression by Statius: *Primus in orbe deos fecit timor,* "At the beginning of the world, fear created the gods."[46] When humans encounter the divine, commonly referred

---

43 See W. Schottroff, *Der altisraelitische Fluchspruch. WMANT,* 30 (1969); H. Schulz, *Das Todesrecht im AT. BZAW,* 114 (1969); V. Wagner, *Rechtssätze in gebundener Sprache und Rechtssatzreihen im israelitischen Recht. BZAW,* 127 (1972); C. M. Carmichael, *The Laws of Deuteronomy* (Ithaca, N.Y., 1974).

44 R. H. Pfeiffer, 41.

45 *De rerum natura* v.1161-1240.

46 *Thebais* iii.661.

to since Otto as the "numinous,"[47] one effect is fear. Fear of the numinous embraces an inner polarity: terror, retreat, and flight on the one hand; attraction, trust, and love on the other. In Otto's terminology, the numinous appears as *tremendum* but also *fascinans,* revealing itself in concrete personal form as God or as a divine incarnation, for example in the person of the king (Egypt). Thus the numinous can be experienced as a powerful helper and a guarantor of life. This internal polarity and dynamic gives rise to a semantic development in the fear of God: when the element of literal fear recedes, "fear of God" becomes tantamount to "religion" or "spirituality";[48] i.e., fear of God becomes synonymous with reverence, worship, and obedience to God's command. This semantic development is found in all the Semitic languages. There is, however, no analogous historical development such as many scholars postulate,[49] as we see when we examine the concept of the fear of God in the ancient Near East.

2. *Egypt.* Like Hebrew, Egyptian has a variety of terms for "fear."[50] The semantic equivalent of Heb. *yrʾ* is *śnḏ,* "fear" (used both absolutely and, more commonly, with a prepositional obj.), with its nominal derviatives *śnḏ/śnḏ.w* or *śnḏ.t/śnḏ.w.t,* "fear," and *śnḏ.w,* "one who fears."[51] The meaning of fear of God in Egyptian religion has not received sufficient attention. Bonnet does not consider it "an important element,"[52] and Morenz discusses it only indirectly.[53] Texts from the Old Kingdom all the way through the New Kingdom bear witness to its importance in Egyptian religion. The divine nature on which all depend is incomprehensible, beyond human ken, hidden in inaccessible darkness.[54] This realization evokes fear of the deity, who appears as the One in Many. "Lord/Lady of fear [in human hearts]" is a common divine epithet. In the context of human history, this deity is revealed as beneficent, "shaper of the earth," "who created all gods, human beings, and animals,"[55] guarantor of the state and of human life, giver of happiness and inward perfection. Such experience evokes trust and love, which find expression in the community's devotion, worship, and service, but also in the prayer and spirituality of the individual. "The house of god—its abomination is tumult. Pray privately with a desirous heart, all of whose words are hidden; then god will carry out your concern, then he will hear your words."[56] In Egypt since the Pyramid texts of the

---

47 Cf. M. Eliade, *The Sacred and the Profane* (Eng. trans., 1961; repr. Magnolia, Mass., 1983), 8-16; van der Leeuw, 23-26, 43-51; S. Mowinckel, *Religion und Kultus* (Ger. trans., Göttingen, 1953), 30-49; F. Heiler, *Erscheinungsformen und Wesen der Religion. RdM,* 1 (1961), 29-33.

48 Becker, *Gottesfurcht im AT,* 75.

49 E.g., A. Weiser, *Religion und Sittlichkeit der Genesis* (Heidelberg, 1928); J. Hempel, *Gott und Mensch im AT. BWANT,* 38[3/2] (^{2}1936), 32f.; L. Nieder, "Gottesfurcht," *LThK*^{2}, IV (1960), 1107.

50 *WbÄS,* II, 460; III, 147, 170; IV, 42, 44, 174, 205, 278.

51 *Ibid.,* IV, 182-85; Derousseaux, 21-42.

52 H. Bonnet, "Frömmigkeit," *RÄR,* 197; cf. Derousseaux, 41f.

53 S. Morenz, *Egyptian Religion* (Eng. trans., Ithaca, N.Y., 1973), chs. 4f.

54 Papyrus Berlin 3048, IX, 10a.

55 *Ibid.,* VIII, 2.

56 A. Erman, "Denksteine aus der thebänischen Gräberstadt," *SPAW,* 1911, 1086f.

Old Kingdom, the fear of God means worship and service, with little emphasis on literal fear. What is uniquely Egyptian is the fact that this service and this worship are owed above all to the king, who is the incarnation of the deity when alive and is identified with Osiris when dead.

3. *Mesopotamia.* The term for fear of God in Mesopotamia is the Akkadian verb *palāḫu(m)* with the noun *puluḫtu.*[57] The noun in particular is used to express numinous fear in the literal sense. Akk. *puluḫtu* "always has the strong sense of 'terror,' spread by the dragons of Tiamat, the scorpion men, or the armor of Marduk. . . . All these divine realities are mighty and terrible, above all Marduk the king when he engages in victorious combat."[58] The primary meaning of the verb is "be afraid" of threatening situations in daily life, especially in battle; then it comes to mean "treat with respect," "serve," "worship." In this sense it is used for fear of God, as many texts bear witness; Hammurabi already calls himself *pāliḫ ilī* in the introduction to his Code.[59] Personal names of the form [DN]-*piluḫ* or *pilaḫ*-[DN] are common. Thus in Mesopotamia, too, the element of literal fear is reduced and fear of God refers to worship, service, and the cult (in the literal sense): "the gods are at peace, fear of god is great, the temples are frequented"; "the fear of god brings prosperity, sacrifice restores life, prayer blots out sin"; "the day I worshipped the gods was joy to my heart."[60] But it is hard to agree with Becker[61] that the ethical element is absent. Derousseaux comes to a different conclusion, discussing *crainte sacrée* against the background of Sumerian religion, which he considers "profoundly characterized by the terrifying aspect of the divine," and arguing that "the early usage of *palaḫu* and *puluḫtu* in Akkadian seems to take their inspiration from this source."[62]

4. *Ugarit.* Some Ugaritic texts speak of the fear gripping people who encounter the deity or other powers. These texts use a variety of terms (e.g., *ʿrṣ, ṯtʿ*).[63] To the extent that their very fragmentary condition permits any conclusion, the emphasis is on *crainte sacrée*; a semantic shift in the direction of service and worship analogous to the development in Egypt and Mesopotamia remains hypothetical. Two texts[64] contain the word *yr'*, which is undoubtedly connected with Heb. *yr'*. Both contain cosmogonic myths describing the rivalry between the gods Baʿal and Mot. In *KTU,* 1.5, it is Baʿal who fears the greatness and power of Mot; in *KTU,* 1.6, it is Mot who fears the power of risen Baʿal.

---

57 *AHw,* II (1972), 812f.; cf. Becker, *Gottesfurcht im AT,* 78f.

58 Derousseaux, 58.

59 CH §1, 31.

60 These quotations and others will be found in *AHw,* II, 812f.

61 *Gottesfurcht im AT,* 79.

62 *Ibid.,* 58f.

63 On Akk. *plḫt* in Ugaritic texts, see C. Virolleaud, "Fragments alphabétiques divers de Ras-Shamra," *Syr,* 20 (1939), 115, 118; originally considered a Ugaritic word by É. P. Dhorme and C. H. Gordon (*UH,* no. 1637; cf. R. H. Pfeiffer, 42; Derousseaux, 63, n. 134), it is no longer cited in later lexica (*UT, WUS,* Whitaker).

64 *KTU,* 1.5 II, 6f.; 1.6 VI, 30f.

In both cases, *yr'* stands in parallel with *ṯt'*; cf. Isa. 41:10,23 (*yr'* par. *št'*).[65] As the parallel *ṯt'*, "be terrified," suggests, *yr'* refers to fear in the literal sense.

IV. Fear of God as Fear of the Numinous.

1. *Holy and Terrible.* The originally numinous nature of fear of God is still clearly visible in several OT passages. This fear is evoked by an attribute of God expressed biblically by → קדשׁ *qdš* and its derivatives: holiness. The definition of the term and its range of meanings have been discussed by many scholars.[66] In essence, they find a distinction between absolute holiness—"holy per se" (i.e., belonging to the divine realm and totally inaccessible to mortals)—and moral holiness—"holy for . . ." (i.e., responsible conduct in response to divine sovereignty). We are speaking here of the former, and in this sense "holy" is identical with "numinous."[67]

An internal association between holiness and numinous fear is documented in several passages: comparison of Gen. 28:17 and Ex. 3:5 shows that *qāḏôš* and *nôrā'* are synonyms; *yr'* occurs in both contexts as an expression of numinous fear. Both appear in parallel in Ps. 99:3; 111:9; cf. Ex. 15:11; Ps. 96:9; Isa. 8:13; 29:23; Sir. 7:29. There are also passages in which *nôrā'* and *gāḏôl* (→ גדל)[68] appear in parallel: Dt. 7:21; 10:17,21; Neh. 1:5; 4:8; 9:32; Ps. 99:3; Dnl. 9:4; cf. Ps. 47:3(2); 96:4; 145:6; Mal. 1:14.

The numinous nature of God, which is identical with his holiness, is termed *nôrā'*, "terrible." In 36 of its 44 occurrences, it is an attribute of Yahweh (Ex. 15:11; Dt. 7:21; 10:17; Neh. 1:5; 4:8[14]; 9:32; Job 37:22; Ps. 47:3[2]; 68:36[35]; 76:8,13[7,12]; 89:8[7]; 96:4 [par. 1 Ch. 16:25]; Dnl. 9:4; Zeph. 2:11), his name (Dt. 28:58; Ps. 99:3; 111:9; Mal. 1:14), his deeds (Ex. 34:10; Dt. 10:21; 2 S. 7:23 [par. 1 Ch. 17:21]; Ps. 65:6[5]; 66:3; 106:22; 145:6; Isa. 64:2[3]), or his eschatological day of judgment (Joel 2:11; 3:4[2:31]; Mal. 3:23[4:5]). According to Hempel,[69] *nôrā'* is characteristic of the diction of the hymns of Zion and of Yahweh as king (cf. Ps. 47:3[2]; 76:8,13[7,12]; 96:4; 99:3) and may probably be considered part of the language of the cult, whence it entered the framework of Deuteronomy (Dt. 7:21; 10:17,21; 28:58).

In the formula *hā'ēl haggāḏôl wᵉhannôrā'* (Neh. 1:5; 9:32; Dnl. 9:4; cf. Neh. 4:8[14]), used as a predicate of the merciful God, *nôrā'* may exhibit a diminution of its numinous element. The same is true in Ps. 45:5(4), where it is used of the "glorious" deeds of the king; cf. the adverbial usage in Ps. 139:14, "wonderfully."[70]

---

65 M. Held, "Philological Notes on the Mari Covenant Rituals," *BASOR*, 200 (1970), 37.

66 J. Hänel, *Die Religion der Heiligkeit* (Gütersloh, 1931); O. Schilling, *Das Heilige und Gute im AT* (Leipzig, 1956); Eichrodt, 270-282; T. C. Vriezen, *An Outline of OT Theology* (Eng. trans., Boston, ²1970), 43f.; Köhler, *OT Theology,* 33f.; W. H. Schmidt, "Wo hat die Aussage: Jahwe 'der Heilige' ihren Ursprung?" *ZAW,* 74 (1962), 62-66; Becker, *Gottesfurcht im AT,* 42ff.; H. Wildberger, "Gottesnamen und Gottesepitheta bei Jesaja," *Zer ligburot. Festschrift B. Z. Shazar* (Jerusalem, 1972/73), 699-728.

67 Cf. Otto, 6.

68 On this word as a term for the numinous, see Becker, *Gottesfurcht im AT,* 48.

69 Hempel, 30; cf. Becker, *ibid.,* 48.

70 Cf. H.-J. Kraus, *Psalms 60–150* (Eng. trans., Minneapolis, 1989), 510.

2. *Yahweh's Presence.* It is well documented that the OT considers encounter with God, the presence of his holiness, to be dangerous, indeed deadly (Gen. 16:13; 32:31[30]; Ex. 19:21; 24:10f.; Jgs. 6:22f.; 13:22; 1 S. 6:19; 1 K. 19:13; Isa. 6:5; above all Ex. 33:18ff.) The same is true of hearing God's voice (Ex. 20:19; Dt. 4:33; 5:23ff.). Fear (of death) is therefore the natural human reaction when someone experiences divine revelation in a theophany, dream, or vision.

This is shown with particular clarity in Ex. 3:6. Moses hides his face, "for he was afraid to look at God." Fear of the deadly sight of the deity includes fear of the numinous, which is recognized as perilous. The context of the verse is the call of Moses, as narrated by J and E. Several scholars have undertaken literary and form-critical analysis of the passage,[71] sometimes ascribing Ex. 3:6b to J,[72] but more usually to E.[73] In conjunction with other E passages, it has been used to draw broad conclusions about the theological concerns that distinguish E from J.[74] The present status of Pentateuchal criticism[75] undoubtedly makes it very difficult to determine lines of theological tradition. Becker's criticism[76] of Derousseaux's attempt seems unjustified in its present form. Until we have firm conclusions within the framework of an overall theory, the results to date—however provisional—may be considered useful working hypotheses.

The people are also seized by fear on the occasion of Yahweh's theophany at Sinai (Ex. 20:18). There is a consensus among scholars to follow the Samaritan Pentateuch, LXX, and Vulg. in reading *yr'* in parallel with *nû^{a}'*, "trembling." The context of this verse is E's recension of the Sinai theophany (Ex. 19:16aβ,b,17,19; 20:18b-21).[77] According to E, the fear of the people is triggered by Yahweh's appearance in a storm; the unusual parallelism of thunder and increasingly loud trumpet blasts gives an air of distance to the original theophany account. Ex. 19:19 goes on to explain that God's voice could be heard answering Moses in the thunder. Ex. 20:18a (redactional), which combines the versions of J and E, explicitly adds the phenomena of the J account (the smoking mountain, Yahweh's coming down in fire, earthquake) to the causes of the people's fear.

An individual may experience the terrifying aspect of God's presence in a dream or vision as well as in a theophany. This is especially clear in Gen. 28:17. In the present

---

71 See W. Richter, *Die sogenannte vorprophetischen Berufungsberichte. FRLANT,* N.S. 83[101] (1970), 57-133; L. Perlitt, "Mose als Prophet," *EvTh,* 31 (1971), 588-608; K. Reichert, *Der Jehowist und die sogenannten deuteronomistischen Erweiterungen im Buch Exodus* (diss., Tübingen, 1972); H. H. Schmid, *Der sogenannten Jahwist* (Zurich, 1976), 19-43.

72 Holzinger, Richter.

73 Baentsch, Beer, Noth, Wolff, *EvTh,* 29 (1969), 66.

74 Cf. Wolff, *ibid.,* 59-72, and esp. Derousseaux, ch. IV, with the theory that the moral concept of fear of God originated in the northern kingdom.

75 See H. H. Schmid; R. Rendtorff, *Das überlieferungsgeschichtliche Problem des Pentateuch. BZAW,* 147 (1977); E. Otto, "Stehen wir vor einem Umbruch in der Pentateuchkritik?" *Verkündigung und Forschung,* 1 (1977), 82-97.

76 *Bibl,* 53 (1972), 283f.

77 See Beer and Noth, contra W. Beyerlin, *Origins and History of the Oldest Sinai Traditions* (Eng. trans., Oxford, ²1965); for a discussion of the entire passage, see E. Zenger, *Die Sinaitheophanie. FzB,* 3 (1971), 170ff., 208ff.; Reichert, 115f.; H. H. Schmid, 97ff.

redactional combination of the ancient Bethel traditions (Gen. 28:11-22), Jacob's fear, expressed in his exclamation *mah-nnôrā'*, represents his reaction to his dream; not until he awakens does he realize that he has been in God's presence and that the place where he happens to be is holy. But Gen. 28:17 belongs to the E version, along with vv. 11, 12, 18-20, 21a, 22;[78] i.e., according to E, Jacob's experience of God's presence in his dream fills him with fear.

The descriptions of visions associated with prophetic calls ordinarily avoid mentioning numinous fear, since they downplay the visionary experience in order to emphasize the imparting of God's word.[79] Exceptions include Isa. 6 (fear expressed in the 1st person) and Ezk. 1 (the prophet's falling on his face). Job 4:12-16 vividly describes the fear occasioned by a visionary experience. This passage, however, is most likely a literary composition and does not reflect a personal experience. Dnl. 10 is similar.

3. *Yahweh's Intervention in History and the Natural Realm.* It is not only in sensory experiences of God's presence that the numinous is encountered, but also in God's actions in history and the natural world. Hebrew has a highly differentiated vocabulary to designate specific aspects of God's activity: its miraculous nature, its efficacy, its greatness and power, its judgment. The words *nôrā'ôṯ* and *môrā'îm* underline explicitly its numinous and terrifying aspect (Dt. 10:21; 2 S. 7:23 [par. 1 Ch. 17:21]; Ps. 65:6[5]; 106:22; 139:14; 145:6; Isa. 64:2[3]; and Dt. 4:34). In Ex. 34:10; Ps. 66:3, the adj. *nôrā'* is used as an epithet of Yahweh's deeds; according to Ex. 15:11; Ps. 66:5, Yahweh himself is *nôrā' tᵉhillōṯ* and *nôrā' ʿᵃlîlâ*.

For Israel, the deliverance of the people from Egypt is the deed of Yahweh par excellence. It is the reason Israel fears the Lord (Ex. 14:31, undoubtedly with a semantic nuance of "revere"); it is the reason the nations are filled with terror and dread (Ex. 15:14-16). The mere recollection of the event engenders fear in the Philistines (1 S. 4:7f.). Cf. also Dt. 26:8; Jer. 32:21; Mic. 7:15-17.

Yahweh's intervention on behalf of his people evokes fear. Ps. 65:6(5) says that Israel's prayers were answered by dread deeds; according to v. 10(9), the reference is to the gift of fertility. Taken as a whole, Ps. 76, an archaic cult psalm, is a hymn to Yahweh's power and glory, expressed in his universal judgment, which brings fear upon the whole earth. Yahweh's mighty act of judgment is also the object of the petition in Ps. 9:21(20) that Yahweh will bring terror upon the nations. Cf. also Ps. 67:8(7); Isa. 19:16; 25:3; 41:5,23; Hab. 3:2; Zec. 9:5. According to Ps. 40:4(3), the prayer of the individual causes many to fear; *rabbîm* refers to the assembled congregation (cf. vv. 10f.[9f.]). Yahweh's intervention to deliver the worshipper causes all who see (*r'h*) it to fear (*yr'*). Fear in the face of Yahweh's deeds awakens trust. In Ps. 52:8(6); 64:10(9), the fear of the righteous before God's judgment of the wicked goes hand in hand with joy and understanding of what he has done.

---

78 Most recently E. Otto, "Jakob in Bethel," *ZAW,* 88 (1976), 165-190; for a different analysis, see A. de Pury, *Promesse divine et légende cultuelle dans le cycle de Jacob,* II. *ÉtB* (1975), 389ff.

79 Cf. Fuhs.

Yahweh's power is revealed not only in his shaping of history but also, albeit less markedly,[80] in his deeds as Creator and lord of nature; this power conveys a sense of the numinous and evokes fear (cf. 1 K. 18:39; Job 37:1,24; Ps. 33:8; Jer. 5:22,24; 10:7; Jon. 1:16). In Ps. 65:6-9(5-8), the two notions are intertwined.

Finally, even a human agent may convey a sense of the numinous. The appearance of God's messenger is "terrible" (Jgs. 13:6; cf. Dnl. 8:17f.; 10:7-11,15-19; Tob. 12:16). Encounter with a man of God or charismatic leader evokes reverential fear: Moses (Ex. 34:30), Joshua (Josh. 4:14), Samuel (1 S. 12:18; 16:4; cf. 28:20f.), Yahweh's anointed king (2 S. 1:14; 1 K. 3:28). Yahweh's people are feared because they are called by his name (Dt. 28:10; cf. Neh. 6:16). Finally, numinous fear is associated with certain places and objects: the crystal canopy or pediment (Ezk. 1:22),[81] the desert (Dt. 1:19; 8:15), the sanctuary (Lev. 19:30; 26:2; cf. Gen. 28:17).

4. *Divine Panic.* Numinous fear in the face of God's deeds must be distinguished from divine panic, which is not terror evoked by God's presence but terror instilled by God. The distinct nature of this phenomenon is reflected in the Hebrew vocabulary;[82] a similar terminological difference is found in Akk. *palāḫu/ḫattu,* "panic."[83] The noun *môrāʾ* (< *yrʾ*) refers exclusively to such divinely inspired panic. It is associated with the deliverance formula in credal sections of Deuteronomy (Dt. 4:34; 26:8; 34:12; cf. Jer. 32:21).[84] "The holy war is the occasion par excellence of divine panic."[85]

5. *Fear and Joy.* The polarity of *tremendum* and *fascinans* inherent in the numinous holiness of God[86] explains why people react to the experience of God's presence with both fear and flight on the one hand and acceptance, trust, and joy on the other. This is clear in several passages where fear and joy, though polar opposites, stand in parallel (Ps. 40:4[3]; 52:8[6]; 64:10[9]; 96:11-13). According to Ex. 14:31, Yahweh's deeds evoke both fear and belief. Ps. 119:120,161 express numinous fear before the God who is present in the law. This same law is also a source of joy. Numinous fear thus becomes the starting point of a semantic development that reduces the element of literal fear to a "moral fear of God" and through affirmation and confession of Yahweh approaches the "cultic concept" (fear = worship).

---

80 Vriezen, *Theology,* 162f., 331-341.

81 W. Zimmerli, *Ezekiel 1. Herm* (Eng. trans. 1979), 87. Eichrodt and others consider *nôrāʾ* here a later gloss.

82 See I.3 above.

83 See *CAD,* VI (1956), 151; *AHw,* I (1972), 336; Becker, *Gottesfurcht im AT,* 66-74; Derousseaux, 97f.

84 See E. Zenger, "Funktion und Sinn der ältesten Herausführungsformel," *ZDMGSup,* 1 (1969), 334-342; W. Gross, "Die Herausführungsformel—Zum Verhältnis von Formel und Syntax," *ZAW,* 86 (1974), 425-452.

85 Derousseaux, 98; cf. Becker, *Gottesfurcht im AT,* 67, and earlier G. von Rad, *Der heilige Krieg im alten Israel* (Göttingen, [5]1969), 10ff., 63ff., 72ff., 82f.; Köhler, *Hebrew Man,* 116-19.

86 See IV.1 above.

V. "Fear Not." The formula *'al-tîrā'* (*'al-tîre'î, 'al-tîre'û*) appears in a wide range of literary and sociological contexts.

1. *Everyday Life.* It occurs 15 times as an idiom in everyday contexts: Gen. 35:17; 43:23; 50:19, 21; Jgs. 4:18; Ruth 3:11; 1 S. 4:20; 22:23; 23:17; 28:13; 2 S. 9:7; 2 K. 6:16; Ps. 49:17(16); Prov. 3:25 (?); Jer. 42:11. Usually no object is specified. The reason is stated in an independent clause (e.g., Gen. 43:23; 50:21; Ruth 3:11) or in a causal subordinate clause introduced by *kî* (Gen. 35:17; 1 S. 4:20; 22:23; 2 S. 9:7; 2 K. 6:16). In Gen. 35:17, the midwife reassures Rachel: "Fear not; for now you will have another son." Joy over the birth of a son will alleviate the fear of the mother, who is fighting for her life; cf. 1 S. 4:20. Joseph's brothers are afraid of death for quite different reasons; therefore they are encouraged by a servant (Gen. 43:23) and by Joseph himself (Gen. 50:19,21). Jonathan uses the phrase to enhearten David while he is being persecuted (1 S. 23:17); David uses it to reassure Abiathar and Meribaal, who are afraid that they will be put to death (1 S. 22:23; 2 S. 9:7). In 2 K. 6:16, it counters fear of military defeat, and in 2 K. 25:24 (= Jer. 40:9) fear of servitude. In ordinary usage, "Fear not" can be called a "banal formula of reassurance,"[87] which serves the purpose of encouraging someone in trouble, alleviating his fear (of death), strengthening his resolve. It can even be used casually as a rhetorical flourish, "Take it easy" (Ruth 3:11; possibly also Jgs. 4:18; Ps. 49:17[16]).

2. *Holy War.* The phrase occurs frequently in the context of war and battle, especially in the wars of Yahweh (Ex. 14:13; Nu. 14:9; 21:34; Dt. 1:21,29; 3:2,22; 7:18; 20:1,3; 31:6,8; Josh. 8:1; 10:8,25; 11:6; 2 Ch. 20:15,17; 32:7; Neh. 4:8[14]; Isa. 7:4). For the most part it appears in discourses before battle ("battle speeches"[88]), in which the leader encourages his host to be fearless and courageous when facing the enemy (Moses: Ex. 14:13; Dt. 1:21,29; 3:22 to Joshua; 7:18; 20:1; 31:6; 31:8 to Joshua in the presence of Israel; Joshua: Nu. 14:9; Josh. 10:25; a priest: Dt. 20:3; Hezekiah: 2 Ch. 32:7; Nehemiah: Neh. 4:8[14]). The inclusion of multiple synonyms is striking: *'mṣ* (Dt. 31:6; Josh. 10:25; 2 Ch. 32:7), *ḥzq* (Dt. 31:6; Josh. 10:25; 2 Ch. 32:7); *ḥtt* niphal (Dt. 1:21; 31:8; Josh. 8:1; 10:25; 2 Ch. 32:7); *'rṣ* (Dt. 1:29; 20:3; 31:6), *rkk* (Dt. 20:3; Isa. 7:4). In all cases, the exhortation to be fearless is motivated more or less formulaically by the assurance that Yahweh will be with them. In the other passages, the formula is placed in God's mouth; the regular form of the motivation is: "I will give . . . into your hand" (Nu. 21:34; Dt. 3:2; Josh. 10:8; 11:6). According to von Rad, this formula is associated with the institution of the oracle obtained at the outset of a holy war. It has been suggested[89] that the formula *'al-tîrā'* had its original *Sitz im Leben* in this ancient battle oracle.

Extrabiblical parallels have been cited. Heintz[90] calls the formula part of the

87 Derousseaux, 90; cf. Plath, 114f.

88 H. W. Wolff, *Frieden ohne Ende. BSt,* 35 (1962), 18ff.

89 Most recently by Derousseaux, 97.

90 J.-G. Heintz, "Oracles prophétiques et 'guerre sainte' selon les archives royales de Mari et l'AT," *Congress Volume, Rome 1968. SVT,* 17 (1969), 112-128, citing G. Dossin, *et al., Textes*

"stereotyped phraseology"[91] of the holy war. Dion, however, points out[92] that several of the passages cited[93] do not appear in the context of a battle oracle and that the formula *ʾal-tîrāʾ* is almost never found in really early OT texts, i.e., those dating from a period when Yahweh war was not just a theologoumenon but a reality. The clearest passages are Ex. 14:13 (J); Josh. 10:8; 11:6. Derousseaux, however, considers the latter two passages Deuteronomistic.[94] Nu. 14:9 is generally assigned to P.[95] All in all, there does not appear to be enough evidence to "establish 'fear not' as a distinctive and original holy war formula,"[96] notwithstanding the fact that the promise of victory was given by oracle before battle and the passages containing the "fear not" formula still reflect this institution.[97] These passages are now integrated into Deuteronom(ist)ic language and theology; the exhortation not to fear is based on the experience of Yahweh at work in history.[98]

3. *Oracles of Salvation.* The formula does, however, appear to have a firm *Sitz im Leben* in the so-called priestly oracle of salvation, as is shown by a variety of extrabiblical texts.[99] In the name of the deity, the priest addresses the supplicant with the "fear not" formula, followed by the self-predication of the deity ("I am . . .") introducing the oracle. Gressmann[100] recognized this form in numerous passages in Deutero-Isaiah (Isa. 41:10,13,14; 43:1,5; 44:2; 54:4; cf. 44:8; 51:12) and termed *ʾal-tîrāʾ* a revelation formula, having its original *Sitz im Leben* in the priestly oracle of salvation. Begrich[101] later demonstrated that the salvation oracle was also a cultic institution in Israel. It is found, for example, in the late passage Lam. 3:57. We may therefore assume that the salvation oracle influenced Deutero-Isaiah, especially since it usually appears in conjunction with

---

divers. Festschrift A. Parrot. ARM, XIII (1964), 114; Dossin, *Correspondance féminine. ARM,* X (1978), 80; other passages include *ANET*[3], 449-451, 605; *KAI,* 202 A, 12-14; RS 17.132, 3-5 (*PRU,* IV, 35f.); cf. H. Cazelles, "Connexions et structure de *Gen.,* XV," *RB,* 69 (1962), 321-349; H. Wildberger, "'Glauben' im AT," *ZThK,* 65 (1968), 129-159; O. Kaiser, "Traditionsgeschichtliche Untersuchung von Genesis 15," *ZAW,* 70 (1958), 107-126.

91 P. 122.

92 H. M. Dion, "The Patriarchal Traditions and the Literary Form of the 'Oracle of Salvation'," *CBQ,* 29 (1967), 198-206; also *CBQ,* 32 (1970), 565-570.

93 *ARM,* XIII, 114; X, 80; RS 17.132, 3-5.

94 P. 93.

95 Noth; N. Lohfink, "Darstellungskunst und Theologie in Dtn 1,6–3,29," *Bibl,* 41 (1960), 107, n. 2; Wagner, "Die Kundschaftergeschichten im AT," *ZAW,* 76 (1964), 262, n. 8; G. W. Coats, *Rebellion in the Wilderness* (Nashville, 1968), 138.

96 P.-E. Dion, 567.

97 Von Rad, 7f.; R. Smend, *Yahweh War and Tribal Confederation* (Eng. trans., Nashville, 1970); F. Stolz, *Jahwes und Israels Kriege. AThANT,* 60 (1972); M. Weippert, "'Heiliger Krieg' in Israel und Assyrien," *ZAW,* 84 (1972), 460-493.

98 Becker, *Gottesfurcht im AT,* 54.

99 Cf. *ANET*[3], 449-451, 605.

100 H. Gressmann, "Die literarische Analyse Deuterojesajas," *ZAW,* 34 (1914), 254-297.

101 G. Begrich, "Das priesterliche Heilsorakel," *ZAW,* 52 (1934), 81-92 = *GSAT. ThB,* 21 (1964), 217-231.

a self-predication[102] (Isa. 41:10,13,14; 43:3,5; 44:6,8; 51:12). It may also have influenced 2 K. 19:6 (par. Isa. 37:6); Isa. 10:24; Jer. 30:10f. (par. 46:27f.); the latter two passages also include self-predication. It probably lies behind Gen. 15:1; 26:24; 46:3 (all with self-predication) and Gen. 21:17; 28:13 LXX. It may be that *ʾal-tîrāʾ* as a revelation formula in salvation oracles gradually found its way into exhortations to be fearless in the context of the Yahweh war.[103]

4. *Theophanies.* Finally, we may cite the use of the revelation formula *ʾal-tîrāʾ* in theophanies (Ex. 20:20; Jgs. 6:23; Dnl. 10:12,19; cf. Gen. 15:1; 21:17; 26:24; 28:13 LXX; 46:3). According to Köhler,[104] the numinous experience of theophany or of the divine presence in general should be considered the original locus of this revelation formula. The God who reveals himself directly or through a messenger calms the terrified recipient of the revelation by saying, "Do not fear." This is clearly the case in Jgs. 6:23; Richter's hypothesis[105] that the fear motif is redactional makes no difference.[106] Ex. 20:20; Dnl. 10:12,19 are discussed in IV.2 above. We may agree with the scholars who reject Köhler's position,[107] in that the passages from Deutero-Isaiah that he cites are irrelevant (see above) and Gen. 15:1; 26:24; 46:3 have been influenced by the literary form of the salvation oracle. Weiser and Kaiser[108] therefore suggest that the salvation oracle was associated originally with a (cultic) theophany. We must leave the question of its original *Sitz im Leben* unresolved. In any case, *ʾal-tîrāʾ* appears as a revelation formula in the context of theophany; in this function it also influenced the NT.

VI. Loyalty to the God of the Covenant.

1. *Deuteronom(ist)ic Literature.* As Becker and Derousseaux observe, the use of "to fear Yahweh" for fearing God is remarkably uniform, both grammatically and semantically, in Deuteronomic and Deuteronomistic literature. It is therefore unnecessary to discuss in detail the *yrʾ* passages in the various strata or schools.[109] The relevant passages

---

102 See K. Elliger, "Ich bin der Herr—euer Gott," *Theologie als Glaubenswagnis. Festschrift K. Heim* (Hamburg, 1954), 9-34 = *KlSch. ThB,* 32 (1966), 211-231; W. Zimmerli, "I am Yahweh," *I Am Yahweh* (Eng. trans., Atlanta, 1982), 1-28; *idem,* "The Word of Divine Self-Manifestation (Proof-Saying): A Prophetic Genre," *I Am Yahweh,* 99-110; R. Rendtorff, *Offenbarung als Geschichte. KuD, Beiheft,* 1 (1961), 32-38.

103 Becker, *Gottesfurcht im AT,* 52, contra Derousseaux, 97, who postulates exactly the opposite development, since he considers the priestly salvation oracle a "derivative and late form."

104 *SchThZ,* 36 (1919), 33-39.

105 W. Richter, *Traditionsgeschichtliche Untersuchungen zum Richterbuch. BBB,* 18 (^{2}1966), 203f.

106 For a recent discussion of this passage, see Y. Zakovitch, "The Sacrifice of Gideon (Jud. 6:11-24) and the Sacrifice of Manoaḥ (Jud. 13)," *ShnatMikr,* 1 (1975), 151-54 [Heb.], XXV [Eng.].

107 Plath, 120f.; Becker, *Gottesfurcht im AT,* 51ff.; Derousseaux, 91; Stähli, 773.

108 Pp. 111-16.

109 M. Noth, *Überlieferungsgeschichtliche Studien,* I (Tübingen, ^{3}1967); G. von Rad, "The Form-critical Problem of the Hexateuch," *The Problem of the Hexateuch* (Eng. trans. 1966; repr. London, 1984), 1-78; G. Minette de Tillesse, "Sections 'tu' et sections 'vous' dans le Deutéronome," *VT,* 12 (1962), 29-87; N. Lohfink, *Das Hauptgebot. AnBibl,* 20 (1963); J. G. Plöger,

are Dt. 4:10; 5:29; 6:2,13,24; 8:6; 10:12,20; 13:5(4); 14:23; 17:19; 28:58; 31:12,13; Josh. 4:24; 24:14; Jgs. 6:10; 1 S. 12:14,24; 1 K. 8:40,43 par. 2 Ch. 6:31,33; 2 K. 17:7,25,28,32-39,41. Scholars generally assign the *yrʾ* passages to later hands, but Lohfink ascribes the passages in Dt. 5–11 (except for 8:6) to the author of the basic document. The grammatical uniformity is evidenced by the appearance of verbal forms exclusively,[110] typically the infinitive construct in Deuteronomy. The object of the verb is always "Yahweh"—in Deuteronomy, "Yahweh your/our God."

A central theologoumenon of Deuteronom(ist)ic literature is Yahweh's covenant with Israel. Baltzer has attempted to analyze the structure of the covenant formulary more precisely.[111] Von Rad proposes the attractive theory that the covenant formulary took on literary form in Deuteronomy. Whether or not this is true in detail, the Yahweh covenant and its specific implications—cultic worship of Yahweh, fidelity to the Covenant Code (not the same thing as observance of the law, as we shall see below)—are very important for interpretation of the *yrʾ* passages.

Dt. 6:13,24 are part of what Lohfink calls the great "setting of the law" (Dt. 6:10-25). They constitute formally the statement of substance or "general clause" of the covenant and provide a commentary on the primary commandment: "fear" means "worship," specifically sole and faithful worship of Yahweh. This is shown also by the synonyms in the surrounding context, all of which refer to fidelity to the covenant and worship of Yahweh: *škḥ* (v. 12), *ʿbd* (v. 13),[112] *šbʿ bšmw* (v. 13), *hlk ʾḥry ʾlhym ʾḥrym* (v. 14).[113]

Whether Dt. 5 and 6 were a single unit from the beginning or Dt. 6:2 is a transitional verse introducing a new unit that begins with 6:4ff., there is a structural association between 5:29 and 6:2 in the present form of the text. The connection with 6:4ff. makes it clear that *yrʾ* means "worship" in the sense of fidelity to the covenant God; the element of obedience to the law is secondary to that of faithfulness to the covenant. According to 5:29, the people should "fear" Yahweh with their heart; according to 6:2, they should "love" him. In other words, *yrʾ* and *ʾhb* belong to the terminology of the general clause in the covenant treaty and are to this extent synonymous (→ אהב *ʾāhaḇ* [*ʾāhabh*]). "Heart" (RSV) or "mind" in 5:29 does not refer to feelings or emotions, but to the conscious and deliberate decision to be faithful to Yahweh and Yahweh's covenant.[114]

In Dt. 10:12,20 we find the source for the passages in chs. 5f., especially since 10:20 is formulated in the same way as 6:13, assuming that the author of chs. 5f. drew on

---

Literarkritische, formgeschichtliche und stilkritische Untersuchungen zum Deuteronomium. BBB, 26 (1967); J. Floss, *Jahwe dienen, Göttern dienen. BBB,* 45 (1975); S. Mittmann, *Deuteronomium 1 1–6 3* literarkritisch und traditionsgeschichtlich untersucht. *BZAW,* 139 (1975).

110 On 2 K. 17:32-34, see Becker, *Gottesfurcht im AT,* 87.

111 Baltzer, 22f., 46f.; cf. D. J. McCarthy, *Der Gottesbund im AT. SBS,* 13 (²1967); *idem, OT Covenant* (Oxford, 1972); E. Kutsch, *Verheissung und Gesetz. BZAW,* 131 (1973).

112 See F. Horst, "Der Eid im AT," *EvTh,* 17 (1951), 366ff. = *Gottes Recht. GSAT. ThB,* 12 (1961), 297f.

113 Antithetical; see Köhler, *Hebrew Man,* 99, n. 1; F. J. Helfmeyer, *Die Nachfolge Gottes im AT. BBB,* 29 (1968).

114 J. B. Bauer, "De 'Cordis' Notione Biblica et Iudaica," *VD,* 40 (1962), 27-32.

10:12–11:17. Here, too, especially if we follow Baltzer[115] in assigning both passages to the general clause, *yr'* means to worship Yahweh faithfully as the covenant God. We may interpret Dt. 8:6; 13:5, which belong to later strata, in the same sense.

The fear of Yahweh is something that can be learned (Dt. 4:10; 14:23; 17:19; 31:12f.). We may note that what is learned in 14:23; 17:19 is behavior appropriate to fear or worship, whereas in 4:10 and 31:12f. it is the law. Even if one sees in these passages "reemphasis on the typical Deuteronomistic notion of what it means to worship Yahweh faithfully," they at least pave the way for the legalistic understanding of the fear of Yahweh.[116]

The Deuteronomistic passages outside of Deuteronomy exhibit the same meaning for *yr'*. This is best illustrated by 2 K. 17:7-41, basically a Deuteronomistic meditation on the relationship between fear of Yahweh and observance of the law. Although the *yr'* passages may belong to various strata,[117] they all have the same meaning,[118] which can appropriately be rendered as "worship" (Vulg. *colere*; cf. Jgs. 6:10).

The concept "fear of God" appears in Deuteronom(ist)ic literature almost exclusively in the cultic sense ("fear" = "worship"). With Yahweh as object, it refers to worship of Yahweh, faithfulness to the covenant, which finds expression in the cult of Yahweh alone and observance of the Covenant Code. The Deuteronomistic authors make use of the cultic terminology common throughout the ancient Near East, including Israel, drawing on it in service of their central concern: faithfulness to Yahweh.[119]

2. *Psalms.* The phrase *yir'aṯ YHWH* in the Psalms constitutes an independent development, both grammatically and semantically, of the fear of Yahweh concept. It is typified by the exclusive use of the plural as well as the divine name "Yahweh" or the appropriate suffix (Ps. 66:16 is no exception, since the name "Yahweh" was probably used in the original version of the Elohistic Psalter). Equivalent to the suffix forms are *yir'ê šᵉmeḵā* (Ps. 61:6[5]) and *yir'ê šᵉmî* (Mal. 3:20[4:2]). The construct phrase uses the verbal adjective to modify Yahweh as subject; *yir'ê YHWH* does not mean "those who worship Yahweh" but "the worshippers who belong to Yahweh." In other words, this idiom expresses possession. "Yahweh-fearers" always refers to the community that worships Yahweh.

The texts nevertheless exhibit some semantic nuances. Originally, "Yahweh-fearers" referred to the cultic community assembled in the sanctuary (Ps. 22:24,26[23,25]; 31:20[19]; 66:16). As this meaning was extended, the entire people of Yahweh could be so designated (Ps. 15:4; 60:6[4]; 61:6[5]; 85:10[9]). In certain late psalms, all influenced

115 P. 38.

116 See below.

117 O. Eissfeldt, *The OT: An Intro.* (Eng. trans., New York, 1965), 359; Šanda; Noth, 85; A. Jepsen, *Die Quellen des Königsbuches* (Halle, ²1956) [2. K. 2, 21, 23b: R^1; 7-10, 22, 23a, 34-40: R^2; 24-33, 41: R^3]; etc.

118 Contra Olivier, 41f.

119 Becker, *Gottesfurcht im AT,* 85; Derousseaux, 255. It is unlikely, however, that the development took the course outlined by the latter, 255ff.

by the wisdom tradition, it comes to mean "those who are faithful to Yahweh," the "devout" (Ps. 25:14; 33:18; 34:8,10[7,9]; 103:11,13,17; 111:5; 119:74,79; 145:19; 147:11). The notion of a cultic community assembled in the sanctuary yields to that of faithfulness to Yahweh evidenced by a life of devotion. Here we see the influence of the ethical (Ps. 25:14; 34:8,10[7,9]) or nomistic (103:17; 119:74,79) concept of the fear of God.[120] It is still a matter of debate whether "those who fear Yahweh" in Ps. 115:11,13; 118:4; 135:20 are so-called "proselytes"[121] or (more likely) the various groups of participants in the postexilic cult.[122]

3. *Other Texts.* Finally we come to a few non-Deuteronomistic texts that use "fear" in the sense of "worship Yahweh faithfully."

The meaning "worship" is certain in Neh. 1:11. This verse concludes the prayer of Nehemiah (Neh. 1:5-11), which has long been recognized to echo Deuteronomistic language (cf. Dt. 3:26-45; 9:5-37).[123] It is reasonable to follow Baltzer[124] in positing a common setting for Deuteronomistic preaching and this penitential prayer. Jer. 32:39f. is concerned with faithfulness to Yahweh as the God of the covenant (cf. the covenant formula in v. 38 and mention of the covenant in v. 40), evidenced in constant, undivided worship.[125] Other passages include 2 Ch. 26:5; Ps. 5:8(7); 86:11; 130:4; Isa. 63:17. Simple cultic worship is probably intended in Josh. 22:25; Isa. 29:13,[126] while Jon. 1:9 has the weakened sense of "belonging to a particular cult or religion."

VII. Fear of God as Moral Response.

1. *Northern Prophecy. The root yr'* appears 3 times in the Elijah/Elisha cycle: 1 K. 18:3,12; 2 K. 4:1. Although the grammatical form (verbal adj. in periphrastic conjugation) also appears in Deuteronomistic passages (1 K. 17:3–2 K. 24:41), they cannot be considered Deuteronomistic, since 1 K. 17–19 was incorporated almost entirely from an existing source.[127] Becker[128] argues nevertheless that there is a semantic connection with Deuteronom(ist)ic passages and that *yr'* is used in the cultic sense of "fearing God":

---

120 See VII and VIII below.

121 A. Bertholet, *Die Stellung der Israeliten und der Juden zu den Fremden* (Freiburg, 1896), 182; Briggs; Kittel; Gunkel; Knabenbauer; Hänel, 125; Calès; cf. Pannier; Weiser; Kraus. On proselytes in general, see E. Schürer, *The History of the Jewish People in the Age of Jesus Christ (175 B.C.–A.D. 135),* III/1 (Eng. trans., Edinburgh, ²1986), 150-176; K. Kuhn, "προσήλυτος," *TDNT,* VI, 727-744.

122 Plath, 102f.; Becker, *Gottesfurcht im AT,* 160; cf. Herkenne, Schmidt, Nötscher, Castellino.

123 Rudolph, 105.

124 Pp. 46f.

125 On the relationship of this passage to Jer. 24:4-7; 31:31-34; Ezk. 36:22-32; 37:15-28; 11:17-21, see J. W. Miller, *Das Verhältnis Jeremias und Hesekiels sprachlich und theologisch untersucht* (Assen, 1955), 97-100.

126 Duhm, Fohrer.

127 Šanda, Eissfeldt; cf. R. de Vaux, *Elie le Prophète,* I (Paris, 1956), 53-83; G. Fohrer, *Elia. AThANT,* 53 (²1968); O. H. Steck, *Überlieferung und Zeitgeschichte in den Elia-Erzählungen. WMANT,* 26 (1968).

128 *Gottesfurcht im AT,* 163f.

Obadiah and the prophet's disciples are true worshippers of Yahweh, unlike the devotees of Baʿal. This is true, but the question remains whether the context does not suggest a moralistic nuance.[129]

The same is true for Hos. 10:3, the only place *yrʾ* occurs in Hosea. Some scholars[130] omit *kî lōʾ yārēʾnû ʾeṯ-YHWH* as a gloss. Becker,[131] interpreting *yrʾ* in the cultic sense, understands Hos. 10:3 as the people's lament: absence of a king is their punishment for practicing forbidden cults instead of worshipping Yahweh alone. Weiser takes the verse to be the people's admission that failure to fear God is the source of all evil. Wolff sees it as a confession of sin. Both interpret "fear of God" as the moral response of the people to Yahweh's demands.

2. *Elohist.* The Elohistic fragments in the Pentateuch[132] uniformly exhibit an ethical sense of the "fear of God" concept. In the E version of Sarah's peril (Gen. 20:1-18), fear of God is a central theme.[133] Here it has the general sense of ethical conduct: reverence and obedience toward God's commandments coupled with respect for the rights and freedom of strangers. Thus E reinterprets the ancient story (cf. Gen. 12:10-20; 26:7-11) and gives it a new accent.

This is also the case in Gen. 22. E characterizes the ancient narrative as a story of testing (v. 1); with an artful play on words, he transforms the original theme *ʾᵉlōhîm yirʾeh* (vv. 8, 14) into *yᵉrēʾ ʾᵉlōhîm* (v. 12). E here defines fear of God as obedience to God, trust that makes it possible to take the ultimate risk.

The disobedience of the Hebrew midwives (Ex. 1:15-21) is a story unique to E, according to whom fear of God was with the people of Israel from the cradle: "And because the midwives feared God he gave them families" (v. 21). But here to fear God means to disobey the command of the Egyptian king: "Obedience to God teaches disobedience to the will of political oppressors who command death where God's will is life."[134]

Fear of God likewise plays a crucial role in E's version of the Sinai narrative. In the first instance it is the people's numinous fear in the presence of a theophany (Ex. 20:18b),[135] which E seizes upon with reverent awe to underline the distance between God and mortals (cf. Ex. 3:6b). But then E gives the event an entirely new interpretation: "Do not fear; for God has come to prove you, and that the fear of him may be before your eyes, that you may not sin" (Ex. 18:20).

One of E's central concerns is thus the fear of God in the specifically ethical sense of the term. E took an existing concept and applied it to the concrete situation of Israel in his own day. It has been suggested that E was influenced by an "ethical movement"

---

129 Derousseaux, 160f.

130 Marti, Sellin (*Das Zwölfprophetenbuch. KAT,* XII [1922, but not ²1929]), Deissler.

131 *Gottesfurcht im AT,* 172.

132 For a discussion, see IV.2 above.

133 Wolff, *ThB,* 22 (²1973), 405f.; P. Weimar, *Untersuchungen zur Redaktionsgeschichte des Pentateuch. BZAW,* 146 (1977), 73.

134 Wolff, *ibid.,* 409.

135 See IV.2 above.

emanating from prophetic circles of the ninth century.[136] But the grammatical forms and the ethical universalism of the concept show that it was a typical term common to Wisdom Literature.

3. *Wisdom.* Fear of God (or Yahweh), expressed by the phrases *yᵉrēʾ YHWH* and especially *yirʾaṯ YHWH,*[137] is a key concept in Wisdom Literature. This tradition encountered a secular world in which natural processes obeyed their own inner laws, and values such as life, possessions, and honor were esteemed for their own sake; at the same time, it had a strong sense of Yahweh's sovereign governance of this world and its history. It therefore undertook to analyze and explain this complex reality so that people might have guidelines for proper conduct in response. Wisdom calls this conduct *yirʾaṯ YHWH.* The problems and questions dealt with by wisdom traditions are quite diverse, and so the resulting picture of what fear of Yahweh means is highly differentiated.

a. In Proverbs, we must distinguish the meanings found in the early collections (Prov. 10–29) from those in the redactional framework (chs. 1–9, 30, 31).[138] If we take Prov. 1:7 as a thematic statement and 31:30b (*ʾiššâ yirʾaṯ-YHWH*) as the climax of the poem in 31:10-31, the entire book is framed by the motif of fear of God; this is true even if *yirʾaṯ YHWH* is considered a gloss.[139]

Fear of Yahweh is mentioned 9 times in 10:1–22:16, 7 of which are associated with the idea of retribution (10:27; 14:26,27; 15:16; 16:6; 19:23; 22:4). Fear of Yahweh is rewarded with a long and secure life (14:26f.; 19:23); it is the source of life (14:27). Poverty with it is better than riches without it (15:16). It helps avoid evil (16:6; 19:23) and therefore deserves high esteem (14:2). According to 15:33, it teaches wisdom, including proper conduct toward God, the king, and those in authority (24:21). It encourages caution (14:16; 28:14).

"The fear of Yahweh is the beginning of wisdom" (Prov. 1:7). This proverbial-sounding statement appears in several variations (Job 28:28; Ps. 111:10; Prov. 1:29; 2:5; 9:10; 15:33; cf. Isa. 11:2; 33:6); it reflects the fundamental relationship between fear of Yahweh and wisdom (*daʿaṯ* or *ḥoḵmâ*). The word *rēʾšîṯ* should not be understood in the sense of "heart" or "essence," but "beginning" (cf. Prov. 9:10). If the fear of Yahweh is the beginning of wisdom, a statement is being made about the origin of wisdom. The question addressed is not the locus of fear of God, but the locus of wisdom. Wisdom is here set in an intimate relationship with fear of God, which precedes all wisdom as its necessary condition and instructs in wisdom. In other words, all human knowledge can be traced back to its divine roots. No one can be expert in the complexities of life who does not begin with the knowledge of Yahweh and dependence on him.[140]

---

136 Jepsen, Cazelles, Plath, Derousseaux.

137 See I.4 above.

138 For detailed analysis, see U. Skladny, *Die ältesten Spruchsammlungen in Israel* (Göttingen, 1962); H. H. Schmid, *Wesen und Geschichte der Weisheit. BZAW,* 101 (1966); B. Lang, *Die weisheitliche Wehrrede. SBS,* 54 (1972); *idem, Frau Weisheit* (Düsseldorf, 1975).

139 Toy, Oesterley, Gemser.

140 Von Rad.

The question of what is required for authentic knowledge was also asked and answered in detail by early wisdom; scholars no longer maintain that it was "utilitarian and eudaimonistic"[141] or "an ethics of prudence."[142] "While later wisdom answered the question about the prerequisite for acquiring wisdom in theological terms (wisdom comes from God), the answer here [in early wisdom] is an anthropological one. Wisdom stands and falls according to the right attitude of man to God."[143]

b. Job uses the traditional terminology of the ethical concept of fear of God found in the wisdom tradition. The phrase *ye rē' ^e lōhîm* appears in Job 1:1,8; 2:3. Unique to Job is the association of *yir'â* with *šadday* (6:14) and *'^a d̲ōnāy* (28:28); both phrases, however, are equivalent semantically to *yir'at̲ YHWH*. Some scholars[144] emend the absolute *yir'â* in the speeches of Eliphaz (4:6; 15:4; 22:4) to *yir'at̲ ^e lōhîm*, but the absolute usage might represent a shorthand form.[145] Parallel terms include *tām, yāšar,* and *sûr mēra'* (1:1,8; 2:3). For grammatical and semantic reasons, Job 28:28, which concludes the Wisdom poem in ch. 28, is considered a later addition by many scholars;[146] but it represents the real point of the passage. Elsewhere the poem insists explicitly that wisdom resides with God alone and is inaccessible to mortals; v. 28, however, states that only the fear of God enables anyone to achieve wisdom, which is by nature totally inaccessible. In other words, wisdom itself is in a sense called into question. Unlike Proverbs, this passage does not espouse wisdom for its own sake but makes it secondary to the fear of God. Here we have hints of an understanding of the fear of God that plays an important role in Ecclesiastes.

c. Ecclesiastes disputes the concept of the fear of God basic to the wisdom tradition (Eccl. 3:14; 5:6[7]; 7:18; 8:12a,b,13; 9:2; 12:5,13). Earlier scholars[147] proposed radical analyses of the book, finding a variety of redactors and glossators who were responsible for the *yr'* passages. Today the literary unity of Ecclesiastes is emphasized, and only a very few passages are considered late additions. Except for Eccl. 12:13, all the *yr'* passages probably derive from the original author of the book.

According to Eccl. 3:14, since God's ordinances are immutable and God is beyond human knowledge, "to fear God" (with *millipnê*!) means that mortals have no choice but absolute submission and strict obedience,[148] relying on whatever God vouchsafes to grant and ready "to bear whatever riddles and afflictions God may decree."[149] Here *yr'* once more has its original sense: terror of the incomprehensible numinous.[150]

---

141 Gemser.

142 Baumgartner.

143 G. von Rad, *Wisdom in Israel* (Eng. trans., Nashville, 1972), 69.

144 Plath, 55; G. Fohrer, *Das Buch Hiob. KAT,* XVI (1963), 138, 267, 355.

145 Becker, *Gottesfurcht im AT,* 247.

146 Duhm, Driver-Gray, Dhorme; G. von Rad, *OT Theology,* I (Eng. trans., New York, 1962), 447, calls the verse "a positive ending . . . dictated by a pastoral concern."

147 Siegfried, Podchard, etc.

148 Wildeboer; similarly Hertzberg, Galling, Oosterhoff.

149 Zimmerli.

150 J. Fichtner, *Die altorientalische Weisheit in ihrer israelitisch-jüdischen Ausprägung. BZAW,* 62 (1933), 52.

Eccl. 5:6(7) is similar. Verse 6b(7b) is a positive admonition concluding the cautionary discourse in 4:17–5:6(5:1-7): "But do you fear God." This imperative must be understood against the background of God's terrifying majesty and power and a corresponding sense of human dependence and futility: fear of God is the only appropriate expression of human finitude.

The situation is more complex in Eccl. 7:18, which concludes the section that begins with v. 15.[151] A wisdom commonplace in v. 18a is given a theological twist by v. 18b: "He who fears God shall come forth from them all." Some scholars[152] therefore consider 18b secondary, but it is the real point of the passage.[153] There is little sense here of the numinous aspect of the fear of God, which is to be understood in the ethical sense of traditional wisdom.

Many scholars consider Eccl. 8:12b-13 a secondary addition.[154] The verses constitute an aside, a personal statement of faith on the part of the Preacher. Paronomasia in the relative clause adds emphasis: "those who fear God particularly"; the antithesis in v. 13 reinforces the statement. Here the Preacher is clearly attacking a superficial understanding of what it means to fear God. "God-fearers" are those who truly live up to their name; contrary to all expectations, only they will attain happiness.

All these passages bear witness to a profound notion of fearing God. Especially in the personal statement of Eccl. 8:12b-13, the author radicalizes the ethical interpretation of traditional wisdom, tracing fear of God to its original numinous and powerful source. "If 'fear of God' is of any avail, it cannot be ordinary fear, but only the fear that makes people tremble in the presence of the holy God."[155]

4. *Fear of God as Obedience.* Certain texts reflect a specialized development of the ethical concept of fear of God. The Holiness Code contains 5 occurrences of the formula "You shall fear your God; I am Yahweh" (Lev. 19:14,32; 25:17,36,43). It lends weight to requirements of mercy or social justice; they cease to be merely general ethical norms but enshrine instead the declared will of the covenant God and thus demand obedience. Neh. 5:9,15 should probably be interpreted in the same sense, as practical consequences of what the Holiness Code requires. Fear of God as obedience to the revealed will of Yahweh appears also in the commandment to revere father and mother (Lev. 19:3; cf. Mal. 1:6a), formulated to reflect the Decalog.

VIII. Fear of God as Devotion to Torah. In some late Wisdom psalms there is a special relationship between fear of Yahweh and Yahweh's torah. Ps. 19b extols Yahweh's torah, describing its perfection and its beneficent effects. Several synonyms for torah appear: *ʿēḏûṯ YHWH* (Ps. 19:8b[7b]), *piqqûḏê YHWH* (v. 9a[8a]), *miṣwaṯ*

---

151 Delitzsch, Wildeboer; for a different analysis, see Hitzig, Galling, Zimmerli, Hertzberg (through v. 22); Volz, Budde (v. 24).

152 Volz, Budde, Fichtner, Galling.

153 Gordis.

154 Volz: "a pious corrective"; Budde: "an orthodox gloss"; cf. Rudolph, Fichtner, Galling.

155 E. Pfeiffer, 151.

YHWH (v. 9b[8b]), *mišpᵉṭê-YHWH* (v. 10b[9b]), *yir'aṯ YHWH* (v. 10a[9a]). It would be wrong to evade the grammatical and semantic difficulties by interpreting the last expression as meaning subjective obedience to the law[156] or "religious devotion" in general[157] or by emending it to *'imraṯ YHWH.*[158] We are dealing rather with an instance of metonymy, which uses *yir'aṯ YHWH* as a term for torah. This may also be the case in Ps. 111:10. Verse 10a cites the familiar Wisdom aphorism (Prov. 1:7; etc.), but Ps. 111:7f. as well as the reference to a rich reward in v. 10 (cf. Ps. 19:12[11]!) suggest this interpretation. Ps. 119:63 uses "fear Yahweh" and "keep his precepts" in parallel. Ps. 112:1; 128:1,4 sing the praises of those who fear Yahweh; here this fear consists in delight in Yahweh's commandments (112:1) or walking in his ways (128:1).

The question is how we should understand this relationship between fear of Yahweh and devotion to torah. Becker,[159] followed by Stähli,[160] interprets it "nomistically"; in other words, citing Noth,[161] he contrasts the Deuteronom(ist)ic understanding of the law as embodying the covenant to a nomistic understanding shaped by late wisdom, which sees in torah the "absolute entity" of the late period (Noth). To each there corresponds a specific understanding of fear of God: faithfulness to the covenant God versus observance of the law. Derousseaux[162] correctly points out that there is little textual support for such a distinction. In addition, there is more reluctance today than in the period between Duhm and Noth to criticize or reject the "legalism" of "late Judaism." This change is linked with a different understanding of torah.[163] Kraus states:[164] "In man's attitude toward the תורה (the translation 'law' should be avoided as much as possible) we ought to consider presuppositions that exclude every thought of nomism, Judaism, and narrow observance." Becker also sees this, pointing out explicitly that he does not want "nomistic" understood in the pejorative sense of "legalistic."[165] It marks not simply a decline, but in some ways a high point.[166]

IX. Qumran. Of the many OT terms for fear,[167] only 4 occur in the Dead Sea scrolls: *pḥd, ḥtt, 'rṣ,* and *yr'*. The last is the most frequent. It is noteworthy that "the idea of the

156 Duhm, Schmidt, Weiser, Castellino.

157 Kittel, Pannier, Nötscher, Oosterhoff, 75f.

158 Gunkel, Briggs, Kraus.

159 *Gottesfurcht im AT,* 262ff.

160 Pp. 777f.

161 M. Noth, "The Laws in the Pentateuch," in *The Laws in the Pentateuch and Other Studies* (Eng. trans. 1967, repr. London, 1984), 1-107.

162 Pp. 348f.

163 See G. Östborn, *Tōrā in the OT* (Lund, 1945); H.-J. Kraus, "Freude an Gottes Gesetz," *EvTh,* 10 (1950/51), 337-351; *idem, Psalms 1-59* (Eng. trans., Minneapolis, 1988), *Psalms 60-150,* on Pss. 1, 19, 119; von Rad, *OT Theology,* I, 221f.; II (Eng. trans., New York, 1965), 388-409; W. Zimmerli, "Das Gesetz im AT," *Gottes Offenbarung. Gesammelte Aufsätze,* 1. *ThB,* 19 (²1969), 249-276.

164 *Psalms 1-59,* 274.

165 *Gottesfurcht im AT,* 262, n. 1.

166 *Ibid.,* 266f.

167 See I.3 above.

fear of God is not among the themes frequently found in the Qumran documents."[168] The few passages where it does appear draw on various forms of the OT concept, such as the exhortation to be fearless in the context of the holy war (1QM 10:3; 15:8; 17:4), the quotation of Isa. 11:2 in 1QSb 5:25, and the quotation of Mal. 3:16 in CD 20:19. In CD 10:2, *yr' 't 'l* means "able to participate in the cult."[169]

Fuhs

---

168 Romaniuk, 29; cf. H. Braun, *Spätjüdisch-häretischer und frühchristlicher Radikalismus. BHTh,* 24 (1957), II, 25f.; W. Pesch, "Zur Formgeschichte und Exegese von Lk 12,32," *Bibl,* 41 (1960), 31, n. 2.

169 Cf. J. Maier, *Die Texte vom Toten Meer* (Munich, 1960), II, 54.

יָרַד *yāraḏ*

Contents: I. General: 1. Etymology, Occurrences, Meaning; 2. LXX. II. Literal Usage: 1. General; 2. Natural Phenomena; 3. Topographical; 4. Nautical. III. Figurative Usage: 1. Threats and Curses; 2. Individual Prayers; 3. Prov. 18:8. IV. Descent to the Underworld: 1. General; 2. Prayers; 3. Prophetic Dirges; 4. Judgment and Judgment Oracles; 5. The Strange Woman. V. Yahweh's Descent: 1. Theophany; 2. J. VI. Dead Sea Scrolls.

I. General.

1. *Etymology, Occurrences, Meaning.* The common Semitic verb *yrd/wrd*[1] appears 380 times in the OT: 307 in the qal, 67 in the hiphil, and 6 in the hophal. It always denotes the direction from above to below. It usually also expresses motion, but it can sometimes merely state a connection between two points at different levels (cf. Neh. 3:15; Prov. 7:27).[2] Many passages suggest that the word might mean simply "go" or "climb" (either

---

yāraḏ. J. Barr, *Comparative Philology and the Text of the OT* (Oxford, 1968), 174f.; G. R. Driver, "Mistranslations," *PEQ,* 79 (1947), 123-26; *idem,* "On עלה 'went up country' and ירד 'went down country'," *ZAW,* 69 (1957), 74-77; O. Eissfeldt, *Baal Zaphon, Zeus Kasios und der Durchzug der Israeliten durchs Meer. BRA,* 1 (1932); *idem, Die Komposition der Samuelisbücher* (Leipzig, 1931), 31; K. Galling, "Bethel und Gilgal," *ZDPV,* 66 (1943), 140-155; *idem,* "Der Ehrenname Elisas und die Entrückung Elias," *ZThK,* 53 (1956), 129-148, esp. 136, n. 1; J. Jeremias, *Theophanie. WMANT,* 10 (^{2}1972); W. Leslau, "An Ethiopian Parallel to Hebrew עלה 'Went Up Country' and ירד 'Went Down Country'," *ZAW,* 74 (1962), 322f.; J. Schneider, "καταβαίνω," *TDNT,* I, 522f.; F. Schnutenhaus, "Das Kommen und Erscheinen Gottes im AT," *ZAW,* 76 (1964), 1-22, esp. 5f.; J. C. VanderKam, "The Theophany of Enoch I 3b-7, 9," *VT,* 23 (1973), 133; G. Wehmeier, "עלה *'lh* hinaufgehen," *THAT,* II, 272-290; J. V. K. Wilson, "Hebrew and Akkadian Philological Notes," *JSS,* 7 (1962), 173-183, esp. 173-75.

1 *KBL*^{3}, 415.

2 See also II.3.d below.

up or down). This interpretation is accepted by several scholars,[3] but is contradicted by the frequent appearance of *yāraḏ* with *ʿālâ* (Gen. 28:12; Dt. 28:43; 1 S. 2:6; 6:21; 14:36f.,46; 2 Ch. 20:16; Job 7:9; Ps. 104:8; 107:26; Prov. 21:22; 30:4; Eccl. 3:21; Am. 9:2). More likely the usage reflects a local or technical idiom that cannot be traced further; see, for example, Jgs. 11:37 or the phrase *yāraḏ laṭṭeḇaḥ* unique to Jeremiah.[4] Neither the hiphil nor the hophal exhibits grammatical or semantic peculiarities distinct from the qal (compare Lev. 9:22 with 1 K. 1:53).

2. *LXX.* To the extent that the LXX reflects the MT, the verb *katabaínō* is used to translate the qal about 80 percent of the time. An additional 7 compounds use the prefix *katá*: *katágō* (8 times), *kathairéomai* (twice), *synkatabaínō, katabibázō, katadýomai, katapēdáō,* and *kataspáō* (once each), as well as the prepositional phrase *eis katábosin.* The remainder of the passages are distributed among 15 different verbs, among which the only distinguishable group comprises *érchomai, diérchomai, eisérchomai,* and *parérchomai,* with a total of 6 occurrences. The translation *anabaínō* in Ruth 3:3 (but not v. 6) is discussed by Rudolph.[5] For the hiphil, we find *katágō* (35 times), *kathairéō* (10), *katabibázō* (8), *kataphérō* (2), *kararréō,* and *katachaláō* (once each), as well as 10 other verbs that occur once each. Noteworthy are *anabibázō* in 2 Ch. 23:20 and *anaphérō* in 1 S. 6:15. For the hophal, we find *katabaínō, katabibázomai* (twice each), *kathairéō,* and *aphairéomai* (once each).

II. Literal Usage.

1. *General.* The action is either repeatable with respect to the subject (qal, hophal) or object (hiphil), or else it means the death or destruction of the subject (qal) or object (hiphil). The first group includes (a) qal: going down a ladder (Gen. 28:12), alighting from an ass (1 S. 25:23) or a chariot (Jgs. 4:15), getting out of bed (2 K. 1:4,6,16), descending the steps of the altar (Lev. 9:22), stepping down from a throne (Ezk. 26:16), and (of birds) swooping down upon prey (Gen. 15:11); (b) hiphil: setting a water jar down from one's shoulder (Gen. 24:18,46), lowering sacks to the ground (Gen. 44:11), taking off jewelry (Ex. 33:5), taking down the tabernacle (Nu. 1:51; cf. 10:17 [hophal]) or its veil (Nu. 4:5), lowering someone out a window (Josh. 2:15,18), taking a body down from a "tree" (Josh. 8:29; 10:27), taking something off a cart (1 S. 6:15), taking someone from the altar (1 K. 1:53) or from the upper chamber of a house (1 K. 17:23), removing the "sea" from the bronze oxen (2 K. 16:17), bringing down those who sit on thrones (Isa. 10:13) or birds in flight (Hos. 7:12), or bowing one's head (Lam. 2:10).

The second group includes (a) qal: destruction of cities (Dt. 20:20), fortified walls (Dt. 28:52), or pillars (Ezk. 26:11), overthrowing horses and riders (Hag. 2:22), leveling of forests (Isa. 32:19; Zec. 11:2), slaughter of oxen (Isa. 34:7), the fall of a crown from a royal head (Jer. 13:18 conj.[6]), and going down to slaughter (Jer. 48:15; 50:27); (b)

---

3 Eissfeldt, *Baal-Zaphon,* 3, n. 3; Barr, 174f.; and others.

4 See II.1 below.

5 W. Rudolph, *Das Buch Ruth. KAT,* XVII/1 (1962), 52.

6 K. Elliger, *Deuterojesaja. BK,* XI/1 (1978), 335-38.

hiphil: breaking down the bars of a gate (Isa. 43:14 conj.), destroying a fortress (Prov. 21:22; Am. 3:11), and bringing to slaughter (Jer. 51:40). This survey shows that the second group is concentrated primarily in prophetic threats of disaster. Isa. 32:19; 34:7; Jer. 48:15; 50:27; 51:40; Zec. 11:2, which use *yrd* in comparisons, come close to figurative usage.[7] In fact, there is not always a sharp line between figurative and literal usage. When Yahweh brings Edom down from its mountains, where it thought it would be secure forever, the prophet probably has in mind both its having to leave its dwelling place and the ensuing humiliation it will experience (Jer. 49:16; Ob. 3f.).

2. *Natural Phenomena.* a. Many natural phenomena are expressed by means of *yrd*: the day draws to a close (Jgs. 19:11 conj.) and shadows fall (2 K. 20:11 = Isa. 38:8). Above all, various forms of precipitation "fall": hail (Ex. 9:19), dew (Nu. 11:9; Ps. 133:3), rain (Isa. 55:10 [*gešem*]; Ps. 72:6 [*māṭār*]), snow (Isa. 55:10). As punishment it rains powder and dust (Dt. 28:24) and fire comes down from heaven (2 K. 1:10,12,14). God's merciful presence is demonstrated by the manna that falls with the dew (Nu. 11:9) and the fire that comes down to consume Solomon's sacrifice (2 Ch. 7:1,3). Just as God causes the rain to fall (hiphil; Ezk. 34:26; Joel 2:23), so other meteorological phenomena have him as their source. The natural and the miraculous are not antithetical.

b. Water flows downhill: a brook (Dt. 9:21), the water of the Jordan (Josh. 3:13,16), the water that issues from the temple (Ezk. 47:1,8). The order established by God's creation vanquished chaos, causing the valleys to sink to their appointed place (Ps. 104:8). If God so desires, he can even cause water to flow plentifully through the desert (hiphil; Ps. 78:16).

Just as water flows down, so do oil (Ps. 133:2), spittle (1 S. 21:14[Eng v. 13]), and juice from the winepress, as in Trito-Isaiah's image of the destruction of the nations (Isa. 63:6).

The similarity of tears to flowing water lies behind the variety of metaphors for unrestrained weeping found in laments. Only in 2 passages, however, does the construction of *yrd* follow the above pattern: Ps. 119:136 ("streams flow from my eyes") and Lam. 2:18 ("let tears stream down [hiphil] like a torrent"). More commonly the construction is patterned after that used by verbs of abundance:[8] eyes (sg. or pl.) overflow with tears (*dimʿâ*: Jer. 9:17[18]; 13:17; 14:17), water (Lam. 1:16), or streams of water (*palgê-mayim*: Lam. 3:48). This suggests a similar interpretation for *yōrēḏ babbeḵî* in Isa. 15:3, especially since the expression appears in a lament: "overflowing in tears."[9]

3. *Topographical.* a. The root *yrd* describes movement that is downhill topographically. One comes down from higher terrain. Several points of origin are named explicitly: the hill country (Nu. 14:45; Jgs. 3:27f.; 5:11; 7:24; 1 S. 25:20), mountaintops (Jgs. 9:36; 2 K. 1:9,11,15), (cultic) high places (1 S. 9:25; 10:5), Sinai (Ex. 19:14, etc.; 32:1, etc.;

7 See III below.
8 *GK*, §117z; Joüon, §125d.
9 H. Wildberger, *Jesaja. BK*, X/2 (1978), 591, contra Driver, *PEQ*, 79 (1947), 124; *KBL*³.

34:29), Tabor (Jgs. 4:14), Gerizim (Jgs. 9:37), Lebanon (hiphil; 1 K. 5:23[9]). One comes down to lower terrain. Destinations include valleys (*ʿēmeq*: Jgs. 1:34; 5:13-15; cf. 1 S. 17:28), low plains (*biqʿâ*: Isa. 63:14), the valley of Jehoshaphat (Joel 4:2[3:2]), the plain of Ono (Neh. 6:2f.).

Since the natural occurrences of water are usually found in valleys or at the bottom of a slope, and since wells and cisterns are dug in the ground, one goes (qal) or brings (hiphil) down: to water (Jgs. 7:4f. [hiphil]), a spring (Gen. 24:16,45 [qal]), a well (*beʾēr*: 2 S. 17:18; 23:20), a cistern (*bôr*: 1 Ch. 11:22), a valley with running water (*naḥal ʾêṯān*: Dt. 21:4 [hiphil]), the Gihon (1 K. 1:33 [hiphil],38), the Kishon (1 K. 18:40 [hiphil]), the Jordan (1 K. 2:8; 2 K. 5:14), and the Nile (Ex. 2:5). The reference in 1 K. 1:25 is to the Kidron valley.

One comes down from Jerusalem (1 K. 22:2 = 2 Ch. 18:2). Lower places are named as destinations: Ashkelon (Jgs. 14:19), Beth-shemesh (1 S. 6:21), Etam (Jgs. 15:8,11,12), Gath (1 Ch. 7:21; Am. 6:2), Gaza (Jgs. 16:21 [hiphil]), Gilgal (1 S. 10:8; 13:12; 15:12), Joppa (Jon. 1:3), Jezreel (1 K. 18:44; 21:16,18; 2 K. 8:29), Timna (Jgs. 14:1,5,7,10).

The verb *yrd* describes the approach to certain persons or groups, obviously on account of where they live or carry on their work. The Philistines dwell in the coastal plain (Jgs. 16:31; 1 S. 13:20; 14:36f.; 2 S. 21:15). Elisha resides in the Jordan depression near Gilgal (2 K. 3:12; 6:18,33; 13:14). In these cases it does not matter whether one's point of departure is actually at a higher elevation or not.

If possible, cities were located on heights in order to make them more defensible. In order to protect their water supply, the inhabitants were forced to include within the city walls the springs, etc., that were lower down.[10] As a consequence, there were different elevations within cities, so that it was easily possible to go/bring down inside a city: 1 S. 9:27; 2 S. 11:8,9,13; 2 K. 11:19 (hiphil); Jer. 18:2f.; 22:1; 36:12). This also means that someone "goes down" to leave the city. Gardens and threshing floors lie outside the city, so that one must "go down" to reach them. This usage appears to be illustrated by Cant. 6:2,11; Ruth 3:3,6. There is no need for speculation as to why Ruth should go down to the threshing floor although one usually goes up to that destination. The translation need say only: "go to the threshing floor."

b. Travel from north to south is usually thought of as going down (qal: Jgs. 1:9; 2 K. 10:13; 2 Ch. 20:16; hiphil: Dt. 1:25; 1 S. 30:15f.). The journey south may pass through Keilah (1 S. 23:4,6,8,11), Bethel (2 K. 2:2), the cave of Adullam (1 S. 22:1; 2 S. 23:13; cf. 5:17[11]), the steppe of Ziph (1 S. 23:20; 26:2), of Maon (1 S. 23:25), or of Paran (1 S. 25:1).

Most typical, however, is the road to Egypt. It is travelled by the patriarchs (qal: Gen. 12:10; 42:2,etc.; Nu. 20:15; Dt. 10:22; 26:5; Josh. 24:4; Isa. 52:4; hiphil: Gen. 43:7,etc.; hophal: Gen. 39:1). The Ishmaelites take Joseph to Egypt (Gen. 39:1 [hiphil]). In oracles of judgment addressed to Hezekiah, Isaiah attacks going down to Egypt as a mistaken policy (Isa. 30:2; 31:1).

---

[10] H. Weippert, "Standanlage," *BRL*², 314.

[11] Driver, *ZAW*, 69 (1957), 76, n. 13.

c. The military usage of *yrd* depends on the basic tactical principle that a camp should be built on a height to make it more defensible. The battle itself is joined in the open countryside (1 S. 26:10; 29:4; 30:24). This is also where representatives of both sides come down to engage in single combat (1 S. 17:8; 2 S. 23:21 par. 1 Ch. 11:23). Attackers must attempt to attack the camp from above (Jgs. 7:9-11; 1 S. 26:6).

d. The texts in Joshua describing the tribal borders of Judah (Josh. 15:10), Joseph (16:3), Ephraim (16:7), Manasseh (17:9), and Benjamin (18:13,16,18) speak of a boundary[12] that "goes down" to indicate that it runs from a fixed point to one that is lower. In Nu. 34:11f. we probably have a remnant of the description of Dan's borders.[13]

e. The verb *yrd* can also be used for departure from a particular region (Gen. 38:1; 1 S. 15:6; cf. Ezk. 31:12).

4. *Nautical.* The root *yrd* is a technical term for boarding (Jon. 1:3) and disembarking from (Ezk. 27:29) a ship. On the ship itself one goes down below decks (Jon. 1:5). Hymns speak of sailors as *yôrᵉd̲ê hayyām* (Isa. 42:10 MT; Ps. 107:23). On the cosmic scale, the tossing of ships on a stormy sea is described in terms of *ʿlh* and *yrd* (Ps. 107:26); *yrd* is used for sinking into the depths (Ex. 15:5).

III. Figurative Usage.

1. *Threats and Curses.* Threats and curses use *yrd* to describe the humiliation and death of the nations (qal: Dt. 28:43; Isa. 47:1; Jer. 48:18; Ezk. 30:6; hophal: Zec. 10:11). Lam. 1:9 uses it for the fall of Jerusalem. Yahweh uses the hiphil to proclaim his decision to "bring down" the nations (Jer. 49:16; Hos. 7:12; Am. 9:2; Ob. 3f.). Pharaoh's officials will have to come down (qal of *yrd*) and bow before Moses (Ex. 11:8).

2. *Individual Prayers.* In the prayers of individuals we find the hiphil in both pleas of the persecuted for deliverance (Ps. 56:8[7]; 59:12[11]) and expressions of trust (2 S. 22:48). The worshipper is certain that injustice will necessarily descend (qal; par. *šûb̲*) upon those who cause it, just as a stone falls back on the head of someone who throws it into the air (Ps. 7:17[16]).[14]

3. *Prov. 18:8.* It is a piece of proverbial wisdom that wicked words about others can be swallowed like delicacies that go down easily (Prov. 18:8).

IV. Descent to the Underworld.

1. *General.* Death is described as descent to the underworld (Gen. 37:35). The hiphil expresses the responsibility of a second party for someone's untimely death (Gen. 42:38; 1 K. 2:6,9). Various terms are used for the destination: the underworld or Sheol (*šᵉʾôl*: Gen. 37:35; Nu. 16:30,33; Job 7:9; 17:16; etc.), the pit (*bôr*: Ps. 28:1; Isa. 38:18; Ezk.

---

12 → גבול *gᵉb̲ûl* (*gᵉbhûl*).

13 M. Noth, *Numbers. OTL* (Eng. trans. 1968), 250.

14 H.-J. Kraus, *Psalms 1–59* (Eng. trans., Minneapolis, 1988), 175.

31:14,16; 32:18; etc.) as the entrance to Sheol,[15] the grave (*šaḥaṯ*: Job 33:24; Ps. 30:10[9]; Ezek. 28:8), the stones of the pit (*ʾaḇnê-ḇôr*: Isa. 14:19), the depths of the pit (*yarkᵉṯê-ḇôr*: Isa. 14:15), the well of the pit (*bᵉʾēr šaḥaṯ*: Ps. 55:24[23]), silence (*dûmâ*: Ps. 115:17), dust (*ʿāp̄ār*: Ps. 22:30[29]), death (*māweṯ*: Prov. 5:5), the chambers of death (*ḥaḏrê-māweṯ*: Prov. 7:27), the people of old (*ʿam ʿôlām*: Ezk. 26:20), the land (*hāʾāreṣ*: Jon. 2:7[6]), the nether land (*ʾereṣ taḥtiyyôṯ*: Ezk. 26:20; 31:18; 32:18). No destination is stated in Ps. 49:18(17). There is no return from this descent (Job 7:9). The bars of this land are closed forever (Jon. 2:7[6]). Worldly goods cannot be brought along, but remain behind (Job 17:16; Ps. 49:18[17]). The people who dwell below have dwelt there for ages and will remain there forever (Ezk. 26:20). But 1 S. 2:6 voices the hope that that Yahweh, who brings down (cf. Ps. 55:24[23]), is able also to raise up (cf. also Ps. 22:30[29]). Doubts concerning the descent are reflected in Eccl. 3:21.

2. *Prayers.* Descent into the underworld is a recurring stylistic element in the prayers of the individual, where those who are sick or unjustly persecuted describe the situation from which they seek deliverance: although still alive, they have come within the sway of death.[16] They dwell amongst "those who go down to the pit" (*yôrᵉḏêā-ḇôr*: Ps. 28:1; 30:4[3] [*K*]; 88:5[4]; 143:7; Isa. 38:18; cf. Ps. 30:10[9]) or "those who go down into silence" (*yôrᵉḏê ḏûmâ*: Ps. 115:17). On the other hand, this fate befalls one's enemies, so that it can be the substance of a curse (Ps. 55:16[15]) or an expression of confidence (Ps. 55:24[23]). In the first case we find the 3rd person plural of the qal jussive; in the second, the 2nd person singular of the hiphil imperfect. Contrary to the usual view (Ps. 30:10[9]; Isa. 38:18), Ps. 22:30(29) maintains that God is worshipped even by "all who go down to the dust" (*yôrᵉḏê ʿāp̄ār*).

3. *Prophetic Dirges.* The motif of descent into the underworld is also a standard element of the prophetic dirge, which mockingly anticipates the downfall of the enemy. In Isa. 14:4-21, a song celebrating the fall of the world ruler (identified with Babylon by the addition of vv. 22f.), the hophal in vv. 11 and 15 suggests that Yahweh is responsible for the ruler's descent into Sheol, which is the consequence of his attempt to storm the heavens like a god (vv. 12-15). Not only is he mocked upon his arrival in Sheol (v. 10), but his disgrace is increased by his exclusion from the company of "those who go down to the stones of the Pit" (v. 19).

Ezekiel develops this motif at length, albeit in stereotyped language. In Ezek. 32:17-32, the descent of proud Egypt to the "nether world" (vv. 18,24) brings it down to "those who have gone down to the Pit" (vv. 18,24,25,29,30). There it enjoys the degrading company[17] of the uncircumcised and those slain by the sword (vv. 19,20,21,28,30,32), who have preceded it (vv. 21,24). The prose lament in Ezk. 31:15-18 over the descent to the underworld of the great tree (= Egypt) is couched in similar terms.

---

15 J.-G. Heintz, "בְּאֵר *bᵉʾēr*," *TDOT*, I, 465f.

16 C. F. Barth, *Die Errettung vom Tode in den individuellen Klage- und Dankliedern des ATs* (Zollikon, 1947), 100ff.

17 W. Zimmerli, *Ezekiel 2. Herm* (Eng. trans. 1983), 173f.

It has gone down to Sheol (vv. 15,17), cast down violently into the "nether world" (vv. 16,18) among the *yôrᵉd̲ê ḇôr* (v. 16), where it is assigned a dwelling place in the realm of the uncircumcised and those slain with the sword (v. 18).

4. *Judgment and Judgment Oracles.* In Ezekiel's oracles of judgment against Tyre (Ezek. 26:19-21) and its prince (28:1-10), the prophet uses the same motif, employing almost the same terminology as in the dirge. Even those slain by the sword and the uncircumcised are included (28:8,10). There is also a variant with features fully represented in Nu. 16:30,33: (1) the earth or Sheol opens its mouth to devour; (2) those in question go down alive into Sheol. This form provides the basis for the threat against Jerusalem in Isa. 5:14 and the curse in Ps. 55:16(15). It serves as a simile in Prov. 1:12.

5. *The Strange Woman.* Wisdom tradition finds a close connection between the "strange woman" and death, warning against having dealings with her. To do so means going down to death (Prov. 5:5) or the chambers of death (7:17; cf. also 2:18). The mythological language raises doubts as to whether the "strange woman" is really just the wife of someone else. She may in fact stand for folly, the rival of wisdom, or the reference may be to a temple prostitute as representative of an alien cult.[18]

V. Yahweh's Descent.

1. *Theophany.* The genre of poetic theophany as defined by Jeremias comprises two elements: Yahweh's coming and its effect on the natural realm. The basic brief form is subject to elaboration, and sometimes one of the elements may be omitted. Yahweh leaves his heavenly dwelling place to intervene on earth, aiding or punishing. The genre, including the imperfect of *yrd* to describe Yahweh's coming, has been incorporated into prophetic threats and proclamations of judgment: Mic. 1:3, the short form, a threat against the northern kingdom; Isa. 31:4, the short form with the first element given independent status, an oracle of deliverance for Jerusalem that is at the same time a threat against Assyria. The descent of Yahweh's sword (Isa. 34:5) and of evil (*raʿ*: Mic. 1:12) in proclamations of judgment probably also derive from the language of theophany. Strictly speaking, Mic. 1:10-16 is a prophetic lament; this explains the perfect tense *yārad̲*. Since, however, the lament is proleptic, it should be interpreted as a threat.[19] In laments, the language of theophany may be transformed into a prayer (Isa. 63:19[64:1] [short form]; Ps. 144:5f. [long form]). The equivalent in thanksgiving is a narrative description (Ps. 18:10[9] [long form]).

2. *J.* a. J's account of the Sinai theophany uses *yrd.* As always, however, when speaking of God's descent, J is scrupulous to avoid mentioning Yahweh's heavenly dwelling place; this puts all the emphasis on Yahweh's destination, Sinai, the site of the divine revelation (Ex. 19:11,18,20; 34:5; cf. Neh. 9:13). Volcanic phenomena accompany

---

18 H. Ringgren, *Sprüche. ATD,* XVI/1 (^{3}1980), 19, 36f.
19 W. Rudolph, *Micha. KAT,* XIII/3 (1975), 43.

Yahweh's coming instead of describing its effect, which is the fear shared by the people.[20] J has also assimilated the episode of the burning bush (Ex. 3:1-5) to the Sinai theophany, in part by the use of *yrd.*[21]

b. Another theophany in the present literary context of J[22] uses *yrd* (without naming the place from which Yahweh comes), speaks of a pillar of cloud, and names the tent of meeting outside the camp as the destination (Ex. 33:9; Nu. 11:17,25; 12:5). It is important to note that Yahweh's descent is pictured not as a single past event but as something that happens repeatedly. This theophany probably derives from the traditions surrounding the → אהל *ʾōhel.*[23]

c. Without any hint of theophany, J uses *yrd* in Gen. 11:5; 18:21 to suggest that the distance separating the divine realm from the human is overcome. For J, Yahweh's mythological dwelling place in heaven is no longer relevant; all that matters is this separation, which only Yahweh is able to transcend (cf. also Prov. 30:4).

VI. Dead Sea Scrolls. The semantic range of *yrd* is preserved in the Dead Sea scrolls. While the Temple scroll uses it solely in technical descriptions (11QT 32:13; 34:15; 46:15), in CD 11:1 it means "descending" to the source. In 1QH 8:28 it refers to the underworld, and in 3:14 it is used for sailing upon the sea. Those who are unclean may not "go down" to battle (1 QM 7:6). According to 1QM 11:7, the Messiah "comes" from Jacob (*yrd*; cf. Nu. 24:17: *dārak*).

G. Mayer

---

20 Jeremias, 109.

21 Cf. M. Noth, *Exodus. OTL* (Eng. trans. 1962), 39f.; W. H. Schmidt, *Exodus. BK,* II (1977), 120.

22 Schmidt, *ibid.*

23 *TDOT,* I, 124f.

יַרְדֵּן yardēn

Contents: I. 1. Etymology; Extrabiblical Evidence; 2. Definite Article; 3. Cultic Role. II. 1. Metaphorical References; 2. Boundaries; 3. "Theological Geography." III. 1. Crossing the Jordan; 2. Josh. 3f.; 3. The Jordan and the Reed Sea.

---

yardēn. R. Dussaud, "Cultes cananéens aux sources du Jordain, d'après les textes de Ras Shamra," *Syr,* 17 (1936), 283-295; M. Fraenkel, "Zur Deutung von biblischen Flur- und Ortsnamen," *BZ,* N.S. 5 (1961), 83-86; B. Gemser, "*Beʿēber hayyardēn*: In Jordan's Borderland," *VT,* 2 (1952), 349-355; N. Glueck, *The River Jordan* (Philadelphia, 1946); A. R. Hulst, "Der Jordan in den alttestamentlichen Überlieferungen," *OTS,* 14 (1965), 162-188; L. Koehler, "Lexi-

I. 1. *Etymology; Extrabiblical Evidence.* The use of "Jordan" as the name of a river is not limited to the onomasticon of Palestine; neither is it restricted to biblical literature. Homer mentions a Jordan river in Crete[1] and another river of the same name in Elis.[2] There are still other rivers called by the same name or something similar,[3] which fuel the debate as to whether the name is of Semitic or non-Semitic (possibly Indo-European) origin. In the Semitic context, various etymologies have been suggested: the "patristic" interpretation ("the river of Dan"), a root *rdn* meaning "roar," and above all the root → ירד *yrd,* "go down."[4] The Indo-European interpretation favors an Iranian etymology (**yardan/us/*), in which case the Jordan would have a name "describing it as a 'year-round' river, a river flowing with water throughout the entire year."[5] More likely, however, the name is "an ancient Mediterranean term that has survived from a period long antedating Indo-European or Semitic settlement."[6] The earliest phonetic equivalents are found in the Egyptian sphere. The form *yrdn* appears in Papyrus Anastasi I, 23.1[7] and the Great List of Shishak I.[8] The use of the "land" determinative in both cases does not absolutely rule out the possibility of a river, since various regions in the ancient Near East can be named for their major rivers.[9] Only in the earlier citation does the formula *p3 ḫd n yrdn* ("the ford of the Jordan") positively indicate that a river is meant. The statement that the name "Jrd(n)" appears on a stela of Seti I from Beth-shan[10] is erroneous; the correct reading is "Jrmt."[11] Analysis of the geographical information in the Satirical papyrus shows only that a crossing of the Jordan (probably

---

kologisch-Geographisches," *ZDPV,* 62 (1939), 115-120: "Der Jordan"; F. Langlamet, *Gilgal et les récits de la traversée du Jordain (Jos III–IV). CahRB,* 11 (1969), M. Noth, "Der Jordan in der alten Geschichte Palästinas," *ZDPV,* 72 (1956), 123-148; E. Otto, *Das Mazzotfest in Gilgal. BWANT,* 107[6/7] (1975); K. H. Rengstorf, "ποταμός," *TDNT,* VI, 595-623, esp. "Ἰορδάνης," 608-623; W. von Soden, "Zur Herkunft des Flussnamens Jordan," *ZAW,* 57 (1939), 153f.; E. Vogt, "*ʿēber hayyardēn* = regio finitima Iordani," *Bibl,* 34 (1953), 118f.; *idem,* "Die Erzählung vom Jordanübergang Josue 3–4 (Literarkritik)," *Bibl,* 46 (1965), 125-148.

1 *Odyssey* iii.292.

2 *Iliad* vii.135.

3 See Koehler, 118f.; Rengstorf, 609f.

4 This and other proposed etymologies are discussed by Koehler, 116-18.

5 *Ibid.,* 120.

6 Von Soden, 154.

7 See, e.g., A. H. Gardiner, *Egyptian Hieratic Texts* (Leipzig, 1911), 24, n. 16; H. W. Helck, *Die Beziehungen Ägyptens zu Vorderasien im 3. und 2. Jahrtausend v. Chr. ÄgAbh,* 5 (^{2}1971), 318.

8 J. J. Simons, *Handbook for the Study of Egyptian Topographical Lists Relating to Western Asia* (Leiden, 1937), xxxiv, 180; for discussion, see M. Noth, "Die Wege der Pharaonenheere in Palästina und Syrien," *ZDPV,* 61 (1938), 303; B. Mazar, "The Campaign of Pharaoh Shishak to Palestine," *Volume du Congrès, Strasbourg 1956. SVT,* 4 (1957), 66; Helck, 244; K. A. Kitchen, *The Third Intermediate Period in Egypt (1100-650 B.C.)* (Warminster, 1973), 441.

9 See, e.g., W. Eilers, "Kyros: Eine namenkundliche Studie," *Beiträge zur Namenforschung,* 15 (1964), 189f.; E. Edel, *Studien zur altägyptischen Kultur,* 3 (Hamburg, 1975), 54; M. Görg, "Das Ratespiel um *Mw-Ḳd,*" *Göttinger Miszellen,* 32 (1979), 22.

10 *KBL*^{3}, 416a.

11 Cf. M. Görg, *Untersuchungen zur hieroglyphischen Wiedergabe palästinischer Ortsnamen. Bonner Orientalische Studien,* 29 (1974), 132.

of commercial importance) was considered a detail of Palestinian geography well worth knowing.[12]

2. *Definite Article.* Except in Job 40:23; Ps. 42:7(Eng. v. 6), *yrdn* is always determined by the definite article (177 times). The absence of the article may reflect poetic style: in Job 40:23, it stands in parallel with *nhr* in v. 23a; in Ps. 42:7(6), it is in a construct phrase following *'rṣ* used in parallel with other toponyms. In Job 40:23, *yrdn* can thus function as "a synonym for 'river' ";[13] but it may also be a later interpolation.[14] The phrase *'ereṣ yardēn* in Ps. 42:7(6) probably means "quite generally the region where the Jordan rises";[15] in other words, it does not refer to the actual watercourse that functions as a boundary.[16] This usage may explain the absence of the article. This identification with the sources of the Jordan is disputed by Dahood,[17] who translates the phrase as "the land of descent,"[18] taking *yrdn* as deriving from *yrd* with the suf. *-ān* (analogously to *māḡēn* for *māḡōn*). There are phonological and semantic problems with this interpretation, however. It is also worth noting that 11QtgJob uses the determined form *yrdn'*,[19] undoubtedly meaning the river. The use of the article everywhere else clearly indicates that the word is more than a name; it has become an appellative.[20]

3. *Cultic Role.* Unlike the Euphrates and Tigris in Mesopotamia and the Nile in Egypt, which dominate and fructify their regions, the Jordan does not play a vital role in Palestine. Palestine is not an oasis dependent on a river. Neither was the Jordan divinized; its name was never used for a deity in the Canaanite pantheon. It would seem, however, that even in the pre-Israelite period at least the region where the Jordan rises took on the character of being "the object of an important cult."[21]

Dussaud would trace the bull cult of Dan promoted under Jeroboam (1 K. 12:25ff.) to a Canaanite cult in the same locality; he cites a text[22] in which the phrase *'ḫ šmk,* "prairie of Samak" or "marsh of Samak," is used as a name of the region around Lake Huleh, inhabited by wild oxen.[23] It is more likely, however, that the name Samachonitis

[12] Cf. Helck, 318.

[13] *KBL*³, 416b.

[14] G. Fohrer, *Das Buch Hiob. KAT,* XVI (1963), 523; E. Ruprecht, "Das Nilpferd im Hiobbuch: Beobachtungen zu der sogenannten zweiten Gottesrede," *VT,* 21 (1971), 220; cf. O. Keel-Leu, *Jahwes Entgegnung an Ijob. FRLANT,* 121 (1978), 130, n. 362.

[15] H.-J. Kraus, *Psalms 1–59* (Eng. trans., Minneapolis, 1988), 440.

[16] See below.

[17] M. Dahood, *Psalms I. AB,* 16 (1965), 258f.

[18] As does N. J. Tromp, *Primitive Conceptions of Death and the Nether World in the OT. BietOr,* 21 (1969), 145.

[19] Cf. T. Muraoka, "Notes on the Old Targum of Job from Qumran Cave XI," *RevQ,* 9 (1977), 124.

[20] Rengstorf, 610.

[21] Cf. Dussaud, 283ff.

[22] *KTU,* 1.10 II, 9, 12.

[23] G. R. Driver supports a similar interpretation; cf. *CML,* 148. A different approach, which does not identify *šmk* with Samachonitis, is found in *UT,* no. 2434; *WUS,* 308. See also K. L. Vine,

derives from the Amarna name *Šamḫuna,*[24] so that the identification of *šmk* with the sources of the Jordan is still uncertain.

II. 1. *Metaphorical References.* When speaking of the Jordan river and its valley or plain,[25] the OT does not provide geographical information for its own sake. The point of reference is always to be found in the immediate or extended context of the statement. For example, Jgs. 3:28; 12:5f. speak of the fords (*maʿbārôṯ*) of the Jordan because of their strategic importance. The jungle or thicket (*gāʾôn*) of the Jordan (Jer. 12:5; 49:19; 50:44; Zec. 11:3) is used as a metaphor. Also metaphorical is the calm confidence of Behemoth even when the Jordan rushes against his mouth (Job 40:23). The so-called plain of the Jordan (*kikkar hayyardēn* or *kikkār* alone in 2 S. 18:23), which the OT views as "the wide lower portion of what is now called the *ġōr* extending north for an undefined distance,"[26] is of interest because a bronze foundry was located there (1 K. 7:46), which produced the extensive bronzework for the temple. The importance of this region was more than merely industrial, however;[27] because of its abundant water supply, it could be likened to the "land of Egypt" and even the "garden of Yahweh" (Gen. 3:10b).[28] The Elisha narratives locate several miracles at the Jordan (2 K. 2:7ff.,13f.; 6:1ff.) and even speak of Naaman's washing in the Jordan seven times to be cured (2 K. 5:10). These stories do not, however, ascribe any special powers to the water of the Jordan,[29] although it is not impossible that they contain overtones of its traditio-historical importance.[30]

2. *Boundaries.* Any analysis of the geographical texts mentioning the Jordan in the context of Israel's settlement must remember that "the division of the land initially dealt solely with the tribes west of the Jordan; only later were the eastern tribes included thematically in this tradition."[31] On the one hand, the Jordan was one of the series of points defining the southern boundary of Joseph (Josh. 16:1), which it is clear was originally identical with the northern boundary of Benjamin (Josh. 18:12).[32] On the other hand, it was also part of the common border shared by Issachar and Naphtali (Josh.

The Establishment of Baal at Ugarit (diss., Michigan, 1965), 259f., with n. 40; P. J. van Zijl, *Baal. AOAT,* 10 (1972), 253, n. 6.

24 EA 225, 4; cf. most recently M. Görg, *Untersuchungen,* 182; for another view, see A. F. Rainey, "Toponymic Problems," *Tel Aviv,* 3 (1976), 62.

25 Cf. G. Wagner, "Vom Jordangraben," *Naturwissenschaftliche Monatsschrift,* 47 (1934); H. Peuker, "Jordan," *BHHW,* II (1964), 884f.

26 M. Noth, *Könige 1–16. BK,* IX/1 (1968), 164.

27 See also E. Würthwein, *Das erste Buch der Könige. ATD,* XI/1 (1976), 84.

28 According to R. Kilian, *Die vorpriestlichen Abrahams-Überlieferungen. BBB,* 24 (1966), 22, this passage is "a secondary addition."

29 This point is also made by Rengstorf, 611; and Hulst, 165, with n. 2.

30 Cf. III.3 below.

31 M. Wüst, *Untersuchungen zu den siedlungsgeographischen Texten des ATs,* I: *Ostjordanland. Beihefte zum Tübinger Atlas des Vorderen Orients,* ser. B, 9 (Wiesbaden, 1975), 239.

32 Cf. M. Noth, *Das Buch Josua. HAT,* VII (^{3}1971), 101, 109.

19:22,33f.).[33] The charge that the Ammonites east of the Jordan claimed the Jordan as their own borderland (Jgs. 11:13) is to be likened to the fictive extension of Sihon's territory (Josh. 12:2), described as including the entire Jordan valley from Lake Tiberias to the Dead Sea (12:3).[34] Analogously to this secondary integration of the Jordan into the territory of Sihon, a later textual phase assigned all the territory east of the Jordan to Gad (Josh. 13:27); the Jordan valley is referred to by the complex expressions "the Jordan as a boundary" and "eastward beyond the Jordan."[35] According to Josh. 13:23a, only the southernmost region of the Jordan valley belonged to Reuben.

Apparently the "settlement" of the half-tribe of Manasseh east of the Jordan in what had been the territory of Og, king of Bashan, was also accomplished by literary means.[36] Here as elsewhere in descriptions of Manasseh's borders (Josh. 17:7-11) the Jordan is not mentioned by name.[37] Only in passages dealing with the half-tribe such as Josh. 17:5; 18:7; 20:8 (22 is discussed below); 2 K. 10:32f.,[38] all of which are probably based on Josh. 13:29f., do we find explicit references. An earlier stage is represented by Josh. 13:32, which (without mentioning Manasseh) summarizes the portions assigned to Reuben and Gad, which are "in the plains of Moab, beyond the Jordan east of Jericho."[39]

According to Nu. 34:12, the course of the Jordan from the Sea of Chinnereth to the "Salt Sea" represents the eastern boundary of the land of Canaan divided among "the Israelites." The similar passages in Dt. 3:17;[40] 4:49[41] are redactional additions. Later reflection represented the loss of the territory east of the Jordan as a reduction of Israel but also as the restoration of the Jordan boundary (cf. 2 K. 10:32f.). Thus literary composition is responsible for the majority of the "geographical" references to the Jordan as a boundary river.

3. *"Theological Geography."* In addition to its function in boundary definitions and related texts, the Jordan had the nature of a dialectal boundary line separating the Ephraimites from the Gileadites; life or death judgment could be made at the fords of the Jordan (Jgs. 12:5f.). The Jordan could also be misinterpreted as a God-given boundary excluding the eastern tribes from a portion in Yahweh (Josh. 22:25). According to the statement of the Reubenites and Gadites (together with the half-tribe of Manasseh), the altar ("of great size") they built by the Jordan[42] upon their arrival at the *gᵉlîlôṯ hayyardēn* (22:10) was to serve as a witness (*ʿēḏ*; → עוד *ʿûḏ*) to the legitimate cultic worship of

---

[33] See *ibid.,* 116, 120.

[34] For more details, see Wüst, 20f.

[35] *Ibid.,* 21.

[36] On Josh. 13:29-31, cf. *ibid.,* 79ff.

[37] See Noth, *HAT,* VII, 104.

[38] For a literary analysis, see Wüst, 89f.

[39] Cf. *ibid.,* 179.

[40] See S. Mittmann, *Deuteronomium 1₁–6₃* literarkritisch und traditionsgeschichtlich untersucht. *BZAW,* 139 (1975), 84; Wüst, 17, 23.

[41] For the dependence of this passage on Josh. 12:3, see Wüst, 23.

[42] According to Noth, *HAT,* VII, 128, *ʿal* here "clearly means a site on the steep bank of the Jordan."

Yahweh on both sides of the border and at the same time to counter the accusation of alienation from Yahweh on the part of the eastern tribes (22:27).

This narrative, which has undergone redaction,[43] has an apologetic purpose. It may be based on an etiology associated with a geographical site no longer identifiable with certainty. Since Josh. 22:10 and 11 are mutually contradictory, the original location of the altar is disputed. Noth[44] claims that v. 11 is an addition; in this case, v. 10 would have referred initially to an altar on the west bank of the Jordan. Otto[45] maintains that it is vv. 9f. that are secondary: the altar originally stood on the east bank. Möhlenbrink[46] proposes associating the altar with Gilgal as an ancient amphictyonic sanctuary (in addition to Shiloh). This theory is rejected by Noth;[47] but it has recently been revived by Otto,[48] who postulates observance of a "crossing festival" with a "pilgrimage procession."[49]

The river Jordan takes on a special dimension as the future eastern boundary in the vision of Ezekiel, where it separates Gilead from "the land of Israel" (Ezk. 47:18). Its southern limit is "the eastern sea" (cf. also Joel 2:20; Zec. 14:8). It is worth considering a connection with the immediately preceding section, which describes the course of the eschatological river flowing from the temple: according to Ezk. 47:8, it fills the Jordan valley (*ʿᵃrāḇâ*) and transforms the Salt Sea into fresh water. Here, too, the dominant purpose is not geographical, correctly descriptive of topography, but theological, transcending the realm of nature. The tiny Gihon brook of Jerusalem becomes a mighty river flowing directly into the Jordan valley and filling the Dead Sea with living water.[50] Although it is not mentioned by name, the Jordan appears here as the "vehicle" of the temple river, providing its motive power.

III. 1. *Crossing the Jordan.* The most important feature of the Jordan tradition is the "crossing" of the Jordan before Israel's occupation of Canaan. The substantial body of texts in Nu. 22–36 describes the events that took place in the *ʿarḇôṯ môʾāḇ*, "a locale that marks the turning point between the period in the desert and the occupation."[51] The location is defined more precisely by the expressions *mēʿēḇer lᵉyardēn yᵉrēḥô* (Nu. 22:1) and *ʿal-yardēn yᵉrēḥô* (Nu. 26:3,63; 31:12; 33:48,50; 35:1; 36:13). This site is also associated with the instructions given by Yahweh before the crossing of the Jordan (Nu. 33:50). The phrase *kî ʾattem ʿōḇᵉrîm ʾeṯ-hayyardēn* looks forward to the coming event, which is described as initiating a string of military conflicts leading to possession of the land (33:51) and also the selection of cities of refuge (Nu. 35:10). Already in Nu.

43 Cf. *ibid.,* 133f.
44 P. 134.
45 E. Otto, *Das Mazzotfest in Gilgal,* 171.
46 K. Möhlenbrink, "Die Landnahmesagen des Buches Josua," *ZAW,* 56 (1938), 248.
47 *HAT,* VII, 135.
48 P. 171, following A. Soggin, "Gilgal, Passah und Landnahme," *Volume de Congrès, Genève 1965. SVT,* 15 (1966), 272f., and others.
49 → מזבח *mizbēaḥ.*
50 See W. Zimmerli, *Ezekiel 2. Herm* (Eng. trans. 1983), 1512f.; M. Görg, "Wo lag das Paradies?" *BN,* 2 (1977), 32.
51 Wüst, 213.

32, the present text of which includes many later additions,[52] the theme of crossing the Jordan is associated with the theme of going into battle (vv. 5,21,29,32), a battle in which the tribes east of the Jordan must join with those to the west. Depending on the orientation of the speaker, the formulaic phrase *ʿēḇer hayyardēn* can refer to the territory either west (Nu. 32:19; cf. also Dt. 3:20,25; 11:30; etc.)[53] or east (Nu. 32:32; cf. also Gen. 50:10f.; Nu. 22:1; Dt. 1:5; Josh. 1:14; Isa. 8:23[9:1]; etc.) of the Jordan. In Deuteronomic usage, *ʿāḇar* is practically a technical term for the occupation of Canaan,[54] with (Dt. 9:1; 11:31; 12:10; 27:2,4,12) or without (6:1; 11:8,11; 27:3) explicit mention of the Jordan. The Israelites cross the Jordan in order to conquer the Canaanites and occupy the land by force (Dt. 9:1), but even more clearly in order to possess the land, without any clear statement of how they are to achieve this possession (11:31; 12:10). According to Dt. 27:2-4, the crossing is to be followed by a permanent record of the law on stone, and according to 27:12 by a ritual of blessing and cursing. Dt. 9:3 even has Yahweh himself go over as "a devouring fire," a statement making it perfectly clear that it is really Yahweh who directs the military campaign. The Deuteronomistic perspective on the crossing of the Jordan is no different (cf. Dt. 2:29; 3:18,27; 4:26; 30:18; 31:13; 32:47; Josh. 1:2,11; 24:11). Dt. 3:27 puts special emphasis on Yahweh's decree that Moses will not be permitted to cross "this Jordan" (cf. also Dt. 4:21f.; 31:2).[55] There can be no doubt that the Deuteronom(ist)ic tradition "considers the land west of the Jordan to be the land bestowed by Yahweh."[56] An important illustration of this understanding is the fact that Josh. 1:12-18 has even Gad, Reuben, and the half-tribe of Manasseh cross the Jordan.

The threat implied by a hostile crossing of the Jordan is exemplified by the Ammonites (Jgs. 10:8f.): they oppress not only the Gileadites "beyond the Jordan" (cf. Jgs. 5:17) but also the tribes on the west bank. Here, as in other scattered mentions of crossing the Jordan in either direction (e.g., 1 S. 13:7; 2 S. 2:29; 10:17; 17:22; 24:5), there is no suggestion of any theological implication. It should be noted, however, that crossing from west to east tends to indicate retreat (cf. 1 S. 13:7), whereas crossing from east to west suggests assertion of sovereignty, as we saw above all in the Shimei episode (2 S. 19:16,19[15,18]).

2. *Josh. 3f.* Central to the traditions concerning the crossing of the Jordan is the section Josh. 3f., which depicts the event itself. The background and history of the two chapters are disputed. We shall outline the most familiar theories.

According to Keller,[57] we must distinguish a "stone circle tradition" (Josh. 4:1-9,20-24; nucleus in 4:2-3,8*,20) and a "crossing tradition" (3:1-17; 4:10-19; nucleus in

---

52 For a detailed discussion, see *ibid.*, 91ff., 213ff.

53 Cf. H. P. Stähli, "עבר *ʿbr* vorüber, hinübergehen," *THAT,* II, 203; but see also Gemser, 355.

54 P. Diepold, *Israels Land. BWANT,* 95[5/15] (1972), 29.

55 On the use of the demonstrative, cf. also Hulst's discussion (166) of Gen. 32:11(10), although his interpretation "in the vicinity of" is not convincing.

56 Hulst, 168; Diepold, 29f., 56f.

57 C. A. Keller, "Über einige alttestamentliche Heiligtumslegenden II," *ZAW,* 68 (1956), 85ff.

3:14a,16; 4:19b); 4:9 represents an independent etiology. Dus[58] finds five different strata: an old legend about the crossing as an etiology for the stones in the Jordan (Josh. 3:1a,7aα,8,9aα,11,13aαβ,14*,15,16a,17abα; 4:9; 3:17b; 4:11abα,18b) which has been expanded by inclusion of an etiology for the Gilgal stones and the introduction of Joshua and has also undergone quasi-Deuteronomistic and Priestly redaction. Maier[59] identifies six strata: an early etiology of the stones in the Jordan (3:14a,16; 4:9), an etiology of the Gilgal stones, the introduction of Joshua, an association with the exodus tradition, and finally a redaction associated with the ark and a Deuteronomistic redaction. Langlamet[60] finds a Deuteronomistic redactor working several traditions: a Shittim-Gilgal narrative, an ark narrative, two distinct etiologies of the Gilgal stones, an etiology of the Jordan stones, and two Gilgal "catecheses."[61]

Otto[62] himself distinguishes a source A in Josh. 3:1,5,9-12; 4:4-7,9,10aαb,11bβ from a source B in 1:1b*,2b,10-11; 3:2-3,4bβγ,6,7aα,8,13abγ,14-16,17abα; 4:1b,2-3,8,11abα, 18b,19*,20-24. He claims that sources A and B go back to a tradition according to which priests bearing the ark preceded the people into the Jordan, whereupon the waters dried up. While the ark bearers stood in the Jordan, twelve men were appointed to set up twelve stones at the feet of the priests. After this was done, the priests and the people went to Gilgal, where twelve massebahs were set up and a narrative was recited instructing the people in the etiology of the cult.[63] The earliest tradition reflects a cultic ceremony, a procession with the ark from Shittim to Gilgal, where a "festival of unleavened bread" (cf. Josh. 5:2-12) was celebrated.[64]

Reconstruction of the literary development of Josh. 3f., best undertaken with the aid of literary criticism and redaction analysis, suggests caution with regard to historical conclusions until the literary independence of the narratives in question is assured. This caution extends for the time being not only to the theory that the original narrative recorded a spectacular crossing at the time of the occupation but also to the presumption of cultic ceremonies and observances. In any case, it seems appropriate to postulate a pre-Deuteronomistic tradition that saw the Jordan as a boundary enshrining local traditions, whose importance extended beyond the central Palestinian tribes.

3. *The Jordan and the Reed Sea.* The traditio-historical locus of the association between the "crossing motif" and the "miracle at the Reed Sea" of the exodus (cf. Ex. 14f.) must therefore remain hypothetical. (According to Otto,[65] the themes of the occupation and exodus were linked at the "feast of unleavened bread" at Gilgal.) Joshua's

---

58 J. Dus, "Die Analyse zweier Ladeerzählungen des Josuabuches (Jos 3-4 und 6)," *ZAW*, 72 (1960), 120ff.

59 J. Maier, *Die altisraelitische Ladeheiligtum. BZAW*, 93 (1965), 18ff.

60 Langlamet, *Gilgal et les récits de la traversée du Jourdain.*

61 These and other theories are presented and criticized by Otto, 104ff.; for earlier theories, see Hulst, 169ff.

62 Pp. 120, 136.

63 *Ibid.*, 162f.

64 *Ibid.*, 175ff.

65 *Ibid.*, 186ff.

speech in Josh. 4:21-23 contains an allusion with a poetic counterpart in Ps. 114 (esp. vv. 3,5): the drying up of the Jordan parallels the parting of the sea. According to Kraus,[66] the motif of the mythological battle with chaos is here transferred in its rudimentary features to the crossing of the Jordan: Yahweh's epiphany causes the powers opposing his people to flee in fear. When Josh. 4:21-23 is compared form-critically with Ps. 114:3,5 (with the context of each), we note the appearance in both texts of the epithet *'ᵃḏôn kol-hā'āreṣ* (Josh. 3:11,13; Ps. 114:7).[67] The question whether the parallel between the crossing of the Jordan and the miracle at the Reed Sea had its *Sitz im Leben* in recitation of a cultic etiology narrative at a festival in Gilgal[68] or first achieved literary expression through a combination of traditions at Jerusalem requires further study. To all appearances, a Jerusalemite redaction is responsible for the present version of the hymn in Ex. 15, which clearly associates the miracle of the Reed Sea (vv. 8,10) with the "crossing" (v. 16: *'br* used twice!) of the people before their "entrance" (v. 17) even though the Jordan is not mentioned by name. Here we have surely reached a stage at which, in line with Deuteronomic usage, the "crossing" has simply become a theologoumenon.

Görg

66 H.-J. Kraus, *Psalmen. BK,* XV/2 (⁵1978), 958.
67 Otto, 188.
68 *Ibid.,* 190.

יָרָה *yārâ* I; יוֹרֶה *yôreh*; מוֹרֶה *môreh*

Contents: I. Root, Occurrences, and Meaning. II. General Usage: 1. Literal Sense; 2. Figurative Sense. III. Theological Usage. IV. Summary.

I. Root, Occurrences, and Meaning. The root *yrh* is not limited to the OT. It appears in Ugaritic with the meaning "throw" or "shoot,"[1] in Old South Arabic ("throw," "fight"), in Ethiopic and Tigré ("throw"), and finally in Middle Hebrew. The meaning "throw" remains constant, modified semantically by the modality of throwing; for example, "throwing" with a bow is "shooting." The root is used 25 times in the OT as a verb, not including the reasonable conjecture in Jer. 50:14 (see below), attested by four manuscripts. Substantive forms occur 6 times. The verb appears in the qal, niphal, and hiphil; the qal and hiphil represent the active voice, the niphal the passive, all with the same meaning. The translation "throw" well represents the meaning of the Hebrew verb, which refers to the movement of someone or something brought about by exertion of force. The nature of the movement is defined more closely by the context. The nouns,

1 *WUS*³, no. 1241.

meaning "archer," are simply nominalized forms of the verb. Although *yārâ* I does not occur frequently, it is widely distributed, appearing in poetry and prose, both early and late. It is not a term characteristic of a particular period or literary stratum.

II. General Usage.

1. *Literal Sense.* In a whole series of OT passages, *yārâ* I is used in the technical military sense of "shoot"; in most cases, it refers to the shooting of arrows (*hiṣṣîm* → חץ *ḥṣ*). This meaning is not entirely explicit in the familiar story of David and Bathsheba in 2 S. 11, but it is very likely. Uriah is to meet his death at a dangerous spot near the besieged Ammonite city of Rabbah; Uriah himself carries the order in a letter to Joab. The artful narrative uses a message from Joab to David to describe how the order was carried out; Joab himself instructs the messenger how to parry David's potential objections to the disastrous skirmish with well-chosen words. In these hypothetical reproaches we learn that one should not approach a besieged city too closely, since the defenders are apt to shoot down from the wall (2 S. 11:20: "Did you not know *'ēṯ 'ᵃšer-yōrû* [hiphil defective] *mē'al haḥômâ?*"). The following comparison in v. 21 to the death of Abimelech at the hands of a woman who threw a millstone down upon him from the besieged fortress at Thebez (although it uses the expression *hišlîḵâ 'ālāyw*) suggests that *yārâ* might refer to any projectile dangerous to a besieger near the wall of a besieged city. Verse 24, however, mentions archers explicitly (*wayyōr'û hammôri'ym,* following the *qere*), suggesting that bowmen may in fact be meant. Although absolute certainty is impossible, parallels might support this theory. Such a parallel may appear in the account of Saul's death in battle with the Philistines on Mt. Gilboa (1 S. 31:3), where the *môrîm* are associated with *qešeṯ*. It would be reasonable to recognize this as a regular association, although it must be confessed that the verse involves serious textual problems.[2]

For example, the middle word in the phrase *hammôrîm 'ᵃnāšîm baqqešeṯ* (1 S. 31:3) is difficult. The Chronicler's version simply omits it (1 Ch. 10:3). The expression in the MT must be translated "those shooting people with the bow," unless a differentiation is intended by the epexegetical addition of *'ᵃnāšîm baqqešeṯ* to *hammôrîm,* defining the term "archer" more precisely as "bowmen." In this case, allowance must be made for the absence of the definite article with *'ᵃnāšîm.* The Masoretic accentuation may further support this interpretation. If so, *môreh* would not necessarily mean "archer" but would be a more general term meaning "one who throws," "slinger," "marksman." Unfortunately, the phrase *wayyāḥel mᵉ'ōḏ mēhammôrîm* at the end of 1 S. 31:3 is also difficult.[3] The parallel in 1 Ch. 10:3, *wayyāḥel min-hayyôrîm,* does not help.[4] There is, nevertheless, a reasonably satisfactory solution proposed by the commentaries: Saul's ability to fight is so reduced by the marksmen or bowmen that he breaks off battle and asks to die (1 S. 31:4f.; 1 Ch. 10:4).

The Chronicler's account of Josiah's death at the battle of Megiddo (2 Ch. 35:23) also

---

2 Cf. H. J. Stoebe, *Das erste Buch Samuelis. KAT,* VIII/1 (1973), 520f.

3 *Ibid.;* cf. also H. W. Hertzberg, *I & II Samuel. OTL* (Eng. trans. 1964), *in loc.*

4 W. Rudolph, *Chronikbücher. HAT,* XII (³1968), 92.

uses the expression *wayyôrû hayyōrîm lammelek̲* (*l*ᵉ = "in the direction of"), which suggests archers. The Egyptian archers of Pharaoh Necho hit the king of Judah on his chariot. Possibly a chariot battle was fought; archers were posted on the chariots.[5] The Syriac version elaborates the passage, stating that Pharaoh Necho himself struck and wounded King Josiah with two arrows.[6] The version in 2 K. 23:29f. says only that Josiah went to battle against Necho and was killed by him (*mûṯ* hiphil).

The Isaiah stories of Isa. 36f. (par. 2 K. 18:13–20:19), which purport to take place during the period when Hezekiah was threatened by Sennacherib, include Isaiah's assurance that the Assyrian will not be allowed to enter besieged Jerusalem. He will not even be able to shoot arrows into the city *welō'-yôreh šām ḥēṣ* [2 K. 19:32 par. Isa. 37:33]) or advance against it with shields. Here the verb *yārâ* I (hiphil) is clearly associated with the object *ḥēṣ* ("arrow"). That military terminology does not use the hiphil of *yārâ* I exclusively for the shooting of arrows by archers is clear from the Chronicler's account of Uzziah's military preparations (2 Ch. 26:6-15, esp. v. 15). We are told that ingeniously designed machines were placed on the towers and battlements of Jerusalem, which were able to shoot arrows and great stones (*lîrô' baḥiṣṣîm ûḇā'ᵃḇānîm gᵉḏōlôṯ*; an infinitive form ending in *aleph* for a verb ending in *he* is found occasionally;[7] either *gᵉḏōlôṯ* must be emended by the addition of the article or the prep. *b*ᵉ must be repointed). The use of *b*ᵉ is to be taken as instrumental: shoot "by means of" arrows or great stones.

A wisdom aphorism (Prov. 26:18f.) in the second collection of Solomonic proverbs (Prov. 25–29, possibly preexilic[8]) likens the damage done by those who deceive their neighbors to that done by arrows shot by a lunatic (*kᵉmiṯlahlēah hayyōreh ziqqîm ḥiṣṣîm wāmāweṯ* /v. 19/ *kēn-'îš . . .*).

Finally, the meaning of *yārâ* I is illuminated by Jer. 50:14, where the text has *yᵉḏû* (from *yāḏâ*, "shoot"), but a few manuscripts read *yᵉrû* (from *yārâ* I). There is no difference in meaning. This oracle of disaster against Babylon calls on those who bend the bow (*kol-dōrᵉk̲ê qešeṯ*) to set themselves up round about the city and shoot into the city (*yᵉrû 'ēleyhā*, i.e., "toward the city"), sparing no arrows (*ḥēṣ*). If this reading is correct, we have another instance of *yārâ* I used with *ḥēṣ*.

The shooting of arrows, albeit for a different purpose, is also the subject of 1 S. 20 (4 occurrences) and 2 K. 13 (2 occurrences). In 1 S. 20:20,36,37, an arrow shot a certain distance and in a certain direction by Jonathan is to inform David secretly whether Saul is friendly or hostile. The prearranged sign (*dāḇār*) has the nature of a pact (v. 23). There are undeniable echoes of a kind of primitive arrow-oracle. The passage uses *yārâ* I (qal and hiphil) in conjunction with *ḥēṣ*, and Jonathan is described as an archer. The problem of whether the textual tradition refers to one arrow or to several need not concern us here.[9]

The story in 2 K. 13:14-21 is part of the Elisha cycle. It describes the death of the prophet, before which he addresses an oracle of salvation to Joash king of Israel. The

---

5 *AncIsr*; *BRL*; *BHHW*; *AOB*, nos. 62, 105, 130, 132; *ANEP*, nos. 172, 314-16, 318f., 365, 390.
6 See the apparatus in *BHK*³.
7 *BLe*, § 443k.
8 See the intros. and comms.
9 Stoebe, *KAT*, VIII/1, *in loc.*

prophetic word is accompanied by a symbolic act or more precisely a series of acts, in which a bow and arrows play a role (v. 15). In the course of one of these, Elisha has the window to the east opened and gives the order to shoot (*y^e^rēh wayyôr,* "'Shoot'; and he shot" [v. 17]). This action is associated with a message of success (Israel's victory over Aram, v. 17). This use of archery (the presence of an archer being presupposed) may also be based on a primitive arrow-oracle.[10]

Josh. 18:6 clearly describes the casting of lots; here, however, it is not arrows that are thrown but "oracular stones" (probably the original meaning of *gôrāl*[11]): *yārîṯî lāḵem gôrāl pōh lip̄nê YHWH ʾelōhênû.* The subject of the action is Joshua, who casts lots to determine how the land is to be divided among the Israelite tribes. The casting of lots was principally a priestly prerogative.[12]

"Throwing" or "shooting" in the military sense without mention of a specific weapon appears in a saying preserved in the Elohistic context of Nu. 21 (vv. 27-30). The passage looks back on the occupation of the territory east of the Jordan by immigrant Israelites, telling how "we threw them" and Heshbon was taken: *wannîrām* [i.e., *wannîrēm*] *ʾāḇaḏ ḥešbôn* (v. 30). Here *yārâ* I takes on the meaning "gain the upper hand over."[13] The object of *yārâ* I is personal. It is nevertheless silently assumed that the inhabitants were "thrown" by being shot at and hit by the Israelites.

Finally, *yārâ* I is used in its general literal sense for the setting up of a boundary marker (Gen. 31:51 [J]) and for the laying of the "cornerstone" of a building (Job 38:6). In the first passage, the mention of a *gal* ("heap of stones"; *maṣṣēḇâ* is probably secondary [cf. Gen. 31:52b]) may explain the usage: stones were thrown up onto a heap to mark a boundary (Laban says to Jacob: *hinnēh haggal hazzeh . . . ʾašer yārîṯî bênî ûḇêneḵā*). The Job passage may involve a technical architectural term: "throw foundation stones," i.e., lay a firm foundation for the building.[14]

2. *Figurative Sense.* The verb *yārâ* I meaning "shoot with bow and arrow" is also used figuratively. The most prominent example is v. 2 of Ps. 11, an individual hymn of trust[15] that may be preexilic. The wicked (*r^e^šāʿîm*) bend the bow and fit arrows to the string "to shoot in the dark at the upright in heart" (*lîrôṯ b^e^mô-ʾōp̄el l^e^yišrê-lēḇ; l^e^* = "in the direction of"; cf. Ps. 64:4,5,11[Eng. vv. 3,4,10]). The phrase expresses metaphorically the persecutions and snares of the wicked to which one who is devout feels exposed, impelling him to flee for refuge to the sanctuary, where he hopes and prays to find help, protection, and justice from Yahweh.[16]

The figurative language of Ps. 64, an individual lament, is to be understood in the

10 → חץ *hēṣ*; cf. "Pfeil" in *BRL*² and *BHHW,* III; G. Fohrer, *Die symbolischen Handlungen der Propheten. AThANT,* 54 (²1968); H.-C. Schmitt, *Elisa* (Gütersloh, 1972).

11 See *KBL*³; → גורל *gôrāl*; *AncIsr*; *BHHW,* II.

12 M. Noth, *Das Buch Josua. HAT,* VII (³1971), *in loc.*

13 See also M. Noth, *Numbers. OTL* (Eng. trans. 1968), 160-66.

14 See G. Fohrer, *Das Buch Hiob. KAT,* XVI (1963), 501, with bibliog.

15 G. Fohrer, *Intro. OT* (Eng. trans., Nashville, 1968), 286; H.-J. Kraus, *Psalms 1–59* (Eng. trans., Minneapolis, 1988), 201f.; L. Delekat, *Asylie und Schutzorakel* (Leiden, 1967), 154ff. Delekat calls the psalm an assurance of protection.

16 Cf. Kraus, Delekat.

same sense. The arrows aimed at the blameless (*tām,* v. 5(4); compare v. 11[10] with Ps. 11:2) likewise stand for the secret persecutions to which the petitioner is exposed. Ps. 64:4(3) shows that the sharp arrows and swords symbolize bitter words (*dāḇār*) and a sharp tongue (*lāšôn*). This may refer specifically to vicious rumors, libel, unjust accusations, or even strong language like a malediction or curse. The expression need not stand for acts of violence.[17] There is no need here to discuss the awkward expression "bend arrows" (*dārᵉḵû hiṣṣîm*) in v. 4(3).

There is also a figurative sense to the simile in Prov. 26:18. The effect is the same whether a man deceives his neighbor or a lunatic throws firebrands and shoots arrows; the outcome is a general sense of existential uncertainty.[18] Finally, in Job 38:6 and its context the use of architectural terminology ("throwing a cornerstone") for the establishment of God's creation can be understood as a metaphor.

III. Theological Usage. In Ps. 64 (discussed in II.2 above), v. 8(7) and its context speak of God as an archer. He shoots his arrow at the enemies of the petitioner (*wayyōrēm ʾᵉlōhîm ḥēṣ*) and makes them stumble on account of their tongue (v. 9[8]).[19] Parallel to this figurative use of *yārâ* I, God will use a word of power to put an end to the (verbal) attacks of the wicked upon the innocent (cf. the context). This reflects the ancient Near Eastern understanding of words as dangerous weapons, to be confronted like massive concrete objects.

In Job's lament (Job 30:19), the hiphil of *yārâ* I with God as subject again describes violence against a mortal. All the disasters that have befallen him—sickness, suffering, reversals of fortune—Job sums up by saying that God has cast him into the mire (*hōrānî laḥōmer*; exegetes often emend to *hôrîḏanî,* from *yāraḏ*;[20] but *yārâ* I also yields a vivid sense: "he has hurled me"), so that he himself has become like dust and ashes. The verb is used here without an instrumental object such as an arrow or stone. The language is a vivid expression of brute force. That this usage is not unique is shown by Ex. 15:4, where the context is a victory song of unknown date.[21] Here Yahweh destroys the chariotry of Pharaoh by hurling them into the sea (*yārâ bayyām*).

In the Yahwist's description of the preparations for Yahweh's theophany at Sinai (Ex. 19:10-15), the people are warned not to come near the mountain and above all not to touch it (*loʾ-tiggaʿ bô yāḏ kî-sāqôl yissāqēl ʾô-yārōh,* "whether beast or human being, none shall live" [v. 13]). The holiness of the mountain due to God's presence means that any unauthorized approach involves mortal danger.[22] Nothing is said that would enable us to picture how the offender would be stoned or "hurled" (RSV: "shot"). There seem to be two possibilities for interpretation: either the irrational element of the natural

---

17 Cf. also H.-J. Kraus, *Psalmen. BK,* XV/2 (⁵1978), 604-7.

18 See II.1 above.

19 For restoration of the text, see Kraus, *BK,* XV/2, 604f.

20 Fohrer, *KAT,* XVI, 414.

21 See M. Noth, *A History of Pentateuchal Traditions* (Eng. trans. 1972; repr. Chico, Calif., 1981), 30f., n. 107; *idem, Exodus. OTL* (Eng. trans. 1962), 123.

22 *Ibid.,* 153f., 158.

phenomena accompanying the theophany (whether thunderstorm or earthquake), which imperils any unauthorized person entering the region, or punishment as an act of sacral justice. In either case, the ultimate subject responsible for the deadly shooting or stoning is Yahweh's holiness.

It is undeniable that the uses of *yārâ* I cited in section II sometimes have clear theological overtones. The oracle recorded in the Isaiah narratives (2 K. 19:32 par. Isa. 37:33) illustrates Yahweh's power over history, which can permit or forbid the Assyrians to shoot arrows into the city. Jer. 50:14 shows that Yahweh can loose arrows against Babylon if his judgment upon the transgressions of the Babylonians so requires. The arrow to be shot is not merely the pointed weapon that can be fired or not at Yahweh's command; it is also a sign anticipating Israel's victory over its enemies, made manifest by Yahweh in symbolic act and prophetic word (2 K. 13:17).

Besides Yahweh's power over history, which extends to the use of military technology (*YHWH ʾîš milḥāmâ* declares Ex. 15:3, immediately before v. 4 celebrates his victory over the Egyptian army), there is also Yahweh's power over nature, revealed in his work of creation. This power is illustrated in part by the metaphor of Yahweh as a skilled architect and builder. In Job 38:6, Job is asked where he, a mere mortal, was when God established the world and laid its foundations: "Who cast down its cornerstone?" The answer—"No one!"—demonstrates the unquestionable power of Yahweh as creator, to which all must submit. The word *yārâ* I with God as subject is a plastic term, able to express the massive powers and perils at God's disposal to bring judgment or salvation upon his people and upon individuals. The enemies of Yahweh and his people are also exposed to these destructive powers.

IV. Summary. Although the notion of archery appears to dominate the use of *yārâ* I (even if only by implication), it is not possible to claim that "shoot arrows" is the basic meaning of the verb. Early passages use the root without the object *ḥēṣ* in the more general sense of "throw" or "hurl." It may, however, be possible to maintain that the term is used primarily in the context of conflicts, if we ignore the few passages that speak of throwing stones, whether to mark a boundary, lay a foundation, or cast lots. The evidence does not suggest that we are dealing with a military term, from which the other usages are derived. Marking a boundary by piling up a heap of stones or erecting a massebah (Gen. 31:51 [J]) presumably goes back to the dawn of time. This confirms our statement at the outset that the root has the general meaning "throw." Its figurative and theological usage does not go beyond this range of meanings.

S. Wagner

יָרָה *yārâ* II; יוֹרֶה *yôreh*; מוֹרֶה *môreh*

Contents: I. Etymology. II. Verb. III. Substantive. IV. Summary.

I. Etymology. It is not universally agreed that *yārâ* II is a separate root. Contrary to rabbinic tradition,[1] recent lexicography[2] has convinced many that this *yārâ* II is merely a by-form of *rāwâ* I, "drink one's fill," with a transitive hiphil meaning "soak."[3] Rabbinic interpretations of its occurrences suggest derivation from *yārâ* I, "throw" (hiphil "shoot") or even the hiphil of *yārâ* III, "instruct": the early rain (*yôreh*; *môreh*) is an "archer" shooting fructifying moisture at the earth or a "teacher" giving instruction on how to gather in the produce of the field.[4] The decision must be based on exegesis of the passages in question. An occurrence of *yr,* "rain(drop)," has been found in Ugaritic.[5]

II. Verb. The root *yārâ* II occurs only 3 times as a verb in the OT: twice in the hiphil (Hos. 6:3; 10:12) and once in the hophal (Prov. 11:25). In Hos. 6:3, *yôreh* clearly functions as predicate for the subj. *malqôš* ("latter rain"), with *ʾereṣ* as its object; the meaning must be connected with what the rain does to the earth. The nature of this activity can be determined from the context. The passage appears in a penitential hymn (Hos. 6:1-3) that belong to a cycle of Hoseanic oracles focusing on the themes of judgment, repentance, and salvation. The hymn is clearly quoting the words of Hosea's audience;[6] the prophet's response follows in vv. 4ff. The hymn is characterized by motifs of total confidence and trust in Yahweh: he may indeed afflict, but only to heal; he may indeed turn away from his people in judgment, but he will return to "revive" those who repent. This salvific return is compared (k^e) to the sure coming of the dawn and the annual arrival of *gešem* and *malqôš yôreh ʾāreṣ,* the rain that "waters" or "revives" (Wolff) the earth. The Targ. and Syr. appear to read *yarweh,* hiphil of *rāwâ* I,[7] which would in fact mean "soak."

The second Hosea passage appears in the context of a temotivated oracle of disaster. (The extent of the oracle is not certain; Wolff treats Hos. 10:9-15 as a unit, whereas Rudolph limits it to 10:11-13a.) It describes the loyalty Yahweh expects Israel to show toward its God, which would (or might) have its counterpart in Yahweh's love bestowed on Israel. The continuation shows, however, that Israel has been disloyal and is therefore unable to escape judgment. In the description of this mutual loyalty ("righteousness"

---

1 See *AuS,* I/1 (1928), 122.

2 See *KBL*³.

3 See H. W. Wolff, *Hosea. Herm* (Eng. trans. 1974),105, 180; W. Rudolph, *Hosea. KAT,* XIII/1 (1966), 132, 201.

4 See *AuS,* I/1.

5 *WUS,* no. 1233.

6 See the comms.

7 Cf. *BHS*.

based on the covenant) between God and people, we find the statement: "It is the time to seek (*liḏrōš*) Yahweh, *'aḏ-yāḇô' weyōreh ṣeḏeq lāḵem* ('that he may come and rain righteousness [salvation] upon [or "for"] you')." Here *yārâ* II is used figuratively.[8]

The third passage also appears to be early. It belongs to the so-called first collection of the proverbs of Solomon (Prov. 10:1–22:16), and may be preexilic. Like the other proverbs in this collection, Prov. 11:25 comprises two stichs; it extols the virtues of generosity in very general terms: "One who blesses will be blessed [lit., 'made fat'] in turn, and one who waters (*ûmarweh*) will certaintly be watered in turn (*gam-hû' yôre'*)." The latter form is a mistake for *yôreh*[9] and can be interpreted as a hophal of *yārâ* II.[10] An association with *rāwâ* I is suggested, however, by the preceding ptcp. *marweh*. The verb *yārâ* II is used literally here, but its literal sense serves as an image of prosperity in a universal wisdom aphorism: ultimately, greed does not pay.[11]

The Hosea passages serve a theological purpose, describing figuratively the gracious favor and love God shows to those who repent or remain loyal.

III. Substantive. There are two substantives that derive from our assumed root: *yôreh* (Dt. 11:14; Jer. 5:24 [*K* written defectively, *Q* plene]) and *môreh* (Joel 2:23; Ps. 84:7[Eng. v. 6]). The context of the passages in which they appear indicates that they mean "early rain." These nouns are not used figuratively, but serve to illustrate the bountiful favor Yahweh shows his people. It is Yahweh who creates the fructifying early rain and makes it fall, although he also can withhold this favor. The specific instances are as follows:

Dt. 11:14 belongs to the homiletic or parenetic framework of the Deuteronomic law code. Yahweh's gift of *yôreh* (par. *maṭar* and *malqôš*) is dependent on Israel's obeying Yahweh's commandments (*miṣwoṭay*, v. 13). If Israel turns aside and worships other gods, the necessary conditions are not fulfilled and Yahweh's anger will be kindled (v. 16). He will shut up the heavens (*'āṣar*, v. 17) and there will be no rain. The very possession of the land will be imperiled (v. 17). When Yahweh gives rain, the "right time" plays a critical role (v. 14: *nāṭan be'ittô*, "give in its season"). The early rain falls around the end of October and the beginning of November. Here Saadia translates *yôreh* as "timely" rain.[12] Rain that comes too late or too early disrupts agriculture and can lead to crop failure.[13]

The same theological perspective lies behind Jer. 5:24, where the motivation for a prophecy of disaster includes the charge that the people have not given Yahweh's power as Creator sufficient due (cf. also v. 22): "They did not say in their hearts, 'Let us fear Yahweh our God, who gives the rain in its season, the autumn rain and the spring rain

---

8 Contra Wolff, *in loc.*
9 See the apparatus in *BHK*[3].
10 *KBL*[3].
11 Cf. its context and all of ch. 11. H. Ringgren, *Sprüche. ATD,* XVI/1 ([3]1980), *in loc.*; B. Gemser, *Sprüche Salomos. HAT,* XVI ([2]1963), *in loc.*
12 *AuS,* I/1, 122.
13 *Ibid.*

(*hannōṯēn gešem wᵉyōreh ûmalqôš bᵉʿittô*), and keeps for us the weeks appointed for the harvest." The oracle in Jer. 5:20-25 is obscure in origin,[14] but Jeremianic authorship is not out of the question, given the strangeness of the themes dealt with in ch. 5.

Rain in general, including both autumn and spring rain, is reason (*kî-nāṯan*) to rejoice in Yahweh (Joel 2:23; cf. vv. 21-24: *gîl* and *śāmaḥ bᵉ-YHWH*). A hymn of thanksgiving is appropriate, above all if the natural catastrophe of a drought has evoked a communal act of penance and Yahweh has been merciful, granting a plenteous harvest (v. 24).[15]

The phrase *hammôreh liṣdāqâ* in Joel 2:23 has raised the question of a connection with the "teacher of righteousness" in the Dead Sea scrolls. Present scholarship has rightly rejected the earlier theory that the expressions are related, even if only through a misunderstanding.[16] The mention of *gešem môreh* in the same verse establishes the meaning "early rain." The phrase in question means the early rain coming at the proper time (or perhaps better: the regular rain that is "right" with the natural order) and in the proper amount.[17] Wolff[18] emends the text and translates: "food according to covenant righteousness." In fact this emendation amounts to the same thing: "according to covenant righteousness" means nothing more nor less than the regular climatic sequence, on which the economic and therefore general welfare depend. In the background is the agrarian economic and social structure of Palestine.[19]

In Ps. 84:7(6), unfortunately, the text of the line containing *môreh* is corrupt.[20] With care, however, one can make out the meaning. Among other things, the Zion hymn[21] sings of the pilgrims' longing for the sanctuary and depicts the blessings already experienced along their arduous route, which passes through the valley of Baca. It is unfortunately impossible to determine what this expression refers to—a particularly harsh and arid region or just the reverse, an especially fertile area. In any case, the pilgrims find springs there and experience the blessing of the early rain (*gam-bᵉrāḵōṯ yaʿṭeh môreh*). However the passage is to be interpreted in detail, there is a clear relationship between *môreh* and *bᵉrāḵâ*. Whether it is used in its literal or figurative sense, *môreh* stands for something positive, something that ultimately comes from God through the mediation of the temple or the holy place. The date of the psalm is uncertain. Kraus thinks that it is preexilic, Fohrer postexilic. There is no compelling evidence against a preexilic date.

IV. Summary. In the OT, the situations described by *yārâ* II involve the rain that farmers look for to water their soil; coming at the right time and in the right amount, it

14 Cf. W. Rudolph, *Jeremia. HAT,* XII (³1968), *in loc.*; A. Weiser, *Das Buch Jeremia 1–25,14. ATD,* XX (⁸1981), *in loc.*

15 T. H. Robinson, *Die zwölf kleinen Propheten: Hosea bis Micha. HAT,* XIV (³1964), 64f.

16 H. W. Wolff, *Joel and Amos. Herm* (Eng. trans. 1977), *in loc.,* with bibliog.

17 Robinson, 64.

18 *Joel and Amos,* 55.

19 Cf. R. B. Y. Scott, "Meteorological Phenomena and Terminology in the OT," *ZAW,* 64 (1952), 11-25.

20 See *BHS*.

21 H. Gunkel; H.-J. Kraus, *Psalmen. BK,* XV/2 (⁵1975), *in loc.*; G. Fohrer, *Intro. OT* (Eng. trans., Nashville, 1968), § 43.

is necessary for a successful harvest. A bountiful crop from field and vineyard means wealth and prosperity, the visible sign of a blessing. It is Yahweh who creates and sends this rain. (In the noun, the root takes on the special meaning "early rain.") His loving favor toward the human race and his own people can be seen in his gift of rain; his alienation, wrath, and judgment, however, can take the form of withholding the fructifying precipitation. The result is drought and hunger, misery and death. The term *yārâ* II can also be used figuratively for the salvation or devastation God brings; but the metaphor draws its strength from the concrete reality and is based on Yahweh's power over nature, upon which one must always depend.

S. Wagner

יָרָה *yārâ* III; מוֹרֶה *môreh*

Contents: I. Root, Distribution, Usage, Meaning. II. Usage with Human Subjects: 1. Secular Contexts; 2. Psalms; 3. Priestly Instruction. III. God as Teacher. IV. *môreh.*

I. Root, Distribution, Usage, Meaning. The root *yārâ* III is found in several Semitic languages, albeit not in the earlier ones. It appears in Middle Hebrew, Jewish Aramaic, Old South Arabic, Amharic, Tigré, and possibly also in Arabic.[1] Its meaning is roughly equivalent to "proclaim." In Old South Arabic, however, it means the opposite: "keep secret."

The verb appears 45 times in the OT, always in the hiphil. There are also 9 occurrences of the derived substantive *môreh.* The other derivative, *tôrâ,* occurs much more frequently; it is treated in a separate article.

In nearly every occurrence the verb can be translated "teach" or "instruct," almost always with a double object: "teach someone something." The root represents a concept with a *Sitz im Leben* in teaching and catechesis. It presupposes a relationship between two personal (or personally conceived) entities: the instructor possesses or claims authority over the other; the recipient of instruction has or should have certain expectations of the teacher. It is clear that only when this mutual relationship is present with its readiness to give and to receive that the functional context denoted by *yārâ* III is given its (full) due. The root implies nothing about any particular method of instruction. The element of mutual personal relationship should always be kept in mind when *yārâ* III is

---

yārâ III. G. Jeremias, *Der Lehrer der Gerechtigkeit. StUNT,* 2 (1963); G. Sarfatti, "Semantics of Mishnaic Hebrew and Interpretation of the Bible by the Tannaim: Nota d," *Lešonénû,* 29 (1964/65), 238-244; 30 (1965), 29-40 [Heb.; Eng. summary]; J. Weingreen, "The Title *Môrēh Ṣédek* (Teacher of Righteousness?)," *From Bible to Mishna* (Manchester, 1946), 100-114; *idem,* "The Title *môrēh ṣeḏeḵ,*" *JSS,* 6 (1961), 162-174; R. B. Zuck, "Hebrew Words for 'Teach,'" *BS,* 121 (1964), 228-235.

1 *KBL*[3].

used. The noun *môreh* can be translated "teacher." This term plays a special role in the Dead Sea scrolls in the person of *môreh haṣṣeḏeq,* the "teacher of righteousness."[2] The suggestion that this figure appears in Joel 2:23 is discussed under *yārâ* II.

The occurrences of *yārâ* III in the OT appear to fall into three functional groups: poetry and wisdom literature, specifically Psalms (8 times), Job (7 times), and Proverbs (4 times); legal passages; and accounts of priestly instruction. It would nevertheless be wrong to say that *yārâ* III was used only in the late literary strata of the OT. There is a marked theological element in the usage of the root.

The word *lᵉhôrōṯ* in Gen. 46:28 is not even supported by the versions.[3] Following Gunkel, von Rad attempts to interpret the text as it stands, but is unable to propose a convincing meaning. As is well known, the passage deals with the departure of Jacob for Egypt. Judah is sent ahead to Joseph "to show the way before him to Goshen."[4] The text is undoubtedly corrupt and may safely be ignored.[5]

II. Usage with Human Subjects.

1. *Secular Contexts.* The "secular usage" of *yārâ* III is clearest in Wisdom Literature. A father instructs his son in the proper conduct of life, imparting sensible bits of wisdom, which, if taken to heart, should lead to a good, successful, and prosperous life. See, for example, Prov. 4:4, from the perspective of the son: *wayyōrēnî wayyōʾmer lî,* "He taught me and said to me, 'Let your heart hold fast my words; keep my commandments, and live.'" There follow in v. 5 further admonitions to seek and use "wisdom." In v. 11, the father states that he has taught his son "the way of wisdom" (*bᵉḏereḵ ḥoḵmâ hōrēṯîḵā*) and led him "in the paths of uprightness." The context suggests that wisdom instruction includes explicitly ethical elements. Demonstration that the ethical maxims make sense argues for their observance (see vv. 14ff.). A typical motif is the warning against the "foreign woman," to whose enticements the youth must not respond, lest he fall into ruin and have to say: *wᵉlōʾ-šāmaʿtî bᵉqôl môrāy,* "I did not listen to the voice of my teachers" (Prov. 5:13; the parallel stich speaks of *mᵉlammᵉḏîm*). The father-son relationship is probably a metaphor for the teacher-student relationship, in which the teacher is a wisdom instructor.[6] These 3 passages appear in a mixed collection of Wisdom poems and individual maxims dating from the postexilic period (Prov. 1–9).[7]

Thematically difficult to place is Prov. 6:13, where *yārâ* III is used in the context of pointing with fingers, feet, and eye movements. A wicked and worthless person uses devious words and gestures to deceive his neighbor with respect to his real evil intentions. Punishment—according to the wisdom instructor—follows such conduct immediately (vv. 12-15; v. 13: *mōreh bᵉʾṣbᵉʿōṯāyw,* "one who instructs or points with his fingers").

---

2 → צדק *ṣeḏeq.*

3 See *BHK*³ and the apparatus of *BHS*.

4 G. von Rad, *Genesis. OTL* (Eng. trans.²1972), *in loc.*

5 See also the earlier comms. of H. Gunkel and O. Procksch.

6 See also H. Ringgren, *Sprüche. ATD,* XVI/1 (³1980), 25; B. Gemser, *Sprüche Salomos. HAT,* XVI (²1963), 33.

7 G. Fohrer, *Intro. OT* (Eng. trans., Nashville, 1968), § 49.

Instruction was undoubtedly reinforced by gestures (pointing, for example); this passage castigates the abuse of such means.

The use of *yārâ* III in the Job dialogues is basically the same as in Proverbs, even though the theme is different: debate over the question of God's justice. Here the "secular" usage of the root suddenly takes on theological overtones. Job asks whether his friends can "teach" him by showing him his error (Job 6:24: *hôrûnî,* "teach me," "instruct me"). His bitter experiences in turn enable him to teach his friends about God's ways (Job 27:11: *'ôreh 'eṯkem beyaḏ-'ēl*), which he still finds unjust. Fohrer appends 27:1-5,11f. to 26:1-4, reconstructing a ninth discourse of Job.[8] The wisdom instructor appeals not only to his own experience but to the experience and teaching of earlier generations (Job 8:8), telling Job in the question of God's actions, which are just by definition, to follow the *dōr rî'šôn* and the *'āḇôṯ* (8:10, Bildad to Job: *halō'-hēm yôrûḵā yō'merû lāḵ* . . . , "Will they not teach you, and tell you, and utter words out of their understanding?").

The created world can also teach: the animals, for example, teach that God has created everything and is omnipotent (Job 12:7-25, esp. 7-11; v. 7: *we'ûlām še'al-nā' behēmôṯ weṯōrekkā,* "But ask the beasts, and they will teach you"; v. 8: *'ô ḥayyaṯ hā'āreṣ weṯōrekka,* "Or the wild animals, and they will teach you" [*śîaḥ lā'āreṣ* makes no sense in the context[9]]). The parallel stichs speak of birds and fish, using the hiphil of *ngd,* "declare," and the piel of *spr,* "tell." God's creatures instruct and declare by virtue of their very existence, demonstrating God's power in creating and preserving the world, a power that is beyond question. We have here an expression of natural theology, of revelation through nature. The entire passage (12:7-25) is probably an interpolation in Job's discourse (chs. 12–14); it bears all the marks of the wisdom tradition.[10]

In Elihu's speeches, Job is accused of expecting God to charge himself with having offended against Job and therefore needing Job to teach him (Job 34:32 in context). The text is probably corrupt; cf. the Vulg. and the comms. *in loc.*; in any case, the phrase *'attâ hōrēnî,* "you teach me," is clear. The argumentation in the poetic discourses of Job is shot through with persiflage, irony, and accusations. Elihu in response speaks of God as the one incomparable teacher (Job 36:22: *mî kāmōhû môreh,* "Who is a teacher like him?"); to claim to teach God would be blasphemous presumption.[11] Of course the notion of God as a teacher is not unique to the wisdom tradition.

2. *Psalms.* Above all in individual laments we find the plea that Yahweh will "teach" the petitioner the right way (Ps. 27:11; 86:11). The trust motif of the laments expresses confidence that Yahweh does in fact instruct people in the "right way" (25:8,12). The same idiom may be observed in the individual hymns of thanksgiving (32:8). All these

---

8 G. Fohrer, *Das Buch Hiob. KAT,* XVI (1963), 376ff.; see also G. Hölscher, *Das Buch Hiob. HAT,* XVII (^{2}1952), 66f., who considers ch. 27 a miscellaneous collection.

9 The emendation is proposed by *BHK*^{3}; cf. the comms.

10 See Fohrer, *KAT,* XVI, 244ff.; Hölscher, *HAT,* XVII, 32f., brackets only vv. 7-10. A. Weiser, *Das Buch Hiob. ATD,* XIII (^{5}1968), 92ff., includes the whole passage.

11 On the skillful structure and the form (disputation), see Fohrer, *KAT,* XVI, 474ff.

expressions depend on our understanding of *dereḵ* ("way") and *'ōraḥ* ("path"), which must be determined from the context. In Ps. 25:8, it is reasonable to understand the "right way" as meaning proper (loyal) behavior toward God. The prayer to be shown the way stands in parallel with a prayer for forgiveness of sins (cf. vv. 4,6,7,9-11; the verbs used in parallel with *yārâ* III are *yāḏaʿ* hiphil and *lāmaḏ* piel). The nature of God's way, which Yahweh is asked to teach the worshipper, is described in terms of steadfast love (*ḥeseḏ*) and faithfulness (*'ᵉmeṯ*; v. 10). Verse 12 associates the way with fear of God. God instructs the man who fears the Lord in the *dereḵ*. The nouns *sôḏ* and *bᵉrîṯ* are almost synonymous with *dereḵ* (v. 14). Central to this postexilic individual lament is the prayer for instruction in God's will (v. 8: *yôreh ḥaṭṭā'îm badderek*; v. 12: *yôrennû bᵉḏereḵ yiḇḥar,* "Him will he instruct in the way that he should choose").

Ps. 27 (possibly not a single unit) probably represents the lament of an accused victim of persecution, who feels separated from Yahweh. His despair leads him to the sanctuary, where he hopes for instruction through an oracle of salvation that will show him the way out. This can only consist in God's justification of the worshipper's conduct, so that his accusers are put to shame (v. 11: *hôrēnî YHWH darkeḵā ûnᵉḥēnî bᵉ'ōraḥ mîšôr,* "Teach my thy way, Yahweh; and lead me on a level [right] path"). A preexilic origin of this psalm is not impossible.

These associations are clearly visible in v. 11 of Ps. 86, a late individual lament that is somewhat obscure as a whole. A prayer for instruction (*hôrēnî YHWH darkeḵā*) is followed by a purpose clause: ". . . that I may walk (*hālaḵ*) in thy truth (*'ᵉmeṯ*)." As in Ps. 25, sin and forgiveness are also spoken of in v. 8 of Ps. 32, a postexilic individual hymn of thanksgiving. The worshipper cites God's words from an oracle of salvation: *'ôrᵉḵā bᵉḏereḵ-zû tēlēḵ,* "I will teach you the way you should go." The parallel terms (*'aśkîl,* "I will instruct," and *'îʿᵃṣâ,* "I will counsel") have wisdom overtones, which might suggest that this psalm became part of the wisdom tradition.

What is implied by the context in these passages is stated explicitly in Ps. 119: *hôrēnî YHWH dereḵ ḥuqqeyḵā,* "Teach me, Yahweh, the way of thy statutes" (v. 33). This late anthology of didactic wisdom,[12] inculcating devotion to the law, frequently uses a variety of words for "way" (*dereḵ, 'ōrâ,* etc.), often modified by or in parallel with words like "testimonies," "commandments," *tôrâ,* etc. (cf. v. 33: "the way of thy statutes"). The speaker's love for the law finds expression, for example, in vv. 97-104. This love leads the devout psalmist to observe God's commandments: *mimmišpāṭeyḵā lō'-sartî kî-'attâ hôrēṯānî,* "I do not turn aside from thy ordinances, for thou hast taught me" (v. 102). Thus *dereḵ* (the only noun used with *yārâ* III, surely by accident) proves to mean "divine instruction"; it derives from the priestly and cultic context of the salvation oracle and the proclamation of God's will through priestly *tôrâ* and affects even the everyday ethical conduct of the devout. To walk in this way signifies the worshipper's loyalty to God.[13]

Ps. 45:5(Eng. v. 4) has long been a crux interpretum.[14] The MT reads: *wᵉṯôrᵉḵā nôrā'ôṯ*

---

[12] Fohrer, *Intro. OT.*

[13] For a discussion of all the passages, see Fohrer, *ibid.,* 285ff.; H.-J. Kraus, *Psalmen. BK,* XV/2 (⁵1978); and the articles on *dereḵ* (*derekh*) in *TDOT* and *THAT.*

[14] Cf. the uncertainty regarding the text as noted in the apparatus of *BHK*³ and *BHS.*

y^emîneḵā, "Let your right hand teach you dread deeds." In this royal psalm, which Kraus calls an epithalamium for the king, this clause appears in the context of appeals calling on the king to intervene mightily on behalf of truth and right, defending the cause of those who are deprived of justice. In this context the clause can be interpreted meaningfully. It calls on the king's right hand or right arm to teach the king to bestir himself and act with power, successfully exerting his sovereignty. It is an appeal for an act of will, asking the king to exercise his power as ruler. The clause is a metaphor for such action (cf. v. 6[5]).

3. *Priestly Instruction.* From early times, instruction was one of the functions of the priesthood. The nature of the instruction might vary. In 2 K. 17:27f., a priest teaches the *mišpāṭ* of the local deity (*w^eyōrēm ʾeṯ-mišpaṭ ʾ^elōhê hāʾāreṣ*), or more specifically how to fear Yahweh (*way^ehî môreh ʾêḵ yîr^eʾû ʾeṯ-YHWH*). On account of a plague of lions in the territory of Samaria, under Assyrian hegemony, a priest is sent back from exile to instruct the aliens settled in the former territory of Israel how to worship Yahweh properly. The natural disaster was blamed on insufficient knowledge (*yāḏaʿ*) of *mišpāṭ YHWH* (v. 26).

The motivation for an oracle of disaster pronounced by Micah against the Jerusalem leadership includes the venality of the priests in their teaching office: *w^ekōh^aneyhā bimḥîr yôrû,* "Its priests teach for hire" (Mic. 3:11). Isaiah, too, castigates the priests who are too drunk (possibly through abuse of sacrificial meals in the Jerusalem temple[15]) to impart clear instruction: *ʾeṯ-mî yôreh dēʿâ,* "Whom will he teach knowledge?" (Isa. 28:9; cf. v. 7). Another passage lists the prophets who teach lies among the reasons for the coming disaster: *nāḇîʾ môreh-šeqer* (Isa. 9:14[15]).

In P we find references to priestly instruction in cultic matters on the basis of statutes (*ḥuqqîm*); see, for example, Lev. 10:11 (*ul^ehôrōṯ ʾeṯ-b^enê yiśrāʾēl*) and more specifically Lev. 14:57, which speaks of instruction in what is clean and what is unclean (*l^ehôrōṯ b^eyôm haṭṭāmēʾ ûḇ^eyôm haṭṭāhōr*).[16] Here also belongs the secondary addition to Dt. 24 requiring priestly instruction in cases of leprosy (v. 8: *k^eḵōl ʾ^ašer-yôrû ʾeṯḵem hakkōh^anîm hal^ewiyyim*).[17] Ezekiel's program for reconstruction of the temple also contains regulations governing the duties of priests, including instruction in the distinction between what is clean and what is unclean (Ezk. 44:23: *w^eʾeṯ-ʿammî yôrû* par. *yôḏiʿum*[18]).

Dt. 17:8f. requires serious legal cases to be brought before the "Levitical priests" at the cultic center and before "the judge who is in office in those days"; their decision is binding: "You shall be careful to do according to all *ʾ^ašer yôrûḵā. ʿal-pî hattôrâ ʾ^ašer yôrûḵā w^eʿal-hammišpāṭ ʾ^ašer-yoʾm^erû l^eḵā ta^{ʿa}śeh*" (17:10f.). Alongside *yārâ* III and *ʾāmar* we also find the hiphil of *ngd.* Clearly the priests are responsible for cases arising out of sacral law. In the familiar Deuteronomistic appraisal of the kings of Israel and Judah, the passage concerning Jehoash, king of Judah, states that he "did what was right in the eyes of Yahweh" because he was instructed by Jehoiada the priest (2 K. 12:3[2]:

---

15 G. Fohrer, *Das Buch Jesaja,* II. *ZBK* (²1967), 49ff.

16 On both passages, see K. Elliger, *Leviticus. HAT,* IV (1966).

17 See G. von Rad, *Deuteronomy. OTL* (Eng. trans. 1966), *in loc.*

18 See W. Zimmerli, *Ezekiel II. Herm* (Eng. trans. 1983), p. 460.

ʾᵃšer hôrāhû yᵉhôyāḏāʿ hakkōhēn). In the view of the Deuteronomistic historian, this "instruction" consisted in teaching how to worship Yahweh alone in the right way. In the Chronicler's message, the presence of priests capable of giving instruction (*kōhēn môreh*) is necessary for the well-being of the body politic (2 Ch. 15:3; cf. 15:1-7).

The blessing of Levi in the so-called Blessing of Moses (Dt. 33:10) may be among the earliest passages illustrating the functional association of the priesthood with instruction (here mentioned alongside the offering of sacrifice: *yôrû mišpāṭeyḵā lᵉyaʿᵃqōḇ wᵉṯôrāṯᵉḵā lᵉyiśrāʾēl*). This would bear witness to a long period during which the OT used *yārâ* III for priestly instruction.[19]

Finally, we may note the woes in Hab. 2:18f., a passage pointing out the uselessness of an idol made by human hands. It is "a teacher of lies" (v. 18: *môreh šeqer*). It is likewise dangerous to turn to a tree or stone as though it were able to prophesy: "Woe to him who says to a wooden thing, Awake; to a dumb stone, Arise! as though such a thing might teach (*hûʾ yôreh*)!" (v. 19). Exegetes usually omit the last clause, probably without good reason. Recourse to idols and cultic objects for guidance was a familiar abuse. Probably v. 19 refers to the same phenomenon as v. 18; it is hardly likely that the latter represents a primitive stage of religion when sacred trees and stones were worshipped.

III. God as Teacher. In Wisdom Literature, as in the Psalms, God may be the indirect subject of *yārâ* III: it is ultimately God who teaches wisdom or imparts an oracle of salvation. But there are also several OT passages in which God is the explicit subject of *yārâ* III. Typical is the tradition ascribed to the Yahwist that tells how Moses and Aaron were sent to Pharaoh (Ex. 4:12,15). Yahweh will teach Moses (and Aaron) what they are to say or do: *wᵉhôrêṯîḵā ʾᵃšer tᵉḏabbēr*; *wᵉhôrêṯî ʾeṯkem ʾeṯ ʾᵃšer taʿᵃśûn*. This promise is reinforced by the promise of Yahweh's presence: *ʾānōḵî ʾehyeh ʿim-pîḵā/ʿim-pîhû*. In Ex. 24:12, the real subject is also Yahweh, even though the text can refer to Moses as the agent: on the mountain of God, Yahweh gives Moses the tablets of stone *ʾᵃšer kāṯaḇtî lᵉhôrōṯām*, "which I have written for their instruction," or possibly "which I have written so that you may instruct them." Source criticism is uncertain about this passage. Noth[20] suggests a secondary stratum of J, with the later addition of "law and commandment," which may be a gloss.[21] However the case may be—whether Yahweh's writing is itself an act of instruction or Moses serves as mediator—Yahweh is ultimately the logical subject of the action. The subject matter is the corpus of covenant stipulations that enshrine Yahweh's will with respect to his people.

A similar mediated act on the part of Yahweh plays a role in the story of Samson's birth (Jgs. 13:8). After the miraculous announcement of Samson's birth by the *malʾaḵ YHWH*,[22] Samson's father prays once more for the coming of the *ʾîš hāʾᵉlōhîm* to teach

---

[19] See von Rad, *Deuteronomy*, 204-8; H.-J. Zobel, *Stammesspruch und Geschichte. BZAW*, 95 (1965), 29ff., 67ff.

[20] M. Noth, *A History of Pentateuchal Traditions* (Eng. trans. 1972; repr. Chico, Calif., 1981), 31, n. 115.

[21] M. Noth, *Exodus. OTL* (Eng. trans. 1962), 200.

[22] See V. Hirth, *Gottes Boten im AT*/ *ThArb*, 32 (1975).

the parents what to do with the boy about to be born (*wᵉyôrēnû mah-naʿᵃśeh lannaʿar hayyûllād*). It is clear that Yahweh is responsible for this act as well; he appoints his agents and equips them to do his will. Thus *yārâ* III has a certain place in call narratives, at least in giving instruction for specific actions.

The Deuteronomistic passages presuppose that God instructs his people in the right way—as defined by Deuteronomistic theology, the right way to worship Yahweh exclusively at the central sanctuary (1 K. 8:36). The Chronicler's version of this passage in Solomon's prayer at the dedication of the temple follows its Deuteronomistic original: *kî tôrēm ʾeṯ-hadderek̲ haṭṭôḇâ ʾᵃšer yēlᵉkû-ḇâ* (1 K. 8:36; the same words appear in 2 Ch. 6:27 with *ʾel* instead of *ʾeṯ*). Just as this passage places Deuteronomistic theology in the mouth of Solomon, so 1 S. 12:23 places it in the mouth of Samuel in his "farewell discourse." He addresses the people with the voice of a Deuteronomistic theologian: *wᵉhôrêṯî ʾeṯkem bᵉḏerek̲ haṭṭôḇâ wᵉhayyᵉšārâ*, "and I will instruct you in the good and the right way."

Among the loveliest ideas associated with God's salvific function as teacher are the hopes expressed in Isa. 2 and Mic. 4, in the context of the people's eschatological pilgrimage to Zion. There, they say, Yahweh will "teach us [one of] his ways, that we may walk in his paths" (*yōrēnû middᵉrāk̲āyw wᵉnēlᵉk̲â bᵉʾōrᵉḥōṯāyw*). Again *derek̲* is defined by the parallel terms *tôrâ* and *dᵉḇar-YHWH* (Isa. 2:3; Mic. 4:2). At the end of time, Yahweh's mediation, which has international force, and the torah on Zion in Jerusalem will solve all the problems of the world and of humanity. The root *yarâ* III has transcendent significance; it goes beyond pedagogy: it means instruction in the way to peace and salvation. Most exegetes are inclined to a late date for both passages, which probably come from an independent eschatological document that was incoporated into the prophetic books.[23]

That God is the source of all the achievements of civilization and has taught the human race how to use them was a widespread conviction in the ancient Near East. Isaiah preserves a wisdom aphorism illustrating this view: God teaches the farmer how to farm his land correctly (Isa. 28:26 [in context]: *ʾᵉlōhāyw yôrennû*, "his God teaches him"; the preceding stich reads: *wᵉyissᵉrô lammišpāṭ*, "he is instructed aright"). The passage must be seen as a parable implying that Isaiah is taught by God to exercise his ministry (v. 29). The Yahwist's account of the bitter water at Marah (Ex. 15:25) provides an earlier illustration of the same idea: Moses is "taught" by Yahweh how to make the water potable by means of a piece of wood (*wayyôrēhû YHWH ʿēṣ*; the Sam. and other versions read *wayyarʾēhû*, "and he showed him"). P's description of the builders of the sanctuary speaks of the inspiration and ability that enabled them to carry out all the work as Yahweh intended. In particular, the Judahite Bezalel is said to have had the God-given ability to instruct others in the craftsmanship needed for the job (Ex. 35:34: *ûlᵉhôrōṯ nāṯan bᵉlibbô*).

IV. *môreh*. The noun *môreh*, derived from *yārâ* III, does not play the role in the OT

---

23 See H. Wildberger, *Jesaja. BK*, X/1 (1972), 75ff.

that it plays in the Dead Sea scrolls, where it refers to the "Teacher of Righteousness" (*môreh haṣṣeḏeq*).[24]

Of its 9 occurrences in the OT, we shall discuss first the 3 passages where the noun is associated with a place: Gen. 12:6 (J); Dt. 11:30; Jgs. 7:1. Gen. 12:6, the earliest of these, tells how Abraham goes to Shechem *ʿaḏ ʾēlôn môreh* ("to the oracle terebinth"[25]), understood to be a Canaanite sacred tree. This terebinth near Shechem is mentioned in other OT passages, albeit without the noun *môreh*: e.g., Josh. 24:26; Jgs. 9:37; Gen. 35:4 (E). The expression in Dt. 11:30 also purports to refer to the vicinity of Shechem; but other phrases in v. 30 create problems (*mûl haggilgāl,* "over against Gilgal"), while v. 29 clearly points to Shechem. In v. 30, *ʾēlônê mōreh* is surely to be read as a singular;[26] the Sam. reads: *mōreʾ šᵉḵem.* In Jgs. 7:1, the Midianite army before battle is encamped north of Gideon's position, at a *giḇʿaṯ hammôreh* in the valley. This hill of Moreh must have been near the spring of Harod (*ʿēn-jālūd*) northwest of Mt. Gilboa at the entrance to the plain of Jezreel.[27] While the terebinth (or "oak") might still be interpreted as referring to a former oracular shrine (compare Gen. 35:8 with Jgs. 4:5), this is much less likely in the case of *giḇʿaṯ hammôreh,* a totally unique expression. In the former case, the root *yārâ* III from which the noun derives still has overtones of meaning: it would stand for instruction in an oracular sense.

In the other 6 occurrences, the meaning "teacher" is clear. Isa. 30:20 uses *môreh* twice, each time referring to God. This late eschatological announcement of salvation looks forward to a time when the people "in" Zion and Jerusalem will once more be able to "see" their teacher (= God) and their teacher (= God) will not hide himself any more. Verse 21 speaks of showing the "way" (*dereḵ*) and v. 22 of turning from idolatry. Verse 20 has its own problems. The noun *môreh* is in fact in the plural (although *BHK*³ cites a few manuscripts with a singular in pause); at least the first occurrence is linked with a singular verb. The second stich expresses God's visible presence on Zion (*wᵉhāyû ʿêneyḵā rōʾôṯ ʾeṯ-môreyḵā*). This idea is not unusual in the context of late apocalyptic thought; we are reminded of Isa. 2 and Mic. 4.

In Hab. 2:18, the *môreh šeqer* appears in a passage introduced by *hôy* attacking the manufacture of idols; vv. 18 and 19 should probably be reversed. The idol and the teacher (oracle) of lies are identical.[28]

Closest to the Isaiah passage discussed above is Job 36:22, which sings the praises of God as the *môreh* par excellence (*mî kāmōhû môreh*). Here, too, however, the verbal origin of the noun must be emphasized (cf. v. 23).

The debated passage Joel 2:23 is discussed under *yārâ* II above.

In wisdom traditions we find the figure of the (wisdom) instructor who teaches the learner, to whom he imparts knowledge to be taken to heart (Prov. 5:13; regrettably, the learner might have to say, "I did not listen to the voice of my teachers [*môrāy*])."[29]

---

24 See *KBL*³ and Jeremias, with bibliog.

25 See von Rad, *Genesis,* 162.

26 *BHK*³.

27 See Y. Aharoni, *The Land of the Bible* (Eng. trans., Philadelphia, ²1979), 263.

28 See II.3 above.

29 See *môreh* in *KBL*³, with bibliog.

With the possible exception of the wisdom instructor, then, *môreh* does not suggest a particular institution. Its semantic range does not extend beyond the range of *yārâ* III. Even in Prov. 5:13, *môreh* need not be understood as a technical term; the par. *m^e lamm^e day* is a verb in the form of a noun. Alongside the wisdom instructor we find the giver of oracles (a priest, or occasionally a prophet). The meaning of *môreh* is heavily dependent on the activity designated by *yārâ* III.

S. Wagner

יְרוּשָׁלַם *ye rûšālēm/ye rûšālayim*

Contents: I. Preliminary: 1. Orthography, Etymology; 2. Jerusalem/Zion/Israel (Judah); 3. Sources. II. The Jebusite Hypothesis. III. Origin and Development of Jerusalem's Importance. IV. Jerusalem Founded and Chosen by Yahweh. V. Holy City and Holy Mountain. VI. Spring, River, and Sea of Chaos. VII. The Future to Come. VIII. Jerusalem and the Individual.

---

ye rûšālayim. Y. Aviram, ed., *Yerushalayim le-doroteha (Jerusalem through the Ages)* (Jerusalem, 1968) [Heb.]; A. Causse, "La vision de la nouvelle Jérusalem (Esaïe LX) et la signification sociologique des assemblées de fête et des pèlerimages dans l'orient sémitique," *Mélanges syriens. Festschrift R. Dussaud,* II. *BAH,* 30 (1939), 739-750; R. J. Clifford, *The Cosmic Mountain in Canaan and the OT. HSM,* 4 (1972), esp. 131-160; H. Donner, "Jerusalem," *BRL*², 157-165; J. Ebach, "Jerusalem," *LexÄg,* III, 267f.; D. Flusser, "Jerusalem in the Literature of the Second Temple Period," *Sefer Reubin Mass* (Jerusalem, 1974), 263-284 (repr. *Immanuel,* 6 [1976], 43-46); G. Fohrer, "Zion-Jerusalem," *Studien zur alttestamentlichen Theologie und Geschichte (1949-1969). BZAW,* 115 (1969), 195-241 (rev. of "Σιών, Ἰερουσαλήμ," *TDNT,* VII, 292-319); H. Gunkel and J. Begrich, *Einl. in die Psalmen. HKAT,* sup. (1939), 309-311 ("Das Wallfahrtslied"); F. Huber, *Jahwe, Juda und die anderen Völker beim Propheten Jesaja. BZAW,* 137 (1976), 233-240 (Exkurs IV: "Die Vorstellung vom Schutz Jerusalems durch Jahwe und ihre Bedeutung für die Aussagen Jesajas über andere Völler"); M. Join-Lambert, *Jérusalem israélite, chrétienne, musulmane* (Paris, 1957); H. Kosmala, "Jerusalem," *BHHW,* II (1964), 820-850; H.-J. Kraus, *Psalms 1–59* (Eng. trans., Minneapolis, 1988), 81-89 ("Excursus 1: The Cultic Traditions of Jerusalem"), 89-92 ("Excursus 2: The Glorification of the City of God"); *idem, Psalmen. BK,* XV/2 (²1978), 1057-1061 ("Psalm 132"); É. Lamirande, "Jérusalem céleste," *Dictionnaire de spiritualité,* VIII (Paris, 1974), 944-958; H.-M. Lutz, *Jahwe, Jerusalem und die Völker. WMANT,* 27 (1968); R. A. F. MacKenzie, "The City and Israelite Religion," *CBQ,* 25 (1963), 60-70; W. Müller, *Die heilige Stadt: Roma quadrata, himmlisches Jerusalem und die Mythe vom Weltnabel* (Stuttgart, 1961); G. Neville, *City of Our God: God's Presence among His People* (London, 1971); M. Noth, "Jerusalem and the Northern Kingdom," in Aviram, *ye rûšālayim l^e dôrôteyhā,* *33-*38; *idem,* "Jerusalem and the Israelite Tradition," *The Laws in the Pentateuch and Other Essays* (Eng. trans. 1967; repr. London, 1984), 132-144; E. Otto, *Jerusalem—Die Geschichte der Heiligen Stadt* (Stuttgart, 1980); J. Pedersen, *ILC,* III/IV, 524-534; N. W. Porteous, "Jerusalem-Zion: The Growth of a Symbol," *Verbannung und Heimkehr. Festschrift W. Rudolph* (Tübingen, 1961), 235-252; G. von Rad, "The City on the Hill," *The Problem of the Hexateuch and Other Essays* (Eng. trans. 1966; repr. London, 1984), 232-242; *idem, OT Theology,* II (Eng.

I. Preliminary.

1. *Orthography, Etymology.* The name is almost always written יְרוּשָׁלַםִ in the OT, with the qere perpetuum y^e*rûšālayim* (exceptions are 1 Ch. 3:5; 2 Ch. 25:1; Est. 2:6; Jer. 26:18, with ירושלים, as well as y^e*rûšālayimāh* with *he*-locale in 2 Ch. 32:8). The LXX form Ιερουσαλημ (cf. NT Ἱεροσόλυμα) and the cuneiform equivalents *Urusalim* (EA) and *Ursalimmu* (Sennacherib prism) obviously presuppose the reading y^e*rûšālēm.* The writing *r*( )*w-u-š*( )*l-m-m* in the Egyptian Execration texts probably represents a form *Urušalimum.*[1] Etymologically, the name may mean something like "foundation (→ ירה *yārâ* I) of the god Shalem."[2] This would be a pre-Israelite name.

Ringgren

2. *Jerusalem/Zion/Israel (Judah).* The distinction between Jerusalem and Zion on the one hand and (the people of) Israel (or the state of Judah) on the other confronts the treatment of the cultural and religious significance of the city with several difficulties. The noun y^e*rûšālayim* occurs 660 times in the OT, → צִיּוֹן *ṣiyyôn* 154 times. The words are unevenly distributed. "Jerusalem" is common in 2 Samuel (30 occurrences), 1–2 Kings (90), 1–2 Chronicles (151), Ezra (48), Nehemiah (38), Isaiah (49), Jeremiah (102), Ezekiel (26), and Zechariah (39); it is rare in Joshua (9), Judges (5), 1 Samuel (1), Esther (1), Pss. 51–147 (17), Ecclesiastes (5), Song of Solomon (8), Lamentations (7), Daniel (10), Joel (6), Amos (2), Obadiah (2), Micah (8), Zephaniah (4), and Malachi (2). It is not found in the other books. Gen. 14:18, however, speaks of "Salem" (*šālēm*), which refers to Jerusalem, as Ps. 76:3(Eng. v. 2); 110:4 show (the latter indirectly by speaking of Melchizedek, who is also mentioned in Genesis), albeit without mentioning it explicitly. "Zion" is relatively common in Psalms (38), Isaiah (47), Jeremiah (17), Lamentations (15), Joel (7), Micah (9), and Zechariah 1–8 (6); it appears once or twice in 2 Samuel, 1–2 Kings, 1–2 Chronicles, Song of Solomon, Amos, Obadiah, and Zephaniah. It is not found in the other books.[3]

"Jerusalem" is used in both poetry and prose; "Zion" is found almost exclusively in

---

trans., New York, 1965), 292-97; *idem,* " 'Righteousness' and 'Life' in the Cultic Language of the Psalms'," *The Problem of the Hexateuch,* 243-266; H. Schmid, "Jahwe und die Kulttraditionen von Jerusalem," *ZAW,* 67 (1955), 168-197; K. L. Schmidt, "Jerusalem als Urbild und Abbild," *Aus der Welt der Urbilder. Festschrift C. G. Jung. ErJB,* 18 (1950), 207-248; J. Schreiner, *Sion-Jerusalem Jahwes Königssitz. StANT,* 7 (1963); J. J. Simons, *Jerusalem in the OT. StFS,* 1 (1952); F. Stolz, *Strukturen und Figuren im Kult von Jerusalem. BZAW,* 118 (1970); S. Talmon, "Die Bedeutung Jerusalems in der Bibel," in W. P. Eckerdt, N. P. Levinson, and M. Stöhr, eds., *Jüdisches Volk—Gelobtes Land. Abhandlungen zum christlich-jüdischen Dialog,* 3 (Munich, 1970), 135-152; R. de Vaux, *Jerusalem and the Prophets* (Cincinnati, 1965); L.-H. Vincent and M.-A. Steve, *Jérusalem de l'AT,* I-III (Paris, 1954-1956); E. K. Vogel, *Bibliography of Holy Land Sites* (repr. Cincinnati, 1982) (= *HUCA,* 42 [1971], 1-96), esp. 44-49; E. Vogt, "Das Wachstum des alten Stadtgebietes von Jerusalem," *Bibl,* 48 (1967), 337-358; T. C. Vriezen, *Jahwe en zijn Stad* (Amsterdam, 1962).

1 Cf. A. Alt, "The Formation of the Israelite State in Palestine," *Essays on OT History and Religion* (Eng. trans., Garden City, 1966), 222f.

2 Stolz, 181ff.

3 These figures are from Fohrer, 195, 198, where further details may be found.

poetry. But since poetry and prose for the most part do not speak of topographically different entities, the former often uses "Zion" where the latter would say "Jerusalem." The difference between the two names can hardly be theological, as their frequent use in parallelism shows. In such use, furthermore, "Zion" is usually the first of the pair, a position that is theologically irrelevant. The choice of words is based instead on stylistic considerations. We arrive at the same conclusion if we note the comparatively small number of occurrences of "Jerusalem" in the Psalms and Lamentations; prayers, including in part Lamentations, have their own preferred vocabulary. The name "Zion" lost its exclusive reference to the oldest part of the city, south of the temple area, and became by and large a synonym for "Jerusalem." In order not to prejudice the discussion that follows, however, we shall only very rarely cite passages in which "Zion" alone appears.

As the capital of Israel or Judah and the most important locale in Israel, Jerusalem often stands for the state or the people, just as the Bible uses "Damascus," "Babylon," and "Memphis" by metonymy for their lands and peoples. The representation is not just stylistic; the city can symbolize the people in many ways. When a passage mentions a people, the city is often included, and vice versa—a feature of the sources that tends to reduce the precision of discussions based on them.

3. *Sources.* More than many other topics, discussion of Jerusalem's intellectual and cultural importance demands historical treatment. The ideas refer to a concrete city, but the city and its destiny have been subject to constant change, which should be reflected in the ideas. Unfortunately, the scattered references often cannot be dated; and, since the evidence as a whole is scanty and not helpfully distributed, the earliest datable literary references may be far distant in time from the appearance of the ideas and their linguistic expression. With respect to the formative early period, we are largely dependent on hypothetical reconstruction—theories that do not propose certain ideas as (contributing) factors helping explain observed facts but instead derive theoretical facts from hypothetical ideas.

II. The Jebusite Hypothesis. According to our present knowledge, the importance of Jerusalem for the religion of Israel is not to be traced to the Jebusite prehistory of the city, as is often done. The undertaking depends on two theories, both of which are dubious: the identification of Jebus with Jerusalem and the inclusion of the Jebusites among the Canaanite (or Amorite) peoples.[4] The second theory is no less important than the first; without it the Jebusite hypothesis is left without support. If it is to say anything of importance, it must constantly substitute "Canaanite" for "Jebusite," since we know practically nothing about the Jebusites. Apart from these uncertainties, the hypothesis is beset with other weaknesses. It is based in part on the story of David's purchase of a

---

[4] On the first of these theories, see J. M. Miller, "Jebus and Jerusalem: A Case of Mistaken Identity," *ZDPV,* 90 (1974), 115-127; on the second, see, e.g., B. Maisler (Mazar), *Untersuchungen zur alten Geschichte und Ethnographie Syriens und Palästinas* (Giessen, 1930), 81; also Y. Aharoni in B. Mazar, ed., *Historiyāh šel ʿam Yiśrāʾēl,* vol. 2: *Hāʾāḇôṯ wᵉhaššōpᵉṭîm* (1967), 346, n. 5; also the bibliog. in *KBL*³, 366.

threshing floor and building of an altar (2 S. 24; → גֹּרֶן *gōren*) and in part on onomastics: a divine name or epithet and an element in the names of two kings, the legendary king of Salem and—on the basis of uncertain evidence—a king of Jerusalem. But interpretation of the threshing floor narrative is so fraught with problems that it cannot be considered seriously as a source for a hypothesis of this importance. The divine name or epithet *ʿelyôn* (Gen. 14:18-22), which appears primarily in the Psalter but has no particular association with Jerusalem, is well attested in the ancient Near East outside Israel;[5] furthermore, it appears in the Bible without any association with Jerusalem and apparently before Jerusalem entered the story (Nu. 24:16).[6] The element *ṣdq* in *malkî-ṣeḏeq* (Gen. 14:18) and *ʾaḏōnî-ṣeḏeq* (Josh. 10:1,3), which some scholars likewise claim to have associations with Jerusalem, is so common in Northwest Semitic names that it proves nothing.[7] The Jebusite hypothesis was given its deathblow by Roberts.[8]

III. Origin and Development of Jerusalem's Importance. At the outset, the ark, which David had brought to Jerusalem (2 S. 6), was permanently installed in the temple by Solomon (1 K. 6–8). The only religious symbol common to all the tribes began to share its symbolism with the city; the decreasing importance of ideas associated with a portable sanctuary necessarily benefited the city, an ideological development that proceeded at some remove from the sociological development in which the nomadic way of life vanished almost totally. This event on both the human and the divine plane is enshrined in the word *menûḥâ*, "rest," used in a similar way for both Israel (Dt. 12:9) and Yahweh (Ps. 132:14; see also 95:11) with reference to Palestine and Jerusalem. Although the installation of the ark and the building of the temple were acts of kings, the election[9] of Jerusalem as the site of God's rest and presence was always understood as an act of God's free will. There are also signs that, as time went on, Jerusalem the city of God grew in importance at the expense of Jerusalem the city of David. As 1 K. 12:26-29(ff.) suggests, within two generations of David Jerusalem was primarily the site of the sanctuary and only secondarily the seat of the Davidic line. The northern tribes had indeed broken with the house of David and elevated Jeroboam to the throne; but Jeroboam had to say to himself that they had by no means dissolved their ties with Jerusalem and the temple,[10] even though Jerusalem had probably entered into Israel's history as Davidic crown property and David and Solomon had planned and built the temple.

What we are saying here and in the discussion to follow should not be understood to suggest that the concept of Jerusalem as the city of David vanished from OT theology at

5 F. M. Cross, "אֵל *ʾēl*," *TDOT*, I, 256.

6 For further details, see R. Rendtorff, "El, Baʿal und Jahwe," *ZAW*, 78 (1966), 277-292; Stolz, 134-37, 157-163.

7 Cf. F. M. Cross, *Canaanite Myth and Hebrew Epic* (Cambridge, Mass., 1973), 209-215, with bibliog., for a thorough discussion of the Jebusite hypothesis.

8 J. J. M. Roberts, "The Davidic Origin of the Zion Tradition," *JBL*, 92 (1973), 329-344.

9 H. Seebass, "בחר *bāḥar* (*bāchar*)," *TDOT*, II, 80f.

10 Cf. M. Noth, *Könige 1–16. BK*, IX/1 (1968), 282.

an early date; various factors kept it alive and reinforced it. Wherever the text says in one breath that Yahweh chose or will restore Jerusalem and the house of David, it is understood as a single divine act: the appointment of Jerusalem as the city of David (e.g., 1 K. 8:16 [Deuteronomistic]; Jer. 33:14-22 [post-Jeremianic]; Ps. 78:68-72[67-71]).

This agrees with another observation made by Noth.[11] The preexilic prophets speak not infrequently of the Davidic kings of their period, and they speak no less often of Jerusalem; but they never combine the two themes. Jerusalem as the royal seat was a matter of their everyday experience, often painful, but it was not crucial. The crucial thing was the prophetic experience of Jerusalem as the city of God. It was not the ark but the city, at least in the time of the prophets, that had this importance, although if what we have said above is correct the city derived its holiness and dignity from the ark within it. The fate of the ark after Solomon, the date and circumstances of its disappearance, are unknown.[12] In any case, it had vanished by the time of Jeremiah (Jer. 3:16f.; 14:21); its function, particularly its status as the throne of Yahweh, were taken over by Jerusalem.

The notion of a city as a (divine) throne appears also to be a Hittite (or Proto-Hattian?) theologoumenon: "The gods took charge of the lands and appointed them—for Ḫattusas [the Hittite capital] they appointed them."[13]

The ark is responsible not only for the holiness of Jerusalem but also, as one might well suppose, for its unique and exclusive status. Noth[14] has good reason to trace Jerusalem's claim to be the only legitimate cultic center back beyond Josiah and Hezekiah to the period of the northern kingdom. The man of God from Judah goes to Bethel to proclaim the desecration of its altar, thereby attacking the Bethel temple as well: if the altar is desecrated, the Bethel cult has come to an end. He does not cite any political or religious reasons—the division of the kingdom, the golden calf, the nonlevitical priesthood (1 K. 13:2f.); his reason is simply the very existence of the temple at Bethel. No temple but the temple of Jerusalem has any right to exist.

IV. Jerusalem Founded and Chosen by Yahweh. The temple was built by human hands, but the city was established by Yahweh (Isa. 14:32; possibly Ps. 87:1, and similarly 48:9[8]). This idea is admittedly hard to reconcile with the never-forgotten fact that Jerusalem, a city totally unassociated with any ancient Israelite tradition, was conquered relatively late ("the city David besieged" [Isa. 29:1]). But the idea might be justified as an antithesis to the notion expressed in the city's name: "foundation of [the god] Shalem."[15]

Much more common and more important than the notion of Jerusalem's divine foundation is the idea of its divine election.[16] The book of Kings frequently qualifies this by adding the phrase ". . . out of all the tribes of Israel" (1 K. 8:16; 11:32; 14:21; 2 K.

---

11 Noth, *The Laws in the Pentateuch,* 137-141.
12 H.-J. Zobel, "אָרוֹן *'^arôn,*" *TDOT,* I, 373f.
13 *KUB,* II, 2, 43f.
14 Aviram, *36-*38.
15 *KBL*³, 417.
16 Seebass, 79-82.

21:7, plus 3 passages in Chronicles), which derives from Dt. 12:5 and represents an institutional refinement of 1 S. 2:28. These passages clearly insist that Jerusalem is the concern of all Israel.

V. Holy City and Holy Mountain. The notion of Jerusalem as a holy city, the city of Yahweh, is especially emphasized in Isa. 40–66 and some of the Psalms (Isa. 45:13; 48:2; 52:1; 60:14; Ps. 46:5[4]; 48:2,9[1,8]; 101:8), but it is not limited to these passages. It is associated with the image of the mountain of Yahweh and the sacred mountain. The count in the following list includes repetitions: *har-YHWH,* 5 times (Ps. 24:3; Isa. 2:3; 30:29; Mic. 4:2; Zec. 8:3 [+ *ṣᵉḇāʾôṯ*]); *har/harᵃrê (haq)qōḏeš,* 3 times (Ps. 87:1; Isa. 27:13; Zec. 8:3); *har qoḏš-î/-eḵā/-ô,* 14/15 times (Ps. 2:6; 3:5[4]; 15:1; 43:3; 48:2[1]; Isa. 56:7; 65:11; 66:20; Ezk. 20:40; Dnl. 9:16 [and 20]; Joel 2:1; 4:17[3:17]; Ob. 16; Zeph. 3:11). In Isa. 57:13; Jer. 31:23, *har haqqōḏeš* probably refers to Palestine, not Jerusalem, as in Isa. 11:9; 65:25.[17] The simple phrase *bāhār hazzeh,* "on this mountain" (Isa. 25:6f.), is also quite clear. The image has little basis in reality. With respect to the geological and geographical evidence, Karmon has pointed out that the Jerusalem of the OT was situated in a steeply declining depression;[18] and so also the discerning eye of Jeremiah saw it, uninfluenced by mythology (Jer. 21:13). The image is either a product of mythology or strongly influenced by it. Except for the late passage in Daniel, the citations are all from poetic texts; the same is true of *har (baṯ) ṣiyyôn* (19 times). The language of Hebrew poetry is open to mythology, but makes use of only a few of the theoretical possibilities: **har yᵉrûšālayim* is not found, and *har (ha)ʾᵉlōhîm* (significantly?) is not used of Jerusalem.[19]

The article on → הר *har*[20] mentions several motifs that contributed to the myth of the sacred mountain, which became associated with Jerusalem. There is also a more general consideration: Palestine—the "goodly mountain" (Dt. 3:25) par excellence—can be called "my [= Yahweh's] holy mountain"; among the passages listed above, see Isa. 11:9; 65:25, and probably also Isa. 57:13; Jer. 31:23; cf. also Ex. 15:17: *har naḥᵃlāṯᵉḵā,* "the mountain that is thine [= Yahweh's] own." It is equally appropriate to use this title of honor for the place where his temple stands and to which his people makes pilgrimage.

The expression *har-ṣiyyôn yarkᵉṯê ṣāp̄ôn,* "Mount Zion, highest [lit., 'furthest'] Zaphon," found only in Ps. 48:3(2), is clearly mythological in origin. Here one of the two names of the mountain of the gods in northern Syria (the other being *ḫa(z)zi*) has become an appellative, a shift comparable to the development that led to our use of "Parnassus." The cases are also comparable in that the use of "Zaphon" has no more bearing on the religious beliefs of the author of Ps. 48 than the use of "Parnassus" has

---

17 G. Westphal, *Jahwes Wohnstätten nach den Anschauungen der alten Hebräer. BZAW,* 15 (1908), 93.

18 Y. Karmon, "The Mountains Round About Jerusalem," in Aviram, 102-4, 106, with maps [Heb.].

19 For a detailed discussion of the sacred mountain, see R. L. Cohn, *The Sacred Mountain in Ancient Israel* (diss., Stanford, 1974).

20 S. Talmon, "הר *har,*" *TDOT,* III, 436ff.

on those of whoever applies it in the realm of poetry.[21] The exaltation of the temple and its city at the end of time (Isa. 2:2f.; Ezk. 40:2) represents the eschatological extension of this mythological line.

It is worth noting that the idea of Jerusalem as the city of Yahweh or God, strengthened by the mountain of Yahweh, cannot be inverted: Israel's God is not the God of Jerusalem. No verb (*yšb, škn,* or even *bḥr*) is able to designate the kind of intimate relationship between God and Jerusalem that a construct phrase would be able to do, but such a phrase just does not occur. Its absence might reflect a nomadic element preserved in the later faith of Israel. It is well said of the Assyrians that "they spoke of the God of Jerusalem as they spoke of the gods of the peoples of the earth" (2 Ch. 32:19); that is how the Assyrians think and speak, and similar expressions are found in the decrees of the Achaemenids (Ezr. 1:3; 7:19). The biblical view is expressed indirectly but unmistakably in Ps. 121:1f.: "I lift up my eyes to the mountains [the dwelling place of the gods]. From whence does my help come? My help comes from Yahweh . . ."—we would expect the psalmist to continue with "the God of Jerusalem" or "who dwells in Jerusalem" (Ps. 135:21) or "who dwells on Mount Zion" (Isa. 8:18). Instead, we find: ". . . who made heaven and earth." It would seem that the author reacts to the potential provocation in the responses mentioned by implicitly rejecting all gods of cities and mountains.

The phrase "your God" with the antecedent "Zion" (more rarely "Jerusalem") appears some 5 times in Deutero-Isaiah (e.g., Isa. 52:7), twice in the Psalms (Ps. 146:10; 147:12), and once in Zephaniah (Zeph. 3:16f.). This expression, in conjunction with many other stylistic devices, contributes to a highly developed personification of Zion in Deutero-Isaiah (similarly Ps. 147:12 and Zeph. 3:17; Ps. 146:10 may borrow from Isa. 52:7).

VI. Spring, River, and Sea of Chaos. The image of spring and river points to the future—quite understandably, since it has even less connection than the image of the mountain with the geography of the present. Four passages (with minor variants) speak of a stream springing from the temple mountain: Ezk. 47:1-12; Joel 4:18(3:18); Zec. 14:8; Ps. 46:5(4).[22] In the first, it quickly swells to become a mighty river. In Isa. 33:21,23 (a somewhat obscure passage), a broad river forms a moat protecting Jerusalem. The origin of this image is debated. Ps. 46 (vv. 3f.[2f.]) links it with the image of Yahweh's battle with chaos (river, sea, serpent), suggesting a connection of the latter with Jerusalem (vv. 5f.[4f.]). Usually, however,[23] there is no such association. It is not uncommon to find this mythological theme historicized (and eschatologized); the hostile powers then appear as nations taking the field against Yahweh, his people, and his city. Sometimes, as in Ps. 46, the two images are combined. The attack of the nations upon Jerusalem is discussed below.

That Yahweh protects his city (e.g., 2 K. 19:34; Ps. 147:13f.; Isa. 31:5) goes without

---

21 On *ṣāpôn,* see M. Dahood and T. Penar, "Ugaritic-Hebrew Parallel Pairs," *RSP,* I (1972), 321f.; M. C. Astour and D. E. Smith, "Place Names," *RSP,* II (1975), 318-324; M. Dietrich, O. Loretz, and J. Sanmartín, "Zur ugaritischen Lexikographie (VII)," *UF,* 5 (1973), 96-99.

22 → גיחון *gîḥôn* (*gîchôn*).

23 Cf. the 19 passages mentioning the battle with chaos cited by Stolz, 61-63.

saying: Jerusalem's inviolability appears guaranteed (Ps. 48:4; Mic. 3:11). The strength of this conviction can be measured by the depth of the dismay we hear in Lamentations when God removes his protection—although even here it is not forgotten that God surrendered Jerusalem on account of the people's many sins (Lam. 1:18; 3:42; etc.), carrying out a decision reached long before (2:17).

It is not always clear whether passages expressing confidence in God's absolute protection are referring to the present or past or to the future; the future is likely when this protection defends against a terrible attack mounted by many nations, and even more so when the attack is described in cosmic and universal terms, as when wild seas rage against the fortress (cf. above). Such passages include Ps. 2:1ff.; 46:7,9f.(6,8f.); 48:5-8(4-7); 76:3-7(2-6); Isa. 8:9f.; 17:12-14; Zec. 12:1-9; the Isaiah passages do not mention Jerusalem explicitly, but clearly refer to it. The attack upon Jerusalem is doomed to fail because Yahweh himself will be a wall of fire around the open city (Zec. 2:8f.[4f.]).

Now several passages, which one is inclined to quote, speak in contradictory terms. These include Jer. 6:22-24 (esp. if read in conjunction with 5:15-17); Joel 2:1-20; Mic. 4:11-14(5:1); and parts of Zec. 14. (Sections of Ezk. 38f., where Jerusalem does not play any role, are similar.) Here Yahweh protects the city and repulses the attack of the nations, and yet it is he who has called them to attack. These are not minor literary inconsistencies: the passages reflect a bitter clash of existential and theological opposites. There has been no lack of critical attempts to resolve the problems by deleting one or another group of verses or sections of verses as revisions by a later hand.[24] In some cases this critical approach is undoubtedly correct; in others, however, it is wrong or pointless, because the fabric is so closely woven that it disintegrates when the threads of the unwanted color are removed. A solution covering all cases does not exist; many times it is best to accept the contradictory ideas as they appear without trying to separate them by literary analysis. Alongside the idea that God protects Jerusalem we find others: he himself may attack Israel to punish it (Lam. 2:4f.,[21]; 3:12) or summon hostile nations to attack (Isa. 5:26-29 [without mention of Jerusalem]; 10:5f.; 29:2f.,6; Jer. 6:6; 22:7f.; Ezk. 16:37-41[ff.]; 23:22-26[ff.]; Hab. 1:6-10 [without mention of Jerusalem]). Anyone aware of Yahweh's omnipotence and Israel's sin cannot avoid interpreting the destruction of Jerusalem as being carried out in some sense by Yahweh himself, and this awareness finds frequent expression in the OT. The outstanding importance and constant presence of both ideas forbid the simple resolution of the contradiction by eliminating one or the other. It was probably not uncommon to confront a paradoxical situation in which hopelessness and hope, darkness and light, were inextricably combined. We cannot charge these passages with failing to speak the language of faith.

VII. The Future to Come. One way of resolving this tension leads to eschatology, in which Yahweh forgives the sins of Israel (Isa. 44:22; Jer. 50:20). In Zion/Jerusalem he will then assume the kingship (Isa. 33:22) that seems so dubious in the present (Jer. 8:19), wonderfully adorn the rebuilt city (Isa. 54:11f.), and cause his glory to shine forth

24 Lutz is typical; a first impression is gained from the notes on 111f., 114.

from it (Isa. 60:1f.). Through his proper viceroy he will see that true justice is done (Isa. 16:5), and mighty nations will come to Zion/Jerusalem to learn Yahweh's ways from his own mouth and have all their quarrels resolved (Isa. 2:2-4). The city, now situated on its high mountain (Ezk. 40:2), will endure forever (Joel 4:20[3:20]).

VIII. Jerusalem and the Individual. This city, whether standing or destroyed, has a special meaning for every Israelite of every age. This is illustrated by the heart-rending laments occasioned by its destruction (Lam. 1–5), the love felt even for the stones and dust of its ruins (Ps. 102:15[14]), and the impossibility of forgetting its fate (Ps. 137:1-6). If Israel can ever be consoled, the consolation will come through (or in?) Jerusalem (Isa. 66:13). This personal relationship finds eloquent expression in delight at the city's beauty (Ps. 48:3[2]; 50:2), in praise of its past and the great expectations harbored for its future (Isa. 62:1f.). Jerusalem is the source of blessing (Ps. 128:5; 133:3); it is the place—since Josiah, the only public place—where true worship is offered. Israelites can wish for nothing better than to spend their lives in the temple like the priests and singers (Ps. 27:4; 65:5[4]; 84:5[4]), for there God's praise resounds (Ps. 122:4). Since most cannot share this good fortune, they go—probably regularly—to Jerusalem to worship: the experience of their pilgrimages is preserved in several psalms (Pss. 42f.,84,122; possibly 118) as eternal evidence of their love for Jerusalem.

The theological meaning of Jerusalem is also discussed in the article → **צִיּוֹן** *ṣiyyôn.*

Tsevat

יָרֵחַ *yārēaḥ;* יֶרַח *yeraḥ*

Contents: I. 1. Root and Meaning; 2. Akk. *arḫu*; 3. Ugar. *yrḫ*; 4. Occurrences and Synonyms. II. 1. The Moon as a Heavenly Body; 2. The Moon as a Token of Durability and Brightness; 3. The Day of Yahweh and Other References. III. The Moon as an Object of Illicit Worship. IV. 1. Month; 2. Calendar.

---

yārēaḥ. F.-M. Abel, "Les stratagèmes dans le Livre de Josué," *RB,* 56 (1949), 321-339; M. C. Astour, "Benê-Iamina et Jéricho," *Sem,* 9 (1959), 5-20; A. Caquot, "Remarques sur la fête de la 'néoménie' dans l'ancien Israël," *RHR,* 158 (1960), 1-18; T. H. Gaster, "Moon," *IDB,* III, 436f.; A. Goetze, "The Nikkal Poem from Ras Shamra," *JBL,* 60 (1941), 353-374; A. Herdner, "Ḫiriḫibi et les noces de Yariḫ et de Nikkal dans la mythologie d'Ugarit," *Sem,* 2 (1949), 17-20; W. Herrmann, *Yariḫ und Nikkal und der Preis der Kuṯarāt-Göttinen. BZAW,* 106 (1968); J. S. Holladay, Jr., "The Day(s) the *Moon* Stood Still," *JBL,* 87 (1968), 166-178; A. Jirku, "Der Kult des Mondgottes im altorientalischen Palästina-Syrien," *ZDMG,* 100 (1950), 202-4 = *Von Jerusalem nach Ugarit* (Graz, 1966), 355-57; E. Koffmahn, "Sind die altisraelitischen Monatsbezeichnungen mit den kanaanäisch-phönikischen identisch?" *BZ,* N.S. 10 (1966), 197-219; J. McKay, *Religion in Judah under the Assyrians, 732-609 B.C. SBT,* N.S. 26 (1973); J. C. de Moor, "The Semitic Pantheon of Ugarit," *UF,* 2 (1970), 187-228; J. B. Segal, "*'Yrḥ'* in the Gezer 'Calendar'," *JSS,*

I. 1. *Root and Meaning.* The root *yrḥ* corresponds to a Proto-Semitic **wrḥ* and is related to the root *'rḥ*,[1] with a basic meaning of "wander, travel." Hence the underlying description is of the moon as "traveler, wanderer" (Heb. *yārēaḥ*), with a derivative (*yeraḥ*), "month," having a calendrical meaning. Cf. also Aram. *yarḥā'* and Ethiop. *warḥ*.

2. *Akk. arḫu.* Akk. *arḫu* A[2] is widely attested in Babylonian and Assyrian texts (along with *warḫu, urḫu,* and *barḫu*) with the meaning "moon," "new moon, first of the month," and "month" (as a period of time).

3. *Ugar. yrḫ.* Ugar. *yrḫ* is listed by Whitaker[3] with 92 occurrences; no less than 26 of these, however, involve some reconstruction of fragmentary or incomplete texts, although several may be regarded as more or less certain. The two undisputed meanings are "moon-god" (Yariḫ; so vocalized by Gordon, Gaster, Herdner, and Driver; vocalized as *yāreaḫ* by Virolleaud, as *yaraḫ* by Goetze, and as *yeraḫ* by Eissfeldt) and "month," the latter as a period of time and in recording dates. The role of *yrḫ,* the West Semitic moon-god, is shown most fully in the short hymnic text[4] celebrating the union between Nikkal, the lunar-goddess (cf. the Sumerian lunar-goddess Ningal), and Yariḫ. The text may be a translation from Hurrian and must be regarded as a cultic hymn, possibly intended to secure blessing and fertility for the family and the birth of children.[5] It clearly identifies Yariḫ as a male deity, closely connected with fertility. He is closely linked with *ks'*, "full moon" (Heb. *kese'*: Ps. 81:4[Eng. v. 3]; Prov. 7:20). We also find the proper name *'bdyrḫ,*[6] which is also attested in Phoenician and Punic inscriptions from Carthage.[7] It is now widely accepted that this name of the moon-god is to be seen in the city name "Jericho" (*y^erîḥô*; Josh. 2:1; etc.), although little trace is left of his worship and cult.

4. *Occurrences and Synonyms.* In the OT, there are 27 occurrences of the noun *yārēaḥ* referring to the moon. None of these shows any direct and positive divinization of the moon, although a number of admonitions are found warning against ascribing to it divine power and status. The OT therefore contains no exact counterpart to the Canaanite-Phoenician *yariḫ.* Neither are there any certain Hebrew proper names that contain this theophorous element. The closest synonyms to *yārēaḥ* in the OT are *l^eḇānâ* (3 occurrences: Cant. 6:10; Isa. 24:23; 30:26) and *kese'* (2 occurrences: Ps. 81:4[3]; Prov. 7:20). See also → חדשׁ *ḥdš,* "month," to which *yeraḥ* appears as a synonym 12 times.

---

7 (1962), 212-221; R. B. Y. Scott, "Meteorological Phenomena and Terminology in the OT," *ZAW,* 64 (1952), 11-25.

1 J. Fürst, *A Hebrew & Chaldee Lexicon to the OT* (Eng. trans., Leipzig, ⁴1871), 608; cf. P. A. de Lagarde and F. Buhl.

2 *CAD,* I/2 (1968), 259-263.

3 Whitaker, 319ff.

4 *CTA,* 24 = *KTU,* 1.24.

5 Cf. Herrmann, 106.

6 *PNU,* 145.

7 Benz, 326.

II. 1. *The Moon as a Heavenly Body.* As a prominent and constantly changing feature of the night sky, the moon inevitably has received considerable attention in the OT. This appears most commonly in the use of the noun *ḥōḏeš* to note the "renewing" of the moon and the beginning of a new month.

Significantly, the natural phenomenon most often associated with *yārēaḥ* is the sun (→ **שׁמשׁ** *šmš*; 24 occurrences out of a total of 27). These two phenomena are related as the great source of light by day and the lesser light of the night (Gen. 1:16, where, however, *yārēaḥ* is not used). Frequently they are also associated with the stars, which, like the moon, are seen in the night sky. The moon and stars are related as objects of human wonder, which point to the greatness of god's power in creation (Ps. 8:4[3]). In contrast to such outstanding achievements and witnesses to the divine creativity, mortals appear puny and insignificant. In reality, however, this contrast is only apparent, not real; for mortals share in the divine glory and honor. They have been empowered by God to exercise dominion over all the creatures he has made. The moon figures similarly as an expression of God's creative power in Ps. 136:9, where it is coupled with the stars. In a natural extension of this theme, Ps. 148:3 calls on the sun, moon, and stars to praise God. In Ps. 104:19, sun and moon are regarded as an occasion to praise God because they mark the passage of time and the moon indicates the changing seasons (→ **מועד** *mô'ēḏ*), as in Gen. 1:14.

In Isa. 60:19f., the theme of sun and moon as witnesses to God's greatness becomes the basis for a skillful poetic development. In the prophet's message of comfort to Israel, he describes the peace and salvation that will characterize the restored community. As a mark of the richness of life that will be experienced, the prophet affirms that Israel will no longer receive light from the sun and moon but from God himself. As the Creator is greater than the thing created, so the mark of the time of salvation will be a fullness of light and glory that exceeds that of sun and moon, because such light will come directly from God. A further unusual development of the theme appears in Ps. 121:6, where the collocation of *šemeš* and *yārēaḥ* has given rise to a very distinctive usage. All who put their trust in Yahweh and are consequently set under his providential care and protection will be guarded from natural dangers. The sun will not strike them by day nor the moon by night. The obvious dangers of sunstroke and heat exhaustion have provided the basis for this illustration of Yahweh's care. Many commentators (Gunkel, Anderson, etc.) find here evidence for belief in the harmful effect of the moon's rays, well attested in antiquity (cf. "lunatic"). Others[8] have suggested the emendation *qeraḥ*, "frost." This emendation is inappropriate, however: the basic requirement of poetic balancing of images has occasioned the word picture, and the prevalent belief in the harm caused by the moon has provided sufficient justification.

2. *The Moon as a Token of Durability and Brightness.* The presence of the moon as a permanent feature of the night sky has led to its employment as a token of durability and brightness. Three occurrences of the moon in the Psalter associate its durability with

---

[8] Cf. *BHK*³.

the permanence of the Davidic kingship. In Ps. 72, a prayer for the Davidic king (cf. v. 20), v. 5 expresses the petition: "May he [= the king] live [reading *wᵉyaʼᵃrîḵ* with the LXX] while the sun endures, and as long as the moon, throughout all generations!" In addition, v. 7 offers the prayer that, under the king's rule, righteousness may flourish "till the moon be no more." The obvious element of poetic hyperbole in the expression may be granted, but it has also drawn on traditions regarding the timeless (mythological) benefits derived through the kingship. Ps. 89:38(37) recalls the divine promise of a dynasty to David, recorded in 2 S. 7:1-17, as a permanent feature of God's will for the government of Israel: "Like the moon it [the Davidic dynasty] shall be established for ever." Again the sun and moon are associated (Ps. 89:37[36]). In Jer. 31:35, the "fixed order" (*ḥuqqōṯ* [Rudolph emends to *ḥōqēq*]) of the moon and stars is cited as a token of God's power and immutability. This immutability, an addition to the prophecy of the new covenant (vv. 27-34), is then employed as a basis for asserting the enduring nature of the relationship between Yahweh and Israel (v. 37).

Two passages use the brightness of the moon as an illustration of greatness. In Job 25:5, God's surpassing greatness is shown by the assertion that before him even the moon is not bright (reading *yāhēl* with the ancient versions). In Gen. 37:9, the moon appears with the sun and stars. It figures in Joseph's second dream, which foretells his destiny and that of his brothers. It is stated that the sun, moon, and eleven stars bowed down before Joseph; the stars clearly represent his brothers, and the inclusion of the sun and moon, representing his father and mother (v. 10), enhances the portrayal of the exalted status Joseph is to attain.

3. *The Day of Yahweh and Other References.* In Josh. 10:12, Joshua strikingly invokes the sun and moon during the Israelite battle for Gibeon. According to v. 13, the curse is cited from the ancient Book of Jashar; it may well have stood originally in a totally different context. It draws on a theme widely attested in the ancient world,[9] which is essentially a prayer for victory in battle. Joshua appeals to the sun to be still (lit., "silent"; Heb. *dmm*) in the Valley of Aijalon until the Israelites have obtained victory over their enemies.

The appeal to the moon to stand still so that Israel may obtain victory in the holy war is part of a wider tradition regarding the role played by natural forces and phenomena on Israel's behalf (cf. also → כוכב *kôḵāḇ*). If Yahweh leads the armies of Israel, it is a simple extension of this belief to look for his assistance through the agency of the power he controls. This theme and tradition is developed further in Hab. 3:11. This prophetic psalm weaves together a number of ancient traditions associated with Yahweh's power. His theophany in a thunderstorm, his leadership in the holy war, and his primeval battle against the forces of chaos have all been brought together to form a complex portrayal of his immense power, which he has placed at the disposal of his people (v. 16). The knowledge of this evokes joy and trust on the part of those who worship him.

In 3 passages (Isa. 13:10; Joel 2:10; 4:15[3:15]) the darkening of the moon is

[9] Abel.

associated with the day of Yahweh; Joel 3:4(2:31) also states that the moon is to become blood on this day (cf. → יוֹם *yôm*). The darkening of the natural luminaries (sun, moon, and stars in the first 3 references; sun and moon only in the last) is a sign of Yahweh's wrath and of impending judgment upon his enemies. The basic elements of this feature of the day of Yahweh are clearly associated with natural phenomena: the heavy black clouds of a thunderstorm and the "reddening" of the moon in a dust storm. The moon's turning to blood (*dām*) may involve a conscious echo of its being "silenced" (*dāmam*) in Josh. 10:12. This observation further strengthens the claim that holy war traditions have influenced the idea of the day of Yahweh. The darkening of the heavenly luminaries as an accompaniment to Yahweh's punishment of his enemies is also found in Ezk. 32:7. Here, however, there is no explicit reference to the day of Yahweh, and the enemy threatened in this fashion is the Egyptian Pharaoh.

Eccl. 12:2 also mentions the darkening of the moon together with the sun and the stars, but without suggesting that this is a sign of divine anger. It signifies instead the coming of old age, when sight begins to fail so that even the great sources of light upon earth no longer appear bright.

III. *The Moon as an Object of Illicit Worship.* Five passages in the OT refer to the moon, together with other heavenly bodies, as an object of illicit worship. Four of these emanate from writers of the Deuteronomistic school (Dt. 4:19; 17:3; 2 K. 23:5; Jer. 8:2), so that they clearly point to the religious situation in the last years of the kingdom of Judah and during the Babylonian exile. The widespread popularity of veneration of the moon as a deity, seen in Canaanite-Phoenician religion, makes it evident that this practice was not limited to a relatively brief period of time. In contrast to the great popularity of sun worship in ancient Israel, traces of lunar mythology and cult objects are quite limited, although not entirely absent.

The cultic observance in which this element is clearest is Passover (→ פסח *psḥ*), which exhibits a number of lunar features. The cultic significance of the new moon day supports this observation, as does the early association of the new moon day with the Sabbath (→ שׁבת *šbt*). Further relics of an ancient lunar cult are to be seen in the use of moon pendants as amulets (cf. Jgs. 8:21,26; Isa. 3:18).[10] Even so, the sum total of such relics of lunar imagery and mythology in ancient Israel is not large, so that its being singled out in the admonitions of the Deuteronomistic writers calls for some comment. Dt. 4:19, elaborating the second commandment of the Decalog, contains an admonition against regarding the moon as an object of worship. In similar fashion, Dt. 17:3 raises the possibility that an Israelite might be found guilty of infringing the requirements of the first commandment by worshipping "the sun or the moon or any of the host of heaven." In this case, it may be assumed that the moon is not a token or symbol of Yahweh but amounts to another god. In 2 K. 23:5, it is recorded that Josiah removed the idolatrous priests (*k^e^mārîm*) of the cities of Judah and round about Jerusalem, who had burned incense to the moon, as well as to other heavenly bodies and to Baʿal. Worship of such phenomena, including

---

10 This interpretation is argued by McKay, 115f.

the moon, is reported by Jer. 8:2 as the sin of the kings, priests, prophets, and other inhabitants of Jerusalem, for which they are to be punished with death by Yahweh.

It is not immediately obvious why the Deuteronomic movement should have focused so sharply and directly on the sin of worshipping the moon and other natural phenomena. The popularity of such lunar and astral symbolism in religion may well have increased during Assyrian suzerainty over Judah. The Assyrians may even have imposed such features directly, although this is not confirmed. But the proven antiquity of such lunar, solar, and astral features in Israel's religious inheritance from Canaan makes it the more likely source. Once Josiah's reform had removed the more blatant and obvious features of Canaanite rites and imagery, those features that could not be abolished by official command actually gained in popularity. The sudden emergence of sharp polemic on the part of the Deuteronomistic school against veneration of the moon and other heavenly bodies was necessary to carry out the reforming aims of its leaders. These phenomena were not in themselves images of gods or of Yahweh; but they could be so interpreted, and therefore demanded the special attention of the Deuteronomistic reformers.

A further reference to worship of the moon appears in Job 31:26, as part of Job's oath of clearance. He declares his innocence of all forms of religious or moral offense of which he might possibly be accused. He includes the possibility that he might have looked reverently at the sun on account of its brilliance or at the moon moving across the sky in its splendor. Of any such offense, Job declares that he is totally innocent.

IV. 1. *Month.* That the phases of the moon provided a simple and readily observable method of calculating the passage of time is fundamental to the calendrical reckoning of the ancient world and to its general awareness of the temporal dimension. So impressive, in fact, is the inherent value of the moon as a means of reckoning time that Gen. 1:14 affirms this as the primary purpose of its creation. The lunar month of 29 days, 12 hours, and 44 minutes gives a lunar year of a little more than 354 days, falling approximately 11 days short of the solar year. This fact is responsible for so many of the difficulties of the ancient world in developing a satisfactory calendar that it became the central reason for the development of different calendrical systems.

Within the literature of the OT, the observation of the moon and its use in reckoning the divisions of the year is often indicated by the noun *ḥōḏeš,* which denotes the time when the moon renews itself. For most of the biblical period, it is certain that the calculation of each month was reckoned from the first appearance of the new moon (Ex. 23:15; 34:18). In ancient Egypt, however, the new month was reckoned from the time the moon became full; it has been suggested[11] that this may also have been true for Israel in its earliest period. That ancient Israel borrowed the Canaanite-Phoenician names of the months is shown by the occasional use of these old names (1 K. 6:37: Ziv; 1 K. 6:38: Bul; 1 K. 8:2: Ethanim). Since Ugaritic texts show the use of *yrḥ* for such calendrical dating of months, it may be significant that the OT uses *yeraḥ* for these dates. In later usage, however, it is noteworthy that *ḥōḏeš* is used consistently for recording dates.

---

11 Cf. A. Strobel, "Monat," *BHHW,* II (1964), 1232.

Apart from these references to specific months, there are only 9 other passages in the OT that use *yeraḥ* to describe the duration of the moon's cycle as a period of time. In all of them, the main interest focuses on the entire span of the lunar cycle and thus upon a definite period of time. The duration of this period is expressed by the phrase *yeraḥ yāmîm,* literally "a month of days" (Dt. 21:13; 2 K. 15:13). In Dt. 21:13, it describes the period of mourning during which a captive slave woman is allowed to mourn the loss of her parents and home. After this time has elapsed, she may be taken as a wife by her captor. The second instance, 2 K. 15:13, describes the brief reign of one month exercised in Israel by Shallum ben Jabesh before his murder by Menahem. Ex. 2:2 (J) mentions a similar relatively short period of time: the infant Moses is reported to have been hidden by his parents for three months. In the Blessing of Moses, the blessing for Joseph concerns the fertility of his land and the abundance of its crops, which are described as "the rich yield (*gereš*) of the months" (Dt. 33:14). The poet is evidently concerned to achieve a balanced parallel to the "produce of the sun," so that the link between "moon" and "month" appears intentional. A more obscure reference to a period of a month is found in Zec. 11:8, where the chief shepherd (God) destroys three shepherds (kings) in one month. The background and point of the allusion are far from clear; it may be linked most plausibly with the deaths of Joram ben Jehosaphat and his son Ahaziah, both kings of Judah, and Joram ben Ahab, king of Israel, all of whom died in the space of a month in 841 B.C.[12]

There are 4 other passages that use the noun *yeraḥ,* all in the book of Job. Three appear in contexts where Job laments his sufferings and the weariness of his life. In the first, Job 3:6, the "number of the months" is a poetic parallel to the "days of the year." The context is Job's cursing the day of his birth and adjuring that it no longer be reckoned among the days of the year. In 7:3, Job laments that God has appointed for him *yarᵉḥê-šāwʾ*, "months of emptiness," in which he experiences nothing but suffering and so enjoys no pleasure of any kind. In 29:2, Job expresses the desire to experience once more the happiness he had known in the past, wishing that he might be "as in the months of old." An idiomatic usage occurs in 39:2, where God asks Job whether he knows the time when the mountain goats and hinds give birth to their young or the length of their pregnancy (lit., "the months that they fulfil"). The use of *yeraḥ* for the period of pregnancy has good parallels in Akk. *arḫu.*

2. *Calendar.* In Ugaritic, the month names are recorded in the form *yrḫ N.* One text[13] gives the sequence *rìš yn, nql, mgmr, pgrm*; another[14] gives *ḫyr, ḥlt, gn, ìṯb*; a third[15] gives *nql, mgmr, dbḥm.* The month of *ìṯtbnm*[16] was followed by *rìš yn.*[17]

Besides the three ancient month names already mentioned, the name of the month Abib in the old Israelite calendar is also attested (Ex. 13:4; 23:15; 34:18; Dt. 16:1), but never

---

12 B. Otzen, *Studien über Deuterosacharja. AcThD,* 6 (1964), 156f.
13 *KTU,* 4.182, 32-40.
14 *KTU,* 4.222, 11-15.
15 *KTU,* 4.316.
16 *KTU,* 4.269, 30.
17 *KTU,* 4.387, 13, 21.

with *yeraḥ.*[18] In the later years of the Israelite monarchy, a system of counting the months by use of the ordinal numbers 1-12 was introduced, probably under Assyrian influence (Jer. 28:1,17; etc.). This continued into the exilic period, after which it became usual to define the months by reference to the Assyro-Babylonian month names (Neh. 1:1; 2:1; etc.). The absence of *yeraḥ* in all these passages further underlines the importance attached to the reckoning of the month from the beginning of the new moon (*ḥōḏeš*).

In the OT as a whole, we can see various survivals of an earlier stratum of Canaanite-Phoenician religion, which attached far greater importance to the moon than became the norm for Israelite religion. Similarly—but not necessarily for this reason—we find a marked preference for *ḥōḏeš* in recording the months of the calendar.

Clements

18 See Koffmahn, 200.

יָרֵךְ *yārēḵ* → חֲלָצַיִם *hᵃlāṣayim (chᵃlātsayim)*

יָרַק *yāraq;* יָרוֹק *yārôq;* יָרָק *yārāq;* יֶרֶק *yereq;* יֵרָקוֹן *yērāqôn;* יְרַקְרַק *yᵉraqraq;* יָרְקְעָם *yorqᵒʿām;* יַרְקוֹן *yarqôn*

Contents: I. Etymology: 1. *yāraq* I, "Spit"; 2. *yrq* II. II. Occurrences. III. Nouns: 1. *yārôq*; 2. *yārāq*; 3. *yereq*; 4. *yērāqôn*; 5. *yᵉraqraq*; 6. Names with *yrq.* IV. Summary.

I. Etymology. The Hebrew lexica distinguish two roots *yrq:*[1] *yrq* I, "spit," a by-form of *rqq* (Lev. 15:8; also *rōq,* "sputum" [Job 7:19; 30:10; Isa. 50:6]), and *yrq* II, which denotes the green or yellow color of plants. The latter is attested in the OT only in its derived nouns.

1. *yāraq I, "Spit."* Although *yrq* I can hardly have any connection with *yrq* II,[2]

---

yāraq. R. Gradwohl, *Die Farben im AT. BZAW,* 83 (1963), 27-33; H. Janssens, "Les couleurs dans la Bible hébraique," *AIPH,* 14 (1954/57), 145-171, esp. 148, 150f.

1 *KBL*³, 420.

2 Contrary to the suggestion of P. de Lagarde, *Übersicht über die im aramäischen, arabischen, und hebräischen übliche Bildung der Nomina. AGWG,* 35 (1889), 200.

probably deriving instead from an onomatopoetic root *rq,* we shall discuss *yrq* I briefly here. This root appears in Ethiop. *waraqa,* "spit," and Arab. *rīq,* "sputum," as well as in Jewish Aram. *yrq,* "spit out,"[3] and in Imperial Aramaic in the form *yrwqn,* "they spit."[4] In the OT, *yrq* I occurs in 2 passages: Nu. 12:14 (*yārōq yāraq*) and Dt. 25:9 (*wᵉyārᵉqâ*). Both verses use the act of spitting to express contempt for and rejection of what is spat out. Ahikar[5] similarly affirms that at first a throne is built for the liar; but as soon as his lies are discovered, people spit in his face. In Nu. 12:14 (spoken by Yahweh), Miriam's exclusion for seven days as a punishment for leprosy is justified on the grounds that she would have been shamed (*tikkālēm*) seven days if her father had spat in her face. Lev. 15:8, on the contrary, prescribes that anyone spat upon (*rqq*) by someone who has a discharge must wash his clothes and bathe himself and is unclean only until the evening. According to Dt. 25:9[6], a wife whose husband has died avenges the refusal of levirate marriage by pulling the sandal off the foot of her dead husband's brother and spitting in his face. In the ancient world, even spitting on the ground could be forbidden out of magical considerations: Herodotus[7] reports that Deiokes, the king of the Medes, prohibited laughing and spitting in his presence. In Sophocles' *Antigone,*[8] Haimon refuses to speak to his father Creon, who is to blame for the death of Antigone, his bride: he spits in his face and falls upon his sword.

2. *yrq II.* The meaning of the root identified as *yrq* II in Biblical Hebrew is "be or become green or yellow." Just as Egyp. *w3ḏ,* "green," connected etymologically with Semitic *wrq,*[9] is derived from the papyrus plant[10] and Arab. *aḫḍar,* "green," from *ḫaḍr/ḫuḍir,* "the fresh green of plants"[11] (cf. the etymological connection in English between "green" and "grass"), so in Hebrew the basic use of the root *wrq/yrq* is to describe the "greening" of flora.[12] A similar situation obtains in Akkadian, where the root appears primarily as the adj. (*w*)*arqu*(*m*), "yellow, green," which serves to describe plants (but also animals and clothing and other green objects). We also find the nouns *arqu,* especially with the meaning "greens," and (*w*)*arqūtu*(*m*), "greenness, freshness."[13] The Akkadian verb *warāqu,* "turn yellow" (of a face),[14] can be interpreted naturally as a denominative. In Arabic, too, the verb *warraqa* (also IV) derives from the noun *waraq,*

---

3 Cf. Bab. *Yebam.* 39b < Dt. 25:9.

4 Ahikar 133.

5 Ahikar 133.

6 Cf. T.Zeb. 3:4.

7 *Hist.* i.99.

8 1230ff.

9 O. Rössler, "Das Ägyptische als semitische Sprache," in F. Altheim and R. Stiehl, eds., *Christentum am Roten Meer,* I (1971), 316.

10 H. Kees, *Farbensymbolik in ägyptischen religiösen Texten. NAWG,* 1943/11, 425.

11 W. Fischer, *Farb- und Formbezeichnungen in der Sprache der altarabischen Dichtung* (Wiesbaden, 1965), 116, 306.

12 Gradwohl, 33.

13 *CAD,* I/2 (1968), 300-302.

14 B. Meissner, *Beiträge zum assyrischen Wörterbuch,* II. *AS,* 4 (1932), 27.

"leaf," as its meaning ("blow about like leaves") shows; the same noun lies behind the color adj. *auraq,* "especially like leaves with respect to color."[15] The root is attested with the meaning "greens" in Old Aram. *yrq;*[16] possibly OSA *wrq ʾrḍn;*[17] Middle Heb. *yarqāʾ;* Syr. *yireq, yarqāʾ;* Mand. *yaruqa, yarqa,* and *yurqa.* Egyp. *y3qt,* "leek," a Semitic loanword, should also be cited here.

The verb forms in Middle Hebrew (with the meaning "make yellow" in the Mishnah and Talmud; cf. "become green" in Jewish Aramaic), Syriac, and Mandaic continue to be used, as in Akkadian, of a face's turning pale green or yellow. The color "yellow" is denoted by *yrq* when the root is used of a metal, usually gold. Thus Akk. *ḫurāṣu arqu*[18] and Ugar. *yrq ḥrṣ*[19] recall the *yᵉraqraq ḥārûṣ* of Ps. 68:14(Eng. v. 13). In South Semitic, we find OSA *wrq,* "gold,"[20] and Ethiop. *waraq,* "gold."[21] The latter also means "gold" in Geʿez, Amharic,[22] and Tigriñᵃ. In Tigré, however, it means "silver."[23] For Libyan, one may cite Tuareg *ûreǵ,* "gold." Although the meaning "silver" appears in Tigré, Arab. *warq/wariq,* "silver coin" (found in the sense of "money" in Koran 18:19, e.g.), is probably derived from *waraq,* "leaf"; it is therefore related only indirectly to "green." Tuareg *darûǵ,* "copper," is based on **ḏa-waruqu,* "something yellow."[24]

The corpus of Amorite proper names from the Mari texts yields the name "Yarq" (*ya-ar-qa-A*[*N*]),[25] which may be compared to OSA *ḏwrqn,*[26] a clan name from Qataba, and *ḏt/wrqn.*[27]

The range of meanings from green to yellow inherent in the Semitic root should be no cause for surprise. In the Near East, green plants that spring up without enough water yellow rapidly. In addition, the words for "green" and "yellow" in other (Indo-European) languages frequently derive from the same root, clearly because the boundary between the two is felt to be vague.[28]

II. Occurrences. There are 21 occurrences of the five different nouns derived from

---

15 Fischer, 116.

16 *KAI,* 222 A.28.

17 C. Rathjens–H. V. Wissmann, *Südarabien-reise* (Hamburg, 1931), 69.3; oral communication from W. W. Müller; otherwise, M. Höfner, *Sabaeica,* III (1966), 36.

18 *CAD,* I/2, 300b.

19 E.g., *KTU,* 1.14 III, 22.

20 E.g., *RÉS,* 3946, 7; 3951, 3.

21 *LexLingAeth,* 898.

22 W. Leslau, *Hebrew Cognates in Amharic* (Wiesbaden, 1969), 83.

23 *TigrWB,* 434a.

24 O. Rössler, "Der semitische Charakter der lybischen Sprache," *ZA,* N.S. 16 [50] (1952), 132.

25 *APNM,* 215.

26 *RÉS,* 3566, 29; 3902, no. 162.

27 Ja 288, 2. See G. L. Harding, *An Index and Concordance of Pre-Islamic Arabian Names and Inscriptions* (Toronto, 1971), 640. On the vocalization *warqān* or *waraqān,* see Y. Abdallah, *Die Personennamen in al-Hamdānaīʾ* Al-Iklīl *und ihre Parallelen in den altsüdarabischen Inschriften* (diss., Tübingen, 1975), 96.

28 Cf. C. D. Buck, *A Dictionary of Selected Synonyms in the Principal Indo-European Languages* (Chicago, 1949), nos. 15.68, 69, pp. 1058f.

yrq: *yārôq* once, *yārāq* 3 times, *yereq* 8 times, *yērāqôn* 6 times, and *yᵉraqraq* 3 times. The proper names *yarqôn* and (possibly) *yorqᵒʿām* occur once each. The occurrences are scattered throughout the OT and their distribution does not suggest any conclusions.

III. Nouns.

1. *yārôq.* The hapax legomenon *yārôq* appears in Job 39:8 with the meaning "green thing." The wild ass that pastures in the mountains must work hard to find its food; it searches out every green thing.

2. *yārāq.* The noun *yārāq* has the specialized meaning "(green) vegetables." In the description of the promised land, Dt. 11:10 states that, unlike a vegetable garden (*gan hayyārāq*) in the riverine civilization of Egypt, the land does not need to be irrigated by human labor; because it lies in the rain belt, it is watered "by the rain from heaven." A vegetable garden is also called *gan-yārāq* in 1 K. 21:2. Ahab wants to have Naboth's vineyard for a *kḗpon lachánōn* (LXX 20:2). According to Prov. 15:17, a dinner of vegetables (*ʾᵃruḥaṯ yārāq*; LXX *xenismós lachánōn*) cooked with love is better than a fatted ox served with hatred.

3. *yereq.* The segholate noun *yereq* is used twice with *ʿēśeḇ* (Gen. 1:30; 9:3) to denote the green foliage of plants.[29] Similarly, Ex. 10:15 uses it with *bāʿēṣ* to denote the green leaves of a tree. In Nu. 22:4, it is qualified by *haśśāḏeh*: the green (grass) of the field is devoured by cattle. In 3 passages, *yereq* is qualified by *dešeʾ*.[30] In the oracle to Sennacherib in 2 K. 19:21-31 (par. Isa. 37:22-32), a secondary insertion into the text, 2 K. 19:26 uses the natural image of withering vegetation to describe the fate of the cities taken by Sennacherib: "They have become like plants of the field (*ʿēśeḇ śāḏeh*), and like tender grass (*wîraq dešeʾ*), like grass on the housetops (*ḥᵃṣîr gaggôṯ*), 'dried out' by 'the east wind'." In Ps. 37:2, similarly, the *mᵉrēʿîm* and *ʿōśê ʿawlâ* are threatened with fading like the grass (*ḥāṣîr*) and withering like the green herb (*yereq dešeʾ*). In Isa. 15:6, *yereq* appears without further qualification in a lament over Moab. The grass (*ḥāṣîr*), the new growth (*dešeʾ*), and thus everything green (*yereq*) have withered and vanished—a vivid picture of the destruction of Moab. As punishment for breaking a treaty, one inscription threatens that no more vegetation (*ḥṣr*), greenery (*yrq*), or grass (*ʾḥw*) will be seen.[31]

4. *yērāqôn.* The noun *yērāqôn* is used 5 times in the OT to denote a disease infecting grain; it always follows *šiddāp̱ôn*. It appears in v. 22 of Dt. 28:15-68 (a curse); in 1 K. 8:37 (par. 2 Ch. 6:28), in the prayer of dedication of the temple, as a plague that causes the people to resort to prayer; and in Am. 4:9, in the context of an invective against the cult pilgrims, as a plague that should cause them to repent and return to Yahweh. Hag.

---

29 W. H. Schmidt, *Die Schöpfungsgeschichte der Priesterschrift. WMANT,* 17 (³1973), 150ff.; C. Westermann, *Genesis 1–11* (Eng. trans., Minneapolis, 1984), 161ff.; O. H. Steck, *Der Schöpfungsbericht der Priesterschrift. FRLANT,* 115 (1975), 137f., esp. nn. 558, 560.

30 → דשא *dešeʾ* (*desheʾ*).

31 *KAI,* 222 A. 28f.; cf. also III.4 below.

2:17 is probably borrowed from the Amos passage. The terms *šiddāp̱ôn* and *yērāqôn* constitute a stereotyped pair in the topos of a "catalogue of calamities."[32] Dalman[33] defines *yērāqôn* as "the fading of the tips of the green grain resulting from 'worm growth' during a period of prolonged drought." In Jer. 30:6, *yērāqôn* describes the face of people terrified at the day of Yahweh. The LXX translates here (LXX 37:2) and in 1 K. 8:37 (Origen only); 2 Ch. 6:28; Am. 4:9 with *íkteros*, "jaundice";[34] in Am. 4:9, where *šiddāp̱ôn* is rendered by *pýrōsis*, "fever," the LXX is thinking of human diseases (cf. the Syr. of 2 Ch. 6:28: *šwḥnʾ wšwnqʾ*, "boils and affliction"; the Arabic is similar).[35]

5. *yᵉraqraq*. In the section on leprous garments of the laws governing ritual purity, Lev. 13:47-49 describes the "infection" of wool and linen cloth or leather as a true case of leprosy if the disease shows greenish (*yᵉraqraq*) or reddish (*ʾᵃḏamdām*) spots that are the product of mildew. Lev. 14:37 discusses the infection of houses with leprosy in a similarly systematic way: it is present if the fungus covering the walls consists of "greenish or reddish nests" (*šᵉqaʿᵃrûrōṯ yᵉraqraqqōṯ ʾô ʾᵃḏamdammōṯ*) appearing deeper than the surface. In other words, light gray mildew was not considered dangerous, whereas "an unusual and changing coloration" was a sign of danger requiring protective measures.[36]

The singular of the reduplicating form *yᵉraqraq* appears only in the much-debated Ps. 68.[37] Verse 14(13) is a famous crux interpretum. There is a formal and contextual parallel in Ethiop. *waraqrīq*[38] in the thirty-fifth discourse of "Physiologus," "On the Dove,"[39] describing the various markings of doves. The interpretations of the dove in v. 14(13) that are of significance for defining *yᵉraqraq* divide into two groups: either (1) the description of the dove reflects a real dove, or (2) it describes an artifact. In the first case, we can ignore the question of whether the poet is really thinking of doves, either as carriers of messages (Eerdmans) or as associated with royal courts (Isserlin), or is using a natural image metaphorically, so that the dove represents Israel (the Jewish interpretation). In this case, the author's words (*kanᵉpê yônâ neḥpâ ḇakkesep wᵉʾeḇrôṯeyhā bîraqraq ḥārûṣ*) were inspired by the play of colors on a dove shining in the sunlight. In the second case, the poet is assumed to have been picturing a dove made of some unspecified material covered with metal—silver, gold, or possibly bronze. (Cf. the dove from Susa, now in the Louvre, probably dating from the latter part of the second

---

32 W. Rudolph, *Amos. KAT,* XIII/2 (1971), 179f.; H. W. Wolff, *Joel and Amos. Herm* (Eng. trans. 1977), 212ff.

33 *AuS,* I/2 (1928), 326.

34 Cf. Akk. *awurriqānum, amurriqānu,* "jaundice" (*AHw,* I [1965], 92a), the probable source of Syr. *mᵉrīqānāʾ*.

35 For a different interpretation, see Gradwohl, 31.

36 K. Elliger, *Leviticus. HAT,* IV (1966), 185.

37 See, e.g., E. W. E. Reuss, *Der achtundsechzigste Psalm* (Jena, 1851); also S. Mowinckel, *Der achtundsechzigste Psalm. ANVAO,* II, 1953/1; J. Vlaardingerbroek, *Psalm 68* (diss., Amsterdam, 1973).

38 Erroneously cited by *KBL*³ as *waraqrūq*.

39 Ed. F. Hommel (Leipzig, 1877), 28, 80, and xxvi-xxvii.

millennium B.C.; it is 8 cm. [3 in.] long, made of lapis lazuli, and covered with gold.[40]) The meaning of *yᵉraqraq* in either case would be "glistening yellowish-green";[41] if the dove is covered with metal, neither verdigris nor patina is necessarily involved.

6. *Names with yrq.* There are two proper names that are probably connected with the root *yrq.*

a. *yorqᵒʿām.* The personified toponym *yorqᵒʿām,* cited in 1 Ch. 2:44 as a descendant of Caleb and frequently identified with the toponym *yoqdᵉʿām* in Josh. 15:56,[42] may derive from the root *yrq,* as the Amorite parallel and certain Old South Arabic names suggest.[43] Now the names based solely on the root *wrq/yrq* are easy to interpret; it is more difficult, however, to interpret *yorqᵒʿām* as a phrase name based on the root *yrq* and the element *ʿam.* One might be tempted to posit a different root, for example *rqʿ,* with prefix and suffix; but this approach, too, does little to clarify the meaning of the name.[44] The uncertainty regarding the history and interpretation of the name *yorqᵒʿām* makes it inadvisable to try to derive from it additional information about the root *yrq* or to interpret the name on the basis of the extended semantic field of *yrq.*

b. *yarqôn.* Josh. 19:46, in the description of Dan's territory, uses the phrase *ûmê hayyarqôn wᵉhāraqqôn.* The text appears to be corrupt; most scholars follow the LXX in deleting the second name as dittography. But the remaining expression *mê hayyarqôn,* which today is used for the Nahr el-ʿAujā, still raises questions. It might actually refer to a wadi or watercourse descriptively called "the greenish (stream)." On the other hand, *hayyarqôn* could be a place name,[45] bearing no less eloquent witness to its fertile environment. In this case, the adjacent stream would have been named after the place. There are parallels for both usages: cf. *mê hayyardēn* in Josh. 3:8,13; etc. and *mê mērôm* in Josh. 11:7. Thus if *hayyarqôn* is the original text, it is an appellative describing either the yellowish-green color of a stream or the fertile environment of a village in the "green countryside."

IV. Summary. The Qumran texts contain no derivatives of the root *yrq.*

a. The LXX uses *ptýein* and *emptýein* to translate *yāraq, láchanon* and *chlōrós* to translate *yereq,* and *íkteros* to translate *yērāqôn.*

b. The various terms under discussion refer primarily to phenomena involving vegetation. Originally, the root probably denoted the color of leaves; this meaning best accounts for the various specific usages. The root appears in theologically important passages in Gen. 1:30, where God gives plants to animals and human beings to use as food, and in Gen. 9:3, where God gives human beings permission to eat not only plants

---

40 A. Schäfer and W. Andrae, *Die Kunst des Alten Orients* (Berlin, 1925), no. 482.

41 Cf. also B. Kedar-Kopfstein, "זהב *zāhāḇ (zāhābh),*" *TDOT,* IV, 34.

42 E.g., F.-M. Abel, *Géographie de la Palestine,* II (Paris, ³1967), 365.

43 See I.2 above.

44 For a proposal that emends the consonantal skeleton of the name, see W. F. Albright, "The Jordan Valley in the Bronze Age," *AASOR,* 6 (1926), 22, with n. 36.

45 Cf. OSA *wrq* as the name of an oasis (*CIH,* 375, 1 = Ja 550, 1).

but also the flesh of animals. In Dt. 28:22; 1 K. 8:37 (par.); and Am. 4:9, the unhealthy yellowing of grain is a sign that God has withheld his blessing.

Kellermann

יָרַשׁ *yāraš*; יְרֵשָׁה *yᵉrēšâ*; יְרֻשָּׁה *yᵉruššâ*; מוֹרָשׁ *môrāš*; מוֹרָשָׁה *môrāšâ*

Contents: I. The Word: 1. Distribution in the OT; 2. Qal; 3. Niphal; 4. Piel; 5. Hiphil; 6. Nouns; 7. Other Languages; 8. Etymology. II. Theological Usage: 1. Secular Background; 2. Ethical Judgment; 3. *yrš* in Statements of Omnipotence and Oracles of Judgment; 4. Absence of the Qal in the Pre-Deuteronomistic Theology of the Promised Land in the Pentateuch; 5. Theological Usage of the Hiphil in Early Strata of Joshua and Judges; 6. Deuteronomistic Theology; 7. Jer. 30f.; 8. Ezekiel; 9. Pᵍ, H, and Late Strata of the Pentateuch; 10. Hope for Restoration of the Davidic Empire in the Redactors of the Prophets; 11. Possession of the Land as the Hope of the "Poor" in the Postexilic Period; 12. Deutero- and Trito-Isaiah.

---

yāraš. F. I. Andersen, "The Socio-Juridical Background of the Naboth Incident," *JBL,* 85 (1966), 46-57; M. C. Astour, "Some New Divine Names from Ugarit," *JAOS,* 86 (1966), 277-284, esp. 284; W. Bacher, "Zu Zephanja 2,4," *ZAW,* 11 (1891), 185-87; O. Bächli, *Israel und die Völker. AThANT,* 41 (1962), 159-161; P. A. Bird, YRŠ *and the Deuteronomic Theology of the Conquest* (diss., Harvard, 1972); R. Bohlen, *Der Fall Naboth. TrThSt,* 35 (1978); S. Böhmer, *Heimkehr und neuer Bund. GöttThArb,* 5 (1976); P.-E. Bonnard, *Le Second Isaïe. ÉtB* (1972); G. Braulik, "Literarkritik und archäologische Stratigraphie," *Bibl,* 59 (1978), 351-383; *idem, Die Mittel deuteronomischer Rhetorik. AnBibl,* 68 (1978); A. M. Brown, *The Concept of Inheritance in the OT* (diss., Columbia, 1965); A. Cholewiński, *Heiligkeitsgesetz und Deuteronomium. AnBibl,* 66 (1976); W. M. Clark, *The Origin and Development of the Land Promise Theme in the OT* (diss., Yale, 1964); E. Cortese, *La terra di Canaan nella storia sacerdotale del Pentateuco. RivBiblSup,* 5 (1972); M. Dahood, *Ugaritic-Hebrew Philology. BietOr,* 17 (1965), 25; *idem,* "Hebrew-Ugaritic Lexicography IV," *Bibl,* 47 (1966), 403-419, esp. 404f.; M. Delcor, "De l'origine de quelques termes relatifs au vin en hébreu biblique et dans les langues voisines," *ACLingSémCham,* 228-230 = *Études bibliques et orientales de religions comparées* (Leiden, 1979), 351-53; P. Diepold, *Israels Land. BWANT,* 95[5/15] (1972); F. Dreyfus, "Le thème de l'héritage dans l'AT," *RSPT,* 42 (1958), 3-49, esp. 5-8; K. Elliger, "Sinn und Ursprung der priesterlichen Geschichtserzählung," *ZThK,* 49 (1952), 121-143 = *KlSchr. ThB,* 32 (1966), 174-198; W. Foerster and J. Herrmann, "κλῆρος," *TDNT,* III, 758-785; V. Fritz, *Israel in der Wüste. MarThSt,* 7 (1970); G. Gerleman, "Nutzrecht und Wohnrecht: Zur Bedeutung von אחוה und נחלה," *ZAW,* 89 (1977), 313-325; J. Halbe, *Das Privilegrecht Jahwes: Ex 34,10-26. FRLANT,* 114 (1975); P. Haupt, "Critical Notes on Micah," *AJSL,* 26 (1909/1910), 201-252, esp. 215, 223; F. Horst, "Das Eigentum nach dem AT," *Gottes Recht. GSAT. ThB,* 12 (1961), 203-221; *idem,* "Zwei Begriffe für Eigentum (Besitz): נַחֲלָה und אֲחֻזָּה," *Verbannung und Heimkehr. Festschrift W. Rudolph* (Tübingen, 1961), 135-156; E. Jenni, *Das hebräische Piʿel* (Zurich, 1968), 212f.; R. Kilian, *Die vorpriesterlichen Abrahams-Überlieferungen. BBB,* 24 (1966); L. Köhler, "Archäologisches. Nr. 23: Eine archaistische Wortgruppe," *ZAW,* 46 (1928), 218f.; F. Langlamet, *Gilgal et les récits de la traversée du Jourdain (Jos III-IV). CahRB,* 11 (1969); N. Lohfink, "Die Bedeutungen von hebr. *jrš qal* und *hif,*" *BZ,* N.S.

I. The Word. Whenever possible, the ancient versions translated *yrš* and its derivatives by words referring to inheritance of private property; the LXX, for example, uses *klēronoméō,* which likewise translates → נחל *nḥl* and its derivatives. Scholars have long recognized that this interpretation demands critical reevaluation, but they have been unable to reach a consensus.

Recent exegetical literature often discusses *yrš* only in other contexts, and then frequently from a one-sided perspective. The only thorough study, that of Bird (unfortunately not published), is more useful in its treatment of philological questions than in its analysis of the OT, because the author limits her study to Deuteronomic usage. Recent

---

27 (1983), 14-33; *idem,* "Darstellungskunst und Theologie in Dtn 1,6–3,29," *Bibl,* 41 (1960), 105-134; *idem,* "Die deuteronomistische Darstellung des Übergangs der Führung Israels von Moses auf Josue," *Scholastik,* 37 (1962), 32-34; *idem, Das Hauptgebot. AnBibl,* 20 (1963); *idem,* "Kerygmata des Deuteronomistischen Geschichtswerks," *Die Botschaft und die Boten. Festschrift H. W. Wolff* (Neukirchen-Vluyn, 1982), 87-100; *idem,* "Die Priesterschrift und die Geschichte," *Congress Volume, Göttingen 1977. SVT,* 29 (1978), 189-225; *idem,* "Der Schöpfergott und der Bestand von Himmel und Erde," in G. Altner, *et al., Sind wir noch zu retten?* (Regensburg, 1978), 15-39; *idem,* "Die Sicherung der Wirksamkeit des Gotteswortes durch das Prinzip der Schriftlichkeit der Tora und durch das Prinzip der Gewaltenteilung nach den Ämtergesetzen des Buches Deuteronomium (Dt 16,18–18,22)," in H. Wolter, ed., *Testimonium Veritati. FThS,* 7 (1971); *idem,* "Textkritisches zu *jrš* im AT," *Mélanges Dominique Barthélemy. OBO,* 38 (1981), 273-288; O. Loretz, "Hebräisch *tjrwš* und *jrš* in Mi 6,15 und Hi 20,15," *UF,* 9 (1977), 353f.; G. C. Macholz, *Israel und das Land* (Habilitationsschrift, Heidelberg, 1969); T. N. D. Mettinger, "The Nominal Pattern Q^{e}Tulla in Biblical Hebrew," *JSS,* 16 (1971), 2-14; S. Mittmann, *Deuteronomium 1$_1$–6$_3$ literarkritisch und traditionsgeschichtlich untersucht.* BZAW, 139 (1975); P. A. Munch, "Das Problem des Reichtums in den Psalmen 37. 49. 73," *ZAW,* 55 (1937), 36-46, esp. 38-40; R. D. Nelson, *The Redactional Duality of the Deuteronomistic History* (diss., Union Theological Seminary in Virginia, 1973); J. G. Plöger, *Literarkritische, formgeschichtliche und stilkritische Untersuchungen zum Deuteronomium. BBB,* 26 (1967), 61-87; G. von Rad, "The Promised Land and Yahweh's Land in the Hexateuch," in *The Problem of the Hexateuch and Other Essays* (Eng. trans. 1966; repr. London, 1984), 79-93; W. Richter, "Die Überlieferungen um Jephtah Ri 10,17–12,6," *Bibl,* 47 (1966), 485-556, esp. 543-46; H. H. Schmid, "ירשׁ *jrš* beerben," *THAT,* I, 778-781; G. Schmitt, *Du sollst keinen Frieden schliessen mit den Bewohnern des Landes. BWANT,* 91[5/11] (1970); M. Schwantes, *Das Recht der Armen. BET,* 4 (1977), 16-20; S. M. Schwertner, *Das verheissene Land* (diss., Heidelberg, 1966), 169-177; G. Seitz, *Redaktionsgeschichtliche Studien zum Deuteronomium. BWANT,* 93[5/13] (1971); R. Smend, "Das Gesetz und die Völker," *Probleme biblischer Theologie. Festschrift G. von Rad* (Munich, 1971), 494-509; L. A. Snijders, "Genesis XV: The Covenant with Abram," *OTS,* 12 (1958), 261-279, esp. 267-271; W. von Soden, "Aramäische Wörter in neuassyrischen und neu- und spätbabylonischen Texten," *Or,* 35 (1966), 1-20, esp. 12; J. J. Stamm, "Hebräische Frauennamen," *Hebräische Wortforschung. Festschrift W. Baumgartner. SVT,* 16 (1967), 301-339, esp. 327 = *Beiträge zur hebräischen und altorientalischen Namenkunde. OBO,* 30 [1980]; N. H. Tur-Sinai, *The Book of Job* (Jerusalem, 1957), 314; P. Weimar, *Untersuchungen zur priesterschriftlichen Exodusgeschichte. FzB,* 9 (1973), 150-53; M. Weinfeld, *Deuteronomy and the Deuteronomic School* (Oxford, 1972), 313-15; *idem,* "The Period of the Conquest and of the Judges as Seen by the Earlier and the Later Sources," *VT,* 17 (1967), 93-113; J. N. M. Wijngaards, "The Dramatization of Salvific History in the Deuteronomic Schools," *OTS,* 16 (1969), 84-90; H. W. Wolff, "Das Kerygma des deuteronomistischen Geschichtswerkes," *ZAW,* 73 (1961), 171-186 = *GSAT. ThB,* 22 (^{2}1973), 308-324; H. Zimmern, *Akkadische Fremdwörter als Beweis für babylonischen Kultureinfluss* (^{2}1917), 17.

lexica, such as *KBL*², *KBL*³, and *THAT,* are often less careful than earlier ones in distinguishing meanings. The present article represents a fresh approach to the sources. On questions of textual criticism, the reader is referred to Lohfink's "Textkritisches zu ירשׁ im AT," which will not always be cited for each case.

1. *Distribution in the OT.*

a. *Qal.* The qal of *yrš* occurs 161 times in the OT, counting the following uncertain passages: Lev. 25:46; Nu. 14:24; Josh. 1:11 (*lršth*), 15 (*wyrštm*); Jgs. 14:15; Prov. 30:23; Am. 9:12; Ob. 20a conj. (correction of a homoioteleuton); and not counting Nu. 21:32 (*K*); Dt. 2:31 (*rš*); Mic. 6:15 conj.; Zeph. 2:4 (*ygršwh*). Of these, 62 are in Deuteronomy and 28 in Joshua–2 Kings, so that a total of 90 are in the Deuteronomistic history. An additional 32 occurrences in the other books continue Deuteronomic or Deuteronomistic usage. The remaining 39 are concentrated in Gen. 15; Jer. 49; Obadiah; cf. also Neh. 9; Ps. 37; Ezk. 33. There is only 1 occurrence in Proverbs, and none in Job or the Megilloth. The context is usually prose; the most common literary types are laws, forensic discourse, narrative, and parenesis. The occurrences in blessings (Gen. 24:60; Dt. 33:23) and prophetic oracles appear to reflect ancient usage. Those in Wisdom psalms, psalms recounting *Heilsgeschichte,* prose prayers, and late strata of the prophetic books presuppose Deuteronomic usage. From the diachronic perspective, there are datable occurrences from all periods between the court history of David (2 S. 14:7) and the Chronicler's history. Late shifts in meaning show that the qal was always part of the living language.

b. *Niphal.* The niphal occurs only 3 times in Proverbs and once in the Joseph story in Genesis, where the style is influenced by Wisdom Literature. It is therefore attested only in the language of wisdom. It would be a mistake to emend some or all of these occurrences to a hophal of *rwš.*[1]

c. *Piel.* There is only a single occurrence of the piel, Dt. 28:42—unless Jgs. 14:15 is to be read as piel.

d. *Hiphil.* There are 64 occurrences of the hiphil, counting Nu. 21:32 (*Q*); 33:53a; Josh. 8:7; 1 S. 2:7, and not counting Nu. 14:24; Jgs. 1:19; Ob. 17 (*môrišêhem*). Of these, 7 are from Deuteronomy and 39 from Joshua–2 Kings, so that the Deuteronomistic history accounts for 46. An additional 11 continue Deuteronomistic style. The distribution of the remaining 7 is random. Within the Deuteronomistic history, occurrences are concentrated in Josh. 13–17 (11); Jgs. 1 (12). Other concentrations appear in Nu. 33; Dt. 9; Josh. 23; Jgs. 11. The qal also occurs in these passages. The hiphil usually appears in prose, most often in narrative summaries or lists. It appears in poetry in Ex. 15:9; 1 S. 2:7; Job 13:26; 20:15; Ps. 44:3(Eng. v. 2); Zec. 9:4. Diachronically, there are occurrences antedating Deuteronomic and Deuteronomistic literature, but they cannot be dated precisely; 2 occurrences in poetry (Ex. 15:9; 1 S. 2:7), a few in narrative (Nu. 14:12; 21:32; 32:39; Josh. 14:12), and some of the list material in Jgs. 1; Josh. 13–17 can be assigned more or less probably to the pre-Deuteronomic period. New meanings appear

---

1 Cf. Lohfink, *Mélanges Dominique Barthélemy,* 273-288.

in the latest occurrences (2 Ch. 20:11; Ezr. 9:12; Job 13:26). The hiphil therefore always remained part of the living language.

e. *Nouns.* The nouns *yᵉrēšâ* (2 occurrences) and *môrāš* (2 occurrences, not counting Job 17:11) appear to be rare words, either archaizing or consciously poetic. The nouns *yᵉruššâ* (14 occurrences) and *môrāšâ* (9 occurrences), on the contrary, are attested around the exilic period as elements in the popular language concerning property ownership (Jer. 32:8; Ezk. 11:15; 33:24). They owe their relative frequency, however, solely to the fact that particular groups of writers chose them both as technical terms in their own specialized language: *yᵉruššâ* in the Deuteronomistic material, *môrāšâ* in Ezekiel and P^{g}. The latter appears also in the psalm in which the Blessing of Moses (basically an early text) is set (Dt. 33:4), but in a stratum that is presumably later and hard to assign diachronically.

f. *Names, rešeṯ, tîrôš.* The root *yrš* appears also in the woman's name *yᵉrušâ* (*yᵉrušāʾ*) and the place name *môrešeṯ gaṯ* (gentilic *hammōraštî*). Whether the words *rešeṯ,* "net," and *tîrôš,* "wine" and/or "must," derive from this root is disputed and probably unlikely.

2. *Qal.* The qal of *yrš* occurs only 8 times without a grammatical object. The object is personal (an individual or a people) in 25 cases, inanimate (usually real property or national territory) in 128. Only in Hos. 9:6 do we find both an animate and an inanimate object. There is a semantic difference between the qal with a personal object and the qal with an inanimate object. Considerations of space prevent us from doing more than recording the results of our semantic analysis of the qal.[2]

a. *With Personal Objects.* The passages in which the qal of *yrš* has a personal object include Gen. 21:10; 2 S. 14:7; and Jer. 49:1a, where no object is specified. They date from the court history of David (2 S. 14:7) to the late legislation of the Pentateuch (Nu. 27:11). The central semantic element is "legal succession."

The legal realm in question is the family; what is handed on is family leadership, even when a concrete object appears to be the center of attention: Gen. 15:3f.; 21:10; Nu. 27:11; 2 S. 14:7; Prov. 30:23. Gen. 21:12 contains a quasi-definition: "Through Isaac shall it come to pass that one can speak of Abraham's continuance through generations to come." Normally the first son becomes the father's legal successor; in the absence of such a son, however, there are alternatives (Gen. 15:3; Nu. 27:8-11).

In prophetic oracles, this meaning is transferred metaphorically to the nation: cf. Isa. 54:3; Jer. 49:1f.; Hos. 9:6.

It is probably against this background that a specialized Deuteronomistic usage evolved (Dt. 2:12,21,22; 9:1; 11:23; 12:2,29; 18:14; 19:1; 31:3; Jgs. 11:23,24). Here by right of conquest one people or nation succeeds another in ruling over a territory. This right of conquest is undergirded by divine providence and action, which can be expressed in a play on words using the hiphil of *yrš* (Dt. 9:1; 11:23; 18:14; Jgs. 11:23f.). Here there is more emphasis on the territory than there is on the object in question in the preceding group of passages. A quasi-definition appears in Dt. 11:23f.: "Every place on which the sole of your foot treads shall be yours." For post-Deuteronomistic usage, cf. Am. 9:12.

---

2 For a study of the individual occurrences, see Lohfink, *BZ,* N.S. 27 (1983), 14-33.

b. *With Inanimate Objects.* The passages in which the qal of *yrš* has an inanimate object include Dt. 1:21; 2:24; Jgs. 14:15; Jer. 8:10; Mic. 1:15, where no object is specified. There are 133 occurrences, of which about 100 are Deuteronomic or Deuteronomistic.

In almost every case, an appropriate translation is "take possession of the object named." Only in very late passages does this usage come to refer also to inheritance of the family's wealth by whoever takes over family leadership when the father dies. Earlier contexts always involve "acquisition" of something additional, without stipulating the specific mode of acquisition, usually purchase.

In Jgs. 14:15, *yrš* refers to the wedding guests' receiving presents from the bridegroom or the receiving of the object of a wager (undergarments and festal garments). In 1 K. 21:15,16,18,19, it refers to taking possession of Naboth's vineyard, title to which was disputed. This possession probably involved the act of perambulation or crossing (cf. the associated verb *yrd*). In pre-Deuteronomic passages and those not influenced by Deuteronomistic usage, the most common meaning is probably acquisition through right of conquest after a battle or war (cf. Dt. 33:23). In Gen. 24:60 (as well as Gen. 22:17, which depends on the latter), the object is the "city gate," probably signifying sovereignty over the city; in Ps. 83:13(12), it is "the pastures of God"; in Mic. 1:15, a city; in Jer. 8:10, fields; in Hab. 1:6, "habitations"; and in Isa. 14:21; Ob. 19f., territories. Here, too, the objects clearly can vary and *yrš* is often used by metonymy. Almost everywhere it can be translated "capture."

The situation is different in the early accounts of wars and battles (Nu. 13:30; 14:24; 21:24; Josh. 19:47; Jgs. 3:13; the Mesha inscription[3] belongs in this context typologically). Here other verbs precede and follow in the narrative sequence, so that *yrš* does not mean "capture" in the comprehensive sense. Whether it denotes a juridically significant act (as in the story of Naboth) or confirms the outcome of the preceding battles remains an open question. There is no reference to settlement.

Deuteronomistic usage derives directly from these texts. Here the subject of *yrš* is invariably "all Israel" or at least a group of tribes. The object is the territory promised by Yahweh. A new element is Yahweh's "gift" of the land.[4] The distribution of the land among the tribes and clans comes later.

Deuteronomistic literature and the texts dependent on it then frequently use cliches containing *yrš* to refer to these Deuteronomistic conquest narratives. The semantics remain the same. When the context recalls Yahweh's oath to "give" the land to the patriarchs, the reference is probably to Gen. 15:7-21. The frequent use of *yrš* in conjunction with a verb of motion (*ʿālâ, ʿāḇar, bôʾ*) recalls its use with *yrd* in the story of Naboth. Is there some suggestion that at least originally *yrš* denoted a concrete symbolic act through which possession was taken of a place (cf. also Dt. 11:24; Josh. 1:3)? It is impossible to reach any certain conclusion.

Dt. 30:5; Ezr. 9:11; Jer. 30:3 use the Deuteronomistic idiom for the peaceful resettle-

---

3 *KAI,* 181.7.

4 Cf. II.6.a below.

ment of the ancient Israelite homeland after the exile. Here, however, there are probably also overtones of another usage of *yrš*. Lev. 20:24; 2 K. 17:24; Isa. 61:7; Ezk. 36:12; Ob. 17 appear to indicate that *yrš*, independently of its use in Deuteronomistic literature, could be used without military overtones for the return from exile and even earlier for the possession of land bestowed by royal decree or the comparable redistribution of land in a year of release (cf. also Isa. 34:17). In this case, the Deuteronomistic cliche of human *yrš* in conjunction with divine *ntn* developed not only from early military narratives but also from the language of royal or communal redistribution of property.[5]

Another meaning of the qal with the land as its object is attested only from the time of the exile: "own, enjoy possession of." This meaning is more or less likely in Josh. 1:15b; 1 Ch. 28:8; Ps. 25:13; 37:9,11,22,29,34; 69:36(35); Isa. 34:11,17; 57:13; 60:21; 63:18; 65:9b; Ezk. 33:25,26; 35:10. Its presence should not be posited, however, in the Deuteronomistic passages where the occupation of the land under Joshua and in the period of the judges depends on prior observance of the law (with the possible exception of Dt. 16:20). Instead of *'ereṣ*, the object can be a more or less vague feminine suffix (cf. Ps. 69:36[35]; Isa. 34:17; 65:9b; Ezk. 35:10). This meaning of *yrš* + *'ereṣ* may have arisen through contamination of the Deuteronomistic expression with the wisdom idiom *škn* + *'ereṣ* (cf. the occurrences in Ps. 37).

In postexilic texts, we find traces of Aramaic influence on the semantic development of *yrš*. Here the qal with an inanimate object takes on the meaning "inherit (something)," thus entering the family domain and becoming a parallel term to *nḥl*. It can refer to individual objects or even slaves. The texts in question are: Lev. 25:46; Nu. 36:8; Neh. 9:25; Ps. 25:13(?); Isa. 57:13(?); 65:9a.

3. *Niphal*. As Prov. 30:7-9 suggests, the niphal of *yrš* appears related more closely in meaning to the group of words deriving from → רושׁ *rwš*, "be poor," than to the qal of *yrš*. This presented no problem during the period before triliteral theories had carried the day and influenced the general feeling for the language. In the period of David, the derivatives of *rwš* were part of the general language. Later they clearly became restricted to the specialized language of wisdom—unlike the words for "poor" that subsequently became theologically productive. The distribution of *rwš* parallels that of the niphal of *yrš*. In Gen. 45:11, the subject of the verb is not only Jacob and his family but also *kol-'ᵃšer-lāḵ*, undoubtedly including flocks and herds, as suggested by the longer parallel series in v. 10. In other words, the point is not that people become "poor" through loss of domestic animals and other property. Instead, the niphal of *yrš* denotes a general loss, an overall reduction, affecting human beings, their domestic animals, and their other possessions as a whole. This meaning agrees with the opposite expressed in Prov. 20:13; 30:9: "have plenty of bread." This conclusion is not contradicted by the use of "ragged clothing" in parallel in Prov. 23:21, an effect limited to human beings. In all these passages, there is an association with eating, drinking, and sleeping—the most basic forms of human regeneration and their opposites.

---

5 Cf. II.6.a below.

4. *Piel.* According to Jenni's illuminating explanation,[6] the piel in Dt. 28:42 (its only occurrence) adds the element of regular repetition to the single act expressed by the qal: all your trees and the fruit of your ground the locust shall take possession of, year after year. The metaphorical use of the word with a nonhuman subject is similar to the use of the qal in Isa. 34:11. Cf. also Isa. 14:23; Hos. 9:6.

5. *Hiphil.*[7]

a. *"Make Poor."* In early texts not influenced by Deuteronomistic usage, the meaning "make poor" is apparent from the hiphil of *yrš.* This is certain in 1 S. 2:7 and probable in Ex. 15:9; Job 20:15; Zec. 9:4. Semantically, this usage of the hiphil is associated more closely with *rwš* than with *yrš.* Except in Ex. 15:9, the subject is always God.[8]

b. *"Destroy."* There is a realistic possibility that Nu. 14:12 is pre-Deuteronomistic. The most plausible translation is: "I will strike them with the pestilence and destroy them." In addition to the meaning "make poor," we must therefore also reckon with the pre-Deuteronomistic meaning "destroy." It is possible that this meaning developed out of the former, so that we are still in the semantic field of *rwš.*

Josh. 13:12,13; 14:12; 15:14,63; 16:10; 17:12,13(twice),18; Jgs. 1:19a,19b,20,21,27, 28,29,30,31,32,33 and possibly also Nu. 21:32; 32:39 constitute a relatively self-contained corpus of texts; in each case, it is often difficult to decide whether we are dealing with an early text or an empathic formulation on the part of a Deuteronomistic author, redactor, or glossator. Here the hiphil of *yrš* means "destroy someone so that someone else can possess his property," "do away with someone (as owner)." This meaning is related semantically to the qal of *yrš.* In Josh. 14:12 (admittedly a relatively late passage), we find a formal quotation of a word of Yahweh, which can only be Nu. 14:24, where the textually preferable Samaritan version has the qal of *yrš* with an inanimate object. The variant hiphil, being person-oriented, was obviously felt to be preferable to the object-oriented qal of the pre-Deuteronomistic conquest accounts. The personal use of the qal belonged semantically to the realm of normal family succession and was therefore unavailable. The various texts in this corpus are reports or lists of successful or unsuccessful attempts at conquest. The subject is never Yahweh. Only in two cases is it all Israel; usually it is Moses, Caleb, a clan, or a tribe. The object is never the Canaanites as a group. It is specific peoples, population groups, kings, territories, or cities. When territories or cities are mentioned, their inhabitants are probably meant (compare Jgs. 1:27f. with Josh. 17:12).

The usual translation of the hiphil in these passages (following the tradition of the Targumim) is "drive out"; the tradition stemming from the LXX and Vulg. uses "destroy" or the like. Now "driving out" implies more than simply removing others from a place by force. In a positive sense, it rules out destruction and suggests that those driven out can continue to live somewhere else. None of these texts carries any hint of this second

---

[6] Pp. 212f.

[7] For reasons of space, the following discussion can present only conclusions and the most important references; for the entire semantic analysis of the hiphil, see Lohfink, *BZ,* N.S. 27 (1983), 14-33.

[8] For a fuller discussion of these passages, see *ibid.*

element. In any case, the Deuteronomistic editing of this group of texts assumes the meaning "destroy." Therefore this meaning, supported by Nu. 14:12 as the probable pre-Deuteronomistic meaning, is much more likely here.[9]

In the clearly Deuteronomistic passages using the hiphil of *yrš,* it is even clearer that we are dealing with the meaning "destroy someone so that his property can be taken." Besides the human object (usually the peoples of Canaan), we usually find the qualification *mippᵉnê* + *N* (always the Israelites): Ex. 34:24; Nu. 32:21; 33:52,(53),55; Dt. 4:38; 9:4,5; 18:12; Josh. 3:10; 13:6; 23:9; Jgs. 2:21; 11:23,24b; 1 K. 14:24; 21:26; 2 K. 16:3 par. 2 Ch. 28:3; 2 K. 17:8; 21:2 par. 2 Ch. 33:2. With the same meaning, *millipnê* occurs in Dt. 11:23; Josh. 23:5,13; 2 Ch. 20:7. An equivalent suffix appears in Jgs. 11:24a. With this group we should also include Dt. 7:17; 9:3; Josh. 8:7; Jgs. 2:23; Ps. 44:3(2). There is no clearly Deuteronomic occurrence. With few exceptions, Yahweh is the subject of the verb. In contrast to the preceding group, the action is usually successful. There are 17 passages referring to the future, whereas all but 2 of the passages in the other group refer to the past. We are obviously dealing with an important expression of several Deuteronomistic strata, according to which, at the time of Israel's military occupation of the land ("before Israel's face"; cf. → פנה *pāneh*), Yahweh deprived the peoples of Canaan (who can be listed, described as great and powerful, and characterized in terms of their customs and "abominations") of their rights to possession of the land by destroying them. The destruction of the earlier population is followed by the Israelites' taking possession of the land, which is then distributed as an inheritance. In this context, several passages (Nu. 33:53; Dt. 9:3,4,5; 11:23; 18:12,14; Josh. 23:5; Jgs. 11:23,24; Ps. 44:3f.[2f.]) contain a play on words involving the hiphil and qal of *yrš*. In the context of conquest, the latter also appears with personal objects. Yahweh "destroys" (hiphil) the peoples when Israel attacks; but it is Israel, rather than Yahweh, that takes possession of (qal) their right of succession; the focus of attention is on sovereignty over their territory.

That these passages mean destruction, not ejection, is clear from Dt. 7:17 (referring back to *nšl, nkh,* and *ḥrm* in 7:1f. and looking forward to *'bd, nšl, klh,* and *šmd* in 7:20-24); 9:3-5 (par. *šmd, kn', 'bd*); 2 K. 21:2,9 (the hiphil of *yrš* and *šmd* as corresponding terms framing a text). In Nu. 33:55f., there follows the idea of a "remnant,"[10] which also belongs to the context of military destruction.[11]

c. *Late Meanings.* Only in 3 late passages does the hiphil of *yrš* occur as a regular causative based on the meaning of the qal. In these passages it appropriately takes a double accusative or an accusative of the object with *lᵉ* + the person. The meaning in Job 13:26 is based on the old meaning of the qal, "take possession of (something)," albeit metaphorically. By recording them in his heavenly book, God causes Job to take possession of the sins of his youth—i.e., charges them to his account. Ezr. 9:12 uses the qal's late meaning, "inherit (something)": the Judahites are to be able to "bequeath" the good of the land to their descendants. This same meaning is used by 2 Ch. 20:11 to

---

9 For further discussion, including arguments on both sides, see *ibid.*

10 → יתר *ytr* (hiphil).

11 For further discussion, see Lohfink, *BZ,* N.S. 27 (1983), 14-33.

reformulate Deuteronomistic theology: Yahweh has bequeathed to Israel his (= Yahweh's) *yᵉruššâ* as an inheritance. A causative hiphil is found also in Sir. 15:6: Wisdom, described metaphorically as a mother, causes one who fears God to take possession of an eternal name. This verse may suggest the mother as head of the family, handing on the family's possessions and honor.

6. *Nouns.* The noun *yᵉrēšâ* appears only in Nu. 24:18, in the fourth oracle of Balaam. According to its context, it denotes a territory that has come into the possession of another nation through right of conquest.

The noun *yᵉruššâ* cannot be considered simply a late variant with the same meaning. According to Jer. 32:8, Jeremiah has not only the *gᵉʾullâ*[12] but also the *mišpāṭ hayᵉruššâ* of a field. This is something like a "right of succession to a family's real property." He must purchase the field to which he is entitled, but the opportunity to purchase it must clearly be offered to him before anyone else. "Inheritance" in the usual sense is therefore not involved. Since both *gᵉʾullâ* and *yᵉruššâ* are mentioned, they are not the same thing. In this instance, however, Jeremiah has both rights and obligations. In Dt. 3:20; Ps. 61:6(5), *yᵉruššâ* is synonymous with *naḥᵃlâ,*[13] and possibly also in Josh. 1:15. The same is true of its theological usage in 2 Ch. 20:11. In Dt. 2:5,9(twice),12,19(twice); Josh. 12:6,7, too, a *yᵉruššâ,* like a family *naḥᵃlâ,* appears to be looked upon as one instance among many of the same nature. According to Dt. 2, every nation received its *yᵉruššâ* from Yahweh. In Jgs. 21:17, *yᵉruššaṯ pᵉlêṭâ* may be a technical legal term whose precise meaning is no longer accessible to us; Ob. 17 may cast some light on the expression. Mettinger[14] points out that *yᵉruššâ* is a *qᵉṭullâ* form, a type of noun especially common in the period of the exile, used specifically to form abstract legal terms.

The noun *môrāšâ* (9 occurrences) appears 6 times in the construction *ntn* + *lᵉ* + PN + *môrāšâ* and twice in the analogous construction *hyh* + *le* + PN + *môrāšâ.* The construction with *ṣwh* + *lᵉ* in Dt. 33:4 is probably equivalent to the *ntn* construction. The word designates a territory that an individual, a group, or a nation wishes or is intended to take possession of; it is thus related to Deuteronomistic usage of the qal with an inanimate object. This interpretation also fits Dt. 33:4, but the common interpretation—that the law of Moses is metaphorically the "possession" or "heritage" of the sons of Jacob—is wrong. Instead, the double duty of words in poetic parallelism suggests the translation: "Moses gave us a law, [and in addition he gave to us,] to the assembly of Jacob, a land for possession."

In the 2 occurrences of *môrāš,* either the same meaning or the meaning "inheritance" is possible.

7. *Other Languages.* Apart from Hebrew, the root **wrṯ* appears only in Northwest Semitic and South Semitic. Akk. *yāritu,* "heir," and *yārītūtu,* "inheritance," are Aramaic loanwords;[15] and the only connection of **wrṯ* with Akk. *rašû,* "receive, acquire

---

12 → גאל *g'l.*
13 → נחל *nḥl.*
14 Pp. 11-14.
15 A. L. Oppenheim, "Anzeigen," *WZKM,* 44 (1937), 140.

(property)," and *muršītu,* "chattels, booty,"[16] is indirect, based on the primitive biliteral root **rṯ.*[17]

a. *Aramaic and South Semitic.* In Aramaic and the South Semitic languages, the meaning of all the verb forms derived from **wrṯ* is restricted to the transfer of property through inheritance in its various phases and aspects. Within this semantic sphere, several of these languages have developed numerous nouns based on the root denoting the various subjects, objects, and acts involved in such transfer of property. The clear association of this group of words with inheritance parallels another observation: the root *nḥl,* which (contra Gerleman) in Hebrew is used primarily for the inheritance of real property, either is totally absent (as in Aramaic) or is used outside the semantic field of transfer of property by inheritance (as in Arabic).

The earliest occurrence of *yrt* in Aramaic[18] may still bear witness to an earlier semantic situation: *w'l yrt šr̊[š]h 'šm,* "may his root [the remnant of his destroyed family?] not possess/inherit a name." The reading and interpretation of this curse, however, involve many uncertainties.[19]

b. *Ugaritic.* In Ugaritic, which, like Hebrew, has *nḥl* as well as **wrṯ,* there is a verbal noun *yrṯ,* "heir, successor,"[20] probably vocalized *yāriṯu.* The 2 occurrences of finite verb forms, *'rṯm*[21] (G stem) and *ȝtrṯ*[22] (Gt stem), appear in comparable contexts. Both involve mythical battles among the gods. In each case, the object of the verb appears to be gold, which may possibly be a symbol of sovereignty. The most likely meaning is: "take hold or possession of (something)." There is also a personal name *mrṯd,* which (among other possibilities) might be interpreted as "heritage of Adad."[23]

c. *Moabite.* The single Moabite occurrence of the verb in the Mesha inscription[24] is extraordinarily similar to the Hebrew use of the qal in early conquest reports: *wyrš ʿmry 't k[l 'r]ṣ mhdb' wyšb bh ymh wḥṣy ymy bnh,* "And Omri took possession of all the land of Mahdeba, and he dwelt in it during his days and half the days of his sons." A war has preceded. The object of the verb is a territory. It is followed by *yšb,* "dwell."

d. *Phoenician-Punic.* In contrast, the only occurrence of the root **wrṯ* in Phoenician-Punic, *mqny htršm bmypʿl 'dn*[25] or *mqny htrš mbmypʿl 'dn,*[26] appears to belong to the realm of inheritance. Conversely, the only Phoenician-Punic occurrence of *nḥl*[27] clearly

---

16 First identified by Zimmern, 17.

17 The comparative material is dealt with in detail by Bird, 32-202.

18 Sefire I (*KAI,* 222) C 24.

19 For a detailed discussion, see Bird, 72-77.

20 *KTU,* 1.14, 25; possibly also as a personal name in *KTU,* 4.154, 6; 4.188, 15 and in the Akkadian cuneiform text RS 8.213 in the form *ia-ri-šu-nu.*

21 *KTU,* 1.2 I, 19.

22 *KTU,* 1.3 III, 47.

23 *KTU,* 4.63 I, 13; cf. *PNU,* 160.

24 *KAI,* 181.7.

25 J.-G. Février, "Vir Sidonius," *Sem,* 4 (1951/52), 15.

26 *DISO,* 335f.

27 W. F. Albright, "The Phoenician Inscriptions of the Tenth Century B.C. from Byblus," *JAOS,* 67 (1947), 158.

requires the meaning "take possession of (something)."[28] Because the evidence is slight and obscure, conclusions should be drawn from it only with caution.

8. *Etymology.* The question of the original root meaning of **wrṯ* must remain unanswered. The early evidence, in both Hebrew and the other languages, shows a wide range of meanings hard to reduce to a common denominator, as well as semantic confusion with other roots deriving from the biliteral **rṯ*. It is impossible to reconstruct a genetic schema tracing the root's semantic development, in part because we must also allow for secondary influence of the various languages on each other. The influence of Aramaic, for example, is obvious in the late Hebrew usage of *yrš.* In Aramaic and the South Semitic languages, the apparent clarity of the evidence, which dates from a later period than in the other languages, is more likely due to secondary semantic specialization. That such specialization would lead by accidents of historical linguistics back to the original situation is not out of the question, but it cannot be proved.

The early theory, recently revived, posited an "original" root meaning "inherit." The most recent advocate of this theory is Schmid:[29] ". . . not only because the OT evidence for this meaning, although slight, involves the earliest texts, but also because it most easily explains usage elsewhere in the OT and the evidence of the other Semitic languages." Both reasons are probably wrong.

Also clearly wrong is the theory popular in recent decades that *yrš* was originally a term for the "acquisition of foreign territory through war,"[30] being in fact a "technical military term"[31] or "an expression belonging to the language of war with an inherent element of violence."[32] The association of the root with war and battle can be traced back to Ugaritic mythology, but even at Ugarit this is not the only context in which the root occurs. Furthermore, what is at stake in these instances is not land but gold; neither is it demonstrable that the use of force or violence is an inherent element in the meaning of the word itself. In Hebrew, when wars of conquest are described, the technical military terms come first; the qal of *yrš* is therefore more likely to refer only to juridical seizure of enemy territory after battle. It is equally arbitrary to claim either "capture" or "inherit" as the "original" meaning.

Other etymologies are based on the words *rešeṯ* or *tîrôš,* taken to be nouns derived from this root. Gesenius thinks in terms of an original meaning "seize upon."[33] The word *rešeṯ,* "net," is so called "because it seizes."[34] Koehler,[35] following Haupt[36] and citing

---

28 For a discussion of the problem, see *DISO,* 176.

29 P. 780.

30 Mettinger, 8.

31 Plöger, 83.

32 Bächli, 159.

33 F. H. W. Gesenius, *Thesaurus philologicus criticus linguae hebraeae et chaldaeae Veteris Testamenti,* II (Leipzig, 1853), 632.

34 *Ibid.,* 633.

35 *KBL*^{3}, 219f.

36 Pp. 215, 223.

tîrôš, "new wine," proposes "tread, vinify" as the basic meaning. A conjectural *wᵉtîraš* in Mic. 6:15 provides him with an instance of this meaning. According to Snijders,[37] the meaning "tread down, trample" is even found in the MT, namely in Dt. 28:42; Isa. 63:18 (probably not true). According to Haupt, one arrives at the other meanings of *yrš* via the intermediate senses "oppress" and "deprive of"; according to Snijders, the intermediate link is "set foot upon," which was a symbolic way of claiming possession of a piece of land. Apart from any other arguments, however, it is dubious whether *rešeṯ* and *tîrôš* derive from **wrṯ* at all. The noun *rešeṯ,* "net," has a Ugaritic parallel in *rṯt,* which can be derived more straightforwardly from the root *rṯy,* also found in Ugaritic (cf. Akk. *rašu*). In the case of *tîrôš,* there is evidence for a non-Semitic origin and for association with a divine name.[38]

There is some evidence for "tread (upon)" even apart from any theory about *tîrôš.* In cases where the qal of *yrš* in Hebrew means "take possession of," several passages suggest that there was a concrete action performed to take possession of newly acquired property, consisting in walking through or around it; this might be the origin of the sandal handed symbolically to the new owner. The question whether such a juridically relevant "entrance" might constitute the beginning of the semantic development of *yrš* is considered by Horst,[39] Snijders,[40] and Schwertner.[41] The Hebrew word → כבשׁ *kbš,* comparable in certain respects to *yrš,* seems in fact to have had some such basic meaning. In the case of *yrš,* however, it may be objected that here again an isolated phenomenon, itself not clearly demonstrable and attested only in relatively late passages (the earliest being the story of Naboth), is used to explain a highly complex situation evident much earlier. How does this theory, for example, explain the appearance of gold rather than a piece of land as the object of the verb in Ugaritic? How does it explain the early Hebrew texts with personal objects? It is equally possible that a meaning "take formal possession of real property acquired by virtue of certain rights," arising at some point in the course of the root's semantic development, became associated secondarily with the usually concurrent act of entering or walking through. In this case, the Deuteronomistic authors could equally well have been alluding to this act in their use of *yrš.*

Tur-Sinai,[42] with *tîrôš* in mind, proposes in addition to *yrš* I, "inherit," an independent root *yrš* II, "press (out)," which he then associates with the verb in passages that have the meaning "drive out" (which he assumes). This appears to be an ad hoc hypothesis based on Job 20:15.

II. Theological Usage.

1. *Secular Background.* The qal of *yrš* invariably has a human subject. The only

37 P. 267.
38 For details of this discussion, see Bird, 33-39 (*tîrôš*), 64-66 (*rešeṯ*).
39 *GSAT,* 210.
40 P. 268.
41 Pp. 171-77.
42 P. 314.

exception is Jer. 49:1, where the focus is only Milcom, albeit not as the real subject of the action. The qal is primarily a juridical term denoting secular procedures. Israel clearly did not want to involve Yahweh, its God, directly as the agent in such procedures. Therefore the qal of *yrš* remained in a sense a nontheological term. This holds true also for the derived nouns, although comparable words like *naḥ*ᵃ*lâ* could easily be used in speaking of Yahweh's *naḥ*ᵃ*lâ*. Only on the very fringes of the OT, in 2 Ch. 20:11, does the text speak of Yahweh's *y*ᵉ*ruššâ,* which Yahweh then bequeathed to the Israelites.

The situation is different for the hiphil. Here Yahweh is often the subject, even in the earliest texts. The causative function of the hiphil, originally seemingly more closely related to *rwš* than to *yrš,* obviously lent itself much more easily to theological usage.

Now this does not mean that the qal never found its way into theological contexts. In fact, it even became a key word in such contexts. But the semantic structures are more complex, and God does not appear as the grammatical subject of the action denoted by the qal.

When we discuss the theological usage of the qal, we must never lose sight of its basic secular nature. It is used for succession to family leadership (Gen. 15:3f.; 21:10; 2 S. 14:7; Prov. 30:23), receiving gifts (Jgs. 14:15), taking possession of a field on the basis of dubious legal title (1 K. 21), resettlement of a territory by royal decree (2 K. 17:24), but above all acquisition of sovereignty and territory by right of context (in the original context of Nu. 13:30; 21:24; Josh. 19:47; Jgs. 3:13). All these passages speak of human action without any reference to God. Blessings that wish for conquest of cities (Gen. 24:60) or regions (Dt. 33:23) are likewise not theological statements. The hope of those returning from exile to spread abroad in the the land, as expressed in Ezk. 33:23ff., even though it makes reference to the patriarch Abraham, is a defiant response to fate that reflects trust in the people's own resources.

Even the hiphil, in its primary meanings of "make poor" and "destroy," can easily refer to human actions (Ex. 15:9; Nu. 21:32; 32:39; pre-Deuteronomistic texts describing successful or unsuccessful destruction of the enemy in Joshua and Jgs. 1).

In the late period, when both qal and hiphil begin to have specialized reference to the process of inheritance within the family, the possibilities of secular usage expanded, even though the word had taken on theological overtones in the meantime. In particular, the root now entered the vocabulary of legislation (Lev. 25:46; Nu. 27:11; 36:8; Ezr. 9:12).

The niphal of *yrš* seems never to have been theologically productive; its context remained the realm of wisdom discourse.

2. *Ethical Judgment.* Succession within a family, as when a son succeeds his father, is a good and normal process. But even in this context there are extreme possibilities that make the earth tremble because they would be unendurable: when a maid, for example, succeeds her mistress (Prov. 30:23). Even more easily, taking possession of newly acquired property can lead to injustice, such as provokes Yahweh's reaction in 1 K. 21. Here the injustice consists in disregard for the ancient Israelite system of *naḥ*ᵃ*lâ* (cf. vv. 3f.) as well as the criminal course embarked on (cf. v. 19). The former is expressed indirectly, the latter by direct statement. Above all, Yahweh reacts when groups or nations deprive others unjustly of their territory, in particular when the land of Israel falls into

the wrong hands (Jgs. 3:13; Ps. 83:13[12]; Isa. 14:21; Ezk. 11:15; 33:24-26; 35:10; 36:1-15). Jgs. 11:15-17 contains an argument over the justice or injustice of acquiring territory. According to the principle of talion, Yahweh can use *yrš* to avenge unjust *yrš*: Jer. 49:1 (cf. also the etymological play on words in Mic. 1:15). In Ps. 83:13(12), the psalmist hopes for Yahweh's help because the enemies who covet Israel's land seek to take possession of "the pastures of God"—and that cannot be right. Military conquest of territory is not necessarily unjust in itself, at least in the early period. Deuteronomistic theology, however, seems to be less sure of this; for it feels called upon to legitimate absolutely Israel's taking possession of Canaan.[43] To summarize: depending on the context, *yrš* can be used for actions that are ethically unobjectionable or ethically reprehensible. The relationship between *yrš* and God's intervention in history can therefore vary from case to case.

3. *yrš in Statements of Omnipotence and Oracles of Judgment.* Yahweh is responsible not for specific aspects of reality but for everything. He creates both rich and poor (Prov. 22:9; cf. 29:13). This point can be expressed by applying antithetical predications to Yahweh (cf. Dt. 32:39; Job 5:9-18; Ps. 75:8[7]; 147:6; Isa. 45:7; Hos. 6:1). In the most extensive passage of this sort, 1 S. 2:6-10, the hiphil of *yrš* appears: "Yahweh makes poor and makes rich" (v. 7). The preceding verse states that he kills and brings to life—a frequent Yahweh antithesis. It shows how absolutely the statement that Yahweh makes poor and makes rich can be interpreted. The context refers to Yahweh as a judge (v. 10; cf. Ps. 75:8[7]). This parallels exactly the use of the hiphil in Nu. 14:12 (Yahweh will "strike this nation with pestilence and destroy them" and then will make Moses into a nation); Zec. 9:4;[44] Job 20:15.[45] This fundamentally theological context probably lies behind many occurrences of the qal in prophetic oracles of disaster: Jer. 8:10; 49:1f.; Ezk. 7:24; Am. 9:12; Mic. 1:15; Hab. 1:6; and also (with *môrāšâ*) Ezk. 25:4,10. This is especially clear in passages where it is not other people but weeds or wild beasts that will take over possession from those God has made poor: Isa. 34:11,17; Hos. 9:6; Isa. 14:23 (with *môrāš*); Dt. 28:42 (piel). This background also legitimates the specialized Deuteronomistic use of the hiphil. Job 13:26 associates this motif with that of writing in the heavenly book of fate.

4. *Absence of the Qal in the Pre-Deuteronomistic Theology of the Promised Land in the Pentateuch.* In the early sources of the Pentateuch and even in their early Deuteronomic recension, *yrš* plays only a peripheral theological role. In Gen. 21 (and 15), the qal finds its way into the narrative material associated with the promise of descendants. It is not a crucial key word, however: it refers to the nation as a group and not to the successor of individual leaders (Gen. 21:10; 15:3f.). The incorporation of the blessing from Gen. 24:60 into the promise of the land in 22:17 is probably a post-Deuteronomistic interpretative addition, for 22:16 speaks of Abraham's obedience as its already fulfilled condition.

---

43 See II.6.a below.
44 Cf. I.5.a above.
45 *Ibid.*

Therefore the Deuteronomistic theology of the promised land did not employ the expression "take possession of the enemies' gate." If Gen. 15:7-21 is in fact early, v. 7 contains the first (and, among early texts, the only) use of *yrš* to expand the earlier promise of the land (still cited faithfully in v. 18); as was to become typical later, it appears in conjunction with *ntn.* But the date of this text is disputed. If it is late, there is no occurrence at all of *yrš* as a key word in the promise of the land until the early Deuteronomistic recension of the JE complex. At most, it appears quite peripherally in Nu. 14:24 (J), a promise of land to Caleb. The Yahwistic story of the spies in Nu. 13f. draws on a tradition explaining why Caleb conquered Hebron. The secular nature of this narrative is shown by Caleb's reason for taking taking possession of the region (13:30): *kî-yāḵôl nûḵal lāh,* "for we are well able to overcome it." In the original form of the story, it is possible that Caleb then set out immediately to take it. J's interest, however, focuses on explaining why Israel had to stay in the desert and finally invade the land from the east. Caleb cannot be excluded from this route. He there receives an oracle promising that he will enter the territory of Hebron and his sons will possess it (14:24). If we assume that the stage of pentateuchal theology immediately preceding the early Deuteronomic recension of JE was the Deuteronomic editing of the pre-Deuteronomistic law, we must conclude that it appears impossible to assign even one of the occurrences of the qal or hiphil of *yrš* in the book of Deuteronomy to this stage with assurance. How elegantly the text could speak of the occupation without using *yrš* is illustrated by the "small historical credo" in Dt. 26:9. In contrast, later credal formulas under Deuteronomistic influence could no longer do without *yrš*: cf. Ps. 44:3f.(2f.); 105:44; Jer. 32:23; Am. 2:10. It is clear, therefore, that *yrš* did not really enter into pentateuchal theology until the Deuteronomistic stage.[46] In the earlier language of Deuteronomy, the word *ntn* clearly sufficed to recall the promise of the land to the fathers. Of the 21 passages in Deuteronomy citing God's oath to give the land to the fathers, only 7 contain the word *yrš.*[47]

If the Balaam poems are interpreted as oracles, then Nu. 24:18 should be included in the context of the promise of the land in early sources: formulated with *yᵉrēšâ,* it would be a promise of the conquest of Seir, presumably with David in mind. Deuteronomistic theology did not draw on this passage.

5. *Theological Usage of the Hiphil in Early Strata of Joshua and Judges.* Josh. 13–17 cites sporadically and Jgs. 1 preserves in a single complex the tradition concerning the peoples the individual tribes could not destroy (*yrš* hiphil) during the occupation, which Israel did not destroy later, when it was powerful, but only put to forced labor. This tradition records more than secular history, since it appears to presuppose a divine prohibition against making a treaty with the inhabitants of the land and a promise to

---

46 For a further discussion of the hand at work in Gen. 22:17, see Kilian, 318ff.; for the argument that the text of J in Nu. 14 is probably J's own composition rather than a revision of an earlier version, see Fritz, 83f.

47 On the absence of *yrš* in the pre-Deuteronomistic stages of the Deuteronomic lawbook, see Lohfink, *Festschrift H. W. Wolff,* 87-100.

drive them out.[48] If Halbe[49] is correct in assuming that Jgs. 1 existed in conjunction with Jgs. 2:1-5 long before its incorporation (at a very late date) in the Deuteronomistic history, then this theological background was also made explicit there by the use of the verb *grš* and by repeated references to Yahweh's ancient legal privileges reflected in Ex. 34:10-26. The ancient promise to drive out the inhabitants of the land and the prohibition against making a treaty with them meant that it was not a matter of indifference to Israel's life in the land given by its God whether Israel had destroyed the previous inhabitants or they continued to live on inside Israel (within the territorially organized Davidic state and its successor institutions): this life could be totally corrupted by their presence (Jgs. 2:3).

In a late pre-Deuteronomistic or early Deuteronomistic stage in the redaction of the sources of Joshua and Judges, the hiphil of *yrš* + *mippᵉnê N,* with God as the subject, came to replace *grš* in the promise to drive the inhabitants out: Josh. 3:10; Jgs. 11:21-24.[50] In accordance with the Deuteronomistic systematization of the narrative, the idea of "destruction"[51] replaced that of "ejection." The hiphil of *yrš* joins the other Deuteronomistic words for "destroy" with Yahweh as subject. In a single passage, Jgs. 11:21-24 uses the qal with the conquered territory as its object, the hiphil with the destroyed nation as its object, and the qal with the "successor" nation as its object, deliberately relating all three. The fact that the territory of nation A has been taken possession of by nation B (qal) is legitimated by the destruction of nation A by the god of nation B (hiphil), so that nation B can be the legal successor of nation A (qal). We cannot say here that the possession of territories by right of conquest was suddenly felt to be dubious, so that new reasons had to be found to legitimate such possession. What we are dealing with is merely an explicit theological statement of what the qal of *yrš* already implied in the early conquest accounts. A different approach to legitimation, stemming from a different source, is found in Dt. 1–Josh. 22.

6. *Deuteronomistic Theology.*

a. *Qal of yrš and yᵉruššâ in the Narrative Framework of Dt. 1–Josh. 22.* The qal of *yrš* with the conquered land as its object became a key theological concept in a Deuteronomistic narrative structure, probably dating from the period of expansion under Josiah, that can be observed from Dt. 1 through Josh. 22.[52] The theme of the texts is Israel's occupation of Palestine. They were composed as part of the narrative framework of the Deuteronomic law or added to it secondarily.

The opening chapter of Deuteronomy retells the JE account of Nu. 13f. The promise to Caleb's descendants in Nu. 14:24, which uses *yrš,* is formulated with *ntn* in Dt. 1:36. The verb *yrš,* however, is used in 1:39, which speaks not of a subgroup but of all the

---

48 Schmitt, 46-80.

49 Pp. 385-89.

50 On the various strata, see I.5.b above.

51 → חרם *ḥāram* III.3.

52 For the literary criticism of this block, see Lohfink, *Festschrift H. W. Wolff,* 87-100; on other structures in these texts, see also his *Bibl,* 41 (1960), 105-134, and *Scholastik,* 37 (1962), 32-34.

Israelites of the coming generation. Here it is clear that a term referring to the occupation of the land by all Israel has developed out of the isolated, particularistic tradition of the *yrš* promise found in the early sources. The verb *yrš* is well suited to this purpose, because the purpose of Dt. 1–Josh. 22 is to picture the occupation as the result of military conquests, and *yrš* belonged to the vocabulary of secular conquest accounts. The concept was theologized not only by use in an oracle addressed to Moses borrowed from JE but also through association with the oath by which Yahweh promised the land to the patriarchs: in the divine command to set out from Horeb (Dt. 1:8) and (implicitly: "Yahweh, the God of your fathers") in Moses' repetition of this command at Kadesh-barnea (1:21). Because of Israel's unbelief, Yahweh withdrew his support from the generation of the exodus (1:35); thus *yrš* in 1:39 became the key term for the successful occupation of the land by the following generation, under Moses east of the Jordan in Dt. 2:24,31; 3:12 and under Joshua west of the Jordan in Josh. 1:11 (twice); (18:3?); 21:43. In addition, *yrš* is used specifically when the text speaks of the tribes east of the Jordan joining the tribes west of the Jordan in their campaign of conquest: Dt. 3:18,20; Josh. 1:15a; also Josh. 12:1, at the beginning of the list of conquered kings.

The noun *y^eruššâ* also occurs in both these contexts in Dt. 3:20 and Josh. 12:6,7; it probably also appeared originally in Josh. 1:15b. In these cases, however, it refers not to the land as a whole but rather to the territory possessed by subgroups in Israel, allotted to them by Moses (and Joshua). For Joshua, this stratum elsewhere uses the hiphil of *nḥl* or the piel of *ḥlq* + *b^enaḥ^alâ* in this context: Dt. 1:38; 3:28; 31:7; Josh. 1:6; 13:7.[53] There is thus a terminological distinction between the assignment of territory by Joshua and the assignment of territory by Moses; the term used for Joshua probably derives from the source material utilized in Josh. 13–19, whereas the term used for Moses is based on the use of *yrš* for Yahweh's gift of the entire land to Israel. The noun *y^eruššâ* itself is also used on the national level and with theological intent in Dt. 2:5,9(twice),19(twice); secondarily also in 2:12. Yahweh gave not only Israel but also the neighbors related to Israel through the patriarchs their land as *y^eruššâ*; the basis of this tradition might be the use of *nḥl* in Dt. 32:8. This usage of *y^eruššâ* did not become part of the later stereotyped Deuteronomistic language. In those contexts, *naḥ^alâ* clearly took on its former function, or else the formulation drew on the language suggested by Jgs. 11:23f., as already in the secondary passage Dt. 2:20-22. If *y^eruššâ* could take the place of *naḥ^alâ* for a moment in this stratum, it was clearly not to describe Israel's land as a heritage to be handed down from one generation to another but to characterize it as a territory taken possession of both legitimately and by force.

The association of *yrš* with the promise of the land to the patriarchs in Dt. 1:8 is repeated in 10:11 at the end of the story concerning the breaking and renewal of the covenant at Horeb—in other words, upon reaching the point in the narrative where 1:6-8 had begun. It returns in Josh. 21:43f., framing the entire textual complex. In the passages relating to Joshua in Dt. 31:7; Josh. 1:6, the oath to the patriarchs is associated with *nḥl*.

Theologically, the crucial point in this stratum is the association of Israel's *yrš* with

---

53 See Lohfink, *Scholastik,* 37 (1962), 32-34.

Yahweh's *ntn.* If Gen. 15:7 does not furnish the basis for the tradition, this association is the creative accomplishment of this stratum. The simplest form of the association is narrative juxtaposition: Yahweh gives the land, Israel takes possession of the land (Dt. 1:39; 3:20; Josh. 1:15a; 21:43). Yahweh's gift can be qualified more extensively as a gift sworn to the fathers (Dt. 1:8; 10:11; Josh. 21:43) or a gift in prospect of Israel's taking possession (Josh. 1:11). "Giving" alone can also be used elliptically for Israel's taking possession of the land (Dt. 1:8). This reflects the formulation of the gift as *y^eruššâ* (Dt. 2:5,9[twice],19[twice]).

What do these passages mean by saying that Yahweh "gives" something? In JE, the promise to the fathers may have been based on the model of a donation; here, however,[54] we can see another model at work. If Yahweh, the one God, "gives" various neighboring nations their territories, the "gift" must be interpreted after the analogy of royal allotment of land. This may be conceived as reflecting a feudal privilege, much like enfeoffment (cf. 1 S. 8:14; 22:7; 27:6); or else it presupposes a system in which the entire land is considered the king's property. In this case, a real estate transaction (although in fact representing a purchase agreement, say, between two private parties) must be construed juridically as (appropriation and) a new "gift" on the part of the king. There is cuneiform evidence for such a system, above all in Ugarit. Our texts do not make clear which of the two possible analogies is intended. Possibly the matter was left deliberately vague so as to accommodate both early feudal notions of the relationship between Yahweh and Israel and parallels to notions of ancient Near Eastern property law that had taken hold in Judah. In any case, we have here alongside the "historical" and "cultic" conceptions of the land (identified by von Rad) a third conception, based on the laws of kingship. With respect to their earthly territory, Yahweh's relationship to the nations of the world is that of a king to his subjects with respect to productive land. Yahweh, as king, is lord of every territory. Transfer of title becomes legally valid only through his juridical act, termed "giving." In the case of Israel, he has pledged himself in advance to perform this act. Within this legal structure, Israel's action denoted by the qal of *yrš* is to be understood on the basis of the distinction—clearly laid out, for example, in Babylonian law—between conveying possession and taking possession: it refers to the taking possession of the "given" territory by its new national proprietor once title has been conveyed by Yahweh as king. The verb *yrš* does not carry this precise sense solely by virtue of its inherent meaning but only in the context of the total system. The word itself, however, makes it absolutely clear that the actual case involves a very specific manner of taking possession: through conquest. This meaning is conveyed by *yrš* because it has a fixed role in standard accounts of conquest. In summary, then, the use of *yrš* in this group of texts set Israel's occupation of the land, clearly described in terms of military conquest, in a comprehensive scheme of theological and juridical legitimation.

In the situation obtaining when Dt. 1–Josh. 22 was composed, the ancient theory of possession by right of conquest seems no longer to have sufficed, even when undergirded

---

54 Contra Lohfink, *Bibl,* 41 (1960), 124-27.

theologically by arguments like Jgs. 11:21-24. The new texts may reflect Josiah's efforts to recover Israel's ancient territory. The right of conquest was on Assyria's side. Assyria could take Jephthah's arguments against the king of the Ammonites and turn them against Josiah. What Josiah took from a temporarily weak Assyria could be taken from him, should Assyria become stronger, with the same argument of arms and the national god at work behind those arms. Using the new conception found in these texts, Josiah's propaganda of national restoration could at least hold before the Israelite population a comprehensive juridical structure within which the use of military force represented merely the taking possession (for the first time or once again) of a territory already belonging to Israel as a matter of record by virtue of a royal/divine conveyance. At the same time, this juridical structure meant that the neighbors to the immediate east had nothing to fear from this resurgent Israel.

Ancient Near Eastern parallels documenting the royal "gift" of land will be found in Schwertner.[55] In Nu. 27:8-11, where both *ntn* and the hiphil of *ʿbr* are used, the "people" of Israel exercises this royal prerogative in "democratic" form.

b. *yrš in Cliches.* The Deuteronomic law incorporated in Dt. 1–Josh. 22 and the various strata and recensions of the entire Deuteronomistic history build on these texts, using the qal and hiphil of *yrš* (with the land or the peoples inhabiting it as object) as a cliche in the stereotyped Deuteronomistic vocabulary. This language continues to influence Jeremiah and extensive portions of the whole of postexilic literature.

Within the compass of the Deuteronomic law, *yrš* often simply reactivates the narrative situation in the mind of the hearer (the qal in combination with *bwʾ* or *ʿbr,* particularly in the parenetic framework; also, in later strata, the hiphil and qal with peoples as objects) or to recall the theologico-juridical basis for possession of the land (the qal with *ntn,* esp. in the actual laws; the hiphil along with the qal, recalling the theology of Jgs. 11:21-24, in Dt. 9:1-6; 11:23; 18:12,14; Josh. 23:5). Often a word for "land" or "peoples" is simply expanded ornamentally by means of a phrase containing *yrš.* But the stereotyped use of *yrš* appears above all in a few typical contexts, which we shall now discuss.[56]

c. *yrš in Statements of the Law's Authority.* Introductory and concluding sections of the Deuteronomic law contain clauses defining the extent of its authority. They belong to various strata but agree in substance: the law is in force in the land that Israel takes possession of (*yrš*) and as long as Israel dwells there: Dt. 4:5 (cf. v. 14); 5:31; 6:1; 12:1 (cf. 11:31f.: when the law first takes effect); 31:13. It is not impossible that at least in exilic strata these clauses conceal a debate over whether and to what extent the law was binding on those who had been deported to other lands.

Besides the question of the authority of the law as a whole, there is that of its particular statutes. There are laws that become critical only at a certain point in history

---

55 Pp. 165-69.

56 On the phrases and syntactic patterns with *yrš* in Deuteronomistic language and their rules, see Lohfink, *Das Hauptgebot,* 81-85; Plöger, 61-87; Weinfeld, *Deuteronomy and the Deuteronomic School,* 341-43.

or prescribe behavior on a single occasion. This is usually made clear by "historicizing introductions," which are fond of citing the occupation of the land and the destruction or replacement of the previous inhabitants as the historical starting point. In many cases, these texts are not real "laws" but proleptic sections of the historical work: corresponding texts later in the work record whether or not the requirements were carried out. Here *yrš* helps establish the theologico-historical perspective. These introductions were already present in the early Deuteronomic recension of JE used by the Deuteronomistic writers; they can refer both to the land itself (Ex. 13:5,11) and to its inhabitants (Ex. 23:31b; cf. v. 23). They do not, however, use either the qal or hiphil of *yrš* (cf. still Dt. 6:10 and 8:7, which depends on it; also 27:2,4). Only in Deuteronomistic strata do stereotyped cliches with *yrš* begin to appear in these contexts. The hiphil replaces *grš* from Ex. 23:31 on, as in Dt. 7:1, repeated in v. 17, which prescribes the treatment of the inhabitants during and after the occupation (in a revision of Ex. 23:20-33 with additions and commentary). There follow Dt. 11:29 (blessing and curse to be pronounced immediately after the conquest; cf. Dt. 27; Josh. 8:30-35); Dt. 12:29 (rejection of the cultic practices of the inhabitants; cf. the associated laws in vv. 2f., likewise with *yrš* but lacking a formal historicizing introduction, and the use of the hiphil in 1 K. 14:24; 21:26; 2 K. 16:3; 17:8; 21:2, all from an exilic recension of the Deuteronomistic history, which describe failure to obey the laws of Dt. 12, the real cause of the exile in the eyes of this stratum as a whole); Dt. 17:14 (appointment of a king; cf. 1 S. 8–12); Dt. 18:12,14 (secondary amplifications of the historicizing introduction in v. 9a: rejection of child sacrifice [2 K. 16:3; 17:17; 21:6; 23:10] and pagan divination [2 K. 17:17; 21:6], hearkening to the prophets of Yahweh [2 K. 17:13f.]—all in the exilic stratum of the Deuteronomistic history discussed in the context of Dt. 12:9); Dt. 19:1f. (establishment of cities of refuge; cf. Josh. 20); Dt. 25:19 (destruction of the Amalekites; cf. 1 S. 15). Only Dt. 26:1 introduces a law that—at least as it is usually understood—is not intended to be fulfilled at a particular moment in history but every year once Israel is dwelling in the land: the law of firstfruits.[57]

The historicizing introductions belong to several strata. There seems to be an important association between Dt. 12:2f.,29-31; 18:9-22 and the recension of the books of Kings discussed above in the context of Dt. 12:29, the goal of which—as stated by von Rad—was obviously to explain the exile by means of the Deuteronomistic history in a "great doxology of judgment."[58] The passages from Kings use the hiphil of *yrš* with Yahweh as subject. Probably with the final recension of the laws pertaining to office Dt. 17:14 should also be assigned to this stratum.[59] It is likely that the passages in Deuteronomy were consciously formulated from the perspective of this recension of Kings and thus clearly embody the kerygma of this early exilic recension of the Deuteronomistic history. Dt. 26:2 requires the presentation of firstfruits at the place chosen by Yahweh, probably a central sanctuary. Dt. 12:10, in an historicizing introduc-

---

[57] For a general discussion of the form of the historicizing introductions, see Lohfink, *Das Hauptgebot,* 113f.; Seitz, 95-101.

[58] For further discussion, see Lohfink, *Festschrift H. W. Wolff,* 87-100.

[59] Cf. Lohfink, *Festschrift W. Kempf* (1971).

tion without *yrš,* makes this requirement take effect in the period of David and Solomon; of course they are not mentioned by name, but the implication is clear. Dt. 26:1 avoids this chronology, saying only that the law takes effect when the Israelites are "living in the land." The ambiguity is clearly unresolved, unless the adjacent introductions in Dt. 25:19; 26:1, which are strongly parallel in structure, are meant to be mutually explanatory in a kind of parallelism. If so, Dt. 25:19 points to the time when Yahweh has given Israel rest from all its enemies round about, which can be understood as an allusion to the period of the first kings (cf. 2 S. 7:1,11; Josh. 23:1 probably derives from a later hand). Ex. 34:24a, a secondary addition,[60] also belongs with these texts.

d. *yrš in Statements Relating the Occupation to Observance of the Law.* Deuteronomy promises blessing in return for observance of the law. It is usually assumed that both this observance and the blessing have their locus in Israel's land. This setting can be made explicit in passages that frequently describe the land as being taken into possession through conquest: Dt. 5:33; 15:4; 23:21(20); 30:16; 32:47. Thus *yrš* helps define the nature of the blessing. In Dt. 5:33; 32:47, the blessing is identified with long life in the land. This feature of the blessing parallels the curse pronounced in Dt. 4:26; 28:61,63; 30:18: if the law is not obeyed, the people will be driven out of the land they once possessed. In either case, the sequence is: *yrš*—(non)observance of the law—blessing or curse.

We are dealing with a totally different structure when entrance into and possession of the land themselves become part of the blessing and are therefore dependent on prior observance of the law. This approach is in fact a *reductio ad absurdum* of the historical fiction that sets the proclamation of the law immediately prior to—or actually in the midst of—the events of the conquest. This structure nevertheless appears, making use of *yrš,* in Dt. 6:17-19; 8:1; 11:8,22-25; and possibly also 16:20. If the Israelites intermarry with the peoples that have not yet been destroyed, Josh. 23:12f. threatens that Yahweh will not destroy them; Jgs. 2:20–3:6 records God's final decision and its fulfillment. All these texts except Dt. 8:1; 16:20 probably belong to the Deuteronomistic recension of Joshua and Judges identified by Smend as DtrN. In this stratum, *yrš* appears also in Josh. 13:1,6; 23:5(twice),9; Jgs. 2:6.[61] Although it does not use *yrš,* Josh. 1:7f. is a similar passage belonging to this stratum. Contrary to the expressed views of recent scholars, this stratum does not appear to extend beyond Judges. It is "nomistic" in the strict Pauline sense, since Yahweh's blessing and salvation are made dependent on prior fidelity to the law. This theology does not appear in the books of Kings; it would be out of place there, if the blessing involves occupation of the land. Its most likely setting would be the situation toward the end of the exile. In this period, a redactor might well have worked renewed fidelity to the law and consequent repossession of the land into the situation of Israel in Moab. Such a setting would in fact mitigate the "nomistic" harshness of the kerygma by turning it into parenesis.[62]

---

60 Halbe, 161-170.

61 See also Lohfink, *Festschrift H. W. Wolff,* 87-100.

62 For a different interpretation of all these texts, see the studies by Weinfeld.

The occurrences of *yrš* in Dt. 8:1; 9:1-6 probably belong to an even later stratum of Deuteronomistic editing, which exhibits a critical stance toward the central thesis of DtrN. Dt. 8:1 first states the thesis (using *yrš*) in a parenesis that clearly accepts it. The "argument" in 8:2-6, under the guise of describing Israel's life in the desert, speaks cryptically of the exile and the process of learning and growth possible in that setting, even emphasizing the necessity of obedience to the law. But there follows a warning, a critical distancing in the form of a commentary that imitates 6:10-16: because formerly so much depended on the obedience to the law, when Israel is brought once more into the land by Yahweh and has grown rich, it must not ascribe its success to its own achievements and forget that, despite Israel's prior obedience to the law, it was Yahweh alone who vouchsafed the blessing. A second stage even questions the causal relationship between Israel's return and its prior observance of the law, its "righteousness" (9:4,5,6). There is in fact no such righteousness, since Israel has "provoked" Yahweh fundamentally and repeatedly (9:7,23,24). This, too, is worked back into the desert period and Israel's situation in Moab by Dt. 9:1-8, placed as an interpretative key immediately before the account of Israel's breach of the covenant at Horeb, which probably belongs to the earliest stratum of the Deuteronomistic history. In 9:22-24, the same hand has inserted in this account still other demonstrations of Israel's rebelliousness. Dt. 9:1-8 alludes to 6:17-19 (DtrN) (9:4: *hdp* [cf. 6:19]; 9:5: *yōšer* [cf. 6:18]) and uses *yrš* as a key word in both qal and hiphil (9:1,3,4[twice],5[twice],6). Thus the theme of the destruction of the Canaanites and the possession of the land promised to the fathers (9:5) serves to develop the clearest OT anticipation of the Pauline theology of God's "righteousness," beside which there can be no human "righteousness" (*ṣᵉḏāqâ*[63]).

The stage to which Dt. 4:1-40; 30:1-10 belong may represent the latest redactional stratum, although still dating from the end of the exile. It rejects DtrN's nomism not so much on theological grounds as from the perspective of the actual return from exile. In 4:1, Moses does not simply promise that the Israelites will enter the land and take possession of it, as in the earlier Deuteronomistic strata, but imposes a prior condition: not obedience to the law, as in DtrN, but merely hearing and giving heed to God's will. This is analogous to 4:30, which presents the exiles with the possibility of returning and hearkening to his voice. Then Yahweh will not forget his covenant with the fathers. Nothing more is said in Dt. 4, but 30:1-10 develops the theme. There the stituation of the exile is addressed from the beginning. Both the blessing and the curse of the law have been experienced. Israel is in exile, but can return and hearken to Yahweh's voice *kᵉḵōl ʾᵃšer-ʾānōḵî mᵉṣawwᵉḵā hayyôm* (30:2). The vagueness of the formulation is probably deliberate, since according to Deuteronomy the law is not binding outside the land. Yahweh will then assemble Israel from among all the nations and bring it back to the land that the generation of Moses and Joshua took possession of (*yrš*); they will once more take possession of it (*yrš*), and their prosperity will be greater than before (v. 5). Here, in the land they have once more taken possession of, Yahweh will circumcise their hearts, so that love of God will be possible in a new way. After this transformation, Israel

63 → צדק *ṣdq*.

will be able to observe the entire law (v. 8, further explicated in v. 10). Then the land will be fruitful (the ancient substance of the blessing). Here we have a theology similar to that in the promises of salvation found in the redactional sections of Jeremiah and Ezekiel: assembly and restoration, followed by a new heart, a new covenant, or the like, and consequently by a new possibility of living according to Yahweh's law. A connection between this stratum of Deuteronomy and the "Deuteronomistic" prose of Jeremiah is likely. As in the original Deuteronomistic conception, possession of the land is thus the precondition for observance of the law, not the reverse. It no longer suffices, however, as a definition of Yahweh's salvific work. There must also be a change of heart, brought about solely by Yahweh. But there will be no return and no repossession of the land if the people do not first return to Yahweh and hearken to his voice.[64]

The concept of righteousness based on observance of the law derives from Dt. 6:25. The shift of the covenant idea from Horeb to the patriarchs, which is typical of this stratum (Dt. 8:18; 9:5; cf. 7:8,12), suggests contacts with the intellectual milieu of P.

7. *Jer. 30f.* The passage most closely related to Dt. 30:1-10 in the "Deuteronomistic" sections of Jeremiah is the "Deuteronomistic" framework of Jer. 30f. Yahweh's forgiveness is the basis for his postexilic salvation (chs. 31,34). The first act of God's salvation sees Yahweh bringing Israel and Judah (i.e., the descendants of both kingdoms) back to the land he had given (*ntn*) to their fathers so that they may take possession of it (*yrš*) once more (30:3). Then follows the increase of man and beast (31:27f.) and the establishment of a new covenant, which makes it possible to observe Yahweh's law in a new way from within (31:31-34a).[65]

Several translators (including Luther) have interpreted *wîrēšûhā* in Jer. 30:3 as a result clause introduced by *waw*-consecutive, with the subject *ʾᵃḇôṯām*: "I gave . . . and they took possession." The result is a common idea in Deuteronomistic cliches, but expressed more elegantly by means of an infinitive construction. This interpretation loses the point that the end of the exile is marked not only by a new covenant but also by a new occupation.

8. *Ezekiel.* In an analogous manner, Ezk. 36:12 contains a prediction (formulated by means of *yrš*) of the occupation of the land after the exile preceding a passage concerning the new heart and new spirit that make it possible to live according to the law (36:16-32). But the section of the verse containing *yrš* may belong to a later interpretation, introducing a word that Ezekiel does not commonly use in the context of return from exile.

More important is Ezekiel's use of *yrš* and *môrāšâ* in connection with the question of to whom the land, depopulated by the deportation, belongs in the eyes of Yahweh. This question is examined in three (or possibly four) stages. Each time, the expression

---

[64] For a discussion of the stratum represented in Dt. 8:1-9,22-24, see Lohfink, *Das Hauptgebot,* 189-206. On the stratum in Dt. 4:1-40; 30:1-10 and its relationships with Jeremiah, see Wolff, *ZAW,* 73 (1961), 180-83. On 4:1-40 as a single unit (contra Mittmann, etc.), see Braulik, *Bibl,* 59 (1978), 351-383; on *yrš* 4:1-40, see Braulik, *Die Mittel deuteronomischer Rhetorik,* 83f., 92-95.

[65] For a discussion of these chapters, see Böhmer.

of a claim to the land by a specific group evokes a response from the prophet. After the first deportation in 598/597, those still living in Jerusalem claim the land (Ezk. 11:15: *lānû . . . nittᵉnâ hāʾāreṣ lᵉmôrāšâ*), arguing that those who have been deported are far from Yahweh. Ezekiel disputes their argument. Yahweh is not far from the exiles. It is they to whom he promises return, a new heart, and a new spirit. Again, the promise of return (11:17f.) could be a secondary interpretation. In any case, however, the claim of those who were spared deportation to possess the entire land is rejected. After the destruction of Jerusalem in 586, those still dwelling in ruins in the land of Israel assert the same claim by appealing to the example of Abraham (33:24). For the first time in the OT, we find the statement that Abraham himself took possession of the land (the similar statement in Gen. 15:7f. being interpreted by 15:18 as referring to Abraham's descendants). They say: "Abraham was only one man, yet he took possession of (*wayyîraš*) the land; but we are many—so the land is surely given us to possess (*lānû nittᵉnâ hāʾāreṣ lᵉmôrāšâ*)" (Ezk. 33:24). The argument a fortiori perverts the statment about Abraham. Its point is that Abraham did not receive the land by virtue of his own efforts—he was only a single individual—but through Yahweh. But the argument of those dwelling in the ruins boasts of their numbers and their own efforts. The prophet's response (33:25f.) makes this perversion quite clear. It demolishes any claim to *yrš*: idolatry and bloodshed rule out any right to possess the land. Here *yrš* should probably be translated "enjoy possession of." The curses of the law await those living in the land who do not obey the law. Therefore 33:27-29 predicts that those dwelling in the ruins will perish and the land will become a desolate waste. In a further state, this desolation is then presupposed as having taken place. Now other nations—Edom (35:10,12) and the rest of the surrounding nations together with Edom (36:2,5)—claim "the mountains of Israel" as their possession. They do so "although Yahweh was there" (35:10). Yahweh therefore sees to it that Edom's land is laid waste, while the desolate mountains of Israel are to be repopulated and made fruitful by the return of Israel (35:1–36:15). As in the Deuteronomistic stratum of Dt. 1–Josh. 22, Yahweh appears here as the divine king who rules over the nations, "giving" to all of them their territory. The allotment of territories to Israel and its neighbors to the south and east described there is not abrogated. But the possibility exists for the people to be driven out and to return, for the land to be laid waste and then restored to life. All lies in the power of Yahweh, who rules as king. The prophet rejects the mythological notion of specific territories as inherently "cannibalistic" (36:13-15).[66]

9. *P^g, H, and Late Strata of the Pentateuch.* The basic stratum of P (P^g), even if it was intended to end with the death of Moses, is clearly concerned with the themes of the land and its occupation.[67] This is all the more so if it goes on to record the entrance into

---

66 On 11:17ff.; 36:12 as possible secondary interpretative material, see W. Zimmerli, *Ezekiel. Herm* (Eng. trans. 1979-1983). On 35:10, cf. also Ps. 83:13(12), where the context also inolves Edom and other neighbors.

67 Elliger and Cortese, contra M. Noth, *A History of Pentateuchal Traditions* (Eng. trans. 1972; repr. Chico, Calif., 1981).

Canaan.[68] For these themes it appears deliberately to use words drawn from various traditions: above all *ntn* from the early sources (Gen. 17:8; 28:4; 35:12; 48:4; Ex. 6:4,8; Nu. 13:2; 20:12; Dt. 32:49,52), then *'ᵃḥuzzâ* (Gen. 17:8; 48:4; Dt. 32:49) and *naḥᵃlâ* (Nu. 34:2,14,15; Josh. 14:2; cf. Nu. 34:13; Josh. 14:1; 19:51). The root *kbš,* which Josh. 18:1 uses prominently in concluding position, makes it clear that Israel's occupation of Canaan is the realization of the Creator's blessing given to all the nations of the world: *kbš* appears also in Gen. 1:28. Human well-being is thus the effective outcome of creation.[69] Within this complex and yet homogeneous system of discourse, *yrš* appears in Gen. 28:4, recalling Deuteronomistic language; and *môrāšâ* appears in Ex. 6:8,[70] recalling above all Ezk. 36, which is also in the background of Nu. 13f. (P^g) (cf. the land "devouring" its inhabitants in Nu. 13:32). Possibly this root, which at least in Deuteronomistic usage has military overtones, was deliberately avoided in the later account of the occupation because P^g seems to have eliminated all military features from its presentation of the occupation.[71]

At a crucial point in the redaction of the major parenetic framework passage Lev. 20:22–26:46[72] the Holiness Code (H) uses the verb *yrš* for taking possession of the land—referring, in agreement with the narrative fiction, to the occupation following the events at Sinai. The context clearly excludes all military overtones. Yahweh's actions, despite the attractive play on words involving *yrš* qal, are not denoted by the hiphil of *yrš* or some other word meaning "destroy," but by *šlḥ* piel + *mippᵉnê N* (Lev. 20:23; cf. 18:24 and the image of the land that vomits out its inhabitants [18:25,28; 20:22]). In Lev. 20:24, Yahweh refers to his earlier promise that he would give the Israelites the land that they might take possession of it. If this stratum of H belongs to the literary context of P^g, then there is an allusion to Gen. 28:4; otherwise, the quotation probably refers diffusely to the whole corpus of Deuteronomistic material. For the first time in the OT, the laudatory cliche of the "land flowing with milk and honey" is used in immediate conjunction with the stereotyped usage of *yrš* (the next occasion probably being Dt. 11:8-10). The concern of the entire text—reflecting totally the early postexilic situation—is that the people dwelling once more in the land may be vomited out once again if they do not consider themselves "separate"[73] and "holy"[74] in their conduct with respect to the nations. Israel received the land only because Yahweh was filled with loathing at the conduct of the people (sg.!) dwelling in the land. Here, then, we see one of Yahweh's reasons for making Israel's *yrš* possible (cf. Dt. 9:5 [*bᵉriš*ᵉ*aṯ haggôyim hā*'*ēlleh*; also Gen. 15:16); it is associated closely with the nexus combining observance of the law with possession of the land.

In contrast to P^g and H, 2 passages in the post-P recension of the Pentateuch once

68 Most recently supported by Lohfink, *SVT,* 29 (1978), 198.
69 Lohfink, in Altner, *et al., Sind wir noch zu retten?,* 27-31.
70 Weimar, 150-52.
71 Cf. Lohfink, *SVT,* 29 (1978), 199, n. 30.
72 See most recently Cholewiński, 60-63, 136.
73 → בדל *bdl.*
74 → קדשׁ *qdš.*

more emphasize the hiphil of *yrš* and the violent destruction of those dwelling in the land. Now, however, the subject of *yrš* hiphil + *mippᵉnê N* is no longer Yahweh but Israel or even the individual Israelite warrior. This is true in Nu. 32 (esp. 32:21), an expansion of the account in the early sources of the negotiations between Moses and the tribes east of the Jordan; it draws on the entire range of parallel passages. The traditional wordplay involving the qal of *yrš* (with the land as its object) does not appear, because *yrš* qal has been replaced by *kbš,* introduced from Pᵍ (Nu. 32:22,29; cf. the basic texts in Dt. 3:20; Josh. 1:15a). We see the same usage in Nu. 33:50-55, which incorporates the ancient tradition of feudal privilege from Ex. 23 and 34 but cites as the only formal commandment the destruction of all the inhabitants of the land by the Israelites, using the standard OT term *yrš.* Our great ignorance of the postexilic centuries prevents us from determining whether these texts may reflect a deterioration of the situation in the late period. Perhaps the militant motifs were introduced only to voice a totally different concern in a setting that sounded as archaic as possible: the proper distribution of landed property with respect to the population of the individual groups (cf. Nu. 33:54).[75]

Cortese's attempt[76] to claim Nu. 33:50-55 for Pᵍ I do not find convincing. In Nu. 32:21, the syntax admits the possibility that Yahweh is the subject of *yrš* hiphil. But this would be the only passage depicting Yahweh as destroying nations before himself.

10. *Hope for Restoration of the Davidic Empire in the Redactors of the Prophets.* In the partially interdependent passages representing the final recension of the prophetic books, there are 2 verses that associate *yrš* with the idea of repossessing the Davidic empire, with special emphasis on Edom. Ob. 17, which could be part of the original text, while speaking of Jerusalem says only that the house of Jacob (i.e., the exiles) shall possess their own possessions once more. But a secondary interpretation in two stages, repeating the key word *yrš* several times, defines this statement first as meaning that (starting from Judah) the mountains of Esau, the land of the Philistines, Ephraim-Samaria, and Gilead will be reclaimed (Ob. 19) and then as meaning that the exiles of the northern kingdom will take possession of the Phoenician territory as far as Zarephath and the exiles of Jerusalem in Sepharad (= Sardis in Asia Minor) will take possession of the cities of the Negeb (Ob. 20). Here it is only implicit that the interpreter is envisioning the united kingdom of the earliest monarchy; this is stated explicitly, however, in the conclusion to Amos (Am. 9:12), which probably dates from the exilic period at the earliest. Yahweh will raise up the booth of David and rebuild it as in the days of old, i.e., the days of David. Then the Israelites will dispossess (*yrš* with personal obj.) those in Edom who have escaped the judgment (cf. Am. 1:11f.) and all the other nations called by Yahweh's name (at the establishment of the Davidic empire).[77]

Rudolph is the most recent scholar to support the authenticity of Am. 9:12. His primary

---

75 For the most recent critical analysis of Nu. 32, see Mittmann, 95-104.

76 Pp. 147-150.

77 On the translation of Ob. 19f., see W. Rudolph, *Obadja. KAT,* XIII/2 (1971); on the dating of both texts, see H. W. Wolff, *Joel and Amos. Herm* (Eng. trans. 1977).

argument, that there was a "remnant" of Edom only in the time of Amos, overlooks the fact that in Am. 9:12 *yrš* is used with a personal object.

11. *Possession of the Land as the Hope of the "Poor" in the Postexilic Period.* Ps. 37, an acrostic Wisdom psalm, uses the expression *yrš ᵓereṣ* as a kind of leitmotif (Ps. 37:9,11,22,29,34; synonyms in 18,27,29). Unlike Deuteronomistic literature, it does not promise possession of the land to all Israel. The psalm instead presupposes an Israel already living in the land, Yahweh's beneficent gift; now its conduct is under scrutiny. There are some who are wicked, and there are some who are good, who adhere to Yahweh. The latter, also called the "poor" and the "oppressed" in the land, are exhorted not to fret, but to remain faithful to Yahweh and hope in him. They are promised that they will enjoy possession of the land, whereas the wicked will be exterminated in the end. It is possible that the psalm refers specifically to the peasantry, who faced increasing class differences and were in danger of losing their land to great landowners. It does not speak of people with no possessions at all, promising them the property of their oppressors (cf. v. 3: "dwell in the land"). Furthermore, the phrase *yrš ᵓereṣ,* despite its concrete meaning, seems also to be a kind of shorthand for salvation and prosperity in general. The expression recalls traditions associated with wisdom as well as Deuteronomistic traditions.[78] As a parallel we find: *wᵉhiṯᶜannᵉgû ᶜal-rōḇ šālôm* (v. 11). The relationship between the proper conduct of the poor and the promised possession of the land cannot be reduced to a simple formula of "cause and effect" or even "conduct and reward." The distinction between present and promise becomes blurred. The righteous are to "take delight in Yahweh"; they will then "delight in abundant prosperity" (vv. 4,11). They will possess the land and dwell upon it forever (v. 29) if they trust in Yahweh, do good, and "dwell in the land" (v. 3). The proper ordering of society is already in existence. It may be in distress, but it will be fully established by Yahweh in the future. Here we are undoubtedly dealing with postexilic reflection on the well-being looked for but not yet really visible after the return.

The theme developed broadly in Ps. 37 is summarized tersely in the petitions of Ps. 25:13; 61:6(5); 69:36f.(35f.). In Ps. 25:13ff., *yrš ᵓereṣ* is surrounded by a variety of Deuteronomistic catchwords. In Ps. 69:34-37(35-36), the catchwords *ᵓeḇyônîm*[79] and *ᵓᵃsîrîm* introduce an individual prayer that is then expanded to include all Israel (cf. the similar passage, with *škn* instead of *yrš,* in Ps. 102:29[28]). The parallels in Trito-Isaiah suggest that the "servants" and "those who love his name" are not the returnees as a group but rather those among them who are faithful to Yahweh, for *yrš ᵓereṣ* is used similarly in Isa. 57:13 (as a climax); 60:21; 65:9. Matthew formulated the third beatitude in the Sermon on the Mount strictly after the pattern of Ps. 37:11; it is therefore hardly correct to translate Mt. 5:5 as "for they will take possession of the land" or "for they will inherit the land."

The extant portions of 4QpPs[a], a pesher on selected texts from the Psalms, deal

---

78 See I.2.b above.

79 → אביון *ᵓeḇyôn* (*ᵓebhyôn*).

primarily with Ps. 37; in it the Qumran community identifies itself with the righteous and poor of the psalm. The destruction of the wicked will take place after forty years, i.e., at the end of the eschatological holy war (1-10.II.8). Those who repented in the desert (?) will live in prosperity (?) for a thousand generations, and the entire heritage of Adam (or the human race) will belong to them and their descendants forever (1-10.III.1f.; cf. IV.3). The heritage of all the great (?) will belong to the community of the poor. They will possess the high mountain of Israel. On his holy mountain they will take their delight (1-10.III.10f.). The "holy mountain" reveals the influence of the book of Isaiah.

12. *Deutero- and Trito-Isaiah.* In its message of salvation, Deutero-Isaiah avoids the Deuteronomistic idea that Yahweh will give the land once more to the returnees and that they will take possession of it once more. He speaks of a second exodus, but not a second occupation. It is not necessary. The exiles do indeed depart from Babylon, and Yahweh himself goes with them. But Zion is already waiting for them in the land and experiences their arrival. The desolate *neḥālôṯ* must be reapportioned (Isa. 49:8), but the idea of "taking possession" appears only in a secondary context. Zion, bereft of her children, is suddenly blessed with a multitude of children coming from all the nations. The place has become too narrow for her (Isa. 49:18-23). She is therefore urged to enlarge the space of her tent and spread out in all directions (54:1-3). Then "your descendants will succeed to the inheritance (*yrš* qal) of the nations and will people the desolate cities" (v. 3). It remains unclear whether this passage—like the late strata of other prophetic books—refers to expansion into the old Davidic empire or even further. There is no suggestion of war. Destroyed cities are there for the taking. The miraculous glow that illuminates all of Deutero-Isaiah is not absent here. Trito-Isaiah will draw on this text but develop it more concretely.

Bonnard[80] translates Isa. 54:3 as follows: "Your descendants will inherit nations [i.e., 'people of other nations'; cf. 55:5], and these will settle the desolate cities [of Judah]." The context argues against this interpretation. In addition, Bonnard uses the meaning "inherit," which probably did not develop until later, and assumes to boot that it is used figuratively.

In Trito-Isaiah—in contrast to Proto-Isaiah and almost all of Deutero-Isaiah—*yrš* plays a certain role as a term denoting Israel's salvation and prosperity. Not all its occurrences, however, can be ascribed to a single hand or system of discourse. Isa. 63:7–64:11(12), a communal lament from the time when Jerusalem still lay in ruins, looks back on the monarchy as the period when Israel "possessed" the sanctuary of Yahweh, an all too brief golden age: "Return for the sake of thy servants, the tribes that are thy *naḥalâ*: only for a little while did thy holy people possess thy sanctuary; our adversaries have now trodden it down" (63:17f.). This passage constitutes the basis on which other texts promise renewed possession of the land, often in conjunction with the root → קדשׁ *qdš* (57:13; 65:9 [cf. v. 11]). Ch. 60, which is dominated by the theme of the nations' pilgrimage to Zion, recalls the various motifs of the promises to the

---

80 P. 291.

fathers: the blessing of the nations (vv. 1-18), "Israel's God" (vv. 19f.), the land (v. 21), increase (v. 22). The land has long since been given. But in the age of salvation—in contrast to the present time—the population of Zion will consist solely of *ṣaddîqîm*. Therefore they will "possess the land for ever" (v. 21). Here, then, in a passage that draws above all on the language of Ps. 37, *yrš* becomes an eschatological term for the promise of the land.

Isa. 61:4-7 is a chiastic parallel to 54:3. In the year of Yahweh's favor described by ch. 61, "those who mourn in Zion" will rebuild the desolate cities (61:4; cf. 54:3bβ). Their taking the heritage of the nations (54:3bα) is developed in a complex midrash (61:5-7). Secular labor in Jerusalem is performed by aliens. Zion's inhabitants are priests, and live from the wealth of the nations. Then there is a play on various meanings of *mišneh*. "Instead of your [those who mourn in Zion] shame you shall have a double portion." First: "[Instead of] dishonor, they [the nations] will rejoice in your portion." It is not clear whether "portion" here refers to the property of Zion's inhabitants in their own land (cf. 61:6) or to Yahweh as the "portion" allotted in Israel to the priests. In any case, the other nations rejoice over Zion's fate and, as a concrete result, place their own land at Zion's disposal: "Therefore in their [the nations'] land you shall take possesion of (*yrš*) a second [portion]; yours shall be everlasting joy." Does this passage exalt theoretically the fact that Israel already possesses a large diaspora in addition to those dwelling in the land? Or does it develop the idea of the eschatological pilgrimage of the nations to Jerusalem (cf. Isa. 60) into a kind of interpenetration of Israel and the nations? Perhaps both are true. In any case, it goes beyond what 60:21 says: in the age of salvation, the inhabitants of Jerusalem will have a second portion among the nations, outside their own land.

This possession of the land presupposes the great division within the land. In the context of statements referring to this division, and clearly in related symmetrical positions within chs. 56–66, Isa. 57:13; 65:9 speak of "possessing" the land or the holy mountain of Yahweh. In contrast to the wicked mentioned in the same context, its possession is promised to *ḥôseh ḇî* (57:13), the *yôrēš hāray* newly brought forth from Jacob, the *bᵉḥîray* and *ʿᵃḇāḏay* (65:9). Unlike Ps. 37, however, this passage does not have in mind simply a portion of the Jewish people. In the last redactional strata of Trito-Isaiah, to which both these passages clearly belong, the "aliens" of ch. 56 can also be included (the catch phrase *har qoḏšî* links the two passages [for 65:9, cf. vv. 11,25] with 56:7; 66:20 in the outermost framework). If Israel was the "chosen servant" of Yahweh in Deutero-Isaiah, then here the "chosen ones" and "servants" constitute a group much more subtle and hard to define, profoundly transforming the notion of the people of God. It is they who are promised delight in possessing the holy mountain of Yahweh.

Lohfink

יִשְׂרָאֵל *yiśrā'ēl*

Contents: I. 1. Occurrences; 2. Etymology; 3. Meanings. II. History of the Name: 1. After Division of the Kingdom; 2. In the Time of David and Solomon; 3. In the Time of Saul; 4. Before the Monarchy; 5. Origin of "Israel." III. The Religious Significance of the Name "Israel": 1. El, the God of Israel; 2. Yahweh, the God of Israel; 3. Nationalistic Elements during the Early Monarchy; 4. Israel as the People of God in Preexilic Prophecy; 5. Israel in Deuteronomy; 6. Israel in Exilic and Postexilic Prophecy; 7. Israel in the Chronicler's History; 8. Israel in the Psalter. IV. Israel in Post-OT Jewish Literature: 1. The Apocrypha and Pseudepigrapha; 2. Qumran.

---

yiśrā'ēl. P. R. Ackroyd, "Hosea and Jacob," *VT,* 13 (1963), 245-259; W. F. Albright, "The Names 'Israel' and 'Judah' with an Excursus on the Etymology of Tôdâh and Tôrâh," *JBL,* 46 (1927), 151-185; *idem,* "Syrien, Phönizien, und Palästina vom Beginn der Sesshaftigkeit bis zur Eroberung durch die Achämeniden," in F. Kern, ed., *Historia mundi,* II (Bern, 1953), 331-376; A. Alt-R. Bach, "Israel. I. Geschichte," *RGG*[3], III (1959), 936-942; E. Auerbach, *Wüste und gelobtes Land,* I (Berlin, 1932); O. Bächli, *Amphiktyonie im AT. ThZSond,* 6 (1977); H. Bauer, "Al-Muštarī," *OLZ,* 38 (1935), 477; *idem,* "Die Gottheiten von Ras Schamra," *ZAW,* 51 (1933), 81-101; A. Besters, " 'Israël' et 'Fils d'Israël' dans les livres historiques (Genèse–II Rois)," *RB,* 74 (1967), 5-23; *idem,* "L'expression 'Fils d'Israël' en *Ex.,* I-XIV," *RB,* 74 (1967), 321-355; J. Bright, *A History of Israel* (Philadelphia, [3]1981); W. Caspari, "Sprachliche und religionsgeschichtliche Bedeutung des Namens Israel," *ZS,* 3 (1924), 194-211; H. P. Chajes, "Der Name ישראל," *JQR,* 13 (1901), 344; R. B. Coote, "The Meaning of the Name *Israel,*" *HThR,* 65 (1972), 137-142; F. Crusemann, *Der Widerstand gegen das Königtum. WMANT,* 49 (1978), 95-111; M. Dahood, "Is *'Eben Yiśrā'ēl* a Divine Title?" *Bibl,* 40 (1959), 1002-7; G. A. Danell, *Studies in the Name Israel in the OT* (Eng. trans., Uppsala, 1946); W. Eichrodt, *Israel in der Weissagung des AT* (1951); *idem,* "Religionsgeschichte Israels," in Kern, ed., *Historia mundi,* II (Bern, 1953), 377-448 (repr. separately, Bern, 1969); O. Eissfeldt, "Ein gescheiterter Versuch der Wiedervereinigung Israels (2. Sam. 2,12–3,1)," *NC,* 3 (1951), 110-127 = *KlSchr,* III (1966), 132-146; *idem,* "Jakobs Begegnung mit El und Moses Begegnung mit Jahwe," *OLZ,* 58 (1963), 325-331 = *KlSchr,* IV (1968), 92-98; *idem, Neue keilalphabetische Texte aus Ras Schamra. SDAW,* 1965/6; *idem,* "Non dimittam te, nisi benedixeris mihi," *Mélanges bibliques. Festschrift A. Robert. Travaux de l'Institut Catholique de Paris,* 4 (1957), 77-81 = *KlSchr,* III, 412-16; *idem,* "Palestine in the Time of the Nineteenth Dynasty. (a) The Exodus and Wanderings," *CAH*[3], II/2, XXVI(a), 307-330; *idem,* "Renaming in the OT," *Words and Meanings. Festschrift D. Winton Thomas* (Cambridge, 1968), 69-79 = *KlSchr,* V (1973), 68-76 [Ger.]; S. Feist, "Die Etymologie des Namens יִשְׂרָאֵל," *MGWJ,* 73 (1929), 317-320; J. W. Flanagan, "The Deuteronomic Meaning of the Phrase '*kol yisrā'ēl,*' " *StR,* 6 (1976/77), 159-168; G. Gerleman, "ישראל *Jiśrā'ēl,*" *THAT,* I, 782-85; C. H. J. de Geus, *The Tribes of Israel. SSN,* 18 (1976), 187-192; J. Heller, "Ursprung des Namens Israel," *ComViat,* 7 (1964), 263f.; J. Hempel, "Israel. I. AT," *BHHW,* II (1964), 782-86; S. Herrmann, "Autonome Entwicklungen in den Königreichen Israel und Juda," *Congress Volume, Rome 1968. SVT,* 17 (1969), 139-158; *idem, A History of Israel in OT Times* (Eng. trans., Philadelphia, [2]1981); *idem,* "Das Werden Israels," *ThLZ,* 87 (1962), 561-574; H. W. Hertzberg, "Jeremia und das Nordreich Israel," *Festschrift J. Herrmann. ThLZ,* 77 (1952), 595-602 = *Beiträge zur Traditionsgeschichte und Theologie des ATs* (Göttingen, 1962), 91-100, A. R. Hulst, "Der Name 'Israel' im Deuteronomium," *OTS,* 9 (1951), 65-106; A. Jepsen, "Zur Überlieferung der Vätergestalten," *Festschrift A. Alt. WZ Leipzig,* 3 (1953/54), 265-281 = *Der Herr ist Gott* (Berlin,

I. 1. *Occurrences.* "Israel" is a West Semitic proper name. It appears 2514 times in

---

1978), 46-75; P. Joüon, "Notes des lexicographie hébraïque," *MUSJ,* 10 (1925), 1-47, esp. 42f. ("רה *être fort*"); Z. Kallai, "Judah and Israel—A Study in Israelite Historiography," *IEJ,* 28 (1978), 251-261; R. Kittel, *Geschichte des Volkes Israel,* I (Stuttgart, ^{7}1932), II (^{7}1925); A. Lemaire, "Asriel, *šrʾl,* Israel et l'origine de la conféderation israélite," *VT,* 23 (1973), 239-243; V. Maag, "Der Hirte Israels: Eine Skizze von Wesen und Bedeutung der Väterreligion," *SchThU,* 28 (1958), 2-28 = *Kultur, Kulturkontakt und Religion* (Göttingen, 1980), 111-144; R. Marcus, "The Hebrew Sibilant *Śin* and the Name *Yiśraʾel,*" *JBL,* 60 (1941), 141-150; A. D. H. Mayes, *Israel in the Period of the Judges. SBT,* N.S. 29 (1974), 55-67; *idem,* "Israel in the Pre-monarchy Period," *VT,* 23 (1973), 151-170; E. Meyer, *Die Israeliten und ihre Nachbarstämme* (1906; repr. Darmstadt, 1967); I. Mihalik, "Some Thoughts on the Name Israel," *Theological Soundings,* 1973, 11-19; P. D. Miller, Jr., "El the Warrior," *HThR,* 60 (1967), 411-431; S. Mowinckel, " 'Rahelstämme' und 'Leastämme'," *Von Ugarit nach Qumran. Festschrift O. Eissfeldt. BZAW,* 77 (1958, ^{2}1961), 129-150; M. Naor, "יַעֲקֹב und יִשְׂרָאֵל," *ZAW,* 49 (1931), 317-321; E. Nielsen, *Shechem: A Traditio-Historical Investigation* (Copenhagen, ^{2}1959); M. Noth, *The History of Israel* (Eng. trans., New York, ^{2}1960); *idem,* "Mari und Israel: Eine Personennamenstudie," *Geschichte und AT. Festschrift A. Alt. BHTh,* 16 (1958), 127-152 = *Aufsätze sur biblischen Landes- und Altertumskunde,* II (Neukirchen- Vluyn, 1971), 213-233; *idem, The OT World* (Eng. trans., Philadelphia, 1966); *idem, Das System der zwölf Stämme Israels. BWANT,* 52[4/1] (^{2}1966); D. H. Odendaal, "Israel, die Volk van God, in Bybelse Perspektief," *NedGTT,* 12 (1971), 153-170; E. Otto, *Jakob in Sichem. BWANT,* 110[6/10] (1979); G. von Rad, K. G. Kuhn, and W. Gutbrod, "Ἰσραήλ," *TDNT,* III, 356-391; W. Richter, "Zu den 'Richtern Israels'," *ZAW,* 77 (1965), 40-72, esp. 50-56 ("Israel"); L. Rost, *Israel bei den Propheten. BWANT,* 71[4/19] (1937); E. Sachsse, *Die Bedeutung des Namens Israel: Eine geographisch-geschictliche Untersuchung* (Gütersloh, 1922); *idem, Die Bedeutung des Namens Israel: Eine quellenkritische Untersuchung* (Bonn, 1910); *idem,* "Die Etymologie und älteste Aussprache des Namens ישראל," *ZAW,* 34 (1914), 1-15; *idem,* "Der Ursprung des Namens Israel," *ZS,* 4 (1926), 63-69; G. Sauer, "Bemerkungen zu 1965 edierten ugaritischen Texten," *ZDMG,* 116 (1966), 235-241; J. Scharbert, "Patriarchentradition und Patriarchenreligion," *Verkündigung und Forschung. BEvTh,* 19 (1974), 2-22; H. H. Schmid, "Ich will euer Gott sein, und ihr sollt mein Volk sein," *Kirche. Festschrift G. Bornkamm* (Tübingen, 1980), 1-25; H. Seebass, *Der Erzvater Israel und die Einführung der Jahweverehrung in Kanaan. BZAW,* 98 (1966); R. Smend, *Die Bundesformel. ThSt,* 68 (1963); *idem, Yahweh War and Tribal Confederation* (Eng. trans., Nashville, 1970); *idem,* "Zur Frage der altisraelitischen Amphiktyonie," *EvTh,* 31 (1971), 623-630; W. Staerk, *Studien zur Religions- und Sprachgeschichte des ATs* (Berlin, 1899), II, 50-73 ("I. Jisrael"); C. Steuernagel, "Jahwe, der Gott Israels," *Festschrift J. Wellhausen. BZAW,* 27 (1914), 329-349; E. Täubler, "The First Mention of Israel," *PAAJR,* 12 (1942), 115-120; R. de Vaux, *AncIsr*; *idem, The Early History of Israel* (Eng. trans., Philadelphia, 1978); *idem,* "Israel: Le nom," *DBS,* IV (1949), 730f.; K. Vollers, "Die solare Seite des alttestamentlichen Gottesbegriffes," *ARW,* 9 (1906), 176-184; L. Wächter, "Israel und Jeschurun," *Schalom: Studien zu Glaube und Geschichte Israels. Festschrift A. Jepsen. ArbT,* 1/46 (1971), 58-64; N. Walker, " 'Israel'," *VT,* 4 (1954), 434; G. Wallis, "Die Tradition von den drei Ahnvätern," *ZAW,* 81 (1969), 18-40; *idem,* "Zur Geschichte der Jakob-Tradition," *WZ Halle-Wittenberg,* 13 (1964), 427-440 = "Die Jakobtradition und Geschichte," *Geschichte und Überlieferung. ArbT,* 2/13 (1968), 13-44; G. Wanke, *Die Zionstheologie der Korachiten in ihren traditionsgeschichtlichen Zusammenhang. BZAW,* 97 (1966), 54-58 ("Der Gott Jakobs"); J. Weingreen, "The Theory of the Amphictyony in Pre-Monarchial Israel," *JANES,* 5 (1973), 427-433; J. Wellhausen, *Israelitische und jüdische Geschichte* (Berlin, ^{9}1958); H. G. M. Williamson, *Israel in the Books of Chronicles* (Cambridge, 1977); G. E. Wright, "Israel in the Promised Land: History Interpreted by a Covenant Faith," *Encounter,* 35 (1974), 318-334; S. Yeivin, "The Age of the Patriarchs," *RSO,* 38 (1963), 301; W. Zimmerli, *Ezekiel 2. Herm* (Eng. trans. 1983), 563-65 (" 'Israel' in the Book

the OT.[1] The gentilic form appears an additional 5 times. There are 144 occurrences in the Qumran documents and 6 in the Mesha inscription. The monolithic inscription of Shalmaneser III from Qarqar includes an instance of the masculine gentilic form: "Ahab the Israelite" (*šir-'i-la-ai*).[2] The LXX always transcribes the name as *Israḗl*. The name continues to appear with great frequency in Jewish literature and the NT.

The name "Israel" also appears in a Ugaritic text in the form *yšril*,[3] the name of a charioteer (*mrynm*), and in the form *y-si-r-i'-r* as the name of a people in line 27 of the Merneptah inscription. The former has no connection with the Israel of the OT; the connection in the latter is disputed. It is uncertain whether the name *šr'l* in ostraca nos. 42 and 48 from Samaria is to be read as "Asriel" (cf. Nu. 26:31; Josh. 17:2; 1 Ch. 7:14) and associated with Israel.[4]

2. *Etymology*. The etymology of the name "Israel" has not been explained satisfactorily. Two OT passages play on the name. In Gen. 32:29(Eng. v. 28) (assigned to L by Eissfeldt and to J by Noth), the name is explained as follows: ". . . for you have striven (*śārîtā*) with God and with men, and have prevailed." This etymology associates "Israel" with the root *śrh*, which from the context must mean something like "struggle" or "strive."[5] Hos. 12:4f.(3f.) alludes to Gen. 32:23-33(22-32) or some other tradition,[6] saying—albeit pejoratively—that "in his manhood he strove (*śārâ*) with God and contended (?) (*wayyāśar*) with an angel and prevailed (→ יכל *yāḵōl*)." In Hos. 12:4(3), as in Gen. 32:29(28), the root *śrh* appears again, but the derivation of the verb at the beginning of Hos. 12:5(4) is obscure. It might be a form of *śrr*,[7] but the translation "rule" or "yield" makes no sense. If one does not assume that the text of Hos. 12:5(4) is corrupt,[8] the only other possibility is to assume the meaning "and he contended" for *wayyaśar* on the basis of v. 4(3).

In any case, both are popular etymologies interpreting the name "Israel" as a compound comprising a verb plus a theophorous element. Identification of the latter as the object of the verb is clearly a fiction of the etymology. In fact, the name exemplifies

---

of Ezekiel"); *idem*, "Israel im Buche Ezechiel," *VT*, 8 (1958), 75-90; H.-J. Zobel, "Das Selbstverständnis Israels nach dem AT," *ZAW*, 85 (1973), 281-294; *idem*, *Stammesspruch und Geschichte*. *BZAW*, 95 (1965); *idem*, "Die Stammessprüche des Mose-Segens (Dtn 33,6-25): Ihr 'Sitz im Leben,'" *Klio*, 46 (1965), 83-92.

1 Lisowsky lists 2511 occurrences, to which must be added Gen. 47:31 and the 2 occurrences in 1 K. 9:7; 16:29, as Gerleman notes.

2 II.92.

3 *KTU*, 4.623, 3; on the interchange of *š* and *ś*, see Marcus; for a discussion of the text itself, see Sauer.

4 Lemaire.

5 Danell, 17f.; Wächter, 58f.; Sachsse, *ZAW*, 34 (1914), 1, 5; Heller, 263; cf. also Coote.

6 Cf. L. Ruppert, "Herkunft und Bedeutung der Jakob-Tradition bei Hosea," *Bibl*, 52 (1971), 488-504.

7 Wächter, 62, n. 14.

8 Cf. the divergent views in W. Rudolph, *Hosea*. *KAT*, XIII/1 (1966), 222, and H. W. Wolff, *Hosea*. *Herm* (Eng. trans. 1974), 206.

a widespread type of West Semitic name consisting of the imperfect of a verb plus a theophorous element.[9] The theophorous element is not the object but the subject of the phrase name.[10] And since *'ēl* is probably not an appellative but the name of the God El,[11] "Israel" must mean something like "El strives" or "El contends." Stamm alters this interpretation somewhat by taking the imperfect as a narrative tense and translating the name as referring to the past.[12]

This translation of the verbal element is based entirely on the popular etymologies cited, and is therefore by no means compelling. This obvious fact has led over the years to a wealth of proposed interpretations.[13] Many suggestions need not be taken seriously: the root *yšr*[14] or *'šr,*[15] or even an Aegean *iser,* "holy,"[16] not to mention Steuernagel's theory that "Israel" means *'îš rāḥēl,* "the man from the tribe of Rachel,"[17] or Walker's,[18] that "Israel" is a kind of abbreviation for "Yah from Seir is El." The only realistic root for the etymology is *śrh,* as the OT texts assume. When we turn to the interpretation of this root, the proposal of Vollers and Bauer[19] to postulate a basic meaning "be radiant, shine" (on the basis of Arab. *šariya*) and translate the name as "El shines forth" is implausible. S. R. Driver's translation "El persists," interpreting *śrh* as "persevere, persist," has likewise found no support. Ultimately, the choice is between the translations "contend"[20] and "reign, hold sway."[21] It is noteworthy that the popular etymology that interprets the personal name "Jerubbaal" as meaning "Let Ba'al contend against him" (Jgs. 6:32) resembles our interpretation in taking the verbal element to mean "contend." Now in this latter case there can be no question that the verbal element does not reflect the root *rîḇ,* "contend," but *rbb,* "be exalted, reign."[22] This observation lends support to the theory that the interpretation of *śrh* as "contend" is a fiction of the popular etymology

---

9 Cf. M. Noth, *IPN,* 208; *idem, Aufsätze,* II, 228; *The History of Israel,* 4.

10 As first observed by E. Nestle in Sachsse, *ZAW,* 34 (1914), 4.

11 See most recently Mihalik, 13f.

12 J. J. Stamm, *Beiträge zur hebräischen und altorientalischen Namenkunde. OBO,* 30 (1980), 62f.

13 See the material assembled in Sachsse, *ZAW,* 34 (1914), 1-5, listing 9 variations, and Danell, 22-28, who repeats Sachsse's survey and adds more recent proposals. The most recent suggestion is that of Wächter, who proposes an etymology involving *yāšar* and translates the name as "El is just," an interpretation already proposed by Sachsse.

14 Albright, *JBL,* 46 (1927), 151-185; Sachsse; and Danell; as well as Wächter.

15 Most recently Naor.

16 Feist.

17 Cited by Sachsse, *ZAW,* 34 (1914), 4.

18 P. 434.

19 *OLZ,* 38 (1935), 477; *ZAW,* 51 (1933), 83.

20 Wellhausen, 23: "El contends"; Meyer, 252: "El is one who contends"; Kittel, I, 274, n. 1: " 'God contends', or the like"; Auerbach, 72: "God contends"; Eissfeldt, *KlSchr,* IV, 98: "El fights"; Hempel, 782: " 'El contends' or 'El heals'?"; Heller, 263: "May God contend"; cf. Miller.

21 Joüon, 42f.: "be strong"; Noth, *IPN,* 207: "May God show himself to be lord/ruler"; von Rad, 356, n. 1: "God reigns" (?); Eissfeldt, *Festschrift D. Winton Thomas,* 76: "El is lord"; Sauer, 240 (citing Ugar. *šr,* "prince"): "May El show himself to be lord"; Eichrodt, "Religionsgeschichte Israels," 384 (= 21): "God rules."

22 Eissfeldt, *Festschrift D. Winton Thomas,* 76, n. 2.

and that the basic meaning is "rule, be exalted." In this case, the original meaning of our name would be "El reigns, El is supreme."[23] As the Ugaritic example shows, this is in fact a masculine personal name.

3. *Meanings.* This impression concerning the meaning of the name "Israel" seems to be confirmed if we follow the sequence of the biblical books, beginning with Genesis. The first occurrence is in Gen. 32:29(28), which recounts the solemn renaming of Jacob as Israel; here Jacob is represented as an individual. The text can speak of his right hand or his left, his eyes, his lifetime. Of 43 occurrences in Genesis, 29 refer clearly to the patriarch; another 7 involve the phrase "sons of Israel." It is noteworthy that of 29 occurrences where "Israel" denotes an individual, 22 appear in a version of the Joseph story; similarly, 5 of the 7 occurrences of "sons of Israel" appear in this version. In 5 instances, "Israel" clearly refers to a larger group: Gen. 34:7 ("commit a crime in Israel"; cf. Dt. 22:21; Josh. 7:15; Jgs. 20:6,10,13; etc.); Gen. 48:20 ("pronounce a blessing in Israel"); 49:7 ("scatter in Israel"); 49:16,28 ("the tribes of Israel"). Finally God is called "El, the God of Israel" (Gen. 33:20) and "Shepherd of the rock of Israel" (Gen. 49:24).

Only in Genesis do we find this preponderance of individual over collective usage. In Exodus, the patriarch is mentioned in 2 passages: Ex. 6:14 (P) and 32:13 (redactional). But there are 41 occurrences, beginning with Ex. 4:22, in which "Israel" refers to the people enslaved in Egypt and let go by Pharaoh, who experienced the miracle of the exodus and were brought into covenant with God. Beginning with Ex. 5:1, there are 4 references to "(Yahweh,) the God of Israel" (24:10; 32:27; 34:23; cf. 32:4,8). The phrase "sons of Israel" occurs 123 times.

This picture is repeated in the following biblical books: Leviticus (11 occurrences of the collective, 54 of "sons of Israel"), Numbers (2 occurrences as the father of Reuben [Nu. 1:20; 26:5 (both P)]; 63 occurrences of the collective, 171 of "sons of Israel," 1 of "God of Israel" [Nu. 16:9]), Deuteronomy (51 of the collective, 21 of "sons of Israel"), Joshua (76 of the collective [note the expression "hill country of Israel" in Josh. 11:16,21, which in v. 21 means the hill country of Ephraim in contrast to the hill country of Judah], 69 of "sons of Israel," 14 of "Yahweh, the God of Israel" plus 1 of simply "the God of Israel" [Josh. 22:16]), Judges (1 occurrence as the father of Dan [Jgs. 18:29], 115 of the collective, 61 of "sons of Israel," 7 of "Yahweh, the God of Israel").

The situation is somewhat more complex in 1 Samuel: there are 12 occurrences of "sons of Israel," 9 of "God of Israel" (1 S. 1:17; 5:7,8[3 times],10,11; 6:3,5), and 8 of "Yahweh, the God of Israel"; once the text speaks of Yahweh as "the Glory of Israel" (15:29). For the first time, however, we find "Israel" clearly used to denote an entity different from Judah (17:52; 18:16). This observation supports the notion that in the remaining 119 occurrences "Israel" does not always mean the entire nation but rather a group of tribes in central and northern Palestine distinct from Judah. The phrases "all the tribes of Israel" (2:28; 10:20; cf. 9:21; 15:17) and "all Israel, from Dan to Beer-sheba" (3:20) probably refer to the totality, especially since the threat of judgment against Eli

23 Cf. Yeivin, 301; de Geus, 192.

(2:32) and Samuel's farewell discourse (12:1) exhibit features of Deuteronomistic editing. Even as early as 2:14ff., however, one might ask whether the "Israel" that comes to Shiloh includes Judah; Saul's sovereignty over Israel (9:16,20; 11:2,13; 13:1; 14:22ff.; also 14:47,48) probably implies an Israel without Judah. Finally, the expression "king of Israel" (24:15[14]; 26:20; 29:3)—as distinct from the functional designation "king over (*ʿal*) Israel" (15:17; etc.), which Saul was the first to bear—sounds like a formal title; it appears again only once, when Michal applies it to David (2 S. 6:20).

A general survey of 2 Samuel reveals the following: 5 occurrences of "sons of Israel," 61 occurrences of the collective denoting the Davidic monarchy (2 S. 5:17; 6:1,21; etc.), and 48 designating the territory distinct from Judah, generally identical with the later northern kingdom, or one of its parts (2:9; 5:1,2[3 times],3[2 times]),5; 11:11; 20:1; etc.). There is 1 occurrence each of "Yahweh Sabaoth, the God of Israel" (7:27), "Yahweh, the God of Israel" (12:7), "God of Israel" (23:3[24]), and "Rock of Israel" (23:3). We find the following distribution in 1 Kings: 2 references to the patriarch (1 K. 18:31,36), 21 occurrences of "sons of Israel," 52 occurrences of the collective for all Israel (of which 5 are in "the throne of Israel," used in 2:4; 8:20,25; 9:5 for the kingship of the Davidic line; cf. 2 K. 10:30; 15:12, where the phrase is restricted to the northern kingdom), 108 occurrences referring to the northern kingdom (38 of which are in the phrase "king of Israel" and 8 in the plural of the same phrase), and 20 occurrences of "Yahweh, the God of Israel." It is noteworthy that this formula appears in the mouth of Judahites until 1 K. 11:31, but appears 11 times subsequently only with kings of the northern kingdom. This remains true (2 K. 9:6; 10:31; 14:25) through 2 K. 18:5, after which it is associated once more with Judahites (18:5; 19:15,20; 21:12; 22:15,18). In 2 Kings, there is an allusion to Gen. 32 (2 K. 17:34); there are 11 occurrences of "sons of Israel," 10 occurrences of the collective referring to all Israel, 132 referring to the northern kingdom, and a single occurrence (19:22) of "the Holy One of Israel" (cf. Isaiah).

In the prophets, such a classification is hardly possible or must involve serious reservations. This is because many passages refer clearly to the northern or southern kingdom, but the majority of the occurrences reveal a more comprehensive concept of Israel. In Proto-Isaiah, we find 4 occurrences of "sons of Israel," 13 of all Israel, 6 of the northern kingdom, 21 of various divine appellatives ("the Holy One of Israel" [12]; "Yahweh, the God of Israel" [4]; "Yahweh Sabaoth, the God of Israel" [2]; "the Mighty One of Israel"; "Light of Israel"; and "God of Israel" [1 each]). In Deutero-Isaiah, there are 22 references to the exiles, 20 divine appellatives ("the Holy One of Israel" [11]; "God of Israel" [6]; "Creator of Israel"; "Redeemer of Israel"; and "King of Israel" [1 each]). Trito-Isaiah contains a single reference to the patriarch (Isa. 63:16), 1 occurrence of "sons of Israel," 2 references to the Israel of the prophet's day, and 2 occurrences of "the Holy One of Israel."

Of the 125 occurrences in Jeremiah,[25] 9 involve the "sons of Israel," 28 refer clearly to the former northern kingdom, and 53 appear in various divine appellatives ("Yahweh

---

24 But cf. *BHS*.

25 Cf. Hertzberg, *Beiträge*, 92-99.

Sabaoth, the God of Israel" [35]; "Yahweh, the God of Israel" [14]; "the Holy One of Israel" [2]; "Hope of Israel" [2]); the remaining 35 once more seem to denote a larger entity.

In Ezekiel, "sons of Israel" occurs 11 times, "God of Israel" 6 times, and "Yahweh, the God of Israel" and "the Holy One of Israel" once each. Most of the remaining 167 occurrences refer to an Israel that appears to remain constant in extent through the past, the present, and the future age of salvation. Only in Ezk. 9:9 ("house of Israel and Judah"); 25:3 ("the land of Israel and the house of Judah"); 27:17 ("Judah and the land of Israel"); and 37:16 ("Judah and the sons/house of Israel"), 19 ("tribes of Israel") might one ask whether a distinction is not being made between Judah and Israel. But these expressions either are due to secondary redaction (as in 9:9) or should be interpreted in another sense on the basis of their context (25:3; 27:17; 37:16,19).[26]

In Hosea, a prophet from the northern kingdom, we find "Israel" primarily as a designation of the northern kingdom (33 occurrences; 6 occurrences of "sons of Israel"). Only 4 occurrences refer to all Israel (Hos. 9:10; 11:1; 12:14[13]; 13:1; possibly 7:1 and 10:9). Hos. 12:13(12) refers to the patriarch. The occurrences in the book of Joel refer to postexilic Israel (including 1 instance of "sons of Israel"). Amos uses "Israel" 23 times for the northern kingdom; 5 times he uses "sons of Israel." In Am. 5:25; 9:7, there is a kind of collective reference to all Israel in the context of the past (cf. 3:1). Ob. 20 uses "sons of Israel" for the exiles. In Micah we find once more an ambiguous use of "Israel" that is hard to define precisely. In Mic. 5:2(3), "sons of Israel" refers to the Israel of the future age of salvation, just as 5:1(2) speaks of a "ruler in Israel" who will come from Bethlehem-Ephrathah. In Mic. 3:1,9, the rulers of Zion (= Jerusalem) are called "princes of the house of Israel" (cf. 4:14[5:1]; 1:14). In Mic. 1:5, on the other hand, the contrast between "house of Israel" and "house of Judah," parallel to that between the cities of Samaria and Jerusalem, gives the impression that "Israel" refers to the northern kingdom. This is probably also the case in Mic. 1:13; 3:8, while 1:15; 6:2 sound more comprehensive; 2:12 speaks of the "remnant of Israel." Nah. 2:3(2) probably refers to the northern kingdom,[27] while Zeph. 3:13,14,15 addresses Judah and 2:9 speaks of "Yahweh Sabaoth, the God of Israel." In Proto-Zechariah, we find "house of Judah" and "house of Israel" side by side in Zec. 8:13; 2:2(1:19) contains the sequence "Judah, Israel, and Jerusalem." In Deutero-Zechariah, we find "all the tribes of Israel" (Zec. 9:1), "Judah and Israel" (11:14), and "Israel" (12:1, denoting Jerusalem and the south). In Malachi, finally, "Yahweh, the God of Israel" appears in Mal. 2:16. In Mal. 2:11, we find "Judah," "Israel," and "Jerusalem" side by side, which suggests that "Israel" refers to the northern kingdom; but in Mal. 3:22(4:4), the laws of Moses are addressed to "all Israel," and 1:1,5 also sound more comprehensive.

In the Psalter, "Israel" (along with 2 occurrences of "sons of Israel") denotes primarily (46 times) a comprehensive group; the various divine appellatives (12 occurrences)[28]

---

26 Cf. W. Zimmerli, *Ezekiel 2, in loc.* and 563.

27 F. Horst, *Die zwölf Kleinen Propheten: Nahum bis Maleachi. HAT,* XIV (^{3}1964), *in loc.*

28 See III.8 below.

follow the same usage. The title "Shepherd of Israel" in Ps. 80:2(1) is associated with the group comprising "Ephraim, Benjamin, and Manasseh" mentioned in v. 3(2). The parallelism between Judah and Israel in Ps. 76:2(1); 114:2 likewise might point to an entity distinct from Judah.

In Ruth 2:12, we find the phrase "Yahweh, the God of Israel"; there are also 4 occurrences of "Israel" referring to the whole nation. In Eccl. 1:12, the phrase "king over Israel" refers to Solomon. Lamentations deals with the fate of Judah, Jerusalem, and Zion; "Israel" is mentioned only in Lam. 2:1,3,5. Cant. 3:7 speaks of the "mighty men of Israel" surrounding Solomon's litter. The redactional superscription to the book of Proverbs calls Solomon "king of Israel" (Prov. 1:1). Daniel, too, uses "Israel" in the comprehensive sense (Dnl. 1:3; 9:7,11,20; once "sons of Israel").

In Ezr. 8:18, Levi is called "son of Israel"; there are 4 occurrences of "sons of Israel" in general, and 13 occurrences of "Israel" in a divine appellative ("Yahweh, the God of Israel" [6]; "God of Israel" [4]; "Elah of Israel" [3]). The remaining 22 occurrences refer to postexilic Israel as a national and religious community, and occasionally to the Israel of the past (Ezr. 5:11; 3:10). Nehemiah uses "sons of Israel" 9 times and "Israel" 13 times to refer to his contemporaries as a nation emerging from its historical roots.

In 1 Chronicles,[29] "Israel" appears 9 times and "sons of Israel" 4 times in genealogical contexts. The phrase "Yahweh, the God of Israel" appears 10 times, "God of Israel" twice, and "Yahweh Sabaoth, the God of Israel" once. Only in 1 Ch. 5:17 does "Israel" refer to the northern kingdom. In 87 instances, the name refers to the entire nation. In 2 Chronicles, the phrase "God of Abraham, Isaac, and Israel" appears in 2 Ch. 30:6; "sons of Israel" appears 23 times. The expression "God of Israel" is found 22 times and "Yahweh, the God of Israel" once. There are 75 occurrences referring to all Israel, 61 referring to the northern kingdom, and 4 referring to Judah.

This rough tabulation of the meanings of the name "Israel" in the OT shows that, apart from the 241 instances of divine appellatives and 637 instances of the phrase "sons of Israel,"[30] there are only 49 references to the patriarch Israel, mostly in Genesis. In the great majority of occurrences, "Israel" denotes a collective entity; from a purely statistical point of view, the collective term "Israel" is more than twice as common as the individualizing phrase "sons of Israel."[31] Even if further differentiation is difficult and frequently not totally certain, "Israel" refers some 564 times to the northern kingdom and its people, but only rarely (some 17 times) to the southern kingdom. In by far the largest group of occurrences (1006), "Israel" is primarily a comprehensive term for the people of Yahweh identified by that name since their sojourn in Egypt. After the fall of the northern kingdom, however, "Israel" comes to mean more an ideal entity, instantiated in Judah, the exiles, the postexilic community, and last but not least the nation of the age of salvation.[32]

---

29 See Williamson for a discussion of 1–2 Chronicles.

30 Cf. Besters.

31 Staerk, 50-59.

32 See esp. Danell, 9.

II. History of the Name.

1. *After Division of the Kingdom.* With the division of the empire after Solomon's death, we find in 1 K. 12 a usage of the name "Israel" that is unambiguous, because it refers to an independent entity distinct from Judah: "All Israel" came to Shechem (v. 1), "all the assembly of Israel" asked Rehoboam to lighten their yoke of forced labor (v. 3), "all Israel" reacted negatively to the king's harsh decision (v. 16), heard the cry "To your tents, O Israel!" (v. 16), and obeyed the summons (v. 16); for "all Israel" stoned Adoram (v. 18) and made Jeroboam "king over all Israel" (v. 20). "So Israel rebelled against the house of David" (v. 19). Here this Israel is a homogeneous entity, acting independently in all respects. According to 1 K. 11:31, it comprises ten tribes; their territory is clearly distinguished from that of their neighbors, and they have an independent political authority, which 1 K. 12:20 calls "king over all Israel." The name "Israel" defines both the people and the sphere of influence; the standard political title is clearly "king of Israel." This title is first applied to Jeroboam in 1 K. 15:9, and is then used 79 additional times in 1 and 2 Kings for the rulers of the northern kingdom, down to their last representative, Hoshea, in 2 K. 18:1,9,10; it is also used for Ahab in 21:3, and the Mesha inscription mentions the *mlk yśr'l*.[33] There are in addition 28 occurrences of the plural, "kings of Israel." The expression "sit upon the throne of Israel" (2 K. 10:30; 15:12) is attested only during the period of the northern kingdom; it refers to Jehu and his dynasty. Thus "Israel" is clearly the name of the northern kingdom; it is a political term of constitutional law which, underlined by the use of *kōl,* "all" (esp. frequent in 1 K. 12), is used to distinguish the northern from the southern kingdom.

This conclusion is confirmed by examination of how the formula "Yahweh, the God of Israel," is used in 1–2 Kings: up to 1 K. 11:31, this formula appears also in the mouths of Judahites, but from that point on it appears 14 times solely in association with the kings of the northern kingdom; from 2 K. 18:5 on, it is linked 6 more times with Judahites. Finally, the words with which Jeroboam introduces the two golden images of bulls to his people—"Behold, this is your god, O Israel, who brought you up out of the land of Egypt" (1 K. 12:28)—show that "Israel" here means the people of the northern kingdom apart from the people of the southern kingdom, although this very formula recalling the exodus from Egypt refers elsewhere to all Israel. Thus far the situation is clear: as long as the northern kingdom is in existence, it alone may claim the name "Israel."

In 1 K. 12:17, however, we find the statement that Rehoboam reigned over the Israelites in the cities of Judah. Of course, it would be wrong to attach too much weight to such an isolated passage, and other similar passages like 1 K. 14:24; 21:26; 2 K. 16:3; and 1 K. 14:21 have a Deuteronomistic ring. It is nevertheless not impossible that even during the period of the northern kingdom Israel was thought of ideally as a single whole comprising twelve tribes. And we must not overlook the fact that, although Isaiah uses "Israel" 6 times for the northern kingdom, he uses it much more frequently for the entire people of God, and even speaks in Isa. 8:14 of "the two houses of Israel" (cf. CD 7:12f.) and incorporates the name "Israel" into his favorite term for God, "the Holy One of

---

33 *KAI,* 181.5, 10f., 18.

Israel." And when Amos calls the people God brought out of Egypt (Am. 9:7; 3:1) and led through the desert (5:25) "Israel," he probably has in mind the people of God as a whole, not just the inhabitants of the northern kingdom he is addressing. Thus we see that even during the period of the northern kingdom the comprehensive sense of the name "Israel" is attested. It was obviously able to hold its own against its political restriction to the northern state.

2. *In the Time of David and Solomon.* If we go back a step into history, our conclusions so far are confirmed. Once again, "Israel" is primarily an exclusive term for an independent entity distinct from the "house of Judah." This is clear from the short account of how David, the Judahite king, was made king over Israel at Hebron (2 S. 5:1-5). "All the tribes of Israel" came there (v. 1); David had previously been the leader of "Israel" (v. 2) and had been shepherd over Yahweh's people "Israel" (v. 2). Now he is to be "*nāgîḏ* over Israel" (v. 2). "All the elders of Israel" entered into the royal treaty with David (v. 3) and anointed him "king over Israel" (v. 3). A concluding comment states that at Jerusalem David reigned thirty-three years "over all Israel and Judah" (v. 5). This usage, which distinguishes Israel from Judah, still appears so frequently in the sources relating to the period of David and Solomon that it must be contemporary (cf. only 2 S. 3:19,21; 11:11; 19:41-44[40-43]; 20:1,2; 24:1,9; 1 K. 4:20; 5:5[4:25]): "Israel" designates the group of tribes that by and large constituted the later northern kingdom.

In addition, however, "Israel" is attested also as a term encompassing the people of Judah and Israel as a whole. This is the case in the formula used by Tamar: "Such a thing is not done in Israel" (2 S. 13:12), because here Judah belongs to Israel.[34] The phrase "all Israel" in 2 S. 16:21,22 likewise includes Judah, as is shown by the qualifier in "all Israel, from Dan to Beer-sheba" (2 S. 17:11; similarly 24:2; but cf. 2 S. 3:10: "Israel and Judah, from Dan to Beer-sheba"). Finally, the phrase "all the house of Israel" (2 S. 6:5,15) likewise refers to this totality of Israel, including Judah. These last two passages in particular give the impression that "Israel" means something like "the community of Yahweh," more a religious designation than the much narrower political term referring to what was later to be the northern kingdom. This impression is confirmed by the use of the two expressions "king over (*ʿal*) (all) Israel" and "king of Israel." The first is applied to David in 2 S. 5:12,17; 12:7 (cf. 7:8) and to Solomon in 1 K. 1:34; 4:1; 11:37 (cf. Eccl. 1:12). It is also worth considering whether 2 S. 5:17 may not contain an allusion to 5:3, "king over [northern] Israel." In any case, 5:12 is clear: David looked upon the help he received from Hiram of Tyre in building his Jerusalem palace as proof that Yahweh had established him as "king over Israel" and had exalted his kingship "for the sake of his people Israel." Here "Israel" stands for the people as a whole, including Judah. Another unambiguous passage is 2 S. 12:7, where Yahweh says: "I anointed you king over Israel"; this refers to the entire people of God, as also in the case of Solomon.

But Michal also calls David "king of Israel" (2 S. 6:20; cf. 2 Ch. 8:11; 29:27; 35:4; Ezr. 3:10). Solomon, too, appears to have borne this title (2 Ch. 30:26; 35:3; cf. also Prov.

---

[34] Noth, *System,* 104-6.

1:1). When other kings are called by similar titles—Talmai, king of Geshur (2 S. 3:3); Hiram, king of Tyre (2 S. 5:11); Hadadezer, king of Zobah (2 S. 8:3,5); Mesha, king of Moab (Mesha inscription[35]); Pharaoh, king of Egypt (1 K. 3:1; 9:16; etc.)—the genitive refers to the territory over which they reign, the state or the land. In the analogous expression "king of Israel," therefore, the proper name should probably be interpreted as a political designation for the state of Israel and its territory. David is introduced to Achish, king of Gath, as the "king of the land" (*meleḵ hā'āreṣ*; 1 S. 21:12[11]); this phrase shows that the genitive with *meleḵ* can refer to the state or territory.

Against this background, the different sense of "king over (*ʿal*) Israel" stands out more clearly: it refers to the people over whom the king reigns. And when kingship is understood as a feudal gift from Yahweh (e.g., 1 K. 10:9), the relationship between Yahweh and the people is even clearer. This is absolutely clear in 2 S. 6:21. In replying to Michal's taunts about the conduct of the "king of Israel," David does not repeat the political term but deliberately uses religious language, pointing out that he has been chosen by Yahweh, who appointed him "*nāgîḏ* over the people of Yahweh, over Israel." The "king over Israel" is thus the "king over God's people Israel."

This is also the sense of "Israel" in the phrase "throne of Israel" (1 K. 2:4; 8:20,25; 9:5; 10:9; also 2 Ch. 6:10,16). There is a close connection with the promise spoken by Nathan (2 S. 7) when David is assured that one of his descendants will never fail to sit on the throne of Israel (1 K. 2:4) or when Solomon understands his "sitting on the throne of David" and building the temple as fulfilling the promises made to David (1 K. 8:20; etc.). Because these statements involve religious notions, "Israel" probably also refers here to the people of God as a whole. We have already noted its meaning in the formula "Yahweh (Sabaoth), the God of Israel" (2 S. 7:27; 12:7; cf. also 2 S. 7:26; 23:3; 1 K. 1:30,48; 8:15,17,20,23,25,26; 11:9,31), which is reflected in the use of "Israel" for the people of Yahweh (2 S. 5:2,12; 6:21; 7:8,10,11,23,24; etc.). Finally, we may note the frequent use of "Jacob" and "Israel" in poetic parallelism in the texts of poems from the period of the early monarchy, like the Balaam poems in Nu. 24 (cf. vv. 5,17).

In this period, too, the conclusion is clear: "Israel" can be used in both a narrower and a broader sense. It can be either a political term or a name with religious overtones.

3. *In the Time of Saul.* In 1 S. 9:16, the text speaks pointedly of Saul's being anointed "*nāgîḏ* over my people Israel"; the formula in 1 S. 14:47 speaks of his "kingship over Israel" (cf. 1 S. 13:1), and both David and Achish style Saul the "king of Israel" (1 S. 24:15[14]; 26:20; 29:3). The name "Israel" also appears frequently in other contexts (cf. 1 S. 11:2,13; 14:21ff.), including of course the phrase "(Yahweh,) the God of Israel." The picture is clear: Saul's kingdom is called "Israel"; he reigns as king over God's people Israel. Similarly, David can extol him as the "glory of Israel" (2 S. 1:19). The only point at issue is whether Judah and the south were part of Saul's kingdom.[36]

---

35 *KAI,* 181.1.

36 For: Eissfeldt (emphatically), *KlSchr,* III, 135ff.; K.-D. Schunck, *Benjamin. BZAW,* 86 (1963), 124-27; Mayes, *VT,* 23 (1973), 151-170. Against: Rost, 1; Herrmann, *ThLZ,* 87 (1962), 570; *History,* 147f.; de Vaux, *The Early History of Israel,* 749.

In 2 S. 2:9, there is a list of the territories ruled by Ishbaal, Saul's son: "Gilead, 'Asher', Jezreel, Ephraim, and Benjamin." The next words, "and all Israel," can mean either that the preceding list constitutes "all Israel"—clearly without Judah—or that, while Ishbaal ruled de facto over these territories, his kingship extended de jure to the larger territory of all Israel, including Judah. The next verse, however, speaks of Ishbaal's reign "over Israel," and continues: "Only the house of Judah followed David." It is indisputable that the house of Judah was not part of Ishbaal's kingdom. Considerations of territorial history make it likely also that the house of Judah was not part of Saul's kingdom (cf. also 1 S. 18:16). Insofar as "Israel" is the political designation of this kingdom, it does not include Judah. But is this also the case in the time of Saul when the term "Israel" is used in a religious sense?

Scholars have cited the worship of Yahweh, which was clearly as typical of Judah as of Israel and thus constituted a common bond.[37] But does the name "Israel" go hand in hand with the name "Yahweh," so that worshippers of Yahweh automatically belong or should belong to Israel? We shall see that this conjecture is in fact true. In addition, it can be argued that "Israel" could never have become the political designation of David's kingdom if Judah had not been included in this "Israel."[38]

4. *Before the Monarchy.* Noth's hypothesis of an ancient Israelite amphictyony appeared to solve the problem we are dealing with: "The name 'Israel' is used in the OT tradition only as a *collective* term for a group of twelve tribes" (italics added).[39] Alt said much the same thing: "This tribal league was the first entity to bear the name Israel."[40] This hypothesis, often with modifications, was widely accepted at first;[41] but for some time so many voices have been raised in criticism and opposition that the present tendency is to avoid it entirely. The effect of this change on our interpretation of the term "Israel" is stated by Smend:[42] "Thus the question of what—and who—constituted this [premonarchic] Israel has become more open and more interesting."

The most valuable source for our question is the Song of Deborah (Jgs. 5), which contains 8 occurrences of "Israel." Two of these are in the divine appellative "Yahweh, the God of Israel" (vv. 3,5), and 1 in a genitive phrase, "the commanders (*ḥôqeqê*) of Israel" (v. 9). In all the other occurrences, the name has the prefix *be*, "in": "the leaders took the lead in Israel" (v. 2); "the peasantry rested in Israel" and Deborah "arose as a mother in Israel" (v. 7); "forty thousand in Israel" had no weapons (v. 8); Yahweh performed mighty acts "in Israel" (v. 11). We may note that this is the same usage found in Tamar's protest: "Such a thing is not done in Israel" (2 S. 13:12). This usage generally illuminates the inclusive nature of the entity "Israel." When in addition "Yahweh" is placed in apposition with "the God of Israel," this inclusive Israel is described as the

37 E.g., Herrmann, *ThLZ,* 87 (1962), 573; de Vaux, *The Early History of Israel,* 749.
38 Danell, 287f.
39 *The History of Israel,* 3.
40 P. 938.
41 E.g., by Danell, 287; Hempel, 782.
42 *Die Bundesformel,* 31f.

community of Yahweh, just as conversely Yahweh performs his mighty acts on behalf of this Israel (Jgs. 5:11; cf. v. 7).

In deciding what constituted this entity "Israel," scholars generally cite the tribes listed in Jgs. 5:14-17, which either participated in the battle (Ephraim, Benjamin, Machir [Manasseh?], Zebulun, Issachar, [and Naphtali]) or refrained (Reuben, Gilead [Gad?], Dan, and Asher), noting that Judah and the Judahite south are not mentioned and therefore did not belong to Israel.[43] It must be remembered, however, that the group engaged in battle is called, not "Israel," but "the people of Yahweh" (vv. 11,13; cf. also *ʿam* alone in vv. 2,9), who "come to the help of Yahweh" (v. 23).[44] We must not forget that the terms "Israel" and "people of Yahweh" are not coextensive; it seems that the concept of "Israel" is broader, more extensive, and more comprehensive than that of the "people of Yahweh," and a fortiori than the list of tribes participating. Whether this group of tribes would have been called "Israel" if the nonparticipants had joined the battle[45] is a moot question. It is therefore probably wrong to conclude that the Israel of Jgs. 5 comprised ideally ten tribes.[46]

The tribal oracles take us a step further. Those found in the Blessing of Moses (Dt. 33) for the most part presuppose the same situation: a cultic assembly convened by Zebulun and Issachar on their mountain, Tabor, to worship their God Yahweh (vv. 18f.); we may picture this assembly as including (besides these two tribes) Reuben (v. 6), Benjamin (v. 12), Ephraim and Manasseh (vv. 13-16), Gad (vv. 20f.), Naphtali (v. 23), Asher (vv. 24f.), Levi (vv. 8-11), and probably also Dan (v. 22), already dwelling in its northern territory. The crucial point is that Judah would like to join this group of tribes (v. 7; Schunk[47] even speaks of "Judah's presence"), making a group of twelve, and this association of tribes bears the name "Israel" (cf. vv. 10,21). The text may be dated in the twelfth or eleventh century B.C.[48]

The other evidence that Judah belonged to Israel in the early period of the judges appears in Gen. 49:10. If *šîlōh* here refers to the city Shiloh (still the most likely interpretation), then the oracle depicts what Judah hopes will be its commanding entrance into Shiloh and the obedience of the other tribes, which have Shiloh as their focal point; it bears witness to Judah's efforts to join this group of tribes—more precisely, Israel—and even expresses its claim to supremacy within this association.[49] Other considerations make it likely that here, as in the Blessing of Moses, "Judah" refers to the group constituting "Greater Judah."

In any case, it is clear that even in the early period of the judges the term "Israel" could refer to a totality involving Judah and the south, but also that the real nucleus of this Israel resided not in south, but in central Palestine.

---

43 Most recently, de Vaux, *The Early History of Israel,* 748f.; Herrmann, *History,* 119f., 147f.

44 This point is emphasized by Smend, *Yahweh War and Tribal Confederation,* 13f.; *Die Bundesformel,* 11f.

45 Smend, *Die Bundesformel,* 12.

46 See also Noth, *System,* 5f.

47 *Benjamin,* 72.

48 Zobel, *Klio,* 46 (1965), 83-92.

49 Zobel, *Stammesspruch und Geschichte,* 12-15, 75f.

5. *Origin of "Israel."* The Song of Deborah, which dates from the twelfth century B.C., is familiar with a tradition of "Yahweh's mighty acts on behalf of Israel," presupposing that these acts took place in the past; it also calls Yahweh "God of Israel" and "Lord of Sinai" (Jgs. 5:5). These observations take us back to the earliest history of this "Israel," before the occupation of Canaan. More precisely: the name "Israel" was not simply adopted by the Moses group after its entrance into Canaan; it was known to them previously.[50] It is not possible to demonstrate this, except by giving some weight to the consideration that the Moses group, intimately associated with Yahweh, is most unlikely to have adopted a name compounded with "El." In any case, the Moses group, the later "house of Joseph," which cultivated the traditions concerning Yahweh, is more likely to have been called "Israel" from time immemorial than to have adopted this El-name after entering Canaan, a change that would also have been a remarkable anachronism. If this is true, the ark saying in Nu. 10:36 ("Return, O Yahweh, to the ten thousand thousands of Israel"), generally considered suspect, may well be accurate in using the name "Israel."

It is also noteworthy that the formula "Yahweh, the God of Israel" is used for the first time in the OT in Ex. 5:1 and does not appear again until Ex. 24:10; 32:27; 34:23.[51] This reflects very closely the statements of many of the prophets (e.g., Jer. 2:3; 31:2; Ezk. 20:5,13; Am. 9:7; Hos. 9:10; 11:1; 12:14[13]); for, as Wellhausen well stated,[52] "the prophets were right to say that it was Yahweh who begat and bore Israel."

The divine appellative "Shepherd of the Rock of Israel" (*rōʿeh ʾeḇen yiśrāʾēl*) (Gen. 49:24) must also be discussed in this context. The preceding *miššām,* "from there," clearly associates this name with a place. We can no longer determine whether this is Bethel[53] or Shechem, which Gen. 33:20 associates with the name "Israel";[54] the context makes it clear, however, that the territory of the house of Joseph is involved. This setting is supported by Ps. 80:2(1), which associates *rōʿēh yiśrāʾēl* with Ephraim, Benjamin, and Manasseh (v. 3[2]). As the name "Reuel" ("El is Shepherd"; Gen. 36:4,10,13,17; etc.) also shows, and as the local association of our phrase would lead us to expect, we are dealing here with El or at least with an hypostasis of El. The association of this hypostasis with the house of Joseph and its early identification with Yahweh, suggested by the context, casts significant light on the process involved. The house of Joseph or even the groups that came to constitute the house of Joseph worshipped this El before they came to know Yahweh. Regardless of whether one gives credence to the statements in Ex. 3:6,15,16; 6:2,3 that associate the new God Yahweh with the old God (or gods) of the fathers, there was an undeniable fusion of Yahwism with the earlier worship of El. But this would mean that the Moses group or at least parts of it already knew the name "Israel."

This brings us to the last remaining mentions of the name "Israel" in Gen. 32:29(28)

---

50 Cf. Herrmann, *ThLZ,* 87 (1962), 572; Smend, *Yahweh War and Tribal Confederation,* 23, 78f.; and above all Rost, 105, n. 4, who considers the shared religion of Yahwism the precondition for the adoption of the name "Israel" by all the tribes.

51 Cf. also Auerbach, 72; Eichrodt, "Religionsgeschichte Israels," 384 (= 21).

52 P. 23.

53 Most recently Zobel, *Stammesspruch und Geschichte,* 23.

54 Otto, 132; cf. de Vaux, *The Early History of Israel,* 172f., who suggests both sites.

(L or J; cf. 35:10 [P]) and 33:20 (J): after Jacob's struggle with God at the Jabbok, he is renamed "Israel" and comes to Shechem; there before the city, on a field he buys from its inhabitants, he builds an altar (or a massebah), which he names *'ēl 'elōhê yiśrā'ēl*. Today hardly anyone doubts that the renaming reflects an historical event.[55] It has been suggested repeatedly[56] that behind it lies the coalescence of a Jacob group with an Israel group; this possibility in fact deserves serious consideration. It is nevertheless more likely that this renaming, like others in the OT,[57] reflects a change of sovereignty. In our case, precisely because the new name is theophorous and contains the element "El," a change of religion could be involved.[58] The place of the deity previously worshipped by Jacob and of course his people is now taken by El, the new God of Israel. The name "Jacob" (→ יעקב *ya'aqōḇ*), long felt to be neutral, is replaced with the name "Israel," fraught with religious overtones. In this case—as we should expect in any event—the name given the altar or massebah at Shechem should be interpreted as a confessional statement and translated "El is the God of Israel."[59] Cf. also Josh. 8:30, where the name of an altar near Shechem appears in apposition with "the God of Israel."

There is a striking difference between this name and the names of the other hypostases of El mentioned in Genesis, such as El Olam, El Shaddai, El Elyon, El Roi, or El Bethel. In them, the second element of the name is an attribute or a place name; in "El is the God of Israel," however, we have instead a genitive phrase that associates El with a group of worshippers named "Israel." This name is indeed associated with Shechem; its real locus, however, is not the place but a group for whom acceptance of the worship of El was the most important, the most crucial event in the history of their community. Up to this point, the situation is still relatively clear.

Left totally open is the question of who took part and when this took place. The choice is between the Jacob-Rachel group and the Jacob-Leah group,[60] since it is clear from the outset that this change, which revolves around the name "Israel," antedates Moses and the introduction of Yahwism.[61] In favor of the Rachel group is the location of the event, at Bethel or Shechem, in the center of the territory west of the Jordan. This was the historical homeland of the house of Joseph, which also appears to be especially associated with the name "Israel," as is suggested by the predilection for this name in the Joseph story.[62] One may object that, while these events belong to the period after the house of Joseph settled in its territory, it is unlikely that worshippers of Yahweh adopted the name "Israel." In favor of the Jacob-Leah group[63] are several observations: Gen. 34 at least describes a portion of

---

55 Contra Danell, 287; cf. Mowinckel, 130f.

56 Kittel, I, 272, 298; Hempel, 782; Seebass; Wächter, 60; similarly Mowinckel, 130-32; de Vaux, *The Early History of Israel,* 172f., 649.

57 Cf. Eissfeldt, *Festschrift D. Winton Thomas,* 73-76.

58 Suggested repeatedly by Eissfeldt: *KlSchr,* III, 414-16; IV, 96-99; *Festschrift D. Winton Thomas,* 76; *CAH,* II/2, XXVI(a), 318.

59 Smend, *Die Bundesformel,* 15.

60 Contra Mihalik, 15-17.

61 A point already made by Albright, *JBL,* 46 (1927), 168.

62 De Vaux, *The Early History of Israel,* 649; cf. Steuernagel, 331, 345f.

63 Cf. Smend, *EvTh,* 31 (1971), 626f.

this group as staying at Shechem; the incorporation of Gen. 34 into the tradition of the patriarchs suggests such a dating; and, in contrast to the tomb of Jacob east of the Jordan, the tomb of Israel is located at Hebron, i.e., in the territory of Judah or Caleb.[64] But the figure of Jacob-Israel is obviously redactional in Gen. 34 itself; and the cruel treatment of Shechem on the part of Simeon and Levi does not chime with the normal conduct of the patriarchs, who sought a peaceful accommodation with the Canaanites.[65] Furthermore, the designation of Hebron as the burial place of Israel is meant to indicate that Israel was also honored in the heartland of Greater Judah, so that it, too, was part of Israel.

Thus we can hardly escape the conclusion that these Jacob people who solemnly adopted the name "Israel" constituted a group distinct from the familiar groups of a later period named after their ancestral mothers Leah and Rachel. We must identify them with the predecessors of the people who, in the course of transhumance, came in contact with the central Palestinian region around Shechem—in other words, proto-Israelites, whose neighbors included both the Jacob-Leah people and the Jacob-Rachel people.[66]

It is hardly possible to determine which of the various groups is meant by the "Israel" in line 27 of the Merneptah inscription. On the assumption that *y-si-r-i'-r* is to be read as "Israel" rather than "Jezreel" or some other name, that the sequence of names is geographically significant, and that the text with the determinative for "people" is correct,[67] we should narrow our search to central Palestine and the period around 1230. Then we would not be dealing with the Israelite tribes that entered Canaan around 1200 after the exodus and a period of wandering in the desert (the Jacob-Rachel group),[68] but with the Jacob-Leah people, who entered Canaan at an earlier date.[69] But all these arguments are hypothetical.

III. The Religious Significance of the Name "Israel." Eissfeldt was right in expressing his "feeling that the name 'Israel' has by nature a special religious aura";[70] his statement is generally true. The only question is the nature of this special aura and its historical instantiation in any given period.

1. *El, the God of Israel.* As long as we are dealing with the deity El, we can generally transfer the substance of the patriarchal promises to Israel's religion of El, speaking of El's promise of numerous descendants and possession of the land.[71] The name "El

64 Cf. Jepsen, 48-50.

65 Cf. Eissfeldt, *CAH,* II/2, XXVI(a), 315.

66 Cf. N. K. Gottwald, *The Tribes of Yahweh* (Maryknoll, N.Y., 1979), 494f.

67 Cf. J. A. Wilson in *ANET*³, 378, n. 18; also Eissfeldt, *CAH,* II/2, XXVI(a), 317f.; and E. Otto, "Erwägungen zum Palästinaabschnitt der 'Israel-Stele' des Mernepta," *ZDMGSup,* 4 (1979), 131-33.

68 De Vaux, *The Early History of Israel,* 390f., 490f.

69 See most recently Smend, *Die Bundesformel,* 14f.

70 *KlSchr,* IV, 98.

71 Cf. O. Eissfeldt, "Der kanaanäische El als Geber der den israelitischen Erzvätern geltenden Nachkommenschaft- und Landbesitzverheissungen," *Festschrift C. Brockelmann. WZ Halle-Wittenberg,* 17 (1968), 45-53 = *KlSchr,* V, 50-62.

reigns" (or the like) vouches for Israel's hope in the fulfillment of these promises. And when Jacob, the father of what was to be the people Israel, was given the name enshrining these promises, it was as though the expectation of becoming a great nation and possessing the land had been fulfilled. The fact that the El of Shechem is given the designation "God of Israel," which refers to this group, indicates the intimate, almost personal contact between El and Israel. For the group accepting El as their God, the consequences of adopting such a highly religious name can hardly be measured. In any case, this event almost certainly endued this group with a sense of their own "unity and solidarity."[72] Not only does the name "Israel" in the OT have a "religious aura" from the outset; it also embodies the notion of a totality, united inwardly by common hopes and convictions and defined outwardly by the common confession of "El, the God of Israel."

2. *Yahweh, the God of Israel.* The expression "Yahweh, the God of Israel" is the proper religio-historical equivalent to the earlier expression "El, the God of Israel," for it reflects the identification of El with Yahweh. We are therefore justified in expecting to find associated with it the same two aspects of the totality and the corresponding self-understanding. Now it is immediately clear that the formula "Yahweh, the God of Israel" cannot antedate the revelation of Yahweh's name to Moses. And if we assign the name "Israel" a Canaanite locus in or near Shechem and assume that the group called by this name likewise dwelt exclusively in Canaan, then the formula "Yahweh, the God of Israel" is inconceivable until after the entrance into Canaan of the groups coming from Egypt. It would assume that these groups coalesced with another group that had remained in Canaan and bore the name "Israel."[73] This theory deserves serious consideration; it seems to the author, however, that the adoption of a name compounded with "El" by a group that worshipped Yahweh is harder to explain than the reverse process, and that there are grounds for assuming that the Moses group, already calling itself "Israel" or belonging to this Israel, became acquainted with Yahweh as a new deity and saw the ideas associated with the name "Israel" realized more clearly than before in Yahweh's mighty acts. The parallel collocation of "Yahweh, the one from Sinai" and "Yahweh, the God of Israel" in the Song of Deborah (Jgs. 5:5) is to be understood as reflecting the identity of the terms in apposition.

Our sources still reflect the fact that Yahweh became the God of Israel during the events of the exodus and Sinai. Following Gen. 33:20 with its "El, the God of Israel," the first instance of "Yahweh, the God of Israel" is found in the prophetical formula introducing the words Moses and Aaron address to Pharaoh: "Thus says Yahweh, the God of Israel, 'Let my people go'" (Ex. 5:1); the equivalent in Ex. 4:22f. (J or L) is: "Thus says Yahweh, Israel is my first-born son. . . . 'Let my son go.'" The Yahweh formula appears again in the archaic passage describing the meal Moses and the seventy elders share with the "God of Israel" (Ex. 24:10 [J or L]) and in the equally early narrative

72 Eichrodt, "Religionsgeschichte Israels," 384 (= 21), albeit with reference to Sinai.
73 Smend, *Die Bundesformel,* 14-18.

of the choice of the Levites to serve as priests (Ex. 32:27 [J or L]). It also appears in J's cultic decalog (Ex. 34:23; cf. also 20:2).

This association of the name "Israel" with the fundamental events of Israel's early history explains the special solemnity that, among other things, led to the preference for styling Yahweh "the God of Israel" in ceremonious discourse;[74] it also makes clear the intimate relationship between this Israel and Yahweh. Because Yahweh showed this community his favor, opened for it a new future, and gave it the law entrusted to the Levites (cf. Dt. 33:10), the Moses group became a Yahweh community, standing henceforth under Yahweh's special protection and at the same time obligated to obey his law addressed specifically to it. Thus "Yahweh fights for Israel," as we read in Josh. 10:14,42; but his anger can also be kindled against Israel, as when Israel deserted him for Baʿal of Peor (Nu. 25:3,4). It is irrelevant whether or not the phrase "people of Yahweh" is attested in this early period; the reality is there: the clearly demarcated community of "Israel," religiously defined and devoted to its God.[75]

3. *Nationalistic Elements during the Early Monarchy.* A change appears to take place early in the period of David; at least this is when the sources first allow us to glimpse this change. On the one hand, we find enthusiastic poetry like Nu. 24:3-9; Dt. 33:26-29, extolling the outward power and glory of Israel; the latter concludes with a characteristic shout of jubilation: "Hail, O Israel! Who is your equal?" On the other hand, we find in this period a remarkable wealth of passages using "Jacob" in parallel with "Israel," usually with "Jacob" preceding. As an example, we may cite the Balaam poems once more, and especially Nu. 24:17. If, as the vague imagery of this poem suggests, it is not a *vaticinium ex eventu* but a truly prophetic poem predicting the imminent rise of David, it (like the third poem in Nu. 24:3-9) dates from the time of Saul. As we have seen,[76] the name "Jacob" does more to express the national solidarity of the people as a whole and is therefore a favorite term to express the visible power and greatness of the nation. The parallel use of the two terms "Jacob" and "Israel," both of which convey the sense of a totality, sets in motion a process of mutual semantic influence. The name "Jacob" begins to shine with the reflected religious glow of the term "Israel," and the designation "Israel" begins to have stronger overtones of national solidarity. This is particularly so when Israel is described as comprising twelve tribes, so that no tribe must be cut off from Israel (Jgs. 21:3,6,17), no city and mother must be destroyed in Israel (2 S. 20:19f.), and when the basic form of the Pentateuchal tradition is set forth in terms of all Israel. This probably first took place in J, but in any case during the period of David and Solomon.

4. *Israel as the People of God in Preexilic Prophecy.* The significance of the name "Israel" was not seriously called into question by the division of the kingdom and the adoption of the term "Israel" in a restricted sense to designate the northern kingdom.

---

74 Cf. the list (based on Steuernagel) in Smend, *Die Bundesformel,* 20.

75 Cf. *ibid.,* 21.

76 → יעקב *yaʿaqōḇ.*

"Israel" also continues to designate the whole people of God. In a certain sense, however, we do note a change. In contrast to the Yahwist's Balaam poems, those of the Elohist (Nu. 23:7-10,18-24) exhibit a shift of accent from nationalistic religion to religious nationalism. "Israel" cannot be cursed because it has been blessed by God for all time (vv. 7f.); as a blessed nation, it cannot experience misfortune or trouble (vv. 20f.); there is no enchantment or divination among God's people Jacob/Israel, for whom God has done great things (vv. 22f.).

This notion of the unity of the people of God also shapes the ministry of the prophets. It is the reason why a prophet from the southern kingdom like Amos appears in the northern kingdom, addresses the people of that kingdom as "Israel" (Am. 4:12) or (speaking on behalf of Yahweh) "my people Israel" (7:8,15; 8:2; cf. 9:14 [redactional]), uses the term "Israel" in connection with the exodus from Egypt (3:1; 9:7), the forty years of wandering in the desert (5:25), and the destruction of the Amorites (cf. 2:6-11), and finally announces the end of Israel (3:14; 4:12; 7:9,11,16,17). As Wolff rightly concludes,[77] "Israel" here clearly means "the people of God."

The same is true for Isaiah. The parallelism of "Israel" and "my people" (Isa. 1:3), the prophet's statement that his children are to be "signs and portents in Israel" (8:18), his confidence that the "remnant of Israel," "the survivors of the house of Jacob," will return to "Yahweh, the Holy One of Israel" (10:20-22; note that "Israel" precedes "Jacob"), and last but not least Yahweh's titles "*'ᵃḇîr* of Israel" (1:24), "light of Israel" (10:17), and "the Holy One of Israel" (12 occurrences) all use "Israel" in the sense "the people of God." But because the people Isaiah is addressing have nothing in common with the people of Yahweh—he speaks almost contemptuously of "this people" (e.g., 6:9,10; 8:6,11,12; 9:15[16])—because as the people of God they should have knowledge of Yahweh, they will be unable to escape the judgment imposed by Yahweh in his sovereign majesty as "the Holy One of Israel," a judgment from which only a "remnant of Israel" will escape and turn in faithfulness to their God.

Hosea, the only prophet known to us from the northern kingdom, exhibits similar if not identical notions concerning the import of the name "Israel." Israel is the historical people of God: "like grapes in the wilderness, I found Israel" (Hos. 9:10); "when Israel was a child, I loved him" (11:1); "Yahweh brought Israel up from Egypt" (12:14[13]), perhaps also 10:9: "from the days of Gibeah, you have sinned, O Israel." Israel is the people loved by God as a father loves his son. The abbreviated formula "Yahweh your God from the land of Egypt" (12:10[9]; 13:4) makes it clear that the prophet is addressing this same Israel, calling it to repent and return "to Yahweh your God" (14:2[1]). When Ephraim is said to be "exalted in Israel" (13:1), we can sense a distinction between Ephraim and Israel. It may therefore be correct to follow Wolff[78] in interpreting "Israel" used in parallel with the political designation "Ephraim" (4:15; 5:9; 8:2,3,6,14; 9:1; 10:1; 13:9; 14:2,6[1,5]) to mean the people of Yahweh as a whole, with further specification of the part addressed—Ephraim, Judah, Samaria, or whatever. Just as the name "Israel" is symbolic of God's election, in Hosea it

77 H. W. Wolff, *Joel and Amos. Herm* (Eng. trans. 1977), 165.

78 Wolff, *Hosea,* 164; contra Rost, 105-7.

becomes also a sign of God's will to maintain the covenant. The so-called covenant formula—"Yahweh, the God of Israel, and Israel, the people of Yahweh"—stands behind both the proclamation of judgment in 1:9 and the promise of salvation in 2:25(23).[79] Thus the personal aspect of Yahwism is now fully integrated into the name "Israel" through the personal relationship between God and the people of God.

In general terms, this concludes the development of the meaning of "Israel." The other preexilic prophets do not introduce any major new themes. Israel is the people of God that "was holy" to Yahweh (Jer. 2:3; cf. 10:16), whom he led (Jer. 31:2; 32:21) but now must bring to judgment (Mic. 6:2; cf. 3:1,8,9; also Lam. 2:1,3,5), whose remnant must be gathered (Mic. 2:12; 5:2[3]; cf. Zeph. 3:13; Jer. 31:7; stated more sharply in Jer. 6:9) and will belong to the "ruler in Israel" coming forth from Bethlehem Ephrathah (Mic. 5:1[2]; cf. Zeph. 3:15: "Yahweh, the king of Israel"). Similarly, the call to Israel (Zeph. 3:14; par. "daughter Zion" and "daughter Jerusalem") to rejoice and exult announces the dawn of the age of salvation. This is reflected in the divine appellatives: "Yahweh Sabaoth, the God of Israel" (35 times in Jeremiah), "Yahweh, the God of Israel" (14 times in Jeremiah), "the Holy One of Israel" (Jer. 50:29; 51:5), "the hope of Israel" (Jer. 14:8; 17:13).

5. *Israel in Deuteronomy.* Deuteronomy represents as it were the systematized theological precipitate of all these statements. It frequently speaks with emphasis of "all Israel" (e.g., Dt. 1:1; 11:6; 13:12[11]; 18:6; 31:1,11 [twice]; 34:12). Israel is called on repeatedly to hear the statutes and ordinances and obey them (4:1; 5:1; 6:3,4; 9:1; 13:12; 20:3; 21:21; 27:9) and to purge the evil from its midst (17:12; 22:21,22); for "this day you have become the people of Yahweh, your God" (27:9). The book speaks of "thy people Israel" (21:8 [twice]; 26:15), whom Yahweh "loved" (7:8; cf. also 1 K. 10:9), "redeemed" (Dt. 21:8), "chose" (7:6), and made "his own possession" (26:18). The use of the second person throughout most of Deuteronomy means that the name Israel appears rarely (cf. the last passages); but the notion of a "holy people" (7:6; 14:2,21; 26:19; 28:9) also belongs in this context. "Israel" is the name of "the community for which what matters most is its commitment to Yahweh."[80]

6. *Israel in Exilic and Postexilic Prophecy.* During the exilic period, this extreme concentration on the religious import of the name "Israel" resulted in its being applied to the exiles as a group. It appears with this meaning as early as Jeremiah (e.g., Jer. 50:17,19). Deutero-Isaiah uses "Israel" frequently for the people of the exile, at the same time emphasizing Israel's connection with its past. Yahweh "formed" (*yṣr*) Jacob (Isa. 43:1; par. Israel); he is the "Creator (*bôrē'*) of Israel" (43:15); on account of its misdeeds, Yahweh allowed Jacob/Israel to be destroyed (42:24; 43:22,28). Now, however, Yahweh has redeemed Jacob/Israel (44:23) and called it by name (45:4; cf. 48:12); he is putting salvation in Zion for Israel (46:13; cf. 45:17). Thus Israel is called Yahweh's "chosen" (44:1; 45:4), his "servant" (44:21; 49:3), his "glory" (46:13). Conversely, Yahweh is

---

79 Smend, *Die Bundesformel,* 24f.
80 Hulst, 103.

titled "the God of Israel" (41:17; 45:3,15; 48:1,2; 52:12), the "Creator" (43:15), "Redeemer" (49:7), "King" (44:6), and "Holy One" (41:14) of Israel. As 44:5 says with lapidary accuracy, "Israel" is "a cognomen" by which one may call himself or be called (44:5; 48:1), a name expressing membership in the community of Yahweh and thus representing something like a confession of faith.

In some ways, this differs from the usage of the prophet Ezekiel.[81] Here "Israel" denotes the people of God of the past (Ezk. 20:5,13); in contrast to Jeremiah's usage, however, this unified past lasts until the end of Judah's existence as an independent state (cf. 13:2,9; 18:6; 38:17) and Jerusalem is described as the center of the land of Israel (cf. 12:19; 21:7[2]; ch. 48). But it also denotes the band of exiles to which the prophet is sent, which he calls "the house of Israel" (3:1,4,5,7[twice],17; etc.) or "sons of Israel" (2:3; 4:13; 6:5; etc.). It is this Israel whose elders come to him (14:1; 20:1,3). That this Israel is the people of Yahweh is clear from the phrase "my people Israel" (14:9; 25:14; 36:8,12; 38:14,16; 39:7), as well as references to its election (20:5) and sanctification (37:28), but also its straying (44:10), its guilt (4:4f.; 9:9), its abominations (6:11), and its idols (8:10; 18:6,15). Last but not least, this solidarity of the people of God as homogeneous entity, almost like a family, is emphasized by expressions coined by Ezekiel, such as *'admaṯ yiśrā'ēl* (17 occurrences, only in Ezekiel) and *hārê yiśrā'ēl* (16 occurrences, only in Ezekiel). The unity of God's land reflects the unity of his people: the fertile soil and the mountains together constitute "the land of Israel." There is also the phrase *n^eḇî'ê yiśrā'ēl* (13:2,16; 38:17), found only in Ezekiel, which associates "the phenomenon of prophecy with the people of God."[82] The "mountains of Israel" are to yield fruit for Yahweh's people Israel (36:8), who are to walk upon them (36:12) as a people (37:22); false prophets will never be seen again in the land of Israel (13:9); and "on my holy mountain, the mountain height of Israel, . . . all the house of Israel . . . shall serve [Yahweh] in the land" (20:40; cf. 34:14). But all this is to one end, that "the house of Israel may know that I am Yahweh their God" (39:22), "that I Yahweh sanctify Israel" (37:28), that "my holy name I will make known in the midst of my people Israel" (39:7), "that they may be my people and I may be their God" (14:11), that he is "the Holy One in Israel" (39:7), whose glory as the God of Israel is at stake (8:4; 9:3; 10:19; 11:22; 43:2). "The majesty of the divine name stands over Israel, Yahweh's own people. . . . That is the deepest mystery of Israel."[83]

There is really nothing definite to say about postexilic prophecy. The 2 occurrences of "Israel" in Proto-Zechariah (Zec. 2:2[1:19]; 8:13) refer to the past. Haggai does not use "Israel" at all. Rost's conclusion[84] fits the facts: "The diaspora of its own accord refrained from using 'Israel' to ensure its uniqueness." He is also correct in describing the use of "Israel" in Deutero-Zechariah (Zec. 9:1; 11:14; 12:1) as archaizing.[85] The occurrences in Trito-Isaiah (Isa. 56:8 [= 11:12]; 63:7,16) are obscure.[86]

---

81 On the following discussion, see Zimmerli, *VT,* 8 (1958), 78-90; *Ezekiel 2,* 563-65.
82 Zimmerli, *Ezekiel 2,* 565.
83 Zimmerli, *VT,* 8 (1958), 90.
84 Pp. 113f.
85 *Ibid.,* 115.
86 Cf. *ibid.,* 114.

In contrast, it is noteworthy that Malachi uses the name "Israel" 5 times. The Moses group is called by this name (Mal. 3:22[4:4]). There was a faithless Israel as well as a faithless Judah and Jerusalem (2:11). But the postexilic community addressed by the prophet is also called "Israel" (1:1,5); its God bears the ancient name "Yahweh, the God of Israel" (2:16).

7. *Israel in the Chronicler's History.* This "predilection for Israel"[87] increases in 1–2 Chronicles. As a result, the patriarch who was Esau's brother is called not "Jacob" but "Israel" (1 Ch. 1:34; cf. also 1 Ch. 2:1; 5:1,3; 6:23[38]; 7:29; 16:13), the text speaks of "Israel our father" (1 Ch. 29:10) and "the God of Abraham, Isaac, and Israel, our fathers" (1 Ch. 29:18; 2 Ch. 30:6), "Israel" is used to denote both the former northern kingdom (1 Ch. 5:17; 2 Ch. 16:1; etc.) and Judah (1 Ch. 9:1; 2 Ch. 21:2,4; etc.), and is also the name of premonarchic Israel (1 Ch. 2:7; 17:5; 2 Ch. 24:6,9). This observation alone makes it clear that the Chronicler is concerned to emphasize the continuity and totality of Israel; this concern is further underlined by the use of "all Israel" in 1 Chronicles (21 times) and 2 Chronicles (25 times) (1 Ch. 9:1; 11:1,4,10; 12:39[38] [twice]; 13:5,6,8; 14:8; 15:3,28; 18:14; 19:17; 21:4,5; 28:4; 29:21,23,25,26; 2 Ch. 1:2[twice]; 6:29; 7:6,8; 9:30; 10:1,3,16[twice]; 11:3,13; 12:1; 13:4,15; 18:16; 24:5; 28:23; 29:24[twice]; 30:1,5,6; 31:1; 35:3). The phrases "all the assembly[88] of Israel" (1 Ch. 13:2; 2 Ch. 6:3[twice],12,13) and "all Israel, the assembly (*qᵉhal*) of Yahweh" (1 Ch. 28:8) and also the identification of "all Israel" with "the [entire] assembly" (clear from comparison of 1 Ch. 29:1,10,20 with vv. 21,23,25,26) indicate that the postexilic cultic community constitutes this Israel (cf. the use of *qāhāl* also in 2 Ch. 1:3,5; 7:8; 20:5,14; 23:3; 24:6; 28:14; 29:23,28,31,32; 30:2,4,13,17,23,24[twice],25; 31:18). This is also emphasized by such a statement as: "Yahweh Sabaoth, the God of Israel, is God over Israel" (1 Ch. 17:24), where the original reads only: "Yahweh Sabaoth is God over Israel" (2 S. 7:26). By adding "the God of Israel," the Chronicler establishes historical continuity between the two uses of "Israel" in the formula: the Israel of the past is embodied in the present assembly of Yahweh.

In the books of Ezra and Nehemiah, we observe the following: The exiles returning to Judah are called "Israel" (Ezr. 2:70) or "the people of Israel" (Ezr. 2:2; even 7:13). They are descended "from Israel" (Ezr. 2:59; Neh. 7:61) and also are "Israel" (Ezr. 6:17; 7:10; Neh. 10:34[33]; 11:3; 13:3) or "all Israel" (Neh. 7:73; 12:47), which hears the law of its God and must live by it. It is therefore evident that Yahweh should be called "God of Israel" (Ezr. 1:3; 4:1,3; 6:21; 7:6; 9:15; also 3:2; 5:1; 6:22; 7:15; 8:35; 9:4). "Israel" thus denotes membership in both the people and the cultic community. The two are identical, so that aliens are "separated from Israel" (Neh. 13:3). Others cannot even claim to belong to Israel, for this cultic community is all Israel. It is also striking that, in contrast to Ezra, the book of Nehemiah does not use the title "God of Israel" for Yahweh.[89] The

---

87 *Ibid.*, 114.
88 → קהל *qāhāl*.
89 Cf. Williamson.

book of Daniel, which calls the exiles "Israel" (Dnl. 1:3; cf. 9:7,11,20), likewise does not use the title "Yahweh, the God of Israel."

8. *Israel in the Psalter.* Because the Psalter contains poetry from the entire OT period, it reflects the entire range of meanings of "Israel." In parallel with "Ephraim," "Benjamin," and "Manasseh" (Ps. 80:2f.[1f.]), "Israel" can denote a group of tribes in central Palestine; the rejection of Israel (78:59) in parallel with the rejection of the "tent of Joseph" (v. 67) probably refers to the Israel of Saul's period; the frequent conjunction of "Jacob" and "Israel" denotes the entire people of God (14:7 par. 53:7[6]; 78:5,21,71; 81:5[4]; 98:3[LXX 97:3]; 105:10,23; 114:1; 135:4; 147:19; cf. 22:24[23]). References to Israel as "my [or 'his'] people" (50:7; 81:9,12,14[8,11,13]; 135:12; cf. 148:14), "his inheritance" (78:71; 135:4), "his dominion" (114:2), and "his servant" (136:22) express the intimate ties binding this people to Yahweh its God; for the same reason, the Psalms speak of Yahweh's fundamental acts in history (78:31; 103:7; 105:23; 114:1; 136:11, 14,22; 147:19). All these statements follow the lines already sketched. In addition, Israel appears as the cultic community of God, called to worship and give thanks to their Lord (22:24[23]; 68:27[26]; 118:2; 124:1; 129:1; 135:19f.; 149:2; cf. 122:4), which places its hope and trust in him (14:7 par. 53:7[6]; 25:22; 115:9; 130:7; 131:3; 147:2) and hears the shout "Peace be in Israel!" (125:5; 128:6). Finally, the divine epithets should be mentioned: "El of Israel" (68:36[35]); "Yahweh, the God of Israel" (41:14[13]; 72:18; 106:48; cf. 68:9[8]); "the Holy One of Israel" (71:22; 78:41; 89:19[18]); "Yahweh Sabaoth, the God of Israel" (59:6[5]); "God of Israel" (69:7[6]); "Shepherd of Israel" (80:2[1]); the "keeper of Israel" (121:4), Israel's "Maker" (149:2). They all express the interrelatedness of Israel and Yahweh, given almost classic expression in 22:4(3): "Thou art the Holy One, enthroned on the praises of Israel."

IV. Israel in Post-OT Jewish Literature.

1. *The Apocrypha and Pseudepigrapha.* The tendency observed in Chronicles continues in post-OT Jewish literature. "Israel" is the "typical self-designation of the Jewish people,[90] whereas the non-Jewish world speaks of "Jews" (cf., e.g., 1 Mc. 11:20,30, 33,49-51; 12:3[91]). This literature continues to speak of "Israel," "the people of Israel," and "the whole house of Israel" (Jth. 4:1,8,9,11,15; 5:1; 1 Mc. 13:26,41,42; etc.; Ps.Sol. 8:26,28), as well as the "God of Israel" (Jth. 4:12; 6:21; 10:1; 12:8; 13:7; 14:10; etc.; Ps.Sol. 4:1; 9:8; 16:3; etc.). "Israel" denotes the cultic community (also in Bar. 3:9,10,24,36; 4:4,5; 5:7,8,9) that enjoys the mercy of its God (Jth. 13:14; Ps.Sol. 9:11; 11:1,9) and is his servant (Ps.Sol. 17:21). An alien like Achior can be received into the community by accepting circumcision (Jth. 14:10). "Israel" is the community's name of honor (Sir. 44:23; cf. Ps.Sol. 14:5). As the best portion of the human race, it is under the protection of the angel Michael (1 (Eth.)En. 20:5 conj.). At the eschaton, "Israel" will experience God's punishment of the heathen, rise up in joy, and look down from above

90 A. Strobel, "Israel. III," *BHHW,* II, 786.
91 See the discussion by Kuhn in *TDNT,* III, 360.

upon its enemies, vindicated by its God (As.Mos. 10:8-10). This Israel, belonging to the present and yet timeless, is described most vividly as a religious and cultic community in Ps.Sol. 11:7: "Put on, Jerusalem, the clothes of your glory, for God has determined good things for Israel for ever and ever"; 17:44: "Blessed are those who will live in those days and be able to see the salvation of Israel in the union of the tribes."

2. *Qumran.* In the literature specifically associated with Qumran, the name "Israel" appears with particular frequency in the Damascus document (43 times), the War scroll (28 times), and the Manual of Discipline (16 times). To the extent that the text does not represent an OT quotation or similar reference (as in 1QM 11:6f.; CD 7:19f.), Israel is "the people of God" (1QM 3:13) and the name of its God is "El of Israel" (1QS 3:24; 1QM 1:9f.; 6:6; 10:8; 13:1; etc.). The Qumran community belongs to this Israel (1QS 5:5,22; 6:13; 9:16; CD 3:19). At the same time, one receives the impression that "Israel" as the community of God is set apart within a larger Israel. In lists like that in CD 14:4-6, we find the sequence: "Levites, priests, Israel, and aliens" (cf. CD 10:5). Aaron and Israel are frequently conjoined (1QS 9:11; cf. CD 1:7; 10:5; 1QM 5:1), just as two messiahs are expected, one out of Aaron and one out of Israel (1QS 9:11; CD 13:1; 14:10; 19:11; 20:1; etc.). When God's glory appears, the wicked will be exterminated from Israel (CD 20:6); others will be left "as a remnant for Israel" (CD 1:5), with whom God will "establish his covenant for Israel for ever [cf. 1QS 5:5], to reveal to them the mystery wherein all Israel went astray" (CD 3:13f.). Thus an exclusive Israel is set apart within the larger totality of all Israel (1QS 6:13f.). This is the true Israel, "the house of perfection and truth in Israel" (1QS 8:9), for whom God built "a sure and certain house in Israel" (1QM 10:9). The "simple people of Ephraim" will join this Israel (4QpNah 3:5). This exclusive Israel is the Qumran community, which, as the nucleus of Israel, has a mission to all Israel.

Zobel

יָשַׁב *yāšab̲*; מוֹשָׁב *môšāb̲*

Contents: I. Occurrences: 1. Morphology and Extrabiblical Evidence; 2. Statistics; 3. LXX. II. Human Subjects: 1. Semantics; 2. "Sit Down"/"Sit"; 3. "Settle"/"Dwell"; 4. "Ascend the Throne"/"Reign"; 5. Cultic Usage. III. Divine Subjects: 1. Syntagmemes; 2. The *mkwn* Formula and Allusions; 3. The Epithet *yôšēb̲ kᵉrūb̲îm* and its Semantics; 4. Finite Forms and their Semantics; 5. "Ark" and "Angel" as Subjects.

---

yāšab̲. L. H. Brockington, "The Use of the Hebrew Verb יָשַׁב to Describe an Act in Religious Observance," *Festschrift G. W. Thatcher* (Sydney, 1967), 119-125; A. Feuillet, "'S'asseoir à l'ombre' de l'Époux (*Os.*, XIV, 8ª et *Cant.*, II, 3)," *RB*, 78 (1971), 391-405; M. Haran, "The Ark and the Cherubim: Their Symbolic Significance in Biblical Ritual," *Eretz-Israel*, 5 (1958), 83-90 [Heb.] = *IEJ*, 9 (1959), 30-38, 89-94 [Eng.]; R. Kilian, *Die vorpriesterlichen Abrahams-*

I. Occurrences. 1. *Morphology and Extrabiblical Evidence.* The base *wṯb* that lies behind the West Semitic root *yšb*[1] is morphologically an expansion of the consonant pair *ṯb* by the addition of the prefixed root augment *w.* The semantic nucleus of the biliteral primary base has not been determined beyond all doubt,[2] but probably lies in the realm of change of location, especially in the case of persons. Shift to a lasting or even permanent state appears to be in the foreground.

In Akkadian, *wašābu,* a fientic verb with initial *wa-,* belongs to the group of "verbs of motion with a specific origin or destination."[3] There is also a rare secondary form *tašābu.*[4] Phonological change led to the loss of the root augment (*wašābu* > *ašābu*) in Middle and Late Babylonian.[5] The range of meanings can be grouped into several sections,[6] with a primary distinction between habitual and causative habitual senses. There are causative forms (*šûšubu*) corresponding to the basic meanings "sit down," "reside and live somewhere," and "be settled," all with the common aspect of enduring presence. Of special interest is the semantic nuance of "sitting on a throne," used primarily of kings and gods.[7] Lawhead[8] has recently given a partial explanation of the material in *CAD.* Akk. *ušbu,* "seat," "throne," appears also as a loanword in Egyptian, in the phonological equivalent *ỉsb.t/ỉsp.t,* with the additional meaning "kind of shelter."[9] The Egyptian reflex with the feminine article appears in cuneiform as *ta-as-bu* in the vocabulary of the Amarna letters,[10] where the meaning "chair" reappears. The two contradictory transcriptions of the Amarna period probably represent an unusual phenomenon.

While the cuneiform Amarna literature has only the verb form *nišab*[11] as an example of a West Semitic prefix conjugation,[12] Ugaritic provides a broad range of syntagmemic variants that are relevant to Hebrew, as well as a variety of correlative word pairs that are semantically significant. The root *yṯb,* with the broad basic meanings "sit," "be

---

Überlieferungen. BBB, 24 (1966), 246, 249; A. S. Lawhead, *A Study of the Theological Significance of* yašab *in the Masoretic Text, with Attention to its Translation in the Septuagint* (diss., Boston, 1975; repr. 1977); M. Metzger, "Himmlische und irdische Wohnstatt Jahwes," *UF,* 2 (1970), 139-158; R. de Vaux, "Les chérubins et l'arche d'alliance, les sphinx gardiens et les trônes divins dans l'Ancien Orient," *MUSJ,* 37 (1960/61), 91-124 = *Bible et Orient* (Paris, 1967), 231-259; A. Wuckelt, *Die Basis* YŠB *in Gottesprädikationen des ATs* (1978).

1 P. Marrassini, *Formazione del lessico dell' edilizia militare nel semitico di Siria. QuadSem,* 1 (1971), 16-18.

2 "Turn away," "move away," according to R. L. Cate, *The Theory of Biliteral Roots* (Louisville, 1959), 152; similarly G. Robinson, "The Idea of Rest in the OT and the Search for the Basic Character of Sabbath," *ZAW,* 92 (1980), 41.

3 *GaG,* §103b.

4 *Ibid.,* §103d, h.

5 Cf. *ibid.,* §103i.

6 *CAD,* I/2 (1968), 387ff.

7 *Ibid.,* 396f.

8 Pp. 51-55.

9 W. A. Ward, "Notes on Some Semitic Loan-Words and Personal Names in Late Egyptian," *Or,* 32 (1963), 418.

10 EA 368; cf. A. F. Rainey, *El Amarna Tablets 359-379. AOAT,* 8 (^{2}1978), 38f.

11 EA 363, 21.

12 Cf. the translation "we may dwell" in Rainey, 65.

enthroned," is realized not only in verb forms but also in nominal derivatives such as *ṯbt,* "(the act or state of) sitting," and *mṯb,* "a dwelling."[13] The list of lexical meanings[14] can be improved by classification according to the prepositions used. According to Pardee,[15] we find the combinations *yṯb b/btk,* "sit/live in," *yṯb l,* "sit for (temporal)," *yṯb l,* "sit in order to," *yṯb l,* "sit on," and *yṯb tḫt,* "sit at the feet of." The later neighboring dialects have equivalents for many of these, the Hebrew of the OT for them all. Looking for possible analogies in the OT, Dahood notes a series of word pairs, such as *yṯb // ẓll, nḥl, nḫ, rʿy,* and *ṯpt,*[16] *yṯb // šty,*[17] and even *yṯb // yṯb.*[18] As in Akkadian, the semantic field in Ugaritic[19] exhibits both the central meanings cited and the special sense of "be enthroned," used of a king or god.[20] Baʿal in particular is said to "sit enthroned."[21] Baʿal can also perform the act of *yṯb lks3,* "sitting down on the throne."[22]

The later West Semitic dialects related to OT Hebrew do not appear to add much to the semantic repertory.[23] Even in Phoenician and Punic, besides the use of the base as both verb and noun, we may still observe a differentiation among the aspects of habitual and causative habitual "dwelling," etc.[24]

We may also cite the West Semitic use of *yṯb* to form proper names. Already among the names from Mari we find such forms as *ya-aw-ši-bu*[25] and (in the gen.) *wa-ši-bi-im.*[26] The alleged Ugaritic toponym *yṯbmlk* should be accepted with caution; it certainly does not mean "royal residence"[27] and may possibly represent a verbal clause name (something like "may a king [or '*Mlk*'] sit enthroned" at the place in question). In late West Semitic, it is difficult at best to identify proper names that are clearly based on *yšb.*

---

13 *UT,* no. 1177; according to Gordon, the problem of distinguishing *yṯb* forms from **ṯwb* forms is "due mostly to the orthography."

14 Cf. *WUS,* nos. 140f.

15 D. G. Pardee, "Attestations of Ugaritic Verb/Preposition Combinations in Later Dialects," *UF,* 9 (1977), 216.

16 M. Dahood and T. Penar, "Ugaritic-Hebrew Parallel Pairs," *RSP,* I, nos. 270-75.

17 M. Dahood, "Ugaritic-Hebrew Parallel Pairs," *RSP,* II, no. 25.

18 Dahood-Penar, *RSP,* I, no. 271; cf. also P. C. Craigie, "Parallel Word Pairs in Ugaritic Poetry," *Festschrift C. F. A. Schaeffer. UF,* 11 (1979), 138.

19 Provisionally described by Lawhead, 60-62, on the basis of Whitaker's concordance.

20 Cf. Lawhead, 60-62; also W. H. Schmidt, *Königtum Gottes in Ugarit und Israel. BZAW,* 80 (²1966), 65, n. 9.

21 On the alleged "royal residence" of Baʿal at Astaroth and Edrei (*KTU,* 1.108 rto., 3, as interpreted by B. Margulis, "A Ugaritic Psalm (RŠ 24.252)," *JBL,* 89 [1970], 292-304), see the critical comments of such scholars as M. Görg, "Noch einmal: Edrei in Ugarit?" *UF,* 6 (1974), 474f., with bibliog., and M. C. Astour and D. E. Smith, "Place Names," *RSP,* II, no. 36.

22 See P. J. van Zijl, *Baal. AOAT,* 10 (1972), 218f.

23 Cf. *DISO,* 111f., with the meanings "sit, dwell, reside" and their corresponding causatives; Lawhead (55-60) examines some of the occurrences on the basis of *KAI.*

24 Cf. the citations in R. S. Tomback, *A Comparative Semitic Lexicon of the Phoenician and Punic Languages. SBL Diss.,* 32 (Missoula, 1978), 130.

25 See *APNM,* 68, 185.

26 *Ibid.,* 185; but cf. A. Goetze, "Remarks on Some Names Occurring in the Execration Texts," *BASOR,* 151 (1958), 31f.

27 As suggested by Astour, *RSP,* II, no. 293.

The two uniquely South Semitic meanings, Ethiop. *'awšaba,* "marry," and Arab. *waṯaba,* "leap up from one's seat,"[28] will be mentioned only in passing, since they clearly lie outside the semantic range just delineated. Even here, however, we can identify a useful connection with the semantic nucleus proposed above, if we think in both cases of the persons concerned as undergoing a change of place. The first case may involve something like resettlement in a different kinship group. The possible occurrence of the meaning "marry" in the OT is discussed below.

2. *Statistics.* According to Lawhead's tabulation,[29] the base appears most frequently in Jeremiah (149 occurrences); next, with less than half as many, come Genesis (71), Judges (71), Isaiah (71), Ezekiel (62), and Psalms (60). There are 1090 occurrences in all. More informative is the list of finite and nonfinite verbal realizations of the base,[30] which documents an absolute preponderance of G stem forms; almost half of the 1090 occurrences of the G stem are participial forms (496).[31] The dominant role of the participial forms may confirm the perspective of movement to an enduring state proposed for the semantic nucleus. It is dubious, however, whether Lawhead's purely statistical evidence concerning allegedly parallel passages justifies the conclusion that "there is a continuity in the meaning of various grammatical forms of *yašab* throughout the history of the writing of the OT."[32] He further concludes[33] that the occurrence of the phrase *mē'ên yôšēḇ,* "without inhabitant," exclusively in Jeremiah (9 times) and Zephaniah (twice) is convincing evidence that they were contemporaries and that Zephaniah may even have been a disciple of Jeremiah; this argument, too, must be met with skepticism.

The nominal derivative *môšāḇ,* according to Lawhead, appears 44 times, including 10 occurrences in construct phrases. Its distribution is generally even. A second derivative → תּוֹשָׁב *tôšāḇ* appears 14 times, without exhibiting any noteworthy correlations.[34]

The verbal usages, however, may be classified provisionally according to grammatical subject.[35] Only in 8 passages is the subject an inanimate object; in 5 of these it is the ark.[36] Animals appear as subject only in Job 38:40 (young lions); the statistical difference between the usage of *yšb* and → שׁכן *škn* in this regard appears to be significant. Most of the occurrences appear in passages with human subjects (about 1030). A divine subject appears in 45 passages (50 if the ark passages are included). Lawhead categorizes only these as texts with a "theological significance of the verb," clearly an abridgment that exegetical examination of the remaining passages[37] suggests is unjustified.

---

28 Cf. *KBL*³, 423b.
29 P. 63.
30 *Ibid.,* 64.
31 For additional statistics, see Lawhead, 65f.
32 P. 68.
33 P. 68.
34 *Ibid.,* 70.
35 See the tabulation in Lawhead, 70f.
36 See the discussion below.
37 See below.

3. *LXX.* The translations of *yšb* in the LXX exhibit a broad spectrum of Greek verbs. The comparative frequency of various equivalents permits an ordered list:[38] *katoikéō* (515), *káthēmai* (183), *kathízō* (177), *oikéō* (93), *ménō* (10), and scattered others. An obvious preference for the most common equivalent, *katoikéō,* may be noted in Genesis–Judges (excluding Exodus), the prophetic literature (except for Isaiah, Jonah, and Malachi), and the Writings (except for Psalms and 1–2 Chronicles).[39] Lawhead finds no clear regularity in the rendering of specific stems of *yšb,* since the translators "did not make any conscious or concerted effort to reproduce faithfully each particular grammatical form of *yašab* by a different Greek translation."[40]

II. Human Subjects. 1. *Semantics.* The semantic nucleus of Heb. *yšb* is also composite. According to Schweizer,[41] "two sememes appear to characterize the semantic nucleus": location in a particular place ("mansive") and cessation of movement ("quietive"). The "mansive" sememe can be eliminated, he claims, only at the cost of "effacing the fundamental meaning of the verb." Without prejudice to the emphasis on a sense of intended permanence, however, the lexical evidence and the analogies of extrabiblical usage allow us to posit a combination of "sedative" and "mansive" sememes. This refers not only to a change of aspect ("ingressive"/"durative") but to a range of meaning already inherent in the semantic nucleus, which covers everything from the genesis of the act of "sitting," "dwelling," "being enthroned," etc., to its completion. The phase that brings the condition into being receives its full due. It is impossible to say whether in Hebrew the element that goes beyond the "sedative" meaning, which is undoubtedly present although less clearly emphasized outside the OT, can be associated with the early Israelite experience of a nomadic and a settled phase.

The verb has at least two obligatory actants: a subject and a prepositional specification. In exceptional cases, the latter, which frequently makes the "mansive" element more specific, can be replaced by a "productive" continuation in the form of another verb. In Gen. 27:19, for example, the potential "mansive" specification is merely suspended,[42] and the dominant "sedative" meaning is not even touched upon. The absolute use of *yšb* in this passage[43] is therefore apparent, not real.

In the following discussion of the classemes of *yšb* (the contextual meanings that supplement the nuclear structure), the role of the actants will receive particular attention. At the same time, our interest will focus on how the syntagmemes realize the sememe pair "sedative"/"mansive."

2. *"Sit Down"/"Sit."* The twofold semantic structure of the verb finds significant expression in Gen. 21:16, which describes the actions of the Egyptian Hagar as out of

38 Following Lawhead, 78f.
39 *Ibid.,* 96.
40 P. 103; on the translation of the nominal derivatives, see 100f., with appendices D and E.
41 H. Schweizer, *Elischa in den Kriegen. StANT,* 37 (1974), 188, n. 401.
42 On the process involved, see *ibid.*
43 Noted by *GesB,* 323a.

desperation she exposes her son: first *wattēšeḇ lāh minneḡeḏ* (16a), then *wattēšeḇ minneḡeḏ* (16b). The apparent doublet has led to source-critical analyses;[44] but in the first occurrence the "sedative" element is emphasized by the addition of *lāh* (cf. also the impv. *šeḇû-lāḵem,* "Sit down!" in Gen. 22:5), while the second instance presents the "mansive" side of the verb's meaning. It is noteworthy that in both syntagmemes the verb function (narrative conjugation) and value structure are identical. Both verbal phrases, furthermore, refer to an action that can be qualified semantically as an expression of mourning.[45] This perspective is brought out explicitly in later texts by mention of the ground. Thus Job's friends sit with him upon the ground (*yšb lā'āreṣ*: Job 2:13; cf. also Lam. 2:10) for seven days and seven nights, while Job himself "sits" in the midst of (*beṯôḵ*) the ashes (Job 2:8). Here, too, both semantic elements occur in the same context, except that here, with a change of actant from first to third person, the "sitting down" appears in the narrative tense, the "sitting" in the circumstantial participle. Thus, despite all the sympathy shown by Job's friends, the difference between his fate and theirs is documented.

The verb *yšb* can have positive overtones in contexts that specify the place. This is true in the context of eating (cf. already Gen. 27:19) at table (1 K. 13:20[46]); it is all the more so when the passage speaks of "sitting" in the gate (Gen. 19:1) or "holding a session" (Jer. 39:3[47]) in (*be*) the city gate. "Sitting" in the gate has legal overtones when the text involves furnishing hospitality (Gen. 19:1; cf. also 18:1) or a formal judicial assembly (as in the case of Jeremiah: obviously a "regular court session"[48]). That even these passages are inconceivable apart from the sedative semantic element is clear from analysis of the relationship between Gen. 18:1 and 13:18. While Gen. 13:18[49] speaks of Abraham's "settling" (*yšb* in the narrative form) near (*be*) the terebinth of Mamre, Gen. 18:1 in its present version uses the participle[50] to speak of Abraham's "sitting" at or in the doorway to his tent in the heat of the day. Although the statement appears redundant (according to Kilian and Weimar, Gen. 18:1a belongs to the same literary stratum as 13:8, which it follows), what we really have is a repetition of the catchword *yšb* with both "sedative" and "mansive" meaning; the "sedative" element is indicated formally by use of the narrative form in the context of a verbal triplet ("moved," "came," and "dwelt") and the mention of a new place (with *be*), whereas the "mansive" element is indicated by use of the participle introducing *peṯaḥ-hā'ōhel* without a preposition (probably emphasizing the association with a particular place), together with a specification of place and time.

---

44 Cf. Kilian, 246, 249.

45 Cf. also M. Dahood, "Textual Problems in Isaiah," *CBQ,* 22 (1960), 401ff.

46 On the use of the prep. *'el,* see M. Noth, *Könige 1–16. BK,* IX/1 (1968), 291.

47 Cf. O. Eissfeldt, "Unheils- und Heilsweissagungen Jeremias als Vergeltung für ihm erweisene Weh- und Wohltaten," *WZ Halle-Wittenberg,* 14 (1965), 183f. = *KlSchr,* IV (1968), 187.

48 *Ibid.,* 187, n. 2.

49 Pre-J according to Kilian, but assigned to J by P. Weimar, *Untersuchungen zur Redaktionsgeschichte des Pentateuch. BZAW,* 146 (1977), 50.

50 Kilian (97) claims that an original text can be reconstructed with a form of *yšb* in the suffix conjugation as an introduction to the "plural version."

The use of *yšb* for an individual's action in a particular group (which does duty for the usual specification of place) is still totally imbued with the notion of "sitting" or "sitting down." Thus Ephron "sits" (ptcp.) "in the midst of" (*bᵉṯôḵ*) the Hittites (Gen. 23:10); the upright does not sit "in" (*bᵉ*) the "seat" (*môšāḇ*!) of scoffers (Ps. 1:1) or with (*ʿim*) "those who are false" (Ps. 26:4) or "the wicked" (Ps. 26:5). The striking change of conjugation in Ps. 26 may represent "the fact that the statements are true for all times."[51] In the domain of secular law,[52] sitting down at the city gate[53] among the *bāʾê šaʿar* (Gunkel: "enfranchised citizens"), who act as it were as witnesses, signalizes the beginning of public proceedings. In the domain of sacral law, as shown by the oath of purgation in Ps. 26:4ff., sitting down in the company of evildoers means exclusion from the sphere of the righteous. In addition, the correlation of *yšb* with the verbs *hlk* and *ʿmd* ("take one's place") in Ps. 1:1 and with *bwʾ* in Ps. 26:4b makes it sufficiently clear that the context emphasizes the element of motion, even though the motion aims at an enduring disposition. While "sitting with" reveals agreement and support, "sitting before" can express respect for someone of higher station, as demanded by the disciple-teacher relationship (cf., e.g., 2 K. 4:38).

In the case of both human beings and animals, sitting in hiding can also be a sign of potential danger to others. It is typical of the wicked to sit in ambush (Ps. 10:8), like a lion awaiting its prey (Ps. 17:12; Job 38:40). In these cases, the purpose of the verb is not to express instances of the commonly observed aggressiveness of human beings and animals, but to indicate the permanence of the threat in all its variations. This image addresses a fundamental element of evil: it is always a danger, even when it is not erupting. Inactivity, in either a positive or negative sense, must therefore not be imputed to the "sedative" or "mansive" meaning of *yšb.* This is certainly true of the professional spies involved in the Samson-Delilah affair (Jgs. 16:9,12). Perhaps we may note here a distinction comparable to that in Gen. 21:16,[54] if the specifier *lāh* in the first of the otherwise identical participial clauses serves to underline the potentially "sedative" meaning of *yôšēḇ* in v. 9, while v. 12 depicts the situation described in a "mansive" sense. In Jgs. 16:9, however, unlike Gen. 21:16, *lāh* is not reflexive, and the participial form is generally a means of expressing the "mansive" sense; it is therefore also possible to describe the construction as a dative of reference.

3. *"Settle"/"Dwell."* A level of semantic abstraction beyond the "sit down"/"sit" pair leads to the meanings "settle"/"dwell" or "stay." Since the bodily position originally denoted is no longer part of the picture, the semic composite can be manifested in a more general sense. At first glance, the "mansive" element appears to be the dominant sememe of this level. A woman who has given birth must remain at home for a period of thirty-three days after the infant's circumcision (Lev. 12:4); someone who is forced to

---

51 H.-J. Kraus, *Psalms 1–59* (Eng. trans., Minneapolis, 1988), 327.

52 H. Gunkel, *Genesis* [*HKAT,* I/1] (⁸1969), 276, on Gen. 23:10: "all legal business is transacted sitting"; cf. Ruth 4:1f.,4.

53 See above.

54 See above.

stay at home after being injured must be recompensed (Ex. 21:19). The desire that someone "remain" is often expressed. For example, Rebecca's family request her to remain "a little while, or at least ten days" (Gen. 24:55); the stated length of time makes the requested (jussive) remaining at home specific. Moses requires (impv.) the elders to remain (Ex. 24:14); the added *lānû* is probably to be taken as a dative of reference. Joash of Israel expects (impv.) Amaziah of Judah to stay at home (2 K. 14:10). Hosea insists that his temple prostitute stay at home (*tēšᵉḇî lî*) for "many days" (Hos. 3:3). Since remaining is valued because it enables people to stay together—as in Laban's request that Jacob stay with him (Gen. 29:19; cf. also the possible "sedative" counterpart in Gen. 27:44, without any explicit reference to family ties binding Jacob to Laban)—it is not surprising that the causative of *yšb* can be used for occasioning someone to set up a household (Ps. 68:7[Eng. v. 6]; 113:9). In very late texts, this form can even be used with reference to marriage (Ezr. 10:2,10,14,17f.; Neh. 13:23,27). This development lies behind the meaning of the base in Ethiopic.[55]

The fundamental complex of "sedative" and "mansive" meanings appears above all in contexts involving the phases of "settling" and "dwelling" in a place. Of course the domain of the patriarchal traditions provides generous material of this sort. Gen. 19:30, for example, begins with the narrative form *wayyaʿal* followed by the narrative form *wayyēšeḇ,* meant "sedatively." In the present text, we find the verbal function and semic specification of a "mansive" meaning of *yšb* in vv. 29 (stative) and 30b (inf.); finally, in v. 30b, we return to a "sedative" narrative form: "So he settled in a cave." Kilian[56] is probably correct in seeing doublets here and proposing a source-critical analysis of v. 30; the semiology may support his approach. Also significant for the meaning of the verb is the relationship between the narrative form *wayyēšeḇ* and the following narrative form *wayyāḡor* in Gen. 20:1. The geographical statements in this context are mutually contradictory; the source-critical approach to the problem[57] is corroborated by the sequence *yšb* ("sedative")—*gwr* (provisional semic specification: "be a temporary guest" or "morative"). The opposite relationship appears in Gen. 26:3,6 in the sequence *gwr* (impv.)—*yšb* (narrative), where *yšb* is to be interpreted as meaning "that Isaac dwelt at Gerar."[58] While the impv. *gûr* clearly conveys the exclusive sememe "morative," the "mansive" sememe predominates once again in *yšb* (cf. also v. 17).

Going beyond the immediate context, we may observe that the same syntactical form (narrative) can be used both when the "sedative" sememe is dominant (as in Gen. 4:16; 11:2,31; etc.) and when the "mansive" meaning predominates (as in Gen. 21:20, 21; 22:19; etc.). There does not appear to be a clear preference associated with any literary stratum, even though the phrase *wayyēšeḇ šām* (Gen. 11:31; etc.) has been described as a schematic element of an "emigration account" in P.[59] As Gen. 13:6 clearly shows, the

---

55 See above; cf. also *KBL*³, 424b.

56 P. 128.

57 Cf. *ibid.,* 190; for a different analysis, see Weimar, 56, n. 164.

58 Weimar, *ibid.,* 84.

59 P. Weimar, "Aufbau und Struktur der priesterschriftlichen Jakobsgeschichte," *ZAW,* 86 (1974), 189f., with n. 68.

infinitive tends to convey a "mansive" meaning: it proves impossible for Abraham and Lot to "dwell together" any longer. Ps. 133:1 also speaks of brothers "dwelling together," albeit in laudatory terms.

The participle is naturally well suited to express prolongation of a stay or specify the nature of a residence. The phrase *yōšēḇ bāʾāreṣ* conveys stability of location; with variations, it can be used of the former presence of the Canaanites (Gen. 13:7) as well as of the presence of the patriarchs (Gen. 24:62). Two quasi epithets deserve special attention: *ʾaḇî yōšēḇ ʾōhel,* "father of those who dwell in tents" (Gen. 4:20, with reference to Jabal), and *yōšēḇ ʾōhālîm,* "dweller in tents" (Gen. 25:27, with reference to Jacob). Far from suggesting the periodic change of abode associated with the instability of tent dwelling (for which one would expect the term *škn* with its dominant "morative" semic specification[60]), these expressions denote the qualitative nature of life lived permanently in tents. Jacob is described also as "a quiet man," while his brother and counterpart Esau is described in aggressive terms ("a skilful hunter").

The terminology in Jgs. 5:17 makes clear in a highly original fashion the semiological differentiation of the verbs *yšb* (17b), *škn* (17a,b), and *gwr* (17a). According to Richter,[61] the verse uses "three terms for 'dwell': as a full citizen, as a nomad, and as an alien." Even Täubler[62] would interpret *yšb* as implying a "fixed abode with its own economic base," including "ties of legal ownership that deliberately make the stay permanent." Zobel[63] sees in *yšb* a term "for the settlement of a tribe." It is clear that neither sees the difference between *yšb* and *škn* necessitated by the "morative" semic specification of the latter. With regard to *yšb* (used both here and in Jgs. 5:16a in the *x-qaṭal*), we may observe that it expresses the "abiding" ("mansive") of the tribe (Asher) "at the coast of the sea," however the following *škn* by (*ʿal*) its "inlets" is to be interpreted.[64]

Finally, the "mansive" element takes on a special dimension in texts that speak of "(not) dwelling" or "(not) being inhabited" in the future. When *yšb* is predicated of something that has not yet come to pass, any discernible "sedative" element is totally subordinate to the "mansive." This is illustrated by Dt. 12:10 (from the Deuteronomistic redactor), which speaks of future "settlement" in Israel's heritage and "dwelling in safety" there; the latter will become reality when God gives the people "rest" from their enemies round about. This element of "giving rest," which functions as a "structural signal,"[65] makes it clear on the one hand that *yšb* can embody the optimum human presence on earth, but on the other that such "dwelling in safety" depends on Yahweh, whose presence as conceived by the Deuteronomistic school depends on other criteria (cf. Dt. 12:11 and III below). The category of promise also means that the future perspective brings "mansive" dwelling close in meaning to (repeatable) "morative"

---

60 See provisionally M. Görg, *Das Zelt der Begegnung. BBB,* 27 (1967), 97ff.

61 W. Richter, *Traditionsgeschichtliche Untersuchungen zum Richterbuch. BBB,* 18 (^{2}1966), 90.

62 E. Täubler, *Biblische Studien: Die Epoche der Richter* (Tübingen, 1958), 91.

63 H.-J. Zobel, *Stammessprache und Geschichte. BZAW,* 95 (1965), 49.

64 See provisionally Görg, *Das Zelt der Begegnung,* 100.

65 R. P. Merendino, *Das deuteronomische Gesetz. BBB,* 31 (1969), 322.

sojourning; on this plane, then, *yšb* and *škn* can be considered almost synonymous (see, e.g., Isa. 32:16), but only when Yahweh provides the guarantee for such "dwelling." Jeremiah therefore appeals to Yahweh's initiative in his letter to the exiles, in which he tells them to build houses and live in them (impv. of *yšb*; Jer. 29:5,28).[66] His exhortation is also a challenge to those who consider *yšb* in a foreign land to be the ultimate disaster. Since the Rechabites in Palestine are barred entirely from *yšb* in houses, being intended to *yšb* in tents (Jer. 35:7,9f.), their *yšb* in Jerusalem (v. 11) is a "dwelling as though they did not dwell" as well as a sign to the others. Only a future restoration of Judah will make possible a *yšb* that turns its back on exhaustion and marks the beginning of a new age (Jer. 31:24). The redactor can state that Jerusalem "shall be inhabited forever" (Jer. 17:25), a promise whose context also predicts the entrance of kings and princes who "sit on the throne of David" (ptcp.), people of Judah, and "inhabitants of Jerusalem" (i.e., citizens of the city). As we would expect in a postexilic context, observance of the Sabbath and indeed of the entire law is considered here to be a qualitative prerequisite for "dwelling safely" (cf. Lev. 25:18f.; 26:5). The expression "sit down in the shadow of Yahweh" (Hos. 14:8[7]; "sedative") attests a special intimacy with Yahweh.[67]

"Dwelling safely" must be guaranteed by Yahweh. Any *yšb* is therefore bound to fail if it is based on injustice (cf. Isa. 5:8 with the hophal *hûšaḇtem* and the meaning "property owner"[68]) or contradicts Yahweh's direct command, like the chosen abode of the "Egyptian diaspora" (Jer. 42:10,12ff.). "Uninhabited desolation," finally, is characteristic of the barren desert and of a chaotic situation in general (see, e.g., Jer. 51:43[69]), so that in the last analysis any human *yšb* apart from Yahweh's guarantee is tantamount to "nondwelling," i.e., future nonexistence: the prophecy of disaster predicts concretely that there will be no inhabitants (cf. the phrase *ʾên-yôšēḇ* in Jer. 4:29; etc.).

The semantic planes just discussed appear to be in harmony with the meaning of those proper names that have a good claim to involve the element *yšb,* even though other derivations are not ruled out: *yešeḇʾāḇ* (1 Ch. 24:13: "may the father remain alive"[70]); *yošbᵉqāšâ* (1 Ch. 25:4,24: "sitting in misfortune"[71]), and the toponym *yāšûḇ* (Josh. 17:7: "inhabited"?[72]). The reduplicating expression *yōšēḇ baššeḇeṯ* in 2 S. 23:8 probably represents a distorted form having nothing to do with a name derived from *yšb.*[73] The name *yôšiḇyâ* ("may Yahweh cause to dwell") in 1 Ch. 4:35 betrays a theological interest.[74]

---

66 See T. Seidl, *Texte und Einheiten in Jeremia 27–29. ATS,* 5 (1978), 289, who would see a single complement here despite *bāttîm.*

67 See Feuillet, 391ff.

68 See A. Alt, "Eine syrische Bevölkerungsklasse im ramessidischen Ägypten," *ZÄS,* 75 (1940), 19; *KBL*³, 425a; H. Wildberger, *Jesaja. BK,* X/1 (²1980), 183.

69 See O. Keel-Leu, *Jahwes Entgegnung an Ijob. FRLANT,* 121 (1978), 57f.

70 *IPN,* 247.

71 Cf. W. Rudolph, *Chronikbücher. HAT,* XII (1955), 167.

72 *KBL*³, 425.

73 See *ibid.,* 425a.

74 *IPN,* 202f.; *KBL*³, 386b.

4. *"Ascend the Throne"/"Reign."* The double semiological structure of *yšb* can also be observed in the terminology of accession to the throne and royal residence. Enthronement and sovereignty surely are more than just "aspects" of kingship. The king has automatic claim to a special "seat" (*môšāḇ*), which he regularly occupies (*yšb*) at meals, namely a "seat by the wall" (1 S. 20:25). This is all the more true when he is carrying out the duties of his reign. The "throne" is undoubtedly "the most important symbol of royal authority"; at the same time, "the expression 'to sit on the throne' signifies 'to become king.'"[75] Thus we read in a an oathlike statement that is certainly pre-Deuteronomistic: "Solomon your son shall reign after me, and he shall sit upon my throne *wᵉhuʾ yēšēḇ ʿal-kisʾî*)" (1 K. 1:13,17).[76] The situation envisioned here after David's death has been transformed, apparently by a redactor,[77] so that Solomon accedes to the throne on the very same day (1 K. 1:30,35,46,48). The sequence of "petitives"[78] *ûḇāʾ wᵉyāšaḇ* (v. 35) supports the "sedative" meaning of *yšb,* while the specification *ʿal-kisʾî* insists on its "mansive" side.[79] The two meanings are then realized in a resultative ("he has sat down"; v. 46: "sedative") and a circumstantial participle (v. 48: "mansive"); in each case, *ʿal* appears with the noun *kissēʾ*. There seems to be no definable qualitative difference between these formulas and analogous extrabiblical expressions.[80] The specification of the throne as the "father's throne" signalizes "legitimate succession."[81] The expectation of permanence implicit in enthronement is clearly expressed in 1 K. 2:12. The "throne of David," as "the dynastic symbol of the House of David,"[82] can then be the designation of the seat of subsequent kings of Judah (cf., e.g., Jer. 17:25; 22:2,30). It is therefore not surprising that *yšb* by itself can have the meaning "be king, reign" (cf. Ex. 15:14;[83] 2 S. 5:6;[84] Zec. 9:5f. [probably the latest occurrence]).

"Reigning" or "sitting on the throne" is far from being characteristically Israelite; the expression can be used unhesitatingly of Pharaoh (Ex. 11:5; 12:29), for example, or the Amorite Sihon (Dt. 1:4; etc.). The text that speaks of Jeroboam's *yšb* in Egypt (1 K. 12:2) may reflect the notion of a kind of government in exile.[85] But the *yšb* of a king takes on a special dimension when it is associated with the presence of Yahweh or even defined as being fundamentally dependent on Yahweh. After 2 S. 7:1 has spoken of David's *yšb*

---

75 T. Ishida, *The Royal Dynasties in Ancient Israel. BZAW,* 142 (1977), 104, with reference to 1 K. 10:18-20.

76 See T. Veijola, *Die ewige Dynastie. AnAcScFen,* B, 193 (1975), 17f.

77 Veijola: Deuteronomistic.

78 On this term, see M. Görg, review of W. Gross, *Bileam. StANT,* 38 (1974), *ThRv,* 73 (1977), 19.

79 W. Richter, *Grundlagen einer althebräischen Grammatik. ATS,* 13 (1980), 96, finds here a "locative"/"directive" function.

80 Ishida, *Dynasties,* 104f.

81 *Ibid.,* 105.

82 *Ibid.*

83 See F. Cross and D. N. Freedman, "The Song of Miriam," *JNES,* 14 (1955), 248ff.

84 See W. G. E. Watson, "David Ousts the City Ruler of Jebus," *VT,* 20 (1970), 501f.

85 See most recently J. C. Trebolle Barrera, "Jeroboán y la Asamblea de Siquén," *EstBíb,* 38 (1979/1980), 189-220.

in his house (here probably "sedative"), v. 2 has the king speak critically of the disproportion between his "dwelling" (ptcp.) in a "house" of cedar and the "dwelling" (ptcp.) of the ark of Elohim in a tent. Whether the passage represents a quotation of an earlier accusation[86] or a Deuteronomistic formulation[87] does not detract from the "mansive" interpretation of the repeated *yōšēḇ*. If we use the translation "be enthroned" in both clauses, as would be appropriate with both subjects, the judgmental perspective appears in full force. According to the present context of vv. 5f., a "mansive" *yšb* seems to meet with absolute rejection on the part of Yahweh.[88] The thrust of 2 S. 7:1-7 is to reclaim *yšb* for the king alone, although this tendency is mitigated somewhat in v. 18 by a skilful repetition of the catchword: *wayyēšeḇ lipnê YHWH*.[89]

That Yahweh is the authentic initiator and guarantor of enthronement is attested explicitly in the causative use of the base in 1 K. 2:24, which in its own way serves the Deuteronomistic legitimation argument.[90] According to Isa. 28:6 (cf. also Ps. 122:5), the spirit of divine justice rests upon the future ruler "who sits upon the judgment throne" (*yōšēḇ ʿal-hammišpāṭ*).[91] An extraordinary exaggeration of the divine grace associated with the enthronement of a king appears in the wording of Ps. 110:1, in the imperative addressed by Yahweh to "my lord": "Sit at my right hand (*šēḇ lîmînî*)," a formula that has inspired a search for analogies in other religions, not least because of the assurance that follows: ". . . until I have made your enemies a stool for your feet."[92] The closest analogies are certain Egyptian illustrations[93] and texts.[94] Kraus rightly points out that the "sitting" referred to in Ps. 110:1 is not "limited to the earthly temple";[95] the "cultic chamber is also the image, the reflection, indeed the presence of the heavenly throne room. The king of Jerusalem, too, is enthroned in this heavenly sphere." There can be no doubt that the Israelite perspective places special weight on the unmerited divine election of the king.

5. *Cultic Usage*. The notion that the king's *yšb* is dependent on Yahweh suggests investigating any cultic usage of *yšb*[96] that might be associated with a description of an "act of worship." According to 1 S. 1:9, Eli is sitting (ptcp.: "mansive") *ʿal-hakkissēʾ* beside one of the doorposts of *bêṯ YHWH*. Of course this text cannot be referring to a throne, but it might describe a seat associated with some kind of sacral guardianship. There does not appear to be any clear evidence here for a cultic function in the narrower

---

86 Görg, *Das Zelt der Begegnung*, 94, 96.

87 "Possibly": K. Rupprecht, *Der Tempel von Jerusalem*. *BZAW*, 144 (1977), 75.

88 See below.

89 See below.

90 See Veijola, 133.

91 Cf. W. H. Irwin, "Is 28-33; Translation with Philological Notes," *BietOr*, 30 (1977), 11-13.

92 H.-J. Kraus, *Psalms 60–150* (Eng. trans., Minneapolis, 1989), 344; → הדם *hᵃḏōm* (*hᵃdhōm*).

93 Cf. O. Keel, *The Symbolism of the Biblical World* (Eng. trans., New York, 1978), 255; the seating precedence in Ps. 110, e.g., recalls the cella of the temple of Rameses II at Abu Simbel, where the Pharaoh is depicted sitting to the right of the "father-god" Re-Harakhte.

94 See U. Luft, *Studia Aegyptiaca*, IV (1978), 50ff.

95 *Psalmen*. *BK*, XV/2 (⁴1972), 759.

96 See Brockington.

sense, whereas David's action cited above (2 S. 7:18), despite the unusual appearance of sitting as a gesture of adoration,[97] undoubtedly serves the worship of Yahweh. According to Hertzberg,[98] "the king sits or lies down on the ground." The narrative verb with the formula *lipnê YHWH* does not suggest any concrete meaning for *yšb,* although we may think of David's dropping to the ground before the ark. On the other hand, the repetition of the catchword *yšb,* which dominates 2 S. 7:1-7, may be intended to suggest a semantic shift in opposition to v. 2: David's *yšb* ("mansive") in a house of cedar requires that he *yšb* ("sedative") before Yahweh, which itself intends a stay of some length.[99] Apart from these passages, there does not seem to be any clear evidence requiring us to identify *yšb* as a formal cultic term designating a specific liturgical action. This conclusion applies in particular to "dwelling" in the "house" of God (Ps. 84:5[4]): the enduring stay (ptcp.) in the presence of God is described from the perspective of a metaphorical doxology.

III. Divine Subjects.

1. *Syntagmemes.* An initial morphological and syntactic analysis of the occurrences of *yšb* with Yahweh as the "first syntagmeme"[100] reveals word classes: finite verb (5 occurrences of the suffix conjugation, 11 of the prefix conjugation), infinitive (17 occurrences), and participle (17 occurrences). The (obligatory) syntagmemes of the verb appear primarily in the form of prepositional phrases with "locative/directive" function.[101] The infinitives always appear in "locative" relationships, two of which are expanded by nouns indicating time. The infinitive appears 9 times as *nomen rectum,* once as *nomen regens.* It is introduced by *lᵉ* 7 times. In participial usage, the dependent noun may appear either with a preposition (*bᵉ* [3 times], *ʿal* [4 times]) or without (10 times).[102]

2. *The mkwn Formula and Allusions.* Among the phrases where *yšb* appears, there are two formulaic expressions in which it is not exclusively verbal: *mᵉḵôn šiḇtᵉḵā* (1 K. 8:39,43,49; 2 Ch. 6:30,33,39), with the variants *mᵉḵôn-šiḇtô* (Ps. 33:14), *māḵôn lᵉšiḇtᵉḵā* (Ex. 15:17; 1 K. 8:13; 2 Ch. 6:2), and *mᵉqôm šiḇtᵉḵā* (1 K. 8:30; 2 Ch. 6:21); and *yōšēḇ hakkᵉrū/ûḇîm* (1 S. 4:4; 2 S. 6:2; 2 K. 19:15; 1 Ch. 13:6; Ps. 80:2[1]; Isa. 37:16), with the variant *yôšēḇ kᵉrûḇîm* (Ps. 99:1).

The full form of the first formula appears to be *māḵôn lᵉšiḇtᵉḵā ʿôlāmîm* (1 K. 8:13; 2 Ch. 6:2). This is also its earliest occurrence, in the setting of the so-called "temple dedication formula" (1 K. 8:12f.), a "hymnic song of praise" that, after the analogy of Egyptian texts, "combines a 'cosmic' presentation of the deity with an autobiographical dedication of a cultic building, both pronounced by the king."[103] It exhibits a semantic

---

97 But see H. P. Smith, *Samuel. ICC* (²1953; repr. 1977), 302.

98 H. W. Hertzberg, *I & II Samuel. OTL* (Eng. trans. 1964), 287.

99 Cf. M. Görg, *Gott-König-Reden in Israel und Ägypten. BWANT,* 105 (1975), 202.

100 Cf. Richter, *Grundlagen einer althebräischen Grammatik,* 17.

101 *Ibid.,* 96f.

102 For a tabular synopsis, see Wuckelt, 8ff.

103 M. Görg, "Die Gattung des sogenannten Tempelweihspruchs (1 Kg 8,12f.)," *UF,* 6 (1974), 63.

opposition between *liškōn* (v. 12) and *lᵉšeḇeṯ* (v. 13). This alternation may suggest a differentiated terminology of divine presence, in which *yšb* in *bêṯ-zᵉbûl* ("exalted and princely house") conveys a clearly "mansive" meaning,[104] here emphatically confirmed by the addition of *ʿôlāmîm*. The theory that the change of terminology for the presence of Yahweh between vv. 12 and 13 reflects an (early dynastic) controversy in the temple theology of Jerusalem remains hypothetical, but is supported by recent observations.[105]

The Deuteronomistic redaction shifts Yahweh's *yšb* from the temple to heaven (1 K. 8:30,39,43,49; 2 Ch. 6:21,30,33,39), introducing its own terminology for the presence of "Yahweh's name" and "making a conscious distinction between Yahweh's sitting on his heavenly throne and the presence of his name in an earthly building."[106] Thus the idea expressed in 1 K. 8:12f. is revised and corrected: Yahweh "has moved to a more distant and inaccessible realm."[107] At the same time, the danger that Yahweh's "dwelling" will be conceived in static, physical terms has been averted.[108]

Heaven is "the place of his dwelling," from which Yahweh looks down and beholds those who "dwell" upon earth (Ps. 33:14).[109] Here divine *yšb* corresponds to human *yšb*, although the realms are separated. Thus *yšb* upon earth takes place under the protection of Yahweh's *yšb* in heaven (cf. also Ps. 113:5,8). Closest to the supposed original form and constituting a semantic "bridge" between "dwelling" in the temple and "sitting enthroned" in heaven is the phrase *māḵôn lᵉšiḇtᵉḵā* followed by *pāʿaltā YHWH* in Ex. 15:17; the same context identifies the "place of thine enthronement" with the "mountain of thy heritage" (*har naḥᵃlāṯᵉḵā*).[110] It is noteworthy that this passage refers explicitly to Yahweh's initiative, a note that allows us tentatively to ask whether this passage supports an alternative to the glorification of royal building programs (in response to 1 K. 8:13?). Against the background of the equivalence of *māḵôn* and *har*, we may here discuss also the formulation *hāhār ḥāmaḏ ʾᵉlōhîm lᵉšiḇtô* (Ps. 68:17[16]), an isolated expression that may once have referred to a different mountain[111] but has clearly been applied to the Jerusalem temple by the explanatory phrase *ʾap̱-YHWH yiškōn lāneṣaḥ*.[112] Whether the passage also indicates a replacement of the *yšb* concept by the idea of Yahweh's *škn* cannot be determined.

In 2 S. 7:5, however, the context of the phrase *bayiṯ lᵉšiḇtî* takes us into the midst of the controversy over Yahweh's *yšb* in a permanent house or temple. This expression, too, represents an isolated formulation and cannot be considered merely a variant of the formula above. Its setting is a rebuke of David's building program, which Yahweh counters with the statement that he has never "dwelt" in a house (v. 6). Our phrase appears

---

104 Cf. *ibid.*, 56.
105 See below.
106 Metzger, 158.
107 *Ibid.*, 150.
108 For a discussion of the Deuteronomistic program, see *ibid.*, 149ff.
109 Cf. F. Stolz, *Strukturen und Figuren im Kult von Jerusalem. BZAW*, 118 (1970), 164.
110 Cf. Metzger, 147, 156.
111 Cf. Kraus, *Psalms 60–150*, 50.
112 Görg, *Gott-König-Reden*, 115.

in Yahweh's question in v. 5; it should be interpreted not only against the background of its present relationship to the use of *yšb* in v. 2 but also as an "allusion" to the earlier formula. Furthermore, the absolute statement *lō' yāšabtî bᵉbayiṯ* (v. 6) can be seen as a deliberate contrast to 1 K. 8:13. There is no persuasive reason to ascribe the text of 2 S. 7:6 entirely to Deuteronomistic usage.[113] To all appearances, we have here an example of preexilic or even early dynastic—at any rate, certainly pre-Deuteronomistic—opposition to the notion of Yahweh's "sitting enthroned" in the temple, of which the Deuteronomistic redaction made generous use.

3. *The Epithet yôšēb kᵉrūbîm and its Semantics.* The title *yōšēb (hak)kᵉrūbîm,* using the participle of *yšb,* is a stereotyped epithet applied to Yahweh; grammatically, it is best taken as a construct phrase.[114] While earlier scholars based their interpretation of the title on the information in P,[115] recent discussion reflects two schools of thought: one considers every reference to the cherubim prior to the building of Solomon's temple an anachronism (e.g., 1 S. 4:4; 2 S. 6:2); the other, primarily following Eissfeldt,[116] argues for the existence of a cherubim throne and the corresponding title as early as the sanctuary at Shiloh.[117] Since we lack sufficiently detailed information concerning the interior of the temple at Shiloh, we must reckon with the possibility that the title is of Jerusalemite provenience and that its use in the ark narrative serves a legitimating purpose. Our explanation of the idea reflected in this title must therefore be based on the situation in the Jerusalem temple.

Although 1 K. 6:23-28 makes no mention of a "throne,"[118] the detailed description of the wings of cherubim in the *dᵉbîr* (v. 27) has occasioned the proposal that Yahweh's throne should be pictured as being these outspread wings, touching in the midst of the *dᵉbîr.*[119] A reconstruction may be attempted[120] on the basis of extrabiblical analogies (e.g., a Cypriote group from the 7th century B.C. with a deity enthroned on a seat made by the inner wings of a pair of sphinxes[121]) and biblical statements; the position of the outer wings must remain an open question.

A more important problem related to reconstruction of the *dᵉbîr,* albeit only indirectly relevant to the question of Yahweh's throne, is that of the ark's position. Schmitt[122] postulates a "lengthwise" position of the ark beneath the cherubim "instead of a transverse position in front of the statues"; this would contradict the theory that the ark

---

113 Rupprecht, 70; cf. also W. Gross, "Die Herausführungsformel—Zum Verhältnis von Formel und Syntax," *ZAW,* 86 (1974), 440.

114 But cf. *GesB,* 323a.

115 See R. Schmitt, *Zelt und Lade als Thema alttestamentlicher Wissenschaft* (Gütersloh, 1972), 128f.

116 O. Eissfeldt, *MAB,* II/2 (1950), 146.

117 Schmitt, 130.

118 For an attempt at a theological explanation of this observation, see de Vaux, 93f.

119 Haran, 35f.; O. Keel-Leu, *Jahwe-Visionen und Siegelkunst. SBS,* 84/85 (1977), 24.

120 For an illustration, see Keel-Leu, *ibid.,* 25.

121 *Ibid.,* 26.

122 P. 131.

was the footstool of the one enthroned on the cherubim. According to Keel-Leu,[123] the original statements of 1 K. 8:6-9 about the relative positions of cherubim and ark have been expanded in v. 7 by the addition of a statement concerning the "protective function with respect to the ark of having the ark between the cherubim." The statement, he claims, was derived by implication from the ark's location under the wings of the sphinxes. It is conceivable that the ark, which certainly has no inherent connection with the cherubim throne, came to be thought of as the throne's base after the two became associated.[124] The relationship to the cherubim suggested by P (Ex. 25:17-22) is probably based on a revised original text that may have had some independent idea of the cherubim as protecting the ark; the revision was intended to guard against interpreting the epithet *yôšēḇ hakkᵉrūḇîm* as implying a static presence, i.e., an exclusively "mansive" interpretation of "dwelling."[125] Even though there are cogent reasons to think that the cherubim throne originated in the realm of Canaanite-Phoenician civilization (following an earlier history in Egypt),[126] it is dubious whether the epithet "enthroned on the cherubim," despite its closeness to Canaanite cultic symbolism,[127] points to an "already existing fusion with Israelite ideas."[128] The undoubtedly real resistance to associating the "dwelling" notion of *yšb* with Yahweh emerges most profoundly from "Israelite ideas" that did not have to wait for Deuteronomistic reflection before finding expression. There seems to be no similarity in meaning to the clearly pre-Israelite expression *rōḵēḇ bāʿᵃrāḇôṯ* (Ps. 68:5[4]),[129] even though the latter is a formally similar epithet that also derives from Canaanite ideology. With the connotation of "invisibility," the nonexistence of any image of the deity, the notion of Yahweh "enthroned on the cherubim" takes on in its Israelite context a dimension that, despite all the inherent dangers, could give rise to the idea of a transcendent "throne" surpassing all measure and reaching to the heavens. Thus the title appears in conjunction with two other participial predications of the "Shepherd of Israel" (Ps. 80:2[1]), and even in association with the "King" who reigns over all peoples (Ps. 99:1). In the prayer of Hezekiah, Yahweh, "enthroned on the cherubim," is both the only God "of all the kingdoms of the earth" and the Creator of heaven and earth (2 K. 19:15 par. Isa. 37:16).

For the most part, the other participial predications present Yahweh in his function as cosmic ruler. The epithet *yōšēḇ ṣiyyôn* (Ps. 9:12[11]) clearly reflects the "enthronement" of the "righteous Judge" (v. 5[4]; "sedative") and his eternal "sitting enthroned" upon the "throne of judgment" (v. 8[7]; "mansive"). Here Yahweh's jurisdiction extends beyond his "ancestral" residence in Jerusalem; so, too, his "throne" can be so "exalted" as to be experienced only in a vision. The almost identical appositions to Yahweh in 1 K.

---

123 *Jahwe-Visionen und Siegelkunst,* 29.

124 M. Görg, "Die Lade als Thronsockel," *BN,* 1 (1976), 29f.

125 For further discussion, see M. Görg, "Keruben in Jerusalem," *BN,* 4 (1977), 15ff.

126 Keel-Leu, *Jahwe-Visionen und Siegelkunst,* 29f., with bibliog.

127 Rupprecht, 70.

128 *Ibid.*

129 Keel-Leu, *Jahwe-Visionen und Siegelkunst,* 23f., contra H. J. Stoebe, *Das erste Buch Samuelis. KAT,* VIII/1 (1973), 158.

22:19 and *ʾadōnāy* in Isa. 6:1 describe the regal majesty of God.[130] Isaiah experiences "the otherwise hidden presence of Yahweh in the Jerusalem temple as a presence conveying the same enormous power inherent in Yahweh's unveiled heavenly holiness";[131] Micaiah ben Imlah's vision sees nothing of the earthly temple, beholding Yahweh exclusively in the company of the "host of heaven."[132] The "sitting upon (*ʿal*) a high and exalted throne" in Isaiah presents itself to the prophet as a new experience of Yahweh's presence in the temple; it signifies both direct encounter and distance.

While Ps. 2:4 (*yôšēḇ baššāmayim*); 123:1 (*hayyōšeḇî baššāmayim*) speak of Yahweh's sovereign authority and protective power,[133] the phrases *qāḏôš yôšēḇ tehillôṯ yiśrāʾēl* (Ps. 22:4[3]) and *ʾēl yōšēḇ qeḏem* (Ps. 55:20[19]), each of which occurs only once, bear witness to a distinction between the reign of Yahweh and that of El, even though in their present contexts both refer to Yahweh. Ps. 55:20(19) preserves Canaanite diction ("the Primeval One"[134]), while Ps. 22:4(3) ("the Holy One, enthroned [above] the praises of Israel"[135]) associates Yahweh's *yšb* with the sacral realm of Israel's worship, far from any mythological overtones, thus also making experience of the "Holy One" a present reality (cf. also Isa. 6:1ff.). The extent to which the presentation of Yahweh's cosmic *yšb* can go hand in hand with his establishment and promotion of human *yšb* upon earth is illustrated by Deutero-Isaiah's expression (Isa. 40:22, likewise unique) *hayyōšēḇ ʿal-ḥûg hāʾāreṣ,* "who sits above the circle of the earth," with the associated comparison of earth's inhabitants (*yšb*!) to grasshoppers, which emphasizes the absolute gulf between them and Yahweh, and finally the "reference to Yahweh's use of the heavens as a tent for them—but not him—to dwell in."[136] The expression *kāʾōhel lāšeḇeṯ* is intended to convey the image of a secure abode within the sphere of protection guaranteed by Yahweh, who controls the forces of nature.

Finally, Ps. 113:5,8 expresses an analogy, secured by Yahweh, between human and divine *yšb.* In v. 5, the characteristic formula *hammagbîhî lāšeḇeṯ* denotes the phase of exaltation to the throne ("sedative") by means of a participle combined with an infinitive; the next verse, however, immediately expresses Yahweh's further purpose of a look down upon heaven and earth. This aspect takes significant concrete form in v. 8, which voices Yahweh's will to "enthrone" the needy with princes. The phrase in v. 5 thus takes on special importance: although keeping its distance from its formulaic origins, it is nevertheless well suited to express the genuinely Israelite conception of divine exaltation for the sake of raising the lowly.

There is one more possible reference to divine *yšb* in Nu. 21:14f., clearly not far

---

130 Cf. J. Schreiner, *Sion-Jerusalem, Jahwes Königssitz. StANT,* 7 (1963), 89f.

131 Keel-Leu, *Jahwe-Visionen und Siegelkunst,* 54.

132 *Ibid.,* 48f.

133 Cf. also Metzger, 140.

134 M. Dahood, *Psalms II. AB,* XVII (³1979), 36; contra Kraus, *Psalms 1–59,* who suggests (probably incorrectly) human "inhabitants of the east."

135 H. Schmidt, *Die Psalmen. HAT,* XV (1934), 35, and others; other interpretations are proposed by Kraus (295) and Dahood (*Psalms I. AB,* XVI [1965], 138), but they are not convincing.

136 K. Elliger, *Deuterojesaja. BK,* XI/1 (1978), 84.

advanced along the road to formulaic usage; it appears in Weippert's interpretation of this fragment (probably predynastic) from the "Book of the Wars of Yahweh" as reconstructed by Christensen.[137] In this reading, Yahweh's theophany finds expression in an appearance that overwhelms the forces of nature; it crosses the Arnon in order to "sit [or 'settle'] down at Ar" (*lšbt ʿr*) and stay in Moab. The semantic ambivalence of *yšb* can be seen even here; it could suggest an early articulation of the notion of Yahweh's taking sovereign possession of an alien region.

4. *Finite Forms and their Semantics.* The remaining phrases using a finite verbal form instead of a participle or an infinitive to express Yahweh's *yšb* can be analyzed from the perspective of the mutual relationship between the "sedative" and "mansive" meanings, since the "mansive" function dominates in the formulas cited, their variants, and allusions to them.

The wording of Ps. 29:10 (*YHWH lammabbûl yāšāḇ wayyēšeḇ YHWH meleḵ leʿôlām*) clearly exhibits the double semiological structure of Yahweh's *yšb,* which is confirmed both functionally and syntactically: "Yahweh has taken his seat over the flood, and [therefore now] sits enthroned as king for ever."[138] Verse 10a documents the "sedative" side of the verb's meaning, v. 10b the "mansive" side. This reflects the notion that Yahweh, like the earthly king, takes his seat upon his throne, albeit thenceforth to exercise permanent sovereignty. The enthronement of Yahweh as king is all the more significant because it involves victory over → מבול *mabbûl,* "the upper portion of the primal flood, which spreads out over the firmament of heaven,"[139] and is thus presented as a victory over chaos. (Dahood's translation of *lammabbûl* as "since the flood"[140] can hardly be correct.) It is therefore not surprising that the text does not specify where Yahweh dwells.[141]

The "dwelling" terminology of Ps. 132 appears in the designation of Zion as Yahweh's *môšāḇ* (v. 13; mansive) and in the words *pōh-ʾēšēḇ* (v. 14; sedative) placed in Yahweh's mouth. The context also contains an oath assuring David that one of his sons will always "sit upon the throne" (v. 12).

A "perfective aspect"[142] is expressed by Ps. 47:9a(8a): "God has become king over the nations"; the same is probably true in v. 9b(8b): "God has taken his seat on the throne of his holiness." In both instances, the sedative meaning is conveyed: the beginning of God's reign is pictured as an enthronement. An "imperfective aspect"[143] with "mansive" meaning appears, however, in Lam. 5:19: "Thou dost reign for ever." This *yšb* is seen in

---

137 D. L. Christensen, "Num 21:14-15 and the Book of the Wars of Yahweh," *CBQ,* 36 (1974), 359f.; M. Weippert, "The Israelite 'Conquest' and the Evidence from Transjordan," in F. M. Cross, ed., *Symposia. ZRFOP,* 1-2 (Cambridge, Mass., 1979), 17f.

138 Following W. Gross, *Verbform und Function:* wayyiqṭol *für die Gegenwart? ATS,* 1 (1976), 97.

139 F. Stolz, 165.

140 M. Dahood, *Ugaritic-Hebrew Philology. BietOr,* 17 (1965), 26.

141 Seemingly contra Schmidt, *Königtum Gottes,* 48, who also cites Ugaritic parallels.

142 In the sense meant by A. Denz, *Die Verbalsyntax des neuarabischen Dialektes von Kwayriš. AKM,* 40/1 (1971), 48-50.

143 Cf. W. Gross, "Zur Funktion von *qāṭal,*" *BN,* 4 (1977), 29.

contrast to the desolation of Mt. Zion (v. 18). Ps. 102:13(12) is structured similarly, except that this text expresses a contrast to human impotence (v. 14[13]).

Finally, the critical language of the Deuteronomistic school, which asks whether God really "dwells (*yēšēḇ*) upon earth" (1 K. 8:27 par. 2 Ch. 6:18), brings to light the problem it attempts to solve by introducing different terminology.[144] For this school, a "mansive" interpretation of God's presence upon earth is inconceivable.

5. *"Ark" and "Angel" as Subjects.* When the ark is the subject of *yšb,* Yahweh can be associated with the verb only in a restricted sense. Here the "mansive" element predominates: the prohibition "The ark must not remain (*lōʾ-yēšēḇ*) with us" (1 S. 5:7), the infinitive (1 S. 7:2), and the participle (2 S. 7:2), as well as the narrative conjugation (2 S. 6:11 par. 1 Ch. 13:14), all express the idea of a lengthy stay; the syntagmemes shape the semantics. There is no trace of any "*yšb* formula." Of course this is even more true of the *yšb* of the *malʾaḵ YHWH* who sits down under the oak (*wayyēšeḇ*; Jgs. 6:11). Here, too, the absence of any formal identification with Yahweh prevents us from drawing conclusions about the meaning of divine *yšb.*

Görg

144 See III.2 above.

יָשֵׁן yāšēn; יָשָׁן yāšān; שֵׁנָא šēnāʾ; שֵׁנָה šēnâ

Contents: 1. Etymology and Meaning; 2. OT Usage; 3. Theological Contexts.

1. *Etymology and Meaning.* The individual occurrences of *yšn* in the Semitic languages make it hard to determine[1] whether we are dealing with two roots[2] or one.[3] On the one hand, if we postulate a single root with the basic meaning "be still, sleep," the OT occurrences of the niphal and the derived noun *yāšān* must come from this root; the meaning "grow old" makes good sense as a further development of the basic meaning "be quiet, still"—analogous to Arabic and Ethiopic reflexes with the respective meanings

yāšēn. G. Dalmann, *Aus,* I (1928), 634ff.; E. L. Ehrlich, *Der Traum im AT. BZAW,* 73 (1953); O. Michel, "Zur Lehre vom Todesschlaf," *ZNW,* 35 (1936), 285-290; A. Resch, *Der Traum im Heilsplan Gottes* (Freiburg, 1964); J. G. S. S. Thomson, "Sleep: An Aspect of Jewish Anthropology," *VT,* 5 (1955), 421-433; G. Widengren, *Sakrales Königtum im AT und im Judentum* (Stuttgart, 1955), 67ff.

1 See *KBL*².

2 *KBL*³.

3 Driver.

"become stagnant, putrid" (of water) and "decay, be destroyed."[4] On the other hand, Ugar. *yṯn,* "old," suggests the existence of a second root that would appear to account for the meaning "grow old" found in the niphal forms and *yāšān.* Such an etymology would not, however, cast any new light on the meaning of these forms.

Thus all the OT occurrences of *yšn* can be viewed in a single semantic context based on the fundamental meaning "be still, sleep." The verb *yāšēn* occurs 16 times in the OT (15 qal, 1 piel [Jgs. 16:19]): 5 times in the Psalms, twice each in Genesis and Jeremiah, and once each in Job, Proverbs, Ecclesiastes, Isaiah, and Ezekiel. The adj. *yāšēn,* "asleep," occurs 9 times: 4 in the Deuteronomistic history, twice in the Song of Solomon, and once each in Psalms, Hosea, and Daniel. The noun *šēnâ,* "sleep," occurs 22 times: 7 in Proverbs, 3 each in Psalms and Jeremiah, twice each in Genesis, Judges, and Ecclesiastes, and once each in Esther, Job, Zechariah, and Daniel. The noun *šēnāʾ* occurs only in Ps. 127:2, *šᵉnaṯ* only in Ps. 132:4.

The root occurs only 11 times with the meaning "be old": 6 in Leviticus, twice in Nehemiah, and once each in Deuteronomy, the Song of Solomon, and Isaiah.

In the LXX, the root *yšn* is almost coextensive with Gk. *hýpnos* and its derivatives.[5] The verb *yāšēn* (including Sirach) is translated 13 times by *hypnoún,* 5 times by *katheúdein,* and once each by *koimán* and *koimízein.* The noun *šēnâ* is represented 18 times by *hýpnos,* twice each by *hypnoún* and *nystázein.*

The semantic component "old" is represented in the LXX by *palaiós, archaíos, palaioún,* etc. It is noteworthy that the LXX also often uses *hýpnos* for Heb. → חלום *ḥᵃlôm* (*chᵃlôm*).

The root *yšn* appears only once in the Dead Sea scrolls, in 1QS 7:10; the context is a threat to punish anyone who falls asleep during a meeting of the community,

2. *OT Usage.* The qal of the verb means "be idle, still," "fall asleep," "sleep" (1 K. 18:27; Eccl. 5:11[Eng. v. 12]; Ezk. 34:25) at a specific time for rest (night, midday, or at the onset of fatigue), i.e., what takes place in the interval between lying down (*šāḵaḇ*: 1 K. 19:5; Ps. 4:9) and waking (*yqṣ*: Gen. 41:5; 1 S. 26:12; 1 K. 18:27; Ps. 3:6[5]; 44:24[23]; 78:65; Jer. 51:39; Dnl. 12:2) or getting up (*qûm*: 1 K. 3:20f.; 19:5). In addition, *yšn* can also denote an especially deep sleep (*tardēmâ*: 1 S. 26:12; Ps. 76:6f.[5f.]) or the sleep of death (Ps. 13:4[3]; Jer. 51:57). Therefore *yšn* appears in parallel with *šāḵaḇ,* "lie still" (1 S. 26:7; Ps. 3:6[5]; 4:9[8]; cf. Job 3:13), *ʿālap̱,* "be unconscious" (Jer. 51:39; cf. Ps. 78:65), *rāḏam* (or *tardēmâ*), "be in a deep sleep" (1 S. 26:12; cf. Job 33:15; Prov. 10:5), and *ḥālam,* "dream" (Gen. 41:5). The root → נום *nûm,* "slumber, be sleepy," is also used in parallel. It and its derivatives *nûmâ* and *tᵉnûmâ* appear only in the prophets (Isa. 5:27; 56:10; Nah. 3:18), the Psalms (Ps. 76:6[5]; 121:3f.; 132:4), Job (Job 33:15), and Proverbs (Prov. 6:4,10; 23:21; 24:33), and must be considered a poetic synonym of *yšn.*

The piel of *yšn* is found (with an acc.) with the meaning "make someone go to sleep" (Jgs. 16:19).

---

4 See *KBL*³.

5 H. Balz, "ὕπνος," *TNDT,* VIII, 550f.

The verbal adj. *yāšēn* accordingly describes specific persons as being asleep (1 S. 26:7,12; 1 K. 3:20; 18:27; Ps. 78:65; 22:30[29] [conj.]; Cant. 5:2; Dnl. 12:2). Used metaphorically, it can indicate that a feeling is inactive (Hos. 7:6, of anger). The nouns *šēnā'* and *šēnâ* refer to the sleep from which one awakes, is awakened, or arises (Gen. 28:16; Jgs. 16:14,20; Job 14:12; Ps. 127:2; Prov. 6:9; Zec. 4:1), sweet refreshing sleep (Prov. 3:24; Eccl. 5:11[12]; Jer. 31:26), the sleep that one loses when it flees one's eyes (Gen. 31:40; Est. 6:1; Prov. 4:16; Eccl. 8:16; Dnl. 2:1), that one refuses to one's eyes for a particular reason (Ps. 132:4), that is dangerous (Prov. 6:4,10; 20:13; 24:33), that brings unconsciousness (Ps. 76:6[5]), or from which one never awakes (Jer. 51:39,57; cf. Job 14:12).

The niphal forms of *yšn* (*yšn* II?) and the derived substantive *yāšān* have the meaning "(be) old." When used of human beings, they can refer to extended settlement in a land (Dt. 4:25; cf. also Sir. 9:10). Used of food, they can describe grain stored the previous year (Lev. 25:22; 26:10) or fruit a year old (Cant. 7:14[13]). They can describe long-term chronic leprosy (Lev. 13:11), an ancient gate belonging to the old city (Neh. 3:6; 12:39), or an old pool, long in existence (compared to a newer pool) (Isa. 22:11). In such contexts, therefore, *yšn* appears as the opposite of → חדשׁ *ḥāḏāš* (*chādhāsh*) (Lev. 26:10; Cant. 7:14[13]; cf. also Sir. 9:10 ["old friend"/"new friend").

3. *Theological Contexts.* The OT refers to the phenomenon of sleep in various theological contexts. Sleep can be thought of as sleep in serene security under the protection of Yahweh in contrast to sleepless, fearful anxiety (Ps. 4:9[8]; 3:6[5]). Sweet, refreshing sleep is considered the result of conduct that is righteous in the eyes of Yahweh (Prov. 3:24; Eccl. 5:11[12]). Insomnia, conversely, is associated with a wicked way of life (Prov. 4:16; Eccl. 5:11[12]).

Sleep can also appear in a negative light as a sign of laziness and depravity; idlers, drunkards, and gluttons can be blamed for their sleeping (Prov. 6:4,10; 20:13; 24:33; Isa. 56:10; Nah. 3:18).

Different from ordinary sleep is especially deep sleep (Jgs. 4:21; Prov. 10:5; 19:15; Jon. 1:5f.), a total unconsciousness that can be ascribed also to the direct, miraculous intervention of Yahweh (Gen. 2:21; 15:12; 1 S. 26:12; Job 4:13; 33:15; Ps. 76:6[5]; Isa. 29:10; Dnl. 8:18; 10:9). Yahweh causes a deep sleep to fall on people as a bar to their activity, involvement, and resistance, so that he can do his work undisturbed and unhindered (Gen. 2:21; 1 S. 26:12; Ps. 76:6[5]; Isa. 29:10); he can also use such a deep sleep to reveal his divine word with particular force (Gen. 15:12; Job 4:13; 33:15; Dnl. 8:18; 10:9). Sleep is frequently understood as the locus of revelation, perhaps ultimately because of the Canaanite practice of incubation, which can be glimpsed behind Gen. 28:10-22.[6] The best-known examples of such revelation during sleep are the deep sleeps of Abraham (Gen. 15:12-21), Jacob (Gen. 28:10-22), Solomon at the sanctuary of Gibeon (1 K. 3:4-15), and Balaam's dream (Nu. 22:8-13).[7]

---

6 *Ibid.*, 550; Ehrlich, 13-55.

7 On the topic of dreams in general, see J. Bergman, M. Ottosson, G. J. Botterweck, "חלם *ḥālam* (*chālam*)," *TDOT*, IV, 421-432.

Like other ancient Near Eastern religions, and hence undoubtedly under the influence of the Canaanite fertility cult with its notion of the annual death and resurrection of the deity,[8] the OT uses sleep to represent the state of death, an image that inherently implies rising to life. Thus sleep can be referred to on the one hand as eternal sleep, the sleep of death in the stillness of the grave, where all the turmoil and anxiety of life find their end (Job 3:13; 14:12; Ps. 13:4[3]; Jer. 51:39,57). On the other hand, in the context of eschatological hope, the OT can emphasize rising from this sleep of death (Isa. 26:19). Such rising from death can be interpreted dualistically as bringing a resurrection to everlasting life for some, a resurrection to everlasting shame and contempt for others (Dnl. 12:2).

Finally, we must mention the sleep of Yahweh and of Baʿal; here the mythological Canaanite idea of the sleeping deity clearly stands in the background.[9] When the presence and power of Baʿal do not manifest themselves, Elijah can suggest ironically that the deity is taking a midday siesta (1 K. 18:27). Similarly, in the context of a lament in the face of terrible disaster, the apparent absence of Israel's God can be perceived as Yahweh's sleeping (Ps. 44:24[23]); Yahweh's renewed intervention can be described figuratively as an awakening from sleep (Ps. 78:65). But we also find the contrary statement, that Yahweh does not sleep (Ps. 121:3f.); this text denies Yahweh's passivity while emphasizing his watchful, continuous, unceasing vitality.

Schüpphaus

---

8 See Thomson.

9 See Widengren.

ישׁע *yšʿ*; הוֹשִׁיַע *hôšîaʿ*; יְשׁוּעָה *yešûʿâ*; יֵשַׁע / יֶשַׁע *yēšaʿ* / *yešaʿ*; מוֹשָׁעוֹת *môšāʿôṯ*; תְּשׁוּעָה *tešûʿâ*

Contents: I. 1. Etymology; 2. Semantics of *hôšîaʿ*. II. Distribution: 1. OT; 2. Dead Sea Scrolls. III. Corresponding Terms: 1. LXX; 2. NT; 3. Targumim; 4. Vulgate. IV. OT Usage: 1. Narrative Prose Texts; 2. Wisdom Literature; 3. Prophetic Literature; 4. Psalms.

---

yšʿ. F. Asensio, "La salvación en el AT," *Studia missionalia upsaliensia*, 29 (1980), 1-56; C. F. Barth, *Die Errettung vom Tode in den individuellen Klage- und Dankliedern des ATs* (Zollikon, 1947), 127; M. A. Beek, "Josua und Retterideal," *Near Eastern Studies in Honor of William Foxwell Albright* (Baltimore, 1971), 35-42; H. J. Boecker, *Law and the Administration of Justice in the OT and Ancient East* (Eng. trans., Minneapolis, 1980); *idem, Redeformen des Rechtslebens im AT. WMANT,* 14 (²1970), 61-66; M. Dahood, "Hebrew-Ugaritic Lexicography III: יְשׁוּעוֹת 'Savior'," *Bibl,* 46 (1965), 324; G. Fohrer, "σῴζω. B.2.," *TDNT,* VII, 973-78; H. Goeke, *Das Menschenbild der individuellen Klagelieder* (diss., Bonn, 1970), 168-180; D. Gonzalo-Maeso,

I. 1. *Etymology.* The root *yṯʿ*, in both the simple stem and a causative stem, is attested in a large number of proper names in Amorite, Ugaritic, Nabatean, and Old South Arabian; these correspond closely to Hebrew names containing the root *yšʿ*, in both qal (e.g., "Isaiah") and hiphil (e.g., "Hosea"). It is therefore probable that these proper names as well as the common Hebrew words *hôšîaʿ*, *yᵉšûʿâ,* etc., all go back to Proto-Semitic **yṯʿ*[1] and have nothing to do with Arab. *wasiʿa,* "be spacious" (IV *ʾawsaʿa,* "give room to"), as has been assumed in modern times.[2] A connection with *wasiʿa* is phonologically difficult, because it would involve anomalous correspondences between West Semitic *ṯ* and Arab. *s*[3] as well as South Semitic *y* and Arab. *w.*[4] The association is also semantically unsupportable: other terms are just as frequent in contexts involving *ṣārâ, ṣārōṯ,* etc., "straits, trouble" (terms that in any case may not always retain their original concrete sense of "narrow, confined"), e.g., *hiṣṣîl,* "deliver" (Ps. 34:18[Eng. v. 17]), *ʿāzar,* "help" (Ps. 46:2[1]), *ʿānâ,* "answer" (Ps. 86:7), *pāḏâ,* "ransom, rescue" (Ps. 25:22), and *šāmar,* "keep" (Prov. 21:23). The conception of salvation as "spaciousness," liberation from restricting, oppressive experiences both physical and spiritual, occurs frequently in the OT (e.g., Ps. 4:2[1]; 18:17-20[16-19]; 25:17; 31:9[8]; 118:5;[5] Est. 4:14);[6] this meaning, however, is expressed not by *hôšîaʿ* but by *hirḥîḇ,* "give room to," *merḥāḇ,* "liberating space,"[7] and the like. No trace of the "spaciousness" hypothesis is attested before Schultens,[8] and in practice, apart from brief

---

"Concepto de la *Yᵉšuʿah* ('Salud' o 'salvación') Biblica," *26. Semana Biblica Española,* I (Madrid, 1939), 5-19; K. Gouders, "In Jahwe ist Israels Heil: Exodus, Erlösung und Heil," *Bausteine biblischer Theologie. Festschrift G. J. Botterweck. BBB,* 50 (1977), 303-317; H. Gross, "Die Entwicklung der alttestamentlichen Heilshoffnung," *TrThZ,* 70 (1961), 15-28; A. S. Kapelrud, "Frelse i Det Gamle testamente," *NTT,* 80 (1979), 139-159; A. H. Leon, *The Meaning of the Verb Hošiaʿ in the OT* (diss., Claremont, 1980); J. S. Licht, "יְשׁוּעָה," *EMiqr,* III (1958), 897f.; P. V. P. Sagar, "'Salvation' in the OT," *IJT,* 18 (1969), 197-205; J. F. A. Sawyer, "A Historical Description of the Hebrew Root *yšʿ*," *Hamito-Semitica* (The Hague, 1975), 75-84; *idem, Semantics in Biblical Research. SBT,* N.S. 24 (1972); *idem,* "Spaciousness," *ASTI,* 6 (1967/68), 20-34; *idem,* "What Was a *mošiaʿ*?" *VT,* 15 (1965), 475-486; J. Scharbert, *Heilsmittler im AT und im Alten Orient. QuaestDisp,* 23/24 (1964); I. L. Seeligmann, "Zur Terminologie für das Gerichtsverfahren im Wortschatz des biblischen Hebräisch," *Hebräische Wortforschung. Festschrift W. Baumgartner. SVT,* 16 (1967), 251-278, esp. 274ff.; N. H. Snaith, *The Distinctive Ideas of the OT* (1946; repr. New York, 1964); J. J. Stamm, *Erlösen und Vergeben im AT* (Bern, 1940); J. H. Stek, "Salvation, Justice and Liberation in the OT," *Calvin Theological Journal,* 13 (1978), 133-165; F. Stolz, "ישׁע *jšʿ* hi. helfen," *THAT,* I, 786-790.

1 Sawyer, *Hamito-Semitica,* 75-84; Stolz, 786.

2 Cf. *KBL*³, 427; Fohrer, 970f.; H.-J. Kraus, *Psalms 1–59* (Eng. trans., Minneapolis, 1988), 139. W. W. Müller, "Altsüdarabische Beiträge zum hebräischen Lexikon," *ZAW,* 75 (1963), 310, ignores the West Semitic evidence.

3 *VG,* I, 128; *BDB,* 446.

4 *RyNP,* I, 232.

5 Kraus, 148.

6 Sawyer, *ASTI,* 6 (1967/68), 20-34.

7 Kraus, 253, 262.

8 A. Schultens, *Origines hebraeae, sive, Hebraicae linguae antiquissima natura et indoles ex Arabiae penetralibus revocata* (Leipzig, 1761), 81.

etymological sections, it has played a minor role in comprehensive discussions of the meaning of *hôšîaʿ*, *yᵉšûʿâ*, etc.[9]

The biform *šûaʿ* (cf. *ṭôḇ* beside *yāṭaḇ*, *ṣûq* beside *yāṣaq*, etc.[10]) is also a common element in personal names (e.g., "Joshua," "Elisha").[11] The piel of *šûaʿ*, "cry for help," "is probably to be understood like the piel of *ṣʿq* (found only in 2 K. 2:12) as referring to a succession of cries,"[12] and may be derived from the cry *šaʿ*, "Help!" (qal impv. of **yāšaʿ*).[13]

a. *Proper Names in West Semitic and South Arabian Inscriptions.* The earliest attested occurrence of the root is in the Amorite personal name *la-šu-ʾil* from Ur, *ca.* 2048 B.C.[14] Analyzable as *la-yašuʿ-ʾil*, this name contains an element corresponding to *yašuḫ-/-ešuḫ* in 8 Amorite names from Mari, such as *ia-šu-ḫu-ūm* and *i-li-e-šu-uḫ*,[15] and to *yṯʿ* in the Ugaritic personal name *yṯʿd*, transcribed in Akkadian cuneiform as *ya-aš-ad-du*, "Hadad saves."[16] Ugar. *yṯil*[17] may be a shortened form of *yṯʿ-ʾil*;[18] and *ya-šu-ia*, the name of the leader of a revolt in southern Palestine referred to in an Amarna letter, may be another fourteenth-century example.[19] The evidence for a West Semitic verb *yašaʿ*, impf. *yašuʿ*,[20] although it goes back to the second millennium B.C., is limited to personal names, where it is normally associated with a theophorous element.

In Old South Arabian, there are 20 personal names containing the element *yṯʿ*.[21] Among them can be distinguished the name of a Sabean god *yaṯiʿ* (e.g., *ʿabd-yaṯiʿ*) and a causative verb *hayṯaʿ* (e.g., *hayṯaʿ-ʾil*).[22] The name of Sabean ruler Iṯʾamra (*yiṯiʿ-ʾamara*) occurs only in the annals of Sargon II.[23]

In the OT, there are 14 proper names with the element *yšʿ/šûaʿ*: Abishua, Elishua, Elisha, Bath-shua, Hosea/Hoshea, Hoshaiah, Joshua, Jeshua, Ishi, Isaiah, Malchishua, Mesha, Shua, and Shuah. "Jeshua" is a late form of "Joshua" through dissimilation (cf. "Jehu").[24] The name "Isaiah" occurs at Elephantine,[25] while the full form *yšʿyhw* is attested along with *yšʿ*, *yšʿʾ*, and *yšʿʾl* on seal stamps of uncertain date and provenance.[26]

---

9 Cf. Fohrer, 970-78.
10 Cf. *VG*, I, 604; *BLe*, §496; *KBL*³, 427.
11 *KBL*³, 55, 379f.
12 E. Jenni, *Das hebräische Piʿel* (Zurich, 1968), 248.
13 Cf. W. J. Gerber, *Die hebräischen Verba denominativa* (Leipzig, 1896), 33.
14 G. Buccellati, *The Amorites of the Ur III Period* (Naples, 1966), 165.
15 *APNM*, 215f.
16 *UT*, no. 1179; *PNU*, 147.
17 *UT*, no. 1176.
18 *PNU*, 200.
19 EA 256, 18.
20 I. J. Gelb, *La lingua degli Amoriti. AANLR*, 8/13 (1958), 160.
21 *RyNP*, I, 112.
22 ContiRossini, 165.
23 *ARAB*, II, 7f.; cf. G. W. van Beek, "South Arabian History and Archaeology," *The Bible and the Ancient Near East. Festschrift W. F. Albright* (1961; repr. Winona Lake, 1979), 301.
24 *IPN*, 244f.; *VG*, I, 255.
25 *AP*, index.
26 D. Diringer, *Le iscrizioni antico-ebraïci Palestinesi* (Florence, 1934), 52, 63, 85, 86.

The name *ʾlyš*ʿ, "Elisha," appears on ostraca from Samaria[27] and Nimrud.[28] The name "Mesha" (possibly originally *mōša*ʿ; cf. LXX *Mōsa*[29]) occurs in the Moabite "Mesha inscription" (cf. 2 K. 3:4).

b. *History of the Root in Hebrew.* Apart from the occurrence of the verb *hôšîa*ʿ in the Mesha inscription with the Moabites' god Chemosh as subject and its appearance as a loanword in Aramaic,[30] *yš*ʿ occurs outside proper names only in Hebrew. In the Hebrew Bible, it is one of the most common roots, both in personal names and in common verbs and nouns. It is reserved almost exclusively for theological usage, however, with Yahweh as subject and his people as object (see below). The postbiblical history of these terms confirms their exclusively religious associations.

Already in the later books of the OT (Ruth, Chronicles, Ezra, Esther, Ecclesiastes, Song of Songs, Daniel) the root occurs only rarely and then in direct quotations from the earlier books and deliberate archaisms (e.g., Neh. 9:27). The same is true of rabbinic literature and modern Hebrew. Its place in everyday Hebrew is normally taken by *ʿāzar*, "help," *hiṣṣîl*, "rescue," *niṣṣāḥôn*, "victory," or the like.[31] The contrast between the religious usage of the Bible and later secular usage is illustrated by the story of a pedantic school teacher who was drowned in a lake because no one understood him when he shouted *hôšîʿēnî*, "Help me!"[32] The secular usage of these terms in postbiblical Hebrew is apparently limited to three legal terms: *môšîa*ʿ, "defender, rescuer," preferred to the normal *maṣṣîl* only in the context of talmudic legislation on rape;[33] the idiom *hôšîʿâ yāḏî lî*, "I took the law into my own hands" (cf. 1 S. 25:23-35),[34] found 3 times in the Qumran texts (1QS 6:27; CD 9:9f.); and finally the enigmatic phrase *yᵉšûa*ʿ *habbēn*, "redemption of the first-born,"[35] said to be a cryptic cipher for *piḏyôn habbēn* used in time of persecution.[36] It has been suggested that, as in the case of → גאל *gʾl*, → פדה *pdh*, and → צדק *ṣdq*, the religious and soteriological usage is derived from an original legal usage.[37] But there is not enough evidence from the meaning of the earliest West Semitic occurrences to substantiate this theory; and it may be argued that the usage in this small group of legal contexts, both biblical and postbiblical, is itself ultimately theological, insofar as the legal system in ancient Israel was believed to be sanctioned by God as supreme judge, who could delegate his authority to a king (cf. 2 S. 14:4; 2 K. 6:26f.) or

---

27 *Ibid.*, 42.

28 *Ibid.*, 200.

29 *KBL*³, 548; S. Segert, "Die Sprache der moabitischen Königsinschriften," *ArOr*, 29 (1961), 246.

30 J. T. Milik, " 'Prière de Nabonide' et autres écrits d'un cycle de Daniel," *RB*, 63 (1956), 413; J. H. Petermann, *Brevis linguae samaritanae grammatica* (Karlsruhe, 1873), 50.

31 E. Ben Yehuda, *Thesaurus totius hebraitatis* (repr. New York, 1960), IV, 2182f., cites no modern examples (cf. 2189ff.); cf. Licht, 897f.

32 Sawyer, *Semantics in Biblical Research*, 95f.

33 *Sanh.* 73a; cf. Dt. 22:27: Jastrow, II, 751.

34 See IV.1.b(4) below.

35 *B. Qam.* 80a bottom.

36 Jastrow, I, 600.

37 Sawyer, *VT*, 15 (1965), 483-86.

the community (Dt. 22:27),[38] just as in the period of the judges he appointed *môšî'îm* for his people when they appealed to him for protection against their adversaries (e.g., Jgs. 3:9,15; Neh. 9:27; Ob. 21).[39] However this may be, the peculiarly religious associations of the root *yš'* in almost every context are its most distinctive feature.

2. *Semantics of hôšîa'*. The basic meaning of the verb *hôšîa'* is best defined by establishing oppositions between it and other terms in the same semantic field.[40] The most frequent are *hiṣṣîl* (203 occurrences) and *'āzar* (137). Closely related are terms originally derived from the language of the lawcourt but also common in soteriological contexts: → גאל *gā'al,* "redeem" (113); → פדה *pāḏâ,* "ransom"; → שׁפט *šāpaṭ,* "judge"; → ריב *rîḇ,* "controversy"; and → צדק *ṣeḏeq,* "righteousness." Also associated with *hôšîa'* are numerous words and phrases applied by biblical writers metaphorically (like the forensic terms) to a variety of saving acts: → שׁמר *šāmar,* "watch over"; → גנן *gānan,* "defend"; → סמך *sāmaḵ,* "support"; → רפא *rāpā',* "heal"; → רמם *rāmam,* "rise"; → שׂגב *śāgaḇ,* "raise up"; → משׁה *māšâ,* "pull out"; → זכר *zāḵar,* "remember"; → רחב *rḥb* hiphil, "give room to"; → ענה *'ānâ,* "answer."[41] Against the background of this semantic field, the following distinctive features of *hôšîa'* are evident:

a. *hôšîa'* is the commonest soteriological term in religious contexts, but the rarest in everyday language.[42] The subject of *hôšîa'* is almost without exception Yahweh or his appointed representative, and there are indications that it is deliberately avoided when the speaker is not an Israelite (e.g., Ex. 2:19 [cf. v. 17]; 1 S. 4:8 [cf. v. 3]; 2 K. 19:11 [cf. vv. 19,34]).[43]

b. *hôšîa'* has a relatively large number of noun forms,[44] and acquires colorful associations from construct phrases such as *mimma'ayᵉnê hayᵉšû'â,* "wells of salvation" (Isa. 12:3); *ṣûr yiš'ēnû,* "rock of our salvation" (Ps. 95:1); *māḡēn yiš'eḵā,* "shield of your salvation" (Ps. 18:36)[35]); and *śᵉśôn yiš'eḵā,* "joy of your salvation" (Ps. 51:14[12]). These associations are not so apparent in any of the other terms in this field.

c. *hôšîa'* implies bringing help to those in trouble rather than rescuing them from it. In more than 20 passages it is followed by the prep. *lᵉ,* "to, for" (e.g., Josh. 10:6; Jgs. 10:14; Ps. 72:4; 86:16). Here it resembles *'āzar lᵉ,* "bring help to," *hēnîaḥ lᵉ,* "give rest to," and *hirḥîḇ lᵉ,* "give room to"; it takes *min,* "from," much less frequently than *hiṣṣîl,* "rescue," *gā'al,* "redeem," and the like.[45] It is not one of the regular terms used for the exodus, *hiṣṣîl, heʿᵉlâ, hôṣî',* and *gā'al* being the most common (cf. Ex. 3:7f.; 6:6-8); but it is applied 3 times to the victory of the Egyptians at the Red Sea (Ex. 14:13,30; 15:2).[46]

---

38 See IV.1.b(1) below.
39 Cf. Seeligmann, 272-78.
40 Sawyer, *Semantics in Biblical Research,* 102-111.
41 *Ibid.,* 29-48.
42 Licht, 897.
43 See IV.1.a below.
44 Sawyer, *Semantics in Biblical Research,* 68f.
45 Cf. *ibid.,* 103, 111.
46 Stolz, 789.

d. *hôšîaʿ* is closely related to the legal terms → גאל *gāʾal*, "redeem"; → פדה *pāḏâ*, "ransom"; → שפט *šāpaṭ*, "judge"; → צדק *ṣeḏeq*, "righteousness"; etc., which are attested in general soteriological contexts as well as technical legal passages. This is the only usage attested for *hôšîaʿ*—apart from its exclusively religious usage—in all varieties of Hebrew, and may ultimately depend on a primary theological meaning.[47]

e. The cognate nouns *yešûʿâ*, *yēšaʿ*, *môšāʿôṯ*, and *tešûʿâ* are not distinct semantically from the verb *hôšîaʿ*, even if in some contexts they are translated differently (e.g., "help," save" for the verb, "victory" for the nouns). Noun phrases like *ṣûr yešûʿāṭî*, "rock of my salvation" (Ps. 89:27[26]), and constructions like *nāṯattā ʾeṯ-hatತešûʿâ haggeḏôlâ hazzōʾṯ*, "you have given this great victory" (Jgs. 15:18), or *qerôḇâ yešûʿāṭî lāḇôʾ*, "my salvation is close at hand" (Isa. 56:1), are analyzable as nominalizing constructions generated from the same kernel as, for example, *hôšîaʿ YHWH mešîḥô*, "the Lord has given victory to his anointed king" (Ps. 20:7[6] [NEB]).[48] Thus what has been said of *hôšîaʿ* applies also to *yešûʿâ*, *yēšaʿ*, etc.: *yešûʿâ* comes to those in need, like a light (Isa. 49:6) or like walls and ramparts round a beleaguered city (Isa. 26:1), and does not remove or "rescue" them from it.[49] The noun *yešûʿâ* is also closely associated with *ṣeḏāqâ*, "righteousness," *mišpāṭ*, "justice," *ḥāmās*, "crime, violence," and the like. Like *ṣeḏāqâ*, *yešûʿâ* can denote both a single act or event and a permanent state (e.g., Isa. 51:6,8).[50]

II. Distribution.

1. *OT.* a. *Root.* The root *yšʿ* occurs 354 times in the OT. The largest concentration of occurrences is in the Psalms (136) and the prophetic books (100), especially Deutero-Isaiah (56). Excluding the poetic passages Gen. 49; Ex. 15:1-18; Dt. 32:1-43; 33:2-29; 1 S. 2:1-10; 2 S. 22 (par. Ps. 18); 2 S. 23:2-7; 1 Ch. 16:8-36 (par. Pss. 96:1-13; 105:1-15; 106:1,47f.); 2 Ch. 6:41f. (par. Ps. 132:8-10), it occurs only 8 times in the Pentateuch (3 in Exodus, 1 in Numbers, 4 in Deuteronomy) and 75 times in the historical books, most conspicuously Judges (22) and 1–2 Samuel (40). The remaining occurrences are in Job (8), Proverbs (5), and Lamentations (2).

The root is rare in eighth-century prophecy, occurring 4 times in Hosea and once in Micah; it is absent from Amos and Isa. 1–11. If we count the "Deuteronomistic history" (Joshua–Kings) as an exilic composition,[51] there is a significant concentration of occurrences (44%) in the period of the Babylonian exile: Deutero-Isaiah (56[52]), Jeremiah (20), Ezekiel (3), and the Deuteronomistic history (88). The Psalms and exilic compositions thus account for over 85 percent of the total. It is rare in the later books of the OT. In Nehemiah (2) and Chronicles (14) it occurs only in direct quotations from earlier books or stereotyped archaisms (e.g., Neh. 9:27); it is entirely absent from Ruth, Ezra, Esther,

---

47 See IV.1.b below.
48 Sawyer, *Semantics in Biblical Research*, 61-67.
49 See IV.3.c below.
50 See IV.3.e below.
51 M. Noth, *The Deuteronomistic History. JSOTSup,* 15 (Eng. trans. 1981); P. R. Ackroyd, *Exile and Restoration. OTL* (1968), 62-83.
52 Cf. P. E. Bonnard, *Le Second Isaïe. ÉtB* (1972), 535.

Ecclesiastes, the Song of Songs, Daniel, Joel, and Haggai. The only 2 occurrences in Sirach are in the appended psalm, which is consciously archaic in style (Sir. 51:1,10).

b. *Verb.* The hiphil verb *hôšîaʿ* is the most common term in all contexts: more than half (184) of the total occurrences of the root in Biblical Hebrew are forms of *hôšîaʿ*, and the hiphil stem occurs also in the personal names "Hosea," "Hoshaiah," and "Mesha,"[53] as well as in the noun *môšāʿōṯ*, attested once in the OT (Ps. 68:21[20]). The hiphil act. ptcp. *môšîaʿ* occurs 33 times in the OT and as a technical term in rabbinic literature;[54] it usually functions as an agent noun.[55] The late or anomalous form *yᵉhôšîaʿ* is an aramaism in Ps. 116:6 (cf. *limᵉnûḥāyᵉḵî* [v. 7], *ʿālāyᵉḵî* [v. 7], *tagmûlôhî* [v. 12]).[56] Why it appears also in 1 S. 17:47 is not explained; possibly the text is corrupt.[57] The niphal occurs 21 times in the OT, and the qal only in personal names.[58] The piel of *šwʿ* occurs 21 times, and the cognate noun *šawʿâ*, 11.

c. *Noun.* Not counting the hapax legomenon *môšāʿōṯ*, there are three noun forms: *yᵉšûʿâ*, *yešaʿ*, and *tᵉšûʿâ*. The first, with 78 occurrences, is more than twice as common as the others in the OT, although it is rare in prose (4 occurrences); it is the only one found in the plural (12 occurrences). The form *yᵉšûʿāṯâ*, with the unstressed suffix *-â* (Ps. 3:3[2]; 80:3; Jon. 2:10[9]), beside *ʿezrāṯâ* (Ps. 63:8[7]; 94:17), may originally have had a quasi-verbal function (like Ger. *zu Hilfe!*).[59] The noun *yešaʿ* occurs 35 times, always in poetry, and 5 times in the construct form *yēšaʿ* (with *ṣere*).[60] The form *yôšaʿ* appears in the Babylonian tradition at Job 5:4,11, and possibly also Isa. 35:4 MT.[61] The form *tᵉšûʿâ* occurs 33 times, with a markedly higher proportion in prose (11) than is the case with the other nouns.[62] It is probably derived from the biform *šûaʿ*, but could come from *hôšîaʿ* itself after the analogy of *yᵉšûʿâ* (cf. *tᵉqûp̄â* from *hiqqîp̄*).[63]

Sawyer

2. *Dead Sea Scrolls.* In the Qumran documents, the root *yšʿ* appears in many biblical quotations (e.g., 11QMelch 16:19, from Isa. 52:7[64]; cf. also the rejection of taking the law into one's own hands [*hôšîʿâ yāḏô lô*] in 1QS 6:27; CD 9:9,10, recalling 1 S. 25,[65] as well as some 100 occurrences in 1QIs*ᵃ*). Besides these quotations, there are 15 occurrences of the verb, 18 of the noun *yšwʿh*, 5 of the noun *yšʿ*, and 9 occurrences of

---

53 *IPN*, 176.

54 See IV.1.b below.

55 Boecker, *Redeformen*, 65f.; *KBL*³, 532; Sawyer, *VT*, 15 (1965), 476, n. 1.

56 H.-J. Kraus, *Psalms 60–150* (Eng. trans., Minneapolis, 1989), 388.

57 *BHK;* S. R. Driver, *Notes on the Hebrew Text of the Books of Samuel* (Oxford, ²1913), 147.

58 *IPN*, 36.

59 *BLe*, §528t,u.

60 *KBL*³, 428.

61 *Idem*; P. Wernberg-Møller, "Two Difficult Passages in the OT," *ZAW*, 69 (1957), 73.

62 Driver, 118.

63 *BLe*, §496s; *VG*, I, 383.

64 Cf. A. S. van der Woude, "Melchisedek als himmlische Erlösergestalt in den neugefundenen eschatologischen Midraschim aus Qumran Höhle XI," *OTS*, 14 (1965), 358.

65 See IV.1.b(4) below.

the root in personal names. It is noteworthy that in almost all cases God is the subject and initiator of salvation. Throughout Israel's history, he has given many demonstrations of his *yšwʿh* (1QS 1:19; 1QM 10:4; 11:3; 14:5; 18:7; CD 5:19; 6QCD 3:2; 4Q183 1.II.3), which is now developed as an article of faith in the setting of realized eschatology: the time of the community is considered an "age of salvation" (1QM 1:5; 10:8; 13:13), an occasion for praising God (1QS 10:17; 1QH 11:23; 12:3; 11QPs[a] 22:3,4,8); even the formation of the community happens for the purpose of proclaiming God's *yešaʿ* (11QPs[a] 154:4 [= 11QPs[a] 18:2]); cf. also the inscription on the community's standard in the decisive eschatological battle: *yšwʿwt ʾl*, "God's saving acts" (1QM 4:13).

God brings salvation to his devout followers by the gift of his *tôrâ* (1QH 5:11f.), by demonstrations of his *ḥesed* (1QS 11:12; 1QH 2:23; 11:18; 4Q185 1f.II.13), and by personal intervention against the wicked (4QpPs[a] 37:4,21).[66] The purpose of his whole creation is eternal salvation (1QH 15:16), which is given to those who have true faith.

A member of the Essene community at Qumran can look forward to God's salvation if he himself fears God (CD 20:20), seeks refuge in God's name (CD 20:34), and looks for his salvation (1QH fr. 18:5). The Essenes provide a series of detailed sketches of this future age of salvation,[67] but the term *yšʿ* does not play an important role in them.

A search for significant reinterpretations of the MT in 1QIs[a] yields only 2 passages involving the root *yšʿ*.[68] In Isa. 26:18, the scroll reads *wšwʿtk* instead of MT *yšwʿt*, thus interpreting God as the subject even of the *yᵉšûʿâ* that (according to the MT) the human race has tried in vain to realize on earth. This change clearly illustrates the total devaluation of humanity in the anthropology of Qumran. In Isa. 51:5, against an otherwise unanimous textual tradition, 1QIs[a] reads for *yāṣāʾ yišʿî ûzᵉrōʿay* the 3rd person singular suffix: *wzrwʿw*.[69] Thus *yešaʿ* as a function of God (MT) is personalized as an hypostasis of this divine function; at the same time, it is interpreted messianically,[70] since the text now speaks of "his [the savior's] strong arm."

The occurrences of the TR (Isa. 59:8,11,18; 66:8) clearly reflect OT usage (compare Dt. 28:29; Jgs. 2:18 and Ex. 22:15f.; Dt. 22:28).

Fabry

III. Corresponding Terms.

1. *LXX*. The LXX renders the *yšʿ* group most consistently by *sṓzō, sōtēría, sōtḗrion, sōtḗr, anasṓzō,* and *diasṓzō* (cf. Sir. 51:1). Gk. *sōtḗr* is not the regular translation for *môšîaʿ*, which is rendered by *sṓzōn* (e.g., 1 S. 11:3; Isa. 43:11), *sotēría* (e.g., 2 S. 23:5; Isa. 47:15), and *anasṓzō* (Zec. 8:7), as well as *sotḗr* (e.g., Jgs. 3:9,15; Neh. 9:27). It also represents *yešaʿ* (12 times) and *yᵉšûʿâ* (4 times).[71] Otherwise the LXX has *boēthéō,*

---

66 See also W. Foerster, "σῴζω," *TDNT,* VII, 982ff.

67 See H. W. Kuhn, *Enderwartung und gegenwärtiges Heil. StUNT,* 4 (1966), 176ff.

68 E. Y. Kutscher, *The Language and Linguistic Background of the Isaiah Scroll (1QIsa[a]). STDJ,* 6 (1974), 559.

69 *Ibid.,* 561.

70 Foerster, 1014, n. 59 (G. Bertram).

71 Fohrer, 970ff.

boēthós, boētheía (10 times), *hrýomai* (7 times), and various other terms, including *exaírō* (Jer. 42:11 [LXX 49:11]) and *amýnō* (Isa. 59:16). In 2 S. 22:42, the choice of *boēthós* in the LXX has probably been influenced by the similarity between the words for "shout for help" and "help" in both Greek and Hebrew: *boḗsontai, kaí ouk éstin boēthós, yešawweʿû weʾên môšîaʿ* (*BHK*). The distinction between *hôšîaʿ le*, "bring help to (a person in distress)" and *hiṣṣîl*, "rescue or remove (a person from trouble)"[72] was perceived by the LXX translators, who used *hrýomai*, "rescue,"[73] only 7 times for *hôšîaʿ*, but 84 times for *hiṣṣîl*.[74]

2. *NT.* In the Greek NT, the Hebrew terms underlie the explanations of the name "Jesus" in Mt. 1:21 (cf. Lk. 2:30) and of the loanword *hōsanná* in Mt. 21:9; Mk. 11:10; Jn. 12:13 (cf. Ps. 118:25).[75] Elsewhere in the gospels, "*sṓzō* and *sotēría* are very much in the background."[76] They are frequent, however, in Pauline eschatological language, both in allusions to the OT (e.g., 2 Cor. 6:2 [cf. Isa. 49:8]; see also the OT passages quoted in Paul's speeches in Acts: Ps. 107:19f. in Acts 13:26; Isa. 49:6 in Acts 13:47; Ps. 67:3[2] in Acts 28:28) and in his own Greek, where *sōtēría* is opposed to death in several passages (e.g., 1 Cor. 5:5; 2 Cor. 7:10; Phil. 1:28; 1 Th. 5:8ff.; 2 Th. 2:10) and treated as synonymous with the synoptic expression "inherit the kingdom of God" (cf. esp. Rom. 13:11).

3. *Targumim.* The Aramaic targumim normally render these terms by *peraq, parîq, purqān,* etc., which differ from *šezib*, "rescue," in the same way that *hôšîaʿ* differs from *hiṣṣîl* (cf. 1 S. 4:3,8; 2 K. 19:11,34).[77] Their influence on Hebrew is seen in the aramaism *pāraq,* "rescue," in Ps. 7:3(2); 136:24; Lam. 5:8.[78]

4. *Vulgate.* The Vulg. normally uses *servare, salvus, salus, salvator, salvare,* etc., but occasionally *defendere* (Ex. 2:17), *adiuvare* (Dt. 28:31), *liberare* (Dt. 22:27; 28:29; Prov. 20:22), *magnalia Domini* (Ex. 14:13), *protector salvationum* (Ps. 28:8[Vulg. 27:8]), or the like. In patristic usage, the name "Jesus" was translated as *salvator:* e.g., "Christus Jesus, id est Christus Salvator . . . salvare et salvator non fuerunt haec Latina, antequam veniret Salvator."[79] The peculiarly productive use of these words for "salvation, safety, protection, health," etc., in Christian Latin, consciously deriving from Biblical Hebrew, further illustrates the rich soteriological meaning of *hôšîaʿ, yešûʿâ,* etc. (in contrast to *ʿāzar* [represented by *adiuvare,* etc.] and *hiṣṣîl* [represented by *liberare,* etc.]), and the

---

72 See I.2.c above.

73 W. Bauer, *A Greek-English Lexicon of the NT and Other Early Christian Literature* (Eng. trans., Chicago, ²1979), 737.

74 Cf. W. Kasch, "ῥύομαι," *TDNT,* VI, 999, where a different conclusion is based on this evidence.

75 See IV.4 below.

76 Foerster, 991.

77 See IV.1.a below.

78 *BDB,* 830; Kraus, *Psalms 1–59,* 170; Sawyer, *Semantics in Biblical Research,* 100, 109.

79 Augustine *Sermones* ccxcix.6.

distinction between bringing help, health, or protection to a person (*hôšîaʿ le, salvare*) and rescuing a person from trouble (*hiṣṣîl, liberare*).[80]

IV. OT Usage.

1. *Narrative Prose Texts.* In the narrative prose style of the historical books, to which may be added the 8 occurrences in prose sections of the Pentateuch (Ex. 2:17; 14:13,30; Nu. 10:9; Dt. 20:4; 22:27; 28:29,31), two distinct usages can be identified: one in the context of theological history, in which the terms are applied to acts of divine intervention in the history of Israel (65 occurrences), and a more secular usage in a legal or political context, where the subject is a human being (23 occurrences).

a. *Theological Usage.*

(1) The Victory at the Red Sea. The *locus classicus* of theological usage is Ex. 14, where Israel's spectacular victory over the Egyptians at the Red Sea is described as *yešûʿaṯ YHWH* (v. 13; cf. 15:2): *wayyôšaʿ YHWH bayyôm hahûʾ ʾeṯ-yiśrāʾēl miyyaḏ miṣrāyim,* "Yahweh saved Israel that day from the hand of the Egyptians" (14:30). The subject is the God of Israel, a fact emphasized throughout the chapter: e.g., "Yahweh will fight for you, and you have only to be still" (v. 14; cf. vv. 18,25,27,31). The sequence of events is also typical: the Israelites cry out for help when they see Pharaoh's army advancing on them (vv. 10-12), and they are instructed to "stand firm and see the salvation of Yahweh" (v. 13), which comes to them in the form of "the angel of God," "the pillar of cloud," protecting them from the pursuing Egyptians (vv. 19f.), "the pillar of fire and of cloud" (v. 24), and the unnatural behavior of the waters of the Red Sea (vv. 21-29). The term *hôšîaʿ* is not used of the exodus (Ex. 3:7-10; 6:6-8), which involves removing Israel *from* its distress, but of the coming of divine help *to* the Israelites where they are.[81]

Finally, there are clear indications in the style of this passage that the event described has peculiar significance in the history of Israel: it takes place *bayyôm hahûʾ*, "on that day" (v. 30); Israel "saw the great work (*ʾeṯ-hayyāḏ haggeḏōlâ*) which Yahweh did against the Egyptians" (v. 31); and it led to praise of God (vv. 17f.) and the commitment of the people to faith "in Yahweh and in his servant Moses" (v. 31).

(2) Other Divinely Inspired Victories. This typical usage of *hôšîaʿ*, *yešûʿâ,* etc., in the context of *Heilsgeschichte* is found also in connection with the military successes of Gideon (Jgs. 6:37; 7:7),[82] Samuel (1 S. 7:8), Saul and Jonathan (1 S. 11:13; 14:23,39), David (1 S. 19:5; 2 S. 3:18; 8:6,14), David's heroes (2 S. 23:10,12; cf. 1 Ch. 11:14), Joash (2 K. 13:17), Jeroboam (2 K. 14:27), Jehoshaphat (2 Ch. 20:17), and Hezekiah (2 Ch. 32:22). In the other passages, God is the implied subject, since it is he who sends the *môšîʿîm,* "saviors" (Jgs. 2:16,18; 3:9,15; 13:5; 1 S. 9:16; 2 K. 13:5; Neh. 9:27; cf. also Ob. 21), and "gives the victory" to Samson (Jgs. 15:18) and to Syria "by the hand of

80 See A. Ernout and A. Meillet, *Dictionnaire étymologique de la langue latine* (Paris, 1932), 851.

81 See I.2.c above.

82 W. Beyerlin, "Geschichte und heilsgeschichtliche Traditionsbildung im AT," *VT,* 13 (1963), 1-25.

Naaman" (2 K. 5:1). The obscure minor judges Shamgar (Jgs. 3:31) and Tola (10:1) fall into the same category, although the divine initiative is not made explicit.

(3) The Deuteronomist's Tendentious Use with Human Subjects. Most of these examples occur in the Deuteronomistic historian's comments on events in the history of Israel, either in the "Deuteronomistic framework"[83] or in the speeches of characters, such as angels (Jgs. 13:5) or prophets (1 S. 9:16), introduced into the narrative to provide another vehicle for the author's comments.[84] There are speeches in the Deuteronomistic history where the use of *hôšîa'* highlights the contrast between the power of Yahweh and the illusory appeal of foreign gods or human might. This is the point of the scornful words of Yahweh to the people in Jgs. 10:14: *hēmmâ yôšî'û lākem,* "let them [= foreign gods] save you!" and of the arrogant claim of Israel in Jgs. 7:2: *yādî hôšî'â lî,* "my own hand saved me." Cf. the credal statement *lō' beḥereb ûbaḥanît yehôšîa' YHWH,*[85] "Yahweh saves by neither sword not spear" (1 S. 17:47). In 1 S. 4, the faith of Israel's elders in the power of the ark is clearly expressed by their use of *hôšîa'* (v. 3), in contrast to the frightened Philistines' use of the less highly charged theological term *hiṣṣîl* in the same context (v. 8; cf. 2 K. 19 below).

In two interesting cases, the author implies by using *hôšîa'* that people are attributing to a human agent more credit than is proper. In the first case, Gideon rejects his people's suggestion that, because (in their words) he has "saved" (*hôša'tānû*) them from the Midianites, he should be made king (Jgs. 8:22f.). The second is a piece of flowery rhetoric designed to save Jonathan's life: "Shall Jonathan die, who has wrought this great victory (*'āśâ hayešû'â haggedōlâ hazzō't*)?" (1 S. 14:45). The use of *yešû'â* here for the more normal prose word *tešû'â* (cf. 1 S. 11:13; 19:5; 2 S. 23:10,12; 2 K. 5:1; etc.)[86] may be an indication by the author that the people defending Jonathan are comparing his spectacular exploit against the Philistines to an act of divine intervention (cf. Ex. 14:13; 2 Ch. 20:17). The same victory is attributed to God in 1 S. 14:23 and (in Saul's words) in v. 39.

The peculiar soteriological meaning of these terms is also evident in a number of dialogues where God's power to "save" is at first doubted and then demonstrated dramatically: e.g., *bammâ 'ôšîa' 'eṯ-yiśrā'ēl,* "How can I save Israel?" (Jgs. 6:14f.,36f.; cf. Ex. 14:13; 1 S. 10:27; 2 Ch. 20:17). General Deuteronomistic statements on the saving power of God, in which *hôšîa'*, *tešû'â,* etc. are prominent, can be traced from the priests' exhortations to the Israelite army on the eve of battle (Dt. 20:4; cf. Nu. 10:9) through the historical books (e.g., 1 S. 10:19; 14:6,39; 17:47; 2 Ch. 20:9) to the War scroll from Qumran (1QM 10:4f. [quoting Dt. 20:4]; 1QM 10:7f. [quoting Nu. 10:9]; 1QM 11:2f. [quoting 1 S. 17:47]).

---

83 W. Beyerlin, "Gattung und Herkunft des Rahmens im Richterbuch," *Tradition und Situation. Festschrift A. Weiser* (Göttingen, 1963), 1-29.

84 H. W. Wolff, "Das Kerygma des deuteronomistischen Geschichtswerks," *ZAW,* 73 (1961), 171-186 (= *GSAT. ThB,* 22 [²1973], 308-324); W. Brueggemann, "The Kerygma of the Deuteronomistic Historian," *Int,* 11 (1968), 387-402.

85 See II.1.b above.

86 Driver, 118.

Altogether, *hôšîa'* and *t^e^šû'â* (rarely *y^e^šû'â*[87]) are used 37 times in the Deuteronomistic history in the specific sense of divine intervention on behalf of Israel, to which must be added 8 in Chronicles and Nehemiah (all dependent on Deuteronomistic tradition) and 3 in Deuteronomy itself. This contrasts markedly with the relative infrequency of the two closest synonyms: *'āzar,* "help," occurs only once in this sense (1 S. 7:12, the folk etymology of "Ebenezer"); and *hiṣṣîl,* which occurs 46 times in the Deuteronomistic history, is used in this sense only 14 times. It is always either applied to the rescue of foreigners (Josh. 9:26) and animals (1 S. 17:35) or put in the mouth of foreigners like Philistines (1 S. 4:8) and Assyrians (2 K. 18:29-35; 19:10-13). As in 1 S. 4 (see above), the author contrasts the Assyrians' use of *hiṣṣîl,* referring to Jerusalem's slender chances of being rescued (2 K. 19:11), to Hezekiah's prayer *hôšî'ēnû nā',* "save us, I beseech thee" (v. 19), and God's answer (delivered by the prophet Isaiah): "I will defend the city and save (*hôšîa'*) it" (v. 34).

Two terms that are related to *hôšîa'* in Deuteronomistic usage are *hēnîaḥ,* "give rest to," and *šāp̱aṭ,* "judge." All three imply bringing help to a situation, "salvation" (undefined), peace, and justice respectively, but can be followed in some contexts by *min,* "from"; cf. Dt. 12:10; 25:19; Josh. 23:1; 2 S. 7:1,11 (*hēnîaḥ*); 1 S. 24:16[15]; 2 S. 18:19,31 (*šāp̱aṭ*). The words *šōp̱^e^ṭîm,* "judges," and *môšî'îm* are virtually synonymous in some contexts, e.g., Jgs. 2:16,18 beside 3:9,15.[88] The verb *šāp̱aṭ* can have soteriological overtones (e.g., Jgs. 3:9f.; 1 S. 8:20).[89] The term *hôšîa'* is far more frequent in this sense, however, and may be described as the Deuteronomistic soteriological term par excellence.

b. *Legal Usage.* In the remaining 23 occurrences, the subject of *hôšîa'* is human, not divine; but the context is legal or political in every case. It may be argued that these human agents are acting as God's representatives, like the *môšî'îm* in Judges, to bring divine justice into situations of injustice.[90]

(1) The Law on Rape. The term *môšîa'* is used in the Deuteronomic law on rape (Dt. 22:25-29), where it is apparently a technical term referring to the legal protection a betrothed girl is entitled to expect from the community. In this case, the distinction between adultery and rape hinges on whether or not the assaulted girl's cries for help can be heard by the community: she is assumed to be innocent if the assault takes place in the country out of earshot of her family and friends.[91] The choice of *hôšîa'* in Ex. 2:17—unique in the Pentateuch outside Deuteronomy (excluding the soteriological passages discussed above)—to describe Moses' rescue of Jethro's seven daughters in distress is probably influenced by this usage. Predictably, the word is not used by the Midianites themselves, who employ the more general *hiṣṣîl* in their account of the same

---

87 See II.1.c above.

88 Cf. M. Weinfeld, *Deuteronomy and the Deuteronomistic School* (Oxford, 1972), 120, n. 1; Z. Weismann, "Charismatic Leadership and the Era of the Judges," *Tarbiz,* 45 (1975/76), 1-14 [Heb.], I [Eng. summary].

89 Cf. G. F. Moore, *Judges. ICC* (repr. ²1949), 71, 88.

90 See I.1.b above; cf. Boecker; Seeligmann, 274ff.; Stolz, 786.

91 G. von Rad, *Deuteronomy. OTL* (Eng. trans. 1966), 142f.; Sawyer, *VT,* 15 (1965), 478f.

incident (v. 19).[92] The idiom *wᵉ'ên môšîa'*, "and there shall be no one to help [you]," appears twice in Deuteronomy in a context that emphasizes the helplessness of the Israelites, assaulted by an enemy set on seizing their wives, houses, and possessions (Dt. 28:29-31), a situation not dissimilar to that of the assaulted maiden in the law code.

(2) The Injured Widow's Appeal. The position of the widow in 2 S. 14 is analogous: she appeals to the king for help against her adversaries, using the "usual legal formula":[93] ***hôšîa' hammeleḵ***. The fictitious nature of the situation is significant; the woman of Tekoa, acting on Joab's orders, must therefore use conventional idioms correctly to be convincing. The same formula occurs in 2 K. 6:26f. in a very similar context. In both cases, the assumption is that the king is the official *môšîa'*, appointed (like the judges[94]) by God, and that a defenseless woman is entitled to "appeal" (*ṣā'aq;* cf. Dt. 22:17; Jgs. 3:9,15; 10:12; 12:2; etc.) to him for legal aid or protection. It may be that in so doing she is indirectly addressing God, the proper subject of *hôšîa'*.[95] In Josh. 22:22, *hôšîa'* is used in the sense of defending a just cause. The speakers, accused of treachery (vv. 16-20), begin their defense by calling God to witness and then go on: "If we are guilty, do not defend us (*'al tôšî'ēnû* [2nd person singular, addressed to Phineas, the leader of the mission(?); others emend to the 3rd person singular, referring to God[96]])." Another example is the use in Jgs. 6:31 of *hôšîa'* in conjunction with *rîḇ*, "contend," to describe the defense that Joash challenges his fellow citizens to give to Ba'al: "Will you defend (*tôšî'ûn*) his cause?" The question is whether the community will accept legal responsibility for Ba'al, whose altar has been broken down.[97]

(3) Military Alliances. A third type of legal protection for which *hôšîa'* is used is the assistance to an ally required by some kind of treaty or alliance. Whatever the original content of the treaty between Joshua and the Gibeonites may have been,[98] according to the Deuteronomistic redactor (Josh. 10:1; cf. 9:15) it provides the background for the Amorites' attack on the Gibeonites and their appeal to Joshua for help, in which they use the special term *hôšîa'*: "Come up to us quickly, and bring us protection (*hôšî'â lānû*), and help (*'āzar*) us" (10:6). When the king of Jerusalem addresses a similar request to his Amorite allies, the term is not used (v. 4). It is also noteworthy that in effect the Gibeonites' request is answered not by Joshua but by God (v. 8): their protection comes in the form of spectacular instances of divine intervention (vv. 10-14). Exactly the same kind of situation underlies the use of *hôšîa'* in negotiations between Jephthah and the men of Ephraim (Jgs. 12:2,3); again divine intervention is contrasted with human fallibility (v. 3), between Israel and Jabesh-gilead (1 S. 11:3,9) and between David and Keilah (1 S. 23:2,5).

---

92 See IV.1.a above.

93 J. A. Montgomery and H. S. Gehman, *Kings. ICC* (1951), 385; Boecker.

94 See I.1.b above.

95 See IV.1.a above.

96 Cf. LXX, Syr., Vulg., *BHS;* also M. Noth, *Das Buch Josua. HAT,* VII (³1971), 130.

97 Moore, 195.

98 Noth, *HAT,* VII, 53-59; J. M. Grintz, "The Treaty of Joshua with the Gibeonites," *JAOS,* 86 (1966), 113-126.

Another example is Joab's plan of campaign in conjunction with his brother against the combined forces of Ammon and Syria (2 S. 10:11f. par. 1 Ch. 19:12f.); it may be contrasted with the surprising use of *hôšîaʿ* in the case of the Syro-Ammonite pact referred to at the end of the same chapter (2 S. 10:19; cf. 1 Ch. 19:19). In the first place, with God's help, the plan succeeds (2 S. 10:12f.); in the second, the Syrians' fear leads them to break off their alliance with Ammon. There is one final example of *hôšîaʿ* in the language of political negotiations: 2 K. 16:7. Here the undesirability of the human subject—in this case Assyria (cf. Hos. 14:4[3]), in whom the godless Ahaz (cf. 2 K. 16:2ff.) has chosen to put his faith—is surely implied by the author. Ahaz is represented as addressing Tiglath-pileser as though he were a god; to seal this misdirected alliance, he "took the silver and gold that was found in the house of the Lord . . . and sent [it as] a present to the king of Assyria" (v. 8; cf. vv. 10-18).

(4) "Taking the Law into One's Own Hands." The last idiom that takes a human subject and refers to "meting out justice" is *hôšîaʿ yāḏî lî.* The *locus classicus* of this usage is 1 S. 25:23-35, where the point at issue is whether David will accept Abigail's offer of reparation or "take the law into his own hands" (vv. 26,33; the same idiom probably occurred originally in v. 31, too[99]) and punish her husband Nabal by the sword. The use of the word *yāḏ,* "hand," in this idiom implies not only that the subject is using force[100] but also that he is doing what properly should be done by someone else. This is the significance of Israel's boast in Jgs. 7:2 (see above) and the divine sarcasm in Job 40:14 (cf. Prov. 20:22[101]).

In the Qumran texts, the idiom is applied to the crime of making a person swear an oath, something only judges can do legally (CD 9:9f.).[102] It also occurs in the context of insubordination in 1QS 6:27.[103]

2. *Wisdom Literature.*

a. *Yahwistic Wisdom Sayings.* In Proverbs, the verb *hôšîaʿ* occurs twice and the prose form of the noun *tᵉšûʿâ* 3 times. Here, *tᵉšûʿâ,* "safety" (rather than "victory"[104]), comes from Yahweh, not from the war horse (Prov. 21:31); in a situation of injustice, therefore, it is unnecessary to "take the law into one's own hands":[105] "Wait for Yahweh, and he will help (*hôšîaʿ*) you" (20:22; cf. 1 S. 25:33; etc.).[106] "Safety" is the reward for integrity (Prov. 28:18), a Yahwistic view presupposing divine protection for the blameless;[107] it is achieved by wise counsel rather than physical strength (11:14; 24:5f.). This last proverb is quoted twice, both as a maxim (11:14) and as a motive clause in the instruction section

99 Cf. LXX, *BHK*³, Driver, 202.
100 Driver, 201f.
101 W. McKane, *Proverbs. OTL* (1970), 548.
102 Cf. C. Rabin, *The Zadokite Documents* (Oxford, ²1958), 45f.
103 P. Wernberg-Møller, *The Manual of Discipline. STDJ,* 1 (1957), 112.
104 McKane, 429.
105 *Ibid.,* 548.
106 B. Gemser, *Sprüche Salomos. HAT,* XVI (1937), 63.
107 McKane, 622.

(22:17–24:22); if it comes from "the vocabulary of old wisdom,"[108] it is a rare example in the OT of a neutral usage of *tᵉšûʿâ* in the sense of security that comes through human efforts. Possibly the occurrence of *tᵉšûʿâ* in such a context indicates that the process described by McKane[109] as "a Yahwistic reinterpretation of an older, empirical, mundane wisdom" has already begun in this proverb.

The term does not belong to the "vocabulary of old wisdom":[110] it is relatively rare in Proverbs and Job (see below), and is conspicuously absent from the other "old wisdom" sayings on the same subject, e.g., Prov. 16:32; 21:22;[111] Eccl. 7:19; 10:14-16. The evidence that *hôšîaʿ*, *tᵉšûʿâ*, etc. are primarily theological terms in Wisdom Literature as well as the rest of the OT is in any case overwhelming.

b. *Job.* In Job, the more poetic form *yešaʿ*[112] is used of the protection orphans need in court (Job 5:4) and mourners in their bereavement: *wᵉqōḏᵉrîm śāgᵉḇû yešaʿ*, "and mourners are raised to safety" (5:11). In both cases, God is the implied subject; he withholds protection from the fool and his family (vv. 2-7) and raises the helpless above their troubles (v. 11). He helps (*hôšîaʿ*) the powerless (26:2; cf. 5:15, reading [with Ewald] *moḥᵒrāḇ*, "destitute," or *mēḥarbām yāṯôm*, "the fatherless from their sword" [Budde][113]) and the humble (22:9; cf. 5:11). In 2 cases, *yᵉšûʿâ*, the other predominantly poetic noun form, refers to success in debate: in 30:15, Job looks back to the position of honor he had held in society before his downfall and in particular to his effective participation in court (cf. 29:7-25); in 13:16, he hopes for success in presenting his case before God. The last occurrence in Job is also explicitly forensic: a variant of the idiom *hôšîaʿ yāḏî lî*, "take the law into one's own hands,"[114] is applied ironically to Job's vain attempts throughout the dialogue to play the part reserved for God. This suggests that the 2 occurrences of *yᵉšûʿâ* just mentioned are also intended by the author to emphasize Job's complete dependence on God.[115]

3. *Prophetic Literature.*

a. *Yahweh the Only Proper Subject of hôšîaʿ.* In the prophetic literature, the proper subject of *hôšîaʿ* is always God or *môšîʿîm*, "saviors," under his royal authority (Isa. 19:20; Ob. 21), in contrast to *hiṣṣîl*, which occurs once in Deutero-Isaiah with God as subject and 5 times without.[116] There are no exceptions: passages emphasizing that no other god (Isa. 45:20; Jer. 11:12), idol (Isa. 46:7; Jer. 2:27,28), astrologer (Isa. 47:13), king (Hos. 13:10), or any other power, human or divine (Isa. 26:18; Hos. 14:4[3]), can save (*hôšîaʿ*) confirm it. The term *hôšîaʿ* is avoided when idols are addressed (Isa.

---

108 *Ibid.*, 429, 397f.
109 *Ibid.*, 17-21.
110 *Ibid.*, 17.
111 *Ibid.*, 551.
112 See II.1.c above.
113 S. R. Driver and G. B. Gray, *Job. ICC* (²1927, repr. 1977), II, 32.
114 See IV.1.b(4) above.
115 G. von Rad, *Wisdom in Israel* (Eng. trans., Nashville, 1972), 224.
116 Bonnard, 536.

44:17).[117] There is no *môšîaʿ* apart from God (Isa. 43:11; 45:21; Hos. 13:4[118]). The same exclusiveness is implied by the recurring collocation *YHWH môšîʿēḵ*, "Yahweh your savior" (Isa. 49:26; 60:16 [with fem. sg. suf. referring to Jerusalem]; cf. 43:3; 45:15; Jer. 14:8), in the genitive phrases *ʾelōhê yišʿî* (Isa. 17:10; Mic. 7:7)[119] or *ʾēl yešûʿāṯî*, "God of my salvation" (Isa. 12:2), and in the question, "Why should you be like a mighty man who cannot save (*hôšîaʿ*)?" (Jer. 14:9; cf. Isa. 59:1).

b. *Meaning.* The situations in which God intervenes (*hôšîaʿ*) or for which his *yešûʿâ* (less often *tešûʿâ* or *yešaʿ*) is sought are specified in some passages: an Assyrian invasion (Isa. 37:20; cf. 2 K. 19:19,34); Egyptian oppression (Isa. 19:20); the Babylonian threat of 597 B.C. (Jer. 42:11; Zeph. 3:17); exile (Jer. 30:10f.; 31:7; 46:27; Zec. 8:7; 10:6); sin (Isa. 64:4[5]); ritual impurity (Ezk. 36:29; 37:23); sickness (Jer. 8:20f.; 17:14). Here, too, *hôšîaʿ* denotes bringing something to a person or situation in distress rather than removing him from it. Thus salvation comes to Zion (Isa. 62:11; cf. 56:1) and reaches like a light to the ends of the earth (Isa. 49:6; cf. 62:1); God puts it in Zion (Isa. 46:13; cf. 26:1) and clothes a person in it (Isa. 61:10). Indeed, *yešûʿâ* is like walls and ramparts round a beleaguered city (Isa. 26:1; cf. 60:18) and like water to the thirsty (Isa. 12:3).

In only 7 cases (out of 66) is the verb followed by the prep. *min-*, "from." Two of these (Ezk. 36:29; 37:23) refer to cleansing from ritual impurity; *hôšîaʿ* + *min* becomes a pregnant expression involving sprinkling with clean water (36:25) and the gift of "a new heart and a new spirit" (v. 26),[120] rather than any act of separation. One concerns rescue from an enemy (Isa. 37:20 par. 2 K. 19:19).[121] Four refer to the return from exile (Jer. 30:7,10; 46:27; Zec. 8:7), an expression that may have an eschatological rather than a literal meaning in this context.[122] The distinction between *hôšîaʿ* and *hiṣṣîl* in this respect is nicely illustrated in Jer. 15:20f.: "For I am with you to save (*hôšîaʿ*) you and deliver (*hiṣṣîl*) you. . . . I will deliver you from (*hiṣṣîl min-*) the hand of the wicked, and redeem you from (*pāḏâ min-*) the grasp of the ruthless."[123] The term *hôšîaʿ* is not a regular part of the vocabulary for the ingathering of the exiles or the nations (cf. Isa. 43:5-7; 49:22-26; 56:6-8; 60:8f.; 66:18-21). The hymn (Isa. 52:7-10) describing the moment when news of God's intervention (*yešûʿâ* twice) arrives avoids delineating the return.[124]

c. *Legal Associations.* The association of *hôšîaʿ*, *yešûʿâ*, etc. with the language of the law court and concepts of legal protection is significant. They occur prominently in two of the "trial speeches" in Deutero-Isaiah (Isa. 43:8-15; 45:20-25),[125] where they are associated with *higgîḏ*, "present one's case" (43:11f.; 45:21f.). They also collocate

---

117 Sawyer, *Semantics in Biblical Research,* 71, 81.
118 H. W. Wolff, *Hosea. Herm* (Eng. trans. 1974), 226.
119 Cf. Stolz, 788.
120 G. A. Cooke, *Ezekiel. ICC* (1936), 392.
121 See IV.1.a above.
122 F. Horst, *Die zwölf Kleinen Propheten: Sacharja. HAT,* XIV (^{3}1964), 241-43; Stolz, 787.
123 See I.2.c above.
124 C. Westermann, *Isaiah 40–66. OTL* (Eng. trans. 1969), 249f.
125 *Ibid.,* 119-126, 174-76.

regularly with *rîḇ,* "argue one's case" (Isa. 49:25f.; cf. Jgs. 6:31[126]), *šôpēṭ,* "judge" (noun) (Isa. 33:22; cf. Ezk. 34:22), and *mišpāṭ,* "justice" (Isa. 33:6; 51:6; 59:11; Jer. 23:6; 33:16; Hab. 1:2). The special relationship between *yᵉšûᶜâ* and *ṣᵉḏāqâ* in Deutero-Isaiah is discussed below. In particular, *hôšîaᶜ* is associated with legal processes of various types: redemption (→ גאל *gāʾal;* Isa. 49:26; 60:16; 63:5,8,9), ransom (→ פדה *paḏâ;* cf. Isa. 43:3), recompense (*gᵉmûl,* → גמל *gāmal;* Isa. 35:4; cf. 59:16-18), and legal ownership (Ob. 21). The phrase *wattôšaᶜ lôʾ zᵉrōᶜô* (Isa. 59:16; 63:5) is probably a poetic variant of the legal idiom *hôšîᶜâ yāḏî lî,* "take the law into one's own hands,"[127] especially since in both cases God is represented—with the anthropomorphism typical of Deutero-Isaiah—as first investigating the case to see if anyone is going to intervene and then "taking the law into his own hands" (cf. also Isa. 50:2; 59:1). He is thus represented less as a judge than as a warrior, armed allegorically[128] with *ṣᵉdāqâ, yᵉšûᶜâ, nāqām,* and *qinʾâ* (Isa. 59:17; cf. 42:13; 63:1-6; Jer. 14:9).

In the oracles of salvation,[129] the argument hinges on God's justice as well as his loyalty and love. Thus he will honor his legally binding obligation to provide protection for his kinsfolk (Isa. 41:14; 44:6; 49:7; → גאל *gāʾal*)[130] or pay the price of their freedom (43:3f.). Israel is his people and he is their *môšîaᶜ* (Isa. 63:8), bound to them by an oath (45:22f.), by an everlasting covenant (61:8-10), by his steadfast love (63:7), or by his faithfulness (33:6; cf. Zec. 8:7f.). The popularity of the root *yšᶜ* in Deutero-Isaiah is certainly related to this aspect of the author's concept of the nature of God.

d. *Universal Condition and Single Event.* The noun *yᵉšûᶜâ* (twice *tᵉšûᶜâ*: Isa. 45:17; 46:13) can refer not only to a single, visible event (e.g., Isa. 52:10; cf. Ex. 14:13,31) in one place (e.g., Zion: Isa. 46:13; cf. 26:1) on one day (49:8), but also to a permanent (45:17; 51:6,8; cf. 45:22; 60:18) and universal state or condition (49:6; cf. 62:1). In the celebrated poem on the arrival of news of God's intervention (*yᵉšûᶜâ*) in Isa. 52:7-10, the emphasis is on the completeness and finality of the action. The same applies to Jer. 31:7, which originally read: "Proclaim, give praise, and say, 'Yahweh has saved his people (*hôšîaᶜ YHWH ʾeṯ-ᶜammô*).' "[131]

The words *hôšîaᶜ, yᵉšûᶜâ,* etc., like *ṣᵉḏāqâ,* are used in descriptions of divine intervention "on that day," an expression that in many passages (e.g., Isa. 12:2,3; 19:19f.; 25:9; 26:1;[132] Zec. 9:16; 12:7f.) is eschatological.[133] Deutero-Isaiah's invitation to all to partake in the divine salvation (Isa. 45:22ff.) anticipates a fundamental Christian concept (cf. Rom. 14:11; Phil. 2:10).[134] Jeremiah stresses the lasting peaceful dimension of

---

126 See IV.1.b(2) above.
127 See IV.1.b(4) above.
128 Westermann, 350f.
129 *Ibid.,* 11-15.
130 Bonnard, 113f.
131 W. Rudolph, *Jeremia. HAT,* XII (³1968), 194f.; *BHS.*
132 O. Kaiser, *Isaiah 1–12. OTL* (Eng. trans. ²1983), 269f.; *idem, Isaiah 13–39. OTL* (Eng. trans. 1974), 105, 108f., 202f., 305.
133 Licht, 897; Fohrer, 977f.; Stolz, 788f.; Y. Hoffmann, "The Day of the Lord as a Concept and a Term in the Prophetic Literature," *ZAW,* 93 (1981), 37-50.
134 Westermann, 175f.

salvation, mediated by a scion of David (Jer. 23:6; 33:16). Here the passive verb *nôšā*ᶜ is associated with justice, peace, and security (cf. Jer. 46:27).

e. *Association with Trusting, Rejoicing, etc.* There is a close relationship between *hôšîa*ᶜ, *yᵉšûᶜâ,* etc. and expressions of faith, trust, and rejoicing.[135] The *locus classicus* of this usage in OT prophetic literature[136] is Isa. 30:15, the only occurrence of the root *yš*ᶜ in prophecies of the eighth-century Isaiah:[137] "In returning and rest you shall be saved (*tiwwāšēᶜûn*), in quietness and in trust shall be your strength" (cf. Isa. 12:2; 25:9; 33:2; 51:5; 59:11; Mic. 7:7; Hab. 3:18). In the credal statement *baYHWH ʾᵉlōhênû tᵉšûᶜaṯ yiśrāʾēl,* "in Yahweh our God is the salvation of Israel" (Jer. 3:23; cf. Ps. 3:3[2]), the prep. *bᵉ*, "in," in place of the usual *lᵉ*, "to, for" (e.g., Ps. 3:9[8]; Jon. 2:10[9]), or *min,* "from" (e.g., Ps. 37:39; Prov. 29:26), is to be explained by reference to these and other expressions of trusting, seeking refuge, rejoicing, consulting, taking pride, swearing, and the like, which normally take *bᵉ*: e.g., *lihyôṯ baYHWH mibṭaḥekā,* "that your trust may be in Yahweh" (Prov. 22:19); cf. Ps. 11:1 (*ḥāsâ*); Jgs. 1:1 (*šāʾal*); Isa. 41:16 (*gîl*); 2 S. 19:8(7) (*nišbaᶜ*). Thus *bᵉYHWH,* "in Yahweh," in Jer. 3:23 as opposed to *laššeqer,* "a delusion," denotes both the source of salvation (elsewhere expressed by *lᵉ* or *min*) and the object of hope and trust, as it does in over 80 other passages.[138] Isa. 45:24f. contains an interesting parallel: in the statement that "only in Yahweh (*bᵃYHWH*) . . . are righteousness and strength," *bᵃYHWH* expresses both the source of "righteousness, salvation,"[139] and the reason for Israel's pride (cf. v. 25).

In these expressions, *bᵉ* could conceivably be locative (cf. Josh 22:25,27) or *beth essentiae* (cf. Ex. 6:3).[140] But the rich, peculiarly theological overtones of *tᵉšûᶜâ* and the recurring association of *hôšîa*ᶜ with verbs of trusting, rejoicing, etc. make it more likely that in Jer. 3:23 (as in Ps. 3:3[2][141]) the two distinct but related concepts of salvation and trust overlap in the expression *bᵉYHWH ʾᵉlōhênû tᵉšûaṯ yiśrāʾēl.* Cf. the passive construction *nôšā*ᶜ *bᵉYHWH,* "saved by Yahweh" (Isa. 45:17; Dt. 33:29), alongside Isa. 30:15; Ps. 33:16; etc. The "awkward" *wᵉhôšaᶜtîm bᵉYHWH* in Hos. 1:7 may be explained similarly.[142]

f. *Association with ṣdq.* The soteriological usage of *ṣeḏeq* and *ṣᵉḏāqâ* in Deutero-Isaiah[143] makes these terms virtually synonymous with *yᵉšûᶜâ, yešaᶜ,* and *tᵉšûᶜâ* in that context:[144] e.g., "my righteousness (*ṣiḏqāṯî*) will be for ever, and my salvation (*yᵉšûᶜāṯî*) to all generations" (Isa. 51:8; cf. 45:8; 46:13; 51:6).

This usage, which is to be traced back to early hymnic style (von Rad; cf. Jgs. 5:11;

---

135 Cf. Stolz, 788.

136 Cf. IV.4.b below.

137 Bonnard, 535.

138 Sawyer, *Semantics in Biblical Research,* 66f.

139 Westermann, *Isaiah 40–66,* 176.

140 *GK,* §119i.

141 See II.1.c above.

142 Wolff, *Hosea,* 20f.

143 Snaith, 87-93; Stolz, 788.

144 G. von Rad, *OT Theology,* I (Eng. trans., New York, 1962), 372f.; W. Eichrodt, *Theology of the OT,* I. *OTL* (Eng. trans. 1961), 246f.; C. R. North, *The Second Isaiah* (London, 1964), 208f.

Dt. 33:21; Ps. 103:6), illustrates the application of forensic terminology to the saving relationship between God and his people.[145] Much of what has been written on *ṣᵉḏāqâ* can thus be applied to *yᵉšûʿâ,* e.g., "this righteousness can even be invoked as a basis for the forgiveness of sins."[146] The distinction between these two closely related words can probably best be expressed in terms of the common secular usage of *ṣeḏeq, ṣaddîq,* etc. with a human subject, in contrast to the almost exclusively theological application of *yᵉšûʿâ,* which has less explicitly forensic overtones. In the phrase *ʾēl-ṣaddîq ûmôšîaʿ* (Isa. 45:21), the first epithet stresses the reliability and faithfulness of a just God, true to his word and to the terms of his covenant; the second adds the dimension of his active, unique, and successful intervention in his people's history. Each term, however, carries with it an element of the meaning of the other.[147]

Zec. 9:9 proclaims the arrival of Zion's royal deliverer (cf. Isa. 52:7-10; 62:11) and describes him as *ṣaddîq wᵉnôšāʿ,* a striking juxtaposition strongly reminiscent of the expression used of God in Isa. 45:21, *ṣaddîq ûmôšîaʿ* (LXX, Syr., Targ., and Vulg. hardly distinguish them: *sózon* for the former, *sōtḗr* for the latter), but with the vital difference that in Zec. 9 both terms are passive in meaning. Thus the messianic king has been vindicated (*ṣaddîq*) and, like David (2 S. 8:6,14), made victorious (*nôšāʿ*; cf. Dt. 33:29) by God, who is the only source of *ṣeḏeq* and *yᵉšûʿâ.*[148]

4. *Psalms.* Nearly half of the Psalms contain 1 or more occurrences of *yšʿ*. To these we may add 13 psalmlike passages from the rest of the OT that also contain *yšʿ*: Gen. 49:2-27; Dt. 32:1-43; 33:2-29; 1 S. 2:1-10; 2 S. 22:2-51 (cf. Ps. 18); 2 S. 23:2-7; 1 Ch. 16:8-36 (cf. Ps. 105:1-15; 96:1-13; 106:1,47f.); 2 Ch. 6:41f. (cf. Ps. 132:8-10); Isa. 38:10-20; Lam. 3,4; Jon. 2:3-10(2-9); Hab. 3:2-19. In comparison with the rest of the OT, the nouns *yešaʿ* (27 occurrences out of an OT total of 35), *yᵉšûʿâ* (53 out of 78), pl. *yᵉšûʿôṯ* (10 out of 12), *tᵉšûʿâ* (15 out of 33), and *môšāʿôṯ* (only Ps. 68:21[20]) are proportionately more frequent in the Psalms than the verb (70 out of 105).

The most common verb forms in the Psalms are imperatives, usually with 1st person suffix but also with the modal suffix *-â* (*hôšîʿâ*), a form that occurs only in the Psalms (Ps. 12:2[1]; 20:10[9]; 28:9; 60:7[5]; 86:16; 108:7[6]; 118:25) and in three forensic contexts discussed above.[149] Postbiblical *hôšaʿnāʾ* ("Hosanna") is derived from Ps. 118:25 and may have influenced the MT of Jer. 31:7.[150]

a. *Yahweh Always Subject.* The subject is always God, except where God is contrasted to the vanity of human aid (Ps. 60:13[11]; 108:13[12]; cf. 146:3; Lam. 4:17) or the inadequacy of military might (Ps. 33:16f.; 44:4,6[3,5]). The uniqueness of God's saving power is also expressed in several passages (1 S. 2:1f.; cf. Dt. 33:29), and the same

145 See I.2.d above.

146 Eichrodt, 247.

147 Westermann, *Isaiah 40–66,* 175; Bonnard, 178.

148 Snaith, 88; H. G. Mitchell, *Zechariah. ICC* (1912), 273; otherwise I. L. Seeligmann, "A Psalm from Pre-regal Times," *VT,* 14 (1964), 77.

149 IV.1.b.

150 Rudolph, *HAT,* XII, 179.

exclusiveness is implied in the expression *ʾᵉlōhê yišʿî,* "God of my salvation" (Ps. 18:47[46]; 25:5; 27:9; cf. 88:2[1]), and in metaphors such as *ṣûr yᵉšuʿāṯî,* "rock of my salvation" (Dt. 32:15; Ps. 89:27[26]; cf. 95:1; 31:3[2]; 62:3[2]), *māḡēn yišʿeḵā,* "shield of your salvation" (Ps. 18:36[35]; cf. v. 3[2]; 47:10[9]), and *qeren-yišʿî,* "horn of my salvation" (Ps. 18:3[2]; cf. 1 S. 2:10; Ps. 132:17; Lk. 1:69; the horn symbolizes God's strength, perhaps originally compared to that of a great bull).[151]

b. *Association with Confidence and Triumph.* Particularly striking in the Psalms is the frequent occurrence of *hôšîaʿ*, *yᵉšûʿâ,* etc. in collocation with expressions of confidence and faith,[152] e.g., *wᵉyôšîʿēm kî-ḥāsû ḇô,* "he saves them because they take refuge in him" (Ps. 37:40; cf. 13:6[5]; 17:7; 20:7[6]; 25:5; 27:1; 40:11[10]; 42:6[5]; 43:5; 62:2f.[1f.]; 65:6[5]; 78:22; 86:2; Lam. 3:26). Several of these compositions end with brief credal statements like *laYHWH hayyᵉšûʿâ* (Ps. 3:9[8]; cf. 18:51[50]; 38:23[22]; Gen. 49:16-18; Isa. 38:20; Jon. 2:10[9]). The joy of those who know their prayer will be answered is found in several contexts, e.g.: *ʿālaṣ libbî baYHWH . . . kî śāmaḥtî bîšûʿāṯeḵā,* "my heart exults in Yahweh . . . because I rejoice in your salvation" (1 S. 2:1; cf. Ps. 13:6[5]; 35:9; 40:17[16]; Hab. 3:18). This is probably the explanation for the change in meaning evident in the word *hôšaʿnāʾ*, "Hosanna," which originally (in Ps. 118:25) was an appeal for help but by NT times (Mt. 21:9; Mk. 11:9f.) had become a shout of triumph.[153] The distinction between a cry for help addressed to One who is sure to answer it and an expression of faith and thanksgiving that the cry will be answered is perhaps not very clear-cut.[154]

The rare form *yᵉšûʿāṯâ* in Ps. 3:3(2) might be an additional example of the overlap between an imperative and an expression of faith.[155]

c. *Legal Associations.* The legal associations of these terms, which may offer an explanation of their frequent use in religious language,[156] are evident in many passages in Psalms: they collocate with → גאל *gāʾal* (Ps. 106:10), → שפט *šāp̄aṭ* (7:11f.[10f.]; 72:4; 76:10[9]), *dîn* (54:3[1]), and *ṣᵉḏāqâ* (24:5; 37:39; 40:11[10]; 51:16[14]; 65:6[5]; 118:15; 132:9,16; cf. 25:5). The concept of just retribution (e.g., Ps. 50:23) is expressed by the idiom *hôšîʿâ yᵉmînᵉḵā,* "mete out justice":[157] e.g., Ps. 44:4(3); 60:7(5); 98:1; 108:7(6); 138:7; cf. 20:7b(6b). Very significant is the close association of *yšʿ* with → חסד *ḥeseḏ,* "loyalty," where God's intervention on behalf of his people is, as it were, a legal obligation[158] and therefore for a just God inevitable: "your steadfast love (*ḥeseḏ*) . . . extends to the heavens . . . your righteousness (*ṣᵉḏāqâ*) is like the mountains of God . . . man and beast you save (*hôšîaʿ*)" (Ps. 36:6f.[5f.]; cf. 6:5[4]; 13:6[5]; 17:7; 31:17[16];

---

151 Cf. C. A. Briggs and E. G. Briggs, *Psalms. ICC* (1907), I, 141; A. Weiser, *Psalms. OTL* (Eng. trans. 1962), 196, 782.

152 See IV.3.f above.

153 Kraus, *BK,* XV/2, 984.

154 Cf. J. J. Petuchowski, "'*Hoshiʿah na*'' in Psalm CXVIII,25—A Prayer for Rain," *VT,* 5 (1955), 266-271; also IV.3.f above.

155 See II.1.c above.

156 See I.1.b above.

157 See IV.1.b(4) above.

158 Cf. Kraus, *Psalms 1–59,* 399.

57:4[3]; 85:8[7]; 98:3; 109:26; 1QH 2:23; 11:18; cf. Ps. 69:17[16]). There is also a noticeable correlation between the poverty and helplessness of the victims and the certainty that God will answer their prayer for help (*hôšîa'*), e.g.: "May he defend the cause of (*šāpaṭ*) the poor of the people, and give deliverance (*hôšîa'*) to the needy" (Ps. 72:4; cf. 34:7[6]; 69:30[29]; 76:10[9]; 86:2; 109:31; 116:6; 149:4). The situation of the helpless widow[159] is clearly another (prose) example of the same usage. Finally, *yš'* occurs in law-court scenes (Ps. 17:7; 76:10[9]; 109:31).[160] There are also two related idioms: *w*e*'ên-môšîa'* (Ps. 18:42[41]; cf. 2 S. 22:42) and "they cried (*zā'aq*) to Yahweh in their trouble, and he saved (*hôšîa'*) them from their distress" (Ps. 107:13,19), which have their origin in Deuteronomistic tradition.[161] The author of Ps. 119 seems to have been particularly aware of the legal associations of the *yš'* terms, which he uses frequently. He maintains that he has kept his part of the agreement (vv. 94,166), unlike the wicked (v. 155), and confidently waits for God to keep his word (v. 41).[162]

The brief confessional statement *lîšû'āṯkā qiwwîṯî YHWH* may have been appended to the blessing of Dan in Gen. 49:16-18, partly because of its appropriateness in a legal context.[163] This is the only occurrence of *yš'* in Genesis, and its association with the tribe popularly described as "judging his people" (*dān yāḏîn 'ammô* [Gen. 49:16]) is unlikely to be pure coincidence. Skinner[164] and von Rad[165] offer unsatisfactory explanations for this Yahwistic insertion in the Blessing of Jacob. Emerton[166] removes the legal term by reference to Akk. *danānu,* "be strong," and ignores the late insertion. The "cup of salvation" (Heb. *kôs-y*e*šû'ôṯ*) in Ps. 116:13 may also derive ultimately from an ancient juridical procedure, namely trial by ordeal, in which the guilt or innocence of the accused is established by the effect of a drink (cf. Nu. 5:26ff.). For the guilty, such a cup was the "cup of wrath" (Isa. 51:17,22; Jer. 25:15; Lam. 4:21; Hab. 2:15f.) or "cup of reeling" (Isa. 51:17), while for the innocent, as in Ps. 116, it was a "cup of salvation" (v. 13).[167] In such a trial, justice depends on a form of divine intervention independent of human arguments, evidence, witnesses, and the like; this would explain the choice of terms, both "wrath" and "salvation" (*y*e*šû'ôṯ*) being conspicuously theological in emphasis. Others argue that the origin of this expression is to be found in a thank-offering ceremony (cf. Ps. 116:17).[168]

d. *Situations of Need.* The conventional imagery and metaphorical language in which descriptions of crisis are couched in the Psalms make precise identification of each

---

159 See IV.1.b(2) above.

160 *AncIsr,* 155-57.

161 See IV.1.a above.

162 See Briggs-Briggs, II, 417f.; Weiser, 739-741.

163 Sawyer, *Semantics in Biblical Research,* 95.

164 J. Skinner, *Genesis. ICC* (²1930), 527.

165 G. von Rad, *Genesis. OTL* (Eng. trans. ²1972), 427.

166 J. A. Emerton, "Some Difficult Words in Genesis 49," *Words and Meanings. Festschrift D. W. Thomas* (Cambridge, 1968), 88-91.

167 Weiser, 720; Kraus, *BK,* XV/2, 972.

168 H. Ringgren, "Vredens kalk," *SEÅ,* 17 (1952), 19f.; Briggs-Briggs, II, 400; Kraus, *BK,* XV/2, 972.

situation notoriously difficult.[169] The *yšʿ* terms play a major role in many such descriptions. Several of the hymns containing *yšʿ* celebrate the intervention of Yahweh as a military hero, e.g.: "Who is like you, a people saved (*nôšāʿ*) by Yahweh, the shield of your help (*ʿezreḵā*)?" (Dt. 33:29; cf. Ex. 15:2; Ps. 33:16f.; 95:1; 96:2; 98:1-3).

The difficult phrase *markeḇōṯeyḵā yešûʿâ* in Hab. 3:8 (cf. vv. 13,18) apparently means "your chariots are salvation" (MT possibly influenced by later mystical developments: cf. Ezk. 1; 1 Ch. 28:18; Sir. 49:8[170]). Possibly the text should be emended to *markaḇteḵā yešûʿâ,* "thy riding is to victory."[171] Military imagery occurs a number of times in other Psalms, too: "He will answer him from his holy heaven with mighty victories (*bigeḇūrôṯ yēšaʿ*) by his right hand" (Ps. 20:7f.[6f.]; cf. 18:4,35f.[3,34f.]; 35:3; 44:4-8[3-7]; 106:6-12; 140:8[7]; 144:10). In some cases (e.g., Ps. 20:7-9[6-8]), however, the implication is that God's victory is not by force of arms, which fail in the face of divine intervention (vv. 7f.[6f.]; cf. Hos. 1:7; Jgs. 7:2; etc.[172]).

The terms also occur in contexts of rebuilding (Ps. 69:36[35]), royal victory (21:2[1]; 28:8; 33:16; 144:10; cf. Jgs. 2:16,18; 2 S. 8:6,14), and forgiveness of sins (Ps. 51:14,16[12,14]). In most cases, salvation involves bringing help into a situation of distress or danger, to people where they are and where they need it, not removing them from it.[173]

e. *Eschatological Usage.* The difficulty of identifying the situations underlying the Psalms is particularly acute when we come to the question of the eschatological usage of *yešûʿâ* and the other terms in the Psalms.[174] In some passages, *yešûʿâ* was undoubtedly interpreted eschatologically by NT times: cf. Ps. 67:3(2) in Acts 28:28 and Ps. 107:19f. in Acts 13:26. The identification of "the Lord's anointed" with Christ and probably also the establishment of a connection between *yešûʿâ,* "salvation," and *yēšûaʿ,* "Jesus,"[175] led early Christianity to cite many Psalms in its eschatological discourse.[176] Similarly, there is good evidence for eschatological usage in the sectarian texts from Qumran, e.g., 1QH 5:11f.; 11:23f.; 12:3; 15:16; 1QH fr. 18:15; 1QS 11:11.[177] It seems probable, however, that this development began much earlier, at least in part because of influence from ancient cultic formulas[178] and that therefore *yešûʿâ* could refer in certain contexts to an eschatological event or state.[179]

The meaning of this term is at all events appropriate for such eschatological usage:

---

169 Von Rad, *OT Theology,* I, 414f.; Weiser, 67-69.

170 G. Scholem, *Major Trends in Jewish Mysticism* (³1954; repr. New York, 1961), 40-79.

171 L. H. Brockington, *The Hebrew Text of the OT* (Oxford, 1973), 261; cf. *BHS.*

172 See IV.1.a.

173 See I.2.c above.

174 Cf. Stolz, 790.

175 See III.2 above.

176 Cf. von Rad, *OT Theology,* II, 332-34; Stolz, 790.

177 S. Holm-Nielsen, *Hodayot: Psalms from Qumran. AcThD,* 2 (1960), 296f., n. 41; Foerster, 982f.; Stolz, 790.

178 J. Begrich, *Studien zu Deuterojesaja. BWANT,* 77[4/25] (1938); repr. *ThB,* 20 (1963), 14ff.; *idem,* "Das priesterliche Heilsorakel," *ZAW,* 52 (1934), 81ff. (= *GSAT. ThB,* 21 [1964], 217ff.).

179 See IV.3.e above.

the source of salvation is God alone; the group of colorful construct phrases, which collocate naturally with *šālôm, m^e^nûḥâ, bēṭaḥ,* and the like, are a unique feature of its semantic range[180] and correspond to the wide range of ideas and images associated with eschatological expectation. It is a term implying a dramatic change in the status quo, which only God can achieve.[181] Its legal overtones accord well with the concept of a day of judgment, which was eventually a central element of Jewish eschatology (cf. Dnl. 12:1-3; Lk. 19:44; 1QS 4:18f.[182]). Finally, *hôšîaʿ* expresses the notion of bringing into the human situation something that is not already there rather than "saving" (i.e., "removing") us from it.[183] In this sense it denotes the saving power of God, which brings to this world a kind of "salvation" (incorporating peace, security, health, forgiveness, joy, life, and victory) that properly belongs to the divine sphere.

Sawyer

---

180 See I.2.b above.
181 See I.2.a above.
182 M. Black, *The Scrolls and Christian Origins* (New York, 1961), 135f.
183 See I.2.c above.

יָשַׁר *yāšar;* יֹשֶׁר *yōšer;* יִשְׁרָה *yišrâ;* מִישׁוֹר *mîšôr;* מֵישָׁרִים *mêšārîm*

Contents: I. Etymology. II. Ancient Near East: 1. Akkadian; 2. Ugaritic and Other West Semitic Dialects. III. OT: 1. Occurrences; 2. Literal Meaning; 3. Figurative Meaning; 4. Distinctions; 5. Special Cases. IV. Dead Sea Scrolls.

I. Etymology. Etymologically, Heb. *yšr* corresponds to Ugar. *yšr* (discussed below), Phoen. and Aram. *yšr,* "be just, upright,"[1] Akk. *ešēru* (also discussed below), and probably also Arab. *yasira,* "be easy." OSA *wṯr*[2] would represent Aram. *ytr* and is therefore dubious; *ysr*[3] and the causative *hysr,* "send," suggest otherwise.[4]

Ringgren

---

yāšar. Y. Avishur, "Word Pairs Common to Phoenician and Biblical Hebrew: No. 28: *ṣdq/yšr,*" *UF,* 7 (1975), 28f.; H. S. Cazelles, "De l'idéologie royale," *Festschrift T. H. Gaster. JANES,* 5 (1973), 59-73; G. Liedke, "ישר *jšr* gerade, recht sein," *THAT,* I, 790-94; F. Nötscher, *Gotteswege und Menschenwege in der Bibel und in Qumran. BBB,* 15 (1958), esp. 51f., 83f.; H. Preisker, "ὀρθός," *TDNT,* V, 449-451; R. A. Rickards, "What is Right?" *BT,* 27 (1976), 220-24; R. von Ungern-Sternberg, *Redeweisen der Bibel. BSt,* 54 (1968), esp. 62-82.

1 *DISO,* 112.
2 *KBL*².
3 ContiRossini, 163.
4 W. W. Müller, "Altsüdarabische Beiträge zum hebräischen Lexikon," *ZAW,* 75 (1963), 310.

II. Ancient Near East.

1. *Akkadian.* The root *yšr* is represented primarily by the verb *ešēru,* "be in order, become orderly, move toward,"[5] the adj. *išaru,* "normal, in order, right,"[6] and the subst. *mîšaru,* "righteousness, justice."[7] Various semantic fields can be distinguished:

a. In a local sense: (1) Alongside the rare "be or make straight or upright" (*ešēru* G, Š; *išaru, mušāru,* "penis"), we commonly find the meaning "(cause to) go straight (i.e., without detours or obstacles)" (*ešēru* G, Š, Št, N; *išaru*), often used of a route such as a road or watercourse; the transition to "way of life" is easy. Specialized nuances appear in the meanings "give birth easily (without complications)" (*ešēru* Št) and (of intestines) "evacuate" (*ešēru* G, Š; *išaru*).

(2) With reference to a floor, **yšr* means "flat, swept clean" (*ešēru* Š, "sweep"; *mušēšertu,* "palm broom"; *šūšurtu,* "sweepings"); with reference to water, it means "flowing quietly, without turbulence."[8]

b. In a figurative sense: "in order, right." (1) "Be in order, become orderly, make or keep orderly" (*ešēru* G, Š, Št; *muštēšertu,* "maintenance"); with reference to tools, merchandise, etc., "prepare, process, manufacture" (*ešēru* Š, Št); with reference to ideas, "make (un)clear" (*ešēru* Š). "In order" can also mean "normal" in the sense of "unobjectionable" or "regular" (*išaru, ešēru* G, etc.). When forms of **yšr* are combined with expressions meaning "go" or "way" in the figurative sense (= "walk, live"), often only the context can determine whether **yšr* means "normal," "successful," "upright," or even "legally vindicated" (*išáriš alāku, [m]īšarūtu alāku*; "way" + *išaru, ešēru* Š).

(2) The root can also mean "be favorable" (time, omens, wind); "be or make successful" (persons and actions); "flourish" (plants, animals, human beings) (*ešēru* G, Š, Št, N; *išaru*; *išartu,* "success").

(3) It can have the general ethical sense "(be) upright, righteous" (*išaru*; *ešēru* G) or "(act or treat) rightly, correctly, appropriately" (*išariš, ešēru* Št).

(4) In the forensic realm, *šutēšuru* (Št) can denote the function of a judge: "dispense justice," literally "restore the 'normal' situation upset by the excesses of others."[9] Usually, however, it has the more general meaning "rule rightly" (namely subjects, esp. those with little legal protection). The scepter (*ḫaṭṭu*) of the king is therefore called "righteous" (*išaru*). The "righteousness" or "justice" of (earthly and heavenly) rulers in the administration of justice and exercise of power is called *mîšaru*; the word is often associated with *kittu,* "that which endures: truth and justice." Both terms are often personified.[10]

Whether Lemche[11] is correct that Heb. *mêšārîm* and *mîšôr* reflect Akk. *mīšarum* is

---

5 *AHw,* I (1965), 254ff.; *CAD,* IV (1958), 352-363.

6 *AHw,* I, 392; *CAD,* VII (1960), 224ff.

7 *AHw,* I, 659f.

8 Cf. W. G. Lambert, "Dingír.šá.dib.ba Incantations," *JNES,* 33 (1974), 267-322, esp. I, 58-60 with comm.

9 Cf. F. R. Kraus, *Vom mesopotamischen Menschen. MKAW,* N.S. 36/6 (1973), 143.

10 H. Ringgren, *Word and Wisdom* (Lund, 1947), 53ff.

11 N. P. Lemche, "*Andurārum* and *Mīšarum:* Comments on the Problem of Social Edicts and Their Application in the Ancient Near East," *JNES,* 38 (1979), 11, n. 1, and 22 (top).

difficult to decide. In any case, *ṣeḏeq* appears in parallelism with *mêšārîm/mîšôr* (Ps. 9:9[Eng. v. 8]; 58:2[1]; 98:9; Isa. 11:4; [33:15]; 45:19), like Akk. *kittum* and *mīšarum.*[12]

W. Mayer

2. *Ugaritic and Other West Semitic Dialects.* There is only 1 certain occurrence of the root *yšr* in Ugaritic,[13] where *mtrḫt yšrh,* "his legal spouse," stands in synonymous parallelism with *'ṯt ṣdqh.*

The Phoenician Yeḥimilk inscription[14] contains the phrase *mlk yšr,* "righteous king." In Punic inscriptions, the verb appears in expressions like *myšr* [D stem ptcp.] *'rṣt,* "leader [i.e., 'ruler'] of the lands,"[15] and *p'lt m'šrt* [= *myšrt*], "a righteous act."[16]

In Aramaic, the causative of the verb has the meaning "straighten, attend to, dispatch."[17] The expression *'t p' yšrh* in the Panammuwa I inscription[18] is obscure.

Ringgren

III. OT.

1. *Occurrences.* In the OT (including Sirach), we find the verb *yšr,* the adj. *yāšār,* the substs. *yōšer, yišrâ, mîšôr,* and *mêšārîm,* and the proper names → יְשֻׁרוּן *yešurûn* and *'aḥîšar* (and possibly *šārôn*). The meanings discussed below are represented among all these forms, albeit in varying proportion.

The verb appears 14 times in the qal, almost always with *be'ênê* ("be right in the eyes of someone"); the exceptions are 1 S. 6:12; Hab. 2:4; Sir. 39:24. There are 9 occurrences of the piel, usually with the meaning "make straight" (cf. the specialized meaning "consider right" in Ps. 119:128). The pual occurs once, the hiphil twice.

The adjective is common (120 occurrences). It may be used attributively or as a predicate, often with *dereḵ* or a synonymous word. Nominalized, it appears frequently in the plural and as the object in the expression *'āśâ hayyāšār be'ênê,* "do what is right in the eyes of (someone)." The subst. *yōšer* occurs 17 times; it is also used with *be-* in adjectival or adverbial function. The subst. *yišrâ* occurs only once; *mîšôr* occurs 24 times, often in the topographical sense of "plain"; and *mêšārîm* occurs 19 times, used as an abstract with adverbial function, often with *dîn* or *špṭ.*

2. *Literal Meaning.* The literal meaning of *yšr* refers to a physical quality: the form of an object or movement in relationship to a geometrical prototype. It describes something straight, level, or flat. When the linear dimension is involved, the object is "straight," either horizontally or vertically. When a surface is involved, the object is "flat"

---

12 For the Akkadian evidence, see *CAD,* VIII (1971), *"kittu* A," 1.b.2′, 4′; *CAD,* X (1978), "mīšaru A," 2.b.1′, d. Cf. M. Liverani, "Συδύκ e Μισώρ," *Festschrift E. Volterra,* VI (Milan, 1971), 55-74 (Phoen. *sydýk* and *misṓr,* earlier *ṣdq* and *yšr* // *kittu* and *mīšaru*). See also → צדק *ṣdq.*

13 *KTU,* 1.14 I, 13; cf. *WUS,* no. 1252.

14 *KAI,* 4.6f.

15 *KAI,* 161.2.

16 *KAI,* 123.5.

17 *KAI,* 233.6, 14; also Egyptian Aramaic: *DISO,* 112.

18 *KAI,* 214.33.

or "level." "Straight" or "right" is the antonym of "crooked" or "wrong"; "level" is "not undulating," "not rough." When describing movement, the linear aspect predominates.

a. Since there is no sense of geometrical abstraction in the OT, straightness is judged by a physical standard of comparison, in relation to which an object is "right." Thus the legs of an animal are "straight" or "right," not crooked, with respect to the vertical (Ezk. 1:7); wings are stretched out straight horizontally (Ezk. 1:23). The situation is clearest in the case of movement: "The cows went straight . . . ; they turned neither to the right nor to the left" (1 S. 6:12); this does not mean that their progress was absolutely in a straight line. People similarly go straight on their way (Prov. 9:15). Water flows without diversion through Hezekiah's tunnel (2 Ch. 32:30); wine goes down the throat "directly" (Prov. 23:31).

b. Flatness is characteristic of topographical features: *šārôn* and *mîšôr* are names of plains. It is frequently used to describe roads, with a clear concern for human movement: a level road is one that can be traveled easily without fear of stumbling[19] or falling.[20] It is the opposite of rough or bumpy (*ʿāqōḇ, rᵉḵāsîm* [Isa. 40:4]). A level way is prepared by removal of obstacles; the result is a "highway" (*mᵉsillâ* [Isa. 40:3; cf. also Isa. 26:7, with *pls*]). In the extreme case, a level road may be blocked by a mountain or hill (Zec. 4:7; cf. Isa. 45:2, if *hᵃrārîm* is read for *hᵃḏûrîm*). The root is also used to describe the beaten gold leaf applied to a relief (1 K. 6:35).

3. *Figurative Meaning.* The common symbolism of roads and travel, possibly coupled with the symbolism of simple geometrical forms, makes it easy for *yšr* to take on figurative meanings in the domain of human values, ethics, and religion. These meanings can be classed into two groups: "straight" and "level."

a. The root *yšr* can refer to human conduct (= a person's "way"); in this case, it denotes conduct that is right, honest, upright, conduct that does not go astray or out of bounds. This is the ethical sense, which is common—in fact dominant—in the OT. This usage reflects the dynamic aspect of human movement, although one can also speak of a *line* of action: "The way of the dishonest is crooked, but the conduct of the pure is 'honest' " (Prov. 21:8).

b. As a clear consequence of conduct but without explicit reference to it, *yšr* can denote the "smoothness" that stands for a positive value in human life, the success of an undertaking or action: when in the presence of the people Ezra prays to God for a successful journey, the Hebrew phrase *dereḵ yᵉšārâ* impressively illustrates how the meanings are intertwined: the journey involves a real road, its "smoothness" suggests the success of the undertaking, and the context gives the words religio-historical significance.

c. The double sense of the root *yšr* makes it possible for certain Hebrew expressions to seem imprecise or even ambiguous, as though meant to suggest that ethical conduct not only is right but also leads to success. The terse and elliptical style of proverbs and aphorisms is well suited to this shifting semantic indefiniteness. Prov. 16:17 contains the

---

19 → כשל *kšl.*
20 → נפל *npl.*

following statement: *mᵉsillaṯ yᵉšārîm sûr mērāʿ šōmēr napšô nōṣēr darkô.* When one considers that predicates precede subjects in the schema predicate-subject = predicate-subject, the following relationships are stated if *yᵉšārîm* is taken as an adjective: "turning aside from evil"/"guarding one's way"—"a smooth highway"/"preserving one's life." Thus we arrive at the following translation: "Turning aside from evil is a smooth highway; whoever guards his way preserves his life." The ethics is expressed in the subjects, the result in the predicates; but the word *yᵉšārîm* appears to have taken on an ethical meaning.

In his farewell discourse, Samuel says that he wants to guide his people *bᵉḏereḵ haṭṭôḇâ wᵉhayᵉšārâ* (1 S. 12:23). Is this an hendiadys? Do both adjectives merely denote proper conduct, or do they mean both rightness and its result? The uncertainty is resolved in v. 25, which establishes the following relationships: *ṭôḇâ—raʿ*: *yᵉšārâ—tissāpû,* i.e., the good way leads to success, while wicked conduct leads to destruction. This statement does not alter the fact that at the end of v. 23 the meaning is still vague and ambiguous.

The adj. *yāšār* can also have religious content: people describe God as being *yāšār* (Dt. 32:4; Ps. 92:16[15]); in other words, God gives norms that are "straight" and right, and vouchsafes the success of human undertakings.

This brief sketch can be developed in greater detail. The figurative meanings influence the various realizations of the lexeme *yšr.* The figurative meaning follows the normal laws of lexical actualization: the meaning is actualized by the use of *dereḵ* and its synonyms or by other contextual elements, e.g., the verb *ʿāwâ,* "pervert" (Job 33:27).

4. *Distinctions.* Ethical and religious order can specify its activities and consequently make the meaning of *yšr,* "straight," more precise and nuanced. The change of subject does not alter the meaning of the predicate *yšr,* but sometimes the translation must be differentiated.

a. *Distinctions as to Activity.* In Israel, the power to legislate is, strictly speaking, reserved to God. Laws, decrees, instructions, etc. express and communicate God's will as a guide to human conduct. Threfore they can attract *yšr* as a verbal or adjectival predicate: Yahweh's precepts (*piqqûḏê YHWH* [Ps. 19:9(8), par. *tôrâ tᵉmîmâ,* "perfect law," *ʿēḏûṯ neʾᵉmānâ,* "sure testimony," and *miṣwâ bārâ,* "pure commandment"]), ordinances (*mišpāṭîm* [Neh. 9:13, par. *tôrôṯ ʾᵉmeṯ,* "true laws," and *ḥuqqîm ûmiṣwôṯ ṭôḇîm,* "good statutes and commandments"]), Yahweh's word (*dāḇār* [Ps. 33:4, par. *maʿᵃśēhû beʾᵉmûnâ,* "his working in faithfulness"]), thy judgments (*mišpāṭeyḵā* [Ps. 119:137, par. "thou art righteous (*ṣaddîq*)"]), Yahweh's ways (*darḵê* [Hos. 14:10(9)]). The last example is especially interesting: God offers or shows straight ways; although the upright (*ṣaddiqîm*) walk in them, transgressors (*pōšᵉʿîm*) stumble in them. The text thus expresses God's unlimited goodness and human responsibility for making crooked what God has made straight. Sir. 39:24 says much the same: "The paths of the righteous (*tāmîm*) are smooth (*yišᵉrû*), but they are impassable for the wicked"; cf. Sir. 11:15.

Since wisdom plays a similar or analogous role in guiding human conduct, her word can also be called *yāšār* (Prov. 8:9).

Forensic language predicates *yšr* of actions, judgments, and judges, divine or human. This area exhibits a certain preference for the noun *mêšārîm.* In the following examples, the frequency of the root *špṭ* and its synonyms will be noted: God judges (*yāḏîn*) with *mêšārîm* (Ps. 9:9[8], par. *yišpōṭ beṣeḏeq*; cf. Ps. 96:10); God loves justice (*mišpāṭ*) and has established (*kônēn*) *mêšārîm* (Ps. 99:4); from God comes vindication (*mišpāṭ*), and his eyes see *mêšārîm* (Ps. 17:2); God judges the world with *ṣeḏeq* and the peoples with *mêšārîm* (Ps. 98:9). Of mortals, the psalmist asks: "Do you indeed decree what is right (*ṣeḏeq teḏabbērûn*), . . . do you judge . . . with *mêšārîm?*" (Ps. 58:2[1]). The noun *mîšôr* also appears in forensic contexts (Ps. 67:5[4]; Isa. 11:4).

We shall here single out executive or administrative activity, even though it does not differ clearly from the previous context. A king's scepter is a scepter of equity (*šēḇeṭ mîšōr* [Ps. 45:7(6)]), based on "love of righteousness and hate of wickedness" (v. 8[7]). Mic. 3:9-11 describes the opposite conduct of leaders who abhor justice and pervert all equity (*hamᵃṯa ʿᵃḇîm mišpāṭ weʾēṯ kol-hayešārâ yeʿaqqēšû*). If Job 33:27 refers to Job's function as a sheik, the verse refers to governing and judging. In this group we may also include the cases where *yāšār* is predicated of God (note the parallels): Dt. 32:4, "he is just (*ṣaddîq*) and *yāšār*" par. "a God of faithfulness (*ʾemûnâ*) and without iniquity (*ʿāwel*)"; Ps. 25:8, "Good and *yāšār* is Yahweh" (+ 3 occurrences of the root *drk*); Ps. 92:16(15), "*yāšār* is Yahweh" par. "there is no unrighteousness (*ʿawlâ*) in him."

Acting in history, God makes smooth the way of his people, i.e., brings them success. The shift of meaning can be conditioned or promoted by the traditional experience of desert travel. The most important passages appear in contexts that speak of restoration: that the exiles may return, God will turn *heʿāqōḇ* into *mîšôr* (Isa. 40:4) and make the "rough places into level ground" (*maʿᵃqaššîm lemîšôr* [Isa. 42:16]); he will remove obstacles and smooth the way (*hᵃḏûrîm ʾᵃyaššēr* [Isa. 45:2 (*Q*)[21]]) and lead them *beḏereḵ yāšār,* where they shall not stumble (Jer. 31:9); for Zerubbabel he will level (*lemîšôr*) the "great mountain" (*har-haggāḏôl* [Zec. 4:7]).

b. *Describing Persons.* When describing human beings, *yšr* can refer to the entire person or to a part. Prov. 29:27 describes an entire manner of life, as the word *dereḵ* indicates and the synonym *ṣaddîqîm* and the antonym *ʾîš ʿāwel* show: "An unjust man is an abomination to the righteous, but he whose way is straight is an abomination to the wicked." In Prov. 16:13, the verb *dbr* and the par. *śipeṯê-ṣeḏeq* show that *yšr* refers to uprightness in speech; Prov. 23:16 specifies the nature of uprightness by the phrase *beḏabbēr śepāṯeyḵā mêšārîm.* In Prov. 4:25, it is sight that is straightforward: "Let your eyes look directly forward, and your gaze be straight before you." Prov. 8:6-9 is a context that clearly deals with uprightness in speech: Wisdom speaks noble things (*negîḏîm*) with equity (*mêšārîm*); she speaks words that are righteous (*beṣeḏeq*), true (*neḵōḥîm*), and right (*yešārîm*), which are not twisted or crooked (*niptāl weʿiqqēš*). The uprightness of inward attitudes is the subject of Dt. 9:5 (*beṣiḏqāṯeḵā ûḇeyōšer leḇāḇeḵā*); 1 K. 9:4; Ps. 119:7, as well as 1 Ch. 29:17, where uprightness in giving is based on generosity (*beyōšer leḇāḇî hiṯnaddaḇtî*). Job 6:25, by way of contrast, speaks of forceful and clever words. Job 33:3 is difficult.[22] In his prolix introduction, Elihu stresses the value of his words, the skill of oratory, and the pureness of his lips, which matches his upright purpose (*yōšer-libbî*).

---

21 Cf. *BHS*.
22 See *BHS*.

From its function as a predicate, *yšr* comes to denote the type of the ethically concerned individual, as the subject of various statements or the object of others' actions. In such contexts we find the pl. *yᵉšārîm,* the collective or typical sg. *yāšār,* and the phrase *yišrê-lēḇ*. To indicate what these terms convey, we may note their synonyms and antonyms (in the extended sense) in parallelism, in hendiadys, and in coordination. Thus *yšr* stands in parallel with *ṣaddîq* in Ps. 140:14(13); Prov. 21:18, with *tāmîm* in Prov. 2:21, and with *hālaḵ tōm* in Prov. 2:7; with *nāqî* in Job 4:7; and with *ḥāsîḏ* in Mic. 7:2. Coordination with *tām* appears in Job 1:1,8; 2:3 and with *zaḵ*[23] in Job 8:6; Prov. 20:11. In antithetical parallelism with *yšr* we find *nālôz,* "perverse" (Prov. 3:32; 14:2), *ʿāṣēl,* "sluggard" (Prov. 15:19), *bōgᵉḏîm,* "treacherous" (Prov. 11:3,6), *rᵉšāʿîm,* "wicked" (Prov. 11:11; 12:6; 14:11; 15:8; 21:29), and *ʾᵉwilîm,* "fools" (Prov. 14:9). The phrase *yišrê-lēḇ* stands in parallel with *ṣaddîq* in Ps. 7:11(10); 32:11; [33:1;] 64:11(10); 97:11 and with *yōḏᵉʿeyḵā* in Ps. 36:11(10); *yᵉšārîm bᵉlibbôṯām* stands in parallel with *ṭôḇîm* in Ps. 125:4.

It is normal for the antonyms to exhibit a greater range of meanings and to be more specific, since there are many ways to diverge from the straight path. The *bōgᵉḏîm,* "faithless" or "treacherous," confirm the nuance of upright faithfulness that *yšr* can convey. In this regard, the almost gnomic equation of Prov. 21:18 is interesting: *ṣaddîq—rāšāʿ* par. *yᵉšārîm—bôgēḏ.*

The "upright" are called upon to praise God (Ps. 32:11; 33:1), to pray (Prov. 15:8), to behold God's face (Ps. 11:7), to receive his light (Ps. 112:4), and to rejoice in his intervention (Ps. 64:11[10]; 107:42). They are promised success (Prov. 2:7), permanence (Prov. 2:21), and prosperity (Prov. 14:11); cf. the negative in Job 4:7.

The last examples bring us back to the consequence of uprightness: the way is smooth and has a happy end. In the examples just given to illustrate the ethical meaning of *yšr,* the result is expressed in different terms. In the following examples, the term *yšr* includes the result: *ʾorḥôṯ yōšer* par. *darkê-ḥōšeḵ* (Prov. 2:13); *dereḵ yāšār* par. *darkê-māweṯ* (Prov. 14:12). In the first, "darkness" can denote malicious concealment, but also the darkness that leads to destruction (cf. Ps. 23:4). The former is associated with evil, the latter with failure. Similarly, *yšr* could denote either the straight way as opposed to the way of darkness or success as opposed to failure. The second example speaks expressly of the denouement or end (*ʾaḥᵃrîṯ*); since death is the ultimate failure, its opposite means or implies success. Prov. 11:5 (with the verb in the piel) is very clear: the notion of uprightness appears in the subject (*ṣiḏqaṯ tāmîm*) and its opposite (*ršʿ*); success and failure are expressed by the predicates *tᵉyaššēr* and *yippōl.* Uprightness smoothes the way; wickedness leads to destruction (cf. Prov. 15:9; Isa. 26:7; Jer. 31:9).

The antithesis *ʿāṣēl—yᵉšārîm* in Prov. 15:19 lends laziness an ethical dimension and expresses success and failure. Two passages use *yšr* in parallel with wisdom and astuteness: Prov. 4:11 identifies the way of wisdom with the straight path of uprightness; Prov. 23:15f. establishes a connection between an astute heart and right or upright words.

---

23 → זכך *zkk.*

5. *Special Cases.*

a. *yšr bᵉʿênê.* The expression *yšr bᵉʿênê* deserves special treatment. It occurs in both verbal and adjectival form (plus the formal variant *yšr lip̄nê* in Prov. 14:12; 16:25). Given that for the Hebrews the eyes are the seat of the evaluative faculty, the expression can cover a broad spectrum of judgments and evaluations, from neutral acceptance to formal and final approval.

A Philistine woman "pleases" Samson (Jgs. 14:3,7); some cities do not "please" the king of Tyre (1 K. 9:12). The king or the people approve a proposal, it seems good to them, they find it correct (1 S. 18:20,26; 2 S. 17:4; 1 Ch. 13:4; 2 Ch. 30:4). People act on the basis of such judgments, like the potter in Jer. 18:4.

Such judgment can be in error, as contrastive statements can make clear: when private opinion is not subordinated to monarchic order (Jgs. 17:6; 21:25), when someone rejects another's counsel like a fool (Prov. 12:15), when someone decides to disregard God's choice of a cultic center (Dt. 12:8) or even opposes it.

On the other hand, God's judgment is not only sovereign (Jer. 27:5) but right and absolute; it can therefore serve as a criterion for judging a regime (2 K. 12:3[2]; 14:3; 15:3; 16:2; etc.). Furthermore, what pleases God, what he approves, coincides with what he chooses or commands, or is transformed into an explicit law. Thus in the historical commentaries of the Deuteronomists, we find a formula using the verb "do": *ʿāśâ/laʿᵃśôṯ hayyāšār bᵉʿênê YHWH.* This formula keeps recurring as a stereotyped idiom in rhetorical sequences, in various positions and associated with various members of the sequence. If we call this formula "M," we can illustrate its appearance in several sequences:

Dt. 6:17f.: *šmr miṣwōṯ YHWH wᵉʿēḏōṯāyw wᵉḥuqqāyw ʾᵃšer ṣiwwâ* M
Dt. 12:28: *šᵉmōr wᵉšāmaʿtā ʾēṯ kol-haddᵉḇārîm hāʾēlleh ʾᵃšer ʾānōḵî mᵉṣawweḵā* M
Dt. 13:19(18): *kî tišmaʿ bᵉqôl YHWH ʾᵉlōheyḵā lišmōr ʾeṯ-kol-miṣwôṯāyw* . . . M
1 K. 11:38: *ʾim-tišmaʿ ʾeṯ-kol-ʾᵃšer ʾᵃṣawweḵā wᵉhālaḵtā biḏrāḵay* M *lišmôr ḥuqqôṯay*
1 K. 14:8: *ʾᵃšer šāmar miṣwôṯay waʾᵃšer-hālaḵ ʾaḥᵃray bᵉḵol-lᵉḇāḇô* M

These examples and others that might be cited place the formula in the domain of obedience to the stipulations of the covenant, equivalent to "obey" (*šāmaʿ bᵉqôl*), "walk in the way" (*hālaḵ bᵉḏereḵ*), and "keep the commandments" (*šāmar miṣwôṯ*), without formally distinguishing a psychological element in God prior to the commandment. Since we are dealing with a stereotyped cliche or an idiomatic formula, and since "eye" does not have the same connotations as in our languages, the proper translation should be: "what pleases God," "what God (dis)approves."

The Deuteronomistic usage described here cannot be cited in a discussion of legal positivism. Nevertheless, although the author does not address our theoretical problems, we can state this much: what God considers right he imposes as a commandment, and his judgment cannot be questioned; what God commands pleases him, and therefore those who obey deserve reward (Dt. 12:25; 21:9).

b. *Other Cases.* Hab. 2:4 is a special case: *hinnēh ʿuppᵉlâ lōʾ-yāšᵉrâ nap̄šô bô wᵉṣaddîq beʾᵉmûnāṯô yiḥyeh.* We accept the Masoretic reading. We expect an antithesis and look for its correlative members, which can be schematized as follows:

ʿuppelâ = *lōʾ-yāšerâ*
ʿuppelâ ≠ *ṣaddîq beʾemûnāṯô*
yāšerâ = *ṣaddîq* = *ʾemûnâ*
lōʾ-yāšerâ ≠ *yiḥyeh*

In topographical terminology, we find the antithesis "plain—hill," which corresponds to the pair "smooth—bulging." Both the concrete and figurative senses can refer to the neck or throat (*nepeš*): his neck is distended and stretched not by nature but because he has tried to swallow too much, as v. 5b corroborates: *ʾašer hirḥîḇ kišʾôl napšô*. This is the opposite of the uprightness and confidence of the one who is righteous. Since *yšr* can also denote the result, in our case his throat or appetite will be unsuccessful (as v. 5a states); this stands in contrast to the life that is promised the righteous. In other words, the glutton will choke on his intemperance (cf. the wine that goes down directly [*mêšārîm*] in Prov. 23:31). The author probably played on the ambiguity of the word in order to create a subtle concentration of meaning, concluding with the taunts of the chorus (*māšāl ûmelîṣâ ḥîḏôt* [Hab. 2:6]). We might paraphrase as follows: A swollen appetite is not normal [obvious], is not right [ethical judgment], is doomed to failure [result]. The rest of the chapter confirms this reading.[24]

Eccl. 7:29 reads: *ʿāśâ hāʾelōhîm ʾeṯ-hāʾāḏām yāšār wehēmmâ biqešû hiššeḇōnôṯ rabbîm*. The opposites *ʿāśâ—biqešû, ʾelōhîm—ʾāḏām*, and *yāšār—ḥiššeḇōnôṯ* are clear. The verse is almost a synthesis of the author's meditations: people labor excessively, destroying the meaning of life and its pleasure; the blame does not rest with God, who created "in moderation." This equable moderation stands in contrast both to what the human race has made crooked (*meʿuwwāṯ lōʾ-yûḵal liṯqōn* [Eccl. 1:15]) and to what God himself has made crooked (*mî yûḵal leṯaqqēn ʾēṯ ʾašer ʿiwweṯô* [Eccl. 7:13]).

The name → ישרון *yešurûn* appears in Dt. 32:15; 33:5,26; Isa. 44:2; Sir. 37:25 as a hypocoristicon and title of honor for Israel. The etymological meaning "honest, upright, truthful" may be meant in contrast to the swindler *yaʿaqōḇ*, possibly influenced by alliteration with *yiśrāʾēl*. But in Dt. 32:15 the conduct of *yešurûn* is treacherous, and the context of Isa. 44:2 speaks of election. The ancient versions do not help: LXX: *ho ēgapēménos*; Aquila, Symmachus, and Theodotion: *euthýs*; Vulg.: *dilectus*.

Josh. 10:13; 2 S. 1:18 cite a *sēp̄er hayyāšār*, "Book of the Upright"; some scholars emend the phrase to *sēp̄er haššîr* on the basis of 1 K. 8:53 LXX.

In Dnl. 11:17, *wîšārîm ʿimmô*[25] seems to mean some kind of truce, agreement, or settlement, as in "settle a conflict." In Prov. 10:18; 17:7, some scholars prefer to read *yšr* for *šqr* and *ytr*, respectively, on the basis of LXX *díkaia* and *pistá*. The *yešārîm* of Prov. 29:10, conversely, is often emended to *rešāʿîm*. In Prov. 17:26, the parallelism with *lōʾ-ṭôḇ* appears to support the reading of a negative: *ʾal/lōʾ-yāšār*.[26]

Alonso-Schökel

---

24 On the use of this verse in Rom. 1:17, Gal. 3:11; He. 10:38, see the comms.
25 See the comms.
26 See the comms., esp. McKane.

IV. Dead Sea Scrolls. The Dead Sea scrolls use *yšr* twice in the literal sense: in 1QM 5:12, which speaks of "straight" grooves on swords, and in 1QpHab 3:1, which describes the enemy going off over flat terrain (*mîšôr*).

All other occurrences involve an ethical or religious sense. No one can walk in the right way without divine guidance (1QH 12:34); God "directs" (*yšr* piel) one's feet on the paths of righteousness (*ṣᵉḏāqâ*) (1QH 7:14). In 1QH 6:23f., the Teacher of Righteousness laments that he is like a sailor on the open sea, where he cannot "direct" (*yšr* piel) his course over the waters. But when his enemies set snares to catch him, his foot stood on level ground (*mîšôr*) through God's help (1QH 2:29), and he will walk henceforth on a level path (*mîšôr*). The smooth or level path is easy to travel; it is also brings happiness and success. A similar sense is probably present in 1QH 4:25, which says of the saved community: "Thou [= God] dost bring forth their right (*mišpāṭ*) to victory (*nṣḥ*) and their faithfulness to "*mêšārîm.*"[27] The parallelism with *nṣḥ* shows that *mêšārîm* includes the secondary meaning "success."

Those who do not enter into the "covenant" are not counted among the upright (*yᵉšārîm*) (1QS 3:1). But the members of the community are to "do what is good and right before him [= God] (*ṭôḇ wᵉyāšār lᵉpānāyw*)" (1QS 1:2). God will instruct the "upright" in the knowledge of the Most High and the truth of the sons of heaven (1QS 4:22). Human sin is atoned for by the spirit of uprightness (*yōšer*) (1QS 3:8). The contrite are "established in their counsel" according to the uprightness of God's truth (*yōšer ʾᵃmittᵉḵā*) (1QH 6:10); they are then called *yišrê dereḵ*, "those who walk uprightly."

"Making straight (*yšr* piel) the way" in Isa. 40:3 is interpreted by 1QS 8:4 as meaning study of the law. A purely biblical usage, *yšr bᵉʿênê*, appears in CD 8:7: "Each did what was right in his own eyes."

Ringgren

---

27 Cf. J. Becker, *Das Heil Gottes. StUNT*, 3 (1964), 73.

יְשֻׁרוּן *yᵉšurûn*

Contents: 1. Occurrences and Meaning; 2. Jeshurun/Israel/Jacob; 3. Individual Passages.

---

yᵉšurûn. W. Bacher, "יְשֻׁרוּן," *ZAW*, 5 (1885), 161-63; W. Caspari, "Sprachliche und religionsgeschichtliche Bedeutung des Namens Israel," *ZS*, 3 (1924), 194-211; G. A. Danell, *Studies in the Name Israel in the OT* (Eng. trans., Uppsala, 1946); J. S. Licht, "יְשֻׁרוּן," *EMiqr*, III, 937f.; G. E. Mendenhall, "Jeshurun," *IDB*, II, 868; M. Naor, "יַעֲקֹב und יִשְׂרָאֵל," *ZAW*, 49 (1931), 317f.; E. Sachsse, "Die Etymologie und älteste Aussprache des Namens ישראל," *ZAW*, 34 (1914), 1-15; *idem*, "Der Ursprung des Namens Israel," *ZS*, 4 (1926), 63-69; H. Seebass, "Die Stämmeliste

1. *Occurrences and Meaning.* The name "Jeshurun" occurs only 4 times in the OT: Dt. 32:15; 33:5,26; Isa. 44:2. It is also found in two Hebrew manuscripts of Sir. 37:25.[1] In early rabbinic texts, "Jeshurun" appears frequently when the OT texts in question are cited in the Talmud and Midrash; elsewhere in early Jewish writings the use of this word is limited almost entirely to these OT passages.

There is general agreement that "Jeshurun" is associated with the root *yšr.*[2] What is debated is whether *-ûn* is a diminutive suffix resembling the endings of names like *šimšôn* and *zᵉḇulôn*[3] or a denominative suffix.[4] Whether *-ûn* represents an independent suffix or is merely a dialectal variant of *-ôn* is hard to decide.[5] In the latter case, there would be no etymological reason not to consider "Jeshurun"[6] a diminutive.[7] It is significant that *yšr* appears as an element in Akkadian and especially Amorite personal names, e.g., *i-šar-ra-ma-aš, i-šar-ra-ma šu,* etc.;[8] *i-šar-li-im, ḫu-mu-yl-šar,* etc.[9] In many of these names, *yšr* (in Amorite, the /š/ can alternate with /s/[10]) is a theophorous element.[11] The Akkadian and Amorite parallels to the name "Jeshurun" show that the name itself need not be a neologism. Neither, however, is it necessarily an old hypocoristic name. The occurrences of "Jeshurum" are much too scattered and unusual.

The LXX already translates the name as *ēgapēménos*; in Isa. 44:2, it adds an explanatory "Israel" (cf. Sir. 37:25, where the LXX reads only "Israel"). It clearly already assumed that the name was associated with → ישר *yšr,* "be upright." This interpretation also appears occasionally in later Jewish literature (e.g., in the morning prayer "Jacob . . . , whom thou didst name Israel and Jeshurun"), although it is well known that this literature enjoys wordplay (cf. the play on *šôr* and *šîr* in *Gen. Rab.* lxxvii.1). The

---

von Dtn. XXXIII," *VT,* 27 (1977), 158-169; M. H. Segal, *Sefer Ben Sira* (Jerusalem, ³1972) [Heb.]; F. Vattioni, *Ecclesiastico* (Naples, 1968); L. Wächter, "Israel und Jeschurun," in *Schalom. Festschrift A. Jepsen. ArbT,* 1/46 (1971), 58-64.

1 See 3 below.

2 See 2 below.

3 E.g., F. H. W. Gesenius, *Thesaurus philologicus criticus linguae hebraeae et chaldaeae Veteris Testamenti* (Leipzig, 1853), 642; H. G. A. Ewald, *Ausführliches Lehrbuch der hebräischen Sprache des Alten Bundes* (Göttingen, ⁸1870), §167a; G. Kampffmeyer, "Südarabisches," *ZDMG,* 54 (1900), 660; R. Meyer, *Hebräische Grammatik,* I (Berlin, ³1969), §41, 1c.

4 E.g., *GK,* §86g; *BDB, s.v.,* and other lexica; cf. Wächter, 58.

5 Cf. *BLe,* §61, v´.

6 But cf. 2 below.

7 Cf. J. Barth, *Die Nominalbildung in den semitischen Sprachen* (²1894; repr. Hildesheim, 1967), §212.

8 *AN,* 122.

9 *APNM,* 216; cf. C. J. Gadd, "Tablets from Chagar Bazar and Tall Brak 1937-38," *Iraq,* 7 (1940), 38f.; C.-F. Jean, "Les noms propres de personnes," in A. Parrot, *Studia Mariana. DMOA,* 4 (1950), 83; *CAD,* VII (1960), 225.

10 G. Mendenhall, "Puppy and Lettuce in Northwest-Semitic Covenant Making," *BASOR,* 133 (1954), 29, and n. 14; *APNM,* 212, 216.

11 For the hypocoristicon *yašarum* as a perfect and the element *išar* as a possible imperfect, see M. Noth, "Mari und Israel: Eine Personennamenstudie," *Geschichte und AT. BHTh,* 16 (1953), 139, and n. 45 = *Aufsätze zur biblischen Landes- und Altertumskunde* (Neukirchen-Vluyn, 1971), II, 222, and n. 45.

Vulg. follows the LXX, translating "Jeshurun" as *dilectus* (Dt. 32:15) and *rectissimus* (*Israhel* in Sir. 37:25). In Isa. 44:2, for example, the other ancient Greek versions (Aquila, Symmachus, and Theodotion) have *euthýs* or *euthýatos.*[12] In all the passages (except Sir. 37:25, where it provides no translation[13]), the Syr. maintains the translation "Israel." The Targumim also usually prefer the translation (*bêṯ*) *yiśrāʾēl*; but Targ. Neofiti, for example, has *bêṯ yaʿaqōḇ* in Dt. 32:5, and some manuscripts read *yᵉšurûn* as well as *yiśrāʾēl* in Isa. 44:2.[14]

2. *Jeshurun/Israel/Jacob.* Most scholars[15] consider "Jeshurun" in the OT to be a cognomen for Israel and/or Jacob based on the root *yšr.*[16] The word almost always appears in parallel with or in the context of both names. Bacher[17] has suggested that "Jeshurun" is a neologism coined as a euphemism for "Jacob"; this view has found wide acceptance.[18] According to Bacher, the name "Jacob" is associated with notions of trickery and dishonesty (cf. Gen. 25:26; 27:36; Hos. 12:4[Eng. v. 3]), the opposite of uprightness and honesty (cf. Isa. 40:4; 42:16; Mic. 3:9). Bacher adds two conjectures based on this interpretation: (1) to read "Jeshurun" instead of *yᵉšārîm* in Nu. 23:10 (explaining the sg. *kāmōhû*); and (2) in the title of the book *sēp̄er hayyāšār* (Josh. 10:13; 2 S. 1:18), to treat *hayyāšār* as a title for Israel, "coined for the same reasons as 'Jeshurun.' " In opposition to Bacher, Naor[19] has tried to show that the word "Jeshurun" is in fact a remnant of an early form dating from a time before *ʿqb* had acquired the secondary meaning "deceive." He agrees with Sachsse that "Jeshurun" is important for the earliest etymology and pronunciation of the word "Israel": *yšrʾl,* he claims, means "God is trustworthy, upright." Others, too, find the *š* in "Jeshurun" significant for the etymology and meaning of "Israel."[20] Besides those (e.g., Caspari) who categorically deny the possibility of an original /*š*/ in "Israel," there are others (e.g., Naor) who argue for this possibility, citing, for example, Jgs. 12:6 and 1 Ch. 25:14 as evidence for variation between /*š*/ and /*ś*/ in Hebrew.[21] Whether "Jeshurun" is in fact related to "Israel" and the latter was originally pronounced with /*š*/ instead of /*ś*/ is discussed under → ישראל *yiśrāʾēl.* Here we simply restate our view that "Jeshurun" is associated with the root *yšr.* This etymology is

---

12 Cf. Jerome in *MPL,* 24, 450f.

13 See 3 below.

14 J. F. Stenning, *The Targum of Isaiah* (Oxford, 1949), *in loc.*

15 A. Bertholet, *Deuteronomium. KHC,* V (1899), 97; Liedke, 791; Mendenhall, *IDB,* II, 868; G. von Rad, *Deuteronomy. OTL* (Eng. trans. 1966), 198; Wächter, 58; G. Wallis, "Jesurun," *BHHW,* II (1964), 858; C. Westermann, *Isaiah 40–66. OTL* (Eng. trans. 1969), 135; F. Zorrell, *LexHebAram, s.v.;* etc.

16 Cf. already Calvin's preference for this root stated in his comm. on Isa. 44:2: "Some think that it is derived from ישר (*yāshar*), which means 'to be upright' or 'to please'; others from שור (*shūr*), and others from אשר (*āshar*)."

17 P. 162.

18 Cf. also I. L. Seeligmann, "A Psalm from Pre-regal Times," *VT,* 14 (1964), 89, n. 3.

19 P. 318.

20 E.g., F. M. T. de Liagre Böhl, *Kanaanäer und Hebräer. BWAT,* 9 (1911), 80; Licht, 938; Wächter, 58ff.

21 For a summary of the etymologies proposed for the name "Israel," see Danell, 22-28.

suggested by the ancient versions and supported by the Akkadian and Amorite personal names cited above; the contexts in which the word occurs also argue for this view. Nevertheless, Bacher's theory that "Jeshurun" is a neologism deliberately antithetical to "Jacob" remains dubious. Although there is no consensus respecting the date and *Sitz im Leben* of Dt. 32 and 33, it is quite clear that both in these chapters and in Isa. 44 "Jeshurun" is a word familiar to the author, used in some kind of play on the names "Jacob" and "Israel." There is no hint, however, of a deliberate antithesis.[22] Also unresolved is the question why the word appears so rarely in the OT and outside this book. Bacher has tried to answer this question by arguing that the name "Jacob" was a familiar name with a long history and that "Israel" functioned as a significant and honorable alternative to "Jacob." But this argument holds only if "Jeshurun" always functions as an antithesis to "Jacob." This is not true, however, in Dt. 33:26. If we follow the MT, we even have the reading *kā'ēl* instead of *kᵉ'ēl (yᵉšurûn)*: "the god Jeshurun," like "the god Bethel."[23] The conclusion is obvious: "Jeshurun" is only a rarely used equivalent to "Jacob" and "Israel." It may be a "literary invention, and therefore not part of the real corpus of Israelite names,"[24] or a hypocoristic[25] form of the name "Israel," used as a pet name or cognomen for Israel/Jacob.

3. *Individual Passages.* In Dt. 32, the Song of Moses, and Dt. 33, the Blessing of Moses, "Jacob" appears 4 times in parallel with "Israel" (Dt. 32:9; 33:4,10,28[26]), "Jeshurun" 3 times. This in itself is striking. In addition, after 32:14 has stated that Yahweh fed Israel miraculously with such food as "curds from the herd, and milk from the flock, with fat of lambs," etc., the Samaritan Pentateuch and LXX continue (v. 15) in poetic parallelism: *wayyō'ḵal ya'ᵃqōḇ wayyiśba' wayyišman yᵉšurûn wayyiḇ'āṭ*, etc., with "Jacob" and "Jeshurun" in parallel. Although the interpretation of v. 15 is difficult ("He became cocky, fat, thick, and sleek, and forsook God his maker"), it is clear that Jeshurun was fostered by God and thus became "fat and sleek."[27] The word "Jeshurun" clearly suggests Israel in an ideal situation,[28] with its "uprightness" due more to God's help than his own efforts.

Dt. 33:5, in a context that mentions the assembly of Jacob (v. 4) and the tribes of Israel, says: *wayᵉhî bîšurûn meleḵ*. The text does not say who became king in or over Jeshurun; the Midrash even suggests Moses himself. Many translate: "There was a king in Jeshurun";[29] others think in terms of Yahweh and translate: "And Yahweh became king over Jeshurun" (cf. Nu. 23:21; Jgs. 8:23; Isa. 33:22). The latter interpretation has much

---

22 Wächter.

23 Cf. Danell, 26f.; for "Jeshurun" as a vocative, see S. R. Driver, *Deuteronomy. ICC* (³1902, repr. 1978), 415.

24 *IPN,* 9f.

25 Mendenhall, etc.

26 Cf. Danell, 64.

27 Cf. also E. Baumann, "Das Lied Mose's (Dt. XXXII 1-43) auf seine gedankliche Geschlossenheit untersucht," *VT,* 6 (1956), 417f.

28 Driver, 361; cf. *BDB,* 449.

29 Driver, 394.

to recommend it. In any case, it is clear that here Israel is also presented as a community in its ideal state, while the poet is indulging in some kind of wordplay with "Jacob," "Jeshurun," and "Israel." Seebass[30] thinks that "Jeshurun" here refers originally to Israel's non-Israelite neighbors associated with Judah (Caleb, Cain, Othniel, and Jerahmeel), which were incorporated into the system of the twelve tribes of Israel to compensate for the vanished tribe of Simeon.

Immediately after the blessing of the tribes, in which many of them are promised the rich bounty of heaven and earth, the epilogue begins: "There is none like the God of Jeshurun, who rides through the heavens to your help (*bᵉʿezrᵉḵā*)" (Dt. 33:26). We reject the Masoretic pointing mentioned above (*kāʾēl* instead of *kᵉʾēl*) both because elsewhere "Jeshurun" is another name for Jacob/Israel and also because in the languages in which *yšr* appears in theophorous names it is always a verbal element, not the theophorous element.[31] This verse, too, speaks of Israel's "uprightness" bestowed by God's grace. Again "Jeshurun" is mentioned first, followed later (v. 28) by "Israel" and "Jacob." In Dt. 33:2-5,26-29, a hymn von Rad[32] calls an "informative psalm of praise," not only the verses in question but also the word "Jeshurun" exert a kind of centripetal force, enclosing the tribal oracles of the Blessing of Moses (vv. 6-25). The idealistic promises to the tribes in the oracles are, as it were, guaranteed by an idealistic and promising name for Israel and Jacob: "Jeshurun."

The word appears in 1 other OT passage, in Deutero-Isaiah (Isa. 44:2). The context of this verse is Isa. 43:22–44:4,[33] in which God promises to blot out Israel's transgressions and then tells Israel not to fear, because he will pour out his blessing on Israel's descendants. Isa. 44:2a calls Yahweh "the one who made you, who formed you from the womb and will help you"; v. 2b continues: "Fear not, O Jacob my servant, Jeshurun whom I have chosen." In Deutero-Isaiah, "Israel" appears almost always in parallel with "Jacob."[34] In this regard, we may note Isa. 43:22,28; 44:1,5 in the present pericope. Only in 44:2 does "Jacob" stand in parallel with "Jeshurun." Is Deutero-Isaiah here merely playing with words, using a hypocoristicon for variety? The notion that a diminutive with "benevolent overtones" is inappropriate to the language of divine love[35] is already disproved by Isa. 41:14 ("worm Jacob"). But why does Deutero-Isaiah use the word only here? Apart from the question whether the transitional 44:1 is a secondary addition,[36] clearly placing God's chosen Israel in parallel with Jeshurun, it is immediately apparent that in 43:23ff. God charges Jacob/Israel with having refused to offer him sheep, fat, and other choice sacrifices. Nevertheless, God will bless the people in the future by pouring his spirit upon Israel's offspring and descendants (44:3). This will create an ideal situation, in which new names will be given (44:5). This description constitutes a clear

---

30 P. 161.
31 See 1 above.
32 P. 295.
33 K. Elliger, *Deuterojesaja. BK,* XI/1 (1978), 368f.
34 Danell, 261, n. 44.
35 F. J. Delitzsch, *The Prophecies of Isaiah. KD,* VII, 202.
36 Elliger, 368f.

parallel to the Song of Moses and the Blessing of Moses in Dt. 32 and 33, even to the use of the same words (such as *ʿāśâ* [Dt. 32:15; Isa. 44:2] and *ʿāzar* [Dt. 33:26; Isa. 44:2]). This relationship best accounts for the use of "Jeshurun" here.

Finally, Sir. 37:25 poses a difficult problem. Here "Jeshurun" appears only in ms. D and in the margin of ms. B.[37] Ms. B itself reads *ʿam yiśrāʾēl*, a reading supported by the LXX and Vulg. The Syr. completely omits v. 25.[38] Segal[39] thinks its omission is due to Christian hostility toward the people of Israel. But the varying position and text of this verse in the Hebrew and Greek manuscripts indicate that it is probably a late interpolation into the text of Sirach, as many scholars rightly suggest. But this fact makes it difficult to explain why "Jeshurun" should be used in this particular text. In any event, the word clearly conveys a favorable meaning and is equated with the term "(people of) Israel."

Mulder

---

37 Vattioni, 197.

38 Cf. D. Barthélemy and O. Rickenbacher, *Konkordanz zum hebräischen Sirach* (Göttingen, 1973), 172.

39 P. 242.

יָתוֹם *yāṯôm*

Contents: I. Etymology. II. Ancient Near East: 1. Egyptian; 2. Akkadian; 3. West Semitic. III. OT: 1. Occurrences and Meaning; 2. LXX; 3. God and King as Helpers of Orphans; 4. Law; 5. Wisdom Literature; 6. The Prophets; 7. Being Orphaned as Punishment.

I. Etymology. Heb. *yāṯôm*, "orphan(ed)," has reflexes in Ugaritic (*ytm*, fem. *ytmt*[1]), Phoenician (*ytm*[2]), Aramaic (*yaṯmāʾ*, found in Egyptian Aramaic, Jewish Aramaic, Syriac, and Mandaic), Arabic (*yatīm*, which also means "unique"), and Ethiopic (*yatīm*;[3] cf. the Tigré verb *yattam*[4]). The root does not appear in Akkadian, which uses *ekû* instead.[5]

---

yāṯôm. F. M. T. de Liagre Böhl, "De Zonnegod als de Beschermer der Nooddruftigen," *Opera minora* (Groningen, 1953), 188-206; F. C. Fensham, "Widow, Orphan, and the Poor in Ancient Near Eastern Legal and Wisdom Literature," *JNES*, 21 (1962), 129-139.

1 *WUS*, no. 1254; *UT*, no. 1168.

2 *DISO*, 113.

3 Leslau, *Contributions*, 26.

4 *TigrWb*, 508.

5 See II.2 below.

II. Ancient Near East.

1. *Egyptian.* Egyptian has two words for "orphan": Egyp. *tfn(.t)*, attested as early as *Pyr.* 317 ("N gave relief to *tfn* and *tfn.t*"), and *nmḥw,* attested since the Middle Kingdom, which also means "poor, humble." The latter term shows that orphans were considered especially helpless and needy. To care for such people was the duty of the king and the nomarchs. In the Peasant's Lament, the speaker addresses the chief administrator Rensi as follows: "For you are the father of the orphan (*nmḥw*), the husband of the widow, the brother of the outcast. . . ."[6] It is characteristic that helpless orphans and widows are mentioned in the same breath. In the Instructions for Merikare, we read: "Comfort whoever mourns, do not afflict a widow, dispossess no man of his father's property."[7] The last expression clearly refers to orphans. Pharaoh Amenemhet I similarly boasts that he has "given to the poor and maintained the orphan."[8] Fensham[9] notes that all these passages refer to the social unrest of the First Intermediate period.

Later texts describe Amon as the protector of the poor and of orphans.[10] Rameses III boasts that he has protected widows and orphans.[11]

2. *Akkadian.* In ancient Mesopotamia, concern for widows and orphans begins with the reform of Urukagina (*ca.* 2400 B.C.), who made a pact with Ningirsu including, among other things, the stipulation that "the mighty shall not wrong the widow and the orphan." The same principle appears in the prologue to the Code of Ur-Nammu (*ca.* 2050), where the king says: "The orphan was not left at the mercy of the rich, . . . the man with a shekel was not left at the mercy of the man with a mina."[12] This tradition is continued by Hammurabi. In the epilogue of his code, he states among the goals of his reign: ". . . that the strong might not oppress the weak, and that orphans and widows enjoy their rights."[13]

As is well known, Hammurabi describes himself as representing the sun-god. Therefore texts that speak of Šamaš as protector of the needy are of particular interest,[14] although orphans are not mentioned explicitly.[15] Such protection is also associated with Ninurta: "You hold court over the human race, you help those who have been pushed aside to obtain what is rightfully theirs, [as well as] the orphan boy and girl. You grasp the hand of the weak. . . ."[16]

The word for "orphan" is disputed. The *CAD*[17] cites only the feminine form *ekûtu,*

---

6 B I, 62; *ANET*³, 408.
7 Ll. 47f.; *ANET*³, 415.
8 I, 6f.; *ANET*³, 418.
9 Pp. 132f.
10 Papyrus Anastasi II, 6.5f.; Fensham, 133.
11 Papyrus Harris I; Fensham, 133.
12 Ll. 162-68; *ANET*³, 524.
13 CH Epilogue, 24, 59-62; *AOT,* 407; *ANET*³, 178.
14 Böhl.
15 Fensham, 131; see, e.g., the great Hymn to the Sun in *BWL,* 132f., ll. 99f., 134ff.; *SAHG,* 243ff.
16 *SAHG,* 315.
17 IV (1958), 72f.

"homeless, destitute girl," and comments that there is no masculine form *ekû,* "orphan boy"; *iku,* it states, means only "weak." But elsewhere[18] it cites the Hymn to Ninurta mentioned above, where *ekû* and *ekûtu* appear together, and translates as indicated. It also cites *akû,* "impoverished, weak, humble."[19] Von Soden,[20] however, lists *ekû, ikû* as meaning "impoverished, orphaned," and comments that it often appears together with *almattu,* "widow," "also used of fatherless orphans." The only meaning he gives for *akû* is "cripple."[21]

3. *West Semitic.* Ugar. *ytm* appears in one text[22] together with *'lmnt*: King Danel judges the cause of the widow (*ydn dn 'lmnt*) and decides the right of the orphan (*yṯpṭ ṯpṭ ytm*). Here, therefore, it is the duty of the king to preserve the rights of orphans.[23] A similar statement probably appeared in another fragmentary text.[24] The same conclusion can be drawn from the charge that Keret is unable to "judge" widows and those who are afflicted (*qṣr*) or to feed (*šlḥm*) widows and orphans.[25]

In the Phoenician inscription of Ešmunʿazar,[26] the king refers to himself as "*ytm,* son of a widow"; and in the Kilamuwa inscription,[27] the king says that the *muškabim* felt toward him as an orphan toward its mother, since he held them by the hand.

III. OT. 1. *Occurrences and Meaning.* There are 42 occurrences of *yāṯôm* in the OT. The meaning is clear from Lam. 5:3: "We are *yᵉṯômîm* without a father (*ʾên ʾāḇ*)." More detail is provided by Job 29:12: the orphan has no helper (*ʿōzēr*); cf. Ps. 10:14, which states that God helps orphans.

2. *LXX.* The LXX always translates *yāṯôm* as *orphanós.*

3. *God and King as Helpers of Orphans.* Along with widows, orphans appear as particularly weak and helpless in Israelite society. In Deuteronomy, *gērîm* are added to the list.

Above all it is God who helps orphans. According to Dt. 10:17f., it is the mighty and terrible God, the upright judge, "who executes justice (*ʿōśēh mišpāṭ*) for orphans and widows, and loves sojourners (*gērîm*)." The text goes on to enjoin love of sojourners, while saying nothing further of widows and orphans.

Ps. 68:6(Eng. v. 5) describes triumphant Yahweh as "father of orphans and judge (*dayyan*) of widows"; in the following verse, he helps the desolate (*yᵉḥîḏîm*) and

---

18 VII (1960), 69.
19 *CAD,* I/1 (1964), 283f.
20 *AHw,* I (1965), 195.
21 *AHw,* I, 30.
22 *KTU,* 1.17 V, 8.
23 Fensham, 134.
24 *KTU,* 1.19 I, 23ff.
25 *KTU,* 1.16 VI, 45ff.
26 *KAI,* 14.3, 13.
27 *KAI,* 24.13.

prisoners, and in v. 25(24) he is referred to as "king." Ps. 10:16 also extols Yahweh as king; v. 14 of the same psalm describes him as helper (*ʿôzēr*) of orphans, and v. 18 states that he "judges" (*šāp̱aṭ*) orphans, i.e., helps them secure their rights. According to Ps. 146:9, Yahweh watches over (*šāmar*) the *gērîm* and upholds (*yᵉʿôḏēḏ*) orphans and widows, while leading astray (*ʿiwwēṯ dereḵ*) the wicked. Verse 10 states that he reigns as king (*mālaḵ* qal) forever. Thus Yahweh's care for orphans is almost always associated with his royal office.

In Ps. 82, which exhibits Canaanite influence, "God" (*ʾᵉlōhîm*, probably originally *ʾēl*) addresses the "gods" (*ʾᵉlōhîm*), demanding that they eschew unjust judgment, that they give justice (*šāp̱aṭ*) to the weak (*dal*) and to orphans, and that they maintain the right (*ṣdq* hiphil) of the poor (*ʿānî* and *rāš*) (v. 3). The gods refuse and are condemned to death by God. It is significant that the God of Israel appears here as ruler and judge (v. 8). The *ʾᵉlōhîm* are probably both the gods of the pagans and the rulers who represent these gods. Yahweh thus guarantees justice to the needy, especially orphans and widows.

Hosea also expresses the hope that Israel will no longer need to seek help from Assyria and from idols, but that Yahweh will have mercy on the orphan (Hos. 14:4[3]). When Ps. 72 speaks of the king's care for the poor and needy (vv. 2,4,12f.), it is noteworthy that orphans and widows are not mentioned explicitly. But we would probably not be far wrong in assuming that this omission is accidental and that in Israel, too, orphans were counted among the weak who were the object of special royal protection.

4. *Law.* The Covenant Code already requires that widows and orphans not be oppressed (*ʿānâ* piel) (Ex. 22:21[22]); the punishment for doing so will fit the crime: "Your wives shall become widows and your children orphans" (v. 23[24]). Deuteronomy is particularly concerned for these groups of the weak. It is a general rule that the justice due the sojourner (*gēr*) or orphan must not be perverted (and that a widow's garment must not be taken in pledge) (Dt. 24:17). The curse formulas of ch. 27 include a curse on those who pervert the justice due the *gēr*, widows, and orphans (v. 19). Grain, olives, and grapes left over from the harvest belong to the *gērîm*, orphans, and widows (Dt. 24:19-21). The *gērîm*, orphans, and widows have the right to participate fully in celebrating festivals (Dt. 16:11,14). The *gēr*, the orphan, and the widow receive a portion of the tithe along with the Levites (Dt. 14:29; 26:12).

5. *Wisdom Literature.* Wisdom Literature also speaks of the special needs of the poor and those without families (e.g., Prov. 14:31; 15:25; 19:17; 22:9,22). Only once, in one of the proverbs echoing an Egyptian original, is the *yāṯôm* mentioned explicitly (Prov. 23:10), in a warning against encroaching on the property of an orphan. The parallel stich speaks of displacing the boundary marker of a widow.

The book of Job speaks of orphans much more frequently. Oppression of orphans is one of the marks of the wicked: they even cast lots over orphans (Job 6:27), they send widows away with empty hands and crush orphans (22:9), they take the orphan's ass and the widow's ox (24:3), they snatch the orphan from its mother's breast (24:9). Ps. 94:6 says much the same: the wicked slay widows and *gērîm* and murder orphans.

Conversely, in his concluding discourse (Job 29–31), Job maintains his righteousness, emphasizing that he has helped the poor and the fatherless (29:12; 31:16f.) and that he has treated the fatherless equitably in court (31:21).

6. *The Prophets.* The demand to care for the fatherless also appears occasionally in the message of the prophets. Isaiah exhorts his listeners to forsake evil and do good, amplifying his demand with the words *šip̱ṭû yāṯôm rîḇû ʾalmānâ* (Isa. 1:17). He also illustrates the moral decay of Jerusalem by citing its neglect of these very obligations (1:23). In 10:2, Isaiah castigates the perversion of the law that despoils widows and orphans.

Jeremiah likewise speaks of the wicked at whose hands the fatherless and poor suffer injustice (Jer. 5:28), and in his temple sermon (ch. 7) he calls on the people to amend their ways, to execute justice, and to cease oppressing the sojourner (*gēr,* as in Deuteronomy!), the fatherless, and the widow, since the temple by itself offers no protection (v. 6). A similar warning is heard in Jer. 22:3.

In Jer. 49:7-22, an oracle against Edom, on the other hand, we find the assurance that Yahweh himself will care for the fatherless and widows among his people, so that others need not worry about them. One passage in Ezekiel (Ezk. 22:7) also charges the people of Jerusalem with oppressing the fatherless and widows; the same text speaks of violations against the *gērîm.* Finally, Zec. 7:9f. calls for true judgment, love, and mercy, warning against oppressing widows, orphans, sojourners, and the poor.

7. *Being Orphaned as Punishment.* Finally, the desolation of being orphaned may be cited as a punishment. Ps. 109 curses an enemy by wishing that his children may be made fatherless and his wife a widow (v. 9); this is amplified in v. 12 by the wish that none may have pity on his fatherless children. As a punishment, Isa. 9:16(17) threatens that Yahweh will not have mercy on the fatherless and widows among his people. Ex. 22:23(24) has already been discussed.[28] In Lam. 5:3, the people lament: "We have become orphans, fatherless; our mothers have become widows"—in other words, we are without help or protection. The context of the lament more or less implies that this suffering is a punishment (v. 7).

Ringgren

[28] See III.4 above.

יָתַר *yāṯar* I; יֶתֶר *yeṯer* I; יוֹתֵר/יֹתֵר *yôṯēr/yōṯēr;* יֹתֶרֶת *yōṯereṯ;* יִתְרָה/יִתְרַת *yiṯrâ/yiṯraṯ;* יִתְרוֹן *yiṯrôn;* מוֹתָר *môṯār;* יַתִּיר/יַתִּירָה(א) *yattîr/yattîrâ(ā')*

Contents: I. Etymology, Semantics, OT Occurrences. II. OT Usage: 1. The Verb *yāṯar* I; 2. *yeṯer* I; 3. *yôṯēr/yōṯēr*; 4. *yōṯereṯ;* 5. *yiṯrâ/yiṯraṯ*; 6. *yiṯrôn*; 7. *môṯār*; 8. *yattîr/yattîrâ(ā')*. III. LXX. IV. Dead Sea Scrolls.

I. Etymology, Semantics, OT Occurrences. The root *ytr* I, quite common in the OT, is in all likelihood etymologically distinct from the root *ytr* II, which is represented only by the nouns *yeṯer* II ("string" [Jgs. 16:7-9], "bowstring" [Job 30:11; Ps. 11:2; Hab. 3:9 conj.], "tent-cord" [Job 4:21])[1] and *mêṯār* ("bowstring" [Ps. 21:13(Eng. v. 12)], "tent-cord" [Ex. 35:18; 39:40; Nu. 3:26,37; 4:26,32; Isa. 54:2; Jer. 10:20; Job 17:11 conj.]),[2] as Ibn Barūn already suggested in his *Kitāb al-Muwāzana* (*ca.* A.D. 1100).[3] Ibn Barūn connects *ytr* I with Arab. *'aṯira* and *ytr* II with Arab. *watara.*[4]

The root *ytr* I (or the related *'tr/wtr*) is found in all Semitic languages, and it is not hard to determine its basic meaning: "be extra, surplus." Akk. *wtr* finds frequent use in economic texts, but also appears occasionally in mathematical and astronomical sources, as well as in a few omen texts. It is represented primarily by the verb (*w*)*atāru*: in the G stem, it means "exceed in number or size" or "surpass in importance" or "quality"; in the D stem, it takes on the intensive meaning "become more important or richer," "increase in number or size"; in the causative Š stem (*šuturu*) it means "cause to increase" or "surpass."[5] Other derivatives include the noun *atartu,* "surplus" (in accounting; also

yāṯar. R. Braun, *Kohelet und die frühhellenistische Popularphilosophie. BZAW,* 130 (1973), 47f.; J. C. Campbell, "God's People and the Remnant," *SJT,* 3 (1950), 78-85; S. Garofalo, *La nozione profetica del "Resto d'Israel"* (Rome, 1942), esp. 197-202; W. Günther and H. Krienke, "Remnant, Leave," *NIDNTT,* III (1978), 247-254; G. F. Hasel, *The Origin and Early History of the Remnant Motif in Ancient Israel* (diss., Vanderbilt, 1970), 171-203; *idem, The Remnant. AUM,* 5 (²1974) (literature survey, 1-44); *idem,* "Semantic Values of Derivatives of the Hebrew Root Š'R," *AUSS,* 11 (1973), 152-169; E. W. Heaton, "The Root שׁער and the Doctrine of the Remnant," *JTS,* N.S. 3 (1952), 27-39; V. Herntrich and G. Schrenk, "λεῖμμα," *TDNT,* IV, 194-214; J. Jeremias, "Der Gedanke des 'Heiligen Restes' im Spätjudentum und in der Verkündigung Jesu," *ZNW,* 42 (1949), 184-194 = *Abba* (Göttingen, 1966), 121-132; P. Joüon, "Notes de lexicographie hébraïque, III: Deut racines יתר," *MUSJ,* 6 (1913), 174; J. Meinhold, *Studien zur israelitischen Religionsgeschichte,* I/1 (Bonn, 1903); W. E. L. Müller and H. D. Preuss, *Die Vorstellung vom Rest im AT* (Neukirchen-Vluyn, 1973); L. Rost, "Der Leberlappen," *ZAW,* 79 (1967), 35-41; O. Schilling, *"Rest" in der Prophetie des ATs* (diss., Münster, 1942), esp. 7-16; R. de Vaux, "The 'Remnant of Israel' According to the Prophets," *The Bible and the Ancient Near East* (Eng. trans., London, 1971), 15-30; P. Wechter, *Ibn Barūn's Arabic Works on Hebrew Grammar and Lexicography* (Philadelphia, 1964), 98f.; H. Wildberger, "שׁאר *š'r* übrig sein," *THAT,* II, 844-855.

1 *KBL*³, 431.
2 *KBL*³, 548.
3 Cf. Wechter, 98f.; P. Wernberg-Møller, review of Wechter, *JSS,* 11 (1966), 125.
4 Cf. also Joüon, 174.
5 *CAD,* I/2 (1968), 487-492.

with reference to size, area, etc.) or "exaggeration," i.e., "lie" (cf. *ša atrāti,* "one who lies, liar");[6] the adj. *atru,* "excessive, additional," even "extraordinary," but also "exaggerated, false";[7] and finally the noun *atru,* "supplement," "supplementary payment," also more generally "price, cost," etc.[8]

In some Ugaritic texts, especially in such personal names as *(bn) ytr, ytrhd,* or *ytrʿm,*[9] the element *ytr* probably functions to bring out the unique, extraordinary nature of the bearer; Gordon, for example, suggests that *ytrhd* means "Hadd is Unique."[10] Similarly, *ytr* seems to appear with the meaning "be surpassing" in a series of Amorite personal names.[11] The root is also attested in Ya'udic, Palmyrene, and Imperial Aramaic inscriptions, and possible also in Punic.[12] In an inscription on the statue of Hadad from Zinjirli (mid-8th century B.C.),[13] for example, Panammuwa I, the ruler of Ya'udi, declares that Hadad and other gods "gave abundance" to him (*wytr,* interpreted as a 3rd person masc. sg. qal with *waw copulativum*[14])—indeed, that everything he asked of them they "gave in abundance" (*ytr*; qal perf. or impf.[15]). The noun *ytr*[16] probably appears in a similar text on the statue of Panammuwa II, also from Zinjirli (second half of the 8th century B.C.).[17]

Arab. *watara* and its derivatives, especially in stems I and VI, is unlikely to be cognate with *ytr* I;[18] the first stem does not mean "do something unusual," as stated by *KBL*³, but "isolate something," "make something (numerically) uneven," "span (a bow)," "damage," etc.[19] It is better to follow Ibn Barūn's suggestion of *ʾṯr* (e.g., *ʾaṯāra,* "remainder"; *ʾīṯār,* "preference")[20] or Joüon's suggestion[21] of *ṯrw* (I: "become great in number or quantity," "be/become rich").[22]

In Ethiopic, the verb *tarafa,* which "appears to be related to *ytr,*"[23] has the meaning "be left over, survive, remain."

While the Old Aramaic occurrences of *ytr* I are of course not very numerous (as a verb in the peal, "be abundant," in the pael, "do much," in the haphel, "multiply, make

6 *Ibid.,* 485f.
7 *Ibid.,* 499-501.
8 *Ibid.,* 501f.
9 *UT,* nos. 1170, 1171, 1173; cf. also 1172, 1174, 1175; *WUS,* nos. 1258-1262.
10 *UT,* no. 1171.
11 *APNM,* 217f.
12 J. Cantineau, *Grammaire du palmyrénien épigraphique* (Cairo, 1935), 136; *KAI,* 214.11f.; 215.4; *DISO,* 113.
13 *KAI,* 214.
14 *KAI,* II, 218.
15 *Ibid.,* 219.
16 *Ibid.,* 225.
17 *KAI,* 215.
18 Contra *KBL*³, 431.
19 Lane, VIII, 2917-19; Wehr, 1046.
20 Lane, I, 18-20; Wehr, 4.
21 P. 174.
22 Lane, I, 335f.; Wehr, 102.
23 *LexLingAeth,* 557f.

useful"; as a noun, *ytr,* "remainder"[24]), the root is common in postbiblical Aramaic; the verb appears in the peal ("be left over"), pael ("leave over," "add," "do something too much"), aphel ("leave over," "cause to abound"), (h)ithpaal ("be left over," "be added"), and ishtaphal ("be left over"), and there are such nominal derivatives as *yûṯrān, yattîr,* and *yiṯrāʾ*.[25]

The situation is similar in Mandaic. The verb appears in the peal ("be enlarged"), pael ("multiply"), etpaal ("become rich"), and there are nominal derivatives: *iatir, iatarta, iutrana, iatruta,* and *tiatruta.*[26] In Syriac, the verb *îṯar* in the peal has the basic meaning "be left over or superfluous"; the pael is causative; the aphel means "have an overabundance," "be abundant," also "be useful"; the etpaal means "be abundant," "be superior." Nominal derivatives include *yûṯrān/āʾ, yattîr/ûṯāʾ, mawtrānûṯāʾ, mᵉyattᵉrûṯāʾ,* and *tawtār.*[27]

The root is also common in Postbiblical Hebrew (as a verb, with the nominal derivatives *yāṯēr, yeṯer, yiṯrôn,* etc.).[28]

In OT Hebrew, the root *ytr* I appears both as a verb (81 times in the niphal,[29] 24 times in the hiphil) and in nominal derivatives: *yeṯer* (95 occurrences, 44 of which are in the phrase *yeṯer diḇrê* in Kings and Chronicles), *yôṯēr/yōṯēr* (9 occurrences, 7 in Ecclesiastes), *yōṯereṯ* (11 occurrences, 9 in Leviticus), *yiṯrâ/yiṯraṯ* (once each), *yiṯrôn* (10 occurrences, all in Ecclesiastes), and *môṯār* (3 occurrences). In Biblical Aramaic we find only the adj./adv. *yattîr/yattîrâ(āʾ)*. The proper names involving elements from the semantic field of "be left over"[30] are derived from *ytr,* not *šʾr.*[31] Some personal names derive from the root *ytr*:[32] *ʾeḇyāṯār* (1 S. 22:20–23:9; 30:7; 1 K. 1:7ff.; 1 Ch. 15:11; etc.), *hôṯîr* (1 Ch. 25:4,28),[33] *yeṯer* (Ex. 4:18 [= *yiṯrô* (Ex. 3:1; etc.)]; Jgs. 8:20; 1 K. 2:5,32; 1 Ch. 2:17 [= *yiṯrāʾ* (2 S. 17:25)]; 1 Ch. 7:38 [= *yiṯrān* I], *yiṯrān* II (Gen. 36:26; 1 Ch. 1:41), *yiṯrᵉʿam* (2 S. 3:5; 1 Ch. 3:3). There are also toponyms: *yattîr/yattir* (Josh. 15:48; 1 S. 30:27; etc.) and the gentilic *yiṯrî* or *hayyiṯrî* (2 S. 23:38; 1 Ch. 11:40; 2:53).[34]

The biblical occurrences of *ytr* I generally involve the basic meaning "be abundant," "be left over." The root → שׁאר *šʾr,* which often appears in parallel with it, likewise has the basic meaning "be left over." With 226 OT occurrences, it is by far the most common root in this semantic field,[35] which also includes → פלט *plṭ,* "escape," "be saved," also

---

24 S. Segert, *Altaramäische Grammatik* (Leipzig, 1975), 537.

25 *WTM,* II, 279; Jastrow, 604f.; G. Dalman, *Aramäisch-neuhebräisches Handwörterbuch zu Targum, Talmud und Midrasch* (³1938; repr. Hildesheim, 1967), 190.

26 *MdD,* 194; cf. R. Macuch, *Handbook of Classical and Modern Mandaic* (Berlin, 1965), 309, 419f., 437.

27 R. P. Smith, ed., *Thesaurus Syriacus,* I (Oxford, 1879), 1648-1654; *LexSyr,* 312-14.

28 *WTM,* II, 278f.; Jastrow, 604f.; Dalman, 190.

29 According to Wildberger, 846, 82 times; but cf. *KBL*³, 431.

30 Cf. *KBL*³, 430ff.

31 See below.

32 Cf. *IPN,* nos. 31, 193, 783, 785.

33 Cf. W. W. Müller, "Altsüdarabische Beiträge zum hebräischen Lexicon," *ZAW,* 75 (1963), 308.

34 Cf. *KBL*³, 432a.

35 Cf. Hasel, *The Remnant*; Wildberger, 844-855.

"be left over" (80 occurrences in the OT),[36] and → שׂרד *śrd,* "escape (by fleeing)" (29 occurrences in the OT).[37] The primary antonym to *ytr* I is → חסר *ḥāsēr,* "lack."

II. OT Usage.

1. *The Verb yāṯar I.* a. *Qal.* In Biblical Hebrew, the qal of *ytr* I occurs in the nominalized act. ptcp. *yôṯēr/yōṯēr* (fem. *yōṯereṯ*).[38] The primary meaning "be left over" can be seen especially clearly in 1 S. 15:15, which states that the Israelites spared the best of the sheep and oxen taken from the Amalekites and sacrificially destroyed "the rest."[39]

b. *Niphal.* The niphal of the verb *ytr* I occurs 81 times in the OT (including 2 S. 17:12, where *nwtr* [MT *nôṯar*] should possibly be interpreted as a hiphil [LXX: *hypoleipsómetha*][40]). It is not hard to see that the niphal conveys the passive or reflexive equivalent of the basic meaning: "prove to be superfluous," "be left over." Ex. 10:15, for example, states that after the plague of locusts upon the trees and fields "nothing green was left" (*lō'-nôṯar kol-yereq*). Most instances involve very ordinary matters: Jacob was left alone at the Jabbok (Gen. 32:25[24]); Jotham was the only one of Jerubbaal's sons left alive (Jgs. 9:5); David asks whether there is anyone left of the house of Saul to whom he may show kindness (2 S. 9:1); Asa took all the silver and gold that was left in the temple treasury and gave it to the Aramean king as a gift (1 K. 15:18); Elijah feels that he alone is left as Yahweh's prophet (1 K. 18:22; 19:10,14).

When the ban is carried out, none is left of the Anakim (Josh. 11:22 [cf. v. 11: "no *nᵉšāmâ*"]) or the Amorites (1 K. 9:20f.). After the fall of Samaria, Jerusalem is left "like a booth in a vineyard, like a lodge in a cucumber field" (Isa. 1:8: note the continuation: "Yahweh has left [hiphil] us a small remnant [*śariḏ*]"). Isaiah says to Hezekiah: "All that is in your house . . . shall be carried to Babylon; nothing shall be left" (2 K. 20:17 par. Isa. 39:6).

Isa. 1:8f. introduces the notion of the "remnant,"[41] as does Isa. 4:3: "And he who is left (*niš'ār* → שׁאר *š'r*) in Zion and remains (*nôṯār*) in Jerusalem will be called holy." Cf. also Ezk. 14:22: "There is left a remnant (*pᵉlēṭâ*) in it." According to Amos, contrariwise, ten inhabitants left in Samaria must die (Am. 6:9). Deutero-Zechariah foresees that that two thirds of the population must be exterminated, so that only a third will be left (Zec. 13:8). At the eschaton, however, all that are left among the nations of the world will come to Jerusalem to celebrate the Feast of Booths (Zec. 14:16).

Some cultic regulations use the verb *ytr.* For example, it is forbidden to let any of the Passover lamb remain (hiphil) until morning; anything that remains (niphal) is to be burnt (Ex. 12:10). Similarly, anything left over from the sacrifices offered at the consecration of priests is to be burnt (Ex. 29:34; Lev. 8:32); the same holds true for the *šᵉlāmîm* sacrifice

---

36 Cf. E. Ruprecht, "פלט *plṭ* pi. retten," *THAT,* II, 420-27.
37 Cf. Herntrich-Schrenk, 196-209.
38 See below.
39 H. J. Stoebe, *Das erste Buch Samuelis. KAT,* VIII/1 (1973), 288.
40 Cf. K. Budde, *Die Bücher der Samuel. KHC,* VIII (1902), *in loc.*; cf. also *GK,* §109d.
41 Cf. Müller-Preuss, 44-46.

(Lev. 7:17; 19:6). In the case of other sacrifices, what remains is eaten by the priests (Lev. 2:3,10; 6:9[16]; 10:12).

Dnl. 10:13 presents a problem. The MT reads *wa'ᵃnî nôṯartî šām*. Many scholars[42] emend this to *wᵉ'ōṯô hôṯartî šām* on the basis of the LXX and Theodotion, but this can hardly be right. It is probably best to keep the MT and interpret the words as meaning "I became superfluous there."[43] Also difficult is 2 Ch. 31:10, where the MT (*wᵉhannôṯār 'eṯ-hehāmôn hazzeh*) might possibly be rendered freely as "and so we have this great quantity."[44] Often *hannôṯār* is emended to *wannôṯēr* or *wannôṯar* on the basis of the LXX or else *wᵉhinnēh nôṯar.*[45] All 51 occurrences of the niphal participle are determined.

c. *Hiphil.* The hiphil of *ytr* I occurs 24 times in the OT. Of these occurrences, the majority can be interpreted factitively: "leave over." Thus Ex. 12:10 says of the Passover lamb: *wᵉlō'-ṯôṯîrû mimmennû 'aḏ-bōqer,* "and you shall let none of it remain until the morning." Similar statements are made concerning the manna (Ex. 16:19f.), thanksgiving sacrifices (Lev. 22:30), enemies (Nu. 33:55; 2 S. 17:12; also Isa. 1:9;[46] Jer. 44:7 ["no *šᵉ'ērîṯ*]; Ezk. 6:8; 12:16; 39:28). Some occurrences are probably causative: "cause to abound," as in Dt. 28:11; 30:9. This is clearly the case in the MT of Ps. 79:11;[47] the impv. *hôṯēr* is probably best taken as meaning "give abundance [of life]," "grant survival," or more simply "preserve."[48] Others mean "have something [vouchsafed]," i.e., "have abundance" (Ex. 36:7), often simply "have left" (Dt. 28:54; 2 S. 8:4; 1 Ch. 18:4; also Sir. 10:27). Especially noteworthy is the sequence "eat—[be filled]—have some left" (Ruth 2:14,18; 2 K. 4:43f.; 2 Ch. 31:10). Finally, Gen. 49:4 may involve an elative hiphil: "have precedence," "be first" (cf. Akk. *šūturu*).[49]

2. *yeṯer I.* The masculine noun *yeṯer* I, associated with *ytr* I, occurs 95 times in the OT. It denotes in general terms something that is "left over," the "rest." This remainder is seen primarily from a negative perspective, implying that what is left is less in number or quantity. Ex. 23:11, for example, speaking of the produce of the land during the Sabbatical Year, says that the poor are to eat of it, "and what they leave the wild beasts may eat." The same is true in Ex. 10:5: the locusts are to eat "what is left to you after the hail." This is even clearer in the triple statement of Joel 1:4: "What the biter left, the locust devoured. What the locust left, the hopper devoured. What the hopper left, the jumper devoured."[50] The same is true of the "rest of the vessels" belonging to the

---

42 E.g., R. H. Charles, *A Critical and Exegetical Comm. on the Book of Daniel* (Oxford, 1929), 262.

43 A. Bentzen, *Die fünf Megilloth: Daniel. HAT,* XIX (^{2}1952), 72; O. Plöger, *Das Buch Daniel. KAT,* XVIII (1965), 145.

44 J. M. Myers, *II Chronicles. AB,* XIII (^{2}1979), 181.

45 W. Rudolph, *Chronikbücher. HAT,* XXI (^{2}1968), 305.

46 See above.

47 Cf. H.-J. Kraus, *Psalmen. BK,* XV/2 (^{5}1978), 714.

48 *Ibid.,* 713.

49 E. A. Speiser, *Genesis. AB,* I (^{3}1979), 364; *idem,* "The 'Elative' in West-Semitic and Akkadian," *Oriental and Biblical Studies* (Philadelphia, 1967), 474, n. 26; *KBL*^{3}, 431.

50 H. W. Wolff, *Joel and Amos. Herm* (Eng. trans. 1977), 17.

Jerusalem temple (Jer. 27:19) and the "rest of the firewood" (Isa. 44:19; *yiṯrô* par. *šᵉʾrîṯô* in v. 17). Here also belong Ps. 17:14; Job 22:20. The former can hardly refer to "abundance, affluence,"[51] but rather to "something left for their children";[52] the latter states that the fire consumed what was left. In Job 4:21, *yiṯrām* clearly has nothing to do with *yeṯer* I,[53] but is *yeṯer* II, "tent-cord." Other passages using the noun *yeṯer* associated with *ytr* I often refer to survivors, either individually (Dt. 3:11; 28:54; Josh. 12:4; 13:12) or collectively (Josh. 23:12; 2 S. 21:2; 2 K. 25:11; Jer. 52:15; Ezk. 34:18; Mic. 5:2[3]; Zeph. 2:9).

A weakened sense of "remainder" may be seen in a series of passages where the idea of something left over comes primarily from the perspective of the narrative or the narrator. This is particularly true of the formula *yeṯer diḇrê,* "the rest of the things of . . . ," i.e., "the rest of the matters concerning . . . ," "all the rest about . . . ,"[54] especially common in the Deuteronomistic history and the Chronicler's history. It appears in 1 K. 11:41 and 41 additional times in Kings and Chronicles; there are some variations: *yeṯer kol-diḇrê* (1 K. 15:23), *yeṯer dᵉḇārāyw* (2 Ch. 28:26). The noun *yeṯer* has a similar function in a few passages where it denotes the remainder of a group already named or described; here it is equivalent to "the others" (2 S. 10:10; 12:28; 1 K. 12:23; 1 Ch. 19:11; Neh. 6:1; Jer. 29:1; Ezk. 48:23). It can thus denote a disqualified group, a majority (Jgs. 7:6; 1 S. 13:2), or the common people in contrast to the upper classes (Neh. 2:16; 4:8,13[14,19]). It can also refer to the unspecified portions of a land or region (Dt. 3:13; Josh. 13:27), the rest of other specified things (Lev. 14:17 [oil]; Nu. 31:32 [booty]), or the rest of someone's years (Isa. 38:10).

A different meaning of *yeṯer,* associated with the basic idea of abundance, is clearly present in Prov. 17:7: *śᵉpaṯ-yeṯer* (if the MT is not emended to *śᵉpaṯ-yōšer* on the basis of the LXX[55]), the "lip of (super)abundance," probably does not so much mean "arrogant speech"[56] as exaggerated and therefore "lying speech."[57] A similar nuance is probably present in a few adverbial expressions, e.g., *gāḏôl yeṯer mᵉʾōḏ,* "great beyond measure" (Isa. 56:12), *ʿal-yeṯer,* "exceedingly" (Ps. 31:24[23]; hardly just "in full measure"[58]), and *wattigdal-yeṯer,* "and [the horn] grew exceedingly great" (Dnl. 8:9).

3. *yôṯēr/yōṯēr.* Apart from 1 S. 15:15,[59] the qal ptcp. *yôṯēr/yōṯēr* appears only in relatively late texts (9 times: 7 in Ecclesiastes, once in Esther). Like *yiṯrôn,* which occurs only in Ecclesiastes, and *môṯār,*[60] which occurs only in Wisdom contexts (Proverbs,

---

51 *BDB,* 452; also E. P. Dhorme, *A Comm. on the Book of Job* (Eng. trans. 1967; repr. Nashville, 1984), *in loc.*

52 H.-J. Kraus, *Psalms 1–59* (Eng. trans., Minneapolis, 1988), 244.

53 Cf. Dhorme, *in loc.*

54 M. Noth, *Könige 1–16. BK,* IX/1 (1968), 241.

55 Cf. *BHS.*

56 *BDB,* 452.

57 H. Ringgren, *Sprüche. ATD,* XVI/1 (³1980), 71.

58 Kraus, *Psalms 1–59,* 364f.

59 See 1.a above.

60 See below.

Ecclesiastes), this term has primarily economic overtones: "surplus," "profit," or more generally "advantage." This meaning is clear in Eccl. 7:11, which says that in combination with an inheritance[61] wisdom is "an advantage to those who see the sun" (with *ṭôḇâ* as a parallel term). The sense of "advantage" is also found in Eccl. 6:8: "What advantage has one who is wise over the fool?" which actually means "How much advantage one who is wise has over a fool," for "in Ecclesiastes, *mh-ytrwn* or *mh-ywtr* is always a rhetorical question."[62] Eccl. 6:11 asks similarly: "What is anyone the better?"

Like *yeṯer,*[63] *yôṯēr/yōṯēr* can also function adverbially. This is especially clear in Eccl. 7:16, where *yôṯēr* appears in parallel with *harbēh,* which in Postbiblical Hebrew often means "exceedingly, very":[64] "Be not righteous overmuch, and do not make yourself overwise." This adverbial function may also be observed in Eccl. 2:15. When followed by *min, yōṯēr* means "more than" (Est. 6:6; Eccl. 12:12), as often in Postbiblical Hebrew. Once *yōṯēr* is found with *še*; the clause *weyōṯēr šehāyâ qōheleṯ ḥāḵām* (Eccl. 12:9) can mean either: "Not only was Koheleth a sage himself . . ."[65] or "And in addition: Qohelet was a 'sage'."[66]

4. *yōṯereṯ.* The noun *yōṯereṯ* occurs 11 times in Exodus and Leviticus; it denotes the "appendage [to the liver]," as translated by Saadia (*ziyāda*).[67] It never appears in isolation but only in conjunction with *kāḇēḏ* II, "liver," either in a construct phrase (*yōṯereṯ hakkāḇēḏ*: Ex. 29:22; Lev. 8:16,25; 9:19) or in a prepositional phrase (*hayyōṯereṯ min-hakkāḇēḏ*: Lev. 9:10; *hayyōṯereṯ ʿal-hakkāḇēḏ*: Ex. 29:13; Lev. 3:4,10,15; 4:9; 7:4). The eleven texts refer to the livers of three different animals: sheep, goats, and cattle. Six of these passages (Ex. 29:13,22; Lev. 8:16,25; 9:10,19) include the appendage in a list of the parts to be offered in a *šelāmîm* sacrifice; the appendage is listed both immediately before and immediately after the kidneys. In the five other passages (Lev. 3:4,10,15; 4:9; 7:4), the appendage is modified by an additional clause, which is always the same: "he shall take it away together with the kidneys" (not: "he shall take it away from the kidneys"[68]). Rost's special study has shown that in all its OT occurrences *yōṯereṯ* refers to the *lobus caudatus.*[69] Because the *lobus caudatus* of sheep and goats differs from that of cattle, and furthermore because only the livers of sheep and goats, not the livers of cattle, were used for the hepatoscopy common in the ancient world, especially Mesopotamia,[70] there is support for Rost's theory that "when the sacrificial regulations

61 On *ʿim,* see R. Gordis, *Koheleth—The Man and His World* (New York, ³1968), 273.
62 H. W. Hertzberg, *Der Prediger. KAT,* XVII/4 (1963), 130.
63 See above.
64 Cf. Jastrow, 572.
65 Gordis, 200, citing Bab. *Pesaḥ.* 112a; *Yebam.* 113a.
66 Hertzberg, 215f.
67 Cf. F. H. W. Gesenius, *Thesaurus philologicus criticus linguae hebraeae et chaldaeae Veteris Testamenti,* II (Leipzig, 1853), 645f.
68 K. Elliger, *Leviticus. HAT,* IV (1966), 47; cf. Rost, 35-41.
69 Cf. also Mishnah *Tamid* iv.3.
70 See, e.g., S. R. Driver, *The Book of Exodus. CBSC* (1911, repr. 1953), 317; B. Meissner, *BuA,* II, 267ff.; K. H. Bernhardt, "Leber," *BHHW,* II (1964), 1061.

deal also with the livers of cattle, it represents a secondary extension of a provision that was originally necessary only for the livers of sheep and goats."[71]

5. *yiṯrâ/yiṯraṯ*. The forms *yiṯrâ* and *yiṯraṯ* occur once each, in Isa. 15:7 and Jer. 48:36 (mss.: *yiṯrāṯ*[72]) respectively. On the basis of *ytr* I, *yiṯrâ* can be interpreted as meaning "remainder," e.g., in Isa. 15:7: "Therefore the remainder and what they have laid up they carry away over the Brook of the Willows."[73] The meaning "abundance,"[74] however, is not impossible.

6. *yiṯrôn*. The noun *yiṯrôn* occurs only in Ecclesiastes;[75] its connection with *ytr* I and its economic overtones are easily recognized. Although there is much to suggest "that Kohelet's *yiṯrôn* locutions are influenced by the language of ancient rhetoric,"[76] the meaning of *yiṯrôn* can be defined on the basis of *ytr* I as "'that which remains'—the surplus, if any, of the balance-sheet of life,"[77] a combination of the positive "outcome" of human life and the "profit" or "advantage" left over from it.[78] It is not always possible to maintain a clear differentiation between the two perspectives. The meaning of *yiṯrôn* can also be defined negatively by its antonym *ḥesrôn,* found only in Eccl. 1:15, which means "deficit" in the economic sense.[79] The noun *yiṯrôn* therefore means "surplus" or "return," what the language of trade would call "profit" or "gain."[80] Eccl. 1:3 asks a fundamental existential (albeit rhetorical) question: "What do people gain with all their toil?" (Dahood's attempt[81] to interpret *beḵol-ʿamālô* as "*from* all his toil" is not convincing). A similar question, also rhetorical, appears in 3:9, obviously concluding the section 3:2-8 with its 28 phrases involving *ʿēṯ*: "What, then, is the gain of a worker when he toils?"[82] The question is asked concerning frail mortals, subject to divine fate: "What gain do they have when they have toiled [only] for wind?" (5:15[16]). The answer to questions of this sort is given in 2:11: "There is no [real] profit/gain under the sun," because even "the *yiṯrōn* of the *ḥāḵām* amounts to nothing, and all he has is pain and worries."[83] The relationship

---

71 Rost, 37; cf. also Elliger, 52; G. F. Moore, "הַיֹּתֶרֶת עַל הַכָּבֵד 'Lobus caudatus' and its Equivalents," *Orientalische Studien. Festschrift T. Nöldeke* (Giessen, 1906), II, 761ff.

72 Cf. *BLe,* §62v.

73 Cf. H. Wildberger, *Jesaja. BK,* X/2 (1978), 588.

74 O. Kaiser, *Isaiah 13–39. OTL* (Eng. trans. 1974), 58.

75 Cf. *BLe,* §61nθ; S. J. du Plessis, "Aspects of Morphological Peculiarities of the Language of Qohelet," *De fructu oris sui. Festschrift A. van Selms. POS,* 9 (1971), 164-67.

76 Braun, 48.

77 E. H. Plumptre, *Ecclesiastes. CBSC* (1881), 104.

78 *KBL*³, 432.

79 M. Dahood, "The Phoenician Background of Qoheleth," *Bibl,* 47 (1966), 266; *idem,* "Canaanite-Phoenician Influence in Qoheleth," *Bibl,* 33 (1952), 221; H.-J. Fabry, "*ḥāsēr,*" *TDOT,* V, 80f.; but cf. Braun, 47f.

80 A. Lauha, *Kohelet. BK,* XIX (1978), 33; cf. C. F. Whitley, *Kohelet: His Language and Thought. BZAW,* 148 (1979), 7.

81 *Bibl,* 47 (1966), 265.

82 Cf. J. A. Loader, *Polar Structures in the Book of Qohelet. BZAW,* 152 (1979), 32.

83 *Ibid.,* 41.

between wisdom and folly is viewed similarly as a plus/minus relationship: "wisdom represents a plus with respect to folly, just as light represents a plus with respect to darkness" (2:13);[84] this plus ascribed to wisdom can be defined in terms of preservation: "It preserves the life of those who possess it" (7:12 MT).[85]

The interpretation of *wᵉyiṯrôn hakšēr ḥoḵmâ* in Eccl. 10:10 is uncertain.[86] Hertzberg[87] emends to *hᵃḵišrôn wᵉyiṯrôn ḥoḵmâ,* "there is gain and profit from wisdom." Di Fonzo[88] simply emends *hakšēr* (hiphil inf. abs.) to *hakšîr* (inf. const.), interpreting the expression to mean "thus wisdom helps 'to gain in effectiveness.'" Gordis, *BHS,* and others keep the MT and, citing Postbiblical Hebrew, interpret it to mean: "But it is an advantage to prepare one's skill in advance."[89] Also difficult are the 2 other occurrences of *yiṯrôn.* The first, 10:11, in the context of the preceding statement probably means: "If the serpent bites before it is charmed, the charmer has no advantage."[90] The second, 5:8(9) (*wᵉyiṯrôn ʾereṣ bakkōl hîʾ meleḵ leśāḏeh neʿᵉḇāḏ*), is very difficult.[91] The best interpretation, based on the Targ. and Ibn Ezra, may be: "the advantage of land is paramount; even a king is subject to the soil."[92]

7. *môṯār.* Just as the meaning of *yiṯrôn* can be defined more precisely by contrast with its antonym *ḥesrôn,* the meaning of the parallel term *môṯār* can be determined from its antonym *maḥsôr,*[93] "want," in Prov. 14:23; 21:5: it means "advantage, profit, gain."[94] This also fits its last OT occurrence (Eccl. 3:19), which speaks of the advantage human beings have over beasts.[95]

8. *yattîr/yattîrâ(āʾ).* Biblical Aram. *yattîr,* which derives from *ytr* I, means primarily "extra," "exceptional."[96] Describing the great statue in King Nebuchadnezzar's dream, Dnl. 2:31 says it was *zîwēh yattîr,* "of exceeding brightness." Dnl. 5:12 speaks similarly of Daniel's *rûaḥ yattîrâ,* "extraordinary spirit"; 6:4(3) does the same (*yattîrāʾ*). Daniel's *ḥoḵmâ yattîrâ,* "extraordinary wisdom," is praised in 5:14. Finally, Nebuchadnezzar, in his account of how his faculties were restored, says (Dnl. 4:33[36]): "extra [i.e., 'even greater'] power was given me" (*rᵉḇû yattîrâ hûsᵉpaṯ lî*).[97] We also find *yattîrâ* used

---

84 Cf. *GK,* §24e.
85 On the text, see Hertzberg, 130.
86 For a brief survey of the proposals, see Gordis, 321f.
87 P. 182; similarly K. Galling, *Die fünf Megilloth: Der Prediger. HAT,* XVIII (²1969), 116.
88 L. di Fonzo, *Ecclesiaste. SaBi* (1967), 294.
89 Gordis, 192, 321f.
90 Hertzberg, 182; similarly Lauha, 186.
91 For its discussion, see esp. H. Odeberg, *Qohælæt* (Uppsala, 1929), 47f.; di Fonzo, 204; Gordis, 250; A. T. Varela, "A new approach to Ecclesiastes 5.8-9," *BT,* 27 (1976), 240f.
92 Gordis, 166; cf. 250.
93 → חסר *ḥsr.*
94 Cf. *KBL*³, 534.
95 Hertzberg, 97.
96 Cf. *LexLingAram,* 78; Wildberger, 846; Segert, 537, also 4.3.3.6.5.
97 Plöger, 70.

adverbially (cf. Heb. *yeṯer* I and *yôṯēr/yōṯēr* above),[98] with the meaning "greatly, extremely, very."[99] In Dnl. 3:22, the fiery furnace is described as "extremely overheated" (Aram. *ʾēzēh yattîrāʾ*).[100] In Daniel's first great vision, the fourth beast is described as "very strong" (*taqqîpāʾ yattîrāʾ* [Dnl. 7:7]) and "very terrible" (*deḥîlâ yattîrâ* [v. 19]).

III. LXX. The LXX translates *ytr* I in a great variety of ways, for the most part using some form of *leípein* or *perisseúein* plus a prepositional phrase. The qal is translated by *loipós* (actually only in 1 S. 15:15; see also *yôṯēr/yōṯēr* and *yōṯereṯ* below). The niphal is translated by *apoleípein, enkataleípein, epíloipos, heurískein, kataleípein, katáloipos, loipós, perisseúein, perissós, perittós, hypolambánein, hypoleípein,* and *hypóloipos*; the hiphil, by *apoleípein, enkataleípein, ekzeín, eulogeín, kataleípein, peripoieín, plēthýnein (-úein), polyōreín, proskataleípein,* and *hypoleípein.* The noun *yeṯer* I is usually translated by *loipós* (44 times) or *katáloipos* (17 times); we also find *élleimma, epíloipos, katáleimma(-limma), kataleípein, perissós, perittós, perissṓs, pistós* (?), *pleónasma, hypoleípein,* and *hypóloipos*; *yôṯēr/yōṯēr,* by *perisseía(-ia), perisseúein, perissós,* and *perittós* (*yôṯēr min* in Est. 6:6 by *ei mḗ*); *yōṯereṯ,* by *lobós*; *yiṯraṯ,* by *peripoieín* (Jer. 48:36 [LXX 31:36]; *ʿal-kēn yiṯrâ ʿāśâ* [Isa. 15:7] by *mḗ kaí hoútōs méllei sōthḗnai*); *yiṯrôn,* by *perisseía(-ia)*; *môṯār,* by *perisseúein* or *perissós.* The noun *yattîr/yattîrâ(āʾ),* finally, is translated in a great variety of ways: by *hágios* (Dnl. 5:12,14; 6:4[3]; Theodotion: *perissós*), *hypér* (Dnl. 3:22; Theodotion: *perissós*), *hyperpherḗs* (Dnl. 2:31), *hyperphereín* (Dnl. 7:7; Theodotion: *perissṓs*), and *hypér(phobos)* (Dnl. 7:19; Theodotion: *perissṓs*).

IV. Dead Sea Scrolls. From the Dead Sea scrolls, we can cite only a very few examples of *ytr* I. In 1QpHab 7:7, we find the adverbial phrase *ytr ʿl,* which may be read *yeṯer ʿal* (cf. Ps. 31:24[23]: *ʿal-yeṯer*)[101] or, perhaps better (cf. the par. 1Q22 3:2 [*ywtr ʿl ʾrbʿt*; cf. 1Q30 1:5: /*wʾšr yw/tr l/?/*]), *yōṯēr ʿal.* Discussing Hab. 2:3a, 1QpHab 7:7f. says: "Its interpretation is that the final end time is long delayed, indeed far beyond (*weyōṯēr ʿal*) all that the prophets have said." In 1QM 2:6, we find the niphal ptcp. *hannôṯārôṯ* with its usual meaning, "remaining"; the passage is simply speaking of the "thirty-three remaining years of the war." The same word appears with the same function in 1QM 2:10,14. In CD 2:11, we find *hytr,* which might be read *hōṯēr* (hiphil inf. const. of *ytr* I), in the sense of "remaining," but more likely derives from the root *ntr*;[102] cf. also *ytrh* in 1QIs^a 1:8.[103] The word *nwtrw* in CD 3:13 is almost certainly to be read as the niphal perf. *nôṯerû,* "be left over." The passage deals with the Israelites who were faithful to the covenant, specifically "those of them remaining."

Kronholm

---

98 Cf. Segert, 5.5.8.5.2.

99 Cf. *LexLingAram,* 78; Segert, 537, also 7.2.4.1.2.

100 Plöger, 58.

101 E. Lohse, *Die Texte aus Qumran* (Munich, ²1971), 234.

102 Kuhn, 95.

103 P. Wernberg-Møller, "Studies in the Defective Spellings in the Isaiah-Scroll of St. Mark's Monastery," *JSS,* 3 (1958), 250.